GO! with Microsoft® Office 2010

Volume 2

Shelley Gaskin, Nancy Graviett, Donna Madsen, Suzanne Marks, Carol Martin, and Toni Marucco

Prentice Hall

Boston Columbus Indianapolis New York San Francisco Upper Saddle River
Amsterdam Cape Town Dubai London Madrid Milan Munich Paris Montreal Toronto
Delhi Mexico City Sao Paulo Sydney Hong Kong Seoul Singapore Taipei Tokyo

Associate VP/Executive Acquisitions Editor, Print: Stephanie Wall
Editorial Project Manager: Laura Burgess
Editor in Chief: Michael Payne
Product Development Manager: Eileen Bien Calabro
Development Editors: Jennifer Lynn, Toni Ackley, Linda Harrison, and Ginny Munroe
Editorial Assistant: Nicole Sam
Director of Marketing: Kate Valentine
Marketing Manager: Tori Olson Alves
Marketing Coordinator: Susan Osterlitz
Marketing Assistant: Darshika Vyas
Senior Managing Editor: Cynthia Zonneveld
Associate Managing Editor: Camille Trentacoste
Production Project Manager: Mike Lackey
Operations Director: Alexis Heydt
Operations Specialist: Natacha Moore
Senior Art Director: Jonathan Boylan
Cover Photo: © Ben Durrant
Text and Cover Designer: Blair Brown
Manager, Cover Visual Research & Permissions: Karen Sanatar
Manager, Rights and Permissions: Zina Arabia
AVP/Director of Online Programs, Media: Richard Keaveny
AVP/Director of Product Development, Media: Lisa Strite
Media Project Manager, Editorial: Alana Coles
Media Project Manager, Production: John Cassar
Full-Service Project Management: PreMediaGlobal
Composition: PreMediaGlobal
Printer/Binder: QuadGraphics-Taunton
Cover Printer: Lehigh-Phoenix Color
Text Font: Bookman Light

Credits and acknowledgments borrowed from other sources and reproduced, with permission, in this textbook appear on appropriate page within text.

Library of Congress Cataloging-in-Publication Data
CIP to come

10 9 8 7 6 5 4 3 2

Prentice Hall
is an imprint of

PEARSON

www.pearsonhighered.com

ISBN 10: 0-13-509090-3
ISBN 13: 978-0-13-509090-9

Brief Contents

Contents

Word

Chapter 4 Using Styles and Creating Multilevel Lists and Charts 49

Chapter 5 Creating Web Pages and Using Advanced Proofing Options. 105

Excel

GO! System Contributors

We thank the following people for their hard work and support in making the *GO!* System all that it is!

Instructor Resource Authors

Adickes, Erich	Parkland College
Baray, Carrie	Ivy Tech Community College
Bornstein, Abigail	City College of San Francisco
Bowman, Valeria	National College
Callahan, Michael	Lone Star College
Cleary, Kevin	University at Buffalo
Clausen, Jane	Western Iowa Tech Community College
Colucci, William	Montclair State University
Crossley, Connie	Cincinnati State Technical and Community College
Damanti, Lori	
Edington, Barbara	St. Francis College
Emrich, Stefanie	Metropolitan Community College of Omaha, Nebraska
Faix, Dennis	Harrisburg Area Community College
Hadden, Karen	Western Iowa Tech Community College
Hammerle, Patricia	Indiana University/Purdue University at Indianapolis
Hines, James	Tidewater Community College
Hicks, Janette	Binghamton University / State University of New York
Hollingsworth, Mary Carole	Georgia Perimeter College
Holly, Terri	Indian River State College
Holland, Susan	Southeast Community College-Nebraska
Jacob, Sherry	Kentucky Community and Technical College
Leinbach, Andrea	Harrisburg Area Community College
Lutz, Mary	Southwestern Illinois College
Miller, Abigail	Gateway Community and Technical College
Monson, Shari	Black Hawk College
Landenberger, Toni	Southeast Community College-Nebraska
McMahon, Richard	University of Houston—Downtown
Miller, Sandra	Wenatchee Valley College
Neal, Ruth	Navarro College
Niebur, Katherine	Dakota County Technical College
Nowakowski, Anthony	Buffalo State
Pierce, Tonya	Ivy Tech Community College
Reynolds, Mark	Lone Star College
Roselli, Diane	Harrisburg Area Community College
Shing, Chen-Chi	Radford University
St. John, Steve	Tulsa Community College
Sterr, Jody	Blackhawk Technical College
Thompson, Joyce	Lehigh Carbon Community College
Tucker, William	Austin Community College
Volker, Bonita	Tidewater Community College
Walters, Kari	Louisiana State University

Technical Editors

Matthew Bisi
Mary Corcoran
Lori Damanti
Barbara Edington
Sarah Evans
Adam Layne
Elizabeth Lockley
Joyce Nielsen
Janet Pickard
Sean Portnoy
Jan Snyder
Sam Stamport
Mara Zebest

Student Reviewers

Albinda, Sarah Evangeline	Phoenix College
Allen, John	Asheville-Buncombe Tech Community College
Alexander, Steven	St. Johns River Community College
Alexander, Melissa	Tulsa Community College
Bolz, Stephanie	Northern Michigan University
Berner, Ashley	Central Washington University
Boomer, Michelle	Northern Michigan University
Busse, Brennan	Northern Michigan University
Butkey, Maura	Central Washington University
Cates, Concita	Phoenix College
Charles, Marvin	Harrisburg Area Community College
Christensen, Kaylie	Northern Michigan University
Clark, Glen D. III	Harrisburg Area Community College
Cobble, Jan N.	Greenville Technical College
Connally, Brianna	Central Washington University
Davis, Brandon	Northern Michigan University
Davis, Christen	Central Washington University
De Jesus Garcia, Maria	Phoenix College
Den Boer, Lance	Central Washington University
Dix, Jessica	Central Washington University
Downs, Elizabeth	Central Washington University
Elser, Julie	Harrisburg Area Community College
Erickson, Mike	Ball State University
Frye, Alicia	Phoenix College
Gadomski, Amanda	Northern Michigan University
Gassert, Jennifer	Harrisburg Area Community College
Gross, Mary Jo	Kirkwood Community College
Gyselinck, Craig	Central Washington University
Harrison, Margo	Central Washington University
Hatt, Patrick	Harrisburg Area Community College
Heacox, Kate	Central Washington University
Hedgman, Shaina	Tidewater College
Hill, Cheretta	Northwestern State University
Hochstedler, Bethany	Harrisburg Area Community College Lancaster
Homer, Jean	Greenville Technical College
Innis, Tim	Tulsa Community College
Jarboe, Aaron	Central Washington University
Key, Penny	Greenville Technical College
Klein, Colleen	Northern Michigan University
Lloyd, Kasey	Ivy Tech Bloomington
Moeller, Jeffrey	Northern Michigan University
Mullen, Sharita	Tidewater Community College
Nelson, Cody	Texas Tech University
Nicholson, Regina	Athens Tech College
Niehaus, Kristina	Northern Michigan University
Nisa, Zaibun	Santa Rosa Community College
Nunez, Nohelia	Santa Rosa Community College
Oak, Samantha	Central Washington University

Oberly, Sara	Harrisburg Area Community College Lancaster
Oertii, Monica	Central Washington University
Palenshus, Juliet	Central Washington University
Pohl, Amanda	Northern Michigan University
Presnell, Randy	Central Washington University
Reed, Kailee	Texas Tech University
Ritner, April	Northern Michigan University
Roberts, Corey	Tulsa Community College
Rodgers, Spencer	Texas Tech University
Rodriguez, Flavia	Northwestern State University
Rogers, A.	Tidewater Community College
Rossi, Jessica Ann	Central Washington University
Rothbauer, Taylor	Trident Technical College
Rozelle, Lauren	Texas Tech University
Schmadeke, Kimberly	Kirkwood Community College
Shafapay, Natasha	Central Washington University
Shanahan, Megan	Northern Michigan University
Sullivan, Alexandra Nicole	Greenville Technical College
Teska, Erika	Hawaii Pacific University
Torrenti, Natalie	Harrisburg Area Community College
Traub, Amy	Northern Michigan University
Underwood, Katie	Central Washington University
Walters, Kim	Central Washington University
Warren, Jennifer L.	Greenville Technical College
Wilson, Kelsie	Central Washington University
Wilson, Amanda	Green River Community College
Wylie, Jimmy	Texas Tech University

Series Reviewers

Abraham, Reni	Houston Community College
Addison, Paul	Ivy Tech Community College
Agatston, Ann	Agatston Consulting Technical College
Akuna, Valeria, Ph.D.	Estrella Mountain Community College
Alexander, Melody	Ball Sate University
Alejandro, Manuel	Southwest Texas Junior College
Alger, David	Tidewater Community College Chesapeake Campus
Allen, Jackie	Rowan-Cabarrus Community College
Ali, Farha	Lander University
Amici, Penny	Harrisburg Area Community College
Anderson, Patty A.	Lake City Community College
Andrews, Wilma	Virginia Commonwealth College, Nebraska University
Anik, Mazhar	Tiffin University
Armstrong, Gary	Shippensburg University
Arnold, Linda L.	Harrisburg Area Community College
Ashby, Tom	Oklahoma City Community College
Atkins, Bonnie	Delaware Technical Community College
Aukland, Cherie	Thomas Nelson Community College
Bachand, LaDonna	Santa Rosa Community College
Bagui, Sikha	University of West Florida
Beecroft, Anita	Kwantlen University College
Bell, Paula	Lock Haven College
Belton, Linda	Springfield Tech. Community College
Bennett, Judith	Sam Houston State University
Bhatia, Sai	Riverside Community College
Bishop, Frances	DeVry Institute—Alpharetta (ATL)
Blaszkiewicz, Holly	Ivy Tech Community College/Region 1
Boito, Nancy	HACC Central Pennsylvania's Community College
Borger-Boglin, Grietje L.	San Antonio College/Northeast Lakeview College
Branigan, Dave	DeVry University
Bray, Patricia	Allegany College of Maryland
Britt, Brenda K.	Fayetteville Technical Community College
Brotherton, Cathy	Riverside Community College
Brown, Judy	Western Illinois University
Buehler, Lesley	Ohlone College
Buell, C	Central Oregon Community College
Burns, Christine	Central New Mexico Community College
Byars, Pat	Brookhaven College
Byrd, Julie	Ivy Tech Community College
Byrd, Lynn	Delta State University, Cleveland, Mississippi
Cacace, Richard N.	Pensacola Junior College
Cadenhead, Charles	Brookhaven College
Calhoun, Ric	Gordon College
Cameron, Eric	Passaic Community College
Canine, Jill	Ivy Tech Community College of Indiana
Cannamore, Madie	Kennedy King
Cannon, Kim	Greenville Technical College
Carreon, Cleda	Indiana University—Purdue University, Indianapolis
Carriker, Sandra	North Shore Community College
Casey, Patricia	Trident Technical College
Cates, Wally	Central New Mexico Community College
Chaffin, Catherine	Shawnee State University
Chauvin, Marg	Palm Beach Community College, Boca Raton
Challa, Chandrashekar	Virginia State University
Chamlou, Afsaneh	NOVA Alexandria
Chapman, Pam	Wabaunsee Community College
Christensen, Dan	Iowa Western Community College
Clay, Betty	Southeastern Oklahoma State University
Collins, Linda D.	Mesa Community College
Cone, Bill	Northern Arizona University
Conroy-Link, Janet	Holy Family College
Conway, Ronald	Bowling Green State University
Cornforth, Carol G.	WVNCC
Cosgrove, Janet	Northwestern CT Community
Courtney, Kevin	Hillsborough Community College
Coverdale, John	Riverside Community College
Cox, Rollie	Madison Area Technical College
Crawford, Hiram	Olive Harvey College
Crawford, Sonia	Central New Mexico Community College
Crawford, Thomasina	Miami-Dade College, Kendall Campus
Credico, Grace	Lethbridge Community College
Crenshaw, Richard	Miami Dade Community College, North
Crespo, Beverly	Mt. San Antonio College
Crooks, Steven	Texas Tech University
Crossley, Connie	Cincinnati State Technical Community College

Curik, Mary	Central New Mexico Community College
De Arazoza, Ralph	Miami Dade Community College
Danno, John	DeVry University/Keller Graduate School
Davis, Phillip	Del Mar College
Davis, Richard	Trinity Valley Community College
Davis, Sandra	Baker College of Allen Park
Dees, Stephanie D.	Wharton County Junior College
DeHerrera, Laurie	Pikes Peak Community College
Delk, Dr. K. Kay	Seminole Community College
Denton, Bree	Texas Tech University
Dix, Jeanette	Ivy Tech Community College
Dooly, Veronica P.	Asheville-Buncombe Technical Community College
Doroshow, Mike	Eastfield College
Douglas, Gretchen	SUNYCortland
Dove, Carol	Community College of Allegheny
Dozier, Susan	Tidewater Community College, Virginia Beach Campus
Driskel, Loretta	Niagara Community College
Duckwiler, Carol	Wabaunsee Community College
Duhon, David	Baker College
Duncan, Mimi	University of Missouri-St. Louis
Duthie, Judy	Green River Community College
Duvall, Annette	Central New Mexico Community College
Ecklund, Paula	Duke University
Eilers, Albert	Cincinnati State Technical and Community College
Eng, Bernice	Brookdale Community College
Epperson, Arlin	Columbia College
Evans, Billie	Vance-Granville Community College
Evans, Jean	Brevard Community College
Feuerbach, Lisa	Ivy Tech East Chicago
Finley, Jean	ABTCC
Fisher, Fred	Florida State University
Foster, Nancy	Baker College
Foster-Shriver, Penny L.	Anne Arundel Community College
Foster-Turpen, Linda	CNM
Foszcz, Russ	McHenry County College
Fry, Susan	Boise State University
Fustos, Janos	Metro State
Gallup, Jeanette	Blinn College
Gelb, Janet	Grossmont College
Gentry, Barb	Parkland College
Gerace, Karin	St. Angela Merici School
Gerace, Tom	Tulane University
Ghajar, Homa	Oklahoma State University
Gifford, Steve	Northwest Iowa Community College
Glazer, Ellen	Broward Community College
Gordon, Robert	Hofstra University
Gramlich, Steven	Pasco-Hernando Community College
Graviett, Nancy M.	St. Charles Community College, St. Peters, Missouri
Greene, Rich	Community College of Allegheny County
Gregoryk, Kerry	Virginia Commonwealth State
Griggs, Debra	Bellevue Community College
Grimm, Carol	Palm Beach Community College
Guthrie, Rose	Fox Valley Technical College
Hahn, Norm	Thomas Nelson Community College
Haley-Hunter, Deb	Bluefield State College
Hall, Linnea	Northwest Mississippi Community College
Hammerschlag, Dr. Bill	Brookhaven College
Hansen, Michelle	Davenport University
Hayden, Nancy	Indiana University—Purdue University, Indianapolis
Hayes, Theresa	Broward Community College
Headrick, Betsy	Chattanooga State
Helfand, Terri	Chaffey College
Helms, Liz	Columbus State Community College
Hernandez, Leticia	TCI College of Technology
Hibbert, Marilyn	Salt Lake Community College
Hinds, Cheryl	Norfolk State University
Hines, James	Tidewater Community College
Hoffman, Joan	Milwaukee Area Technical College
Hogan, Pat	Cape Fear Community College
Holland, Susan	Southeast Community College
Holliday, Mardi	Community College of Philadelphia
Hollingsworth, Mary Carole	Georgia Perimeter College
Hopson, Bonnie	Athens Technical College
Horvath, Carrie	Albertus Magnus College
Horwitz, Steve	Community College of Philadelphia
Hotta, Barbara	Leeward Community College
Howard, Bunny	St. Johns River Community
Howard, Chris	DeVry University
Huckabay, Jamie	Austin Community College
Hudgins, Susan	East Central University
Hulett, Michelle J.	Missouri State University
Humphrey, John	Asheville Buncombe Technical Community College
Hunt, Darla A.	Morehead State University, Morehead, Kentucky
Hunt, Laura	Tulsa Community College
Ivey, Joan M.	Lanier Technical College
Jacob, Sherry	Jefferson Community College
Jacobs, Duane	Salt Lake Community College
Jauken, Barb	Southeastern Community
Jerry, Gina	Santa Monica College
Johnson, Deborah S.	Edison State College
Johnson, Kathy	Wright College
Johnson, Mary	Kingwood College
Johnson, Mary	Mt. San Antonio College
Jones, Stacey	Benedict College
Jones, Warren	University of Alabama, Birmingham
Jordan, Cheryl	San Juan College
Kapoor, Bhushan	California State University, Fullerton
Kasai, Susumu	Salt Lake Community College
Kates, Hazel	Miami Dade Community College, Kendall
Keen, Debby	University of Kentucky
Keeter, Sandy	Seminole Community College
Kern-Blystone, Dorothy Jean	Bowling Green State
Kerwin, Annette	College of DuPage
Keskin, Ilknur	The University of South Dakota
Kinney, Mark B.	Baker College
Kirk, Colleen	Mercy College
Kisling, Eric	East Carolina University
Kleckner, Michelle	Elon University
Kliston, Linda	Broward Community College, North Campus

Knuth, Toni	Baker College of Auburn Hills
Kochis, Dennis	Suffolk County Community College
Kominek, Kurt	Northeast State Technical Community College
Kramer, Ed	Northern Virginia Community College
Kretz, Daniel	Fox Valley Technical College
Laird, Jeff	Northeast State Community College
Lamoureaux, Jackie	Central New Mexico Community College
Lange, David	Grand Valley State
LaPointe, Deb	Central New Mexico Community College
Larsen, Jacqueline Anne	A-B Tech
Larson, Donna	Louisville Technical Institute
Laspina, Kathy	Vance-Granville Community College
Le Grand, Dr. Kate	Broward Community College
Lenhart, Sheryl	Terra Community College
Leonard, Yvonne	Coastal Carolina Community College
Letavec, Chris	University of Cincinnati
Lewis, Daphne L, Ed.D.	Wayland Baptist University
Lewis, Julie	Baker College-Allen Park
Liefert, Jane	Everett Community College
Lindaman, Linda	Black Hawk Community College
Lindberg, Martha	Minnesota State University
Lightner, Renee	Broward Community College
Lindberg, Martha	Minnesota State University
Linge, Richard	Arizona Western College
Logan, Mary G.	Delgado Community College
Loizeaux, Barbara	Westchester Community College
Lombardi, John	South University
Lopez, Don	Clovis-State Center Community College District
Lopez, Lisa	Spartanburg Community College
Lord, Alexandria	Asheville Buncombe Tech
Lovering, LeAnne	Augusta Technical College
Lowe, Rita	Harold Washington College
Low, Willy Hui	Joliet Junior College
Lucas, Vickie	Broward Community College
Luna, Debbie	El Paso Community College
Luoma, Jean	Davenport University
Luse, Steven P.	Horry Georgetown Technical College
Lynam, Linda	Central Missouri State University
Lyon, Lynne	Durham College
Lyon, Pat Rajski	Tomball College
Macarty, Matthew	University of New Hampshire
MacKinnon, Ruth	Georgia Southern University
Macon, Lisa	Valencia Community College, West Campus
Machuca, Wayne	College of the Sequoias
Mack, Sherri	Butler County Community College
Madison, Dana	Clarion University
Maguire, Trish	Eastern New Mexico University
Malkan, Rajiv	Montgomery College
Manning, David	Northern Kentucky University
Marcus, Jacquie	Niagara Community College
Marghitu, Daniela	Auburn University
Marks, Suzanne	Bellevue Community College
Marquez, Juanita	El Centro College
Marquez, Juan	Mesa Community College
Martin, Carol	Harrisburg Area Community College
Martin, Paul C.	Harrisburg Area Community College
Martyn, Margie	Baldwin-Wallace College
Marucco, Toni	Lincoln Land Community College
Mason, Lynn	Lubbock Christian University
Matutis, Audrone	Houston Community College
Matkin, Marie	University of Lethbridge
Maurel, Trina	Odessa College
May, Karen	Blinn College
McCain, Evelynn	Boise State University
McCannon, Melinda	Gordon College
McCarthy, Marguerite	Northwestern Business College
McCaskill, Matt L.	Brevard Community College
McClellan, Carolyn	Tidewater Community College
McClure, Darlean	College of Sequoias
McCrory, Sue A.	Missouri State University
McCue, Stacy	Harrisburg Area Community College
McEntire-Orbach, Teresa	Middlesex County College
McKinley, Lee	Georgia Perimeter College
McLeod, Todd	Fresno City College
McManus, Illyana	Grossmont College
McPherson, Dori	Schoolcraft College
Meck, Kari	HACC
Meiklejohn, Nancy	Pikes Peak Community College
Menking, Rick	Hardin-Simmons University
Meredith, Mary	University of Louisiana at Lafayette
Mermelstein, Lisa	Baruch College
Metos, Linda	Salt Lake Community College
Meurer, Daniel	University of Cincinnati
Meyer, Colleen	Cincinnati State Technical and Community College
Meyer, Marian	Central New Mexico Community College
Miller, Cindy	Ivy Tech Community College, Lafayette, Indiana
Mills, Robert E.	Tidewater Community College, Portsmouth Campus
Mitchell, Susan	Davenport University
Mohle, Dennis	Fresno Community College
Molki, Saeed	South Texas College
Monk, Ellen	University of Delaware
Moore, Rodney	Holland College
Morris, Mike	Southeastern Oklahoma State University
Morris, Nancy	Hudson Valley Community College
Moseler, Dan	Harrisburg Area Community College
Nabors, Brent	Reedley College, Clovis Center
Nadas, Erika	Wright College
Nadelman, Cindi	New England College
Nademlynsky, Lisa	Johnson & Wales University
Nagengast, Joseph	Florida Career College
Nason, Scott	Rowan Cabarrus Community College
Ncube, Cathy	University of West Florida
Newsome, Eloise	Northern Virginia Community College Woodbridge
Nicholls, Doreen	Mohawk Valley Community College
Nicholson, John R.	Johnson County Community College
Nielson, Phil	Salt Lake Community College
Nunan, Karen L.	Northeast State Technical Community College

O'Neal, Lois Ann	Rogers State University
Odegard, Teri	Edmonds Community College
Ogle, Gregory	North Community College
Orr, Dr. Claudia	Northern Michigan University South
Orsburn, Glen	Fox Valley Technical College
Otieno, Derek	DeVry University
Otton, Diana Hill	Chesapeake College
Oxendale, Lucia	West Virginia Institute of Technology
Paiano, Frank	Southwestern College
Pannell, Dr. Elizabeth	Collin College
Patrick, Tanya	Clackamas Community College
Paul, Anindya	Daytona State College
Peairs, Deb	Clark State Community College
Perez, Kimberly	Tidewater Community College
Porter, Joyce	Weber State University
Prince, Lisa	Missouri State University-Springfield Campus
Proietti, Kathleen	Northern Essex Community College
Puopolo, Mike	Bunker Hill Community College
Pusins, Delores	HCCC
Putnam, Darlene	Thomas Nelson Community College
Raghuraman, Ram	Joliet Junior College
Rani, Chigurupati	BMCC/CUNY
Reasoner, Ted Allen	Indiana University—Purdue
Reeves, Karen	High Point University
Remillard, Debbie	New Hampshire Technical Institute
Rhue, Shelly	DeVry University
Richards, Karen	Maplewoods Community College
Richardson, Mary	Albany Technical College
Rodgers, Gwen	Southern Nazarene University
Rodie, Karla	Pikes Peak Community College
Roselli, Diane Maie	Harrisburg Area Community College
Ross, Dianne	University of Louisiana in Lafayette
Rousseau, Mary	Broward Community College, South
Rovetto, Ann	Horry-Georgetown Technical College
Rusin, Iwona	Baker College
Sahabi, Ahmad	Baker College of Clinton Township
Samson, Dolly	Hawaii Pacific University
Sams, Todd	University of Cincinnati
Sandoval, Everett	Reedley College
Santiago, Diana	Central New Mexico Community College
Sardone, Nancy	Seton Hall University
Scafide, Jean	Mississippi Gulf Coast Community College
Scheeren, Judy	Westmoreland County Community College
Scheiwe, Adolph	Joliet Junior College
Schneider, Sol	Sam Houston State University
Schweitzer, John	Central New Mexico Community College
Scroggins, Michael	Southwest Missouri State University
Sedlacek, Brenda	Tidewater Community College
Sell, Kelly	Anne Arundel Community College
Sever, Suzanne	Northwest Arkansas Community College
Sewell, John	Florida Career College
Sheridan, Rick	California State University-Chico
Silvers, Pamela	Asheville Buncombe Tech
Sindt, Robert G.	Johnson County Community College
Singer, Noah	Tulsa Community College
Singer, Steven A.	University of Hawai'i, Kapi'olani Community College

Sinha, Atin	Albany State University
Skolnick, Martin	Florida Atlantic University
Smith, Kristi	Allegany College of Maryland
Smith, Patrick	Marshall Community and Technical College
Smith, Stella A.	Georgia Gwinnett College
Smith, T. Michael	Austin Community College
Smith, Tammy	Tompkins Cortland Community Collge
Smolenski, Bob	Delaware County Community College
Smolenski, Robert	Delaware Community College
Southwell, Donald	Delta College
Spangler, Candice	Columbus State
Spangler, Candice	Columbus State Community College
Stark, Diane	Phoenix College
Stedham, Vicki	St. Petersburg College, Clearwater
Stefanelli, Greg	Carroll Community College
Steiner, Ester	New Mexico State University
Stenlund, Neal	Northern Virginia Community College, Alexandria
St. John, Steve	Tulsa Community College
Sterling, Janet	Houston Community College
Stoughton, Catherine	Laramie County Community College
Sullivan, Angela	Joliet Junior College
Sullivan, Denise	Westchester Community College
Sullivan, Joseph	Joliet Junior College
Swart, John	Louisiana Tech University
Szurek, Joseph	University of Pittsburgh at Greensburg
Taff, Ann	Tulsa Community College
Taggart, James	Atlantic Cape Community College
Tarver, Mary Beth	Northwestern State University
Taylor, Michael	Seattle Central Community College
Terrell, Robert L.	Carson-Newman College
Terry, Dariel	Northern Virginia Community College
Thangiah, Sam	Slippery Rock University
Thayer, Paul	Austin Community College
Thompson, Joyce	Lehigh Carbon Community College
Thompson-Sellers, Ingrid	Georgia Perimeter College
Tomasi, Erik	Baruch College
Toreson, Karen	Shoreline Community College
Townsend, Cynthia	Baker College
Trifiletti, John J.	Florida Community College at Jacksonville
Trivedi, Charulata	Quinsigamond Community College, Woodbridge
Tucker, William	Austin Community College
Turgeon, Cheryl	Asnuntuck Community College
Turpen, Linda	Central New Mexico Community College
Upshaw, Susan	Del Mar College
Unruh, Angela	Central Washington University
Vanderhoof, Dr. Glenna	Missouri State University-Springfield Campus
Vargas, Tony	El Paso Community College
Vicars, Mitzi	Hampton University
Villarreal, Kathleen	Fresno
Vitrano, Mary Ellen	Palm Beach Community College
Vlaich-Lee, Michelle	Greenville Technical College
Volker, Bonita	Tidewater Community College
Waddell, Karen	Butler Community College
Wahila, Lori (Mindy)	Tompkins Cortland Community College
Wallace, Melissa	Lanier Technical College
Walters, Gary B.	Central New Mexico Community College

Waswick, Kim	Southeast Community College, Nebraska
Wavle, Sharon M.	Tompkins Cortland Community College
Webb, Nancy	City College of San Francisco
Webb, Rebecca	Northwest Arkansas Community College
Weber, Sandy	Gateway Technical College
Weissman, Jonathan	Finger Lakes Community College
Wells, Barbara E.	Central Carolina Technical College
Wells, Lorna	Salt Lake Community College
Welsh, Jean	Lansing Community College Nebraska
White, Bruce	Quinnipiac University
Willer, Ann	Solano Community College
Williams, Mark	Lane Community College
Williams, Ronald D.	Central Piedmont Community College
Wilms, Dr. G. Jan	Union University
Wilson, Kit	Red River College
Wilson, MaryLou	Piedmont Technical College
Wilson, Roger	Fairmont State University
Wimberly, Leanne	International Academy of Design and Technology
Winters, Floyd	Manatee Community College
Worthington, Paula	Northern Virginia Community College
Wright, Darrell	Shelton State Community College
Wright, Julie	Baker College
Yauney, Annette	Herkimer County Community College
Yip, Thomas	Passaic Community College
Zavala, Ben	Webster Tech
Zaboski, Maureen	University of Scranton
Zlotow, Mary Ann	College of DuPage
Zudeck, Steve	Broward Community College, North
Zullo, Matthew D.	Wake Technical Community College

About the Authors

Shelley Gaskin, Series Editor, is a professor in the Business and Computer Technology Division at Pasadena City College in Pasadena, California. She holds a bachelor's degree in Business Administration from Robert Morris College (Pennsylvania), a master's degree in Business from Northern Illinois University, and a doctorate in Adult and Community Education from Ball State University. Before joining Pasadena City College, she spent 12 years in the computer industry where she was a systems analyst, sales representative, and Director of Customer Education with Unisys Corporation. She also worked for Ernst & Young on the development of large systems applications for their clients. She has written and developed training materials for custom systems applications in both the public and private sector, and has written and edited numerous computer application textbooks.

This book is dedicated to my students, who inspire me every day.

Nancy Graviett is a professor in the Business and Computer Science department at St. Charles Community College in Cottleville, Missouri, where she is the program coordinator for the Business Administrative Systems program and teaches within the program. Nancy is also very active with distance learning and teaches in face-to-face, hybrid, and online formats. She holds a master's degree from University of Missouri. Nancy holds Microsoft® Certified Application Specialist certification in multiple applications and provides training both on and off campus. In her free time, Nancy enjoys quilting and spending time with family and friends.

I dedicate this book to my husband, David, my children (Matthew and Andrea), and my parents, whose love and support I cherish more than they could ever know.

Donna Madsen is a retired professor from Kirkwood Community College in Cedar Rapids, Iowa. She has B.A. and M.A. degrees in Business Education from the University of Northern Iowa and advanced studies in Instructional Design at the University of Iowa. In addition to teaching classes at Kirkwood, she managed a business computer learning center and coordinated a microcomputer specialist program. She served as an Education Instruction Specialist for IBM, was named Kirkwood Innovator of the Year sponsored by the League for Innovation, and received a Tribute to Women of Achievement from Waypoint. She enjoys traveling, reading, and quilting.

I dedicate this book to Ruth Rasmussen, my sister and best friend, and to all my family—David, Mary, Sophie, Bill, and Jim; Scott, Colleen, Dan, Sean, Jack, and especially my great-niece Maggie Rasmussen for her great ideas. I also dedicate this book to Kay Forest, my writing partner at Kirkwood Community College, who says that we "think on the same wave length."

Suzanne Marks is a faculty member in Business Technology Systems at Bellevue Community College, Bellevue, Washington. She holds a bachelor's degree in business education from Washington State University, and was project manager for the first IT Skills Standards in the United States.

This book is dedicated to my son, Jeff, and to my sisters, Janet Curtis and Joan Wissmann, for their brilliance, wisdom, and encouragement.

Carol L. Martin is a faculty member at Harrisburg Area Community College. She holds a bachelor's degree in Secondary Education—Mathematics from Millersville (PA) University and a master's degree in Training and Development from Pennsylvania State University. For over 35 years she has instructed individuals in the use of various computer applications. She has co-authored several training manuals for use in Pennsylvania Department of Education in-service courses and has written an Outlook textbook.

This book is dedicated to my husband Ron—a constant source of encouragement and technical support; and to my delightful grandsons, Tony and Josh, who keep me young at heart.

Toni Marucco recently retired from Lincoln Land Community College in Springfield, Illinois, where she was a professor of business and technologies. She holds a bachelor's degree in merchandising, a master's degree in education, and a Ph.D. in educational administration and higher education. Earlier in her career she served as an Education Industry Specialist with IBM for 10 years. She has also served as a contributing author on several textbooks. She continues to teach several online classes and serves as a faculty advocate for Pearson Education. Currently she serves as interim director for the Illinois Office of Educational Services.

This book is dedicated to my husband, John, to my mother, Dorothy, and to my children, Kori, Gia, and Charlie, who supported the pursuit of my dream.

Teach the Course You Want in Less Time

A Microsoft® Office textbook designed for student success!

GO!

- **Project-Based –** Students learn by creating projects that they will use in the real world.
- **Microsoft Procedural Syntax –** Steps are written to put students in the right place at the right time.
- **Teachable Moment –** Expository text is woven into the steps—at the moment students need to know it—not chunked together in a block of text that will go unread.
- **Sequential Pagination –** Students have actual page numbers instead of confusing letters and abbreviations.

Student Outcomes and Learning Objectives – Objectives are clustered around projects that result in student outcomes.

Project Activities – A project summary stated clearly and quickly.

Project Files – Clearly shows students which files are needed for the project and the names they will use to save their documents.

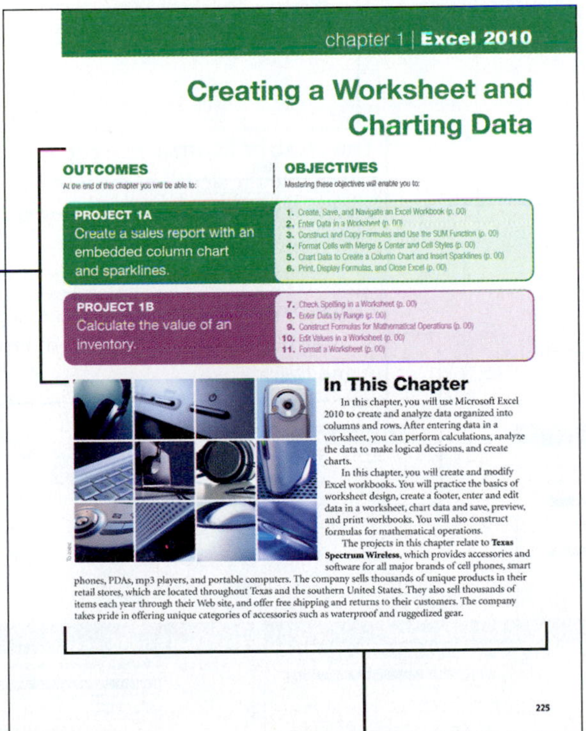
chapter 1 | **Excel 2010**

Creating a Worksheet and Charting Data

OUTCOMES
At the end of this chapter you will be able to:

PROJECT 1A
Create a sales report with an embedded column chart and sparklines.

PROJECT 1B
Calculate the value of an inventory.

OBJECTIVES
Mastering these objectives will enable you to:

1. Create, Save, and Navigate an Excel Workbook (p. 00)
2. Enter Data in a Worksheet (p. 00)
3. Construct and Copy Formulas and Use the SUM Function (p. 00)
4. Format Cells with Merge & Center and Cell Styles (p. 00)
5. Chart Data to Create a Column Chart and Insert Sparklines (p. 00)
6. Print, Display Formulas, and Close Excel (p. 00)
7. Check Spelling in a Worksheet (p. 00)
8. Enter Data by Range (p. 00)
9. Construct Formulas for Mathematical Operations (p. 00)
10. Edit Values in a Worksheet (p. 00)
11. Format a Worksheet (p. 00)

In This Chapter

In this chapter, you will use Microsoft Excel 2010 to create and analyze data organized into columns and rows. After entering data in a worksheet, you can perform calculations, analyze the data to make logical decisions, and create charts.

In this chapter, you will create and modify Excel workbooks. You will practice the basics of worksheet design, create a footer, enter and edit data in a worksheet, chart data and save, preview, and print workbooks. You will also construct formulas for mathematical operations.

The projects in this chapter relate to **Texas Spectrum Wireless**, which provides accessories and software for all major brands of cell phones, smart phones, PDAs, mp3 players, and portable computers. The company sells thousands of unique products in their retail stores, which are located throughout Texas and the southern United States. They also sell thousands of items each year through their Web site, and offer free shipping and returns to their customers. The company takes pride in offering unique categories of accessories such as waterproof and ruggedized gear.

225

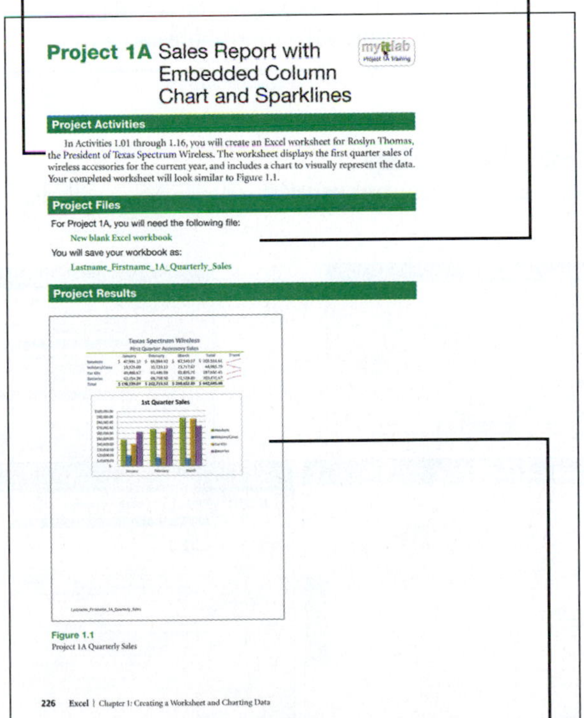
Project 1A Sales Report with Embedded Column Chart and Sparklines

Project Activities

In Activities 1.01 through 1.16, you will create an Excel worksheet for Roslyn Thomas, the President of Texas Spectrum Wireless. The worksheet displays the first quarter sales of wireless accessories for the current year, and includes a chart to visually represent the data. Your completed worksheet will look similar to Figure 1.1.

Project Files

For Project 1A, you will need the following file:
New blank Excel workbook
You will save your workbook as:
Lastname_Firstname_1A_Quarterly_Sales

Project Results

Figure 1.1
Project 1A Quarterly Sales

226 Excel | Chapter 1: Creating a Worksheet and Charting Data

Scenario – Each chapter opens with a story that sets the stage for the projects the student will create.

Project Results – Shows students how their final outcome will appear.

Key Feature

Microsoft Procedural Syntax – Steps are written to put the student in the right place at the right time.

Color Coding – Color variations between the two projects in each chapter make it easy to identify which project students are working on.

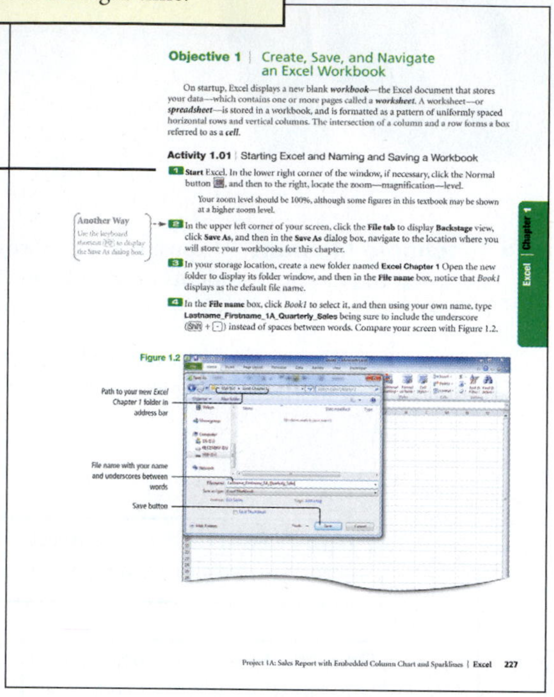
Objective 1 | Create, Save, and Navigate an Excel Workbook

On startup, Excel displays a new blank *workbook*—the Excel document that stores your data—which contains one or more pages called a *worksheet*. A worksheet—or *spreadsheet*—is stored in a workbook, and is formatted as a pattern of uniformly spaced horizontal rows and vertical columns. The intersection of a column and a row forms a box referred to as a *cell*.

Activity 1.01 | Starting Excel and Naming and Saving a Workbook

1 Start Excel. In the lower right corner of the window, if necessary, click the Normal button, and then to the right, locate the zoom—magnification—level.

Your zoom level should be 100%, although some figures in this textbook may be shown at a higher zoom level.

2 In the upper left corner of your screen, click the File tab to display Backstage view, click Save As, and then in the Save As dialog box, navigate to the location where you will store your workbooks for this chapter.

3 In your storage location, create a new folder named Excel Chapter 1 Open the new folder to display its folder window, and then in the File name box, notice that *Book1* displays as the default file name.

4 In the File name box, click *Book1* to select it, and then using your own name, type Lastname_Firstname_1A_Quarterly_Sales being sure to include the underscore (Shift + -) instead of spaces between words. Compare your screen with Figure 1.2.

Figure 1.2

Project 1A: Sales Report with Embedded Column Chart and Sparklines | Excel 227

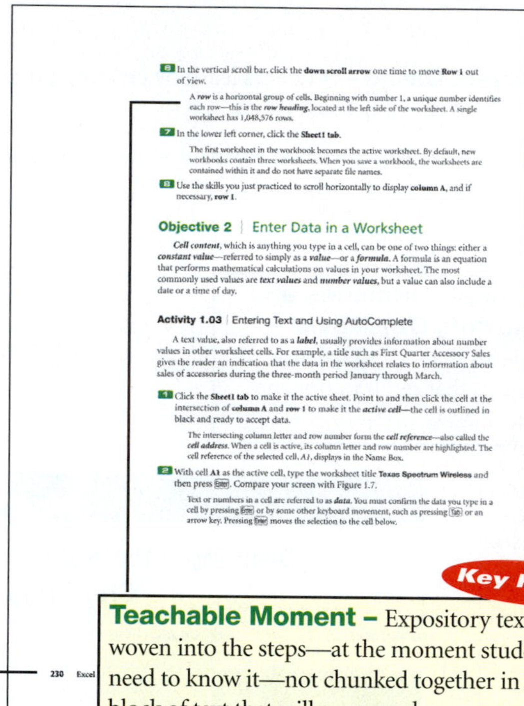
6 In the vertical scroll bar, click the down scroll arrow one time to move Row 1 out of view.

A *row* is a horizontal group of cells. Beginning with number 1, a unique number identifies each row—this is the *row heading*, located at the left side of the worksheet. A single worksheet has 1,048,576 rows.

7 In the lower left corner, click the Sheet1 tab.

The first worksheet in the workbook becomes the active worksheet. By default, new workbooks contain three worksheets. When you save a workbook, the worksheets are contained within it and do not have separate file names.

8 Use the skills you just practiced to scroll horizontally to display column A, and if necessary, row 1.

Objective 2 | Enter Data in a Worksheet

Cell content, which is anything you type in a cell, can be one of two things: either a *constant value*—referred to simply as a *value*—or a *formula*. A formula is an equation that performs mathematical calculations on values in your worksheet. The most commonly used values are *text values* and *number values*, but a value can also include a date or a time of day.

Activity 1.03 | Entering Text and Using AutoComplete

A text value, also referred to as a *label*, usually provides information about number values in other worksheet cells. For example, a title such as First Quarter Accessory Sales gives the reader an indication that the data in the worksheet relates to information about sales of accessories during the three-month period January through March.

1 Click the Sheet1 tab to make it the active sheet. Point to and then click the cell at the intersection of column A and row 1 to make it the *active cell*—the cell is outlined in black and ready to accept data.

The intersecting column letter and row number form the *cell reference*—also called the *cell address*. When a cell is active, its column letter and row number are highlighted. The cell reference of the selected cell, *A1*, displays in the Name Box.

2 With cell A1 as the active cell, type the worksheet title Texas Spectrum Wireless and then press Enter. Compare your screen with Figure 1.7.

Text or numbers in a cell are referred to as *data*. You must confirm the data you type in a cell by pressing Enter or by some other keyboard movement, such as pressing Tab or an arrow key. Pressing Enter moves the selection to the cell below.

230 Excel

Key Feature

Sequential Pagination – Students are given actual page numbers to navigate through the textbook instead of confusing letters and abbreviations.

Key Feature

Teachable Moment – Expository text is woven into the steps—at the moment students need to know it—not chunked together in a block of text that will go unread.

End-of-Chapter

Content-Based Assessments – Assessments with defined solutions.

Objective List - Every project includes a listing of covered objectives from Projects A and B.

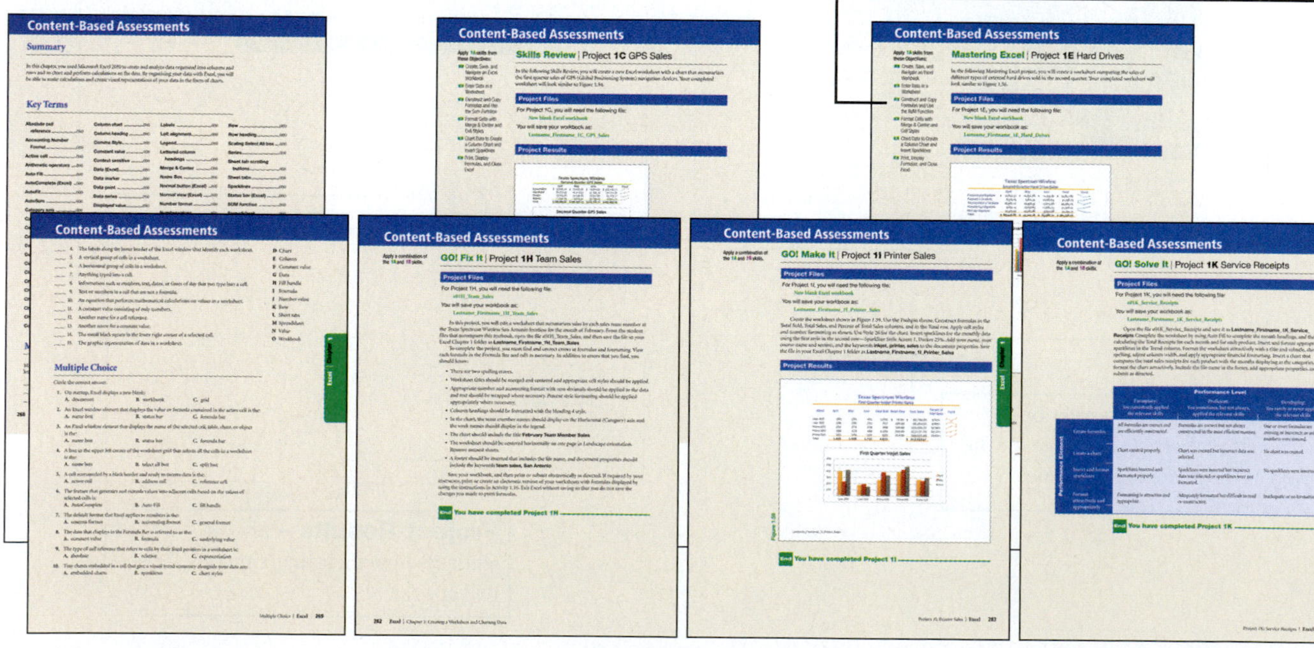

End-of-Chapter

Outcomes-Based Assessments – Assessments with open-ended solutions.

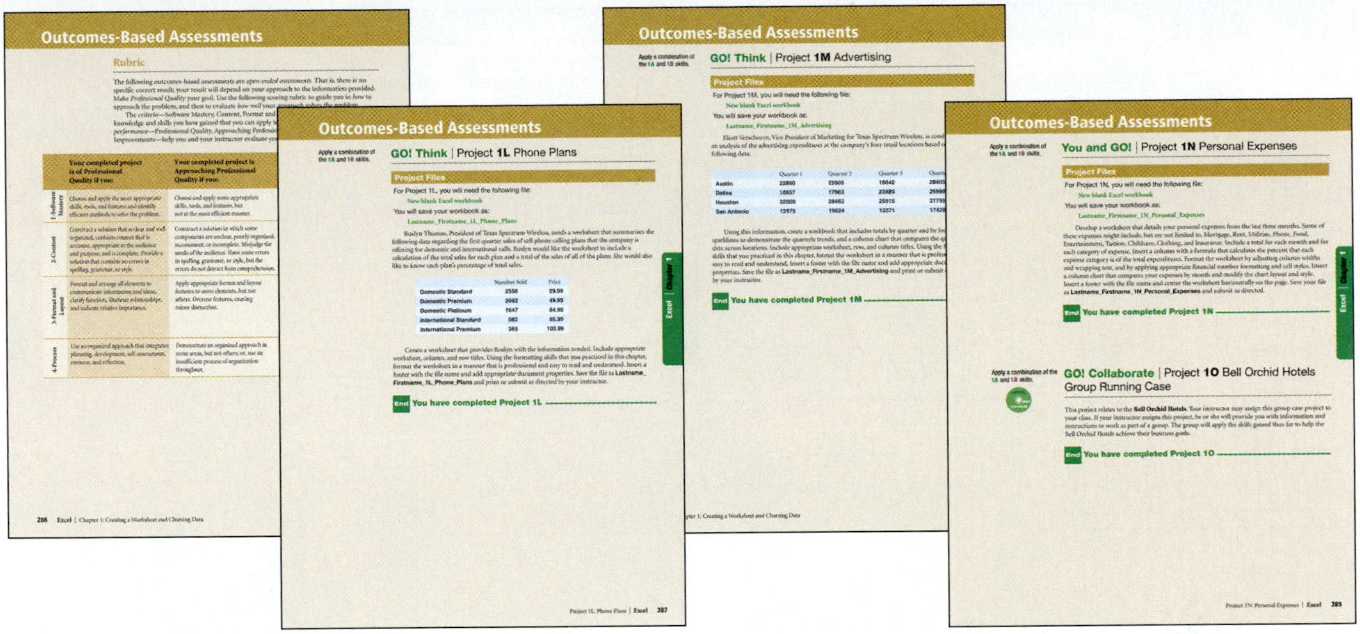

Task-Specific Rubric – A matrix specific to the **GO! Solve It** projects that states the criteria and standards for grading these defined-solution projects.

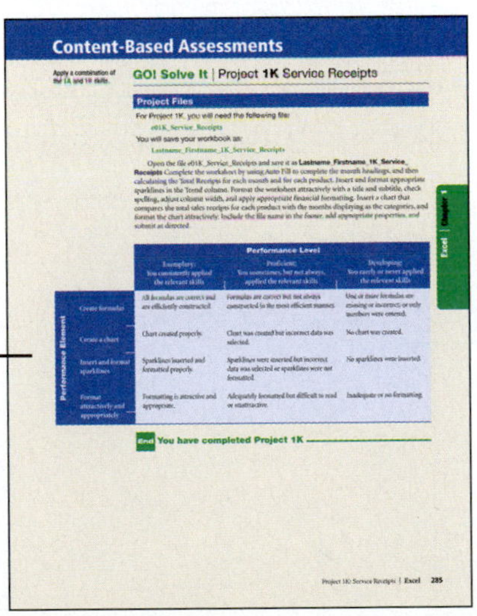

Outcomes Rubric – A matrix specific to the **GO! Think** projects that states the criteria and standards for grading these open-ended assessments.

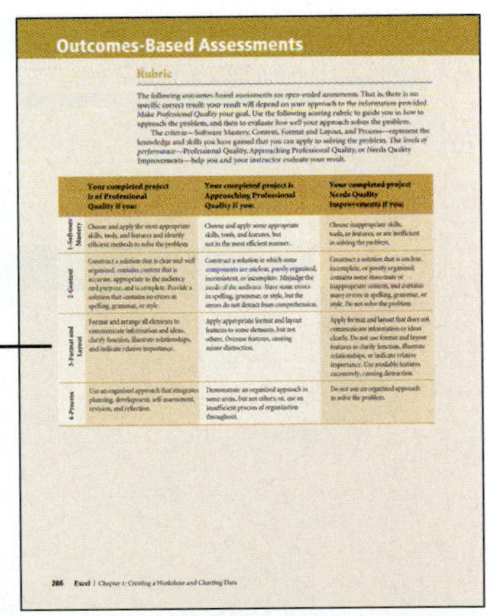

Student CD – All student data files readily available on a CD that comes with the book.

Podcasts – Videos that teach some of the more difficult topics when working with Microsoft applications.

Student Videos – A visual and audio walk-through of every A and B project in the book (see sample images on following page).

End-of-Chapter

Outcomes-Based Assessments – Assessments with open-ended solutions.

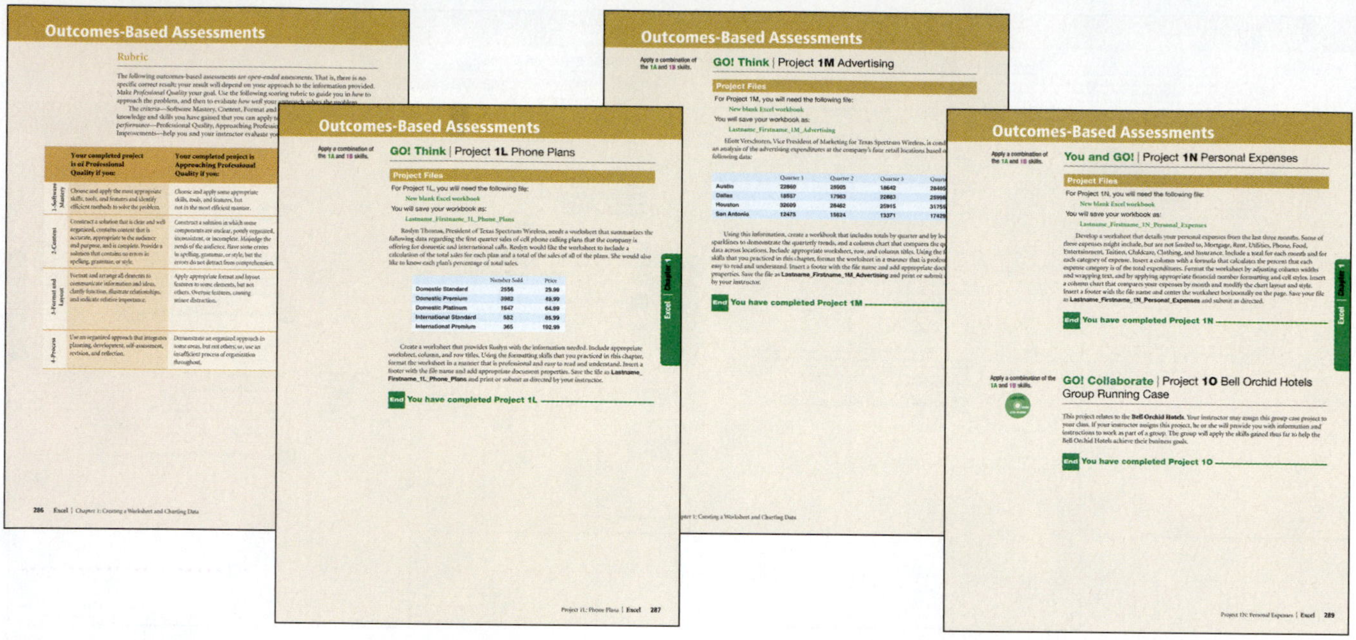

Task-Specific Rubric – A matrix specific to the **GO! Solve It** projects that states the criteria and standards for grading these defined-solution projects.

Outcomes Rubric – A matrix specific to the **GO! Think** projects that states the criteria and standards for grading these open-ended assessments.

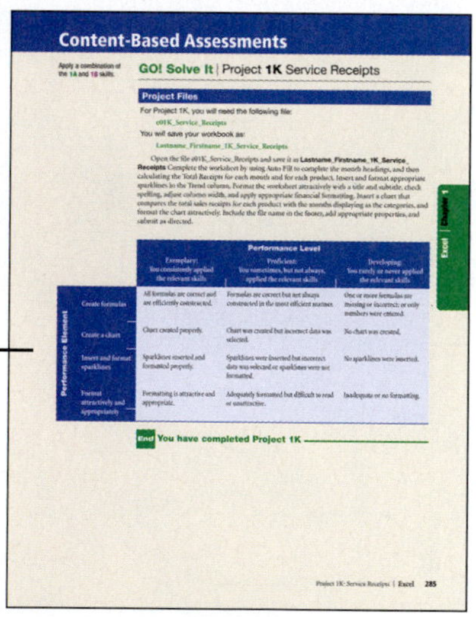

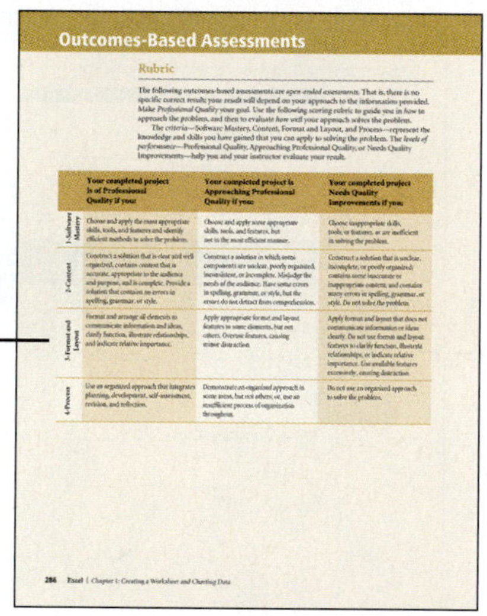

Student CD – All student data files readily available on a CD that comes with the book.

Student Videos – A visual and audio walk-through of every A and B project in the book (see sample images on following page).

Using the Common Features of Microsoft Office 2010

OUTCOMES

At the end of this chapter you will be able to:

OBJECTIVES

Mastering these objectives will enable you to:

PROJECT 1A

Create, save, and print a Microsoft Office 2010 file.

1. Use Windows Explorer to Locate Files and Folders (p. 3)
2. Locate and Start a Microsoft Office 2010 Program (p. 6)
3. Enter and Edit Text in an Office 2010 Program (p. 9)
4. Perform Commands from a Dialog Box (p. 11)
5. Create a Folder, Save a File, and Close a Program (p. 13)
6. Add Document Properties and Print a File (p. 18)

PROJECT 1B

Use the Ribbon and dialog boxes to perform common commands in a Microsoft Office 2010 file.

7. Open an Existing File and Save It with a New Name (p. 22)
8. Explore Options for an Application (p. 25)
9. Perform Commands from the Ribbon (p. 26)
10. Apply Formatting in Office Programs (p. 32)
11. Use the Microsoft Office 2010 Help System (p. 43)
12. Compress Files (p. 44)

olly/Shutterstock

In This Chapter

In this chapter, you will use Windows Explorer to navigate the Windows folder structure, create a folder, and save files in Microsoft Office 2010 programs. You will also practice using the features of Microsoft Office 2010 that are common across the major programs that comprise the Microsoft Office 2010 suite. These common features include creating, saving, and printing files.

Common features also include the new Paste Preview and Microsoft Office Backstage view. You will apply formatting, perform commands, and compress files. You will see that creating professional-quality documents is easy and quick in Microsoft Office 2010, and that finding your way around is fast and efficient.

The projects in this chapter relate to **Oceana Palm Grill**, which is a chain of 25 casual, full-service restaurants based in Austin, Texas. The Oceana Palm Grill owners plan an aggressive expansion program. To expand by 15 additional restaurants in North Carolina and Florida by 2018, the company must attract new investors, develop new menus, and recruit new employees, all while adhering to the company's quality guidelines and maintaining its reputation for excellent service. To succeed, the company plans to build on its past success and maintain its quality elements.

Project 1A PowerPoint File

myitlab
Project 1A Training

Project Activities

In Activities 1.01 through 1.06, you will create a PowerPoint file, save it in a folder that you create by using Windows Explorer, and then print the file or submit it electronically as directed by your instructor. Your completed PowerPoint slide will look similar to Figure 1.1.

Project Files

For Project 1A, you will need the following file:

New blank PowerPoint presentation

You will save your file as:

Lastname_Firstname_1A_Menu_Plan

Project Results

Oceana Palm Grill Menu Plan
Prepared by Firstname Lastname
For Laura Hernandez

Figure 1.1
Project 1A Menu Plan

Objective 1 | Use Windows Explorer to Locate Files and Folders

A ***file*** is a collection of information stored on a computer under a single name, for example, a Word document or a PowerPoint presentation. Every file is stored in a ***folder***—a container in which you store files—or a ***subfolder***, which is a folder within a folder. Your Windows operating system stores and organizes your files and folders, which is a primary task of an operating system.

You ***navigate***—explore within the organizing structure of Windows—to create, save, and find your files and folders by using the ***Windows Explorer*** program. Windows Explorer displays the files and folders on your computer, and is at work anytime you are viewing the contents of files and folders in a ***window***. A window is a rectangular area on a computer screen in which programs and content appear; a window can be moved, resized, minimized, or closed.

Activity 1.01 | Using Windows Explorer to Locate Files and Folders

1 Turn on your computer and display the Windows ***desktop***—the opening screen in Windows that simulates your work area.

> **Note | Comparing Your Screen with the Figures in This Textbook**
>
> Your screen will match the figures shown in this textbook if you set your screen resolution to 1024 × 768. At other resolutions, your screen will closely resemble, but not match, the figures shown. To view your screen's resolution, on the Windows 7 desktop, right-click in a blank area, and then click Screen resolution. In Windows Vista, right-click a blank area, click Personalize, and then click Display Settings. In Windows XP, right-click the desktop, click Properties, and then click the Settings tab.

2 In your CD/DVD tray, insert the **Student CD** that accompanies this textbook. Wait a few moments for an **AutoPlay** window to display. Compare your screen with Figure 1.2.

AutoPlay is a Windows feature that lets you choose which program to use to start different kinds of media, such as music CDs, or CDs and DVDs containing photos; it displays when you plug in or insert media or storage devices.

> **Note | If You Do Not Have the Student CD**
>
> If you do not have the Student CD, consult the inside back flap of this textbook for instructions on how to download the files from the Pearson Web site.

Figure 1.2

3 In the upper right corner of the **AutoPlay** window, move your mouse over—***point*** to—the **Close** button, and then ***click***—press the left button on your mouse pointing device one time.

4 On the left side of the **Windows taskbar**, click the **Start** button to display the **Start menu**. Compare your screen with Figure 1.3.

The ***Windows taskbar*** is the area along the lower edge of the desktop that contains the ***Start button*** and an area to display buttons for open programs. The Start button displays the ***Start menu***, which provides a list of choices and is the main gateway to your computer's programs, folders, and settings.

Figure 1.3

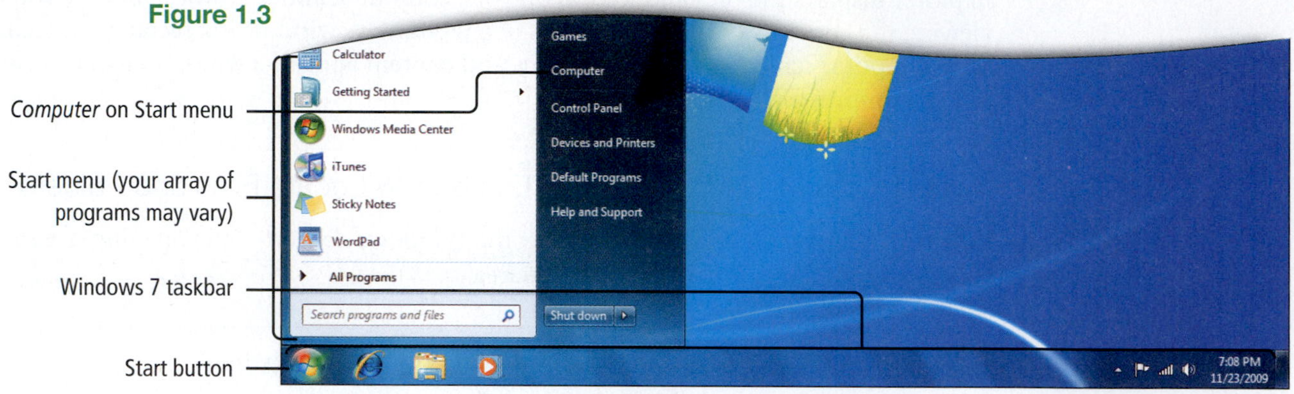

5 On the right side of the **Start menu**, click **Computer** to see the disk drives and other hardware connected to your computer. Compare your screen with Figure 1.4, and then take a moment to study the table in Figure 1.5.

The ***folder window*** for *Computer* displays. A folder window displays the contents of the current folder, ***library***, or device, and contains helpful parts so that you can navigate within Windows.

In Windows 7, a library is a collection of items, such as files and folders, assembled from *various locations*; the locations might be on your computer, an external hard drive, removable media, or someone else's computer.

The difference between a folder and a library is that a library can include files stored in *different locations*—any disk drive, folder, or other place that you can store files and folders.

Figure 1.4

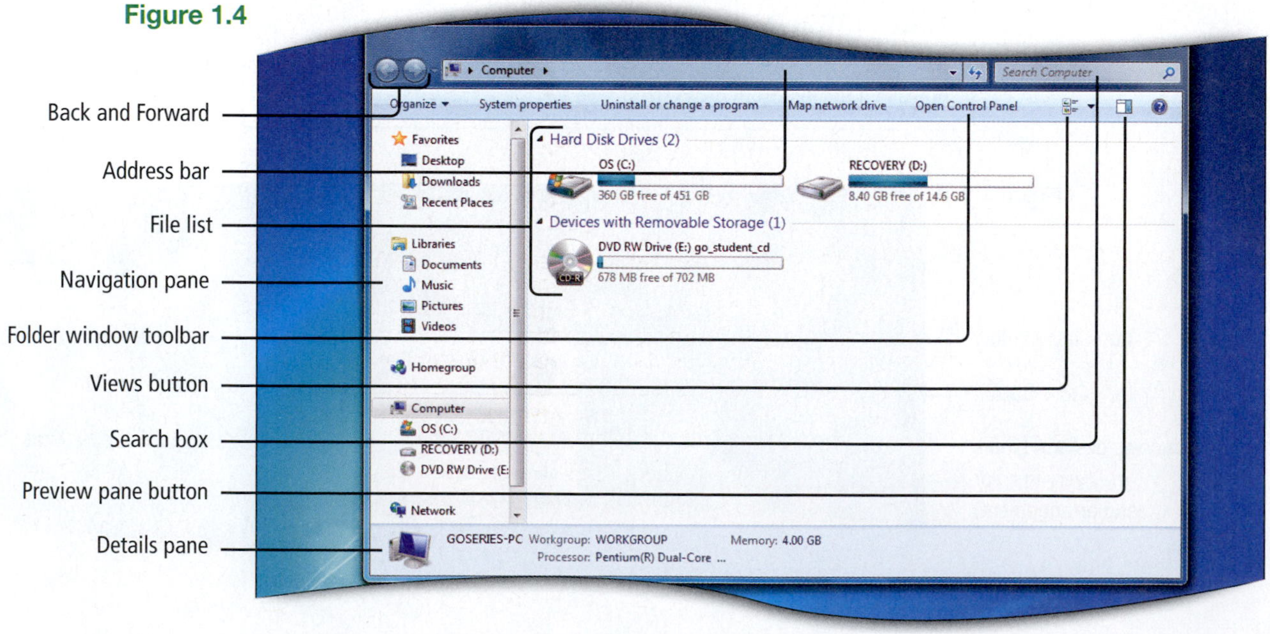

Window Part	Use to:
Address bar	Navigate to a different folder or library, or go back to a previous one.
Back and Forward buttons	Navigate to other folders or libraries you have already opened without closing the current window. These buttons work in conjunction with the address bar; that is, after you use the address bar to change folders, you can use the Back button to return to the previous folder.
Details pane	Display the most common file properties—information about a file, such as the author, the date you last changed the file, and any descriptive ***tags***, which are custom file properties that you create to help find and organize your files.
File list	Display the contents of the current folder or library. In Computer, the file list displays the disk drives.
Folder window for *Computer*	Display the contents of the current folder, library, or device. The Folder window contains helpful features so that you can navigate within Windows.
Folder window toolbar	Perform common tasks, such as changing the view of your files and folders or burning files to a CD. The buttons available change to display only relevant tasks.
Navigation pane	Navigate to, open, and display favorites, libraries, folders, saved searches, and an expandable list of drives.
Preview pane button	Display (if you have chosen to open this pane) the contents of most files without opening them in a program. To open the preview pane, click the Preview pane button on the toolbar to turn it on and off.
Search box	Look for an item in the current folder or library by typing a word or phrase in the search box.
Views button	Choose how to view the contents of the current location.

Figure 1.5

6 On the toolbar of the **Computer** folder window, click the **Views button arrow**—the small arrow to the right of the Views button—to display a list of views that you can apply to the file list. If necessary, on the list, click **Tiles**.

The Views button is a ***split button***; clicking the main part of the button performs a ***command*** and clicking the arrow opens a menu or list. A command is an instruction to a computer program that causes an action to be carried out.

When you open a folder or a library, you can change how the files display in the file list. For example, you might prefer to see large or small ***icons***—pictures that represent a program, a file, a folder, or some other object—or an arrangement that lets you see various types of information about each file. Each time you click the Views button, the window changes, cycling through several views—additional view options are available by clicking the Views button arrow.

Another Way

Point to the CD/DVD drive, right-click, and then click Open.

7 In the **file list**, under **Devices with Removable Storage**, point to your **CD/DVD Drive**, and then ***double-click***—click the left mouse button two times in rapid succession—to display the list of folders on the CD. Compare your screen with Figure 1.6.

When double-clicking, keep your hand steady between clicks; this is more important than the speed of the two clicks.

Figure 1.6

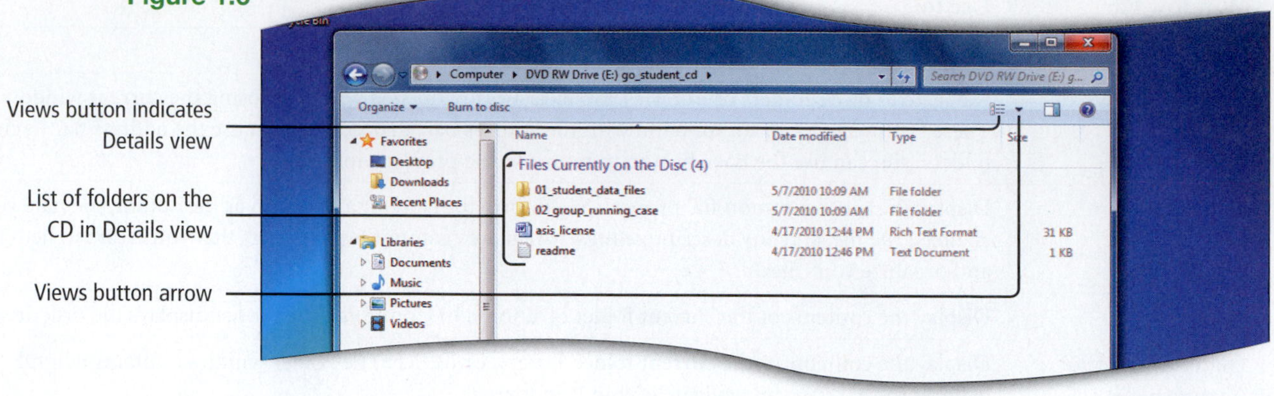

8 In the **file list**, point to the folder **01_student_data_files** and double-click to display the list of subfolders in the folder. Double-click to open the folder **01_common_features**. Compare your screen with Figure 1.7.

The Student Resource CD includes files that you will use to complete the projects in this textbook. If you prefer, you can also copy the **01_student_data_files** folder to a location on your computer's hard drive or to a removable device such as a ***USB flash drive***, which is a small storage device that plugs into a computer USB port. Your instructor might direct you to other locations where these files are located; for example, on your learning management system.

Figure 1.7

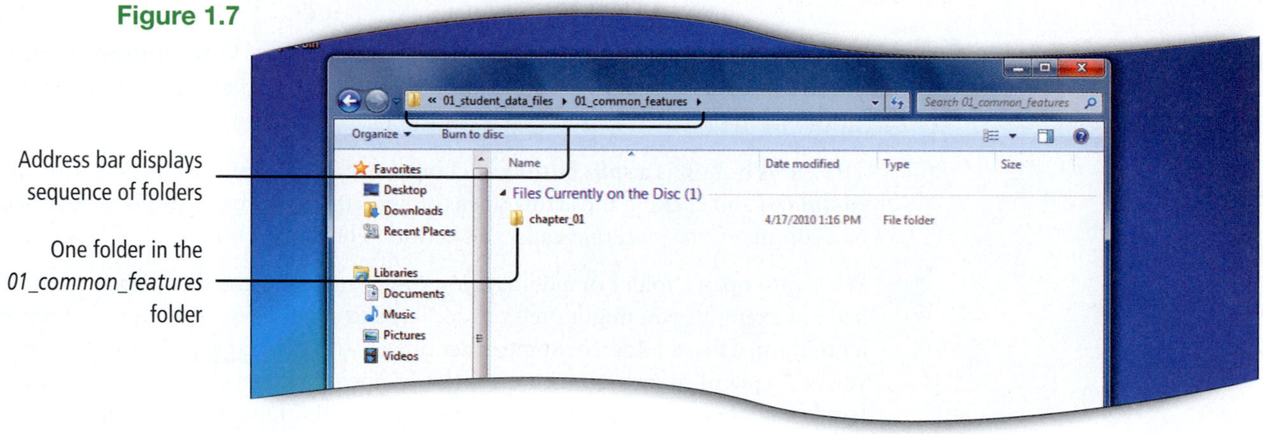

9 In the upper right corner of the **Computer** window, click the **Close** button to redisplay your desktop.

Objective 2 | Locate and Start a Microsoft Office 2010 Program

Microsoft Office 2010 includes programs, servers, and services for individuals, small organizations, and large enterprises. A ***program***, also referred to as an ***application***, is a set of instructions used by a computer to perform a task, such as word processing or accounting.

Activity 1.02 | Locating and Starting a Microsoft Office 2010 Program

1 On the **Windows taskbar**, click the **Start** button to display the **Start** menu.

2 From the displayed **Start** menu, locate the group of **Microsoft Office 2010** programs on your computer—the Office program icons from which you can start the program may be located on your Start menu, in a Microsoft Office folder on the **All Programs** list, on your desktop, or any combination of these locations; the location will vary depending on how your computer is configured.

All Programs is an area of the Start menu that displays all the available programs on your computer system.

3 Examine Figure 1.8, and notice the programs that are included in the Microsoft Office Professional Plus 2010 group of programs. (Your group of programs may vary.)

Microsoft Word is a word processing program, with which you create and share documents by using its writing tools.

Microsoft Excel is a spreadsheet program, with which you calculate and analyze numbers and create charts.

Microsoft Access is a database program, with which you can collect, track, and report data.

Microsoft PowerPoint is a presentation program, with which you can communicate information with high-impact graphics and video.

Additional popular Office programs include ***Microsoft Outlook*** to manage e-mail and organizational activities, ***Microsoft Publisher*** to create desktop publishing documents such as brochures, and ***Microsoft OneNote*** to manage notes that you make at meetings or in classes and to share notes with others on the Web.

The Professional Plus version of Office 2010 also includes ***Microsoft SharePoint Workspace*** to share information with others in a team environment and ***Microsoft InfoPath Designer and Filler*** to create forms and gather data.

Figure 1.8

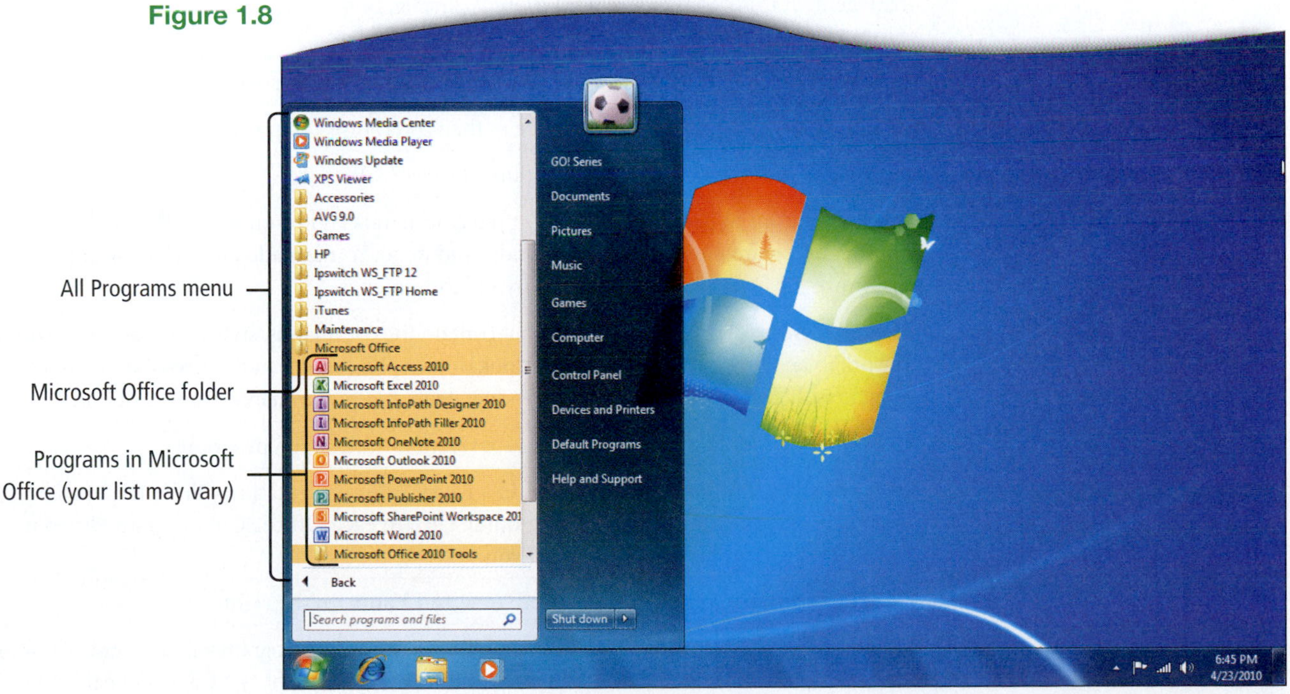

4 Click to open the program **Microsoft PowerPoint 2010**. Compare your screen with Figure 1.9, and then take a moment to study the description of these screen elements in the table in Figure 1.10.

Figure 1.9

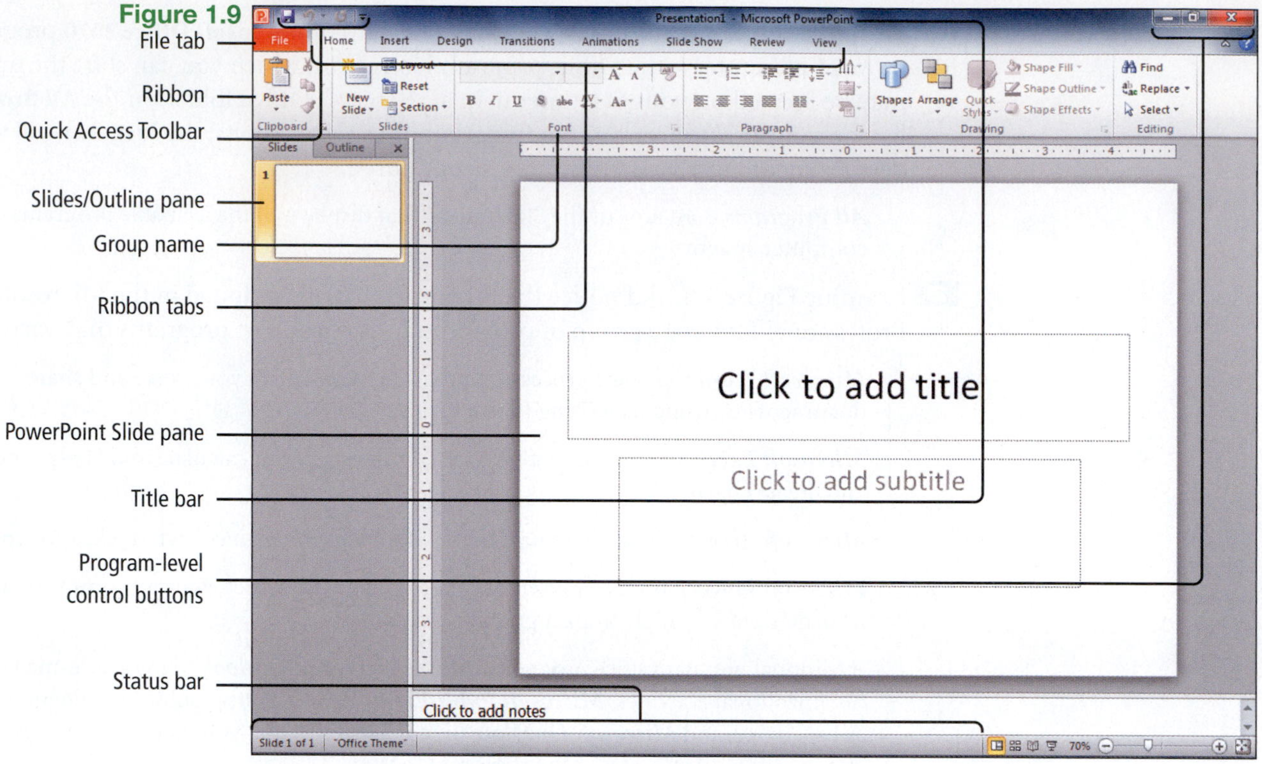

Screen Element	Description
File tab	Displays Microsoft Office Backstage view, which is a centralized space for all of your file management tasks such as opening, saving, printing, publishing, or sharing a file—all the things you can do *with* a file.
Group names	Indicate the name of the groups of related commands on the displayed tab.
PowerPoint Slide pane	Displays a large image of the active slide in the PowerPoint program.
Program-level control buttons	Minimizes, restores, or closes the program window.
Quick Access Toolbar	Displays buttons to perform frequently used commands and resources with a single click. The default commands include Save, Undo, and Redo. You can add and delete buttons to customize the Quick Access Toolbar for your convenience.
Ribbon	Displays a group of task-oriented tabs that contain the commands, styles, and resources you need to work in an Office 2010 program. The look of your Ribbon depends on your screen resolution. A high resolution will display more individual items and button names on the Ribbon.
Ribbon tabs	Display the names of the task-oriented tabs relevant to the open program.
Slides/Outline pane	Displays either thumbnails of the slides in a PowerPoint presentation (Slides tab) or the outline of the presentation's content (Outline tab). In each Office 2010 program, different panes display in different ways to assist you.
Status bar	Displays file information on the left and View and Zoom on the right.
Title bar	Displays the name of the file and the name of the program. The program window control buttons—Minimize, Maximize/Restore Down, and Close—are grouped on the right side of the title bar.

Figure 1.10

Objective 3 | Enter and Edit Text in an Office 2010 Program

All of the programs in Office 2010 require some typed text. Your keyboard is still the primary method of entering information into your computer. Techniques to ***edit***—make changes to—text are similar among all of the Office 2010 programs.

Activity 1.03 | Entering and Editing Text in an Office 2010 Program

1 In the middle of the PowerPoint Slide pane, point to the text *Click to add title* to display the [I] pointer, and then click one time.

The ***insertion point***—a blinking vertical line that indicates where text or graphics will be inserted—displays.

In Office 2010 programs, the mouse ***pointer***—any symbol that displays on your screen in response to moving your mouse device—displays in different shapes depending on the task you are performing and the area of the screen to which you are pointing.

2 Type **Oceana Grille Info** and notice how the insertion point moves to the right as you type. Point slightly to the right of the letter *e* in *Grille* and click to place the insertion point there. Compare your screen with Figure 1.11.

Figure 1.11

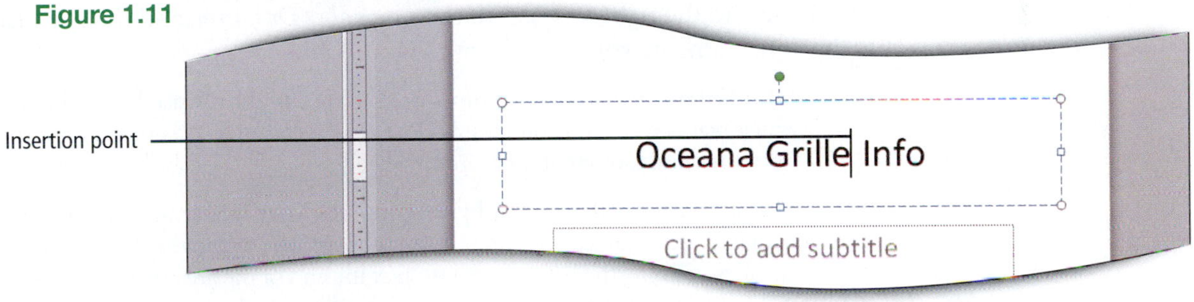

3 On your keyboard, locate and press the [Backspace] key to delete the letter *e*.

Pressing [Backspace] removes a character to the left of the insertion point.

4 Point slightly to the left of the *I* in *Info* and click one time to place the insertion point there. Type **Menu** and then press [Spacebar] one time. Compare your screen with Figure 1.12.

By ***default***, when you type text in an Office program, existing text moves to the right to make space for new typing. Default refers to the current selection or setting that is automatically used by a program unless you specify otherwise.

Figure 1.12

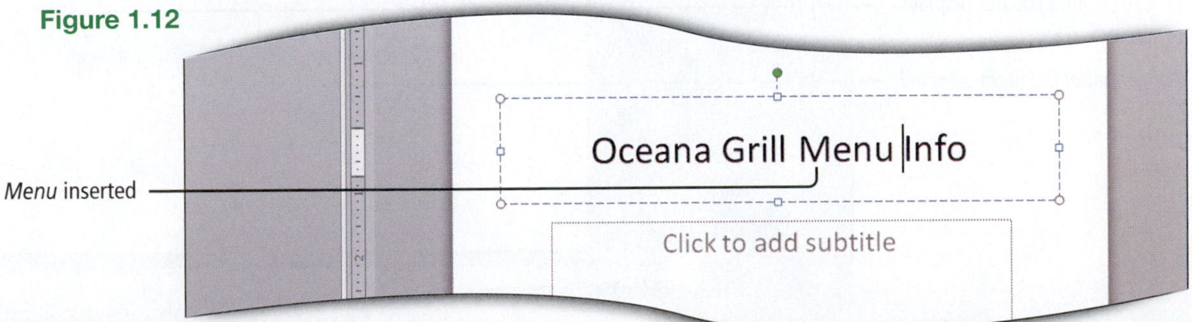

5 Press [Del] four times to delete *Info* and then type **Plan**

Pressing [Del] removes—deletes—a character to the right of the insertion point.

6 With your insertion point blinking after the word *Plan*, on your keyboard, hold down the [Ctrl] key. While holding down [Ctrl], press [←] three times to move the insertion point to the beginning of the word *Grill*.

This is a ***keyboard shortcut***—a key or combination of keys that performs a task that would otherwise require a mouse. This keyboard shortcut moves the insertion point to the beginning of the previous word.

A keyboard shortcut is commonly indicated as [Ctrl] + [←] (or some other combination of keys) to indicate that you hold down the first key while pressing the second key. A keyboard shortcut can also include three keys, in which case you hold down the first two and then press the third. For example, [Ctrl] + [Shift] + [←] selects one word to the left.

7 With the insertion point blinking at the beginning of the word *Grill*, type **Palm** and press [Spacebar].

8 Click anywhere in the text *Click to add subtitle*. With the insertion point blinking, type the following and include the spelling error: **Prepered by Annabel Dunham**

9 With your mouse, point slightly to the left of the *A* in *Annabel*, hold down the left mouse button, and then ***drag***—hold down the left mouse button while moving your mouse—to the right to select the text *Annabel Dunham*, and then release the mouse button. Compare your screen with Figure 1.13.

The ***Mini toolbar*** displays commands that are commonly used with the selected object, which places common commands close to your pointer. When you move the pointer away from the Mini toolbar, it fades from view.

To ***select*** refers to highlighting, by dragging with your mouse, areas of text or data or graphics so that the selection can be edited, formatted, copied, or moved. The action of dragging includes releasing the left mouse button at the end of the area you want to select. The Office programs recognize a selected area as one unit, to which you can make changes. Selecting text may require some practice. If you are not satisfied with your result, click anywhere outside of the selection, and then begin again.

Figure 1.13

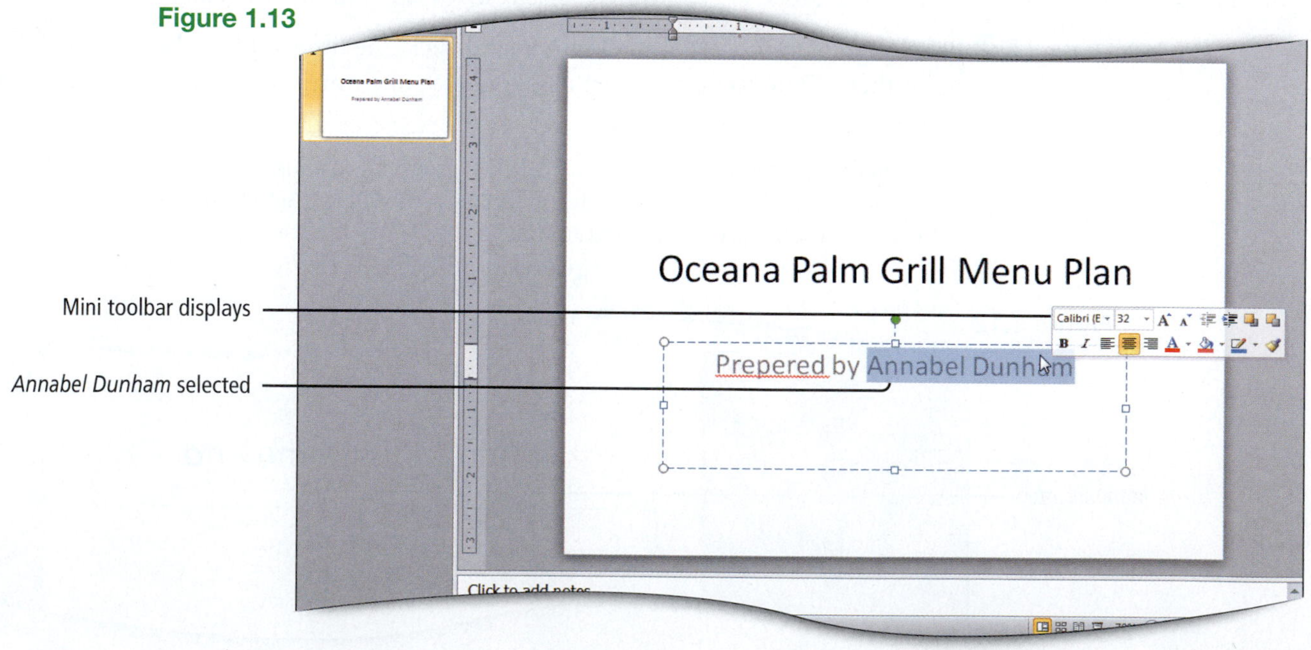

10 With the text *Annabel Dunham* selected, type your own firstname and lastname.

In any Windows-based program, such as the Microsoft Office 2010 programs, selected text is deleted and then replaced when you begin to type new text. You will save time by developing good techniques to select and then edit or replace selected text, which is easier than pressing the Del key numerous times to delete text that you do not want.

11 Notice that the misspelled word *Prepered* displays with a wavy red underline; additionally, all or part of your name might display with a wavy red underline.

Office 2010 has a dictionary of words against which all entered text is checked. In Word and PowerPoint, words that are *not* in the dictionary display a wavy red line, indicating a possible misspelled word or a proper name or an unusual word—none of which are in the Office 2010 dictionary.

In Excel and Access, you can initiate a check of the spelling, but wavy red underlines do not display.

12 Point to *Prepered* and then ***right-click***—click your right mouse button one time.

The Mini toolbar and a ***shortcut menu*** display. A shortcut menu displays commands and options relevant to the selected text or object—known as ***context-sensitive commands*** because they relate to the item you right-clicked.

Here, the shortcut menu displays commands related to the misspelled word. You can click the suggested correct spelling *Prepared*, click Ignore All to ignore the misspelling, add the word to the Office dictionary, or click Spelling to display a ***dialog box***. A dialog box is a small window that contains options for completing a task. Whenever you see a command followed by an ***ellipsis*** (...), which is a set of three dots indicating incompleteness, clicking the command will always display a dialog box.

13 On the displayed shortcut menu, click **Prepared** to correct the misspelled word. If necessary, point to any parts of your name that display a wavy red underline, right-click, and then on the shortcut menu, click Ignore All so that Office will no longer mark your name with a wavy underline in this file.

More Knowledge | Adding to the Office Dictionary

The main dictionary contains the most common words, but does not include all proper names, technical terms, or acronyms. You can add words, acronyms, and proper names to the Office dictionary by clicking Add to Dictionary when they are flagged, and you might want to do so for your own name and other proper names and terms that you type often.

Objective 4 | Perform Commands from a Dialog Box

In a dialog box, you make decisions about an individual object or topic. A dialog box also offers a way to adjust a number of settings at one time.

Activity 1.04 | Performing Commands from a Dialog Box

1 Point anywhere in the blank area above the title *Oceana Palm Grill Menu Plan* to display the pointer.

2 Right-click to display a shortcut menu. Notice the command *Format Background* followed by an ellipsis (...). Compare your screen with Figure 1.14.

Recall that a command followed by an ellipsis indicates that a dialog box will display if you click the command.

Figure 1.14

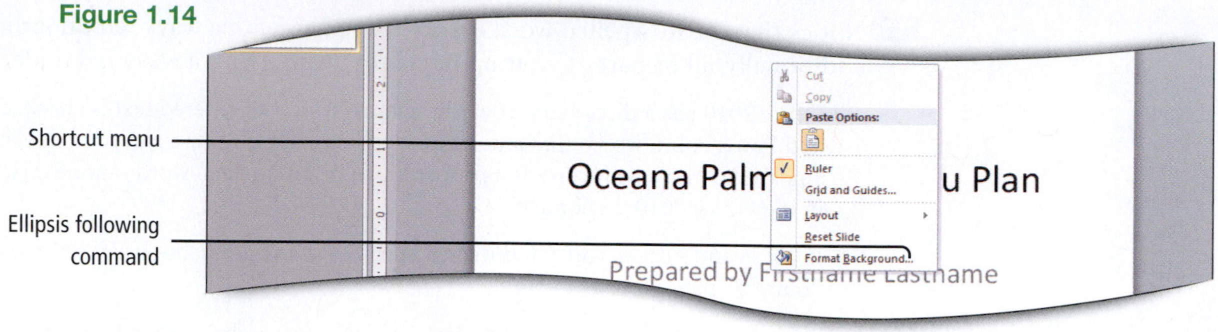

3 Click **Format Background** to display the **Format Background** dialog box, and then compare your screen with Figure 1.15.

Figure 1.15

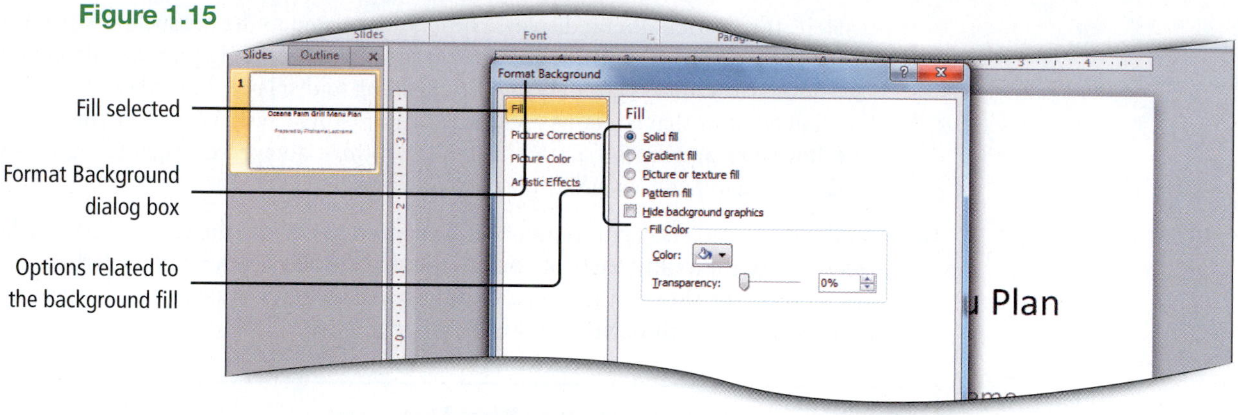

4 On the left, if necessary, click **Fill** to display the **Fill** options.

Fill is the inside color of an object. Here, the dialog box displays the option group names on the left; some dialog boxes provide a set of tabs across the top from which you can display different sets of options.

5 On the right, under **Fill**, click the **Gradient fill** option button.

The dialog box displays additional settings related to the gradient fill option. An ***option button*** is a round button that enables you to make one choice among two or more options. In a gradient fill, one color fades into another.

6 Click the **Preset colors arrow**—the arrow in the box to the right of the text *Preset colors*—and then in the gallery, in the second row, point to the fifth fill color to display the ScreenTip *Fog*.

A ***gallery*** is an Office feature that displays a list of potential results. A ***ScreenTip*** displays useful information about mouse actions, such as pointing to screen elements or dragging.

7 Click **Fog**, and then notice that the fill color is applied to your slide. Click the **Type arrow**, and then click **Rectangular** to change the pattern of the fill color. Compare your screen with Figure 1.16.

Figure 1.16

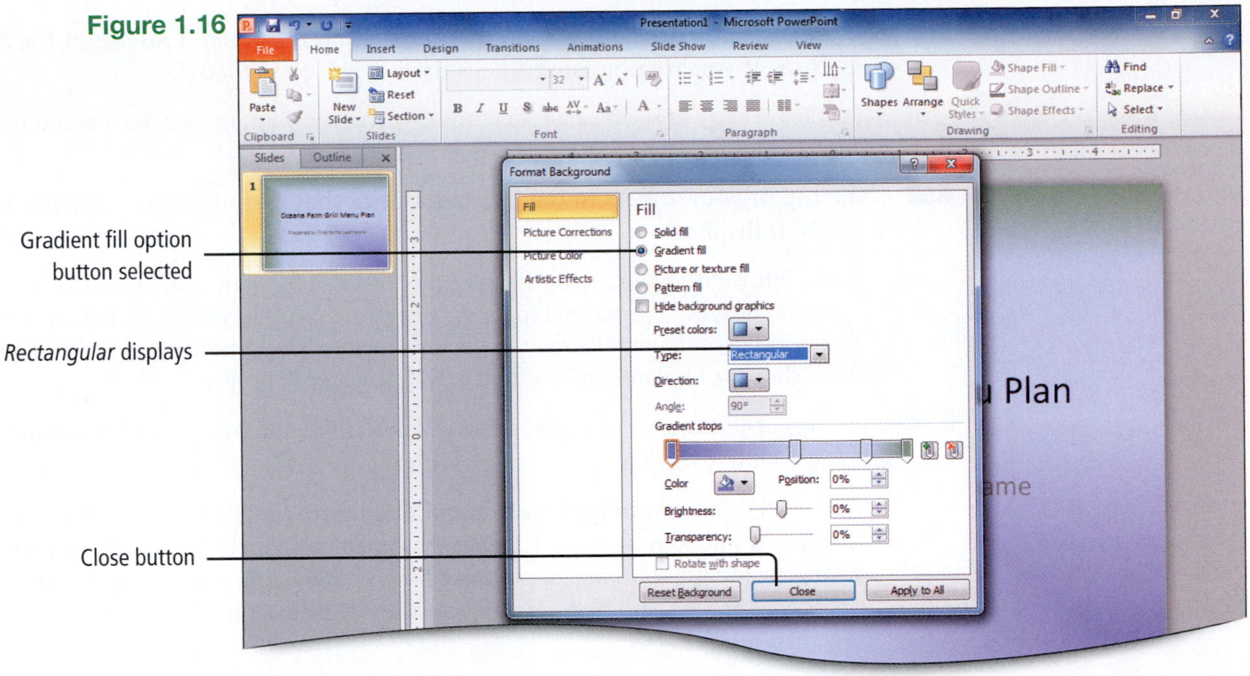

8 At the bottom of the dialog box, click **Close**.

As you progress in your study of Microsoft Office, you will practice using many dialog boxes and applying dramatic effects such as this to your Word documents, Excel spreadsheets, Access databases, and PowerPoint slides.

Objective 5 | Create a Folder, Save a File, and Close a Program

A ***location*** is any disk drive, folder, or other place in which you can store files and folders. Where you store your files depends on how and where you use your data. For example, for your classes, you might decide to store primarily on a removable USB flash drive so that you can carry your files to different locations and access your files on different computers.

If you do most of your work on a single computer, for example your home desktop system or your laptop computer that you take with you to school or work, store your files in one of the Libraries—Documents, Music, Pictures, or Videos—provided by your Windows operating system.

Although the Windows operating system helps you to create and maintain a logical folder structure, take the time to name your files and folders in a consistent manner.

Activity 1.05 | Creating a Folder, Saving a File, and Closing a Program

A PowerPoint presentation is an example of a file. Office 2010 programs use a common dialog box provided by the Windows operating system to assist you in saving files. In this activity, you will create a folder on a USB flash drive in which to store files. If you prefer to store on your hard drive, you can use similar steps to store files in your My Documents folder in your Documents library.

1 Insert a USB flash drive into your computer, and if necessary, **Close** [x] the **AutoPlay** dialog box. If you are not using a USB flash drive, go to Step 2.

As the first step in saving a file, determine where you want to save the file, and if necessary, insert a storage device.

2 At the top of your screen, in the title bar, notice that *Presentation1 – Microsoft PowerPoint* displays.

Most Office 2010 programs open with a new unsaved file with a default name—*Presentation1*, *Document1*, and so on. As you create your file, your work is temporarily stored in the computer's memory until you initiate a Save command, at which time you must choose a file name and location in which to save your file.

3 In the upper left corner of your screen, click the **File tab** to display **Microsoft Office Backstage** view. Compare your screen with Figure 1.17.

Microsoft Office ***Backstage view*** is a centralized space for tasks related to *file* management; that is why the tab is labeled *File*. File management tasks include, for example, opening, saving, printing, publishing, or sharing a file. The ***Backstage tabs***—*Info*, *Recent*, *New*, *Print*, *Save & Send*, and *Help*—display along the left side. The tabs group file-related tasks together.

Above the Backstage tabs, ***Quick Commands***—*Save*, *Save As*, *Open*, and *Close*—display for quick access to these commands. When you click any of these commands, Backstage view closes and either a dialog box displays or the active file closes.

Here, the ***Info tab*** displays information—*info*—about the current file. In the center panel, various file management tasks are available in groups. For example, if you click the Protect Presentation button, a list of options that you can set for this file that relate to who can open or edit the presentation displays.

On the Info tab, in the right panel, you can also examine the ***document properties***. Document properties, also known as ***metadata***, are details about a file that describe or identify it, such as the title, author name, subject, and keywords that identify the document's topic or contents. On the Info page, a thumbnail image of the current file displays in the upper right corner, which you can click to close Backstage view and return to the document.

More Knowledge | Deciding Where to Store Your Files

Where should you store your files? In the libraries created by Windows 7 (Documents, Pictures, and so on)? On a removable device like a flash drive or external hard drive? In Windows 7, it is easy to find your files, especially if you use the libraries. Regardless of where you save a file, Windows 7 will make it easy to find the file again, even if you are not certain where it might be.

In Windows 7, storing all of your files within a library makes sense. If you perform most of your work on your desktop system or your laptop that travels with you, you can store your files in the libraries created by Windows 7 for your user account—Documents, Pictures, Music, and so on. Within these libraries, you can create folders and subfolders to organize your data. These libraries are a good choice for storing your files because:

- From the Windows Explorer button on the taskbar, your libraries are always just one click away.
- The libraries are designed for their contents; for example, the Pictures folder displays small images of your digital photos.
- You can add new locations to a library; for example, an external hard drive, or a network drive. Locations added to a library behave just like they are on your hard drive.
- Other users of your computer cannot access your libraries.
- The libraries are the default location for opening and saving files within an application, so you will find that you can open and save files with fewer navigation clicks.

Figure 1.17

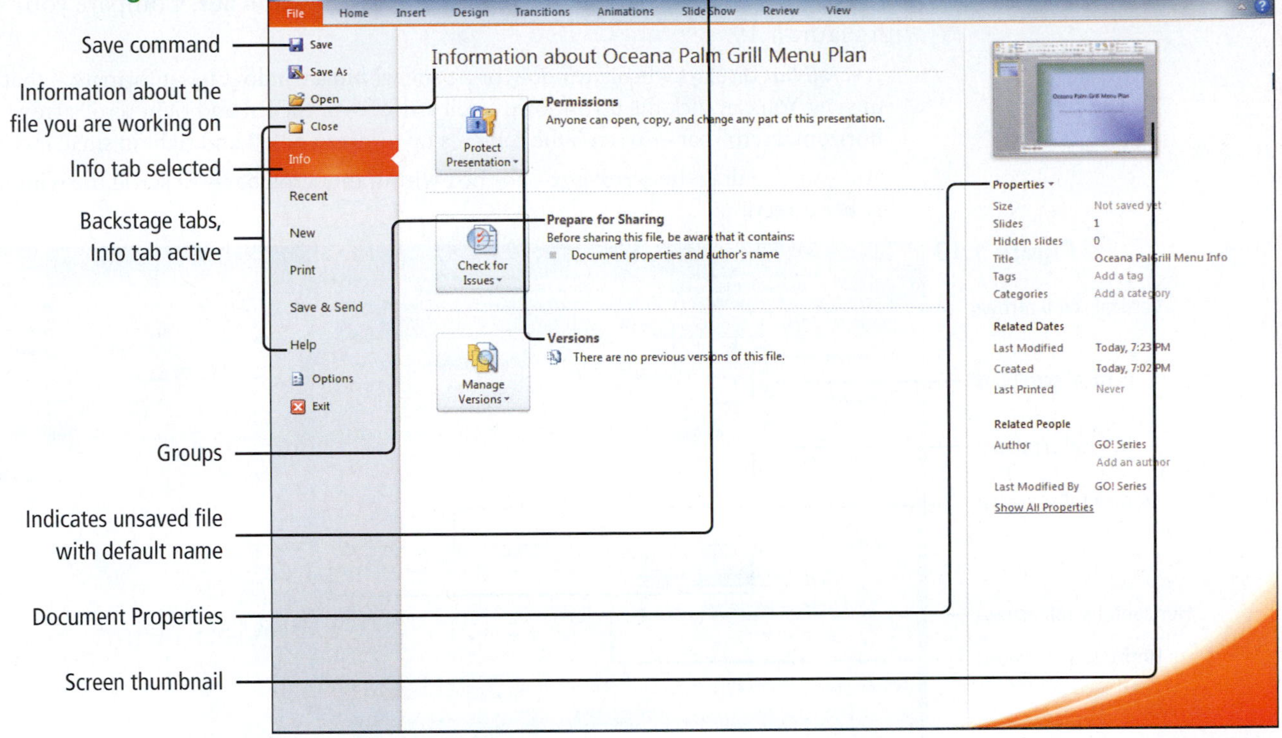

4 Above the **Backstage tabs**, click **Save** to display the **Save As** dialog box.

Backstage view closes and the Save As dialog box, which includes a folder window and an area at the bottom to name the file and set the file type, displays.

When you are saving something for the first time, for example a new PowerPoint presentation, the Save and Save As commands are identical. That is, the Save As dialog box will display if you click Save or if you click Save As.

Note | Saving Your File

After you have named a file and saved it in your desired location, the Save command saves any changes you make to the file without displaying any dialog box. The Save As command will display the Save As dialog box and let you name and save a new file based on the current one—in a location that you choose. After you name and save the new document, the original document closes, and the new document—based on the original one—displays.

5 In the **Save As** dialog box, on the left, locate the **navigation pane**; compare your screen with Figure 1.18.

By default, the Save command opens the Documents library unless your default file location has been changed.

Figure 1.18

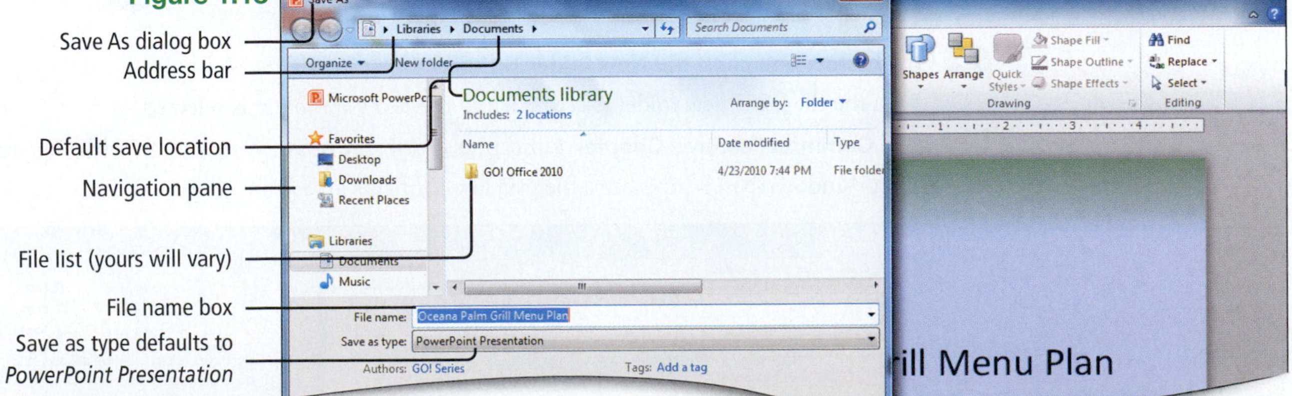

6. On the right side of the **navigation pane**, point to the **scroll bar**. Compare your screen with Figure 1.19.

   A ***scroll bar*** displays when a window, or a pane within a window, has information that is not in view. You can click the up or down scroll arrows—or the left and right scroll arrows in a horizontal scroll bar—to scroll the contents up or down or left and right in small increments.

   You can also drag the ***scroll box***—the box within the scroll bar—to scroll the window in either direction.

Figure 1.19

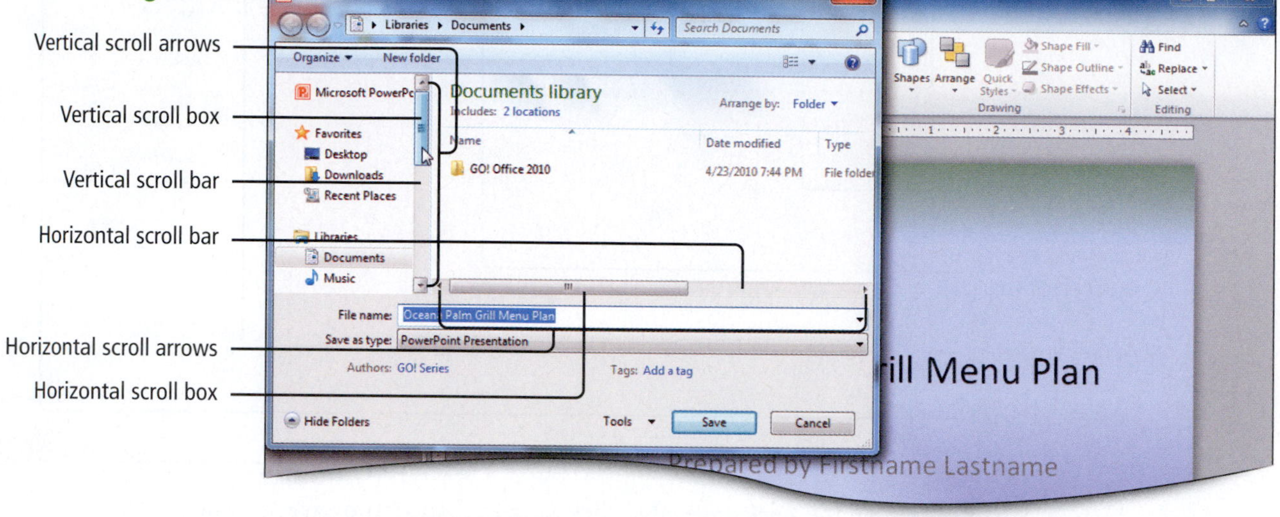

7. Click the **down scroll arrow** as necessary so that you can view the lower portion of the **navigation pane**, and then click the icon for your USB flash drive. Compare your screen with Figure 1.20. (If you prefer to store on your computer's hard drive instead of a USB flash drive, in the navigation pane, click Documents.)

Figure 1.20

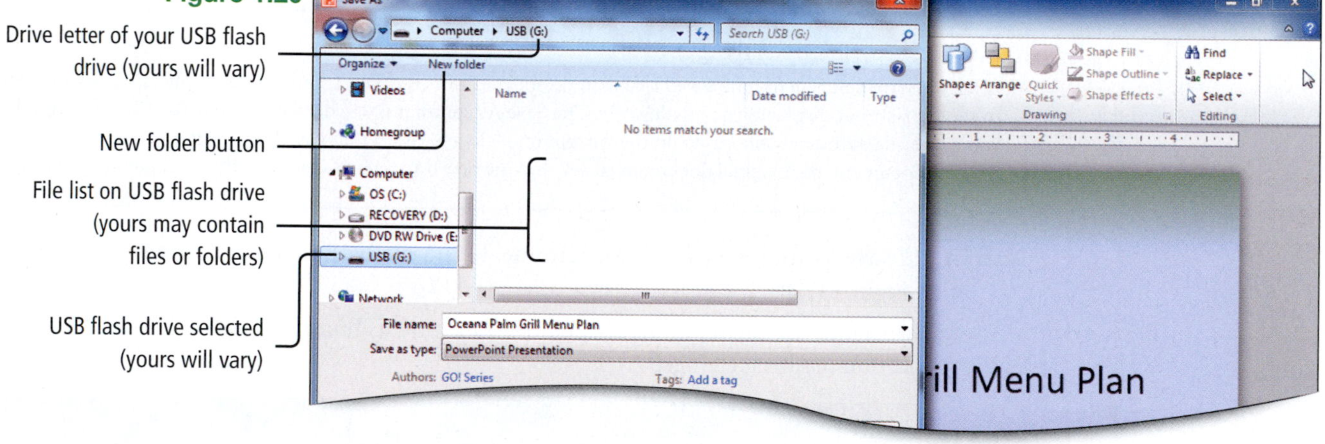

8. On the toolbar, click the **New folder** button.

   In the file list, a new folder is created, and the text *New folder* is selected.

9. Type **Common Features Chapter 1** and press Enter. Compare your screen with Figure 1.21.

   In Windows-based programs, the Enter key confirms an action.

Figure 1.21

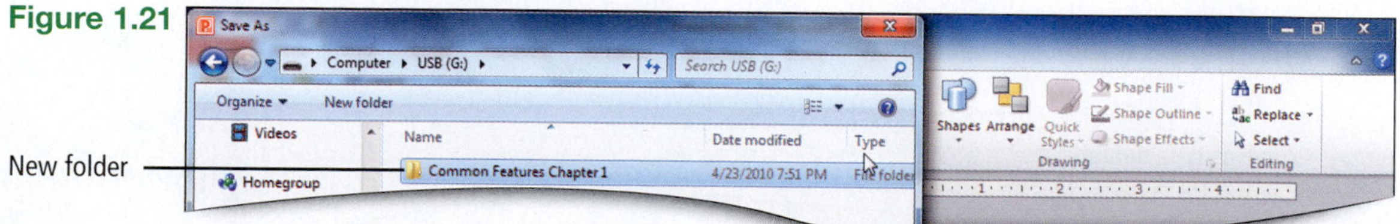

10 In the **file list**, double-click the name of your new folder to open it and display its name in the **address bar**.

11 In the lower portion of the dialog box, click in the **File name** box to select the existing text. Notice that Office inserts the text at the beginning of the presentation as a suggested file name.

12 On your keyboard, locate the [-] key. Notice that the Shift of this key produces the underscore character. With the text still selected, type **Lastname_Firstname_1A_Menu_Plan** Compare your screen with Figure 1.22.

You can use spaces in file names, however some individuals prefer not to use spaces. Some programs, especially when transferring files over the Internet, may not work well with spaces in file names. In general, however, unless you encounter a problem, it is OK to use spaces. In this textbook, underscores are used instead of spaces in file names.

Figure 1.22

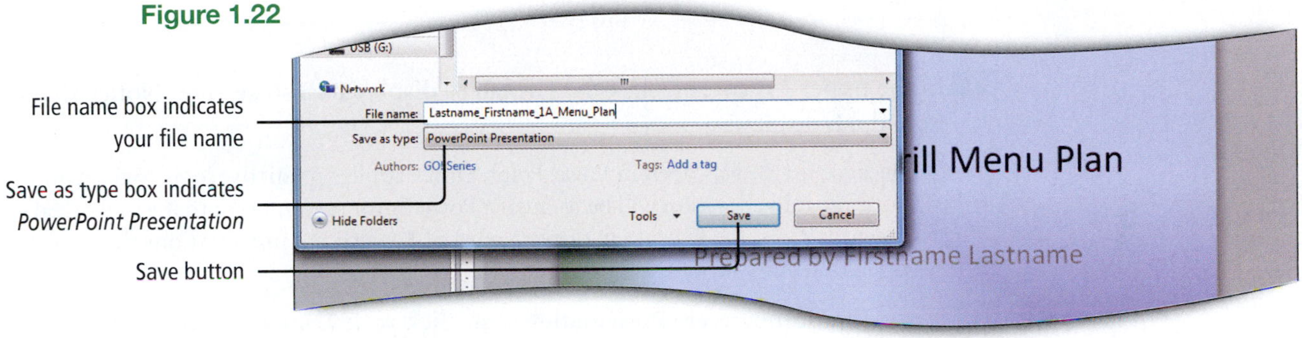

13 In the lower right corner, click **Save**; or press [Enter]. See Figure 1.23.

Your new file name displays in the title bar, indicating that the file has been saved to a location that you have specified.

Figure 1.23

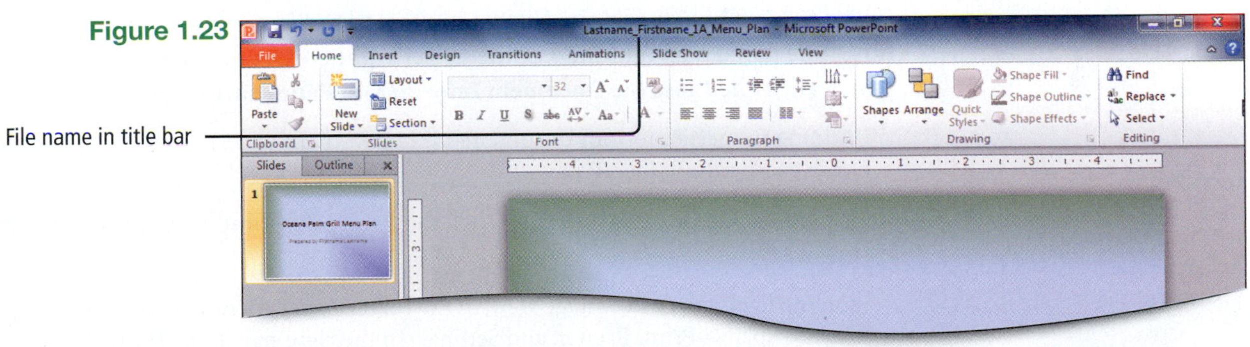

14 In the text that begins *Prepared by*, click to position the insertion point at the end of your name, and then press [Enter] to move to a new line. Type **For Laura Hernandez**

15 Click the **File tab** to display **Backstage** view. At the top of the center panel, notice that the path where your file is stored displays. Above the Backstage tabs, click **Close** to close the file. In the message box, click **Save** to save the changes you made and close the file. Leave PowerPoint open.

PowerPoint displays a message asking if you want to save the changes you have made. Because you have made additional changes to the file since your last Save operation, an Office program will always prompt you to save so that you do not lose any new data.

Objective 6 | Add Document Properties and Print a File

The process of printing a file is similar in all of the Office applications. There are differences in the types of options you can select. For example, in PowerPoint, you have the option of printing the full slide, with each slide printing on a full sheet of paper, or of printing handouts with small pictures of slides on a page.

Activity 1.06 | Adding Document Properties and Printing a File

> **Alert! | Are You Printing or Submitting Your Files Electronically?**
>
> If you are submitting your files electronically only, or have no printer attached, you can still complete this activity. Complete Steps 1-9, and then submit your file electronically as directed by your instructor.

1. In the upper left corner, click the **File tab** to display **Backstage** view. Notice that the **Recent tab** displays.

   Because no file was open in PowerPoint, Office applies predictive logic to determine that your most likely action will be to open a PowerPoint presentation that you worked on recently. Thus, the Recent tab displays a list of PowerPoint presentations that were recently open on your system.

2. At the top of the **Recent Presentations** list, click your **Lastname_Firstname_1A_Menu_Plan** file to open it.

3. Click the **File tab** to redisplay **Backstage** view. On the right, under the screen thumbnail, click **Properties**, and then click **Show Document Panel**. In the **Author** box, delete the existing text, and then type your firstname and lastname. Notice that in PowerPoint, some variation of the slide title is automatically inserted in the Title box. In the **Subject** box, type your Course name and section number. In the **Keywords** box, type **menu plan** and then in the upper right corner of the **Document Properties** panel, click the **Close the Document Information Panel** button [×].

   Adding properties to your documents will make them easier to search for in systems such as Microsoft SharePoint.

> **Another Way**
>
> Press [Ctrl] + [P] or [Ctrl] + [F2] to display the Print tab in Backstage view.

4. Redisplay **Backstage** view, and then click the **Print tab**. Compare your screen with Figure 1.24.

   On the Print tab in Backstage view, in the center panel, three groups of printing-related tasks display—Print, Printer, and Settings. In the right panel, the ***Print Preview*** displays, which is a view of a document as it will appear on the paper when you print it.

   At the bottom of the Print Preview area, on the left, the number of pages and arrows with which you can move among the pages in Print Preview display. On the right, ***Zoom*** settings enable you to shrink or enlarge the Print Preview. Zoom is the action of increasing or decreasing the viewing area of the screen.

Figure 1.24

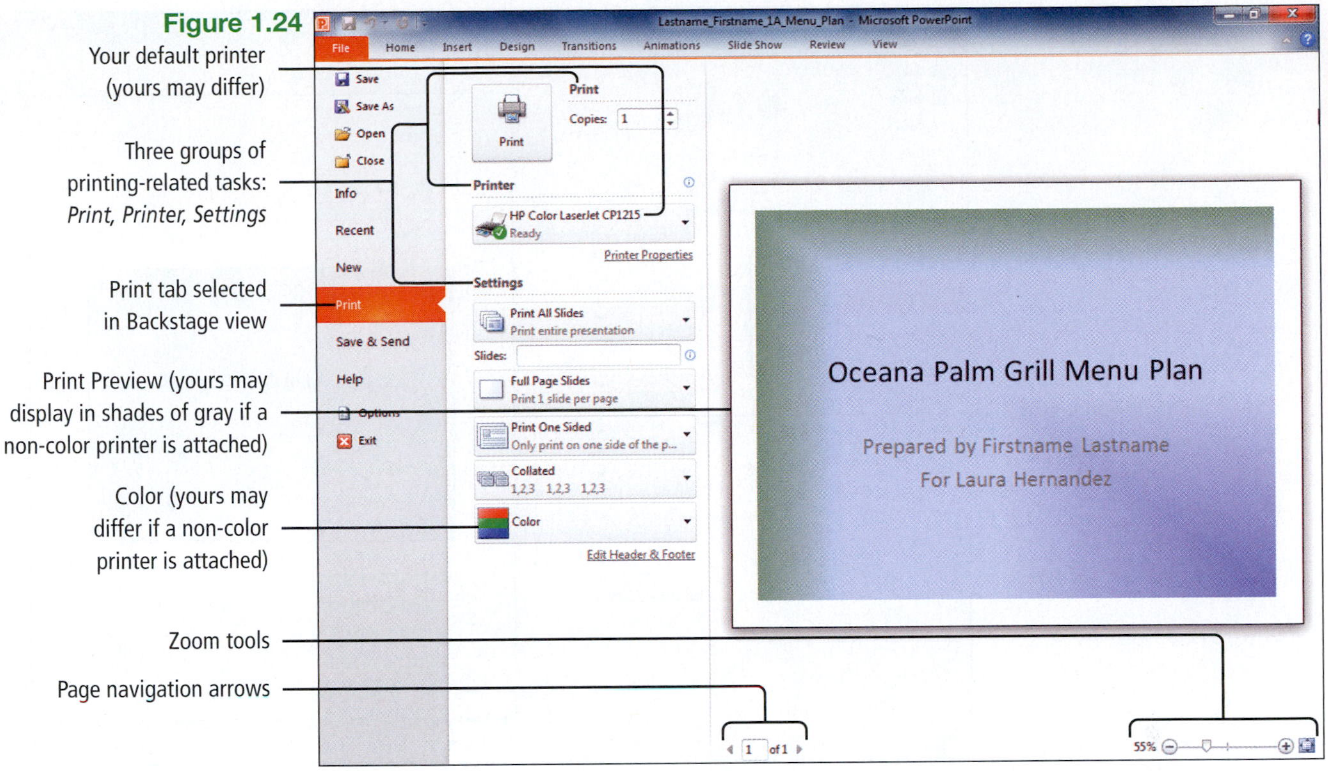

5. Locate the **Settings group**, and notice that the default setting is to **Print All Slides** and to print **Full Page Slides**—each slide on a full sheet of paper.

6. Point to **Full Page Slides**, notice that the button glows orange, and then click the button to display a gallery of print arrangements. Compare your screen with Figure 1.25.

Figure 1.25

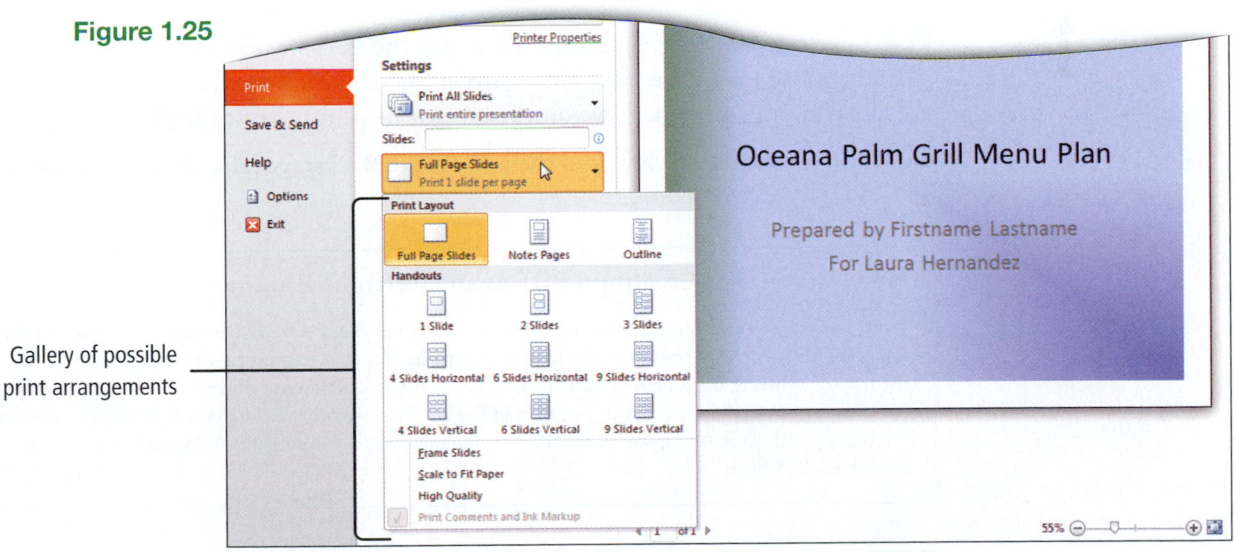

7. In the displayed gallery, under **Handouts**, click **1 Slide**, and then compare your screen with Figure 1.26.

The Print Preview changes to show how your slide will print on the paper in this arrangement.

Figure 1.26

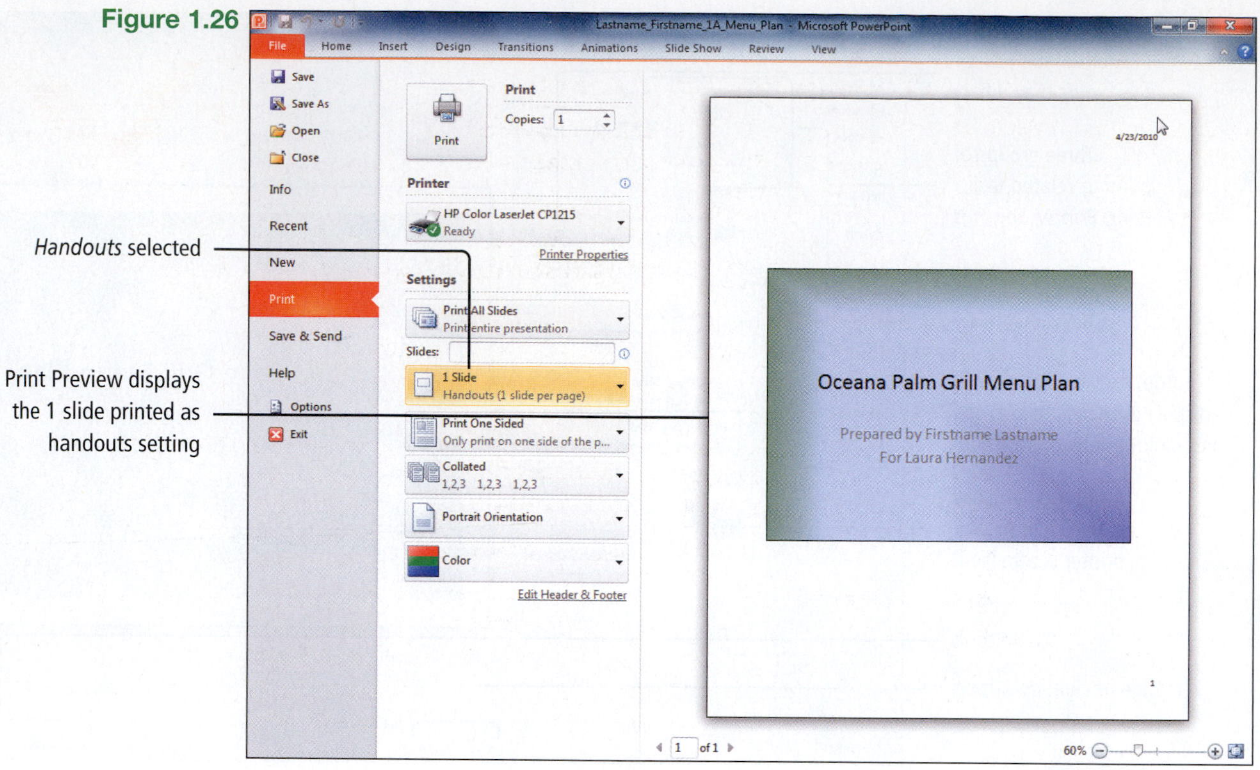

8 To submit your file electronically, skip this step and move to Step 9. To print your slide, be sure your system is connected to a printer, and then in the **Print group**, click the **Print** button. On the Quick Access Toolbar, click **Save**, and then move to Step 10.

The handout will print on your default printer—on a black and white printer, the colors will print in shades of gray. Backstage view closes and your file redisplays in the PowerPoint window.

9 To submit your file electronically, above the **Backstage tabs**, click **Close** to close the file and close **Backstage** view, click **Save** in the displayed message, and then follow the instructions provided by your instructor to submit your file electronically.

Another Way

In the upper right corner of your PowerPoint window, click the red Close button.

10 Display **Backstage** view, and then below the **Backstage tabs**, click **Exit** to close your file and close PowerPoint.

More Knowledge | Creating a PDF as an Electronic Printout

From Backstage view, you can save an Office file as a ***PDF file***. ***Portable Document Format*** (PDF) creates an image of your file that preserves the look of your file, but that cannot be easily changed. This is a popular format for sending documents electronically, because the document will display on most computers. From Backstage view, click Save & Send, and then in the File Types group, click Create PDF/XPS Document. Then in the third panel, click the Create PDF/XPS button, navigate to your chapter folder, and then in the lower right corner, click Publish.

End You have completed Project 1A

Project 1B Word File

myitlab
Project 1B Training

Project Activities

In Activities 1.07 through 1.16, you will open, edit, save, and then compress a Word file. Your completed document will look similar to Figure 1.27.

Project Files

For Project 1B, you will need the following file:

cf01B_Cheese_Promotion

You will save your Word document as:

Lastname_Firstname_1B_Cheese_Promotion

Project Results

Memo

TO:	Laura Mabry Hernandez, General Manager
FROM:	Donna Jackson, Executive Chef
DATE:	December 17, 2014
SUBJECT:	Cheese Specials on Tuesdays

To increase restaurant traffic between 4:00 p.m. and 6:00 p.m., I am proposing a trial cheese event in one of the restaurants, probably Orlando. I would like to try a weekly event on Tuesday evenings where the focus is on a good selection of cheese.

I envision two possibilities: a selection of cheese plates or a cheese bar—or both. The cheeses would have to be matched with compatible fruit and bread or crackers. They could be used as appetizers, or for desserts, as is common in Europe. The cheese plates should be varied and diverse, using a mixture of hard and soft, sharp and mild, unusual and familiar.

I am excited about this new promotion. If done properly, I think it could increase restaurant traffic in the hours when individuals want to relax with a small snack instead of a heavy dinner.

The promotion will require that our employees become familiar with the types and characteristics of both foreign and domestic cheeses. Let's meet to discuss the details and the training requirements, and to create a flyer that begins something like this:

Oceana Palm Grill Tuesday Cheese Tastings

Lastname_Firstname_1B_Cheese_Promotion

Figure 1.27
Project 1B Cheese Promotion

Objective 7 | Open an Existing File and Save It with a New Name

In any Office program, use the Open command to display the ***Open dialog box***, from which you can navigate to and then open an existing file that was created in that same program.

The Open dialog box, along with the Save and Save As dialog boxes, are referred to as ***common dialog boxes***. These dialog boxes, which are provided by the Windows programming interface, display in all of the Office programs in the same manner. Thus, the Open, Save, and Save As dialog boxes will all look and perform the same in each Office program.

Activity 1.07 | Opening an Existing File and Saving it with a New Name

In this activity, you will display the Open dialog box, open an existing Word document, and then save it in your storage location with a new name.

1 Determine the location of the student data files that accompany this textbook, and be sure you can access these files.

For example:

If you are accessing the files from the Student CD that came with this textbook, insert the CD now.

If you copied the files from the Student CD or from the Pearson Web site to a USB flash drive that you are using for this course, insert the flash drive in your computer now.

If you copied the files to the hard drive of your computer, for example in your Documents library, be sure you can locate the files on the hard drive.

2 Determine the location of your **Common Features Chapter 1** folder you created in Activity 1.05, in which you will store your work from this chapter, and then be sure you can access that folder.

For example:

If you created your chapter folder on a USB flash drive, insert the flash drive in your computer now. This can be the same flash drive where you have stored the student data files; just be sure to use the chapter folder you created.

If you created your chapter folder in the Documents library on your computer, be sure you can locate the folder. Otherwise, create a new folder at the computer at which you are working, or on a USB flash drive.

3 Using the technique you practiced in Activity 1.02, locate and then start the **Microsoft Word 2010** program on your system.

Another Way

In the Word (or other program) window, press Ctrl + F12 to display the Open dialog box.

4 On the Ribbon, click the **File tab** to display **Backstage** view, and then click **Open** to display the **Open** dialog box.

5 In the **navigation pane** on the left, use the scroll bar to scroll as necessary, and then click the location of your student data files to display the location's contents in the **file list**. Compare your screen with Figure 1.28.

For example:

If you are accessing the files from the Student CD that came with your book, under Computer, click the CD/DVD.

If you are accessing the files from a USB flash drive, under Computer, click the flash drive name.

If you are accessing the files from the Documents library of your computer, under Libraries, click Documents.

Figure 1.28

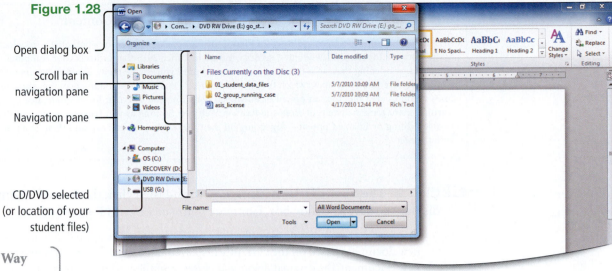

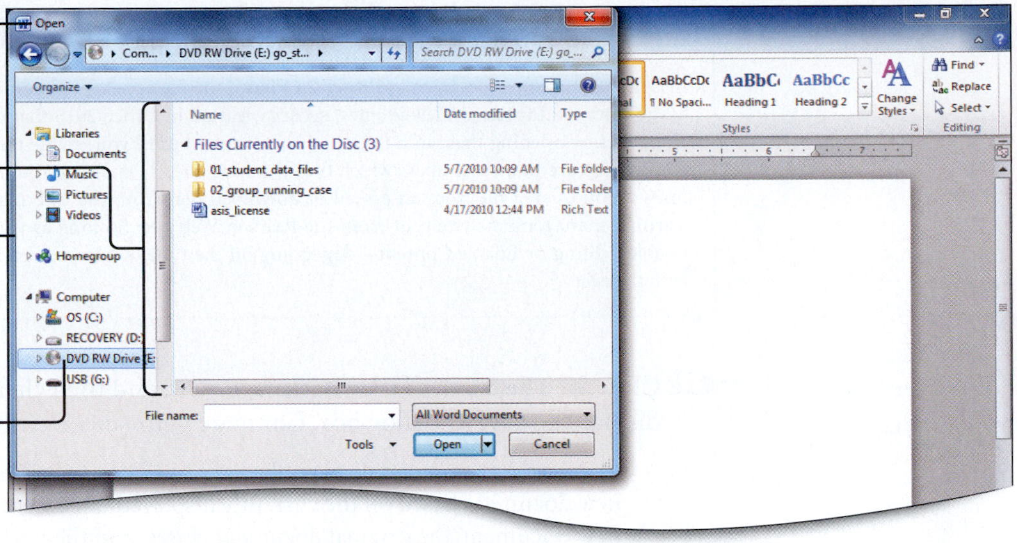

Another Way

Point to a folder name, right-click, and then from the shortcut menu, click Open.

6 Point to the folder **01_student_data_files** and double-click to open the folder. Point to the subfolder **01_common_features**, double-click, and then compare your screen with Figure 1.29.

Figure 1.29

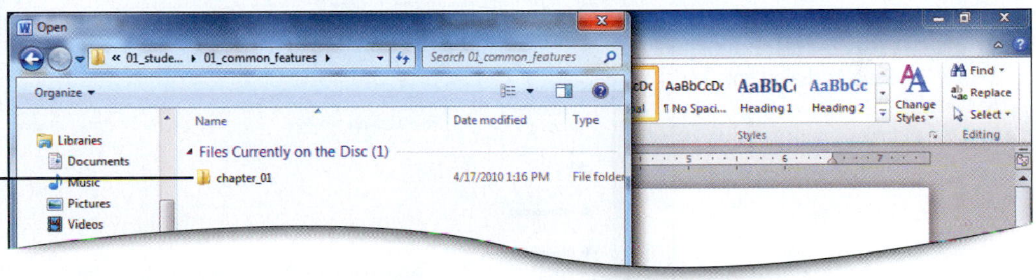

Another Way

Click one time to select the file, and then press Enter or click the Open button in the lower right corner of the dialog box.

7 In the **file list**, point to the **chapter_01** subfolder and double-click to open it. In the **file list**, point to Word file **cf01B_Cheese_Promotion** and then double-click to open and display the file in the Word window. On the Ribbon, on the **Home tab**, in the **Paragraph group**, if necessary, click the **Show/Hide** button ¶ so that it is active—glowing orange. Compare your screen with Figure 1.30.

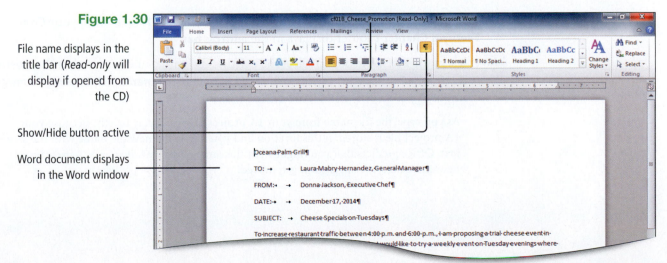

On the title bar at the top of the screen, the file name displays. If you opened the document from the Student CD, (*Read-Only*) will display. If you opened the document from another source to which the files were copied, (*Read-Only*) might not display. ***Read-Only*** is a property assigned to a file that prevents the file from being modified or deleted; it indicates that you cannot save any changes to the displayed document unless you first save it with a new name.

Figure 1.30

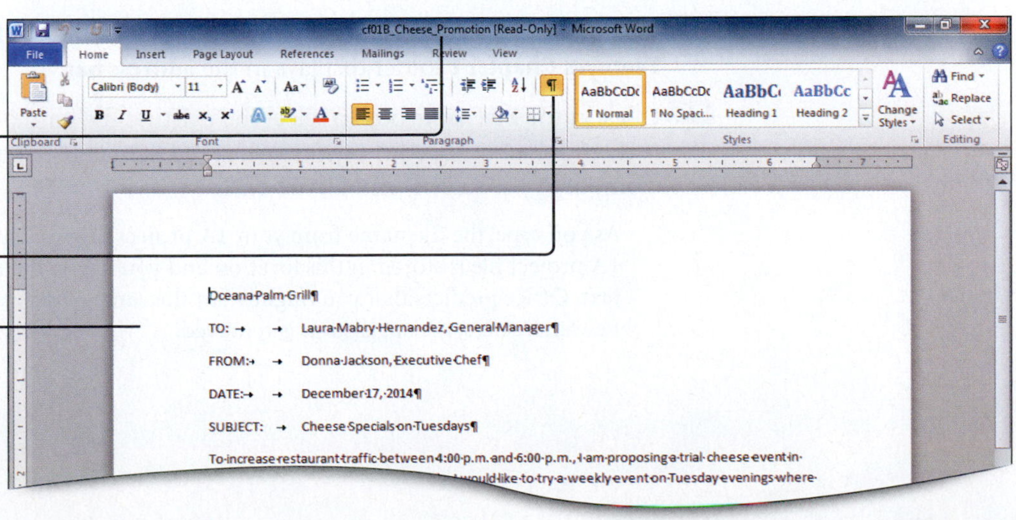

> **Alert! | Do You See a Message to Enable Editing or Enable Content?**
>
> In Office 2010, some files open in ***Protected View*** if the file appears to be from a potentially risky location, such as the Internet. Protected View is a new security feature in Office 2010 that protects your computer from malicious files by opening them in a restricted environment until you enable them. ***Trusted Documents*** is another security feature that remembers which files you have already enabled. You might encounter these security features if you open a file from an e-mail or download files from the Internet; for example, from your college's learning management system or from the Pearson Web site. So long as you trust the source of the file, click Enable Editing or Enable Content—depending on the type of file you receive—and then go ahead and work with the file.

Another Way
Press F12 to display the Save As dialog box.

8 Click the **File tab** to display **Backstage** view, and then click the **Save As** command to display the **Save As** dialog box. Compare your screen with Figure 1.31.

The Save As command displays the Save As dialog box where you can name and save a *new* document based on the currently displayed document. After you name and save the new document, the original document closes, and the new document—based on the original one—displays.

Figure 1.31

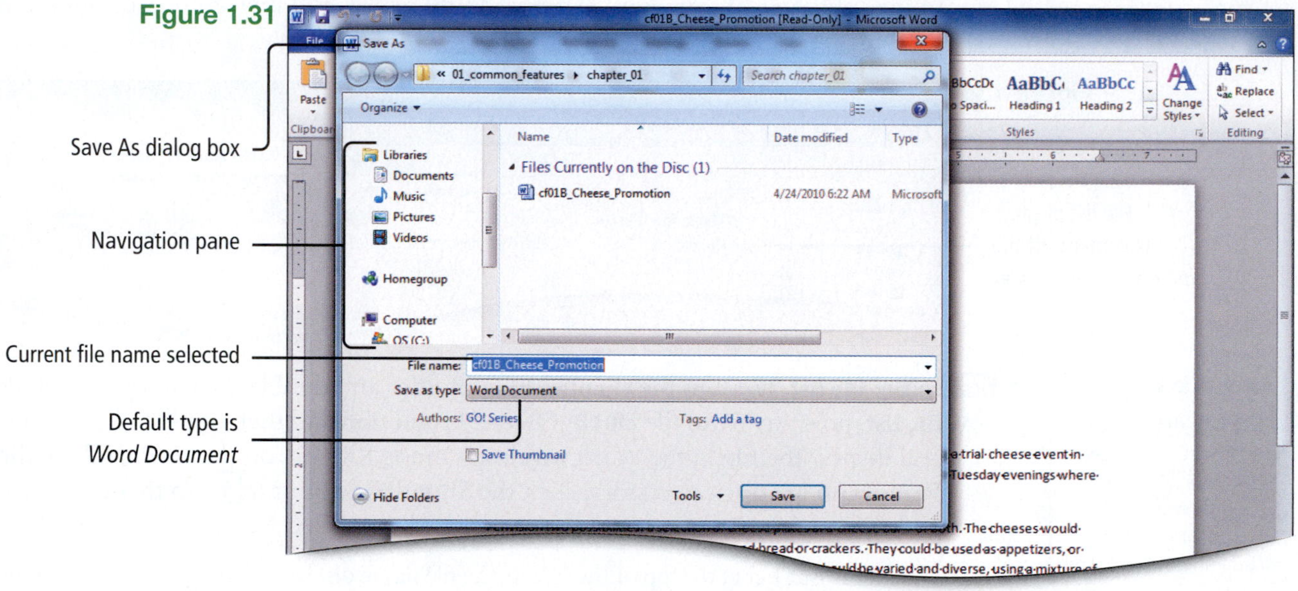

9 In the **navigation pane**, click the location in which you are storing your projects for this chapter—the location where you created your **Common Features Chapter 1** folder; for example, your USB flash drive or the Documents library.

10 In the **file list**, double-click the necessary folders and subfolders until your **Common Features Chapter 1** folder displays in the **address bar**.

11 Click in the **File name** box to select the existing file name, or drag to select the existing text, and then using your own name, type **Lastname_Firstname_1B_Cheese_Promotion** Compare your screen with Figure 1.32.

As you type, the file name from your 1A project might display briefly. Because your 1A project file is stored in this location and you began the new file name with the same text, Office predicts that you might want the same or similar file name. As you type new characters, the suggestion is removed.

Figure 1.32

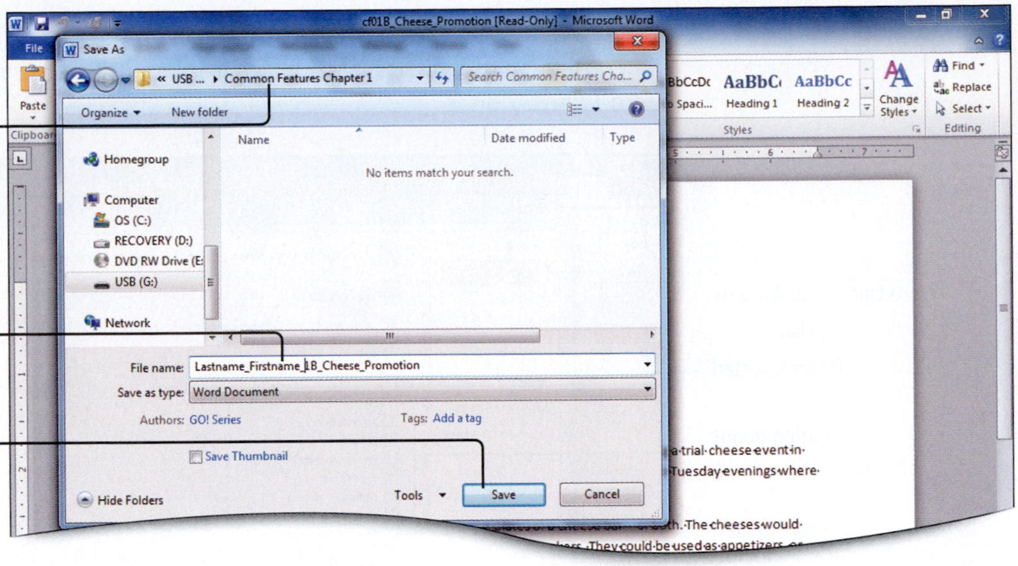

Your folder name in address bar

File name box displays your new file name

Save button

12 In the lower right corner of the **Save As** dialog box, click **Save**; or press Enter. Compare your screen with Figure 1.33.

The original document closes, and your new document, based on the original, displays with the name in the title bar.

Figure 1.33

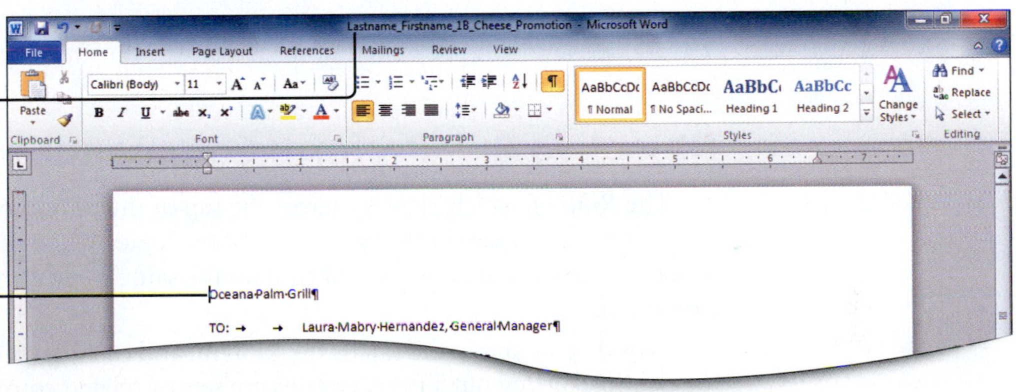

New document name in title bar

Insertion point at beginning of document

Objective 8 | Explore Options for an Application

Within each Office application, you can open an ***Options dialog box*** where you can select program settings and other options and preferences. For example, you can set preferences for viewing and editing files.

Activity 1.08 | Viewing Application Options

1 Click the **File tab** to display **Backstage** view. Under the **Help tab**, click **Options**.

2 In the displayed **Word Options** dialog box, on the left, click **Display**, and then on the right, locate the information under **Always show these formatting marks on the screen**.

When you press Enter, Spacebar, or Tab on your keyboard, characters display to represent these keystrokes. These screen characters do not print, and are referred to as ***formatting marks*** or ***nonprinting characters***.

3 Under **Always show these formatting marks on the screen**, be sure the last check box, **Show all formatting marks**, is selected—select it if necessary. Compare your screen with Figure 1.34.

Figure 1.34

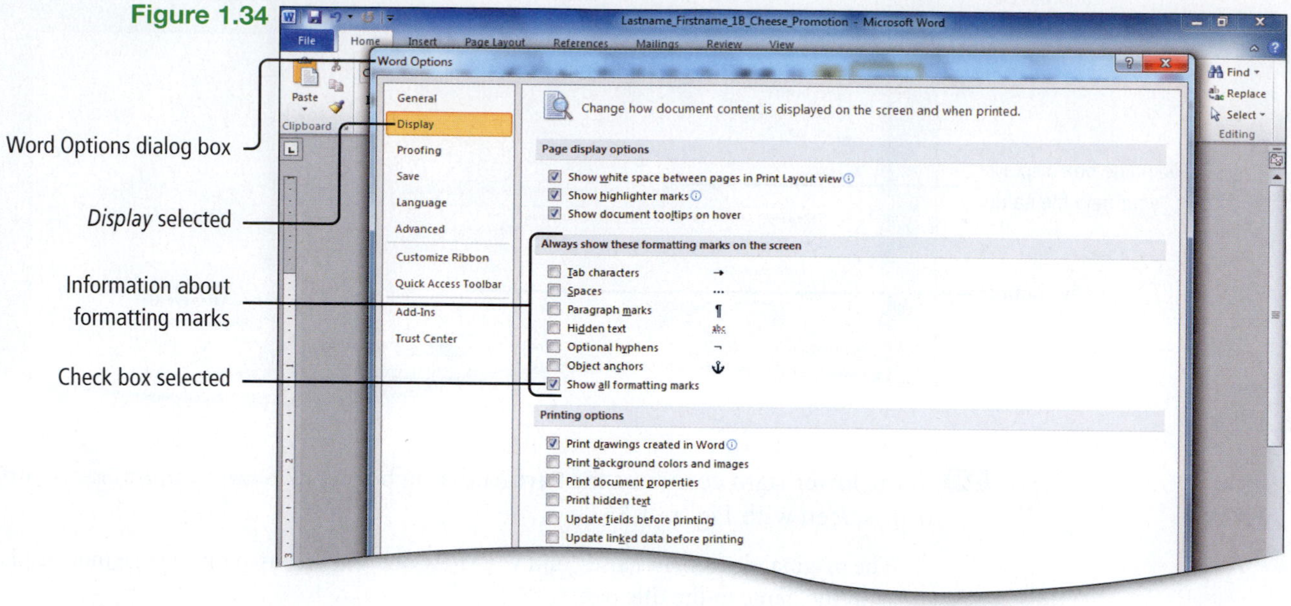

4 In the lower right corner of the dialog box, click **OK**.

Objective 9 | Perform Commands from the Ribbon

The ***Ribbon***, which displays across the top of the program window, groups commands and features in a manner that you would most logically use them. Each Office program's Ribbon is slightly different, but all contain the same three elements: ***tabs***, ***groups***, and ***commands***.

Tabs display across the top of the Ribbon, and each tab relates to a type of activity; for example, laying out a page. Groups are sets of related commands for specific tasks. Commands—instructions to computer programs—are arranged in groups, and might display as a button, a menu, or a box in which you type information.

You can also minimize the Ribbon so only the tab names display. In the minimized Ribbon view, when you click a tab the Ribbon expands to show the groups and commands, and then when you click a command, the Ribbon returns to its minimized view. Most Office users, however, prefer to leave the complete Ribbon in view at all times.

Activity 1.09 | Performing Commands from the Ribbon

1 Take a moment to examine the document on your screen.

This document is a memo from the Executive Chef to the General Manager regarding a new restaurant promotion.

2 On the Ribbon, click the **View tab**. In the **Show group**, if necessary, click to place a check mark in the **Ruler** check box, and then compare your screen with Figure 1.35.

When working in Word, display the rulers so that you can see how margin settings affect your document and how text aligns. Additionally, if you set a tab stop or an indent, its location is visible on the ruler.

Figure 1.35

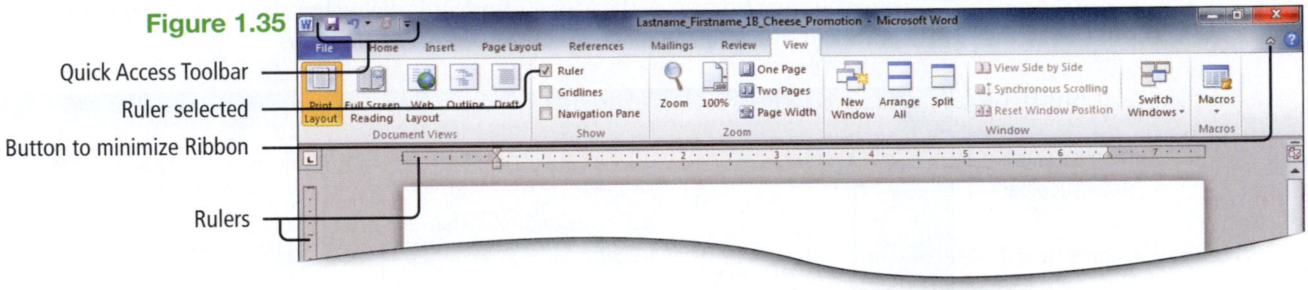

3 On the Ribbon, click the **Home tab**. In the **Paragraph group**, if necessary, click the **Show/Hide** button [¶] so that it glows orange and formatting marks display in your document. Point to the button to display information about the button, and then compare your screen with Figure 1.36.

When the Show/Hide button is active—glowing orange—formatting marks display. Because formatting marks guide your eye in a document—like a map and road signs guide you along a highway—these marks will display throughout this instruction. Many expert Word users keep these marks displayed while creating documents.

Figure 1.36

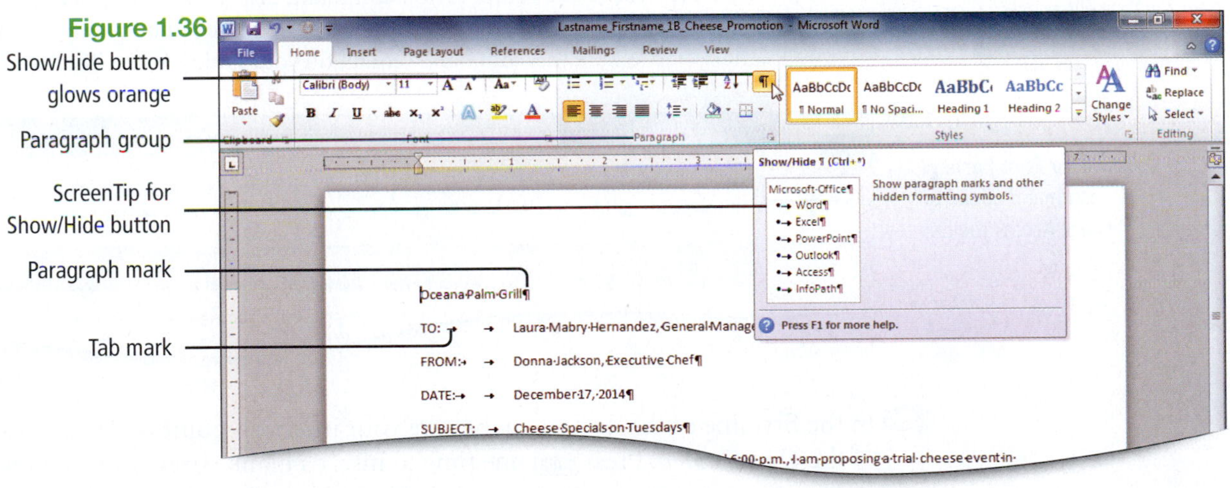

4 In the upper left corner of your screen, above the Ribbon, locate the **Quick Access Toolbar**.

The ***Quick Access Toolbar*** contains commands that you use frequently. By default, only the commands Save, Undo, and Redo display, but you can add and delete commands to suit your needs. Possibly the computer at which you are working already has additional commands added to the Quick Access Toolbar.

5 At the end of the Quick Access Toolbar, click the **Customize Quick Access Toolbar** button [▾].

6 Compare your screen with Figure 1.37.

A list of commands that Office users commonly add to their Quick Access Toolbar displays, including *Open*, *E-mail*, and *Print Preview and Print*. Commands already on the Quick Access Toolbar display a check mark. Commands that you add to the Quick Access Toolbar are always just one click away.

Here you can also display the More Commands dialog box, from which you can select any command from any tab to add to the Quick Access Toolbar.

Figure 1.37

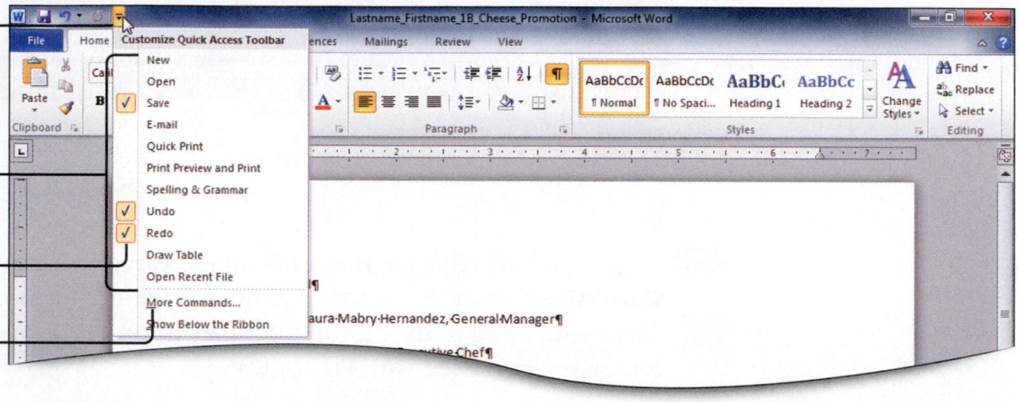

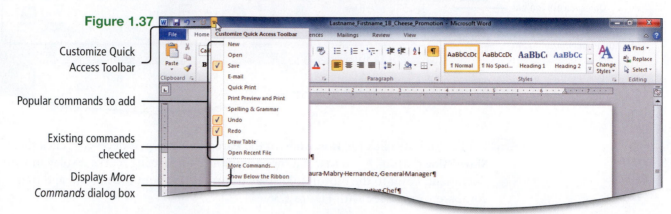

> **Another Way**
>
> Right-click any command on the Ribbon, and then on the shortcut menu, click Add to Quick Access Toolbar.

7 On the displayed list, click **Print Preview and Print**, and then notice that the icon is added to the **Quick Access Toolbar**. Compare your screen with Figure 1.38.

The icon that represents the Print Preview command displays on the Quick Access Toolbar. Because this is a command that you will use frequently while building Office documents, you might decide to have this command remain on your Quick Access Toolbar.

Figure 1.38

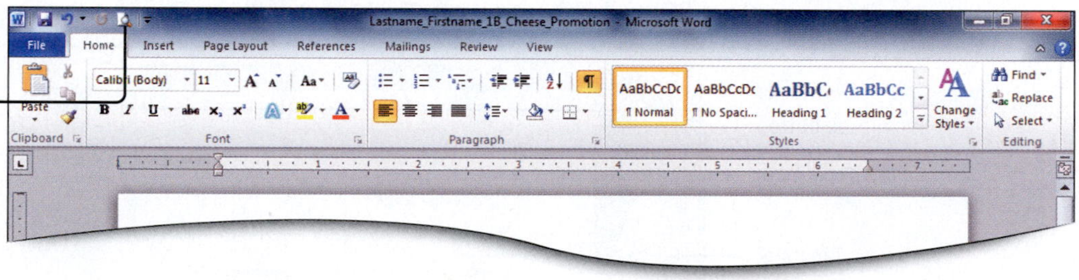

8 In the first line of the document, be sure your insertion point is blinking to the left of the *O* in *Oceana*. Press Enter one time to insert a blank paragraph, and then click to the left of the new paragraph mark (¶) in the new line.

The ***paragraph symbol*** is a formatting mark that displays each time you press Enter.

9 On the Ribbon, click the **Insert tab**. In the **Illustrations group**, point to the **Clip Art** button to display its ScreenTip.

Many buttons on the Ribbon have this type of ***enhanced ScreenTip***, which displays more descriptive text than a normal ScreenTip.

10 Click the **Clip Art** button.

The Clip Art ***task pane*** displays. A task pane is a window within a Microsoft Office application that enables you to enter options for completing a command.

11 In the **Clip Art** task pane, click in the **Search for** box, delete any existing text, and then type **cheese grapes** Under **Results should be:**, click the arrow at the right, if necessary click to *clear* the check mark for **All media types** so that no check boxes are selected, and then click the check box for **Illustrations.** Compare your screen with Figure 1.39.

Figure 1.39

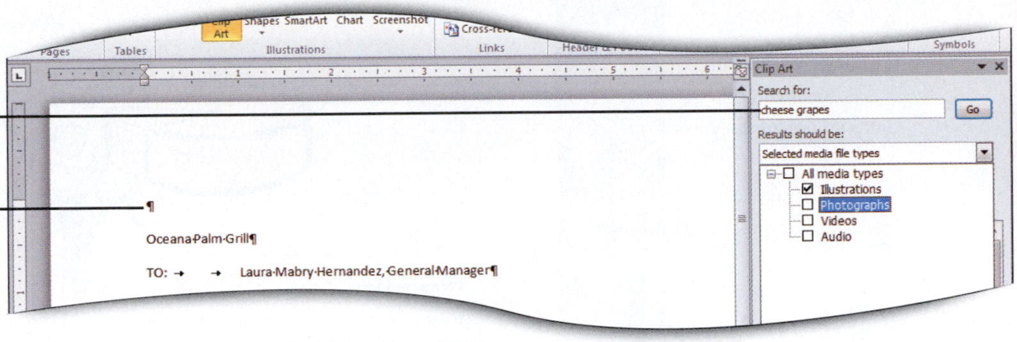

12 Click the **Results should be arrow** again to close the list, and then if necessary, click to place a check mark in the **Include Office.com content** check box.

By selecting this check box, the search for clip art images will include those from Microsoft's online collections of clip art at www.office.com.

13 At the top of the **Clip Art** task pane, click **Go.** Wait a moment for clips to display, and then locate the clip indicated in Figure 1.40.

Figure 1.40

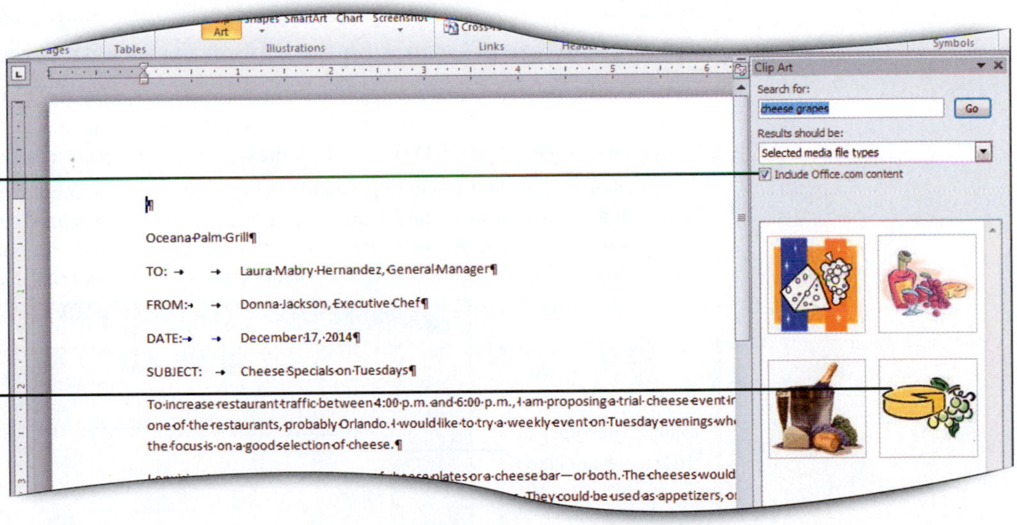

14 Click the image indicated in Figure 1.40 one time to insert it at the insertion point, and then in the upper right corner of the **Clip Art** task pane, click the **Close** [X] button.

Alert! | If You Cannot Locate the Image

If the image shown in Figure 1.40 is unavailable, select a different cheese image that is appropriate.

15 With the image selected—surrounded by a border—on the Ribbon, click the **Home tab**, and then in the **Paragraph group**, click the **Center** button. Click anywhere outside of the bordered picture to ***deselect***—cancel the selection. Compare your screen with Figure 1.41.

Figure 1.41

16 Point to the inserted clip art image, and then watch the last tab of the Ribbon as you click the image one time to select it.

The *Picture Tools* display and an additional tab—the *Format* tab—is added to the Ribbon. The Ribbon adapts to your work and will display additional tabs—referred to as ***contextual tabs***—when you need them.

17 On the Ribbon, under **Picture Tools**, click the **Format tab**.

> **Alert! | The Size of Groups on the Ribbon Varies with Screen Resolution**
>
> Your monitor's screen resolution might be set higher than the resolution used to capture the figures in this book. In Figure 1.42 below, the resolution is set to 1024 × 768, which is used for all of the figures in this book. Compare that with Figure 1.43 below, where the screen resolution is set to 1280 × 1024.
>
> At a higher resolution, the Ribbon expands some groups to show more commands than are available with a single click, such as those in the Picture Styles group. Or, the group expands to add descriptive text to some buttons, such as those in the Arrange group. Regardless of your screen resolution, all Office commands are available to you. In higher resolutions, you will have a more robust view of the commands.

Figure 1.42

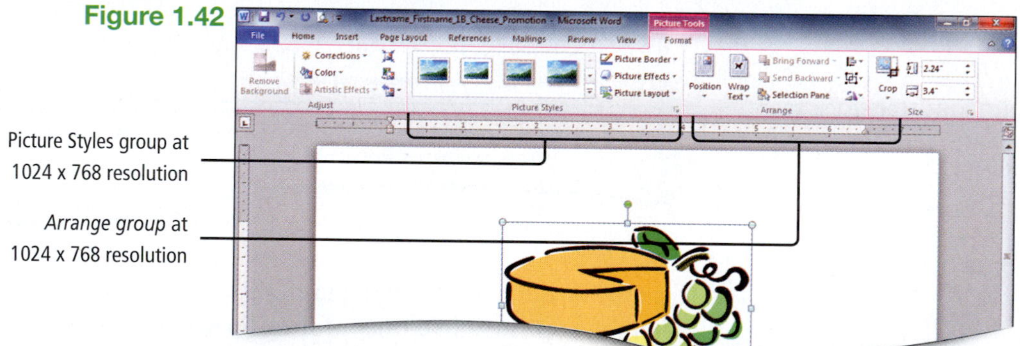

Figure 1.43

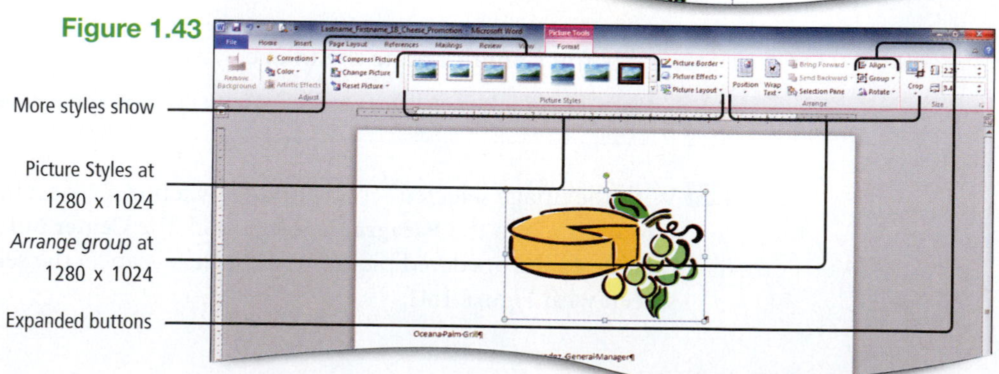

18 In the **Picture Styles group**, point to the first style to display the ScreenTip *Simple Frame, White*, and notice that the image displays with a white frame.

19 Watch the image as you point to the second picture style, and then to the third, and then to the fourth.

This is ***Live Preview***, a technology that shows the result of applying an editing or formatting change as you point to possible results—*before* you actually apply it.

20 In the **Picture Styles group**, click the fourth style—**Drop Shadow Rectangle**—and then click anywhere outside of the image to deselect it. Notice that the Picture Tools no longer display on the Ribbon. Compare your screen with Figure 1.44.

Contextual tabs display only when you need them.

Figure 1.44

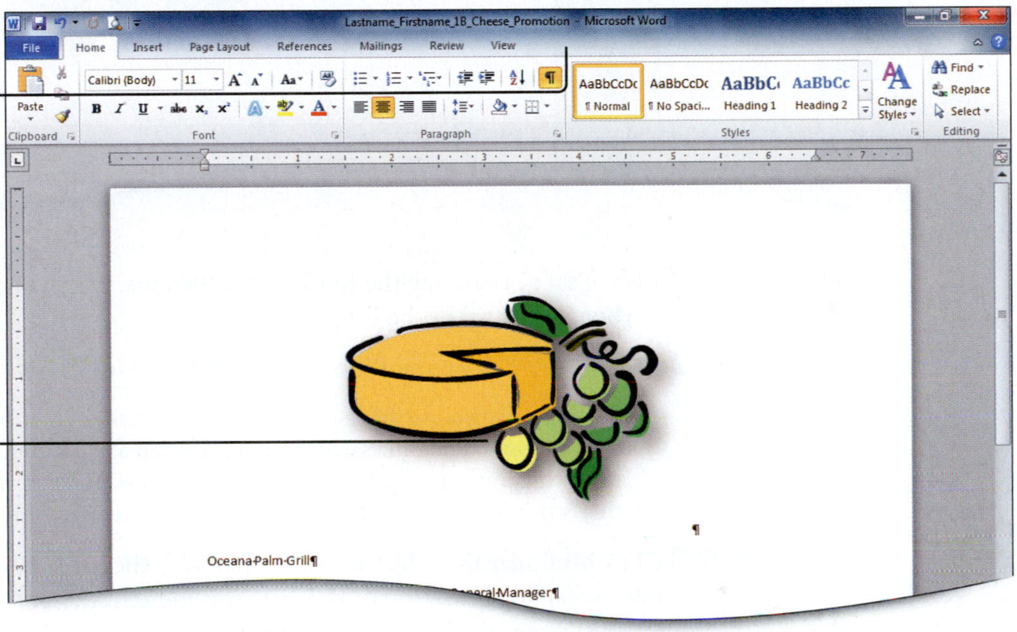

21 In the upper left corner of your screen, on the Quick Access Toolbar, click the **Save** button to save the changes you have made.

Activity 1.10 | Minimizing and Using the Keyboard to Control the Ribbon

Instead of a mouse, some individuals prefer to navigate the Ribbon by using keys on the keyboard. You can activate keyboard control of the Ribbon by pressing the Alt key. You can also minimize the Ribbon to maximize your available screen space.

1 On your keyboard, press the Alt key, and then on the Ribbon, notice that small labels display. Press N to activate the commands on the **Insert tab**, and then compare your screen with Figure 1.45.

Each label represents a ***KeyTip***—an indication of the key that you can press to activate the command. For example, on the Insert tab, you can press F to activate the Clip Art task pane.

Figure 1.45

KeyTips indicate that keyboard control of the Ribbon is active

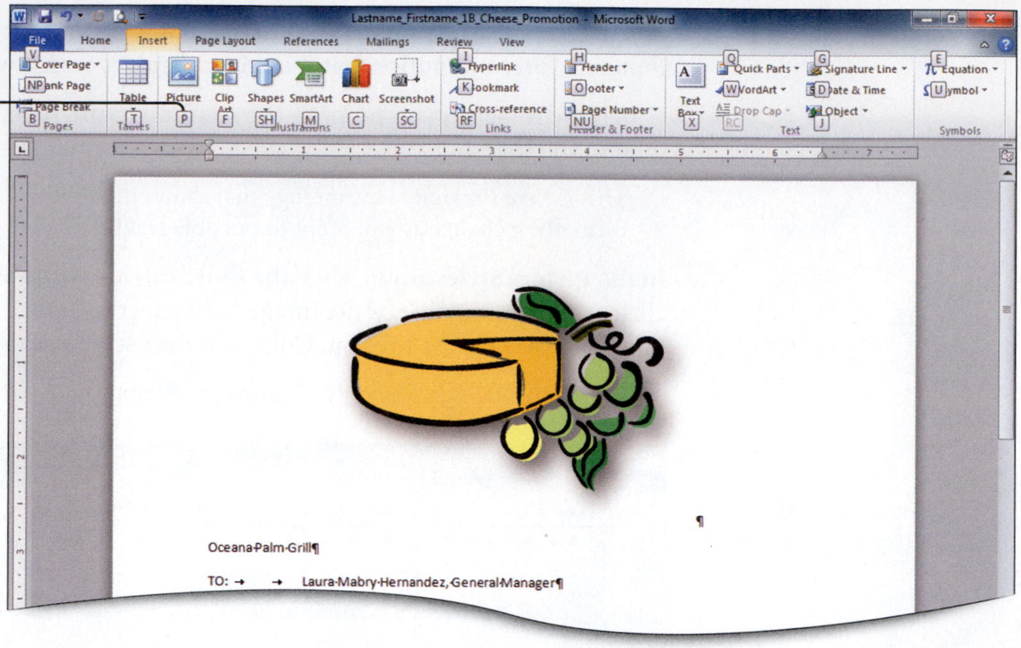

2 Press Esc to redisplay the KeyTips for the tabs. Then, press Alt again to turn off keyboard control of the Ribbon.

3 Point to any tab on the Ribbon and right-click to display a shortcut menu.

Here you can choose to display the Quick Access Toolbar below the Ribbon or minimize the Ribbon to maximize screen space. You can also customize the Ribbon by adding, removing, renaming, or reordering tabs, groups, and commands on the Ribbon, although this is not recommended until you become an expert Office user.

> **Another Way**
>
> Double-click the active tab; or, click the Minimize the Ribbon button at the right end of the Ribbon.

4 Click **Minimize the Ribbon**. Notice that only the Ribbon tabs display. Click the **Home tab** to display the commands. Click anywhere in the document, and notice that the Ribbon reverts to its minimized view.

> **Another Way**
>
> Double-click any tab to redisplay the full Ribbon.

5 Right-click any Ribbon tab, and then click **Minimize the Ribbon** again to turn the minimize feature off.

Most expert Office users prefer to have the full Ribbon display at all times.

6 Point to any tab on the Ribbon, and then on your mouse device, roll the mouse wheel. Notice that different tabs become active as your roll the mouse wheel.

You can make a tab active by using this technique, instead of clicking the tab.

Objective 10 | Apply Formatting in Office Programs

Formatting is the process of establishing the overall appearance of text, graphics, and pages in an Office file—for example, in a Word document.

Activity 1.11 | Formatting and Viewing Pages

In this activity, you will practice common formatting techniques used in Office applications.

1 On the Ribbon, click the **Insert tab**, and then in the **Header & Footer group**, click the **Footer** button.

> **Another Way**
>
> On the Design tab, in the Insert group, click Quick Parts, click Field, and then under Field names, click FileName.

2 At the top of the displayed gallery, under **Built-In**, click **Blank**. At the bottom of your document, with *Type text* highlighted in blue, using your own name type the file name of this document **Lastname_Firstname_1B_Cheese_Promotion** and then compare your screen with Figure 1.46.

Header & Footer Tools are added to the Ribbon. A ***footer*** is a reserved area for text or graphics that displays at the bottom of each page in a document. Likewise, a ***header*** is a reserved area for text or graphics that displays at the top of each page in a document. When the footer (or header) area is active, the document area is inactive (dimmed).

Figure 1.46

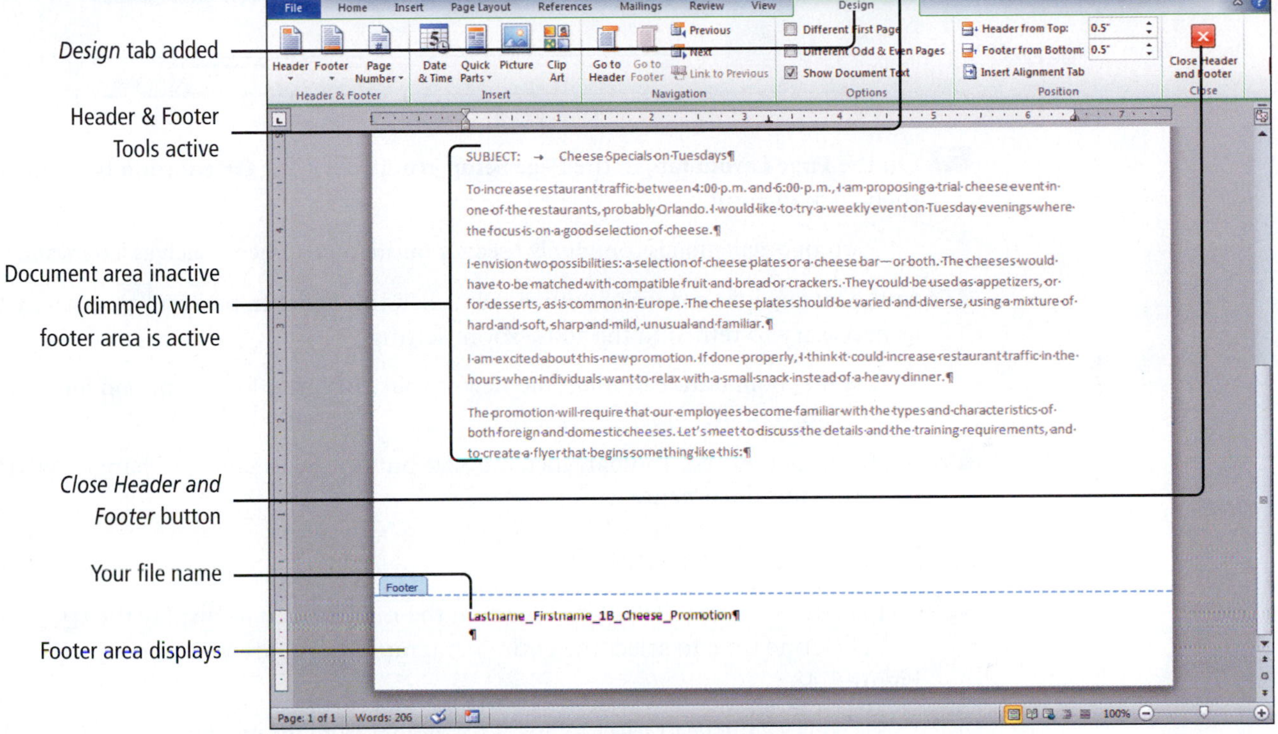

3 On the Ribbon, on the **Design tab**, in the **Close group**, click the **Close Header and Footer** button.

4 On the Ribbon, click the **Page Layout tab**. In the **Page Setup group**, click the **Orientation** button, and notice that two orientations display—*Portrait* and *Landscape*. Click **Landscape**.

In ***portrait orientation***, the paper is taller than it is wide. In ***landscape orientation***, the paper is wider than it is tall.

5 In the lower right corner of the screen, locate the **Zoom control** buttons 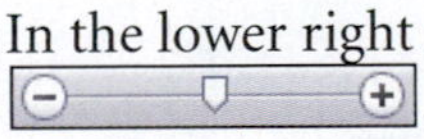.

To ***zoom*** means to increase or decrease the viewing area. You can zoom in to look closely at a section of a document, and then zoom out to see an entire page on the screen. You can also zoom to view multiple pages on the screen.

6 Drag the **Zoom slider**  to the left until you have zoomed to approximately *60%*. Compare your screen with Figure 1.47.

Figure 1.47

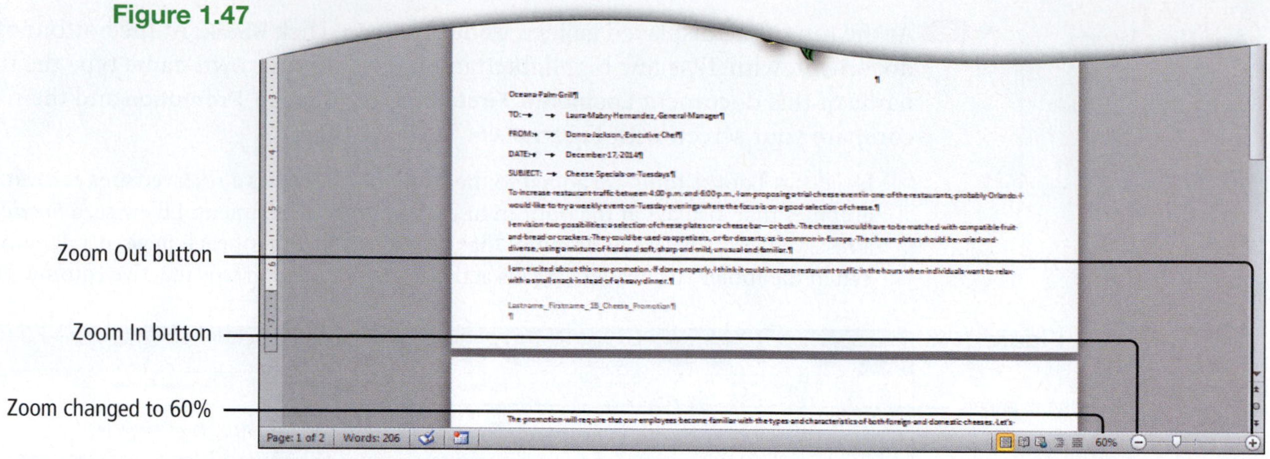

7 On the **Page Layout tab**, in the **Page Setup group**, click the **Orientation** button, and then click **Portrait**.

Portrait orientation is commonly used for business documents such as letters and memos.

8 In the lower right corner of your screen, click the **Zoom In** button as many times as necessary to return to the **100%** zoom setting.

Use the zoom feature to adjust the view of your document for editing and for your viewing comfort.

9 On the Quick Access Toolbar, click the **Save** button to save the changes you have made to your document.

Activity 1.12 | Formatting Text

1 To the left of *Oceana Palm Grill*, point in the margin area to display the pointer and click one time to select the entire paragraph. Compare your screen with Figure 1.48.

Use this technique to select complete paragraphs from the margin area. Additionally, with this technique you can drag downward to select multiple-line paragraphs—which is faster and more efficient than dragging through text.

Figure 1.48

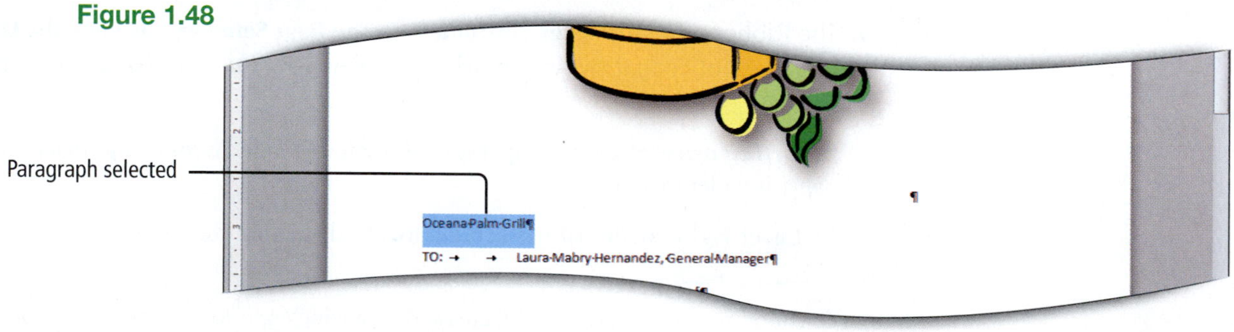

2 On the Ribbon, click the **Home tab**, and then in the **Paragraph group**, click the **Center** button to center the paragraph.

Alignment refers to the placement of paragraph text relative to the left and right margins. ***Center alignment*** refers to text that is centered horizontally between the left and right margins. You can also align text at the left margin, which is the default alignment for text in Word, or at the right margin.

3 On the **Home tab**, in the **Font group**, click the **Font button arrow** [Calibri (Body)]. At the top of the list, point to **Cambria**, and as you do so, notice that the selected text previews in the Cambria font.

A ***font*** is a set of characters with the same design and shape. The default font in a Word document is Calibri, which is a ***sans serif*** font—a font design with no lines or extensions on the ends of characters.

The Cambria font is a ***serif*** font—a font design that includes small line extensions on the ends of the letters to guide the eye in reading from left to right.

The list of fonts displays as a gallery showing potential results. For example, in the Font gallery, you can see the actual design and format of each font as it would look if applied to text.

4 Point to several other fonts and observe the effect on the selected text. Then, at the top of the **Font** gallery, under **Theme Fonts**, click **Cambria**.

A ***theme*** is a predesigned set of colors, fonts, lines, and fill effects that look good together and that can be applied to your entire document or to specific items.

A theme combines two sets of fonts—one for text and one for headings. In the default Office theme, Cambria is the suggested font for headings.

5 With the paragraph *Oceana Palm Grill* still selected, on the **Home tab**, in the **Font group**, click the **Font Size button arrow** [11], point to **36**, and then notice how Live Preview displays the text in the font size to which you are pointing. Compare your screen with Figure 1.49.

Figure 1.49

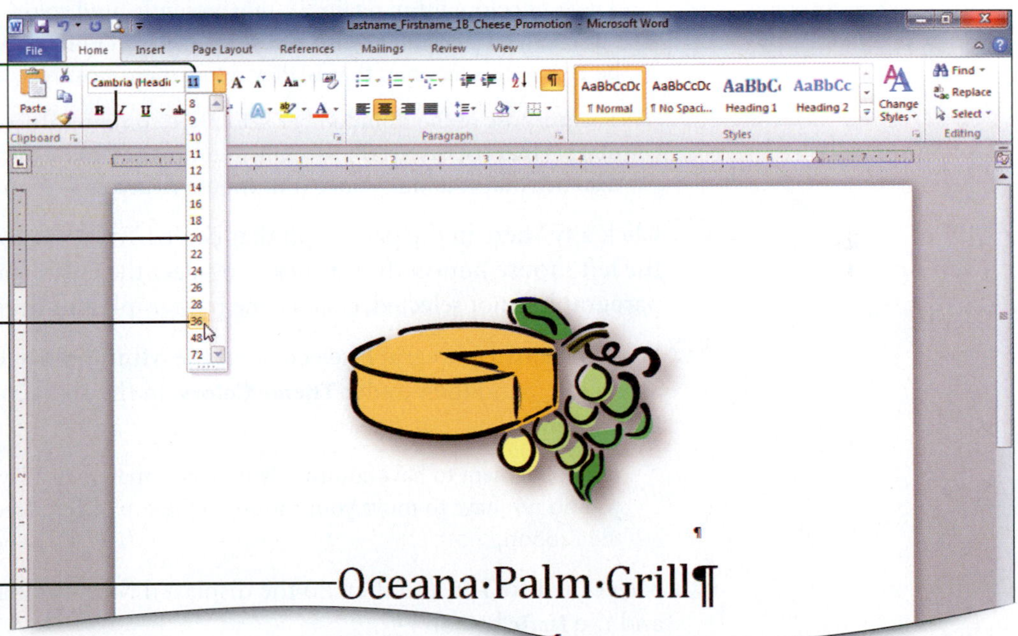

6 On the displayed list of font sizes, click **20**.

Fonts are measured in ***points***, with one point equal to 1/72 of an inch. A higher point size indicates a larger font size. Headings and titles are often formatted by using a larger font size. The word *point* is abbreviated as ***pt***.

7 With *Oceana Palm Grill* still selected, on the **Home tab**, in the **Font group**, click the **Font Color button arrow** [A]. Under **Theme Colors**, in the seventh column, click the last color—**Olive Green, Accent 3, Darker 50%**. Click anywhere to deselect the text.

8 To the left of *TO:*, point in the left margin area to display the [pointer] pointer, hold down the left mouse button, and then drag down to select the four memo headings. Compare your screen with Figure 1.50.

Use this technique to select complete paragraphs from the margin area—dragging downward to select multiple-line paragraphs—which is faster and more efficient than dragging through text.

Figure 1.50

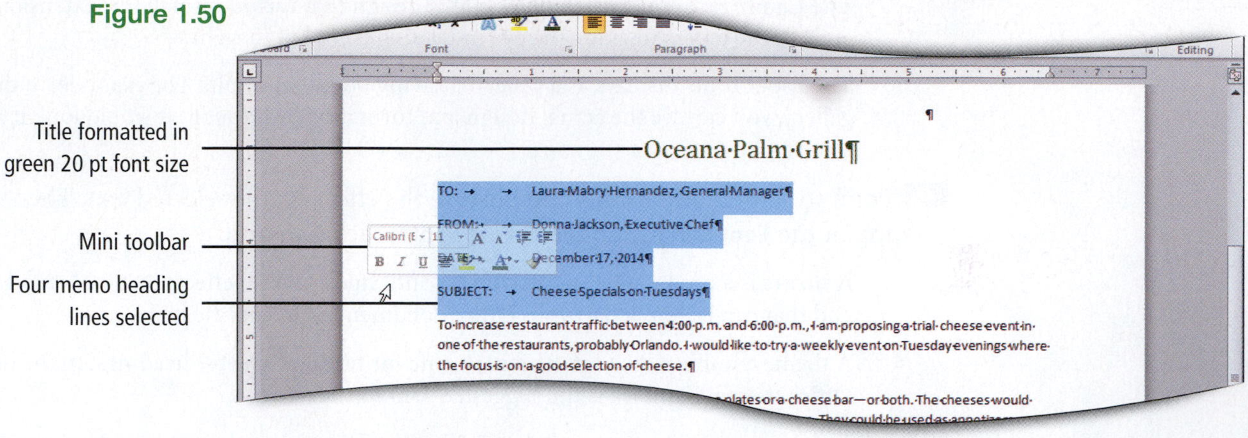

9 With the four paragraphs selected, on the Mini toolbar, click the **Font Color** button [A], which now displays a dark green bar instead of a red bar.

The font color button retains its most recently used color—Olive Green, Accent 3, Darker 50%. As you progress in your study of Microsoft Office, you will use other buttons that behave in this manner; that is, they retain their most recently used format.

The purpose of the Mini toolbar is to place commonly used commands close to text or objects that you select. By selecting a command on the Mini toolbar, you reduce the distance that you must move your mouse to access a command.

10 Click anywhere in the paragraph that begins *To increase*, and then ***triple-click***—click the left mouse button three times—to select the entire paragraph. If the entire paragraph is not selected, click in the paragraph and begin again.

11 With the entire paragraph selected, on the Mini toolbar, click the **Font Color button arrow** [A], and then under **Theme Colors**, in the sixth column, click the first color—**Red, Accent 2.**

It is convenient to have commonly used commands display on the Mini toolbar so that you do not have to move your mouse to the top of the screen to access the command from the Ribbon.

12 Select the text *TO:* and then on the displayed Mini toolbar, click the **Bold** button [B] and the **Italic** button [I].

Font styles include bold, italic, and underline. Font styles emphasize text and are a visual cue to draw the reader's eye to important text.

13 On the displayed Mini toolbar, click the **Italic** button [I] again to turn off the Italic formatting. Notice that the Italic button no longer glows orange.

A button that behaves in this manner is referred to as a ***toggle button***, which means it can be turned on by clicking it once, and then turned off by clicking it again.

14 With *TO:* still selected, on the Mini toolbar, click the **Format Painter** button. Then, move your mouse under the word *Laura*, and notice the mouse pointer. Compare your screen with Figure 1.51.

You can use the ***Format Painter*** to copy the formatting of specific text or of a paragraph and then apply it in other locations in your document.

The pointer takes the shape of a paintbrush, and contains the formatting information from the paragraph where the insertion point is positioned. Information about the Format Painter and how to turn it off displays in the status bar.

Figure 1.51

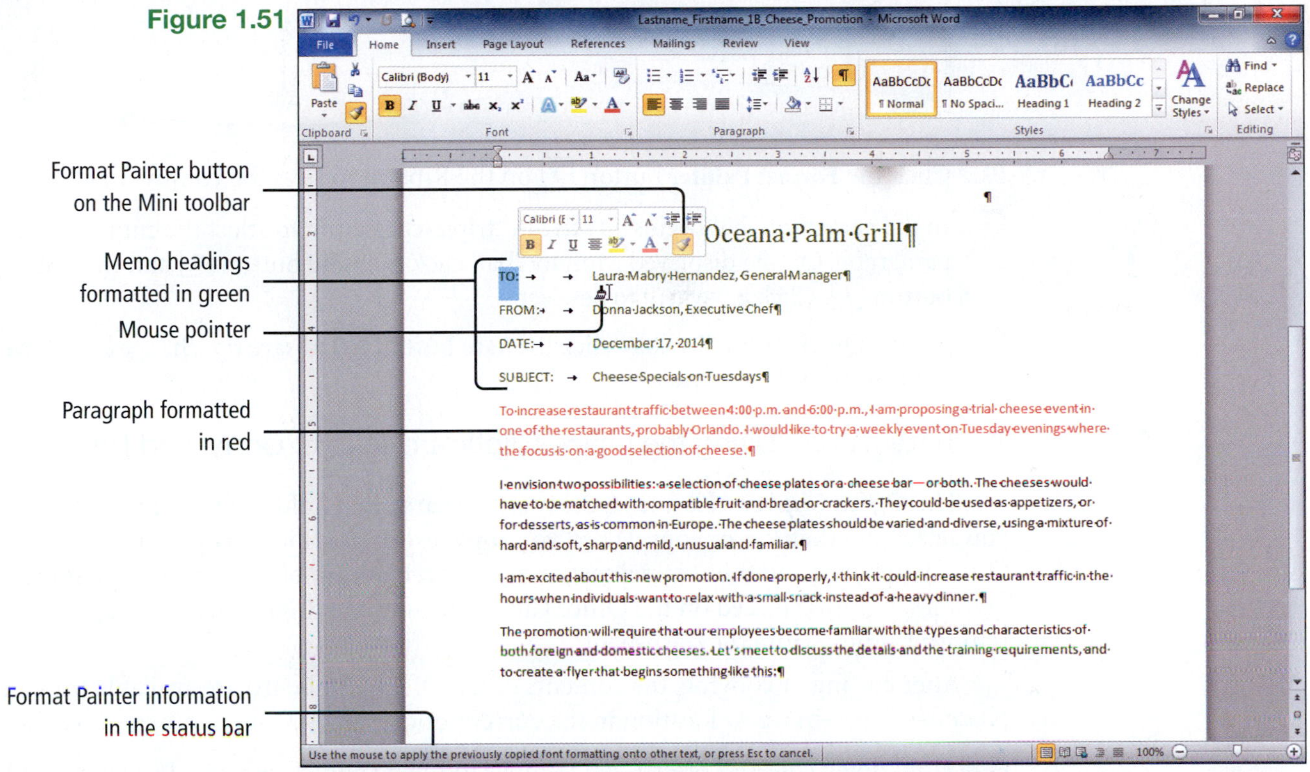

15 With the pointer, drag to select the text *FROM:* and notice that the Bold formatting is applied. Then, point to the selected text *FROM:* and on the Mini toolbar, *double-click* the **Format Painter** button.

16 Select the text *DATE:* to copy the Bold formatting, and notice that the pointer retains the shape.

When you *double-click* the Format Painter button, the Format Painter feature remains active until you either click the Format Painter button again, or press Esc to cancel it—as indicated on the status bar.

17 With Format Painter still active, select the text *SUBJECT:*, and then on the Ribbon, on the **Home tab**, in the **Clipboard group**, notice that the **Format Painter** button is glowing orange, indicating that it is active. Compare your screen with Figure 1.52.

Figure 1.52

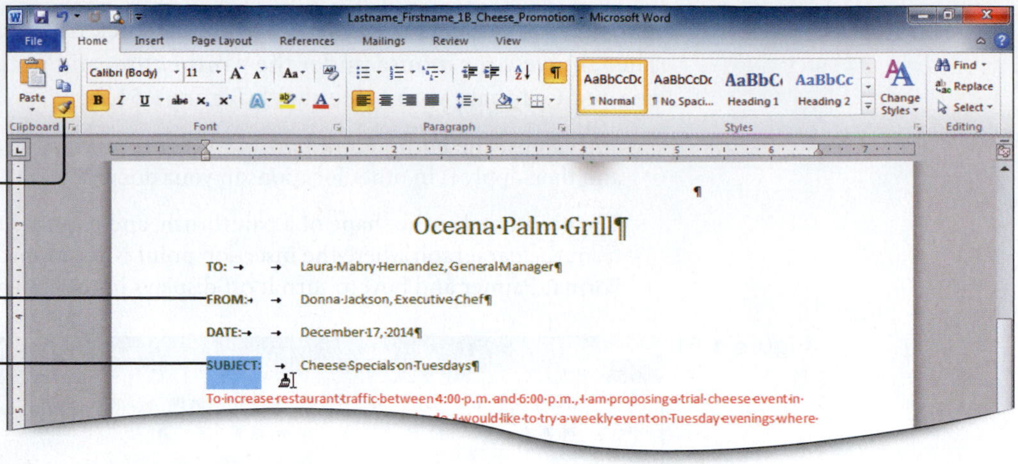

18 Click the **Format Painter** button on the Ribbon to turn the command off.

19 In the paragraph that begins *To increase*, triple-click again to select the entire paragraph. On the displayed Mini toolbar, click the **Bold** button **B** and the **Italic** button *I*. Click anywhere to deselect.

20 On the Quick Access Toolbar, click the **Save** button to save the changes you have made to your document.

Activity 1.13 | Using the Office Clipboard to Cut, Copy, and Paste

The ***Office Clipboard*** is a temporary storage area that holds text or graphics that you select and then cut or copy. When you ***copy*** text or graphics, a copy is placed on the Office Clipboard and the original text or graphic remains in place. When you ***cut*** text or graphics, a copy is placed on the Office Clipboard, and the original text or graphic is removed—cut—from the document.

After cutting or copying, the contents of the Office Clipboard are available for you to ***paste***—insert—in a new location in the current document, or into another Office file.

1 Hold down Ctrl and press Home to move to the beginning of your document, and then take a moment to study the table in Figure 1.53, which describes similar keyboard shortcuts with which you can navigate quickly in a document.

To Move	Press
To the beginning of a document	Ctrl + Home
To the end of a document	Ctrl + End
To the beginning of a line	Home
To the end of a line	End
To the beginning of the previous word	Ctrl + ←
To the beginning of the next word	Ctrl + →
To the beginning of the current word (if insertion point is in the middle of a word)	Ctrl + ←
To the beginning of a paragraph	Ctrl + ↑
To the beginning of the next paragraph	Ctrl + ↓
To the beginning of the current paragraph (if insertion point is in the middle of a paragraph)	Ctrl + ↑
Up one screen	PgUp
Down one screen	PageDown

Figure 1.53

Another Way

Right-click the selection, and then click Copy on the shortcut menu; or, use the keyboard shortcut Ctrl + C.

2 To the left of *Oceana Palm Grill*, point in the left margin area to display the pointer, and then click one time to select the entire paragraph. On the **Home tab**, in the **Clipboard group**, click the **Copy** button.

Because anything that you select and then copy—or cut—is placed on the Office Clipboard, the Copy command and the Cut command display in the Clipboard group of commands on the Ribbon.

There is no visible indication that your copied selection has been placed on the Office Clipboard.

3 On the **Home tab**, in the **Clipboard group**, to the right of the group name *Clipboard*, click the **Dialog Box Launcher** button, and then compare your screen with Figure 1.54.

The Clipboard task pane displays with your copied text. In any Ribbon group, the ***Dialog Box Launcher*** displays either a dialog box or a task pane related to the group of commands.

It is not necessary to display the Office Clipboard in this manner, although sometimes it is useful to do so. The Office Clipboard can hold 24 items.

Figure 1.54

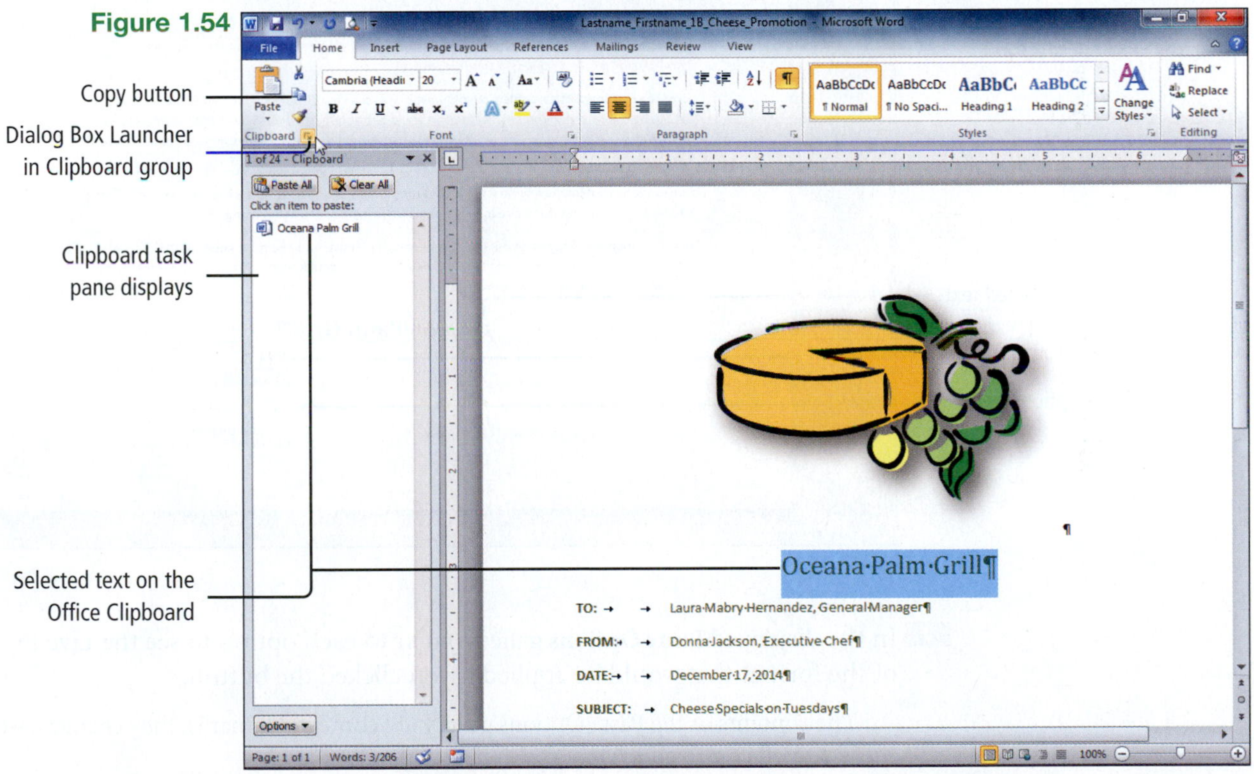

4 In the upper right corner of the **Clipboard** task pane, click the **Close** button.

Another Way

Right-click, on the shortcut menu under Paste Options, click the desired option button.

5 Press Ctrl + End to move to the end of your document. Press Enter one time to create a new blank paragraph. On the **Home tab**, in the **Clipboard group**, point to the **Paste** button, and then click the *upper* portion of this split button.

The Paste command pastes the most recently copied item on the Office Clipboard at the insertion point location. If you click the lower portion of the Paste button, a gallery of Paste Options displays.

6 Click the **Paste Options** button that displays below the pasted text as shown in Figure 1.55.

Here you can view and apply various formatting options for pasting your copied or cut text. Typically you will click Paste on the Ribbon and paste the item in its original format. If you want some other format for the pasted item, you can do so from the ***Paste Options gallery***.

The Paste Options gallery provides a Live Preview of the various options for changing the format of the pasted item with a single click. The Paste Options gallery is available in three places: on the Ribbon by clicking the lower portion of the Paste button—the Paste button arrow; from the Paste Options button that displays below the pasted item following the paste operation; or, on the shortcut menu if you right-click the pasted item.

Figure 1.55

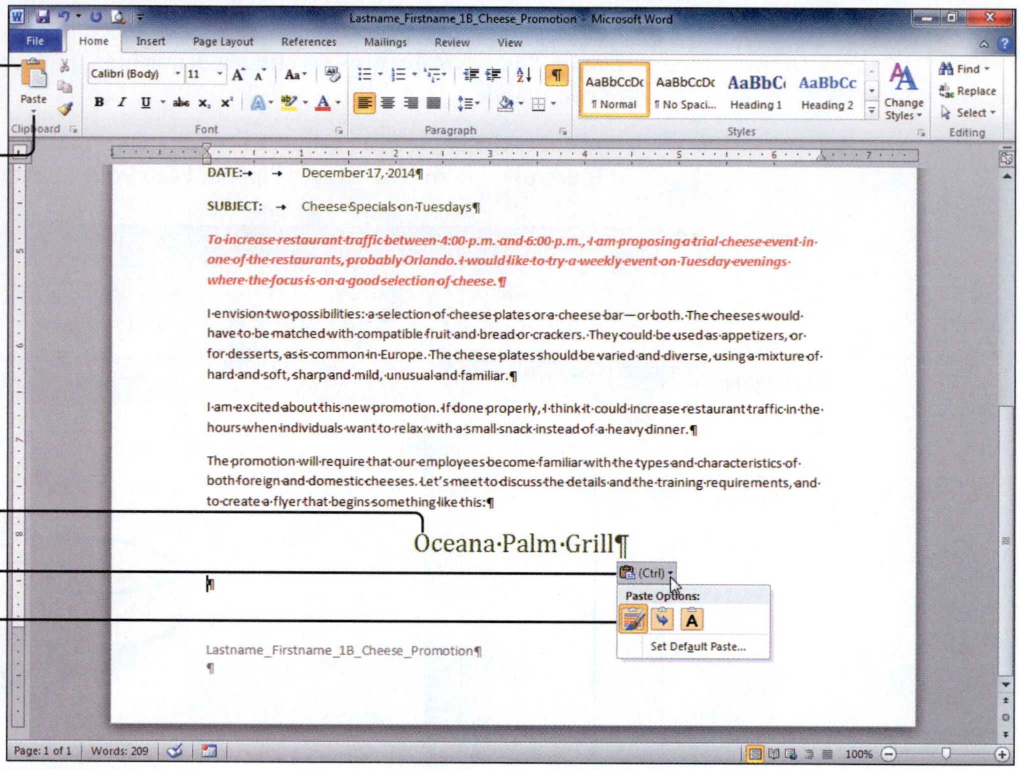

7 In the displayed **Paste Options** gallery, *point* to each option to see the Live Preview of the format that would be applied if you clicked the button.

The contents of the Paste Options gallery are contextual; that is, they change based on what you copied and where you are pasting.

8 Press Esc to close the gallery; the button will remain displayed until you take some other screen action.

Another Way

On the Home tab, in the Clipboard group, click the Cut button; or, use the keyboard shortcut Ctrl + X.

9 Press Ctrl + Home to move to the top of the document, and then click the **cheese image** one time to select it. While pointing to the selected image, right-click, and then on the shortcut menu, click **Cut**.

Recall that the Cut command cuts—removes—the selection from the document and places it on the Office Clipboard.

10 Press Del one time to remove the blank paragraph from the top of the document, and then press Ctrl + End to move to the end of the document.

11 With the insertion point blinking in the blank paragraph at the end of the document, right-click, and notice that the **Paste Options** gallery displays on the shortcut menu. Compare your screen with Figure 1.56.

Figure 1.56

Paste Options on shortcut menu

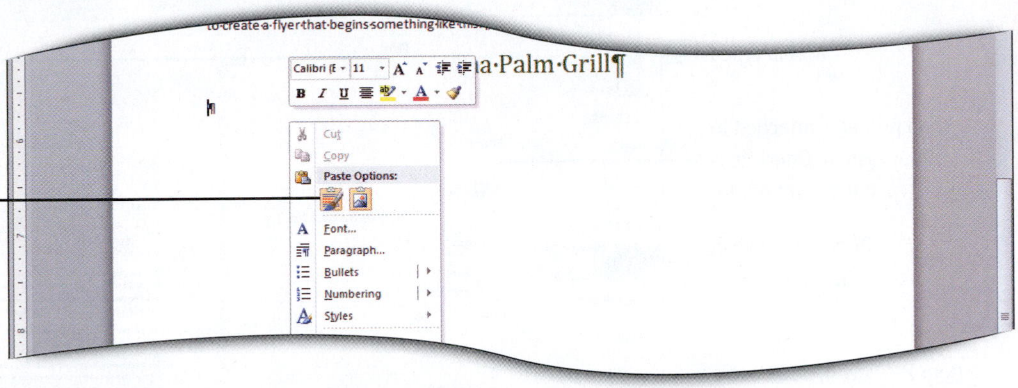

12 On the shortcut menu, under **Paste Options**, click the first button—**Keep Source Formatting**.

13 Click the picture to select it. On the **Home tab**, in the **Paragraph group**, click the **Center** button.

14 Above the cheese picture, click to position the insertion point at the end of the word *Grill*, press Spacebar one time, and then type **Tuesday Cheese Tastings** Compare your screen with Figure 1.57.

Figure 1.57

Heading

Picture inserted and centered

Activity 1.14 | Viewing Print Preview and Printing a Word Document

1 Press Ctrl + Home to move to the top of your document. Select the text *Oceana Palm Grill*, and then replace the selected text by typing **Memo**

2 Display **Backstage** view, on the right, click **Properties**, and then click **Show Document Panel**. Replace the existing author name with your first and last name. In the **Subject** box, type your course name and section number, and then in the **Keywords** box, type **cheese promotion** and then **Close** the **Document Information Panel**.

Another Way

Press Ctrl + F2 to display Print Preview.

3 On the Quick Access Toolbar, click **Save** to save the changes you have made to your document.

4 On the Quick Access Toolbar, click the **Print Preview** button that you added. Compare your screen with Figure 1.58.

Figure 1.58

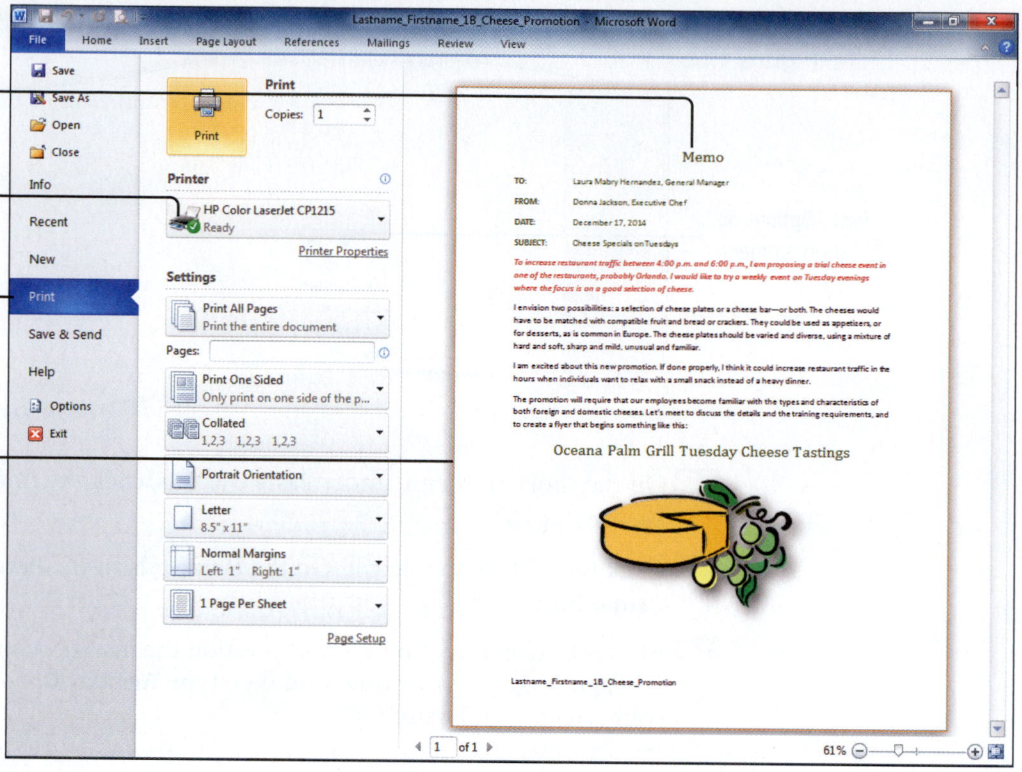

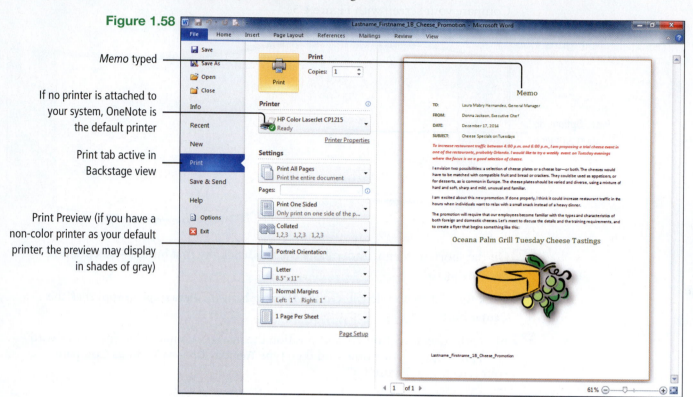

5 Examine the **Print Preview**. Under **Settings**, notice that in **Backstage** view, several of the same commands that are available on the Page Layout tab of the Ribbon also display.

For convenience, common adjustments to Page Layout display here, so that you can make last-minute adjustments without closing Backstage view.

6 If you need to make any corrections, click the Home tab to return to the document and make any necessary changes.

It is good practice to examine the Print Preview before printing or submitting your work electronically. Then, make any necessary corrections, re-save, and redisplay Print Preview.

7 If you are directed to do so, click Print to print the document; or, above the Info tab, click Close, and then submit your file electronically according to the directions provided by your instructor.

If you click the Print button, Backstage view closes and the Word window redisplays.

8 On the Quick Access Toolbar, point to the **Print Preview icon** you placed there, right-click, and then click **Remove from Quick Access Toolbar**.

If you are working on your own computer and you want to do so, you can leave the icon on the toolbar; in a lab setting, you should return the software to its original settings.

9 At the right end of the title bar, click the program **Close** button [X].

10 If a message displays asking if you want the text on the Clipboard to be available after you quit Word, click **No**.

This message most often displays if you have copied some type of image to the Clipboard. If you click Yes, the items on the Clipboard will remain for you to use.

Objective 11 | Use the Microsoft Office 2010 Help System

Within each Office program, the Help feature provides information about all of the program's features and displays step-by-step instructions for performing many tasks.

Activity 1.15 | Using the Microsoft Office 2010 Help System in Excel

In this activity, you will use the Microsoft Help feature to find information about formatting numbers in Excel.

> **Another Way**
> Press F1 to display Help.

1 **Start** the **Microsoft Excel 2010** program. In the upper right corner of your screen, click the **Microsoft Excel Help** button [?].

2 In the **Excel Help** window, click in the white box in upper left corner, type **formatting numbers** and then click **Search** or press Enter.

3 On the list of results, click **Display numbers as currency**. Compare your screen with Figure 1.59.

Figure 1.59

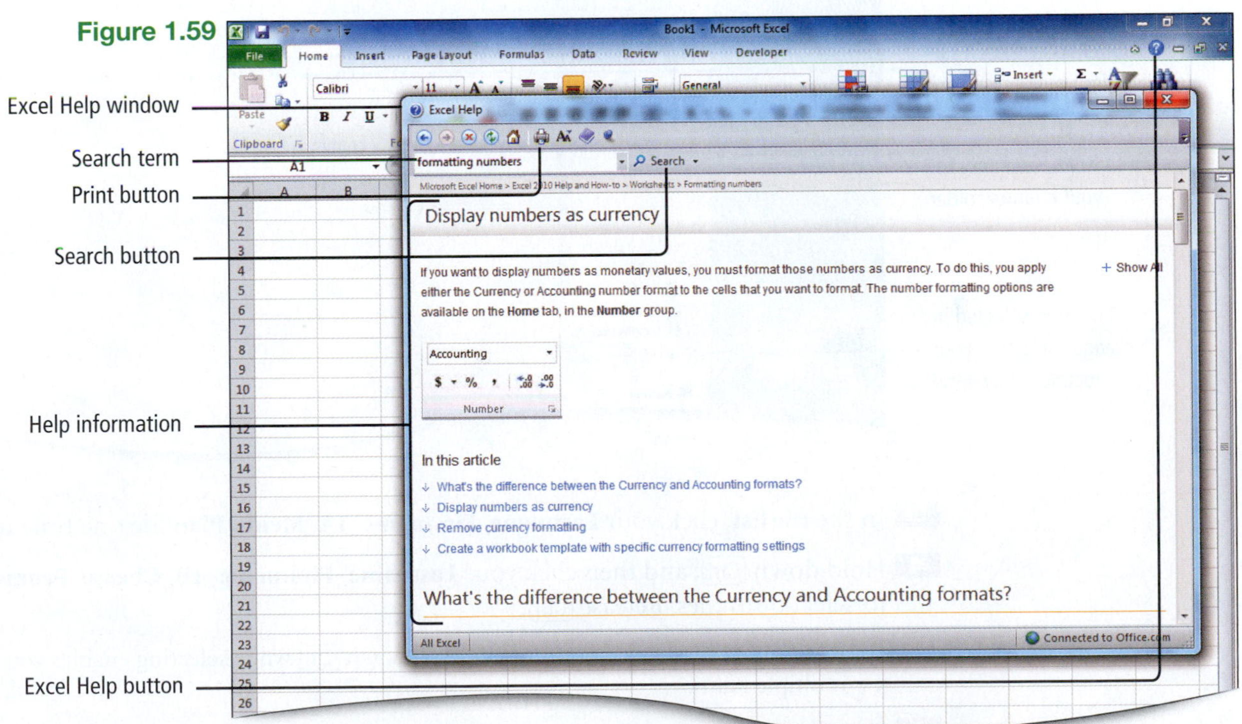

4 If you want to do so, on the toolbar at the top of the **Excel Help** window, click the Print [printer] button to print a copy of this information for your reference.

5 On the title bar of the Excel Help window, click the **Close** button. On the right side of the Microsoft Excel title bar, click the **Close** button to close Excel.

Objective 12 | Compress Files

A ***compressed file*** is a file that has been reduced in size. Compressed files take up less storage space and can be transferred to other computers faster than uncompressed files. You can also combine a group of files into one compressed folder, which makes it easier to share a group of files.

Activity 1.16 | Compressing Files

In this activity, you will combine the two files you created in this chapter into one compressed file.

1 On the Windows taskbar, click the **Start** button, and then on the right, click **Computer**.

2 On the left, in the **navigation pane**, click the location of your two files from this chapter—your USB flash drive or other location—and display the folder window for your **Common Features Chapter 1** folder. Compare your screen with Figure 1.60.

Figure 1.60

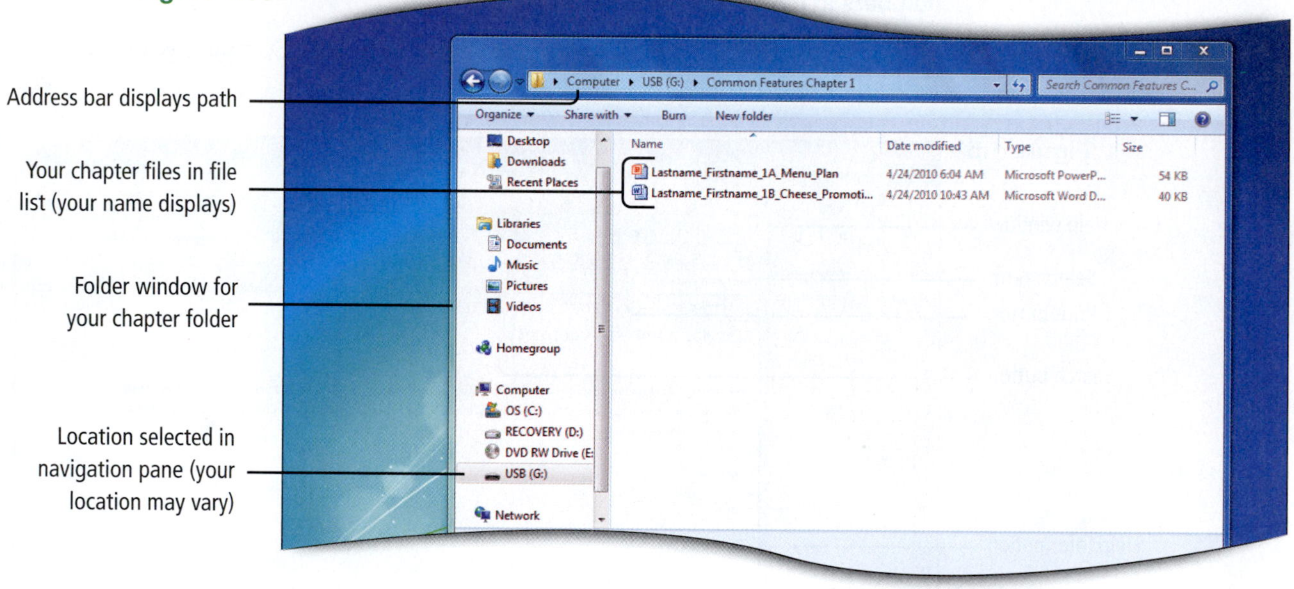

3 In the **file list**, click your **Lastname_Firstname_1A_Menu_Plan** file one time to select it.

4 Hold down Ctrl, and then click your **Lastname_Firstname_1B_Cheese_Promotion** file to select both files. Release Ctrl.

In any Windows-based program, holding down Ctrl while selecting enables you to select multiple items.

5 Point anywhere over the two selected files and right-click. On the shortcut menu, point to **Send to**, and then compare your screen with Figure 1.61.

Figure 1.61

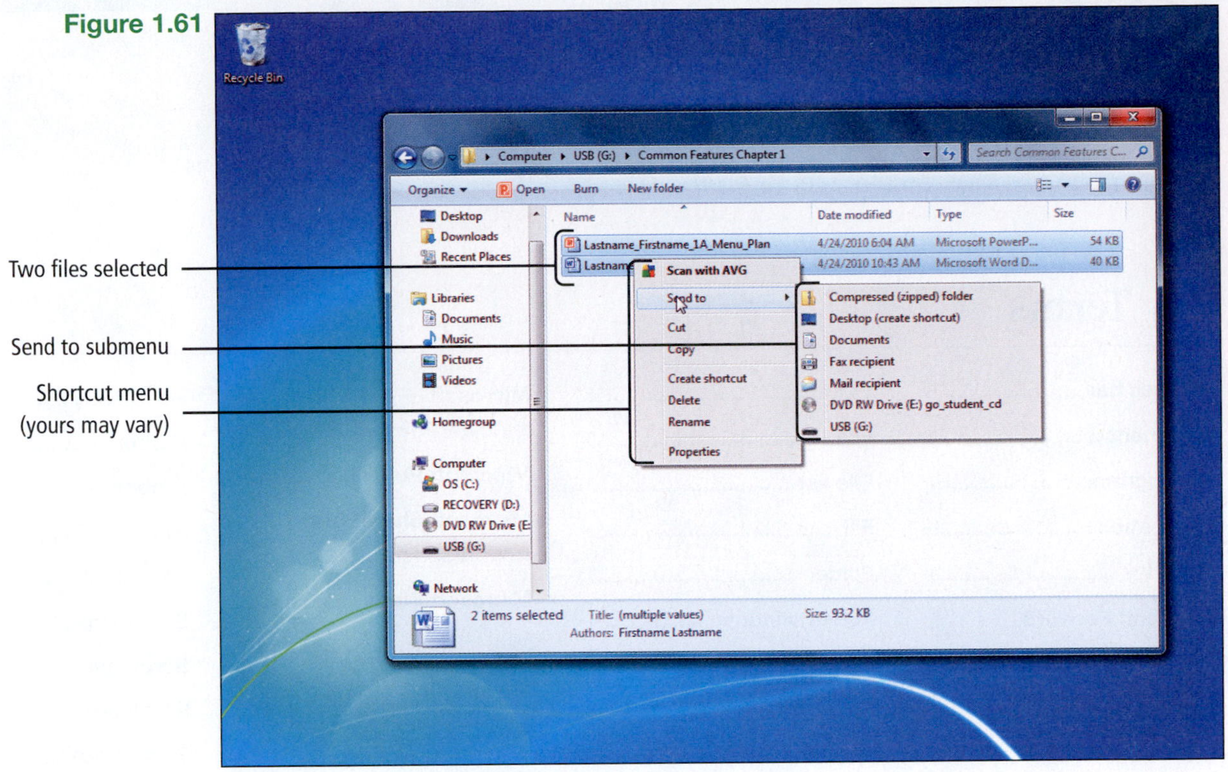

6 On the shortcut submenu, click **Compressed (zipped) folder**.

Windows creates a compressed folder containing a *copy* of each of the selected files. The folder name is the name of the file or folder to which you were pointing, and is selected—highlighted in blue—so that you can rename it.

7 Using your own name, type **Lastname_Firstname_Common_Features_Ch1** and press Enter.

The compressed folder is now ready to attach to an e-mail or share in some other electronic format.

8 **Close** [X] the folder window. If directed to do so by your instructor, submit your compressed folder electronically.

> **More Knowledge | Extracting Compressed Files**
>
> ***Extract*** means to decompress, or pull out, files from a compressed form. When you extract a file, an uncompressed copy is placed in the folder that you specify. The original file remains in the compressed folder.

End **You have completed Project 1B**

Content-Based Assessments

Summary

In this chapter, you used Windows Explorer to navigate the Windows file structure. You also used features that are common across the Microsoft Office 2010 programs.

Key Terms

Address bar 5
Alignment 34
All Programs 7
Application 6
AutoPlay 3
Back and Forward buttons 5
Backstage tabs 14
Backstage view 14
Center alignment 34
Click 4
Command 5
Common dialog boxes 22
Compressed file 44
Context sensitive command 11
Contextual tabs 30
Copy 38
Cut 38
Default 9
Deselect 29
Desktop 3
Details pane 5
Dialog box 11
Dialog Box Launcher 39
Document properties 14
Double-click 5
Drag 10
Edit 9
Ellipsis 11
Enhanced ScreenTip 28
Extract 45
File 3
File list 5
Fill 12
Folder 3
Folder window 4
Font 35
Font styles 36
Footer 33
Format Painter 37
Formatting 32
Formatting marks 25
Gallery 12
Groups 26
Header 33
Icons 5
Info tab 14
Insertion point 9
Keyboard shortcut 10
KeyTip 31
Landscape orientation 33
Library 4
Live Preview 31
Location 13
Metadata 14
Microsoft Access 7
Microsoft Excel 7
Microsoft InfoPath 7
Microsoft Office 2010 6
Microsoft OneNote 7
Microsoft Outlook 7
Microsoft PowerPoint 7
Microsoft Publisher 7
Microsoft SharePoint Workspace 7
Microsoft Word 7
Mini toolbar 10
Navigate 3
Navigation pane 5
Nonprinting characters 25
Office Clipboard 38
Open dialog box 22
Option button 12
Options dialog box 25
Paragraph symbol 28
Paste 38
Paste Options 40
PDF (Portable Document Format) file 20
Point 4
Pointer 9
Points 35
Portrait orientation 33
Preview pane button 5
Print Preview 18
Program 6
Program-level control buttons 8
Protected View 24
Pt 35
Quick Access Toolbar 27
Quick Commands 14
Read-Only 23
Ribbon 26
Ribbon tabs 8
Right-click 11
Sans serif 35
ScreenTip 12
Scroll bar 16
Scroll box 16
Search box 5
Select 10
Serif 35
Shortcut menu 11
Split button 5
Start button 4
Start menu 4
Status bar 8
Subfolder 3
Tabs 26
Tags 5
Task pane 28
Theme 35
Title bar 8
Toggle button 36
Triple-click 36
Trusted Documents 24
USB flash drive 6
Views button 5
Window 3
Windows Explorer 3
Windows taskbar 4
Zoom 18

Content-Based Assessments

Matching

Match each term in the second column with its correct definition in the first column by writing the letter of the term on the blank line in front of the correct definition.

A	Address bar
B	Command
C	File
D	Folder
E	Folder window
F	Icons
G	Keyboard shortcut
H	Library
I	Microsoft Excel
J	Program
K	Ribbon
L	Start menu
M	Subfolder
N	Title bar
O	Windows Explorer

_____ 1. A collection of information stored on a computer under a single name.

_____ 2. A container in which you store files.

_____ 3. A folder within a folder.

_____ 4. The program that displays the files and folders on your computer.

_____ 5. The Windows menu that is the main gateway to your computer.

_____ 6. In Windows 7, a window that displays the contents of the current folder, library, or device, and contains helpful parts so that you can navigate.

_____ 7. In Windows, a collection of items, such as files and folders, assembled from various locations that might be on your computer.

_____ 8. The bar at the top of a folder window with which you can navigate to a different folder or library, or go back to a previous one.

_____ 9. An instruction to a computer program that carries out an action.

_____ 10. Small pictures that represent a program, a file, a folder, or an object.

_____ 11. A set of instructions that a computer uses to perform a specific task.

_____ 12. A spreadsheet program used to calculate numbers and create charts.

_____ 13. The user interface that groups commands on tabs at the top of the program window.

_____ 14. A bar at the top of the program window displaying the current file and program name.

_____ 15. One or more keys pressed to perform a task that would otherwise require a mouse.

Multiple Choice

Circle the correct answer.

1. A small toolbar with frequently used commands that displays when selecting text or objects is the:
   A. Quick Access Toolbar **B.** Mini toolbar **C.** Document toolbar

2. In Office 2010, a centralized space for file management tasks is:
   A. a task pane **B.** a dialog box **C.** Backstage view

3. The commands Save, Save As, Open, and Close in Backstage view are located:
   A. above the Backstage tabs **B.** below the Backstage tabs **C.** under the screen thumbnail

4. The tab in Backstage view that displays information about the current file is the:
   A. Recent tab **B.** Info tab **C.** Options tab

5. Details about a file, including the title, author name, subject, and keywords are known as:
   A. document properties **B.** formatting marks **C.** KeyTips

6. An Office feature that displays a list of potential results is:
   A. Live Preview **B.** a contextual tab **C.** a gallery

7. A type of formatting emphasis applied to text such as bold, italic, and underline, is called:
   A. a font style B. a KeyTip C. a tag

8. A technology showing the result of applying formatting as you point to possible results is called:
   A. Live Preview B. Backstage view C. gallery view

9. A temporary storage area that holds text or graphics that you select and then cut or copy is the:
   A. paste options gallery B. ribbon C. Office clipboard

10. A file that has been reduced in size is:
    A. a compressed file B. an extracted file C. a PDF file

Using Styles and Creating Multilevel Lists and Charts

OUTCOMES

At the end of this chapter you will be able to:

OBJECTIVES

Mastering these objectives will enable you to:

PROJECT 4A

Edit a handout using Quick Styles and arrange text into an organized list.

1. Apply and Modify Quick Styles (p. 51)
2. Create New Styles (p. 54)
3. Manage Styles (p. 56)
4. Create a Multilevel List (p. 60)

PROJECT 4B

Change a style set, and create and format a chart.

5. Change the Style Set and Paragraph Spacing of a Document (p. 68)
6. Insert a Chart and Enter Data into a Chart (p. 71)
7. Change a Chart Type (p. 77)
8. Format a Chart (p. 78)

© Steve Murray / Alamy

In This Chapter

In this chapter you will apply styles, create multilevel lists, and display numerical data in charts. You can draw attention to text by using formatting tools. The theme and style set features in Word provide a simple way to coordinate colors, fonts, and effects used in a document. For example, if you publish a monthly newsletter, you can apply styles to article headings and modify lists to ensure all editions of the newsletter maintain a consistent and professional look.

Charts display numerical data in a visual format. You can use charts to show a comparison among items, to show the relationship of each part to a whole, or to show trends over time. Formatting chart elements adds interest and assists the reader in interpreting the displayed data.

The projects in this chapter relate to **Lehua Hawaiian Adventures**. Named for the small, crescent-shaped island that is noted for its snorkeling and scuba diving, Lehua Hawaiian Adventures offers exciting but affordable adventure tours. Hiking tours go off the beaten path to amazing remote places on the islands. If you prefer to ride into the heart of Hawaii, try the cycling tours. Lehua Hawaiian Adventures also offers Jeep tours. Whatever you prefer—mountain, sea, volcano—our tour guides are experts in the history, geography, culture, and flora and fauna of Hawaii.

Project 4A Customer Handout

myitlab
Project 4A Training

Project Activities

In Activities 4.1 through 4.10, you will create a handout for Lehua Hawaiian Adventures customers who are interested in scuba diving tours. You will use styles and multilevel list formats so that the document is attractive and easy to read. Your completed document will look similar to Figure 4.1.

Project Files

For Project 4A, you will need the following file:

w04A_Customer_Handout

You will save your document as:

Lastname_Firstname_4A_Customer_Handout

Project Results

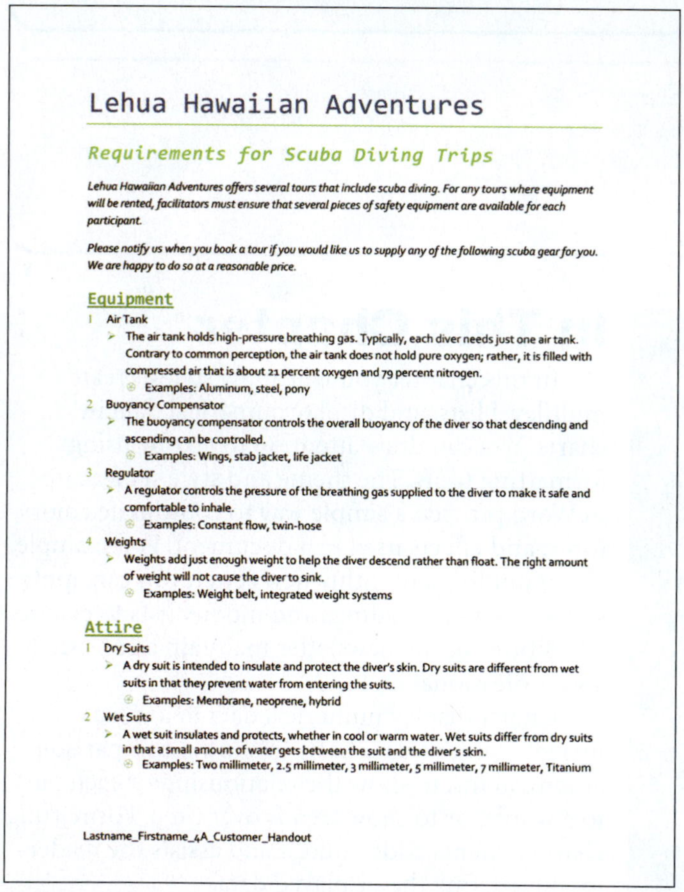

Lehua Hawaiian Adventures

Requirements for Scuba Diving Trips

Lehua Hawaiian Adventures offers several tours that include scuba diving. For any tours where equipment will be rented, facilitators must ensure that several pieces of safety equipment are available for each participant.

Please notify us when you book a tour if you would like us to supply any of the following scuba gear for you. We are happy to do so at a reasonable price.

Equipment

1 Air Tank
- The air tank holds high-pressure breathing gas. Typically, each diver needs just one air tank. Contrary to common perception, the air tank does not hold pure oxygen; rather, it is filled with compressed air that is about 21 percent oxygen and 79 percent nitrogen.
  - Examples: Aluminum, steel, pony

2 Buoyancy Compensator
- The buoyancy compensator controls the overall buoyancy of the diver so that descending and ascending can be controlled.
  - Examples: Wings, stab jacket, life jacket

3 Regulator
- A regulator controls the pressure of the breathing gas supplied to the diver to make it safe and comfortable to inhale.
  - Examples: Constant flow, twin-hose

4 Weights
- Weights add just enough weight to help the diver descend rather than float. The right amount of weight will not cause the diver to sink.
  - Examples: Weight belt, integrated weight systems

Attire

1 Dry Suits
- A dry suit is intended to insulate and protect the diver's skin. Dry suits are different from wet suits in that they prevent water from entering the suits.
  - Examples: Membrane, neoprene, hybrid

2 Wet Suits
- A wet suit insulates and protects, whether in cool or warm water. Wet suits differ from dry suits in that a small amount of water gets between the suit and the diver's skin.
  - Examples: Two millimeter, 2.5 millimeter, 3 millimeter, 5 millimeter, 7 millimeter, Titanium

Lastname_Firstname_4A_Customer_Handout

Figure 4.1
Project 4A Customer Handout

Objective 1 | Apply and Modify Quick Styles

A ***style*** is a group of formatting commands, such as font, font size, font color, paragraph alignment, and line spacing. You can retrieve a style by name and apply it to text with one click.

Using styles to format text has several advantages over using ***direct formatting***—the process of applying each format separately; for example, bold, then font size, then font color, and so on. Styles are faster to apply, result in a consistent look, and can be automatically updated in all instances in a document, which can be especially useful in long documents.

Activity 4.01 | Applying Quick Styles

Quick Styles are combinations of formatting options that work together and look attractive together. A collection of frequently used Quick Styles is available from the Quick Styles gallery on the Ribbon. Each Quick Style option has a name—for example, *Subtitle* or *Heading 1*. A Quick Style can be applied to any selected text.

1 **Start** Word. Click the **File tab** to display **Backstage** view, and then click **Open**. From your student files, locate and open the document **w04A_Customer_Handout**.

2 Click the **File tab**, and then click **Save As**. In the **Save As** dialog box, navigate to the location where you are saving your files for this chapter. Create a new folder named **Word Chapter 4** Save the document as **Lastname_Firstname_4A_Customer_Handout**

3 Scroll to the bottom of **Page 1**, right-click in the footer area, click **Edit Footer**, and then using **Quick Parts**, insert the file name. **Close** the footer area. If necessary, display the rulers and formatting marks.

4 Press Ctrl + Home to move to the top of the document. If *Lehua* is flagged as a spelling error, point to the first occurrence, right-click, and then click **Ignore All**.

5 On the **Home tab**, in the **Styles group**, notice that the **Normal** style is selected—outlined in orange. Compare your screen with Figure 4.2.

The ***Normal Quick Style*** is the default style for new documents and includes default styles and customizations that determine the basic look of a document. For example, the Normal Quick Style includes the Calibri font, 11 point font size, multiple line spacing at 1.15, and 10 pt spacing after a paragraph.

Figure 4.2

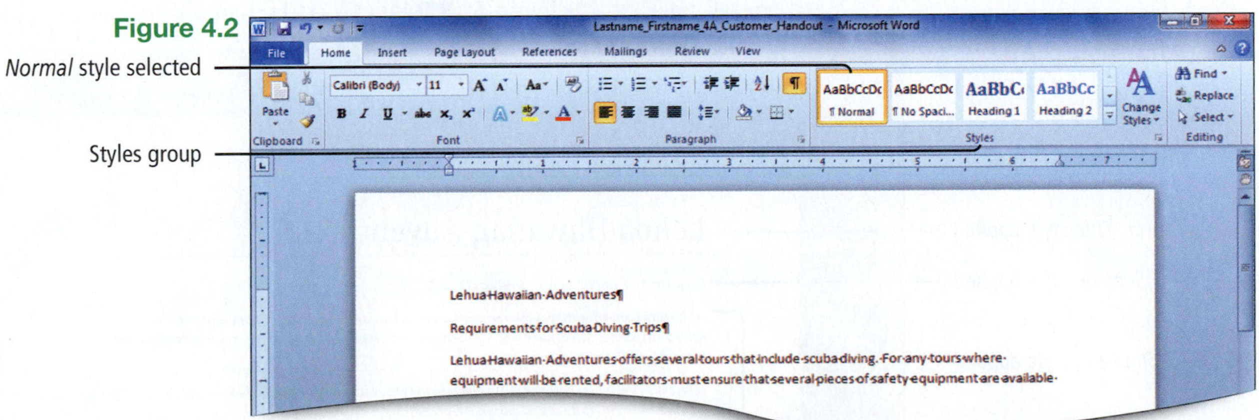

6 Including the paragraph mark, select the first paragraph, which forms the title of the document. On the **Home tab**, in the **Styles group**, click the **More** button [▾] to display the **Quick Styles** gallery. Point to the **Quick Style** named **Title**, and then compare your screen with Figure 4.3.

Live Preview displays how the text will look with this style applied.

Figure 4.3

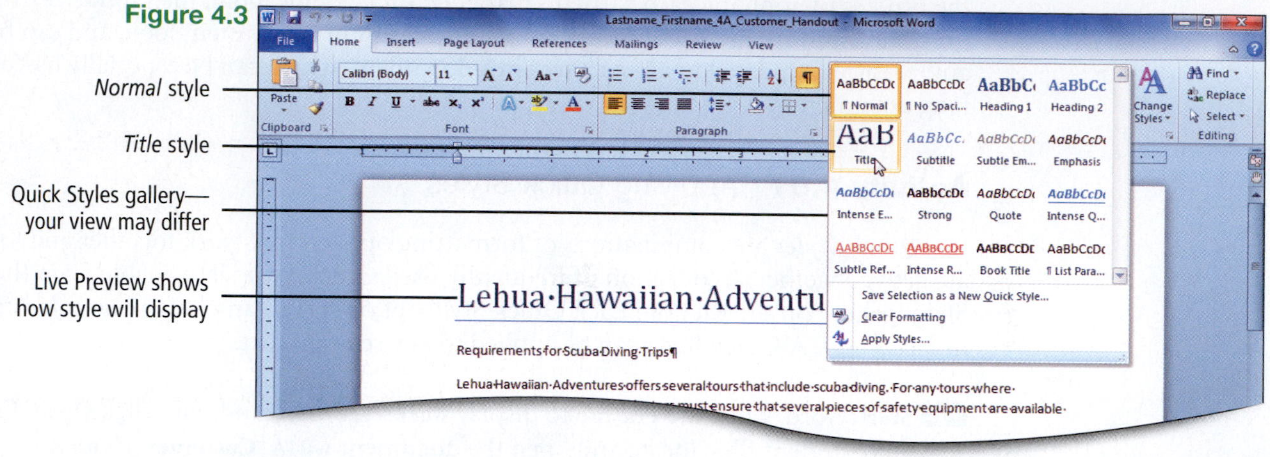

7 Click the **Title** style, and then click anywhere in the document to deselect the title.

The Title style includes the 26 point Cambria font, a dark blue font color, and a line that spans the width of the document.

8 Select the second paragraph, which begins *Requirements for* and is the subtitle of the document. In the **Styles group**, click the **More** button [▾], and then from the displayed **Quick Styles** gallery, click the **Subtitle** style.

The Subtitle style includes the 12 point Cambria font, italic emphasis, and a blue font color.

9 Select the third and fourth paragraphs, beginning with *Lehua Hawaiian Adventures offers* and ending with the text *at a reasonable price*. In the **Styles group**, click the **More** button [▾], and then from the displayed **Quick Styles** gallery, click the **Emphasis** style. Click anywhere to deselect the text, and then compare your screen with Figure 4.4.

Figure 4.4

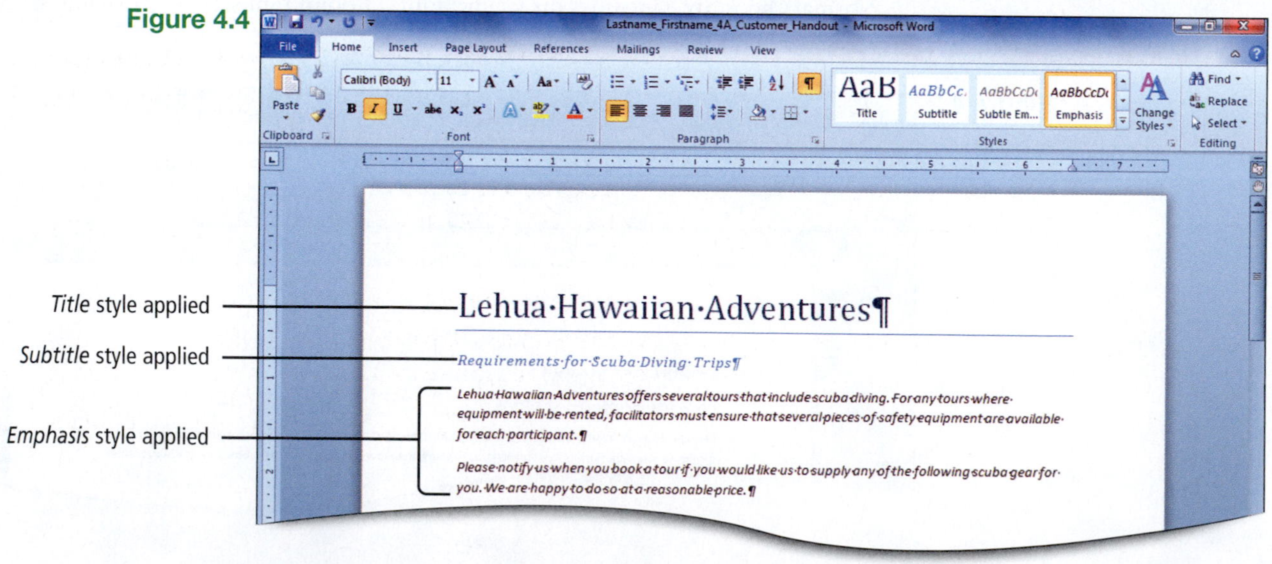

10 **Save** your document.

Activity 4.02 | Modifying Quick Styles

You are not limited to the exact formatting of a Quick Style—you can change it to suit your needs. For example, you might like the effect of a Quick Style with the exception of the font size. If you plan to use such a customized style repeatedly in a document, it's a good idea to modify the style to look exactly the way you want it, and then save it as a *new* Quick Style.

1 Select the heading *Equipment.* Using the technique you practiced, display the **Quick Styles** gallery, and then click the **Heading 1** style.

The Heading 1 style includes the 14 point Cambria font, bold emphasis, a blue font color, and 24 pt spacing before the paragraph.

A small black square displays to the left of the paragraph indicating that the Heading 1 style also includes the ***Keep with next*** and ***Keep lines together*** formatting—Word commands that keep a heading with its first paragraph of text on the same page, or prevent a single line from displaying by itself at the bottom of a page or at the top of a page.

2 With the paragraph selected, on the displayed Mini toolbar, change the **Font Size** to **16**.

3 Click the **Page Layout tab**, and then in the **Paragraph group**, change the **Spacing Before** to **12 pt**.

4 With the paragraph still selected, click the **Home tab**. Display the **Quick Styles** gallery, and then right-click the **Heading 1** style to display a shortcut menu. Compare your screen with Figure 4.5.

Figure 4.5

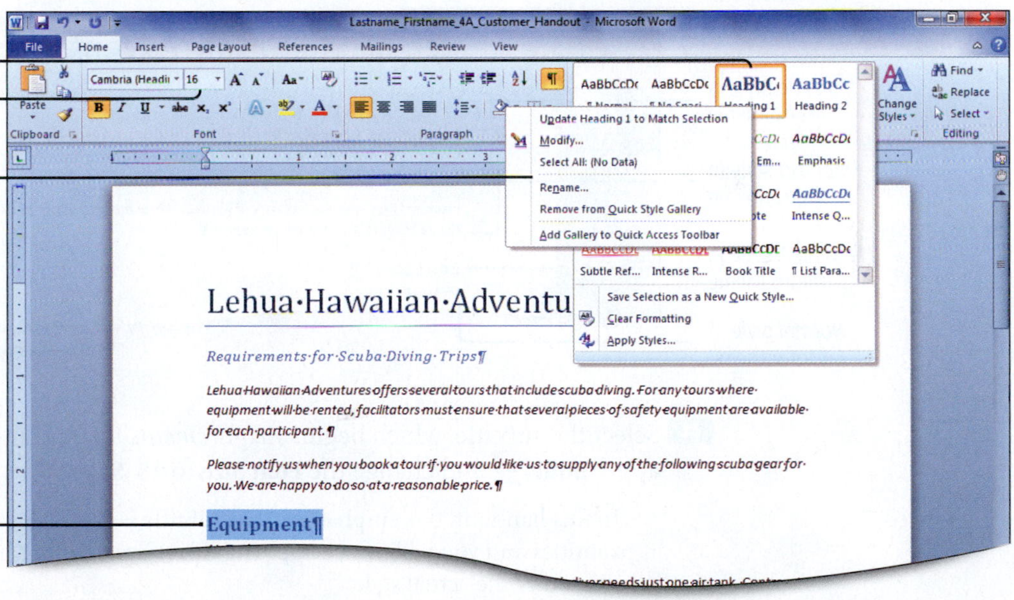

5 From the displayed shortcut menu, click **Update Heading 1 to Match Selection**, and then click anywhere to deselect the text.

By updating the heading style, you ensure that the next time you apply the Heading 1 style in *this* document, it will retain these new formats. In this manner, you can customize a style. The changes to the Heading 1 style are stored *only* in this document and will not affect the Heading 1 style in any other documents.

6 Scroll down to view the lower portion of **Page 1**, and then select the heading *Attire.* In the **Styles group**, click **Heading 1**, and notice that the *modified* **Heading 1** style is applied to the paragraph. Click anywhere in the document to deselect the text. **Save** your document.

Activity 4.03 | Changing the Theme

Recall that a theme is a predefined combination of colors, fonts, and effects; the *Office* theme is the default setting. Quick Styles use the color scheme, font scheme, and effects associated with the current theme. If you change the theme, the Quick Styles adopt the fonts, colors, and effects of the new theme.

1 Press Ctrl + Home. Click the **Page Layout tab**, and then in the **Themes group**, click the **Themes** button.

2 Point to various themes and notice the changes in your document.

Live Preview enables you to see the effect a theme has on text with Quick Styles applied.

3 Scroll as necessary, click the **Metro** theme, and then compare your screen with Figure 4.6.

The Metro theme's fonts, colors, and effects display in the document. All the Quick Styles now use the Metro theme.

Figure 4.6

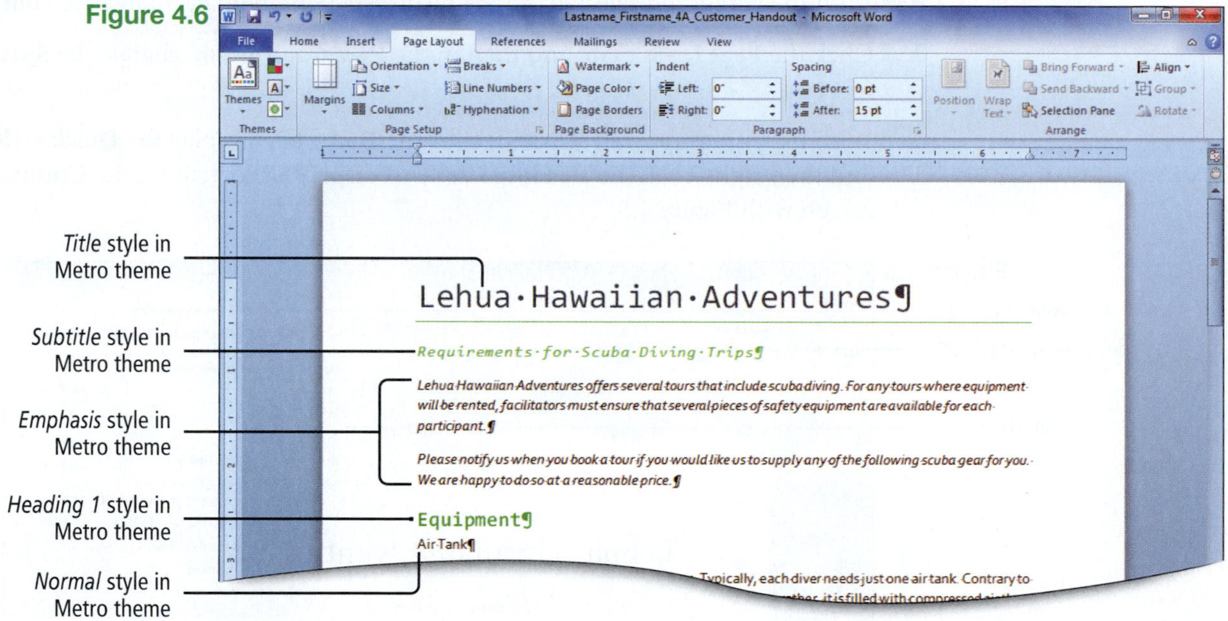

4 Select the subtitle, which begins *Requirements for*, and then on the Mini toolbar, apply **Bold** B and change the **Font Size** to **18**. **Save** your document.

In this handout, this emphasis on the subtitle is useful. Because the handout has no other subtitles and you will not be applying this style again in this document, it is not necessary to modify the actual style.

Objective 2 | Create New Styles

You can create a new style based on formats that you specify. For example, if you frequently use a 12 pt Verdana font with bold emphasis and double spacing, you can create a style to apply those settings to a paragraph with a single click, instead of using multiple steps each time you want that specific formatting. Any new styles that you create are stored with the document and are available any time the document is open.

Activity 4.04 | Creating New Styles

1 Select the paragraph that begins *Examples: Aluminum*, and then on the Mini toolbar, change the **Font Size** to **12** and apply **Bold** [B] and **Italic** [I].

2 With the paragraph still selected, click the **Home tab**, and then in the **Styles group**, click the **More** button [▾] to display the **Quick Styles** gallery. In the lower portion of the gallery, click **Save Selection as a New Quick Style**.

3 In the **Create New Style from Formatting** dialog box, in the **Name** box, type **Examples** Compare your screen with Figure 4.7.

Select a name for your new style that will remind you of the type of text to which the style applies. A preview of the style displays in the Paragraph style preview box.

Figure 4.7

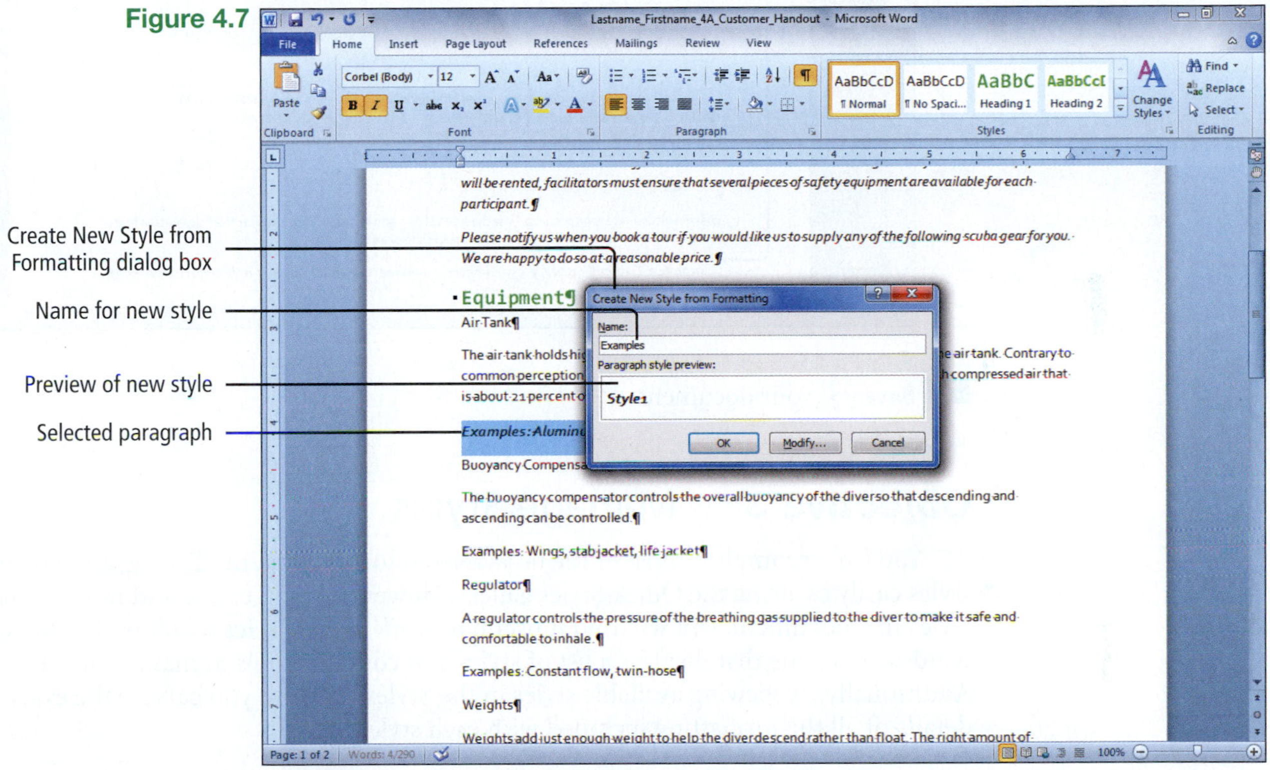

4 Click **OK** to add your *Examples* style to the available styles for this document and display it in the Quick Styles gallery.

5 Scroll down as necessary and select the paragraph that begins *Examples: Wings*. In the **Quick Styles** gallery, click the **Examples** style to apply the new style.

6 Using the technique you just practiced, select the four remaining paragraphs that begin *Examples:*, and then apply the **Examples** style. Click anywhere to deselect the text, and then compare your screen with Figure 4.8.

Figure 4.8

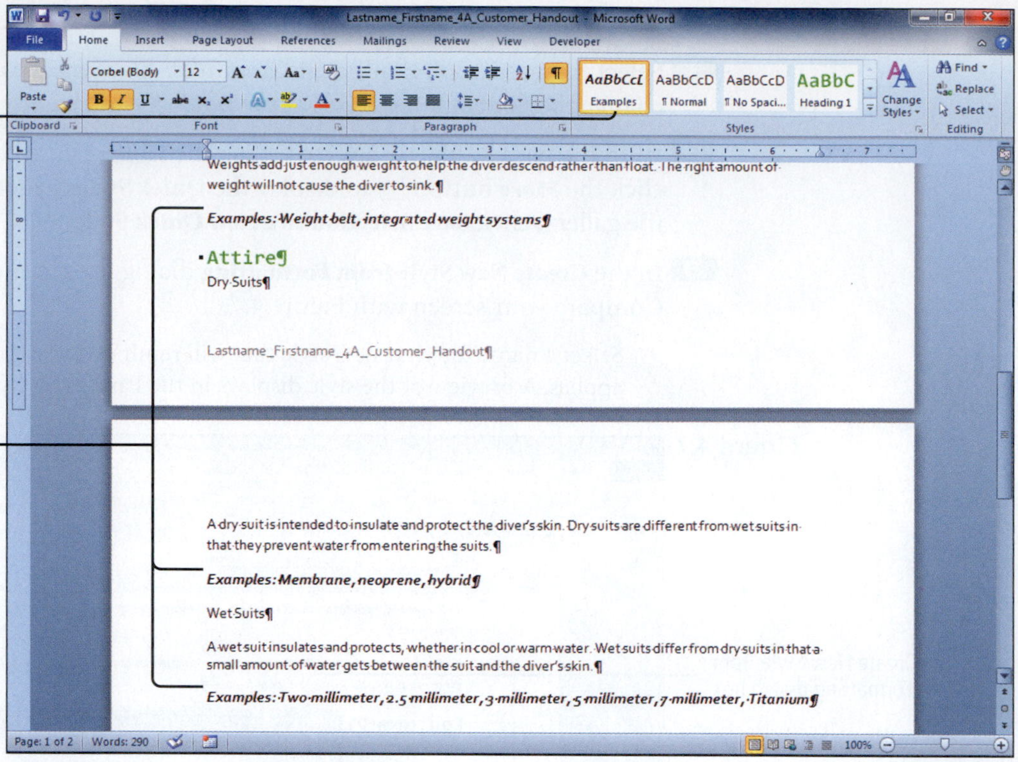

7 **Save** your document.

Objective 3 | Manage Styles

You can accomplish most of the tasks related to applying, modifying, and creating styles easily by using the Quick Styles gallery. However, if you create and modify many styles in a document, you will find it useful to work in the ***Styles window***. The Styles window is a pane that displays a list of styles and contains tools to manage styles. Additionally, by viewing available styles in the Styles window, you can see the exact details of all the formatting included with each style.

Activity 4.05 | Modifying a Style in the Styles Window

1 Press Ctrl + Home, and then click anywhere in the title *Lehua Hawaiian Adventures*. On the **Home tab**, in the lower right corner of the **Styles group**, click the **dialog box launcher button** to display the **Styles** window. Compare your screen with Figure 4.9.

The Styles window displays the same group of available styles found in the Quick Styles gallery, including the new *Examples* style that you created.

Figure 4.9

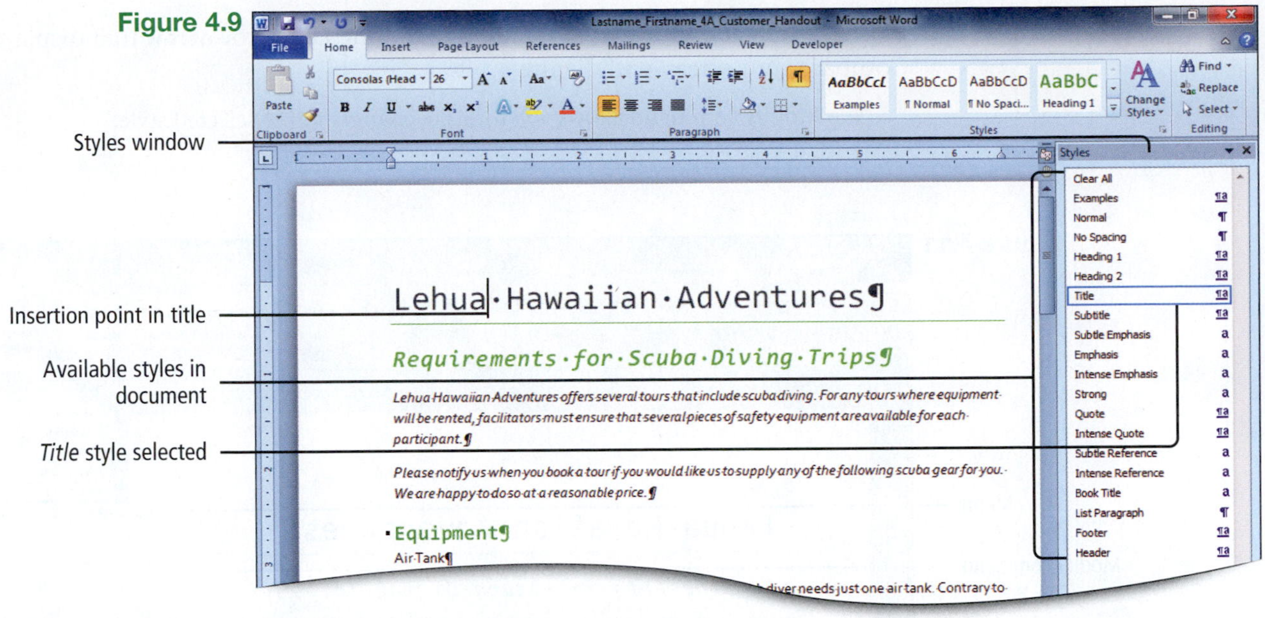

2 In the **Styles** window, point to **Title** to display a ScreenTip with the details of the formats associated with this style. In the displayed ScreenTip, under **Style**, notice that *Style Linked* is indicated.

By displaying a style's ScreenTip in this manner, you can verify all the information associated with the style.

3 Move your mouse pointer into the document to close the ScreenTip. In the **Styles** window, examine the symbols to the right of each style, as shown in Figure 4.10.

A ***character style***, indicated by the symbol **a**, contains formatting characteristics that you apply to text—for example, font name, font size, font color, bold emphasis, and so on.

A ***paragraph style***, indicated by the symbol ¶, includes everything that a character style contains *plus* all aspects of a paragraph's appearance—for example, text alignment, tab stops, line spacing, and borders.

A ***linked style***, indicated by the symbol **¶a**, behaves as either a character style or a paragraph style, depending on what you select.

List styles, which apply formats to a list, and ***table styles***, which apply a consistent look to the borders, shading, and so on of a table, are also available but do not display here.

Figure 4.10

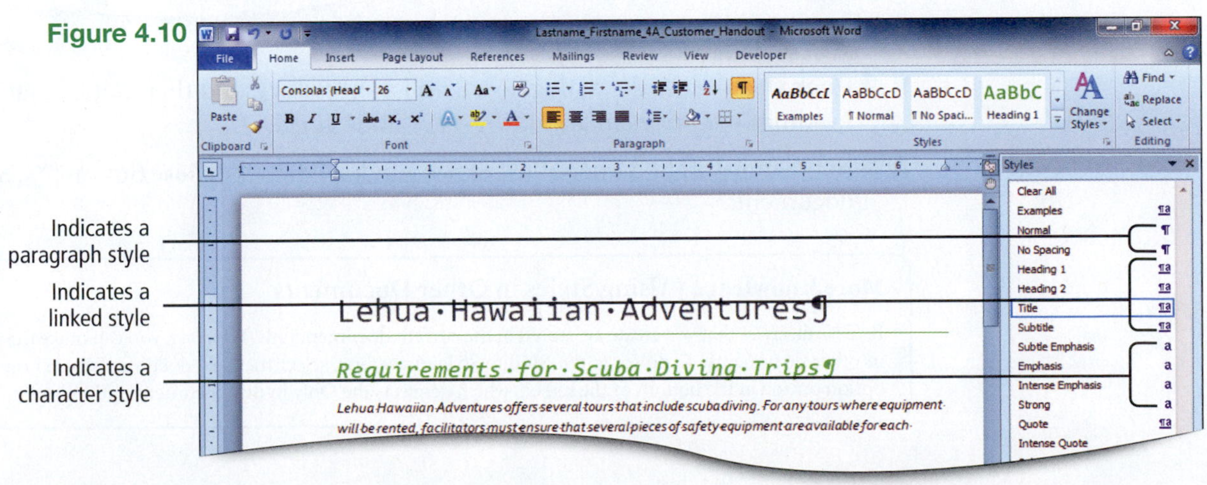

> **Another Way**
>
> In the **Quick Styles** gallery, right-click the style name, and then click **Modify**.

4 In the **Styles** window, point to **Heading 1**, and then click the **arrow** that displays. Compare your screen with Figure 4.11.

The Modify command allows you to make changes to the selected style.

Figure 4.11

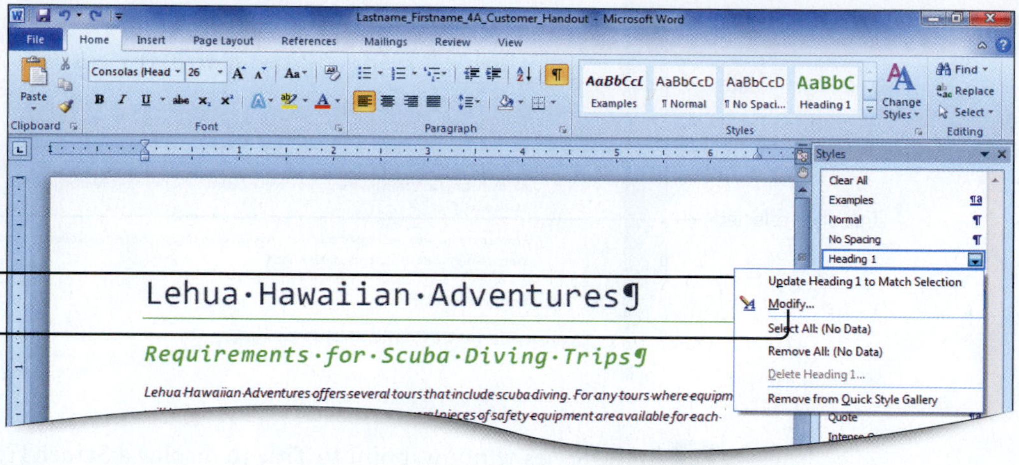

5 From the displayed menu, click **Modify** to display the **Modify Style** dialog box. In the **Modify Style** dialog box, under **Formatting**, click the **Underline** button [U] to add underline emphasis to the style. Compare your screen with Figure 4.12.

Figure 4.12

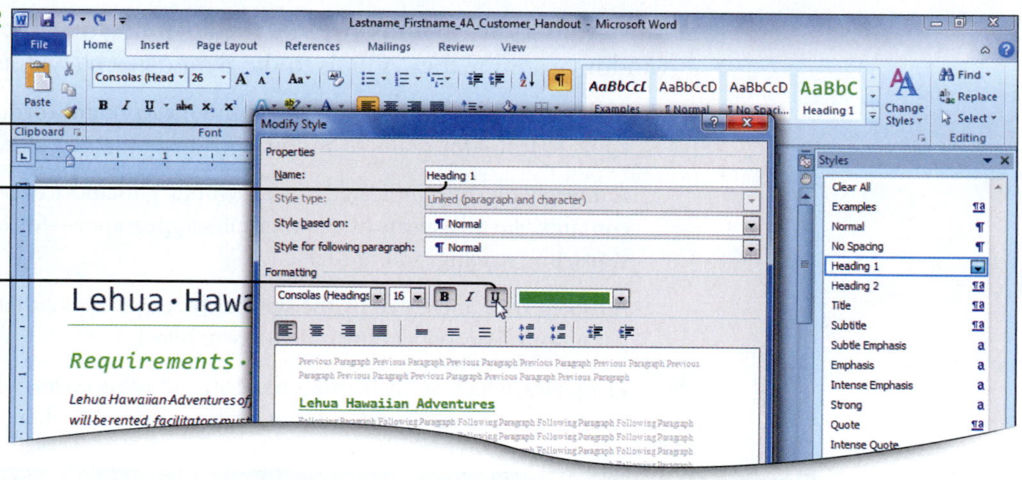

6 Click **OK** to close the dialog box. Scroll as necessary, and then notice that both headings—*Equipment* and *Attire*—are underlined.

7 In the upper right corner of the **Styles** window, click the **Close** button [×]. **Save** your document.

> **More Knowledge** | **Using Styles in Other Documents**
>
> By default, styles that you create are stored in the current document only. However, you can make the style available in other documents. To do so, in the Modify Style dialog box, select the New documents based on this template option button at the bottom of the screen, which deselects the Only in this document option button.

Activity 4.06 | Clearing Formats

There may be instances where you wish to remove all formatting from existing text—for example, when you want to create a multilevel list.

Another Way

Display the **Styles** window, and then at the top of the window, click the **Clear All** command.

1 Scroll to view the upper portion of **Page 1**, and then select the paragraph that begins *Examples: Aluminum*. On the **Home tab**, in the **Font group**, click the **Clear Formatting** button. Compare your screen with Figure 4.13.

The Clear Formatting command removes all formatting and applied styles from the selected text. The text returns to the *Normal* style for the current theme.

Figure 4.13

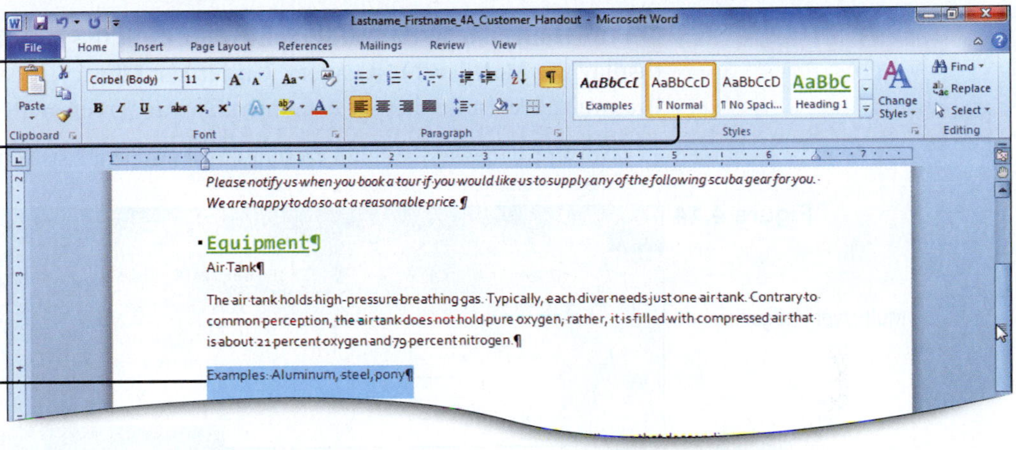

2 In the **Styles group**, point to the **Examples** style, and then right-click. From the displayed shortcut menu, click **Update Examples to Match Selection**.

The Examples style is removed from all text in the document. In this manner, you can clear the formatting for all instances with the applied style in the document.

3 **Save** your document.

Activity 4.07 | Removing a Quick Style

If a style that you created is no longer needed, you can remove it from the Quick Styles gallery.

1 In the **Styles group**, display the **Quick Styles** gallery. Right-click **Examples**, and then click **Remove from Quick Style Gallery**.

The Examples style is removed from the Quick Styles gallery. The style is no longer needed because all the paragraphs that are examples of scuba gear will be included in the multilevel list. Although the Examples style is removed from the Quick Styles gallery, it is not deleted from the document.

More Knowledge | Removing Built-in Styles

Built-in styles are predefined in Word, displaying in the Quick Styles gallery whenever you open a new document. Although you can remove a built-in style from a single document, the built-in style is not deleted from the Word program; the built-in style will be available in all other documents.

2 **Save** your document.

Objective 4 | Create a Multilevel List

When a document includes a list of items, you can format the items as a bulleted list, as a numbered list, or as a ***multilevel list***. Use a multilevel list when you want to add a visual hierarchical structure to the items in the list.

Activity 4.08 | Creating a Multilevel List

1 On **Page 1**, scroll to position the heading *Equipment* near the top of your screen. Beginning with the paragraph *Air Tank*, select the 12 paragraphs between the headings *Equipment* and *Attire*.

2 On the **Home tab**, in the **Paragraph group**, click the **Multilevel List** button to display the **Multilevel List** gallery. Under **List Library**, locate the ❖, ➢, ■ style, which is the multilevel bullet list style. Compare your screen with Figure 4.14.

Word provides several built-in styles for multilevel lists. You can customize any style.

Figure 4.14

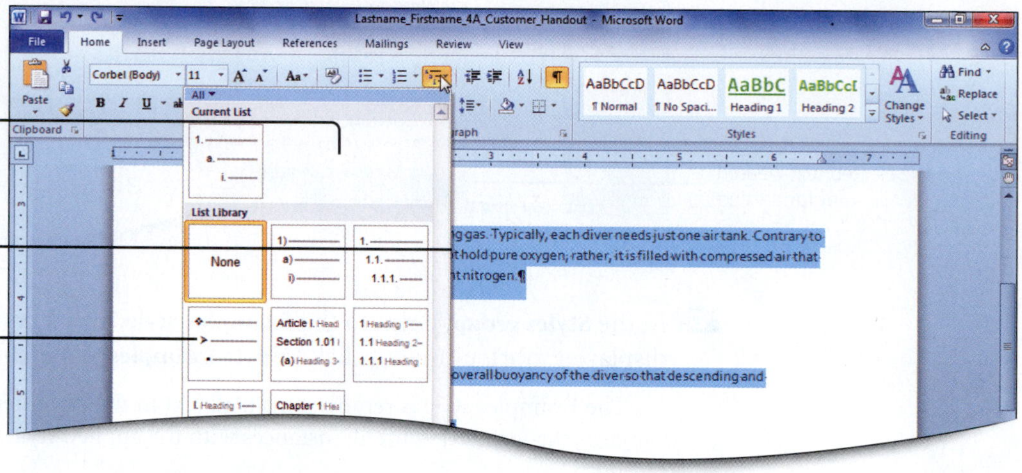

3 Click the **multilevel bullet list** style. Compare your screen with Figure 4.15.

All the items in the list display at the top level; the items are not visually indented to show different levels.

Figure 4.15

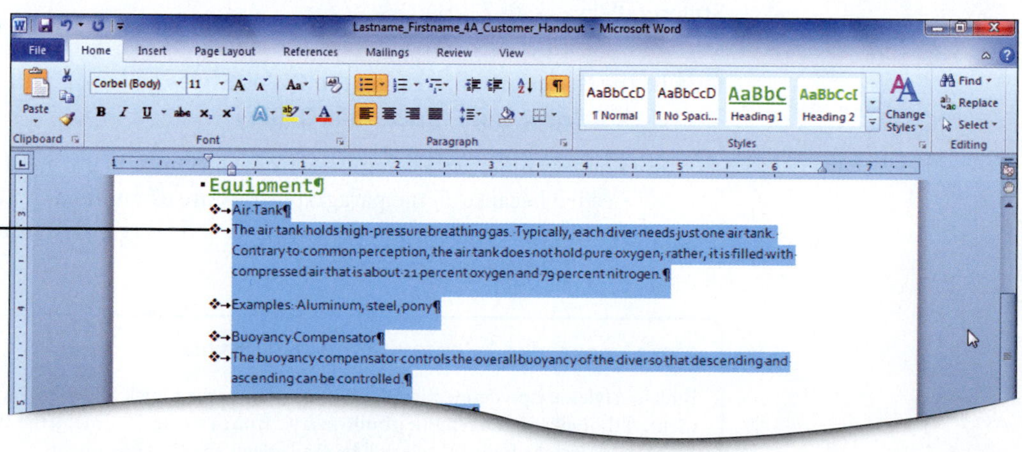

> **Another Way**
>
> Select the paragraph, and then press Tab to demote an item in a list, or press Shift + Tab to promote an item.

4 Click anywhere in the second list item, which begins *The air tank*. In the **Paragraph group**, click the **Increase Indent** button one time, and then compare your screen with Figure 4.16.

The list item displays at the second level, which uses the ➢ symbol. The Increase Indent button demotes an item to a lower level; the Decrease Indent button promotes an item to a higher level. To change the list level using the Increase Indent button or Decrease Indent button, it is not necessary to select the entire paragraph.

Figure 4.16

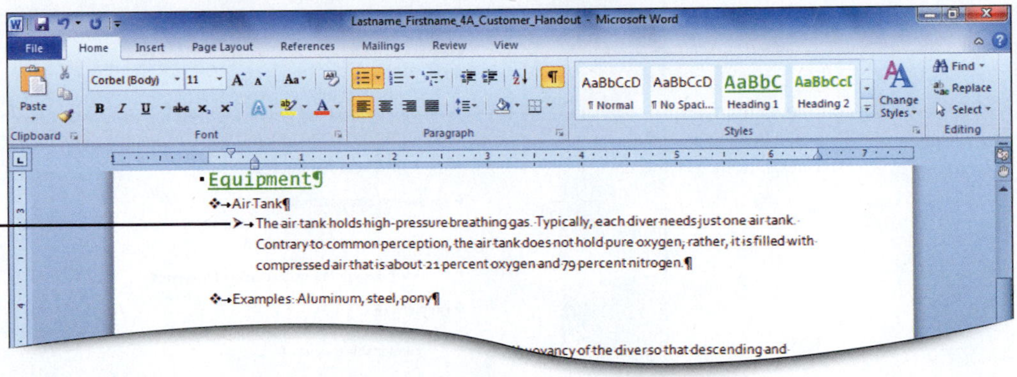

5 Click in the third item in the list, which begins *Examples: Aluminum*. In the **Paragraph group**, click the **Increase Indent** button two times, and then compare your screen with Figure 4.17.

The list item displays at the third level, which uses the ■ symbol.

Figure 4.17

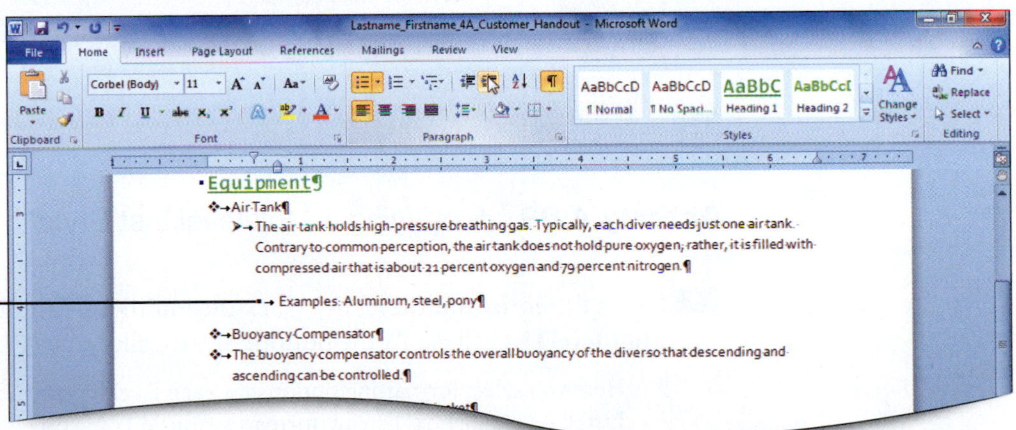

6 Using the technique you just practiced, continue setting levels for the remainder of the multilevel list as follows: Apply the second-level indent for the descriptive paragraphs that begin *The buoyancy*, *A regulator*, and *Weights add*. Apply the third-level indent for the paragraphs that begin *Examples*.

> **More Knowledge | Selecting List Items**
>
> To select several items in a document that are ***contiguous***—adjacent to one another—click the first item, hold down Shift, and then click the last item. To select several items that are ***noncontiguous***—not adjacent to one another—hold down Ctrl, and then click each item. After items are selected, you can format all the selected items at the same time.

7 Compare your screen with Figure 4.18. If necessary, adjust your list by using the Increase Indent or Decrease Indent buttons so that your list matches the one shown in Figure 4.18.

Figure 4.18

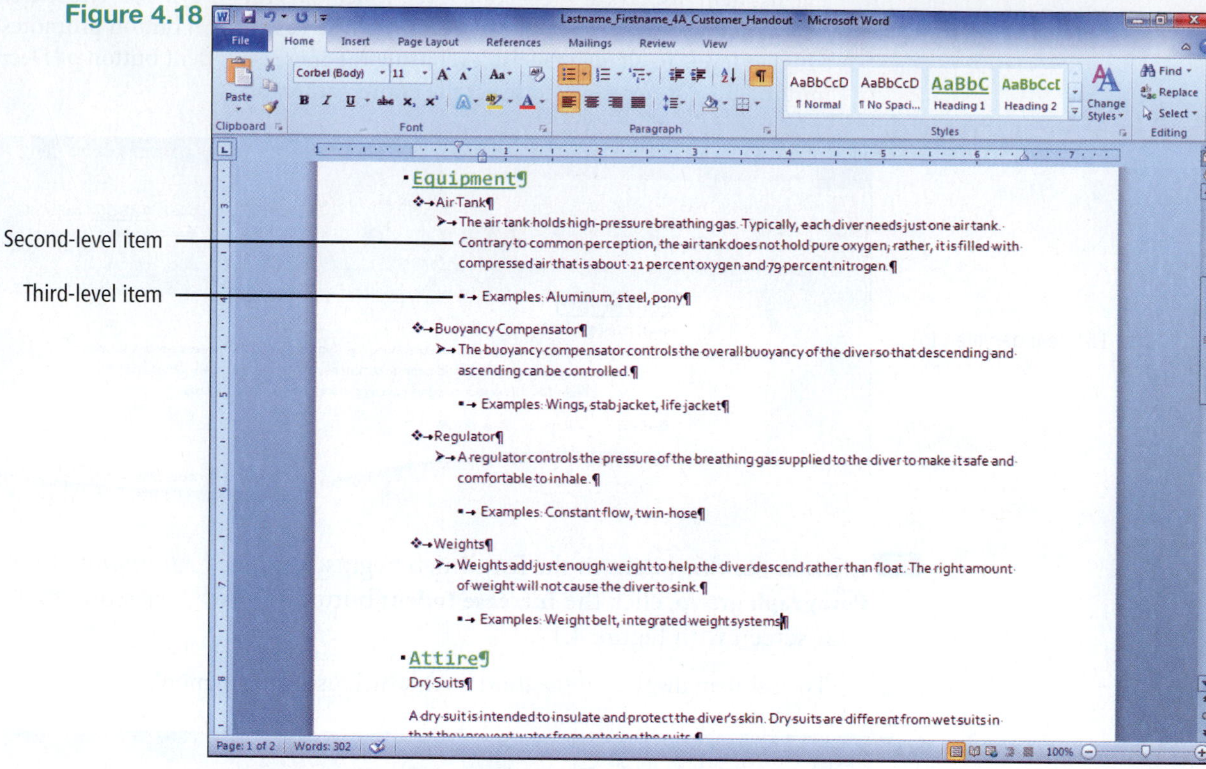

8 **Save** your document.

Activity 4.09 | Modifying a Multilevel List Style

1 Select the entire multilevel list. Click the **Multilevel List** button to display the **Multilevel List** gallery. At the bottom of the gallery, click **Define New List Style**.

Here you select formatting options for each level in your list. By default, the Define New List Style dialog box displays formatting options starting with the *1st level*.

2 Under **Properties**, in the **Name** box, type **Equipment List** Under **Formatting**, in the small toolbar above the preview area, to the right of *Bullet:* ❖, click the **Numbering Style arrow**.

3 In the displayed list, scroll to the top of the list, and then click the **1, 2, 3** style. Click the **Font Color arrow**, which currently displays black, and then in the fifth column, click the fifth color—**Green, Accent 1, Darker 25%**. Compare your screen with Figure 4.19.

The numbering style and font color change will be applied only to first-level items. The style changes are visible in the preview area.

Figure 4.19

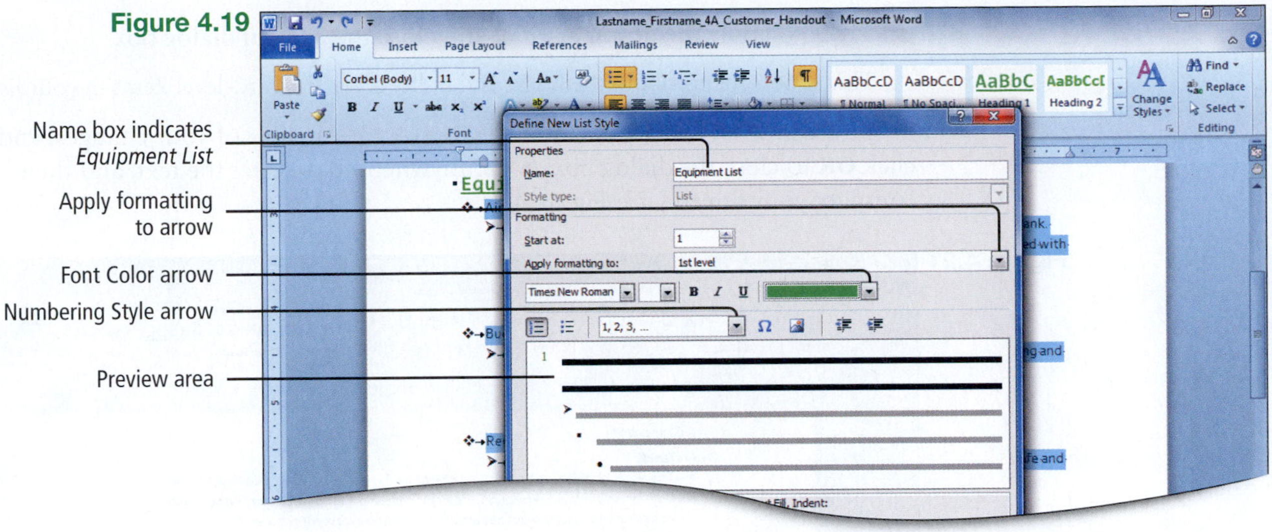

4 Under **Formatting**, click the **Apply formatting to arrow**, and then click **2nd level**. Click the **Font Color arrow**, and then in the fifth column, click the fifth color—**Green, Accent 1, Darker 25%**—to change the bullet color for the second-level items.

5 Click the **Apply formatting to arrow**, and then click **3rd level**. Click the **Font Color arrow**, and then in the fifth column, click the first color—**Green, Accent 1**.

> **Another Way**
>
> If you know a symbol's character code, in the **Symbol** dialog box, select the number that displays in the **Character code** box, and then type the desired number.

6 Click the **Insert Symbol** button. In the **Symbol** dialog box, click the **Font arrow** and display the **Wingdings** font, if necessary, and then scroll to the top of the icons list. In the sixth row, click the twelfth symbol—❁. Compare your screen with Figure 4.20.

The character code for this symbol—123—displays in the Character code box.

Figure 4.20

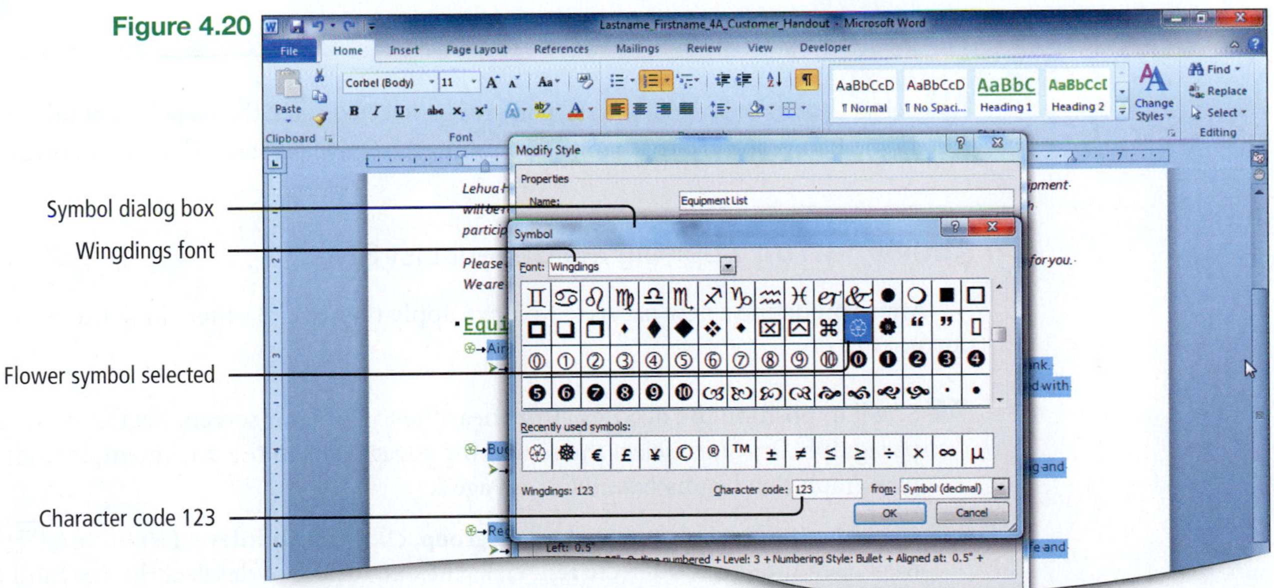

7 Click **OK** to apply the flower symbol and close the **Symbol** dialog box.

This action changes both the bullet and bullet color for third-level items in your list.

8 In the **Define New List Style** dialog box, notice the preview of your changes, and then click **OK** to close the dialog box. Click anywhere to deselect the text, and then compare your screen with Figure 4.21.

Figure 4.21

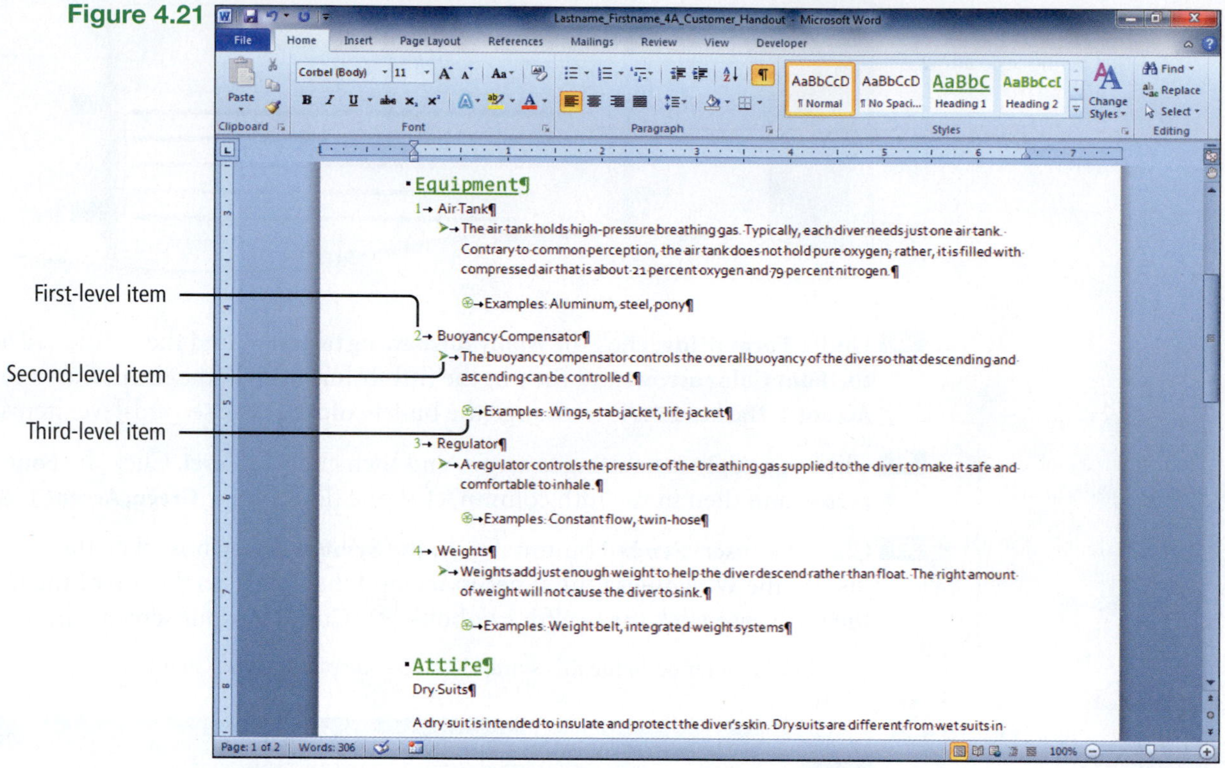

9 Select the entire list. With all 12 paragraphs selected, click the **Page Layout tab**, and then in the **Paragraph group**, change the **Spacing After** to **0 pt**. **Save** your document.

Activity 4.10 | Applying the Current List Style

After you define a new list style, you can apply the style to other similar items in your document.

1 Scroll to position the heading *Attire* near the top of your screen. Beginning with the paragraph *Dry Suits*, select the remaining paragraphs in the document, including the paragraph that begins *Examples* on **Page 2**.

2 Click the **Home tab**. In the **Paragraph group**, click the **Multilevel List** button, and then click the style under **Current List**. Click anywhere to deselect the text, and then compare your screen with Figure 4.22.

The current list style formats each paragraph as a first-level item.

Figure 4.22

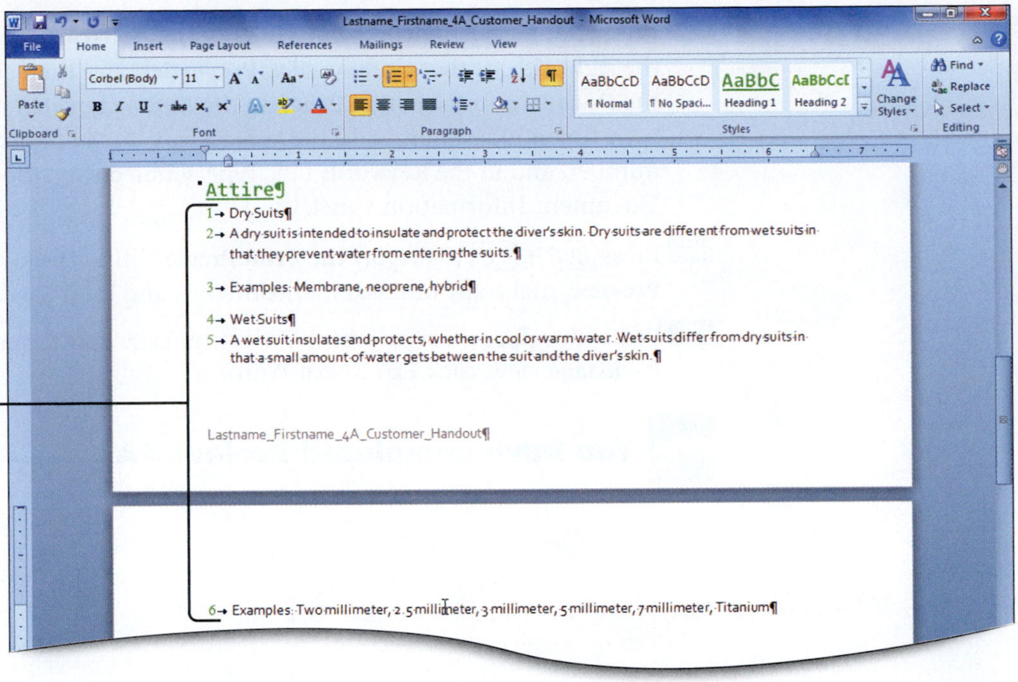

Current list style applied, first-level items

3 Under the **Attire** heading, select the two descriptive paragraphs that begin *A dry suit* and *A wet suit*, and then click the **Increase Indent** button one time. Select the two paragraphs that begin *Examples*, and then click the **Increase Indent** button two times. Deselect the text, and then compare your screen with Figure 4.23.

Figure 4.23

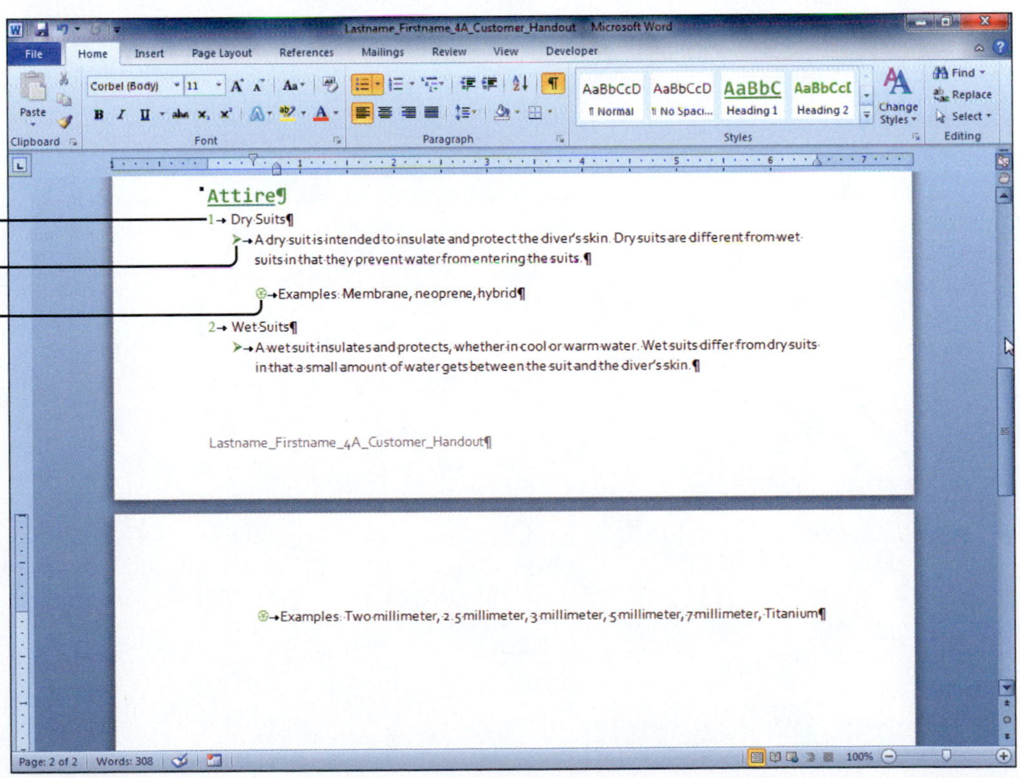

First-level item

Second-level item

Third-level item

4 Select the entire list. With all six paragraphs selected, click the **Page Layout tab**, and then in the **Paragraph group**, change the **Spacing After** to **0 pt**. Click anywhere to deselect the list.

5 Press Ctrl + Home. Click the **File tab** to display **Backstage** view, and then click **Info**. On the right side of the window, click **Properties**, and then click **Show Document Panel**. In the **Document Information Panel**, in the **Author** box, delete any text, and then type your first and last names. In the **Subject** box, type your course name and section number, and in the **Keywords** box, type **scuba diving, trip handout** **Close** the Document Information Panel.

6 Press Ctrl + F2 to display the **Print Preview** in **Backstage** view. Examine the **Print Preview**, make any necessary adjustments, and then **Save** your document.

7 Print your document or submit it electronically as directed by your instructor. From **Backstage** view, click **Exit** to exit Word.

End **You have completed Project 4A**

Project 4B Planning Memo with a Chart

myitlab
Project 4B Training

Project Activities

In Activities 4.11 through 4.20, you will edit a memo to all the company tour guides regarding the planning session. The Tour Operations Manager of Lehua Hawaiian Adventures is preparing for a planning session in which he and other key decision makers will discuss the types of tours the company will offer in the coming year. They want to use information gathered from customer research to provide an appropriate mix of tour types that will appeal to a wide audience. You will add a chart to illustrate plans for tour types in the coming year. Your completed document will look similar to Figure 4.24.

Project Files

For Project 4B, you will need the following file:

w04B_Planning_Memo

You will save your document as:

Lastname_Firstname_4B_Planning_Memo

Project Results

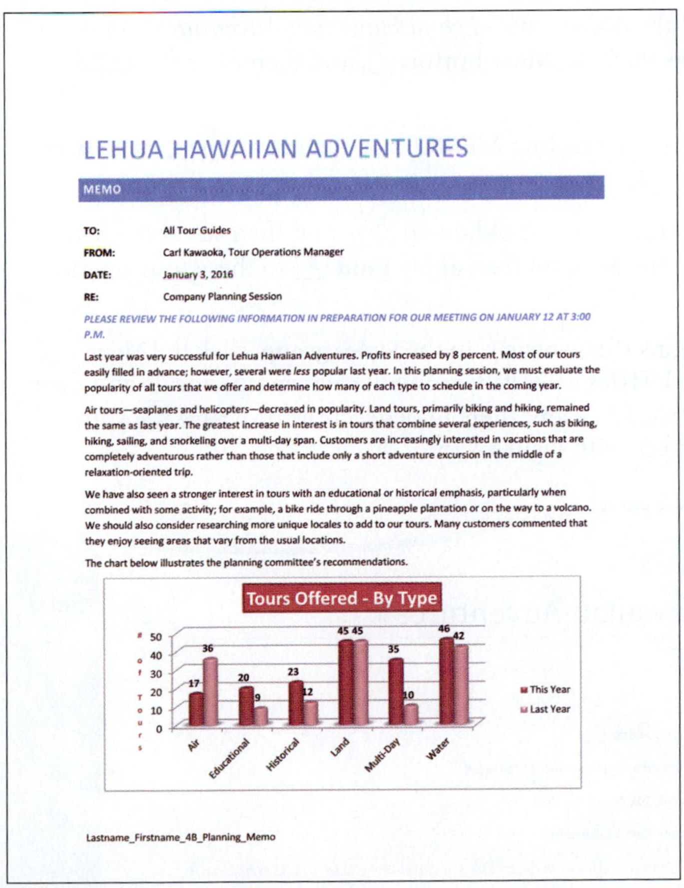
LEHUA HAWAIIAN ADVENTURES

MEMO

TO: All Tour Guides

FROM: Carl Kawaoka, Tour Operations Manager

DATE: January 3, 2016

RE: Company Planning Session

PLEASE REVIEW THE FOLLOWING INFORMATION IN PREPARATION FOR OUR MEETING ON JANUARY 12 AT 3:00 P.M.

Last year was very successful for Lehua Hawaiian Adventures. Profits increased by 8 percent. Most of our tours easily filled in advance; however, several were *less* popular last year. In this planning session, we must evaluate the popularity of all tours that we offer and determine how many of each type to schedule in the coming year.

Air tours—seaplanes and helicopters—decreased in popularity. Land tours, primarily biking and hiking, remained the same as last year. The greatest increase in interest is in tours that combine several experiences, such as biking, hiking, sailing, and snorkeling over a multi-day span. Customers are increasingly interested in vacations that are completely adventurous rather than those that include only a short adventure excursion in the middle of a relaxation-oriented trip.

We have also seen a stronger interest in tours with an educational or historical emphasis, particularly when combined with some activity; for example, a bike ride through a pineapple plantation or on the way to a volcano. We should also consider researching more unique locales to add to our tours. Many customers commented that they enjoy seeing areas that vary from the usual locations.

The chart below illustrates the planning committee's recommendations.

Lastname_Firstname_4B_Planning_Memo

Figure 4.24
Project 4B Planning Memo

Objective 5 | Change the Style Set and Paragraph Spacing of a Document

Recall that formatting commands that are grouped together comprise a style. Likewise, styles that are grouped together comprise a ***style set***. A style set is a group of styles that is designed to work together. A style set is useful when you want to change the look of *all* the styles in a document in one step rather than modifying individual styles. The styles grouped together in each style set reflect the font scheme and color scheme of the current theme, including paragraph spacing formats.

Activity 4.11 | Formatting a Memo

A ***memo***, also referred to as a ***memorandum***, is a written message to someone working in the same organization. Among organizations, memo formats vary, and there are many acceptable memo formats. Always consult trusted references or the preferences set by your organization when deciding on the proper formats for your professional memos.

1. **Start** Word. From your student files, locate and open the file **w04B_Planning_Memo**.
2. Save the document in your **Word Chapter 4** folder as **Lastname_Firstname_4B_Planning_Memo** Scroll to the bottom of the page, right-click in the footer area, click **Edit Footer**, and then using **Quick Parts**, insert the file name. **Close** the footer area. If necessary, display the rulers and formatting marks.
3. Press Ctrl + Home. If *Lehua* or *Kawaoka* are flagged as spelling errors, point to the first occurrence of each, right-click, and then click **Ignore All**.
4. Select the first paragraph of the document—*Lehua Hawaiian Adventures*. On the **Home tab**, in the **Styles group**, click the **More** button, and then from the **Quick Styles** gallery, click **Title**.
5. Select the second paragraph—the heading *MEMO*, and then from the **Quick Styles** gallery, apply the **Heading 1** style.
6. Select the text *TO:*—include the colon—hold down Ctrl, and then select the text *FROM:*, *DATE:*, and *RE:*. On the Mini toolbar, apply **Bold** to these four memo headings.
7. Select the paragraph that begins *Please review*. In the **Styles group**, click the **More** button to display the **Quick Styles** gallery. By using the ScreenTips, locate and then click the **Intense Reference** style. Click anywhere to deselect the text. **Save** your document. Compare your screen with Figure 4.25.

Figure 4.25

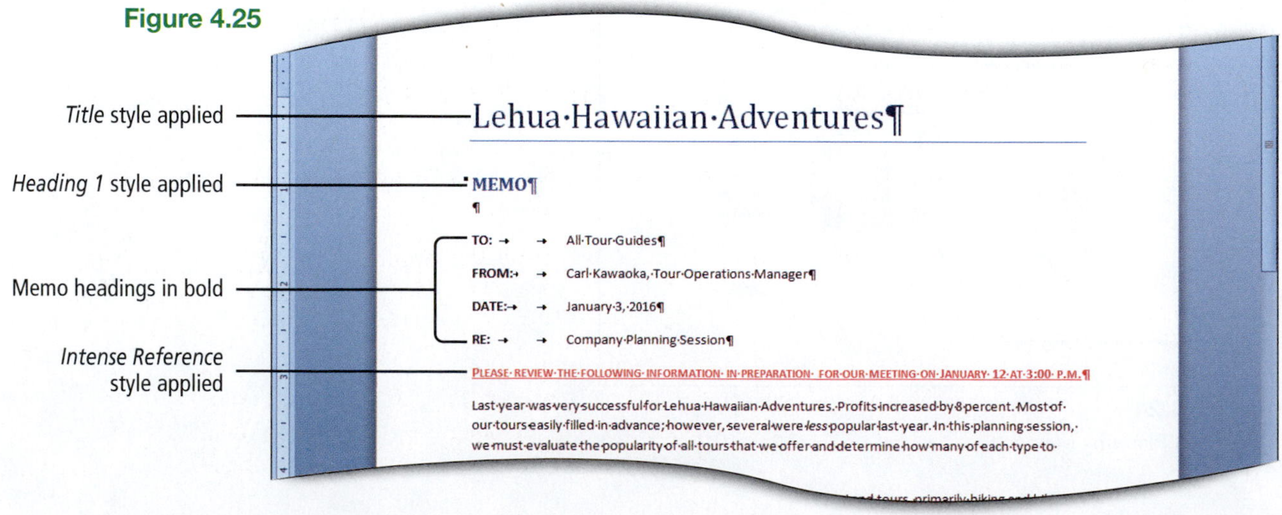

Activity 4.12 | Changing the Style Set

By changing a style set, you can apply a group of styles to a document in one step.

1 In the **Styles group**, click the **Change Styles** button, and then point to **Style Set**. Compare your screen with Figure 4.26.

All available style sets are listed by name in the Style Set menu; there are 13 predefined style sets. The default style set is *Word 2010*.

Figure 4.26

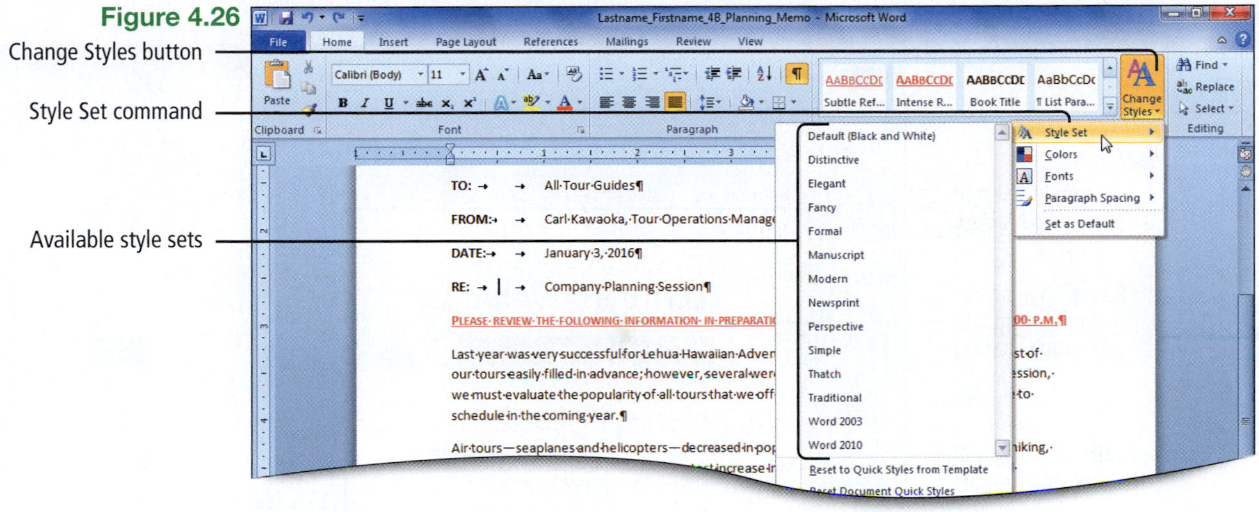

2 From the **Style Set** menu, point to **Fancy**, and notice that **Live Preview** displays how the text would look with this style set applied.

3 From the **Style Set** menu, click **Modern**, compare your screen with Figure 4.27, and then **Save** your document.

Modern is the name of a particular style set. Applying *Modern* causes styles—such as Title, Heading 1, and Intense Reference—to display a different format.

Figure 4.27

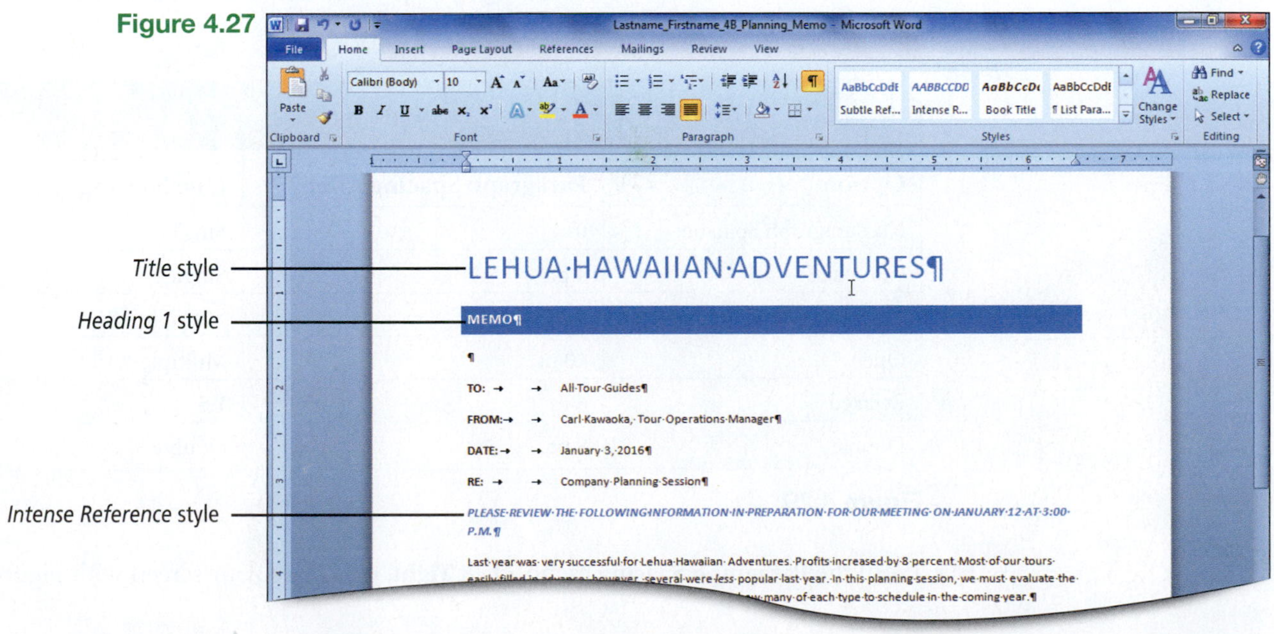

Activity 4.13 | Changing the Paragraph Spacing of a Document

Built-in paragraph spacing formats allow you to change the paragraph spacing and line spacing for an entire document in one step.

1 In the **Styles group**, click the **Change Styles** button, and then point to **Paragraph Spacing**. Under **Style Set**, point to **Modern**. Compare your screen with Figure 4.28.

Word provides six built-in styles for paragraph spacing. The *Modern* style set uses paragraph spacing that includes line spacing of 1.15 and 10 pt spacing before and after a paragraph.

Figure 4.28

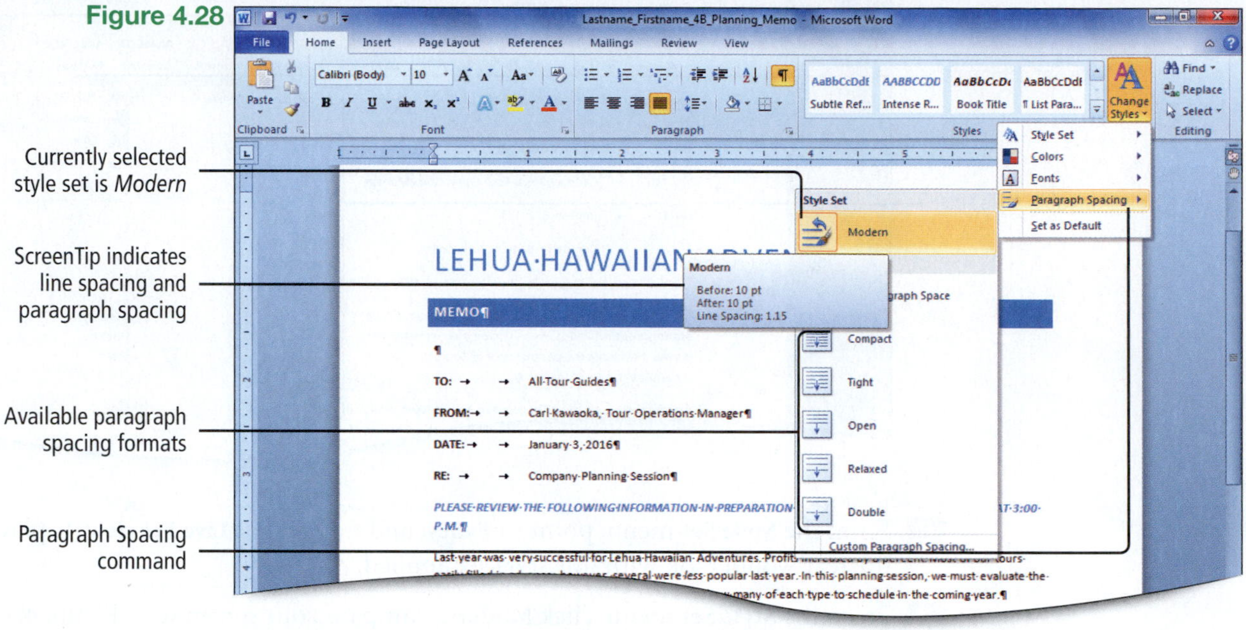

2 From the **Paragraph Spacing** menu, point to **Double**. Notice the **ScreenTip** that describes the paragraph spacing format and that **Live Preview** displays how the document would look with this paragraph spacing format applied. Take a moment to study the table shown in Figure 4.29.

Paragraph Spacing Formats

Option	Paragraph Spacing After	Line Spacing
No Paragraph Spacing	0	Single
Compact	4 pt	Single
Tight	6 pt	Multiple 1.15
Open	10 pt	Multiple 1.15
Relaxed	6 pt	1.5
Double	8 pt	Double

Figure 4.29

3 From the **Paragraph Spacing** menu, click **Tight**. Compare your screen with Figure 4.30.

Figure 4.30

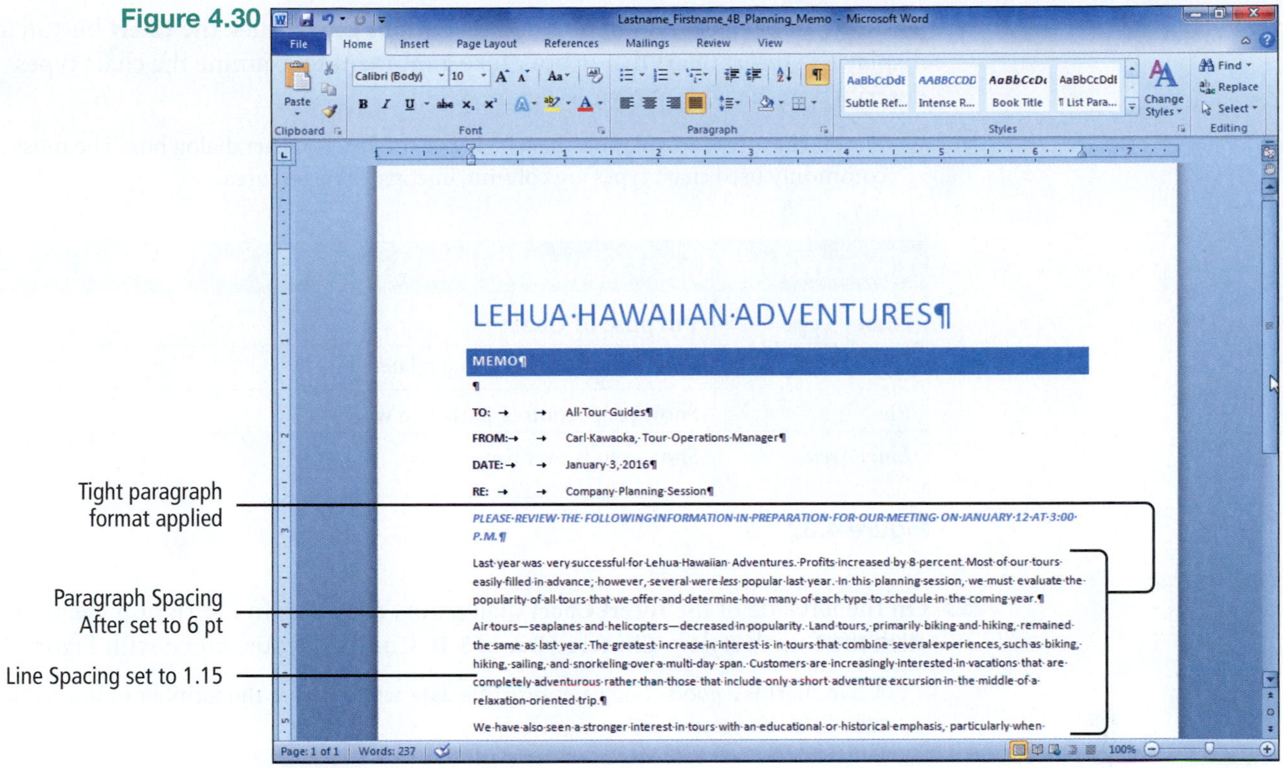

4 **Save** your document.

Objective 6 | Insert a Chart and Enter Data into a Chart

A ***chart*** is a visual representation of ***numerical data***—numbers that represent facts. Word provides the same chart tools that are available in Excel. A chart that you create in Word is stored in an Excel worksheet, and the worksheet is saved with the Word document. Excel, which is part of Microsoft Office 2010, is a spreadsheet application that makes calculations on numbers. An Excel worksheet is a set of cells, identified by row and column headings, that is part of a spreadsheet. Charts make numbers easier for the reader to understand.

Activity 4.14 | Selecting a Chart Type

1 Press Ctrl + End, and then press Enter one time. Compare your screen with Figure 4.31.

Figure 4.31

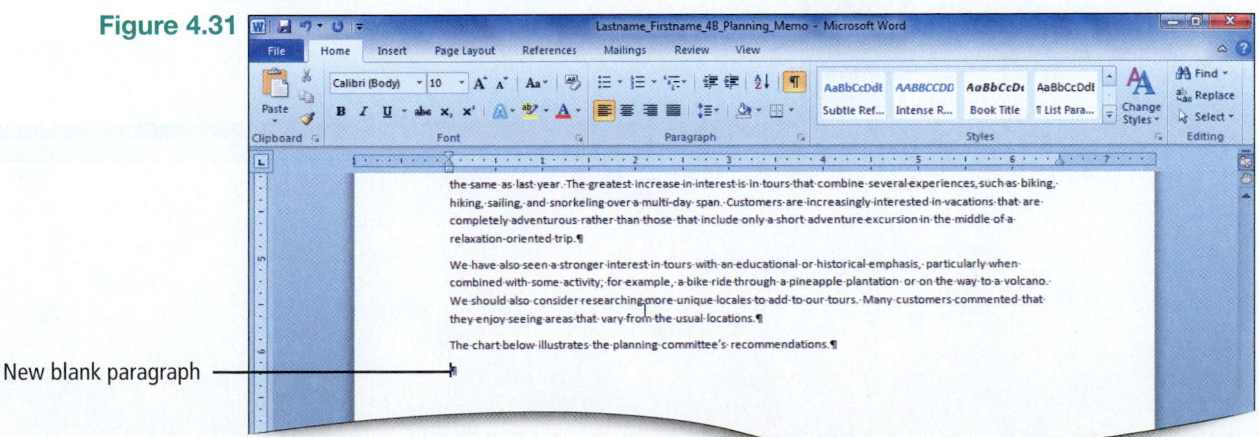

2 Click the **Insert tab**, and then in the **Illustrations group**, click the **Chart** button to display the **Insert Chart** dialog box. Take a moment to examine the chart types described in the table shown in Figure 4.32.

Eleven chart types display on the left side of the Insert Chart dialog box. The most commonly used chart types are column, line, pie, bar, and area.

Commonly Used Chart Types Available in Word

Chart Type	Purpose of Chart
Column, Bar	Show comparison among related data
Pie	Show proportion of parts to a whole
Line, Area	Show trends over time

Figure 4.32

3 On the left side of the **Insert Chart** dialog box, click **Bar**. In the right pane, under **Bar**, click the fourth style—**Clustered Bar in 3-D**. Compare your screen with Figure 4.33.

A bar chart is a good choice because this data will *compare* the number of tours offered in two different years.

Figure 4.33

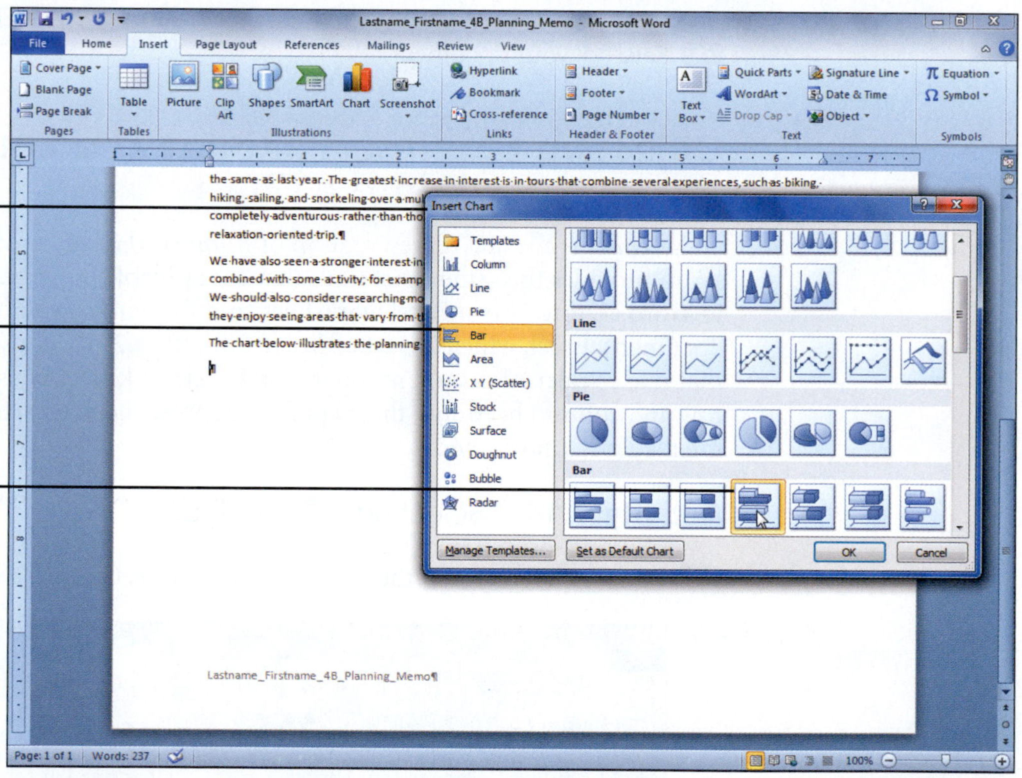

4 Click **OK** to insert the chart in your document and open the related Excel worksheet. Compare your screen with Figure 4.34.

The chart displays on page 2 of your Word document. Excel opens in a split window and displays sample data in a worksheet.

The process of inserting a chart in your document in this manner is referred to as ***embedding***—the object, in this case a chart, becomes part of the Word document. When you edit the data in Excel, the chart in your Word document updates automatically.

Figure 4.34

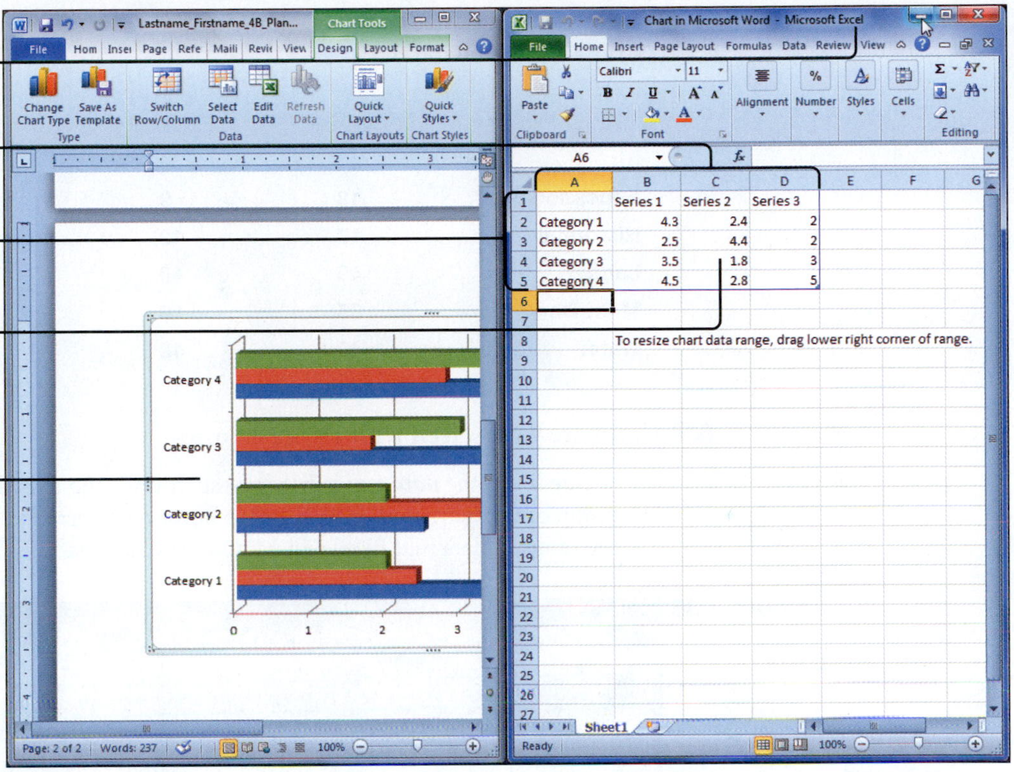

Activity 4.15 | Entering Chart Data

You can replace the sample data in the Excel worksheet with specific tour data for your chart.

1 In the Excel worksheet window, point to the box where **column B** and **row 1** intersect—referred to as cell **B1**—and click one time. Compare your screen with Figure 4.35.

A ***cell*** is the location where a row and column intersect. The cells are named by their column and row headings. For example, cell B1, containing the text *Series 1*, is in column B and row 1.

Figure 4.35

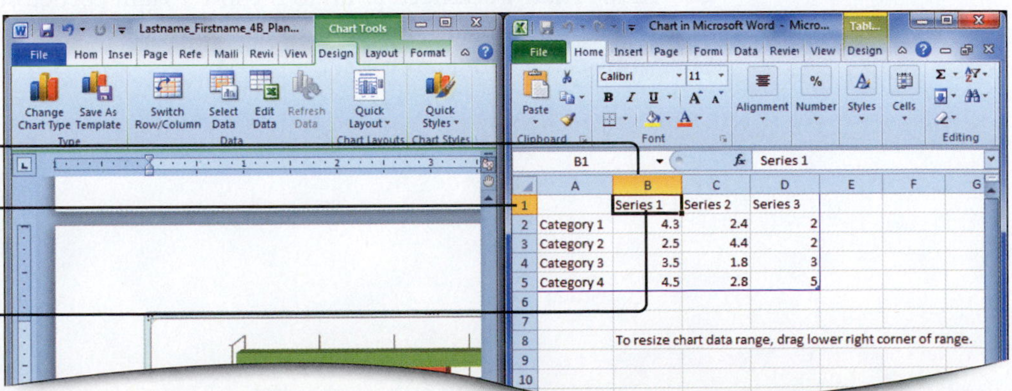

2 With cell **B1** selected, type **This Year** and then press [Tab]. With cell **C1** selected, type **Last Year** and then click cell **A2**—which displays the text *Category 1*.

3 With cell **A2** selected, type **Air** and then press [Tab] to move to cell **B2**. Type **17** and then press [Tab]. In cell **C2**, type **36** and then press [Tab] two times to move to **row 3**.

As you enter data in the Excel worksheet, the chart is automatically updated in the Word document. When entering a large amount of data in a cell, it may not fully display. If necessary, the data worksheet or chart can be modified to display the data completely.

4 Using the technique you just practiced, and without changing any values in **column D**, type the following data:

	This Year	Last Year	Series 3
Air	17	36	2
Educational	**13**	**9**	2
Historical	**17**	**12**	3
Land	**45**	**45**	5
Multi-Day	**35**	**10**	
Water	**46**	**42**	

5 Compare your screen with Figure 4.36.

A blue line—the ***data range border***—surrounds the cells that display in the chart. The group of cells surrounded by the blue border is referred to as the ***chart data range***—the range of data that Excel will use to create the chart.

Figure 4.36

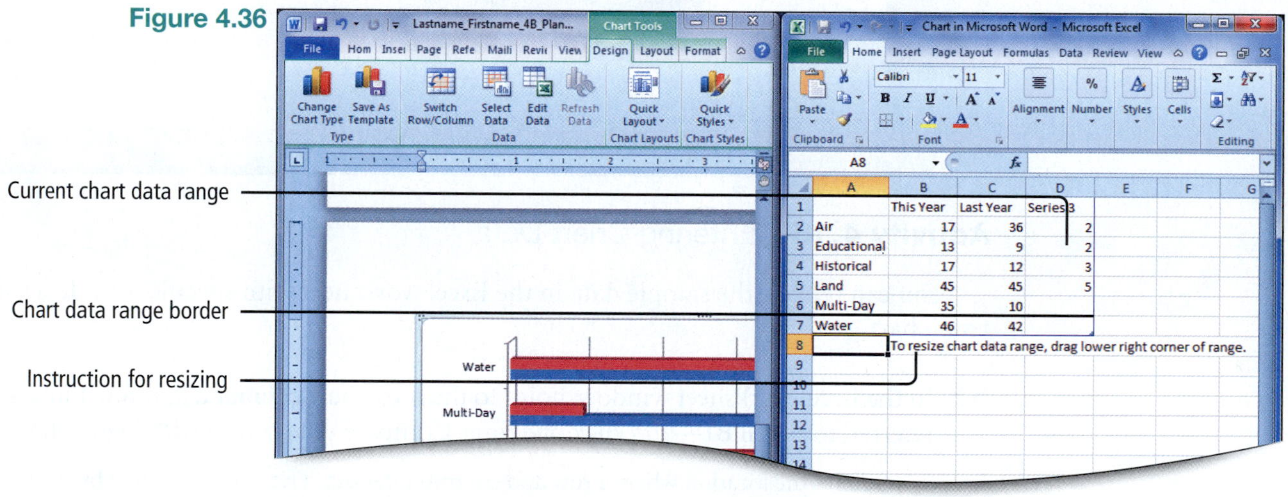

6 In the **Excel** worksheet, point to the lower right corner of the blue border to display the [pointer icon] pointer, and then drag to the left to select only cells **A1** through **C7**. Compare your screen with Figure 4.37.

Figure 4.37

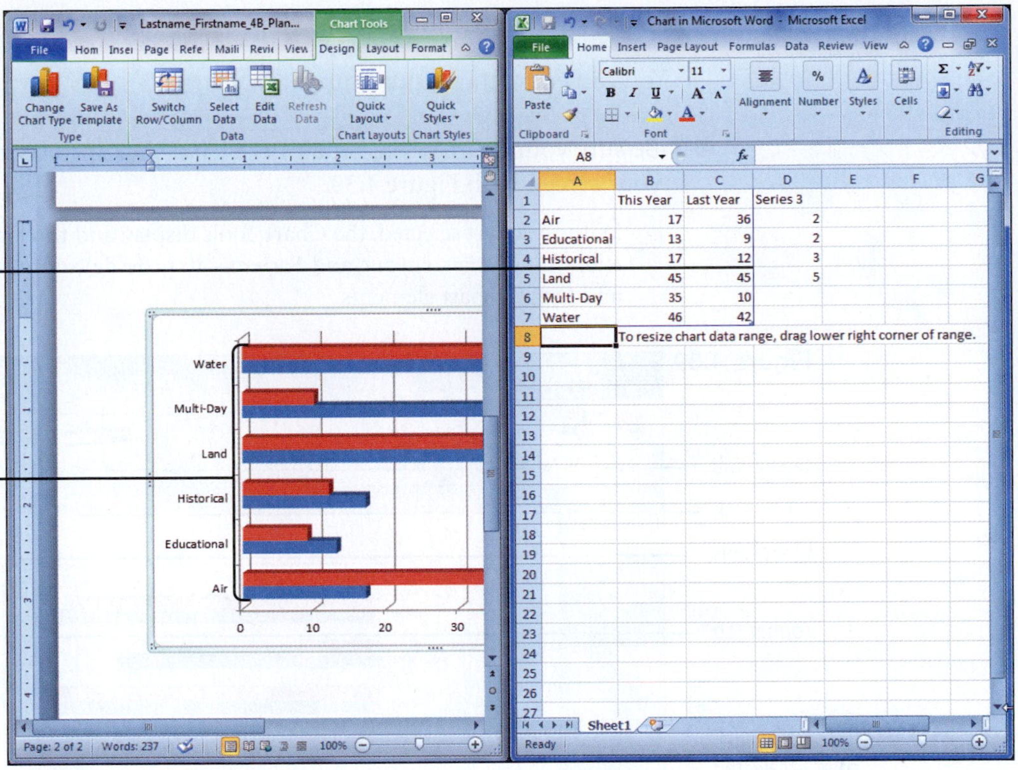

7 In the upper right corner of the **Excel** window, click the **Close** button, and then **Save** your Word document. Scroll if necessary to display the chart, on **Page 2** of your document. Compare your screen with Figure 4.38.

The ***chart area*** refers to the entire chart and all its elements. The categories—the tour type names—display on the ***vertical axis***, which is also referred to as the ***Y-axis***. The scale, based on the numerical data, displays on the ***horizontal axis***, which is also referred to as the ***X-axis***.

Data markers, the bars in the chart, are the shapes representing each of the cells that contain data, referred to as the ***data points***. A ***data series*** consists of related data points represented by a unique color. For example, this chart has two data series—*This Year* and *Last Year*. The ***legend*** identifies the colors assigned to each data series or category.

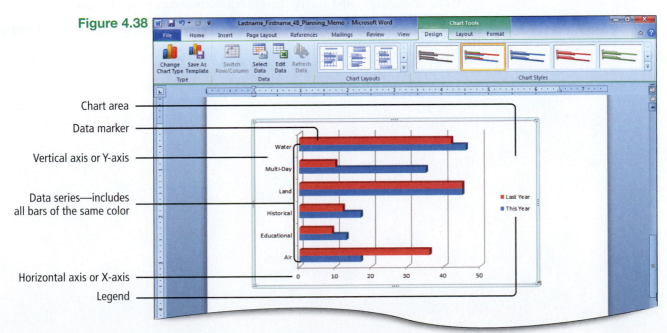

Figure 4.38

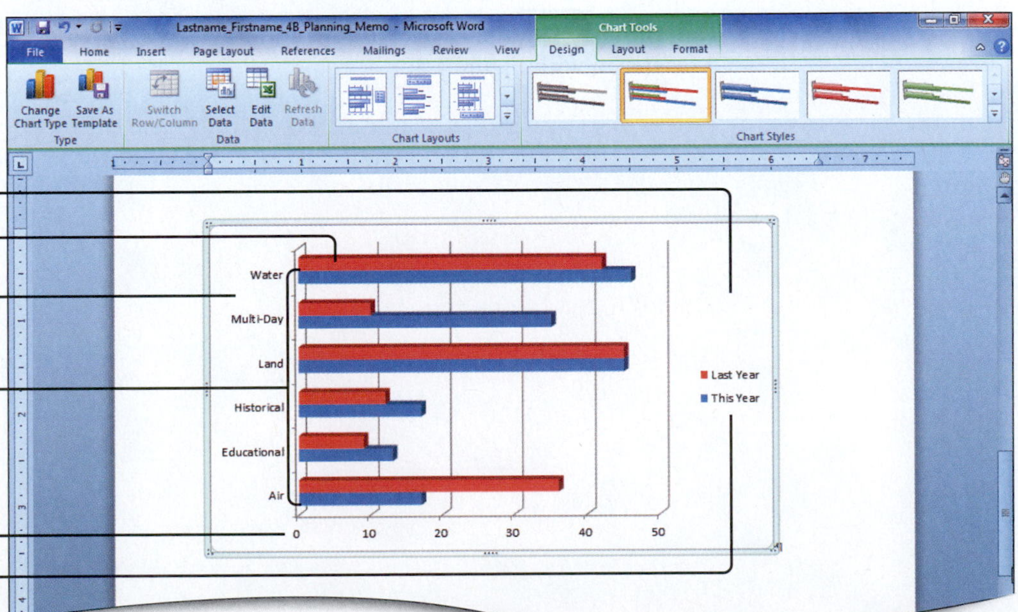

Activity 4.16 | Editing Data

You can edit data points to update a chart.

1 Be sure your chart is selected; if necessary, click the chart border to select it. Compare your screen with Figure 4.39.

With the chart selected, the Chart Tools display and three additional tabs display on the Ribbon—*Design*, *Layout*, and *Format*—to provide commands with which you can modify and format chart elements.

Figure 4.39

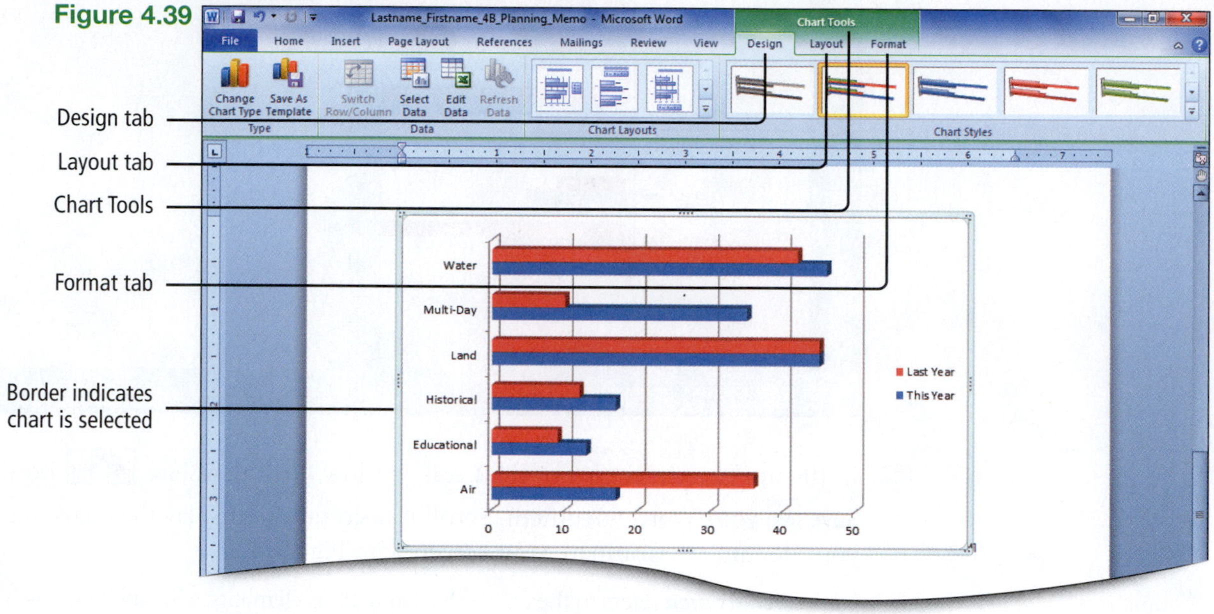

2 On the **Design tab**, in the **Data group**, click the **Edit Data** button to redisplay the embedded Excel worksheet.

3 In the **Excel worksheet**, click cell **B3**, and then type **20** Click cell **B4**, and then type **23** Press Enter.

Word automatically updates the chart to reflect these data point changes.

4 **Close** the Excel window, and then **Save** your Word document. Compare your screen with Figure 4.40.

Figure 4.40

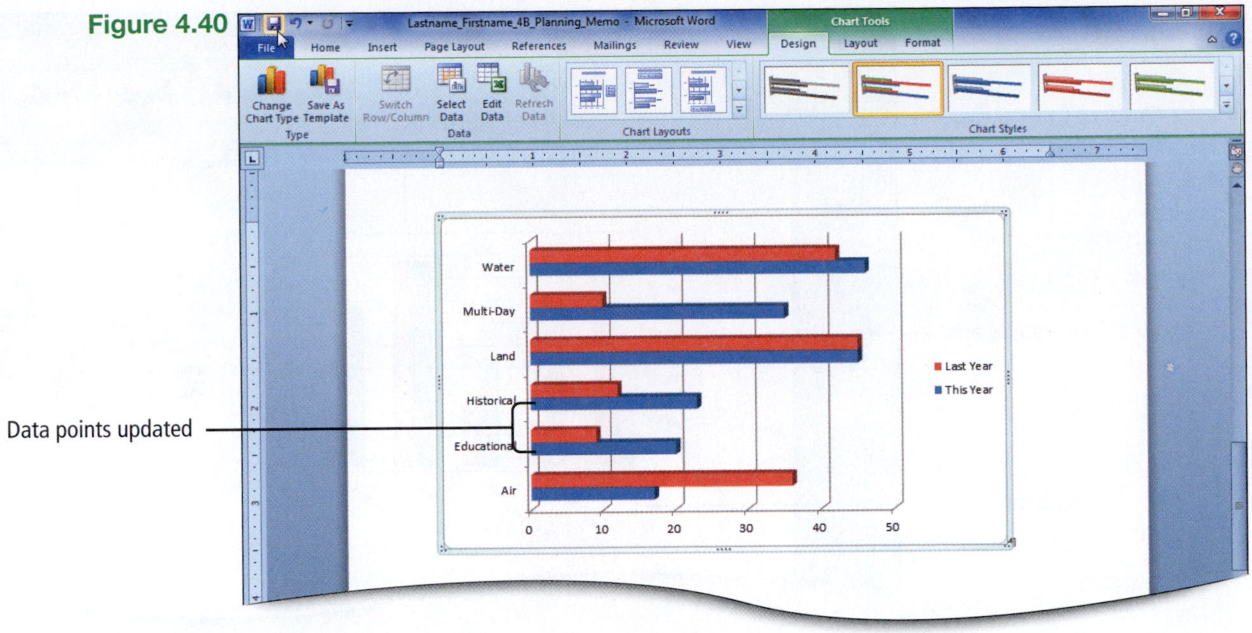

Objective 7 | Change a Chart Type

A chart commonly shows one of three types of relationships—a comparison among data, the proportion of parts to a whole, or trends over time. You may decide to alter a chart type—for example, change a bar chart to a column chart—so that the chart displays more attractively in the document.

Activity 4.17 | Changing the Chart Type

The data in the Tour Types chart compares tour numbers for two years and is appropriately represented by a bar chart. A column chart is also appropriate to compare data.

1. With the chart selected, on the **Design tab**, in the **Type group**, click the **Change Chart Type** button.
2. In the displayed **Change Chart Type** dialog box, on the left, click **Column**, and then on the right, under **Column**, in the second row, click the first chart type—**Clustered Cylinder**. Click **OK**, and then compare your screen with Figure 4.41.

   The category names display in alphabetical order on the horizontal axis; the number scale displays on the vertical axis.

Figure 4.41

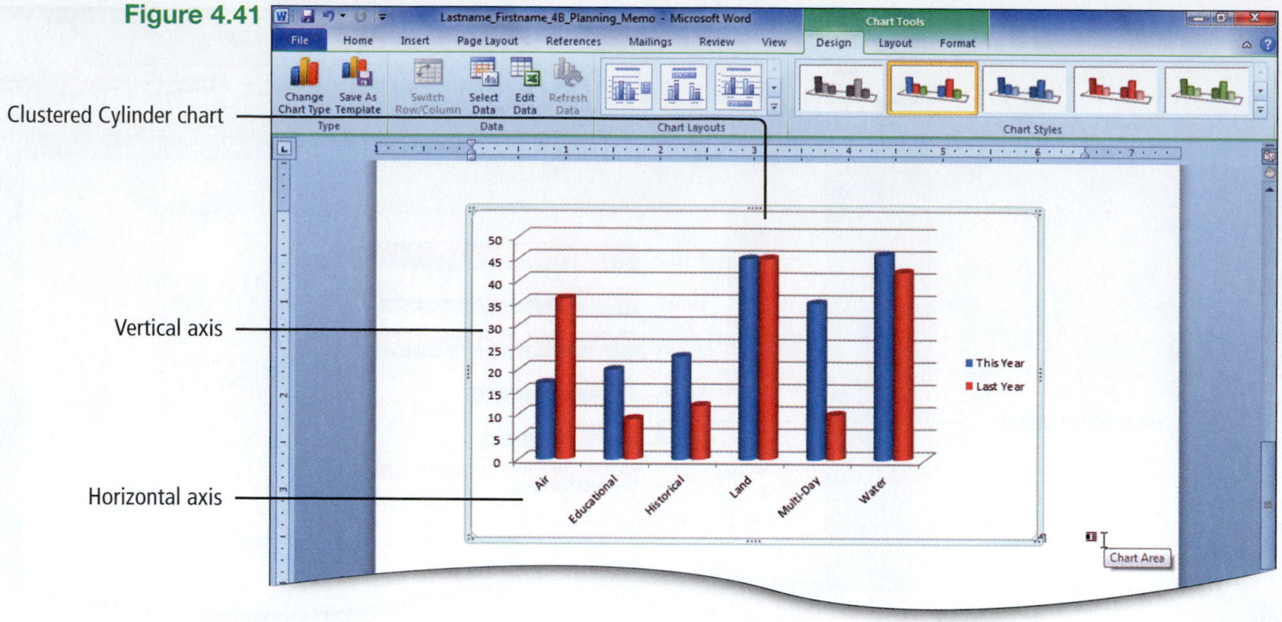

3 **Save** your document.

Objective 8 | Format a Chart

You can modify, add, or delete chart elements such as the chart title, data labels, and text boxes. You can also format a chart to change its size and color.

Activity 4.18 | Adding Chart Elements

Add chart elements to help the reader understand the data in your chart. For example, you can add a title to the chart and to individual axes, or add ***data labels***, which display the value represented by each data marker.

1 Click the **Layout tab.** In the **Labels group**, click the **Chart Title** button, and then from the displayed menu, click **Above Chart.**

A text box containing the text *Chart Title* displays above the chart.

2 In the text box, select the text *Chart Title*, and then type **Tours Offered - By Type**

3 On the **Layout tab**, in the **Labels group**, click the **Axis Titles** button, point to **Primary Vertical Axis Title**, and then click **Vertical Title.**

The text *Axis Title* displays in a text box to the left of the vertical axis.

4 Select the text *Axis Title*, type **# of Tours** and then notice that the text displays vertically in the text box.

5 Click in an empty corner inside the chart to deselect the vertical text box. On the **Layout tab**, in the **Labels group**, click the **Data Labels** button, and then click **Show.** Compare your screen with Figure 4.42. **Save** your document.

The data point values display above each data marker column in the chart. In addition to the scale on the vertical axis, data labels are helpful for the reader to understand the values represented by the columns.

Figure 4.42

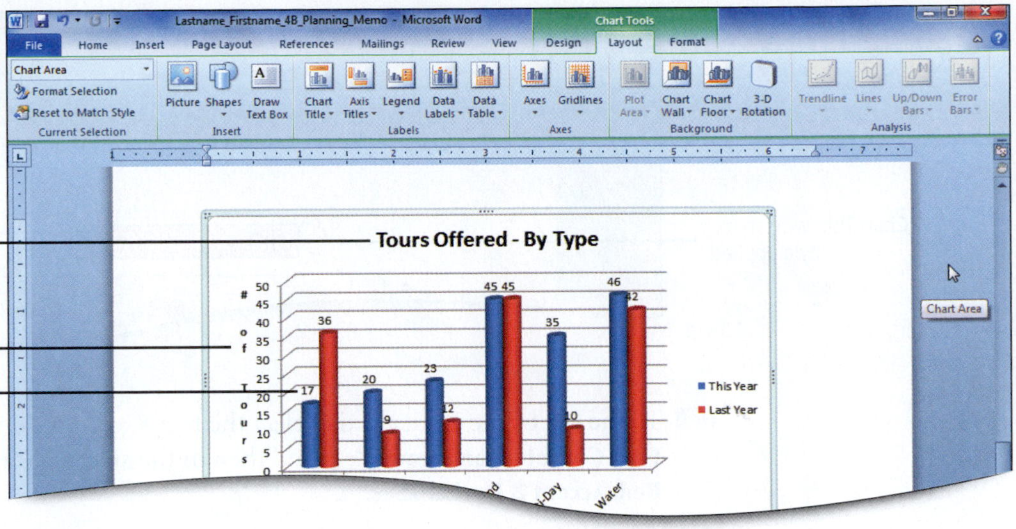

Activity 4.19 | Changing the Chart Style and Formatting Chart Elements

A ***chart style*** refers to the overall visual look of a chart in terms of its graphic effects, colors, and backgrounds; for example, you can have flat or beveled columns, colors that are solid or transparent, and backgrounds that are dark or light.

1 With the chart selected, click the **Design tab**. In the **Chart Styles group**, click the **More** button. In the displayed **Chart Styles** gallery, in the fourth row, click the fourth chart style—**Style 28**. Compare your screen with Figure 4.43.

Figure 4.43

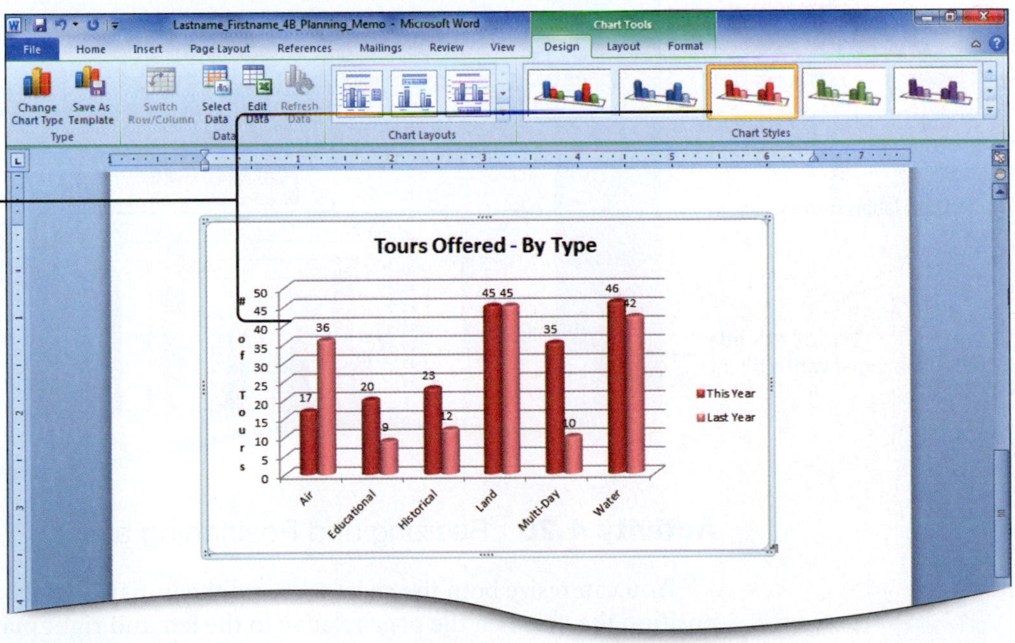

2 Select the chart title text. Click the **Format tab**, and then in the **Shape Styles group**, click the **More** button. In the displayed **Shape Styles** gallery, in the second row, click the third style—**Colored Fill – Red, Accent 2**. Click in an empty corner of the chart to deselect the chart title. Compare your screen with Figure 4.44.

Figure 4.44

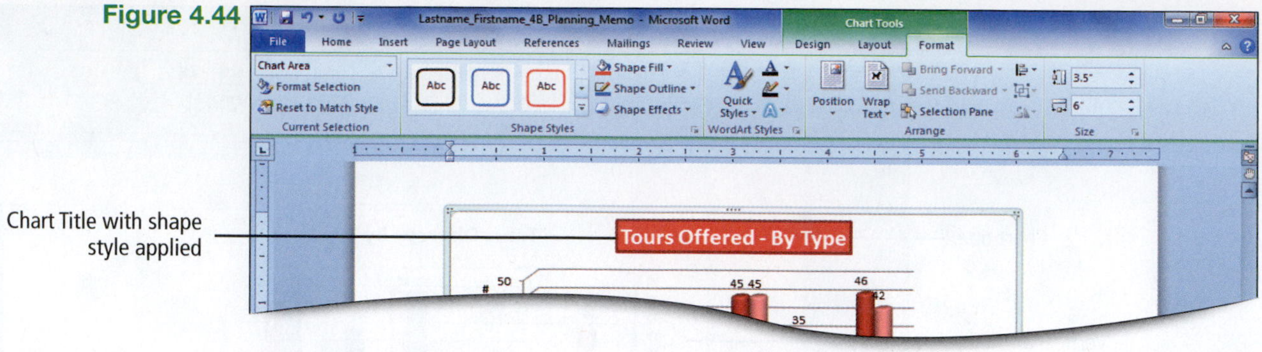

3 To the left of the vertical axis, select the text *# of Tours*. On the Mini toolbar, click the **Font Color button arrow** [A], and then in the sixth column, click the fifth color—**Red, Accent 2, Darker 25%**.

4 Above the **Air** columns, click **17** to select the data labels for each data marker in the *This Year* data series.

5 Point to **17** and right-click, and then on the Mini toolbar, click **Bold** [B].

All the numbers in the *This Year* data series display with bold.

6 Using the technique you just practiced, apply **Bold** [B] to the data labels in the *Last Year* data series. Compare your screen with Figure 4.45, and then **Save** [Save] your document.

Figure 4.45

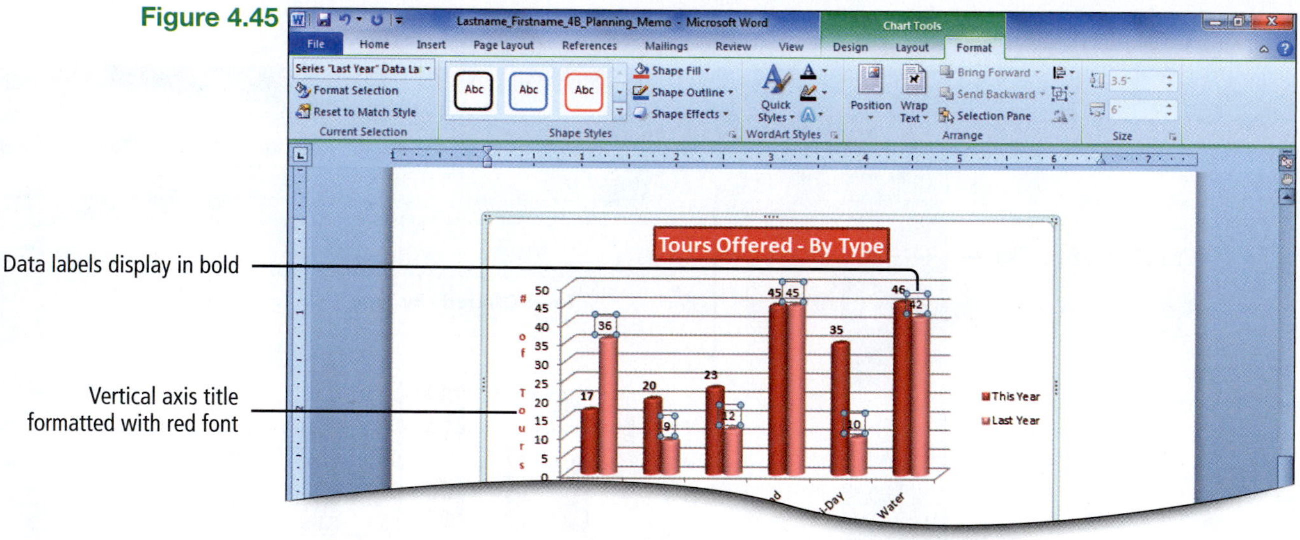

Activity 4.20 | Resizing and Positioning a Chart

You can resize both the chart area and the individual chart elements. You can also position the chart on the page relative to the left and right margins.

1 Click in an empty corner inside the chart so that the chart, and not the data labels, is selected. On the **Format tab**, in the **Size group**, click the **Shape Height spin box down arrow** to **2.7″**. Scroll up as necessary to view your document.

The resized chart moves to the bottom of the first page. Resizing a chart might also require specific chart elements to be resized or repositioned.

2 To the left of the vertical axis, select the text *# of Tours*. On the Mini toolbar, change the **Font Size** to **8**. Click in an empty corner of the chart to deselect the text.

3 Click the **Home tab**. In the **Paragraph group**, click the **Center** button to center the chart between the left and right margins. Compare your screen with Figure 4.46.

Figure 4.46

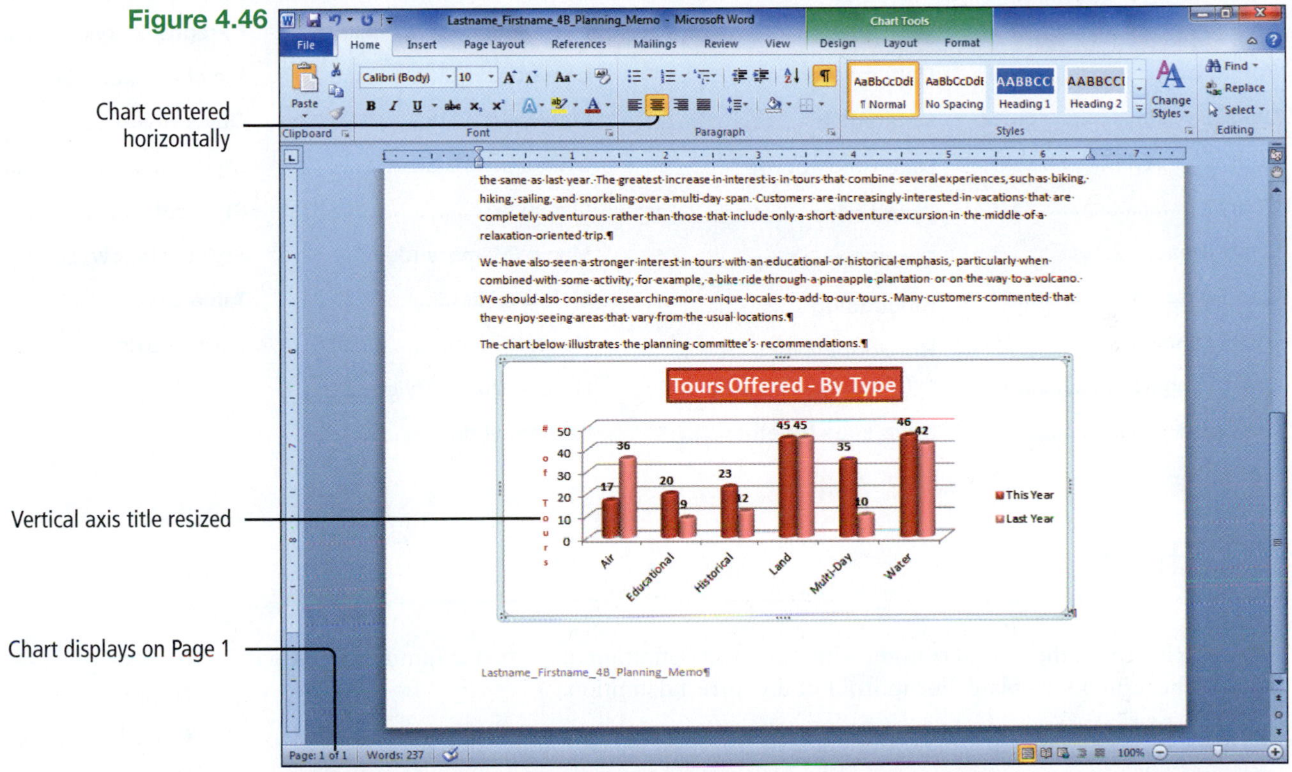

4 Press Ctrl + Home. In **Backstage** view, click **Info**. On the right side of the window, click **Properties**, and then click **Show Document Panel** to display the **Document Information Panel**. In the **Author** box, delete any text, and then type your first and last names. In the **Subject** box, type your course name and section number, and in the **Keywords** box, type **planning memo, tours data Close** the Document Information Panel.

5 Press Ctrl + F2 to display the **Print Preview** in **Backstage** view. Examine the **Print Preview**, and make any necessary adjustments. **Save** your document.

6 Print your document or submit it electronically as directed by your instructor. Click the **File tab**, and then click **Exit** to exit Word.

End **You have completed Project 4B**

Content-Based Assessments

Summary

In this chapter, you used predefined styles, and created your own styles, to apply uniform formatting in a document. You also customized a multilevel list to organize information and inserted and edited a chart to display numerical data in a graphical format within a Word document.

Key Terms

Area chart 72
Bar chart 72
Cell....................................73
Character style 57
Chart 71
Chart area 75
Chart data range 74
Chart style........................79
Column chart 72
Contiguous 61
Data labels 78
Data markers 75
Data points 75
Data range border 74
Data series 75
Direct formatting 51
Embedding 73
Horizontal axis (X-axis).........................75
Keep lines together 53
Keep with next 53
Legend 75
Line chart 72
Linked style.....................57
List style 57
Memo (Memorandum)......68
Multilevel list....................60
Noncontiguous 61
Normal Quick Style 51
Numerical data 71
Paragraph style 57
Pie chart 72
Quick Styles 51
Style.................................51
Style set 68
Styles window 56
Table style 57
Vertical axis (Y-axis) 75

Matching

Match each term in the second column with its correct definition in the first column by writing the letter of the term on the blank line in front of the correct definition.

____ 1. A group of formatting commands, such as font, font size, font color, paragraph alignment, and line spacing.

____ 2. The process of applying each format separately to text—for example, bold, then font size, then font color, and so on.

____ 3. Combinations of formatting options that work together and look attractive together.

____ 4. A formatting feature that keeps a heading with its first paragraph of text on the same page.

____ 5. A formatting feature that prevents a single line from displaying by itself at the bottom of a page or at the top of a page.

____ 6. A pane that displays a list of styles and contains tools to manage styles.

____ 7. A style, indicated by the symbol **a**, that contains formatting characteristics that you apply to text—for example, font name, font size, font color, bold emphasis, and so on.

____ 8. A style, indicated by the symbol ¶, that includes everything that a character style contains, plus all aspects of a paragraph's appearance—for example, text alignment, tab stops, or line spacing.

A Area
B Bar
C Cell
D Character style
E Chart
F Direct formatting
G Keep lines together
H Keep with next
I Memo
J Multilevel
K Paragraph style
L Quick Styles
M Style
N Style set
O Styles window

_____ 9. A list in which the items display in a visual hierarchical structure.

_____ 10. A group of styles that are designed to work together.

_____ 11. A written message sent to someone working in the same organization.

_____ 12. A visual representation of numerical data.

_____ 13. A chart type used to show a comparison among related data.

_____ 14. A chart type used to show trends over time.

_____ 15. In Excel, the location where a row and column meet.

Multiple Choice

Circle the correct answer.

1. What is the default style in Word for new documents that determines the basic look of document?
A. Word Quick Style **B.** Normal Template Style **C.** Normal Quick Style

2. A style, indicated by the symbol **¶a**, that behaves as either a character style or a paragraph style is:
A. an embedded style **B.** a linked style **C.** a Quick Style

3. Numbers that represent facts are referred to as:
A. numerical data **B.** data points **C.** information

4. To show a comparison among related data, use a:
A. pie chart **B.** line chart **C.** column chart

5. The process of inserting an object, such as a chart, into a Word document so that it becomes part of the document is:
A. embedding **B.** linking **C.** attaching

6. In Excel, the group of cells that is used to create a chart is the:
A. cell range **B.** chart data range **C.** chart point range

7. The Y-axis that displays along the left side of a chart is also referred to as the:
A. primary axis **B.** horizontal axis **C.** vertical axis

8. The shapes in a chart that represent each of the cells that contain data are:
A. data labels **B.** data markers **C.** chart styles

9. The part of a chart that identifies the colors assigned to each data series or category is the:
A. legend **B.** vertical axis **C.** horizontal axis

10. The overall visual look of a chart in terms of its graphic effects, colors, and backgrounds is the:
A. chart format **B.** chart style **C.** chart theme

Content-Based Assessments

Apply 4A skills from these Objectives:

1. Apply and Modify Quick Styles
2. Create New Styles
3. Manage Styles
4. Create a Multilevel List

Skills Review | Project 4C Training Classes

In the following Skills Review, you will add styles and a multilevel list format to a document that describes training classes for Lehua Hawaiian Adventures tour guides. Your completed document will look similar to Figure 4.47.

Project Files

For Project 4C, you will need the following file:

w04C_Training_Classses

You will save your document as:

Lastname_Firstname_4C_Training_Classes

Project Results

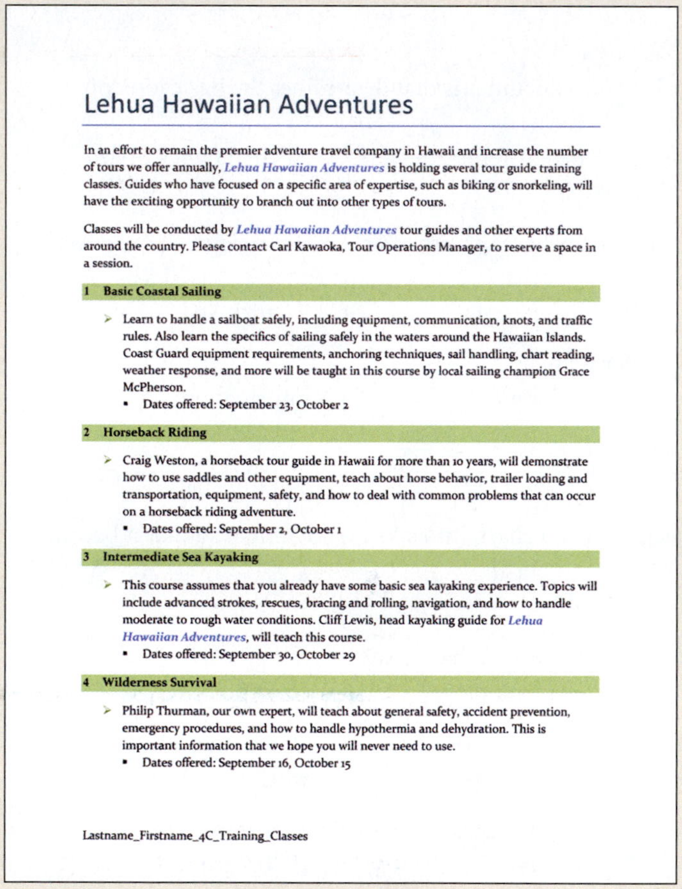
Lehua Hawaiian Adventures

In an effort to remain the premier adventure travel company in Hawaii and increase the number of tours we offer annually, *Lehua Hawaiian Adventures* is holding several tour guide training classes. Guides who have focused on a specific area of expertise, such as biking or snorkeling, will have the exciting opportunity to branch out into other types of tours.

Classes will be conducted by *Lehua Hawaiian Adventures* tour guides and other experts from around the country. Please contact Carl Kawaoka, Tour Operations Manager, to reserve a space in a session.

1 **Basic Coastal Sailing**

- Learn to handle a sailboat safely, including equipment, communication, knots, and traffic rules. Also learn the specifics of sailing safely in the waters around the Hawaiian Islands. Coast Guard equipment requirements, anchoring techniques, sail handling, chart reading, weather response, and more will be taught in this course by local sailing champion Grace McPherson.
  - Dates offered: September 23, October 2

2 **Horseback Riding**

- Craig Weston, a horseback tour guide in Hawaii for more than 10 years, will demonstrate how to use saddles and other equipment, teach about horse behavior, trailer loading and transportation, equipment, safety, and how to deal with common problems that can occur on a horseback riding adventure.
  - Dates offered: September 2, October 1

3 **Intermediate Sea Kayaking**

- This course assumes that you already have some basic sea kayaking experience. Topics will include advanced strokes, rescues, bracing and rolling, navigation, and how to handle moderate to rough water conditions. Cliff Lewis, head kayaking guide for *Lehua Hawaiian Adventures*, will teach this course.
  - Dates offered: September 30, October 29

4 **Wilderness Survival**

- Philip Thurman, our own expert, will teach about general safety, accident prevention, emergency procedures, and how to handle hypothermia and dehydration. This is important information that we hope you will never need to use.
  - Dates offered: September 16, October 15

Lastname_Firstname_4C_Training_Classes

Figure 4.47

(Project 4C Training Classes continues on the next page)

Skills Review | Project 4C Training Classes (continued)

1 **Start** Word. From your student files, open the file **w04C_Training_Classes**. **Save** the document in your **Word Chapter 4** folder as **Lastname_Firstname_4C_Training_Classes** Scroll to the bottom of the page, right-click in the footer area, click **Edit Footer**, and then using **Quick Parts**, insert the file name. **Close** the footer area.

- **a.** If any proper names are flagged as a spelling error, point to the first occurrence, right-click, and then click **Ignore All**.
- **b.** Select the first paragraph, and in the **Styles group**, click the **More** button. In the **Quick Styles** gallery, click **Title**.
- **c.** In the second paragraph, in the second line, select the text *Lehua Hawaiian Adventures*. Display the **Quick Styles** gallery, and then click the **Strong** style.
- **d.** With *Lehua Hawaiian Adventures* selected, right-click the selection, and then on the Mini toolbar, click the **Font Color button arrow**. In the fifth column, click the first color—**Blue, Accent 1**.
- **e.** With the text still selected, display the **Quick Styles** gallery, right-click the **Strong** style, and then from the displayed shortcut menu, click **Update Strong to Match Selection**.
- **f.** In the third paragraph, in the first line, select the text *Lehua Hawaiian Adventures* and apply the **Strong** style. Using the same technique, in the eleventh paragraph that begins *This course*, in the third line, select *Lehua Hawaiian Adventures*—do not include the comma—and then apply the **Strong** style.

2 On the **Page Layout tab**, in the **Themes group**, click the **Themes** button, and then click the **Flow** theme.

- **a.** Including the paragraph mark, select the fourth paragraph of the document—*Basic Coastal Sailing*. On the Mini toolbar, apply **Bold**. On the **Home tab**, in the **Paragraph group**, click the **Shading button arrow**, and then in the last column, click the fourth color—**Lime, Accent 6, Lighter 40%**.
- **b.** With the paragraph still selected, display the **Quick Styles** gallery, and then click **Save Selection as a New Quick Style**. In the **Name** box, type **Class Title** and then click **OK**.
- **c.** Scroll down as necessary, select the paragraph *Horseback Riding*, and then apply the **Class Title** style.
- **d.** Using the same technique, apply the **Class Title** style to the paragraphs *Intermediate Sea Kayaking* and *Wilderness Survival.*

3 Press Ctrl + Home. On the **Home tab**, in the **Styles group**, click the **dialog box launcher** button to display the **Styles** window.

- **a.** In the **Styles** window, point to **Strong**, click the **arrow** that displays, and then click **Modify**.
- **b.** In the **Modify Style** dialog box, under **Formatting**, click the **Italic** button. Click **OK** to close the dialog box and update all instances of the **Strong** style. **Close** the **Styles** window.

4 Click to position the insertion point to the left of the paragraph *Basic Coastal Sailing*, and then from this point, select all remaining text in the document.

- **a.** On the **Home tab**, in the **Paragraph group**, click the **Multilevel List** button. Under **List Library**, locate and then click the ❖, ➢, ■ style.
- **b.** Click in the first paragraph following *Basic Coastal Sailing*, and then in the **Paragraph group**, click the **Increase Indent** button one time. Click in the second paragraph following *Basic Coastal Sailing*, which begins *Dates*, and then click the **Increase Indent** button two times. Under *Horseback Riding*, *Intermediate Sea Kayaking*, and *Wilderness Survival*, format the paragraphs in the same manner.

5 Select the entire multilevel list. Click the **Multilevel List** button to display the **Multilevel List** gallery. At the bottom of the gallery, click **Define New List Style**.

- **a.** Name the style **Training Class** Under **Formatting**, in the **Apply formatting to** box, be sure **1st level** displays. In the small toolbar above the preview area, click the **Numbering Style arrow**, and in the displayed list, scroll to locate and then click the **1, 2, 3** style.
- **b.** Under **Formatting**, click the **Apply formatting to arrow**, and then click **2nd level**. In the small toolbar above the preview area, make certain the **Bullet: ➢** style displays. Click the **Font Color arrow**, and then in the last column, click the fifth color—**Lime, Accent 6, Darker 25%**. Click **OK** to close the dialog box.

6 Press Ctrl + Home. Click the **File tab** to display **Backstage** view, and then click **Info**. On the right side of the window, click **Properties**, and then click **Show**

(Project 4C Training Classes continues on the next page)

Skills Review | Project 4C Training Classes (continued)

Document Panel to display the **Document Information Panel**. In the **Author** box, delete any text, and then type your first and last names. In the **Subject** box, type your course name and section number, and then in the **Keywords** box, type **training classes, description Close** the Document Information Panel.

7 Press Ctrl + F2 to display the **Print Preview** in **Backstage** view. **Examine** the **Print Preview**, and make any necessary adjustments. **Save** your changes. Print your document or submit electronically as directed by your instructor. From **Backstage** view, **Exit** Word.

End **You have completed Project 4C**

Apply 4B skills from these Objectives:

- **5** Change the Style Set and Paragraph Spacing of a Document
- **6** Insert a Chart and Enter Data into a Chart
- **7** Change a Chart Type
- **8** Format a Chart

Skills Review | Project 4D Strategy Session

In the following Skills Review, you will create a memo for Katherine Okubo, President of Lehua Hawaiian Adventures, which details the company's financial performance and provides strategies for the upcoming year. Your completed document will look similar to Figure 4.48.

Project Files

For Project 4D, you will need the following file:

w04D_Strategy_Session

You will save your document as:

Lastname_Firstname_4D_Strategy_Session

Project Results

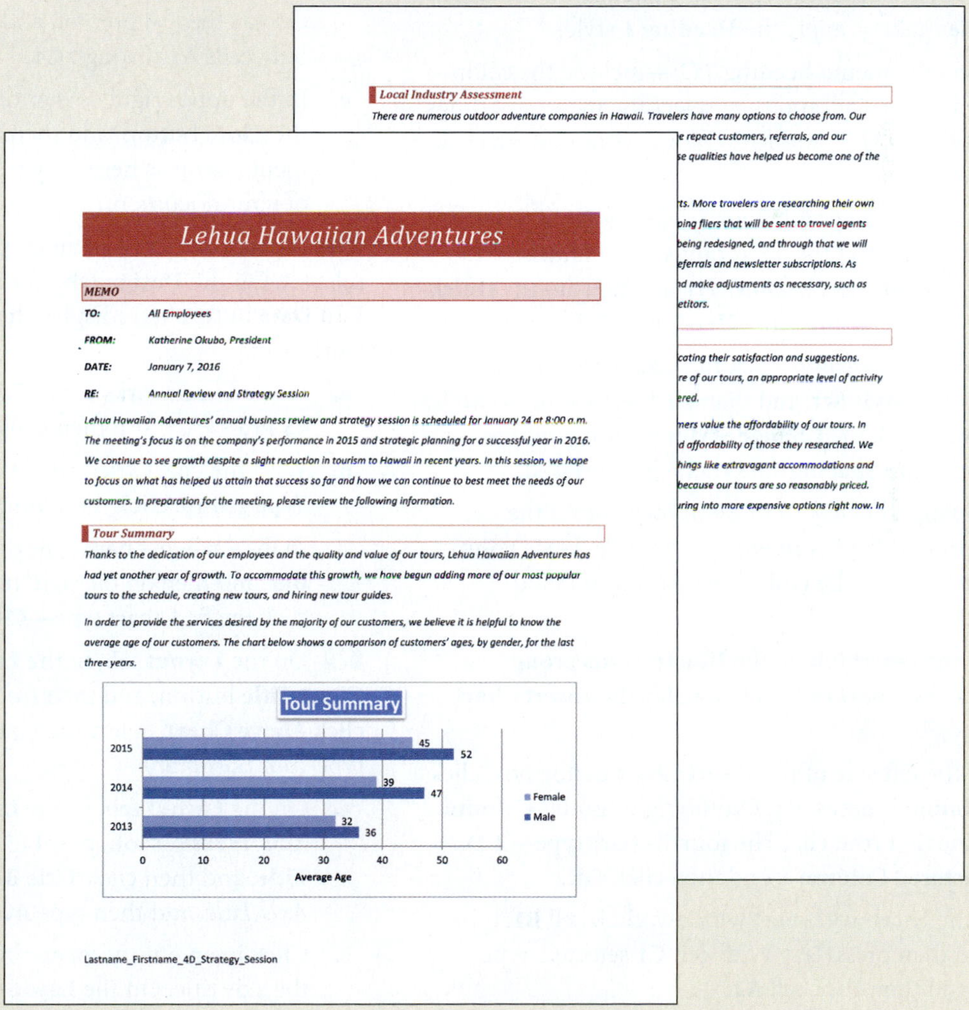

Figure 4.48

(Project 4D Strategy Session continues on the next page)

Content-Based Assessments

Skills Review | Project 4D Strategy Session (continued)

1 **Start** Word. From your student files, locate and open the file **w04D_Strategy_Session**. Save the document in your **Word Chapter 4** folder as **Lastname_Firstname_4D_Strategy_Session** Scroll to the bottom of **Page 1**, right-click in the footer area, click **Edit Footer**, and then using **Quick Parts**, insert the file name. **Close** the footer area.

- **a.** If *Lehua* and *Okubo* are flagged as spelling errors, point to the first occurrence, right-click, and then click **Ignore All**.
- **b.** Select the first paragraph of the document—*Lehua Hawaiian Adventures*. Display the **Quick Styles** gallery, and then click **Title**. Select the second paragraph, the heading *Memo*, and then from the **Quick Styles** gallery, apply the **Heading 1** style.
- **c.** Select the memo heading *TO:*—include the colon—hold down Ctrl, and then select the memo headings *FROM:*, *DATE:*, and *RE:*. On the Mini toolbar, click **Bold**.
- **d.** Select the paragraph *Tour Summary*, hold down Ctrl, and then select the paragraphs *Local Industry Assessment* and *Customer Feedback*. From the **Quick Styles** gallery, apply the **Heading 2** style.
- **e.** In the **Styles group**, click the **Change Styles** button, point to **Style Set**, and then click **Fancy**. In the **Styles group**, click the **Change Styles** button, point to **Paragraph Spacing**, and then click **Relaxed**.

2 On **Page 1**, below *Tour Summary*, locate the paragraph that begins *In order to provide*. Place your insertion point at the end of the paragraph, and then press Enter.

- **a.** On the **Insert tab**, in the **Illustrations group**, click the **Chart** button to display the **Insert Chart** dialog box.
- **b.** On the left side of the **Insert Chart** dialog box, click **Column**, if necessary. On the right, under **Column**, in the first row, click the fourth chart type—**3-D Clustered Column**—and then click **OK**.

3 In the Excel worksheet window, click cell **B1**, type **Male** and then press Tab. With cell **C1** selected, type **Female** and then click cell **A2**.

- **a.** With cell **A2** selected, type **2013** and then press Tab to move to cell **B2**. Type **36** and then press Tab. In cell **C2**, type **32** and then press Tab two times to move to **row 3**.
- **b.** Using the technique you just practiced, and without changing any values in **column D**, type the following data:

	Male	Female	Series 3
2013	36	32	2
2014	**47**	**39**	2
2015	**52**	**43**	3

- **c.** Point to the lower right corner of the blue border to display the pointer, and then drag to the left to select only cells **A1** through **C5**.
- **d.** Point to the lower right corner of the blue border to display the pointer, and then drag up to select only cells **A1** through **C4**.
- **e.** In the upper right corner of the Excel window, click the **Close** button, and then **Save** your Word document. Scroll as necessary to view the chart on **Page 2** of your document.

4 If necessary, click in an empty area of the chart to select it. On the **Design tab**, in the **Data group**, click the **Edit Data** button to redisplay the embedded Excel worksheet.

- **a.** In the Excel worksheet, click cell **C4**, and then type **45** Press Enter, and then **Close** the Excel window.
- **b.** With the chart selected, on the **Design tab**, in the **Type group**, click the **Change Chart Type** button.
- **c.** In the **Change Chart Type** dialog box, on the left, click **Bar**, and then on the right under **Bar**, in the first row, click the first chart type—**Clustered Bar**. Click **OK**.

5 On the **Layout tab**, in the **Labels group**, click the **Chart Title** button, and then from the displayed menu, click **Above Chart**. Select the text *Chart Title*, and then type **Tour Summary**

- **a.** On the **Layout tab**, in the **Labels group**, click the **Axis Titles** button, point to **Primary Horizontal Axis Title**, and then click **Title Below Axis**. Select the text *Axis Title*, and then type **Average Age**
- **b.** Click in an empty corner inside the chart to deselect the axis title. On the **Layout tab**, in the **Labels group**, click the **Data Labels** button, and then click **Outside End**.
- **c.** With the chart selected, on the **Design tab**, in the **Chart Styles group**, click the **More** button to display

(Project 4D Strategy Session continues on the next page)

Skills Review | Project 4D Strategy Session (continued)

the **Chart Styles** gallery. In the first row, click the third chart style—**Style 3**.

d. Select the chart title text. On the **Format tab**, in the **Shape Styles group**, click the **More** button to display the **Shape Styles** gallery. In the third row, click the second style—**Light 1 Outline, Colored Fill – Blue, Accent 1**.

e. Click in an empty corner of the chart so that the chart, and not the title, is selected. On the **Format tab**, in the **Size group**, click the **Shape Height spin box down arrow** to **2.7"** to display the chart on **Page 1** of the document.

f. Click the **Home tab**. In the **Paragraph group**, click the **Center** button.

6 Press Ctrl + Home. Click the **File tab** to display **Backstage** view, and then click **Info**. On the right side of the window, click **Properties**, and then click **Show Document Panel** to display the **Document Information Panel**. In the **Author** box, delete any text, and then type your first and last names. In the **Subject** box, type your course name and section number, and in the **Keywords** box, type **strategy session, memo Close** the Document Information Panel.

7 Press Ctrl + F2 to display the **Print Preview** in **Backstage** view. Examine the **Print Preview**, and make any necessary adjustments. **Save** your document. Print your document or submit electronically as directed by your instructor. From **Backstage** view, **Exit** Word.

End **You have completed Project 4D**

Content-Based Assessments

Apply 4A skills from these Objectives:

1. Apply and Modify Quick Styles
2. Create New Styles
3. Manage Styles
4. Create a Multilevel List

Mastering Word | Project 4E Trip Tips

In the following Mastering Word project, you will create a handout for Carl Kawaoka, Tour Operations Manager of Lehua Hawaiian Adventures, which details tips for tour participants. Your completed document will look similar to Figure 4.49.

Project Files

For Project 4E, you will need the following file:

w04E_Trip_Tips

You will save your document as:

Lastname_Firstname_4E_Trip_Tips

Project Results

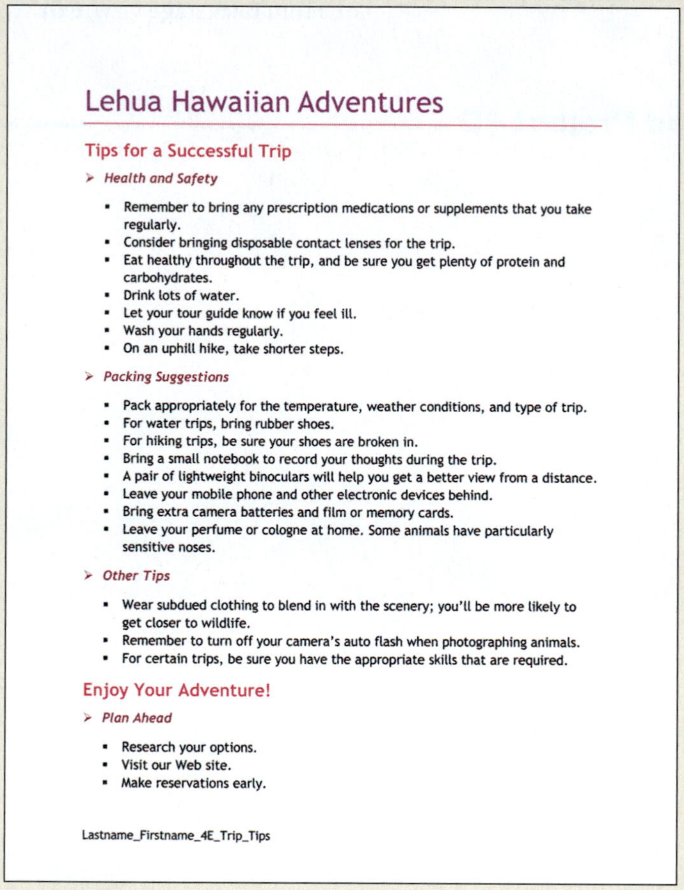

Lehua Hawaiian Adventures

Tips for a Successful Trip

➢ *Health and Safety*

- Remember to bring any prescription medications or supplements that you take regularly.
- Consider bringing disposable contact lenses for the trip.
- Eat healthy throughout the trip, and be sure you get plenty of protein and carbohydrates.
- Drink lots of water.
- Let your tour guide know if you feel ill.
- Wash your hands regularly.
- On an uphill hike, take shorter steps.

➢ *Packing Suggestions*

- Pack appropriately for the temperature, weather conditions, and type of trip.
- For water trips, bring rubber shoes.
- For hiking trips, be sure your shoes are broken in.
- Bring a small notebook to record your thoughts during the trip.
- A pair of lightweight binoculars will help you get a better view from a distance.
- Leave your mobile phone and other electronic devices behind.
- Bring extra camera batteries and film or memory cards.
- Leave your perfume or cologne at home. Some animals have particularly sensitive noses.

➢ *Other Tips*

- Wear subdued clothing to blend in with the scenery; you'll be more likely to get closer to wildlife.
- Remember to turn off your camera's auto flash when photographing animals.
- For certain trips, be sure you have the appropriate skills that are required.

Enjoy Your Adventure!

➢ *Plan Ahead*

- Research your options.
- Visit our Web site.
- Make reservations early.

Lastname_Firstname_4E_Trip_Tips

Figure 4.49

(Project 4E Trip Tips continues on the next page)

Mastering Word | Project 4E Trip Tips (continued)

1 **Start** Word. From your student files, open the document **w04E_Trip_Tips**. **Save** the file in your **Word Chapter 4** folder as **Lastname_Firstname_4E_Trip_Tips** Insert the file name in the footer. For any proper names flagged as spelling errors, right-click, and **Ignore All**.

2 Select the first paragraph—*Lehua Hawaiian Adventures*, and then apply the **Title** style. Select the second paragraph that begins *Tips for*, apply the **Heading 2** style, change the **Font Size** to **16**, and then change the **Spacing After** to **6 pt**. Display the **Quick Styles** gallery, right-click **Heading 2**, and then click **Update Heading 2 to Match Selection**.

3 Scroll to view **Page 2**, and then select the paragraph *Enjoy your Adventure!* Apply the **Heading 2** style. Change the document **Theme** to **Opulent**.

4 Near the top of **Page 1**, select the third paragraph, *Health and Safety*, apply **Italic**, and change the **Font Color** to **Pink, Accent 1, Darker 25%**—in the fifth column, the fifth color. With the text selected, display the **Quick Styles** gallery. Click **Save Selection as a New Quick Style**, and then name the new style **Tip Heading** Apply the **Tip Heading** style to the paragraphs *Packing Suggestions*, *Other Tips*, and *Plan Ahead*. **Modify** the **Tip Heading** style by applying **Bold**.

5 Select the block of text beginning with *Health and Safety* and ending with *that are required* on **Page 2**. Apply a **Multilevel List** with the ❖, ➢, ■ style. Select the paragraphs below each tip heading, and **Increase Indent** one time.

6 Select the entire list, and then display the **Define New List Style** dialog box. Name the list style **Tips List** If necessary, change the **1st level** to **Bullet:** ➢ and set the **Font Color** to **Pink, Accent 1**—in the fifth column, the first color. Set the **2nd level** to **Bullet:** ■. Be sure the bullet ■ displays in black. Click **OK**.

7 At the bottom of **Page 1**, beginning with *Plan Ahead*, select the last four paragraphs. Apply the **Tips List** multilevel list style. Select the last three paragraphs, and then click **Increase Indent** one time.

8 From **Backstage** view, click **Properties**, and then click **Show Document Panel**. In the **Document Information Panel**, in the **Author** box, type your name. In the **Subject** box, type your course name and section, and in the **Keywords** box, type **trip tips, multilevel list**

9 Check your document in **Print Preview**, and then make any necessary corrections. **Save** your document, and then print the document or submit electronically as directed by your instructor. **Exit** Word.

End **You have completed Project 4E**

Content-Based Assessments

Apply **4B** skills from these Objectives:

- 5 Change the Style Set and Paragraph Spacing of a Document
- 6 Insert a Chart and Enter Data into a Chart
- 7 Change a Chart Type
- 8 Format a Chart

Mastering Word | Project 4F Hiking FAQ

In the following Mastering Word project, you will create a document that provides frequently asked questions (FAQs) and includes a chart about hiking trips offered by Lehua Hawaiian Adventures. Your completed document will look similar to Figure 4.50.

Project Files

For Project 4F, you will need the following file:

w04F_Hiking_FAQ

You will save your document as:

Lastname_Firstname_4F_Hiking_FAQ

Project Results

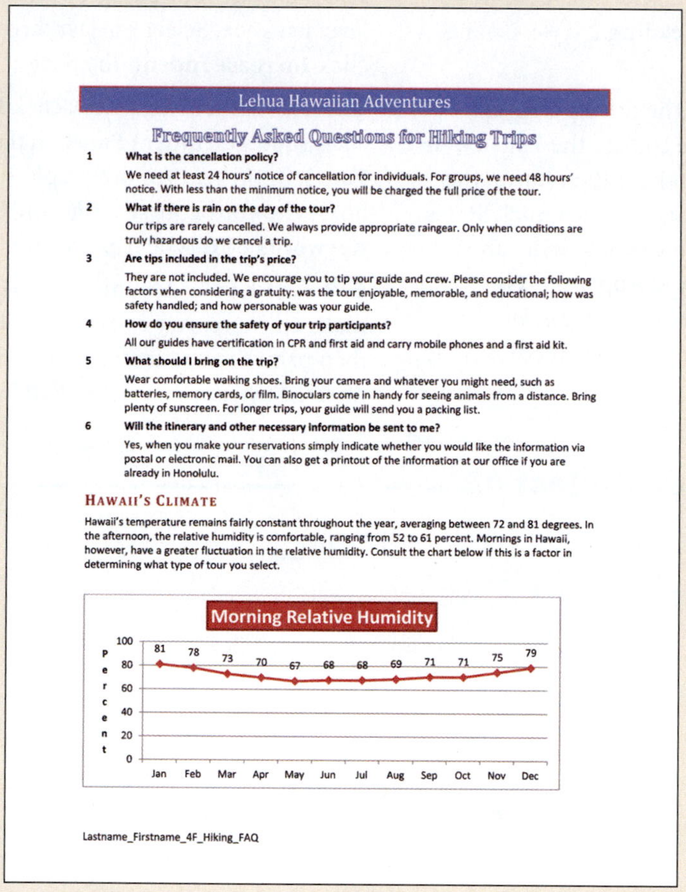

Lehua Hawaiian Adventures

Frequently Asked Questions for Hiking Trips

1 **What is the cancellation policy?**

We need at least 24 hours' notice of cancellation for individuals. For groups, we need 48 hours' notice. With less than the minimum notice, you will be charged the full price of the tour.

2 **What if there is rain on the day of the tour?**

Our trips are rarely cancelled. We always provide appropriate raingear. Only when conditions are truly hazardous do we cancel a trip.

3 **Are tips included in the trip's price?**

They are not included. We encourage you to tip your guide and crew. Please consider the following factors when considering a gratuity: was the tour enjoyable, memorable, and educational; how was safety handled; and how personable was your guide.

4 **How do you ensure the safety of your trip participants?**

All our guides have certification in CPR and first aid and carry mobile phones and a first aid kit.

5 **What should I bring on the trip?**

Wear comfortable walking shoes. Bring your camera and whatever you might need, such as batteries, memory cards, or film. Binoculars come in handy for seeing animals from a distance. Bring plenty of sunscreen. For longer trips, your guide will send you a packing list.

6 **Will the itinerary and other necessary information be sent to me?**

Yes, when you make your reservations simply indicate whether you would like the information via postal or electronic mail. You can also get a printout of the information at our office if you are already in Honolulu.

HAWAII'S CLIMATE

Hawaii's temperature remains fairly constant throughout the year, averaging between 72 and 81 degrees. In the afternoon, the relative humidity is comfortable, ranging from 52 to 61 percent. Mornings in Hawaii, however, have a greater fluctuation in the relative humidity. Consult the chart below if this is a factor in determining what type of tour you select.

Lastname_Firstname_4F_Hiking_FAQ

Figure 4.50

(Project 4F Hiking FAQ continues on the next page)

Mastering Word | Project 4F Hiking FAQ (continued)

1 **Start** Word. From your student files, open the file **w04F_Hiking_FAQ**, and then save the document in your **Word Chapter 4** folder as **Lastname_Firstname_4F_Hiking_FAQ** Insert the file name in the footer. For any proper names flagged as spelling errors, right-click, and **Ignore All**.

2 Format the first paragraph—the title *Lehua Hawaiian Adventures*—with the **Heading 1** style. Change its **Font Size** to **16**, and then **Center** the title. Select the second paragraph, apply the **Heading 2** style, and then **Center** the paragraph. Select the paragraph *Hawaii's Climate*, and then apply the **Heading 3** style. Change the **Style Set** to **Thatch**. Change the **Paragraph Spacing** style to **Compact**. Select all the numbered paragraphs, and then apply **Bold**. For each single paragraph following a numbered paragraph, click the **Increase Indent** button one time.

3 Move the insertion point to the end of the document, and then press Enter two times. **Insert** a **Clustered Column** chart, and then beginning in cell **B1**, and without changing any values in **column C** or **column D**, type the following data, pressing Tab to move from one cell to the next. Note: As you type, the displayed instructions will automatically move to a new row.

	Morning Relative Humidity	Series 2	Series 3
Jan	81	2.4	2
Feb	78	4.4	2
Mar	73	1.8	3
Apr	70	2.8	5
May	67		
Jun	68		
Jul	68		
Aug	69		
Sep	71		
Oct	71		
Nov	75		
Dec	79		

4 Select the chart data range **A1** through **B13**, and then **Close** Excel. Change the chart type to a **Line** chart using the **Line with Markers** style. Display **Data Labels Above** the data points. Add a **Primary Vertical Axis Title** in the style **Vertical Title** with the text **Percent** and **Delete** the legend.

5 Change the chart style to **Style 4**. Format the chart title as a shape style, using the **Colored Fill – Red, Accent 2 Shape Style**. Change the **Shape Height** of the chart to **2.4"**.

6 Display the **Document Information Panel**, add your name, course name and section, and the keywords **FAQ, hiking** Check your document in **Print Preview**, and then make any necessary corrections. **Save** your document, and then print the document or submit electronically as directed by your instructor. **Exit** Word.

End **You have completed Project 4F**

Content-Based Assessments

Apply **4A** and **4B** skills from these Objectives:

1. Apply and Modify Quick Styles
2. Create New Styles
3. Manage Styles
4. Create a Multilevel List
5. Change the Style Set and Paragraph Spacing of a Document
6. Insert a Chart and Enter Data into a Chart
7. Change a Chart Type
8. Format a Chart

Mastering Word | Project 4G Expense Reduction

In the following Mastering Word project, you will create a memo for Paulo Alvarez, Vice President of Finance for Lehua Hawaiian Adventures, which includes ideas for reducing expenses. Your completed document will look similar to Figure 4.51.

Project Files

For Project 4G, you will need the following file:

w04G_Expense_Reduction

You will save your document as:

Lastname_Firstname_4G_Expense_Reduction

Project Results

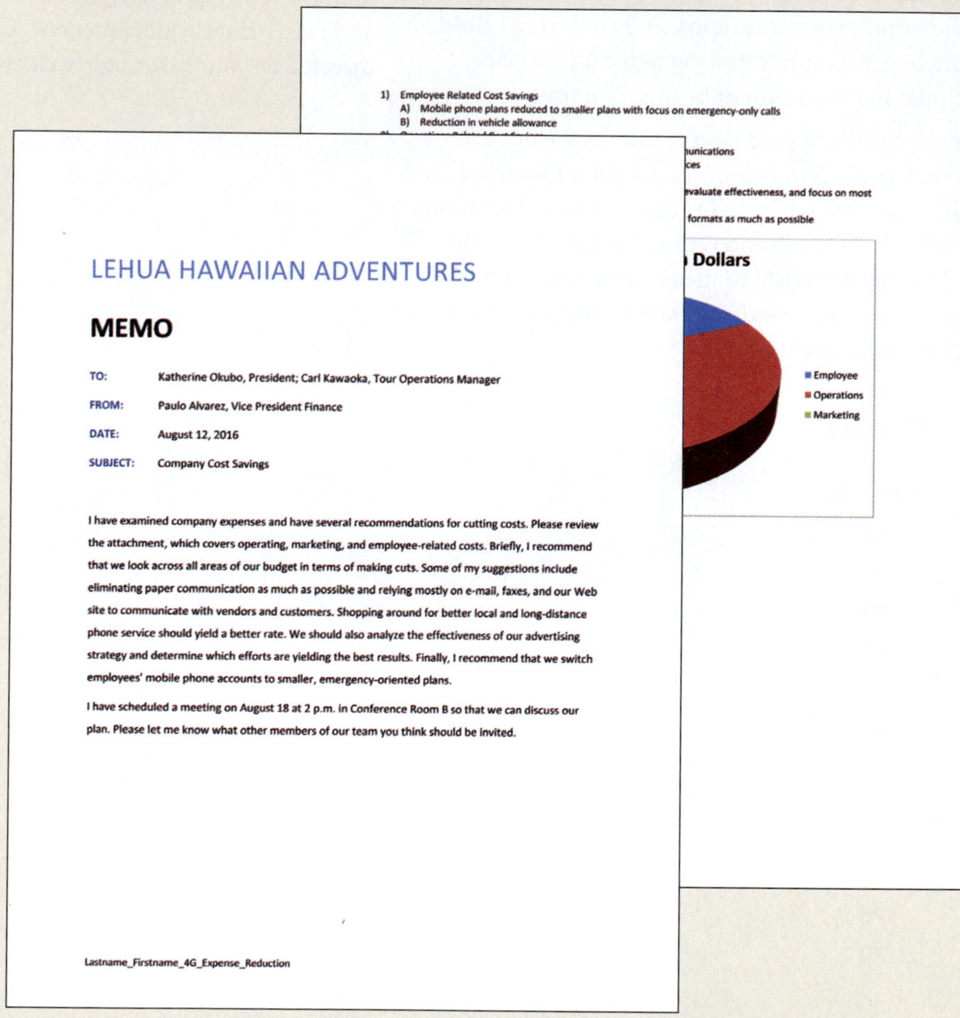

LEHUA HAWAIIAN ADVENTURES

MEMO

TO: Katherine Okubo, President; Carl Kawaoka, Tour Operations Manager

FROM: Paulo Alvarez, Vice President Finance

DATE: August 12, 2016

SUBJECT: Company Cost Savings

I have examined company expenses and have several recommendations for cutting costs. Please review the attachment, which covers operating, marketing, and employee-related costs. Briefly, I recommend that we look across all areas of our budget in terms of making cuts. Some of my suggestions include eliminating paper communication as much as possible and relying mostly on e-mail, faxes, and our Web site to communicate with vendors and customers. Shopping around for better local and long-distance phone service should yield a better rate. We should also analyze the effectiveness of our advertising strategy and determine which efforts are yielding the best results. Finally, I recommend that we switch employees' mobile phone accounts to smaller, emergency-oriented plans.

I have scheduled a meeting on August 18 at 2 p.m. in Conference Room B so that we can discuss our plan. Please let me know what other members of our team you think should be invited.

Lastname_Firstname_4G_Expense_Reduction

Figure 4.51

(Project 4G Expense Reduction continues on the next page)

Mastering Word | Project 4G Expense Reduction (continued)

1 **Start** Word. From your student files, open the file **w04G_Expense_Reduction**, and then save the document in your **Word Chapter 4** folder as **Lastname_Firstname_4G_Expense_Reduction** Insert the file name in the footer. For any proper names flagged as spelling errors, right-click, and **Ignore All**.

2 Apply the **Title** style to the first paragraph. Apply the **Strong** style to *MEMO*, and then change the **Font Size** to **26**. Select *TO:*—include the colon—and then apply **Bold** and change the **Font Color** to **Dark Blue, Text 2**. Save the selection as a new Quick Style with the name **Memo Heading** and then apply the new style to *FROM:*, *DATE:*, and *SUBJECT:*.

3 Change the **Style Set** to **Modern**, and then change the **Paragraph Spacing** style to **Relaxed**. On **Page 1**, beginning with the heading *TO:*, change the **Font Size** of all the remaining text to **11**. Select the text on **Page 2**, and apply a **Multilevel List** with the format **1., a., i.**. For the paragraphs beginning *Mobile phone*, *Reduction*, *Focus*, *Research*, *Evaluate*, and *Utilize*, **Increase Indent** one time.

4 Select the entire list, and then display the **Define New List Style** dialog box. Name the style **Reduction List** Change the **2nd level** letter style to **A, B, C, ...**.

5 Position the insertion point at the end of the document. **Insert** a **Pie in 3-D** chart. Type the following chart data:

	Projected Savings in Dollars
Employee	15,000
Operations	43,000
Marketing	26,000

6 Select the chart data range **A1** through **B4**, and then **Close** Excel. Display **Data Labels** in the **Center** position on the data points. Format the data labels with **Bold** emphasis and a **Font Size** of **12**. **Center** the chart horizontally on the page.

7 Display the **Document Information Panel**, add your name, course name and section, and the keywords **expenses, reduction** Check your document in **Print Preview**, and then make any necessary corrections. **Save** your document, and then print or submit electronically as directed. **Exit** Word.

End **You have completed Project 4G**

Apply a combination of the **4A** and **4B** skills.

GO! Fix It | Project 4H New Tours

Project Files

For Project 4H, you will need the following file:

w04H_New_Tours

You will save your document as:

Lastname_Firstname_4H_New_Tours

In this project, you will edit a flyer from James Gilroy, a guide for Lehua Hawaiian Adventures, to tour guides indicating new tours and tour popularity by gender. From the student files that accompany this textbook, open the file **w04H_New_Tours**, and then save the file in your **Word Chapter 4** folder as **Lastname_Firstname_4H_New_Tours**

To complete the project, you must make changes to the file including formatting text, formatting a multilevel list, and editing a chart. Correct the following:

- The title should have an appropriate style applied.
- The remaining paragraphs should be formatted as a logical multilevel list of two basic tour types—*Full Day Tours* and *Half Day Tours*.
- A custom list style should be created and applied to the first-level list items.
- The chart data for *One Week* should display as 30 percent for *Men* and 10 percent for *Women*.
- The chart title should display as *Tour Popularity by Gender*, a legend should display at the bottom, and the chart type should be Clustered Column with an appropriate chart style applied.

Things you should know to complete this project:

- Displaying formatting marks will assist in formatting the document.
- The final document should fit on one page.

Save your document and add the file name to the footer. In the Document Information Panel, type your first and last names in the Author box and your course name and section number in the Subject box. In the Keywords box, type **new tours, tour popularity** Save your file, and then print or submit electronically as directed by your instructor.

End You have completed Project 4H

Apply a combination of the **4A** and **4B** skills.

GO! Make It | Project 4I Newsletter

Project Files

For Project 4I, you will need the following file:

w04I_Newsletter

You will save your document as:

Lastname_Firstname_4I_Newsletter

From the student files that accompany this textbook, open the file **w04I_Newsletter** and create the document shown in Figure 4.52. Use the Office theme and Word 2010 style set. Apply existing styles to the date and three tour headings. Create a new style and apply it to the four article headings. Apply any other text and paragraph formatting as shown and insert the chart using the percentages as the data in column B. Add your name, your course name and section number, and the keywords **newsletter, chart** to the document properties. Save the file in your **Word Chapter 4** folder as **Lastname_Firstname_4I_Newsletter** and then print or submit electronically as directed by your instructor.

Project Results

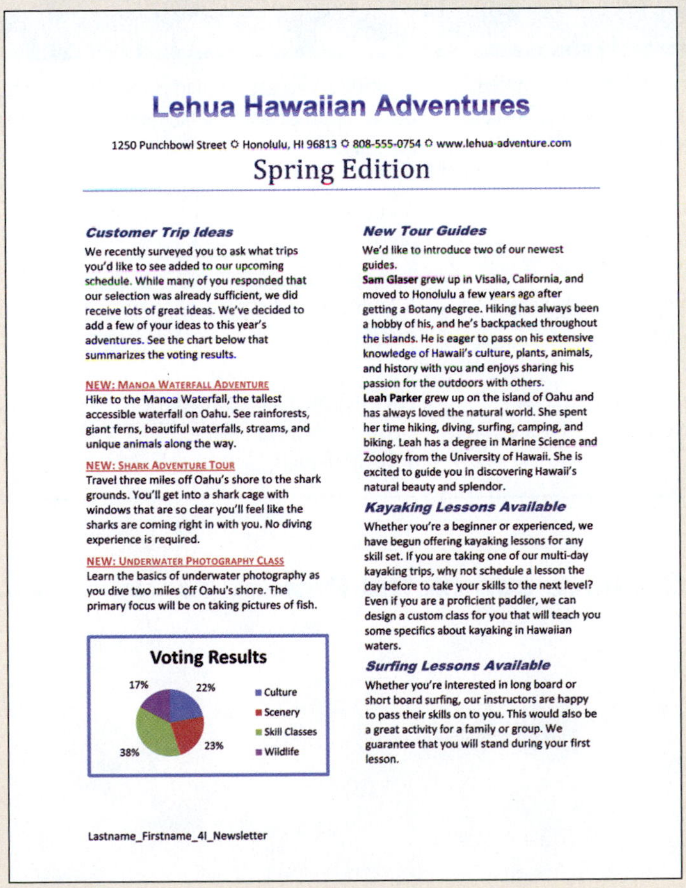

Lehua Hawaiian Adventures

1250 Punchbowl Street ○ Honolulu, HI 96813 ○ 808-555-0754 ○ www.lehua-adventure.com

Spring Edition

Customer Trip Ideas

We recently surveyed you to ask what trips you'd like to see added to our upcoming schedule. While many of you responded that our selection was already sufficient, we did receive lots of great ideas. We've decided to add a few of your ideas to this year's adventures. See the chart below that summarizes the voting results.

NEW: MANOA WATERFALL ADVENTURE

Hike to the Manoa Waterfall, the tallest accessible waterfall on Oahu. See rainforests, giant ferns, beautiful waterfalls, streams, and unique animals along the way.

NEW: SHARK ADVENTURE TOUR

Travel three miles off Oahu's shore to the shark grounds. You'll get into a shark cage with windows that are so clear you'll feel like the sharks are coming right in with you. No diving experience is required.

NEW: UNDERWATER PHOTOGRAPHY CLASS

Learn the basics of underwater photography as you dive two miles off Oahu's shore. The primary focus will be on taking pictures of fish.

New Tour Guides

We'd like to introduce two of our newest guides.

Sam Glaser grew up in Visalia, California, and moved to Honolulu a few years ago after getting a Botany degree. Hiking has always been a hobby of his, and he's backpacked throughout the islands. He is eager to pass on his extensive knowledge of Hawaii's culture, plants, animals, and history with you and enjoys sharing his passion for the outdoors with others.

Leah Parker grew up on the island of Oahu and has always loved the natural world. She spent her time hiking, diving, surfing, camping, and biking. Leah has a degree in Marine Science and Zoology from the University of Hawaii. She is excited to guide you in discovering Hawaii's natural beauty and splendor.

Kayaking Lessons Available

Whether you're a beginner or experienced, we have begun offering kayaking lessons for any skill set. If you are taking one of our multi-day kayaking trips, why not schedule a lesson the day before to take your skills to the next level? Even if you are a proficient paddler, we can design a custom class for you that will teach you some specifics about kayaking in Hawaiian waters.

Surfing Lessons Available

Whether you're interested in long board or short board surfing, our instructors are happy to pass their skills on to you. This would also be a great activity for a family or group. We guarantee that you will stand during your first lesson.

Lastname_Firstname_4I_Newsletter

Figure 4.52

End **You have completed Project 4I**

Content-Based Assessments

Apply a combination of the 4A and 4B skills.

GO! Solve It | Project 4J Custom Adventure

Project Files

For Project 4J, you will need the following file:

w04J_Custom_Adventure

You will save your document as:

Lastname_Firstname_4J_Custom_Adventure

Open the file **w04J_Custom_Adventure** and save it as **Lastname_Firstname_4J_Custom_Adventure** in your **Word Chapter 4** folder. Change the style set, and apply existing styles to the first two and last two paragraphs of the document. Create a new style for *Choose an Island*, and apply the style to *Choose Your Favorite Activities* and *Develop Your Skills*. Define a multilevel list style and apply the style to all lists in the document. Adjust paragraph and text formats to display the information appropriately in a one-page document. Include the file name in the footer, add appropriate document properties, and print your document or submit electronically as directed by your instructor.

Performance Element	Performance Level: Exemplary: You consistently applied the relevant skills	Proficient: You sometimes, but not always, applied the relevant skills	Developing: You rarely or never applied the relevant skills
Change style set and apply existing styles	All existing styles are applied correctly using an appropriate style set.	Existing styles are applied correctly but an appropriate style set is not used.	One or more styles are not applied properly.
Create a style	A new style is created and applied properly.	A new style is created but not applied properly.	A new style is not created.
Create a multilevel list	A multilevel list style is created and applied correctly.	A multilevel list style is applied correctly but the default style is used.	A multilevel list style is not applied correctly.
Format attractively and appropriately	Document formatting is attractive and appropriate.	The document is adequately formatted but is unattractive or difficult to read.	The document is formatted inadequately.

End **You have completed Project 4J**

Apply a combination of the **4A** and **4B** skills.

GO! Solve It | Project 4K Fall Newsletter

Project Files

For Project 4K, you will need the following file:

w04K_Fall_Newsletter

You will save your document as:

Lastname_Firstname_4K_Fall_Newsletter

Open the file **w04K_Fall Newsletter** and save it as **Lastname_Firstname_4K_Fall_Newsletter** to your **Word Chapter 4** folder. Apply appropriate styles to the first five paragraphs of the document. Create and apply styles for the four article headings and three trip titles. Apply a multilevel list style to the trip titles and their descriptions. Change the chart type to display the proportion of parts to a whole. Modify and format the chart so that it clearly explains the represented data. Make other formatting changes to create a one-page document. Include the file name in the footer, add appropriate document properties, and print your document or submit electronically as directed by your instructor.

Performance Element	Performance Level: Exemplary: You consistently applied the relevant skills	Proficient: You sometimes, but not always, applied the relevant skills	Developing: You rarely or never applied the relevant skills
Apply existing styles	All existing styles are applied correctly.	Some existing styles are not applied correctly.	No existing styles are applied.
Create and apply new styles	Two new styles are created and applied properly.	Only one new style is created, or new styles are not applied properly.	No new styles are created.
Apply a multilevel list style	The multilevel list style is applied correctly.	The multilevel list style is applied but no second level items are created.	The multilevel list style is not applied.
Modify a chart	The chart is changed to a pie chart, and data labels and legend display.	The chart is modified but incorrect chart type is used or data labels and legend do not display.	The chart is not modified.
Format attractively and appropriately	Document formatting is attractive and appropriate.	The document is adequately formatted but is unattractive or difficult to read.	The document is formatted inadequately.

End **You have completed Project 4K**

Outcomes-Based Assessments

Rubric

The following outcomes-based assessments are *open-ended assessments*. That is, there is no specific correct result; your result will depend on your approach to the information provided. Make *Professional Quality* your goal. Use the following scoring rubric to guide you in *how* to approach the problem and then to evaluate *how well* your approach solves the problem.

The *criteria*—Software Mastery, Content, Format and Layout, and Process—represent the knowledge and skills you have gained that you can apply to solving the problem. The *levels of performance*—Professional Quality, Approaching Professional Quality, or Needs Quality Improvements—help you and your instructor evaluate your result.

	Your completed project is of Professional Quality if you:	**Your completed project is Approaching Professional Quality if you:**	**Your completed project Needs Quality Improvements if you:**
1-Software Mastery	Choose and apply the most appropriate skills, tools, and features and identify efficient methods to solve the problem.	Choose and apply some appropriate skills, tools, and features, but not in the most efficient manner.	Choose inappropriate skills, tools, or features, or are inefficient in solving the problem.
2-Content	Construct a solution that is clear and well organized, contains content that is accurate, appropriate to the audience and purpose, and is complete. Provide a solution that contains no errors in spelling, grammar, or style.	Construct a solution in which some components are unclear, poorly organized, inconsistent, or incomplete. Misjudge the needs of the audience. Have some errors in spelling, grammar, or style, but the errors do not detract from comprehension.	Construct a solution that is unclear, incomplete, or poorly organized; contains some inaccurate or inappropriate content; and contains many errors in spelling, grammar, or style. Do not solve the problem.
3-Format and Layout	Format and arrange all elements to communicate information and ideas, clarify function, illustrate relationships, and indicate relative importance.	Apply appropriate format and layout features to some elements, but not others. Overuse features, causing minor distraction.	Apply format and layout that does not communicate information or ideas clearly. Do not use format and layout features to clarify function, illustrate relationships, or indicate relative importance. Use available features excessively, causing distraction.
4-Process	Use an organized approach that integrates planning, development, self-assessment, revision, and reflection.	Demonstrate an organized approach in some areas, but not others; or, use an insufficient process of organization throughout.	Do not use an organized approach to solve the problem.

Apply a combination of the **4A** and **4B** skills.

GO! Think | Project 4L Training Memo

Project Files

For Project 4L, you will need the following file:

New blank Word document

You will save your document as:

Lastname_Firstname_4L_Training_Memo

Carl Kawaoka, Tour Operations Manager, wants to send a memo to all tour guides concerning upcoming training opportunities.

Date	Training	Location	Length
June 6	Horseback Riding	Hamilton Stables	4 hours
June 17	Orienteering	Kapiolani Regional Park	8 hours
June 29	Basic Coastal Sailing	Waikiki Beach	6 hours
July 7	Intermediate Sea Kayaking	Waimea Bay	5 hours

Using this information, create the memo. Include a multilevel list for the four training sessions. Insert a chart to compare class length. Format the entire memo in a manner that is professional and easy to read and understand. Save the file as **Lastname_Firstname_4L_Training_Memo** Insert the file name in the footer and add appropriate document properties. Print or submit as directed.

End **You have completed Project 4L**

Outcomes-Based Assessments

Apply a combination of the **4A** and **4B** skills.

GO! Think | Project **4M** Waterfalls Handout

Project Files

For Project 4M, you will need the following file:

New blank Word document

You will save your document as:

Lastname_Firstname_4M_Waterfalls_Handout

Lehua Hawaiian Adventures is promoting a three-day tour of Hawaii's waterfalls. The tour includes hiking, riding in a four-wheel drive vehicle, and a helicopter ride. Available dates are June 20, July 15, and August 3. Cost is $1,500, which includes hotel and a daily continental breakfast.

Waterfall	Location	Access	Height in feet
Akaka Falls	Big Island	Paved Road	422
Hi'ilawe Falls	Big Island	Paved road	1600
Wai'ilikahi Falls	Big Island	Helicopter	1080
Opaekaa Falls	Kauai	Visible from overlook	151
Waipo'o Falls	Kauai	Visible from overlook	800
Makahiku Falls	Maui	Hiking trail	180
Waimoku Falls	Maui	Hiking trail	400

Create the promotional handout. Include a multilevel list using the waterfall, location, and access data shown. Insert a chart to compare the waterfall heights by location. Format the flyer, list, and chart in a manner that is professional and easy to read and understand. Save the file as **Lastname_Firstname_4M_Waterfalls_Handout** Insert the file name in the footer and add appropriate document properties. Print or submit electronically as directed.

End **You have completed Project 4M**

Apply a combination of the **4A** and **4B** skills.

You and GO! | Project 4N Cover Letter

Project Files

For Project 4N, you will need the following file:

New blank Word document

You will save your document as:

Lastname_Firstname_4N_Cover_Letter

Create a cover letter to be sent with a resume to potential employers. Add a multilevel list that includes the types of college courses you have taken, such as Computer Applications, English, Mathematics, and Psychology. Below each course type, list the names of specific courses. Insert a chart that displays the total number of credit hours earned for each subject. Format the letter, multilevel list, and chart appropriately to create a professional appearance. Save the file as **Lastname_Firstname_4N_Cover_Letter** Insert a footer with the file name, and add appropriate document properties. Print the document or submit electronically as directed.

End **You have completed Project 4N**

Creating Web Pages and Using Advanced Proofing Options

OUTCOMES

At the end of this chapter you will be able to:

OBJECTIVES

Mastering these objectives will enable you to:

PROJECT 5A

Create a Web page from a Word document.

PROJECT 5B

Use proofing tools and save a document in RTF format.

kwest/Shutterstock

In This Chapter

In this chapter you will use text, graphic, and document formatting features in Word to create a professional-looking Web page that includes hyperlinks. You will also create a blog post, which can contain text, images, and links to related blogs or Web pages.

You will also examine Word settings so that you can use Word in the most productive way for you. You will locate information on the Internet by using research features, translate foreign-language text, and use the Office Clipboard to collect and organize information. Finally, you will save documents in other useful formats.

The projects in this chapter relate to **Texas Spectrum Wireless**, which provides accessories and software for all major brands of cell phones, smart phones, PDAs, MP3 players, and laptop computers. The company sells thousands of unique products in their retail stores, which are located throughout Texas and the southern United States. They also sell thousands of items each year through their Web site, and offer free shipping and returns to their customers. The company takes pride in offering unique categories of accessories such as waterproof and ruggedized gear.

Project 5A Web Page

myitlab
Project 5A Training

Project Activities

In Activities 5.01 through 5.12, you will assist Eliott Verschoren, Vice President of Marketing for Texas Spectrum Wireless, in creating a new home page for the online store and a new blog post for the company's customer service blog. Your completed documents will look similar to Figure 5.1.

Project Files

For Project 5A, you will need the following files:

w05A_Home_Page
w05A_Features_Guide

You will save your documents as:

Lastname_Firstname_5A_Home_Page
Lastname_Firstname_5A_Features_Guide
Lastname_Firstname_5A_Blog_Post

Project Results

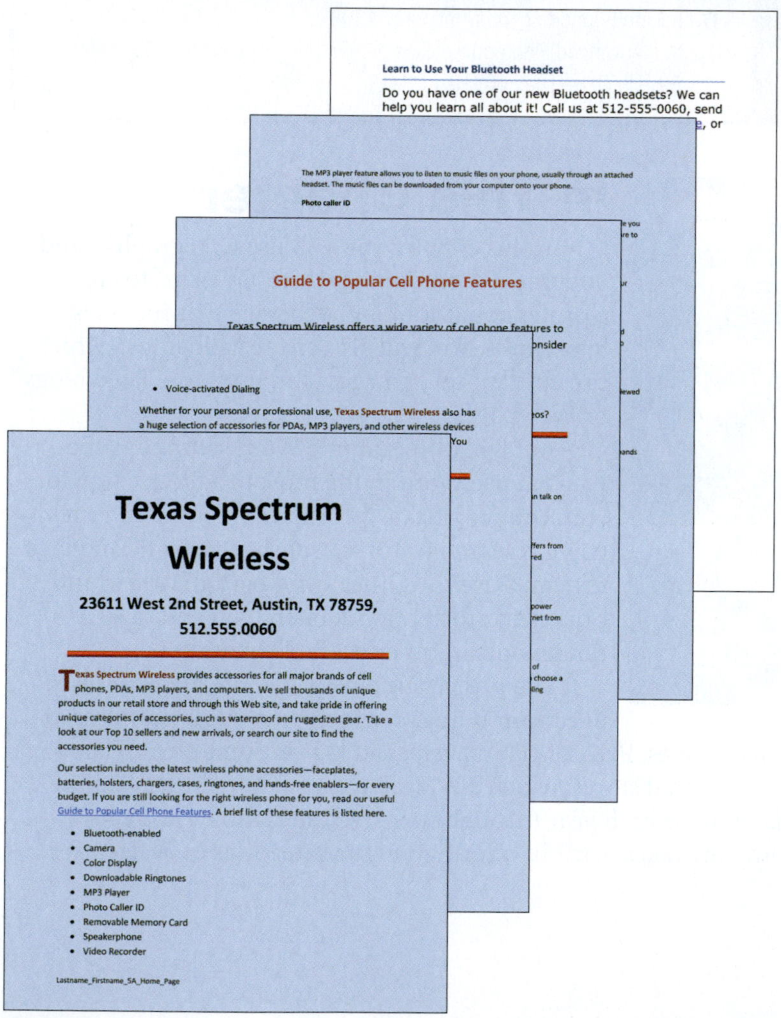

Figure 5.1
Project 5A Home Page

Objective 1 | Create a Web Page from a Word Document

You can create a ***Web page*** from a Word document. A Web page is a file coded in ***HyperText Markup Language***—referred to as ***HTML***—that can be viewed on the Internet by using a ***Web browser***. A Web browser—also referred to as just a ***browser***—is software that interprets HTML files, formats them into Web pages, and then displays them. HTML is a markup language that communicates color and graphics in a format that all computers can understand.

Activity 5.01 | Saving a Document as a Web Page

For a Word document to display in a browser, you must save it in HTML. In this activity, you will save a Word document in the Web Page format so it can be added to the company's Web site.

1 **Start** Word. From your student files, locate and open the file **w05A_Home_Page**. If necessary, display formatting marks and rulers.

2 Click the **File tab**, and then click **Save As**. In the **Save As** dialog box, navigate to the location where you are saving your files for this chapter. Create a new folder named **Word Chapter 5** In the lower portion of the **Save As** dialog box, click the **Save as type arrow**, and then in the displayed list, click **Web Page**.

In this project, you will use the ***Web Page format***, a file type that saves a Word document as an HTML file, with some elements of the Web page in a folder, separate from the Web page. This format is useful if you want to access individual elements, such as pictures, separately.

3 Near the bottom of the dialog box, click the **Change Title** button, and then in the displayed **Enter Text** dialog box, in the **Page title** box, type **Texas Spectrum Wireless** Compare your screen with Figure 5.2.

By creating this title, when the document is viewed as a Web page with a browser, *Texas Spectrum Wireless* will display on the title bar. Because Internet search engines locate the content of Web pages by title, it is important to create a title that describes the content of the Web page.

Figure 5.2

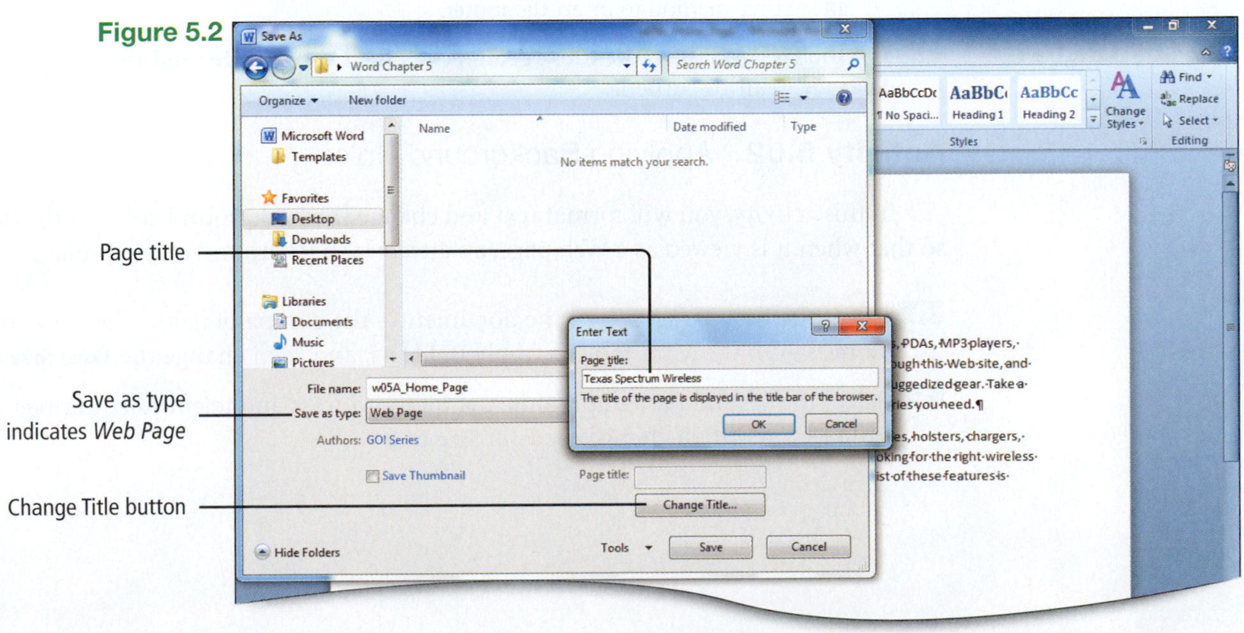

4 Click **OK**. In the displayed **Save As** dialog box, in the **File name** box, type **Lastname_Firstname_5A_Home_Page** and then click **Save**. Compare your screen with Figure 5.3.

Because you saved the document as a Web Page, the document displays in Web Layout view, and on the status bar, the Web Layout button is active. The Zoom level may change to display text according to the size of your screen.

Figure 5.3

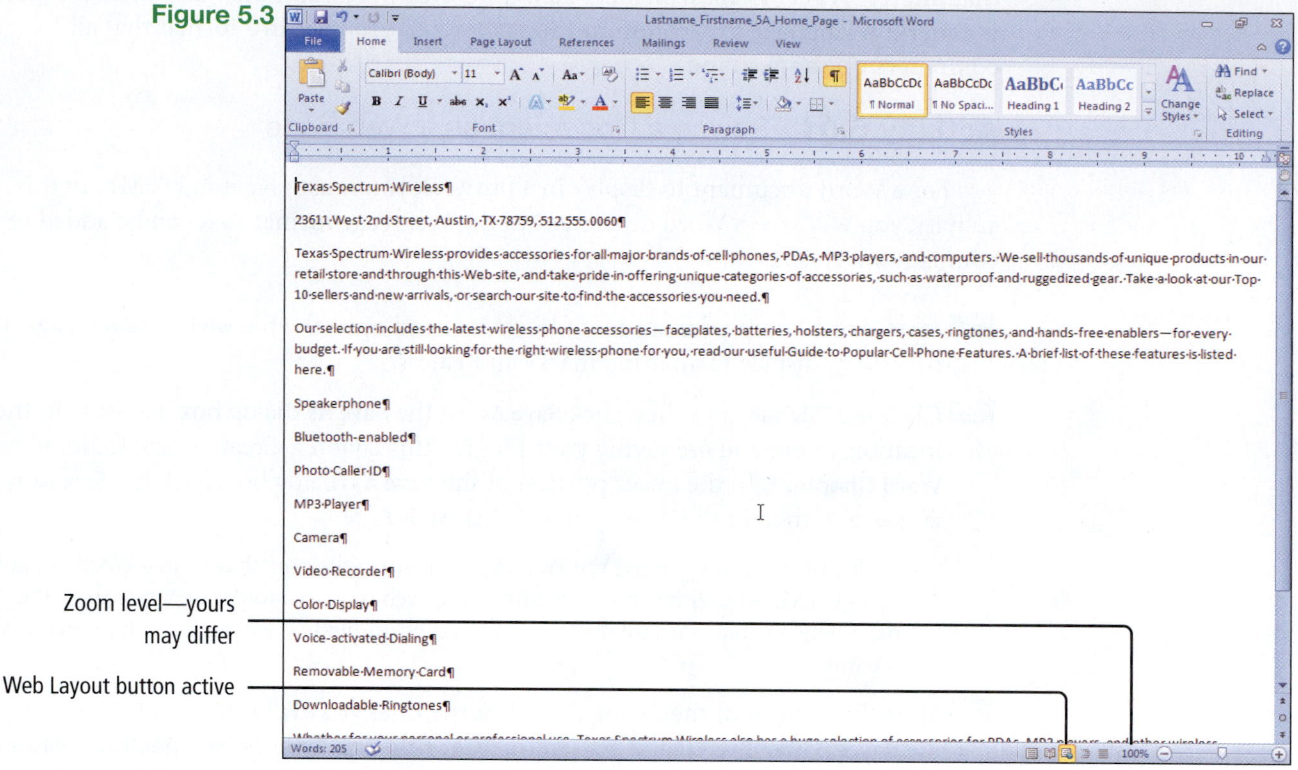

5 On the **Insert tab**, in the **Header & Footer group**, click the **Footer** button. At the bottom of the displayed list, click **Edit Footer**, and then use **Quick Parts** to insert the file name in the footer.

In Web Layout view, headers and footers do not display on the screen, so you used this alternative method to insert the footer.

6 On the **Design tab**, in the **Close group**, click the **Close Header and Footer** button. **Save** your document.

Activity 5.02 | Applying Background Color

In this activity, you will format text and change the background color of the document so that when it is viewed as a Web page, an attractive background color displays.

1 Select the first paragraph of the document—the company name *Texas Spectrum Wireless*. On the Mini toolbar, apply **Bold** **B**, and then change the **Font Size** to **48**.

2 Select the second paragraph—the company address and telephone number. Apply **Bold** **B**, and then change the **Font Size** to **24**.

3 Select the first and second paragraphs, and then click the **Center** button. Click anywhere to deselect the text, and then compare your screen with Figure 5.4.

Figure 5.4

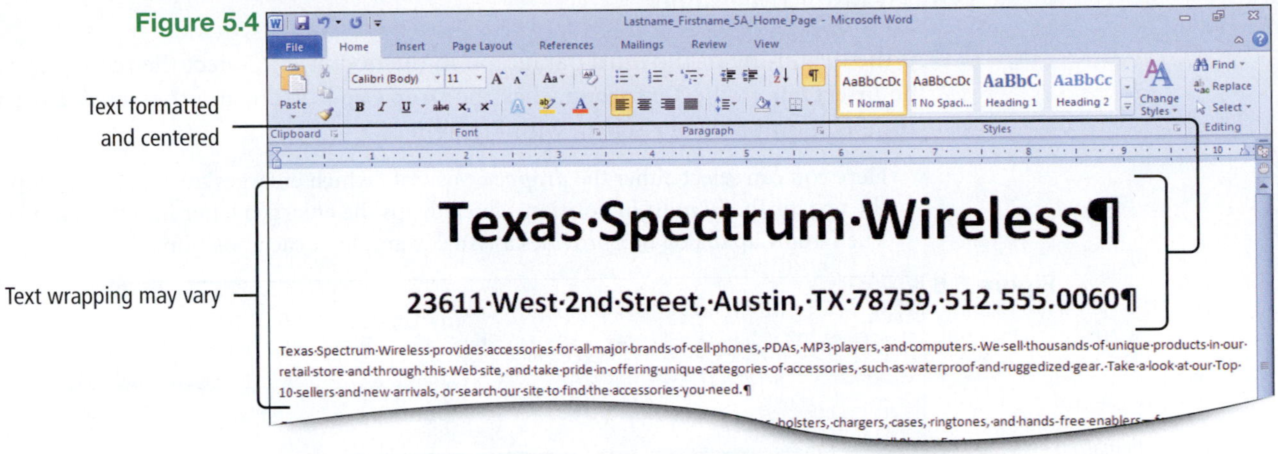

4 Beginning with the paragraph that begins *Texas Spectrum Wireless provides*, select all the remaining text in the document, and then change the **Font Size** to **14**.

5 At the beginning of the third paragraph, select the text *Texas Spectrum Wireless*. Apply **Bold**, click the **Font Color button arrow**, and then under **Theme Colors**, in the sixth column, click the last color—**Red, Accent 2, Darker 50%**.

6 Press Ctrl + End. In the paragraph that begins *Whether*, select the text *Texas Spectrum Wireless*. Apply **Bold**, and then click the **Font Color** button.

7 Select the last paragraph, apply **Bold**, and then deselect the text.

8 On the **Page Layout tab**, in the **Page Background group**, click the **Page Color** button, and then in the fifth column, click the third color—**Blue, Accent 1, Lighter 60%**. **Save** your document, and then compare your screen with Figure 5.5.

Figure 5.5

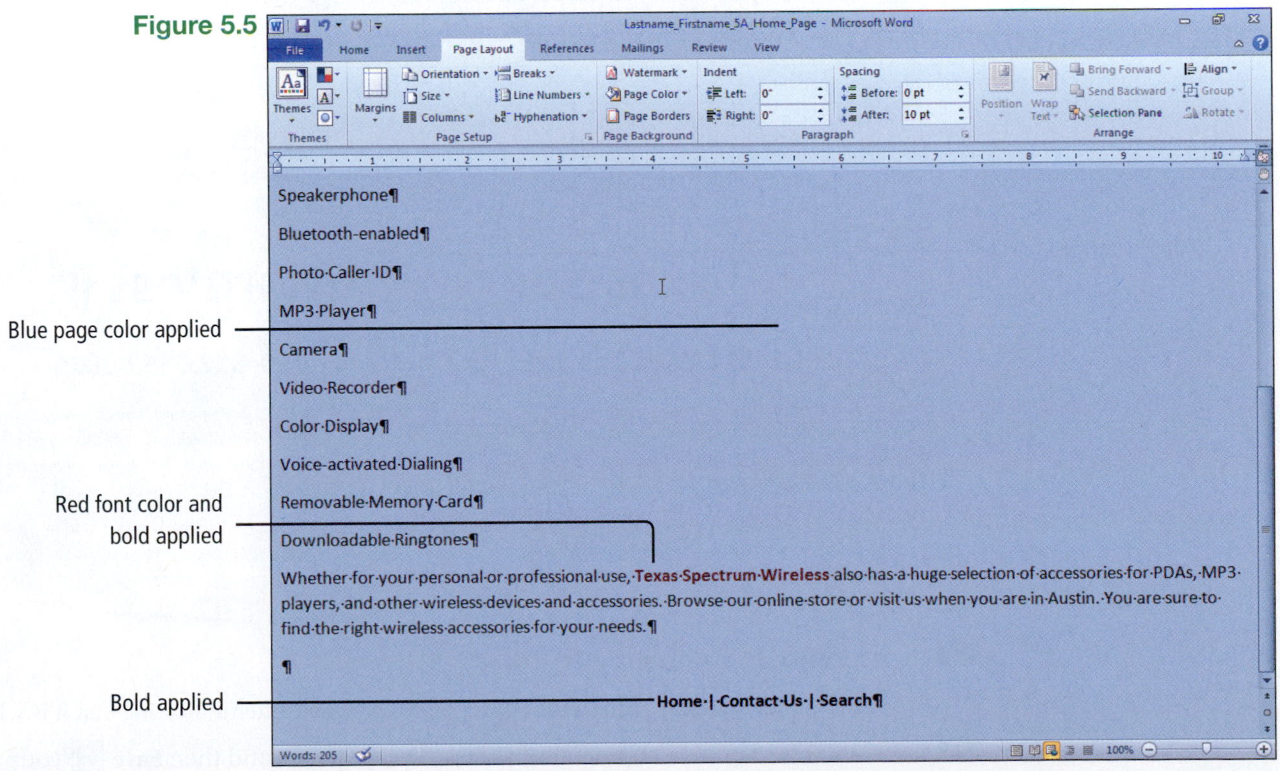

Activity 5.03 | Inserting a Drop Cap in Text

A ***drop cap*** is a large capital letter at the beginning of a paragraph that formats text in a visually distinctive manner.

1 At the beginning of the third paragraph in the document, select the red letter *T*. On the **Insert tab**, in the **Text group**, click the **Drop Cap** button, and then click **Drop Cap Options**. Compare your screen with Figure 5.6.

Here you can select either the ***dropped*** position, which enlarges the letter and drops it into the text, or the ***in margin*** position, which drops the enlarged letter into the left margin. The Drop Cap dialog box provides a visual example of each position.

Figure 5.6

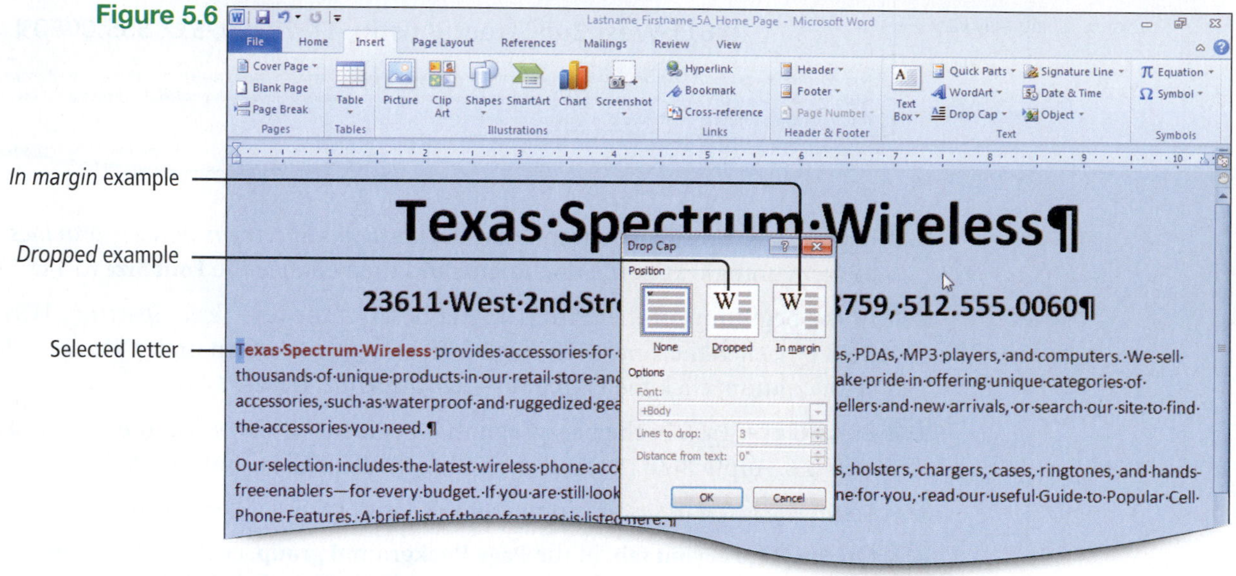

2 In the **Drop Cap** dialog box, under **Position**, click **Dropped**. Under **Options**, click the **Lines to drop spin box down arrow** one time to change the number of lines by which to drop to **2** lines. Compare your screen with Figure 5.7.

Figure 5.7

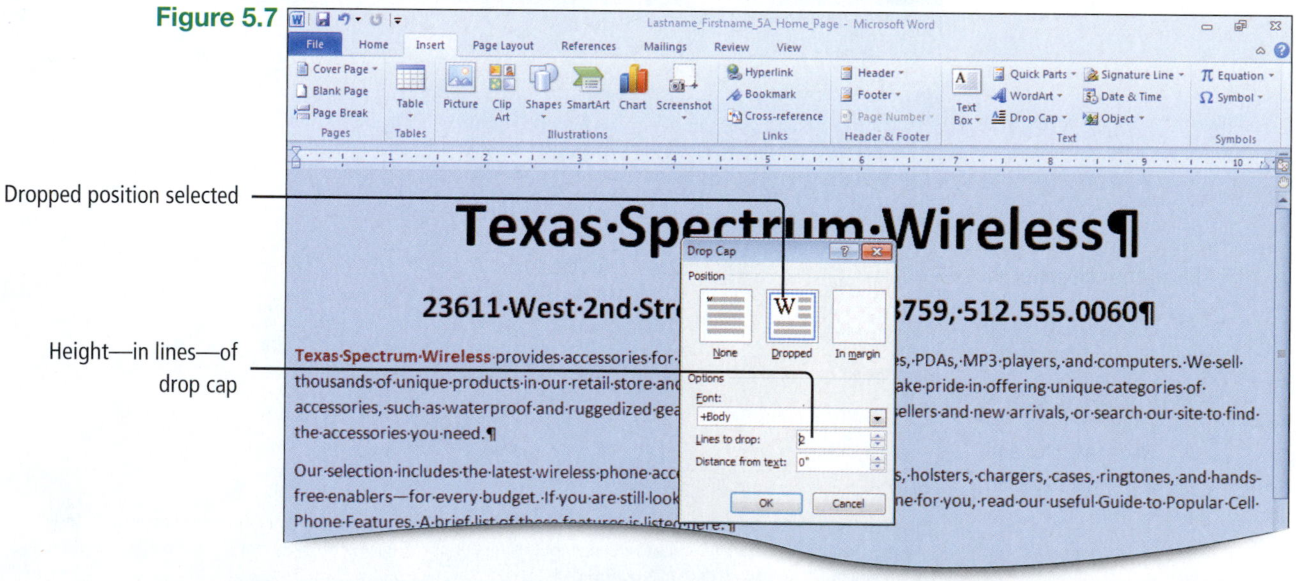

3 In the **Drop Cap** dialog box, click **OK**.

Resize handles display around the border of the dropped letter indicating that it is selected.

4 Click anywhere in the document to deselect the drop cap, and then **Save** your document.

Activity 5.04 | Sorting Paragraphs

Use the ***Sort*** command to alphabetize selected text or to order numerical data. ***Ascending*** refers to sorting alphabetically from A to Z or ordering numerically from the smallest to the largest. ***Descending*** refers to sorting alphabetically from Z to A or ordering numerically from the largest to smallest.

1. Scroll to display the ten paragraphs that comprise the cell phone features—beginning with *Speakerphone* and ending with *Downloadable Ringtones*. Click to position the insertion point to the left of *Speakerphone*, and then select the ten paragraphs.
2. On the **Home tab**, in the **Paragraph group**, click the **Sort** button to display the **Sort Text** dialog box. Compare your screen with Figure 5.8.

   Here you can select what you want to sort by, which in this instance is *Paragraphs*; the type of data to sort, which in this instance is *Text*; and the type of sort—ascending or descending.

Figure 5.8

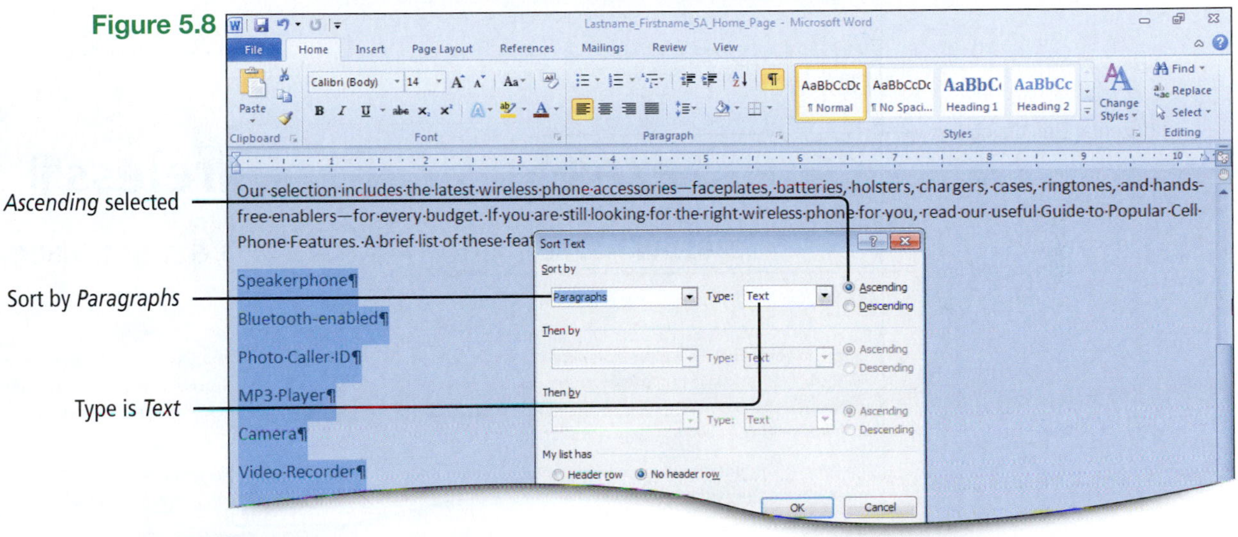

3. Click **OK** to accept the default settings. Notice the paragraphs are arranged alphabetically.
4. With the paragraphs still selected, in the **Paragraph group**, click the **Bullets** button, and then click anywhere to deselect the bulleted text. Compare your screen with Figure 5.9. **Save** your document.

Figure 5.9

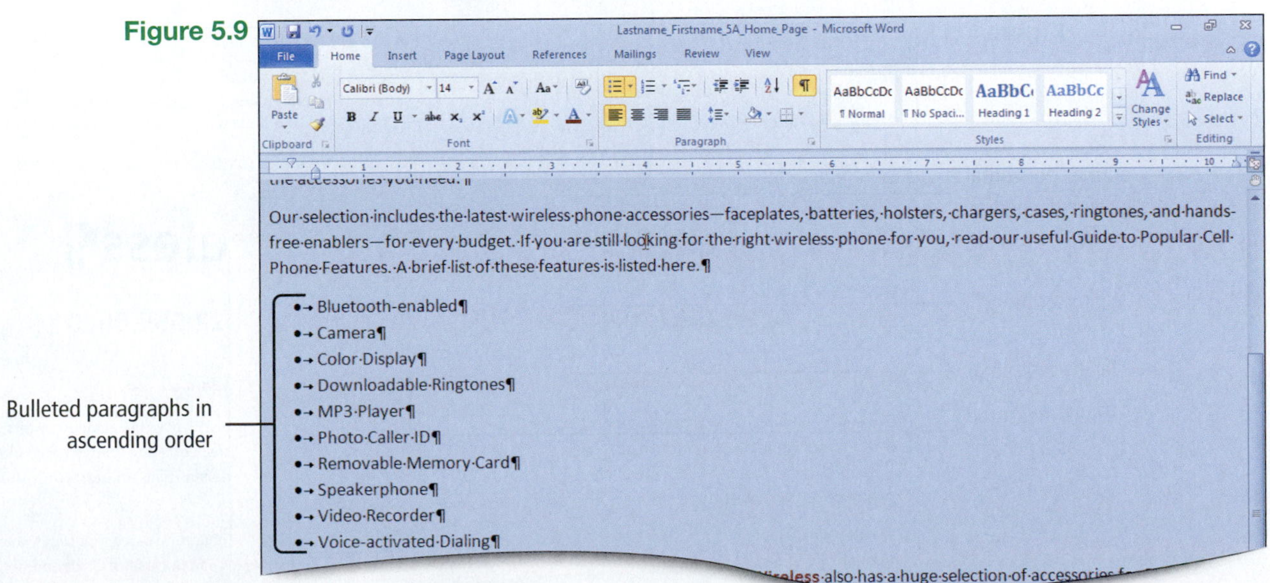

Activity 5.05 | Inserting a Horizontal Line

Word includes a variety of graphical horizontal lines that can add visual interest to and differentiate sections of a Web page.

1 Press Ctrl + Home. In the second paragraph, click to position the insertion point to the right of the last *0* in the telephone number.

2 Press Enter. On the **Home tab**, in the **Paragraph group**, click the **Border button arrow**, and then click **Borders and Shading**. In the **Borders and Shading** dialog box, if necessary, click the **Borders** tab, and then in the lower left corner, click the **Horizontal Line** button.

3 In the **Horizontal Line** dialog box, scroll down until a thick bright red line displays in the first column. Click the red line, and then compare your screen with Figure 5.10.

Figure 5.10

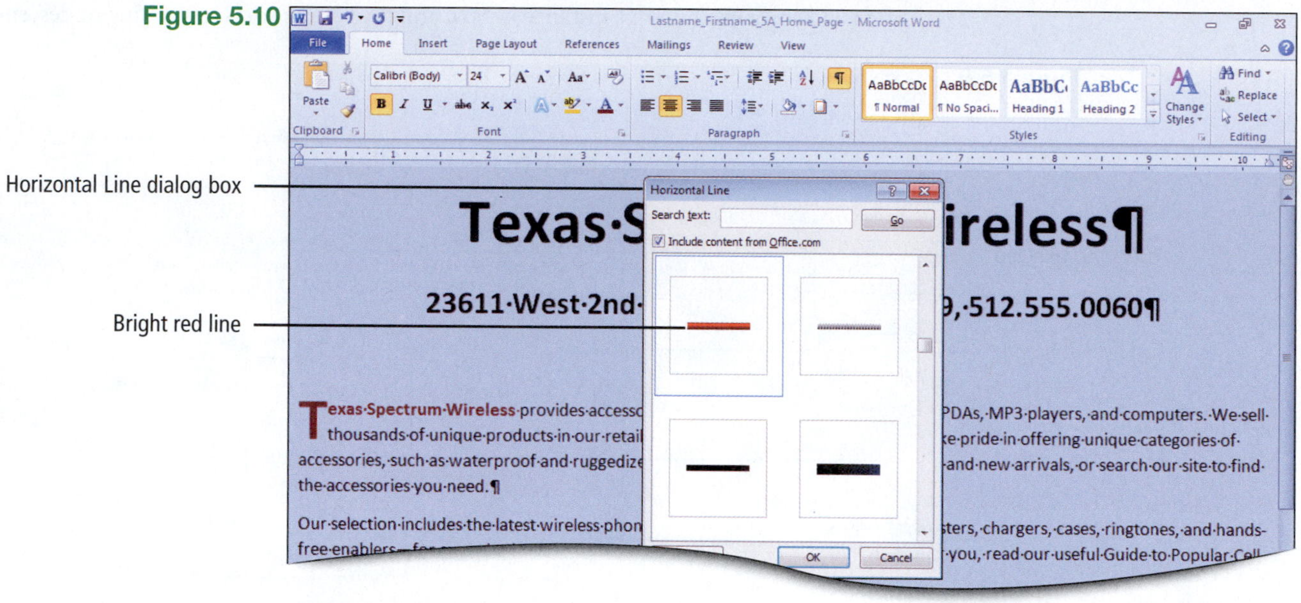

4 In the **Horizontal Line** dialog box, click **OK**. In your document, point to the red line, and then right-click. From the displayed shortcut menu, click **Format Horizontal Line**.

5 In the **Format Horizontal Line** dialog box, click the **Measure in arrow**, and then click **Percent**. Set the **Width** to **95%** and the **Height** to **8 pt**. Compare your screen with Figure 5.11.

Figure 5.11

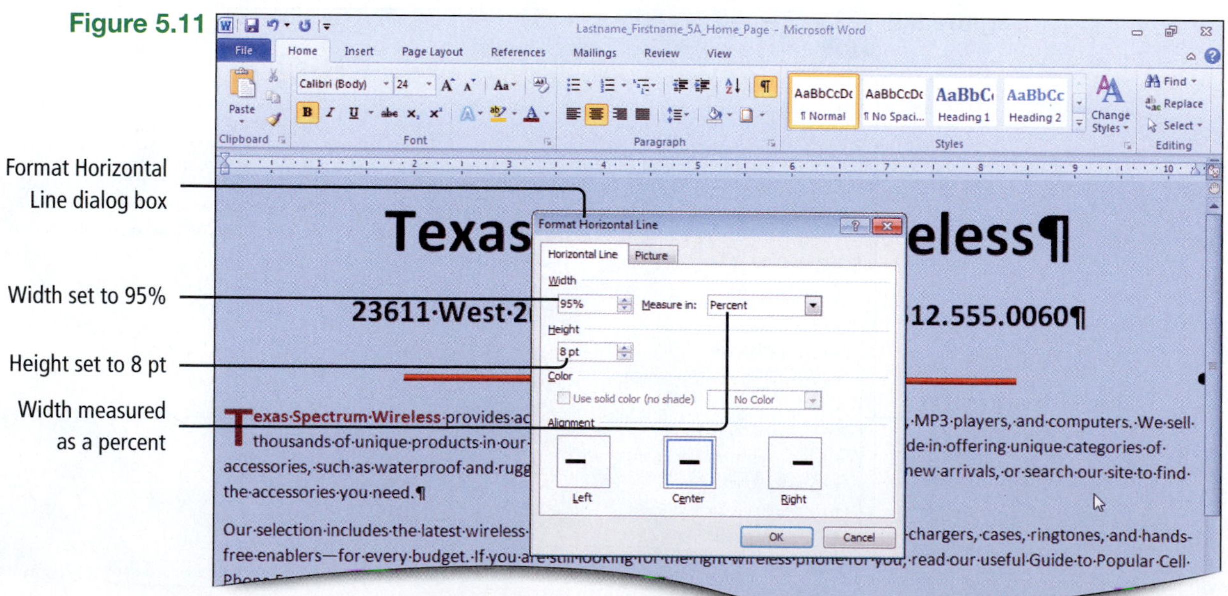

6 Click **OK**. Point to the line and right-click, and then from the displayed shortcut menu, click **Copy**.

7 In the blank paragraph immediately above the last paragraph of the document that begins *Home*, click to position the insertion point. Right-click, and from the displayed shortcut menu, under **Paste Options**, click the first button—**Keep Source Formatting**—to insert a copy of the red line. **Save** your document.

Objective 2 | Insert and Modify Hyperlinks in a Web Page

A Web browser—for example, ***Internet Explorer*** developed by Microsoft—can transfer files, play sound or video files that are embedded in Web pages, and follow ***hyperlinks***—text, buttons, pictures, or other objects displayed on Web pages that, when clicked, access other Web pages, other sections of the active page, or another file.

Activity 5.06 | Inserting a Hyperlink

By inserting hyperlinks, individuals who view your Web page can move to other Web pages inside your ***Web site*** or to pages in another Web site. A Web site is a group of related Web pages published to a specific location on the Internet. The most common type of hyperlink is a ***text link***—a link applied to a selected word or phrase. Text links usually display as blue underlined text.

1 Press Ctrl + End, and notice that the last paragraph consists of a series of words and phrases.

Web sites commonly have a ***navigation bar***—a series of text links across the top or bottom of a Web page that, when clicked, link to another Web page in the same Web site.

Another Way

Alternatively, right-click the selected text, and then from the displayed shortcut menu, click **Hyperlink**.

2 Select the first word in the paragraph—*Home*—and then on the **Insert tab**, in the **Links group**, click the **Hyperlink** button. Compare your screen with Figure 5.12.

Figure 5.12

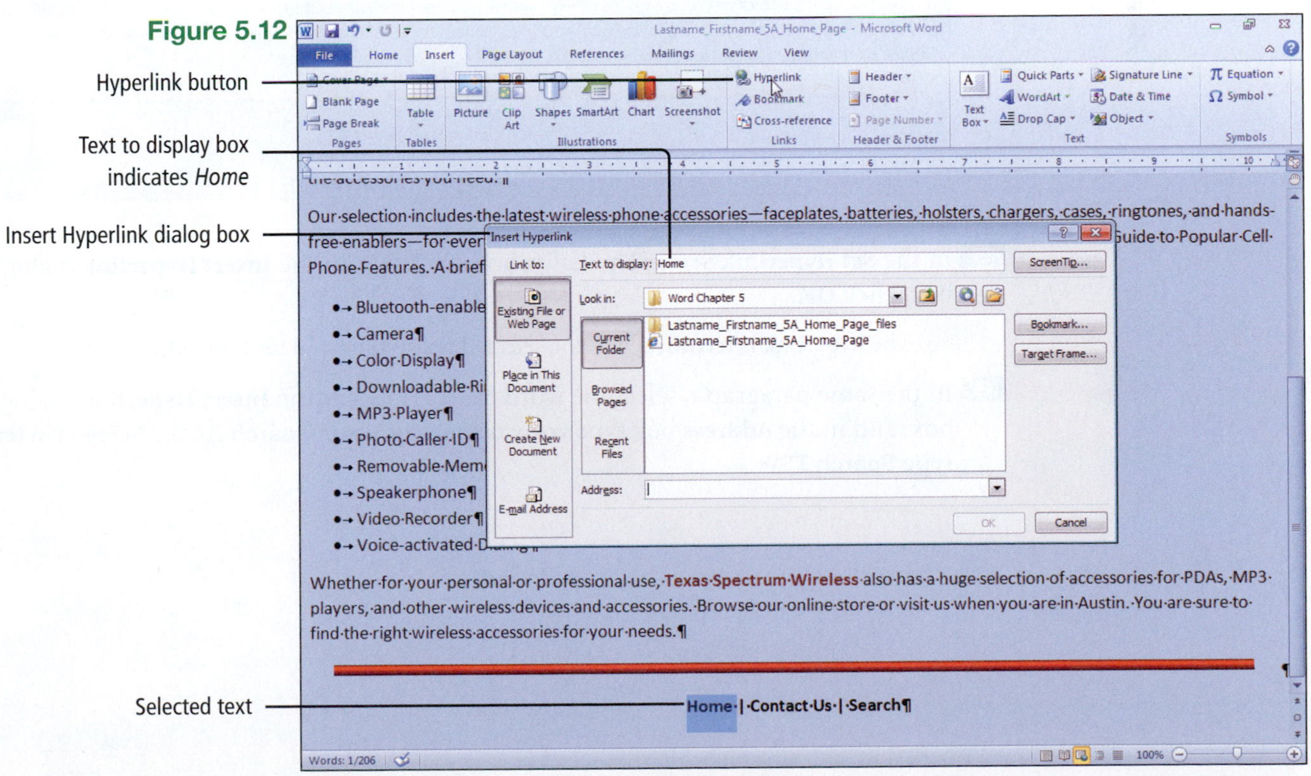

3 Under **Link to**, click **Existing File or Web Page**, if necessary. In the **Address** box, delete any existing text, and then type **www.txspectrum.com** If another address displays while you are typing, continue typing to replace it. When you are finished typing, if any other characters display, delete them.

As you type an Internet address, Word automatically inserts *http://*. An address may display in the Address box as you type. This is a result of the AutoComplete feature, which displays the most recently used Web address from your computer.

4 In the upper right corner, click the **ScreenTip** button. In the **Set Hyperlink ScreenTip** dialog box, in the **ScreenTip text** box, type **Texas Spectrum Wireless** Compare your screen with Figure 5.13.

Text that you type here will display as a ScreenTip when an individual viewing your site points to this hyperlink.

Figure 5.13

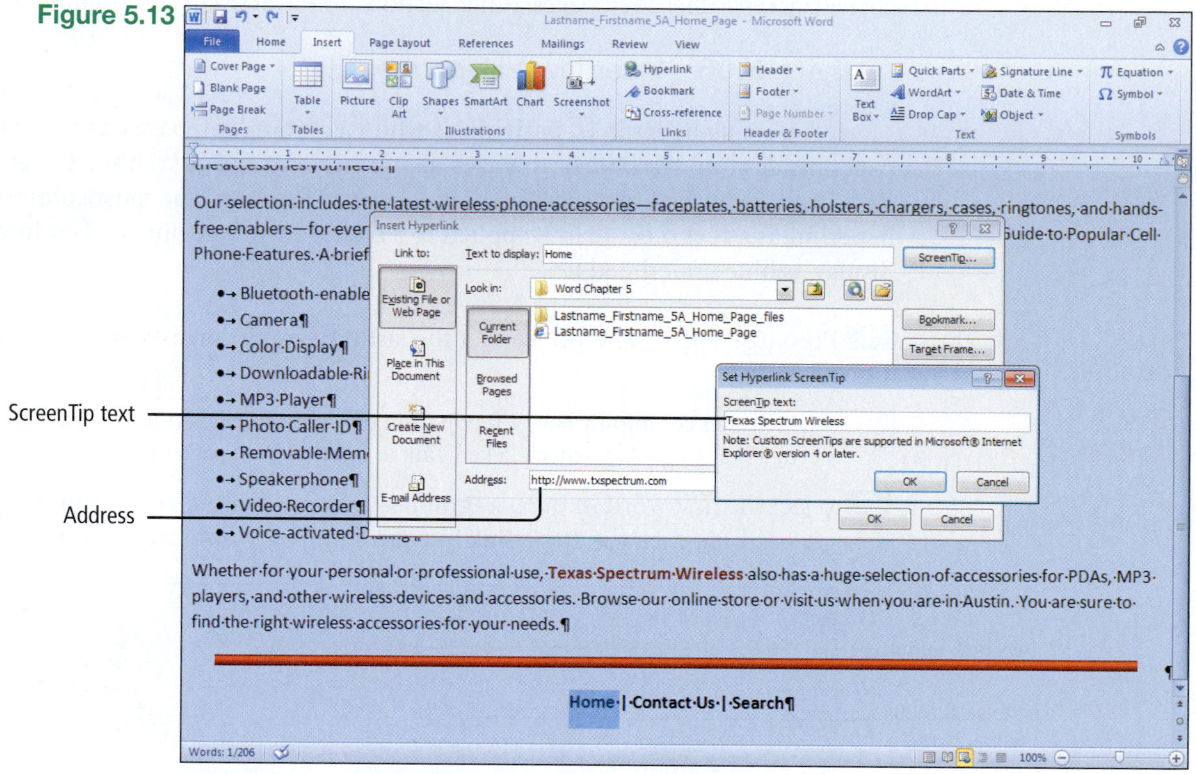

5 In the **Set Hyperlink ScreenTip** dialog box, click **OK**. In the **Insert Hyperlink** dialog box, click **OK**.

The hyperlink is recorded, and the selected text is blue and underlined.

6 In the same paragraph, select the word *Search*. Display the **Insert Hyperlink** dialog box, and in the **Address** box type **www.txspectrum.com/search** As the **ScreenTip text**, type **Search TSW**

7 Click **OK** two times to close the dialog boxes, and then compare your screen with Figure 5.14.

Figure 5.14

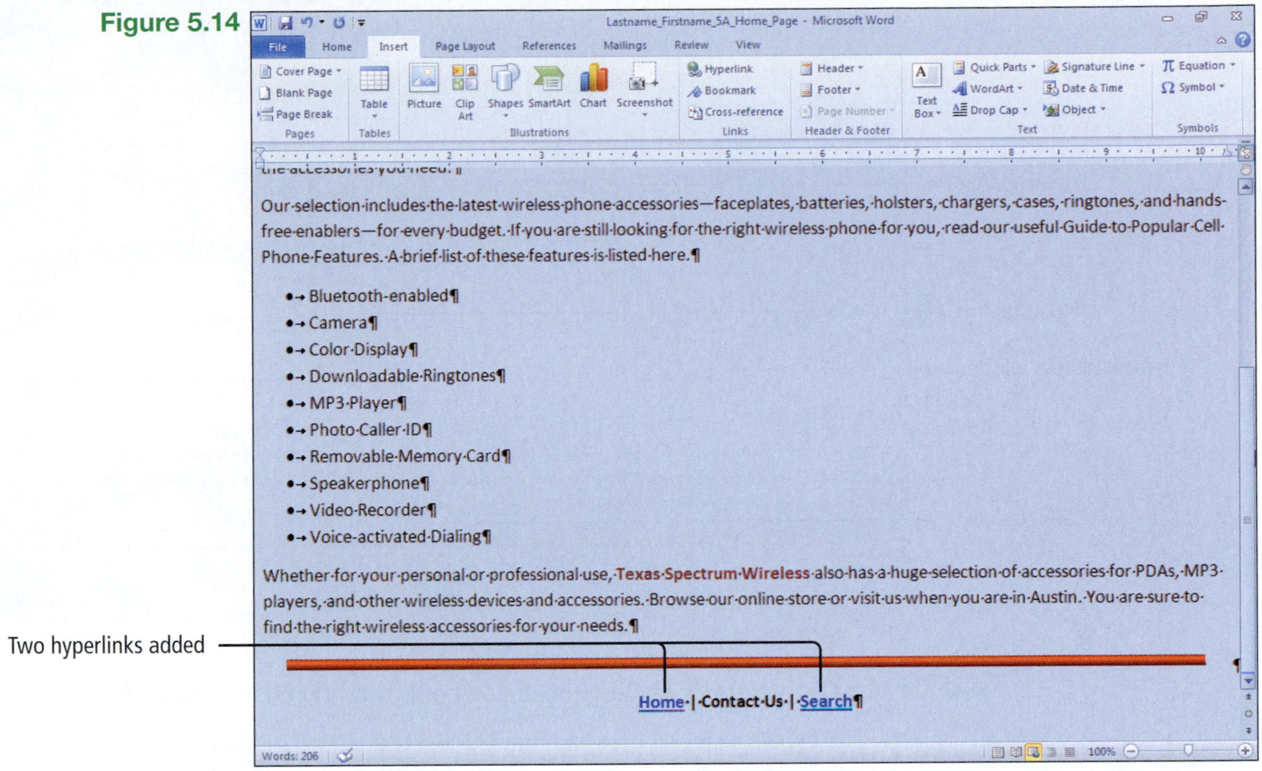

8 **Save** your document.

Activity 5.07 | Inserting a Hyperlink That Opens a New E-mail Message

Another common type of hyperlink is an ***e-mail address link***, which opens a new message window so that an individual viewing your site can send an e-mail message.

1 At the end of the document, select the text *Contact Us*, and then display the **Insert Hyperlink** dialog box. Under **Link to**, click **E-mail Address**.

2 In the **E-mail address** box, type **jlovrick@txspectrum.com** As the **ScreenTip text**, type **Operations Manager** and then compare your screen with Figure 5.15.

As you type an e-mail address, Word automatically inserts *mailto:*. Other e-mail addresses may display in the Recently used e-mail addresses box.

Figure 5.15

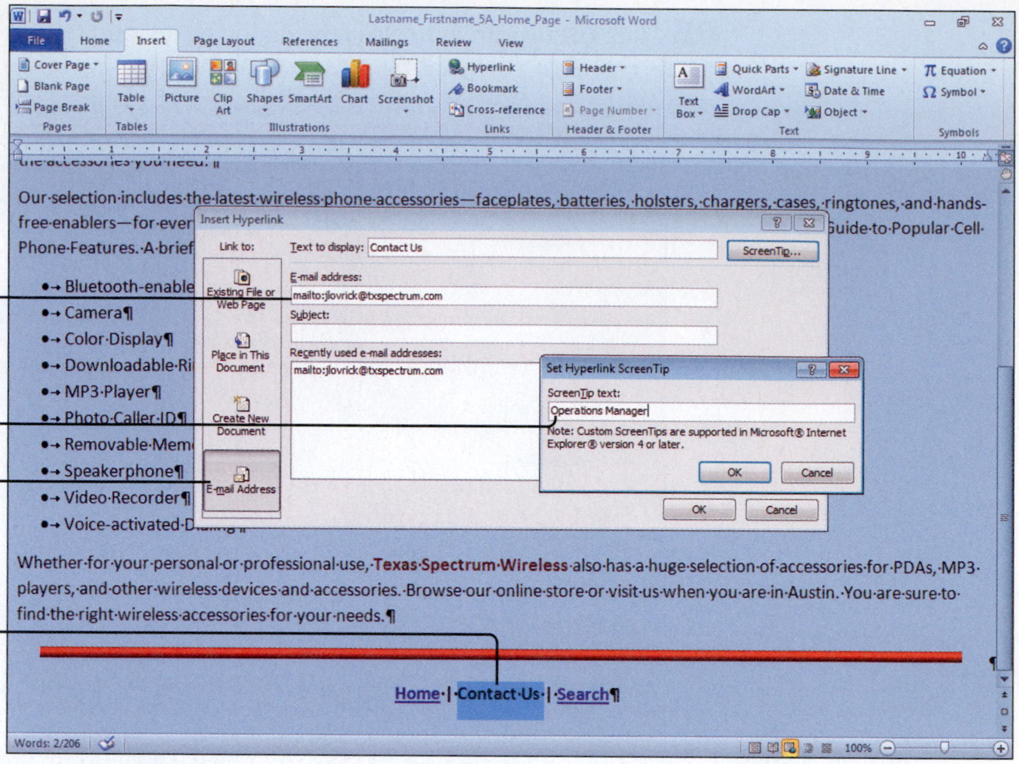

3 Click **OK** two times to close the dialog boxes, and then click **Save**.

The hyperlink is recorded, and the selected text changes to blue and is underlined.

Activity 5.08 | Creating a Web Page for an Internal Link

An ***internal link*** is a hyperlink that connects to another page in the same Web site. In this activity, you will create a second Web page for the Web site and create a link to this page from the home page.

1 Without closing your displayed **Lastname_Firstname_5A_Home_Page** document, from your student files, locate and open the file **w05A_Features_Guide**.

Because you are currently working in Web Layout view, the document opens in Web Layout view.

2 Display **Backstage** view, and then click **Save As**. Navigate to your **Word Chapter 5** folder. Click the **Save as type arrow**, and then click **Web Page**.

3 Click the **Change Title** button to display the **Enter Text** dialog box, and then in the **Page title** box, type **Features Guide** Click **OK**. In the **Save As** dialog box, in the **File name** box, type **Lastname_Firstname_5A_Features_Guide** and then click **Save**.

When viewed with a browser, *Features Guide* will display on the title bar.

4 On the **Insert tab**, in the **Header & Footer group**, click the **Footer** button, click **Edit Footer**, and then use **Quick Parts** to insert the file name in the footer. Close the footer area.

Recall that when viewing documents in Web Layout view, footers do not display.

5 Display **Backstage** view. With the **Info** section selected, on the right under the document thumbnail, click **Properties**, and then click **Show Document Panel**. Below the Ribbon, under the displayed message *The Document Information Panel cannot show properties for this file type.*, click **View properties**. Notice the **Lastname_Firstname_5A_Features_Guide Properties** dialog box displays.

When a document is saved as a Web Page, the Document Information Panel does not display.

6 If necessary, click the **Summary tab**. In the **Subject** box, type your course name and section number. In the **Author** box, delete any existing text, and type your first and last names. In the **Keywords** box, type **web site, features guide** Compare your screen with Figure 5.16.

Figure 5.16

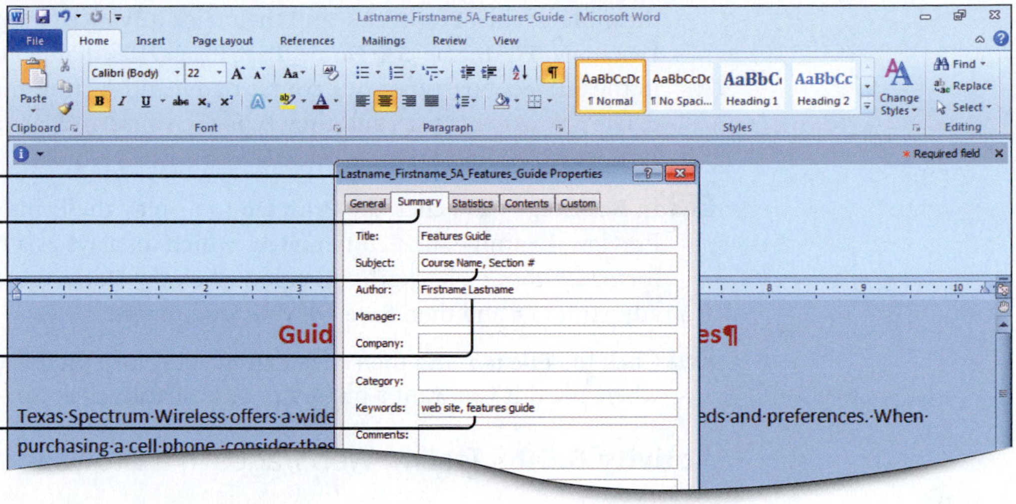

7 Click **OK**, click **Save**, and then **Close** your **Lastname_Firstname_5A_Features_Guide** document.

8 With your **Lastname_Firstname_5A_Home_Page** document displayed, in the paragraph that begins *Our selection includes*, select the text *Guide to Popular Cell Phone Features*. On the **Insert tab**, in the **Links group**, click the **Hyperlink** button.

9 Under **Link to**, click **Existing File or Web Page**. In the **Look in** box, be sure that the name of your **Word Chapter 5** folder displays, and then in the list below, click your file—*not* the folder—named **Lastname_Firstname_5A_Features_Guide**. Compare your screen with Figure 5.17.

Figure 5.17

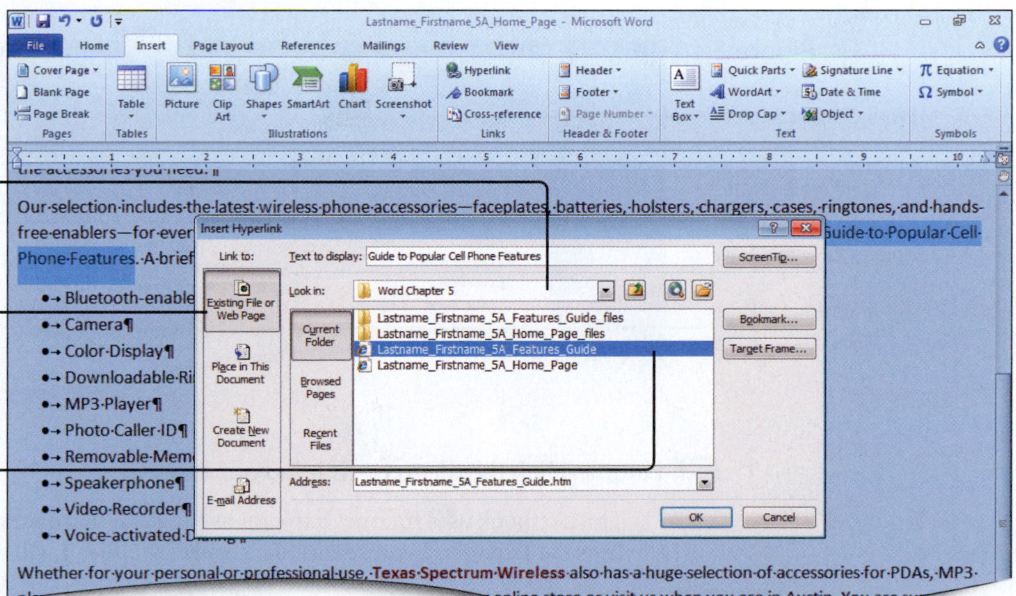

10 Click the **ScreenTip** button, type **Features Guide** and then click **OK** two times to close the dialog boxes.

The selected text displays in blue and is underlined.

11 From **Backstage** view, with the **Info tab** selected, on the right under the document thumbnail, click **Properties**, and then click **Advanced Properties**. In the displayed **Lastname_Firstname_5A_Home_Page Properties** dialog box, on the **Summary** tab, click in the **Subject** box, type your course name and section number. In the **Author** box, delete any existing text, and then type your first and last names. In the **Keywords** box, type **web site, home page** Click **OK**.

12 In **Backstage** view, click the **Print tab** to display the Print commands and the Print Preview. Examine the **Print Preview**, which displays as a two-page document in Word format without a background color. Click the **Home tab**, make any necessary adjustments, and then **Save** your document.

13 Click the **File tab**, and then click **Exit** to exit Word. In the **Microsoft Word** message box, when asked if you want a picture to be available, click **No**.

Activity 5.09 | Testing Web Pages in a Browser

In this activity, you will display and test the Texas Spectrum Wireless Web pages in your browser.

Alert! | I Cannot Connect to the Internet

If the system on which you are working is not connected to the Internet, skip this activity and move to Activity 5.10.

1 From your taskbar, start **Windows Explorer**. Alternatively, click **Start**, and then click **Computer**—or My Computer on Windows XP. Navigate to your **Word Chapter 5** folder, and then select your **Lastname_Firstname_5A_Home_Page** HTML document. Compare your screen with Figure 5.18.

Figure 5.18

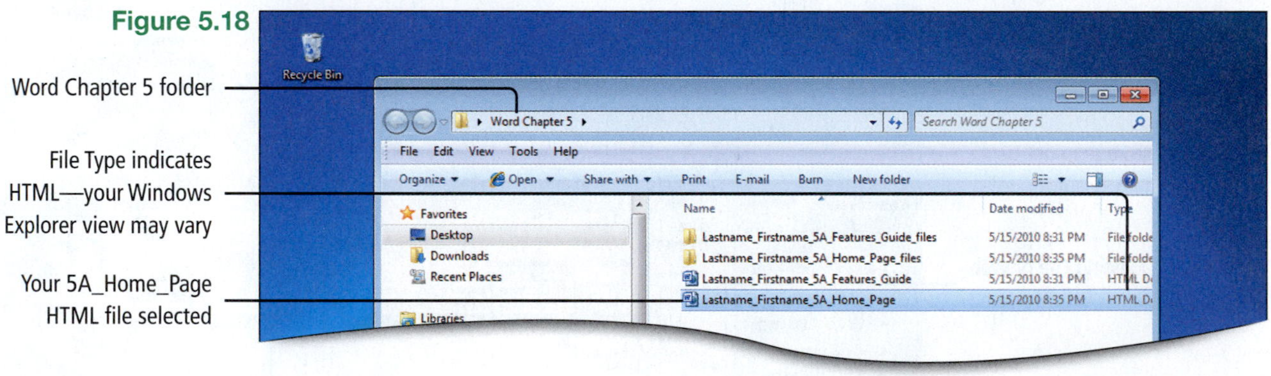

2 Double-click the file to open it in your browser.

This textbook uses Internet Explorer as the default browser, but it is not necessary to use Internet Explorer. Because this file is an HTML file, it will display in any browser.

3 If necessary, scroll to the bottom of the Web page, and then point to the text *Home* to display the pointer and the ScreenTip that you created. Compare your screen with Figure 5.19.

Figure 5.19

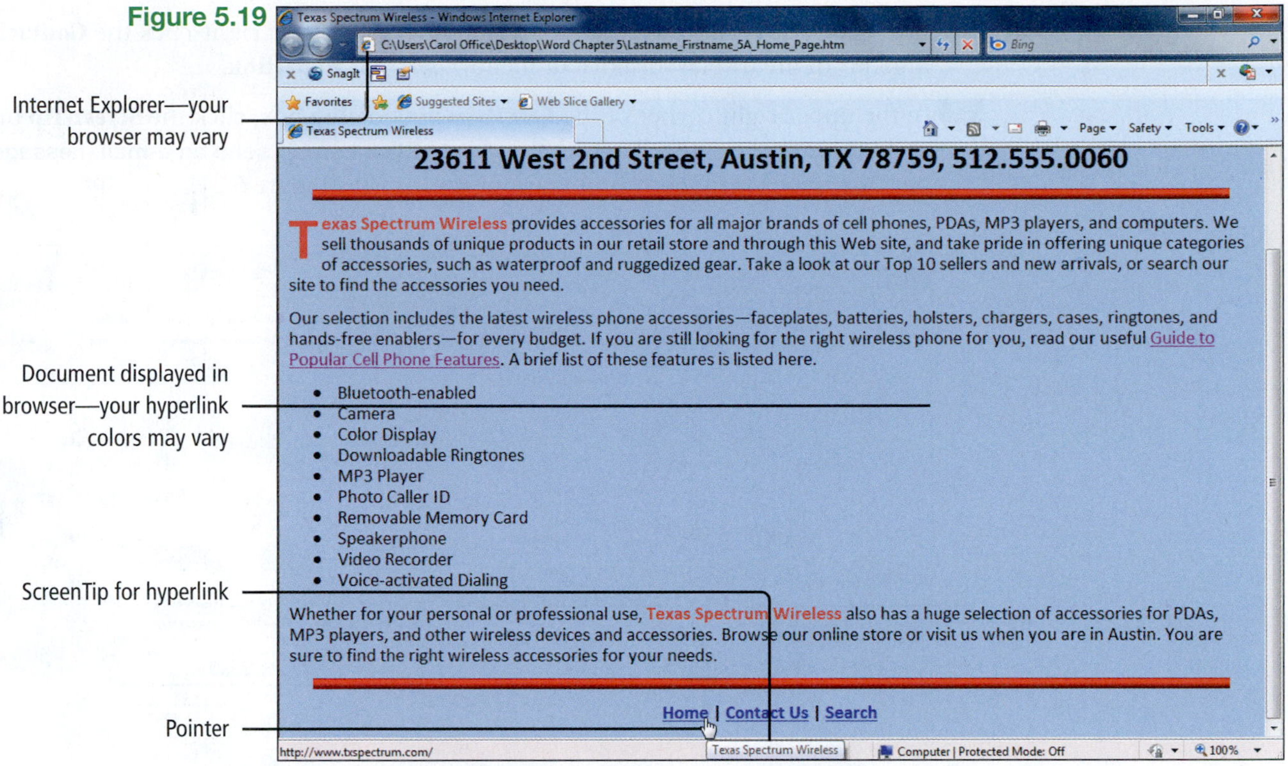

4 On the same line, point to the text *Contact Us* and *Search* to display the ScreenTips.

5 Locate and then click the **Guide to Popular Cell Phone Features** link to display the linked page. Compare your screen with Figure 5.20.

The browser displays the Features Guide Web page.

Figure 5.20

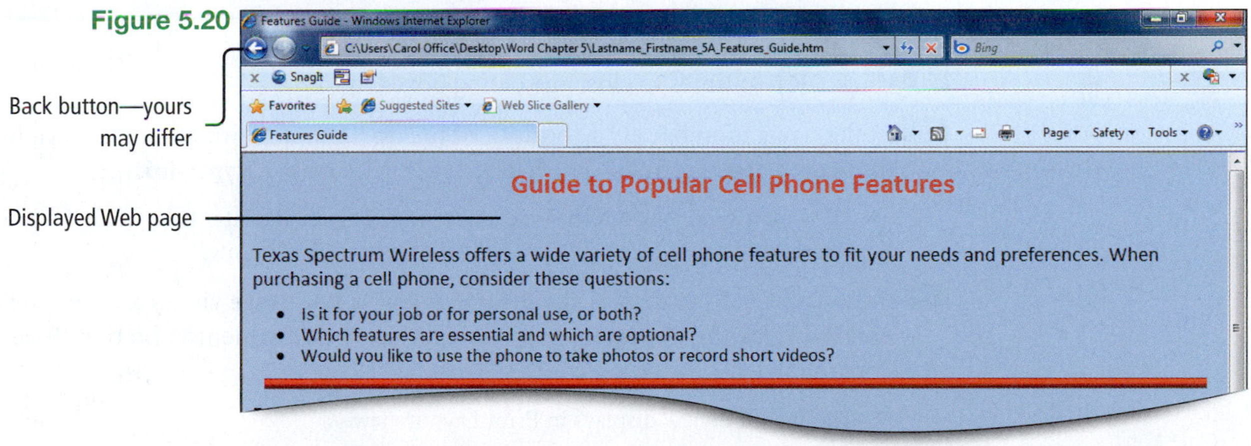

6 In your browser, locate and then click the **Back** button to return to the previously displayed page.

7 **Close** the browser window. If necessary, close any Windows Explorer windows.

Activity 5.10 | Editing and Removing Hyperlinks

You can modify the hyperlinks in your Web page—for example, to change an address or ScreenTip—and you can also remove a hyperlink.

1 Start **Word.** From **Backstage** view, display the **Open** dialog box. Navigate to your **Word Chapter 5** folder, and then open your **Lastname_Firstname_5A_Home_Page** HTML file.

2 Press Ctrl + End. In the navigation bar, point to and then right-click the **Contact Us** link. From the displayed shortcut menu, click **Edit Hyperlink**.

3 In the upper right corner of the **Edit Hyperlink** dialog box, click the **ScreenTip** button, and then edit the ScreenTip text to indicate **Click here to send an e-mail message to our Operations Manager** Compare your screen with Figure 5.21.

Figure 5.21

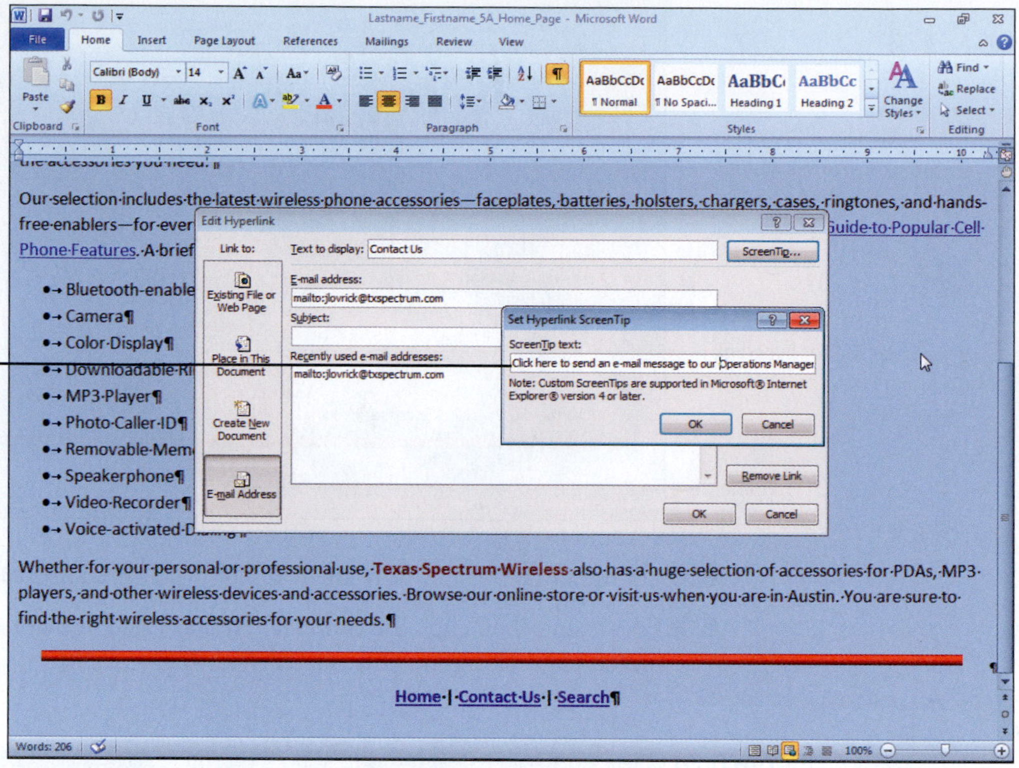

New ScreenTip text—not all text may display

4 Click **OK** two times to close the dialog boxes.

5 In the navigation bar at the bottom of the document, point to and then right-click the **Search** link. From the shortcut menu, click **Remove Hyperlink**.

The link is removed, but the link can be added again at a later time when Texas Spectrum Wireless decides how customers will be able to search the site.

6 Press Ctrl + F2 to display the **Print Preview** in **Backstage** view. Examine the **Print Preview**, click the **Home tab**, make any necessary adjustments, and then **Save** your document.

The Print Preview displays in Print Layout view.

7 Open your **Lastname_Firstname_5A_Features_Guide** HTML file, view the **Print Preview**, and make any necessary adjustments.

8 **Save** and then **Close** both documents. Leave Word open.

Objective 3 | Create a Blog Post

A ***blog***, short for *Web log*, is a Web site that displays dated entries. Blogs are fast-changing Web sites and usually contain many hyperlinks—links to other blogs, to resource sites about the topic, or to photos and videos.

Blogs exist for both individuals and organizations. For example, a blog can function as an individual's personal journal or as a way for a business or organization to provide news on new products or information about customer service.

Microsoft employees post to a blog site about using Word. The site is a good example of a professional blog, and you can view it at http://blogs.msdn.com/microsoft_office_word/.

Activity 5.11 | Creating a Blog Post

A ***blog post*** is an individual article entered in a blog with a time and date stamp. Blog posts commonly display with the most recent post first. Texas Spectrum Wireless has a blog to address customer service questions. In this activity, you will create a new blog post for the customer service blog.

1 Click the **File tab**, click **New**, click **Blog post**, and then in the lower right portion of the screen, click **Create**. If the **Register a Blog Account** dialog box displays, click the **Register Later** button, and then compare your screen with Figure 5.22.

A new document, formatted as a blog post, displays, and the Blog Post and Insert tabs display on the Ribbon. Here you can enter a title for the blog post and then type the text.

Some of the commands are inactive until you register at an actual blog site.

Figure 5.22

Available tabs

New blog post document

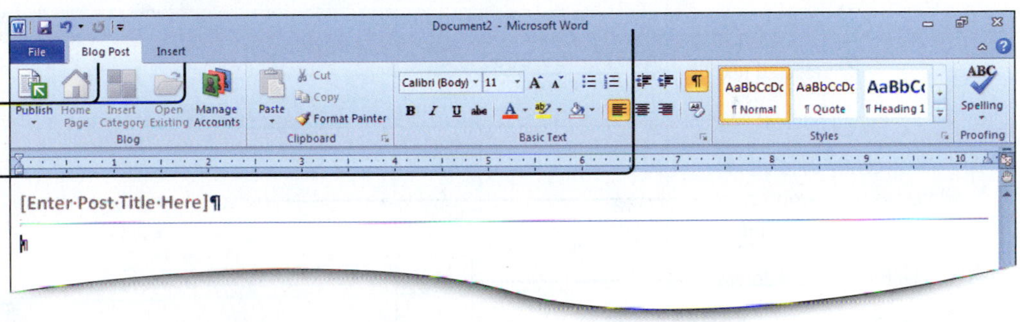

2 Click the **File tab**, click **Save As**, and then in the **Save As** dialog box, navigate to your **Word Chapter 5** folder. In the **File name** box, type **Lastname_Firstname_5A_Blog_Post** and then click **Save**.

This file is saved as a Word Document, not as an HTML file.

3 At the top of the document, click anywhere in the text **Enter Post Title Here** field to select the placeholder text, and then type **Learn to Use Your Bluetooth Headset**

4 Under the thin blue line, click in the body text area, and then type the following text:

Do you have one of our new Bluetooth headsets? We can help you learn all about it! Call us at 512-555-0060, send us an e-mail, download user guides from our Web site, or visit our Austin store for hands-on assistance.

5 Select all the text you typed in the previous step, and then on the Mini toolbar, change the **Font** to **Verdana** and the **Font Size** to **16**. **Save** your blog post.

Although it is not required, you can use Word's formatting tools to change the font, size, color, or alignment of text.

Activity 5.12 | Inserting Hyperlinks in a Blog Post

Blog posts are not limited to text. You can link to pictures, graphics, other Web sites, and to e-mail addresses.

> **Another Way**
>
> Alternatively, right-click the selected text, and then click **Hyperlink**.

1 In the last sentence, select the text *e-mail*. Click the **Insert tab**, and then in the **Links group**, click the **Hyperlink** button.

2 In the **Insert Hyperlink** dialog box, under **Link to**, click **E-mail Address**, if necessary. In the **E-mail address** box, type **jlovrick@txspectrum.com** Compare your screen with Figure 5.23.

Recall that when you create an e-mail hyperlink, Word automatically inserts *mailto:*. Because this is the same e-mail address you typed previously, it may display in the Recently used e-mail addresses box.

Figure 5.23

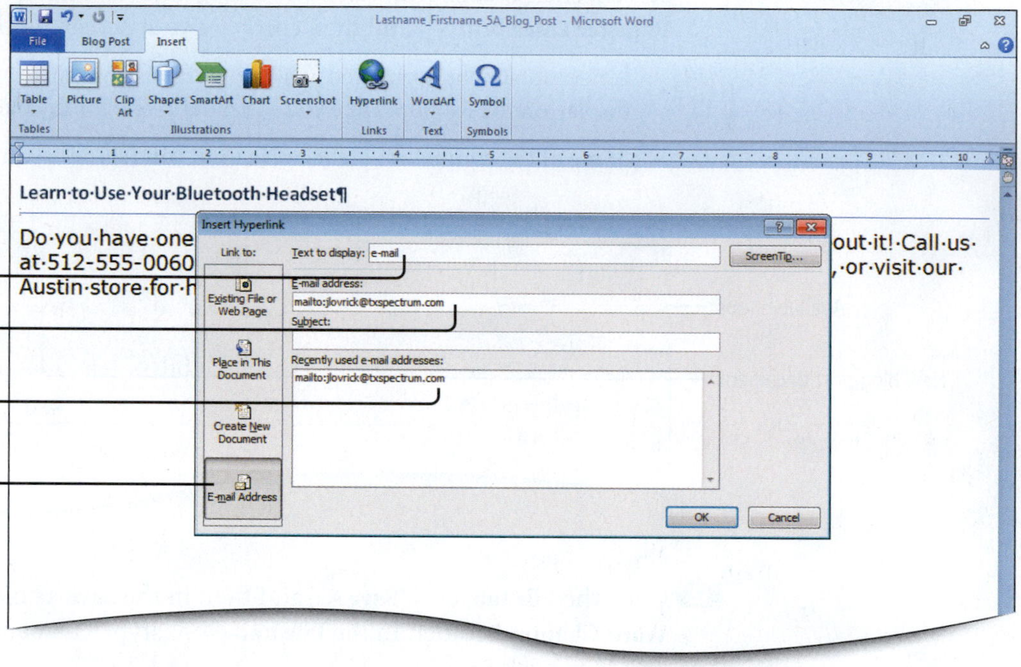

3 Click **OK**. Notice that the text *e-mail* displays with hyperlink formatting.

4 In the last sentence, select the text *Web site*, and then create a hyperlink to link to an existing Web page. As the **Address,** type **www.txspectrum.com** When you are finished typing, if any other characters display, delete them. As the **ScreenTip**, type **Texas Spectrum Wireless** Click **OK** two times to close the dialog boxes.

5 Click to position your insertion point at the end of the paragraph, press Enter two times, and then type your first name and last name.

6 Select your name that you just typed. On the **Blog Post tab**, in the **Styles group**, click the **More** button, and then apply the **Heading 5** style. Click anywhere to deselect the text, and then compare your screen with Figure 5.24.

Figure 5.24

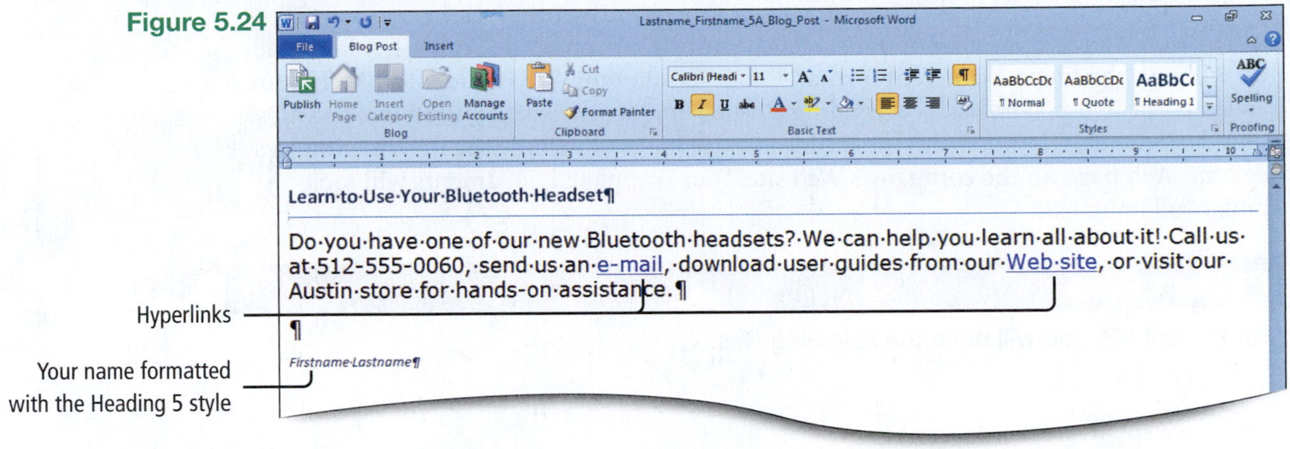

7 From **Backstage** view, display the **Document Information Panel.** In the **Author** box, type your first and last names, if necessary. In the **Subject** box, type your course name and section number, and then in the **Keywords** box, type **web page, blog, Bluetooth** **Close** the Document Information Panel.

8 **Save** your document.

9 Print, or submit electronically, your two HTML files and your blog post as directed by your instructor. In **Backstage** view, click **Exit** to exit Word.

End **You have completed Project 5A**

Project 5B FAQ List

Project Activities

In Activities 5.13 through 5.22, you will examine Word settings, gather supporting information, and use proofing options to create a draft version of the FAQ list. Additionally, you will save the file in a different format. Eliott Verschoren, Vice President of Marketing for Texas Spectrum Wireless, is compiling a list of Frequently Asked Questions, or FAQs, from customers who shop from the online site. He plans to include the information in a separate Web page on the company's Web site. Your completed documents will look similar to Figure 5.25.

Project Files

For Project 5B, you will need the following files:

w05B_FAQ_List
w05B_Images
w05B_Packaging

You will save your documents as:

Lastname_Firstname_5B_FAQ_List
Lastname_Firstname_5B_FAQ_RTF

Project Results

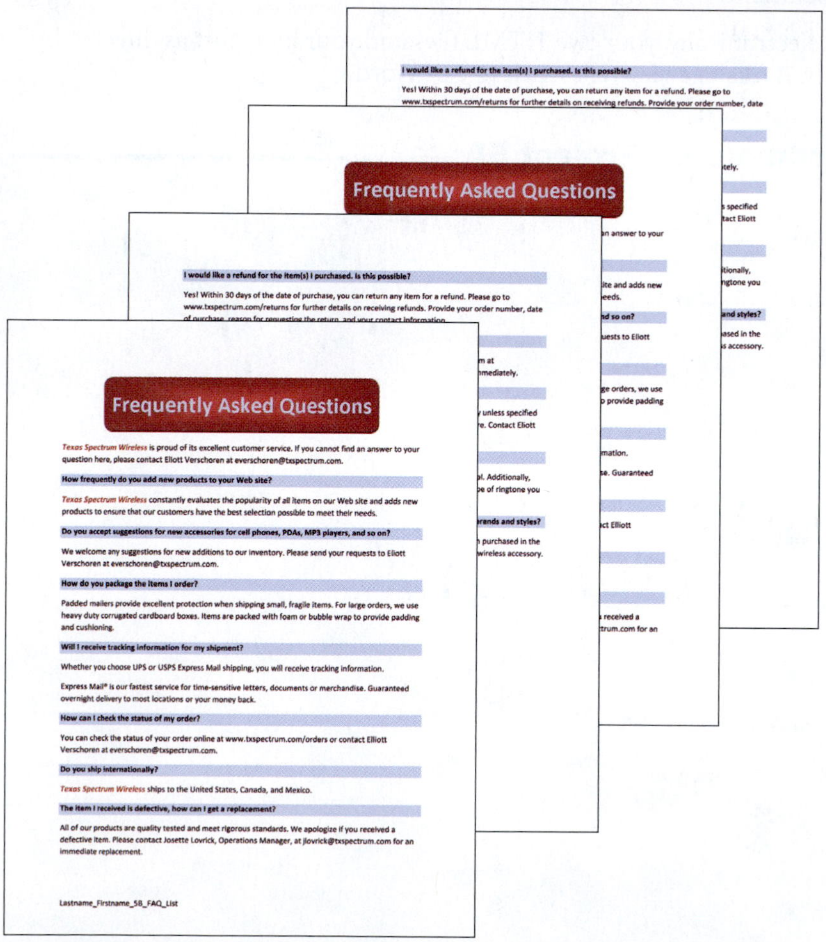

Frequently Asked Questions

Texas Spectrum Wireless is proud of its excellent customer service. If you cannot find an answer to your question here, please contact Elliott Verschoren at everschoren@txspectrum.com.

How frequently do you add new products to your Web site?

Texas Spectrum Wireless constantly evaluates the popularity of all items on our Web site and adds new products to ensure that our customers have the best selection possible to meet their needs.

Do you accept suggestions for new accessories for cell phones, PDAs, MP3 players, and so on?

We welcome any suggestions for new additions to our inventory. Please send your requests to Eliott Verschoren at everschoren@txspectrum.com.

How do you package the items I order?

Padded mailers provide excellent protection when shipping small, fragile items. For large orders, we use heavy duty corrugated cardboard boxes. Items are packed with foam or bubble wrap to provide padding and cushioning.

Will I receive tracking information for my shipment?

Whether you choose UPS or USPS Express Mail shipping, you will receive tracking information.

Express Mail® is our fastest service for time-sensitive letters, documents or merchandise. Guaranteed overnight delivery to most locations or your money back.

How can I check the status of my order?

You can check the status of your order online at www.txspectrum.com/orders or contact Elliott Verschoren at everschoren@txspectrum.com.

Do you ship internationally?

Texas Spectrum Wireless ships to the United States, Canada, and Mexico.

The item I received is defective, how can I get a replacement?

All of our products are quality tested and meet rigorous standards. We apologize if you received a defective item. Please contact Josette Lovrick, Operations Manager, at jlovrick@txspectrum.com for an immediate replacement.

Lastname_Firstname_5B_FAQ_List

Figure 5.25
Project 5B FAQ List

Objective 4 | Locate Word Settings to Personalize Word 2010

When you install Microsoft Office, default settings are created for many features. For example, when you save a file, the default location that displays in the Save As dialog box is *Documents*. You can personalize Word by displaying and changing default settings in the ***Word Options*** dialog box. Word Options form a collection of settings that you can change if you have permission to do so. In the Word Options dialog box, you can also customize some Word features.

Activity 5.13 | Examining the Word Options Dialog Box

Most individuals are satisfied with the default settings in Word. If you find some defaults that you want to change to create a personalized work environment, use the Word Options dialog box to do so. In this activity, you will examine the default settings in the Word Options dialog box.

1 **Start** Word. From your student files, locate and then open the file **w05B_FAQ_List**. If necessary, display formatting marks and rulers.

2 Save the document in your **Word Chapter 5** folder as **Lastname_Firstname_5B_FAQ_List** Scroll to view the bottom of **Page 1**, and then using **Quick Parts**, insert the file name in the footer. Note: Names flagged as spelling errors will be addressed in a later activity.

3 Display **Backstage** view, and then on the left, click **Options** to display the **Word Options** dialog box.

Recall that in an organizational environment such as a college or business, you may not have access or permission to change some or all of the settings.

4 Compare your screen with Figure 5.26, and then take a few moments to study the table in Figure 5.27 to examine the categories of Word options.

Figure 5.26

Word Options dialog box—your settings may vary

Options categories

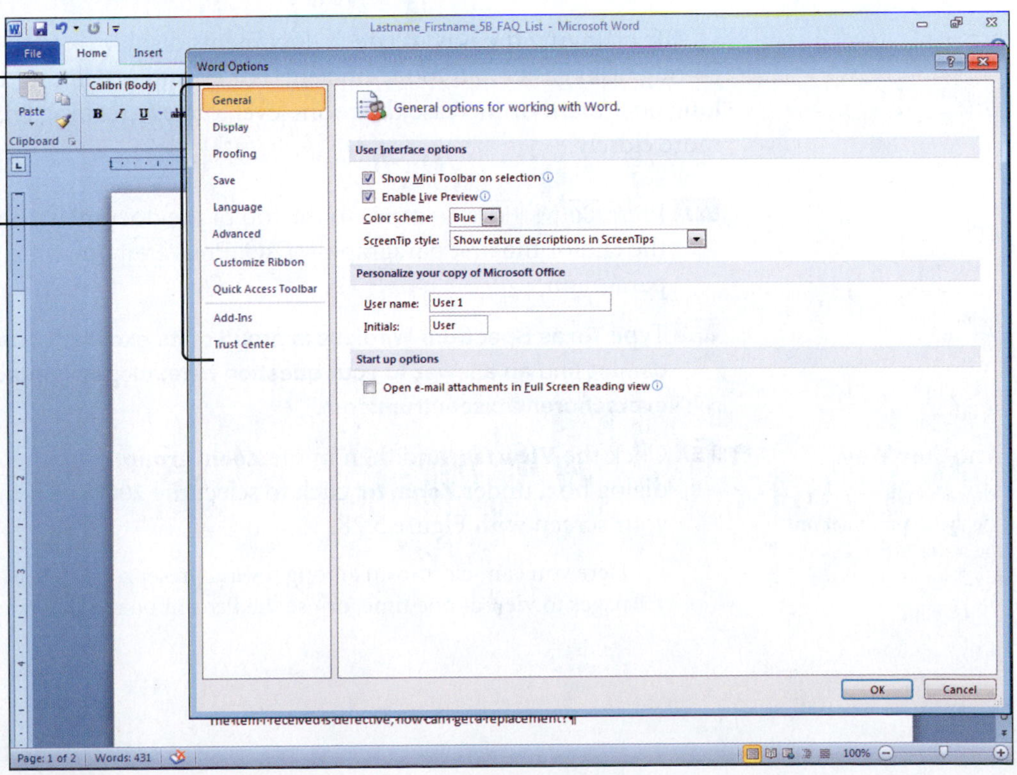

Word Options

Category	Options
General	Set up Word for your personal way of working—for example, changing the color scheme—and personalize Word with your user name and initials.
Display	Control the way Word displays pages on the screen and prints.
Proofing	Control how Word corrects and formats your text—for example, how AutoCorrect and spell checker perform.
Save	Specify where you want to save your Word documents by default and set the AutoRecover time for saving information.
Language	Set the default language and add additional languages for editing documents.
Advanced	Control advanced features related to editing and printing.
Customize Ribbon	Add commands to existing tabs, create new tabs, and set up your own keyboard shortcuts.
Quick Access Toolbar	Customize the Quick Access Toolbar by adding commands.
Add-Ins	View and manage add-in programs that come with the Word software or ones that you add to Word.
Trust Center	Control privacy and security when working with files from other sources or when you share files with others.

Figure 5.27

5 Click **Cancel** to close the dialog box without changing any settings.

Activity 5.14 | Zooming from the View Tab

By changing the way in which documents display on your screen, you make your editing tasks easier and more efficient. For example, you can display multiple pages of a long document or increase the zoom level to make reading text easier or examine graphics more closely.

1 Press Ctrl + Home to move to the top of the document, if necessary, and then click at the end of the first paragraph—*FAQ*. Press Enter one time to insert a new blank paragraph.

2 Type **Texas Spectrum Wireless is proud of its excellent customer service. If you cannot find an answer to your question here, please contact Eliott Verschoren at everschoren@txspectrum.com.**

Another Way

Alternatively, you can use the Zoom slider on the status bar to change the Zoom percentage.

3 Click the **View tab**, and then in the **Zoom group**, click the **Zoom** button. In the **Zoom** dialog box, under **Zoom to**, click to select the **200%** option button, and then compare your screen with Figure 5.28.

Here you can select from among several preset zoom levels, select a specific number of pages to view at one time, or use the Percent box to indicate a specific zoom level.

Figure 5.28

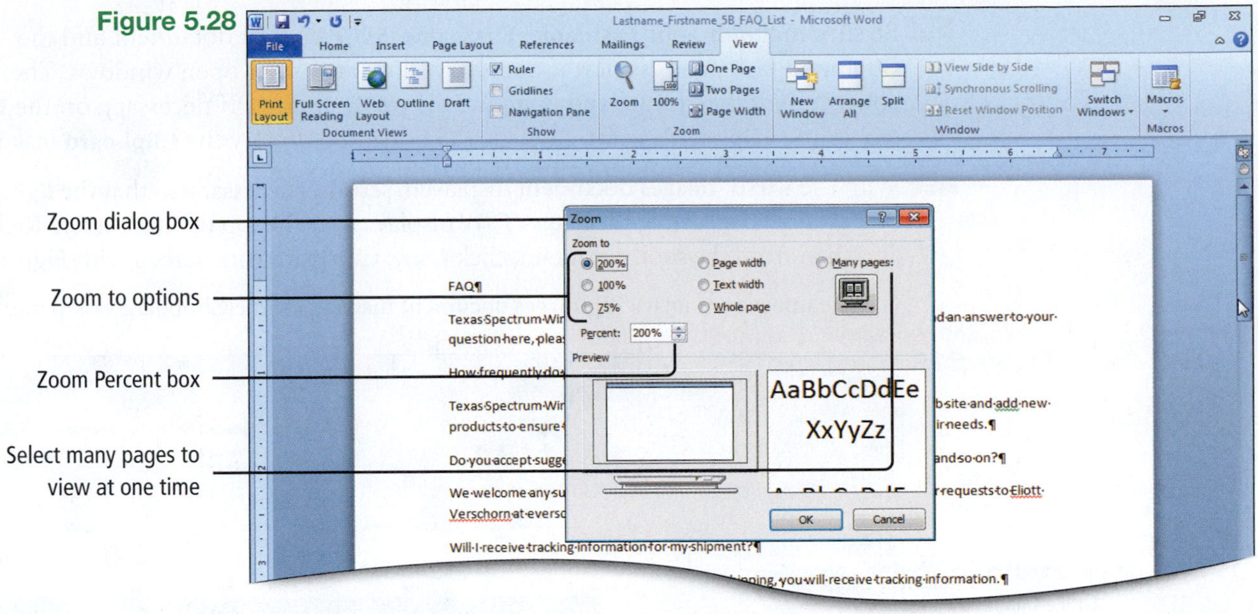

4 Click **OK**, and notice that the document displays in a magnified view.

5 Scroll as necessary, and in the paragraph that begins *We welcome*, notice that the e-mail address has an extra *r* after the letter *p*—the text should be *txspectrum*. **Delete** the character *r*.

A magnified view is useful when you want to make a close inspection of characters—for example, when typing e-mail addresses or scientific formulas.

6 On the **View tab**, in the **Zoom group**, click the **Two Pages** button to display **Page 1** and **Page 2** on your screen.

The ***Two Pages*** zoom setting decreases the magnification to display two pages of a document. Although the text is smaller, you have an overall view of the page arrangement.

7 On the **View tab**, in the **Zoom group**, click the **100%** button to return to the default zoom setting. **Save** your document.

Objective 5 | Collect and Paste Images and Text

As you are writing, you may want to gather material—for example, text and pictures—related to your topic. This supporting information may be located in another document or on the Internet. Recall that you can use the Office Clipboard to collect a group of graphics or selected text blocks and then paste them into a document.

Activity 5.15 | Collecting Images and Text from Multiple Documents

In this activity, you will copy images and text from two different documents and then paste them into your current document.

1 On the **Home tab**, in the lower right corner of the **Clipboard group**, click the button to display the **Clipboard** task pane. If necessary, at the top of the task pane, click the **Clear All** button to delete anything currently on the Clipboard.

2 Be sure that *only* your **Lastname_Firstname_5B_FAQ_List** document and the **Clipboard** task pane display; if necessary, close any other open windows. Then, from your student files, locate and open the file **w05B_Images**. If necessary, on the **Home tab**, in the **Clipboard group**, click the [button] button to display the **Clipboard** task pane.

3 With the **w05B_Images** document displayed, scroll as necessary so that the **lightning bolt** graphic containing the letters *TSW* displays near the top of your screen. Right-click, and then from the shortcut menu, click **Copy**. Compare your screen with Figure 5.29.

The image in your w05B_Images document displays on the Clipboard task pane.

Figure 5.29

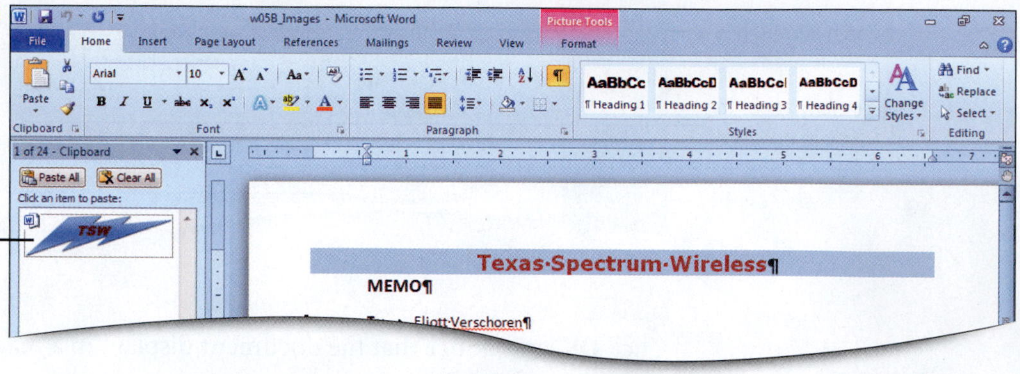

4 Using the technique you just practiced, **Copy** the **Frequently Asked Questions** graphic to the Clipboard. **Close** [X] the **w05B_Images** file.

The copied images display on the Clipboard in your Lastname_Firstname_5B_FAQ_List document.

5 From your student files, open the file **w05B_Packaging**. If necessary, on the **Home tab**, in the **Clipboard group**, click the [button] button to display the **Clipboard** task pane. Without selecting the paragraph mark at the end, select the entire paragraph text that begins *Padded mailers*, and then **Copy** the selection to the Clipboard.

At the top of the Clipboard task pane, notice *3 of 24*, which indicates that 3 of 24 items are now on the Clipboard.

6 **Close** [X] the **w05B_Packaging** document, and then notice the first few lines of the copied text display on the Clipboard. **Save** [save] your document, and then compare your screen with Figure 5.30.

When copying multiple items to the Clipboard, the most recently copied item displays at the top of the list.

Figure 5.30

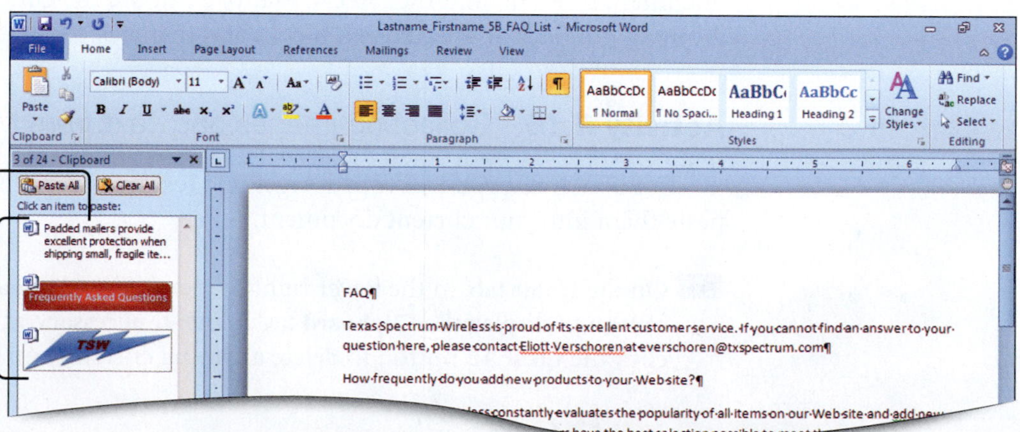

Activity 5.16 | Pasting Information from the Clipboard Task Pane

After you have collected text items or images on the Office Clipboard, you can paste them into a document in any order.

1 Press Ctrl + Home. Without selecting the paragraph mark, select only the text *FAQ*. In the **Clipboard** task pane, click the graphic *Frequently Asked Questions*.

The graphic replaces the selected text.

2 Click the inserted graphic one time to select it, and then on the **Home tab**, in the **Paragraph group**, click the **Center** button.

3 Locate the sixth text paragraph of the document, which begins *Will I receive*. Click to position the insertion point to the left of the paragraph, press Enter, and then press ↑. In the new paragraph, type **How do you package the items I order?** and then press Enter.

4 In the **Clipboard** task pane, click the text entry that begins *Padded mailers* to paste the entire block of text at the insertion point. Compare your screen with Figure 5.31.

Figure 5.31

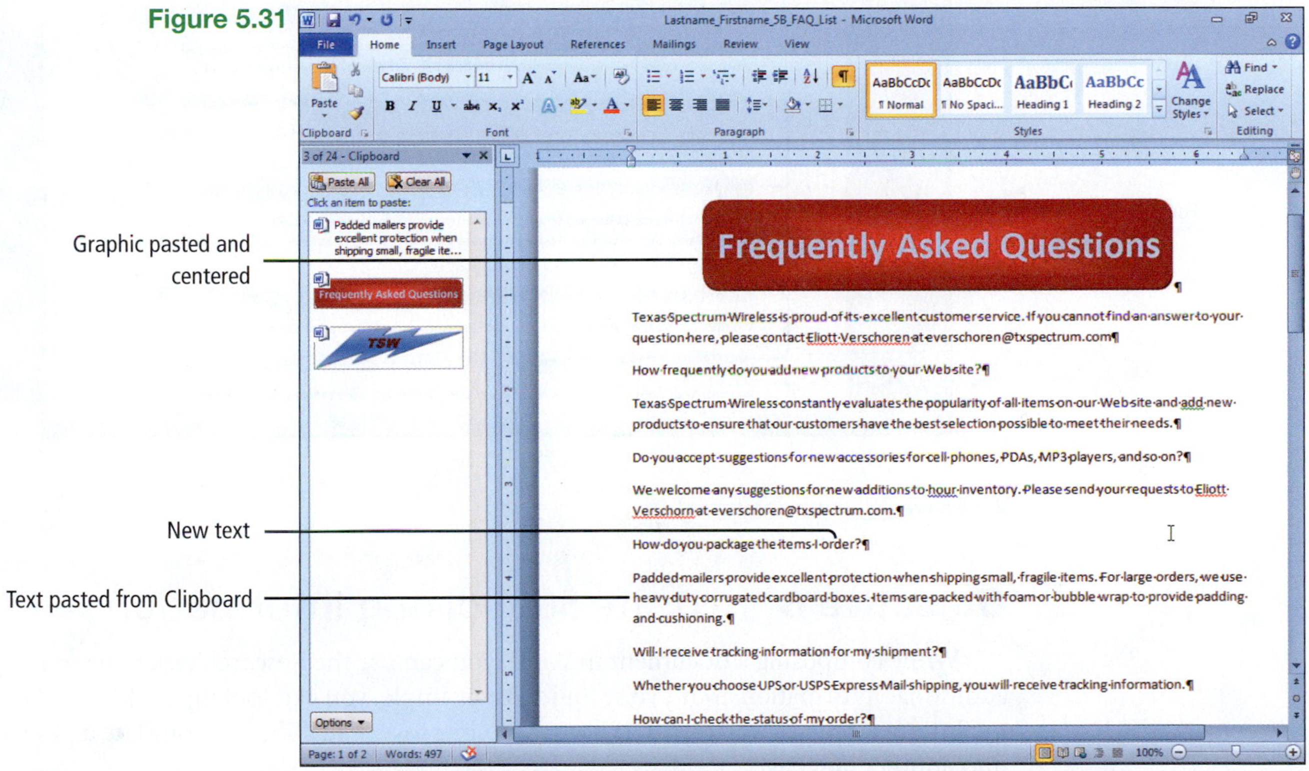

5 Press Ctrl + End to move to the end of the document, and then press Enter. In the **Clipboard** task pane, click the image containing the lightning bolt graphic to paste it at the insertion point, and then using the technique you practiced, **Center** it.

6 At the top of the **Clipboard** task pane, click the **Clear All** button to remove all items from the Office Clipboard, and then **Close** the **Clipboard** task pane.

7 Press Ctrl + Home. Locate and then select, including the paragraph mark, the paragraph that begins *How frequently*. Hold down Ctrl and then select the next question—the paragraph that begins *Do you accept*.

8 Continue to hold down Ctrl, and then select all the remaining paragraphs that end in a question mark, scrolling down with the scroll bar or **down scroll arrow** as necessary to move through the document.

9 With all the questions selected, apply **Bold** [B]. On the **Home tab**, in the **Paragraph group**, click the **Shading button arrow**, and then in the fourth column, click the second color—**Dark Blue, Text 2, Lighter 80%**.

10 Click anywhere to deselect the text, scroll through the document to be sure you have shaded each question, and then scroll so that the Frequently Asked Questions graphic displays at the top of your screen. Compare your screen with Figure 5.32.

Figure 5.32

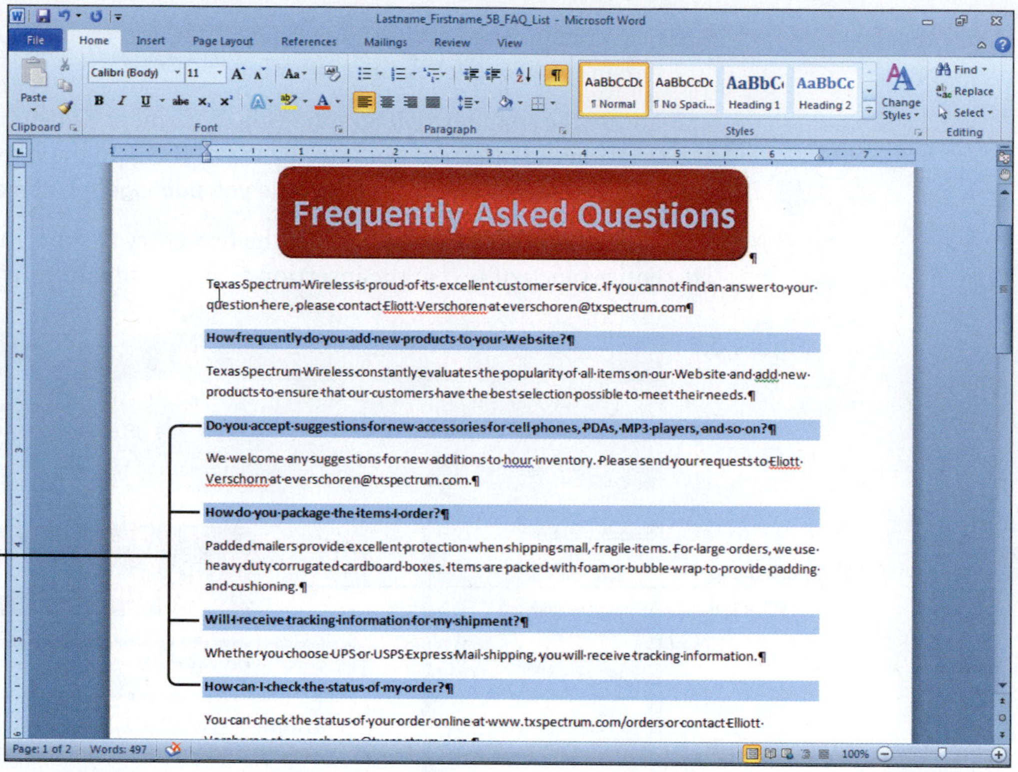

11 **Save** your document.

Objective 6 | Locate Supporting Information

While composing a document in Word, you can use the Research task pane to locate additional information about your topic. For example, you can look up additional facts on the Internet, replace words with synonyms to improve readability, or translate a phrase into another language.

Activity 5.17 | Using the Research Task Pane to Locate Information

In this activity, you will use the Research Sites and Thesaurus features in the Research task pane to search for additional information for and make changes to the FAQ list.

1 In the middle of **Page 1**, locate the paragraph that begins *Whether you choose*, and then click to position the insertion point at the end of the paragraph. Press Enter to add a blank paragraph.

2 Click the **Review tab**, and then in the **Proofing group**, click the **Research** button to display the **Research** task pane.

3 In the **Research** task pane, click in the **Search for** box, type **USPS Express** Under the **Search for** box, in the second box—the **Search location** box—click the **arrow**, point to **Bing**, and then compare your screen with Figure 5.33.

In the Search location box, you can specify the type of reference source from which you want to locate information. For example, you might want to use the Microsoft search engine Bing as a reference source.

> **Alert! | What If Bing Does Not Display?**
>
> If Bing does not display, you may be running an older version of Windows. Consult your instructor.

Figure 5.33

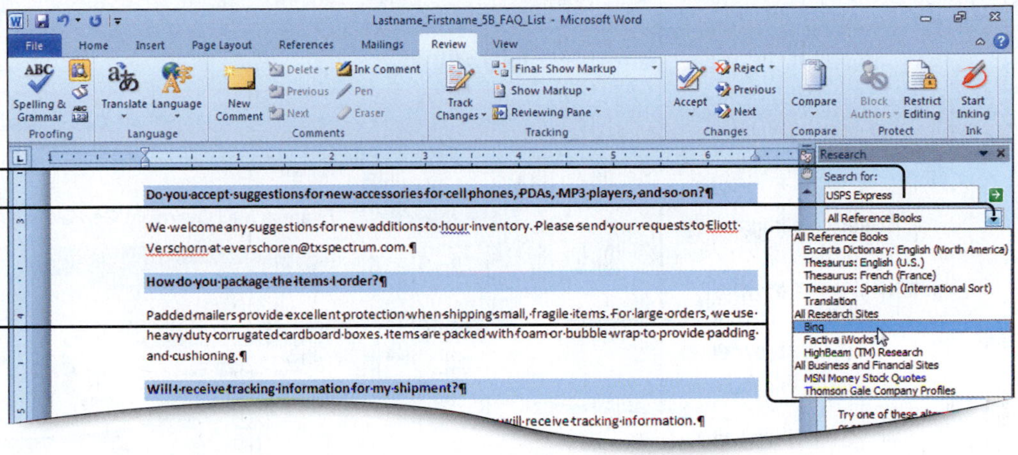

4 In the displayed list, click **Bing**. In the list of results, locate the item titled *USPS - Express Mail Overnight Guaranteed*, and then compare your screen with Figure 5.34.

The search results include Web sites containing information about your search term—*USPS Express*. Each item contains the title of the Web page, a brief summary of the Web page, and a link to the Web page. Because the information on Web sites changes often, the information on your screen may differ.

Figure 5.34

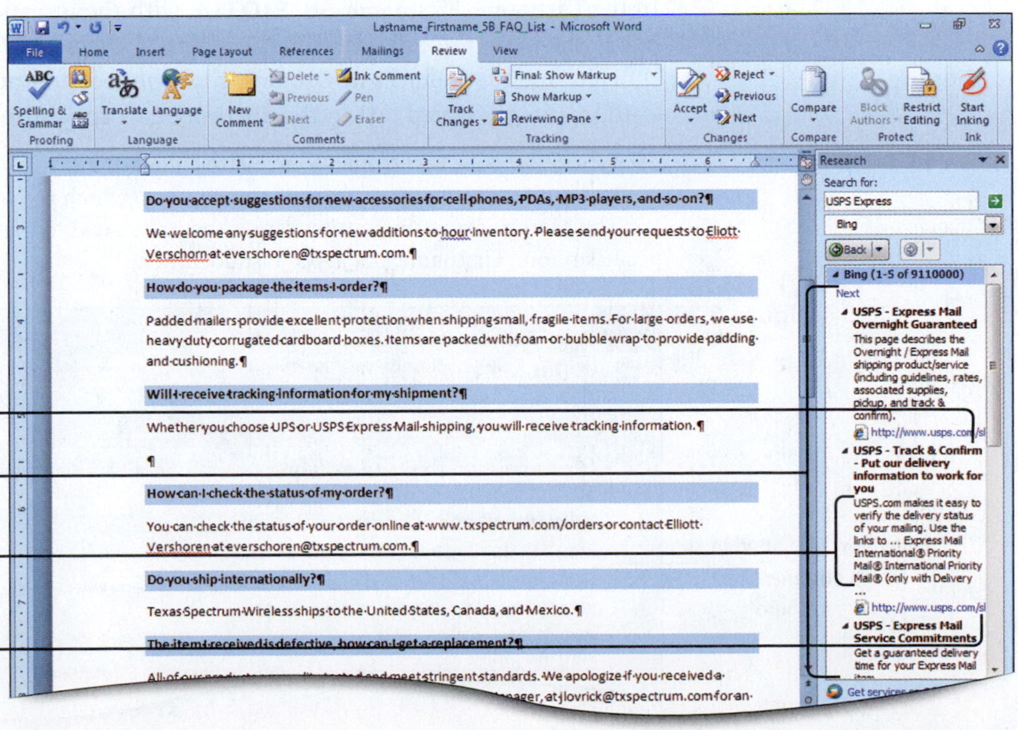

5 For the item titled *USPS - Express Mail Overnight Guaranteed*, click the related hyperlink to open your browser. If necessary, maximize your browser window. Locate and then select the entire paragraph that begins *Express Mail® is our fastest* and ends with *or your money back.* Compare your screen with Figure 5.35.

A blue arrow, called an *accelerator*, displays when you select text in Internet Explorer 8. Because Web pages change frequently, consult your instructor if your results do not look similar to Figure 5.35.

Figure 5.35

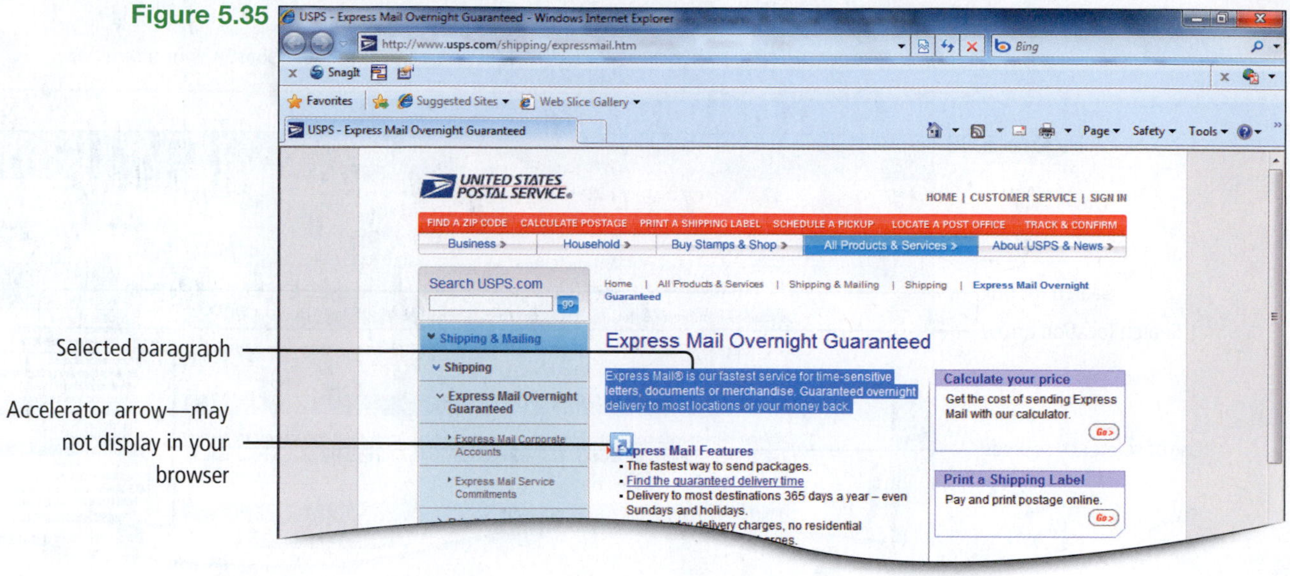

6 On the Web page, right-click the selection, and then from the shortcut menu, click **Copy**. **Close** the browser window.

Alert! | **If Your Browser Displays Differently**

Depending on your operating system—Windows 7, Windows Vista, or Windows XP—you might need to open or close additional browser windows to locate the information from the USPS site.

7 In the **Lastname_Firstname_5B_FAQ List**, with the insertion point in the blank line below the paragraph that begins *Whether you choose*, right-click, and then from the shortcut menu, under **Paste Options**, click the second button—**Merge Formatting** —to insert the copied text in the document. Compare your screen with Figure 5.36.

When you paste text from a source into a document, you will typically want to format the text in the same manner as the document into which you are pasting—the destination. The Merge Formatting option causes the pasted text to match the formatting in your Lastname_Firstname_5B_FAQ_List document.

Figure 5.36

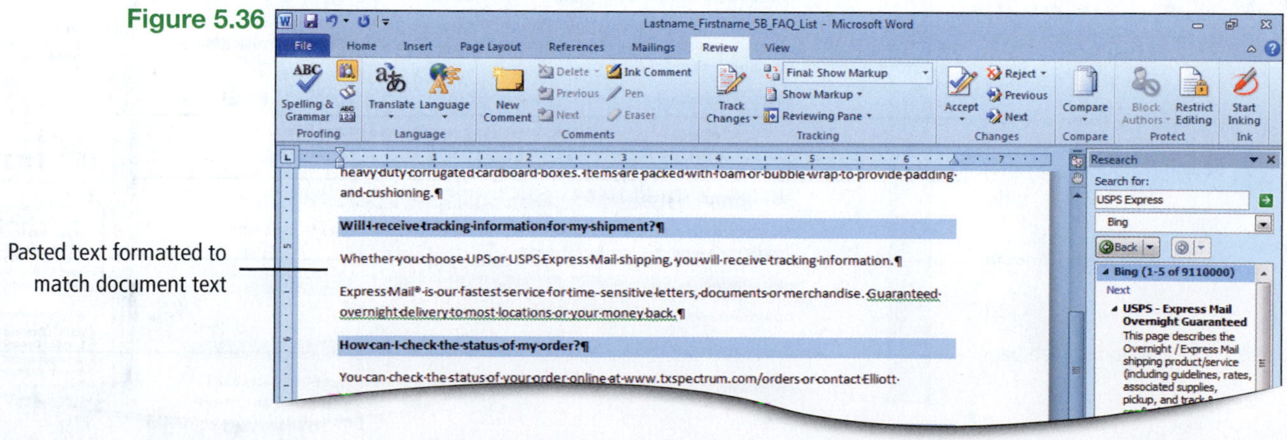

> **Note | Be Careful of Copyright Issues**
>
> Nearly everything you find on the Internet is protected by copyright law, which protects authors of original works, including text, art, photographs, and music. If you want to use text or graphics that you find online, you will need to get permission. One of the exceptions to this law is the use of small amounts of information for educational purposes, which falls under Fair Use guidelines. As a general rule, however, if you want to use someone else's material, always get permission first.

8 In the lower portion of **Page 1**, in the paragraph that begins *All of our products*, point to and then right-click the word *stringent*. Point to **Synonyms**, and then click **Thesaurus**. Compare your screen with Figure 5.37.

In the Research task pane, *stringent* displays in the Search for box, and synonyms for the word *stringent* display under Thesaurus.

Figure 5.37

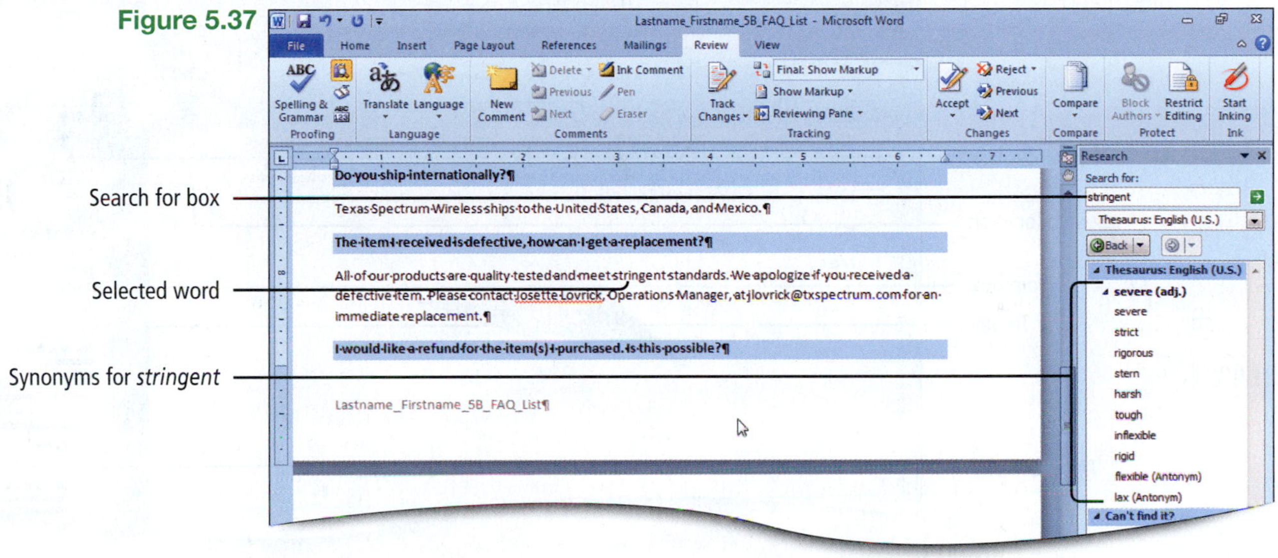

9 In the **Research** task pane, point to **rigorous**, click the displayed **arrow**, and then click **Insert** to replace *stringent* with *rigorous*.

> **Another Way**
>
> Alternatively, on the **Page Layout tab**, in the **Page Setup group**, click the **Breaks** button, and then under **Page Breaks**, click **Page**.

10 At the bottom of **Page 1**, click to position the insertion point to the left of the paragraph that begins *I would like*. Hold down Ctrl, and then press Enter, which is the keyboard shortcut to insert a page break. **Save** your document.

Because the document contains questions and answers, it is good document design to keep the question and answer together on the same page.

> **More Knowledge | Using the Research Options Command**
>
> The option to add or remove research sources does not display in the Word Options dialog box; rather, this command is located at the bottom of the Research task pane. To add or remove a source, click Research Options, and then in the Research Options dialog box, select or clear its check box, and then click OK.

Activity 5.18 | Translating Text from the Research Task Pane

You can translate a word or phrase into a different language from the Research task pane. Because Texas Spectrum Wireless has customers outside of the United States, the FAQ will include text for Spanish-speaking and French-speaking customers that can eventually be linked to FAQ pages written in those languages. In this activity, you will add Spanish and French text to the FAQ list.

Another Way

Alternatively, on the **Review tab**, in the **Language group**, you can click the **Translate** button, and click **Translate Selected Text**.

1 On **Page 2**, locate the paragraph that begins *Our wireless accessories*, and then click to position the insertion point at the end of the paragraph.

2 Press Enter two times, type **FAQ** and then press Spacebar.

3 In the **Research** task pane, in the **Search for** box, delete any existing text if necessary, and then type **Spanish** In the **Search location** box, click the **arrow**, and then click **Translation**.

Here you can select the type of reference you want to search, including online references.

4 If necessary, under **Translation**, click the **From arrow**, and then click **English (U.S.)**. Click the **To box arrow**, and then click **Spanish (International Sort)**. Compare your screen with Figure 5.38.

The translated text—español—displays in the Translation area of the task pane.

Figure 5.38

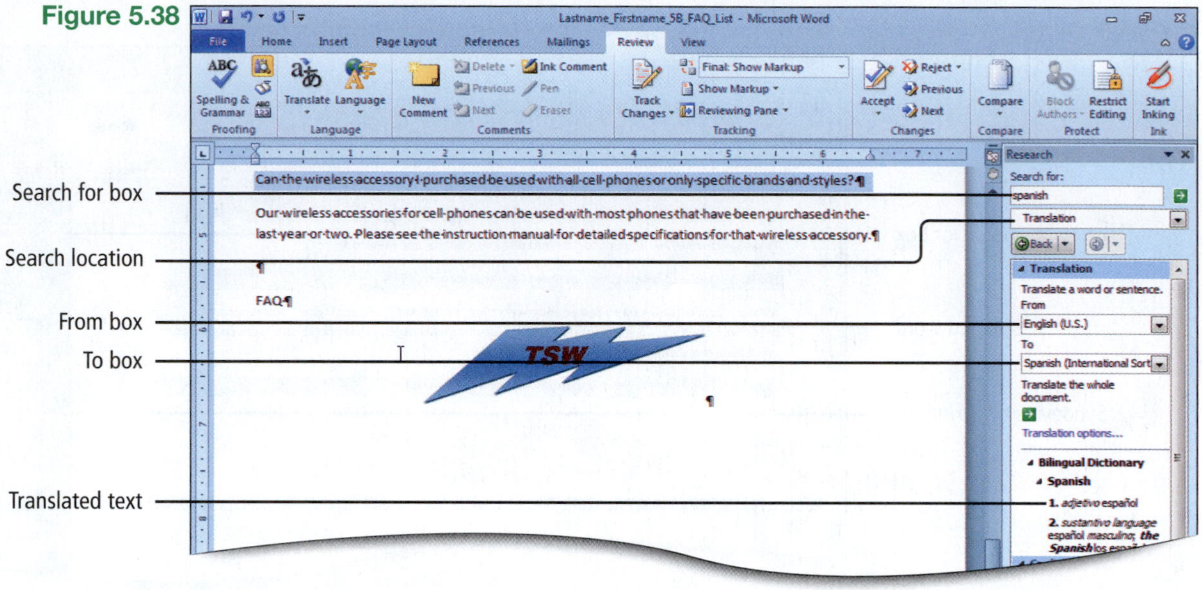

5 In the lower portion of the **Research** task pane, select the translated text *español*, right-click, and then from the shortcut menu, click **Copy**. In your document, locate the paragraph *FAQ*, and then click to position the insertion point at the end of the paragraph. Right-click, and from the shortcut menu, under **Paste Options**, click the **Keep Text Only** A button. In the pasted text, select the first letter *e*, type **E** and then compare your screen with Figure 5.39.

Word uses a machine translation service—not a human being—to translate text, which can result in slight discrepancies in the translated phrases. The main idea is captured, but an accurate translation may differ slightly.

Figure 5.39

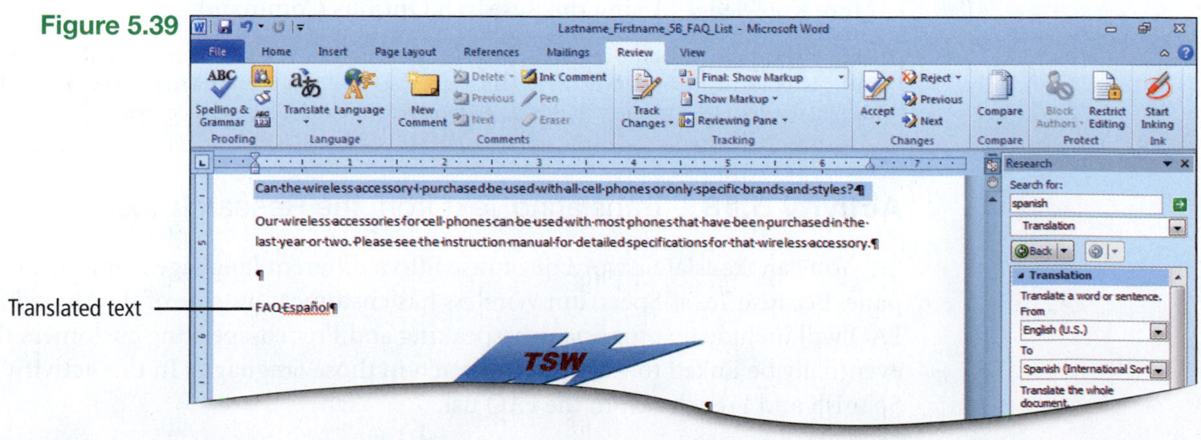

6 Position the insertion point at the end of the paragraph, press Enter, type **FAQ** and then press Spacebar.

7 In the **Research** task pane, in the **Search for** box, type **French** Click the **To box arrow**, and then click **French (France)**.

8 Using the technique you just practiced, insert the French text *français* at the insertion point location. Select the first letter *f*, and then type **F**

9 Select both paragraphs that begin *FAQ*, and then on the Mini toolbar, change the **Font Size** to **14**, and apply **Bold** B.

Mr. Verschoren will develop specific FAQs in both languages to link here.

10 **Close** × the **Research** task pane, and then **Save** your document.

More Knowledge | Using the Translation Language Tools

On the Review tab, in the Language group, you can choose your translation language, translate an entire document, translate selected text, or use the Mini Translator. The Mini Translator provides an instant translation when you point to a word or selected phrase. When you click the Play button in the Mini Translator, the text is read back to you.

Objective 7 | Use Advanced Find and Replace and Proofing Options

From the Find and Replace dialog box, you can locate occurrences of words that sound the same although spelled differently, find phrases that are capitalized in exactly the same way, and find different forms of a word—such as *work*, *worked*, and *working*.

Activity 5.19 | Using Find and Replace to Change Text Formatting

You can change the formatting of a word or phrase that is repeated throughout a document easily by using the Find and Replace dialog box. In this activity, you will change the formatting of the company name that displays numerous times in the FAQ list.

1 Press Ctrl + Home. On the **Home tab**, in the **Editing group**, click the **Replace** button to display the **Find and Replace** dialog box.

2 In the **Find what** box, type **Texas Spectrum Wireless** and then in the **Replace with** box, type the exact same text **Texas Spectrum Wireless**

3 Below the **Replace with** box, click the **More** button to expand this dialog box.

The More button exposes advanced settings, such as formatting, with which you can refine this command.

4 Near the bottom of the **Find and Replace** dialog box, under **Replace**, click the **Format** button, and then in the displayed list, click **Font**.

5 In the displayed **Replace Font** dialog box, under **Font style**, click **Bold Italic**. Click the **Font color arrow**, and then in the sixth column, click the fifth color—**Red, Accent 2, Darker 25%**. Compare your screen with Figure 5.40.

Figure 5.40

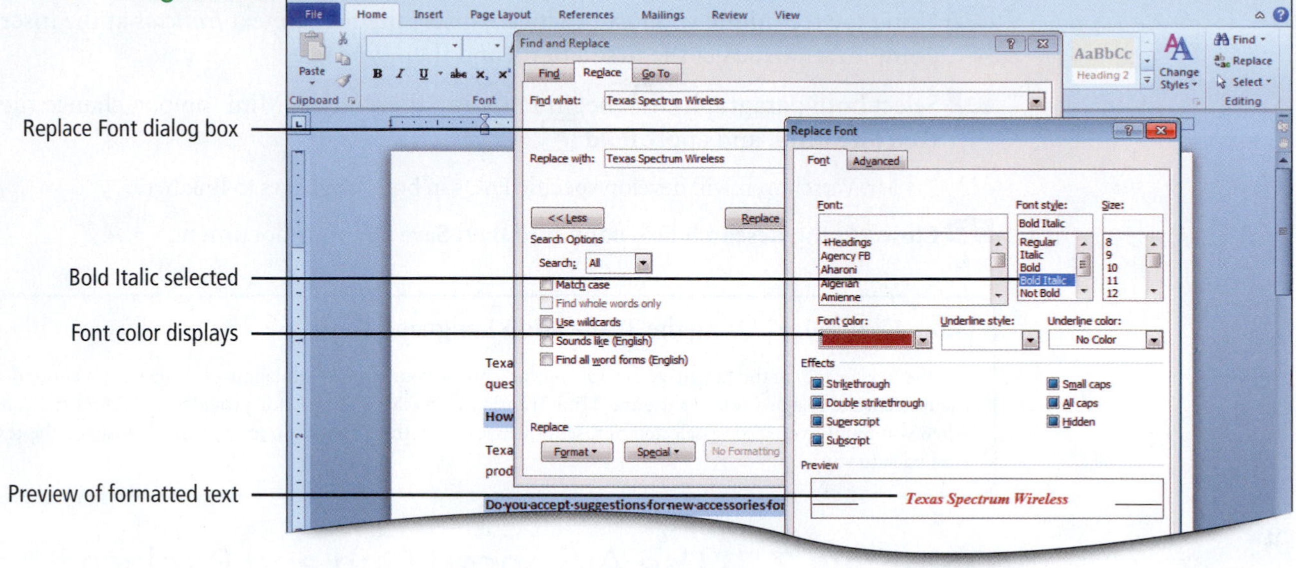

6 Click **OK** to close the **Replace Font** dialog box, and then in the middle of the **Find and Replace** dialog box, click the **Replace All** button. When a **Microsoft Office Word** message displays indicating that you have made 4 replacements, click **OK**. Leave the expanded dialog box displayed.

This action finds each instance of the text *Texas Spectrum Wireless*, and then replaces the font format with bold italic in the red color that you selected.

7 Click anywhere in the document, and then **Save** the document.

Activity 5.20 | Using Wildcards in Find and Replace

Use a ***wildcard*** in the Find and Replace dialog box when you are uncertain of the exact term you want to find. A wildcard is a special character such as * or ? inserted with a Find what term. For example, searching a document for the term *b*k* could find *blink*, *book*, *brick*, or any other word in the document that begins with *b* and ends with *k*. Using a wildcard can save time when you do not know the specific characters in the search term. In this activity, you will use a wildcard to search for e-mail and Web page addresses that may be spelled incorrectly.

1 In the **Find and Replace** dialog box, in the **Find what** box, delete the existing text, and then type **V*n**

2 Press Tab to move to and select the text in the **Replace with** box, and then type **Verschoren** At the bottom of the **Find and Replace** dialog box, click the **No Formatting** button to remove the formatting settings from the previous activity.

3 Under **Search Options**, select the **Use wildcards** check box. Compare your screen with Figure 5.41.

Mr. Verschoren's name may have been spelled incorrectly. By using the Find command to locate each instance that begins with *V* and ends with *n*, you can find, and then verify, the correct spelling of his name in every instance.

Figure 5.41

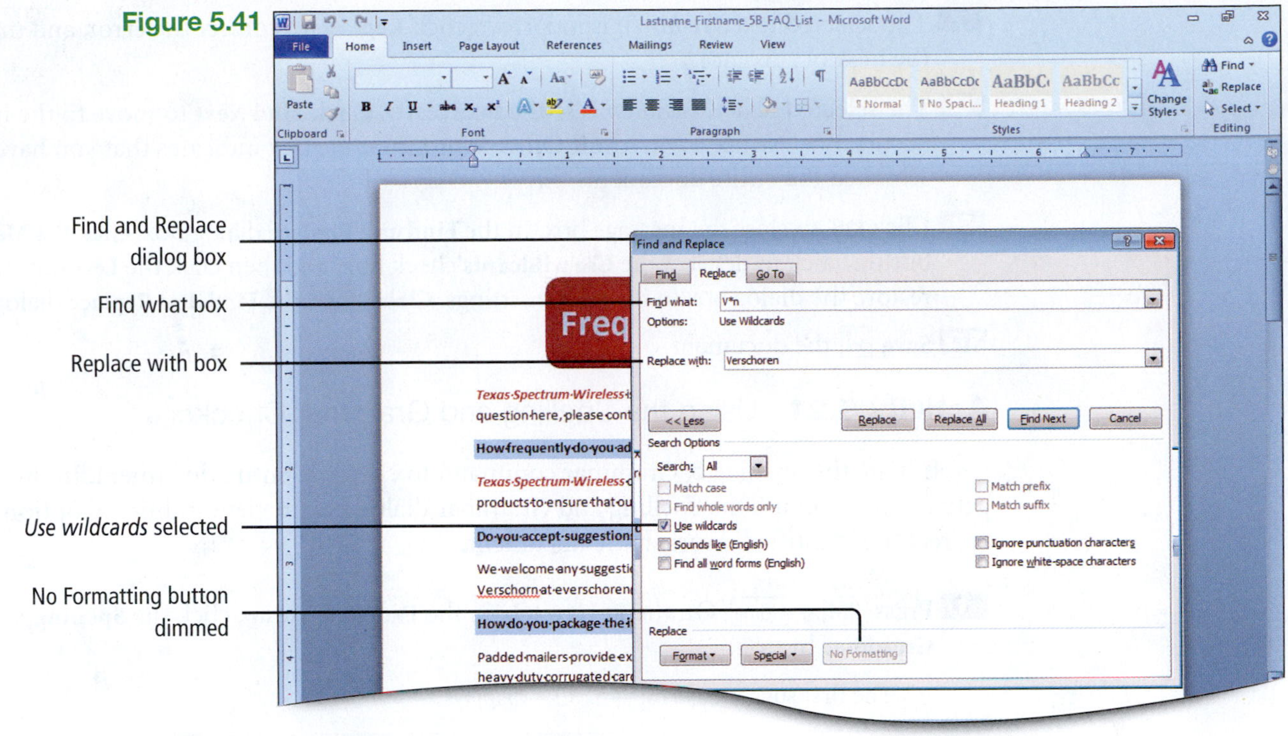

4 In the **Find and Replace** dialog box, click the **Less** button so that the dialog box is smaller. Then, click the **Find Next** button. The text *Verschoren* is selected in the document. If necessary, move the Find and Replace dialog box to view the selection.

This instance is spelled correctly—no changes are required.

5 In the **Find and Replace** dialog box, click the **Find Next** button again, and notice that this occurrence is not spelled correctly.

6 Click the **Replace** button, and then compare your screen with Figure 5.42.

The text *Verschoren* is now spelled correctly, and Word selects the next occurrence of text that begins with *V* and ends with *n*.

Figure 5.42

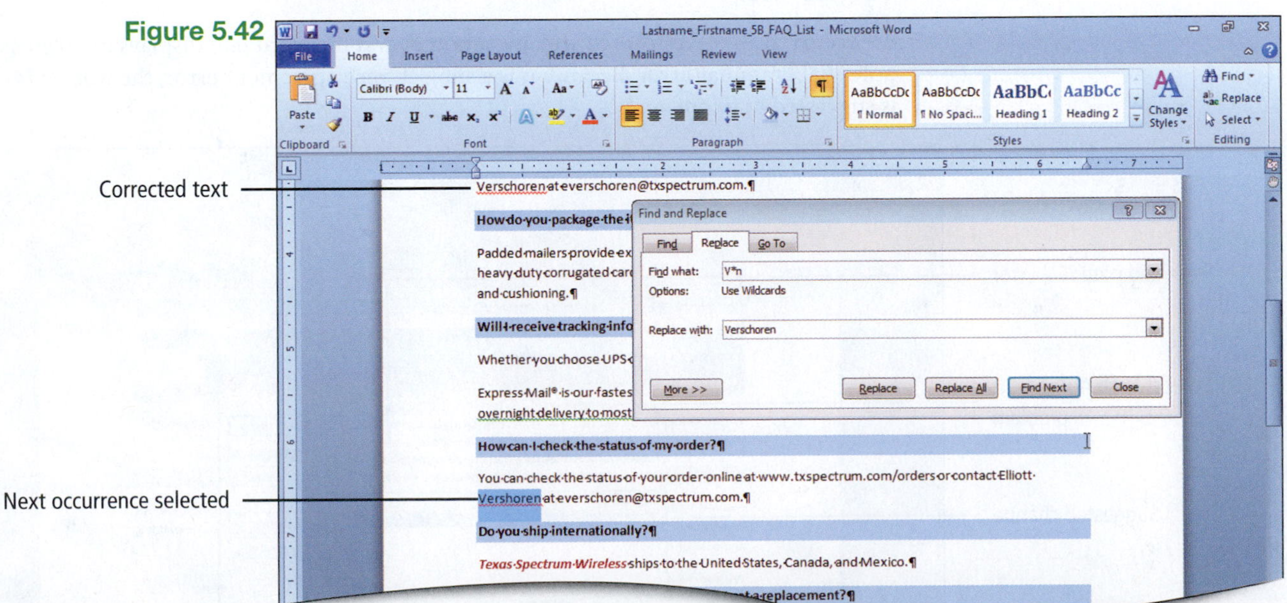

7 The selected text *Vershoren* is incorrect; click **Replace** to correct the error, and move to the next occurrence.

8 The selected text *Verschoren* is spelled correctly. Click **Find Next** to move to the next occurrence. Notice a Microsoft Office Word message box indicates that you have searched the entire document.

9 Click **OK** to close the message box. In the **Find and Replace** dialog box, click the **More** button, click to deselect the **Use wildcards** check box, and then click the **Less** button to restore the dialog box to its default settings. **Close** the **Find and Replace** dialog box.

10 **Save** the document.

Activity 5.21 | Using the Spelling and Grammar Checker

Initiate the Spelling & Grammar command to check an entire document. In this activity, you will use the Spelling and Grammar dialog box to view additional options and correct the identified errors in the document.

1 Press Ctrl + Home. On the **Review tab**, in the **Proofing group**, click the **Spelling & Grammar** button.

The first suggested error—*Eliott*—displays.

> **Alert! | Spelling and Grammar Selections May Differ**
>
> Flagged errors depend on the Proofing settings in the Word Options area, or on the actions of others who might have used the computer at which you are working. Not all of the potential errors listed in this activity may display in your spelling and grammar check. Your document may also display errors not noted here. If you encounter flagged words or phrases that are not included here, take appropriate action.

2 If *Eliott* is indicated as a spelling error, in the **Spelling and Grammar** dialog box, click **Ignore All**.

All occurrences of *Eliott* are now ignored, and the word *Verschoren* displays in red as a potential spelling error.

3 If *Verschoren* is indicated as a spelling error, click **Ignore All**. Compare your screen with Figure 5.43.

All occurrences of *Verschoren* are now ignored, and the word *add* displays in green as a potential grammar error. Because it is a subject-verb agreement error, the word *adds* is suggested to fix the error.

Figure 5.43

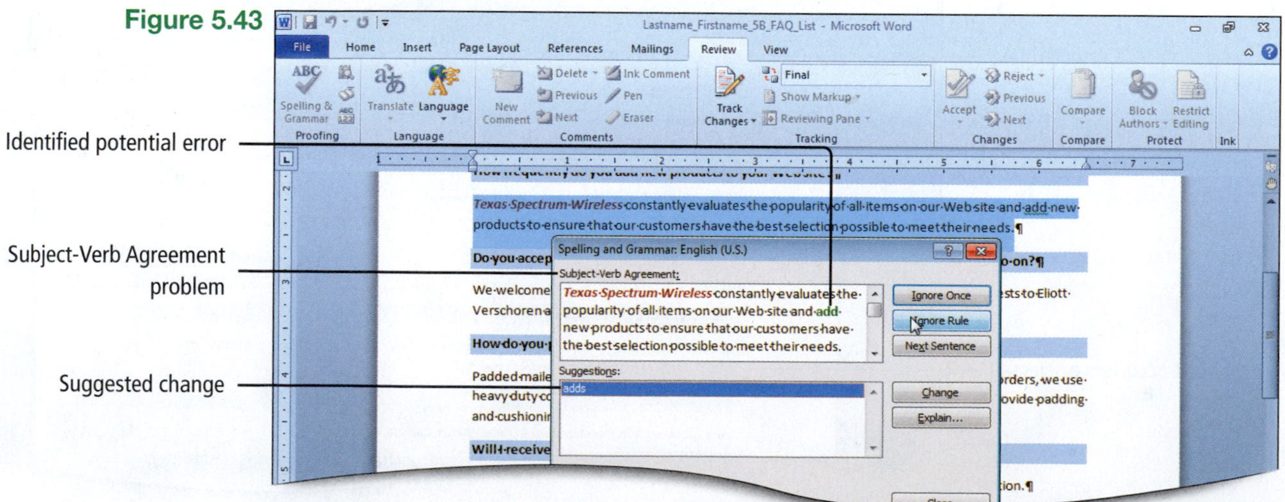

4 In the **Spelling and Grammar** dialog box, click the **Explain** button. In the displayed **Word Help** dialog box, read the displayed text.

When Word detects a potential grammatical error, you can read a detailed explanation of the problem.

5 **Close** [button] the **Word Help** dialog box. In the **Spelling and Grammar** dialog box, if necessary, under **Suggestions**, select *adds*, and then click the **Change** button.

The correction is made and the next identified error is highlighted.

6 Near the bottom of the **Spelling and Grammar** dialog box, click the **Options** button to display the **Proofing** category of the **Word Options** dialog box.

7 In the **Word Options** dialog box, under **When correcting spelling and grammar in Word**, notice that the option **Use contextual spelling** is selected. Compare your screen with Figure 5.44.

When this option is selected, Word will flag potential word usage errors and display with a blue underline.

Figure 5.44

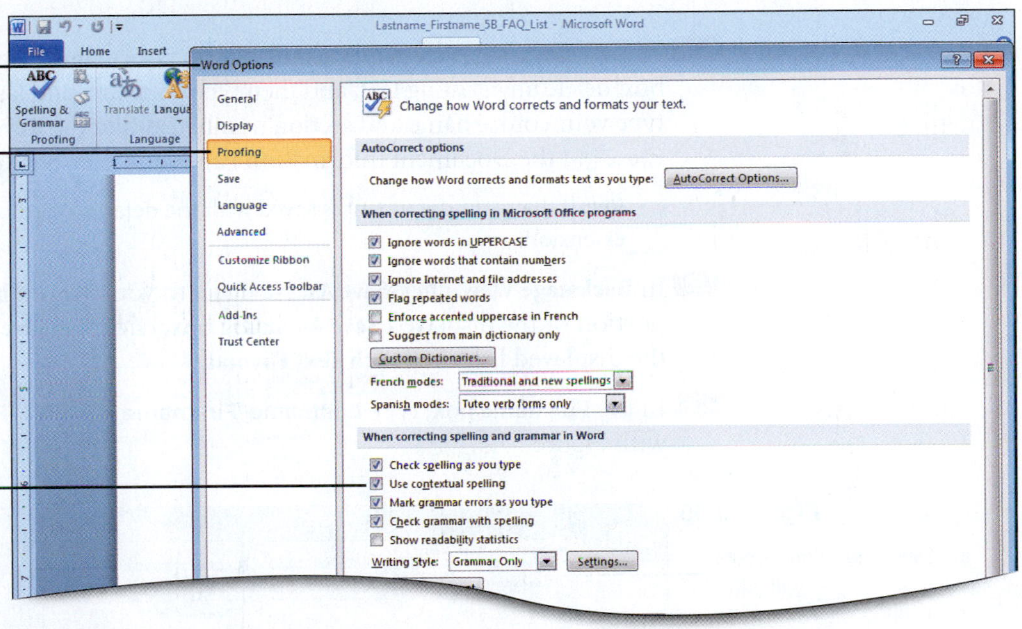

8 Click **OK** to close the **Word Options** dialog box.

9 In the **Spelling and Grammar** dialog box, if *hour* is highlighted as a contextual error, under **Suggestions**, select *our*, and then click the **Change** button. If *hour* is not identified as an error, proceed to Step 10.

In this case, Word identified *hour* as a word that is spelled correctly but used in the wrong context.

10 Click **Ignore All** as necessary to ignore the proper names *Josette* and *Lovrick*.

11 Continue to the end of the document, and click **Ignore Once** for the foreign words.

A message indicates that the spelling and grammar check is complete.

12 Click **OK** to close the message box. **Save** [icon] the document.

Objective 8 | Save in Other File Formats

If you send a Word document to someone who uses a word processing program *other* than Microsoft Word, he or she may not be able to read the document. If you expect that your document must be read or edited in another word processing program, save your Word document in ***Rich Text Format***, or ***RTF***, which is a universal document format that can be read by nearly all word processing programs, and that retains most text and paragraph formatting. Saving a document in the RTF file format adds the *.rtf* extension to the document file name. An RTF file that you might receive can be easily converted to the Word file format.

Activity 5.22 | Saving a Document in RTF Format

When you save a Word document as an RTF file, all but the most complex formatting is translated into a format usable by most word processing programs. Eliott Verschoren is sending the FAQ list to his sales managers for review before saving it as a Web page. In this activity, you will save the FAQ list as an RTF file to ensure that all the managers can review the document.

1 Display **Backstage** view, and then display the **Document Information Panel**. In the **Author** box, delete any existing text, and then type your first and last names. In the **Subject** box, type your course name and section number, and in the **Keywords** box, type **faq list** **Close** [×] the Document Information Panel, and then **Save** [💾] your document.

Recall that your document is saved with the default Word file format with the *.docx* file extension.

2 In **Backstage** view, click **Save As**. Navigate to your **Word Chapter 5** folder. In the lower portion of the displayed **Save As** dialog box, click the **Save as type arrow**, and then in the displayed list, click **Rich Text Format**.

3 In the **File name** box, type **Lastname_Firstname_5B_FAQ_RTF** Compare your screen with Figure 5.45.

Figure 5.45

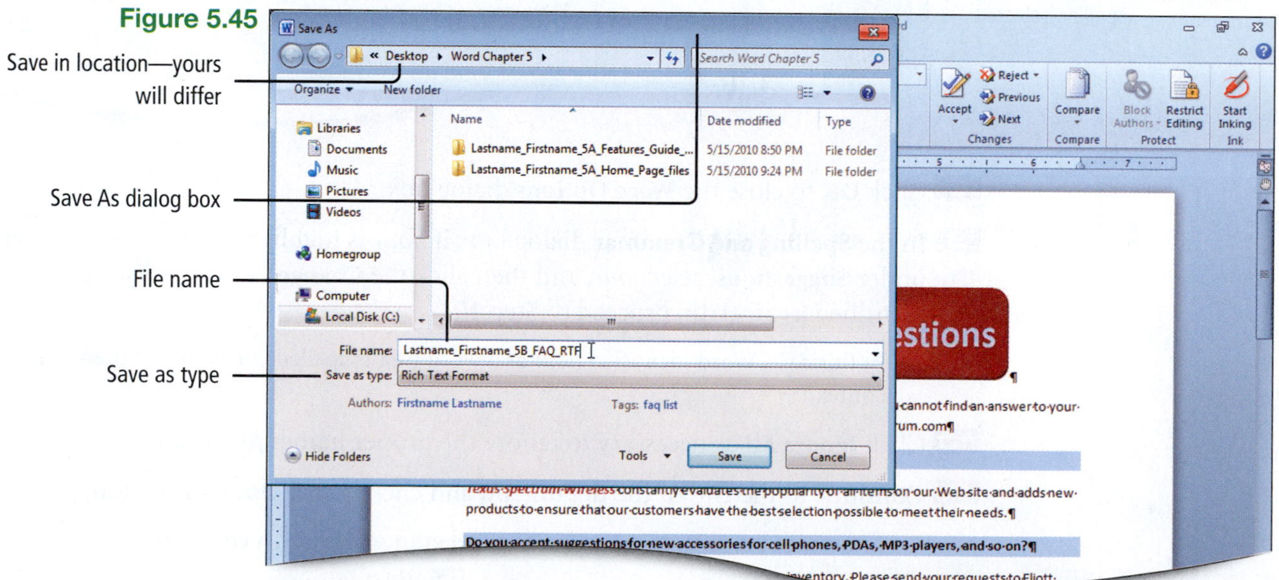

4 Click **Save**. Scroll to the bottom of **Page 1**, and then double-click the footer. Right-click the file name, and then from the shortcut menu, click **Update Field** to update the file name and format. **Close** the footer area.

5 Display **Backstage** view, click **Properties**, and then click **Advanced Properties**.

Because the document is saved as an RTF file, a Properties dialog box displays instead of the Document Information Panel.

6 Click the **Summary tab**, if necessary, and then in the **Keywords** box, position the insertion point to the right of the existing text and type **, rtf** Compare your screen with Figure 5.46.

Figure 5.46

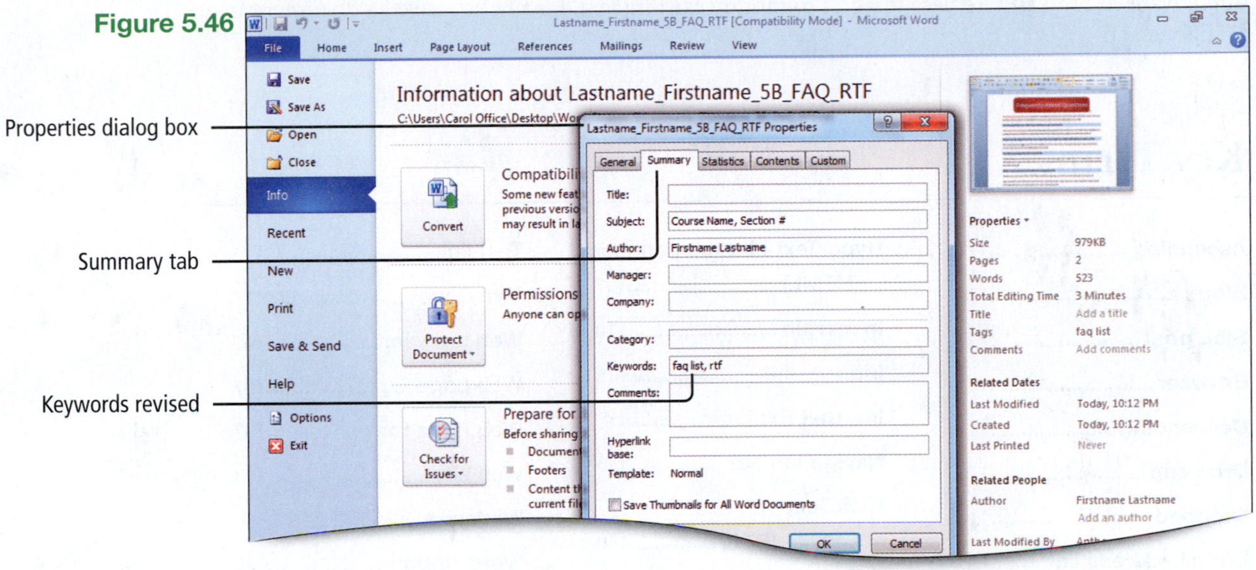

7 Click **OK** to close the **Properties** dialog box, and then click **Save**. Print, or submit electronically, your two files as directed by your instructor. Click **Exit** to exit Word.

More Knowledge | Saving in PDF or XPS Formats

Microsoft Word enables you to save documents in other file formats such as PDF—Portable Document Format—and XPS—XML Paper Specification. Click the File tab, and then click Share. On the Send screen, under File Types, click Create PDF/XPS Document. On the displayed screen, click Create a PDF/XPS.

End You have completed Project 5B

Content-Based Assessments

Summary

In this chapter you saved documents as Web pages, added hyperlinks, and inserted a page background, a drop cap, and graphics. You created a blog post. You examined Word options to identify how you can personalize Word settings. To facilitate using the Office Clipboard to copy and paste text, you changed the view and zoom settings. You used the Research task pane to locate new information and advanced Find and Replace features to modify existing text. Finally, you saved a document in an RTF format.

Key Terms

Matching

Match each term in the second column with its correct definition in the first column by writing the letter of the term on the blank line in front of the correct definition.

____ 1. A file coded in HTML that can be viewed using a browser.
____ 2. The markup language that communicates color and graphics in a format that all computers can understand and that is used to display documents on the Internet.
____ 3. The software that interprets files and displays them as Web pages.
____ 4. The position of a drop cap when it is within the text of the paragraph.
____ 5. The position of a drop cap when it is in the left margin of a paragraph.
____ 6. The action of ordering data, usually in alphabetical or numeric order.
____ 7. Text, buttons, or pictures that, when clicked, access other Web pages.
____ 8. A group of related Web pages.
____ 9. A hyperlink applied to a word or phrase.
____ 10. A hyperlink that connects to another page in the same Web site.
____ 11. A Web site that displays dated entries.
____ 12. An individual article entered on a Web site with a time and date stamp.
____ 13. A collection of settings you can change to personalize Word.
____ 14. A Word feature used to find synonyms for selected text.
____ 15. A file format that can be read by many word processing programs.

A Blog
B Blog post
C Dropped
D HTML
E Hyperlinks
F In margin
G Internal link
H RTF
I Sort
J Text link
K Thesaurus
L Web browser
M Web page
N Web site
O Word Options

Multiple Choice

Circle the correct answer.

1. The file type used to save a document in HTML format, with some elements saved in a separate folder, is:
   A. PDF **B.** Single File Web Page **C.** Web Page
2. A large, capital letter at the beginning of a paragraph that displays on several lines is:
   A. a drop cap **B.** a Quick Part **C.** an embedded cap
3. Numerical data that is arranged from largest to smallest is in:
   A. ascending order **B.** descending order **C.** reverse order
4. The Web browser developed by Microsoft is:
   A. Explorer **B.** Internet Explorer **C.** Windows Explorer
5. A series of text links across the top or bottom of a Web page is called the:
   A. command bar **B.** navigation bar **C.** site map
6. The hyperlink type that causes an e-mail message window to open when clicked is:
   A. a contact link **B.** an e-mail address link **C.** an e-mail message link
7. A zoom setting that decreases the magnification of a document is:
   A. Two Page **B.** 300% **C.** 200%
8. Copyrighted information may be used for educational purposes according to the:
   A. Copied Works guidelines **B.** Educational Research guidelines **C.** Fair Use guidelines
9. A special character such as * or ? that can be part of a search term is called a:
   A. search card **B.** search symbol **C.** wildcard
10. The term RTF stands for:
    A. Rich Text File **B.** Rich Text Format **C.** Rich Type Format

Content-Based Assessments

Apply 5A skills from these Objectives:

1. Create a Web Page from a Word Document
2. Insert and Modify Hyperlinks in a Web Page
3. Create a Blog Post

Skills Review | Project 5C Awards Information

In the following Skills Review, you will modify and add hyperlinks to the Web page containing nomination information for the Employee of the Year Award that is given to outstanding individuals at Texas Spectrum Wireless. You will also create a blog related to the nomination process. Your completed documents will look similar to Figure 5.47, although your text wrapping may vary.

Project Files

For Project 5C, you will need the following files:

w05C_Awards_Information
w05C_Nomination_Form

You will save your documents as:

Lastname_Firstname_5C_Awards_Information
Lastname_Firstname_5C_Nomination_Form
Lastname_Firstname_5C_Awards_Blog

Project Results

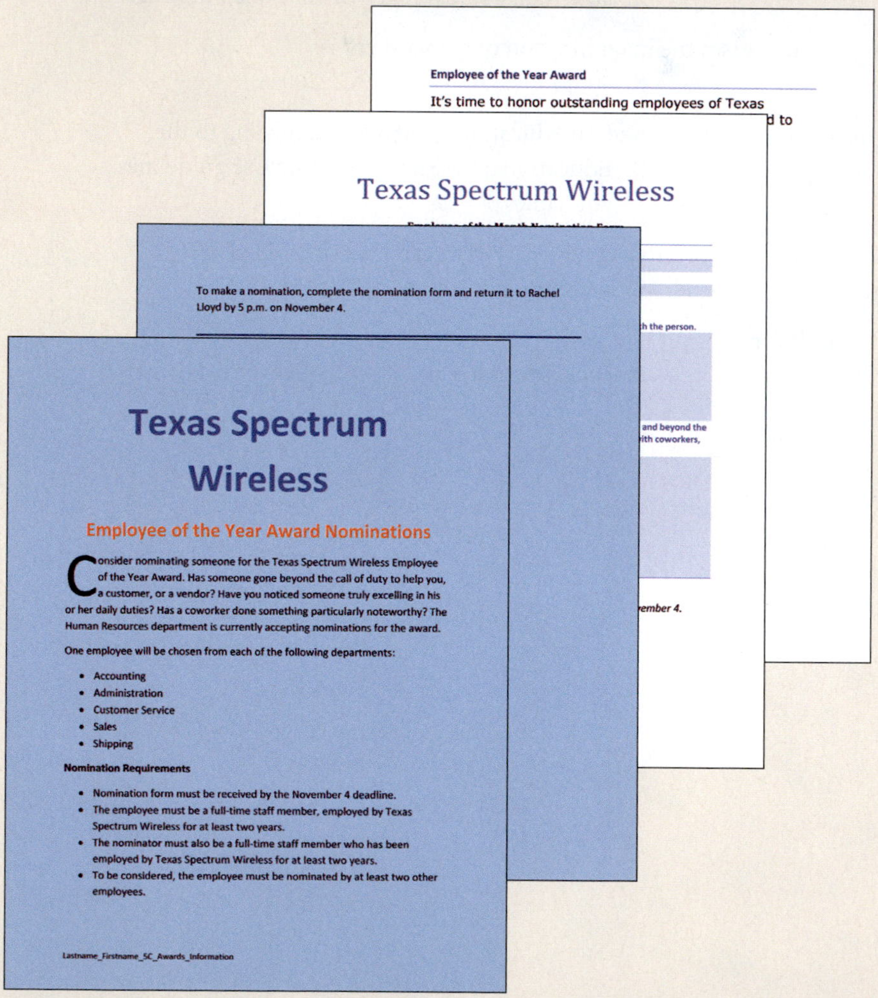

Figure 5.47

(Project 5C Awards Information continues on the next page)

Skills Review | Project **5C** Awards Information (continued)

1 **Start** Word, and then open the file **w05C_Awards_Information**. From **Backstage** view, display the **Save As** dialog box, navigate to your **Word Chapter 5** folder, and then click the **Save as type arrow**. In the displayed list, click **Web Page**. Near the bottom of the dialog box, click the **Change Title** button, and then in the displayed **Enter Text** dialog box, in the **Page title** box, type **Awards Information** Click **OK**. In the **File name** box, using your own name, type **Lastname_Firstname_5C_Awards_Information** and then press Enter.

a. On the **Insert tab**, in the **Header & Footer group**, click the **Footer** button, click **Edit Footer**, and then use **Quick Parts** to insert the file name. **Close** the footer area.

b. Select the first paragraph—*Texas Spectrum Wireless*. On the Mini toolbar, change the **Font Size** to **48**, apply **Bold** and **Center**. Click the **Font Color button arrow**, and then in the fifth column, click the fifth color—**Blue, Accent 1, Darker 25%**.

c. Select the second paragraph, which begins *Employee*. Change the **Font Size** to **24**, apply **Bold**, and then click **Center**. Click the **Font Color button arrow**, and then in the last column, click the fifth color—**Orange, Accent 6, Darker 25%**.

d. Select the remaining text in the document, and then change the **Font Size** to **14**.

2 On the **Page Layout tab**, in the **Page Background group**, click the **Page Color** button, and then in the fourth column, click the second color—**Dark Blue, Text 2, Lighter 80%**.

a. Click to position the insertion point to the left of the paragraph that begins *Consider*. On the **Insert tab**, in the **Text group**, click the **Drop Cap** button, and then click **Dropped**.

b. Click to position the insertion point to the left of the paragraph that begins *Administration*. Beginning with the paragraph *Administration*, select the five paragraphs that comprise the departments—ending with the paragraph *Customer Service*. On the **Home tab**, in the **Paragraph group**, click the **Sort** button. In the **Sort Text** dialog box, click **OK** to accept the default settings. With the paragraphs still selected, in the **Paragraph group**, click the **Bullets** button, and then click anywhere to deselect the list.

c. Select the paragraph *Nomination Requirements* and apply **Bold**. Click to position the insertion point to the left of the paragraph that begins *Nomination form must be*. Beginning with the paragraph *Nomination form*, select the four paragraphs that comprise the requirements—ending with the paragraph that begins *To be considered*. On the **Home tab**, in the **Paragraph group**, click the **Bullets** button, and then click anywhere to deselect. **Save** your changes.

3 In the paragraph that begins *To make a nomination*, click to position the insertion point to the right of the period at the end of the sentence, and then press Enter. On the **Home tab**, in the **Paragraph group**, click the **Border button arrow**, and then click **Horizontal Line**.

a. Point to the inserted line and right-click. From the shortcut menu, click **Format Horizontal Line**. In the **Format Horizontal Line** dialog box, change the **Height** to **2 pt**. Under **Color**, click the **arrow**, and then in the fourth column, click the fifth color—**Dark Blue, Text 2, Darker 25%**. Click **OK**, and then click anywhere to deselect the line. **Save** your changes.

b. From **Backstage** view, display the **Open** dialog box, and navigate to your student files. If necessary, click the Files of type arrow, and then click All Word Documents. Open the file **w05C_Nomination_Form**. From **Backstage** view, display the **Save As** dialog box, and then navigate to your **Word Chapter 5** folder. In the lower portion of the **Save As** dialog box, click the **Save as type arrow**, and then click **Web Page**.

c. Near the bottom of the dialog box, click the **Change Title** button, and then as the **Page title**, type **Nomination Form** Click **OK**, and then in the **File name** box, type **Lastname_Firstname_5C_Nomination_Form** Click **Save**.

d. On the **Insert tab**, in the **Header & Footer group**, click the **Footer** button, click **Edit Footer**, and then use **Quick Parts** to insert the file name in the footer. **Close** the footer area. In **Backstage** view, click **Properties**, and then click **Advanced Properties**. In the displayed dialog box, on the **Summary tab**, in the **Author** box, delete any existing text, and then type your first and last names. In the **Subject** box, type your course name and section number, and in the **Keywords** box, type **awards, nomination form** Click **OK**, click **Save**, and then **Close** the document.

(Project 5C Awards Information continues on the next page)

Skills Review | Project 5C Awards Information (continued)

4 With your **Lastname_Firstname_5C_Awards_Information** document displayed, press Ctrl + End. Select the text *Nomination Form*. On the **Insert tab**, in the **Links group**, click the **Hyperlink** button. In the **Insert Hyperlink** dialog box, under **Link to**, click **Existing File or Web Page**, if necessary.

a. In the **Look in** box, if necessary navigate to your **Word Chapter 5** folder, click your **Lastname_Firstname_5C_Nomination_Form** document, and then click the **ScreenTip** button. In the **ScreenTip text** box, type **Nomination Form** and then click **OK** two times.

b. Select the text *Rachel Lloyd*, and then display the **Insert Hyperlink** dialog box. Under **Link to**, click **E-mail Address**. In the **E-mail address** box, type **rlloyd@txspectrum.com** As the **ScreenTip text**, type **Human Relations Director** Click **OK** two times.

c. At the bottom of the Web page, point to *Rachel Lloyd* to display the ScreenTip. Right-click the **Rachel Lloyd** hyperlink, and then from the shortcut menu, click **Edit Hyperlink**. Click the **ScreenTip** button, and then edit the **ScreenTip text** to indicate **Click here to send an e-mail message to Rachel Lloyd** Click **OK** two times, and then point to the **Rachel Lloyd** link to display the ScreenTip.

d. Press Ctrl + Home. In **Backstage** view, click **Properties**, and then click **Advanced Properties**. In the displayed dialog box, on the **Summary** tab, in the **Author** box, delete any existing text, and then type your first and last names. In the **Subject** box, type your course name and section number, and in the **Keywords** box, type **awards information, Web page** Click **OK**.

e. **Save** your changes, and **Close** the document.

5 If necessary, start **Word**. In **Backstage** view, click the **New tab**, click **Blog post**, and then on the right, click **Create**. If the **Register a Blog Account** dialog box displays, click the **Register Later** button.

a. From **Backstage** view, display the **Save As** dialog box, navigate to your **Word Chapter 5** folder, name the file **Lastname_Firstname_5C_Awards_Blog** and then click **Save**.

b. Click anywhere in the **Enter Post Title Here** field to select the placeholder text, and then type **Employee of the Year Award** Click under the thin blue line in the body text area, and then type **It's time to honor outstanding employees of Texas Spectrum Wireless. Nominations must be submitted to Rachel Lloyd by 5 p.m. on November 4.**

c. Select all the body text, and then change the **Font** to **Verdana** and the **Font Size** to **16**. In the second sentence, select *Rachel Lloyd*. Click the **Insert tab**, and then in the **Links group**, click the **Hyperlink** button. Under **Link to**, click **E-mail Address**, and then in the **E-mail address** box, type **rlloyd@txspectrum.com** Click **OK**.

d. Click to position your insertion point at the end of the paragraph, press Enter two times, and then type your first and last names.

e. From **Backstage** view, display the **Document Information Panel**. In the **Author** box, delete any existing text, and then type your first and last names. In the **Subject** box, type your course name and section number, and in the **Keywords** box, type **awards nominations, blog** **Close** the Document Information Panel. **Save** your document, and then **Exit** Word.

6 As directed by your instructor print, or submit electronically, the three files—the blog post and two Web pages—that are the results of this project.

End **You have completed Project 5C**

Apply **5B** skills from these Objectives:

- **4** Locate Word Settings to Personalize Word 2010
- **5** Collect and Paste Images and Text
- **6** Locate Supporting Information
- **7** Use Advanced Find and Replace and Proofing Options
- **8** Save in Other File Formats

Skills Review | Project 5D Outdoor Accessories

In the following Skills Review, you will create a document for Eliott Verschoren, Marketing Vice President of Texas Spectrum Wireless, which details the waterproof and ruggedized accessories sold by the company. Your completed documents will look similar to Figure 5.48.

Project Files

For Project 5D, you will need the following files:

w05D_Outdoor_Accessories
w05D_Product_Info
w05D_Product_Images

You will save your documents as:

Lastname_Firstname_5D_Outdoor_Accessories
Lastname_Firstname_5D_Accessories_RTF

Project Results

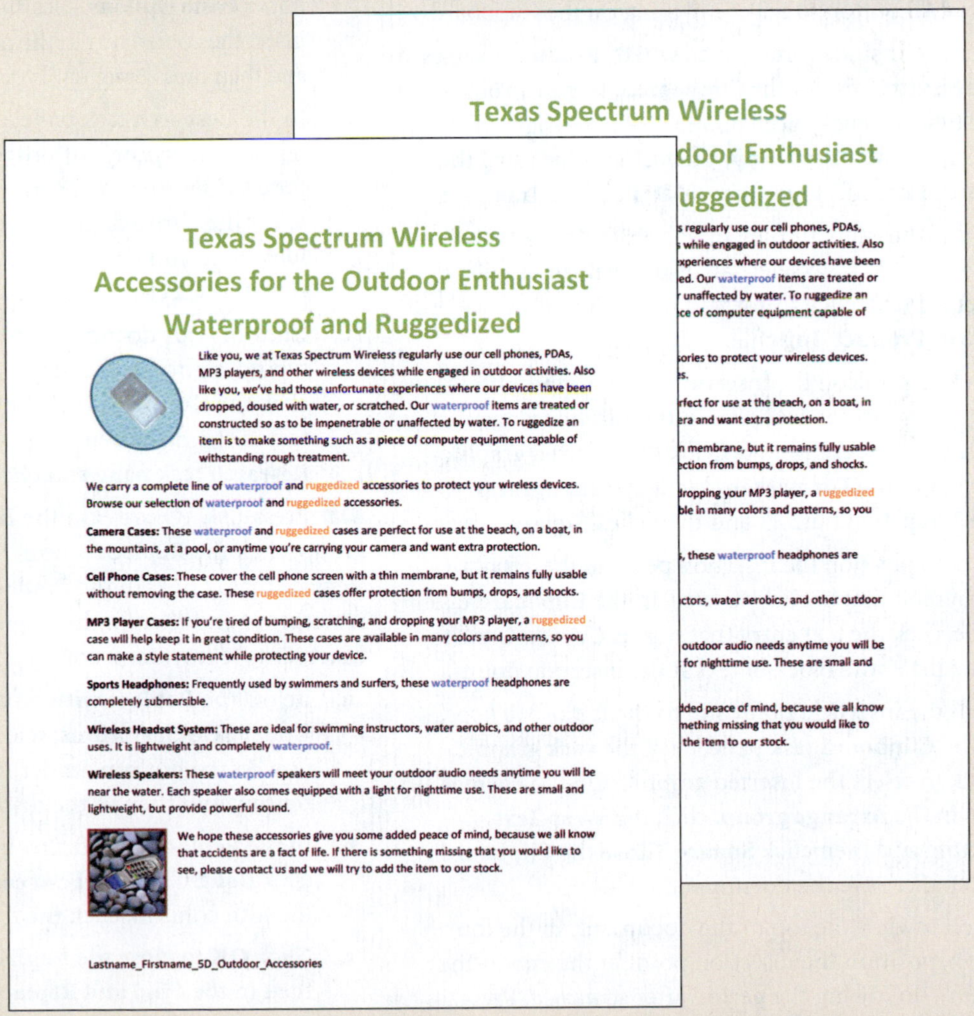

Texas Spectrum Wireless

Accessories for the Outdoor Enthusiast

Waterproof and Ruggedized

Like you, we at Texas Spectrum Wireless regularly use our cell phones, PDAs, MP3 players, and other wireless devices while engaged in outdoor activities. Also like you, we've had those unfortunate experiences where our devices have been dropped, doused with water, or scratched. Our waterproof items are treated or constructed so as to be impenetrable or unaffected by water. To ruggedize an item is to make something such as a piece of computer equipment capable of withstanding rough treatment.

We carry a complete line of waterproof and ruggedized accessories to protect your wireless devices. Browse our selection of waterproof and ruggedized accessories.

Camera Cases: These waterproof and ruggedized cases are perfect for use at the beach, on a boat, in the mountains, at a pool, or anytime you're carrying your camera and want extra protection.

Cell Phone Cases: These cover the cell phone screen with a thin membrane, but it remains fully usable without removing the case. These ruggedized cases offer protection from bumps, drops, and shocks.

MP3 Player Cases: If you're tired of bumping, scratching, and dropping your MP3 player, a ruggedized case will help keep it in great condition. These cases are available in many colors and patterns, so you can make a style statement while protecting your device.

Sports Headphones: Frequently used by swimmers and surfers, these waterproof headphones are completely submersible.

Wireless Headset System: These are ideal for swimming instructors, water aerobics, and other outdoor uses. It is lightweight and completely waterproof.

Wireless Speakers: These waterproof speakers will meet your outdoor audio needs anytime you will be near the water. Each speaker also comes equipped with a light for nighttime use. These are small and lightweight, but provide powerful sound.

We hope these accessories give you some added peace of mind, because we all know that accidents are a fact of life. If there is something missing that you would like to see, please contact us and we will try to add the item to our stock.

Lastname_Firstname_5D_Outdoor_Accessories

Figure 5.48

(Project 5D Outdoor Accessories continues on the next page)

Skills Review | Project **5D** Outdoor Accessories (continued)

1 **Start** Word. From your student files, open the file **w05D_Outdoor_Accessories.** In **Backstage** view, display the **Save As** dialog box, navigate to your **Word Chapter 5** folder, and then save the document as **Lastname_Firstname_5D_Outdoor_Accessories**

a. At the bottom of **Page 1**, use **Quick Parts** to insert the file name in the footer.

b. Select the first three paragraphs, and then on the Mini toolbar, change the **Font Size** to **28**, apply **Bold**, and click **Center**. Click the **Font Color button arrow**, and then in the seventh column, click the first color—**Olive Green, Accent 3**.

c. On the **Home tab**, in the **Clipboard group**, click the **Dialog Box Launcher** to display the **Clipboard** task pane. If necessary, at the top of the task pane, click the **Clear All** button to delete anything on the Clipboard.

d. From your student files, open **w05D_Product_Images**. If necessary, display the **Clipboard** task pane. Point to the first graphic—a cell phone in water—right-click, and then click **Copy**. **Copy** the *rock* graphic using the same technique. **Close** the **w05D_Product_Images** file.

e. From your student files, open **w05D_Product_Info**. Press Ctrl + A to select all of the text, right-click the selected text, click **Copy**, and then **Close** the **w05D_Product_Info** file.

2 Click to position the insertion point to the left of the paragraph that begins *Like you*. In the **Clipboard** task pane, click the **water** graphic. Click the inserted graphic to select it. On the **Format tab**, in the **Arrange group**, click the **Wrap Text** button, and then click **Square**.

a. Click to position the insertion point to the left of the paragraph that begins *We hope*. In the **Clipboard** task pane, click the text entry that begins *Camera Cases* to paste the entire block of text at the insertion point.

b. With the insertion point still to the left of *We hope*, in the **Clipboard** task pane, click the **rock** graphic. Click to select the inserted graphic. On the **Format tab**, in the **Arrange group**, click the **Wrap Text** button, and then click **Square**. **Close** the **Clipboard** task pane. **Save** the document.

3 Scroll to view the top of the document. In the fourth paragraph, position the insertion point at the end of the paragraph—following the period after *scratched*. Press Spacebar, type **Our waterproof items are** and then press Spacebar.

a. On the **Review tab**, in the **Proofing group**, click the **Research** button to display the **Research** task pane on the right.

b. In the **Research** task pane, click in the **Search for** box, delete any text, and then type **waterproof** Under the **Search for** box, in the second box—the **Search location** box—click the **arrow**. In the displayed list, click **Encarta Dictionary: English (North America)**. Under **Encarta Dictionary**, locate the text *impervious to water*. Indented and immediately below the definition, select the text that begins *treated or constructed* and ends with *by water*. Right-click the selection and then from the shortcut menu, click **Copy**.

c. Click in your document at the point you stopped typing, right-click, and then from the shortcut menu, under **Paste Options**, click the **Keep Text Only** button to insert the copied text in the document. Type a period, and then press Spacebar. Type **To ruggedize an item is**

d. In the **Research** task pane, in the **Search for** box, replace *waterproof* with **ruggedize** and then press Enter. Under **Encarta Dictionary**, locate and then select the entire definition that begins *to make something* and ends with *rough treatment*. Right-click the selection and click **Copy**.

e. Click in your document at the point you stopped typing, right-click, and then under **Paste Options**, click the **Keep Text Only** button to insert the copied text in the document. Type a period. **Close** the **Research** task pane and click **Save**.

4 Press Ctrl + Home. On the **Home tab**, in the **Editing group**, click the **Replace** button to display the **Find and Replace** dialog box. In the **Find what** box, type **waterproof** and then in the **Replace with** box, type the exact same text **waterproof**

a. Below the **Replace with** box, click the **More** button. Under **Search Options**, select the **Match case** check box. At the bottom, under **Replace**, click the **Format** button, and then in the displayed list, click **Font**.

b. In the **Replace Font** dialog box, under **Font style**, click **Bold**. Click the **Font color arrow**, and then in the fifth column, click the first color—**Blue, Accent 1**.

c. Click **OK** to close the **Replace Font** dialog box, and then in the **Find and Replace** dialog box, click **Replace All**. When a **Microsoft Office Word** message displays indicating that you have made *7* replacements, click **OK**.

(Project 5D Outdoor Accessories continues on the next page)

Skills Review | Project 5D Outdoor Accessories (continued)

d. Using the same technique, replace all instances of *ruggedized* and select **Match case**. For the replaced text, change the **Font style** to **Bold** and for the **Font color**, in the last column, click the first color—**Orange, Accent 6**. When a **Microsoft Office Word** message displays indicating that you have made *5* replacements, click **OK**.

e. In the **Find and Replace** dialog box, **Delete** the text in the **Find what** and **Replace with** boxes. Deselect **Match case**, click the **No Formatting** button, and then click the **Less** button. **Close** the **Find and Replace** dialog box.

5 Press Ctrl + Home. On the **Review tab**, in the **Proofing group**, click the **Spelling & Grammar** button.

a. For any contextual errors, select the suggestion if necessary, and then click **Change**. Click **Ignore Once** for all other errors. When a message indicates that the spelling and grammar check is complete, click **OK** to close the dialog box. Note: If Word does not identify *weave* and *their* as contextual errors, change the words to *we've* and *there* respectively.

b. From **Backstage** view, display the **Document Information Panel**. In the **Author** box, delete any existing text, and then type your first and last names. In the **Subject** box, type your course name and section number, and in the **Keywords** box, type **waterproof, ruggedized Close** the Document Information Panel. **Save** your document.

c. From **Backstage** view, display the **Save As** dialog box. If necessary, navigate to your **Word Chapter 5** folder. In the lower portion of the **Save As** dialog box, click the **Save as type arrow**, and then in the displayed list, click **Rich Text Format**. In the **File name** box, type **Lastname_Firstname_5D_Accessories_RTF** and then click **Save**.

d. Scroll to the bottom of the document and double-click in the footer area. Right-click the file name, and then from the shortcut menu, click **Update Field**. **Close** the footer area.

e. Display **Backstage** view, click **Properties**, and then click **Advanced Properties**. Click the **Summary tab** if necessary, and then in the **Keywords** box, position the insertion point to the right of the existing text and type **, rtf** Click **OK** to close the **Properties** dialog box, and then **Save** your document.

6 As directed by your instructor, print or submit electronically the two files—the Word document and the RTF file—that are the results of this project. **Exit** Word.

End You have completed Project 5D

Apply 5A skills from these Objectives:

1. Create a Web Page from a Word Document
2. Insert and Modify Hyperlinks in a Web Page
3. Create a Blog Post

Mastering Word | Project 5E Phone Accessories

In the following Mastering Word project, you will create a Web page for Eliott Verschoren, Marketing Vice President of Texas Spectrum Wireless, which describes the types of cell phone accessories available for purchase. You will also create a blog announcing savings on purchases. Your completed documents will look similar to Figure 5.49, although text wrapping may vary.

Project Files

For Project 5E, you will need the following files:

w05E_Phone_Accessories
w05E_Phone_Cases

You will save your documents as:

Lastname_Firstname_5E_Phone_Accessories
Lastname_Firstname_5E_Phone_Cases
Lastname_Firstname_5E_Newsletter_Offer

Project Results

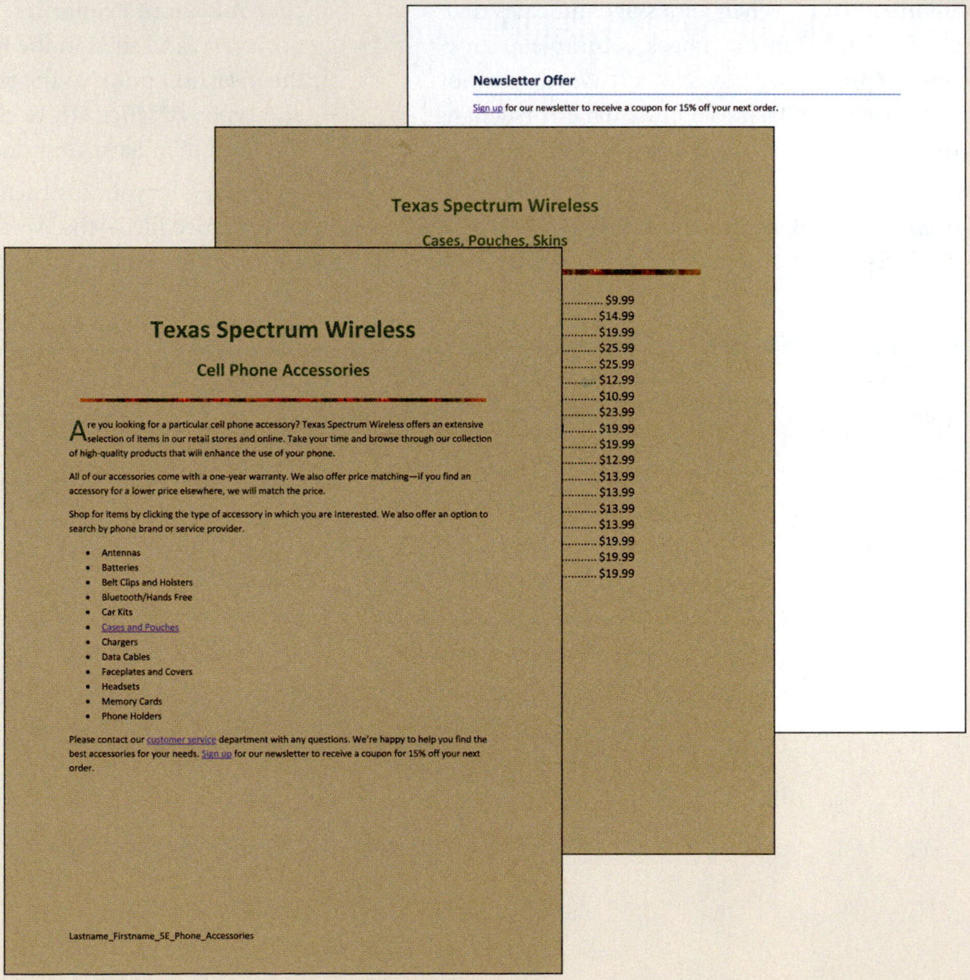

Figure 5.49

(Project 5E Phone Accessories continues on the next page)

Mastering Word | Project 5E Phone Accessories (continued)

1 **Start** Word, open the document **w05E_Phone_Accessories**, display the **Save As** dialog box, and then navigate to your **Word Chapter 5** folder. Change the **Save as type** to **Web Page**, change the title to **Cell Phone Accessories** and then save the file as **Lastname_Firstname_5E_Phone_Accessories** Insert the file name in the footer.

2 Select the first paragraph, change the **Font Size** to **28**, apply **Bold** and **Center**, and then change the **Font Color** to **Olive Green, Accent 3, Darker 50%**. Select the second paragraph, change the **Font Size** to **20**, apply **Bold** and **Center**, and then change the **Font Color** to **Olive Green, Accent 3, Darker 50%**. Set the **Page Color** to **Tan, Background 2, Darker 25%**. Click to the left of the fourth paragraph that begins *Are you looking*. Insert a **Drop Cap**, change **Lines to drop** to **2**, and then change the **Font Color** of the dropped cap to **Olive Green, Accent 3, Darker 50%**.

3 Click in the third paragraph, which is blank, display the **Borders and Shading** dialog box, and then click the **Horizontal Line** button. In the fifth row, select the first line—shades of gold, green, and red. Change the **Width** of the line to **95%** and the **Height** to **10 pt**. Click to the left of the paragraph *Cases and Pouches*. Select the next 12 paragraphs, ending with *Memory Cards*. **Sort** the list in ascending order, and then apply bullets. **Save** your document.

4 Open the document **w05E_Phone_Cases**, display the **Save As** dialog box, navigate to your **Word Chapter 5** folder, and then change the **Save as type** to **Web Page**. Change the page title to **Cases and Pouches** and then save the file as **Lastname_Firstname_5E_Phone_Cases** Insert the file name in the footer.

5 Display the **Document Information Panel**, and then click **View Properties** to display the **Properties** dialog box. If necessary, click the **Summary tab**. In the **Author** box, type your first and last names. In the **Subject** box, type your course name and section number, and in the **Keywords** box type **cases, Web page Save** your changes and **Close** the document.

6 In your displayed **Lastname_Firstname_5E_Phone_Accessories** document, in the bulleted list, select the text *Cases and Pouches*. Insert a hyperlink to the existing file in your **Word Chapter 5** folder named **Lastname_Firstname_5E_Phone_Cases**. In the last paragraph of the document, select the text *customer service department*, and insert a hyperlink to the e-mail address **service@txspectrum.com** In the last sentence, select the text *Sign up*, and insert a hyperlink to the e-mail address **newsletter@txspectrum.com**

7 Display the **Document Information Panel**, and then click **View Properties** to display the **Properties** dialog box. If necessary, click the **Summary tab**. In the **Author** box, type your first and last names. In the **Subject** box, type your course name and section number, and in the **Keywords** box, type **accessories, Web page Close** the **Properties** dialog box. **Save** your changes and **Close** the document.

8 **Create** a new **Blog post**. If necessary, in the displayed message box, click **Register Later**. Save the document in your **Word Chapter 5** folder as **Lastname_Firstname_5E_Newsletter_Offer** In the **Enter Post Title Here** field, type **Newsletter Offer** In the body text area, type **Sign up for our newsletter to receive a coupon for 15% off your next order.** Select the text *Sign up*, and then insert a hyperlink to the e-mail address **newsletter@txspectrum.com** At the end of the typed text, press Enter two times, and then type your first and last names.

9 From **Backstage** view, display the **Document Information Panel**, type your name in the **Author** box, type your course name and section number in the **Subject** box, and as the **Keywords**, type **newsletter, blog Save** and **Close** the blog post.

10 Print, or submit electronically the three files—the blog post and two Web pages—as directed by your instructor. **Exit** Word.

End **You have completed Project 5E**

Apply 5B skills from these Objectives:

4. Locate Word Settings to Personalize Word 2010
5. Collect and Paste Images and Text
6. Locate Supporting Information
7. Use Advanced Find and Replace and Proofing Options
8. Save in Other File Formats

Mastering Word | Project 5F Sale Flyer

In the following Mastering Word project, you will create an RTF document for Eliott Verschoren, Marketing Vice President of Texas Spectrum Wireless, which announces an upcoming sale. Your completed document will look similar to Figure 5.50.

Project Files

For Project 5F, you will need the following files:

w05F_Sale_Flyer
w05F_Sale_List

You will save your document as:

Lastname_Firstname_5F_Sale_Flyer

Project Results

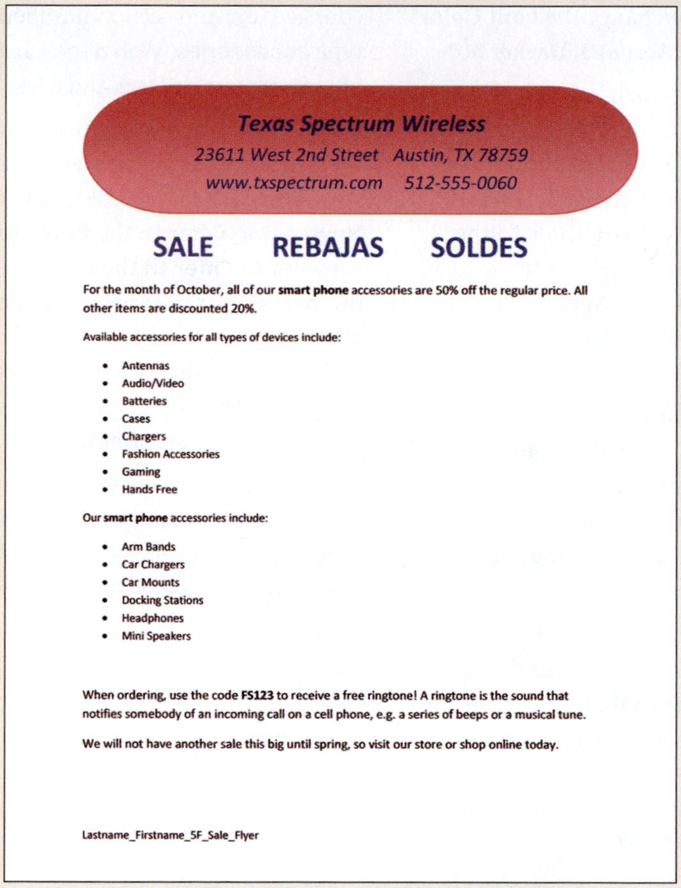
Texas Spectrum Wireless
23611 West 2nd Street Austin, TX 78759
www.txspectrum.com 512-555-0060

SALE REBAJAS SOLDES

For the month of October, all of our **smart phone** accessories are 50% off the regular price. All other items are discounted 20%.

Available accessories for all types of devices include:

- Antennas
- Audio/Video
- Batteries
- Cases
- Chargers
- Fashion Accessories
- Gaming
- Hands Free

Our **smart phone** accessories include:

- Arm Bands
- Car Chargers
- Car Mounts
- Docking Stations
- Headphones
- Mini Speakers

When ordering, use the code **FS123** to receive a free ringtone! A ringtone is the sound that notifies somebody of an incoming call on a cell phone, e.g. a series of beeps or a musical tune.

We will not have another sale this big until spring, so visit our store or shop online today.

Lastname_Firstname_5F_Sale_Flyer

Figure 5.50

(Project 5F Sale Flyer continues on the next page)

Mastering Word | Project 5F Sale Flyer (continued)

1 **Start** Word, open the file **w05F_Sale_Flyer**, and then save it in your **Word Chapter 5** folder as a **Rich Text Format** file with the name **Lastname_Firstname_5F_Sale_Flyer** Insert the file name in the footer.

2 Display the **Clipboard** task pane, and then open the document **w05F_Sale_List**. If necessary, display the **Clipboard** task pane. **Copy** the **Texas Spectrum Wireless** graphic to the Clipboard. Beginning with the text *Available accessories*, select the remaining text in the document, and then **Copy** it to the Clipboard. **Close** the **w05F_Sale_List** file.

3 Click in the blank paragraph at the top of the document, and then from the **Clipboard** task pane, **Paste** the **Texas Spectrum Wireless** graphic. Click in the blank line following the paragraph that begins *For the month*, and then from the **Clipboard** task pane, paste the text that begins *Available accessories*. In the **Clipboard** task pane, **Clear All** entries, and then **Close** the **Clipboard** task pane.

4 Click at the end of the paragraph that begins *When ordering*, press Spacebar, and then type **A ringtone is** Display the **Research** task pane, in the **Search for** box, type **ringtone** and then using the **Encarta Dictionary**, search for the definition. In the **Research** task pane, select and copy the text that begins *the sound that notifies* and ends with *a musical tune*. Paste the text in the document. Type a period.

5 At the top of the document, click to the right of *SALE*, and then press Tab two times. In the **Research** task pane, type **sale** and then translate the text to Spanish. Using the translation for *reduced prices*, copy and paste the translated text. Format the text as uppercase letters. Press Tab two times. Using the same technique, translate the text to French. Copy and paste the translated text, and then format the text as uppercase letters. **Close** the **Research** task pane.

6 Press Ctrl + Home, and then display the **Find and Replace** dialog box. In the **Find what** box, type **smart phone** In the **Replace with** box, type **smart phone** Click the **More** button, and then change the **Font style** to **Bold**. Click **OK**, and then click **Replace All**. In the **Microsoft Office Word** message box, click **OK**. In the **Find and Replace** dialog box, click in the **Replace with** box, and then click the **No Formatting** button. Click the **Less** button, and then **Close** the **Find and Replace** dialog box.

7 Display **Backstage** view, click **Properties**, and then click **Advanced Properties**. On the **Summary** tab, as the **Title**, type **Sale Flyer** In the **Author** box, type your first and last names, as the **Subject**, type your course name and section number, and then as the **Keywords**, type **sale flyer, rtf**

8 **Save** your document, print or submit electronically as directed by your instructor, and then **Exit** Word.

End **You have completed Project 5F**

Content-Based Assessments

Apply 5A and 5B skills from these Objectives:

1. Create a Web Page from a Word Document
2. Insert and Modify Hyperlinks in a Web Page
3. Create a Blog Post
4. Locate Word Settings to Personalize Word 2010
5. Collect and Paste Images and Text
6. Locate Supporting Information
7. Use Advanced Find and Replace and Proofing Options
8. Save in Other File Formats

myitlab grader

Mastering Word | Project 5G Returns Policy

In the following Mastering Word project, you will create a Web page and blog post for Josette Lovrick, Operations Manager of Texas Spectrum Wireless, that explain the return and exchange policy for the company. Your completed documents will look similar to Figure 5.51, although text wrapping may vary.

Project Files

For Project 5G, you will need the following files:

w05G_Returns_Policy
w05G_Returns_Image
w05G_Shipping_Policy

You will save your documents as:

Lastname_Firstname_5G_Returns_Policy
Lastname_Firstname_5G_Shipping_RTF
Lastname_Firstname_5G_Returns_Blog

Project Results

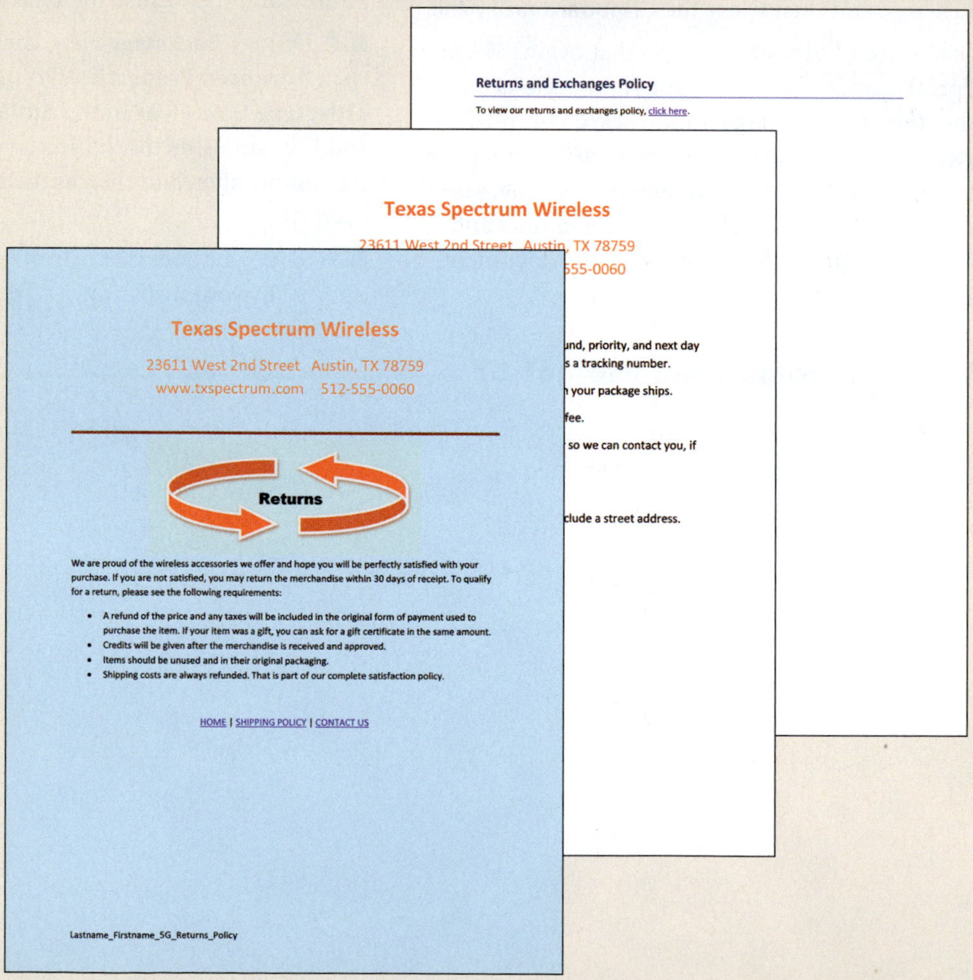

Figure 5.51

(Project 5G Returns Policy continues on the next page)

Mastering Word | Project 5G Returns Policy (continued)

1 **Start** Word, open the document **w05G_Returns_Policy**, display the **Save As** dialog box, navigate to your **Word Chapter 5** folder, and then set the document type to **Web Page**. Change the title to **Returns and Exchanges** and then save the file as **Lastname_Firstname_5G_Returns_Policy** Insert the file name in the footer.

2 Change the **Page Color** to **Aqua, Accent 5, Lighter 80%**. In the second paragraph, which is blank, display the **Borders and Shading** dialog box, and then insert a **Horizontal Line**, using the first style in the **Horizontal Line** dialog box. Format the line by changing the **Height** to **3 pt** and the **Color** to **Orange, Accent 6, Darker 50%**. Beginning with *Items*, select the next four paragraphs. **Sort** the list alphabetically and apply bullets. Display the **Clipboard** task pane and clear it if necessary.

3 Open the file **w05G_Returns_Image**. **Copy** the image to the Clipboard, and then **Close** the document. Open the file **w05G_Shipping_Policy**, display the **Save As** dialog box, navigate to your **Word Chapter 5** folder, set the file type to **Rich Text Format**, and then save as **Lastname_Firstname_5G_Shipping_RTF** Add the file name to the footer. Select and then copy to the Clipboard the first three paragraphs—the company information.

4 Display the **Document Information Panel** and click **View Properties** to display the **Properties** dialog box. If necessary, click the **Summary tab**. In the **Author** box, type your first and last names. In the **Subject** box, type your course name and section number, and then in the **Keywords** box, type **shipping policy, RTF** **Save** and **Close** the document.

5 In your **5G_Returns_Policy** document, press Ctrl + Home. In the **Clipboard** task pane, paste the text in the document. In the blank paragraph below the horizontal line, paste the image, and then clear all items and **Close** the **Clipboard** task pane. At the bottom of the document, select *HOME*, and then insert a hyperlink to **www.txspectrum.com** In the same paragraph, select the text *SHIPPING POLICY*, and then insert a hyperlink to the file in your **Word Chapter 5** folder named **Lastname_Firstname_5G_Shipping_RTF**. Select the text *CONTACT US*, and then insert a hyperlink to the e-mail address **service@txspectrum.com** Display the **Spelling and Grammar Checker**, and then take appropriate action to correct any errors.

6 Display the **Document Information Panel** and click **View Properties** to display the **Properties** dialog box. If necessary, click the **Summary tab**. As the **Author** type your first and last names, as the **Subject** type, your course name and section number, and then as the **Keywords**, type **returns, exchanges, Web page** **Save** and **Close** the document.

7 Create a new **Blog post**; if necessary, click **Register Later**. Save the blog post in your **Word Chapter 5** folder as **Lastname_Firstname_5G_Returns_Blog** As the title, type **Returns and Exchanges Policy** In the body text area, type **To view our returns and exchanges policy, click here.** Press Enter two times, and then type your name. Select the text *click here*, and then insert a hyperlink to your **Lastname_Firstname_5G_Returns_Policy** file.

8 Display the **Document Information Panel**. As the **Author**, type your first and last names. As the **Subject** type, your course name and section number, and then as the **Keywords**, type **returns, exchanges, blog** **Save** your blog post. Print or submit electronically your three files—the blog, the Web page, and the RTF document—as directed by your instructor. **Exit** Word.

End **You have completed Project 5G**

Content-Based Assessments

Apply a combination of the **5A** and **5B** skills.

GO! Fix It | Project 5H Company Overview

Project Files

For Project 5H, you will need the following file:

w05H_Company_Overview

You will save your document as:

Lastname_Firstname_5H_Company_Overview

Open the file **w05H_Company_Overview**, save the file in your **Word Chapter 5** folder as a Web Page, change the page title to **About TSW** and then for the file name, type **Lastname_Firstname_5H_Company_Overview**

This document requires additional formatting and contains errors. Read and examine the document, and then make modifications to improve the overall appearance and correct the errors. Include the following changes and make any other necessary corrections:

- Use the Module theme.
- Apply the Title and Heading 1 styles to the first two paragraphs, respectively.
- Insert and format a drop cap as the first character in the third paragraph, dropped two lines and using the font color Gold, Accent 1.
- Set the page color to Green, Accent 4, Lighter 80%.
- For the horizontal line under the fourth paragraph, set the width to 95%.
- Sort the last five paragraphs of the document alphabetically.
- Replace all occurrences of *TSW* with *Texas Spectrum Wireless* using the Match Case option and Bold font style.
- Create hyperlinks for the last five paragraphs as follows:

Contact Us	**jlovrick@txspectrum.com**
Customer Service	**www.txspectrum.com/service**
Payment Methods	**www.txspectrum.com/payment**
Returns and Exchanges	**www.txspectrum.com/returns**
Shipping Policies	**www.txspectrum.com/shipping**

Things you should know to complete this project:

- Displaying formatting marks will assist in editing the document.
- There are no errors in fonts or font sizes.

Save your document, and add the file name to the footer. In the Document Information Panel, type your first and last names in the Author box and your course name and section number in the Subject box. In the Keywords box, type **Web page, overview** Save your document, and then print or submit electronically as directed by your instructor.

End You have completed Project 5H

Apply a combination of the **5A** and **5B** skills.

GO! Make It | Project 5I Screen Protectors

Project Files

For Project 5I, you will need the following file:

w05I_Screen_Protectors

You will save your document as:

Lastname_Firstname_5I_Screen_Protectors

From the student files that accompany this textbook, open the file **w05I_Screen_Protectors** and create the document shown in Figure 5.52. The page color is Blue, Accent 1, Lighter 60%. The three headings are centered and formatted with styles based on the Office theme. Use **www.txspectrum.com** and **yreynolds@txspectrum.com** for the Home and Contact Us hyperlinks. The displayed clip art is 1" high—if necessary, substitute another image. Add your name, your course name and section, and the keywords **screen protectors** to the document properties. Save the file in your **Word Chapter 5** folder as **Lastname_Firstname_5I_Screen_Protectors** Add the file name to the footer, and then print or submit electronically as directed by your instructor.

Project Results

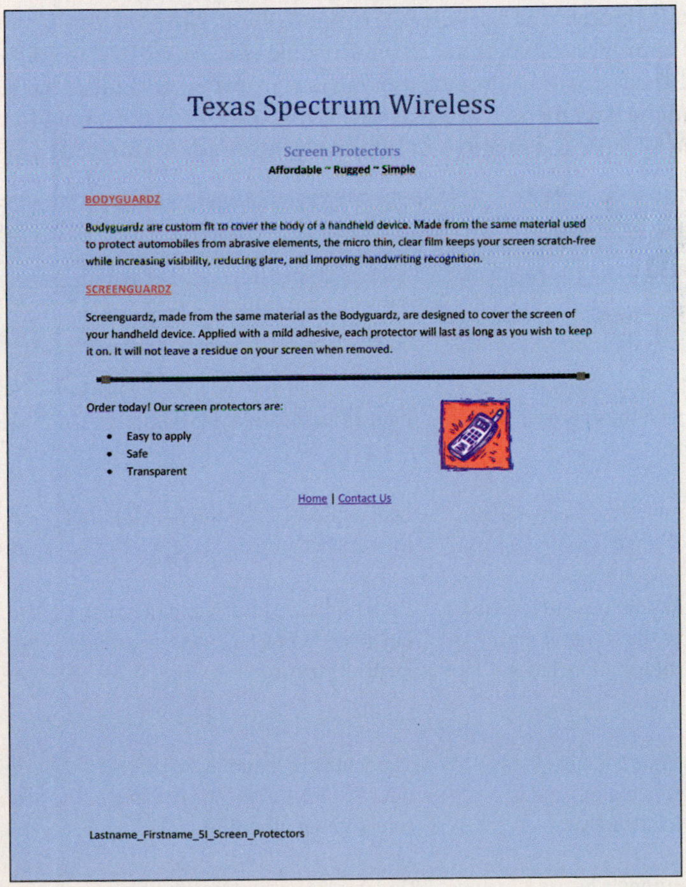

Texas Spectrum Wireless

Screen Protectors

Affordable ~ Rugged ~ Simple

BODYGUARDZ

Bodyguardz are custom fit to cover the body of a handheld device. Made from the same material used to protect automobiles from abrasive elements, the micro thin, clear film keeps your screen scratch-free while increasing visibility, reducing glare, and improving handwriting recognition.

SCREENGUARDZ

Screenguardz, made from the same material as the Bodyguardz, are designed to cover the screen of your handheld device. Applied with a mild adhesive, each protector will last as long as you wish to keep it on. It will not leave a residue on your screen when removed.

Order today! Our screen protectors are:

- Easy to apply
- Safe
- Transparent

Home | Contact Us

Lastname_Firstname_5I_Screen_Protectors

Figure 5.52

End You have completed Project 5I

Apply a combination of the **5A** and **5B** skills.

GO! Solve It | Project 5J Staff Increase

Project Files

For Project 5J, you will need the following files:

New blank Word document
w05J_Staff_Increase

You will save your files as:

Lastname_Firstname_5J_Staff_Schedule
Lastname_Firstname_5J_Staff_Increase

Create a new RTF document and save it as **Lastname_Firstname_5J_Staff_Schedule** in your **Word Chapter 5** folder. Use the following information to create an attractive document:

Sales Manager Yolanda Reynolds is sending a memo to President Roslyn Thomas with an *Employee Schedule for December* attached. The memo should explain that four additional sales associates must be scheduled at the Austin store during the holiday season for the following times: Monday through Friday 9 a.m. to 3 p.m. and 3 p.m. to 9 p.m., Saturday 10 a.m. to 6 p.m., and Sunday 11 a.m. to 5 p.m. Employees will work the same hours throughout December. No employee can be scheduled for two different time periods. Using fictitious employee names, arrange the time periods in an alphabetical list that includes the employee names as bulleted items.

Add appropriate document properties including the keywords **staff, schedule** Open the file **w05J_Staff_Increase** and save it as **Lastname_Firstname_5J_Staff_Increase** Using the existing text, add appropriate hyperlinks to the schedule you created and to contact Ms. Reynolds at yreynolds@txspectrum.com. Add appropriate properties including the keywords **staff, increase** Proofread the documents, correcting any errors. Insert the file names in the footers. Print both files—the RTF file and memo—or submit electronically as directed by your instructor.

Performance Element	Performance Level		
	Exemplary: You consistently applied the relevant skills	**Proficient:** You sometimes, but not always, applied the relevant skills	**Developing:** You rarely or never applied the relevant skills
Save in RTF format	The schedule is saved in RTF format with the appropriate file name.	The schedule is saved in RTF format, but has an incorrect file name.	The schedule is saved in the wrong format.
Insert lists	Sorted, bulleted lists are inserted in the schedule.	Lists are inserted in the schedule, but they are not sorted.	No lists are inserted in the schedule.
Insert hyperlinks	Hyperlinks are inserted in the memo for the schedule and contact information, using existing text.	Hyperlinks are inserted in the memo, but at the wrong locations or include incorrect text.	No hyperlinks are inserted in the memo.
Insert and format text	The schedule contains the correct information and is formatted attractively.	The schedule contains the correct information, but the format is not consistent or attractive.	The schedule does not contain the correct information.
Correct errors	Both documents have no spelling or grammar errors.	One document contains spelling or grammar errors.	Both documents contain spelling or grammar errors.

End You have completed Project 5J

Apply a combination of the **5A** and **5B** skills.

GO! Solve It | Project 5K Wholesalers

Project Files

For Project 5K, you will need the following files:

New blank Word document
w05K_Benefits

You will save your file as:

Lastname_Firstname_5K_Wholesalers

Create a new document and save it in your **Word Chapter 5** folder as a Web page, using **Wholesale Information** for the page title and the file name **Lastname_Firstname_5K_Wholesalers** Use the following information to create a document that includes at least one graphic, a sorted bulleted list, and hyperlinks to the company's home page and contact e-mail address.

Texas Spectrum Wireless is beginning a new venture—selling to wholesalers. Participation is limited to valid companies already in the business of reselling wireless phones or accessories. A company must register with Texas Spectrum Wireless to receive a wholesale account. New accounts are activated within 24 hours. The company will not set up reseller accounts for consumers. Information regarding benefits to wholesalers and contact information to register can be found in the student file **w05K_Benefits**.

Proofread the document, and correct any errors. Add the file name to the footer. In the Properties area, add your name, your course name and section number, and the keywords **wholesalers, Web page** Print your file, or submit electronically, as directed by your instructor.

	Performance Level		
Performance Element	**Exemplary:** You consistently applied the relevant skills	**Proficient:** You sometimes, but not always, applied the relevant skills	**Developing:** You rarely or never applied the relevant skills
Insert and format text	Text explains the purpose of the document with no spelling or grammar errors.	Text explains the purpose, but the document contains spelling or grammar errors.	The purpose of the document is unclear due to insufficient text.
Insert list	A sorted, bulleted list is inserted.	A list is inserted, but it is not sorted.	No list is inserted in the document.
Insert hyperlinks	Hyperlinks are inserted for the company's home page and contact information.	Hyperlinks are inserted, but contain the wrong information.	No hyperlinks are inserted in the document.
Insert graphics	Graphics are inserted to create an attractive document.	Graphics are inserted, but do not enhance the appearance of the document.	No graphics are inserted in the document.
Save as Web page	The document is saved in Web Page format with the appropriate title.	The document is saved in Web Page format, but has an incorrect title.	The document is saved in the wrong format.

End **You have completed Project 5K**

Outcomes-Based Assessments

Rubric

The following outcomes-based assessments are *open-ended assessments*. That is, there is no specific correct result; your result will depend on your approach to the information provided. Make *Professional Quality* your goal. Use the following scoring rubric to guide you in *how* to approach the problem and then to evaluate *how well* your approach solves the problem.

The *criteria*—Software Mastery, Content, Format and Layout, and Process—represent the knowledge and skills you have gained that you can apply to solving the problem. The *levels of performance*—Professional Quality, Approaching Professional Quality, or Needs Quality Improvements—help you and your instructor evaluate your result.

	Your completed project is of Professional Quality if you:	**Your completed project is Approaching Professional Quality if you:**	**Your completed project Needs Quality Improvements if you:**
1-Software Mastery	Choose and apply the most appropriate skills, tools, and features and identify efficient methods to solve the problem.	Choose and apply some appropriate skills, tools, and features, but not in the most efficient manner.	Choose inappropriate skills, tools, or features, or are inefficient in solving the problem.
2-Content	Construct a solution that is clear and well organized, contains content that is accurate, appropriate to the audience and purpose, and is complete. Provide a solution that contains no errors in spelling, grammar, or style.	Construct a solution in which some components are unclear, poorly organized, inconsistent, or incomplete. Misjudge the needs of the audience. Have some errors in spelling, grammar, or style, but the errors do not detract from comprehension.	Construct a solution that is unclear, incomplete, or poorly organized; contains some inaccurate or inappropriate content; and contains many errors in spelling, grammar, or style. Do not solve the problem.
3-Format and Layout	Format and arrange all elements to communicate information and ideas, clarify function, illustrate relationships, and indicate relative importance.	Apply appropriate format and layout features to some elements, but not others. Overuse features, causing minor distraction.	Apply format and layout that does not communicate information or ideas clearly. Do not use format and layout features to clarify function, illustrate relationships, or indicate relative importance. Use available features excessively, causing distraction.
4-Process	Use an organized approach that integrates planning, development, self-assessment, revision, and reflection.	Demonstrate an organized approach in some areas, but not others; or, use an insufficient process of organization throughout.	Do not use an organized approach to solve the problem.

Apply a combination of the 5A and 5B skills.

GO! Think | Project 5L Phone Jewelry

Project Files

For Project 5L, you will need the following file:

New blank Word document

You will save your file as:

Lastname_Firstname_5L_Phone_Jewelry

The marketing director at Texas Spectrum Wireless wants to create a flyer to advertise their latest product line—cell phone bling, a variety of jewelry accessories. The categories include butterfly, tiger, seashore, carnation, and mountain. This document will be reviewed by others because it includes Spanish and French translations of the styles.

Create a flyer with basic information about the new product line. Include a brief paragraph describing cell phone bling and accessories. Use the Research task pane to locate the descriptive information, adding a hyperlink to the Web site where you obtained the data. Display the individual styles in an organized list. Use the Translation tool to create two additional style lists—in Spanish and French. Be sure the document has an attractive design and is easy to read. Correct all spelling and grammar errors, excluding the translated text.

Save the file in Rich Text Format, with the file name **Lastname_Firstname_5L_Phone_Jewelry** Add appropriate information in the Properties area, and then add the file name to the footer. Print your file, or submit electronically, as directed by your instructor.

End **You have completed Project 5L**

Apply a combination of the 5A and 5B skills.

GO! Think | Project 5M Memory Cards

Project Files

For Project 5M, you will need the following files:

New blank Word document
w05M_TSW_Cards

You will save your file as:

Lastname_Firstname_5M_Memory_Cards

Eliott Verschoren, Marketing Vice President, wants to create a Web page advertising the different types of memory cards sold by Texas Spectrum Wireless. The Web page will include the company name, brief explanations of memory cards, SD cards, and microSD cards, and a list of specific cards available.

Create the Web page, using the Research task pane to find definitions for the types of cards. Open the document **w05M_TSW_Cards** to collect the information for the specific cards that are sold by the company. Be sure the Web page has an attractive design and is easy to read and understand. The list of memory cards should be arranged in a logical order. Include a hyperlink **sales@txspectrum.com** to contact the sales department. Correct all spelling and grammar errors.

Save the file as a Web Page, using **TSW Memory Cards** for the page title and **Lastname_Firstname_5M_Memory_Cards** for the file name. Add appropriate information to the Properties area, and add the file name to the footer. Print your file, or submit electronically, as directed by your instructor.

End **You have completed Project 5M**

Apply a combination of the 5A and 5B skills.

You and GO! | Project 5N Personal Web Page

Project Files

For Project 5N, you will need the following file:

New blank Word document

You will save your files as:

Lastname_Firstname_5N_Personal_Webpage
Lastname_Firstname_5N_Courses

Create a personal Web page that includes information about yourself—such as family, school, interests, accomplishments, and goals. Save the file as a Web Page, using your name for the page title and **Lastname_Firstname_5N_Personal_Webpage** the file name. Add the file name to the footer. In the Properties area, add your name, your course name and section number, and the keywords **Web page** and **personal**

Create a second document that contains the courses you are taking this semester. For each course, include the name of the course, when it meets, and a brief description. Save this second document as an RTF file, with the file name **Lastname_Firstname_5N_Courses** Add the file name to the footer. In the Properties area, add your name, your course name and section number, and the keyword **course schedule**

On the Web page, be sure to include a page background, horizontal line, and hyperlinks to your college's Web site, your *5N_Courses* file, and an e-mail address link to contact you. Format the document in an attractive manner and check for spelling errors.

Print your two files, or submit electronically, as directed by your instructor.

End You have completed Project 5N

Building Documents from Reusable Content and Revising Documents Using Markup Tools

OUTCOMES

At the end of this chapter you will be able to:

OBJECTIVES

Mastering these objectives will enable you to:

PROJECT 6A

Create reusable content and construct a document with building blocks and theme templates.

1. Create Building Blocks (p. 165)
2. Create and Save a Theme Template (p. 172)
3. Create a Document by Using Building Blocks (p. 175)

PROJECT 6B

Collaborate with others to edit, review, and finalize a document.

4. Use Comments in a Document (p. 182)
5. Track Changes in a Document (p. 187)
6. View Side by Side, Compare, and Combine Documents (p. 195)

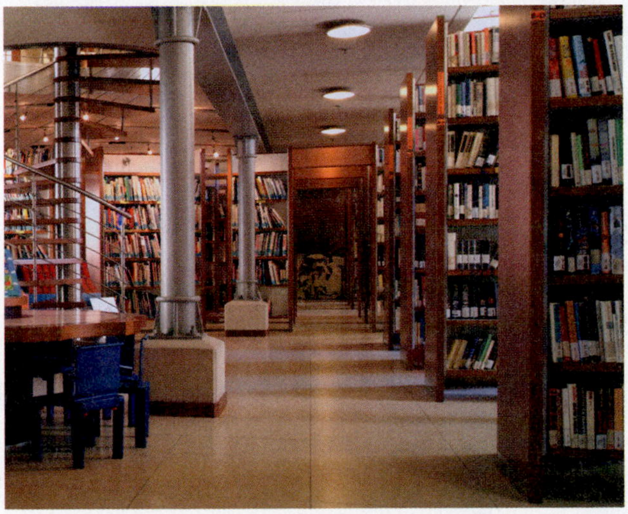

newphotoservice/Shutterstock

In This Chapter

In this chapter you will use building blocks, which save time and give consistency to your documents. You can use predefined building blocks or create your own custom building blocks. To give documents a customized appearance, you can create a theme by defining the colors, fonts, and effects. You will create building blocks and a custom theme template, and then build a document from reusable content.

You will also use the Track Changes feature, which makes it easy to work with a team to collaborate on documents. Because several people may need to review a document, you can track changes made to a document and add comments. You will track changes and insert comments, review changes made by others, and accept or reject changes.

The projects in this chapter relate to the **Lakefield Public Library**, which serves the local community at three locations—the Main library, the East Branch, and the West Branch. The collection includes books, audio books, music CDs, videos and DVDs, and magazines and newspapers—for all ages. The library also provides sophisticated online and technology services, youth programs, and frequent appearances by both local and nationally known authors. The citizens of Lakefield support the Lakefield Public Library with local taxes, donations, and special events fees.

Project 6A Newsletter with Reusable Content and Custom Theme

myitlab
Project 6A Training

Project Activities

In Activities 6.01 through 6.08, you will assist Benedetta Herman, Director of Operations at Lakefield Public Library, in designing a custom look for documents that the library produces by creating a custom theme and building blocks for content that can be reused. Your completed documents will look similar to Figure 6.1.

Project Files

For Project 6A, you will need the following files:

- Two new blank Word documents
- w06A_February_Articles
- w06A_Classes

You will save your files as:

- Lastname_Firstname_6A_Building_Blocks
- Lastname_Firstname_6A_Library_Theme—not shown in figure
- Lastname_Firstname_6A_February_Newsletter

Project Results

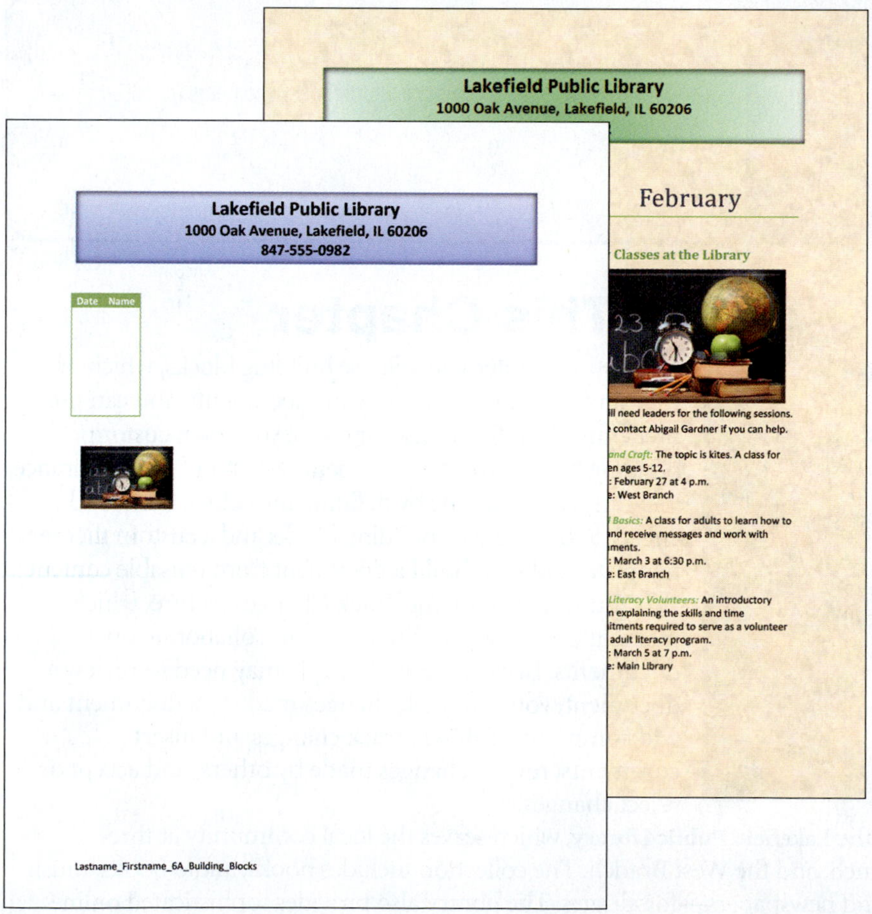

Figure 6.1
Project 6A February Newsletter

Objective 1 | Create Building Blocks

Building blocks are reusable pieces of content or other document parts—for example, headers, footers, page number formats—that are stored in galleries. The Headers gallery, the Footers gallery, the Page Numbers gallery, and the Bibliographies gallery, some of which you have already used, are all examples of building block galleries. You can also create your own building blocks for content that you use frequently.

> **Alert! | Completing This Project in One Working Session**
>
> If you are working in a college lab, plan to complete Project 6A in one working session. Building blocks are stored on the computer at which you are working. Thus, in a college lab, if you exit Word before completing the project, the building blocks might be deleted and will be unavailable for your use—you will have to re-create them. On your own computer, you can exit Word, and the building blocks will remain until you delete them.

Activity 6.01 | Creating a Building Block in the Text Box Gallery

Recall that a ***text box*** is a movable, resizable container for text or graphics. In this activity, you will create a distinctive text box building block that the library can use for any documents requiring the library's contact information.

1 **Start** Word. From **Backstage** view, display the **Save As** dialog box, navigate to the location where you are saving your files for this chapter, and then create a folder named **Word Chapter 6** Save the document as **Lastname_Firstname_6A_Building_Blocks** Using **Quick Parts**, insert the file name in the footer. If necessary, display the rulers and formatting marks.

2 On the **Insert tab**, in the **Text group**, click the **Text Box** button. Notice that predesigned, built-in building blocks display in the **Text Box** gallery. Click the first text box—**Simple Text Box**.

A text box containing placeholder text displays at the top of your document. Text boxes can be formatted like other graphic elements in Word and saved as building blocks.

3 On the **Format tab**, in the **Shape Styles group**, click the **More** button. In the **Shape Styles** gallery, in the fourth row, click the second style—**Subtle Effect – Blue, Accent 1**.

4 On the **Format tab**, if the **Size group** is visible, change the **Shape Width** 1.37" to **6.5"**; otherwise, to the right of the **Arrange group**, click the **Size** button, and then change the **Shape Width** 1.37" to **6.5"**. Compare your screen with Figure 6.2.

Depending on the resolution setting of your monitor, either the Size group or the Size button will display.

Figure 6.2

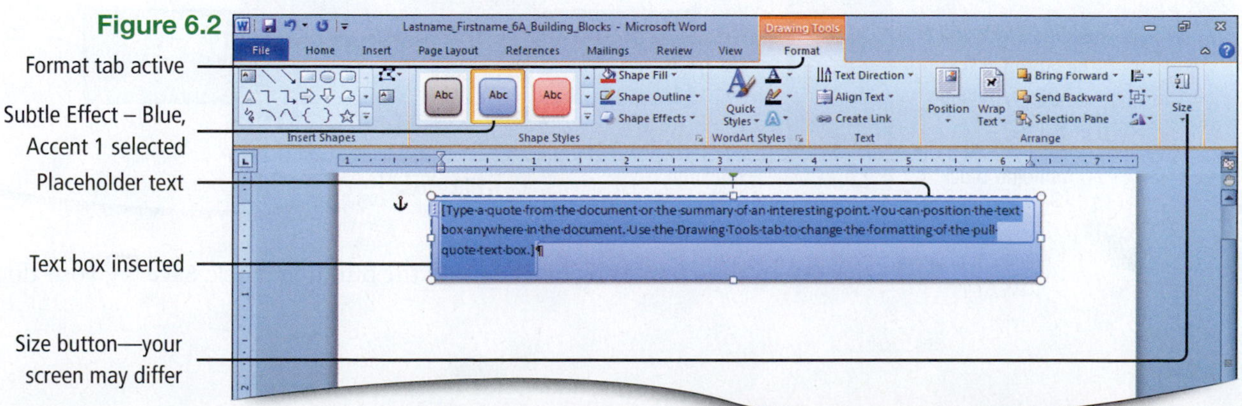

5 On the **Format tab**, in the **Shape Styles group**, click the **Shape Effects** button, and point to **Shadow**. Under **Inner**, in the second row, click the second style—**Inside Center**.

6 In the text box, type the following to replace the placeholder text: **Lakefield Public Library** Press Enter, and then type **1000 Oak Avenue, Lakefield, IL 60206** Press Enter, and then type **847-555-0982**

7 Select all three paragraphs, click the **Home tab**, and then in the **Styles group**, click the **No Spacing** style. Select the first paragraph, change the **Font Size** to **20**, and then apply **Bold** and **Center**. Select the second and third paragraphs, change the **Font Size** to **16**, and then apply **Bold** and **Center**. Notice the height of the text box automatically adjusts to accommodate the text.

8 Click in the first paragraph to cancel the selection. Click the outer edge of the text box so that none of the text is selected, but that the text box itself is selected and displays sizing handles. Compare your screen with Figure 6.3.

Figure 6.3

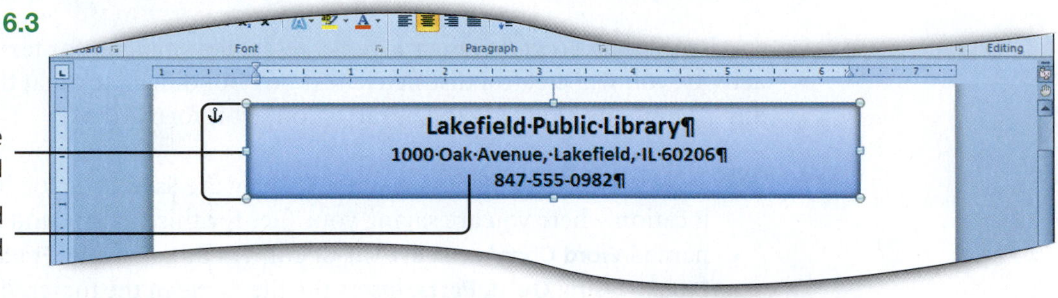

9 On the **Insert tab**, in the **Text group**, click the **Text Box** button, and then click **Save Selection to Text Box Gallery**. In the **Create New Building Block** dialog box, in the **Name** box, type **Library Information** Notice that the **Gallery** box displays *Text Boxes*.

By selecting the Text Boxes gallery, this building block will display in the gallery of other text box building blocks.

10 In the **Description** box, type **Use as the library contact information in newsletters, flyers, public meeting agendas, and other publications** Compare your screen with Figure 6.4.

Figure 6.4

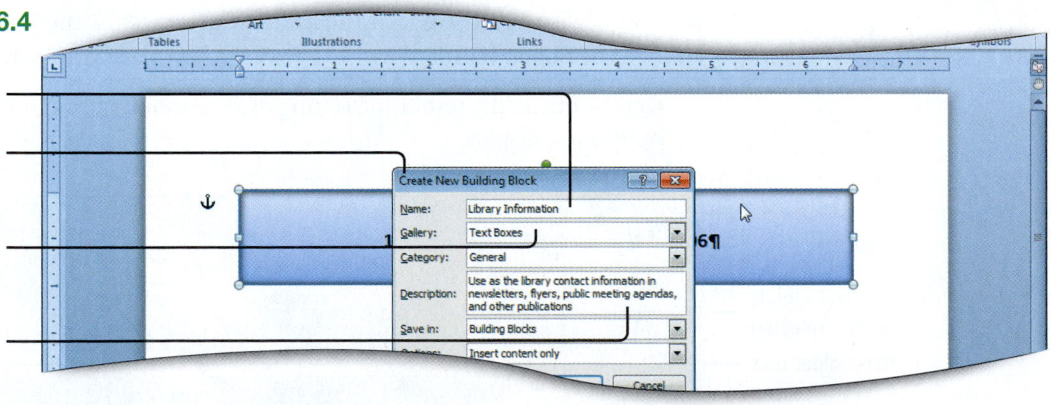

11 Click **OK** to close the dialog box and save the building block. **Save** your document.

> **Alert! | Saving Building Blocks**
>
> Building blocks that you create in a gallery are saved in the Word software on the computer at which you are working. The document you are creating here is only for the purpose of submitting it to your instructor or to distribute to someone else who would like to use the building blocks on his or her computer.

Activity 6.02 | Viewing Building Blocks in the Building Blocks Organizer

The ***Building Blocks Organizer*** enables you to view—in a single location—all of the available building blocks from all the different galleries.

1 On the **Insert tab**, in the **Text group**, click the **Quick Parts** button.

Quick Parts refers to all of the reusable pieces of content that are available to insert into a document, including building blocks, document properties, and fields. Recall that you have used the Quick Parts button to insert the field containing the file name into footers.

2 From the displayed list, click **Building Blocks Organizer**. In the displayed **Building Blocks Organizer** dialog box, in the upper left corner, click **Name** to sort the building blocks alphabetically by name.

Here you can view all of the building blocks available in Word. In this dialog box, you can also delete a building block, edit its properties—for example, change the name or description or gallery location—or select and insert it into a document.

3 By using the scroll bar in the center of the **Building Blocks Organizer** dialog box, scroll down until you see your building block that begins *Library*, and then click to select it. Compare your screen with Figure 6.5.

You can see that Word provides numerous building blocks. In the preview area on the right, notice that under the preview of the building block, the name and description that you entered displays.

Figure 6.5

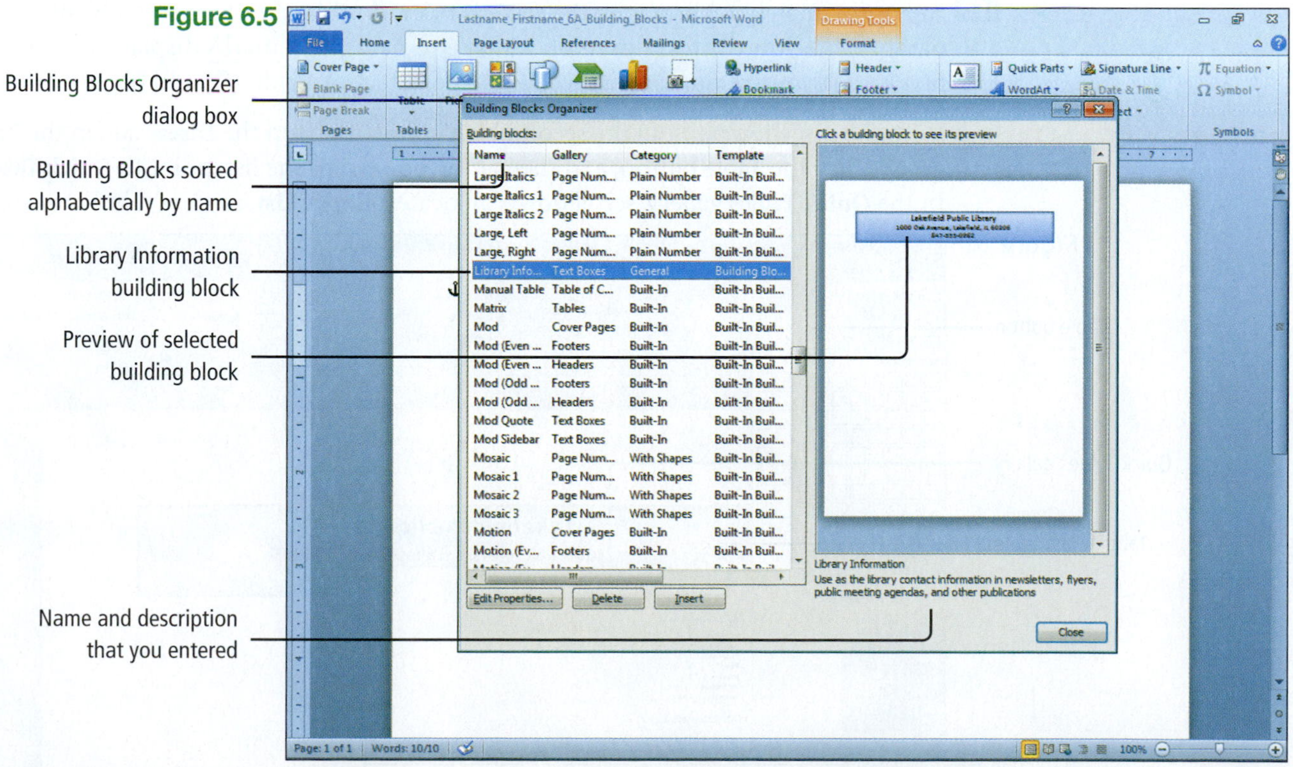

4 In the lower right corner, click **Close**.

Activity 6.03 | Creating a Building Block in the Quick Tables Gallery

Quick Tables are tables that are stored as building blocks. Word includes many predesigned Quick Tables, and you can also create your own tables and save them as Quick Tables in the Quick Tables gallery. In this activity, you will modify an existing Quick Table and then save it as a new building block. Ms. Herman will use this table to announce staff birthdays in the quarterly newsletter and in the monthly staff bulletin.

1 Click anywhere outside of the text box to deselect it, and then point slightly under the lower left corner of the text box to display the [I≡] pointer at approximately **1.5 inches on the vertical ruler**, as shown in Figure 6.6.

The ***click and type pointer*** is the text select—I-beam—pointer with various attached shapes that indicate which formatting—left-aligned, centered, or right-aligned—will be applied when you double-click in a blank area of a document. In this case, if you double-click, a new paragraph will be inserted with a left-aligned format.

Figure 6.6

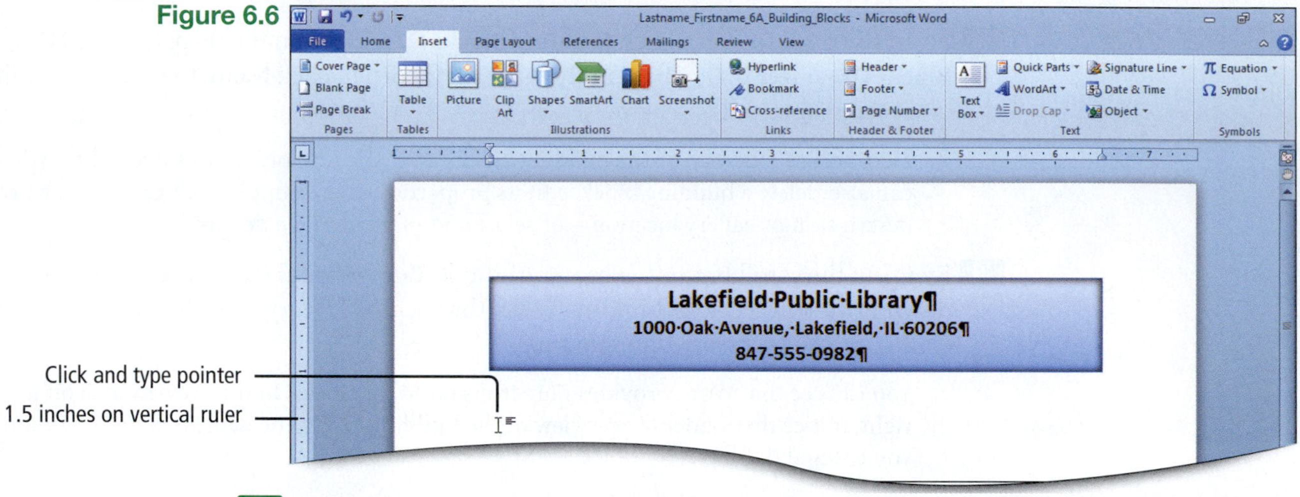

2 At approximately **1.5 inches on the vertical ruler**, double-click to insert a blank paragraph below the text box. Notice that two paragraph marks display below the text box. If you are not satisfied with your result, click Undo [↶] and begin again.

3 With the insertion point in the second blank paragraph, on the **Insert tab**, in the **Tables group**, click the **Table** button, and then at the bottom of the list, point to **Quick Tables**. In the **Quick Tables** gallery, scroll down to locate **Tabular List**, as shown in Figure 6.7.

Figure 6.7

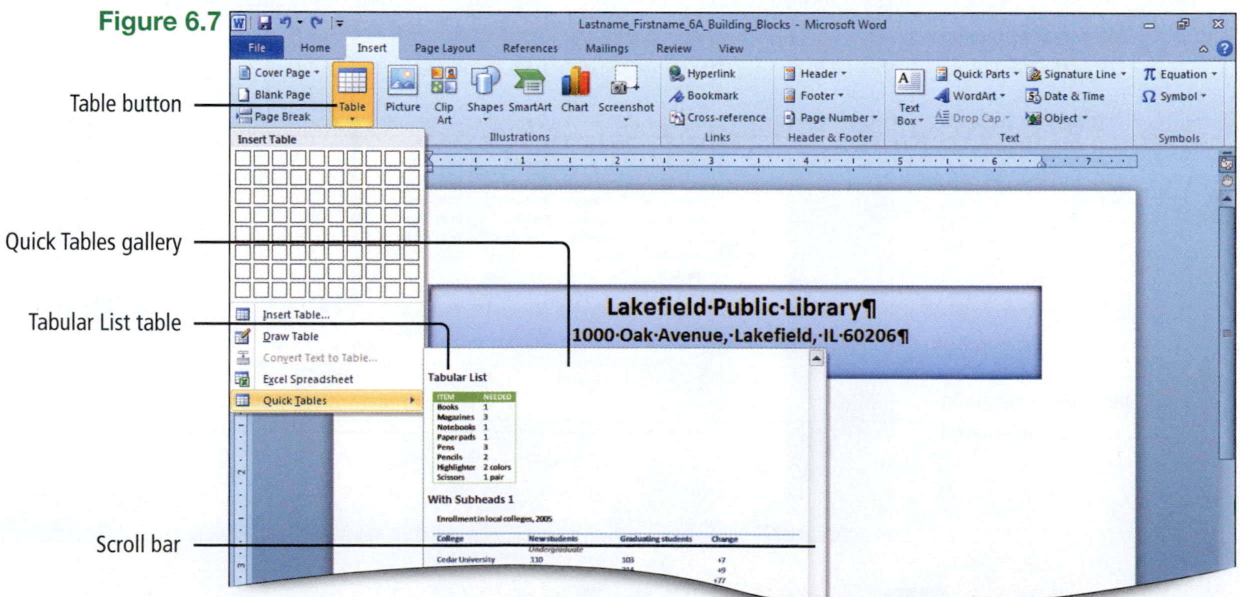

4 Click **Tabular List**. In the first row of the table, click in the first cell, select the text *ITEM*, and then type **Date**

5 Press Tab to move to the second cell, and with *NEEDED* selected, type **Name** Select all the remaining cells of the table, and then press Del. Compare your screen with Figure 6.8.

Because this table will be used as a building block to enter birthday information, the sample text is not needed.

Figure 6.8

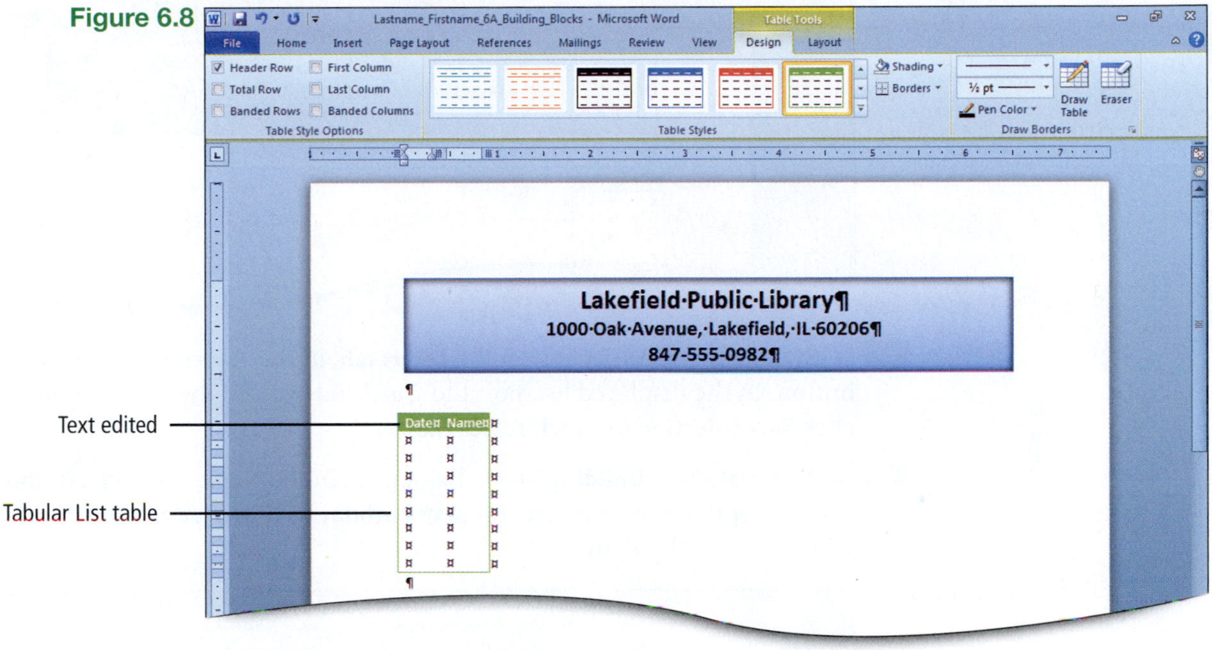

6 Click in the table, point slightly outside of the upper left corner of the table, and then click the **table move handle** to select the entire table.

7 With the table selected, move your pointer to the left end of the horizontal ruler, and then point to the first **Move Table Column** marker to display the pointer, as shown in Figure 6.9.

Figure 6.9

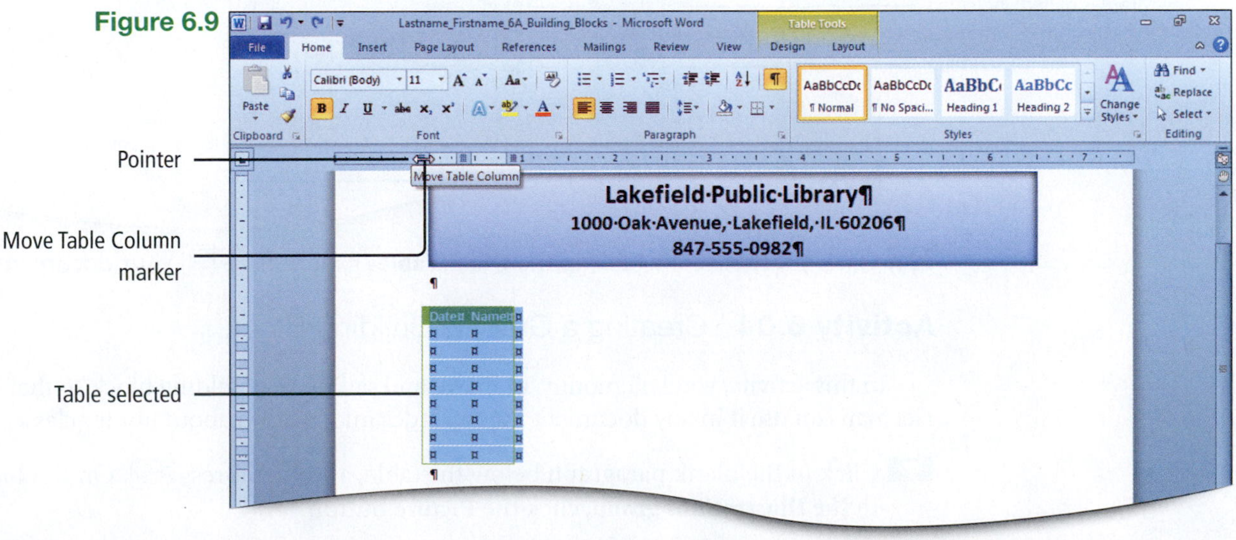

8 Drag the **Move Table Column** marker slightly to the right until the displayed vertical dotted line aligns with the left edge of the text box, as shown in Figure 6.10, and then release the left mouse button.

This action aligns the left edge of the table with the left edge of the text box.

Figure 6.10

Pointer

Dotted vertical line aligns with left edge of text box

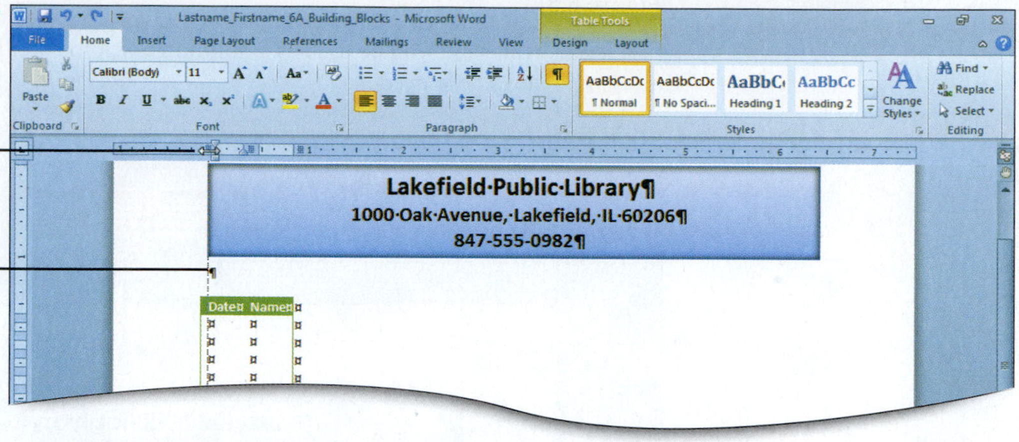

9 With the table still selected, on the **Insert tab**, in the **Tables group**, click the **Table** button. In the displayed list, point to **Quick Tables**, and then at the bottom of the list, click **Save Selection to Quick Tables Gallery**.

10 In the **Create New Building Block** dialog box, in the **Name** box, type **Birthday Table** In the **Description** box, type **Use for staff birthdays in newsletters and bulletins** Compare your screen with Figure 6.11.

Figure 6.11

Name of new building block

Tables gallery indicated

Description

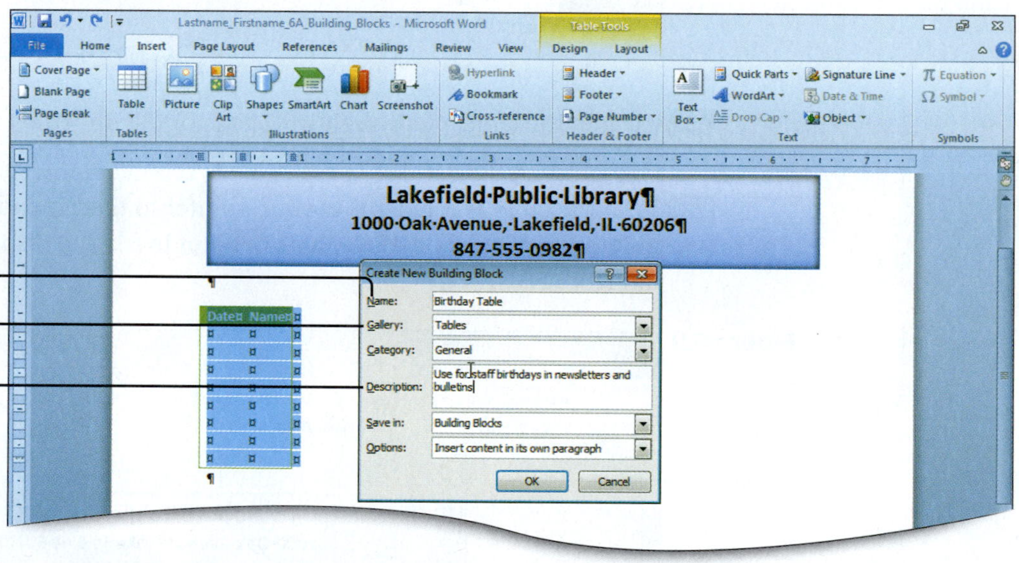

11 Click **OK** to save the table in the **Quick Tables** gallery. **Save** your document.

Activity 6.04 | Creating a Graphic Building Block

In this activity, you will modify an image and save it as a building block so that Benedetta Herman can use it in any document that includes information about library classes.

1 Click in the blank paragraph below the table, and then press Enter. On the **Insert tab**, in the **Illustrations group**, click the **Picture** button.

2 In the **Insert Picture** dialog box, navigate to your student files, select the file **w06A_Classes**, and then click **Insert**.

3 With the picture selected, on the **Format tab**, in the **Picture Styles group**, click the **Picture Effects** button, point to **Bevel**, and then under **Bevel**, in the first row, click the fourth bevel—**Cool Slant**.

4 On the **Format tab**, in the **Size group**, change the **Shape Width** [1.37"] to **1.3"**.

5 With the picture selected, click the **Insert tab**, and then in the **Text group**, click the **Quick Parts** button. From the displayed list, click **Save Selection to Quick Part Gallery**.

By choosing the Save Selection to Quick Parts Gallery command, building blocks that you create are saved in the Quick Parts gallery and assigned to the General category. However, you can save the building block in any of the other relevant galleries, or create your own custom gallery. You can also create your own category if you want to do so.

6 In the **Create New Building Block** dialog box, in the **Name** box, type **Classes Picture** and then in the **Description** box, type **Use this picture in documents containing information about library classes.** Compare your screen with Figure 6.12.

You can create and then select any content and save it as a building block in this manner.

Figure 6.12

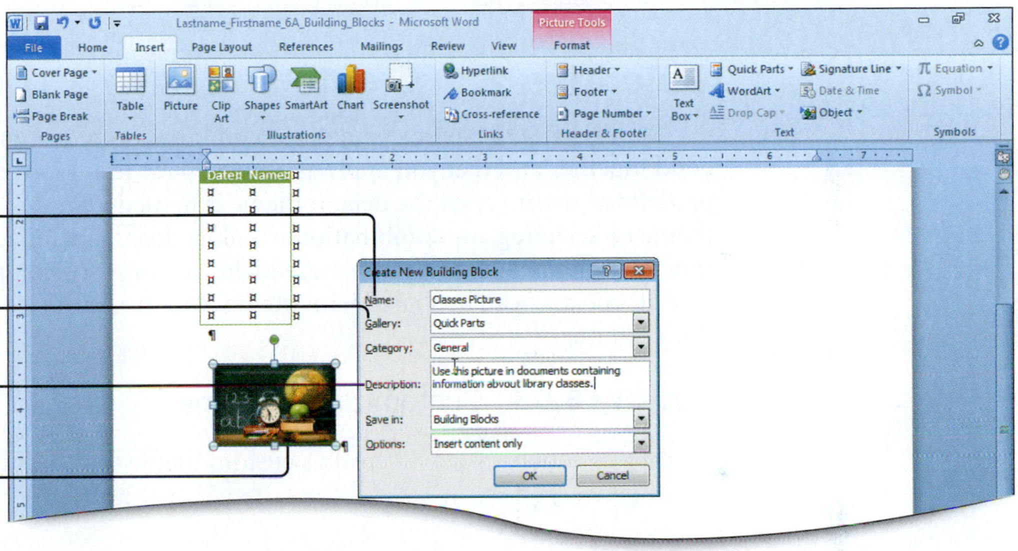

7 Click **OK** to close the dialog box and save the **Classes Picture** building block.

Your new building block is saved, and you can insert it in a document by selecting it from the Quick Parts gallery.

8 On the **Insert tab**, in the **Text group**, click the **Quick Parts** button, and then point to **Classes Picture**. Compare your screen with Figure 6.13.

Your picture displays under General in the Quick Parts gallery.

Figure 6.13

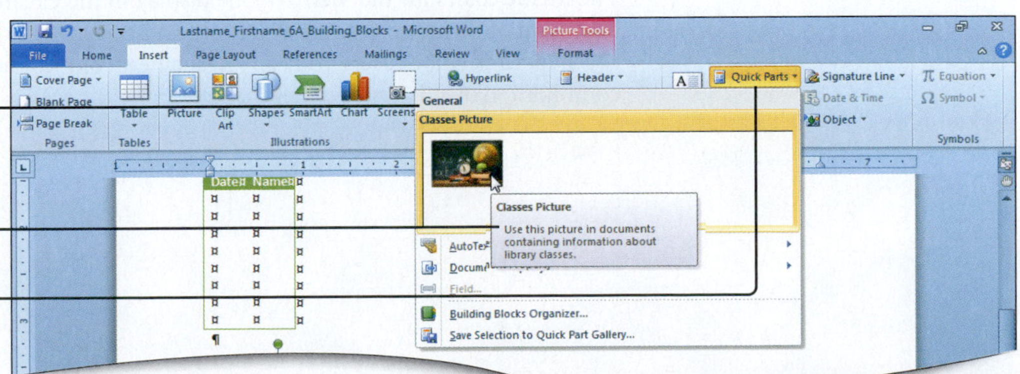

9 Click anywhere in the document to close the **Quick Parts** gallery.

10 Display the **Document Information Panel**. In the **Author** box, type your first and last names. In the **Subject** box, type your course name and section number, and in the **Keywords** box, type **library newsletter, building blocks Close** [×] the Document Information Panel.

11 **Save** [icon] your document, display **Backstage** view, and then **Close** the document. Leave Word open for the next activity.

The purpose of this document is to submit a copy of your building blocks to your instructor. After the building blocks are stored in a gallery, they are saved on your system and no document is required unless you want to distribute your building blocks to someone else who would like to use the building blocks on his or her computer.

> **Alert! | What Happens If I Accidentally Close Word?**
> If you accidently close Word, in the dialog box regarding changes to building blocks, click Save to accept the changes.

Objective 2 | Create and Save a Theme Template

Recall that a ***theme*** is a predefined combination of colors, fonts, and effects that look good together and that you apply as a single selection. Word comes with a group of predefined themes, and the default theme is named *Office*. You can also create your own theme by selecting any combination of colors, fonts, and effects that, when saved, creates a ***theme template***. A theme template, which stores a set of colors, fonts, and effects—lines and fill effects—can be shared with other Office programs, for example, Excel and PowerPoint.

Activity 6.05 | Customizing a Theme

In this activity, you will create a custom theme that the library will use for all documents.

1 Press [Ctrl] + [N] to display a new blank document.

2 On the **Page Layout tab**, in the **Themes group**, click the **Theme Colors** button [icon]. Under **Built-In**, take a moment to examine the groups of colors for each of the predefined themes, scrolling as needed.

3 From the list, click **Metro**. Click the **Theme Colors** button [icon] again, and then at the bottom, click **Create New Theme Colors**. Compare your screen with Figure 6.14.

The theme colors for the Metro theme display in the Create New Theme Colors dialog box. A set of theme colors contains four text and background colors, six accent colors, and two hyperlink colors. Here you can select a new color for any category and save the combination of colors with a new name.

Figure 6.14

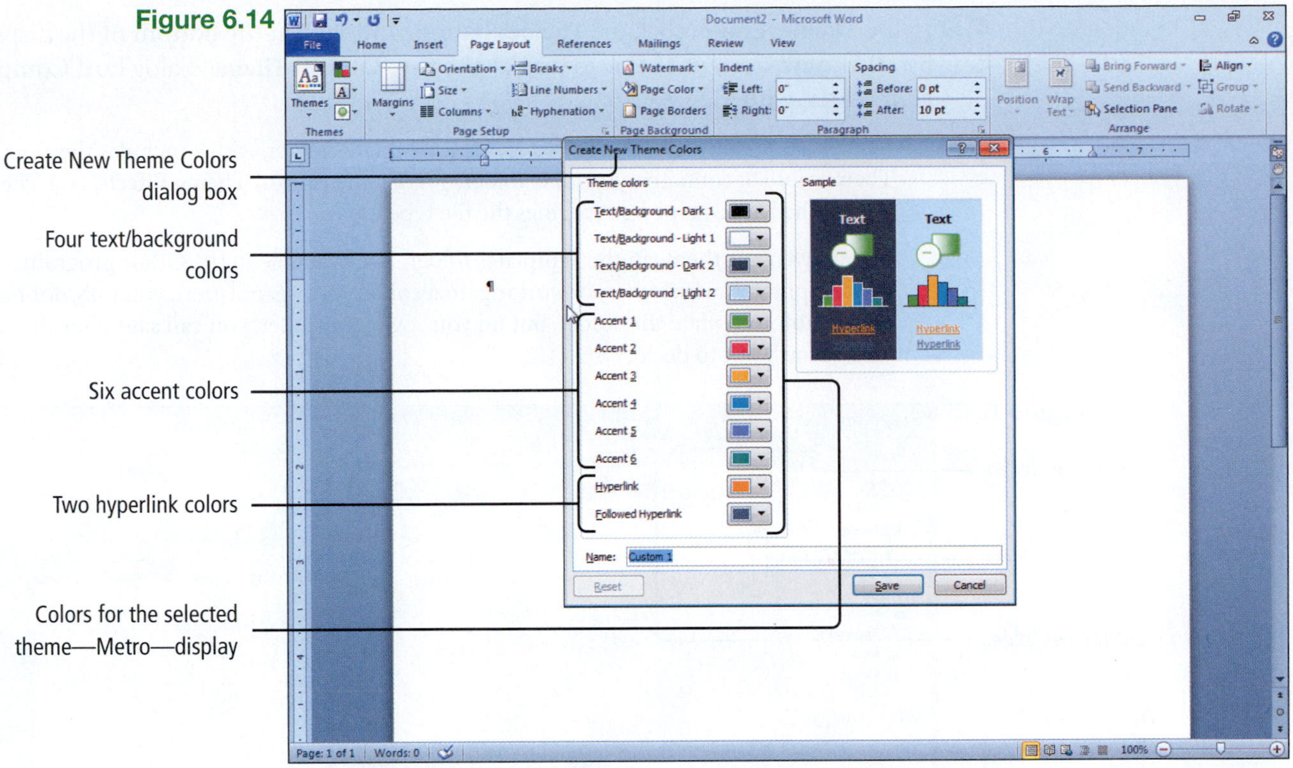

4 Click **Cancel** to keep the current group of color definitions. In the **Themes group**, click the **Theme Fonts** button.

Theme fonts contain a heading font—the upper font—and a body text font—the lower font. You can use an existing set of Built-In fonts for your new theme, or define new sets of fonts.

5 Under **Built-In**, click the **Office** font set. In the **Themes group**, click the **Theme Effects** button.

Theme effects are sets of lines and fill effects. Here you can see the lines and fill effects for each predefined theme. You cannot create your own set of theme effects, but you can choose any set of effects to combine with other theme colors and theme fonts.

6 Under **Built-In**, click **Flow** as the theme effects. Leave Word open—you will save your document in the next activity.

Your custom theme—a combination of the Metro colors, the Office fonts, and the Flow effects—is complete, with no further customization to the Metro color combination or the Office font combination.

Activity 6.06 | Saving a Theme Template

To use your custom theme in other Microsoft Office files, you can save it as a theme template.

1 In the **Themes group**, click the **Themes** button, and then at the bottom of the displayed list, click **Save Current Theme** to display the **Save Current Theme** dialog box. Compare your screen with Figure 6.15.

By default, saving a new theme displays the Templates folder, which includes the Document Themes folder, containing separate folders for Theme Colors, Theme Effects, and Theme Fonts. The Save as type box specifies the file type *Office Theme*.

If you save your theme in the Templates folder, it is available to the Office programs on the computer at which you are working. In a college or organization, you may not have permission to update this folder, but on your own computer, you can save your themes here if you want to do so.

Figure 6.15

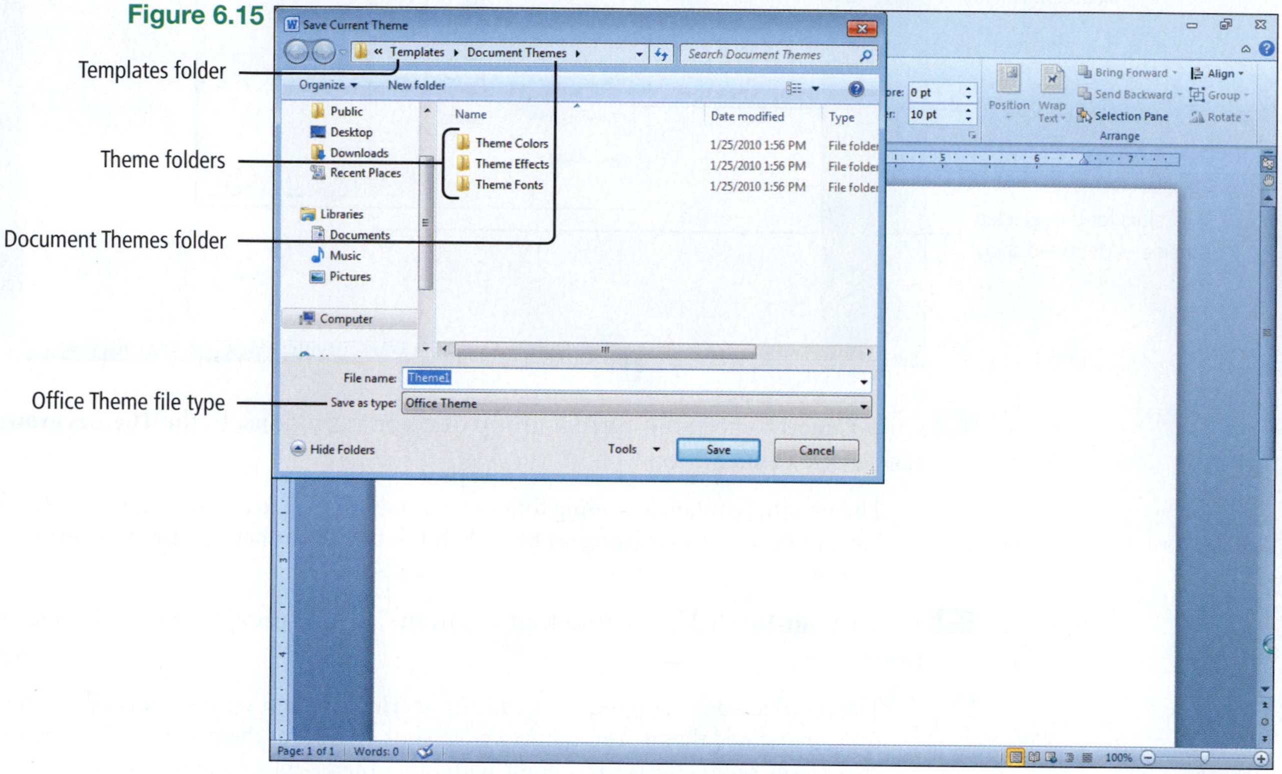

2 In the **Save Current Theme** dialog box, navigate to your **Word Chapter 6** folder. In the **File name** box, type **Lastname_Firstname_6A_Library_Theme** and then click **Save**.

For the purposes of this instruction, you are saving the theme to your Word Chapter 6 folder.

3 In the **Themes group**, click the **Themes** button, and then click **Browse for Themes**. In the **Choose Theme or Themed Document** dialog box, navigate to your **Word Chapter 6** folder, right-click your file **Lastname_Firstname_6A_Library_Theme**, and from the shortcut menu, click **Properties**. Compare your screen with Figure 6.16.

The Properties dialog box for the Theme displays. A Microsoft Office theme is saved with the file extension *.thmx*. By default, a theme template is set to open with PowerPoint; however, the theme can also be applied in Word or Excel.

Figure 6.16

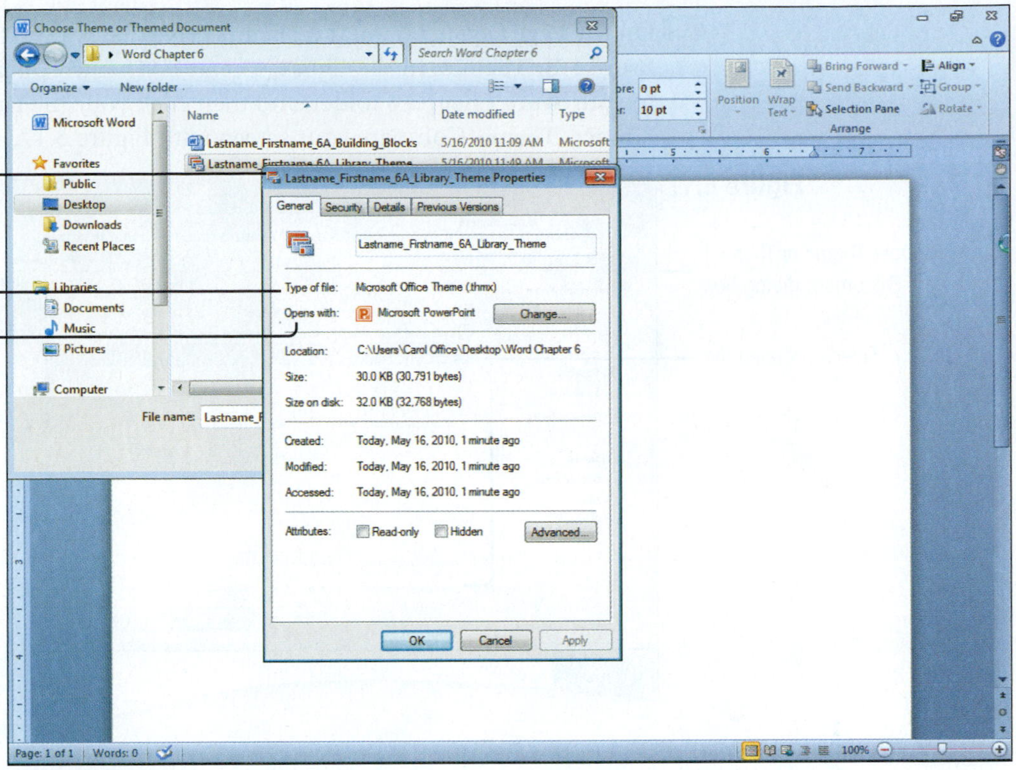

4 **Close** the **Properties** dialog box, and then **Close** the **Choose Theme or Themed Document** dialog box.

5 From **Backstage** view, **Close** the blank document on your screen without saving changes.

Objective 3 | Create a Document by Using Building Blocks

One of the benefits of creating building blocks and theme templates is that they can be used repeatedly to create individual documents. The building blocks ensure consistency in format and structure, and the theme template provides consistency in colors, fonts, and effects.

Activity 6.07 | Creating a Document Using Building Blocks

Benedetta Herman sends a monthly newsletter to all library staff. In this activity, you will create the February newsletter by using the building blocks that you created.

1 Press Ctrl + N to display a new blank document, and then save it in your **Word Chapter 6** folder as **Lastname_Firstname_6A_February_Newsletter** Scroll to the bottom of the page, and then using **Quick Parts**, insert the file name in the footer. If necessary, display the rulers and formatting marks.

2. On the **Page Layout tab**, in the **Themes group**, click the **Themes** button, and then click **Browse for Themes**. In the **Choose Theme or Themed Document** dialog box, navigate to your **Word Chapter 6** folder, and then click your file **Lastname_Firstname_6A_Library_Theme**. Compare your screen with Figure 6.17.

Figure 6.17

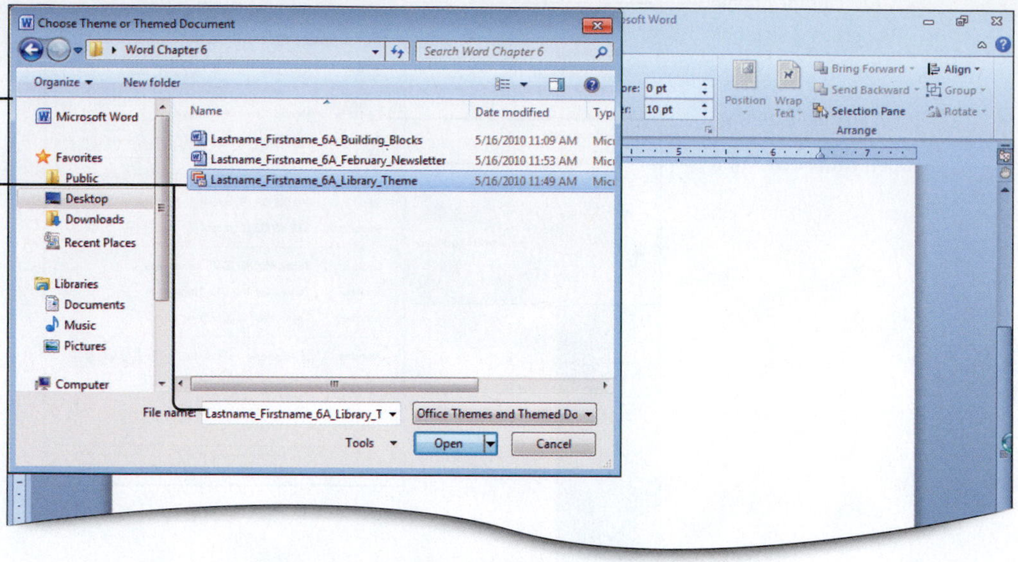

3. Click **Open** to apply the theme, and notice that the colors on the buttons in the **Themes group** change to reflect the new theme.

4. On the **Page Layout tab**, in the **Page Background group**, click the **Page Color** button, and then click **Fill Effects**. In the **Fill Effects** dialog box, click the **Texture tab**, and then in the fourth row, click the third texture–**Parchment**. Compare your screen with Figure 6.18.

Figure 6.18

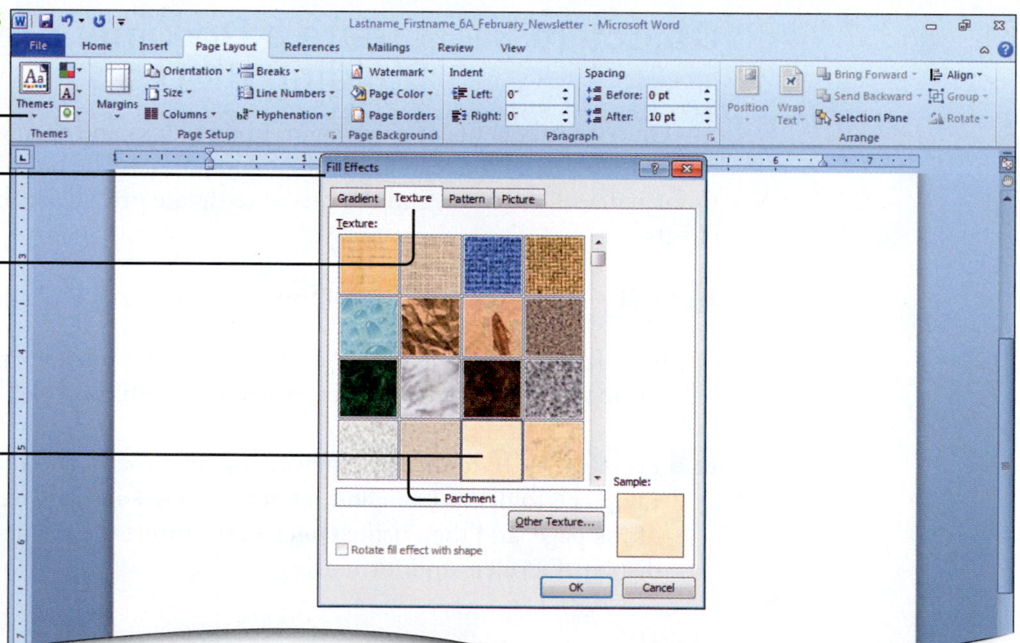

5. Click **OK** to apply the textured background.

6. On the **Insert tab**, in the **Text group**, click the **Text Box** button. Scroll to the bottom of the **Text Box** gallery, and then under **General**, click your **Library Information** building block.

   The theme colors of your custom theme are applied to the building block.

7 Click anywhere outside of the text box to deselect it, and then point slightly under the lower left corner of the text box to display the [I≡] pointer at approximately **1.5 inches on the vertical ruler**. Double-click to insert two blank paragraphs under the text box. If you are dissatisfied with your result, click **Undo** [↶].

8 On the **Home tab**, in the **Styles group**, click the **More** button [▾] to display the **Styles** gallery, and then apply the **Title** style. Type **Staff Newsletter** press Tab two times, and then type **February** Select and then **Center** [≡] the paragraph you just typed.

9 Position the [I≡] pointer at the left margin at approximately **2.25 inches on the vertical ruler**, and then double-click to insert a new blank paragraph. In the **Styles group**, click the **More** button [▾], and then if necessary, apply the **Normal** style to the new paragraph. Select the paragraph mark, and then compare your screen with Figure 6.19.

Figure 6.19

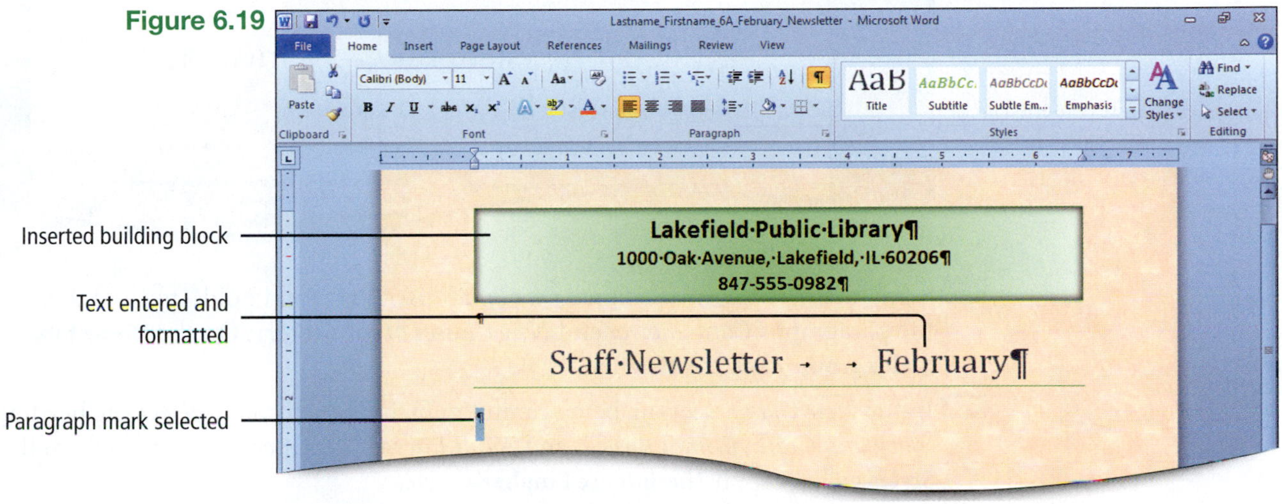

10 With the paragraph mark selected, on the **Page Layout tab**, in the **Page Setup group**, click the **Columns** button, and then click **Two**. Click to the left of the paragraph mark, and then compare your screen with Figure 6.20.

A continuous section break is inserted at the end of the previous paragraph. The remainder of the document will be formatted in two columns.

Figure 6.20

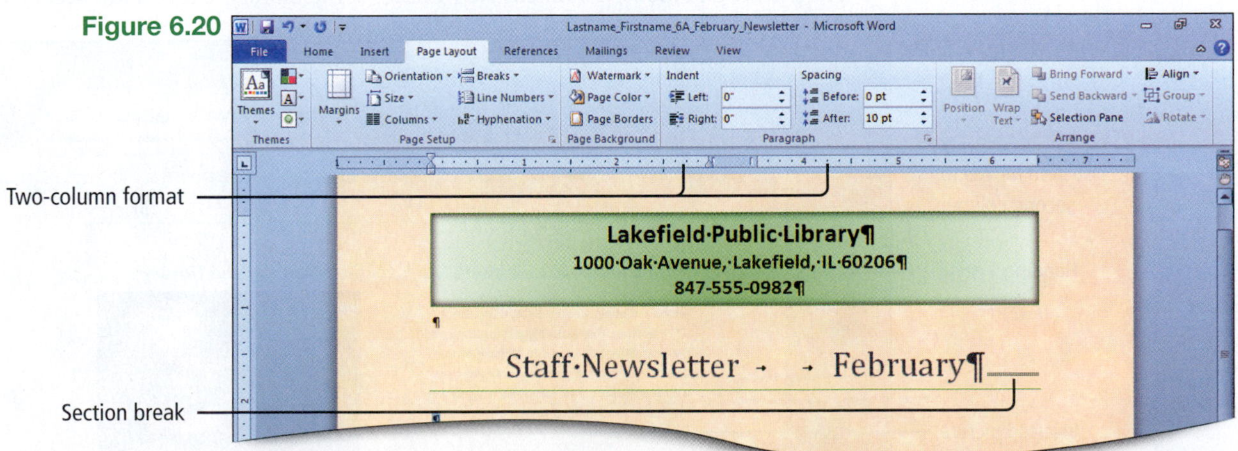

11 On the **Insert tab**, in the **Text group**, click the **Object button arrow**, and then click **Text from File**. In the **Insert File** dialog box, navigate to your student files, click **w06A_February_Articles**, and then click **Insert**. Compare your screen with Figure 6.21.

Word inserts the text in two columns.

Figure 6.21

Text inserted in two-column format

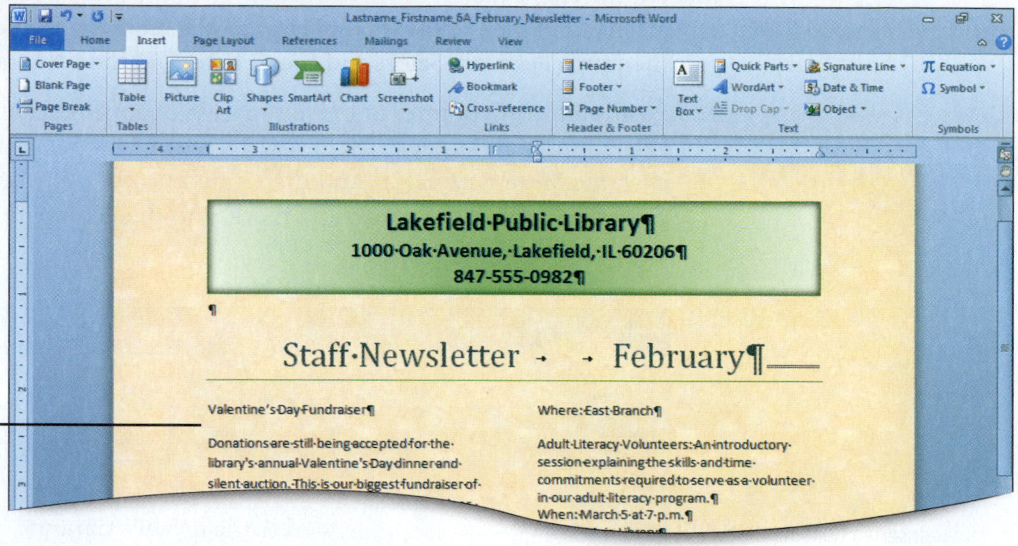

12 Select the paragraph *Valentine's Day Fundraiser*. Press and hold Ctrl, and then select the paragraphs *Card Shower* and *New Classes at the Library*. On the **Home tab**, in the **Styles group**, click the **Heading 1** style.

13 In the *New Classes* section, being careful to include each colon, select the headings *Story and Craft:*, *E-mail Basics:*, and *Adult Literacy Volunteers:*, and then from the **Styles** gallery, apply the **Intense Emphasis** style.

14 In the first column, click to position the insertion point to the left of the paragraph that begins *We still need*. On the **Insert tab**, in the **Text group**, click the **Quick Parts** button. Under **General**, click the **Classes Picture** building block.

15 Click to select the picture, and then on the **Format tab**, in the **Size group**, change the **Shape Height** [1.5"] to **1.85"**. Deselect the picture, and then compare your screen with Figure 6.22.

The picture and the section titled "New Classes at the Library" move to the second column.

Figure 6.22

New Classes at the Library section moves to second column

Heading 1 style

Inserted picture

Intense Emphasis style

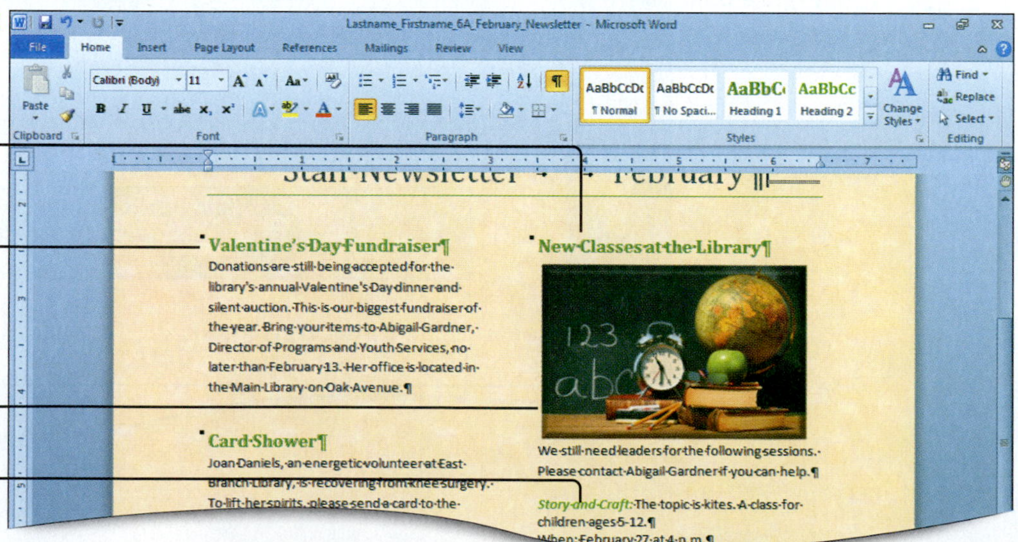

16 At the bottom of the first column, click at the end of the last paragraph—following *60206*—and then press Enter to insert a new paragraph.

17 Type **February Birthdays** and then press Enter. Select the text you just typed, and then from the **Styles** gallery, apply the **Heading 1** style.

18 Click in the blank paragraph below *February Birthdays*. On the **Insert tab**, in the **Tables group**, click the **Table** button, point to **Quick Tables**, scroll toward the bottom of the list, and then under **General**, click **Birthday Table**.

19 In the second row of the table, position the insertion point in the first cell, and then type **11** Press Tab, and then type **Mary Margolis** Using the same technique, type the following text in the table:

17	**Antonio Ramirez**
18	**Lydia Zimmerman**
20	**Eleanor Robinson**
27	**Stefan Richards**

20 Select the last three empty rows of the table. On the **Layout tab**, in the **Rows & Columns group**, click the **Delete** button, and then click **Delete Rows**.

21 Press Ctrl + End, and then select the blank paragraph mark at the bottom of the second column. With the paragraph mark selected, on the **Page Layout tab**, in the **Page Setup group**, click the **Columns** button, and then click **One**. Compare your screen with Figure 6.23, and then **Save** your document.

The existing text remains formatted in two columns; however, the bottom of the document returns to one column—full page width.

Figure 6.23

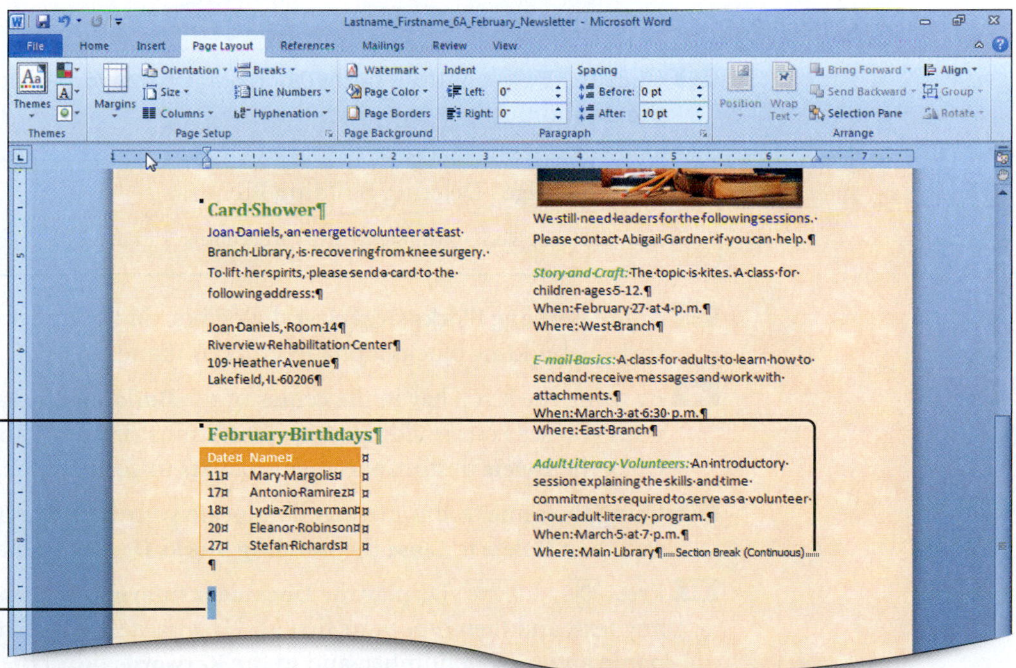

Activity 6.08 | Managing Files and Restoring Settings

You can delete user-created building blocks and user templates if they are no longer needed. If you are sharing a computer with others, you should restore Word to its default settings. In this activity, you will delete the building blocks you created.

1 Click the **Insert tab**, and then in the **Text group**, click the **Quick Parts** button. Right-click the **Classes Picture** building block, and then on the shortcut menu, click **Organize and Delete**. Compare your screen with Figure 6.24.

The Classes Picture building block is selected in the Building Blocks Organizer dialog box. A preview of the building block displays on the right. The name and description of the building block display below the preview.

Figure 6.24

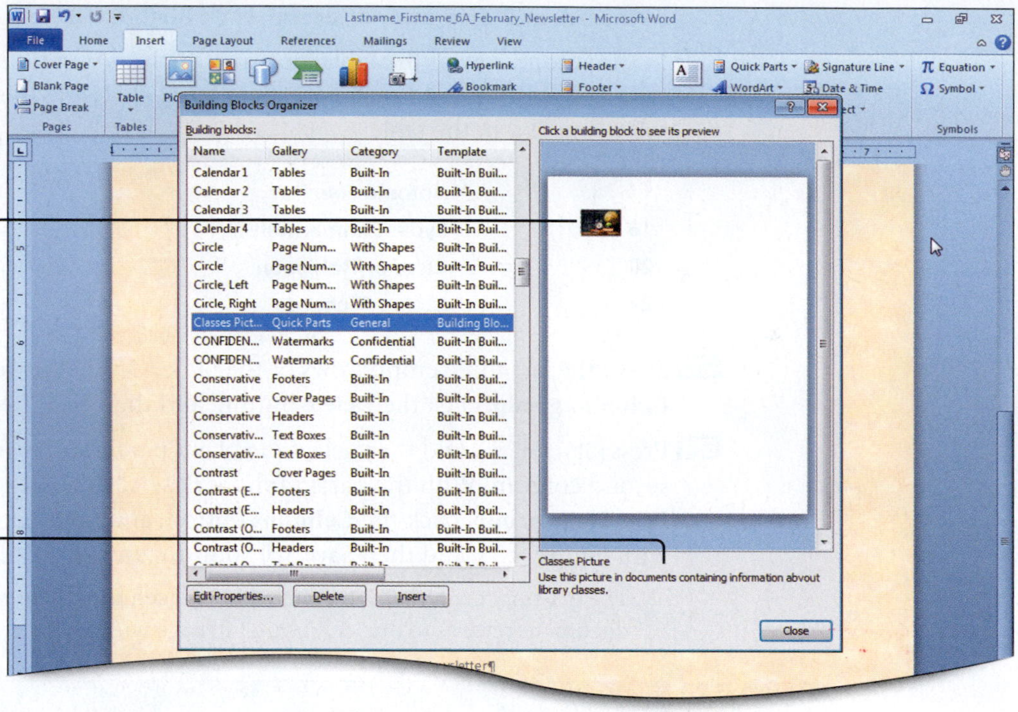

2 Click the **Delete** button. In the **Microsoft Office Word** dialog box, click **Yes** to confirm the deletion.

> **More Knowledge** | Deleting Building Blocks
>
> To delete a building block, you must have an open document. This allows the Quick Parts command to become active.

3 In the **Building Blocks Organizer** dialog box, in the upper left corner, click **Name** to sort the building blocks alphabetically by name.

4 By using the scroll bar in the center of the **Building Blocks Organizer** dialog box, scroll until you see your building block that begins *Birthday*, and then click to select it. Click the **Delete** button, and then click **Yes** to confirm the deletion.

5 Using the same technique, scroll to locate your building block that begins *Library*, and then **Delete** it. **Close** the **Building Blocks Organizer** dialog box.

6 Press Ctrl + Home. Display the **Document Information Panel**. In the **Author** box, delete any text, and then type your first and last names. In the **Subject** box, type your course name and section number, and in the **Keywords** box, type **library newsletter, February** **Close** the Document Information Panel.

7 **Save** your document. Print your two Word documents—you cannot print the theme file—or submit all three files electronically as directed by your instructor. **Close** Word. In the dialog box regarding changes to building blocks, click **Save** to accept the changes.

End **You have completed Project 6A**

Project 6B Events Schedule with Tracked Changes

myitlab
Project 6B Training

Project Activities

In Activities 6.09 through 6.17, you will assist Abigail Gardner, Director of Programs and Youth Services, in using the markup tools in Word to add comments and make changes to a schedule of events. You will accept or reject each change, and then compare and combine your document with another draft version to create a final document. Your completed documents will look similar to Figure 6.25.

Project Files

For Project 6B, you will need the following files:

w06B_Events_Schedule
w06B_Schedule_Revisions

You will save your documents as:

Lastname_Firstname_6B_Events_Schedule
Lastname_Firstname_6B_Schedule_Combined

Project Results

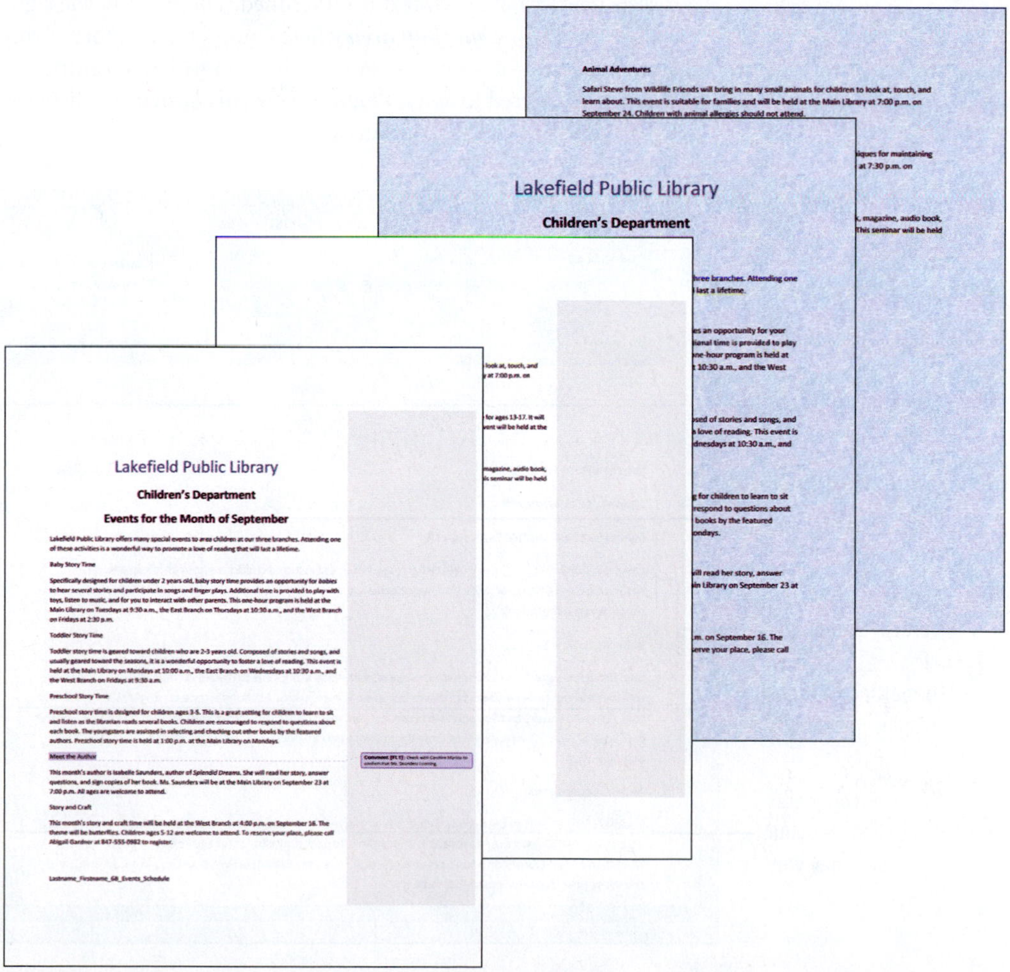

Figure 6.25
Project 6B Events Schedule

Objective 4 | Use Comments in a Document

Building a final document often involves more than one person. One person usually drafts the original and becomes the document ***author***—or *owner*—and then others add their portions of text and comment on, or propose changes to, the text of others. A ***reviewer*** is someone who reviews and marks changes on a document.

A ***comment*** is a note that an author or reviewer adds to a document. Comments are a good way to communicate when more than one person is involved with the writing, reviewing, and editing process. Comments are like sticky notes attached to the document—they can be viewed and read by others, but are not part of the document text.

Activity 6.09 | Inserting Comments

For the library's monthly schedule of events, Abigail Gardner has created a draft document; edits and comments have been added by others. In this activity, you will insert a comment to suggest confirming a scheduled guest.

1 **Start** Word. From your student files, locate and open the file **w06B_Events_Schedule**. If necessary, display the rulers and formatting marks. Compare your screen with Figure 6.26.

The document displays with ***revisions***—changes—shown as ***markup***. Markup refers to the formatting Word uses to denote the revisions visually. For example, when a reviewer changes text, the original text displays with strikethrough formatting by default. When a reviewer inserts new text, the new text is underlined. The space to the right or left of the document is the nonprinting ***markup area*** where comments and formatting changes—for example, applying italic—display. The outline shape in which a comment or formatting change displays is referred to as a ***balloon***. A ***vertical change bar*** displays in the left margin next to each line of text that contains a revision.

Figure 6.26

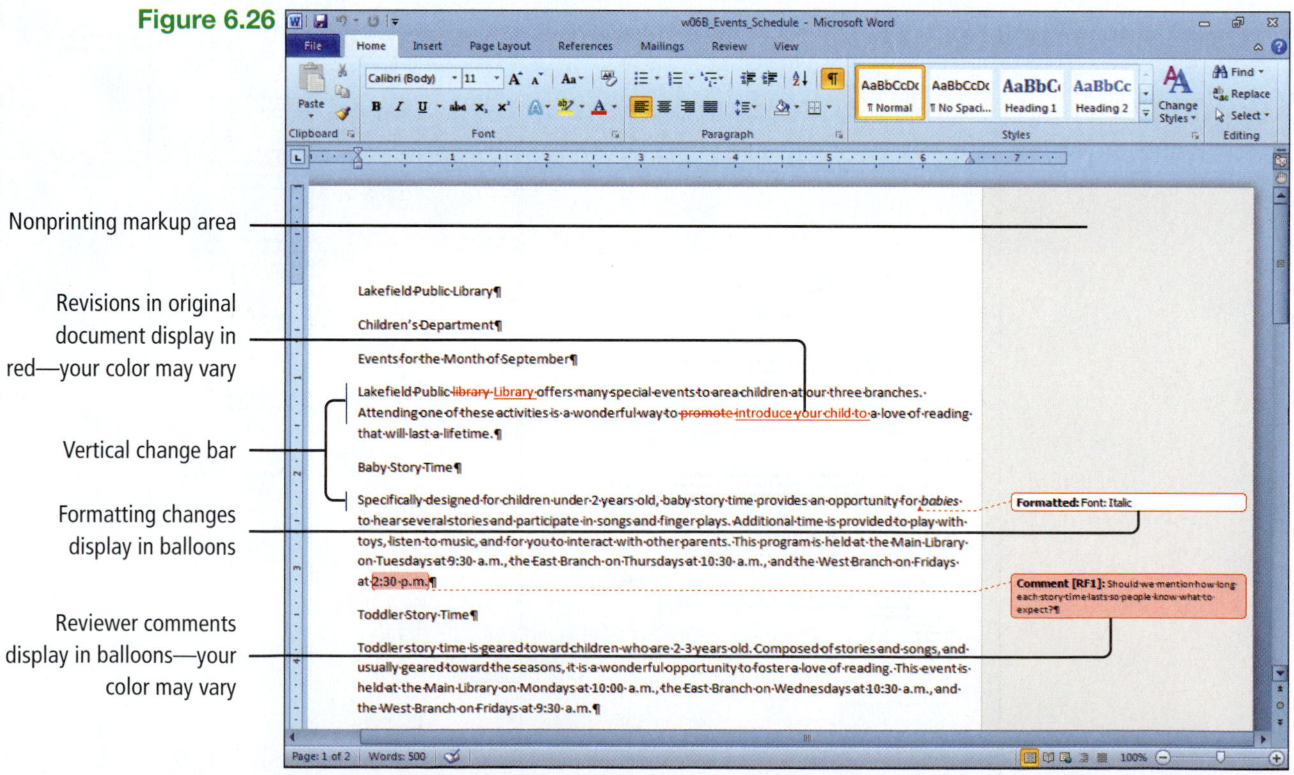

> **Note | Balloons Might Display Instead of Strikethrough Formatting**
>
> Depending on how Word was installed on the computer you are using, you may see balloons instead of strikethrough formatting for some revisions.

2 From **Backstage** view, display the **Save As** dialog box, and then save the document in your **Word Chapter 6** folder as **Lastname_Firstname_6B_Events_Schedule** Using **Quick Parts**, insert the file name in the footer.

3 Click the **Review tab**, and then in the **Tracking group**, notice that *Final: Show Markup* displays, indicating that the markup area is visible and proposed revisions display.

Final: Show Markup is the default view, because you probably do not want to distribute a document that still contains comments or other markup. Thus, Word automatically displays any revisions or comments when you open a document.

4 In the **Tracking group**, click the **Track Changes button arrow**. From the list, click **Change User Name**. Under **Personalize your copy of Microsoft Office**, on a piece of paper, make a note of the **User name** and **Initials**—if you are using your own computer, your own name and initials may display.

The user name identifies the person who makes comments and changes in a document.

> **Alert! | Changing the User Name and Initials**
>
> In a college lab or organization, you may be unable to change the user name and initials, so make a note of the name and initials currently displayed so that you can identify your revisions in this document.

5 If you are able to do so, in the **User name** box, delete any existing text, and then type your own first and last names. In the **Initials** box, delete any existing text, and then type your initials, if necessary. Compare your screen with Figure 6.27. If you are unable to make this change, move to Step 6.

Figure 6.27

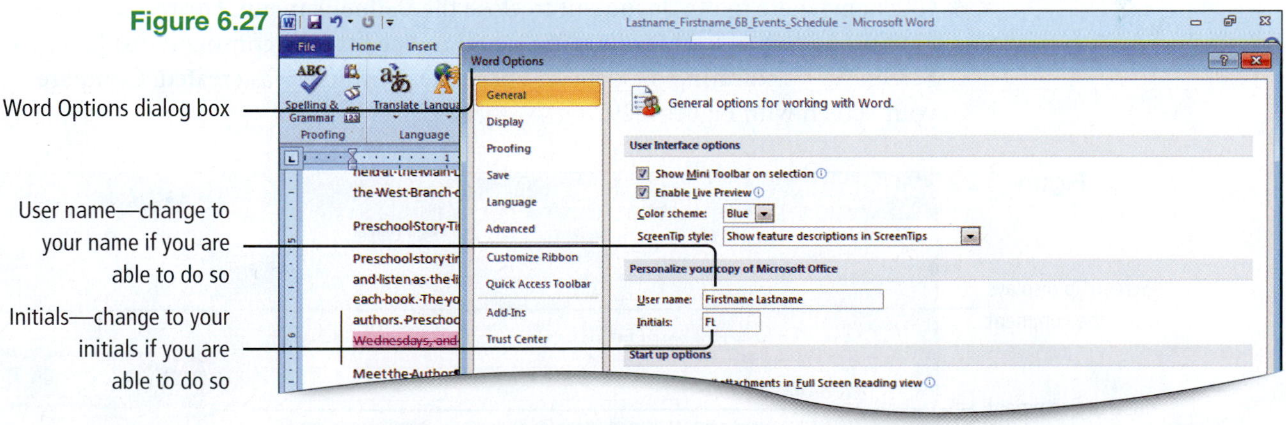

6 Click **OK**. In the lower portion of **Page 1**, select the paragraph *Meet the Author*.

7 On the **Review tab**, in the **Comments group**, click the **New Comment** button, and notice that the comment balloon displays in the markup area with the user initials. Type **Check with Barry Smith to confirm that Ms. Saunders is coming.** Click anywhere outside of the comment, and then compare your screen with Figure 6.28.

You can insert a comment at a specific location in a document or to selected text, such as an entire paragraph. Your initials—or those configured for the computer at which you are working—display at the beginning of the comment, followed by the number *3*, which indicates that this is the third comment in the document. When a new comment is added to a document, existing comments are automatically renumbered. Each reviewer's comments are identified by a distinct color.

Figure 6.28

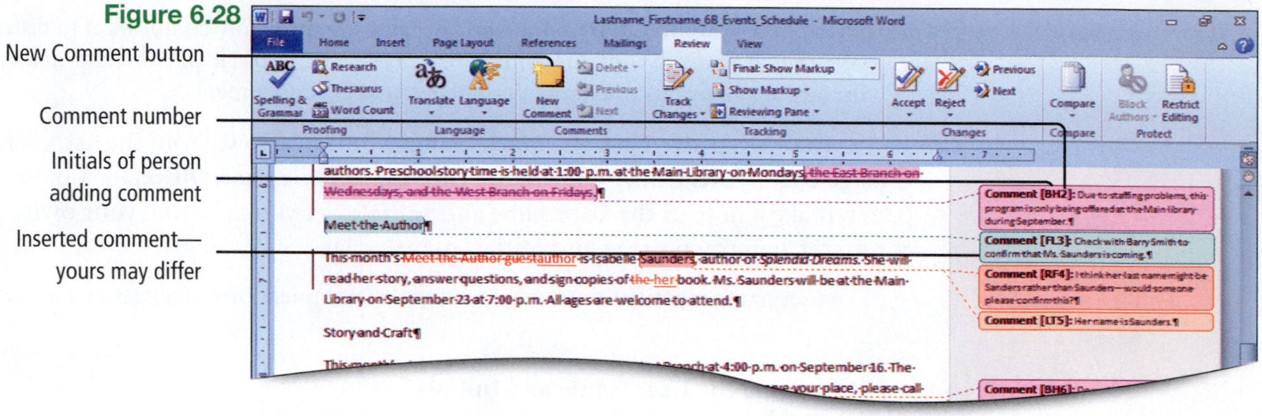

8 On the **Review tab**, in the **Tracking group**, click the **Show Markup** button, and then point to **Balloons**.

The default setting is *Show Only Comments and Formatting in Balloons*. In this default setting, insertions and deletions *do not* display in balloons. Rather, insertions and deletions display directly in the text with insertions underlined and deletions struck out with a line. Comments and formatting *do* display in balloons.

9 Click anywhere in the document to close the **Balloons** menu. For the comment you just added, point to your initials, and notice that the comment displays as a ScreenTip—indicating the date and time the comment was created. Compare your screen with Figure 6.29.

Figure 6.29

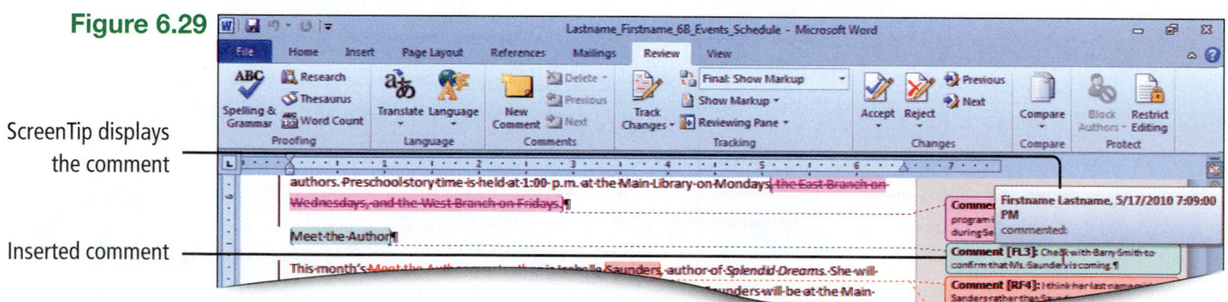

10 Scroll upward as necessary and locate **Comment** **[RF1]**, which begins *Should we mention*. Point to the question mark at the end of the comment text, and then click to position your insertion point after the question mark.

11 In the **Comments group**, click the **New Comment** button, and notice that a new comment displays in the markup area. Compare your screen with Figure 6.30.

The comment includes your initials, the number *2*, and the additional characters *R1*, indicating that this is a *reply* to comment *1*.

Figure 6.30

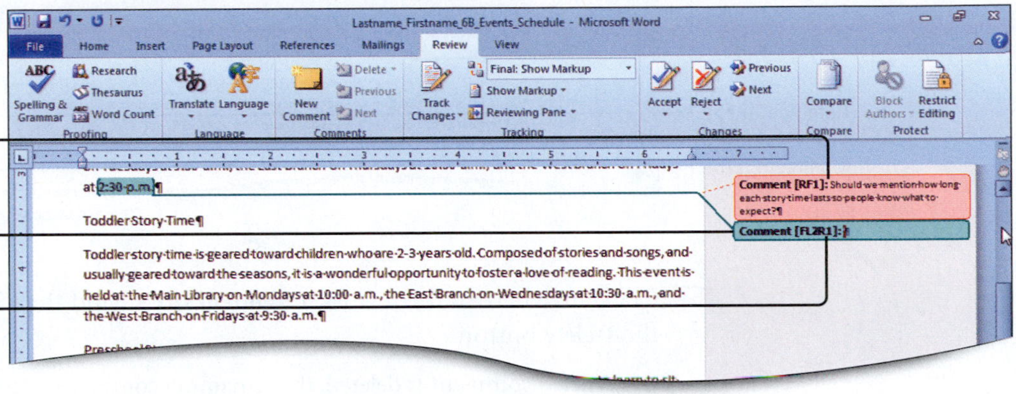

12 With the insertion point in the new comment, type **The program is scheduled for approximately one hour.** and then compare your screen with Figure 6.31.

Figure 6.31

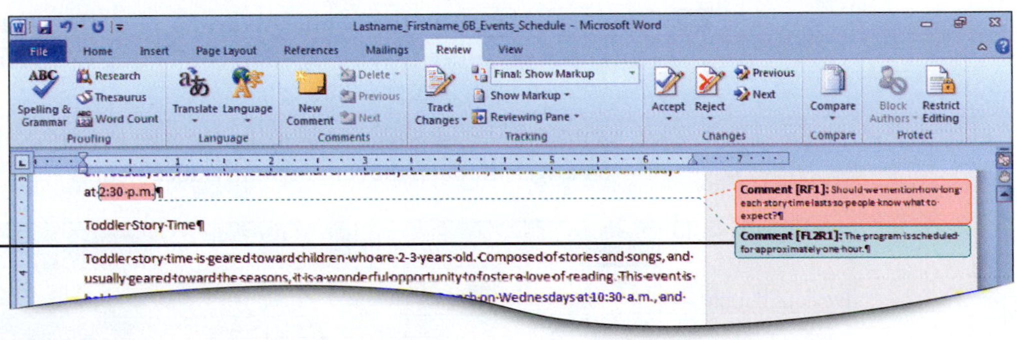

13 **Save** your document.

Activity 6.10 | Editing and Deleting Comments

Typically, comments are temporary. One person inserts a comment, another person answers the question or clarifies the text based on the comment—and then the comments are removed before the document is final. In this activity, you will replace text in your comment and delete comments.

1 Locate the comment you inserted referencing **Barry Smith**, which was comment **4**. Delete the text *Barry Smith*, and then with the insertion point to the left of *to*, type **Caroline Marina** If necessary, press Spacebar.

In this manner, you can edit your comments.

2 Scroll as necessary to locate the **Comment [RF5]** that begins *I think her last name* and the following comment—**Comment [LT6]**. Compare your screen with Figure 6.32.

Because the question asked in *Comment [RF5]* has been answered in *Comment [LT6]*, both comments can be deleted.

Figure 6.32

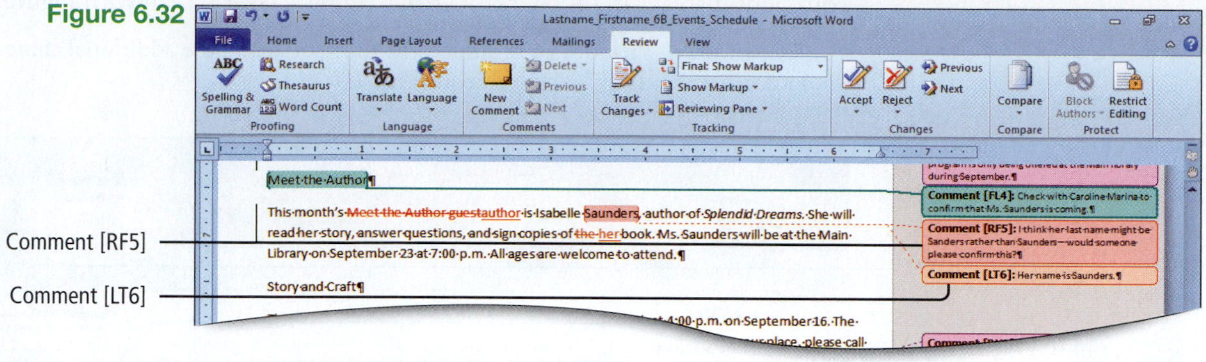

3 Click anywhere in the text for **Comment [RF5]**, and then in the **Comments group**, click the **Delete** button.

When a comment is deleted, the remaining comments are renumbered.

4 Point to **Comment [LT5]**, right-click, and then from the shortcut menu, click **Delete Comment**.

Use either technique to delete a comment.

5 Press Ctrl + Home. In the **Comments group**, click the **Next** button three times. In the markup area, notice that the balloon containing **Comment [BH3]** is selected. Compare your screen with Figure 6.33.

In the Comments group, you can use the Next button and Previous button in this manner to navigate through the comments in a document.

Figure 6.33

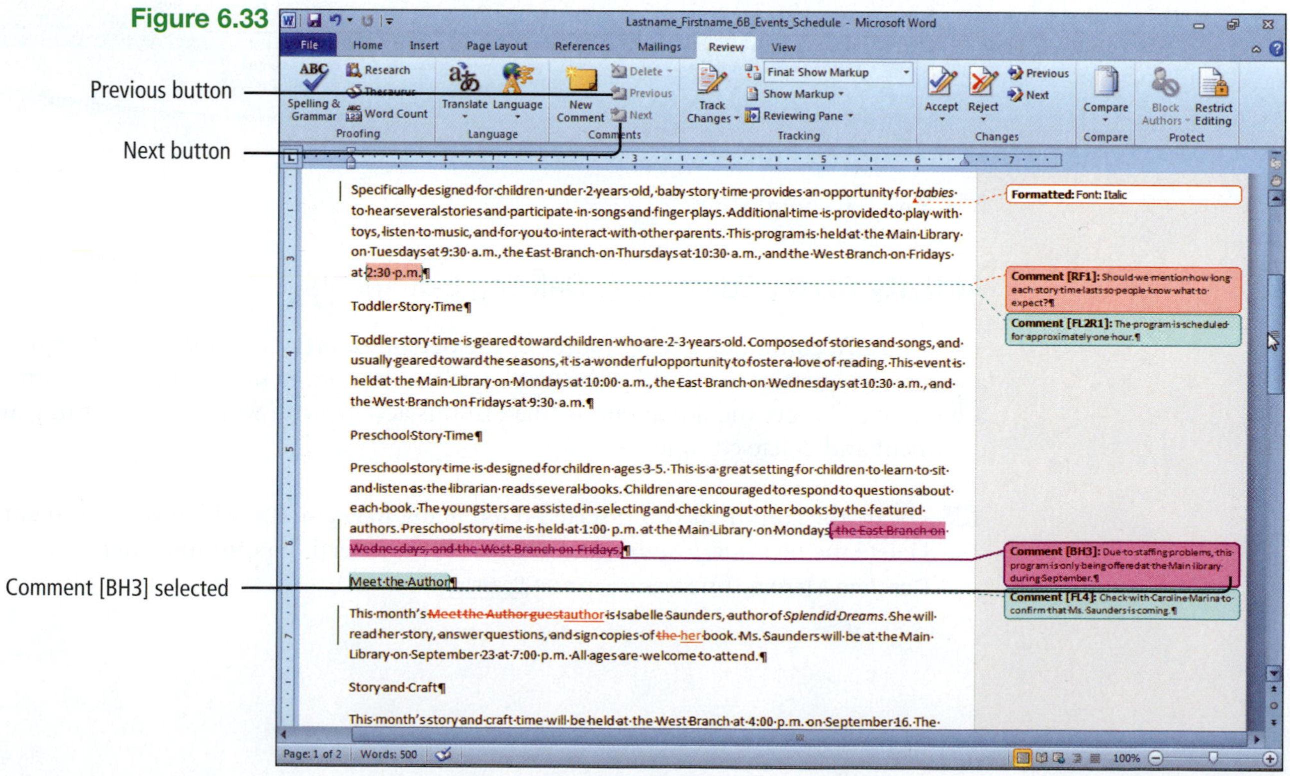

6 With **Comment [BH3]** selected, right-click, and then click **Delete Comment**.

7 In the **Comments group**, click the **Next** button two times to select **Comment [BH4]**, and then using any technique you have practiced, **Delete** the comment.

8 Scroll as necessary, delete **Comment [RF4]**, and then delete **Comment [RF5]**—four comments remain. **Save** your document.

Objective 5 | Track Changes in a Document

When you turn on the ***Track Changes*** feature, Word makes a record of—*tracks*—the changes made to a document. As you revise the document, Word uses markup to visually indicate insertions, deletions, comments, formatting changes, and content that has moved.

Each reviewer's revisions and comments display in a different color. This is useful if, for example, you want to quickly scan only for edits made by a supervisor or only for edits made by a coworker. After the document has been reviewed by the appropriate individuals, you can locate the changes and accept or reject the revisions on a case-by-case basis or globally in the entire document.

Activity 6.11 | Managing Tracked Changes

In this activity, you will change the way insertions and comments display.

1 Press Ctrl + Home to move to the top of the document.

2 In the **Tracking group**, click the **Track Changes button arrow**, and then from the list, click **Change Tracking Options**. Take a moment to study Figure 6.34 and the table shown in Figure 6.35.

Here you can change how markup, moved text, table revisions, formatting changes, and balloons display.

Figure 6.34

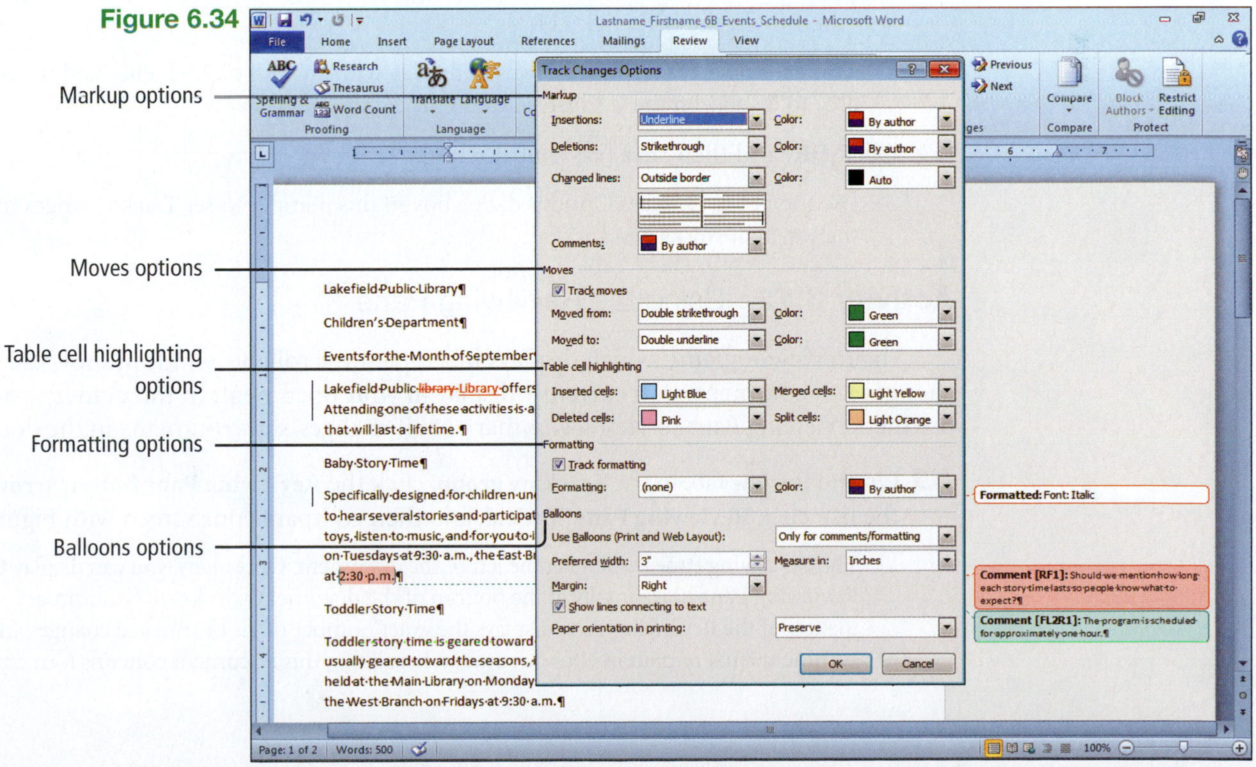

Settings in the Track Changes Options Dialog Box

Options	Settings You Can Adjust
Markup	Specify the format and color of inserted text, deleted text, and changed lines. By default, inserted text is underlined, deleted text displays with strikethrough formatting, and the vertical change bar displays on the outside border—left margin. Click an arrow to select a different format, and click the Color arrow to select a different color. By author, the default, indicates that Word will assign a different color to each person who inserts comments or tracks changes.
Moves	Specify the format of moved text. The default is green with double strikethrough in the moved content and a double underline below the content in its new location. To turn off this feature, clear the check box.
Table cell highlighting	Specify the color that will display in a table if cells are inserted, deleted, merged, or split.
Formatting	Specify the formatting and color of format changes, such as applying italic to a word. By default, no formatting is applied; instead, the formatting change displays in a balloon in the markup area, color coded by author. To turn off this feature, clear the check box.
Balloons	Specify the size and placement of balloons and whether lines should connect the balloon to text. You can also control balloon width and location for online viewing and for printing.

Figure 6.35

3 In the **Track Changes Options** dialog box, under **Balloons**, click the **Preferred width spin box down arrow** as necessary to change the width to **2.5"**. Click the **Margin arrow**, and then from the list, click **Left**.

This action will cause the balloons to display with a width of 2.5 inches and the markup area to display on the left instead of on the right.

4 Click **OK**, and then **Save** your document.

Use the Track Changes Options dialog box in this manner to set Track Changes to display the way that works best for you.

Activity 6.12 | Using the Reviewing Pane

The ***Reviewing Pane***, which displays in a separate scrollable window, shows all of the changes and comments that currently display in your document. In this activity, you will use the Reviewing Pane to view a summary of all changes and comments in the document.

1 On the **Review tab**, in the **Tracking group**, click the **Reviewing Pane button arrow**. From the list, click **Reviewing Pane Vertical**, and then compare your screen with Figure 6.36.

The Reviewing Pane displays at the left of the document. Optionally, you can display the Reviewing Pane horizontally at the bottom of the document window. The summary section at the top of the Reviewing Pane displays the exact number of visible tracked changes and comments that remain in your document. Recall that this document contains four comments.

Figure 6.36

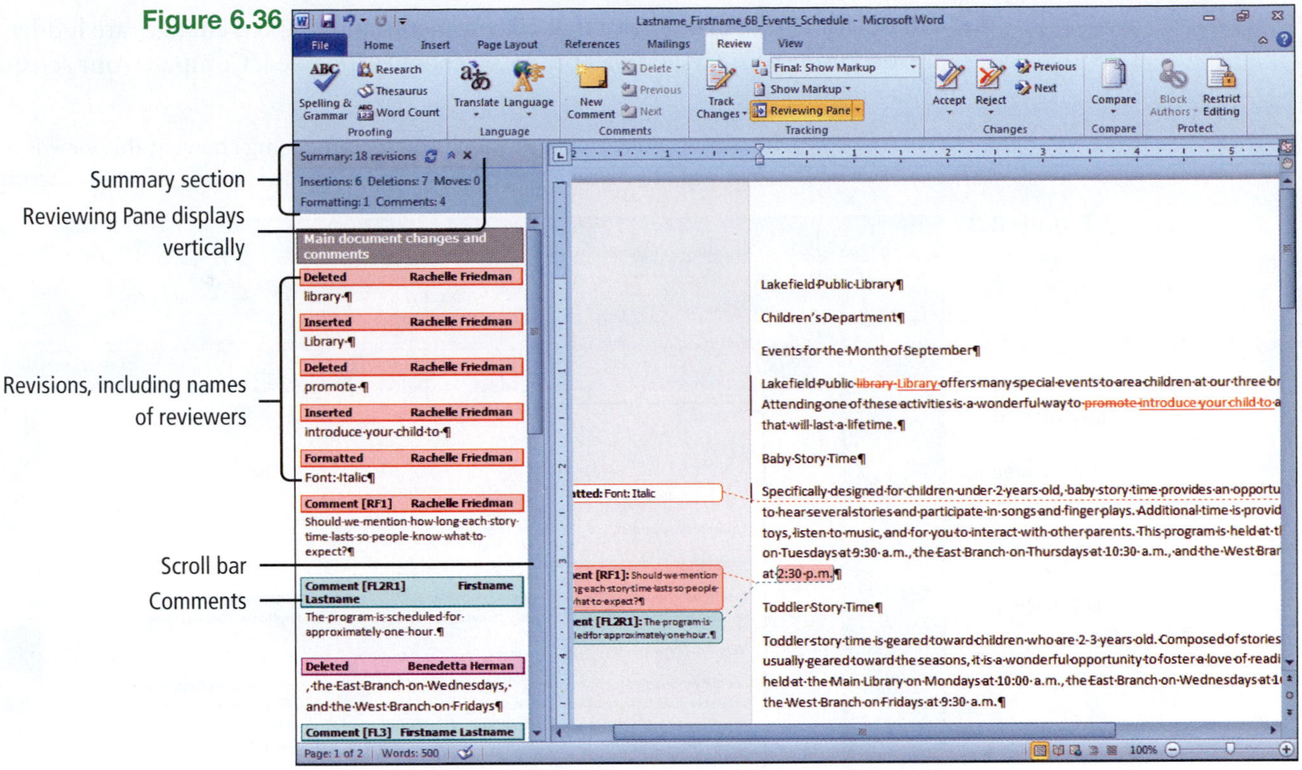

2 Take a moment to read the comments in the **Reviewing Pane**.

In the Reviewing Pane, you can view each type of revision, the name of the reviewer associated with each item, and read long comments that do not fit within a comment bubble. The Reviewing Pane is also useful for ensuring that all tracked changes have been *removed* from your document when it is ready for final distribution.

3 At the top of the **Reviewing Pane**, click the **Close** button [×].

Activity 6.13 | Viewing Revisions in a Document

After one or more reviewers have made revisions and inserted comments, you can view the revisions in various ways. You can display the document in its original or final form, showing or hiding revisions and comments. Additionally, you can choose to view the revisions and comments by only some reviewers or view only a particular type of revision—for example, only formatting changes.

1 On the **Review tab**, in the **Tracking group**, locate the **Display for Review** box that displays the text *Final: Show Markup*. Click the **Display for Review arrow** to display a list.

Final view displays the document with all proposed changes included and comments hidden.

Final: Show Markup view, which is the default view, displays the final document with all revisions and comments visible.

Original view hides the tracked changes and shows the original, unchanged document with comments hidden.

Original: Show Markup view displays the original document with all revisions and comments visible.

2 On the list, click **Final**. Notice that all comments and marked changes are hidden, and the document displays with all proposed changes included. Compare your screen with Figure 6.37.

When you are editing a document in which you are proposing changes, this view is useful because the revisions of others or the markup of your own revisions is not distracting.

Figure 6.37

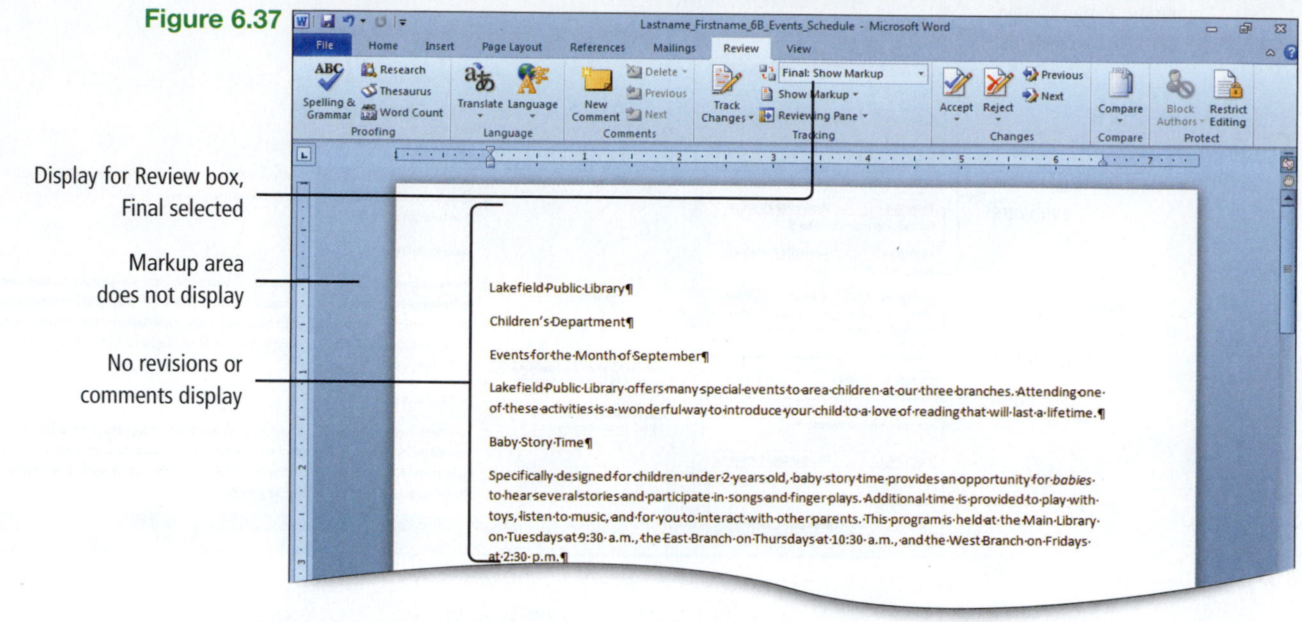

3 In the **Tracking group**, click the **Display for Review arrow**, and then from the list, click **Final: Show Markup**.

At the stage where you, the document owner, must decide which revisions to accept or reject, you will find this view to be the most useful.

4 In the **Tracking group**, click the **Show Markup** button. Point to **Reviewers** to see the name of each individual who proposed changes to this document. Compare your screen with Figure 6.38.

Here you can turn off the display of revisions by one or more reviewers. For example, you might want to view only the revisions proposed by a supervisor—before you consider the revisions proposed by others—by clearing the check box for all reviewers except the supervisor.

Here you can also determine which changes display by deselecting one or more check boxes. ***Ink***, if displayed, refers to marks made directly on a document by using a stylus on a Tablet PC.

Figure 6.38

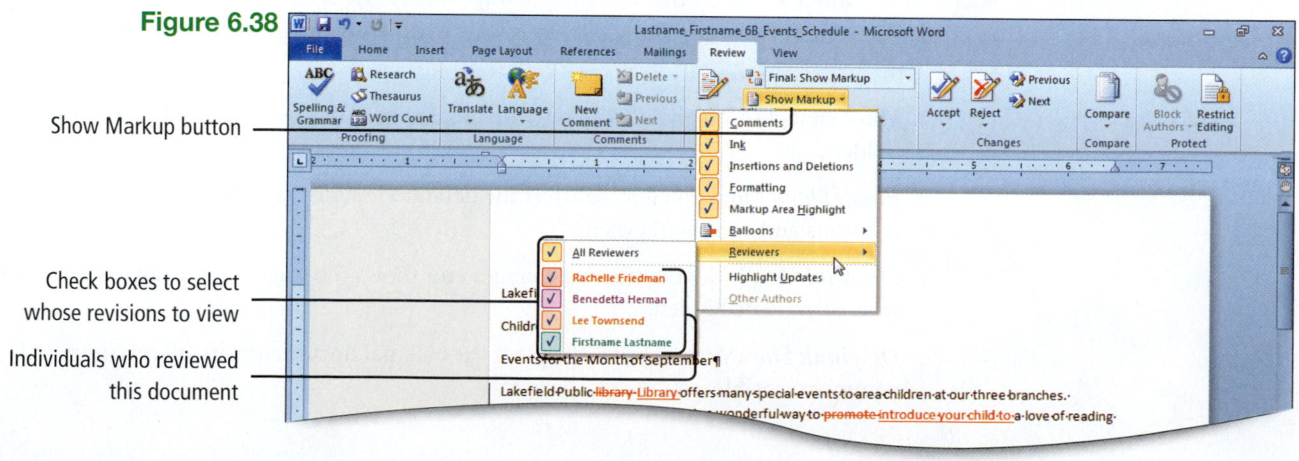

5 Click anywhere in the document to close the **Show Markup** menu and leave all revision types by all reviewers displayed.

Activity 6.14 | Turning on Track Changes

The Track Changes feature is turned off by default; you must turn on the feature each time you want to begin tracking changes in a document.

1 Press Ctrl + Home, if necessary, to move to the top of the document. In the **Tracking group**, click the upper portion of the **Track Changes** button to enable tracking; notice that the button glows orange to indicate that the feature is turned on.

2 Select the first paragraph—the text *Lakefield Public Library*. On the Mini toolbar, change the **Font Size** to **28**, apply **Center** alignment, and change the **Font Color** to **Dark Blue, Text 2**—in the fourth column, the first color.

As you make each change, the markup displays in the markup area, and the vertical change bar displays. The types of changes—formatted text and center alignment—are indicated in balloons, and lines point to the location of the revisions.

3 Click anywhere in the document to cancel the selection. Point to the formatted text, and then compare your screen with Figure 6.39.

A ScreenTip displays, indicating who made the change, when it was made, and the type of change.

Figure 6.39

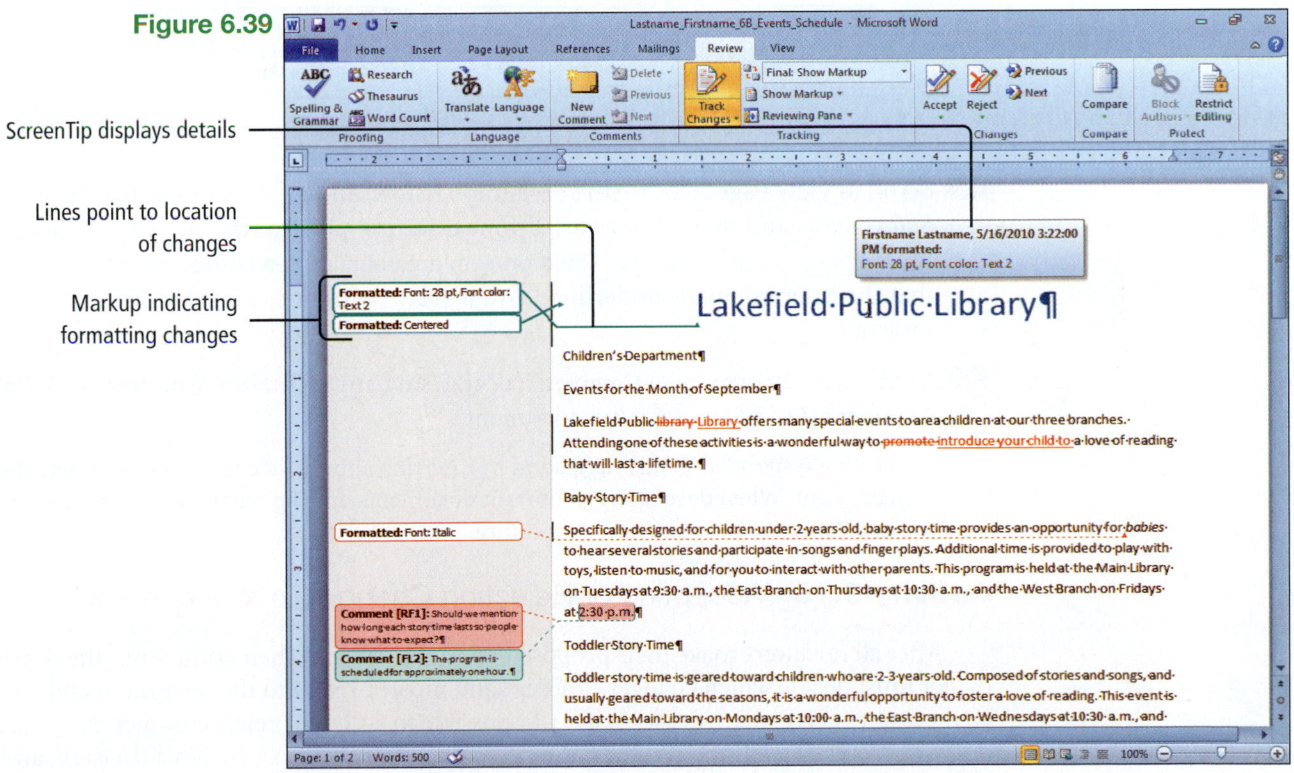

4 Select the second and third paragraphs, change the **Font Size** to **20**, apply **Bold** [B], and then **Center** [≡] the paragraphs.

5 Select the paragraph heading *Baby Story Time*, hold down Ctrl, and then by using the **down scroll arrow** [▾], move through the document and select the remaining paragraph headings—*Toddler Story Time*, *Preschool Story Time*, *Meet the Author*, *Story and Craft*, *Animal Adventures*, *Internet Safety*, and *Seek and Find at the Library*. Apply **Bold** [B] to the selected headings.

6 Scrolling as necessary, locate the paragraph below *Baby Story Time* that begins *Specifically designed*. In the third line, click to place your insertion point to the left of *program*, type **one-hour** and then press Spacebar.

The inserted text is underlined and displays with your designated color.

7 Point to the inserted text, and then compare your screen with Figure 6.40.

A ScreenTip displays, showing the revision that was made, which reviewer made the change, and the date and time of the change.

Figure 6.40

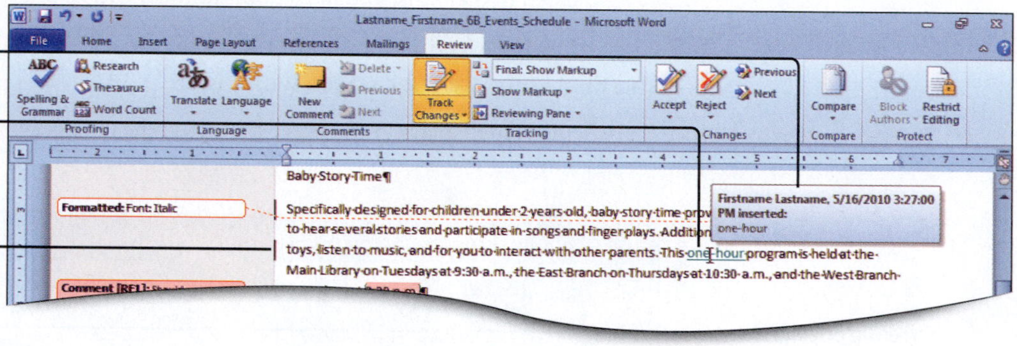

8 Scroll to view **Page 2**, locate the paragraph below *Animal Adventures* that begins *Safari Steve*, and then click to place your insertion point at the end of the paragraph. Press Spacebar, and then type **Children with animal allergies should not attend.** Notice that the inserted text is underlined and displays with the same color as your previous insertion.

9 In the markup area, read **Comment [LT4]**. Using any technique you practiced, **Delete Comment [LT4]**. **Save** [💾] your document.

Having responded to this suggestion by inserting appropriate text, you can delete the comment. When developing important documents, having others review the document can improve its content and appearance.

Activity 6.15 | Accepting or Rejecting Changes in a Document

After all reviewers make their proposed revisions and add their comments, the document owner must decide which changes to accept and incorporate into the document and which changes to reject. Unlike revisions, it is not possible to accept or reject comments; instead, the document owner reads the comments, takes appropriate action or makes a decision, and then deletes each comment. In this activity, you will accept and reject changes to create a final document.

1 Press Ctrl + Home to move to the top of the document.

When reviewing comments and changes in a document, it is good practice to start at the beginning of the document to be sure you do not miss any comments or revisions.

2 On the **Review tab**, in the **Changes group**, click the **Next** button—be careful to select the **Next** button from the **Changes group**, *not* the **Comments group**. Notice the first paragraph is selected.

The Next button and the Previous button in the Changes group enable you to navigate from one revision or comment to the next or previous one.

3 In the **Changes group**, click the upper portion of the **Accept** button.

The text formatting is accepted for the first paragraph, the related balloon no longer displays in the markup area, and the next change—center alignment for the first three paragraphs—is selected. When reviewing a document, changes can be accepted or rejected individually, or all at one time.

> **Another Way**
>
> Right-click the selection, and on the shortcut menu, click **Accept**.

4 In the **Changes group**, click the upper portion of the **Accept** button to accept the alignment change.

The centering change is applied to all three paragraphs.

5 In the **Changes group**, click the **Accept** button to accept the text formatting for the second and third paragraphs.

6 In the next paragraph, point to the strikethrough text *library* and notice the ScreenTip that indicates Rachelle Friedman deleted *library*. Then, point to the underline directly below *Library* to display a ScreenTip. Compare your screen with Figure 6.41.

When a reviewer replaces text—for example, when Rachelle replaced *library* with *Library*—the inserted text displays with an underline and in the color designated for the reviewer. The original text displays with strikethrough formatting.

Figure 6.41

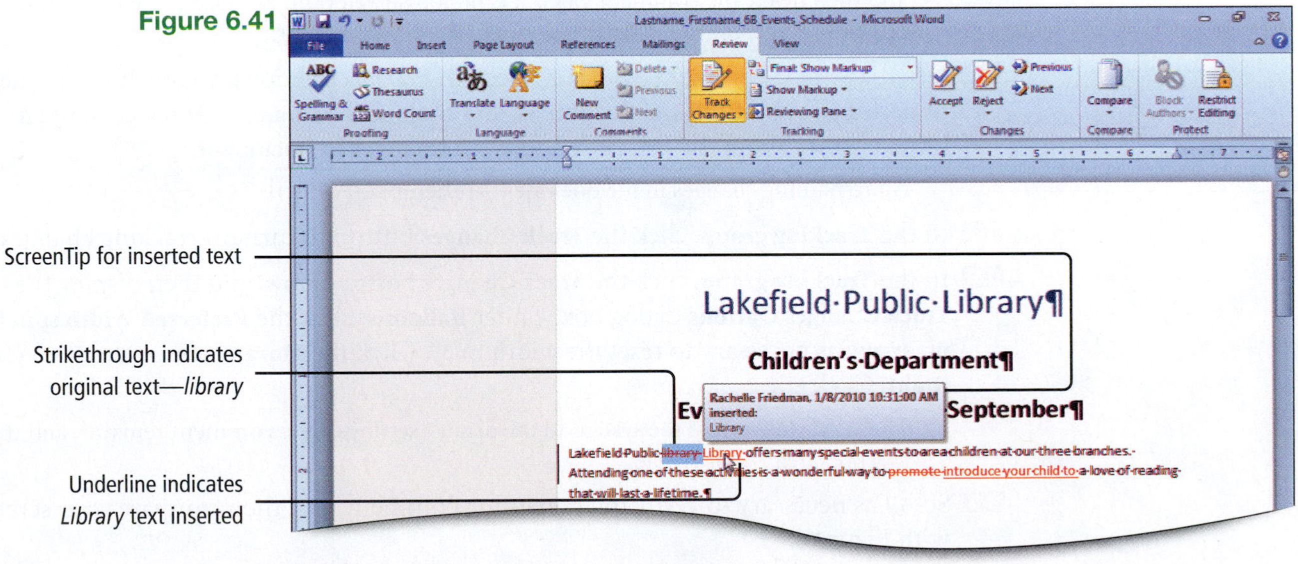

7 In the **Changes group**, click the **Accept** button two times to accept the deletion of *library* and the insertion of *Library*.

The next change, the deletion of *promote* is selected.

8 In the **Changes group**, click the **Reject** button, and then point to the selected text *introduce your child to*, to display a ScreenTip. Compare your screen with Figure 6.42.

The original text *promote* is reinserted in the sentence. As the document owner, you decide which proposed revisions to accept; you are not required to accept every change in a document.

Figure 6.42

9 Click the **Reject** button again to reject the insertion of *introduce your child to* and to select the next change.

10 Click the **Accept** button three times, and then notice that **Comment [RF1]**, suggesting that the program length be mentioned, is selected. Right-click the comment, and then click **Delete Comment**.

Recall that you cannot accept or reject comments. Rather, you take appropriate action, and then delete the comment when it is no longer relevant. Because you entered text indicating the program length, you can delete the comment.

11 Delete the next comment, which is selected. Then, scroll down to quickly scan the remaining revisions in the document, and then in the **Changes group**, click the **Accept button arrow**. From the list, click **Accept All Changes in Document**.

All remaining changes in the document are accepted.

12 In the **Tracking group**, click the **Track Changes** button to turn off tracking changes.

13 In the **Tracking group**, click the **Track Changes button arrow**, and then display the **Track Changes Options** dialog box. Under **Balloons**, click the **Preferred Width spin box up arrow** as necessary to reset the width to **3"**. Click the **Margin arrow**, and then click **Right**. Click **OK**.

These actions restore the system to the default settings. One comment remains, and the markup area is still visible.

14 Scroll as necessary to verify the remaining comment, and then compare your screen with Figure 6.43.

Figure 6.43

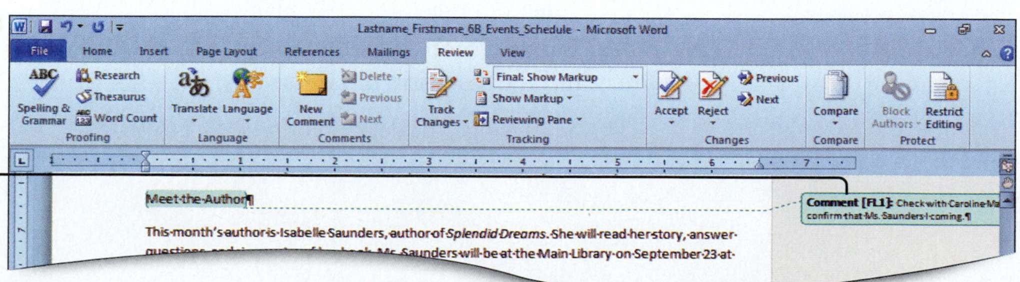

15 Display the **Document Information Panel**. In the **Author** box, delete any text, and then type your first and last names. In the **Subject** box, type your course name and section number, and in the **Keywords** box, type **events schedule, reviewed Close** the Document Information Panel.

16 **Save** your document, and leave it open for the next activity.

Objective 6 | View Side by Side, Compare, and Combine Documents

It is not always possible for reviewers to make their comments and edits on a single Word file. Each reviewer might edit a copy of the file, and then the document owner must gather all of the files and combine all the revisions into a single final document. One method to examine the changes is to use the ***View Side by Side*** command. Using the View Side by Side command displays two open documents, in separate windows, next to each other on your screen.

Word has two other features, ***Compare*** and ***Combine***, which enable you to view revisions in two documents and determine which changes to accept and which ones to reject. Compare is useful when reviewing differences between an original document and the latest version of the document. When using Compare, Word assumes all revisions were made by the same individual. The Combine feature enables you to review two different documents containing revisions—both based on an original document—and the individuals who made the revisions are identified.

Activity 6.16 | Using View Side by Side

Abigail Garner has received another copy of the original file, which contains revisions and comments from two additional reviewers—Angie Harper and Natalia Ricci. In this activity, you will use View Side by Side to compare the new document with the version you finalized in the previous activity.

1 With your file **Lastname_Firstname_6B_Events_Schedule** open and the insertion point displaying at the top of the document, navigate to your student files, and then locate and open the file **w06B_Schedule_Revisions**.

2 On the **View tab**, in the **Window group**, click the **View Side by Side** button to display both documents.

This view enables you to see if there have been any major changes to the original document that should be discussed by the reviewers before making revisions. Both documents contain the same basic text.

> **Alert! | Why Doesn't the Entire Window Display?**
> Depending upon your screen resolution, the entire window may not display.

3 In the **w06B_Schedule_Revisions** document, drag the horizontal scroll bar to the right so that you can see the markup area. Notice that both documents scroll. Compare your screen with Figure 6.44. Depending on your screen resolution, your view may differ.

Edits and comments made by Ms. Harper and Ms. Ricci display in the w06B_Schedule_Revisions file. When View Side by Side is active, ***synchronous scrolling***—both documents scroll simultaneously—is turned on by default.

Figure 6.44

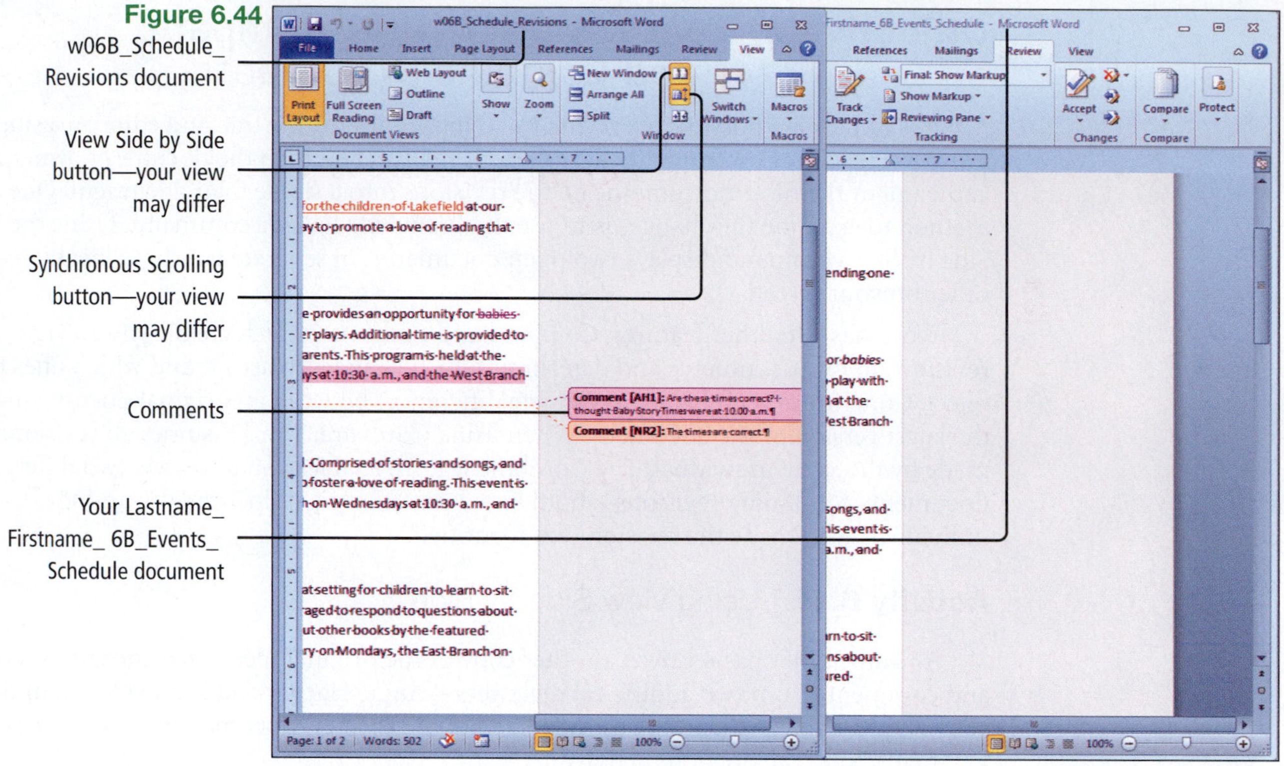

4 **Close** the **w06B_Schedule_Revisions** document. Notice your **Lastname_Firstname_6B_Events_Schedule** document displays in full screen view.

5 Display **Backstage** view, and then **Close** your **Lastname_Firstname_6B_Events_Schedule** without closing Word.

Activity 6.17 | Combining Documents

In this activity, you will combine the document containing revisions and comments by Angie Harper and Natalia Ricci with your finalized version of the events schedule. Then, you will accept or reject the additional revisions to create a final document ready for distribution to the public.

1 On the **Review tab**, in the **Compare group**, click the **Compare** button. From the displayed list, click **Combine** to display the **Combine Documents** dialog box.

When using the Combine feature, it is not necessary to have an open document.

Another Way

To the right of the **Original document** box, click the **Browse** button.

2 In the **Combine Documents** dialog box, click the **Original document arrow**, and then click **Browse**. In the **Open** dialog box, navigate to your student files, select the file **w06B_Schedule_Revisions**, and then click **Open**.

Recall that this file includes revisions and comments from two additional reviewers. *Original document* usually refers to a document without revisions or, in this case, the document that you have not yet reviewed.

3 Under **Original document**, in the **Label unmarked changes with** box, delete the existing text, and then type your first and last names.

4 Click the **Revised document arrow**, and then click **Browse**. Navigate to your **Word Chapter 6** folder, select **Lastname_Firstname_6B_Events_Schedule**, and then click **Open**.

Revised document refers to the latest version of the document—in this case, the document where you accepted and rejected changes.

5 Under **Revised document**, in the **Label unmarked changes with** box, if your name does not display, delete the existing text, and then type your first and last names.

6 In the **Combine Documents** dialog box, click the **More** button, and then under **Show changes in**, be sure the **New document** option button is selected. Compare your screen with Figure 6.45.

The More button expands the dialog box to display additional settings. By selecting the New Document option, all changes in both files display in a new document.

Figure 6.45

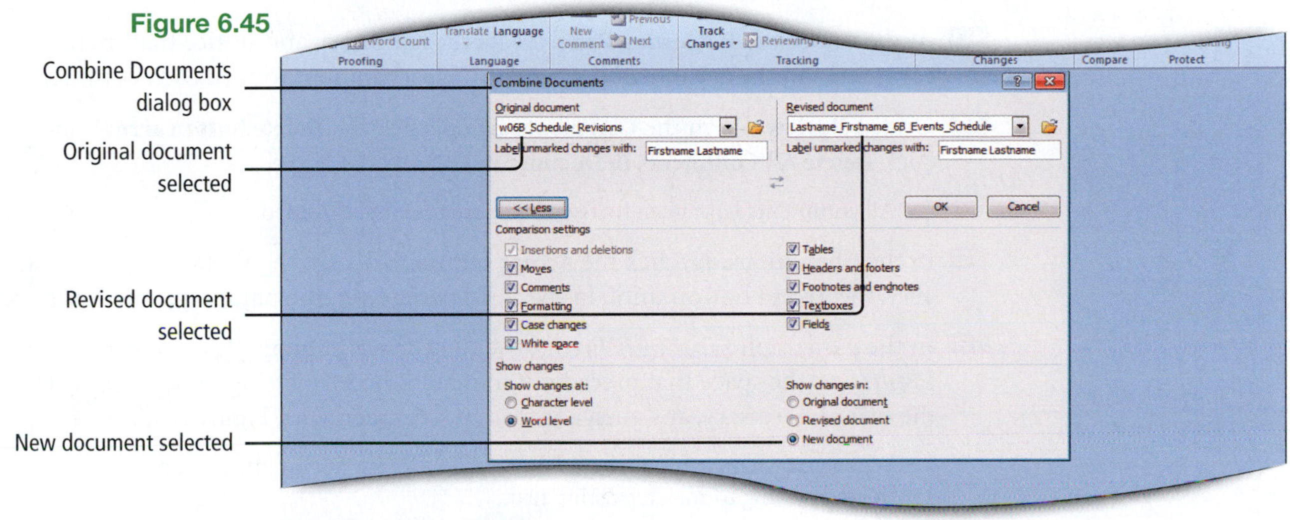

7 In the **Combine Documents** dialog box, click the **Less** button, and then click **OK**. Compare your screen with Figure 6.46.

The Tri-Pane Review Panel displays with the combined document in the left pane, the original document in the top right pane, and the revised document in the bottom right pane. The Reviewing Pane displays to the left of your screen, indicating all accepted changes in your Lastname_Firstname_6B_Events_Schedule file with your user name.

Figure 6.46

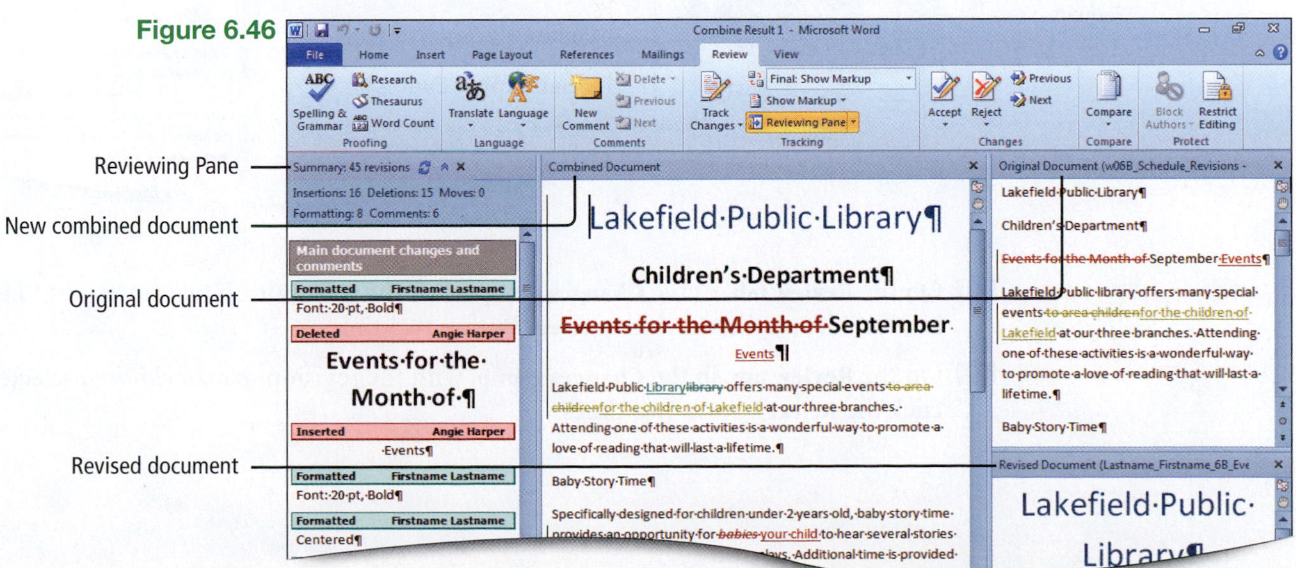

Alert! | Should Both Documents Display?

If only the combined document displays, in the Compare group, click the Compare button, click Show Source Documents, and then click Show Both. If the Reviewing Pane does not display, in the Tracking group, click the Reviewing Pane button arrow, and then click Reviewing Pane Vertical.

8. If necessary, click to place the insertion point at the beginning of the **Combined Document**. **Save** the document in your **Word Chapter 6** folder as **Lastname_Firstname_6B_Schedule_Combined**

9. On the **Insert tab**, in the **Header & Footer group**, click the **Footer** button, and then click **Edit Footer**. Delete any existing text, and then use **Quick Parts** to insert the file name in the footer. At the right end of the Ribbon, click the **Close Header and Footer** button.

10. At the top of the **Reviewing Pane**, locate the summary and notice that there are six comments in the combined document. Take a moment to read each comment.

11. On the **Review tab**, in the **Comments group**, click the **Delete button arrow**, and then click **Delete All Comments in Document**. Press Ctrl + Home.

    All comments have been reviewed and are no longer needed.

12. In the **Changes group**, click the **Accept** button to accept the first change. Continue to click the **Accept** button until, in the third paragraph, the paragraph mark is selected.

13. In the paragraph *September Events*, use the **Format Painter** to format the text *Events* and the space that precedes it to match the formatting of *September*. Deselect the text, if necessary, and then compare your screen with Figure 6.47.

    When new changes are accepted from two different documents, you may need to modify the formatting to match existing text.

Figure 6.47

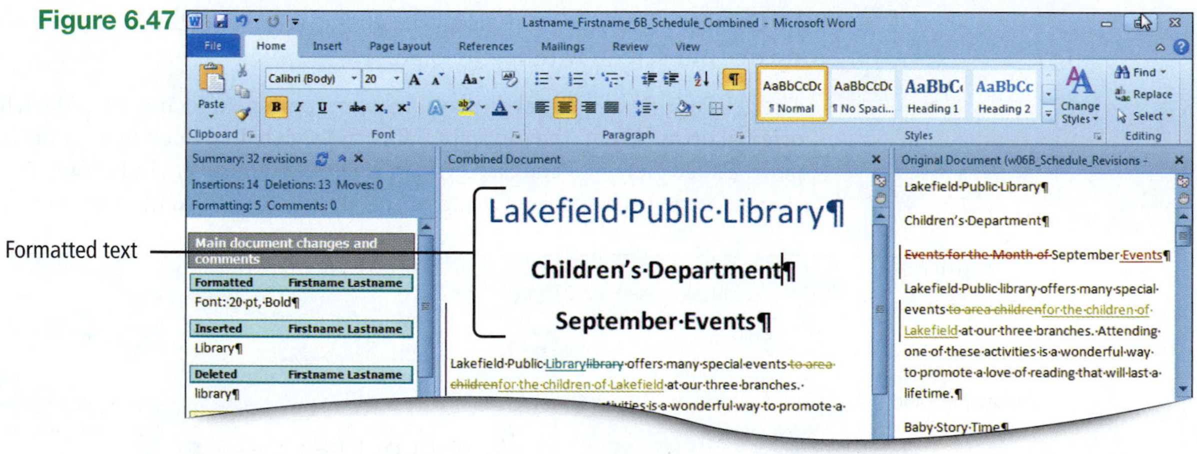

14. On the **Review tab**, in the **Changes group**, click the **Next** button two times until *Library* is selected, and then click the **Accept** button two times.

15. On the **Review tab**, in the **Changes group**, with the revision *to area children* selected, click the **Reject** button two times.

16 In the **Changes group**, click the **Accept button arrow**, and then click **Accept All Changes in Document**. In the **Reviewing Pane**, notice that no further revisions or comments remain. On the right of your screen, **Close** [×] the two panes—the original and revised documents. **Close** [×] the Reviewing Pane.

Because all remaining revisions in the document are accepted, there is no longer a need to view the original or revised documents.

17 In the **Tracking group**, click the **Track Changes button arrow**, and then click **Change User Name**. If you made changes to the user name, delete your name and initials and type the name and initials that displayed originally. Click **OK** to close the dialog box.

When sharing a computer with others, if you have made any changes, it is good practice to restore the settings when you are finished.

18 Press Ctrl + Home. On the **Page Layout tab**, in the **Page Background group**, click the **Page Color** button, and then click **Fill Effects**. In the **Fill Effects** dialog box, click the **Texture** tab, and then scroll to the bottom of the displayed textures. In the next to last row, click the first texture—**Blue tissue paper**. Click **OK**.

The page background is added to improve the final appearance of the document. Because you have been assigned the task of preparing the final document for distribution, it is appropriate to make this formatting change.

Note | Printing Page Backgrounds

Page backgrounds do not display in Print Preview and do not print by default.

19 From **Backstage** view, display the **Document Information Panel**. In the **Author** box, delete any existing text, and then type your first and last names. In the **Subject** box, type your course name and section number, and in the **Keywords** box, type **events schedule, reviewed, combined** **Close** [×] the Document Information Panel.

20 Press Ctrl + F2 to display the **Print Preview** in **Backstage** view. Examine the **Print Preview**, make any necessary adjustments, and then **Save** your document. Print both documents or submit electronically as directed by your instructor. **Exit** Word.

More Knowledge | Printing Page Backgrounds

To print the background color or fill effect of a document, display the Word Options dialog box, select Display, and then under Printing Options, select the Print background colors and images check box. Click OK.

End **You have completed Project 6B**

Content-Based Assessments

Summary

You created text box, graphic, and Quick Table building blocks and reused them in a document. Then you created and applied a theme template to enhance the appearance of the final document. You also used comments and edited and combined documents by use the Track Changes feature in Word.

Key Terms

Author 182
Balloon 182
Building blocks 165
Building Blocks Organizer....................167
Click and type pointer....168
Combine 195
Comment.......................182
Compare 195
Final 189
Final: Show Markup 189
Ink 190
Markup 182
Markup area 182
Original 189
Original: Show Markup.......................189
Quick Parts 167
Quick Tables 168
Reviewer 182
Reviewing Pane 188
Revisions.......................182
Synchronous scrolling.....................196
Text box 165
Theme 172
Theme template 172
Track Changes 187
Vertical change bar 182
View Side by Side 195

Matching

Match each term in the second column with its correct definition in the first column by writing the letter of the term on the blank line in front of the correct definition.

_____ 1. Reusable pieces of content or other documents parts.
_____ 2. A movable, resizable container for text or graphics.
_____ 3. A stored, user-defined set of colors, fonts, and effects.
_____ 4. The owner, or creator, of the original document.
_____ 5. A note that an author or reviewer adds to a document.
_____ 6. Changes made to a document.
_____ 7. The space to the left or right of a document where comments and formatting changes display in balloons.
_____ 8. The outline shape in which a comment or formatting change displays.
_____ 9. Identifies the person who makes comments and changes in a document.
_____ 10. A feature that makes a record of the revisions made to a document.
_____ 11. A separate scrollable window that displays all of the changes and comments that currently display in a document.
_____ 12. A Track Changes view that displays the document with all proposed changes included and comments hidden.
_____ 13. A Track Changes view that hides the tracked changes and shows the original, unchanged document with comments hidden.

A Author
B Balloon
C Building blocks
D Combine
E Comment
F Compare
G Final
H Markup area
I Original
J Reviewing Pane
K Revisions
L Text box
M Theme template
N Track Changes
O User name

_____ 14. A Track Changes feature that enables you to review differences between an original document and the latest version of the document.

_____ 15. A Track Changes feature that allows you to review two different documents containing revisions, both based on an original document.

Multiple Choice

Circle the correct answer.

1. You can view all available building blocks in the:
   A. Quick Tables gallery **B.** Building Blocks Organizer **C.** Quick Parts gallery
2. All of the reusable content pieces including building blocks, properties, and fields are:
   A. Quick Tables **B.** Quick Parts **C.** Text boxes
3. A predefined combination of colors, fonts, and effects that can be applied as a single selection is a:
   A. Quick Part **B.** theme **C.** style
4. In Word, an individual who marks changes in another person's document is referred to as:
   A. a reviewer **B.** an editor **C.** an author
5. The formatting Word uses to denote a document's revisions visually is called:
   A. markup **B.** balloons **C.** comments
6. When a line of text contains revisions, the left margin displays a:
   A. vertical change bar **B.** horizontal change bar **C.** balloon
7. When a reviewer makes a comment, the beginning of the comment displays:
   A. the reviewer's name **B.** the reviewer's initials **C.** the date of the comment
8. The view in which all revisions and comments are visible is:
   A. Combine **B.** Final: Show All **C.** Final: Show Markup
9. To display two documents next to each other in separate windows use the:
   A. Combine setting **B.** View Side by Side setting **C.** Two Pages view
10. To cause two displayed documents to scroll simultaneously, turn on:
    A. Track Changes **B.** synchronous viewing **C.** synchronous scrolling

Content-Based Assessments

Apply **6A** skills from these Objectives:

1. Create Building Blocks
2. Create and Save a Theme Template
3. Create a Document by Using Building Blocks

Skills Review | Project 6C Literacy Program

In the following Skills Review project, you will create and save building blocks and create a theme to be used in a flyer seeking volunteers for Lakefield Public Library's Adult Literacy Program. Your completed documents will look similar to Figure 6.48.

Project Files

For Project 6C, you will need the following files:

Two new blank Word documents
w06C_Literacy_Information

You will save your files as:

Lastname_Firstname_6C_Literacy_Blocks
Lastname_Firstname_6C_Literacy_Theme—not shown in figure
Lastname_Firstname_6C_Literacy_Program

Project Results

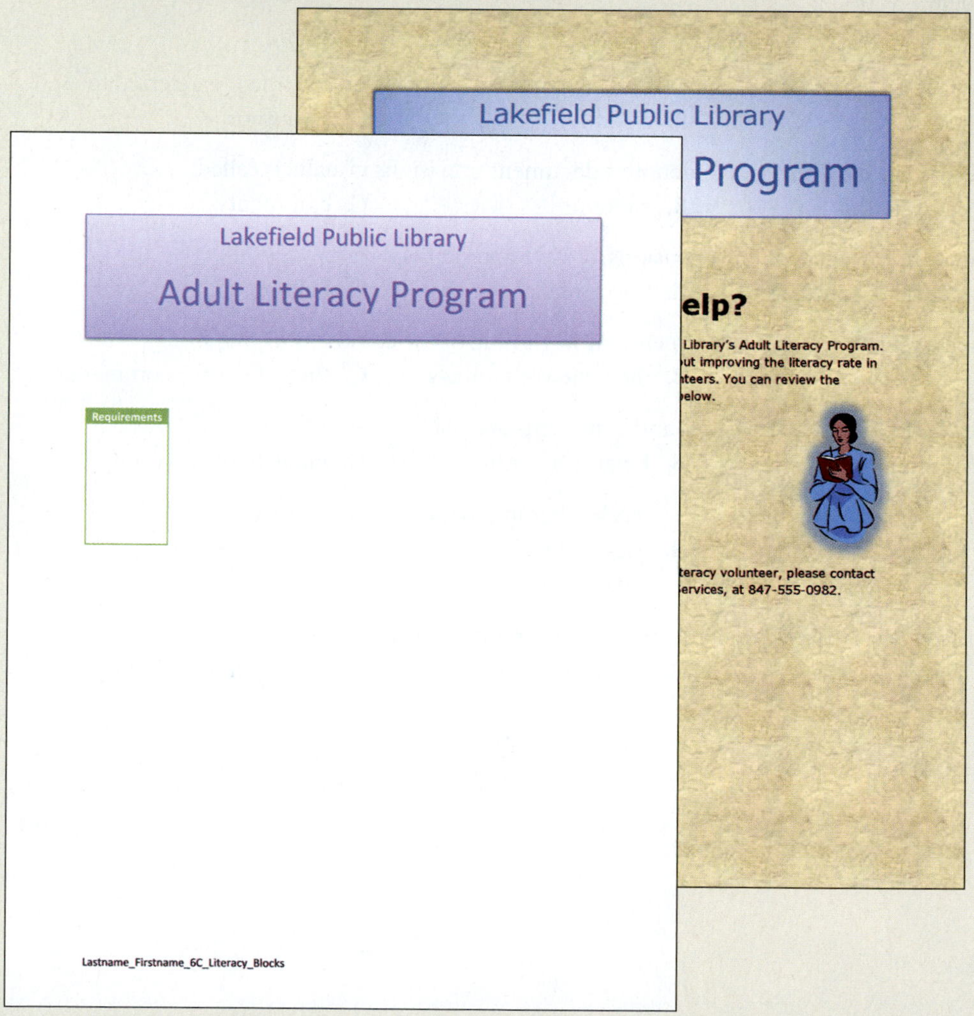

Figure 6.48

(Project 6C Literacy Program continues on the next page)

Skills Review | Project 6C Literacy Program (continued)

1 **Start** Word to display a new blank document. If necessary, display the ruler and formatting marks. From **Backstage** view, display the **Save As** dialog box, navigate to your **Word Chapter 6** folder, and **Save** the document as **Lastname_Firstname_6C_Literacy_Blocks** Insert the file name in the footer.

a. On the **Insert tab**, in the **Text group**, click the **Text Box** button, and then locate and click **Simple Text Box**. On the **Format tab**, in the **Shape Styles group**, click the **More** button. In the fourth row, click the fifth style—**Subtle Effect – Purple, Accent 4**. If the **Size group** is visible, change the **Shape Width** to **6.5"**. Otherwise, to the right of the **Arrange group**, click the **Size** button, and then change the **Shape Width** to **6.5"**.

b. Replace the placeholder text by typing **Lakefield Public Library** Press Enter, and then type **Adult Literacy Program** Select both lines of text, change the **Font Color** to **Purple, Accent 4**, and then apply **Center**. Set the **Font Size** of the first line of text to **24**. Set the **Font Size** of the second line of text to **36**.

c. Click the outside edge of the text box to select it. On the **Insert tab**, in the **Text group**, click the **Text Box** button, and then click **Save Selection to Text Box Gallery**. As the **Name**, type **Literacy Heading** As the **Description**, type **Use as the heading for all literacy documents** Click **OK**.

2 Click outside the text box to deselect it, and then point slightly under the lower left corner of the text box to display the **click and type pointer** at approximately **2.5 inches on the vertical ruler**. Double-click to insert three blank paragraphs under the text box. With the insertion point in the third blank paragraph, on the **Insert tab**, in the **Tables group**, click the **Table** button, point to **Quick Tables**, scroll down, and then click **Tabular List**.

a. Select the text *ITEM*, and then type **Requirements** Press Tab, right-click, and then click **Delete Cells**. In the displayed **Delete Cells** dialog box, select the **Delete entire column** option button. Click **OK**. Select the text in all the remaining cells of the table, and then press Del.

b. Point slightly outside of the upper left corner of the table, and then click the **table move handle** to select the entire table. On the **Insert tab**, in the **Tables group**, click the **Table** button. Point to **Quick Tables**, and then at the bottom, click **Save Selection to Quick Tables Gallery**. As the **Name**, type **Job Information** As the **Description**, type **Use for listing job requirements** Click **OK**.

c. With the table selected, move your pointer up to the left end of the horizontal ruler, and then point to the first **Move Table Column** marker. Drag the **Move Table Column** marker slightly to the right until the vertical dotted line aligns with the left edge of the text box, and then release the left mouse button.

d. From **Backstage** view, display the **Document Information Panel**, and type your first and last names as the **Author**. In the **Subject** box, type your course name and section number, and in the **Keywords** box, type **literacy, building blocks** **Close** the **Document Information Panel**. Click **Save**. Display **Backstage** view and **Close** the document but leave Word open.

3 Press Ctrl + N to display a new blank document.

a. On the **Page Layout tab**, in the **Themes group**, click the **Theme Colors** button, and then click **Concourse**. Click the **Theme Fonts** button, and then click **Aspect**. Click the **Theme Effects** button, and then click **Verve**. Click the **Themes** button, and then click **Save Current Theme**.

b. Navigate to your **Word Chapter 6** folder, and save the theme as **Lastname_Firstname_6C_Literacy_Theme** Display **Backstage** view and **Close** the document, without saving changes, but leave Word open.

4 Press Ctrl + N. Save the document in your **Word Chapter 6** folder as **Lastname_Firstname_6C_Literacy_Program** Insert the file name in the footer, and display rulers and formatting marks, if necessary.

a. On the **Page Layout tab**, in the **Themes group**, click the **Themes** button, and then click **Browse for Themes**. Navigate to your **Word Chapter 6** folder, select your **Lastname_Firstname_6C_Literacy_Theme**, and then click **Open**. In the **Page Background group**, click the **Page Color** button, and then click **Fill Effects**. In the **Fill Effects** dialog box, click the **Texture tab**, and then in the fourth row, click the fourth texture—**Stationery**. Click **OK**.

b. On the **Insert tab**, in the **Text group**, click the **Text Box** button. Scroll to the bottom of the list, and then under **General**, click your **Literacy Heading** building block. Click outside of the text box to deselect it, and

(Project 6C Literacy Program continues on the next page)

Skills Review | Project 6C Literacy Program (continued)

then point slightly under the lower left corner of the text box to display the [I≡] pointer at approximately **2.5 inches on the vertical ruler**. Double-click to insert three blank paragraphs under the text box.

c. On the **Insert tab**, in the **Text group**, click the **Object button arrow**, and then click **Text from File**. Navigate to your student files, click **w06C_Literacy_Information**, and then click **Insert**. At the end of the paragraph that ends *in the table below*, press Enter two times.

5 On the **Insert tab**, in the **Tables group**, click the **Table** button, point to **Quick Tables**, scroll toward the bottom of the list, and then under **General**, click **Job Information**.

a. On the **Design tab**, in the **Table Styles group**, click the **More** button, and then under **Built-In**, in the second row, click the fifth style—**Light List - Accent 4**.

b. Point slightly outside of the upper left corner of the table, and then click the **table move handle** [⊕] to select the entire table. Move your pointer to the left end of the horizontal ruler, and then point to the first **Move Table Column** marker. Drag the **Move Table Column** marker slightly to the right until the vertical dotted line aligns with the left edge of the text box, and then release the left mouse button.

c. Position the insertion point in the second row of the table. Type the following text in the table, pressing Tab after each line:

Possess a high school diploma or GED.
Pass a background check.
Be 21 years of age or older.
Attend all training sessions.
Tutor a minimum of two hours a week.

d. Select the last three empty rows of the table. On the **Layout tab**, in the **Rows & Columns group**, click the **Delete** button, and then click **Delete Rows**.

6 Position the insertion point in the blank paragraph below the table, if necessary. On **the Insert tab**, in the **Illustrations group**, click the **Clip Art** button. In the **Clip Art** task pane, search for **reading** Be sure **All media file types** displays and the **Include Office.com content** box is selected, and then click **Go**. Locate the graphic shown in Figure 6.48, and then click to insert it—or select a similar graphic. **Close** the **Clip Art** task pane. On the **Format tab**, change the **Shape Height** to **1.8"**.

a. With the picture selected, on the **Format tab**, in the **Picture Styles group**, click the **Picture Effects** button, point to **Glow**, and then in the fourth row, click the fourth effect—**Blue, 18 pt glow, Accent color 4**. In the **Arrange group**, click the **Wrap Text** button, and then click **In Front of Text**. Drag to position the graphic at the right margin, spaced evenly between the two paragraphs of text, as shown in Figure 6.48.

b. Delete the blank paragraph at the end of the document, and then press Ctrl + Home. From **Backstage** view, display the **Document Information Panel**. In the **Author** box, type your first and last names. In the **Subject** box, type your course name and section number, and in the **Keywords** box, type **literacy program, volunteers** **Close** the **Document Information Panel**.

c. On the **Insert tab**, in the **Text group**, click the **Quick Parts** button, and then click **Building Blocks Organizer**. In the **Building Blocks Organizer** dialog box, in the upper left corner, click **Name** to sort the building blocks alphabetically by name. Locate your building block **Job Information**, click to select it, click the **Delete** button, and then click **Yes** to confirm the deletion. Using the same technique, scroll to locate your building block **Literacy Heading**, and then **Delete** it. **Close** the dialog box.

7 Print your two documents—you cannot print a theme—or submit all three files electronically as directed by your instructor. **Exit** Word. In the dialog box regarding changes to building blocks, click **Save** to accept the changes.

End **You have completed Project 6C**

Apply 6B skills from these Objectives:

- 4 Use Comments in a Document
- 5 Track Changes in a Document
- 6 View Side by Side, Compare, and Combine Documents

Skills Review | Project 6D User Guide

In the following Skills Review project, you will edit a user guide for Lakefield Public Library by creating and deleting comments, inserting text, applying formatting, and accepting changes made by others. Your completed documents will look similar to Figure 6.49.

Project Files

For Project 6D, you will need the following files:

w06D_User_Guide
w06D_Reviewed_Guide

You will save your documents as:

Lastname_Firstname_6D_User_Guide
Lastname_Firstname_6D_Combined_Guide

Project Results

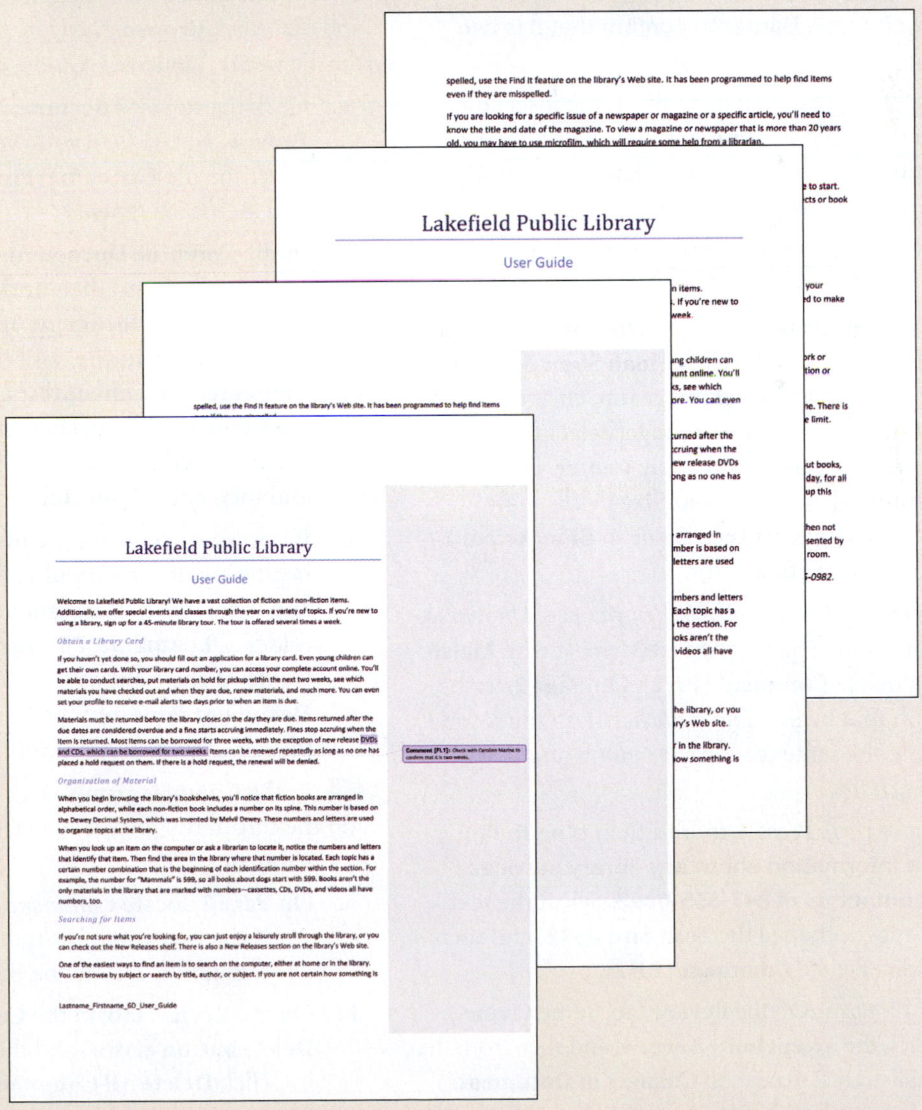

Figure 6.49

(Project 6D User Guide continues on the next page)

Skills Review | Project 6D User Guide (continued)

1 **Start** Word. Navigate to your student files and open the file **w06D_User_Guide. Save** the document in your **Word Chapter 6** folder as **Lastname_Firstname_6D_User_Guide** Insert the file name in the footer.

a. On the **Review tab**, in the **Tracking group**, click the **Track Changes button arrow**. From the list, click **Change User Name**. Under **Personalize your copy of Microsoft Office**, on a piece of paper, make a note of the **User name** and **Initials**. In the **User name** box, type your own first and last name, and then in the **Initials** box, type your initials, if necessary. Click **OK**.

b. In the paragraph beginning *Materials must be*, select the text *DVDs and CDs, which can be borrowed for two weeks.* On the **Review tab**, in the **Comments group**, click the **New Comment** button. In the comment, type **Check with Angie Harper to confirm that it is two weeks.**

c. Press Ctrl + Home. Click to position the insertion point in the text for **Comment [BH1]**, and then in the **Comments group**, click the **Delete** button. Using the same technique, delete **Comment [CM1]**.

d. Locate your comment, and then replace *Angie Harper* with **Caroline Marina**

2 In the **Tracking group**, click the **Display for Review arrow**, and then, if necessary, click **Final: Show Markup**. To enable tracking, in the **Tracking group**, click the **Track Changes** button so that it glows orange. Select the first paragraph—the title—and then apply **Center**. Select the second paragraph, change the **Font Size** to **18**, apply **Center**, and then change the **Font Color** to **Blue, Accent 1**—in the fifth column, the first color.

a. In the paragraph that begins *When you begin browsing*, in the third line, replace the text *Melville* with **Melvil** and then delete **Comment [BH2]**. On **Page 2**, in the paragraph that begins *The branches of*, in the second line, delete the sentence *We have many comfortable desks and chairs.*

b. Press Ctrl + End. Press Enter, and then type **To find out more information about any library services, please contact us at 847-555-0982.** Select the text you just typed, change the **Font Size** to **12**, and then apply **Italic**. Delete **Comment [BH2]**.

c. Press Ctrl + Home. On the **Review tab**, in the **Changes group**, click the **Accept button arrow**, and then from the displayed list, click **Accept All Changes in Document**.

d. In the **Tracking group**, click the **Track Changes button arrow**, and then click **Change User Name**. If you made changes to the user name, delete your name and initials and type those that displayed originally. Click **OK**. Click the **Track Changes** button to turn off the **Track Changes** feature.

e. Display the **Document Information Panel**. Type your first and last names as the **Author**. In the **Subject** box, type your course name and section number, and in the **Keywords** box, type **user guide, edited Save** your document. Display **Backstage** view, and then **Close** the document but leave Word open.

3 On the **Review tab**, in the **Compare group**, click the **Compare** button, and then click **Combine**. In the **Combine Documents** dialog box, click the **Original document arrow**, and then click **Browse**. Navigate to your student files, select the file **w06D_Reviewed_Guide**, and then click **Open**.

a. Click the **Revised document arrow**, and then click **Browse**. Navigate to your **Word Chapter 6** folder, select the file **Lastname_Firstname_6D_User_Guide**, and then click **Open**.

b. In the **Combine Documents** dialog box, click the **More** button, and then under **Show changes in**, select the **New document** option button, if necessary. Click the **Less** button, and then click **OK**. If only the **Combined Document** displays, on the **Review tab**, in the **Compare group**, click the **Compare** button. From the displayed list, point to **Show Source Documents**, and then click **Show Both**.

c. If necessary, position the insertion point at the beginning of the **Combined Document**. Click **Save**, and then save the document in your **Word Chapter 6** folder as **Lastname_Firstname_6D_Combined_Guide** At the right of your screen, close the **Original Document Pane** and the **Revised Document Pane**. At the left of your screen, close the **Reviewing Pane**.

4 In the **Changes group**, click the **Accept button arrow**, and then from the displayed list, click **Accept All Changes in Document**.

a. On **Page 2**, locate *Comment [AH4]*. In the document, select the two sentences that begin *Be aware*, and end *wireless device*. **Delete** the two sentences.

b. On the **Review tab**, in the **Comments group**, click the **Delete button arrow**, and then from the displayed list, click **Delete All Comments in Document**.

(Project 6D User Guide continues on the next page)

Skills Review | Project 6D User Guide (continued)

5 Right-click in the footer area, and then click **Edit Footer**. Right-click the existing text, and then from the shortcut menu, click **Update Field**. **Close** the footer area.

a. Press Ctrl + Home. Display the **Document Information Panel**. In the **Author** box, delete any existing text, and type your first and last names. In the **Subject** box, type your course name and section number, and in the **Keywords** box, type **user guide, reviewed, combined** **Close** the **Document Information Panel**.

b. **Save** your document.

6 Print both documents or submit them electronically as directed by your instructor. **Exit** Word.

End **You have completed Project 6D**

Apply **6A** skills from these Objectives:

1. Create Building Blocks
2. Create and Save a Theme Template
3. Create a Document by Using Building Blocks

Mastering Word | Project 6E Seminar Agenda

In the following Mastering Word project, you will create and save building blocks and create a theme for an agenda for Lakefield Public Library's seminar on Public Libraries and the Internet. Your completed documents will look similar to Figure 6.50.

Project Files

For Project 6E, you will need the following files:

New blank Word document
w06E_Seminar_Agenda

You will save your files as:

Lastname_Firstname_6E_Seminar_Blocks
Lastname_Firstname_6E_Seminar_Theme—not shown in figure
Lastname_Firstname_6E_Seminar_Agenda

Project Results

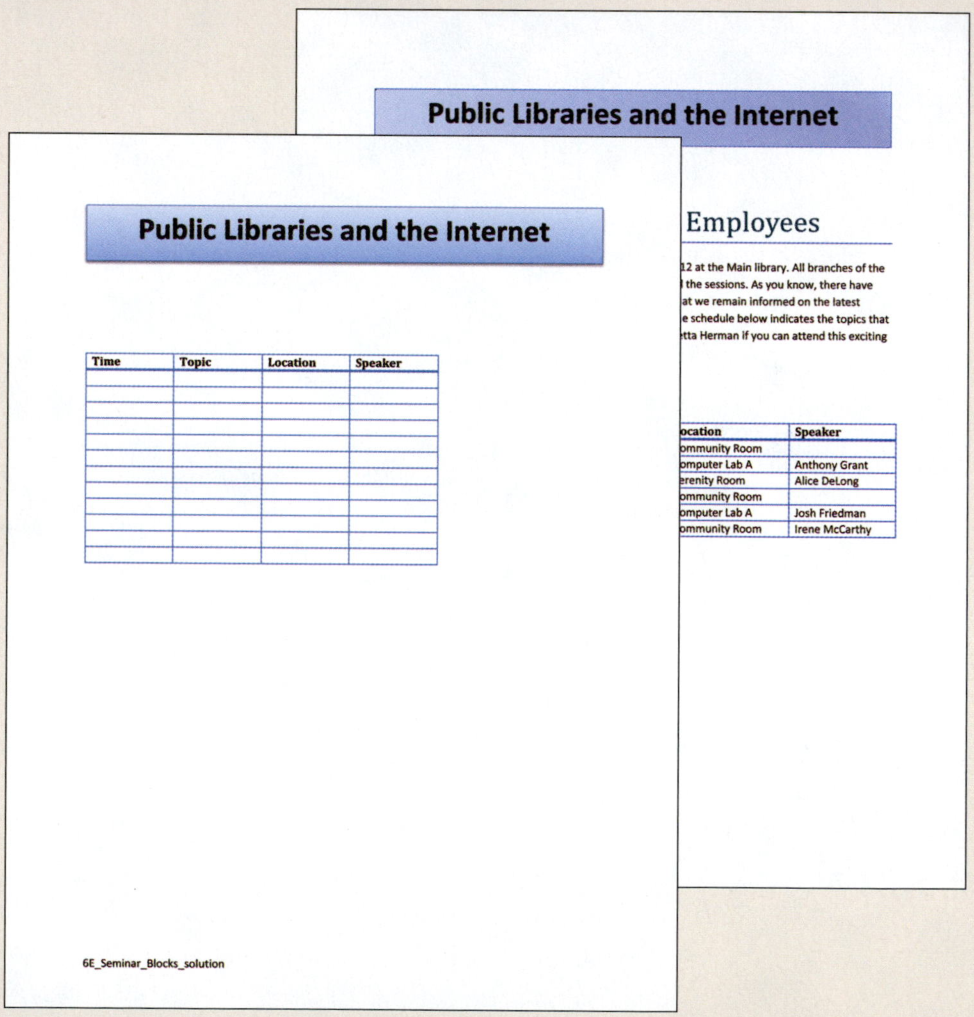

Figure 6.50

(Project 6E Seminar Agenda continues on the next page)

Mastering Word | Project 6E Seminar Agenda (continued)

1 **Start** Word; display rulers and formatting marks. Display the **Save As** dialog box, navigate to your **Word Chapter 6** folder, and save the document as **Lastname_Firstname_6E_Seminar_Blocks** Insert the file name in the footer.

2 **Insert** a **Simple Text Box**, set the **Shape Height** to **0.7"**, set the **Width** to **6.5"**, and then apply the shape style **Subtle Effect - Blue, Accent 1**—in the fourth row, the second style. If necessary, move the text box so that it is centered horizontally in the document. As the text, type **Public Libraries and the Internet** and then format the text with **Font Size 28** and **Bold** and **Center**. Select and then save the text box in the **Text Box** gallery with the name **Internet Seminar** and the **Description Use in all Internet Seminar documents**

3 Insert two or three blank paragraphs under the text box, and then from the **Quick Tables** gallery, click **Double Table**. **Delete** the text *The Greek Alphabet*. Change *Letter name* to **Time** and then press Tab. Change *Uppercase* to **Topic** Change *Lowercase* to **Location** Change *Letter name* to **Speaker** **Delete** the remaining columns, and then delete the remaining text. Apply the table style **Light Grid – Accent 1**. Select the entire table, and then align the left edge of the table with the left edge of the text box. Save the selected table in the **Quick Tables** gallery with the name **Seminar Schedule** and the **Description Use to display schedules for seminars**

4 Display the **Document Information Panel**, type your first and last names as the **Author**, your course name and section number as the **Subject**, and in the **Keywords** box, type **seminar, building blocks** **Save** and then **Close** the document, but leave Word open.

5 Create a new blank document. Change the **Theme Colors** to **Flow**, and then change the **Theme Effects** to **Clarity**. **Save** the custom theme to your **Word Chapter 6** folder as **Lastname_Firstname_6E_Seminar_Theme** From **Backstage** view, **Close** the document without saving changes, but leave Word open.

6 Open the file **w06E_Seminar_Agenda**, save it in your **Word Chapter 6** folder as **Lastname_Firstname_6E_Seminar_Agenda** and then insert the file name in the footer. Apply your custom theme—**Lastname_Firstname_6E_Seminar_Theme**. In the first blank paragraph, from the **Text Box** gallery, insert your **Internet Seminar** text box. On the **Format tab**, in the **Arrange group**, change the text wrapping to **In Line with Text**.

7 Select the text *Spring Seminar for Employees*, apply the **Title** style, and then apply **Center**. On the **Page Layout tab**, in the **Paragraph group**, set the **Spacing Before** to **48 pt**. To the text *AGENDA*, apply the **Heading 1** style, apply **Center**, and then set the **Spacing After** to **12 pt**. Position the insertion point in the blank paragraph following *AGENDA*, and then from the **Quick Tables** gallery, insert your **Seminar Schedule** table. Create the table using the text shown in Table 1 below, deleting empty rows as necessary.

8 Select the table, right-click, point to **AutoFit**, and then click **AutoFit to Contents**. Right-click, point to **AutoFit**, and then click **AutoFit to Window**. Press Ctrl + Home.

9 Display the **Document Information Panel**. Type your name as the **Author** and your course name and section number as the **Subject**. In the **Keywords** box, type **seminar, agenda** **Close** the **Document Information Panel**. Click **Save**.

10 Display the **Building Blocks Organizer** dialog box, and then delete your building blocks **Internet Seminar** and **Seminar Schedule**. In the **Building Blocks Organizer** dialog box, click the **Close** button.

11 Print your two documents—you cannot print a theme—or submit all three files electronically as directed by your instructor. **Exit** Word; in the dialog box regarding changes to building blocks, click **Save** to accept the changes.

Table 1

Time	Topic	Location	Speaker
8 a.m. – 9 a.m.	Continental Breakfast	Community Room	
9 a.m. – 10 a.m.	Innovative Internet Librarians	Computer Lab A	Anthony Grant
10 a.m. – Noon	Privacy versus Technology	Serenity Room	Alice DeLong
Noon – 1 p.m.	Lunch	Community Room	
1 p.m. – 3 p.m.	Virtual Reference Desks	Computer Lab A	Josh Friedman
3 p.m. – 5 p.m.	Fair Use in the Digital Age	Community Room	Irene McCarthy

(Return to Step 7)

End **You have completed Project 6E**

Content-Based Assessments

Apply **6B** skills from these Objectives:

- **4** Use Comments in a Document
- **5** Track Changes in a Document
- **6** View Side by Side, Compare, and Combine Documents

Mastering Word | Project 6F Library Classes

In the following Mastering Word project, you will edit a user guide for Lakefield Public Library by creating and deleting comments, inserting text, applying formatting, and accepting changes made by others. Your completed documents will look similar to Figure 6.51.

Project Files

For Project 6F, you will need the following files:

w06F_Library_Classes
w06F_Classes_Reviewed

You will save your documents as:

Lastname_Firstname_6F_Library_Classes
Lastname_Firstname_6F_Classes_Combined

Project Results

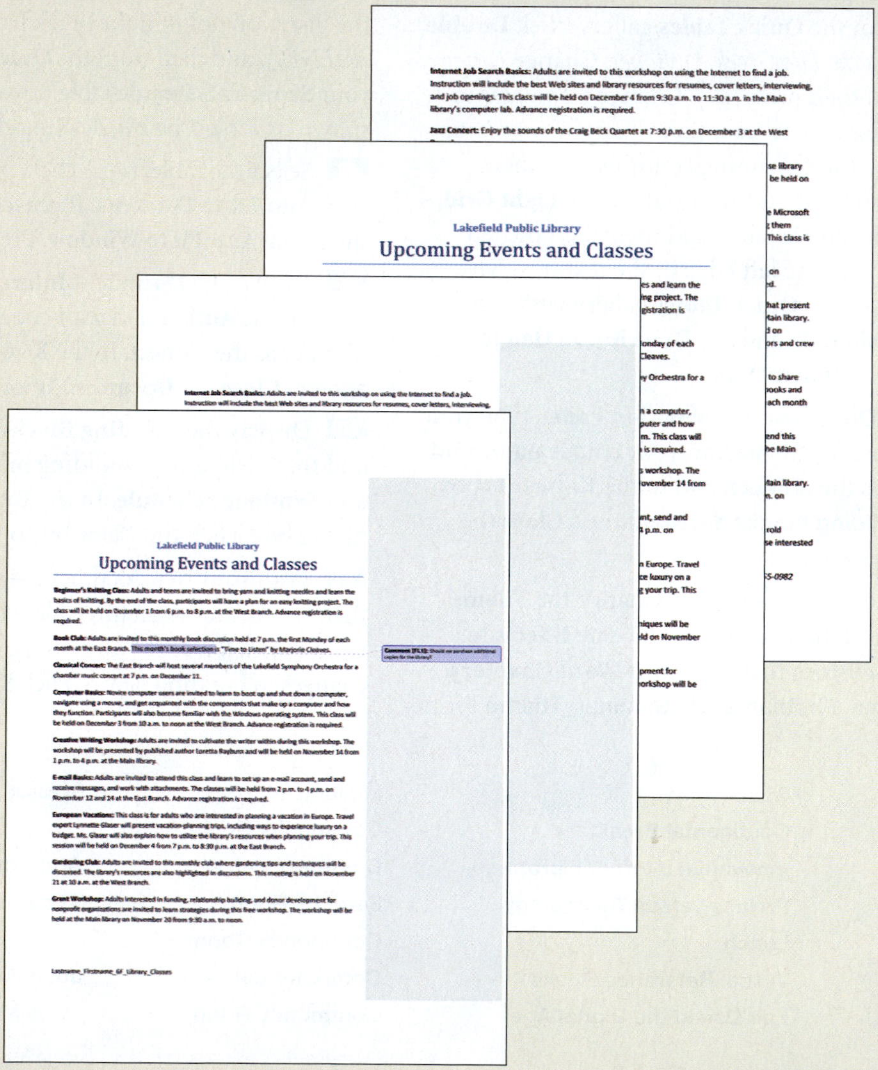

Figure 6.51

(Project 6F Library Classes continues on the next page)

Mastering Word | Project 6F Library Classes (continued)

1 **Start** Word, and then open the file **w06F_Library_Classes**. **Save** the document in your **Word Chapter 6** folder as **Lastname_Firstname_6F_Library_Classes** Insert the file name in the footer. On the **Review tab**, in the **Tracking group**, click the **Track Changes button arrow**, and then click **Change User Name**. Under **Personalize your copy of Microsoft Office**, type your name in the **User name** box, and then type your initials in the **Initials** box, if necessary.

2 In the fourth paragraph, select the text *This month's book selection*. Insert a **New Comment**, and then type **Should we purchase additional copies for the library?** In the markup area, delete **Comment** [**AG2**] and **Comment** [**CM2**].

3 In the **Tracking group**, change the **Display for Review box** to **Final: Show Markup**, and then turn on **Track Changes**. Change the first paragraph to **Heading 1** style, and then apply **Center**. Change the second paragraph to **Title** style, and then apply **Center**. Position the insertion point to the left of the paragraph that begins *Internet*, and then press Ctrl + Enter. Locate the paragraph that begins *Microsoft Word*. **Delete** the text *101*, and then press Ctrl + End. Press Enter, and then type **To register for a class or to obtain more information, contact Abigail Gardner at 847-555-0982.** Select the sentence you just typed, and then apply **Italic** and **Center**.

4 Press Ctrl + Home, and then **Accept All Changes in Document**. Click the **Track Changes button arrow**, and then click **Change User Name**. Delete your name in the **User Name** box, and then delete your initials in the **Initials** box, if necessary. Turn off **Track Changes**. Display the **Document Information Panel**, type your first and last names as the **Author**, and your course name and section number as the **Subject**. In the **Keywords** box, type **library classes, edited Close** the **Document Information Panel**. **Save** your document, and then from **Backstage** view, **Close** the document but leave Word open.

5 Display the **Combine Documents** dialog box. For the **Original document**, from your student data files, select the file **w06F_Classes_Reviewed.** For the **Revised document**, from your **Word Chapter 6** folder, select the file **Lastname_Firstname_6F_Library_Classes.** Click the **More** button, and then select the **New document** option button. Click the **Less** button, and then click **OK**. If a Microsoft Word dialog box displays, click Yes to continue with the comparison.

6 **Save** the document in your **Word Chapter 6** folder as **Lastname_Firstname_6F_Classes_Combined** Then, if displayed, **Close** the two document panes on the right side of your screen, and then **Close** the Reviewing Pane. Click the **Accept button arrow**, and then click **Accept All Changes in Document**. Delete the comment that contains your initials.

7 Double-click in the footer area, right-click the file name field, and then click **Update Field**. **Close** the footer area. Press Ctrl + Home. Display the **Document Information Panel**, type your name as **Author** and your course name and section number as the **Subject**. In the **Keywords** box, type **library classes, reviewed, combined** **Close** the **Document Information Panel**. **Save** your document.

8 Print both documents or submit electronically as directed by your instructor. **Exit** Word.

End **You have completed Project 6F**

Apply **6A** and **6B** skills from these Objectives:

1. Create Building Blocks
2. Create and Save a Theme Template
3. Create a Document by Using Building Blocks
4. Use Comments in a Document
5. Track Changes in a Document
6. View Side by Side, Compare, and Combine Documents

Mastering Word | Project 6G Web Site Flyer

In the following Mastering Word project, you will create a document to announce the launch of Lakefield Public Library's new Web site by creating and inserting building blocks, deleting comments, inserting text, applying formatting, and accepting changes made by others. Your completed documents will look similar to Figure 6.52.

Project Files

For Project 6G, you will need the following files:

New blank Word document
w06G_Website_Flyer

You will save your documents as:

Lastname_Firstname_6G_Website_Block
Lastname_Firstname_6G_Website_Theme—not shown in figure
Lastname_Firstname_6G_Website_Flyer

Project Results

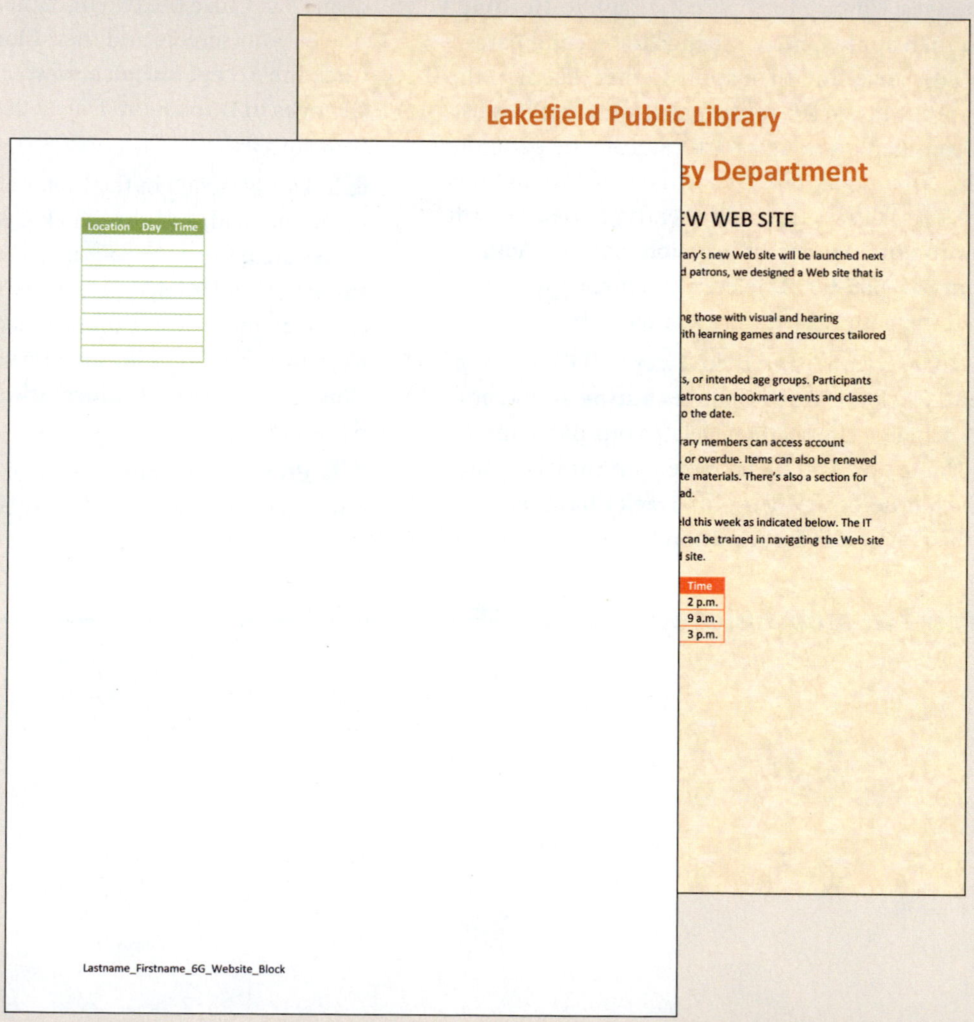

Figure 6.52

(Project 6G Web Site Flyer continues on the next page)

Mastering Word | Project 6G Web Site Flyer (continued)

1 **Start** Word and be sure rulers and formatting marks display. Display the **Save As** dialog box and save the new blank document to your **Word Chapter 6** folder as **Lastname_Firstname_6G_Website_Block** Insert the file name in the footer.

2 From the **Quick Tables** gallery, click **Tabular List**. In the first cell, select *ITEM*, and then type **Location** In the second cell, type **Day** On the **Layout tab**, in the **Rows & Columns group**, click the **Insert Right** button to create a third column. In the first cell of the third column, type **Time** Delete all remaining text in the table, and then apply the **Medium Shading 1 – Accent 3** table style. Select the entire table, and then save it in the **Quick Tables** gallery with the name **Training Schedule** and the **Description** **Use to display schedules for training**

3 Press Ctrl + Home. Display the **Document Information Panel**, type your name as the **Author** and your course name and section number as the **Subject**. In the **Keywords** box, type **IT Department, building block** **Close** the **Document Information Panel**, and then **Save** your changes. From **Backstage** view, **Close** the document but leave Word open.

4 Create a new blank document. Change the **Theme Colors** to **Austin**, and then save the custom theme to your **Word Chapter 6** folder as **Lastname_Firstname_6G_Website_Theme** From **Backstage** view, **Close** the document, without saving changes, but leave Word open.

5 Open the file **w06G_Website_Flyer**, and then save it in your **Word Chapter 6** folder as **Lastname_Firstname_6G_Website_Flyer** Insert the file name in the footer. Apply your custom theme—**Lastname_Firstname_6G_Website_Theme**.

6 Select the first two paragraphs of the document, and then format the text with **Font Size 28**, **Bold** and **Center**, and **Font Color Orange, Accent 6, Darker 25%**. Press Ctrl + End, and then **Insert** the **Training Schedule** Quick Table. Beginning in the first cell of the second row, type the following text in the table.

Item	Location	Day
Main library	**Wednesday**	**2 p.m.**
East Branch	**Thursday**	**9 a.m.**
West Branch	**Friday**	**3 p.m.**

7 Select all empty rows, and then click **Delete Rows**. **Center** the table horizontally in the document. Next, **Accept All Changes in Document**. Change the **Page Color** to the **Parchment Texture Fill Effect**.

8 Press Ctrl + Home. Display the **Document Information Panel**, type your name as the **Author** and your course name and section number as the **Subject**. In the **Keywords** box, type **Website flyer, reviewed** **Close** the **Document Information Panel**. **Save** your document, and then **Close** Word—do not save changes to building blocks.

9 Print both documents—you cannot print a theme—or submit all three files electronically as directed by your instructor. **Exit** Word.

End **You have completed Project 6G**

Apply a combination of the **6A** and **6B** skills.

GO! Fix It | Project 6H Internship Memo

Project Files

For Project 6H, you will need the following file:

w06H_Internship_Memo

You will save your files as:

Lastname_Firstname_6H_Internship_Theme
Lastname_Firstname_6H_Internship_Memo

In this project you will edit a memo from Benedetta Herman, Director of Operations at Lakefield Public Library, to Greta Briggs, IT Director. Navigate to your student files, open the file **w06H_Internship_Memo**, and then save the file in your **Word Chapter 6** folder as **Lastname_Firstname_6H_Internship_Memo**

To complete the project, you must revise the file by changing the theme, inserting a building block, formatting text, and using various Track Changes features. Correct the following:

- The **Theme Colors** should be changed to **Metro**, and the current theme saved in your **Word Chapter 6** folder as **Lastname_Firstname_6H_Internship_Theme**
- The **Title** style should be applied to the first paragraph of text.
- A **Simple Text Box** should be inserted at the top of the document, and formatted **In Line with Text**, with **Shape Width** of **6.5"** and **Subtle Effect – Green, Accent 1** shape style applied. Insert the text **Lakefield Public Library Internship Program** displayed on two lines with **Font Size** of **26**, and apply **Center**.
- The **User Name** and **Initials** should be changed to reflect your own name.
- In the second paragraph of text, a comment should be inserted to check the correct title for Greta Briggs.
- Following the **Date** heading, type the current date.
- In the last paragraph, the day should be changed to **Tuesday**
- All changes in the documents should be accepted.
- A footer should be inserted that includes the file name; document properties should include the keywords **memo, internship**

Save your document, and then print the document—you cannot print a theme—or submit both files electronically as directed by your instructor.

End **You have completed Project 6H**

Apply a combination of the **6A** and **6B** skills.

GO! Make It | Project 6I Request Form

Project Files

For Project 6I, you will need the following files:

w06I_Request_Form
w06I_Library_Logo

You will save your document as:

Lastname_Firstname_6I_Request_Form

From your student files, open the file **w06I_Request_Form**, and create the document shown in Figure 6.53. The Theme Colors is set to Foundry, and Theme Fonts is set to Office Classic. Apply appropriate styles. From your student files, insert the picture **w06I_Library_Logo**. Use building blocks for the table—Matrix style—and the text box—Simple Text Box. Add document properties that include your name and the keywords **loan form, interlibrary** Save the file in your **Word Chapter 6** folder as **Lastname_Firstname_6I_Request_Form** Add the file name to the footer, and then print your document or submit electronically as directed by your instructor. Your completed document will look similar to Figure 6.53.

Project Results

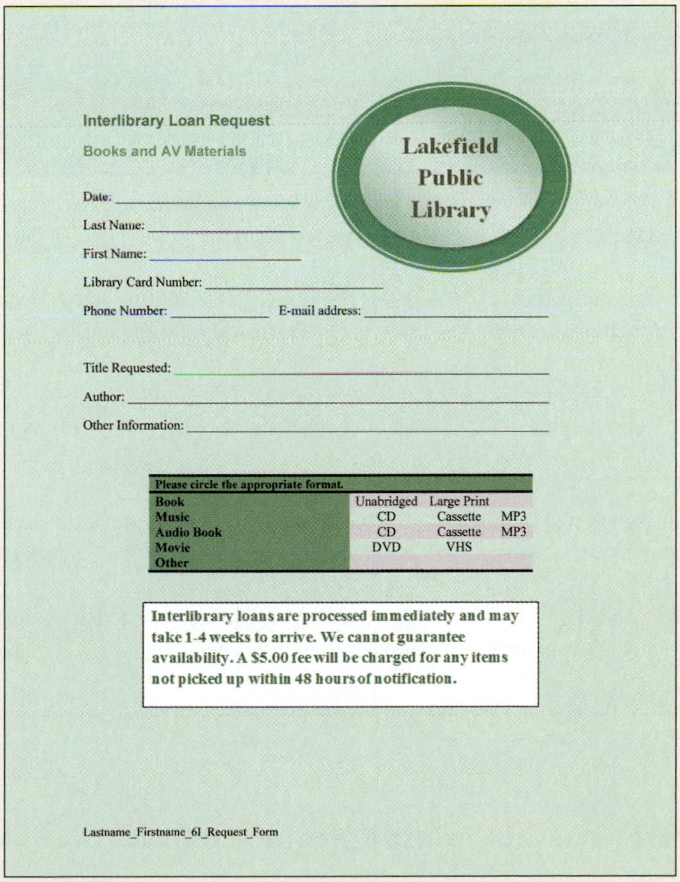

Interlibrary Loan Request

Books and AV Materials

Date: ____________________

Last Name: ________________

First Name: ________________

Library Card Number: ________________

Phone Number: ____________ E-mail address: ____________________

Title Requested: ______________________________

Author: ______________________________

Other Information: ______________________________

Please circle the appropriate format.			
Book	Unabridged	Large Print	
Music	CD	Cassette	MP3
Audio Book	CD	Cassette	MP3
Movie	DVD	VHS	
Other			

Interlibrary loans are processed immediately and may take 1-4 weeks to arrive. We cannot guarantee availability. A $5.00 fee will be charged for any items not picked up within 48 hours of notification.

Lastname_Firstname_6I_Request_Form

Figure 6.53

End You have completed Project 6I

Apply a combination of the 6A and 6B skills.

GO! Solve It | Project 6J Library Rules

Project Files

For Project 6J, you will need the following files:

New blank Word document
w06J_Library_Rules

You will save your documents as:

Lastname_Firstname_6J_Rules_Blocks
Lastname_Firstname_6J_Library_Rules

Display a new blank document and save it to your **Word Chapter 6** folder as **Lastname_Firstname_6J_Rules_Blocks** Insert a graphic related to a library and save it as a building block. Save a text box as a building block that includes the text **Library Rules** Insert the file name in the footer and add appropriate document properties.

From your student files, open the document **w06J_Library_Rules**. Accept all changes. Save the file to your **Word Chapter 6** folder as **Lastname_Firstname_6J_Library_Rules** Modify the theme and format the text to improve readability. Insert the building blocks you created. Adjust the building blocks and text to create an attractive, one-page document. Insert the file name in a footer and add appropriate document properties. Print both documents or submit electronically as directed by your instructor.

Performance Element	Performance Level — Exemplary: You consistently applied the relevant skills	Proficient: You sometimes, but not always, applied the relevant skills	Developing: You rarely or never applied the relevant skills
Create a graphic building block	An appropriate graphic is saved as a building block.	A graphic is saved as a building block, but is not related to the topic.	No graphic is saved as a building block.
Create a text box building block	A text box containing the correct information is saved as a building block.	A text box is saved as a building block but contains incorrect information.	No text box is saved as a building block.
Accept changes	All changes are accepted.	Some changes are accepted but others are not.	No changes are accepted.
Modify theme and format text	The theme is modified and the text is formatted attractively.	The theme is not modified or the text is not formatted attractively.	The theme is not modified and the text is not formatted.
Insert building blocks	Both building blocks are inserted and positioned appropriately.	One building block is not inserted or is positioned inappropriately.	Both building blocks are not inserted or are positioned inappropriately.

End **You have completed Project 6J**

Apply a combination of the 6A and 6B skills.

GO! Solve It | Project 6K Employee Newsletter

Project Files

For Project 6K, you will need the following file:

w06K_Newsletter_Items

You will save your documents as:

Lastname_Firstname_6K_Newsletter_Blocks
Lastname_Firstname_6K_Employee_Newsletter

Display a new blank document and save it to your **Word Chapter 6** folder as **Lastname_Firstname_6K_Newsletter_Blocks** Insert a graphic related to a library and save it as a building block. Save a text box as a building block that includes the text **Lakefield Public Library** Select and format a Quick Table to be used to display the name and department of new employees, and then save it as a building block. Insert the file name in the footer and add appropriate document properties.

Display a new blank document and save it to your **Word Chapter 6** folder as **Lastname_Firstname_6K_Employee_Newsletter** Create a newsletter, using your text box as a heading. Add an appropriate title and comment. Change to a two-column format, and then insert the text from student file **w06K_Newsletter_Items**. Insert the graphic and Quick Table building blocks, adding fictitious data to the table. Adjust paragraph and text formats to display attractively in a one-page document. Insert the file name in the footer, and add appropriate document properties. Print both documents or submit electronically as directed by your instructor.

Performance Element	Performance Level: Exemplary: You consistently applied the relevant skills	Proficient: You sometimes, but not always, applied the relevant skills	Developing: You rarely or never applied the relevant skills
Create building blocks	All three building blocks are saved with appropriate content.	At least one building block is not saved or contains inappropriate content.	No building blocks are saved.
Change to two-column format	Below the title, the document is formatted in two columns.	The entire document is formatted in two columns.	The document is not formatted in two columns.
Insert title and comment	A title is inserted and formatted appropriately, and a comment is inserted.	A title is inserted but is not formatted appropriately or a comment is not inserted.	Neither a title nor a comment is inserted.
Insert building blocks	All building blocks are inserted and formatted appropriately.	At least one building block is not inserted or is formatted inappropriately.	No building blocks are inserted.
Enter data in table	Appropriate and sufficient data is entered in the table.	Inappropriate or insufficient data is entered in the table.	No data is entered in the table.

End **You have completed Project 6K**

Outcomes-Based Assessments

Rubric

The following outcomes-based assessments are *open-ended assessments*. That is, there is no specific correct result; your result will depend on your approach to the information provided. Make *professional quality* your goal. Use the following scoring rubric to guide you in *how* to approach the problem and then to evaluate *how well* your approach solves the problem.

The criteria—Software Mastery, Content, Format and Layout, and Process—represent the knowledge and skills you have gained that you can apply to solving the problem. The levels of performance—Professional Quality, Approaching Professional Quality, or Needs Quality Improvement—help you and your instructor evaluate your result.

	Your completed project is of Professional Quality if you:	**Your completed project is Approaching Professional Quality if you:**	**Your completed project Needs Quality Improvements if you:**
1-Software Mastery	Choose and apply the most appropriate skills, tools, and features and identify efficient methods to solve the problem.	Choose and apply some appropriate skills, tools, and features, but not in the most efficient manner.	Choose inappropriate skills, tools, or features, or are inefficient in solving the problem.
2-Content	Construct a solution that is clear and well organized, contains content that is accurate, appropriate to the audience and purpose, and is complete. Provide a solution that contains no errors in spelling, grammar, or style.	Construct a solution in which some components are unclear, poorly organized, inconsistent, or incomplete. Misjudge the needs of the audience. Have some errors in spelling, grammar, or style, but the errors do not detract from comprehension.	Construct a solution that is unclear, incomplete, or poorly organized; contains some inaccurate or inappropriate content; and contains many errors in spelling, grammar, or style. Do not solve the problem.
3-Format and Layout	Format and arrange all elements to communicate information and ideas, clarify function, illustrate relationships, and indicate relative importance.	Apply appropriate format and layout features to some elements, but not others. Overuse features, causing minor distraction.	Apply format and layout that does not communicate information or ideas clearly. Do not use format and layout features to clarify function, illustrate relationships, or indicate relative importance. Use available features excessively, causing distraction.
4-Process	Use an organized approach that integrates planning, development, self-assessment, revision, and reflection.	Demonstrate an organized approach in some areas, but not others; or, use an insufficient process of organization throughout.	Do not use an organized approach to solve the problem.

Outcomes-Based Assessments

Apply a combination of the **6A** and **6B** skills.

GO! Think | Project 6L Fundraising Flyer

Project Files

For Project 6L, you will need the following file:

New blank Word document

You will save your documents as:

Lastname_Firstname_6L_Fundraising_Blocks
Lastname_Firstname_6L_Fundraising_Flyer

The Lakefield Public Library is conducting a fundraising campaign with a goal of $100,000 needed to upgrade the computer lab at the Main library and fund library programs. Donations can be sent to 1000 Oak Avenue, Lakefield, IL 60206. Benedetta Herman, Director of Operations, is chairing the fundraising committee and can be reached at 847-555-0982. Donor levels include:

Type of Recognition	Amount of Gift
Bronze Book Club	$100 or more
Silver Book Club	$500 or more
Gold Book Club	$1,000 or more

Create a document that includes a text box with the name and address of the library and an appropriate clip art image. Save both objects as building blocks. Save the document as **Lastname_Firstname_6L_Fundraising_Blocks** Create a flyer explaining the campaign and how donors will be acknowledged. Customize the theme, add appropriate text, and insert your building blocks. Include a Quick Table to display the recognition types. Format the flyer in a professional manner. Save the file as **Lastname_Firstname_6L_Fundraising_Flyer** For both documents, insert the file name in the footer and add document properties. Submit both documents as directed.

End You have completed Project 6L

Apply a combination of the **6A** and **6B** skills.

GO! Think | Project 6M Reading Certificate

Project Files

For Project 6M, you will need the following file:

New blank Word document

You will save your documents as:

Lastname_Firstname_6M_Certificate_Blocks
Lastname_Firstname_6M_Reading_Certificate

The Lakefield Public Library conducts a children's summer reading program. Children are encouraged to read one book weekly over a 10-week period. Director of Programs and Youth Services Abigail Gardner keeps a record of books read by registered children. At the end of summer, every child who read at least ten books receives a certificate of achievement.

Create a document that includes an appropriate clip art image and a Quick Table. Edit the table to include places to record ten book titles and the dates read. Save the graphic and Quick Table as building blocks. Save the document as **Lastname_Firstname_6M_Certificate_Blocks** Create the award certificate. Add text appropriate for a certificate, including places to insert a name, date awarded, and signature of the library official. Insert your building blocks. Format the certificate in a professional manner. Insert a comment related to the certificate's design. Save the file as **Lastname_Firstname_6M_Reading_Certificate** For both documents, insert the file name in the footer, and add document properties. Print both documents or submit electronically as directed.

End You have completed Project 6M

Outcomes-Based Assessments

Apply a combination of the **6A** and **6B** skills.

You and GO! | Project 6N Personal Calendar

Project Files

For Project 6N, you will need the following file:

New blank Word document

You will save your documents as:

Lastname_Firstname_6N_Calendar_Block
Lastname_Firstname_6N_Personal_Calendar

In a new document, insert a Quick Table formatted as a calendar. Delete all the dates, and change the design or layout features to suit your taste. Save the table as a building block. Save the document as **Lastname_Firstname_6N_Calendar Block** Insert the file name in the footer and add appropriate document properties. In a new document, insert your Quick Table building block, change the month to the current month, and then insert the appropriate dates. For specific dates, enter scheduled events. These activities should include your current classes and any observed holidays. Add several comments related to particular events. Using the formatting skills you have practiced, format the document in a manner that is professional and easy to read. Save the file as **Lastname_Firstname_6N_Personal_Calendar** Insert the file name in the footer, and add appropriate document properties. Print both documents or submit electronically as directed by your instructor.

End **You have completed Project 6N**

Business Running Case

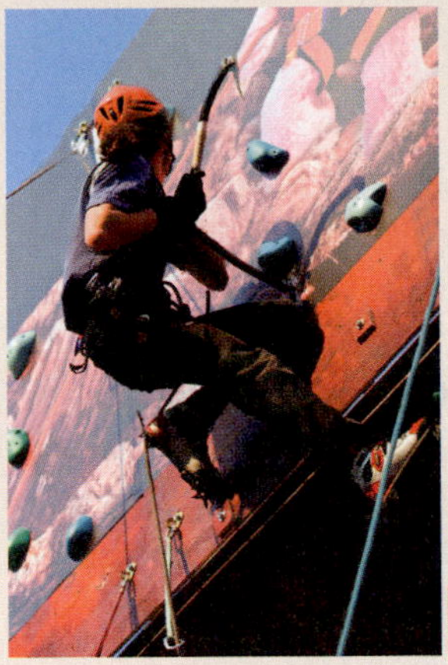

Razvan CHIRNOAGA/Shutterstock

Front Range Action Sports is one of the country's largest retailers of sports gear and outdoor recreation merchandise. The company has large retail stores in Colorado, Washington, Oregon, California, and New Mexico, in addition to a growing online business. Major merchandise categories include fishing, camping, rock climbing, winter sports, action sports, water sports, team sports, racquet sports, fitness, golf, apparel, and footwear.

In this project, you will apply skills you practiced from the Objectives in Chapters 4–6. You will edit and create documents that relate to a new Front Range Action Sports retail store that is opening in Portland, Oregon. The first three documents are a flyer, a Web page, and a blog that announce the opening of the Portland store. The fourth document contains building blocks that are inserted in the final document—a memo to all media outlets announcing the new Portland store opening. Your completed documents will look similar to Figure 2.1.

Project Files

For Project BRC2, you will need the following files:

- New blank Word document
- New blog post—in Word
- wBRC2_Store_Information
- wBRC2_Web_Information
- wBRC2_Portland_Memo

You will save your documents as:

- Lastname_Firstname_BRC2_Portland_Flyer
- Lastname_Firstname_BRC2_Portland_Webpage
- Lastname_Firstname_BRC2_Portland_Blog
- Lastname_Firstname_BRC2_Building_Blocks
- Lastname_Firstname_BRC2_Portland_Memo
- Lastname_Firstname_BRC2_Memo_Theme—not shown in figure

Project Results

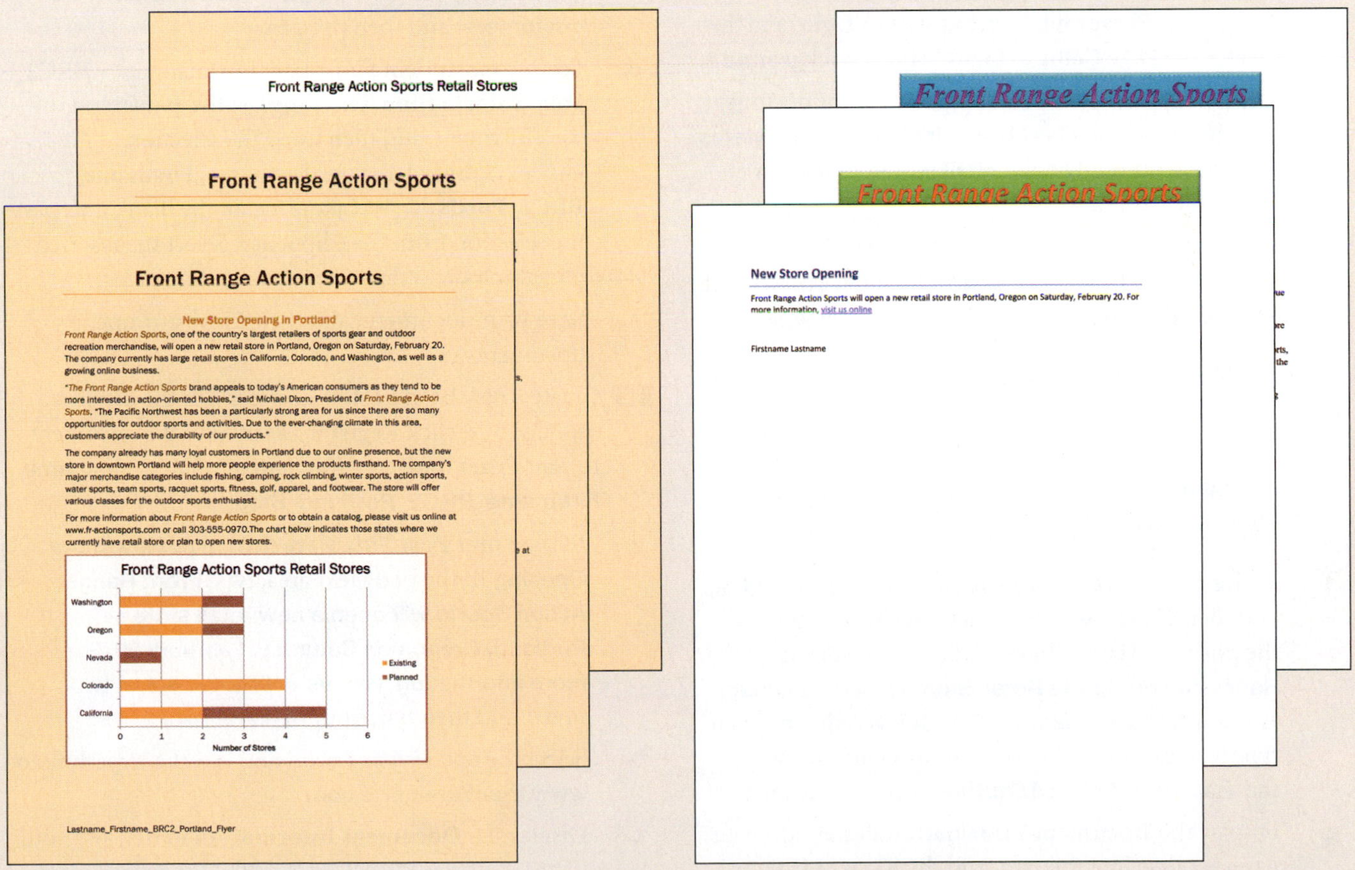

Figure 2.1

Business Running Case 2: Includes Objectives from Word Chapters 4–6

Business Running Case

Front Range Action Sports

1 **Start** Word. From your student files, open **wBRC2_Store_Information**. If necessary, in the location where you are storing your projects, create a new folder named **Front Range Action Sports** or navigate to this folder if you have already created it. **Save** the document as **Lastname_Firstname_BRC2_Portland_Flyer** and then insert the file name in the footer.

a. At the beginning of the document, insert a new paragraph, type **Front Range Action Sports** and then on a new line, type **New Store Opening in Portland** Select the first paragraph, and apply the **Title** style; select the second paragraph, and then apply the **Heading 1** style. **Center** both paragraphs. Change the **Theme** to **Trek**.

b. In the third paragraph, select the text *Front Range Action Sports*. Apply **Bold** and **Italic**, and then change the **Font Color** to **Orange, Accent 1, Darker 50%**. Save the selected text as a **Quick Style** with the name **FRAS** Apply the **FRAS** style to the remaining three occurrences of the company name.

c. Change the **Paragraph Spacing** style to **Tight**, and then change the **Page Color** to **Light Yellow, Background 2**.

d. Position the insertion point at the end of the document, and then type **The chart below indicates those states where we currently have retail stores or plan to open new stores.**

e. On a new line, insert a chart that uses the **Stacked Bar** style. In cell **B1**, type **Existing** and then in cell **C1**, type **Planned** Beginning in cell A2, type the following data:

California	2	3
Colorado	4	0
Nevada	0	1
Oregon	1	2
Washington	2	1

f. Resize the data range to include only **A1** through **C6**, and then **Close** Excel. Insert a **Chart Title** that uses the position **Above Chart**, and then type **Front Range Action Sports Retail Stores** Insert a **Primary Horizontal Axis Title** with **Title Below Axis**, and then type **Number of Stores** Format the chart area with the shape style **Colored Outline – Brown, Accent 2**.

g. Display the **Document Information Panel**, add your name, course information, and the **Keywords flyer, Portland store** **Save** your document.

2 With your **Lastname_Firstname_BRC2_Portland_Flyer** document open, display the **Save As** dialog box. Change **Save as type** to **Web Page**, change the title to **Portland Store Opening** and then save the document to your **Front Range Action Sports** folder as **Lastname_Firstname_BRC2_Portland_Webpage** In **Print Layout** view, update the footer. Display the document properties, and in the **Keywords** box, delete any existing text, and type **Web page, Portland store** If necessary, switch to **Web Layout** view.

a. In the third paragraph, select the first letter, and then insert a **Drop Cap** with **Lines to drop** set to **2**.

b. In the paragraph that begins *For more information*, select the text *www.fr-actionsports.com*, and then insert a **Hyperlink** with the text **Front Range Action Sports** for the **ScreenTip**.

c. After the fifth paragraph, which ends with the text *enthusiast*, insert a blank line. Type **To celebrate the opening of our Portland store, on February 20, we are offering the following discounts to all of our customers:** and then press Enter.

d. From your student files, open the document **wBRC2_Web_Information**, select the last five paragraphs of the document, and then **Copy** the selection to the **Office Clipboard**. In your **Lastname_Firstname_BRC2_Portland_Webpage** file, in the blank line, paste the selection from the Clipboard. Select the inserted paragraphs, and then **Sort** in ascending order.

e. **Save** your document, and then **Close** any open documents.

3 Create a new **Blog post**. If necessary, in the displayed message box, click **Register Later**. Save the document to your **Front Range Action Sports** folder as **Lastname_Firstname_BRC2_Portland_Blog**

a. In the **Enter Post Title Here** field, type **New Store Opening** In the body text area, type **Front Range Action Sports will open a new retail store in Portland, Oregon on Saturday, February 20. For more information, visit us online.** Press Enter two times, and then type your first and last names.

b. Select the text *visit us online*, and insert a hyperlink to **www.fr-actionsports.com**

c. Display the **Document Information Panel**, add your name, course information, and the **Keywords blog, Portland store** **Save** and **Close** your document.

(Business Running Case: Front Range Action Sports continues on the next page)

Front Range Action Sports (continued)

4 Create a new, blank document, and save it to your **Front Range Action Sports** folder as **Lastname_Firstname_BRC2_Building_Blocks** Insert the file name in the footer.

a. Insert a **Text Box** in the style **Simple Text Box**. Change the text wrapping to **In Line with Text**. Change the **Shape Width** to **6.0"** and the **Shape Height** to **0.8"**. Change the shape style to **Intense Effect – Olive Green, Accent 3**. In the text box, type **Front Range Action Sports** Change the **Font Size** to **36**, and then apply **Bold**, **Italic**, and **Center**. Apply the text effect **Gradient Fill – Orange, Accent 6, Inner Shadow**. Save the text box to the **Text Box** gallery with the name **Company Heading**

b. In the document, below the text box, insert a **Quick Table** in the **Tabular List** style. In the first row, in the first cell, change the text to **ITEMS** and then in the second cell, change the text to **DISCOUNT Delete** all remaining text in the table. Save the table to the **Quick Tables** gallery with the name **Discount Table**

c. Display the **Document Information Panel,** add your name, course information, and the **Keywords building blocks, Portland store Save** your changes, and from **Backstage** view, **Close** your document without closing Word.

5 Open the file **wBRC2_Portland_Memo**. Save it to your **Front Range Action Sports** folder as **Lastname_Firstname_BRC2_Portland_Memo** Insert the file name in the footer.

a. Accept all changes in the document, and then **Delete** the comment.

b. Change the **Theme Colors** to **Apex**, and then change the **Theme Fonts** to **Office Classic**. Save the current theme to your **Front Range Action Sports** folder as **Lastname_Firstname_BRC2_Memo_Theme**

c. At the beginning of the document, insert the **Company Heading** building block. If necessary, change text wrapping to **In Line with Text**. If necessary, position the insertion point to the left of *TO:*, and then press Enter.

6 In the paragraph that begins *To celebrate*, immediately to the left of *discounts*, type **the following** and then at the end of the sentence, replace the period with a colon. Press Enter.

a. Insert the **Quick Table** you created—**Discount Table**. Starting in the second row, type the following:

Backpacks	30%
Binoculars	25%
Footwear	20%
GPS Units	10%
Tents	15%

b. **Delete** any empty rows in the table. **Center** the data in the second column, and then **Center** the table horizontally on the page.

c. In the paragraph that begins *The company already*, locate and then select the text *attire*. Using the **Thesaurus**, replace the selected text with an appropriate synonym.

d. Press Ctrl + Home. Display the **Find and Replace** dialog box. In the **Find what** box, type **Front Range Sports** In the **Replace with** box, type **Front Range Action Sports** Display the **Replace Font** dialog box. Select **Bold Italic** and then change the **Font color** to **Lavender, Accent 6, Darker 25%**. Replace all three occurrences.

e. Display the **Document Information Panel**, add your name, course information, and the **Keywords memo, Portland store**

7 **Save** your document, **Delete** your two building blocks from the **Building Blocks Organizer,** and then **Close** Word. In the **Word** message box, **Save** the changes to building blocks.

8 Print all five documents—you cannot print the theme file—or submit electronically as directed by your instructor.

End **You have completed Business Running Case 2**

Use Financial and Lookup Functions, Define Names, and Validate Data

OUTCOMES

At the end of this chapter you will be able to:

OBJECTIVES

Mastering these objectives will enable you to:

PROJECT 4A

Calculate loan options and create a loan amortization schedule.

1. Use Financial Functions (p. 227)
2. Use Goal Seek (p. 230)
3. Create a Data Table (p. 233)

PROJECT 4B

Automate workbooks to look up information automatically and to validate data.

4. Define Names (p. 241)
5. Use Defined Names in a Formula (p. 249)
6. Use Lookup Functions (p. 251)
7. Validate Data (p. 257)

Natalia Barsukova/Shutterstock

In This Chapter

In this chapter, you will use Financial functions and What-If Analysis tools to make your worksheets more valuable for analyzing data and making financial decisions. In addition, you will define names and use them in a formula. You will use the lookup functions to locate information that is needed in a form and create a validation list to ensure that only accurate data is entered.

The projects in this chapter relate to **Rubanne Specialties**, a Montreal-based retailer of quality leather and fabric accessories for men and women. Products include wallets, belts, handbags, key chains, backpacks, business cases, and travel bags. The company distributes its products to department and specialty stores in the United States and Canada.

Project 4A Amortization Schedule

myitlab
Project 4A Training

Project Activities

In Activities 4.01 through 4.05, you will create a worksheet for Yvonne Dubois, International Sales Director for Rubanne Specialties, that details the loan information to purchase furniture and fixtures for a new store in Chicago. Your completed worksheet will look similar to Figure 4.1.

Project Files

For Project 4A, you will need the following file:

e04A_Store_Loan

You will save your workbook as:

Lastname_Firstname_4A_Store_Loan

Project Results

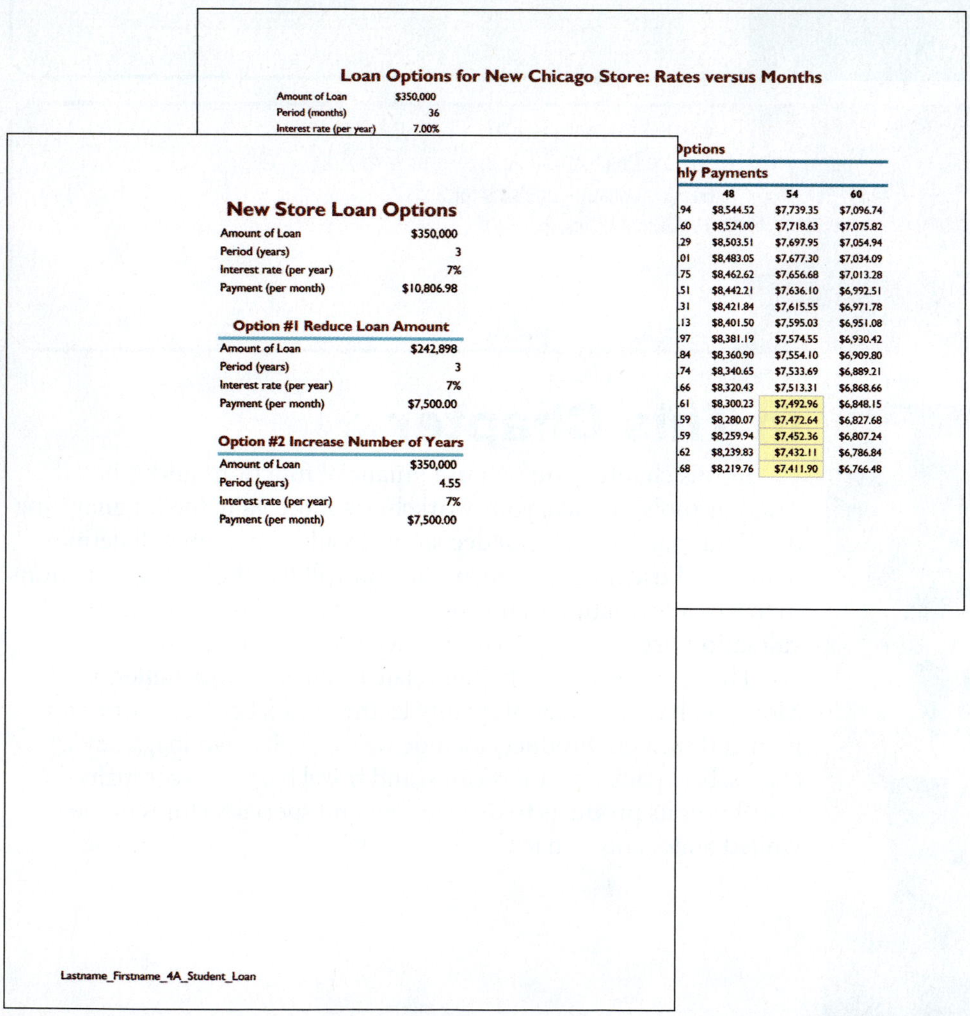

Figure 4.1
Project 4A Amortization Schedule

Objective 1 | Use Financial Functions

Financial functions are prebuilt formulas that make common business calculations such as calculating a loan payment on a vehicle or calculating how much to save each month to buy something. Financial functions commonly involve a period of time such as months or years.

When you borrow money from a bank or other lender, the amount charged to you for your use of the borrowed money is called ***interest***. Loans are typically made for a period of years, and the interest that must be paid is a percentage of the loan amount that is still owed. In Excel, this interest percentage is called the ***rate***.

The initial amount of the loan is called the ***Present value (Pv)***, which is the total amount that a series of future payments is worth now, and is also known as the ***principal***. When you borrow money, the loan amount is the present value to the lender. The number of time periods—number of payments—is abbreviated ***nper***. The value at the end of the time periods is the ***Future value (Fv)***—the cash balance you want to attain after the last payment is made. The future value is usually zero for loans.

Activity 4.01 | Inserting the PMT Financial Function

In this activity, you will calculate the monthly payments that Rubanne Specialties must make to finance the purchase of the furniture and fixtures for the new store in Chicago, the total cost of which is $350,000. You will calculate the monthly payments, including interest, for a three-year loan at an annual interest rate of 4.0%. To stay within Yvonne's budget, the monthly payment must be approximately $7,500.

1 **Start** Excel. From your student files, open **e04A_Store_Loan**. Display the **Save As** dialog box, navigate to the location where you will store your workbooks for this chapter, and then create a new folder named **Excel Chapter 4** Open your new folder, and then **Save** the workbook as **Lastname_Firstname_4A_Store_Loan**

2 In the range **A2:B5**, enter the following row titles and data. Recall that you can format the numbers as you type by typing them with their symbols as shown. Compare your screen with Figure 4.2:

Amount of Loan	**$350,000**
Period (years)	**3**
Interest rate (per year)	**7%**
Payment (per month)	

Figure 4.2

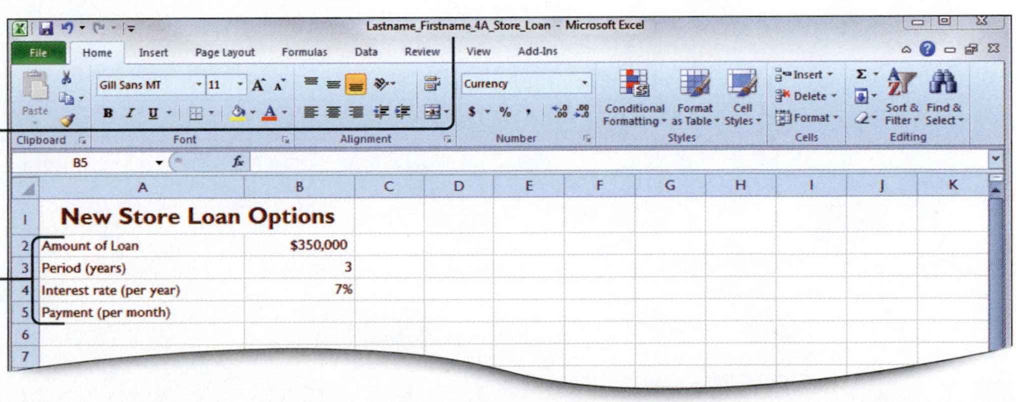

3 Click cell **B5**. On the **Formulas tab**, in the **Function Library group**, click the **Financial** button. In the displayed list, scroll down as necessary, and then click **PMT**.

The Function Arguments dialog box displays. Recall that ***arguments*** are the values that an Excel function uses to perform calculations or operations.

4 If necessary, drag the Function Arguments dialog box to the right side of your screen so you can view columns A:B.

The ***PMT function*** calculates the payment for a loan based on constant payments and at a constant interest rate. To complete the PMT function, first you must determine the total number of loan payment periods (months), which is 12 months x 3 years, or 36 months.

Another Way

Click cell B4 and then type /12.

5 With your insertion point positioned in the **Rate** box, type **b4/12** and then compare your screen with Figure 4.3.

Excel will divide the annual interest rate of 7%, which is 0.07 in decimal notation, located in cell B4 by 12 (months), which will result in a *monthly* interest rate.

When borrowing money, the interest rate and number of periods are quoted in years. The payments on a loan, however, are usually made monthly. Therefore, the number of periods, which is stated in years, and the *annual* interest rate, must be changed to a monthly equivalent in order to calculate the monthly payment amount. You can see that calculations like these can be made as part of the argument in a function.

Figure 4.3

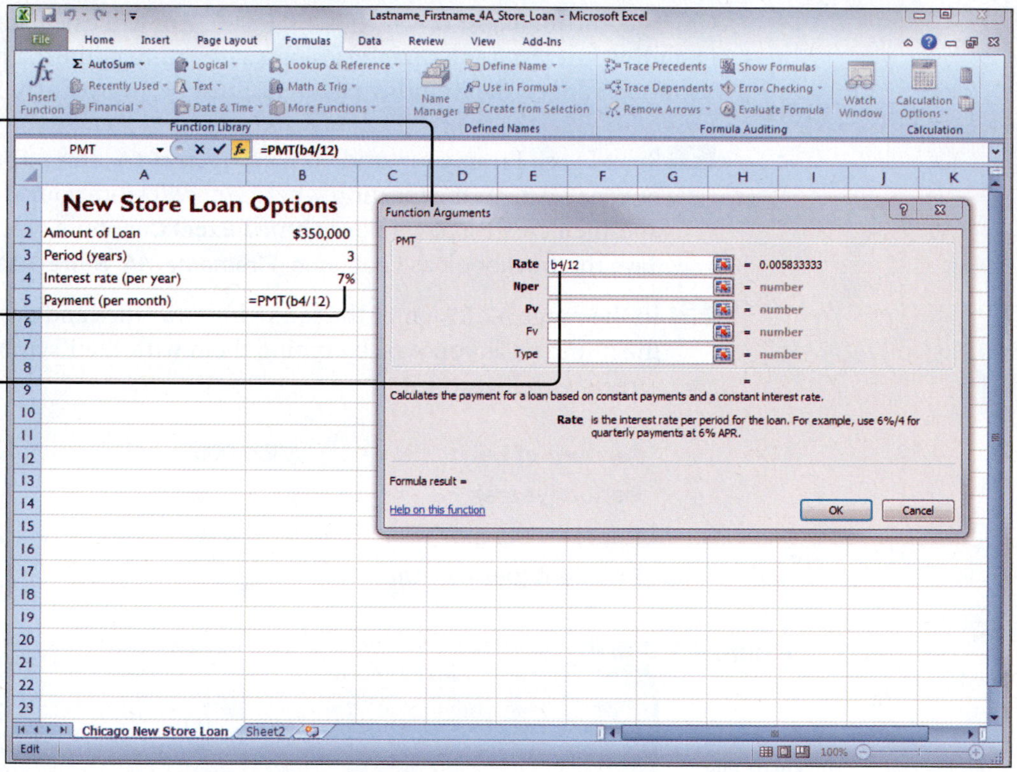

Function Arguments dialog box

Cell B4 contains the interest rate

Rate entered

6 Press [Tab] to move the insertion point to the **Nper** box. In the lower portion of the dialog box, notice Excel points out that *Nper is the total number of payments for the loan* (number of periods).

7 Type **b3*12** to have Excel convert the number of years in the loan in cell B3 (3 years) to the total number of months.

Recall that the PMT function calculates a *monthly* payment. Thus, all values in the function must be expressed in months.

8 Press [Tab] to move to the **Pv** box, and then type **b2** to indicate the cell that contains the amount of the loan.

Pv represents the present value—the amount of the loan before any payments are made—in this instance $350,000.

9 In cell **B5** and on the **Formula Bar**, notice that the arguments that comprise the PMT function are separated by commas. Notice also, in the **Function Arguments** dialog box, that the value of each argument displays to the right of the argument box. Compare your screen with Figure 4.4.

Figure 4.4

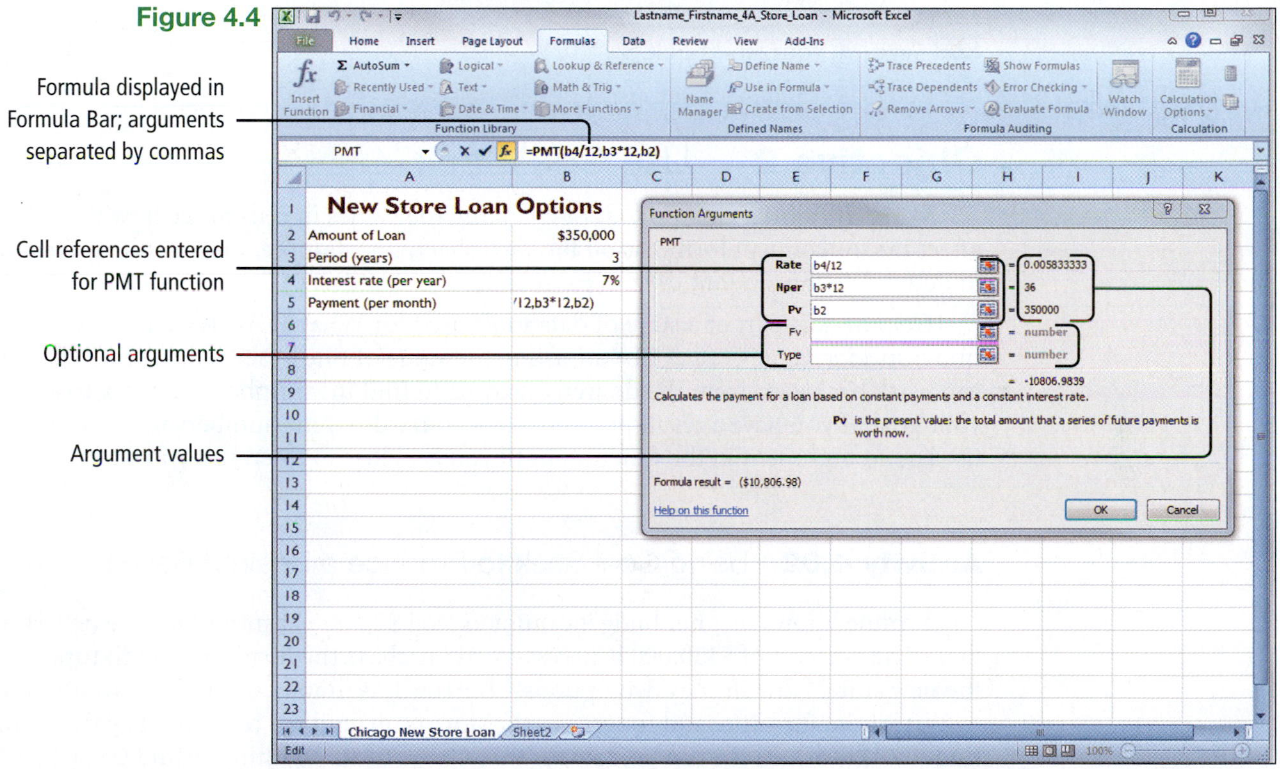

Note | Optional Arguments

The PMT function has two arguments not indicated by bold; these are optional. The Future value (Fv) argument assumes that the unpaid portion of the loan should be zero at the end of the last period. The ***Type argument*** assumes that the payment will be made at the end of each period. These default values are typical of most loans and may be left blank.

10 In the lower right corner of the **Function Arguments** dialog box, click **OK**.

The monthly payment amount—(*$10,806.98*)—displays in cell B5. The amount displays in red and in parentheses to show that it is a negative number, a number that will be *paid out*. This monthly payment of $10,806.98 is over the budget of $7,500 per month that Yvonne has in mind.

11 Click in the **Formula Bar**, and then by using the arrow keys on the keyboard, position the insertion point between the equal sign and *PMT*. Type **-** (minus sign) to insert a minus sign into the formula, and then press Enter.

By placing a minus sign in the formula, the monthly payment amount, $10,806.98, displays in cell B5 as a *positive* number, which is more familiar and less distracting to work with.

12 **Save** your workbook.

Objective 2 | Use Goal Seek

What-If Analysis is a process of changing the values in cells to see how those changes affect the outcome of formulas on the worksheet; for example, varying the interest rate to determine the amount of loan payments.

Goal Seek is part of a suite of data tools used for What-If Analysis. It is a method to find a specific value for a cell by adjusting the value of one other cell. With Goal Seek, you can work backward from the desired outcome to find the number necessary to achieve your goal. If you have a result in mind, you can try different numbers in one of the cells used as an argument in the function until you get close to the result you want.

Activity 4.02 | Using Goal Seek to Produce a Desired Result

Yvonne knows that her budget cannot exceed $7,500 per month for the new store loan. The amount of $350,000 is necessary to purchase the furniture and fixtures to open the new store. Now she has two options—borrow less money and reduce the amount or quality of the furniture and fixtures in the store or extend the time to repay the loan. To find out how much she can borrow for three years to stay within the budget or how much to increase the repayment period, you will use the Goal Seek tool.

1 Click cell **B5**. On the **Data tab**, in the **Data Tools group**, click the **What-If Analysis** button, and then in the displayed list, click **Goal Seek**. In the **Goal Seek** dialog box, in the **Set cell** box, confirm that *B5* displays.

The cell address in this box is the cell that will display the desired result.

2 Press Tab. In the **To value** box, type the payment goal of **7500.00** and press Tab. In the **By changing cell** box, type **b2**, which is the amount of the loan, and then compare your dialog box with Figure 4.5.

Figure 4.5

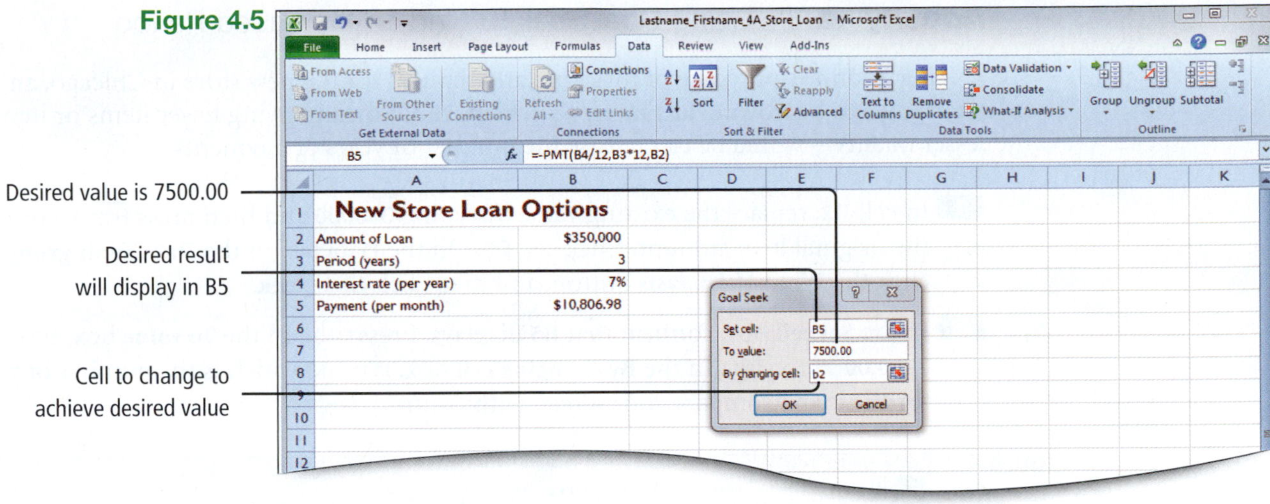

3 Click **OK**, and then in the displayed **Goal Seek Status** dialog box, click **OK**.

Excel's calculations indicate that to achieve a monthly payment of $7,500.00 using a 3-year loan, Yvonne can borrow only *$242,898*—not $350,000.

4 Click cell **A7**. Type **Option #1 Reduce Loan Amount** and then on the **Formula Bar**, click the **Enter** button ✓ to keep the cell active. **Merge and Center** this heading across the range **A7:B7**, on the **Home tab**, display the **Cell Styles** gallery, and then apply the **Heading 2** cell style.

5 Select the range **A2:B5**, right-click, and then click **Copy**. Point to cell **A8**, right-click, point to **Paste Special**, and then under **Paste Values,** click the **second** button—**Values & Number Formatting (A)**. Press Esc to cancel the moving border.

> **Another Way**
>
> Click cell A8, right-click, and then click Paste Special. In the Paste Special dialog box, under Paste, click the Values and number formats option button, and then click OK.

6 **Save** your workbook, click anywhere to deselect, and then compare your worksheet with Figure 4.6.

Recall that by using the Paste Special command, you can copy the *value* in a cell, rather than the formula, and the cell formats are retained—cell B5 contains the PMT function formula, and here you need only the value that *results* from that formula.

Figure 4.6

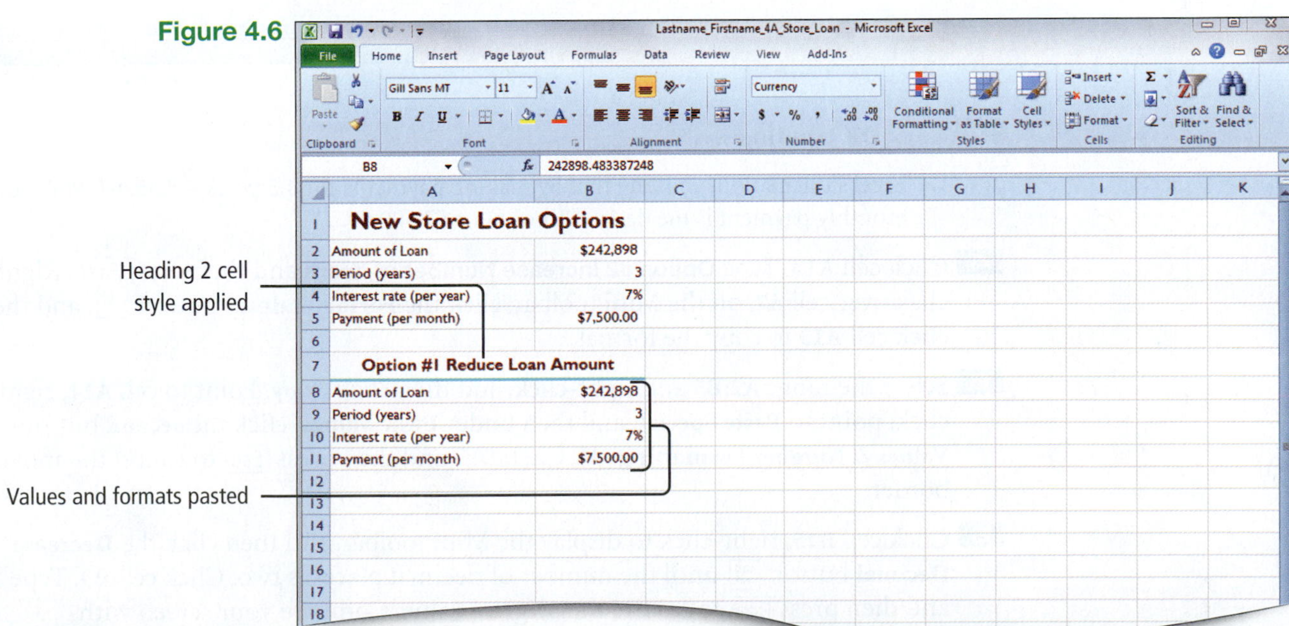

Activity 4.03 | Using Goal Seek to Find an Increased Period

For Yvonne's purchase of furniture and fixtures for the new store in Chicago, an alternative to borrowing less money—which would mean buying fewer items or items of lesser quality—would be to increase the number of years of payments.

1 In cell **B2**, replace the existing value by typing **350000** and then press Enter to restore the original loan amount. Click cell **B5**. On the **Data tab**, in the **Data Tools group**, click the **What-If Analysis** button, and then click **Goal Seek**.

2 In the **Set cell** box, confirm that **B5** displays. Press Tab. In the **To value** box, type **7500.00** Press Tab. In the **By changing cell** box, type **b3** which is the number of years for the loan. Compare your screen with Figure 4.7.

Figure 4.7

Original loan amount $350,000 restored

Cell with the number of payment periods indicated as the *change* cell

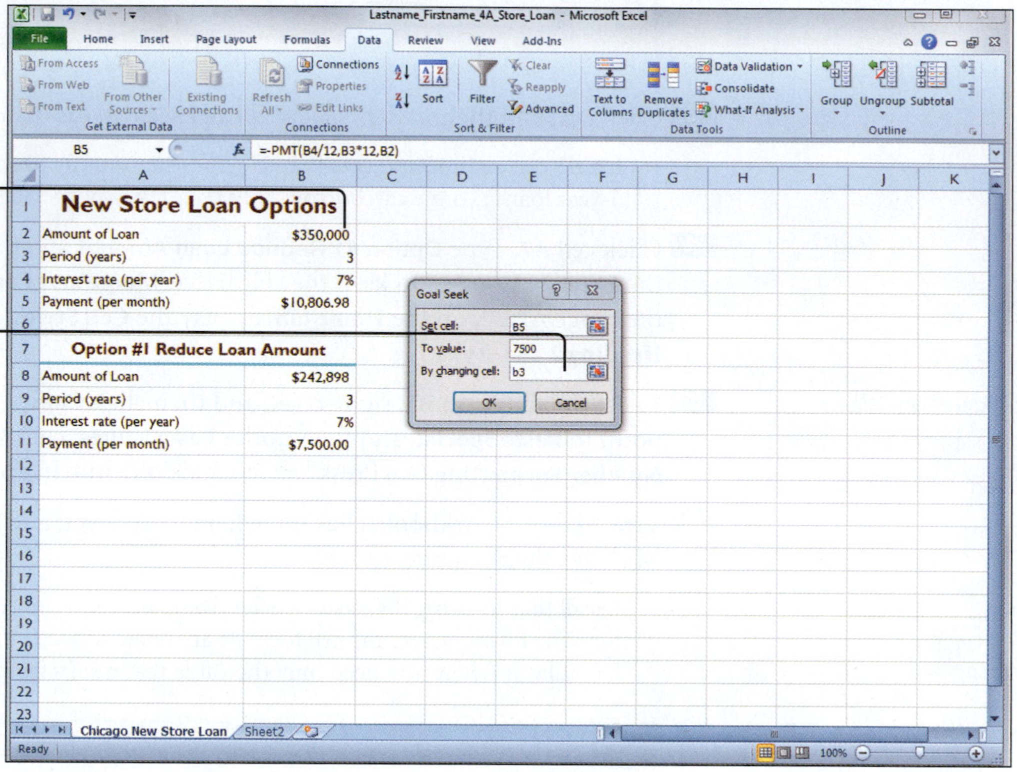

3 Click **OK** two times.

Excel's calculations indicate that by making payments for 4.5 years—*4.552648969*—the monthly payment is the desired amount of $7,500.00.

4 Click cell **A13**. Type **Option #2 Increase Number of Years** and then press Enter. Right-click over cell **A7**, on the Mini toolbar, click the **Format Painter** button, and then click cell **A13** to copy the format.

5 Select the range **A2:B5** and right-click, and then click **Copy**. Point to cell **A14**, right-click, point to **Paste Special**, and then under **Paste Values**, click the **second** button—**Values & Number Formatting (A)**. Click **OK**, and then press Esc to cancel the moving border.

6 Click cell **B15**, right-click to display the Mini toolbar, and then click the **Decrease Decimal** button until the number of decimal places is two. Click cell **B3**. Type **3** and then press Enter to restore the original value. Compare your screen with Figure 4.8.

Figure 4.8

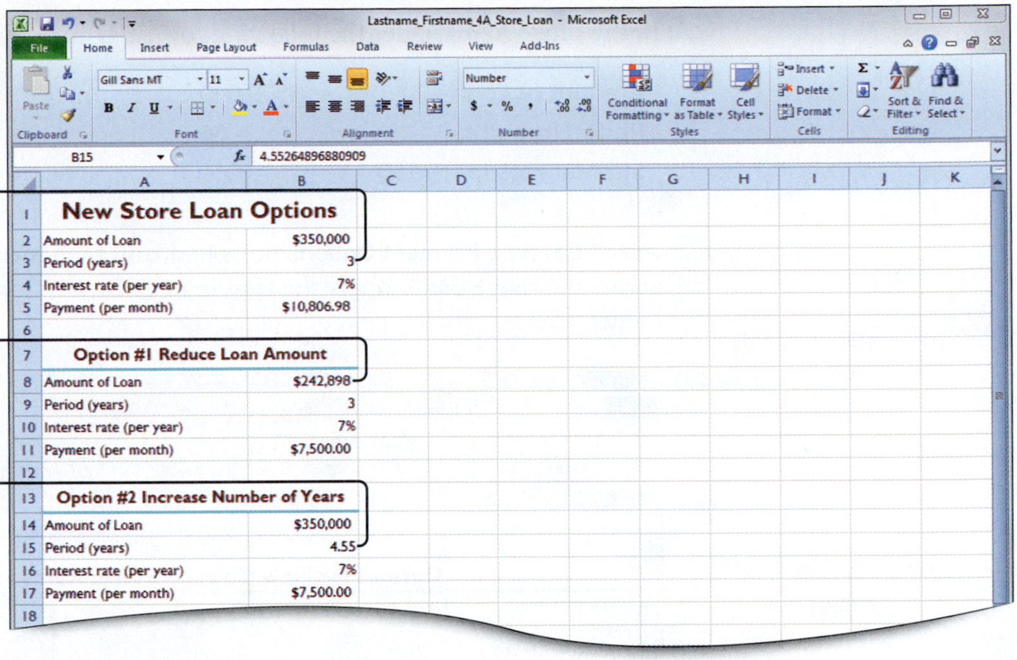

7 **Save** your workbook.

Objective 3 | Create a Data Table

A ***data table*** is a range of cells that shows how changing certain values in your formulas affects the results of those formulas. Data tables make it easy to calculate multiple versions in one operation, and then to view and compare the results of all the different variations.

For example, banks may offer loans at different rates for different periods of time, which require different payments. By using a data table, you can calculate the possible values for each argument.

A ***one-variable data table*** changes the value in only one cell. For example, use a one-variable data table if you want to see how different interest rates affect a monthly payment. A ***two-variable data table*** changes the values in two cells—for example, if you want to see how different interest rates *and* different payment periods will affect a monthly payment.

Activity 4.04 | Designing a Two-Variable Data Table

Recall that the PMT function has three required arguments: Present value (Pv), Rate, and Number of periods (Nper). Because Yvonne would still like to borrow $350,000 and purchase the fixtures and furniture that she has selected for the new store in Chicago, in this data table, the present value will *not* change. The two values that *will* change are the Rate and Number of periods. Possible periods will range from 24 months (2 years) to 60 months (5 years) and the Rate will vary from 8% to 6%.

1 Double-click the **Sheet2 tab**, rename it **Payment Table** and then press Enter.

2 In cell **A1**, type **Loan Options for New Chicago Store: Rates versus Months** and then press Enter. **Merge and Center** this title across the range **A1:I1**, and then apply the **Title** cell style.

3 In the range **A2:B4**, enter the following row titles and data:

Amount of Loan	**$350,000**
Period (months)	**36**
Interest rate (per year)	**7.00%**

4 In cell **C5**, type **Payment Options** press Enter, and then **Merge and Center** this title across the range **C5:I5**. Apply the **Heading 1** cell style. Compare your screen with Figure 4.9.

Figure 4.9

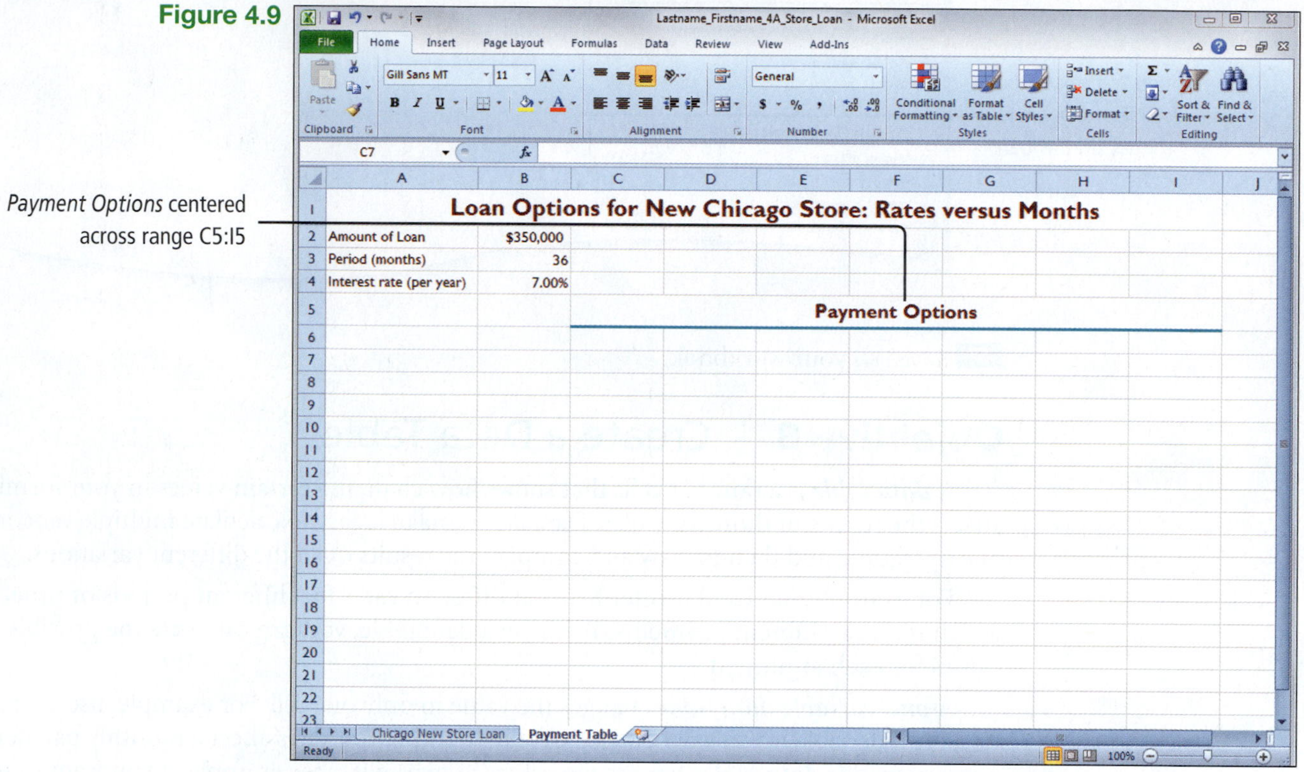

5 In cell **C6**, type **Number of Monthly Payments** press Enter, and then use the **Format Painter** to apply the format of cell **C5** to cell **C6**.

6 In cell **C7**, type **24** and then press Tab. Type **30** and then press Tab. Select the range **C7:D7**, point to the fill handle, and then drag to the right through cell **I7** to fill in a pattern of months from 24 to 60 in increments of six months.

Recall that the Auto Fill feature will duplicate a pattern of values that you set in the beginning cells.

7 In cell **B8**, type **8.000%** and then press Enter. In cell **B9**, type **7.875%** and then press Enter.

Excel rounds both values up to two decimal places.

8 Select the range **B8:B9**. Point to the fill handle, and then drag down through cell **B24** to fill a pattern of interest rates in increments of .125 from 8.00% down to 6.00%.

9 Right-click anywhere over the selected range, and then on the Mini toolbar, click the **Increase Decimal** button one time. **Save** your workbook. Compare your screen with Figure 4.10.

Row 7 represents the number of monthly payments, and column B represents a range of possible annual interest rates. These two arguments will be used to calculate varying payment arrangements for a loan of $350,000.

Figure 4.10

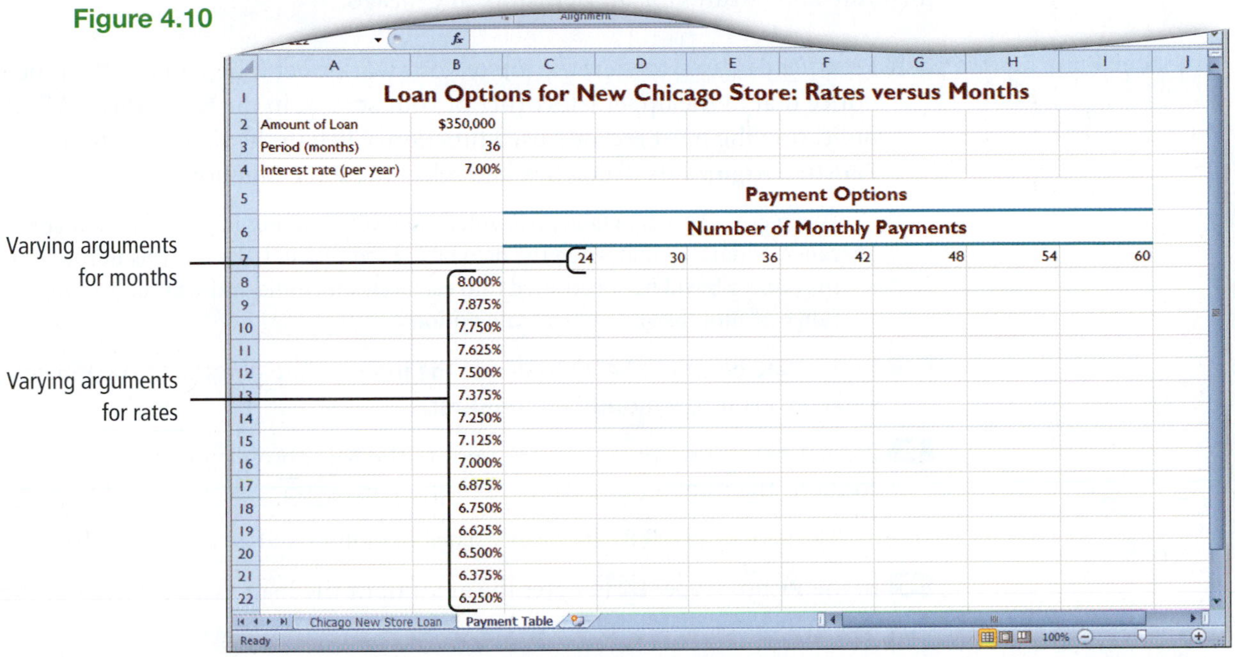

10 In cell **A8**, type **Rates** and then press Enter. Select the range **A8:A24**. On the **Home tab**, in the **Alignment group**, click the **Merge and Center** button, click the **Align Text Right** button, and then click the **Middle Align** button. Display the **Cell Styles** gallery, and then under **Data and Model**, apply the **Explanatory Text** style. Compare your screen with Figure 4.11.

Figure 4.11

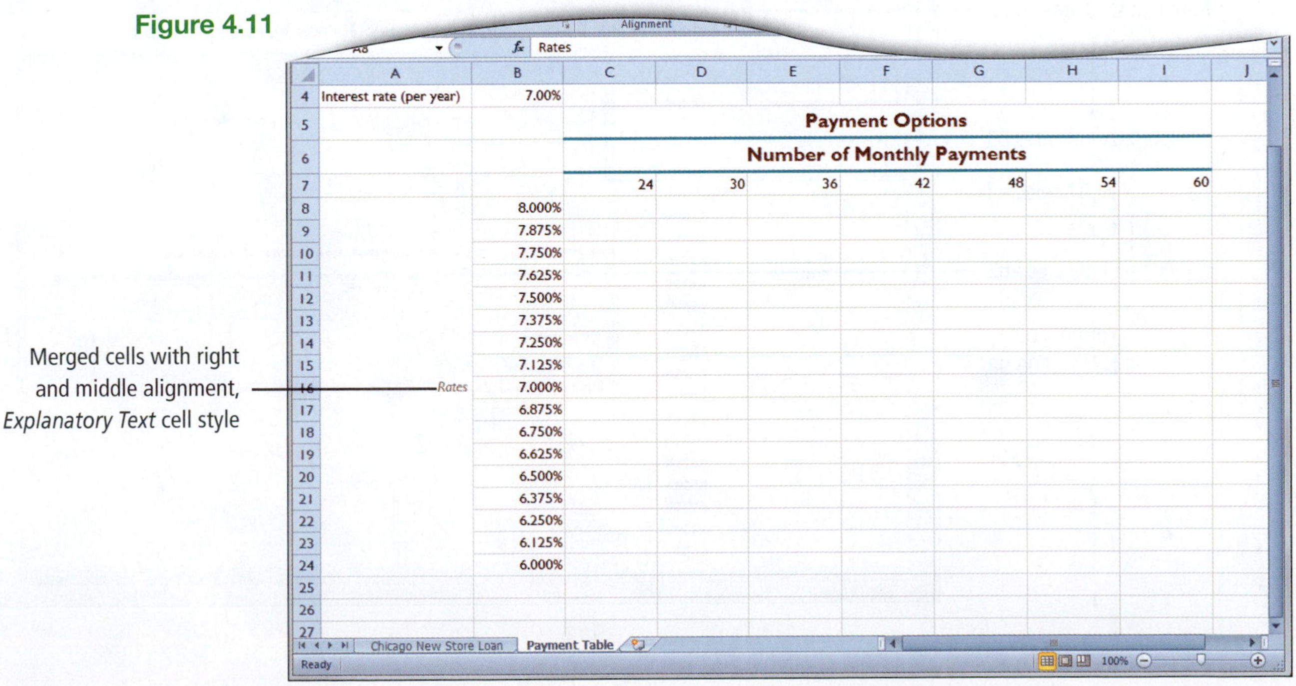

Activity 4.05 | Using a Data Table to Calculate Options

Recall that a data table is a range of cells that shows how changing certain values in your formulas affects the results of those formulas.

In this activity, you will create a table of payments for every combination of payment periods, which are represented by the column titles under *Number of Monthly Payments*, and interest rates, which are represented by the row titles to the right of *Rates*. From the resulting table, Yvonne can find a combination of payment periods and interest rates that will enable her to go forward with her plan to borrow $350,000 to purchase the necessary furniture and fixtures for the new store in Chicago.

> **Another Way**
> Use one of the other methods you have practiced to insert the PMT function.

1 Press Ctrl + Home to view the top of your worksheet. Then, in cell **B7**, type = and notice that in the upper left corner of your screen, in the **Name Box**, *PMT* displays indicating the most recently used function. Click in the **Name Box** to open the **Function Arguments** dialog box and select the **PMT** function.

When creating a data table, you enter the PMT function in the upper left corner of your range of data, so that when the data table is completed, the months in row 7 and the rates in column B will be substituted into each cell's formula and will fill the table with the range of months and interest rate options.

2 In the **Rate** box, type **b4/12** to divide the interest rate per year shown in cell B4 by 12 and convert it to a monthly interest rate.

3 Press Tab to move the insertion point to the **Nper** box. Type **b3** which is the cell that contains the number of months, and then press Tab.

The periods in cell B3 are already stated in months and do not need to be changed.

4 In the **Pv** box, type **-b2** to enter the amount of the loan as a negative number. Compare your dialog box with Figure 4.12.

Figure 4.12

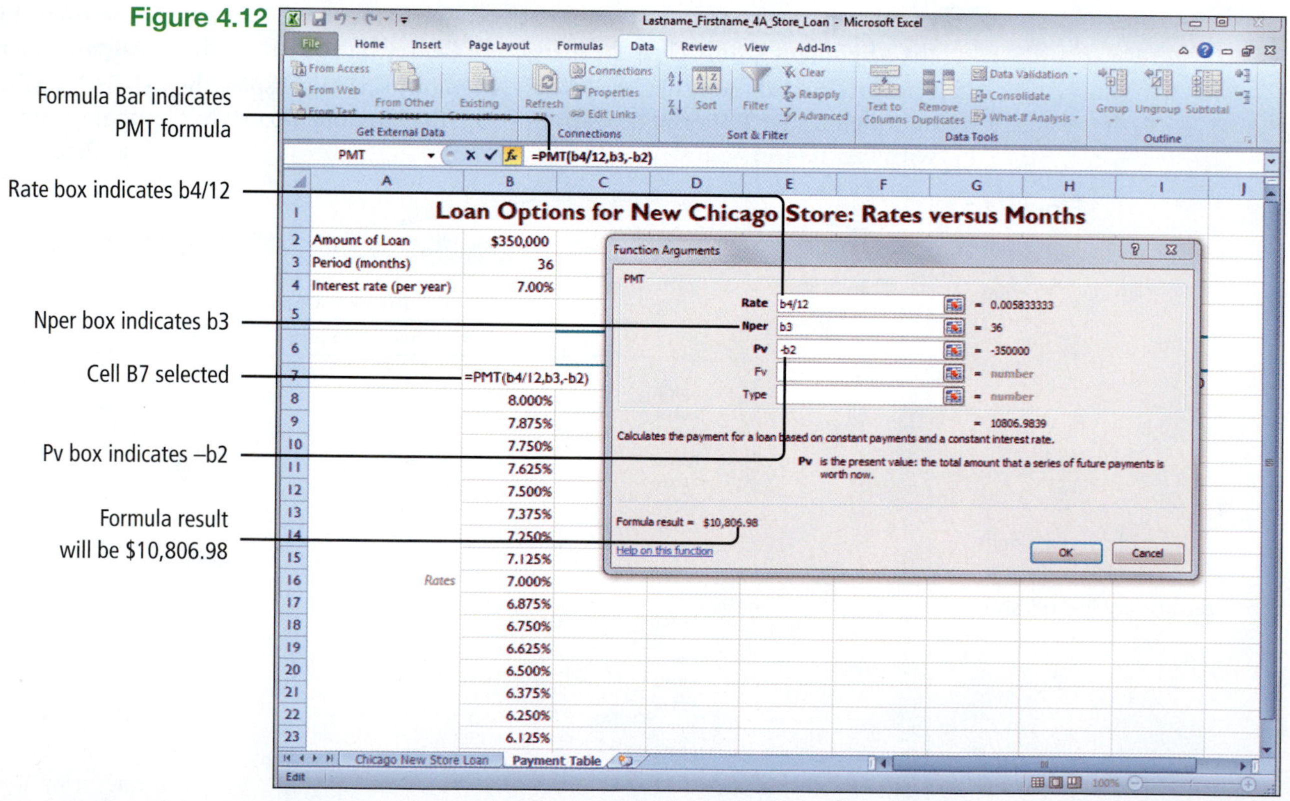

5 Click **OK** to close the **Function Arguments** dialog box and display the result in cell **B7**.

The payment—*10,806.98*—is calculated by using the values in cells B2, B3, and B4. This is the same payment that you calculated on the first worksheet. Now it displays as a positive number because you entered the loan amount in cell B2 as a negative number.

6 Select the range **B7:I24**, which encompasses all of the months and all of the rates. With the range **B7:I24** selected, on the **Data tab**, in the **Data Tools group**, click the **What-If Analysis** button, and then in the displayed list, click **Data Table**.

7 In the **Data Table** dialog box, in the **Row input cell** box, type **b3** and then press Tab. In the **Column input cell** box, type **b4** and then compare your screen with Figure 4.13.

The row of months will be substituted for the value in cell B3, and the column of interest rates will be substituted for the value in cell B4.

Figure 4.13

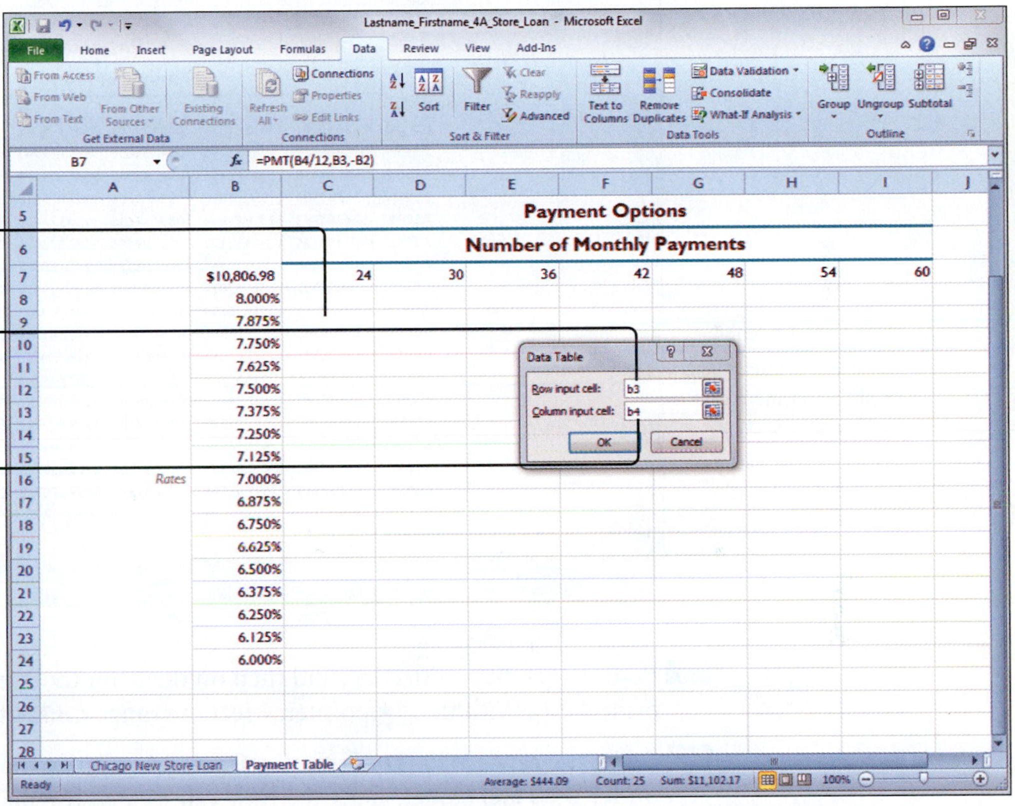

8 Click **OK**. Click cell **H20**, and then examine the formula in the **Formula Bar**. Compare your screen with Figure 4.14.

The table is filled with payment options that use the month and interest rate corresponding to the position in the table. Thus, if Yvonne chooses a combination of 54 months at an interest rate of 6.5%, the monthly payment will be $7,492.96, which is almost the exact monthly payment she wanted. The data table is one of a group of Excel's What-If Analysis tools.

Figure 4.14

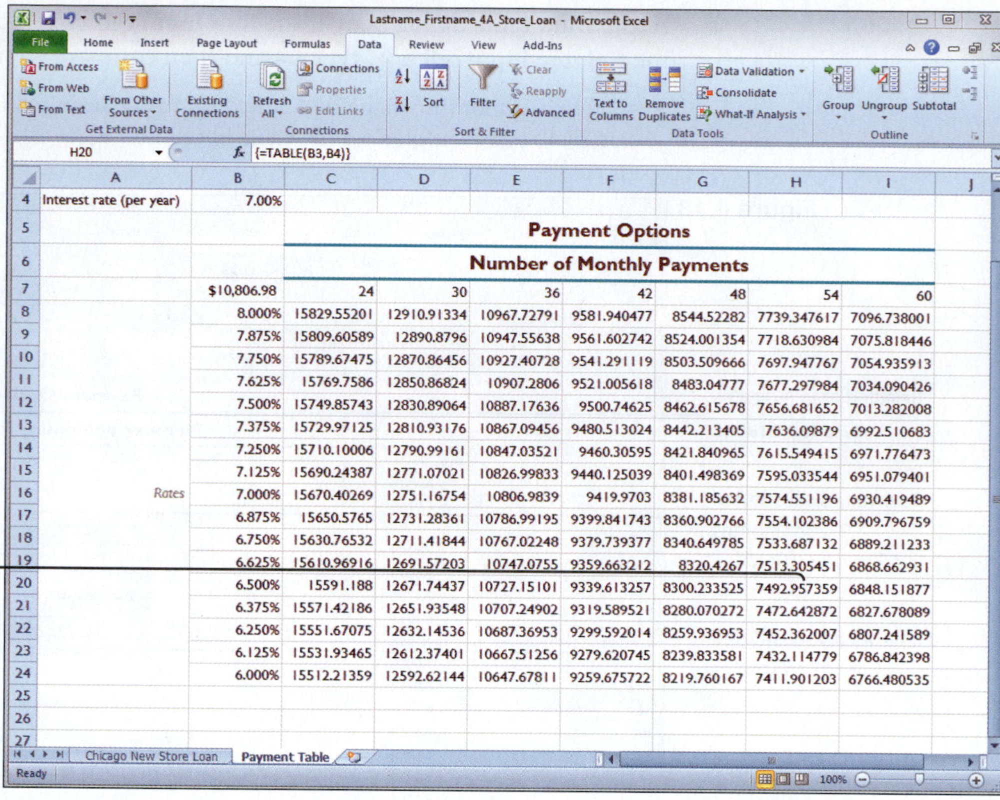

	A	B	C	D	E	F	G	H	I
4	Interest rate (per year)	7.00%							
5			Payment Options						
6			Number of Monthly Payments						
7		$10,806.98	24	30	36	42	48	54	60
8		8.000%	15829.55201	12910.91334	10967.72791	9581.940477	8544.52282	7739.347617	7096.738001
9		7.875%	15809.60589	12890.8796	10947.55638	9561.602742	8524.001354	7718.630984	7075.818446
10		7.750%	15789.67475	12870.86456	10927.40728	9541.291119	8503.509666	7697.947767	7054.935913
11		7.625%	15769.7586	12850.86824	10907.2806	9521.005618	8483.04777	7677.297984	7034.090426
12		7.500%	15749.85743	12830.89064	10887.17636	9500.74625	8462.615678	7656.681652	7013.282008
13		7.375%	15729.97125	12810.93176	10867.09456	9480.513024	8442.213405	7636.09879	6992.510683
14		7.250%	15710.10006	12790.99161	10847.03521	9460.30595	8421.840965	7615.549415	6971.776473
15		7.125%	15690.24387	12771.07021	10826.99833	9440.125039	8401.498369	7595.033544	6951.079401
16	Rates	7.000%	15670.40269	12751.16754	10806.9839	9419.9703	8381.185632	7574.551196	6930.419489
17		6.875%	15650.5765	12731.28361	10786.99195	9399.841743	8360.902766	7554.102386	6909.796759
18		6.750%	15630.76532	12711.41844	10767.02248	9379.739377	8340.649785	7533.687132	6889.211233
19		6.625%	15610.96916	12691.57203	10747.0755	9359.663212	8320.4267	7513.305451	6868.662931
20		6.500%	15591.188	12671.74437	10727.15101	9339.613257	8300.233525	7492.957359	6848.151877
21		6.375%	15571.42186	12651.93548	10707.24902	9319.589521	8280.070272	7472.642872	6827.678089
22		6.250%	15551.67075	12632.14536	10687.36953	9299.592014	8259.936953	7452.362007	6807.241589
23		6.125%	15531.93465	12612.37401	10667.51256	9279.620745	8239.833581	7432.114779	6786.842398
24		6.000%	15512.21359	12592.62144	10647.67811	9259.675722	8219.760167	7411.901203	6766.480535

Period of 54 months, at 6.500% interest, results in payment of 7492.957359

9 Point to cell **B7**, right-click, and then on the Mini toolbar, click the **Format Painter** button. With the pointer, select the range **C8:I24** to apply the same format.

10 Select the range **H20:H24**.From the **Home tab**, display the **Cell Styles** gallery, and then under **Data and Model**, apply the **Note** cell style to highlight the desired payment options.

11 Select the range **B8:B24**, hold down Ctrl, and then select the range **C7:I7**. Right-click over the selection, and then from the Mini toolbar, apply **Bold** B and **Center** ≡. Click anywhere to deselect the range, and then compare your worksheet with Figure 4.15.

By using a data table of payment options, you can see that Yvonne must get a loan for at least 54 months (4.5 years) for any of the interest rates between 6.500% and 6.00% in order to purchase the furniture and fixtures she wants and still keep the monthly payment at approximately $7,500.

Figure 4.15

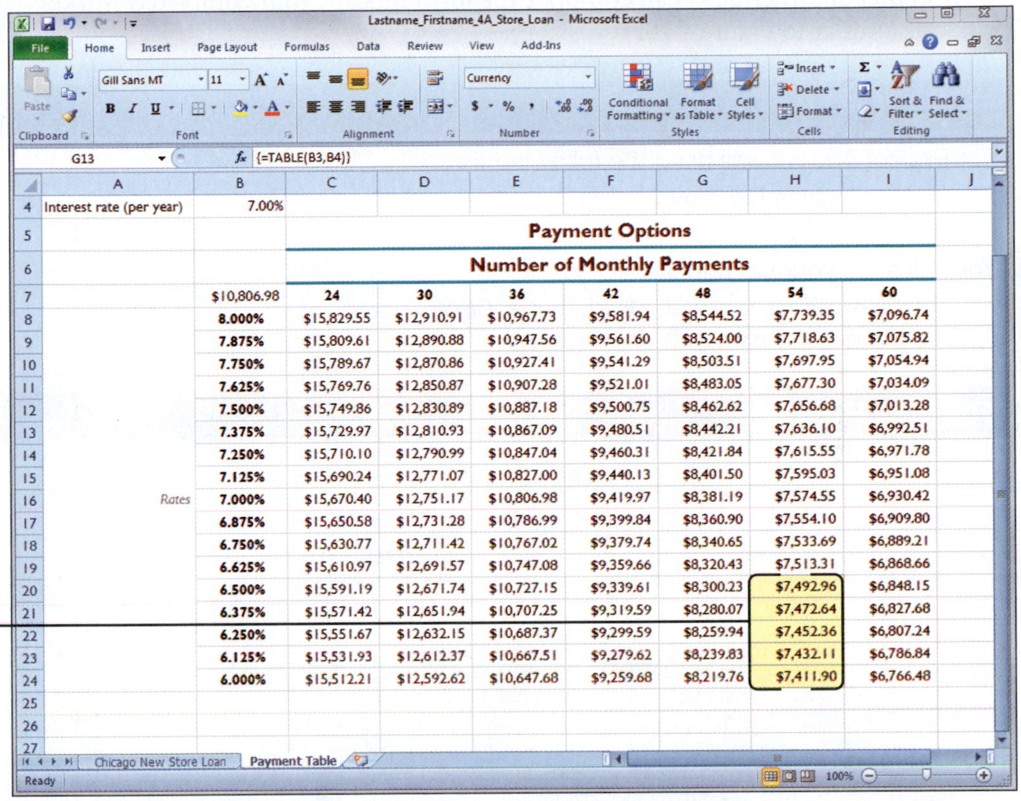

	A	B	C	D	E	F	G	H	I
4	Interest rate (per year)	7.00%							
5			Payment Options						
6			Number of Monthly Payments						
7		$10,806.98	24	30	36	42	48	54	60
8		8.000%	$15,829.55	$12,910.91	$10,967.73	$9,581.94	$8,544.52	$7,739.35	$7,096.74
9		7.875%	$15,809.61	$12,890.88	$10,947.56	$9,561.60	$8,524.00	$7,718.63	$7,075.82
10		7.750%	$15,789.67	$12,870.86	$10,927.41	$9,541.29	$8,503.51	$7,697.95	$7,054.94
11		7.625%	$15,769.76	$12,850.87	$10,907.28	$9,521.01	$8,483.05	$7,677.30	$7,034.09
12		7.500%	$15,749.86	$12,830.89	$10,887.18	$9,500.75	$8,462.62	$7,656.68	$7,013.28
13		7.375%	$15,729.97	$12,810.93	$10,867.09	$9,480.51	$8,442.21	$7,636.10	$6,992.51
14		7.250%	$15,710.10	$12,790.99	$10,847.04	$9,460.31	$8,421.84	$7,615.55	$6,971.78
15		7.125%	$15,690.24	$12,771.07	$10,827.00	$9,440.13	$8,401.50	$7,595.03	$6,951.08
16	Rates	7.000%	$15,670.40	$12,751.17	$10,806.98	$9,419.97	$8,381.19	$7,574.55	$6,930.42
17		6.875%	$15,650.58	$12,731.28	$10,786.99	$9,399.84	$8,360.90	$7,554.10	$6,909.80
18		6.750%	$15,630.77	$12,711.42	$10,767.02	$9,379.74	$8,340.65	$7,533.69	$6,889.21
19		6.625%	$15,610.97	$12,691.57	$10,747.08	$9,359.66	$8,320.43	$7,513.31	$6,868.66
20		6.500%	$15,591.19	$12,671.74	$10,727.15	$9,339.61	$8,300.23	$7,492.96	$6,848.15
21		6.375%	$15,571.42	$12,651.94	$10,707.25	$9,319.59	$8,280.07	$7,472.64	$6,827.68
22		6.250%	$15,551.67	$12,632.15	$10,687.37	$9,299.59	$8,259.94	$7,452.36	$6,807.24
23		6.125%	$15,531.93	$12,612.37	$10,667.51	$9,279.62	$8,239.83	$7,432.11	$6,786.84
24		6.000%	$15,512.21	$12,592.62	$10,647.68	$9,259.68	$8,219.76	$7,411.90	$6,766.48

For a 54-month period, loan options in this range will be within the budget

12 With the two sheets grouped, insert a footer in the **left section** that includes the **file name**. Click outside the footer area, open the **Page Setup** dialog box, click the **Margins tab**, and then center the sheets **Horizontally**. On the status bar, click the **Normal** button ▦. Ungroup the sheets, and click on the **Payment Table sheet**. On the **Page Layout tab**, set the orientation to **Landscape**. Press Ctrl + Home to move to the top of the worksheet.

13 From **Backstage** view, display the **Document Panel**. In the **Author** box, delete any text, and then type your firstname and lastname. In the **Subject** box, type your course name and section number, and in the **Keywords** box, type **amortization schedule, payment table Close** ✕ the **Document Panel**.

14 Press Ctrl + F2, examine the **Print Preview**, make any necessary adjustments, and then **Save** your workbook.

15 Print or submit the two worksheets in this workbook electronically as directed by your instructor. If required, print or create an electronic version of your worksheets with formulas displayed using the instructions in Activity 1.16 in Project 1A.

End **You have completed Project 4A**

Project 4B Quarterly Cost Report and Lookup Form

myitlab Project 4B Training

Project Activities

In Activities 4.06 through 4.13, you will assist Connor Fereday, the Vice President of Marketing at Rubanne Specialties, by defining names for ranges of cells in a workbook containing quarterly merchandise costs and by adding lookup functions to a phone order form so that an order taker can complete the form quickly. Your completed workbooks will look similar to Figure 4.16.

Project Files

For Project 4B, you will need the following files:

e04B_Merchandise_Costs
e04B_Phone_Form

You will save your workbooks as:

Lastname_Firstname_4B_Merchandise_Costs
Lastname_Firstname_4B_Phone_Form

Project Results

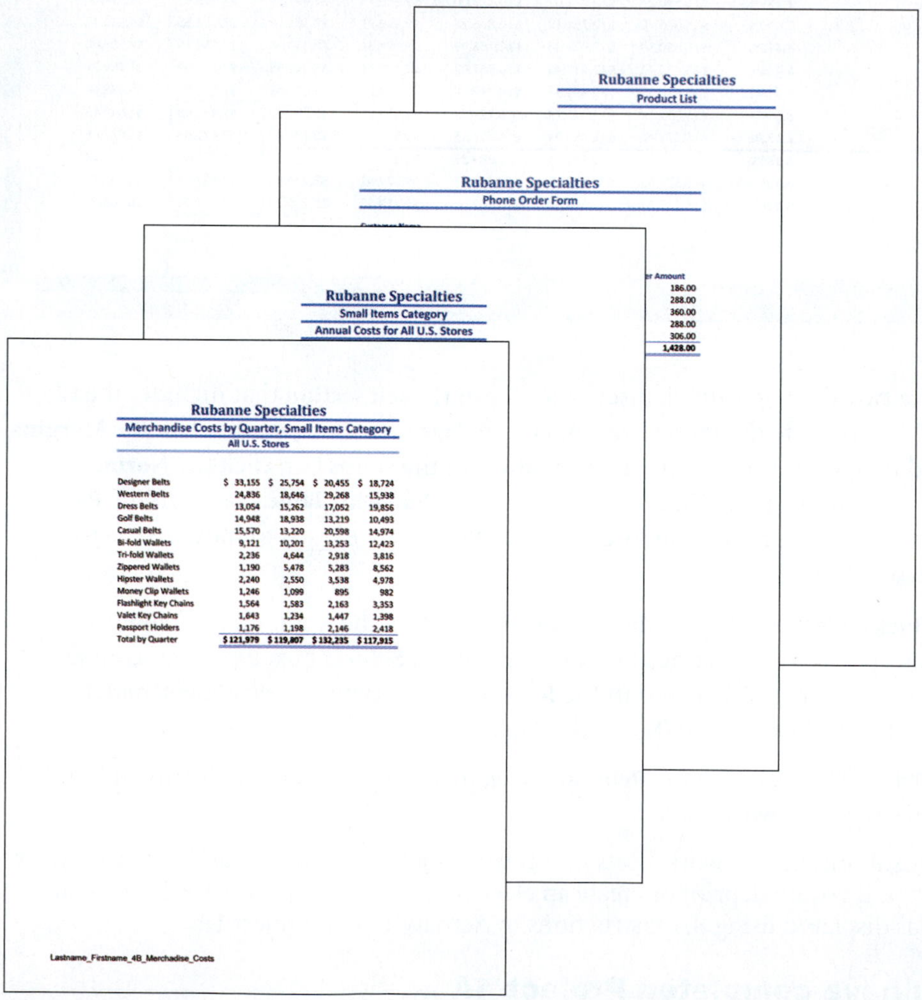

Figure 4.16
Project 4B Quarterly Cost Report and Lookup Form

Objective 4 | Define Names

A ***name***, also referred to as a ***defined name***, is a word or string of characters in Excel that represents a cell, a range of cells, a formula, or a constant value. A defined name that is distinctive and easy to remember typically defines the *purpose* of the selected cells. When creating a formula, the defined name may be used instead of the cell reference.

All names have a ***scope***, which is the location within which the name is recognized without qualification. The scope of a name is usually either to a specific worksheet or to an entire workbook.

Activity 4.06 | Defining a Name

In this activity, you will use three ways to define a name for a cell or group of cells. After defining a name, you can use the name in a formula to refer to the cell or cells. Names make it easier for you and others to understand the meaning of formulas in a worksheet.

1 **Start** Excel. From your student files, open the file **e04B_Merchandise_Costs**, and then **Save** the file in your **Excel Chapter 4** folder as **Lastname_Firstname_4B_Merchandise_Costs**

> **Another Way**
>
> With the range selected, use the keyboard shortcut Alt + = for the SUM function.

2 Select the range **B6:E18**, which includes the adjacent empty cells in **row 18**, and then click the **Sum** button Σ. Click anywhere to cancel the selection.

Use this technique to sum a group of columns or rows simultaneously.

3 Select the range **B6:E6**, hold down Ctrl and select the range **B18:E18**, and then from the **Cell Styles** gallery, under **Number Format**, apply the **Currency [0]** cell style. Select the range **B7:E17**, display the **Cell Styles** gallery, and then under **Number Format**, click **Comma [0]**.

You can use these number formats from the Cell Styles gallery in a manner similar to the Accounting Number Format button and the Comma Style button on the Ribbon. The advantage to using these styles from the Cell Styles gallery is that you can select the option that formats automatically with zero [0] decimal places.

4 Select the range **B18:E18**, and then from the **Cell Styles** gallery, apply the **Total** cell style. Press Ctrl + Home to move to the top of the worksheet, and then compare your screen with Figure 4.17.

Figure 4.17

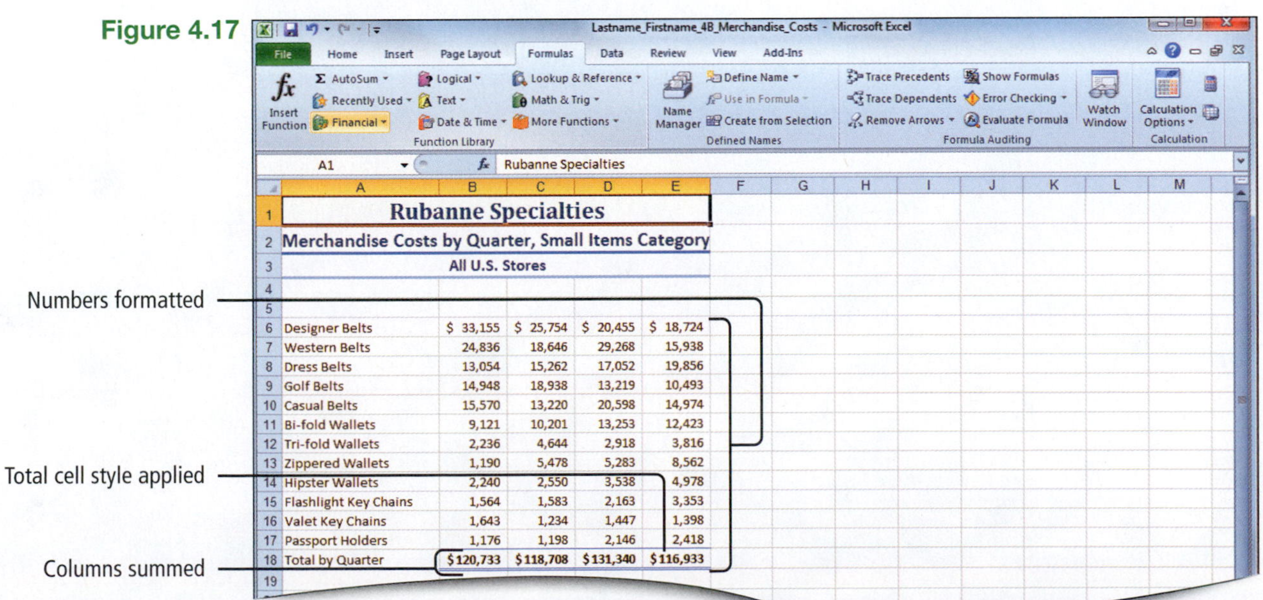

5 Select the range **B6:E9**. On the **Formulas tab**, in the **Defined Names group**, click the **Define Name** button. Compare your screen with Figure 4.18.

The New Name dialog box displays. In the Name box, Excel suggests *Designer_Belts* as the name for this range of cells, which is the text in the first cell adjacent to the selected range. Excel will attempt to suggest a logical name for the selected cells.

Figure 4.18

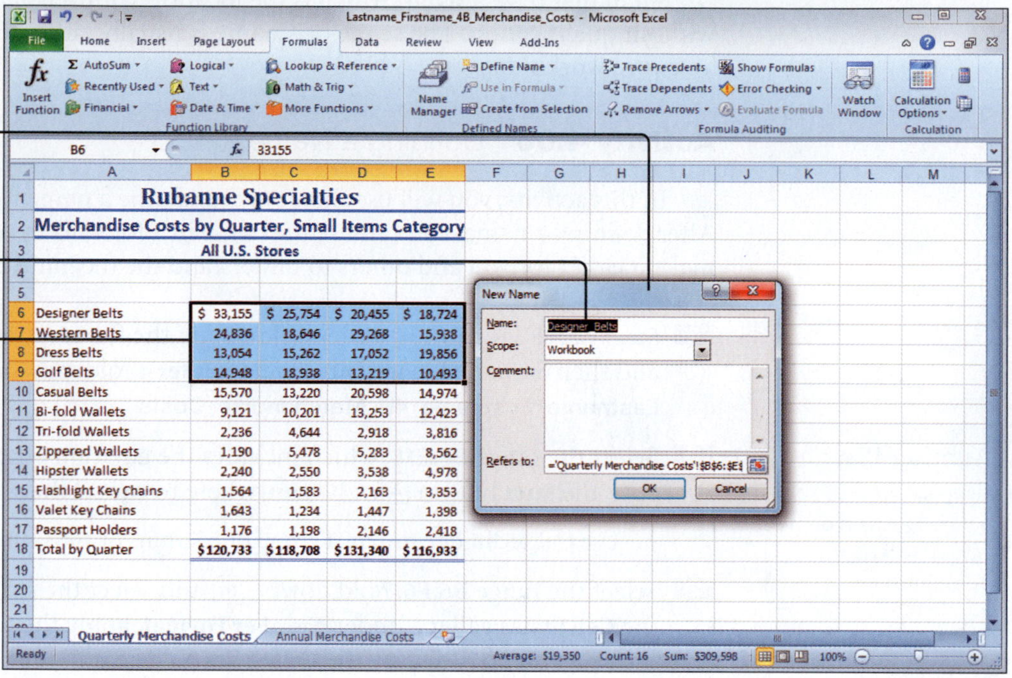

6 With *Designer_Belts* highlighted, type **Belt_Costs** as the name.

Naming cells has no effect on the displayed or underlying values; it simply creates an easy-to-remember name that you can use when creating formulas that refer to this range of cells.

7 At the bottom of the dialog box, at the right edge of the **Refers to** box, point to and click the **Collapse Dialog Box** button. Compare your screen with Figure 4.19.

The dialog box collapses (shrinks) so that only the *Refers to* box is visible, and the selected range is surrounded by a moving border.

When you define a name, the stored definition is an absolute cell reference and includes the worksheet name.

Figure 4.19

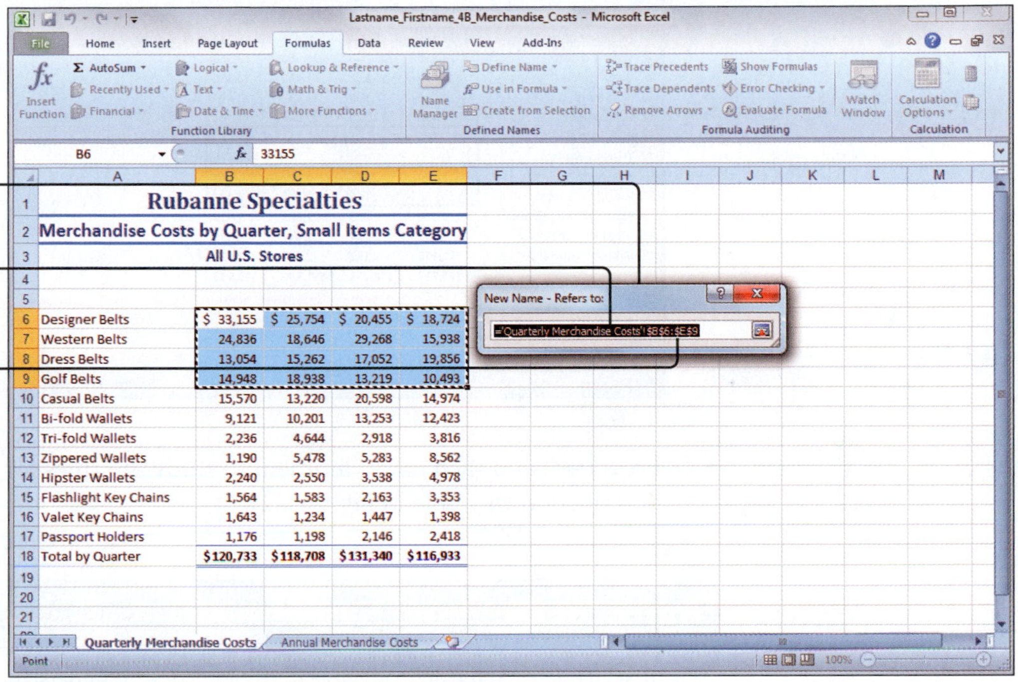

8 If necessary, drag the collapsed dialog box by its title bar to the right of your screen so that it is not blocking the selection. Then, change the range selection by selecting the range **B6:E10**.

A moving border surrounds the new range. The range, formatted with absolute cell references, displays in the *Refers to* box of the collapsed dialog box. In this manner, it is easy to change the range of cells referred to by the name.

9 Click the **Expand Dialog Box** button to redisplay the entire **New Name** dialog box, and then click **OK**.

10 Select the range **B11:E14**. In the upper left corner of the Excel window, to the left of the **Formula Bar**, click in the **Name Box**, and notice that the cell reference *B11* moves to the left edge of the box and is highlighted in blue. Type **Billfold_Costs** as shown in Figure 4.20.

Another Way

Another method to define a name is to select the range, and then type a name in the Name Box.

Figure 4.20

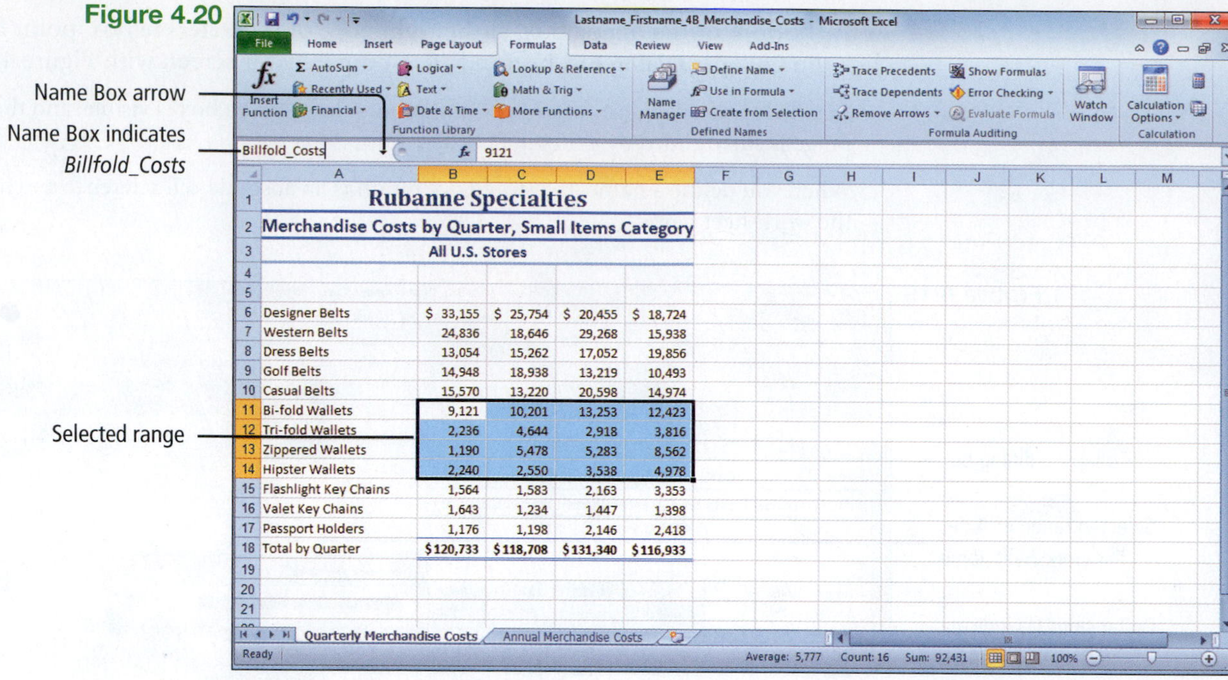

11 Press Enter, and then take a moment to study the rules for defining names, as described in the table in Figure 4.21.

Rules for Defining Names
The first character of the defined name must be a letter, an underscore (_), or a backslash (\).
After the first character, the remaining characters in the defined name can be letters, numbers, periods, and underscore characters.
Spaces are not valid in a defined name; use a period or the underscore character as a word separator, for example *1st.Quarter* or *1st_Qtr*.
The single letter *C* or *R* in either uppercase or lowercase cannot be defined as a name, because these letters are used by Excel for selecting a row or column when you enter them in a Name or a Go To text box.
A defined name can be no longer than 255 characters; short, meaningful names are the most useful.
Defined names cannot be the same as a cell reference, for example M$10.
Defined names can contain uppercase and lowercase letters, however Excel does not distinguish between them. Thus, for example, if you create the name *Sales* and then create another name *SALES* in the same workbook, Excel considers the names to be the same and prompts you for a unique name.

Figure 4.21

12 Click any cell to cancel the selection. Then, click the **Name Box arrow** and compare your screen with Figure 4.22.

Your two defined names display in alphabetical order.

Figure 4.22

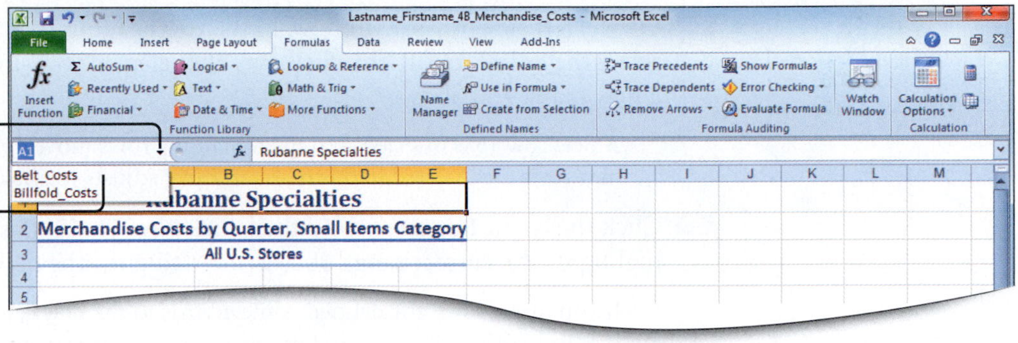

13 From the displayed list, click **Belt_Costs** and notice that Excel selects the range of values that comprise the cost of various Belt styles.

14 Click the **Name Box arrow** again, and then from the displayed list, click **Billfold_Costs** to select the range of values that comprise the Billfold costs.

15 Select the range **B15:E16**. On the **Formulas tab**, in the **Defined Names group**, click the **Name Manager** button, and notice that the two names that you have defined display in a list.

16 In the upper left corner of the **Name Manager** dialog box, click the **New** button. With *Flashlight_Key_Chains* highlighted, type **Key_Chain_Costs** and then click **OK**. Compare your screen with Figure 4.23.

This is another method to define a name—by creating a new name in the Name Manager dialog box. The Name Manager dialog box displays the three range names that you have created, in alphabetical order.

Figure 4.23

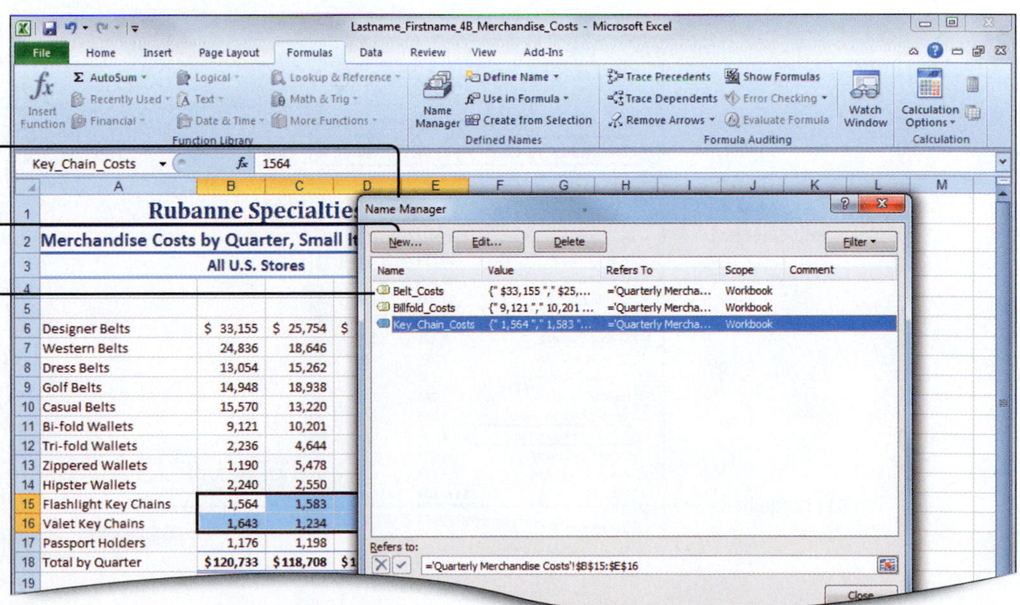

17 **Close** the **Name Manager** dialog box and **Save** your workbook.

Activity 4.07 | Inserting New Data into a Named Range

> **Another Way**
>
> With the row selected, on the Home tab, in the Cells group, click the Insert button arrow, and then click Insert Sheet Rows.

You can insert new data into the range of cells that a name represents. In this activity, you will modify the range named *Billfold_Costs* to include new data.

1 On the left side of your window, in the **row heading area**, click the **row 15** heading to select the entire row. Right-click over the selected row, and then click **Insert** to insert a new blank row above.

A new row 15 is inserted, and the remaining rows move down one row. Recall that when new rows are inserted in this manner, Excel adjusts formulas accordingly.

2 Click the **Name Box arrow**, and then click **Key_Chain_Costs**. Notice that Excel highlights the correct range of cells, adjusting for the newly inserted row.

If you insert rows, the defined name adjusts to the new cell addresses to represent the cells that were originally defined. Likewise, if you move the cells, the defined name goes with them to the new location.

3 In cell **A15**, type **Money Clip Wallets** and then press Tab. In cell **B15**, type **1246** and press Tab. In cell **C15**, type **1099** and press Tab. In cell **D15**, type **895** and press Tab. In cell **E15**, type **982** and press Enter.

The cells in the newly inserted row adopt the Currency [0] format from the cells above.

4 On the **Formulas tab**, from the **Defined Names group**, display the **Name Manager** dialog box.

5 In the **Name Manager** dialog box, in the **Name** column, click **Billfold_Costs**. At the bottom of the dialog box, click in the **Refers to** box and edit the reference, changing **$E$14** to **$E$15** as shown in Figure 4.24.

This action will include the Money Clip Wallet values in the named range.

Figure 4.24

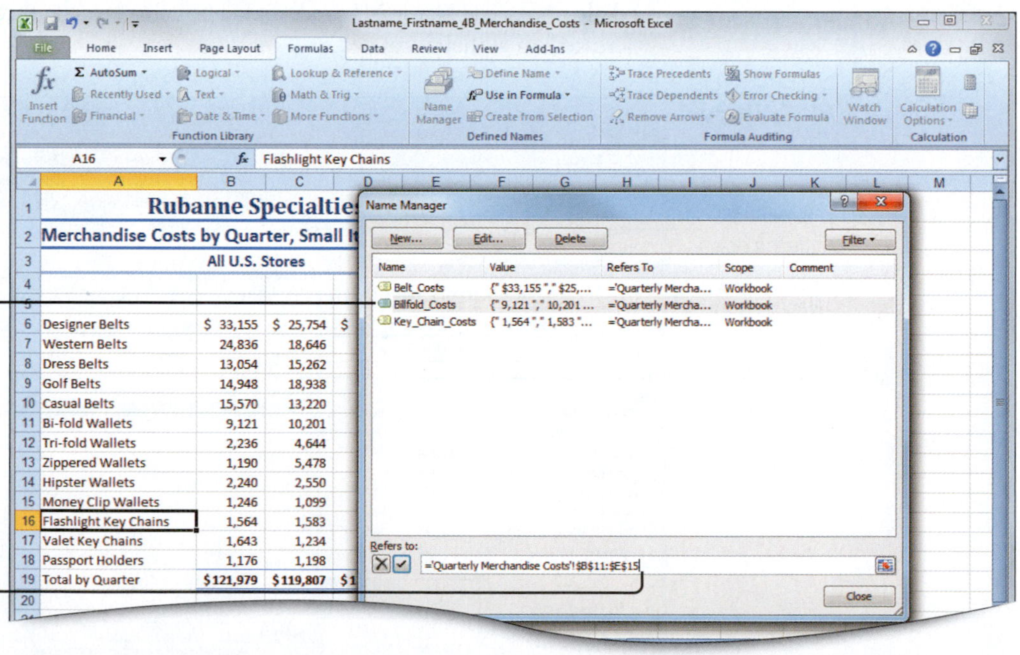

6 **Close** the **Name Manager** dialog box, and click **Yes** to save the changes you made to the name reference.

7 **Save** your workbook.

Activity 4.08 | Changing A Defined Name

You can change a defined name. If the defined name is used in a formula, the new name is automatically changed in any affected formulas. In this activity, you will change the defined name *Billfold_Costs* to *Wallet_Costs*.

1 On the **Formulas tab**, from the **Defined Names group**, display the **Name Manager** dialog box. Click **Billfold_Costs**, and then click the **Edit** button.

2 In the displayed **Edit Name** dialog box, with *Billfold_Costs* highlighted, type **Wallet_Costs** Compare your screen with Figure 4.25.

Figure 4.25

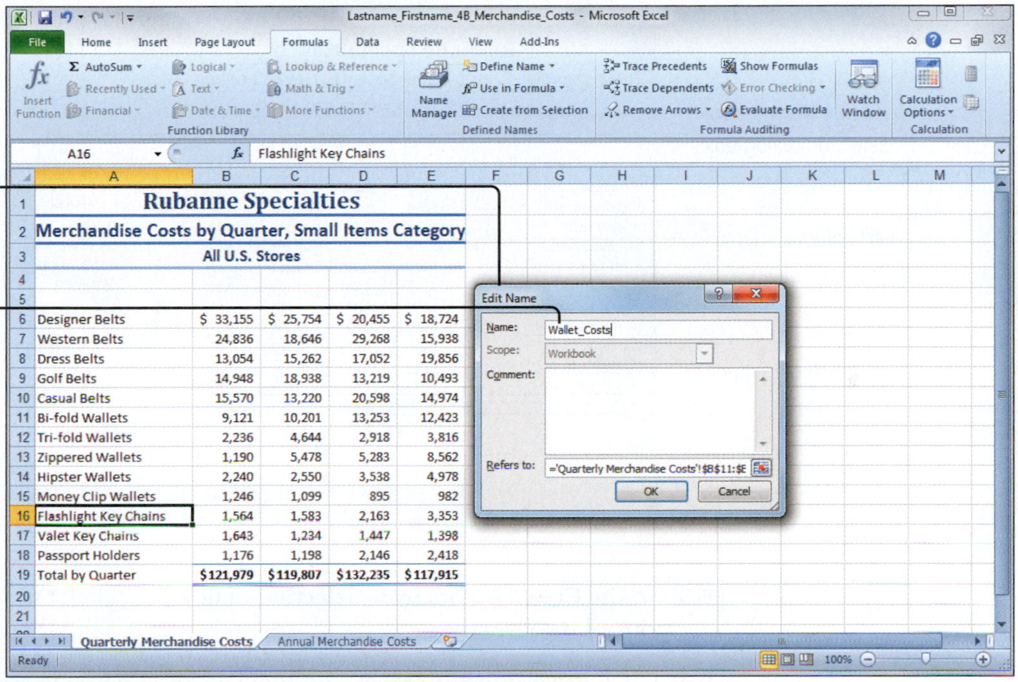

3 Click **OK**, and then **Close** the **Name Manager** dialog box.

4 In the upper left corner of the window, click the **Name Box arrow** and notice the modified range name, *Wallet_Costs*.

5 Click any cell to close the list, and then **Save** your workbook.

Activity 4.09 | Creating a Defined Name by Using Row and Column Titles

You can use the Create from Selection command to use existing row or column titles as the name for a range of cells.

1 Select the range **A18:E18**. On the **Formulas tab**, in the **Defined Names group**, click **Create from Selection**. Compare your screen with Figure 4.26.

The Create Names from Selection dialog box displays. A check mark displays in the *Left column* check box, which indicates that Excel will use the value of the cell in the leftmost column of the selection as the range name, unless you specify otherwise.

Figure 4.26

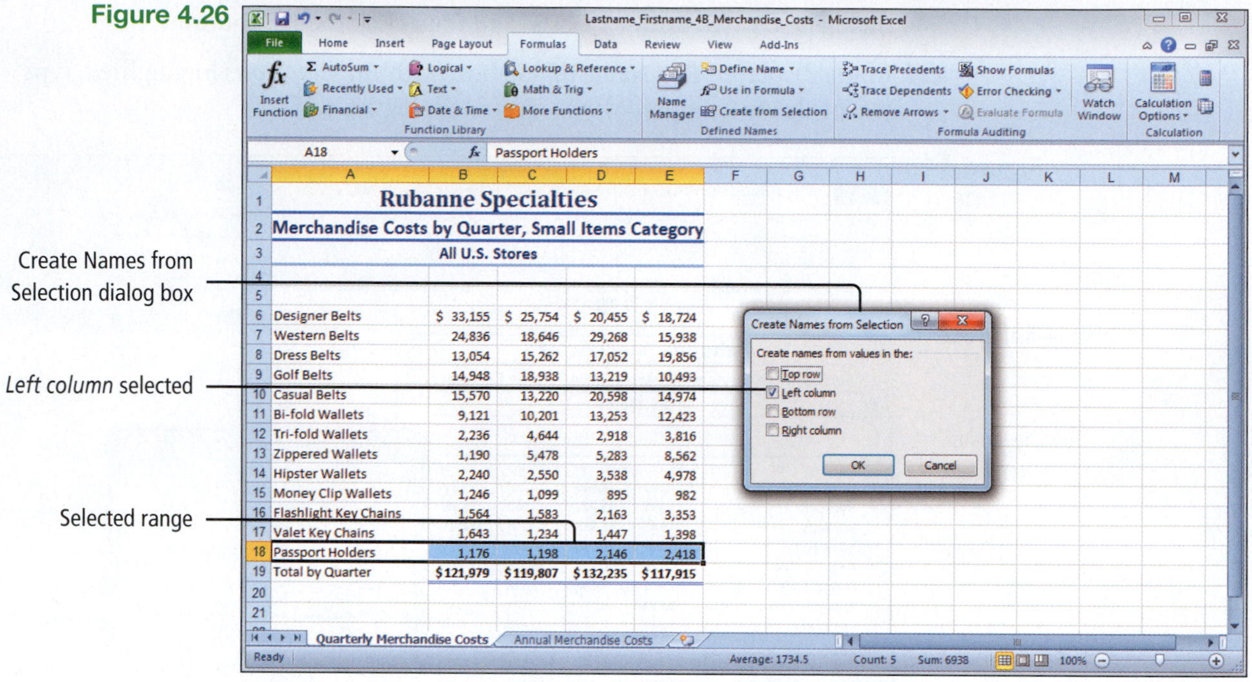

2 In the **Create Names from Selection** dialog box, click **OK**, and then click anywhere to cancel the selection.

3 Click the **Name Box arrow**, and then click the name **Passport_Holders.** Notice that in the new range name, Excel inserted the underscore necessary to fill a blank space in the range name. Also notice that the actual range consists of only the numeric values, as shown in Figure 4.27.

This method is convenient for naming a range of cells without having to actually type a name—Excel uses the text of the first cell to the left of the selected range as the range name and then formats the name properly.

Figure 4.27

Defined name formatted properly by Excel

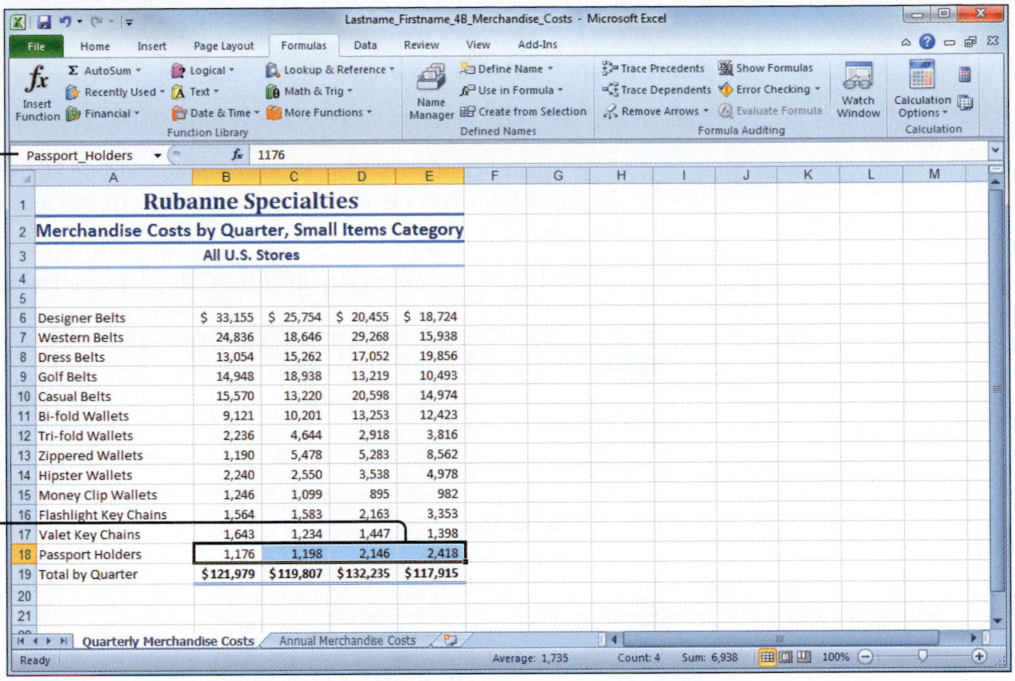

Range consists of numeric values

> **Note | Deleting a Defined Name**
>
> If you create a defined name and then decide that you no longer need it, you can delete the name and its accompanying range reference. Display the Name Manager dialog box, select the defined name, and then at the top of the dialog box, click Delete. Deleting a defined name does not modify the cell contents or formatting of the cells. Deleting a defined name does not delete any cells or any values. It deletes only the name that you have applied to a group of cells. However, any formula that contains the range name will display the #NAME? error message, and will have to be adjusted manually.

4 **Save** your workbook.

Objective 5 | Use Defined Names in a Formula

The advantage to naming a range of cells is that you can use the name in a formula in other parts of your workbook. The defined name provides a logical reference to data. For example, referring to data as *Belt_Costs* is easier to understand than referring to data as *B6:E10*.

When you use a defined name in a formula, the result is the same as if you typed the cell references.

Activity 4.10 | Using Defined Names in a Formula

1 Display the Annual Merchandise Costs worksheet.

2 In cell **B5**, type **=sum(B** and then compare your screen with Figure 4.28.

The Formula AutoComplete list displays containing all of Excel's built-in functions that begin with the letter *B* and any defined names in this workbook that begin with the letter B.

To the left of your defined name *Belt_Costs*, a defined name icon displays.

Figure 4.28

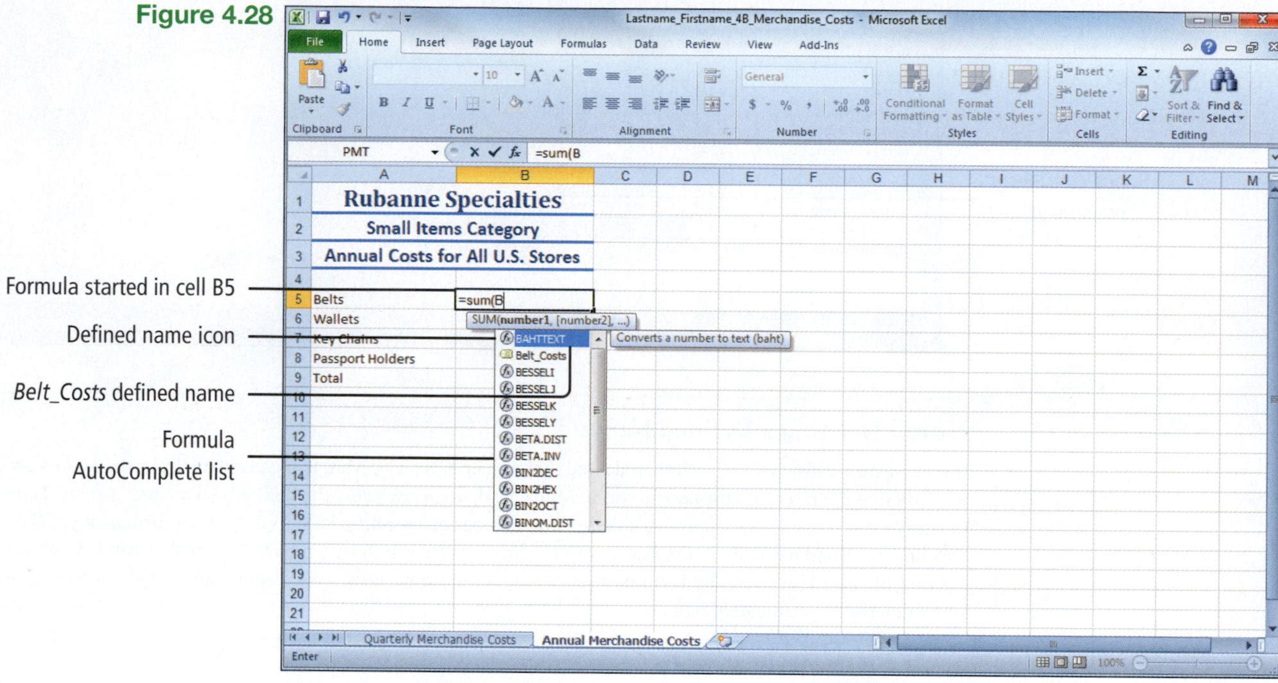

3 Continue typing **elt_Costs** and then press Enter.

Your result is *373960*. Recall that SUM is a function—a formula already built by Excel—that adds all the cells in a selected range. Thus, Excel sums all the cells in the range you defined as Belt_Costs on the first worksheet in the workbook, and then places the result in cell B5 of this worksheet.

4 In cell **B6**, type **=sum(W** and then on the displayed **Formula AutoComplete list**, double-click **Wallet_Costs** to insert the formula. Press Enter to display the result *96653*.

5 Click cell **B7**, type **=sum(** and then on the **Formulas tab**, in the **Defined Names group**, click the **Use in Formula** button. From the displayed list, click **Key_Chain_Costs**, and then press Enter to display the total *14385*.

6 In cell **B8**, use any of the techniques you just practiced to sum the cells containing the costs for **Passport Holders** and to display a result of *6938*. Sum the column in cell **B9** to display a result of *491936*.

7 Select the nonadjacent cells **B5** and **B9**, and then from the **Home tab**, display the **Cell Styles** gallery. Under **Number Format**, apply the **Currency [0]** cell style. Select the range **B6:B8**, display the **Cell Styles** gallery, and then under **Number Format**, click **Comma [0]**.

8 Click cell **B9** and apply the **Total** cell style. Press Ctrl + Home to move to the top of the worksheet. Compare your screen with Figure 4.29.

Figure 4.29

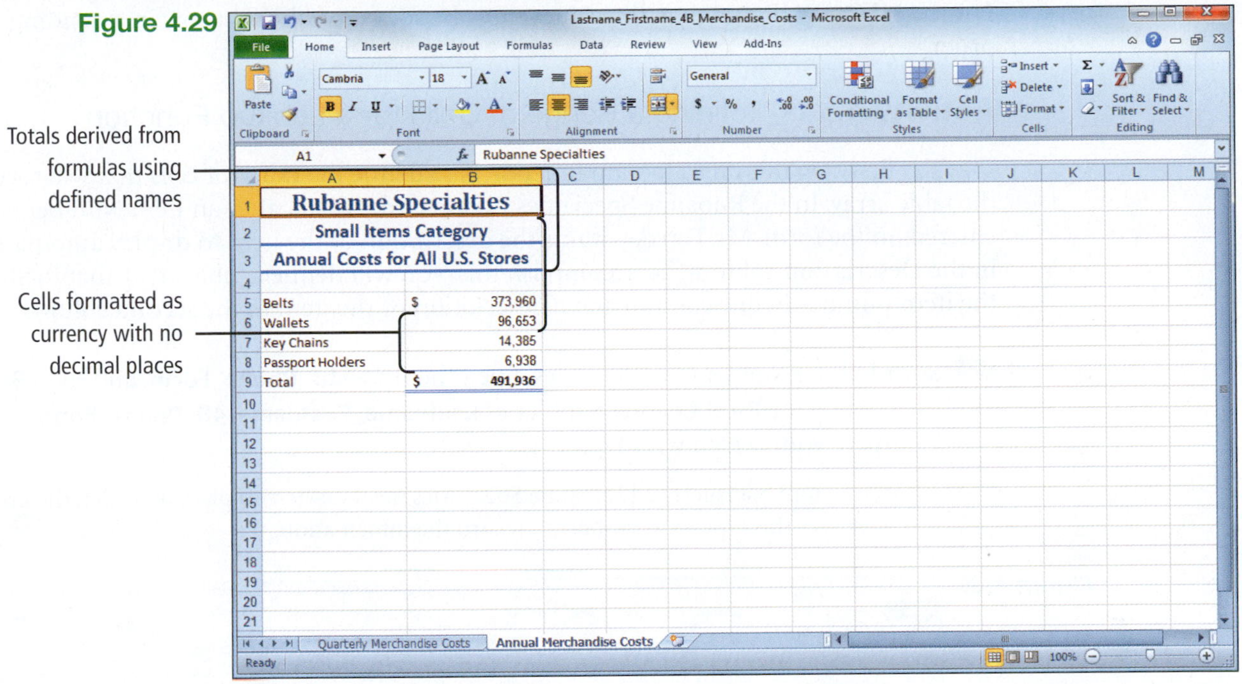

9 Select both worksheets so that *[Group]* displays in the title bar. With the two worksheets grouped, insert a footer in the **left section** that includes the file name. Center the worksheets **Horizontally** on the page.

10 Display the **Document Panel** and in the **Author** box, type your **firstname** and **lastname** In the **Subject** box, type your course name and section number, and in the **Keywords** box, type **Small Items Category, Merchandise Costs Close** the **Document Panel**. Return to **Normal** view and make cell **A1** active, display the grouped worksheets in **Print Preview**, **Close** the **Print Preview**, and then make any necessary corrections or adjustments.

11 **Save** your workbook. Print or submit the two worksheets in this workbook electronically as directed by your instructor. If required, print or create an electronic version of your worksheets with formulas displayed using the instructions in Activity 1.16 in Project 1A. **Close** this workbook.

Objective 6 | Use Lookup Functions

Lookup functions look up a value in a defined range of cells located in another part of the workbook to find a corresponding value. For example, you can define a two-column range of cells containing names and phone numbers. Then, when you type a name in the cell containing the lookup formula, Excel fills in the phone number by looking it up in the defined range. In the lookup formula, the defined range is referred to as the ***table array***.

The ***VLOOKUP*** function looks ups values in a table array arranged as vertical columns. The function searches the first column of the table array for a corresponding value, and then returns a value from any cell on the same row. The ***HLOOKUP*** function looks up values in a table array arranged in horizontal rows. The function searches the top row of the table array for a corresponding value, and then returns a value from any cell in the same column.

There is one requirement for the lookup functions to work properly: *the data in the table array, which can be numbers or text, must be sorted in ascending order.* For the VLOOKUP function, the values must be sorted on the first column in ascending order. For the HLOOKUP function, the values must be sorted on the first row in ascending order.

Activity 4.11 | Defining a Range of Cells for a Lookup Function

The first step in using a lookup function is to define the range of cells that will serve as the table array. In the Rubanne Specialties Phone Order form, after an Item Number is entered on the form, Mr. Fereday wants the description of the item to display automatically in the Description column. To accomplish this, you will define a table array that includes the item number in one column and a description of the item in the second column.

1 **Start** Excel. From your student files, open the file **e04B_Phone_Form**, and then **Save** the file in your **Excel Chapter 4** folder as **Lastname_Firstname_4B_Phone_Form** Compare your screen with Figure 4.30.

When store managers call Rubanne Specialties headquarters to place an order, the order taker uses this type of worksheet to record the information.

Figure 4.30

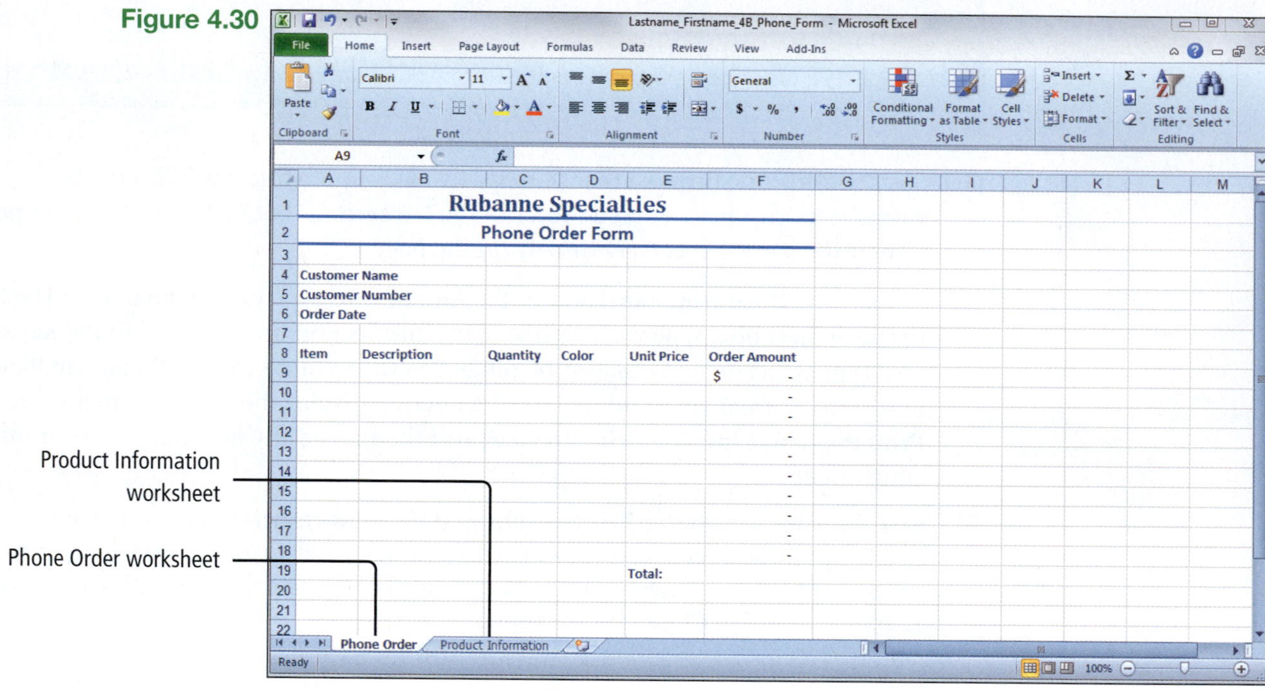

2 Click the **Product Information sheet tab** to display the second worksheet.

The Product Information worksheet contains the Style Code, Description, and Unit Price of specific wallets and belts.

3 On the displayed **Product Information** worksheet, select the range **A4:C11**. On the **Data tab**, in the **Sort & Filter group**, click the **Sort** button. If necessary, drag the **Sort** dialog box to the right side of your screen so you can view **columns A:C**.

To use this list to look up information with the Excel VLOOKUP function, you must sort the list in ascending order by Style Code, which is the column that will be used to look up the matching information.

4 In the **Sort** dialog box, under **Column**, click the **Sort by arrow**. Notice that the selected range is now **A5:C11** and that the column titles in the range **A4:C4** display in the **Sort by** list. Compare your screen with Figure 4.31.

When the selected range includes a header row that should remain in place while the remaining rows are sorted, Excel usually recognizes those column headings, selects the *My data has headers* check box, and then displays the column headings in the Sort by list.

Figure 4.31

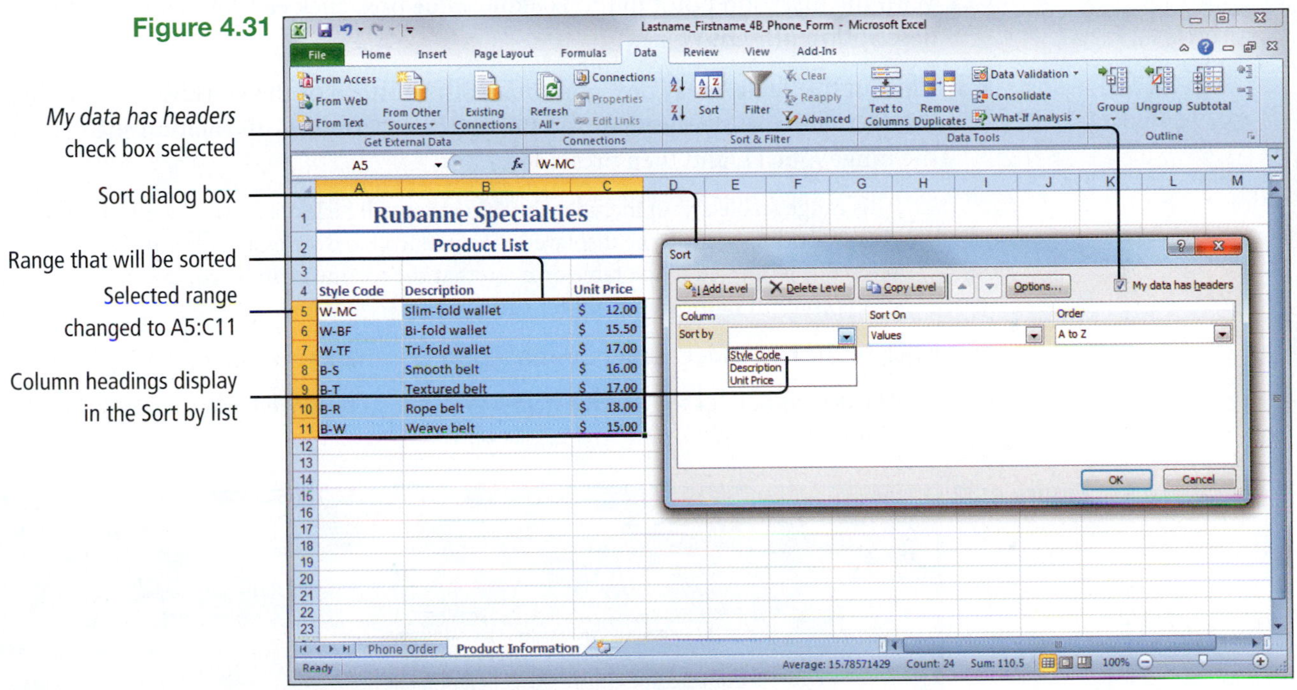

5 From the **Sort by** list, click **Style Code**, which is the first column heading and the column heading that Excel selects by default.

6 Under **Sort On**, verify that *Values* displays, and under **Order**, verify that *A to Z* displays.

Values indicates that the sort will be based on the values in the cells of the first column, rather than cell color or some other cell characteristic. *A to Z* indicates that the cell will be sorted in ascending order.

7 Click **OK** to sort the data by *Style Code* in ascending order.

Excel sorts the data alphabetically by Style Code; *B-R* is first in the list and *W-TF* is last.

8 **Save** your workbook.

Activity 4.12 | Inserting the VLOOKUP Function

Recall that the VLOOKUP function looks ups values in a range of cells arranged as vertical columns. The arguments for this function include *lookup_value*—the value to search in the first column of the table array, *table_array*—the range that contains the data, and *col_index_num*—the column number (1, 2, 3, 4, and so on) in the table array that contains the result you want to retrieve from the table, which in this instance, is the Description.

> **Another Way**
>
> Click the Insert Function button located to the left of the Formula Bar, select the Lookup & Reference category, and then under Select a function, scroll to locate and then click VLOOKUP.

1 Display the **Phone Order** sheet. In cell **A9**, type **W-BF** and press Tab.

2 With cell **B9** as the active cell, on the **Formulas tab**, in the **Function Library group**, click **Lookup & Reference**, and then click **VLOOKUP**.

The Function Arguments dialog box for VLOOKVUP displays.

3 With the insertion point in the **Lookup_value** box, click cell **A9** to look up the description of Item W-BF.

4 Click in the **Table_array** box, and then at the bottom of the workbook, click the **Product Information sheet tab**. On the displayed **Product Information** sheet, select the range **A4:C11**, and then press F4.

This range (table array) includes the value that will be looked up—*W-BF* and the corresponding value to be displayed—*Bi-fold wallet*. By pressing F4, the absolute cell reference is applied to the table array so that the formula can be copied to the remainder of the column in the Phone Order sheet.

5 Click in the **Col_index_num** box and type **2** Compare your screen with Figure 4.32.

The description for the selected item—the value to be looked up—is located in column 2 of the table array.

Figure 4.32

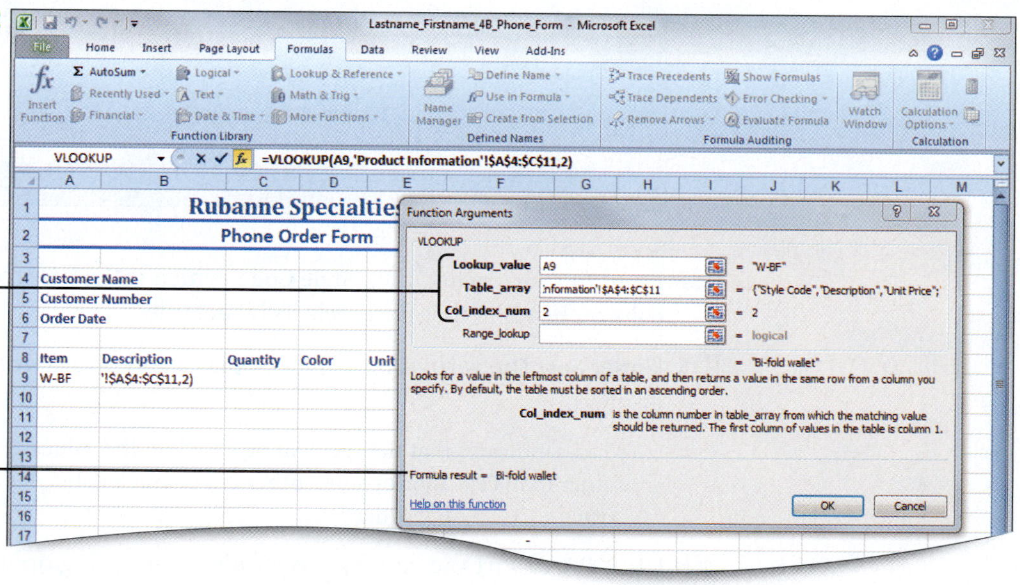

6 Click **OK**.

The description for Item W-BF displays in cell B9.

7 With cell **B9** as the active cell and containing the VLOOKUP formula, point to the fill handle in the lower right corner of the cell, and then drag to fill the VLOOKUP formula down through cell **B18**. Compare your screen with Figure 4.33.

The *#N/A* error notation displays in the cells where you copied the formula. Excel displays this error when a function or formula exists in a cell but has no value available with which to perform a calculation; values have not yet been entered in column A in those rows.

Figure 4.33

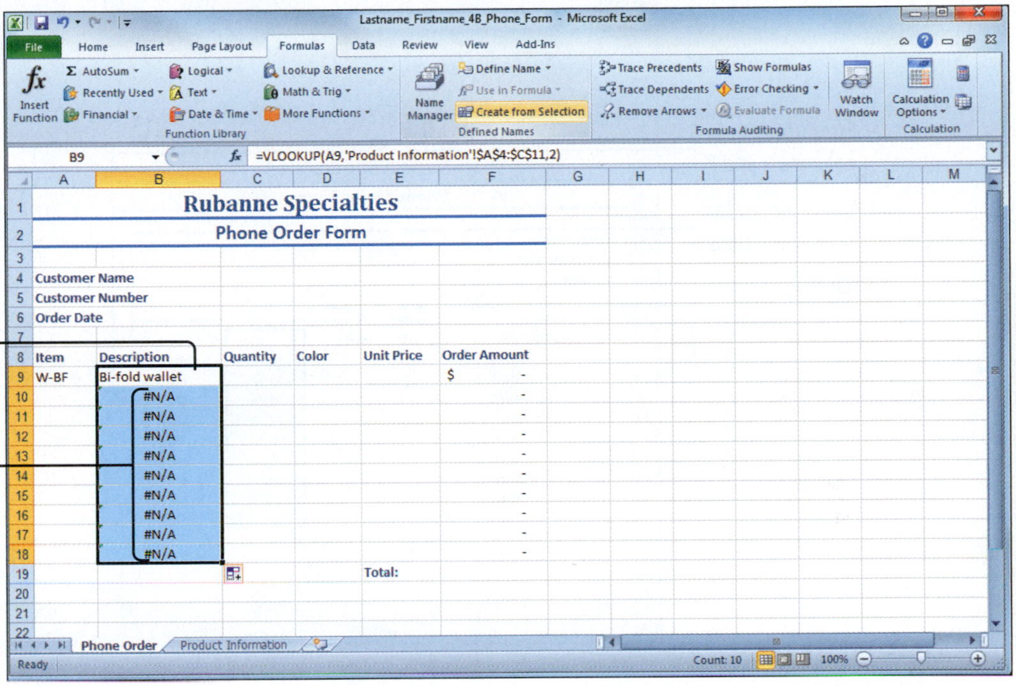

8 Click cell **C9**, type **12** as the quantity ordered and press Tab. In cell **D9,** type **Black** and press Tab.

9 With cell **E9** as the active cell, on the **Formulas tab**, in the **Function Library group**, click **Lookup & Reference**, and then click **VLOOKUP**.

10 With the insertion point in the **Lookup_value** box, click cell **A9** to look up information for Item W-BF. Click in the **Table_array** box, display the **Product Information** sheet, and then select the range **A4:C11**.

11 Press F4 to make the values in the range absolute. In the **Col_index_num** box, type **3** to look up the price in the third column of the range, and then click **OK**.

The Unit Price for the Bi-fold wallet—*$15.50*—displays in cell E9.

12 Click cell **F9**, and notice that a formula to calculate the total for the item, Quantity times Unit Price, has already been entered in the worksheet.

This formula has also been copied to the range F10:F18.

13 Click cell **E9**, and then copy the VLOOKUP formula down through cell **E18**. Compare your screen with Figure 4.34.

The *#N/A* error notation displays in the cells where you copied the formula, and also in cells F10:F18, because the formulas there have no values yet with which to perform a calculation—values have not yet been entered in column A in those rows.

Figure 4.34

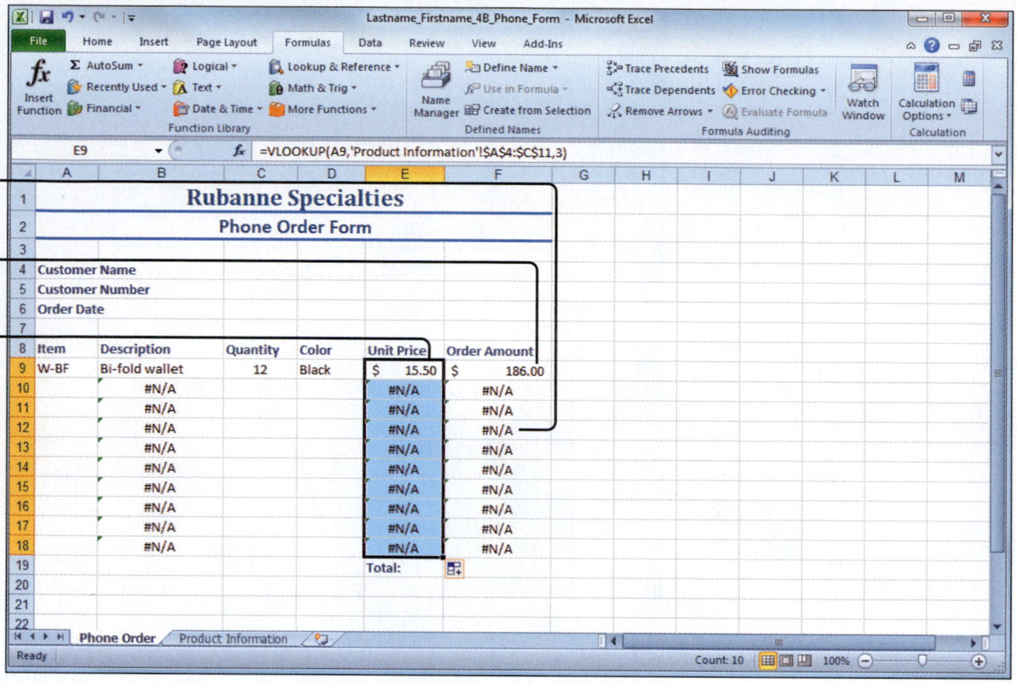

Error notation in columns E and F

Total amount for 12 W-BF items

VLOOKUP formula in cell E9

14 Click cell **A10**, type **W-MC** and press Tab two times.

Excel looks up the product description and the product price in the vertical table array on the Product Information sheet, and then displays the results in cells B10 and E10.

15 In cell **C10**, type **24** and press Tab. Notice that Excel calculates the total for this item in cell **F10**—*288.00*.

16 In cell **D10**, type **Burgundy** and then press Enter. Notice that after data is entered in the row, the error notations no longer display. **Save** your workbook. Compare your screen with Figure 4.35.

Figure 4.35

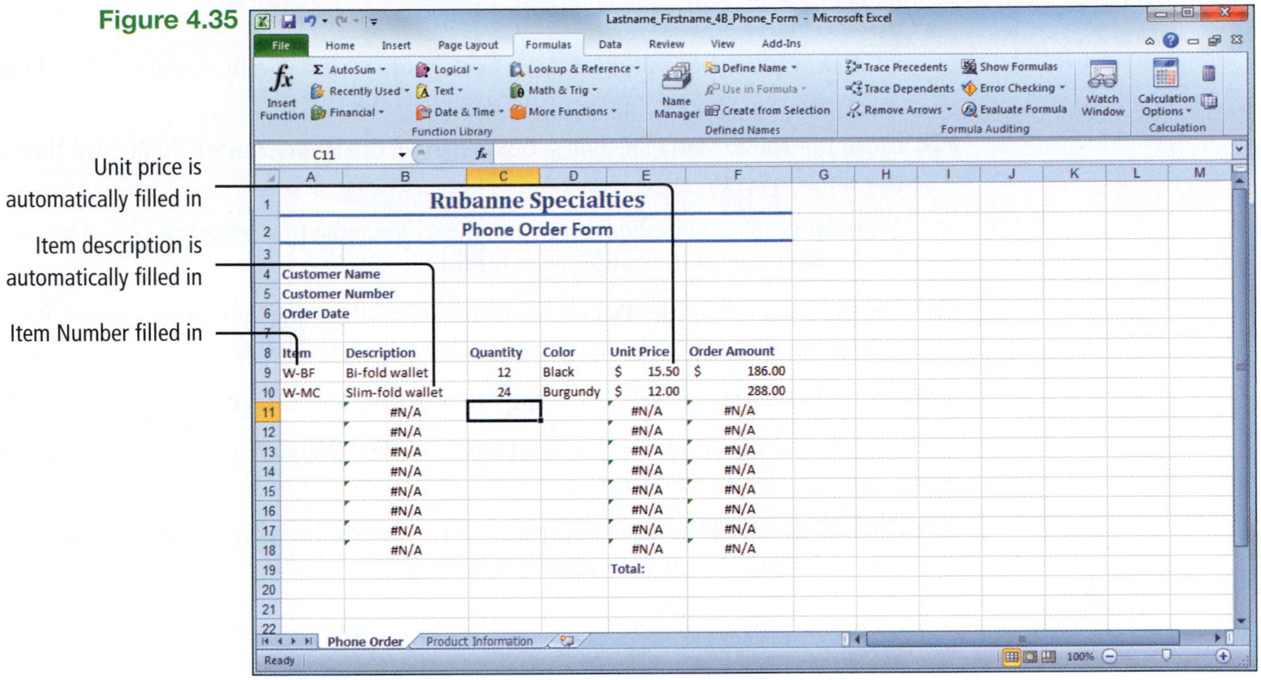

Objective 7 | Validate Data

Another technique to improve accuracy when completing a worksheet is ***data validation***—a technique in which you control the type of data or the values that are entered into a cell. This technique improves accuracy because it limits and controls the type of data an individual, such as an order taker, can enter into the form.

One way to control the type of data entered is to create a ***validation list***—a list of values that are acceptable for a group of cells. Only values on the list are valid; any value *not* on the list is considered invalid. For example, in the Phone Order sheet, it would be useful if in the Item column, only valid Style Codes could be entered.

Activity 4.13 | Creating a Validation List

A list of valid values must either be on the same worksheet as the destination cell, or if the list is in another worksheet, the cell range must be named. In this activity, you will create a defined name for the Style Codes, and then create a validation list for column A of the Phone Order worksheet.

1 Display the **Product Information sheet**. Select the range **A4:A11**. On the **Formulas tab**, in the **Defined Names group**, click **Create from Selection**.

Recall that by using the Create from Selection command, you can automatically generate a name from the selected cells that uses the text in the top row or the leftmost column of a selection.

2 In the **Create Names from Selection** dialog box, be sure the **Top row** check box is selected, and then click **OK** to use *Style Code* as the range name.

3 In the **Defined Names group**, click the **Name Manager** button, and then notice that the new defined name is listed with the name *Style_Code*.

Style_Code displays as the defined name for the selected cells. Recall that Excel replaces spaces with an underscore when it creates a range name.

4 **Close** the **Name Manager** dialog box. Display the **Phone Order** sheet, and then select the range **A9:A18**.

Before you set the validation requirement, you must first select the cells that you want to restrict to only valid entries from the list.

5 On the **Data tab**, in the **Data Tools group**, click the **Data Validation** button. In the **Data Validation** dialog box, be sure the **Settings tab** is selected.

6 Under **Validation criteria**, click the **Allow arrow**, and then click **List**.

A Source box displays as the third box in the Data Validation dialog box. Here you select or type the source data.

7 Click to position the insertion point in the **Source** box, type **=Style_Code** and then compare your screen with Figure 4.36.

Figure 4.36

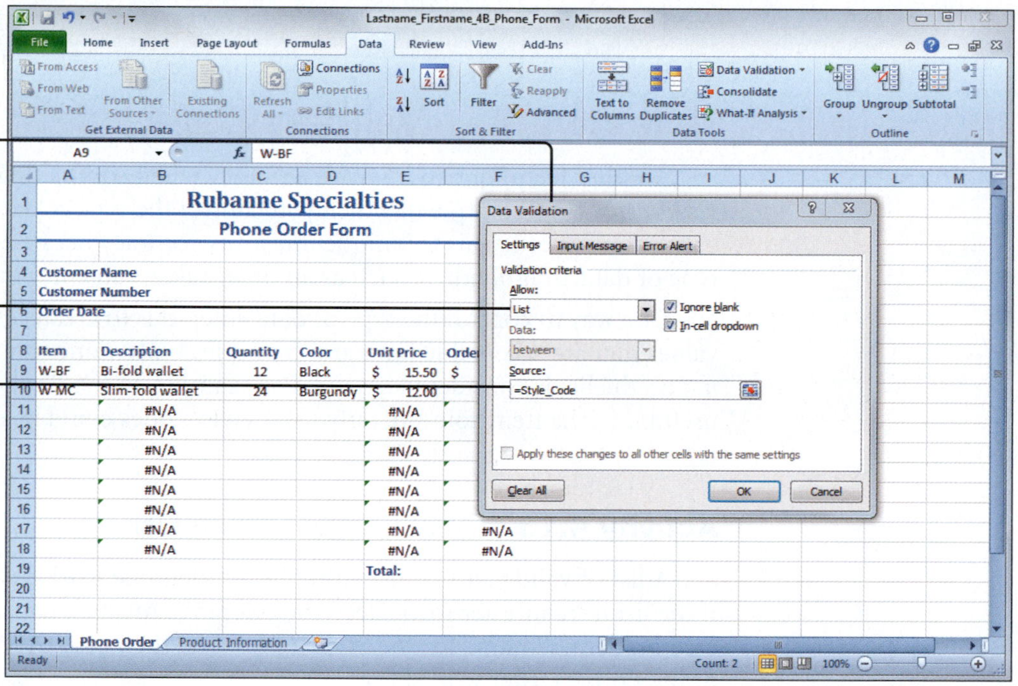

8 Click **OK**. Click cell **A11**, and notice that a list arrow displays at the right edge of the cell.

9 In cell **A11**, click the list arrow to display the list, and then compare your screen with Figure 4.37.

Figure 4.37

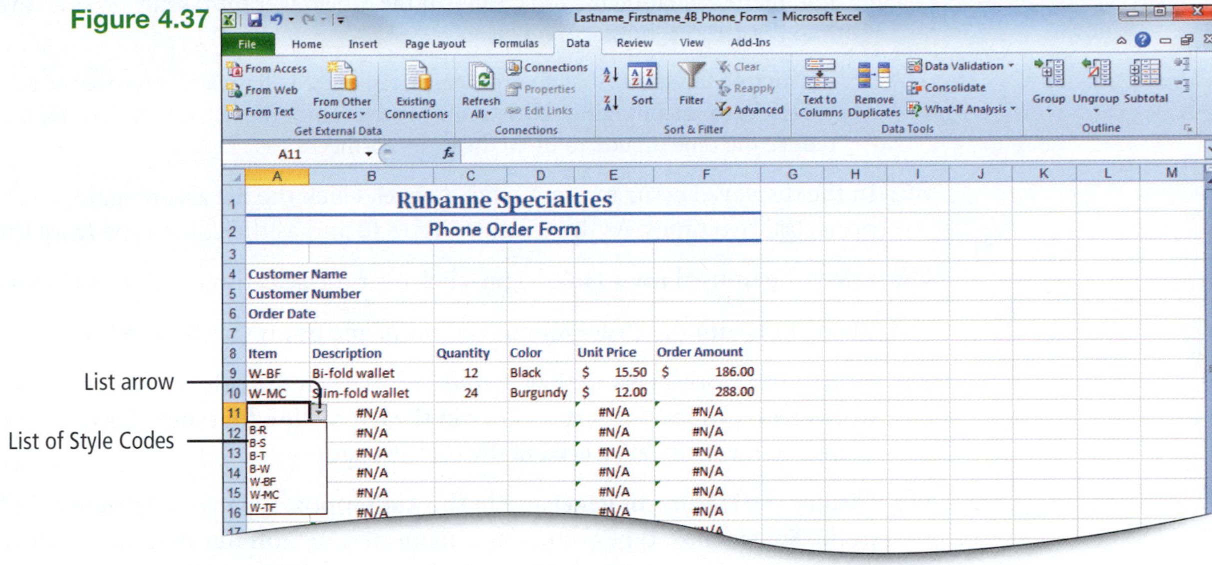

10 From the displayed list, click **B-W**.

The Style Code is selected from the list and the Item, Description, and Unit Price cells are filled in for row 11.

11 Press Tab two times, type **24** and press Tab, type **Brown** and then press Enter to return to the beginning of the next row. Compare your screen with Figure 4.38.

You can see that when taking orders by phone, it will speed the process if all of the necessary information can be filled in automatically. Furthermore, accuracy will be improved if item codes are restricted to only valid data.

Figure 4.38

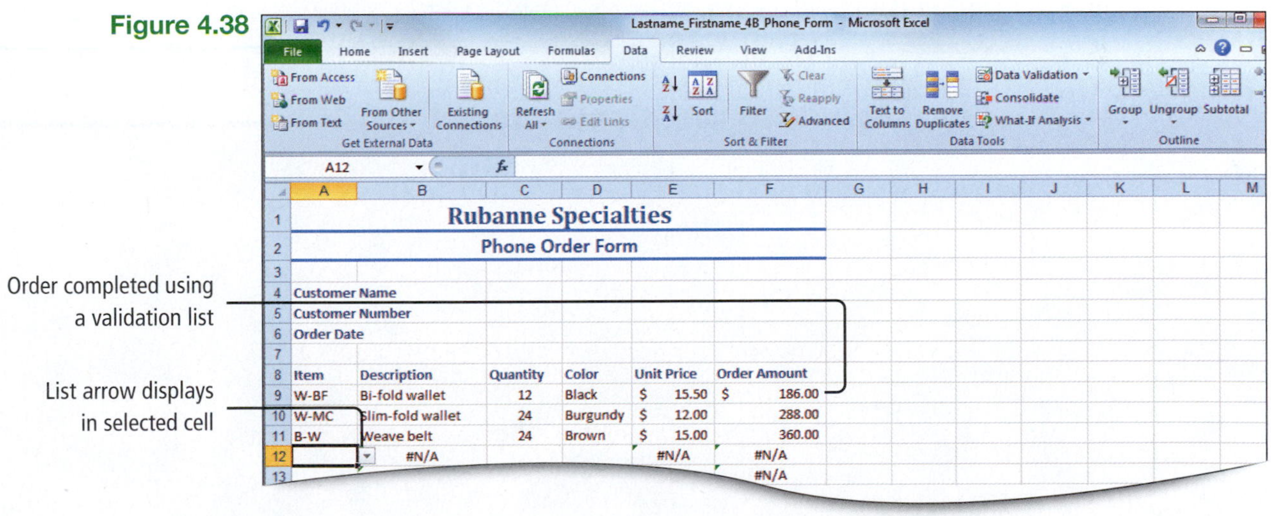

12 With cell **A12** active, click the **list arrow**, and then click **B-S**. As the **Quantity,** type **18** and as the **Color** type, type **Tan** Press Enter.

13 In cell **A13**, type **G-W** and press Tab.

An error message displays indicating that you entered a value that is not valid; that is, it is not on the validation list you created. If the order taker mistakenly types an invalid value into the cell, this message will display.

Restricting the values that an order taker can enter will greatly improve the accuracy of orders. Also, encouraging order takers to select from the list, rather than typing, will reduce the time it takes to fill in the order form.

14 In the displayed error message, click **Cancel**. Click the **list arrow** again, click **W-TF** and press Tab two times. As the **Quantity,** type **18** and as the color, type **Ivory** Press Enter.

15 Select the unused **rows 14:18**, right-click over the selection, and then click **Delete**.

16 In cell **F14**, sum the **Order Amount** column, and apply the **Total** cell style.

17 Select both worksheets so that *[Group]* displays in the title bar. With the two worksheets grouped, insert a footer in the **left section** that includes the file name. Center the worksheets **Horizontally** on the page.

18 Display the **Document Panel** and in the **Author** box, type your **firstname** and **lastname** In the **Subject** box, type your course name and section number, and in the **Keywords** box, type **phone order form** **Close** the **Document Panel**. Return to **Normal** view and make cell **A1** active, display the grouped worksheets in **Print Preview**, **Close** the **Print Preview**, and then make any necessary corrections or adjustments.

19 **Save** your workbook. Print or submit the two worksheets in this workbook electronically as directed by your instructor. If required, print or create an electronic version of your worksheets with formulas displayed using the instructions in Activity 1.16 in Project 1A. **Close** this workbook.

More Knowledge | Creating Validation Messages

In the Data Validation dialog box, you can use the Input Message tab to create a ScreenTip that will display when the cell is selected. The message can be an instruction that tells the user what to do. You can also use the Error Alert tab to create a warning message that displays if invalid data is entered in the cell.

End **You have completed Project 4B**

Content-Based Assessments

Summary

In this chapter, you used the Financial function PMT to calculate the payment for a loan. You also used two of Excel's What-If Analysis tools: Goal Seek to get a result that you want and Data Tables to see the results of many different inputs. You defined names for a range of cells and created a table in which one can look up data. Finally, you used data validation to ensure the accuracy of data entry.

Key Terms

Excel | Chapter 4

Matching

Match each term in the second column with its correct definition in the first column by writing the letter of the term on the blank line in front of the correct definition.

____ 1. Predefined formulas that perform common business calculations, and which typically involve a period of time such as months or years.

____ 2. The amount charged for the use of borrowed money.

____ 3. In the Excel PMT function, the term used to indicate the interest rate for a loan.

____ 4. The total amount that a series of future payments is worth now.

____ 5. Another term for present value.

____ 6. The abbreviation for *number of time periods* in various Excel functions.

____ 7. The value at the end of the time periods in an Excel function; the cash balance you want to attain after the last payment is made—usually zero for loans.

____ 8. The values that an Excel function uses to perform calculations or operations.

____ 9. An Excel function that calculates the payment for a loan based on constant payments and at a constant interest rate.

____ 10. An optional argument in the PMT function that assumes that the payment will be made at the end of each time period.

____ 11. The process of changing the values in cells to see how those changes affect the outcome of formulas in the worksheet.

____ 12. One of Excel's What-If Analysis tools that provides a method to find a specific value for a cell by adjusting the value of one other cell—you can find the right input when you know the result you want.

A Arguments
B Data table
C Financial functions
D Future value (Fv)
E Goal Seek
F Interest
G Nper
H One-variable data table
I PMT function
J Present value (Pv)
K Principal
L Rate
M Two-variable data table
N Type argument
O What-if analysis

_____ 13. A range of cells that shows how changing certain values in your formulas affects the results of those formulas, and which makes it easy to calculate multiple versions in one operation.

_____ 14. A data table that changes the value in only one cell.

_____ 15. A data table that changes the values in two cells.

Multiple Choice

Circle the correct answer.

1. Loans are typically made for a period of:
A. days **B.** months **C.** years

2. The future value at the end of a loan is typically:
A. zero **B.** 100% **C.** loan balance

3. A word or string of characters that represents a cell, a range of cells, a formula, or a constant value is a defined:
A. scope **B.** name **C.** grouping

4. In the Cell Styles gallery, the Currency [0] style and the Comma [0] style format the selected cell with how many decimal places?
A. 0 **B.** 1 **C.** 2

5. When you use a defined name in a formula, the result is the same as if you typed a:
A. column reference **B.** cell reference **C.** row reference

6. A group of Excel functions that look up a value in a defined range of cells located in another part of the workbook to find a corresponding value is referred to as:
A. logical functions **B.** lookup functions **C.** tab

7. An Excel function that looks up values that are displayed vertically in a column is the:
A. VLOOKUP function **B.** HLOOKUP function **C.** Sum function

8. A defined range of cells, arranged in a column or a row, used in a VLOOKUP or HLOOKUP function, is called a table:
A. defined name **B.** list **C.** array

9. When creating a VLOOKUP or an HLOOKUP function, the one requirement is that the data in the table array is sorted in:
A. Ascending order **B.** Descending order **C.** Lookup order

10. A list of values that are acceptable for a group of cells is a:
A. data list **B.** information list **C.** validation list

Content-Based Assessments

Apply 4A skills from these Objectives:

1. Use Financial Functions
2. Use Goal Seek
3. Create a Data Table

Skills Review | Project 4C Auto Loan

In the following Skills Review, you will create a worksheet for Lauren Feeney, U.S. Sales Director, that details loan information for purchasing seven automobiles for Rubanne Specialties sales representatives. The monthly payment for the seven automobiles cannot exceed $3,000. Your completed two worksheets will look similar to Figure 4.39.

Project Files

For Project 4C, you will need the following file:

e04C_Auto_Loan

You will save your workbook as:

Lastname_Firstname_4C_Auto_Loan

Project Results

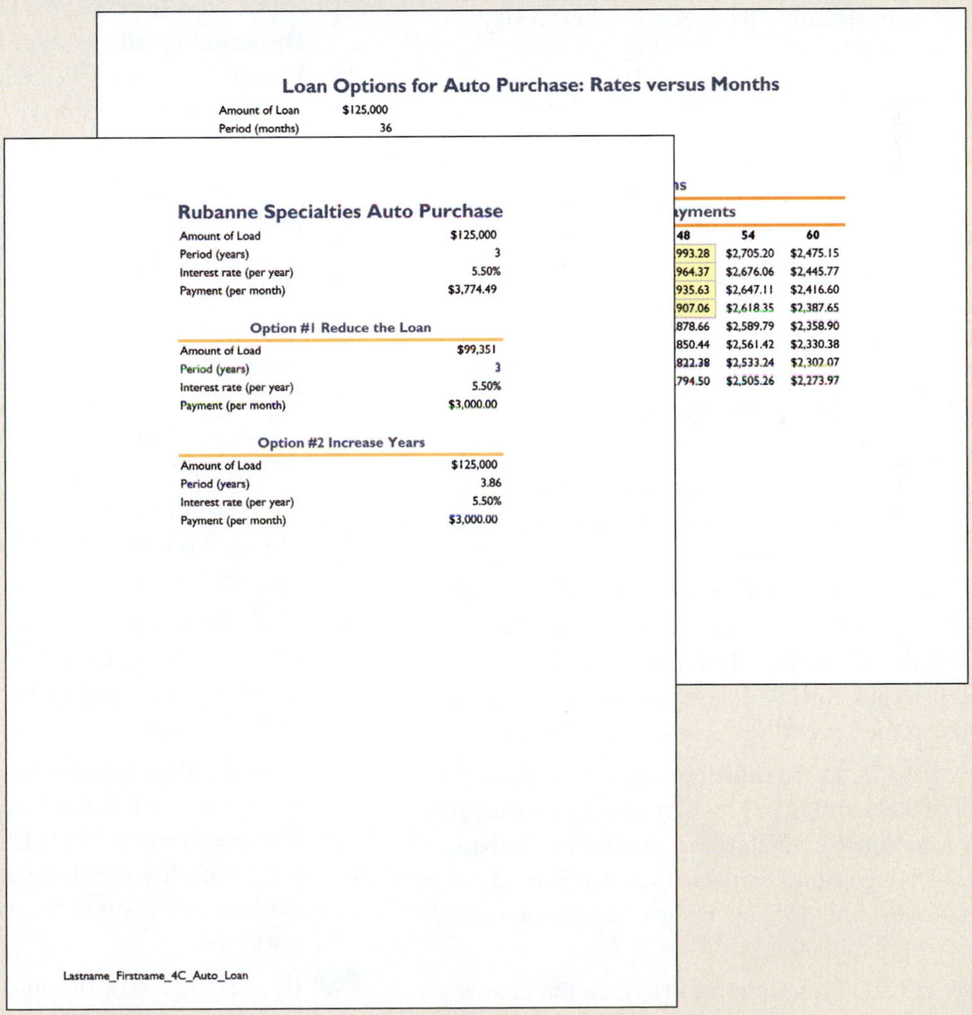

Figure 4.39

(Project 4C Auto Loan continues on the next page)

Skills Review | Project **4C** Auto Loan (continued)

1 **Start** Excel. From your student files, open the file **e04C_Auto_Loan**, and then **Save** the file in your **Excel Chapter 4** folder as **Lastname_Firstname_4C_Auto_Loan**

a. In the range **A2:B5**, enter the following row titles and data.

Amount of Loan	**$125,000**
Period (years)	**3**
Interest rate (per year)	**5.5%**
Payment (per month)	

b. Click cell **B5**. On the **Formulas tab**, in the **Function Library group**, click the **Financial** button, and then click **PMT**. Drag the **Function Arguments** dialog box to the right side of your screen so you can view **columns A:B**.

c. In the **Rate** box, type **b4/12** to convert the annual interest rate to a monthly interest rate. Press Tab, and then in the **Nper** box, type **b3*12** to have Excel convert the number of years in the loan (3) to the total number of months. Press Tab, and then in the **Pv** box, type **b2** to enter the present value of the loan. Click **OK** to create the function. In the **Formula Bar**, between the equal sign and *PMT*, type **–** (minus sign) to insert a minus sign into the formula, and then press Enter to display the loan payment as a positive number.

2 The result of *$3,774.49* is higher than the monthly payment of $3,000 that Lauren wants. One option is to reduce the amount of money that she is going to borrow; she can determine the maximum amount that she can borrow and still keep the payment at $3,000 by using Goal Seek. Click cell **B5**. On the **Data tab**, in the **Data Tools group**, click the **What-If Analysis** button, and then in the displayed list, click **Goal Seek**. In the displayed **Goal Seek** dialog box, in the **Set cell** box, confirm that *B5* displays.

a. Press Tab. In the **To value** box, type the payment goal of **3000** and then press Tab. In the **By changing cell** box, type **b2** which is the amount of the loan. Click **OK** two times. For three years at 5.5%, Lauren can borrow only $99,351 if she maintains a monthly payment of $3,000.

b. Click cell **A7**. Type **Option #1 Reduce the Loan** and then on the **Formula Bar**, click the **Enter** button to keep the cell active. **Merge and Center** the title across the range **A7:B7**, display the **Cell Styles** gallery, and then apply the **Heading 2** cell style.

c. Select the range **A2:B5**, right-click, and then click **Copy**. Point to cell **A8** right-click, point to **Paste Special**, and then under **Paste Values**, click the second button—**Values & Number Formatting**. Press Esc to cancel the moving border.

d. In cell **B2**, type **125000** and then press Enter to restore the original loan amount. Another option that Lauren can explore with Goal Seek is to increase the number of years over which she finances the automobiles. Click cell **B5**. On the **Data tab**, in the **Data Tools group**, click the **What-If Analysis** button, and then click **Goal Seek**.

e. In the **Set cell** box, confirm that **B5** displays. Press Tab. In the **To value** box, type **3000** Press Tab. In the **By changing cell** box, type **b3** which is the number of years for the loan. Click **OK** two times. Extending the loan over 3.8 years will maintain a monthly payment of $3,000 at the current interest rate.

f. Click **A13**. Type **Option #2 Increase Years** and then press Enter. Use the **Format Painter** to copy the format from cell **A7** to cell **A13**. Select the range **A2:B5**, right-click, and then click **Copy**. Point to cell **A14**, right-click, point to **Paste Special**, and then under **Paste Values**, click the second button—**Values & Number Formatting**. Press Esc to cancel the moving border.

g. Point to cell **B15**, right-click to display the Mini toolbar, and then click the **Decrease Decimal** button until the number of decimal places is two. Click cell **B3**. Type **3** and then press Enter to restore the original value.

h. Click the **Insert tab**, insert a footer, and then in the left section, click the **File Name** button. Click in a cell just above the footer to exit the **Footer area** and view your file name.

i. From the **Page Layout tab**. display the **Page Setup** dialog box, and on the **Margins tab**, select the **Horizontally** check box. Click **OK**, and then on the status bar, click the **Normal** button. Press Ctrl + Home to move to the top of the worksheet. **Save** your workbook.

3 To determine how variable interest rates and a varying number of payments affect the payment amount, Lauren will set up a two-variable data table. Double-click the **Sheet2 tab**, rename it **Payment Table** and then press Enter. In cell **A1**, type **Loan Options for Auto Purchase: Rates versus Months** and then press Enter.

(Project 4C Auto Loan continues on the next page)

Skills Review | Project 4C Auto Loan (continued)

Merge and Center this title across the range **A1:I1**, and then apply the **Title** cell style.

a. In the range **A2:B4**, enter the following row titles and data.

Amount of Loan	$125,000
Period (months)	36
Interest rate (per year)	5.5%

b. Click cell **C8**. Type **24** and then press Tab. Type **30** and then press Tab. Select the range **C8:D8**. Drag the fill handle to the right through cell **I8** to fill a pattern of months from 24 to 60 in increments of six months.

c. In cell **B9**, type **7.0%** and press Enter. Type **6.5%** and press Enter. Select the range **B9:B10**, and then drag the fill handle down through cell **B16** to fill a pattern of interest rates in increments of .5% from 7.00% down to 3.50%.

d. Click cell **C6**. Type **Payment Options** and then press Enter. **Merge and Center** this title across the range **C6:I6**. Apply the **Heading 1** cell style. Click cell **C7**. Type **Number of Monthly Payments** and then use the **Format Painter** to apply the format of cell **C6** to cell **C7**.

e. Click cell **A9**, type **Rates** and then press Enter. Select the range **A9:A16**. On the **Home tab**, in the **Alignment group**, click the **Merge and Center** button, click the **Align Text Right** button, and then click the **Middle Align** button. Apply the Explanatory Text cell style.

f. Click cell **B8**. On the **Formulas tab**, in the **Function Library group**, click the **Financial** button, and then click **PMT**. In the **Rate** box, type **b4/12** to divide the interest rate per year by 12 to convert it to a monthly interest rate. Press Tab, and then in the **Nper** box, type **b3** Press Tab. In the **Pv** box, type **-b2** and then click **OK**.

g. Select the range **B8:I16**. On the **Data tab**, in the **Data Tools group**, click the **What-If Analysis** button, and then in the displayed list, click **Data Table**.

In the **Data Table** dialog box, in the **Row input cell** box, type **b3** and then press Tab. In the **Column input cell** box, type **b4** In the **Data Table** dialog box, click **OK** to create the data table. Click in any cell outside of the table to deselect.

h. Right-click cell **B8**, and then on the Mini toolbar, click the **Format Painter** button. Select the range **C9:I16** to apply the same format. Notice that in cell **G9**, the payment is *$2,993.28*, which is close to Lauren's goal of a monthly payment of $3,000. At any of the interest rates, she will have to extend the loan over at least 48 months to stay within her goal of $3,000 per month.

i. Select the range **G9:G12** and apply the **Note** cell style to highlight the desired payment option. Select the nonadjacent ranges **C8:I8** and **B9:B16**, apply **Bold** and **Center**. On the **Page Layout tab**, set the orientation for this worksheet to **Landscape**.

j. Click the **Insert tab**, insert a footer, and then in the left section, click the **File Name** button. Click in a cell just above the footer to exit the **Footer area** and view your file name. From the **Page Layout tab**, display the **Page Setup** dialog box, and on the **Margins tab**, select the **Horizontally** check box. Click **OK**, and then on the status bar, click the **Normal** button. Press Ctrl + Home to move to the top of the worksheet.

k. Display the **Document Panel** and in the **Author** box, type your **firstname** and **lastname**; in the **Subject** box type, your course name and section number; and in the **Keywords** box, type **amortization schedule, payment table.** Return to **Normal** view and make cell **A1** active. Display each worksheet in **Print Preview**, and then make any necessary corrections or adjustments. Close the print preview.

l. **Save** your workbook. Print or submit the two worksheets in this workbook electronically as directed by your instructor. If required, print or create an electronic version of your worksheets with formulas displayed using the instructions in Activity 1.16 in Project 1A.

End **You have completed Project 4C**

Content-Based Assessments

Apply **4B** skills from these Objectives:

- 4 Define Names
- 5 Use Defined Names in a Formula
- 6 Use Lookup Functions
- 7 Validate Data

Skills Review | Project 4D Quarterly Cost Report and Lookup Form

In the following Skills Review, you will assist Connor Fereday, the Vice President of Marketing at Rubanne Specialties, by defining names for ranges of cells in a workbook containing quarterly Store Supply costs and by adding lookup functions to a Packing Slip form so that an order taker can complete the form quickly. Your completed workbooks will look similar to Figure 4.40.

Project Files

For Project 4D, you will need the following files:

e04D_Store_Supplies
e04D_Packing_Slip

You will save your workbooks as:

Lastname_Firstname_4D_Store_Supplies
Lastname_Firstname_4D_Packing_Slip

Project Results

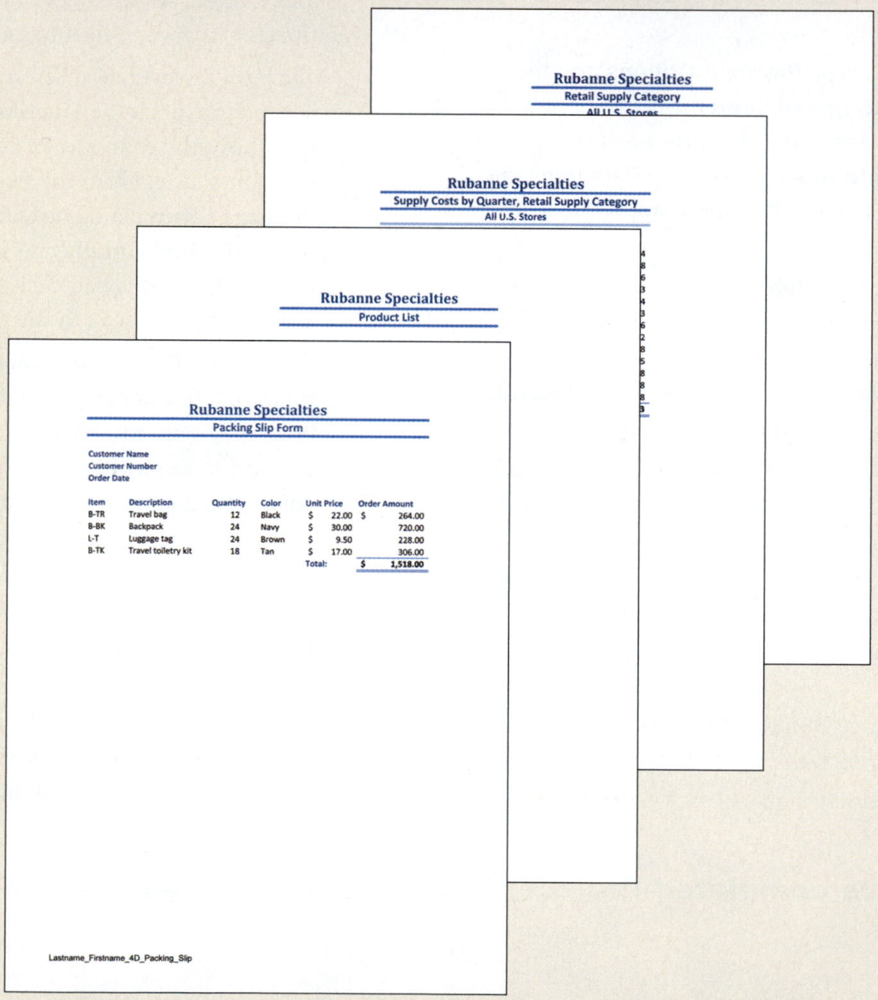

Figure 4.40

(Project 4D Quarterly Cost Report and Lookup Form continues on the next page)

Content-Based Assessments

Skills Review | Project 4D Quarterly Cost Report and Lookup Form (continued)

1 **Start** Excel. From your student files, open the file **e04D_Store_Supplies**, and then **Save** the file in your **Excel Chapter 4** folder as **Lastname_Firstname_4D_Store_Supplies**

a. Select the range **B6:E18**, which includes the empty cells in **row 18**, and then click the **Sum** button. Click anywhere to cancel the selection. Select the range **B6:E6**, hold down Ctrl and select the range **B18:E18**, and then from the **Cell Styles** gallery, under **Number Format**, apply the **Currency [0]** cell style. Select the range **B7:E17**, display the **Cell Styles** gallery, and then under **Number Format**, click **Comma [0]**. Select the range **B18:E18**, and then apply the **Total** cell style.

b. Select the range **B6:E9**. On the **Formulas tab**, in the **Defined Names** group, click the **Define Name** button. With *Revolving_Glass_Towers* selected, type **Showcase_Costs** as the name. At the bottom of the dialog box, at the right edge of the **Refers to** box, point to and click the **Collapse Dialog Box** button. Change the range by selecting the range **B6:E10**.

c. Click the **Expand Dialog Box** button to redisplay the **New Name** dialog box, and then click **OK**. Select the range **B11:E14**. In the upper left corner of the Excel window, to the left of the **Formula Bar**, click in the **Name Box**, and notice that the cell reference *B11* moves to the left edge of the box and is highlighted in blue. Type **Wrapping_Costs** and press Enter.

d. Select the range **B15:E16**. On the **Formulas tab**, in the **Defined Names group**, click the **Name Manager** button. In the upper left corner of the **Name Manager** dialog box, click the **New** button. With *Slant_Back_Counter_Racks* selected, type **Countertop_Costs** and then click **OK**. **Close** the **Name Manager** dialog box and **Save** your workbook.

e. On the left side of your window, in the **row heading area**, point to the **row 15** heading and right-click to select the entire row and display a shortcut menu. Click **Insert** to insert a new blank row above. Click cell **A15**, type **Ribbons and Bows** and then press Tab. In cell **B15**, type **200** and press Tab. In cell **C15**, type **195** and press Tab. In cell **D15**, type **315** and press Tab. In cell **E15**, type **275** and press Enter.

f. On the **Formulas tab**, from the **Defined Names group**, display the **Name Manager** dialog box. In the **Name** Manager dialog box, in the **Name** column, click **Wrapping_Costs**. At the bottom of the dialog box, click in the **Refers to** box and edit the reference, changing **$E$14** to **$15** to include the new row in the range. **Close** the **Name Manager** dialog box, and click **Yes** to save the changes you made to the name reference. **Save** your workbook.

g. On the **Formulas tab**, from the **Defined Names group**, display the **Name Manager** dialog box. Click **Wrapping_Costs**, and then click the **Edit** button. In the displayed **Edit Name** dialog box, with *Wrapping_Costs* highlighted, type **Packaging_Costs** Click **OK**, and then **Close** the **Name Manager** dialog box. In the upper left corner of the window, click the **Name Box arrow** and notice the modified range name, *Packaging_Costs*. Click any cell to close the list, and then **Save** your workbook.

h. Select the range **A18:E18**. On the **Formulas tab**, in the **Defined Names group**, click **Create from Selection**. In the **Create Names from Selection** dialog box, click **OK**, and then click anywhere to cancel the selection. Click the **Name Box arrow**, and then click the name **Tags_and_Labels**. Notice that in the new range name, Excel inserted the underscore necessary to fill a blank space in the range name.

2 Display the **Annual Supply Costs** worksheet. In cell **B5**, type **=sum(S** Continue typing **howcase_Costs** and then press Enter. Your result is *41879*. In cell **B6**, type **=sum(P** and then on the displayed **Formula AutoComplete list**, double-click **Packaging_Costs** to insert the formula. Press Enter to display the result *10984*.

a. In cell **B7**, type **=sum(** and then on the **Formulas tab**, in the **Defined Names group**, click the **Use in Formula** button. From the displayed list, click **Countertop_Costs** and then press Enter to display the total *4475*.

b. In cell **B8**, use any of the techniques you just practiced to sum the cells containing the costs for **Tags and Labels Costs** and to display a result of *5768*. Click cell **B9**, hold down Alt and press = to insert the SUM function, and then press Enter to display a total of *63106*.

c. Select the nonadjacent cells **B5** and **B9**, and then from the **Home tab**, display the **Cell Styles** gallery. Under **Number Format**, apply the **Currency [0]** cell style. To the range **B6:B8**, apply the **Comma [0]** cell style. Click cell **B9** and apply the **Total** cell style.

(Project 4D Quarterly Cost Report and Lookup Form continues on the next page)

Skills Review | Project 4D Quarterly Cost Report and Lookup Form (continued)

d. Select both worksheets so that *[Group]* displays in the title bar. With the two worksheets grouped, insert a footer in the left section that includes the file name. **Center** the worksheets horizontally on the page.

e. Display the **Document Information Panel** and in the **Author** box, type your **firstname** and **lastname** In the **Subject** box, type your course name and section number, and in the **Keywords** box, type **Retail Supply Category, Supply Costs** Return to **Normal** view and make cell **A1** active, display the grouped worksheets in **Print Preview**, **Close** the **Print Preview**, and then make any necessary corrections or adjustments.

f. **Save** your workbook. Print or submit the two worksheets in this workbook electronically as directed by your instructor. If required, print or create an electronic version of your worksheets with formulas displayed using the instructions in Activity 1.16 in Project 1A. **Close** this workbook, but leave Excel open.

3 From your student files, **Open** the file **e04D_Packing_Slip**, and then **Save** the file in your **Excel Chapter 4** folder as **Lastname_Firstname_4D_Packing_Slip**

a. Display the **Product Information** worksheet. Select the range **A4:C11**. On the **Data tab**, in the **Sort & Filter group**, click **Sort**. If necessary, drag the Sort dialog box to the right side of your screen so you can view columns A:C.

b. In the **Sort** dialog box, under **Column**, click the **Sort by arrow**. Notice that the selected range is now **A5:C11** and that the column titles in the range **A4:C4** display in the **Sort by** list. In the **Sort by** list, click **Style Code**, which is the first column heading and the column heading that Excel selects by default. Under **Sort On**, verify that *Values* displays, and under **Order**, verify that *A to Z* displays. Click **OK** to sort the data by *Style Code* in ascending order. **Save** your workbook.

c. Display the **Packing Slip** worksheet. In cell **A9**, type **B-TR** and press Tab. With cell **B9** as the active cell, on the **Formulas tab**, in the **Function Library group**, click **Lookup & Reference**, and then click **VLOOKUP**.

d. With the insertion point in the **Lookup_value** box, click cell **A9** to look up the description of Item B-TR. Click in the **Table_array** box, and then at the bottom of the workbook, click the **Product Information sheet tab**. On the displayed **Product Information** sheet, select the range **A4:C11**, and then press F4. Click in the **Col_index_num** box, type **2** and then click **OK**.

e. With cell **B9** as the active cell and containing the VLOOKUP formula, point to the fill handle in the lower right corner of the cell, and then drag to fill the VLOOKUP formula down through cell **B18**. The *#N/A* error notation displays in the cells where you copied the formula because no values have been entered in Column A in those rows.

f. Click cell **C9**, type **12** as the quantity ordered, and then press Tab. In cell **D9**, type **Black** and press Tab. With cell **E9** as the active cell, on the **Formulas tab**, in the **Function Library group**, click **Lookup & Reference**, and then click **VLOOKUP**.

g. With the insertion point in the **Lookup_value** box, click cell **A9** to look up information for Item B-TR. Click in the **Table_array** box, display the **Product Information** sheet, and then select the range **A4:C11**. Press F4 to make the values in the range absolute.

h. In the **Col_index_num** box, type **3** to look up the price in the third column of the range, and then click **OK**. The Unit Price for the Travel bag displays in cell E9. Click cell **F9**, and notice that a formula to calculate the total for the item, Quantity times Unit Price, was already entered in the worksheet.

i. Click cell **E9**, and then copy the VLOOKUP formula down through cell **E18**. The *#N/A* error notation displays in the cells where you copied the formula, and also in cells F10:F18, because a value is not available to the formulas—values have not yet been entered in column A in those rows.

j. Click cell **A10**, type **B-BK** and press Tab two times. In cell **C10**, type **24** and press Tab. Notice that Excel calculates the total for this item in cell **F10**—*720.00*. In cell **D10**, type **Navy** and then press Enter. Notice that after data is entered in the row, the error notations no longer display. **Save** your workbook.

4 Display the Product Information sheet. Select the range **A4:A11**. On the **Formulas tab**, in the **Defined Names group**, click **Create from Selection**.

a. In the **Create Names from Selection** dialog box, be sure only the **Top row** check box is selected, and then click **OK**.

(Project 4D Quarterly Cost Report and Lookup Form continues on the next page)

Skills Review | Project 4D Quarterly Cost Report and Lookup Form (continued)

b. Display the **Packing Slip** worksheet, and then select the range **A9:A18**. On the **Data tab**, in the **Data Tools group**, click the **Data Validation** button. In the displayed **Data Validation** dialog box, be sure the **Settings tab** is selected.

c. Under **Validation criteria**, click the **Allow arrow**, and then click **List**. Click to position the insertion point in the **Source** box, type **=Style_Code** and then click **OK**.

d. Click cell **A11**, and notice that a list arrow displays at the right edge of the cell. In cell **A11**, click the list arrow to display the list. In the displayed list, click **L-T**. Press Tab two times, type **24** and press Tab, type **Brown** and then press Enter to return to the beginning of the next row.

e. With cell **A12** active, click the **list arrow**, and then click **B-TK**. As the **Quantity**, type **18** and as the **Color**, type **Tan** Press Enter. In cell **A13**, type **B-W** and press Tab. An error message displays indicating that you entered a value that is not valid; that is, it is not on the validation list you created. In the displayed error message, click **Cancel** and then **Save** your workbook.

f. Select the unused **rows 13:18**, right-click over the selected rows, and then click **Delete**. In cell **F13**, **Sum** the order amounts and then apply the **Total** cell style.

5 Select both worksheets so that *[Group]* displays in the title bar. With the two worksheets grouped, insert a footer in the left section that includes the file name. **Center** the worksheets horizontally on the page.

a. Display the **Document Panel** and in the **Author** box, type your **firstname** and type your **lastname** In the **Subject** box, type your course name and section number, and in the **Keywords** box, type **luggage, bag, order, form** Return to **Normal** view and make cell **A1** active, display the grouped worksheets in **Print Preview**, **Close** the **Print Preview**, and then make any necessary corrections or adjustments. **Save** your workbook.

b. Print or submit the two worksheets in this workbook electronically as directed by your instructor. If required, print or create an electronic version of your worksheets with formulas displayed using the instructions in Activity 1.16 in Project 1A.

End **You have completed Project 4D**

Content-Based Assessments

Apply 4A skills from these Objectives:

1. Use Financial Functions
2. Use Goal Seek
3. Create a Data Table

Mastering Excel | Project 4E Condo Loan

In the following Mastering Excel project, you will create a worksheet for Jean Jacques Dupuis, President of Rubanne Specialties, that analyzes loan options for a condo in Montreal that the company is considering purchasing. Jean Jacques wants to provide a lodging facility for company visitors, but would like to keep the monthly loan payment below $6,000. The worksheets of your workbook will look similar to Figure 4.41.

Project Files

For Project 4E, you will need the following file:

e04E_Condo_Loan

You will save your workbook as:

Lastname_Firstname_4E_Condo_Loan

Project Results

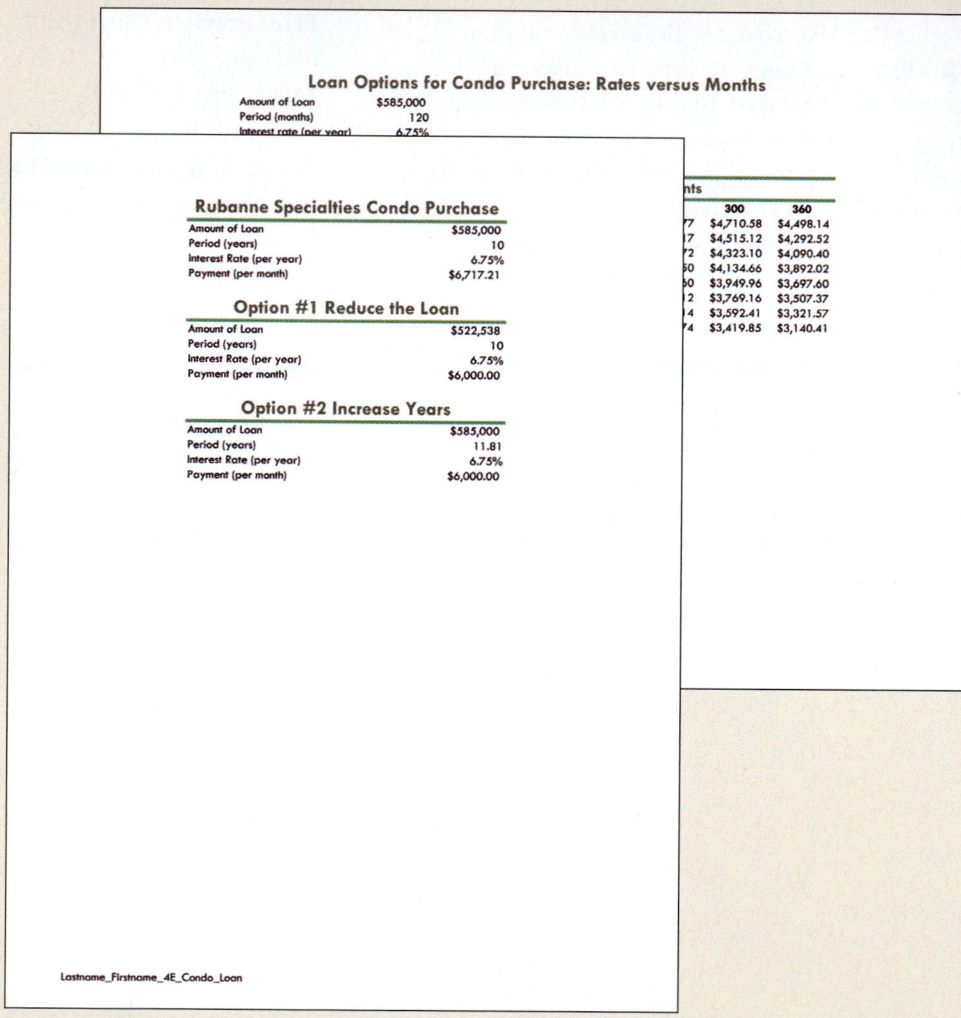

Loan Options for Condo Purchase: Rates versus Months

Amount of Loan	$585,000
Period (months)	120
Interest rate (per year)	6.75%

300	360
$4,710.58	$4,498.14
$4,515.12	$4,292.52
$4,323.10	$4,090.40
$4,134.66	$3,892.02
$3,949.96	$3,697.60
$3,769.16	$3,507.37
$3,592.41	$3,321.57
$3,419.85	$3,140.41

Rubanne Specialties Condo Purchase

Amount of Loan	$585,000
Period (years)	10
Interest Rate (per year)	6.75%
Payment (per month)	$6,717.21

Option #1 Reduce the Loan

Amount of Loan	$522,538
Period (years)	10
Interest Rate (per year)	6.75%
Payment (per month)	$6,000.00

Option #2 Increase Years

Amount of Loan	$585,000
Period (years)	11.81
Interest Rate (per year)	6.75%
Payment (per month)	$6,000.00

Lastname_Firstname_4E_Condo_Loan

Figure 4.41

(Project 4E Condo Loan continues on the next page)

Mastering Excel | Project 4E Condo Loan (continued)

1 Start **Excel**. From your student files, locate and **Open** **e04E_Condo_Loan**. **Save** the file in your **Excel Chapter 4** folder as **Lastname_Firstname_4E_Condo_Loan**. In cell **B5**, insert the **PMT** function using the data from the range **B2:B5**—be sure to divide the interest rate by 12, multiply the years by 12, and display the payment as a positive number. The result, *$6,717.21*, is larger than the payment of $6,000.

2 Use **Goal Seek** so that the payment is under $6,000. Then, in **A7**, type **Option #1 Reduce the Loan** and then **Copy** the format from cell **A1** to cell **A7**. **Copy** the range **A2:B5**, and then **Paste** the **Values & Number Formatting** to cell **A8**. In cell **B2**, type **585000** to restore the original loan amount.

3 Use **Goal Seek** so that the payment does not exceed $6,000. In **A13**, type **Option #2 Increase Years**. Format the cell the same as cell **A7**. **Copy** the range **A2:B5**, and then **Paste** the **Values & Number Formatting** to cell **A14**. Display the value in **B15** with two decimal places, and then in cell **B3**, type **10** to restore the original value. Insert a footer with the **File Name** in the left section, and then **Center** the worksheet **Horizontally** on the page.

4 **Save** and return to **Normal** view. Set up a two-variable data table. Rename the **Sheet2 tab** to **Condo Payment Table** In the range **A2:B4**, enter the following row titles and data.

Amount of Loan	**$585,000**
Period (months)	**120**
Interest rate (per year)	**6.75%**

5 In cell **C8**, type **60**—the number of months in a 5-year loan. In **D8**, type **120**—the number of months in a 10-year loan. Fill the series through cell **H8**; apply **Bold** and **Center**.

6 Beginning in cell **B9**, enter varying interest rates in increments of .5% beginning with **8.5%** and ending with **5%**. Format all the interest rates with two decimal places, and then apply **Bold** and **Center**. In cell **B8**, enter a **PMT** function using the information in cells **B2:B4**. Be sure that you convert the interest rate to a monthly rate and that the result displays as a positive number.

7 Create a **Data Table** in the range **B8:H16** using the information in cells **B2:B4** in which the **Row input cell** is the **Period** and the **Column input cell** is the **Interest rate**. Copy the format from **B8** to the results in the data table. Format the range **E9:E10** with the **Note cell** style as two payment options that are close to but less than $6,000 per month. Change the **Orientation** to **Landscape**. Insert a footer with the **File Name** in the left section, and **Center** the worksheet **Horizontally** on the page. Return to **Normal** view and move to cell **A1**.

8 Display the **Document Panel** and in the **Author** box, type your **firstname** and type your **lastname** In the **Subject** box, type your course name and section number, and in the **Keywords** box, **condo, payment table**. **Print Preview**, make corrections, and **Save**. Print or submit electronically as directed.

End **You have completed Project 4E**

Content-Based Assessments

Apply 4B skills from these Objectives:

- 4 Define Names
- 5 Use Defined Names in a Formula
- 6 Use Lookup Functions
- 7 Validate Data

Mastering Excel | Project 4F Quarterly Cost Report and Lookup Form

In the following Mastering Excel project, you will assist Connor Fereday, the Vice President of Marketing at Rubanne Specialties, by defining names for ranges of cells in a workbook containing quarterly Advertising costs and by adding lookup functions to an Advertising Order form so that an order taker can complete the form quickly. Your completed workbooks will look similar to Figure 4.42.

Project Files

For Project 4F, you will need the following files:

e04F_Advertising_Costs
e04F_Advertising_Form

You will save your workbooks as:

Lastname_Firstname_4F_Advertising_Costs
Lastname_Firstname_4F_Advertising_Form

Project Results

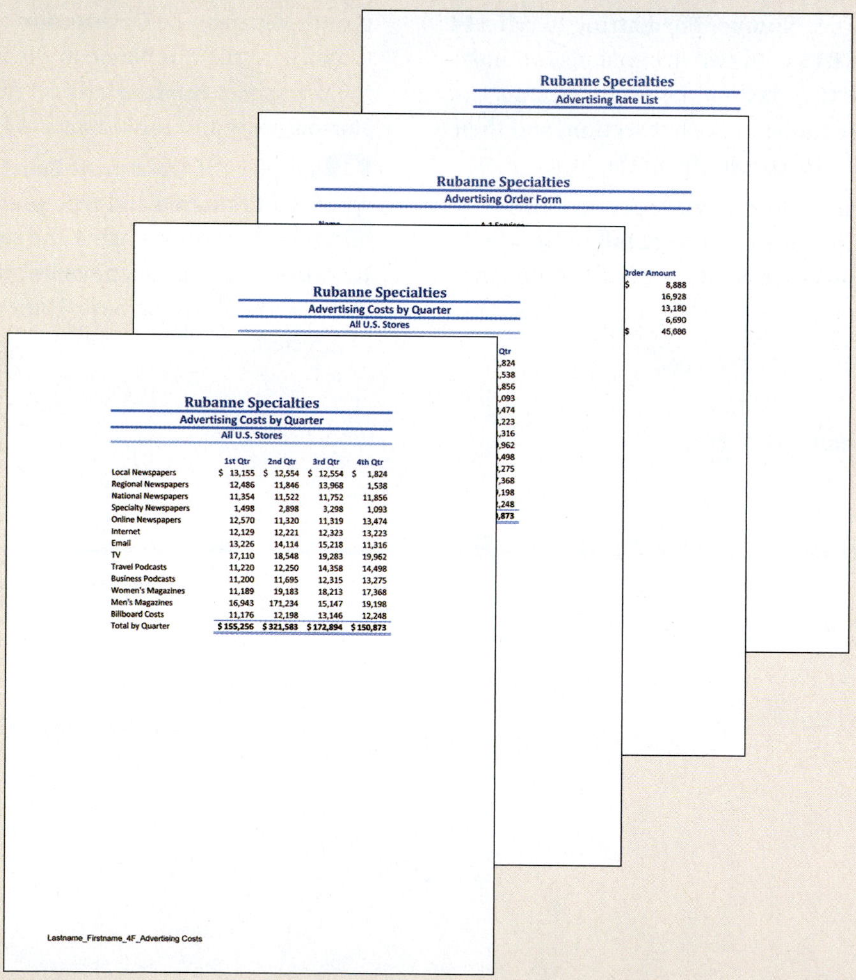

Figure 4.42

(Project 4F Quarterly Cost Report and Lookup Form continues on the next page)

Mastering Excel | Project 4F Quarterly Cost Report and Lookup Form (continued)

1 From your student files, open **e04F_Advertising_Costs**. **Save** it in your **Excel Chapter 4** folder as **Lastname_Firstname_4F_Advertising_Costs** Display the **Advertising Costs by Quarter** worksheet, and then apply appropriate **Currency [0]**, **Comma [0]**, and **Total** cell styles.

2 Name the following ranges: **B6:E9 Newspaper_Costs B10:E14 Digital_Costs B15:B16 Magazine_Costs B17:E17 Billboard_Costs Insert** a new row 15. In cell **A15**, type **Business Podcasts** In cell **B15**, type **11200** In cell **C15**, type **11695** In cell **D15**, type **12315** In cell **E15**, type **13275**.

3 Display **Name Manager**, click **Digital_Costs**, and then include cell **E15**. Select the **Billboard_Costs**, and **Edit** the name to **Outdoor_Costs**. Display the **Annual Advertising Costs** sheet. In cell **B5**, type **=sum(N** and sum the values. Do this for the other named ranges. Apply **Currency [0]**, **Comma [0]**, and **Total** cell styles. Sum all the costs. Group the worksheets, insert a footer that includes the file name and sheet tab name. **Center** the worksheets horizontally on the page. Document properties should include the keywords **advertising costs**. **Save** your file and then print or submit your worksheet electronically as directed by your instructor. **Close** your file.

4 Open **e04F_Advertising_Form**. **Save** in **Excel Chapter 4** folder as **Lastname_Firstname_4F_Advertising_Form** Display the **Advertising Rate Information** sheet, select the range **A4:C11**, and **Sort** by **Code**. Select the range **A4:A11**. In the **Defined Names group**, click **Create from Selection** with **Top row** selected, click **OK**. Display the **Advertising Order Form** sheet; select range **A9:A18**. Display the **Data Validation** button, select **List**, and then in the **Source** box, type **=Code** Click **OK**.

5 Click cell **A9**, click the **list arrow**, click **D-PH**, and then press Tab. With cell **B9** as the active cell, insert the **VLOOKUP** function. As the **Lookup_value** box, click cell **A9**. Click in the **Table_array** box, display the **Advertising Rate Information** sheet, select the range **A4:C11**, and then press F4 to make the cell reference absolute. In the **Col_index_num** box, type **2** and then click **OK**.

6 With cell **B9** as the active cell, fill the VLOOKUP formula through cell **B18**. In cell **C9**, type **4** as the **Quantity ordered** and press Tab. In cell **D9**, type **Regional** and press Tab. With cell **E9** as the active cell, insert the **VLOOKUP** function. As the **Lookup_value** box, click cell **A9**, and then click in the **Table_array** box. Display the **Advertising Rate Information** sheet, select the range **A4:C11**, and then press F4. In the **Col_index_num** box, type **3** and then click **OK**. **Copy** the VLOOKUP formula through cell **E18**. Add the following orders:

Item	Quantity	Type
D-R	8	National
D-IN	10	Internet
B-BB	6	Billboard

7 Delete unused rows, sum the **Order Amount**, and apply **Total** cell style. Group the worksheets, insert a footer that includes the file name and sheet tab name. **Center** the worksheets horizontally on the page. Document properties should include the keywords **advertising costs** and **form** **Save** your file and then print or submit your worksheet electronically as directed by your instructor.

End **You have completed Project 4F**

Content-Based Assessments

Apply 4A and 4B skills from these Objectives:

1. Use Financial Functions
2. Use Goal Seek
3. Create a Data Table
4. Define Names
5. Use Defined Names in a Formula
6. Use Lookup Functions
7. Validate Data

Mastering Excel | Project 4G Warehouse Loan and Lookup Form

In the following Mastering Excel project, you will create a worksheet for Jean Jacques Dupuis, President of Rubanne Specialties, that analyzes loan options for a warehouse that the company is considering purchasing. Jean Jacques wants to establish an additional storage facility in the United States, but would like to keep the monthly loan payment below $8,000. You will also assist Connor Fereday, the Vice President of Marketing at Rubanne Specialties by adding lookup functions to a Staff Planning form so that a manager can complete the form quickly. Your completed workbooks will look similar to Figure 4.43.

Project Files

For Project 4G, you will need the following files:

e04G_Warehouse_Loan
e04G_Staff_Form

You will save your workbooks as:

Lastname_Firstname_4G_Warehouse_Loan
Lastname_Firstname_4G_Staff_Form

Project Results

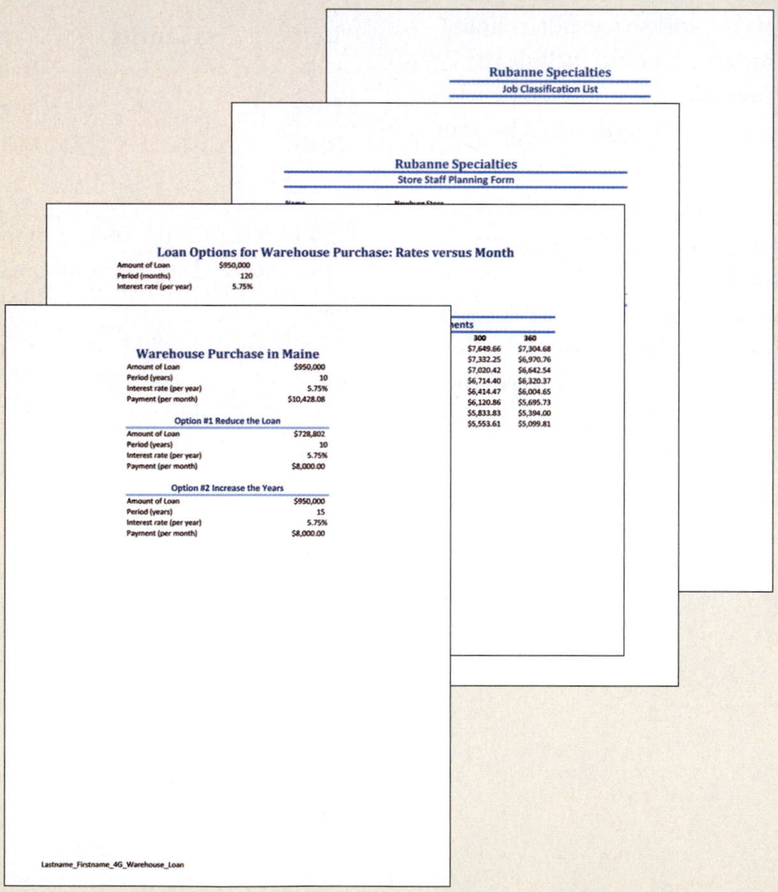

Figure 4.43

(Project 4G Warehouse Loan and Lookup Form continues on the next page)

Mastering Excel | Project 4G Warehouse Loan and Lookup Form (continued)

1 In your student files, locate and **Open** the file **e04G_Warehouse_Loan**, and **Save** it in your **Excel Chapter 4** folder as **Lastname_Firstname_4G_Warehouse_Loan** Display the **Warehouse Payment Table** sheet. In cell **B9**, enter rates in increments of .5% beginning with **8.5%** and ending with **5%** in cell B16. Format rates with two decimal places.

2 In cell **B8**, enter a **PMT** function using the information in cells **B2:B4**. Create a **Data Table** in the range **B8:H16** using the information in cells **B2:B4** in which the **Row input cell** is the **Period** and the **Column input cell** is the **Interest rate**. Apply the format from **B8** to the results in the data table. Select the two payment options closest to $8,000 per month and format the two options with the **Note** cell style.

3 Insert a footer that includes the file name, and document properties that include the keywords **warehouse loan** Change the **Orientation** to **Landscape**, **center** horizontally, and return to **Normal** view. **Print Preview**, **Save**, and then print or submit electronically as directed. **Close** this workbook.

4 Open the file **c04G_Staff_Form**, and **Save** it in your **Excel Chapter 4** folder as **Lastname_Firstname_4G_Staff_Form** On the **Job Information** sheet, select the range **A4:C11**, and then **Sort** the selection by **Job Code**. Name the range **A4:A11** by the name in the top row. Display the **Staffing Plan** sheet, and select the range **A9:A18**. Display the **Data Validation** dialog box, and validate from a **List** using the **Source =Job_Code**

5 Click cell **A9**, and then click **M-MG**. Click cell **B9**, and insert the **VLOOKUP** function. As the **Lookup_value** box, click cell **A9**. Click in the **Table_array** box, display the **Job Information** sheet, select the range **A4:C11**, and then press F4. In the **Col_index_num** box, type **2** and click **OK**.

6 With cell **B9** as the active cell, fill the VLOOKUP formula through cell **B18**. In cell **C9**, type **1** as the **# of Positions** and in cell **D9**, type **Management** as the **Type**. In cell **E9**, insert the **VLOOKUP** function. As the **Lookup_value** box, click cell **A9**, and then click in the **Table_array** box. Display the **Job Information** sheet, select the range **A4:C11**, and then press F4. In the **Col_index_num** box, type **3** and then click **OK**. **Copy** the VLOOKUP formula down through cell **E18**.

7 Beginning in cell **A10**, add these staff positions:

Item	#of Positions	Type
C-CASH	4	Cashier
B-BYR	2	Buyer
M-AMG	2	Assistant Manager

8 Delete any unused rows between the last item and the Total row. Sum the **Budget Amount** column and apply the **Total** cell style. Group the worksheets, insert a footer in the left section with the file name, **center** horizontally, update the document properties with your name and course name and section, and add the **Keywords planning, staff Print Preview**, **Save**, and then submit it as directed. **Close** this workbook.

End **You have completed Project 4G**

Excel | Chapter 4

Apply a combination of the **4A** and **4B** skills.

GO! Fix It | Project 4H Bag Costs by Quarter

Project Files

For Project 4H, you will need the following file:

e04H_Bag_Costs

You will save your workbook as:

Lastname_Firstname_4H_Bag_Costs

In this project, you will edit a worksheet to create range names, apply cell styles formatting, and check spelling on worksheets that display bag merchandise costs by quarter for Rubanne Specialties. From the student files that accompany this textbook, open the file e04H_Bag_Costs, and then save the file in your Excel Chapter 4 folder as **Lastname_Firstname_4H_Bag_Costs**

To complete the project, you must find and correct errors in formulas and formatting. In addition to errors that you find, you should know:

- There are two spelling errors.
- All data should be formatted with zero decimal places.
- There should be a named range for each of the following that should include appropriate data from correct ranges: *Handbag Costs*, *Travel Bag Costs*, *Tote Bag Costs*, and *Computer Bag Costs*. On the Annual Bag Costs worksheet, sum the quarterly costs of each named range.
- A footer should be inserted that includes the file name, and document properties should include the keywords **merchandise, bag category**

Save your file and then print or submit your worksheet electronically as directed by your instructor. To print formulas, refer to Activity 1.16. If you printed formulas, be sure to redisplay the worksheet by pressing Ctrl + `, and then exit Excel without saving.

End You have completed Project 4H

Content-Based Assessments

Apply a combination of the **4A** and **4B** skills.

GO! Make It | Project 4I Ohio Store Loan

Project Files

For Project 4I, you will need the following file:

New blank Excel workbook

You will save your workbook as:

Lastname_Firstname_4I_Ohio_Loan

Start a new blank Excel workbook and create the worksheet shown in Figure 4.44. In cell B7, insert the PMT function using the data in the range B2:B4. Then, create a data table in the range B7:H18 using periods of 6 months as shown, interest rates in .5% increments from 9.00% to 1.00%, and the information in cells B2:B4 in which the Row input cell is the Period and the Column input cell is the Interest rate. Apply the format from B8 to the results in the data table. Select the two payment options closest to $5,500 per month—one above and one below—and format the two options with the Note cell style. Rename Sheet 1 **Ohio Loan** Delete Sheet2 and Sheet3. Add your name, your course name and section number as the Subject, and include the Keywords **Cleveland, loan** Format the worksheet with a footer and centering, and Landscape, check in Print Preview, Save the file in your Excel Chapter 4 folder as **Lastname_Firstname_4I_Ohio_Loan** and then print or submit it electronically as directed.

Project Results

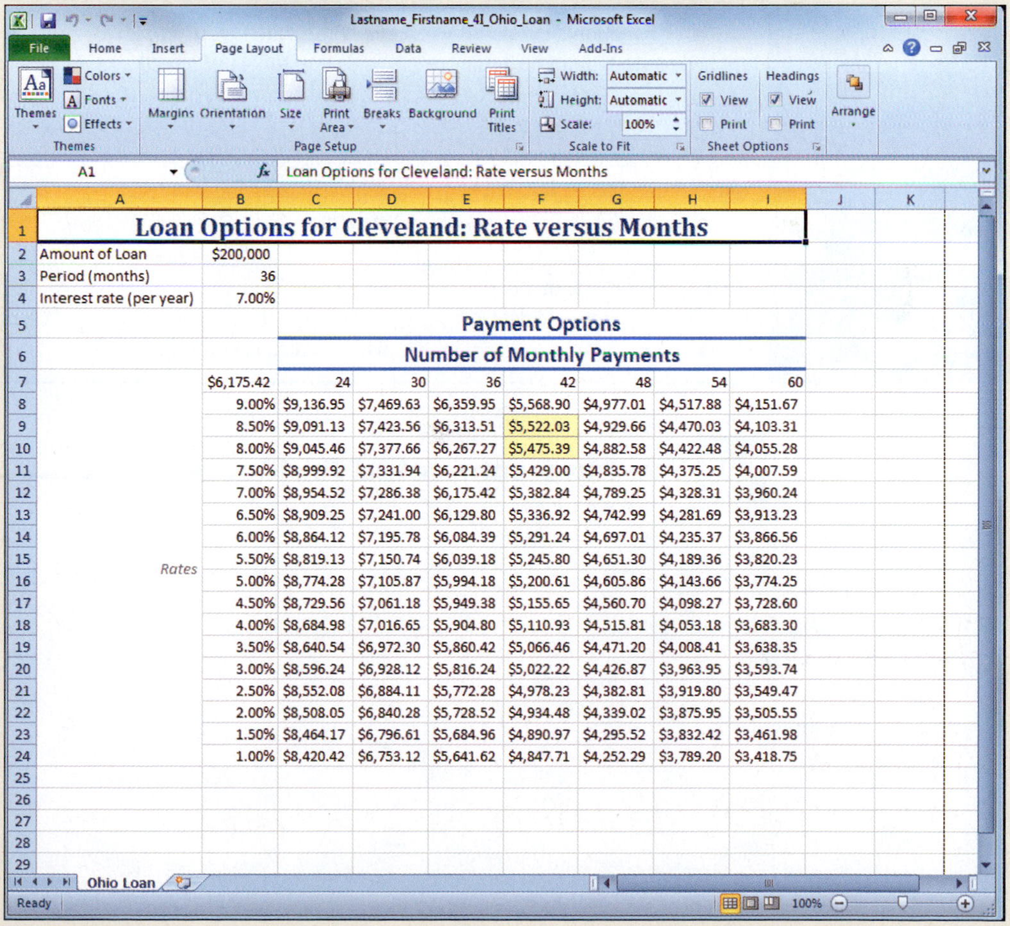

Amount of Loan	$200,000
Period (months)	36
Interest rate (per year)	7.00%

Payment Options

Number of Monthly Payments

	$6,175.42	24	30	36	42	48	54	60
	9.00%	$9,136.95	$7,469.63	$6,359.95	$5,568.90	$4,977.01	$4,517.88	$4,151.67
	8.50%	$9,091.13	$7,423.56	$6,313.51	$5,522.03	$4,929.66	$4,470.03	$4,103.31
	8.00%	$9,045.46	$7,377.66	$6,267.27	$5,475.39	$4,882.58	$4,422.48	$4,055.28
	7.50%	$8,999.92	$7,331.94	$6,221.24	$5,429.00	$4,835.78	$4,375.25	$4,007.59
	7.00%	$8,954.52	$7,286.38	$6,175.42	$5,382.84	$4,789.25	$4,328.31	$3,960.24
	6.50%	$8,909.25	$7,241.00	$6,129.80	$5,336.92	$4,742.99	$4,281.69	$3,913.23
	6.00%	$8,864.12	$7,195.78	$6,084.39	$5,291.24	$4,697.01	$4,235.37	$3,866.56
	5.50%	$8,819.13	$7,150.74	$6,039.18	$5,245.80	$4,651.30	$4,189.36	$3,820.23
Rates	5.00%	$8,774.28	$7,105.87	$5,994.18	$5,200.61	$4,605.86	$4,143.66	$3,774.25
	4.50%	$8,729.56	$7,061.18	$5,949.38	$5,155.65	$4,560.70	$4,098.27	$3,728.60
	4.00%	$8,684.98	$7,016.65	$5,904.80	$5,110.93	$4,515.81	$4,053.18	$3,683.30
	3.50%	$8,640.54	$6,972.30	$5,860.42	$5,066.46	$4,471.20	$4,008.41	$3,638.35
	3.00%	$8,596.24	$6,928.12	$5,816.24	$5,022.22	$4,426.87	$3,963.95	$3,593.74
	2.50%	$8,552.08	$6,884.11	$5,772.28	$4,978.23	$4,382.81	$3,919.80	$3,549.47
	2.00%	$8,508.05	$6,840.28	$5,728.52	$4,934.48	$4,339.02	$3,875.95	$3,505.55
	1.50%	$8,464.17	$6,796.61	$5,684.96	$4,890.97	$4,295.52	$3,832.42	$3,461.98
	1.00%	$8,420.42	$6,753.12	$5,641.62	$4,847.71	$4,252.29	$3,789.20	$3,418.75

Figure 4.44

End You have completed Project 4I

Excel | Chapter 4

Apply a combination of the **4A** and **4B** skills.

GO! Solve It | Project 4J Store Furnishings

Project Files

For Project 4J, you will need the following file:

e04J_Store_Furnishings

You will save your workbook as:

Lastname_Firstname_4J_Store_Furnishings

Open the file **e04J_Store_Furnishings** and save it as **Lastname_Firstname_4J_Store_Furnishings**

Complete the Store Furnishings Loan worksheet by using Goal Seek to explore two options for reducing the loan payment to approximately $7,500—either by reducing the loan or by increasing the number of years. Complete the Payment Table worksheet by creating a data table to calculate payments over 24–60 months with varying interest rates from 6.0% to 8.0% in .5% increments. Use Note cell style to indicate acceptable options. Include the file name in the footer, add appropriate properties, and submit it as directed.

		Performance Level		
		Exemplary: You consistently applied the relevant skills	Proficient: You sometimes, but not always, applied the relevant skills	Developing: You rarely or never applied the relevant skills
Performance Criteria	Use Financial Functions	The PMT Function is properly applied using supplied criteria.	The PMT Function is properly applied to some but not all supplied criteria.	The PMT Function is not properly applied and did not meet the supplied criteria.
	Use Goal Seek	Both Goal Seek outcomes were achieved using the supplied criteria.	One Goal Seek outcome was achieved using the supplied criteria.	No Goal Seek outcomes were achieved using the supplied criteria.
	Create a Data Table	All the criteria were met in the Data Table used to calculate the loan.	Some but not all the criteria were met in the Data Table used to calculate the loan.	The data table was not correctly calculated.

End **You have completed Project 4J**

Apply a combination of the **4A** and **4B** skills.

GO! Solve It | Project 4K Order Form

Project Files

For Project 4K, you will need the following file:

e04K_Order_Form

You will save your workbook as:

Lastname_Firstname_4K_Order_Form

Open the file e04K_Order_Form and save it as **Lastname_Firstname_4K_Order_Form**

Prepare the Product Information worksheet for a *VLOOKUP* function by sorting the items by Style Code, and then create a named range for the Style Code information. On the Order Form worksheet, using the named range, set data validation for the Item column. Insert the VLOOKUP function in column B and column E, referencing the appropriate data in the Product Information worksheet. Then enter the data below.

Item	Description	Quantity	Color
M-TF	**Oversized Bags**	**12**	**Black**
M-MC	**Organizer Bags**	**24**	**Brown**
C-S	**Classic Bags**	**12**	**Black**
C-T	**Fabric Bags**	**36**	**Beige**
C-R	**Designer Bags**	**18**	**Black**

Construct formulas to total the order, and then apply appropriate financial formatting. On both sheets, include your name in the footer, add appropriate properties, and then submit them as directed.

Performance Criteria	Performance Level: Exemplary: You consistently applied the relevant skills	Proficient: You sometimes, but not always, applied the relevant skills	Developing: You rarely or never applied the relevant skills
Use Lookup Functions	The VLOOKUP function correctly looks up data on the validation list.	The VLOOKUP function looks up some but not all the data on the validation list.	The VLOOKUP function does not display or does not look up any of the correct information.
Validate Data	The Validation List is sorted correctly.	Some of the Validation list was sorted.	The Validation List is not sorted.
Calculate and Format the Order Amount	The Order Amount and financial information is properly calculated and formatted.	Some, but not all, of the Order Amount and financial information is properly calculated and formatted.	Incorrect formulas and/or incorrect financial formatting were applied in most of the cells.

End **You have completed Project 4K**

Outcomes-Based Assessments

Rubric

The following outcomes-based assessments are *open-ended assessments*. That is, there is no specific correct result; your result will depend on your approach to the information provided. Make *Professional Quality* your goal. Use the following scoring rubric to guide you in *how* to approach the problem and then to evaluate *how well* your approach solves the problem.

The *criteria*—Software Mastery, Content, Format and Layout, and Process—represent the knowledge and skills you have gained that you can apply to solving the problem. The *levels of performance*—Professional Quality, Approaching Professional Quality, or Needs Quality Improvements—help you and your instructor evaluate your result.

	Your completed project is of Professional Quality if you:	**Your completed project is Approaching Professional Quality if you:**	**Your completed project Needs Quality Improvements if you:**
1-Software Mastery	Choose and apply the most appropriate skills, tools, and features and identify efficient methods to solve the problem.	Choose and apply some appropriate skills, tools, and features, but not in the most efficient manner.	Choose inappropriate skills, tools, or features, or are inefficient in solving the problem.
2-Content	Construct a solution that is clear and well organized, contains content that is accurate, appropriate to the audience and purpose, and is complete. Provide a solution that contains no errors in spelling, grammar, or style.	Construct a solution in which some components are unclear, poorly organized, inconsistent, or incomplete. Misjudge the needs of the audience. Have some errors in spelling, grammar, or style, but the errors do not detract from comprehension.	Construct a solution that is unclear, incomplete, or poorly organized; contains some inaccurate or inappropriate content; and contains many errors in spelling, grammar, or style. Do not solve the problem.
3-Format and Layout	Format and arrange all elements to communicate information and ideas, clarify function, illustrate relationships, and indicate relative importance.	Apply appropriate format and layout features to some elements, but not others. Overuse features, causing minor distraction.	Apply format and layout that does not communicate information or ideas clearly. Do not use format and layout features to clarify function, illustrate relationships, or indicate relative importance. Use available features excessively, causing distraction.
4-Process	Use an organized approach that integrates planning, development, self-assessment, revision, and reflection.	Demonstrate an organized approach in some areas, but not others; or, use an insufficient process of organization throughout.	Do not use an organized approach to solve the problem.

Outcomes-Based Assessments

Apply a combination of the **4A** and **4B** skills.

GO! Think | Project 4L Key Chains

Project Files

For Project 4L, you will need the following file:

e04L_Key_Chains

You will save your workbook as:

Lastname_Firstname_4L_Key_Chains

From your student files, open the file e04L_Key_Chains, and then save it in your chapter folder as **Lastname_Firstname_4L_Key_Chains** So that order takers do not have to type the Style Code, Description, and Unit Price in the Order Form worksheet, use the information on the Product Information sheet to create a validation list for the Item and then insert a VLOOKUP function in the Description and Unit Price columns. Then create an order for two of the Plush Animal Keychains (K-S) and two of the Classic Keychains (M-TF). Delete unused rows, create appropriate totals, apply financial formatting, and then save and submit it as directed.

End **You have completed Project 4L**

Apply a combination of the **4A** and **4B** skills.

GO! Think | Project 4M Delivery Van Purchase

Project Files

For Project 4M, you will need the following file:

New blank Excel document

You will save your document as:

Lastname_Firstname_4M_Van_Purchase

Etienne Alta, Chief Financial Officer for Rubanne Specialties, is exploring financing options for the purchase of four new delivery vans for the company, the cost of which totals $150,000. Using a format similar to the one you used in this chapter, create a worksheet that uses the PMT function to calculate the monthly payment for a loan of $150,000 for 36 months at a rate of 5.25%. Then, create a data table for varying interest rates from 7% to 3.5% in increments of 0.5% and for six periods—from 24 months to 60 months in 6-month increments. Use the Period as the row input and the interest rate as the column input. Apply the Note style to the two closest results to $3,500. Format the worksheet so that it is professional and easy to read and understand. Insert a footer with the file name and add appropriate document properties. Save the file as **Lastname_Firstname_4M_Van_Purchase**

End **You have completed Project 4M**

Outcomes-Based Assessments

Apply a combination of the **4A** and **4B** skills.

You and GO! | Project 4N Vehicle Loan

Project Files

For Project 4N, you will need the following file:

New blank Excel document

You will save your document as:

Lastname_Firstname_4N_Vehicle_Loan

In this chapter, you practiced using Excel to analyze the effect of interest rates and terms on loan payments. From a site such as Kelley Blue Book (www.kbb.com), research a vehicle that you would like to purchase and then begin a new blank workbook. Using a format similar to the one you practiced in this chapter, enter the price of the vehicle and the down payment if any. Subtract the down payment from the purchase price to determine the loan amount. Enter an interest rate of 5% and a loan term of 4 years. If you want to do so, use Goal Seek to determine options for a lower loan amount or a longer payment period, to match the monthly payment that you think you can afford. Insert a footer with the file name and center the worksheet horizontally on the page. Save your file as **Lastname_Firstname_4N_Vehicle_Loan** and submit it as directed.

End **You have completed Project 4N**

Managing Large Workbooks and Using Advanced Sorting and Filtering

OUTCOMES

At the end of this chapter you will be able to:

OBJECTIVES

Mastering these objectives will enable you to:

PROJECT 5A

Manage large workbooks, create attractive workbooks, and save workbooks to share with others.

PROJECT 5B

Analyze information in a database format using advanced sort, filter, subtotaling, and outlining.

Joy Brown/Shutterstock

In This Chapter

In this chapter, you will navigate within a large worksheet, insert a hyperlink in a worksheet, save a worksheet as a Web page, and save worksheets in other file formats to share with others. You will practice applying and modifying themes, styles, lines, and borders to enhance the format of your worksheets.

In this chapter, you will also use Excel's advanced table features and database capabilities to organize data in a useful manner. The skills in this chapter include advanced sorting, sorting on multiple columns, and custom filtering to compare subsets of data. You will also limit data to display records that meet one or more specific conditions, add subtotals, and outline data. These skills will help you visualize and analyze your data effectively.

The projects in this chapter relate to **Capital Cities Community College**, which provides high quality education and professional training to residents in the cities surrounding the nation's capital. Its five campuses serve over 50,000 students and offer more than 140 certificate programs and degrees. Over 2,100 faculty and staff make student success a top priority. CapCCC makes positive contributions to the community through cultural and athletic programs, health care, economic development activities, and partnerships with businesses and non-profit organizations.

Project 5A Large Worksheet for a Class Schedule

myitlab Project 5A Training

Project Activities

In Activities 5.01 through 5.13, you will assist Charles Krasnov, Program Chair for Computer Information Systems, in formatting and navigating a large worksheet that lists the class schedule for the Business Office Systems and Computer Information Systems departments at Capital Cities Community College. You will also save Excel data in other file formats. The worksheets in your completed workbooks will look similar to Figure 5.1.

Project Files

For Project 5A, you will need the following files:

e05A_Class_Schedule
e05A_Faculty_Contacts
e05A_Fall_Classes
e05A_Teaching_Requests

You will save your workbooks as:

Lastname_Firstname_5A_Class_Schedule (Excel Worksheet)
Lastname_Firstname_5A_Faculty_Contacts (Excel Worksheet)
Lastname_Firstname_5A_Fall_PDF (Adobe PDF Document)
Lastname_Firstname_5A_Fall_XPS (XPS Document)
Lastname_Firstname_5A_Schedule_CVS (Microsoft Office Excel Comma Separated Values File)
Lastname_Firstname_5A_Schedule_Webpage (HTML Document)

Project Results

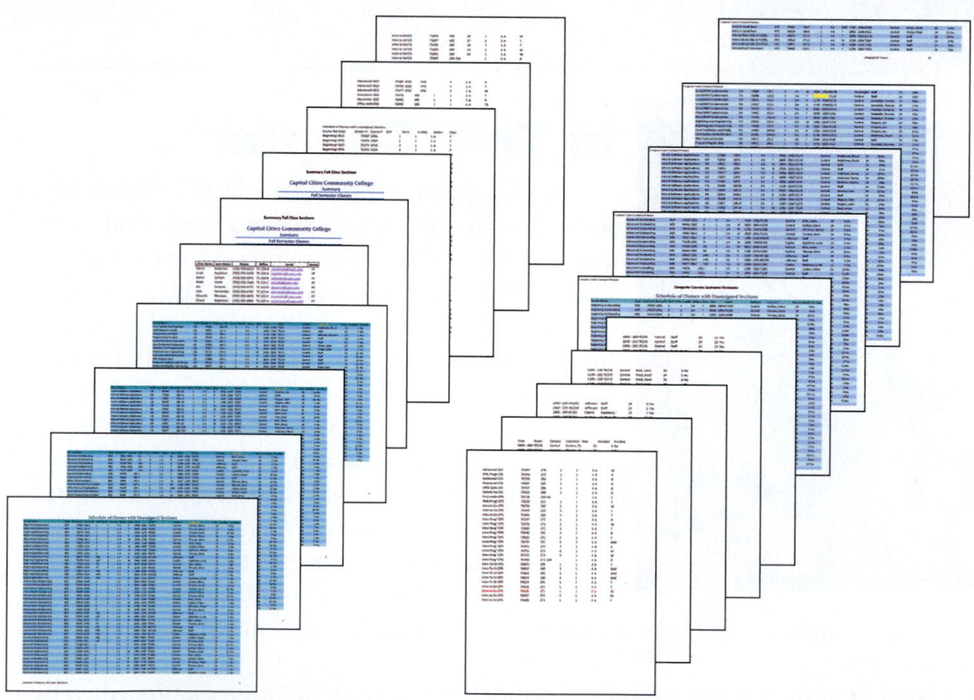

Figure 5.1
Project 5A Large Worksheet

Objective 1 | Navigate and Manage Large Worksheets

Because you cannot view all the columns and rows of a large worksheet on your screen at one time, Excel provides features that help you control the screen display and navigate the worksheet so you can locate information quickly. For example, you can hide columns and use the ***Freeze Panes*** command, which sets the column and row titles so that they remain on the screen while you scroll. The locked rows and columns become separate ***panes***—portions of a worksheet window bounded by and separated from other portions by vertical or horizontal lines.

You can also use the ***Find*** command to find and select specific text, formatting, or a type of information within the workbook quickly.

Activity 5.01 | Using the Go To Special Command

Use the ***Go To Special*** command to move to cells that have special characteristics, for example, to cells that are blank or to cells that contain constants, as opposed to formulas.

1 **Start** Excel. From your student files, open **e05A_Class_Schedule.** In your storage location, create a new folder named **Excel Chapter 5** and then **Save** the file as **Lastname_Firstname_5A_Class_Schedule**

This worksheet lists the computer courses that are available for the upcoming semester in three college departments.

> **Another Way**
>
> Press Ctrl + G, and then in the lower left corner of the dialog box, click the Special button.

2 On the **Home tab**, in the **Editing group**, click the **Find & Select** button, and then click **Go To Special.** Compare your screen with Figure 5.2.

In the Go to Special dialog box, you can click an option button to move to cells that contain the special options listed.

Figure 5.2

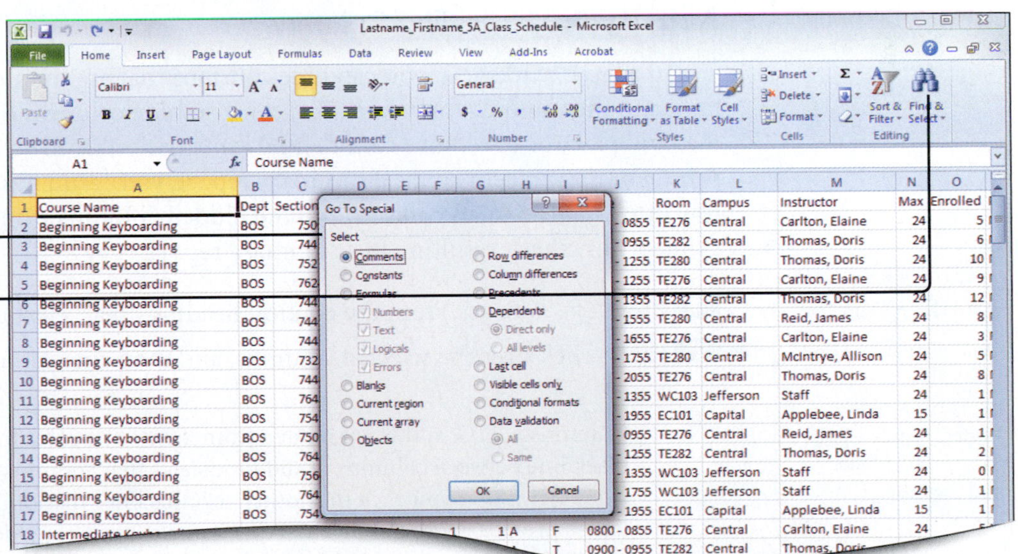

3 In the first column, click the **Blanks** option button, and then click **OK**.

All blank cells in the ***active area*** of the worksheet are located and selected, and the first blank cell—J124—is active. The active area is the area of the worksheet that contains data or has contained data—it does not include any empty cells that have not been used in this worksheet. Cell J124 is missing the time for a Linux/UNIX class held on Tuesday.

4 Point to cell **J124** and right-click. On the Mini toolbar, click the **Fill Color button arrow** and then under **Standard Colors**, click the fourth color—**Yellow**—to highlight the blank cells.

This missing information must be researched before a time can be entered, and the yellow fill color will help locate this cell later, when the correct time for the class is determined.

5 Scroll down and locate the other two cells identified as blank—**J148** and **J160**—and compare your screen with Figure 5.3.

When you initiated the Go To Special command for Blank cells, Excel located and selected *all* blank cells in the active area. Thus, the formatting you applied to the first blank cell, yellow fill, was applied to all the selected cells.

Figure 5.3

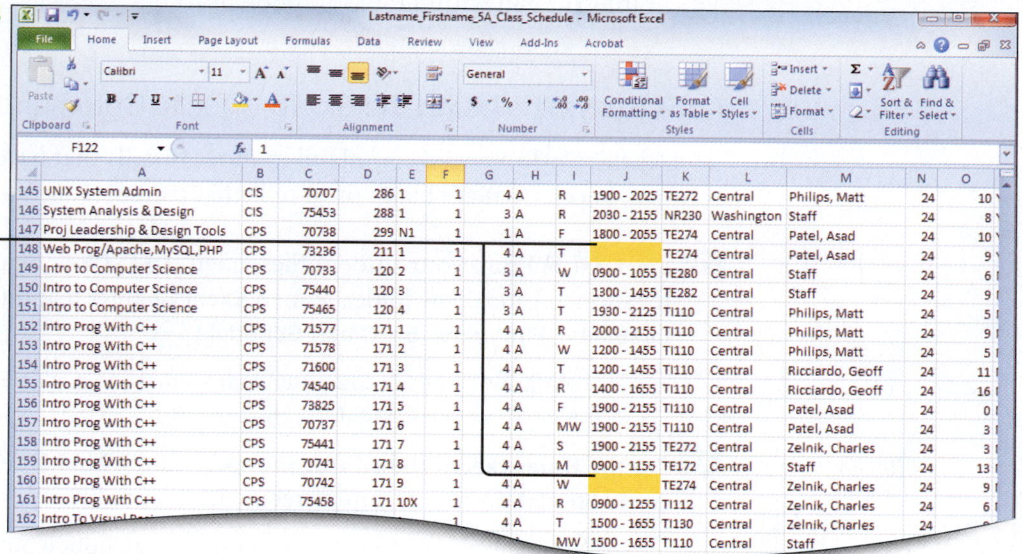

6 **Save** your workbook.

Activity 5.02 | Hiding Columns

In a large worksheet, you can hide columns that are not necessary for the immediate task, and then unhide them later. You can also hide columns or rows to control the data that will print or to remove confidential information from view—hidden data does not print. For example, to create a summary report, you could hide the columns between the row titles and the totals column, and the hidden columns would not display on the printed worksheet, resulting in a summary report.

> **Another Way**
>
> On the Home tab, in the Cells group, click the Format button. Under Visibility, point to Hide & Unhide, and then click Hide Columns.

1 Press Ctrl + Home. From the column heading area, select **columns E:H**.

2 Right-click over the selected columns, and then click **Hide**. Compare your screen with Figure 5.4.

Columns E, F, G, and H are hidden from view—the column headings skip from D to I. A black line between columns D and I indicates that columns from this location are hidden from view. After you click in another cell, this line will not be visible; however, the column letters provide a visual indication that some columns are hidden from view.

Figure 5.4

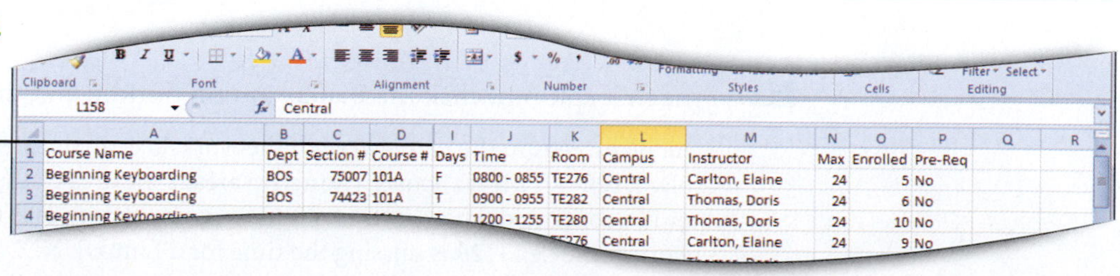

3 Press Ctrl + Home, and then notice that the line between the **column D heading** and the **column I heading** is slightly darker, indicating hidden columns. **Save** your workbook.

Activity 5.03 | Using the Go To Command

Use the ***Go To*** command to move to a specific cell or range of cells in a large worksheet.

1 On the **Home tab**, in the **Editing group**, click the **Find & Select** button, and then click **Go To**. In the **Go To** dialog box, with the insertion point blinking in the **Reference** box, type **m172** and then click **OK**.

2 With cell **M172** active, on the **Formulas tab**, in the **Functions Library group**, click the **More Functions** button, point to **Statistical**, and then click **COUNTIF**. As the **Range**, type **m2:m170** and as the **Criteria**, type **Staff** Click **OK**. Compare your screen with Figure 5.5.

Your result is 47, indicating that 47 courses still indicate *Staff* and need an instructor assigned.

Figure 5.5

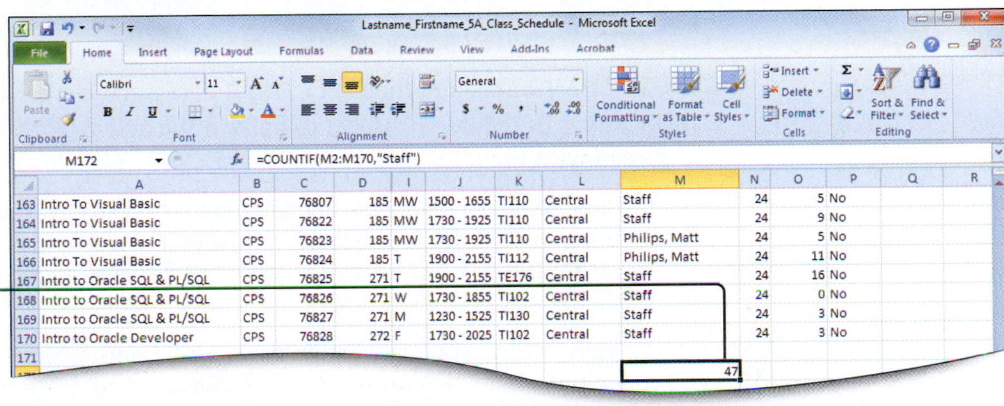

Your result is 47, indicating that 47 courses still indicate *Staff* and need an instructor assigned

3 In cell **K172**, type **Unassigned classes** and press Enter.

4 Press Ctrl + Home, and then **Save** your workbook.

Activity 5.04 | Arranging Multiple Workbooks and Splitting Worksheets

If you need to refer to information in one workbook while you have another workbook open, you can arrange the window to display sheets from more than one workbook—instead of jumping back and forth between the two workbooks from the taskbar. This is accomplished by using the ***Arrange All*** command, which tiles all open program windows on the screen. Additionally, you can view separate parts of the *same* worksheet on your screen by using the ***Split*** command, which splits the window into multiple resizable panes to view distant parts of your worksheet at once.

1 From **Backstage** view, display the **Open** dialog box, and then from your student files, open the file **e05A_Teaching_Requests**.

The e05A_Teaching_Requests file opens, and your 5A_Class_Schedule file is no longer visible on your screen. This worksheet contains a list of instructors who submitted requests for classes they would like to teach. You need not save this file; it is for reference only.

2 On the **View tab**, in the **Window group**, click the **Switch Windows** button, and then at the bottom of the list, click your **5A_Class_Schedule** file to make it the active worksheet.

3 In the **Window group**, click the **Arrange All** button. Compare your screen with Figure 5.6.

Here, in the Arrange Windows dialog box, you can control how two or more worksheets from multiple open workbooks are arranged on the screen.

Figure 5.6

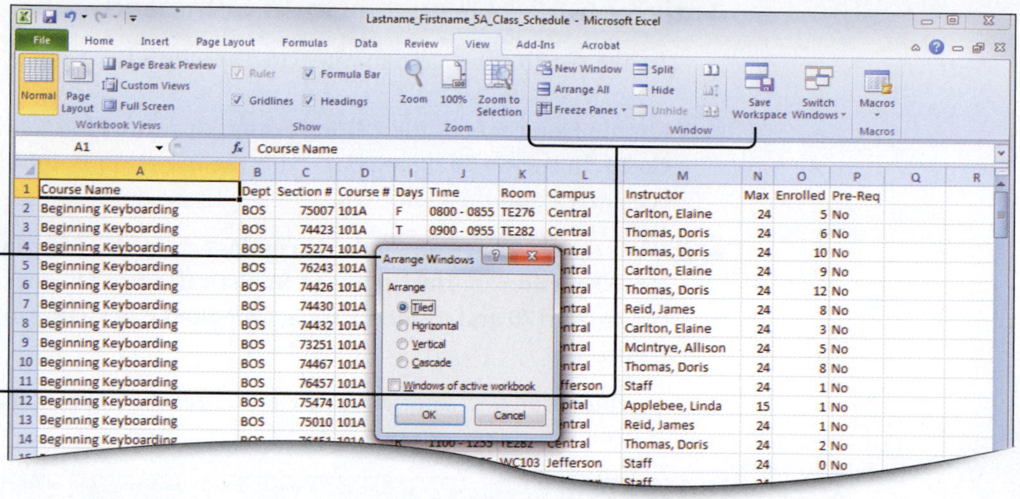

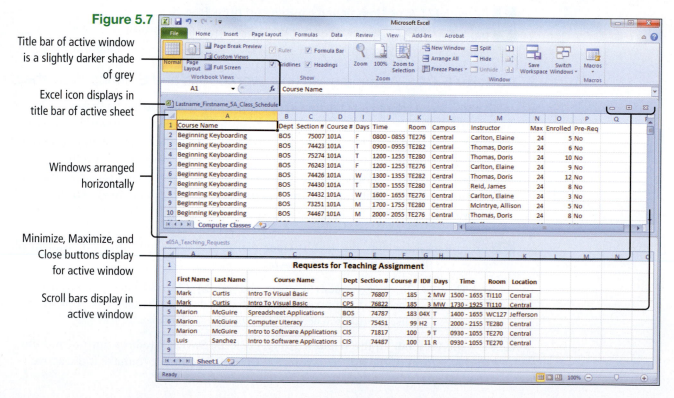

4 Click **Horizontal**, and then click **OK**. If necessary, click the title bar of your **5A_Class_Schedule** worksheet to make it the active worksheet. Compare your screen with Figure 5.7.

The screen is split horizontally, and the e05A_Teaching_Requests worksheet displays below your 5A_Class_Schedule worksheet. The active window displays scroll bars, its title bar displays in a slightly darker shade, and the green Excel icon displays to the left of your 5A_Class_Schedule worksheet title.

Additionally, the active window displays a Minimize, Maximize, and Close button. When multiple worksheets are open on the screen, only one is active at a time. To activate a worksheet, click anywhere on the worksheet or click the worksheet's title bar.

Figure 5.7

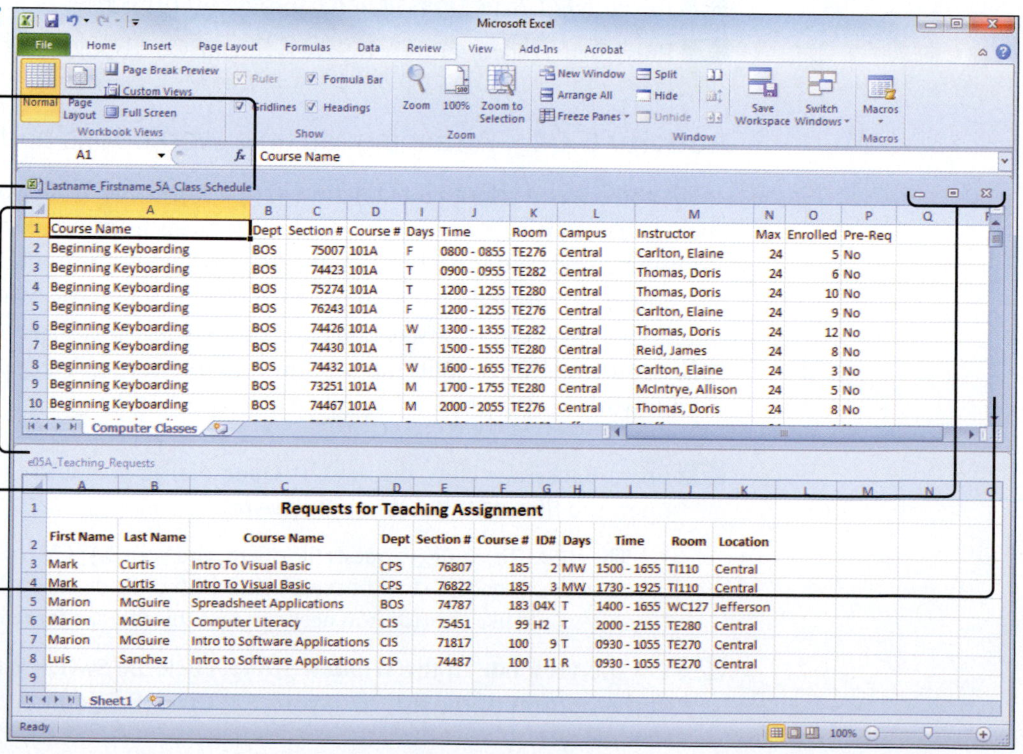

5 Press Ctrl + End to move to cell **P172**, which is now the end of the active area of the worksheet.

6 Click cell **A172**. In the **Window group**, click **Split** to split this upper window horizontally at row 172. Compare your screen with Figure 5.8.

A light blue horizontal bar displays at the top of row 172, and two sets of vertical scroll bars display in the 5A_Class_Schedule worksheet—one in each of the two worksheet parts displayed in this window.

Figure 5.8

5A_Class_Schedule worksheet split into two panes

e05A_Teaching_Requests worksheet displays in lower window

Vertical scroll bars display in both panes of active worksheet

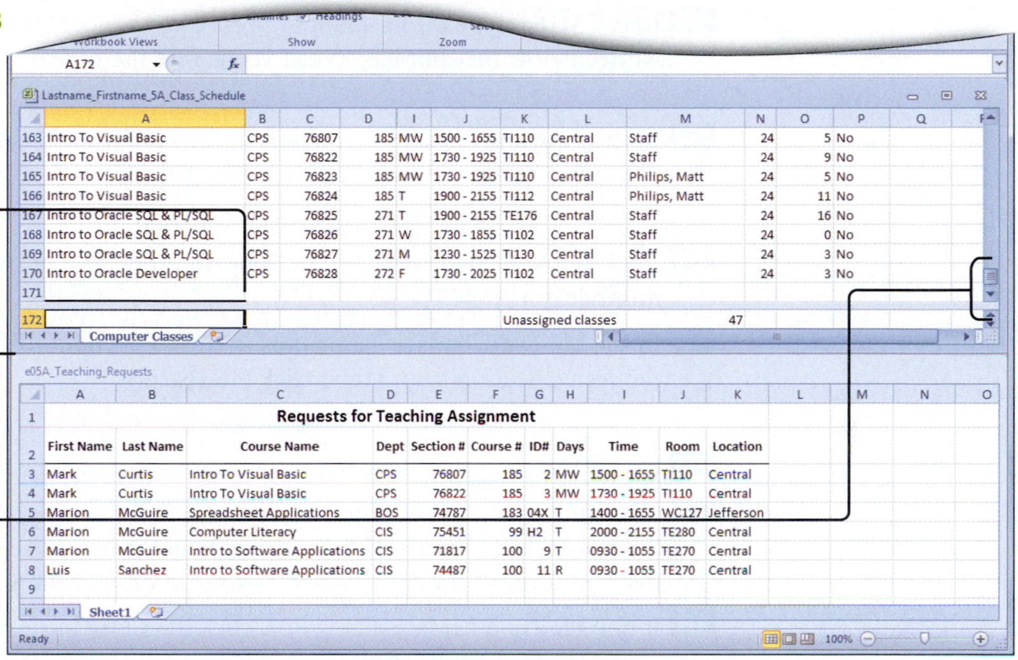

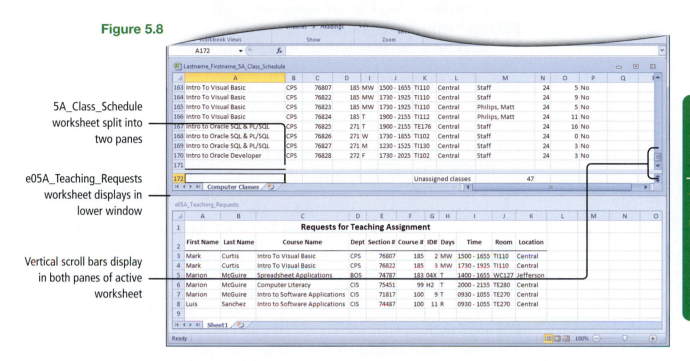

7 Above the **split bar**, click in any cell in **column C**. Press Ctrl + F to display the **Find tab** of the **Find and Replace** dialog box.

Column C lists the Section # for each class. This is a unique number that identifies each class.

8 Drag the title bar of the dialog box into the upper right area of your screen. Then, in the lower half of your screen, look at the first request in the **e05A_Teaching_Requests** worksheet, which is from *Mark Curtis* to teach *Intro to Visual Basic Section # 76807.* In the **Find what** box, type **76807** so that you can locate the course in the **5A_Class_Schedule** worksheet.

9 Click **Find Next**, be sure that you can see the **Name Box**, and then compare your screen with Figure 5.9.

Section # 76807 is located and selected in cell C163 of the Class Schedule worksheet.

Figure 5.9

Find and Replace dialog box

Name Box visible, indicates cell C163 found

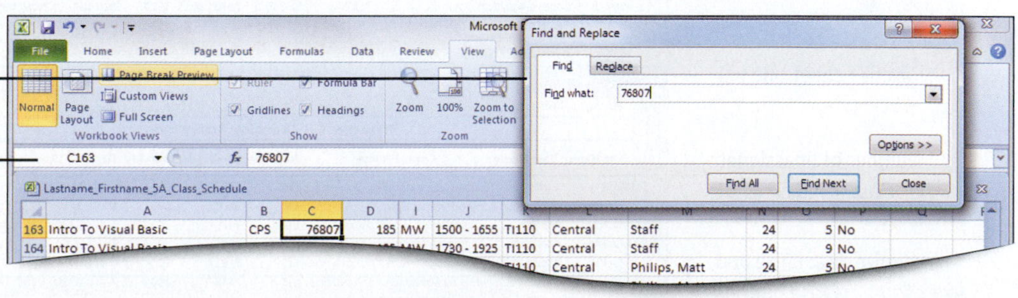

10 In your **5A_Class_Schedule** worksheet, click in cell **M163**, type **Curtis, Mark** to delete *Staff* and assign the class to Mr. Curtis. Press Enter.

The class is assigned to Mr. Curtis, and the number of unassigned classes, which you can view below the split bar, goes down by one, to 46. Use the Split command when you need to see two distant parts of the same worksheet simultaneously.

11 In the **e05A_Teaching_Requests** worksheet, look at **row 4** and notice that the next request, also from Mr. Curtis, is to teach *Section # 76822*.

This class is listed in the next row of your 5A_Class_Schedule worksheet—row 164.

12 In cell **M164**, type **Curtis, Mark** or press Enter to accept the AutoComplete suggestion. Notice below the split bar, in cell **M172**, that the number of unassigned classes goes down to *45*.

13 In the **Find and Replace** dialog box, in the **Find what** box, type **74787** which is the next requested Section #, and then click **Find Next**.

Section # 74787 in cell C66 is selected. Marion McGuire has requested to teach this class.

14 Click cell **M66**, type **McGuire, Marion** and press Enter; notice that the unassigned number is now *44*.

15 In the **Find and Replace** dialog box, in the **Find what** box, type **75451** which is the next requested Section #, and then click **Find Next**.

Section # 75451 in cell C78 is selected. Marion McGuire has requested to teach this class also.

16 In cell **M78**, type **McGuire, Marion** and press Enter; *43* classes remain unassigned.

17 Continue to use the **Find and Replace** dialog box to locate the remaining two **Section #s** listed in the **e05A_Teaching_Requests** worksheet, and enter the appropriate instructor name for each class in **column M** of your **5A_Class_Schedule** worksheet.

18 In the **Find and Replace** dialog box, click the **Close** button. In cell **M172**, notice that *41* classes remain unassigned.

19 Click any cell in the **e05A_Teaching_Requests** worksheet to make it the active sheet, and then on this worksheet's title bar, at the far right end, notice that a **Minimize** button, **Maximize** button, and **Close** button display. Compare your screen with Figure 5.10.

Figure 5.10

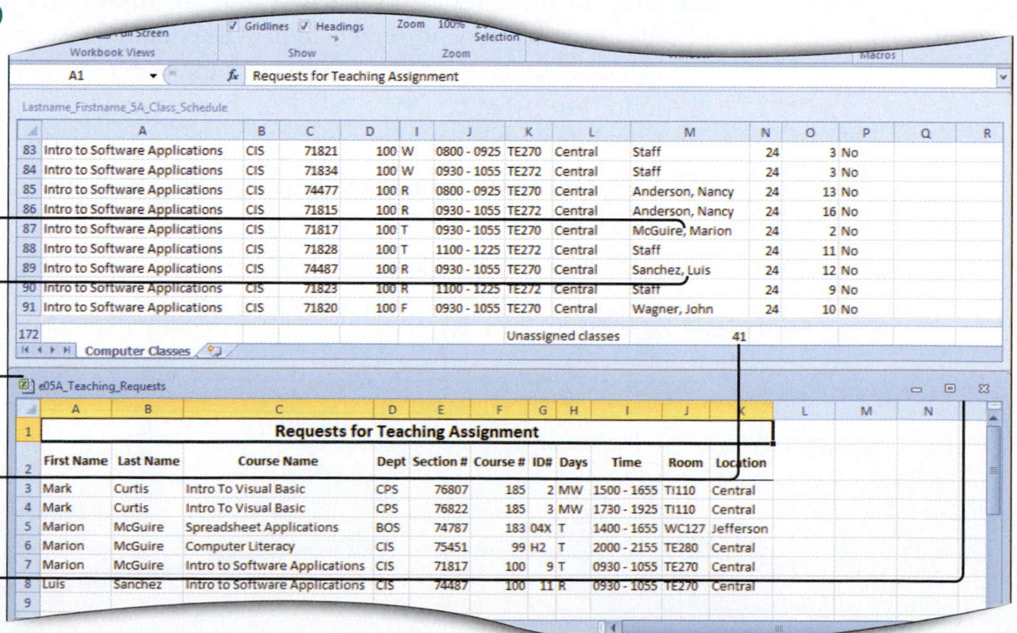

20 On the title bar, click the **Close** button [⊠] to close this workbook. Then, on the title bar of your **5A_Class_Schedule** worksheet, click the **Maximize** button [▣] to restore the size of the worksheet to its full size.

21 On the **View tab**, in the **Window group**, click **Split** to remove the split.

22 Press Ctrl + Home. From the **column heading area**, select **columns D:I**—recall that columns E:H are still hidden. Right-click over the selected area, and then click **Unhide**.

To redisplay hidden columns, first select the columns on either side of the hidden columns—columns D and I in this instance.

23 Press Ctrl + Home, and then **Save** [💾] your workbook.

Objective 2 | Enhance Worksheets with Themes and Styles

Worksheets used to be uninteresting grids of columns and rows viewed primarily on paper by accountants and managers. Now individuals may commonly use worksheets to communicate information both within an organization and to the public. A worksheet might be seen by individuals in an e-mail, in a PowerPoint presentation, or in public blogs and publications. Thus, you will want to use some creative elements when preparing your worksheets.

Recall that a ***theme*** is a predesigned set of colors, fonts, lines, and fill effects that look good together and that can be applied to your entire Office 2010 file or to specific items. A theme combines two sets of fonts—one for text and one for headings. In the default Office theme, Cambria is the font for headings and Calibri is the font for body text.

In Excel, the applied theme has a set of complimentary ***cell styles***—a defined set of formatting characteristics, such as fonts, font sizes, number formats, cell borders, and cell shading. The applied theme also has a set of complimentary table styles for data that you format as a table.

You can create your own themes, cells styles, and table styles.

Activity 5.05 | Changing and Customizing a Workbook Theme

1 Point to the **row 1 heading** to display the [→] pointer, right-click, and then click **Insert** to insert a new blank row. In cell **A1**, type **Schedule of Classes with Unassigned Sections** and press Enter. On the **Home tab**, **Merge & Center** this title across the range **A1:P1**, and then apply the **Title** cell style.

2 On the **Page Layout tab**, in the **Themes group**, click the **Themes** button. Compare your screen with Figure 5.11.

The gallery of predesigned themes that come with Microsoft Office displays. Office—the default theme—is selected.

Figure 5.11

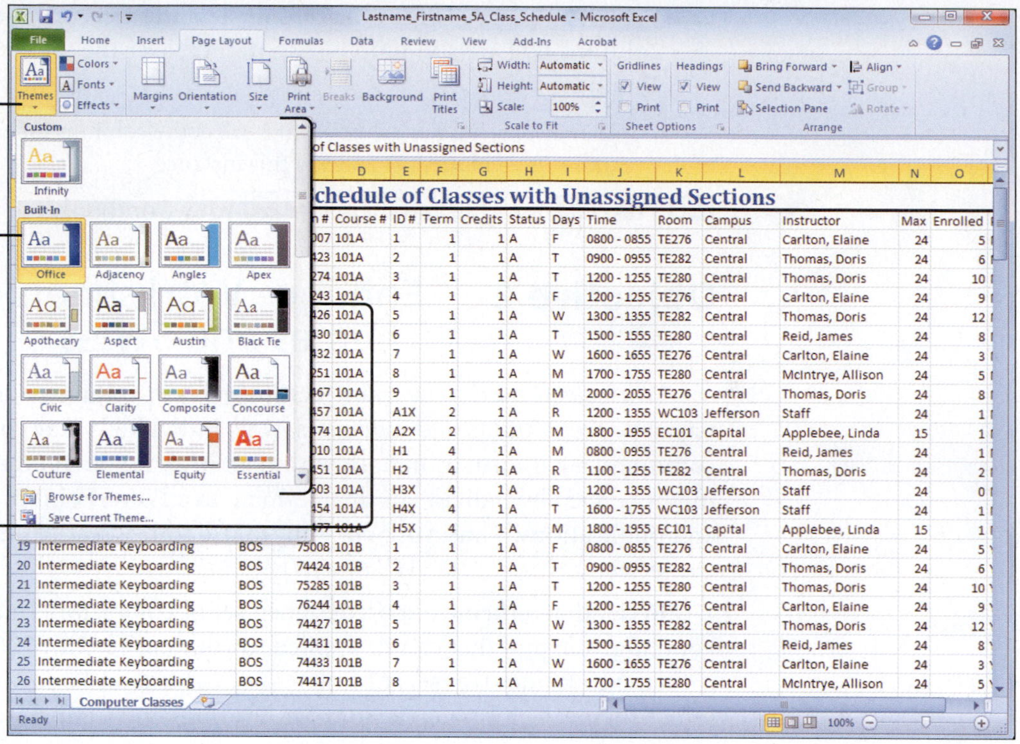

3 Point to several of the themes and notice how Live Preview displays the colors and fonts associated with each theme. Then, click the **Flow** theme.

4 In the **Themes group**, click the **Fonts** button.

The fonts associated with the Flow theme are Calibri and Constantia, but you can customize a theme by mixing the Colors, Fonts, and Effects from any of the supplied themes.

5 Scroll to the top and click the **Office** fonts. **Save** your workbook.

Activity 5.06 | Creating and Applying a Custom Table Style

Excel comes with many predefined table styles, also called quick styles, but if none of those meets your needs, you can also create and apply a custom table of your own design. Custom table styles that you create are stored only in the current workbook, so they are not available in other workbooks.

1 On the **Home tab**, in the **Styles group**, click the **Format as Table** button. At the bottom, click **New Table Style**.

2 In the **New Table Quick Style** dialog box, in the **Name** box, replace the existing text by typing **Class Schedule**

3 In the list under **Table Element**, click **First Row Stripe**, and then compare your screen with Figure 5.12.

Here you can select one or more elements of the table, and then customize the format for each element.

Figure 5.12

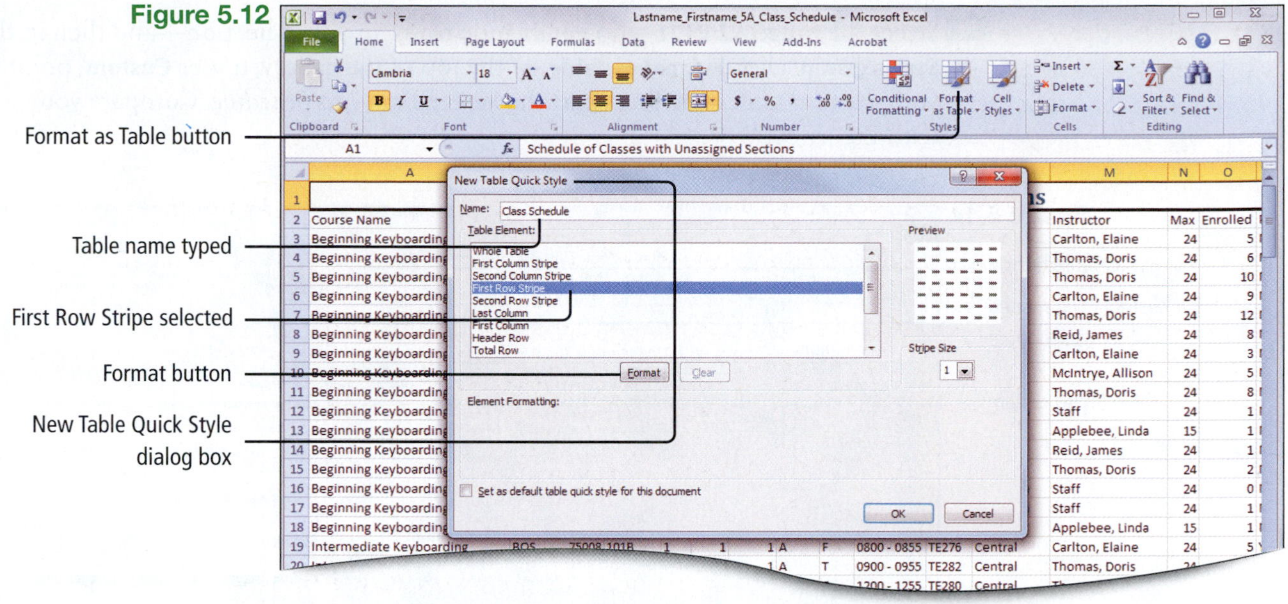

4 Below the list of table elements, click the **Format** button. In the **Format Cells** dialog box, click the **Fill tab**. In the fourth column of colors, click the second color, and notice that the **Sample** area previews the color you selected.

5 In the lower right corner, click **OK**. In the list of table elements, click **Second Row Stripe**, click the **Format** button, and then in the fourth column of colors, click the third color. Click **OK**. Notice the **Preview** that shows the two colors.

6 In the list of table elements, click **Header Row**, click the **Format** button, and then in the third column of colors, click the fourth color.

7 Click **OK**, notice the **Preview**, and then compare your screen with Figure 5.13.

Figure 5.13

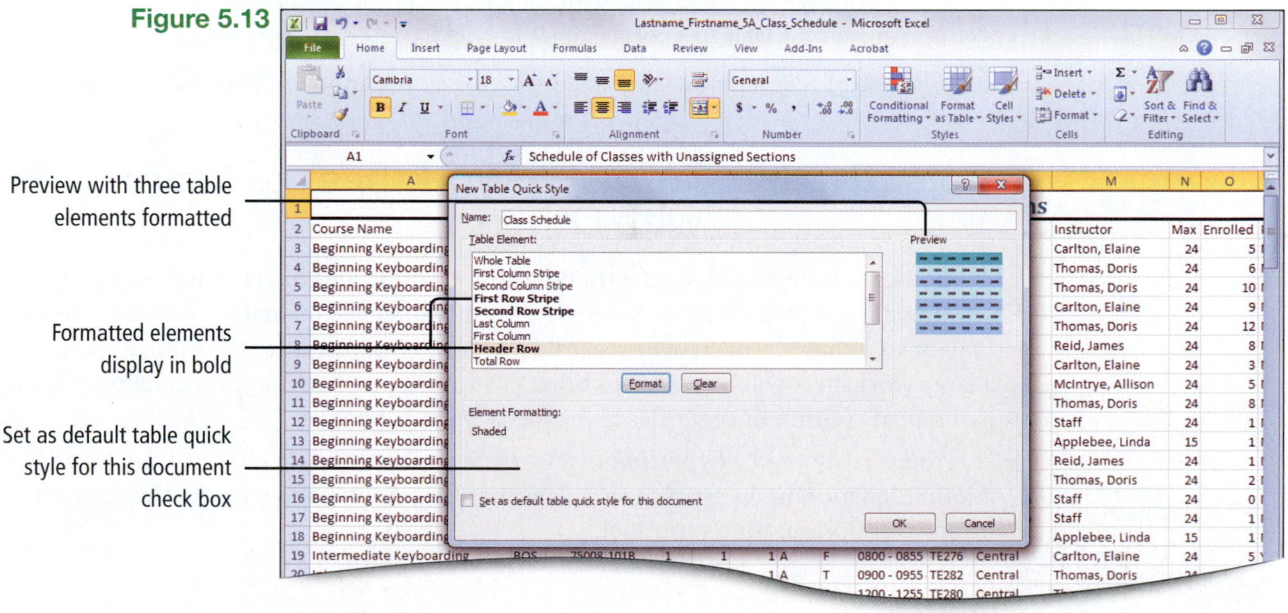

8 In the lower left corner of the dialog box, click to select the check box **Set as default table quick style for this document**. Click **OK**.

You must select this check box to make your table style available in the gallery of table styles.

Excel | Chapter 5

9 Select the range **A2:P171**—do *not* include row 1 in your selection—and then in the **Styles group**, click **Format as Table.** At the top of the gallery, under **Custom**, point to your custom table style to display the ScreenTip *Class Schedule*. Compare your screen with Figure 5.14.

Figure 5.14

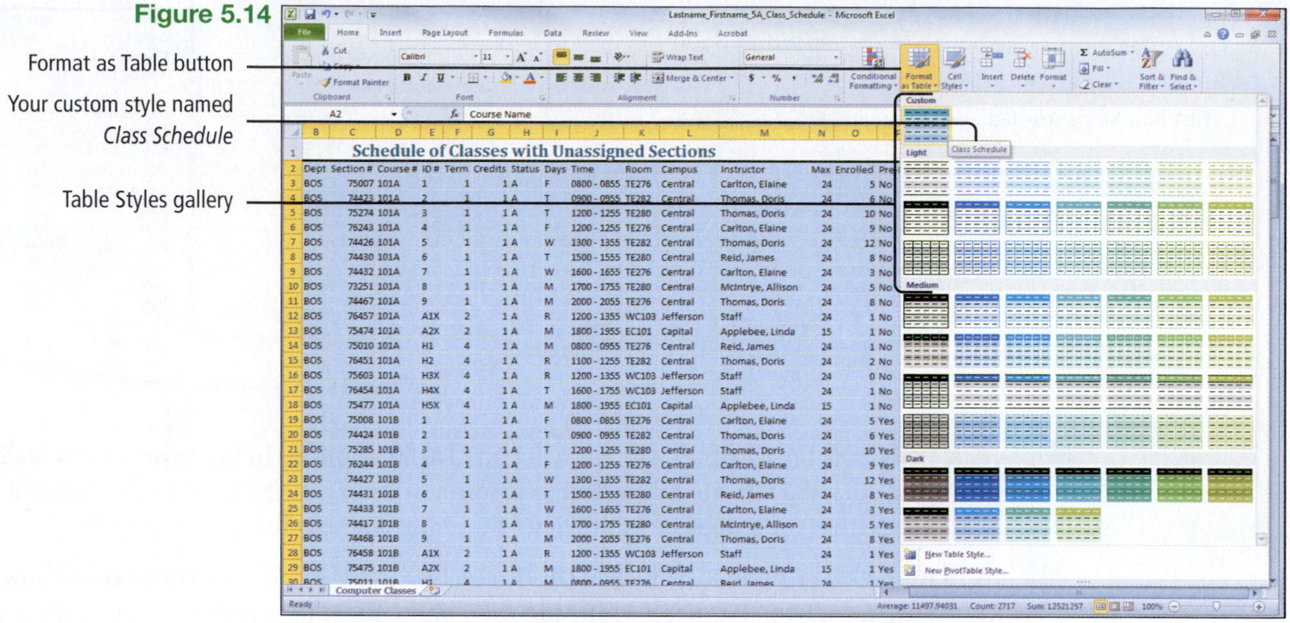

10 Click your **Class Schedule** table style, and then in the **Format As Table** dialog box, click **OK**. Then, because you do not need to filter the table, in the **Tools group**, click **Convert to Range**, and then click **Yes**.

If you do not want to work with your data in a table by filtering and sorting, you can convert the table to a normal range to keep the table style formatting that you applied.

11 Press Ctrl + Home to deselect and move to cell **A1**, and then **Save** your workbook.

Objective 3 | Format a Worksheet to Share with Others

You can share a worksheet with others by printing and distributing paper copies, sending it electronically as an Excel file or some other file format, or posting it to the Web or to a shared workspace. Regardless of how you distribute the information, a large worksheet will be easier for others to view if you insert appropriate page breaks and repeat column or row titles at the top of each page.

You can also add a ***hyperlink*** to a worksheet, which, when clicked, takes you to another location in the worksheet, to another file, or to a Web page on the Internet or on your organization's intranet.

Activity 5.07 | Previewing and Modifying Page Breaks

Before you print or electronically distribute a large worksheet, preview it to see where the pages will break across the columns and rows. You can move the page breaks to a column or row that groups the data logically, and you can change the orientation between portrait and landscape if you want to display more rows on the page (portrait) or more columns on the page (landscape). You can also apply ***scaling*** to the data to force the worksheet into a selected number of pages. Scaling reduces the horizontal and vertical size of the printed data by a percentage or by the number of pages that you specify.

> **Another Way**
> After selecting the columns, in the column heading area, point to any of the column borders and double-click.

1. From the column heading area, select **columns A:P**, in the **Cells group**, click the **Format** button, and then click **AutoFit Column Width**.
2. Click cell **A1**, and then press Ctrl + F2 to view the **Print Preview**. Notice that as currently formatted, the worksheet will print on 8 pages.
3. At the bottom of the **Print Preview**, click the **Next Page** button seven times to view the eight pages required to print this worksheet.

   As you view each page, notice that pages 5 through 8 display the Time, Room, Campus, Instructor, Max, Enrolled, and Pre-Req columns that relate to the first four pages of the printout. You can see that the printed worksheet will be easier to read if all the information related to a class is on the same page.

4. On the Ribbon, click the **View tab** to return to the worksheet, and then in the **Workbook Views group**, click **Page Break Preview**. If the Welcome to Page Break Preview dialog box displays, click OK to close it. Compare your screen with Figure 5.15.

   The Page Break Preview window displays blue dashed lines to show where the page breaks are in the current page layout for this worksheet.

Figure 5.15

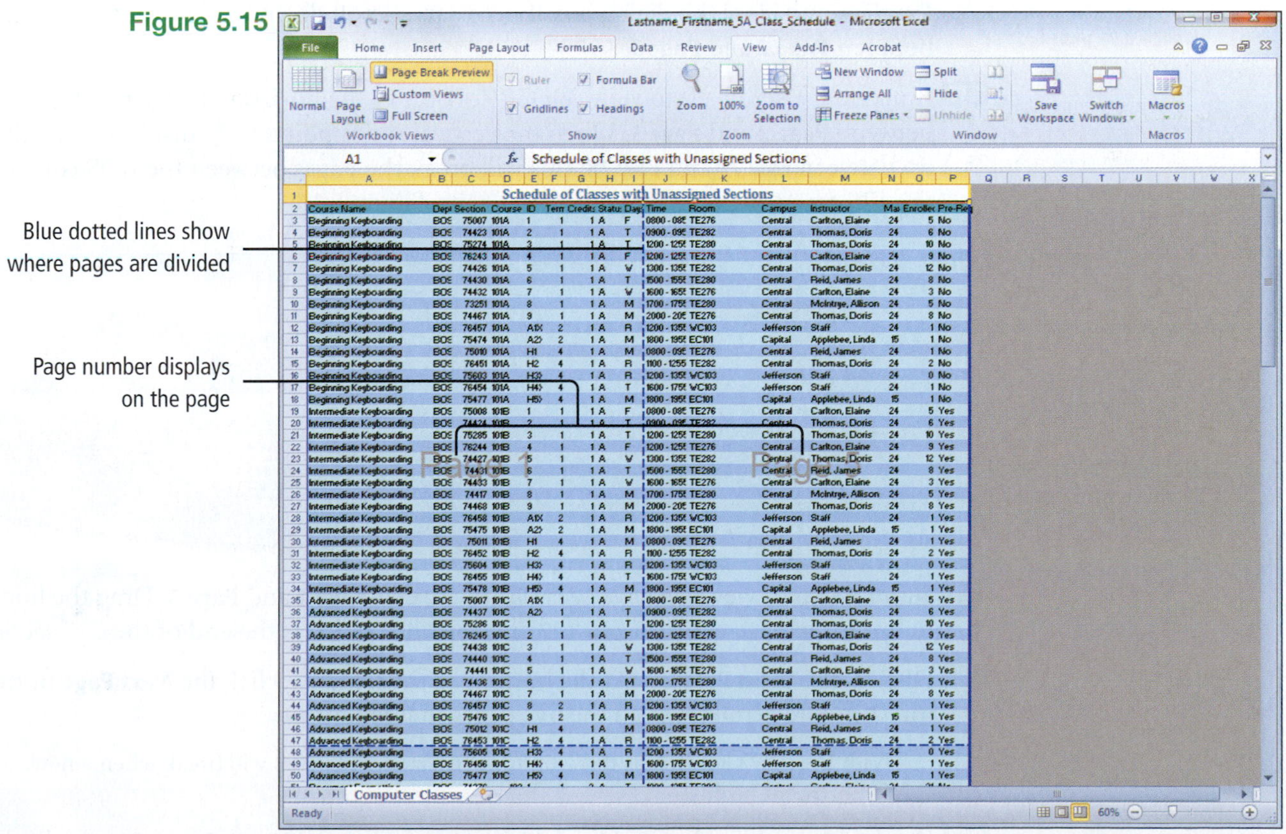

Note | Welcome to Page Break Preview

The Welcome to Page Break Preview dialog box may display with a message informing you that page breaks can be adjusted by clicking and dragging the breaks with your mouse. If this box displays, click OK to close it.

5 Scroll down to view the other pages and see where the page breaks are indicated. Then, in the **Workbook Views group**, click **Normal** to redisplay the worksheet in Normal view.

Dashed lines display at the page break locations on the worksheet.

Another Way

On the Page Layout tab, in the Page Setup group, click the Dialog Box Launcher button to display the Page Setup dialog box.

6 On the **Page Layout tab**, in the **Page Setup group**, set the **Orientation** to **Landscape**. Then, in the **Scale to Fit group**, click the **Width arrow**, and then click **1 page**. Click the **Height arrow** and click **4 pages**.

In the Scale to Fit group, there are two ways to override the default printout size. In the Scale box, you can specify a scaling factor from between 10 and 400 percent. Or, you can use the Width and Height arrows to fit the printout to a specified number of pages. To return to a full-size printout after scaling, in the Scale box, type 100 as the percentage.

7 From the **Insert tab**, insert a footer in the **left section** that includes the file name. Click in the **right section**, and then in the **Header & Footer Elements group**, click the **Page Number** button.

It is good practice to insert any headers or footers *before* making the final page break decisions on your worksheet.

8 Click any cell above the footer to exit the Footer area. Press Ctrl + F2 to display the Print Preview, and at the bottom, notice that the worksheet is now a total of four pages.

By applying the scaling, each complete row of data will fit on one page.

9 On the Ribbon, click the **View tab**, in the **Workbook Views group**, click **Page Break Preview**, and close the dialog box if necessary. Scroll down to view the page break between **Page 2** and **Page 3**.

10 If necessary, scroll left to view column A. Point to the horizontal page break line between **Page 2** and **Page 3**. When the vertical resize pointer displays, drag the line up between **row 77** and **row 78**; this will break the pages between the BOS courses and the CIS courses. Compare your screen with Figure 5.16.

Figure 5.16

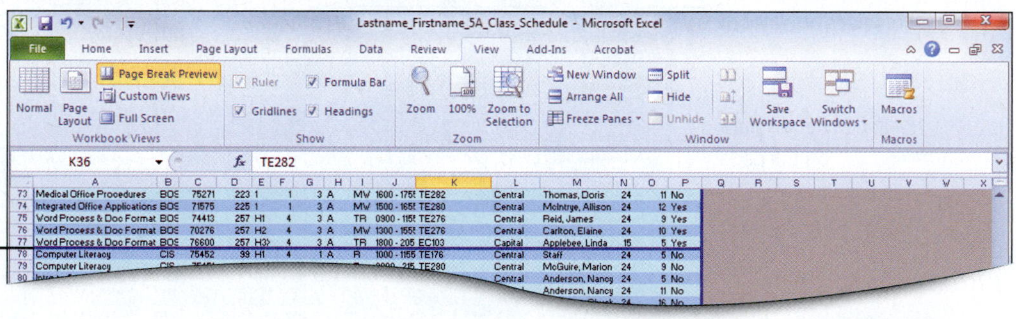

11 Scroll down to view the page break line between **Page 4** and **Page 5**. Drag the line up to break the page between **row 147** and **row 148**, which is the end of the CIS section.

12 Display the **Print Preview**. At the bottom of the window, click the **Next Page** button four times to scroll through the five pages that will print.

With the new page breaks that you have inserted, the pages will break when a new Department begins.

13 On the **View tab**, in the **Workbook Views group**, click the **Normal** button to redisplay the worksheet in Normal view. Press Ctrl + Home, and then click **Save**.

Activity 5.08 | Repeating Column or Row Titles

Recall that when your worksheet layout spans multiple pages, you will typically want to repeat the column titles on each page. If your worksheet is wider than one page, you will also want to repeat the row titles on each page.

1 Display the **Print Preview**, scroll through the pages, and notice that the column titles display only on the first page.

Repeating the column titles on each page will make it easier to understand and read the information on the pages.

2 On the **Page Layout tab**, in the **Page Setup group**, click the **Print Titles** button to display the **Sheet tab** of the **Page Setup** dialog box.

Here you can select rows to repeat at the top of each page or columns to repeat at the left of each page.

3 Under **Print titles**, click in the **Rows to repeat at top** box, and then from the **row heading area**, select **row 2**. Compare your screen with Figure 5.17.

A moving border surrounds row 2, and the mouse pointer displays as a black select row arrow. The absolute reference $2:$2 displays in the Rows to repeat at top box.

Figure 5.17

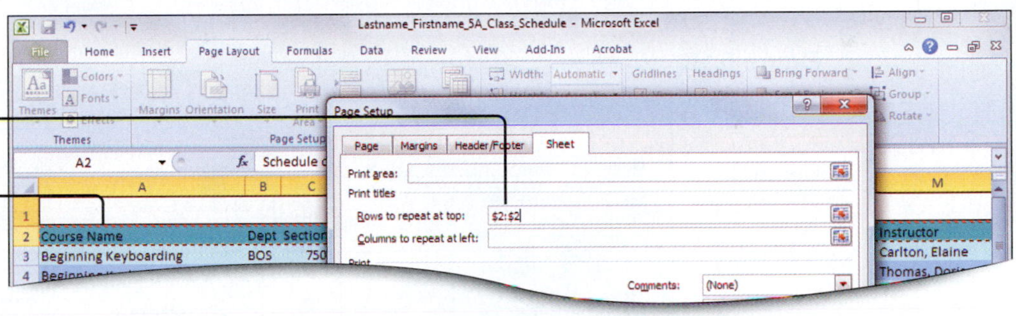

4 Click on **OK**. Display the **Print Preview**, scroll through the pages and notice that the column titles display at the top of each page. Verify that the page breaks are still located between each department. Display **Page 2**, and then compare your screen with Figure 5.18.

Figure 5.18

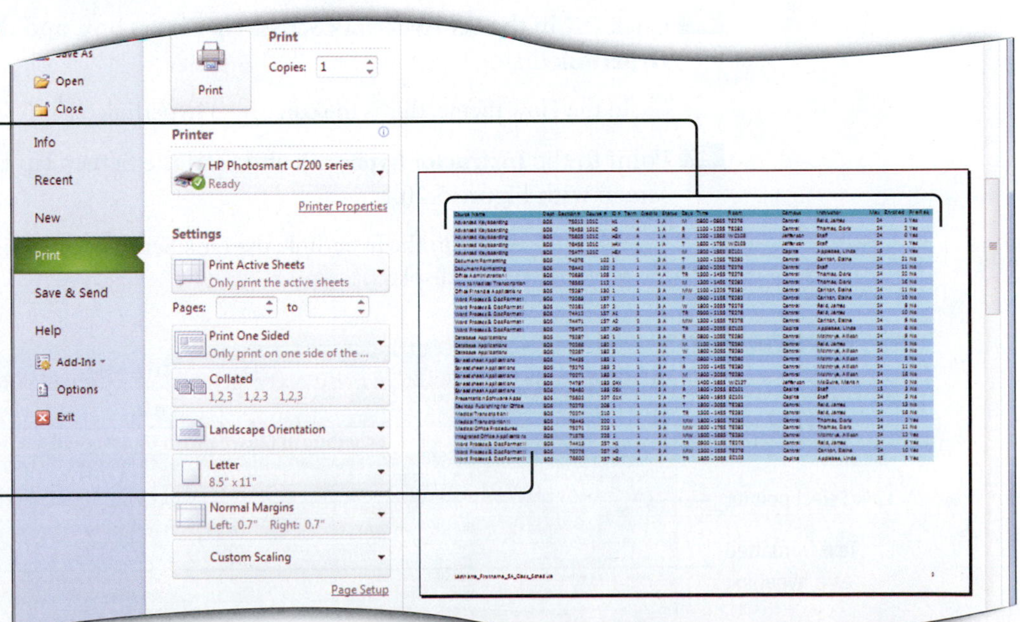

5 Click the **Home tab**, and then click **Save**.

Activity 5.09 | Inserting a Hyperlink in a Worksheet

Recall that a hyperlink is colored and underlined text that you can click to go to a file, a location in a file, a Web page on the Internet, or a Web page on your organization's intranet. Hyperlinks can be attached to text or to graphics. In this activity, you will add a hyperlink that will open a file that contains the contact information for instructors.

> **Another Way**
> Right-click the cell, and then click Hyperlink.

1 Click cell **M2**. On the **Insert tab**, in the **Links group**, click the **Hyperlink** button to display the **Insert Hyperlink** dialog box.

2 Under **Link to**, if necessary, click **Existing File or Web Page**. Click the **Look in arrow**, navigate to your student files, and then select the file **e05A_Faculty_Contacts**, which contains faculty contact information.

3 In the upper right corner of the **Insert Hyperlink** dialog box, click the **ScreenTip** button.

4 In the **Set Hyperlink ScreenTip** dialog box, in the **ScreenTip text** box, type **Click here for contact information** Compare your dialog box with Figure 5.19.

When you point to the hyperlink on the worksheet, this is the text of the ScreenTip that will display.

Figure 5.19

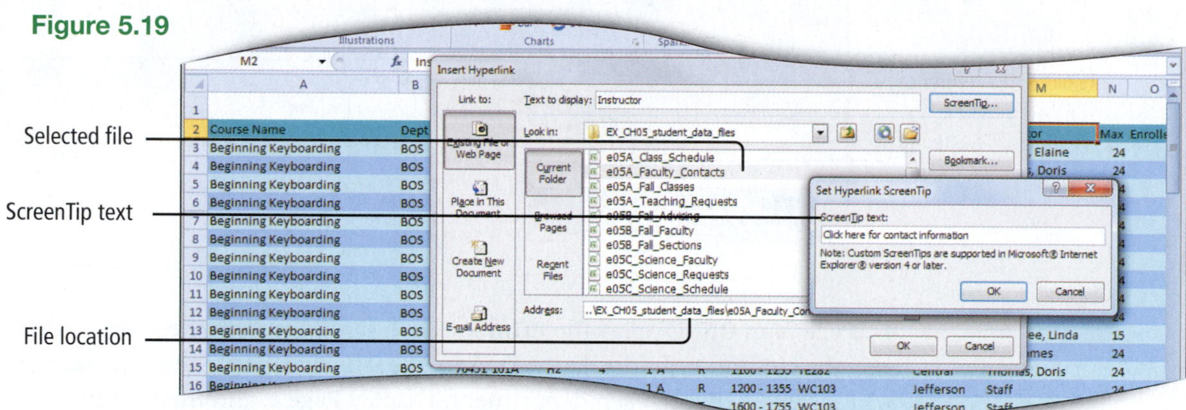

5 Click **OK** in the **Set Hyperlink ScreenTip** dialog box, and then click **OK** in the **Insert Hyperlink** dialog box.

In the Flow theme, this is the color for a hyperlink.

6 Point to the **Instructor hyperlink** and read the ScreenTip that displays. Compare your screen with Figure 5.20.

When you point to the hyperlink, the Link Select pointer displays and the ScreenTip text you entered displays.

Figure 5.20

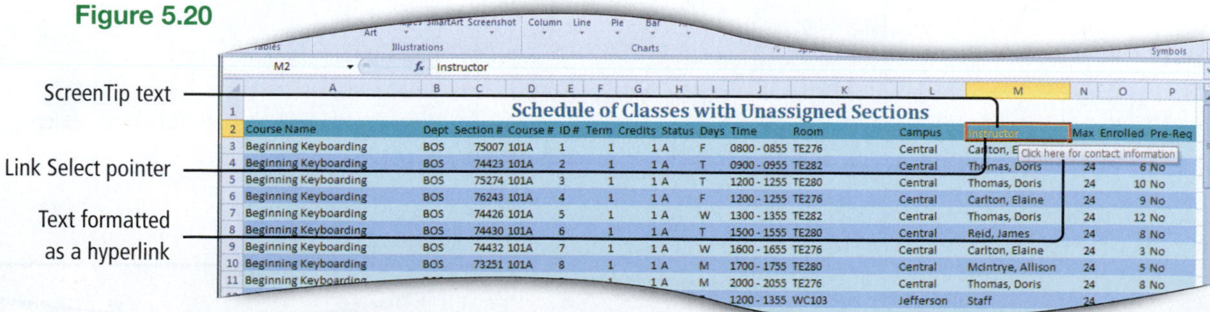

7 Click the **Instructor hyperlink**.

The e05A_Faculty_Contacts file opens and displays the contact information.

8 Click the **Close Window** button to close the **e05A_Faculty_Contacts** file and redisplay your **5A_Class_Schedule** worksheet.

9 On the **Page Layout tab**, in the **Themes group**, click the **Colors arrow**. Notice that the **Flow** color scheme is selected, and then at the bottom of the page, click **Create New Theme Colors**. At the bottom of the dialog box, locate the colors for **Hyperlink** and **Followed Hyperlink**. Compare your screen with Figure 5.21.

Each color scheme uses a set of colors for a hyperlink and for a hyperlink that has been clicked (followed) one time. Now that you have followed your inserted hyperlink one time, the text displays in the Followed Hyperlink color. Here you can also change the colors for any of the colors associated with a theme.

Figure 5.21

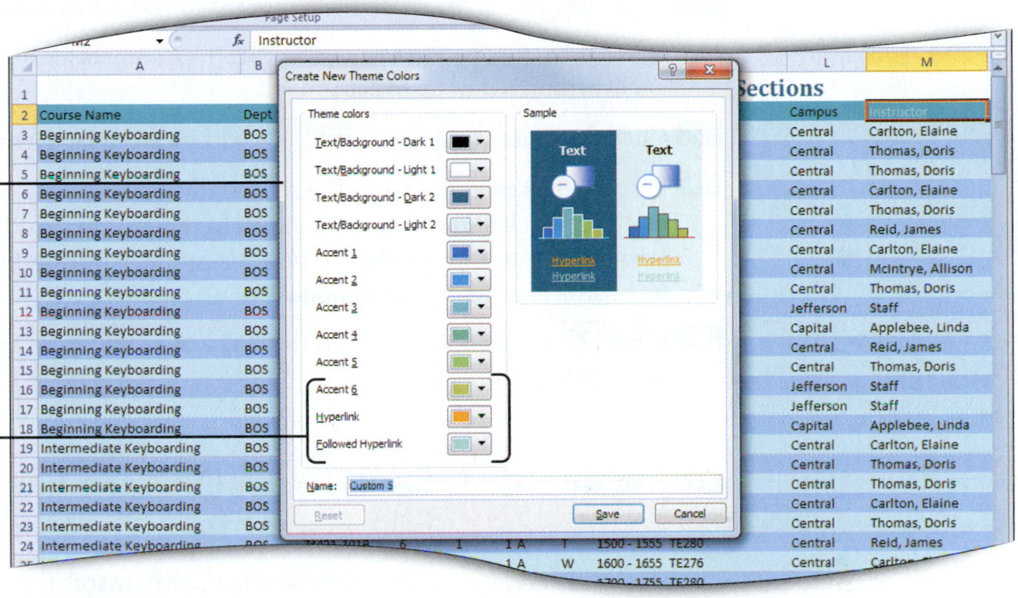

10 In the lower corner of the dialog box, click **Cancel**, and then **Save** your workbook.

Activity 5.10 | Modifying a Hyperlink

If the file to which the hyperlink refers is moved or renamed, or a Web page to which a hyperlink refers gets a new address, the hyperlink must be modified to reflect the change.

1 In cell **M2**, click the **Instructor hyperlink** to display the **e05A_Faculty_Contacts** worksheet.

2 From **Backstage** view, display the **Save As** dialog box, navigate to your **Excel Chapter 5** folder, name this file **Lastname_Firstname_5A_Faculty_Contacts**

3 Insert a footer in the **left section** with the file name, return to **Normal** view, click **Save**, and then click the **Close Window** button to close your **5A_Faculty_Contacts** file and redisplay your **5A_Class_Schedule** file.

4 Right-click cell **M2**—the Instructor hyperlink—and then on the shortcut menu, click **Edit Hyperlink**.

5 In the **Edit Hyperlink** dialog box, click the **Look in arrow**, navigate to your **Excel Chapter 5** folder, and then select your **Lastname_Firstname_5A_Faculty_Contacts** file, as shown in Figure 5.22.

Figure 5.22

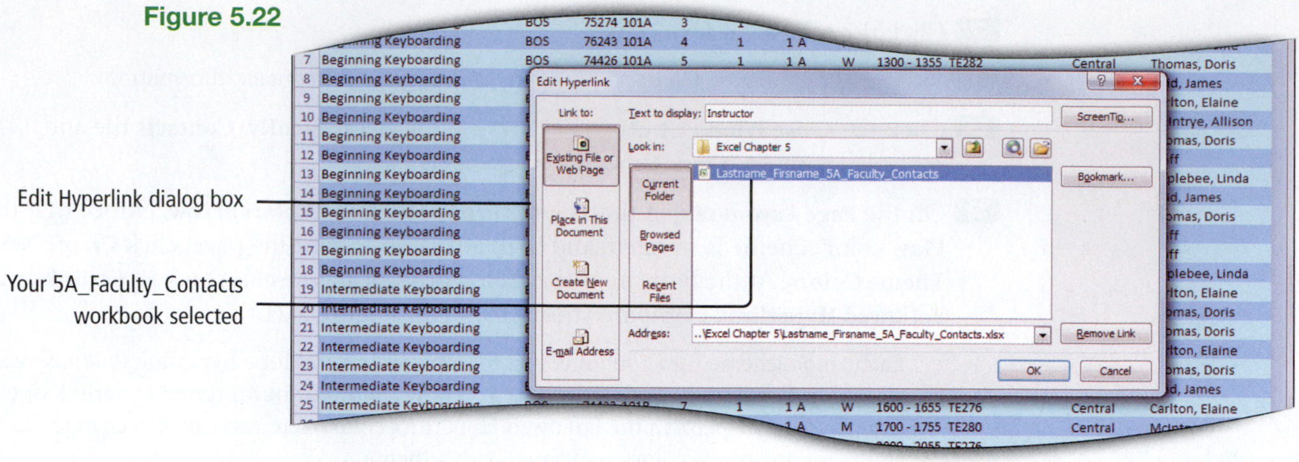

6 Click **OK**. In cell **M2**, click the hyperlinked text—**Instructor**.

Your **Lastname_Firstname_5A_Faculty_Contacts** file displays on your screen, and your hyperlink is now up to date.

7 Click the **Close Window** button [icon] to close **Lastname_Firstname_5A_Faculty_Contacts**.

8 Display **Backstage** view. On the right under the screen thumbnail, click **Properties**, and then click **Show Document Panel**. In the **Author** box, type your firstname and lastname, in the **Subject** box, type your course name and section number, and in the **Keywords** box, type **class schedule**

9 **Close** [icon] the **Document Properties**. Click **Save** [icon]; leave the **5A_Class_Schedule** workbook open.

Objective 4 | Save Excel Data in Other File Formats

By default, Excel 2010 files are saved in the Microsoft Excel Workbook file format with the ***.xlsx file name extension***, which is a set of characters that helps your Windows operating system understand what kind of information is in a file and what program should open it.

Using the Save As command, you can choose to save an Excel file in another file format from the Save as type list. Some frequently used file formats are: Excel 97-2003 Workbook, Excel Template, Single File Web Page, Web Page, Excel Macro-Enabled Workbook, Text (Tab Delimited), or CSV (Comma Delimited).

For the purpose of posting Excel data to a Web site or transferring data to other applications, you can save your Excel file in a variety of other file formats. For example, saving an Excel worksheet as a ***text file*** separates the cells of each row with tab characters. Saving an Excel worksheet as a ***CSV (comma separated values) file*** separates the cells of each row with commas. This format is commonly used to import data into a database program.

You can also save an Excel file in an electronic format that is easy to read for the viewer of the workbook. Such files are not easily modified and are considered to be an electronic printed version of the worksheet.

Recall that you can also add a hyperlink to a worksheet, which, when clicked, takes you to another location in the worksheet, to another file, or to a Web page on the Internet or on your organization's intranet.

Activity 5.11 | Viewing and Saving a Workbook as a Web Page

Before you save a worksheet as a Web page, it is a good idea to view it as a Web page to see how it will display. When saving a multiple-page workbook as a Web page, all of the worksheets are available and can be accessed. You can also save a single worksheet as a Web page. Excel changes the contents of the worksheet into ***HTML*** (***Hypertext Markup Language***), which is a language Web browsers can interpret, when you save a worksheet as a Web page. In this activity, you will save and publish a worksheet as a Web page.

1 Be sure your **Lastname_Firstname_5A_Class_Schedule** workbook is open and displayed on your screen. Display the **Save As** dialog box, navigate to your **Excel Chapter 5** folder, in the lower portion of the dialog box, click the **Save as type arrow**, and then click **Web Page**.

Your Excel files no longer display in the dialog box, because only files with the type Web Page are visible. The file type changes to Web Page and additional Web-based options display below.

2 In the lower portion of the dialog box, click the **Change Title** button.

The text that you type here will become the title when the file displays as a Web page.

3 In the **Enter Text** dialog box, in the **Page title** box, using your own name, type **Computer Courses Lastname Firstname** Compare your screen with Figure 5.23.

Figure 5.23

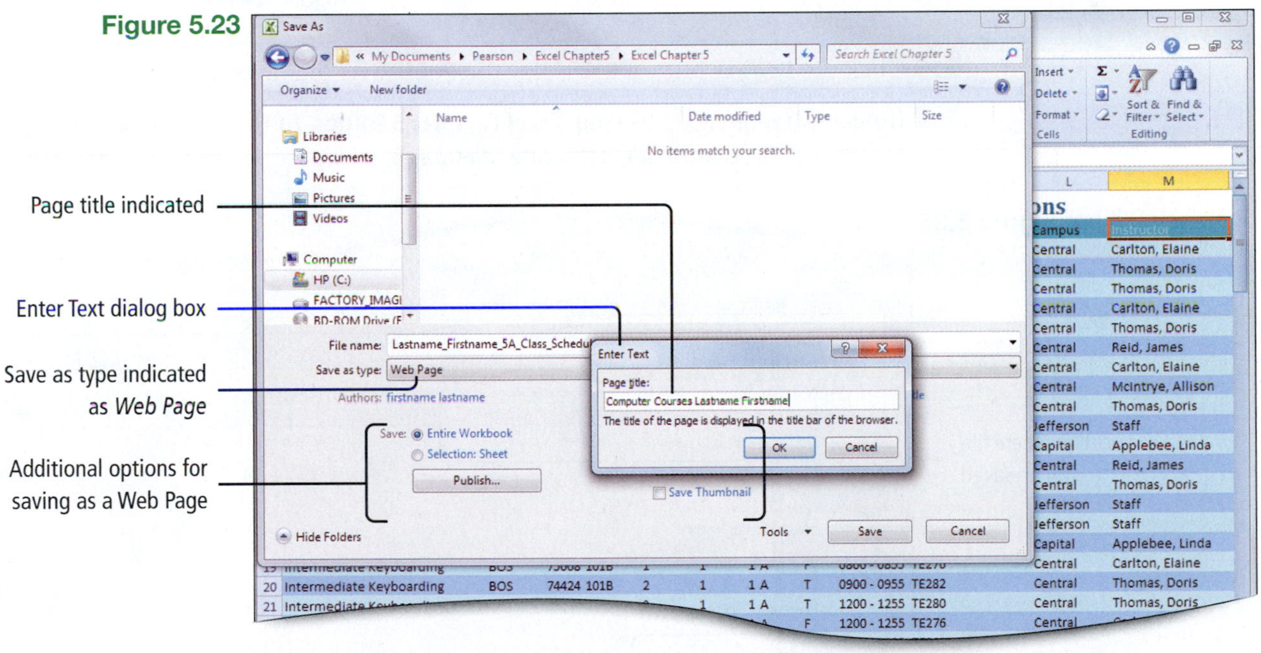

4 In the **Enter Text** dialog box, click **OK**, and notice that in the **Page title** box, your typed text displays.

5 In the **Save As** dialog box, click the **Publish** button.

6 In the **Publish as Web Page** dialog box, click the **Choose arrow**, and then click **Items on Computer Classes**—recall that the worksheet name is *Computer Classes*. In the lower left corner, if necessary, click to select (place a check mark in) the **Open published web page in browser** check box. Compare your screen with Figure 5.24.

Under Item to publish, you can choose which elements to include as part of the Web page. You can select the entire workbook, a specific worksheet in the workbook, a range of cells, or previously published items that you are modifying. The *Open published Web page in browser* selection ensures that the Internet browser software, for example Internet Explorer, will automatically start and display the Web page.

Figure 5.24

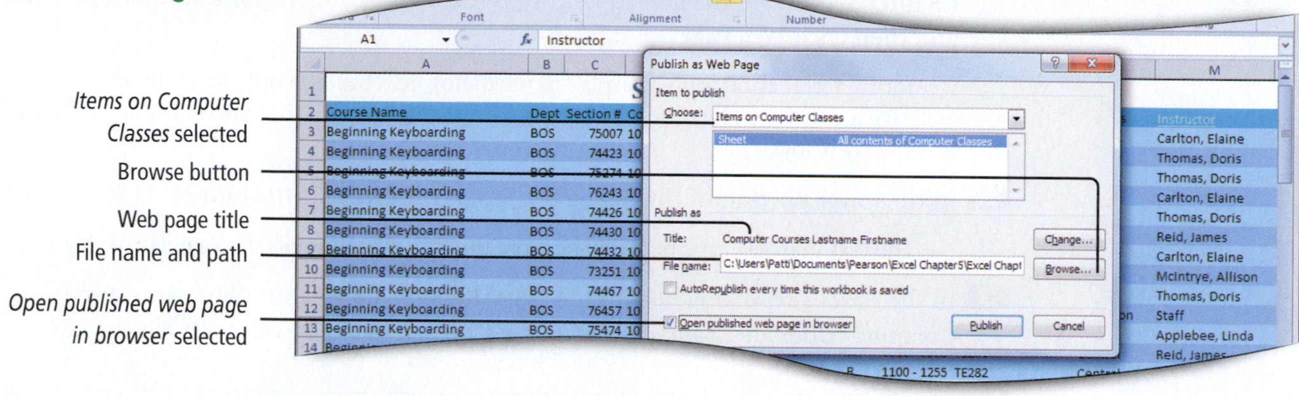

7 Click the **Browse** button to display the **Publish As** dialog box.

8 If necessary, navigate to your **Excel Chapter 5** folder. In the **File name** box, type **Lastname_Firstname_5A_Schedule_Webpage** Compare your screen with Figure 5.25.

Figure 5.25

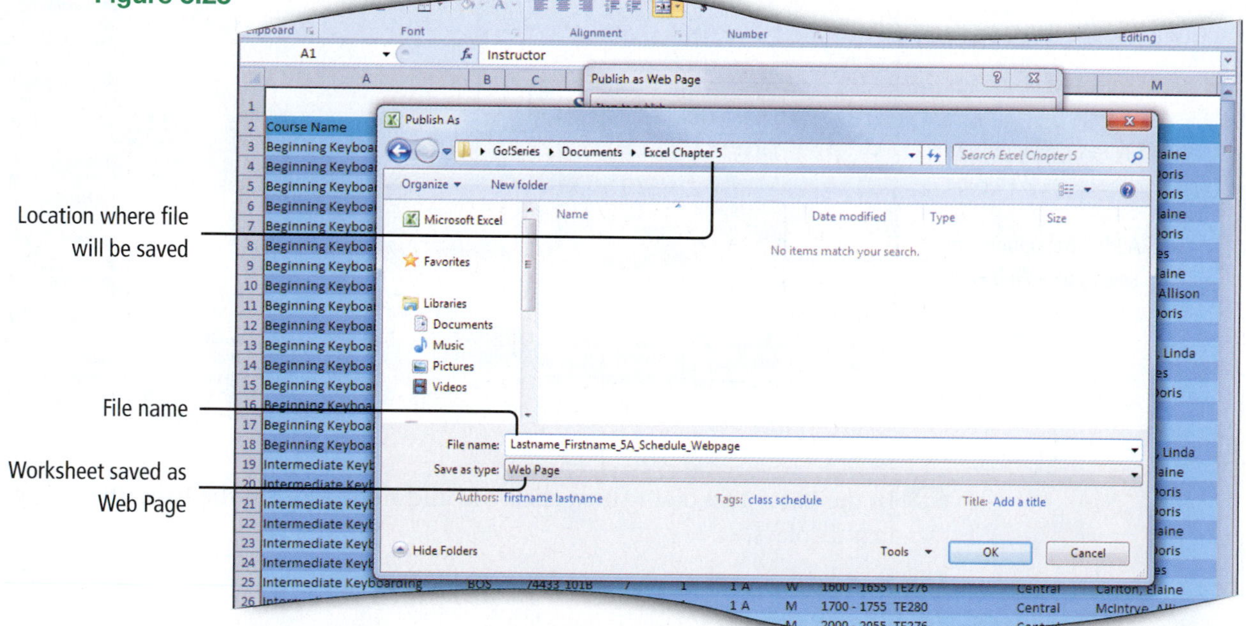

9 Click **OK**, and then on the displayed **Publish as Web Page** dialog box, click **Publish**. Compare your screen with Figure 5.26.

The Web Page is saved in your selected folder, and the Class Schedule file opens in your Internet browser. The browser title bar displays the text you typed in the Enter Text dialog box.

Figure 5.26

Page title

File address

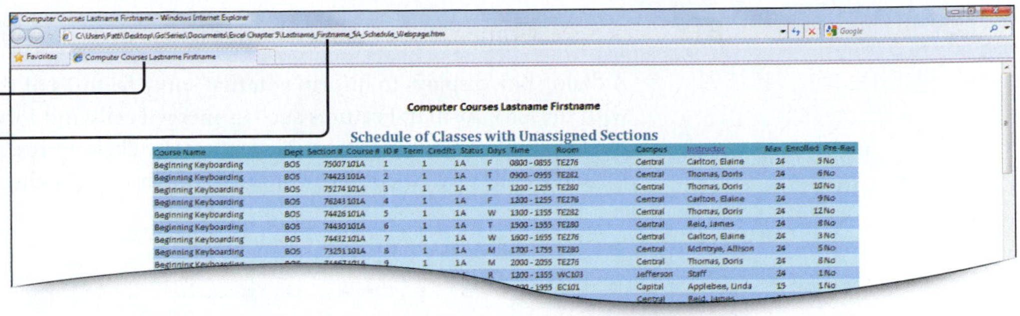

10 If you are instructed to print your Web page on paper, consult the instructions to print from your specific browser software.

Your printed results will vary depending on which browser software you are using. Do not be concerned about the printout; Web pages are intended for viewing, not printing.

11 On the browser title bar, click the **Close** button [Close button]. Leave your **5A_Class_Schedule** Excel workbook open for the next activity.

Activity 5.12 | Saving Excel Data in CSV File Format

You can save an Excel worksheet as a comma separated values (CSV) file, which saves the contents of the cells by placing commas between them and an end-of-paragraph mark at the end of each row. This type of file can be readily exchanged with various database programs, and is also referred to as a ***comma delimited file***.

1 Be sure your **Lastname_Firstname_5A_Class_Schedule** workbook is open and displayed on your screen. Display the **Save As** dialog box, click the **Save as type arrow**, and then click **CSV (Comma delimited)**. Be sure you are saving in your **Excel Chapter 5** folder. In the **File name** box, using your own name, type **Lastname_Firstname_5A_Schedule_CSV** Compare your dialog box with Figure 5.27.

Your Excel files no longer display, because only CSV files are displayed.

Figure 5.27

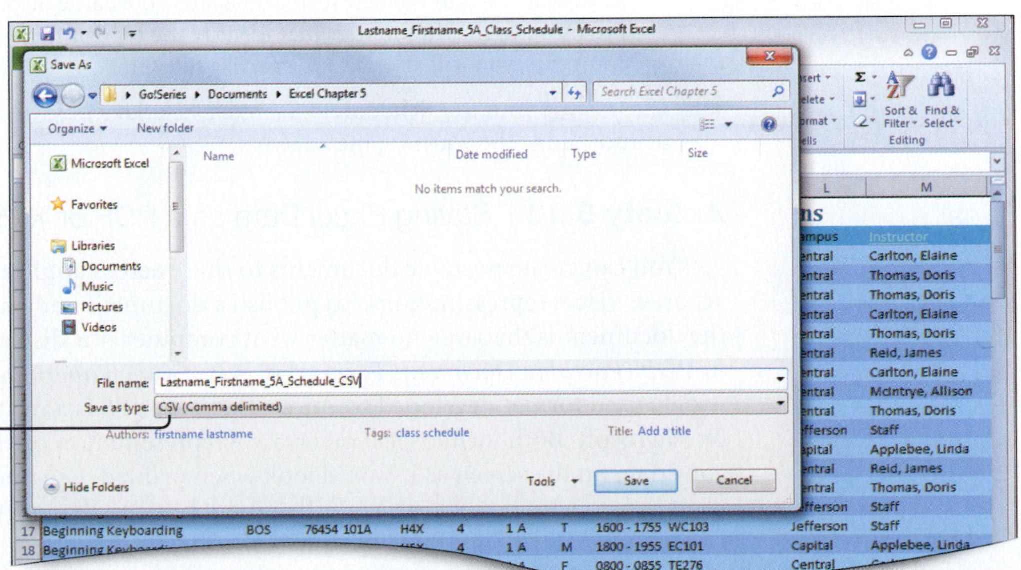

CSV file format selected

2 Click **Save**. Compare your screen with Figure 5.28.

A dialog box displays to inform you that some features of the file may not be compatible with the CSV format. Features such as merged cells and formatting are lost. You can save the file and leave out incompatible features by clicking Yes, preserve the file in an Excel format by clicking No, or see what might be lost by clicking Help.

Figure 5.28

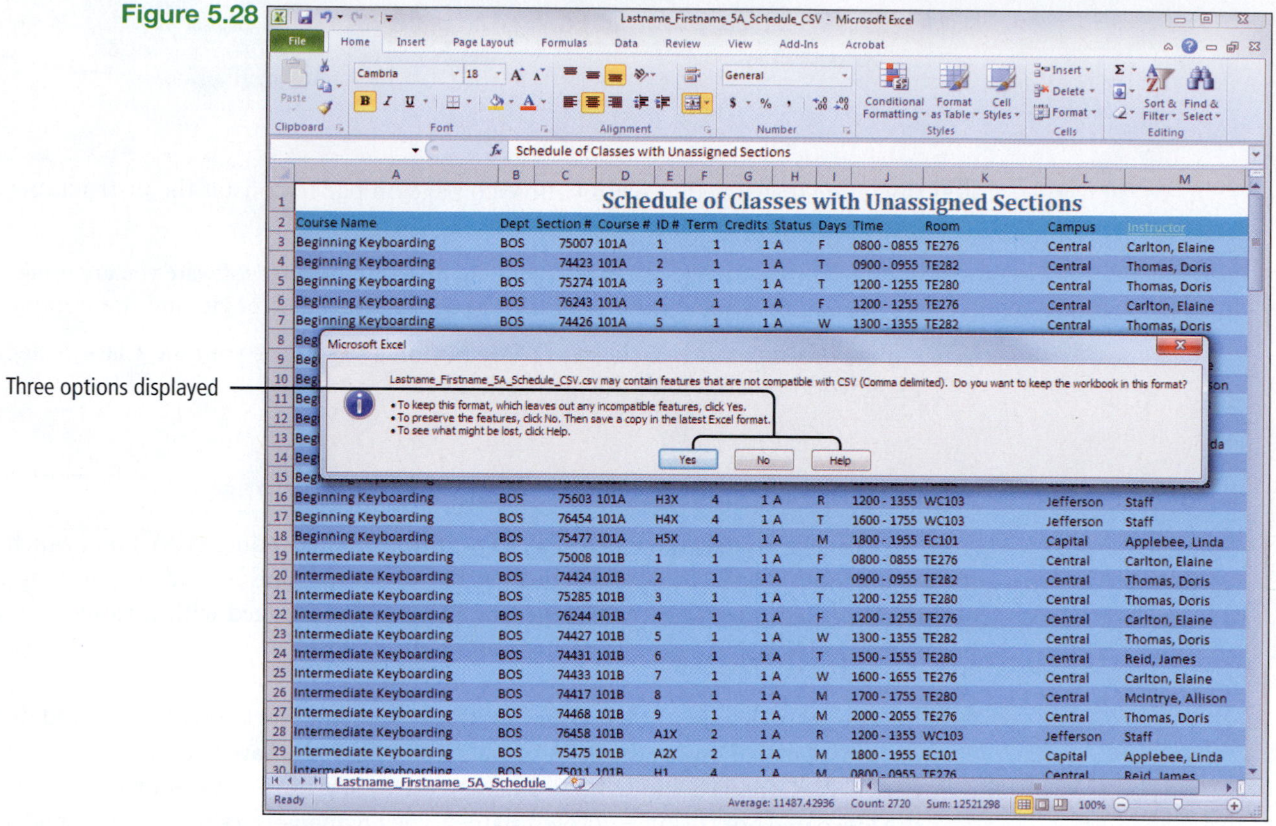

3 Click **Yes** to keep the CSV format.

The file is saved in the new format. The new file name displays in the title bar. If file extensions—the three letters that identify the type of files—are displayed on your computer, you will also see *.csv* after the file name.

4 **Close** [X] your **5A_Schedule_CSV** file. Click **Save** to save changes, and then click **Yes** to acknowledge the warning message.

Activity 5.13 | Saving Excel Data as a PDF or XPS File

You can create portable documents to share across applications and platforms with accurate visual representations. To publish a document and ensure that the appearance of the document is the same no matter what computer it is displayed on, save the document in ***PDF (Portable Document Format)*** or ***XPS (XML Paper Specification)*** format. PDF is a widely used format developed by Adobe Systems. XPS is a relatively new format developed by Microsoft. Both formats let you create a representation of *electronic paper* that displays your data on the screen as it would look when printed. Use one of these formats if you want someone to be able to view a document but not change it. In this activity, you will create PDF and XPS portable documents.

1 In Excel, from your student files, open the file **e05A_Fall_Classes**. Display the footer area, click in the **left section**, and then type **Lastname_Firstname_5A_Fall_PDF** Click in a cell just above the footer to exit the Footer.

2 Display the **Save As** dialog box and navigate to your **Excel Chapter 5** folder. Click the **Save as type arrow**, and then click **PDF**.

3 In the lower right section of the dialog box, if necessary, select the **Open file after publishing** check box. As the file name, type **Lastname_Firstname_5A_Fall_PDF** and then click **Save**.

The file is saved in PDF format, and then opens as a PDF document.

4 **Close** the **Lastname_Firstname_5A_Fall_PDF** document.

5 With the **e05A_Fall_Classes** file open, edit the footer in the left section and type **Lastname_Firstname_5A_Fall_XPS** and then click any cell. In the lower right corner of your screen, on the status bar, click the **Normal** button to return to **Normal** view.

6 Display the **Save As** dialog box, navigate to your **Excel Chapter 5** folder, and then in the **File name** box, type **Lastname_Firstname_5A_Fall_XPS**

7 At the bottom of the **Save As** dialog box, click the **Save as type arrow**, and then click **XPS Document**. In the lower right section of the **Save As** dialog box, if necessary, select the **Open file after publishing** check box, and then compare your screen with Figure 5.29.

Figure 5.29

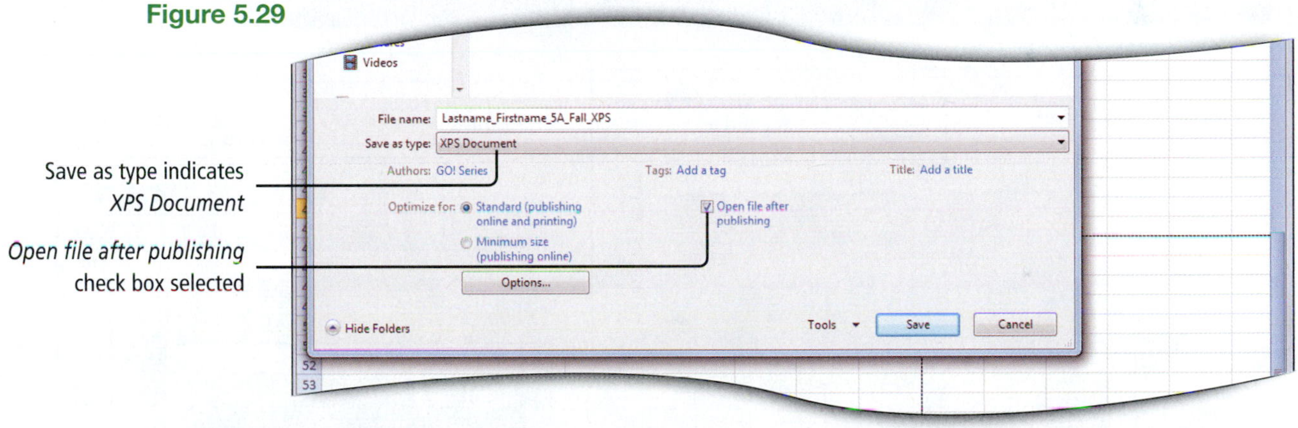

8 Click the **Save** button.

The file is saved in XPS format, and then opens as an XPS document in the XPS Viewer window.

9 **Close** the **XPS Viewer** window. **Close** the **e05A_Fall_Classes** file. **Don't Save** when the message displays—you do not need to save this file.

10 Submit your six files from this project as directed by your instructor, and then **Exit** Excel.

> **More Knowledge | Converting a Tab Delimited Text File to a Word Table**
>
> By choosing Text File as the file type, you can save an Excel worksheet as a text file, which saves the contents of the cells by placing a tab character, rather than commas, between the cells and an end-of-paragraph mark at the end of each row. This type of file can be readily exchanged with various database programs, in which it is referred to as a ***tab delimited text file***. A text file can be converted from tab delimited text to a Word table. Word has a *Convert Text to Table* command that can easily convert a tabbed file into a table. A table displays in a row and column format, like an Excel spreadsheet.

End **You have completed Project 5A**

Project 5B Sorted, Filtered, and Outlined Database

myitlab
Project 5B Training

Project Activities

In Activities 5.14 to 5.21 you will use advanced table features to provide Dr. John Mosier, the Dean of the Computer and Business Systems Division, information about the Fall course sections and assigned faculty in the Division. Your completed worksheets will look similar to Figure 5.30.

Project Files

For Project 5B, you will need the following files:

e05B_Fall_Advising
e05B_Fall_Faculty
e05B_Fall_Sections

You will save your workbooks as:

Lastname_Firstname_5B_Advising
Lastname_Firstname_5B_Faculty
Lastname_Firstname_5B_Sections

Project Results

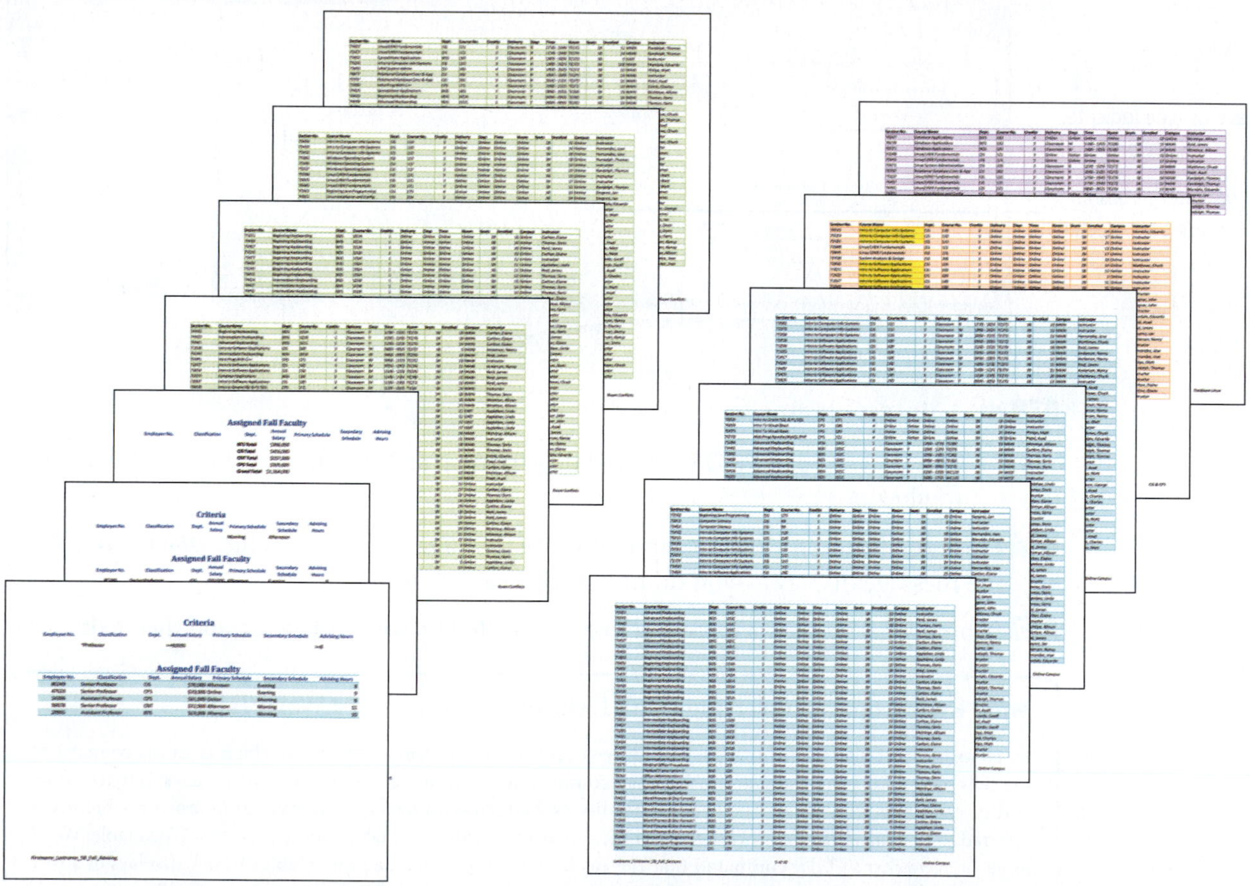

Figure 5.30
Project 5B Advising

Objective 5 | Use Advanced Sort Techniques

Sort means to organize data in a particular order; for example, alphabetizing a list of names. An ***ascending*** sort refers to text that is sorted alphabetically from A to Z, numbers sorted from lowest to highest, or dates and times sorted from earliest to latest. A ***descending*** sort refers to text that is sorted alphabetically from Z to A, numbers sorted from highest to lowest, or dates and times sorted from latest to earliest.

Sorting helps you to visualize your data. By sorting in various ways, you can find the data that you want, and then use your data to make good decisions. You can sort data in one column or in multiple columns. Most sort operations are column sorts, but you can also sort by rows.

Activity 5.14 | Sorting on Multiple Columns

To sort data based on several criteria at once, use the ***Sort dialog box***, which enables you to sort by more than one column or row. For example, Dean Mosier wants to know, by department, how each course is delivered—either online or in a campus classroom. He also wants to examine the data to determine if there are any conflicts in room assignments. In this activity, you will convert the data into an Excel table, and then use the Sort dialog box to arrange the data to see the information the Dean needs.

1 **Start** Excel. From your student files, open **e05B_Fall_Sections**. Display the **Save As** dialog box, navigate to your **Excel Chapter 5** folder, and then save the workbook as **Lastname_Firstname_5B_Fall_Sections**

Another Way

With cell A1 active, insert the table, and Excel will select all the contiguous data as the range.

2 Be sure that the first worksheet, **Room Conflicts**, is the active sheet. In the **Name Box**, type **a1:m170** and press Enter to select this range. On the **Insert tab**, in the **Tables group**, click the **Table** button. In the **Create Table** dialog box, be sure that the **My table has headers** check box is selected, and then click **OK**.

3 On the **Design tab**, in the **Table Styles group**, click the **More** button, and then under **Light**, apply **Table Style Light 18**. Click any cell to deselect, and then compare your screen with Figure 5.31.

A table of data like this one forms a ***database***—an organized collection of facts related to a specific topic. In this table, the topic relates to the Fall course sections for this division of the college.

Each table row forms a ***record***—all of the categories of data pertaining to one person, place, thing, event, or idea. In this table, each course section is a record. Each table column forms a ***field***—a single piece of information that is stored in every record.

When information is arranged as records in rows and fields in columns, then you can ***query***—ask a question of—the data.

Figure 5.31

Sorting and filtering arrows in header row

Table Style Light 18 applied

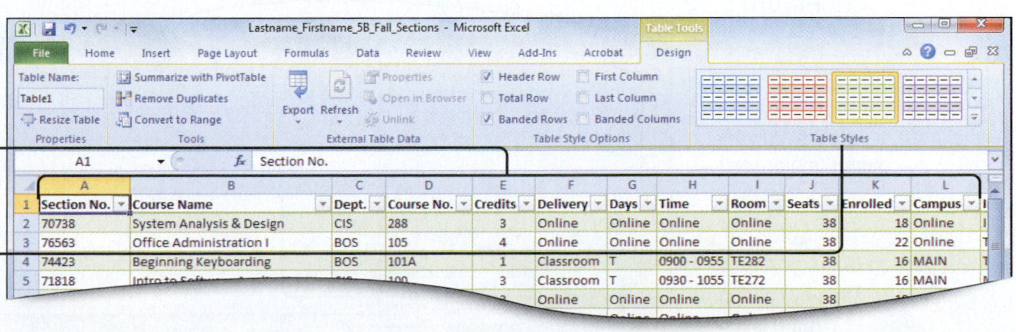

4 On the **Data tab**, in the **Sort & Filter group**, click the **Sort** button.

In the Sort dialog box, you can sort on up to 64 columns (levels) of data.

> **Note | Defining data as a table prior to sort operations is optional.**
>
> Defining your range of data as an Excel table is not required to perform sort operations. Doing so, however, is convenient if you plan to perform sorts on all of the data, because any sort commands will be performed on the entire table. Defining the data as a table also freezes the column titles automatically, so they will not move out of view as you scroll down a worksheet that contains many rows. If you want to sort only part of a list of data, do not convert the data to a table. Instead, select the range, and then click the Sort button.

5 In the **Sort** dialog box, under **Column**, click the **Sort by arrow**. Notice that the list displays in the order of the field names—the column titles. On the displayed list, click **Dept.**

6 Under **Sort On**, click the **arrow**, and then on the displayed list, click **Values**. Under **Order**, click the **arrow**, and then click **A to Z**. Compare your screen with Figure 5.32.

Values indicates that the sort will be based on the values in the cells of the Sort by column—the Dept. column. A to Z indicates that the values in the column will be sorted in ascending alphabetic order.

Figure 5.32

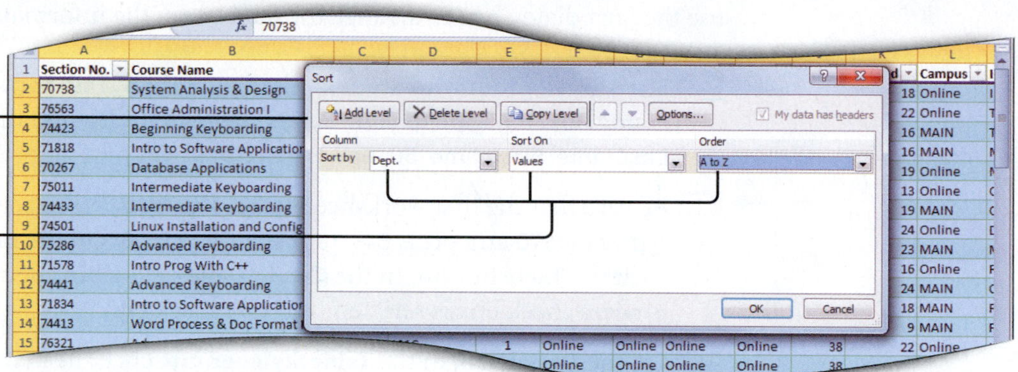

7 In the upper left corner of the **Sort** dialog box, click the **Add Level** button. In the second level row, click the **Then by arrow**, and then click **Course No.** Be sure that **Sort On** indicates *Values* and **Order** indicates *Smallest to Largest*.

When you initiate the sort operation, these numeric values will be sorted from the smallest number to the largest.

8 Click the **Add Level** button again. In the new row, under **Column**, click the **Then by arrow**, and then click **Section No.** Sort on **Values**, from **Smallest to Largest**. Compare your screen with Figure 5.33.

Figure 5.33

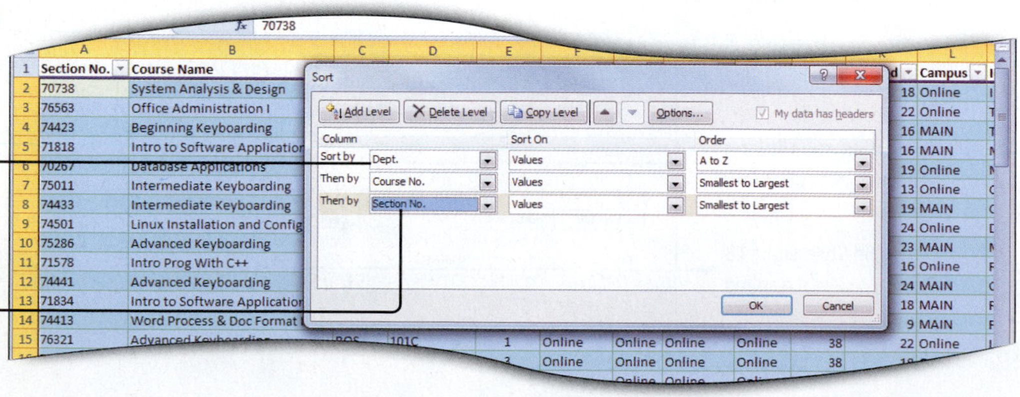

9 Click **OK**. Scroll down until **row 139** is at the top of the worksheet, take a moment to examine the arrangement of the data, and then compare your screen with Figure 5.34.

The first sort level, sometimes referred to as the ***major sort***, is by the Dept. field in alphabetic order, so after the BOS department, the CIS department sections are listed, then the CNT department sections, then the CPS department sections, and so on.

The second sort level is by the Course No. field in ascending order, so within each department, the courses are sorted in ascending order by course number.

The third sort level is by the Section No. field in ascending order, so within each Course No. the section numbers display in ascending order.

Figure 5.34

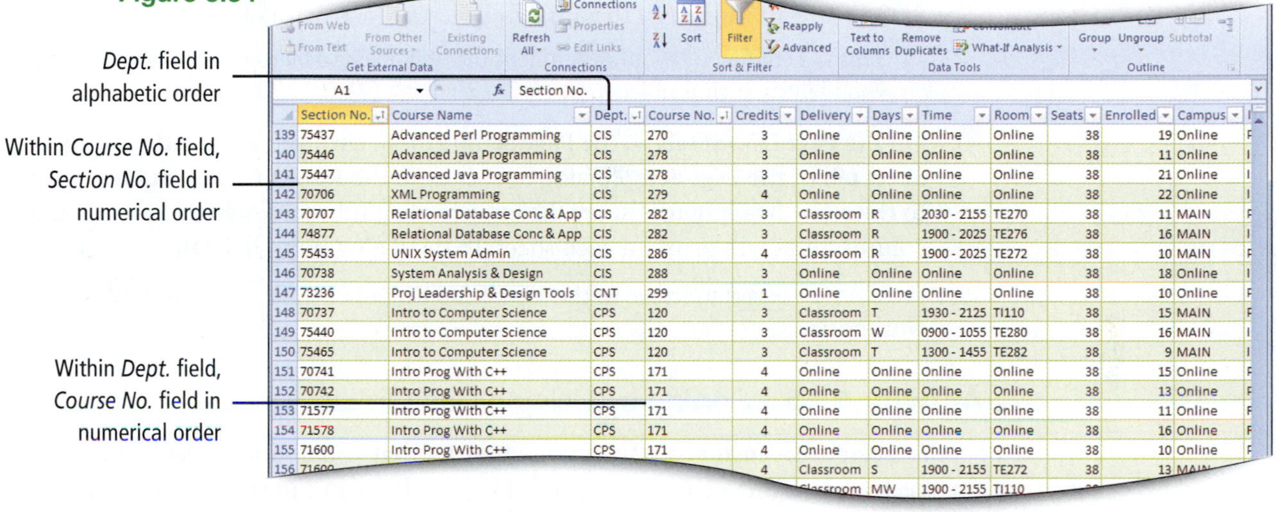

10 From the row heading area, select **rows 148:150**, and then notice that all three sections of the course *CPS 120 Intro to Computer Science* are offered in a campus classroom.

By studying the information in this arrangement, Dean Mosier can consider adding an additional section of this course in an online delivery.

> **Another Way**
>
> Click any row in the dialog box, click Delete Level, and then add new levels.

11 Click any cell to deselect. In the **Sort & Filter group**, click the **Sort** button to redisplay the **Sort** dialog box.

12 Under **Column**, in the first row, click the **Sort by** arrow, and then click **Days**, change the second sort level to **Time**, and change the third sort level to **Room**. For each sort level, sort on **Values** in **A to Z** order. Compare your screen with Figure 5.35.

Figure 5.35

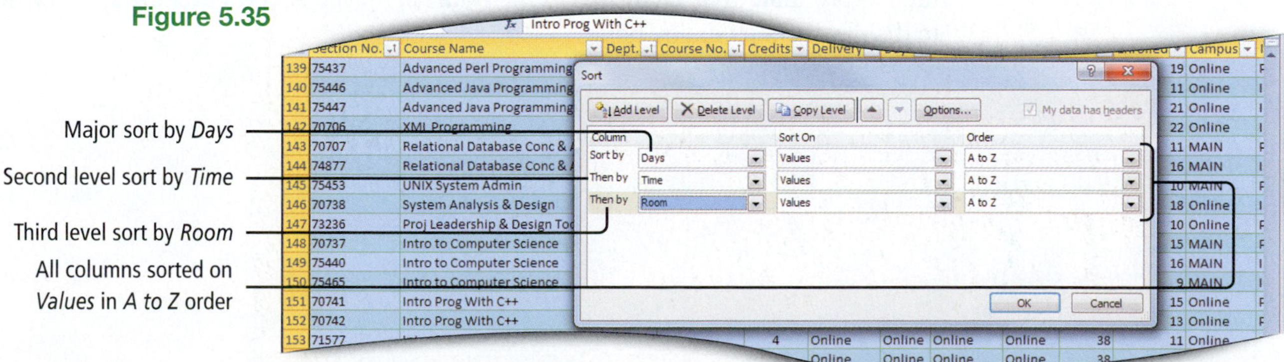

13 Click **OK**, and then scroll to view the top of the worksheet.

Because the days are sorted alphabetically, F (for Friday) is listed first, and then the times for the Friday classes are sorted in ascending order. Within the Friday group, the classes are further sorted from the earliest to the latest. Within each time period, the data is further sorted by room.

14 Examine the sorted data. Notice that the first three classes listed are on *Friday*, at *12:00*, in room *TE276*, with *Elaine Carlton* as the instructor.

These are all keyboarding classes, and the instructor teaches the three levels of keyboarding at the same time, so this is not a room conflict.

15 Notice in **rows 24:25** that two *Intro to Visual Basic* classes are scheduled on *MW* from 8:00 to 9:25 in room *TE110* with two different instructors listed.

This is a conflict of room assignment that will need to be resolved. Sorting data can help you identify such problems.

16 On the **Page Layout tab**, in the **Page Setup group**, click the **Print Titles** button. On the **Sheet tab** of the **Page Setup** dialog box, click in the **Rows to repeat at top** box, point to the **row 1** heading to display the [→] pointer, and click to select **row 1** so that the column titles will print on each sheet. In the dialog box, click **OK**.

17 Press Ctrl + Home to move to the top of the worksheet, and then **Save** your workbook.

Activity 5.15 | Sorting by Using a Custom List

You can use a ***custom list*** to sort in an order that you define. Excel includes a day-of-the-week and month-of-the-year custom list, so that you can sort chronologically by the days of the week or by the months of the year from January to December.

Optionally, you can create your own custom list by typing the values you want to sort by, in the order you want to sort them, from top to bottom; for example, *Fast*, *Medium*, *Slow*. A custom list that you define must be based on a value—text, number, date, or time.

In this activity, you will provide Dean Mosier with a list showing all the Fall sections sorted first by Delivery, with all online courses listed first. Within each delivery type—Online and Classroom—the data will be further sorted by Dept. and then by Course Name.

1 In the **sheet tab area**, click **Online-Campus** to display the *second* worksheet in the workbook.

2 In the **Name Box**, type **a1:m170** and press Enter to select the range, insert a table, and then apply **Table Style Light 20**. On the **Data tab**, in the **Sort & Filter group**, click **Sort** to display the **Sort** dialog box.

3 Set the first (major) level to sort by **Delivery**, and to sort on **Values**. Then, click the **Order arrow** for this sort level, and click **Custom List** to display the **Custom Lists** dialog box.

4 Under **Custom lists**, be sure **NEW LIST** is selected. Then, under **List entries**, click in the empty box and type **Online** Press Enter, and then type **Classroom** Compare your screen with Figure 5.36.

Figure 5.36

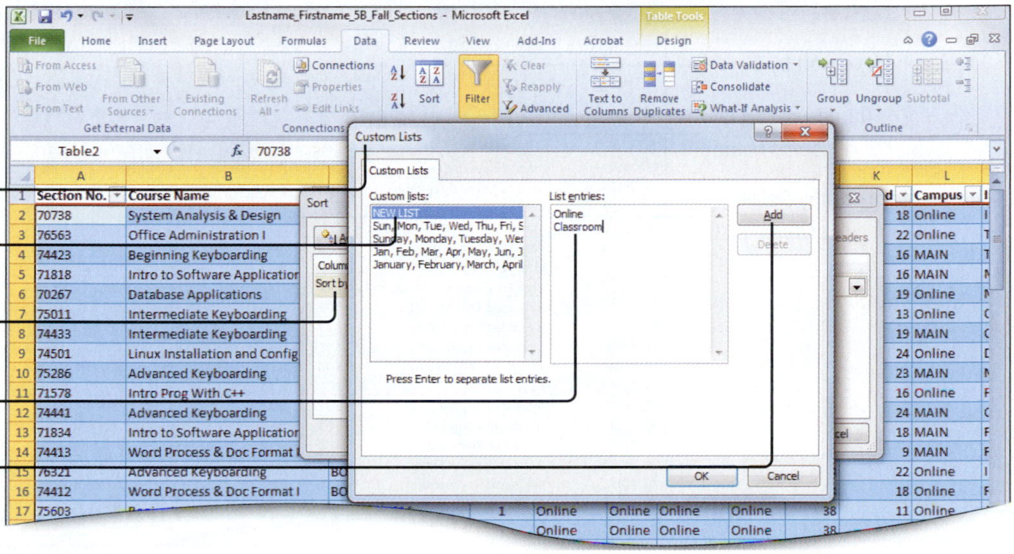

5 In the **Custom Lists** dialog box, click the **Add** button. On the left, under **Custom lists**, select **Online, Classroom**, and then click **OK** to redisplay the **Sort** dialog box.

6 In the **Sort** dialog box, click the **Add Level** button, and then as the second level sort, click **Dept.** Click the **Add Level** button again, and as the third level sort, click **Course Name**. Compare your screen with Figure 5.37.

Figure 5.37

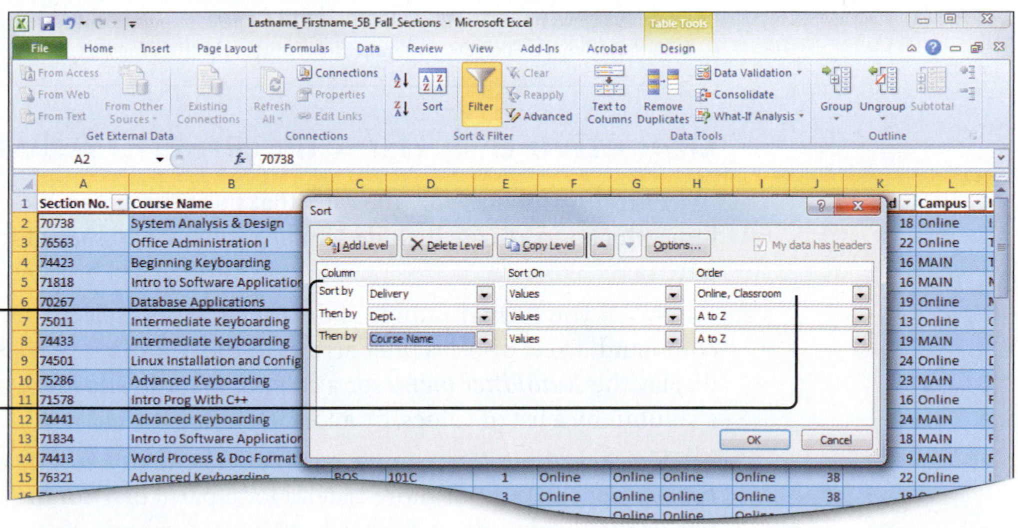

7 Click **OK** and then click any cell to deselect. Scroll down the worksheet, and notice that all of the online courses are listed first, and then scroll down to bring **row 92** into view, which is where the **Classroom** sections begin. Compare your screen with Figure 5.38.

Within each grouping, Online and Classroom, the sections are further sorted alphabetically by *Dept.* and then by *Course Name.*

Figure 5.38

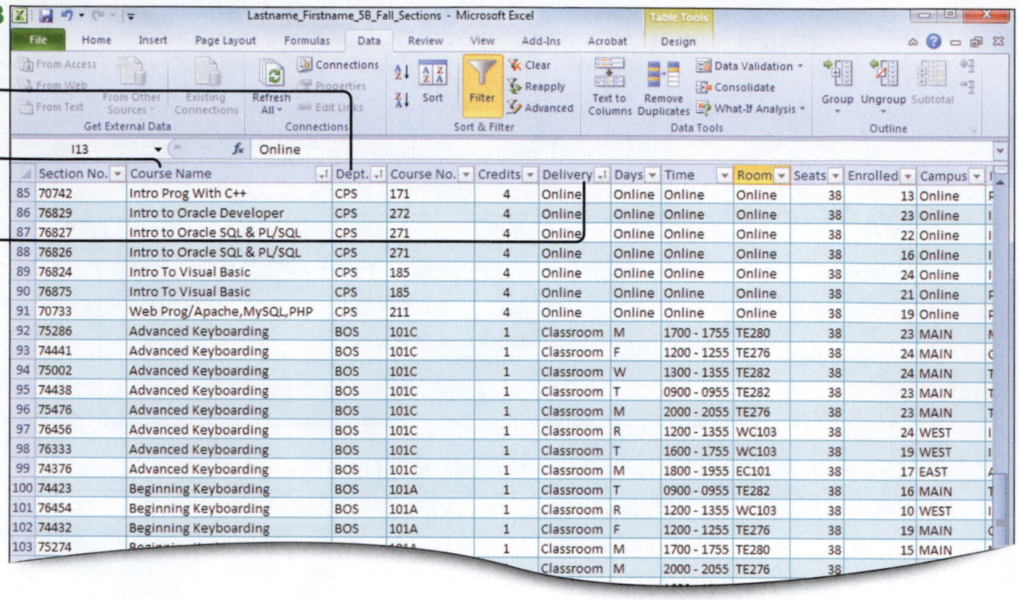

8 Press Ctrl + Home to move to cell **A1**. On the **Page Layout tab**, click the **Print Titles** button, and then set **row 1** to repeat at the top of each page. **Save** your workbook.

> **More Knowledge** | A Custom List Remains Available for All Workbooks in Excel
>
> When you create a custom list, the list remains available for all workbooks that you use in Excel. To delete a custom list, display Excel Options, on the left click Advanced, under Display, click the Edit Custom Lists button, select the custom list, and then click the Delete button to permanently delete the custom list. Click OK to confirm the deletion. Click OK two more times to close both dialog boxes.

Objective 6 | Use Custom and Advanced Filters

Filtering displays only the rows that meet the ***criteria***—conditions that you specify to limit which records are included in the results—and hides the rows that do not meet your criteria.

When you format a range of data as a table, or select a range and click the Filter command, Excel displays filter arrows in the column headings, from which you can display the ***AutoFilter menu*** for a column—a drop-down menu from which you can filter a column by a list of values, by a format, or by criteria.

Use a ***custom filter*** to apply complex criteria to a single column. Use an ***advanced filter*** to specify three or more criteria for a particular column, to apply complex criteria to two or more columns, or to specify computed criteria. You can also use an advanced filter for ***extracting***—copying the selected rows to another part of the worksheet, instead of displaying the filtered list.

Activity 5.16 | Filtering by Format and Value Using AutoFilter

There are three types of filters that you can create with AutoFilter. You can filter by one or more values, for example *CIS* for the CIS department. You can filter by a format, such as cell color. Or, you can filter by criteria; for example, course sections that are greater than 2 credits, which would display courses that have 3 or more credits. Each of these filter types is mutually exclusive for the column; that is, you can use only one at a time.

1 From the **sheet tab area** at the lower edge of your screen, click **CIS & CPS** to display the *third* worksheet in the workbook.

2 Be sure that cell **A1** is the active cell, and then on the **Insert tab**, in the **Tables group**, click **Table**. In the **Create Table** dialog box, be sure that the data indicates the range *$A$1:$M$170*.

The Table command causes Excel to suggest a table range based on the contiguous cells surrounding the active cell.

3 Click **OK** to accept the selection as the table range. Apply **Table Style Light 21** and click cell **A1** to deselect.

4 On the Ribbon, click the **Data tab.** In the **Sort & Filter group**, notice that the **Filter** button is active—it displays orange. In **row 1**, notice the **filter arrows** in each column title.

Recall that when you format a range of data as an Excel table, filter arrows are automatically added in the header row of the table. A filter arrow, when clicked, displays the AutoFilter menu. On the Ribbon, the active Filter button indicates that the data is formatted to use filters.

5 In **column B**, notice that some courses are formatted with a yellow fill color, which indicates courses that have been designated as introductory courses recommended for high school seniors who want to take a college class.

6 In cell B1, click the **Course Name filter arrow**. On the **AutoFilter** menu, point to **Filter by Color**, point to the **yellow block**, and then click one time.

Only courses with a yellow fill color in column B display; the status bar indicates that 79 of the 169 records display.

7 Point to the filter arrow in cell **B1**, and notice the ScreenTip *Course Name: Equals a Yellow cell color*. Notice also that a small funnel displays to the right of the arrow. Compare your screen with Figure 5.39.

The funnel indicates that a filter is applied, and the ScreenTip indicates how the records are filtered.

Figure 5.39

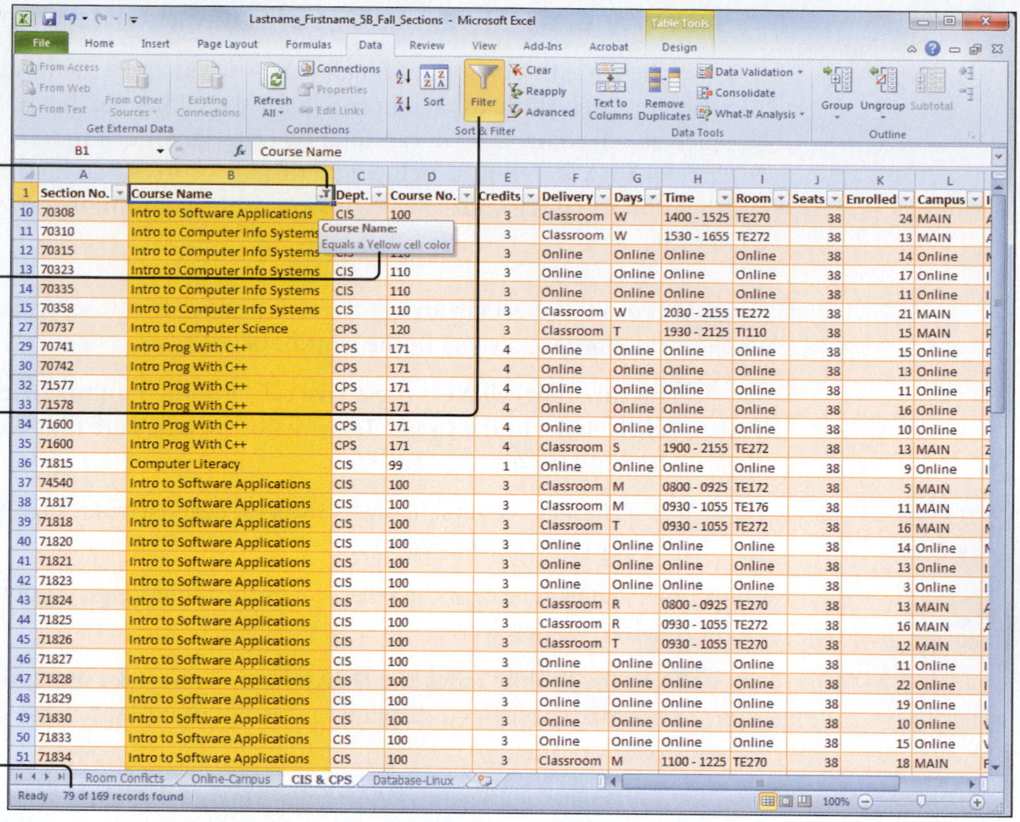

8 In cell **B1**, click the **Course Name filter arrow**, and then click **Clear Filter From "Course Name"**. Then, in cell **B1**, point to the **Course Name filter arrow**, and notice that *(Showing All)* displays.

The funnel no longer displays. The status bar no longer indicates that a filter is active. A filter arrow without a funnel means that filtering is enabled but not applied—if you point to the arrow, the ScreenTip will display *(Showing All)*.

9 Click cell **I5**, which contains the value *TE280*. Right-click over the selected cell, point to **Filter**, and then click **Filter by Selected Cell's Value**. Notice that only the courses that meet in Room TE280 display—all the other records are hidden.

Excel filters the records by the selected value—TE280, and indicates in the status bar that 10 of the 169 records are displayed. This is a quick way to filter a set of records.

10 On the **Data tab**, in the **Sort & Filter group**, click the **Clear** button to clear all of the filters.

Use this command to clear all filters from a group of records. This command also clears any sorts that were applied.

11 In cell **C1**, click the **Dept. filter arrow**. On the displayed list, click the **(Select All)** check box to clear all the check boxes, and then select the **CIS** and **CPS** check boxes. Click **OK**.

The records are filtered so that only course sections in the CIS and CPS departments display. The status bar indicates that 93 of 169 records are found; that is, 93 course sections are either in the CIS or CPS departments.

12 In cell **E1**, click the **Credits filter arrow**, click the **(Select All)** check box to clear all the check boxes, and then select the **3** check box. Click **OK**.

The status bar indicates that 61 of 169 records are found. That is, of the sections in either the CIS or CPS departments, 61 are 3-credit courses. Thus, you can see that filtering actions are ***additive***—each additional filter that you apply is based on the current filter, which further reduces the number of records displayed.

13 In cell **F1**, click the **Delivery filter arrow**, and then using the technique you just practiced, filter the list further by **Online**.

The status bar indicates 30 of 169 records found. That is, 30 course sections that are either in the CIS or CPS departments and that are 3-credit courses are offered online. The filter drop-down lists make it easy to apply filters that provide quick views of your data. For best results, be sure the data in the filtered column has the same data type; for example, in a column, be sure all the values are numbers or text.

14 **Save** your workbook.

Activity 5.17 | Filtering by Custom Criteria Using AutoFilter

By using a custom filter, you can apply complex criteria to a single column. For example, you can use comparison criteria to compare two values by using the ***comparison operators*** such as Equals (=), Greater Than (>), or Less Than (<) singly or in combinations. When you compare two values by using these operators, your result is a logical value that is either true or false.

1 From the **sheet tabs area** at the lower edge of your screen, click **Database-Linux** to display the *fourth* worksheet in the workbook.

2 Be sure that cell **A1** is the active cell, and then on the **Insert tab**, in the **Tables group**, click **Table**. In the **Create Table** dialog box, be sure that the data indicates the range *$A$1:$M$170*. Click **OK**, and then apply **Table Style Light 19**. Click any cell to deselect.

Another Way

Click Custom Filter, click the first arrow in the first row, and then click is less than or equal to.

3 In cell **K1**, click the **Enrolled filter arrow**, point to **Number Filters**, and then click **Less Than Or Equal To**. In the first box, be sure that *is less than or equal to* displays, and then in the second box type **14** Compare your screen with Figure 5.40.

In the displayed Custom AutoFilter dialog box, you can create a ***compound filter***—a filter that uses more than one condition—and one that uses comparison operators.

Figure 5.40

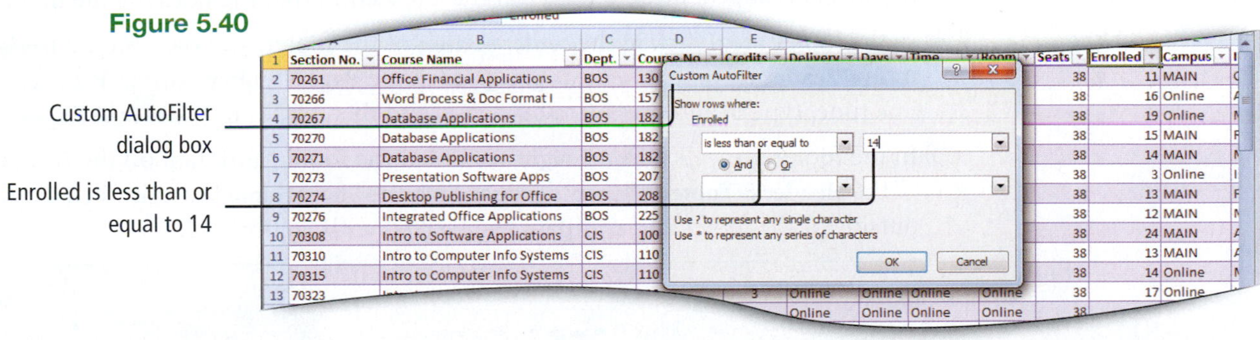

4 Click **OK** to display 69 records.

This filter answers the question, *Which course sections have 14 or fewer students enrolled?*

5 On the **Data tab**, in the **Sort & Filter group**, **Clear** all filters.

6 In cell **B1**, click the **Course Name filter arrow**, point to **Text Filters**, and then click **Contains**.

7 In the **Custom AutoFilter** dialog box, under **Course Name**, in the first box, be sure that *contains* displays. In the box to the right, type **database**

8 Between the two rows of boxes, click the **Or** option button, and then for the second filter, in the first box, click the arrow, scroll down as necessary, and then click **contains**. In the second box, type **linux** and then compare your screen with Figure 5.41.

For the ***Or comparison operator***, only one of the two comparison criteria that you specify must be true. Thus, by applying this filter, only courses that contain the words database or linux will display.

For the ***And comparison operator,*** each and every one of the comparison criteria that you specify must be true.

Figure 5.41

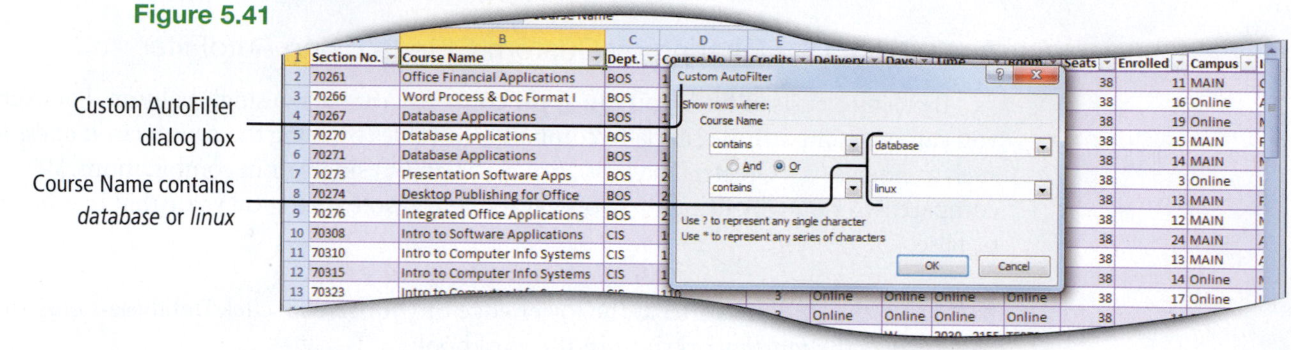

9 Click **OK** to display 14 records.

This filter answers the question, *Which course sections relate to either databases or the Linux operating system?*

Activity 5.18 | Inserting the Sheet Name and Page Numbers in a Footer

You have practiced inserting the file name into the footer of a worksheet. In this activity, you will add the sheet name to the footer.

1 Point to any of the four sheet tabs, right-click, and then click **Select All Sheets**. With the sheets grouped, insert a footer in the left section that includes the file name.

2 In the footer area, click in the **center section** of the footer, and then on the **Design tab**, in the **Header & Footer Elements group**, click the **Page Number** button. Press Spacebar one time, type **of** and press Spacebar again, and then click the **Number of Pages** button.

3 In the footer area, click in the **right section** of the footer, and then on the **Design tab**, in the **Header & Footer Elements group**, click the **Sheet Name** button. Click a cell outside of the footer and compare your screen with Figure 5.42.

Figure 5.42

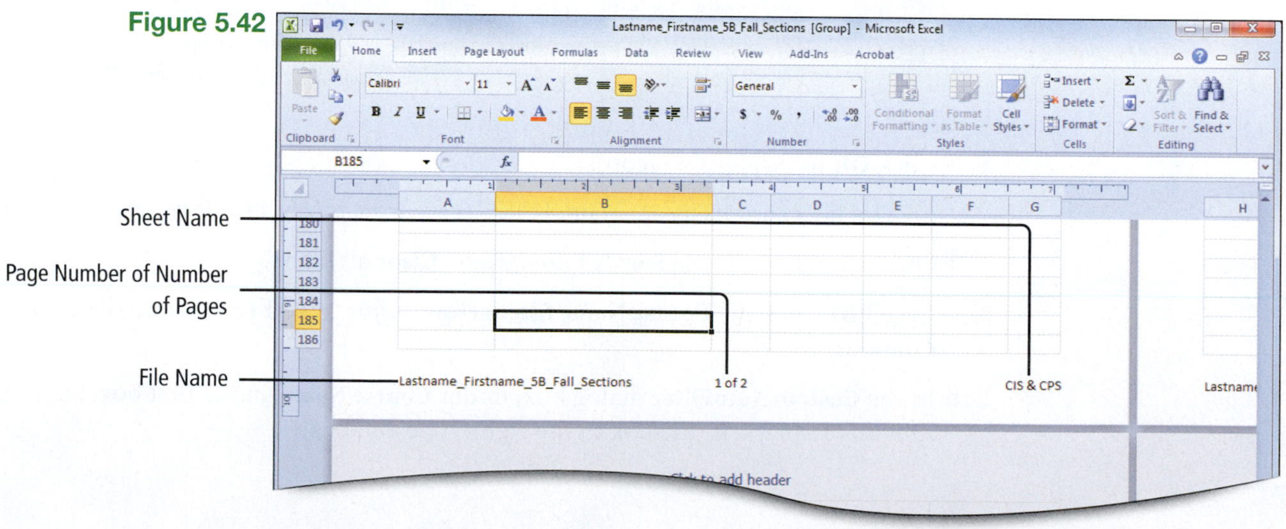

4 On the **Page Layout tab**, set the orientation to **Landscape**, and set the **Width** to **1 page**. On the status bar, click the **Normal** button. Press Ctrl + Home to move to cell **A1**.

You may hear a double chime to alert you that the changes you made will apply to all the sheets in the Group.

5 Display the **Document Panel** and in the **Author** box, type your firstname and lastname, in the **Subject** box, type your course name and section number, and in the **Keywords** box, type **sort, filter, sections Close** the Document Properties. Display **Print Preview**.

Ten pages display in Print Preview. The four worksheets in the workbook result in 10 pages—the first worksheet has four pages (green), the second worksheet has four pages (aqua), the third worksheet has one page (orange), and the fourth worksheet has one page (purple).

6 Redisplay the workbook, and then make any necessary corrections or adjustments.

7 **Save** your workbook. Hold this workbook until the end of this project, and then print or submit the four worksheets—10 total pages—in this workbook electronically as directed by your instructor. There are no formulas in these worksheets. **Close** this workbook, but leave Excel open.

Excel | Chapter 5

Activity 5.19 | Filtering by Using Advanced Criteria

Use an advanced filter when the data you want to filter requires complex criteria; for example, to specify three or more criteria for a particular column, to apply complex criteria to two or more columns, or to specify computed criteria. When you use the Advanced filter command, the Advanced dialog box displays, rather than the AutoFilter menu, and you type the criteria on the worksheet above the range you want to filter.

In this activity, you will create an advanced filter to determine which faculty members whose classification includes *Professor* and that have an annual salary of $60,000 or more, have 8 or more hours of assigned advising hours.

1 From your student files, open **e05B_Fall_Advising**. Display the **Save As** dialog box, navigate to your **Excel Chapter 5** folder, and then save the workbook as **Lastname_Firstname_5B_Fall_Advising**

2 Select the range **A6:G7**, right-click, and then click **Copy**.

The first step in filtering by using advanced criteria is to create a ***criteria range***—an area on your worksheet where you define the criteria for the filter. The criteria range indicates how the displayed records are filtered.

Typically, the criteria range is placed *above* the data. The criteria range must have a row for the column headings and at least one row for the criteria—you will need additional rows if you have multiple criteria for a column. You can also add a title row. Separate the criteria range from the data by a blank row.

3 Point to cell **A1**, right-click, under **Paste Options**, click the first button, **Paste**, and then press Esc to cancel the moving border. Click cell **A1**, type **Criteria** and then press Enter.

4 Select **rows 1:2**, on the **Home tab**, in the **Cells group**, click the **Format** button, and then click **AutoFit Row Height**. Compare your screen with Figure 5.43.

By copying the title and field names, you also copy the formatting that has been applied.

Figure 5.43

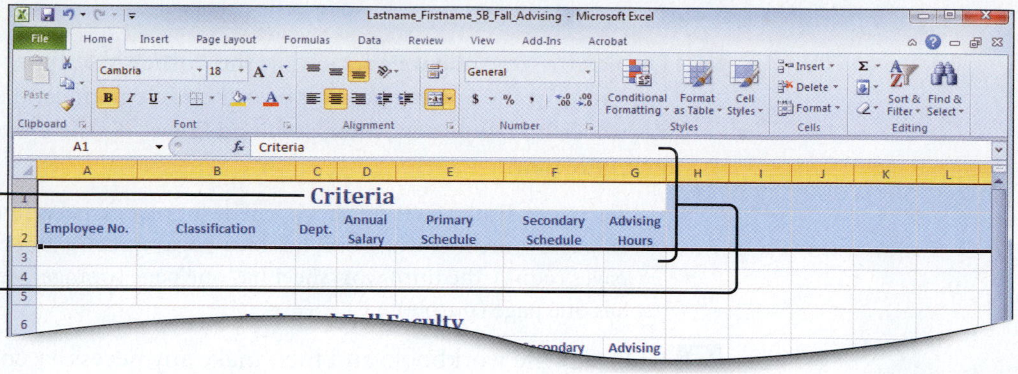

5 Select the range **A2:G3**—the column names and the blank row in the Criteria range. Click in the **Name Box**, and then type **Criteria** as shown in Figure 5.44.

Figure 5.44

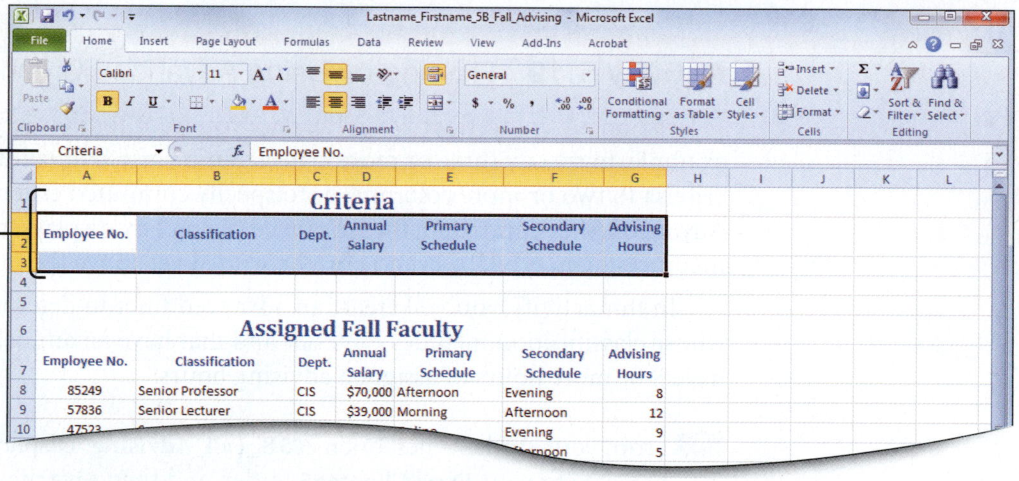

6 Press Enter to name the range.

By naming the range Criteria, which is a predefined name recognized by Excel, the reference to this range will automatically display as the Criteria range in the Advanced Filter dialog box. This defined criteria range includes the field names and one empty row, where the limiting criteria will be placed. It does not include the title *Criteria*.

7 Select the range **A7:G34**, insert a table, and then apply **Table Style Light 6**. Click anywhere in the table to deselect.

8 On the **Formulas tab**, in the **Defined Names** group, click the **Name Manager** button, and then compare your screen with Figure 5.45.

By defining the range as a table, Excel automatically assigns a name to the range. It is not required to format the range as a table—you could select the range and name it Table or Database—however doing so enables you to use the Table Tools, such as formatting and inserting a Total row into the filtered data.

The defined table range will automatically display as the List range in the Advanced Filter dialog box.

Figure 5.45

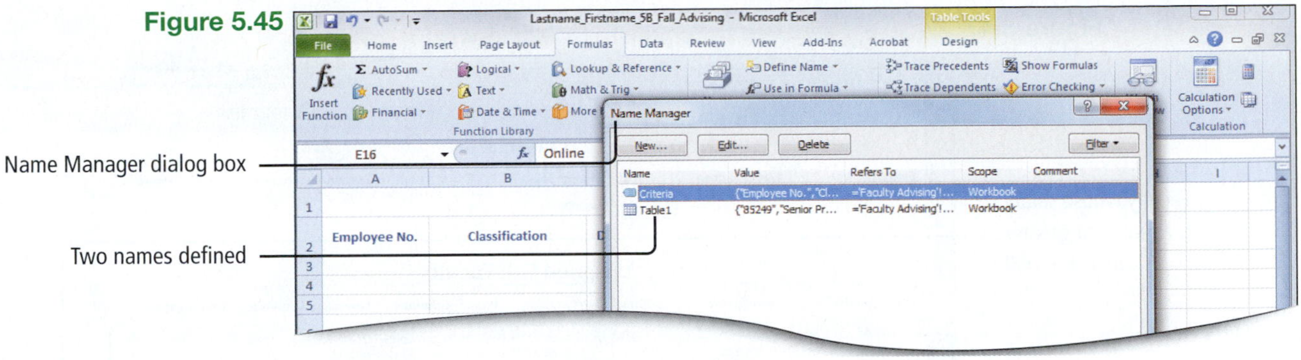

9 **Close** [X] the **Name Manager** dialog box.

10 Scroll to view the top of the worksheet, click cell **D3**, type **>=60000** and then press Enter.

This action creates a criteria using a comparison operator to look for salary values that are greater than or equal to $60,000. Do not include a comma when you type this value, because the comma is a cell format, not part of the value.

11 Click cell **A7**. On the **Data tab**, in the **Sort & Filter group**, click the **Advanced** button.

12 In the displayed **Advanced Filter** dialog box, locate the **List range**, and as necessary edit the range to indicate **$A$7:$G$34** which is your Excel table. Be sure the **Criteria range** is identified as cells **$A$2:$G$3** Compare your screen with Figure 5.46.

Here you define the database area—the List range—and the Criteria range where the results will display. Both ranges use an absolute reference. Under Action, you can choose to display the results in the table—in-place—or copy the results to another location.

Figure 5.46

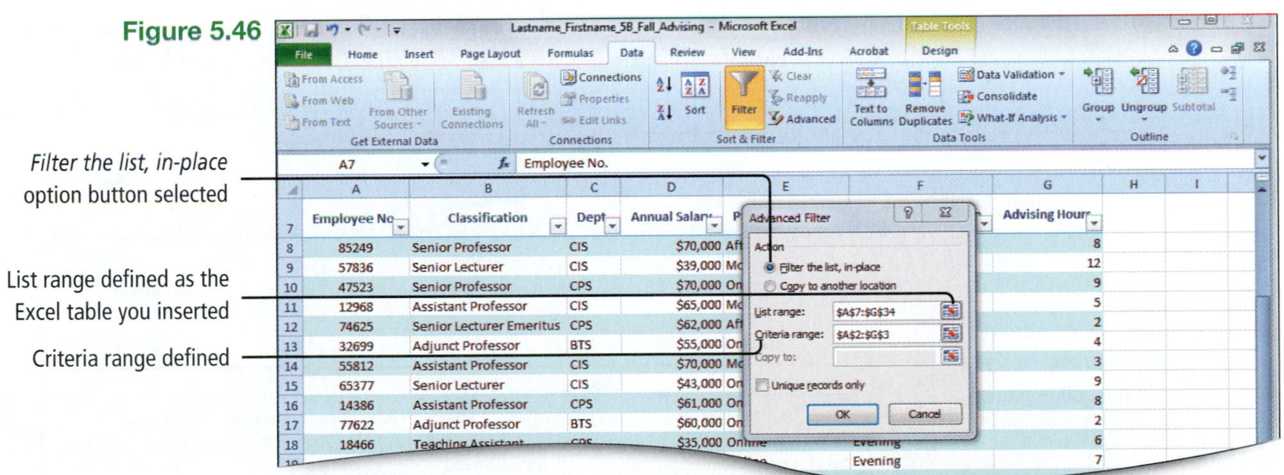

13 Click **OK** to have the filter results display in-place—in the table. At the top of your worksheet, click any blank cell; compare your screen with Figure 5.47.

Only the records for faculty members whose salary is $60,000 or more display. The row numbers for the records that meet the criteria display in blue. The Advanced command disables the AutoFilter command and removes the AutoFilter arrows from the column headings.

Figure 5.47

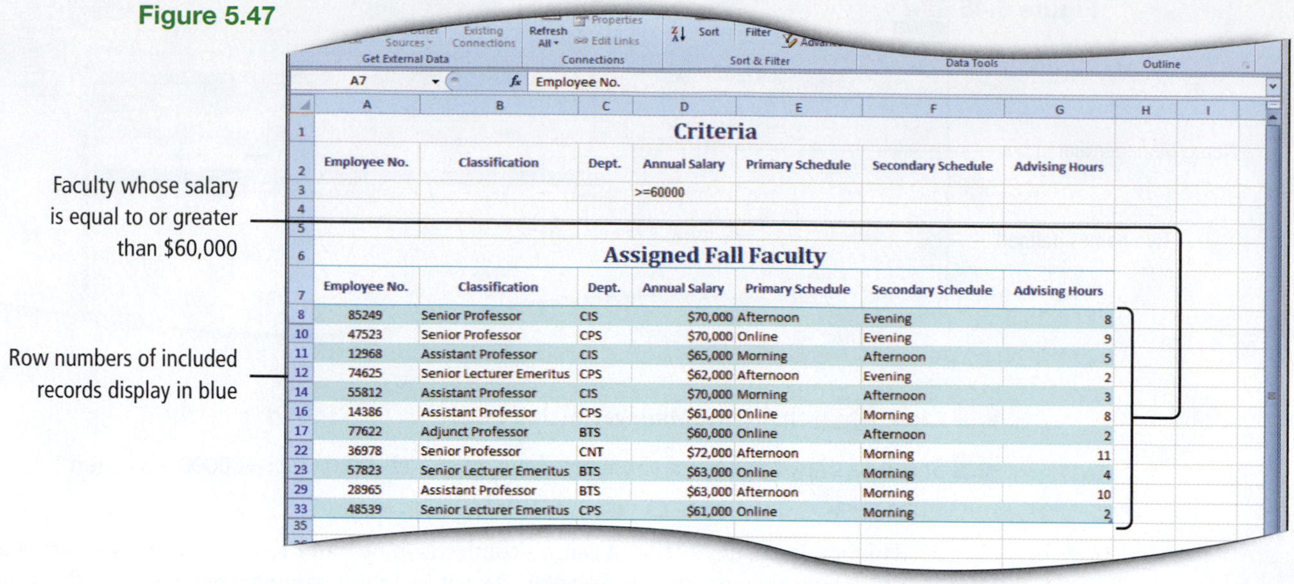

Faculty whose salary is equal to or greater than $60,000
Row numbers of included records display in blue
Get External Data
Existing Connections
Refresh All
Properties
Edit Links
Connections
Sort
Filter
Sort & Filter
Data Tools
Outline
A7
Employee No.
Criteria
Employee No. Classification Dept. Annual Salary Primary Schedule Secondary Schedule Advising Hours
>=60000
Assigned Fall Faculty
Employee No. Classification Dept. Annual Salary Primary Schedule Secondary Schedule Advising Hours
8 85249 Senior Professor CIS $70,000 Afternoon Evening 8
10 47523 Senior Professor CPS $70,000 Online Evening 9
11 12968 Assistant Professor CIS $65,000 Morning Afternoon 5
12 74625 Senior Lecturer Emeritus CPS $62,000 Afternoon Evening 2
14 55812 Assistant Professor CIS $70,000 Morning Afternoon 3
16 14386 Assistant Professor CPS $61,000 Online Morning 8
17 77622 Adjunct Professor BTS $60,000 Online Afternoon 2
22 36978 Senior Professor CNT $72,000 Afternoon Morning 11
23 57823 Senior Lecturer Emeritus BTS $63,000 Online Morning 4
29 28965 Assistant Professor BTS $63,000 Afternoon Morning 10
33 48539 Senior Lecturer Emeritus CPS $61,000 Online Morning 2

14 Click cell **B3**, type ***Professor** and then press Enter.

The asterisk (*) is a ***wildcard***. Use a wildcard to search a field when you are uncertain of the exact value or you want to widen the search to include more records. The use of a wildcard enables you to include faculty whose classification ends with the word Professor. It directs Excel to find Professor and anything before it. The criterion in the Salary field still applies.

The use of two or more criteria on the same row is known as ***compound criteria***—all conditions must be met for the records to be included in the results.

15 Click cell **A7**. On the **Data tab**, in the **Sort & Filter group**, click the **Advanced** button. Verify that the database range is correctly identified in the **List range** box and that the **Criteria range** still indicates *$A$2:$G$3*. Click **OK**. See Figure 5.48.

Only the eight faculty members with a classification containing *Professor* and a salary of $60,000 or more display.

Figure 5.48

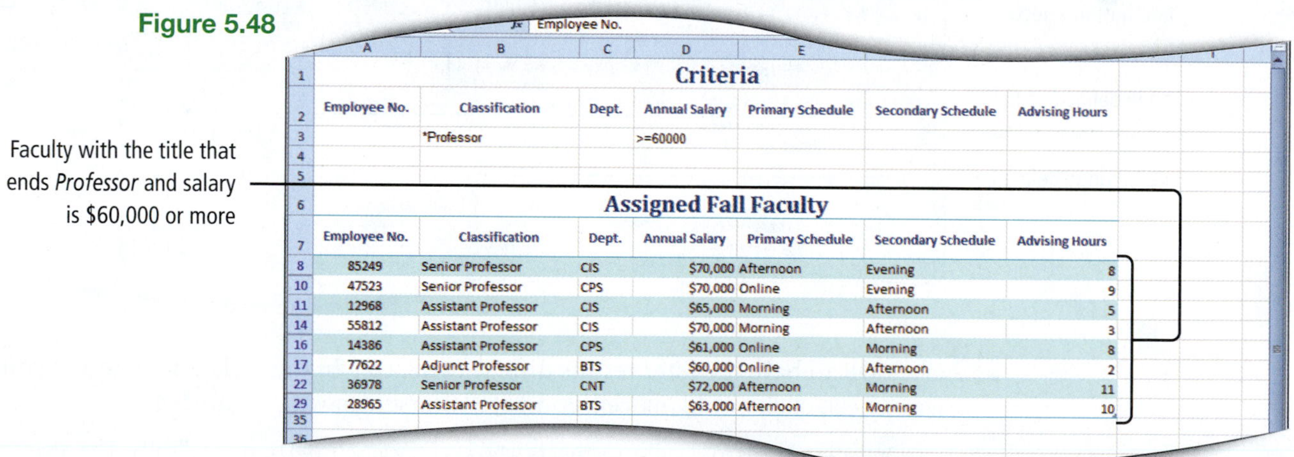

16 Using the techniques you just practiced, filter the data further by adding an additional criteria—faculty who are assigned 8 hours or more of advising. Compare your result with Figure 5.49.

Five faculty members meet all three of the criteria in the Criteria range.

Figure 5.49

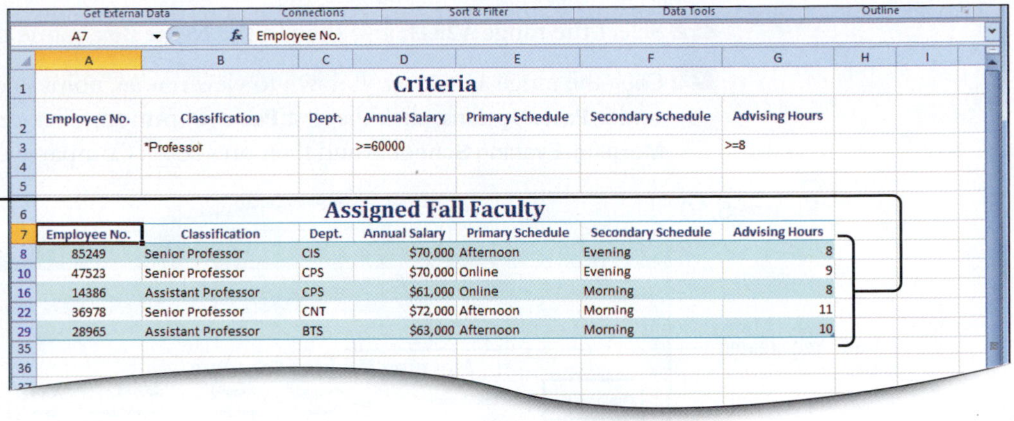

Faculty who have a title that ends *Professor*, a salary of $60,000 or more, and 8 or more advising hours

17 Insert a footer in the **left section** that includes the file name, click outside the footer area, and then on the **Page Layout tab**, set the orientation to **Landscape**. On the status bar, click the **Normal** button. Press Ctrl + Home to move to cell **A1**.

18 Display the **Document Information Panel**, and in the **Author** box, type your firstname and lastname, in the **Subject** box, type your course name and section number, and in the **Keywords** box, type **advanced filter, advising**

19 Display the **Print Preview**. Near the bottom of the window, click **Page Setup** to display the **Page Setup** dialog box. Click the **Margins tab**, center the worksheet horizontally, and then click **OK**. Redisplay the worksheet and make any necessary corrections or adjustments.

20 **Save** your workbook. Hold this workbook until the end of this project, and then print or submit electronically as directed; there are no formulas in this worksheet. **Close** this workbook, but leave Excel open.

More Knowledge | Using Wildcards

A wildcard can help you locate information when you are uncertain how the information might be displayed in your records. The placement of the asterisk in relationship to the known value determines the result. If it is placed first, the variable will be in the beginning of the string of characters. For example, in a list of names if you used **son* as the criteria, it will look for any name that ends in *son*. The results might display *Peterson*, *Michelson*, and *Samuelson*. If the asterisk is at the end of the known value in the criteria, then the variable will be at the end. You can also include the asterisk wildcard at the beginning and at the end of a known value.

A question mark (?) can also be used as part of your search criteria. Each question mark used in the criteria represents a single position or character that is unknown in a group of specified values. Searching for *m?n* would find, for example, *min*, *men*, and *man*; whereas searching for m??d would find, for example, *mind*, *mend*, *mold*.

Activity 5.20 | Extracting Filtered Rows

You can copy the results of a filter to another area of your worksheet, instead of displaying a filtered list as you did in the previous activity. The location to which you copy the records is the ***Extract area***, and is commonly placed below the table of data. Using this technique you can ***extract***—pull out—multiple sets of data for comparison purposes.

In this activity, you will extract data to compare how many faculty have a Morning-Evening schedule and how many have a Morning-Afternoon schedule.

1 From your student files, open **e05B_Fall_Faculty**. Display the **Save As** dialog box, navigate to your **Excel Chapter 5** folder, and then save the workbook as **Lastname_Firstname_5B_Fall_Faculty**

2 Be sure the first worksheet, **Schedule Comparison**, is the active sheet. **Copy** the range **A6:G7**, **Paste** it in cell **A1**, and then change the title in cell **A1** to **Criteria**

3 Select the range **A2:G3**, and then in the **Name Box**, name this range **Criteria**

4 **Copy** the range **A1:G2**, scroll down to view **row 36**, point to cell **A36**, right-click, and then under **Paste Options**, click the first **Paste (P)** button. Click cell **A36**, change the title to **Morning-Evening Schedule** and then press Enter. Compare your screen with Figure 5.50.

Figure 5.50

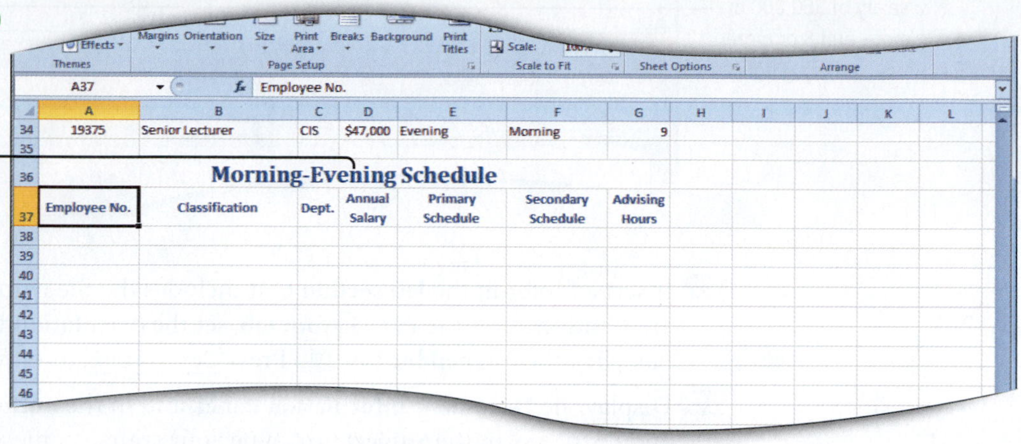

5 Select the range **A37:G37** and then in the **Name Box**, name this range **Extract**

This action defines the Extract area so that the range will display automatically in the Copy to box of the Advanced Filter dialog box. Excel recognizes *Extract* as the location in which to place the results of an advanced filter.

6 Select the range **A7:G34** and then in the **Name Box**, name this range **Database**

Excel recognizes the name *Criteria* as a criteria range, the name *Database* as the range to be filtered, and the name *Extract* for the area where you want to paste the result.

7 At the top of your worksheet, in cell **E3**, type **Morning** and in cell **F3**, type **Evening** and then press Enter.

When applied, the filter will display only those records where the Primary Schedule is Morning and the Secondary Schedule is Evening.

8 On the **Data tab**, in the **Sort & Filter group**, click the **Advanced** button.

9 Under **Action**, click the **Copy to another location** option button. Verify that in the **Copy to** box, the absolute reference to the Extract area—*$A$37:$G$37*—displays. Compare your screen with Figure 5.51.

Figure 5.51

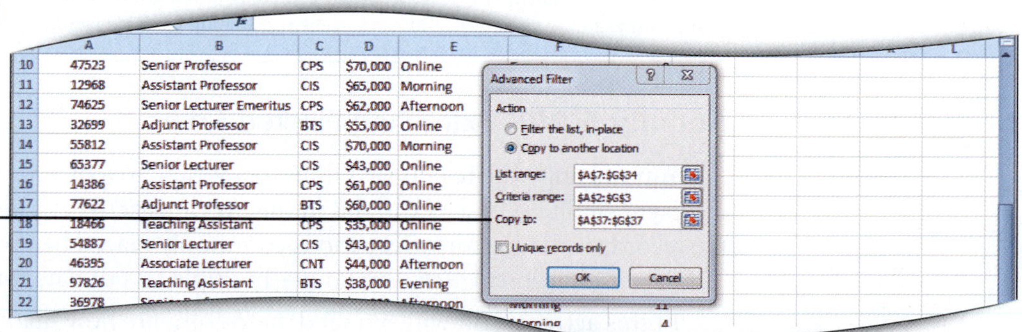

10 Click **OK**, and then scroll to view the lower portion of your worksheet. Compare your screen with Figure 5.52.

Two records meet the criteria and are copied to the extract area on your worksheet. When you use an extract area in this manner, instead of reformatting the table to display the qualifying records, Excel places a copy of the qualifying records in the Extract area.

Figure 5.52

Two records display in the Morning-Evening extract area

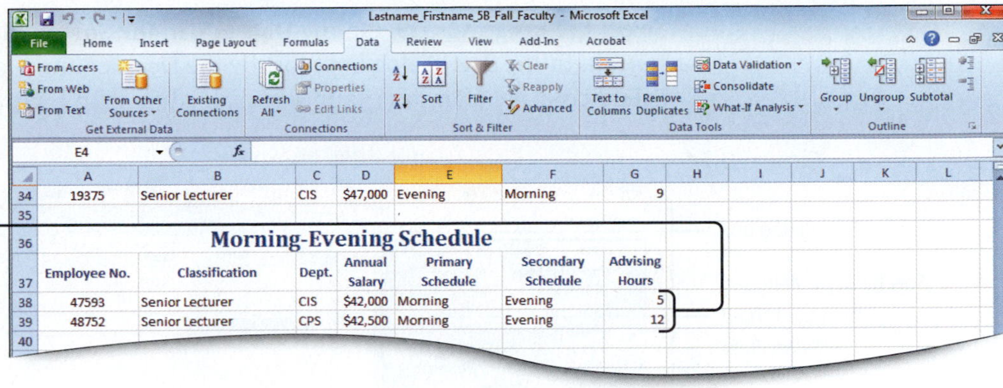

11 **Copy** the range **A36:G37**, and then **Paste** it in cell **A41**. In cell **A41**, change the word *Evening* to **Afternoon**

12 At the top of your worksheet, in cell **F3**, change the criteria to **Afternoon** Display the **Advanced Filter** dialog box, and then click the **Copy to another location** option button.

13 In the **Copy to** box, click the **Collapse Dialog** button, scroll down as necessary, and then select the range **A42:G42**. Click the **Expand Dialog** button, and then click **OK**. Scroll to view the lower portion of the worksheet, and then compare your screen with Figure 5.53.

Three records meet the criteria and are copied to the extract area on your worksheet.

Figure 5.53

Three records display in the Morning-Afternoon extract area

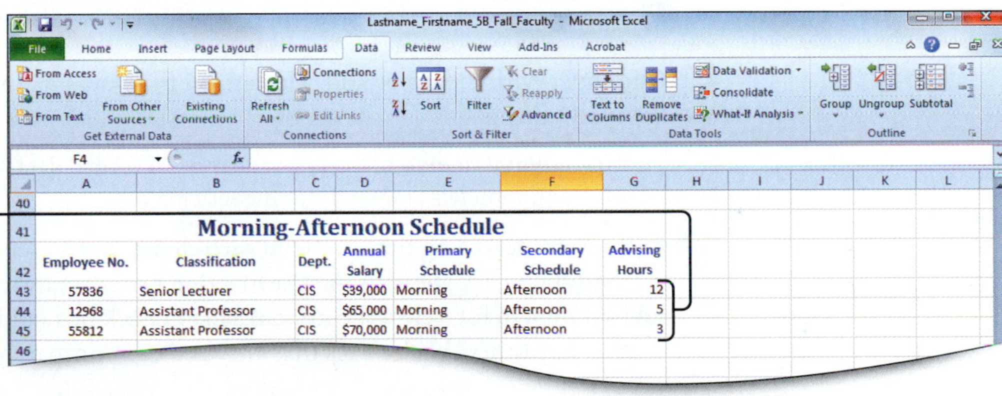

14 **Save** and then leave this workbook open for the next activity.

Objective 7 | Subtotal, Outline, and Group a List of Data

You can group and summarize a ***list***—a series of rows that contains related data—by adding subtotals. The first step in adding subtotals is to sort the data by the field for which you want to create a subtotal.

Activity 5.21 | Subtotaling, Outlining, and Grouping a List of Data

In this activity, you will assist Dean Mosier in summarizing the faculty salaries by department.

1 In your **5B_Fall_Faculty** workbook, display the second worksheet—**Salaries by Department**.

2 Select the range **A2:G29**. On the **Data tab**, in the **Sort & Filter group**, click the **Sort** button. In the **Sort** dialog box, sort by the **Dept.** column, and then by the **Annual Salary** column. Compare your **Sort** dialog box with Figure 5.54.

Figure 5.54

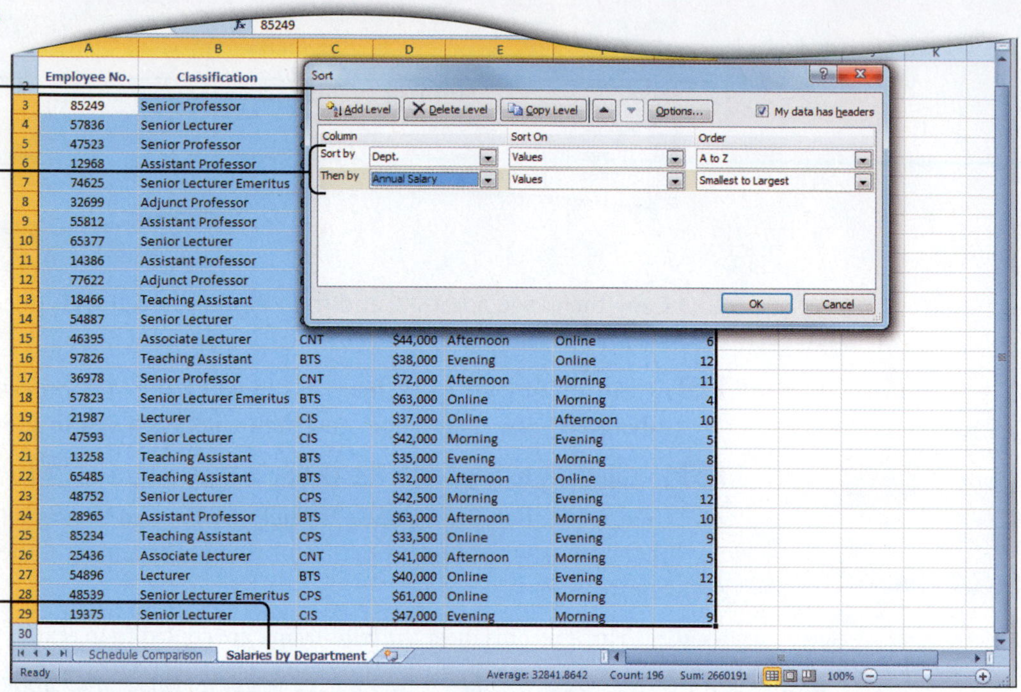

3 Click **OK**. With the range still selected, on the **Data tab**, in the **Outline group**, click the **Subtotal** button.

The ***Subtotal command*** totals several rows of related data together by automatically inserting subtotals and totals for the selected cells.

4 In the **Subtotal** dialog box, in the **At each change in** box, click the arrow to display the list, and then click **Dept.** In the **Use function** box, display the list and click **Sum.** In the **Add subtotal to** list, select the **Annual Salary** check box, and then scroll the list and *deselect* any other check boxes that are selected. Compare your screen with Figure 5.55.

These actions direct Excel to create a group for each change in value in the Dept. field. Excel will then use the Sum function to add a subtotal in the Annual Salary field. The check boxes at the bottom of the dialog box indicate how the subtotals will display.

Figure 5.55

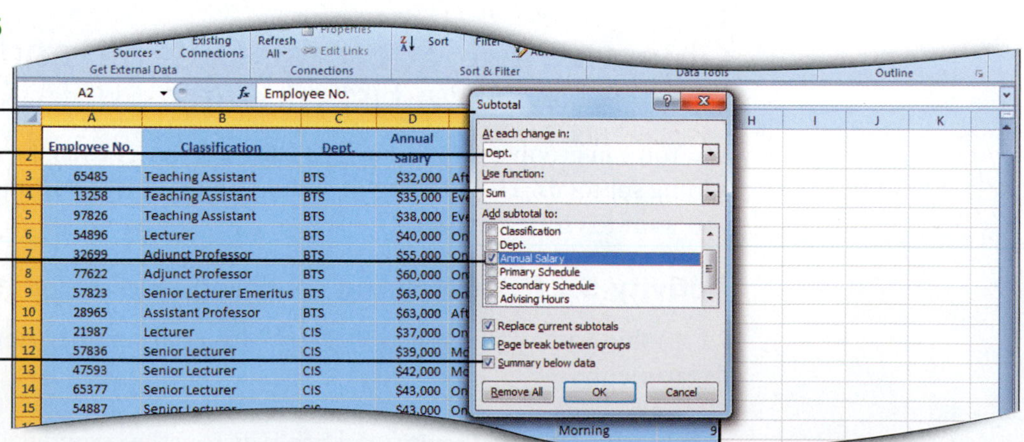

5 Click **OK**, scroll to view the lower portion of the data, and then compare your screen with Figure 5.56.

At the end of each Dept. group, inserted rows containing the subtotals for the salaries within each department display.

Figure 5.56

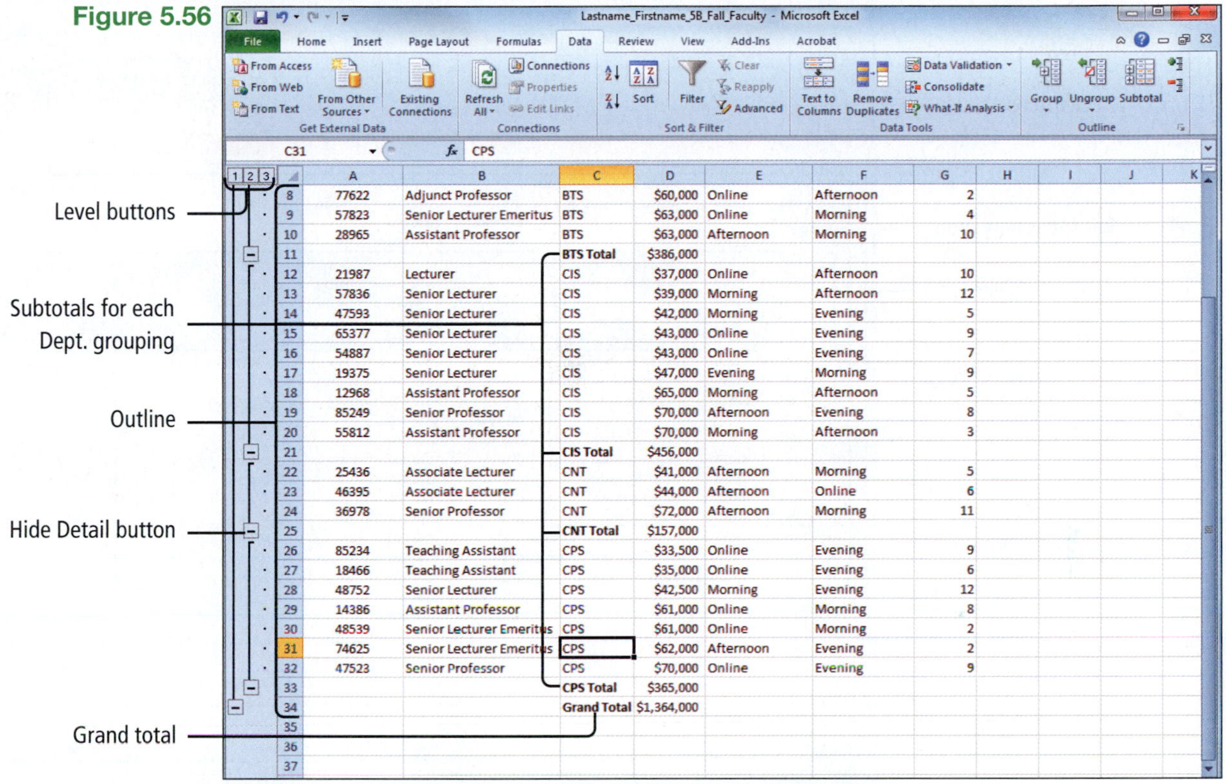

6 Click any cell to deselect, and then along the left edge of your workbook, locate the outline.

When you add subtotals, Excel defines groups based on the rows used to calculate a subtotal. The groupings form an outline of your worksheet based on the criteria you indicated in the Subtotal dialog box, and the outline displays along the left side of your worksheet.

The outline bar along the left side of the worksheet enables you to show and hide levels of detail with a single mouse click. For example, you can show details with the totals, which is the default view. Or, you can show only the summary totals or only the grand total.

There are three types of controls in the outline. Hide Detail (−) collapses a group of cells, Show Detail (+) expands a collapsed group of cells, and the level buttons (1, 2, 3) can hide all levels of detail below the number clicked.

7 To the left of **row 25**, click the **Hide Detail** button (−) to collapse the detail for the **CNT** department.

Detail data refers to the subtotaled rows that are totaled and summarized. Detail data is typically adjacent to and either above or to the left of the summary data.

8 Select **rows 13:17**, and then on the **Data tab**, in the **Outline group**, click the **Group** button. Compare your screen with Figure 5.57.

A fourth group is created and a bar spans the group.

Figure 5.57

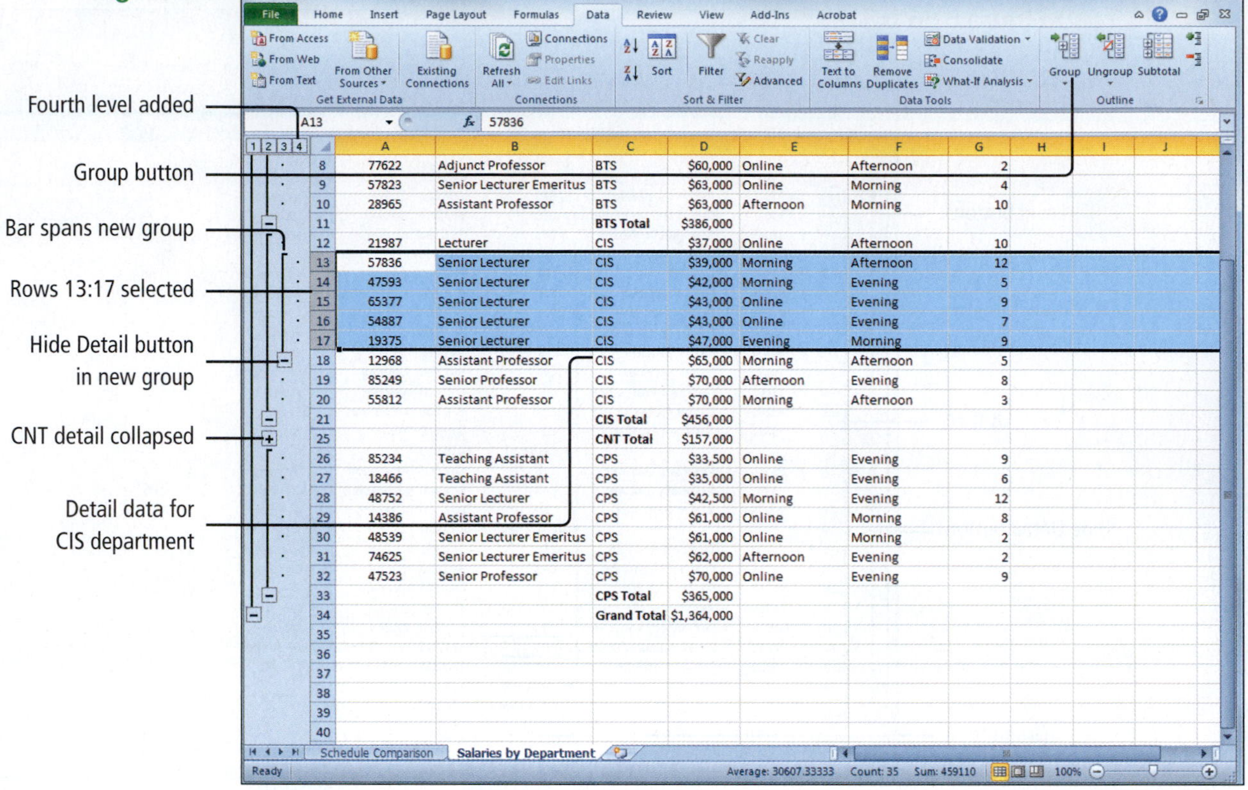

9 To the left of **row 18**, click the **Hide Detail** button (−) for the new group, and notice that the group is collapsed and a break in the row numbers indicates that some rows are hidden from view.

Hiding the detail data in this manner does not change the subtotal for the CIS group—it remains $456,000.

10 At the top of the outline area, click the **Level 2** button to hide all Level 3 and 4 details and display only the Level 2 summary information and the Level 1 Grand Total. Press Ctrl + Home and compare your screen with Figure 5.58.

Figure 5.58

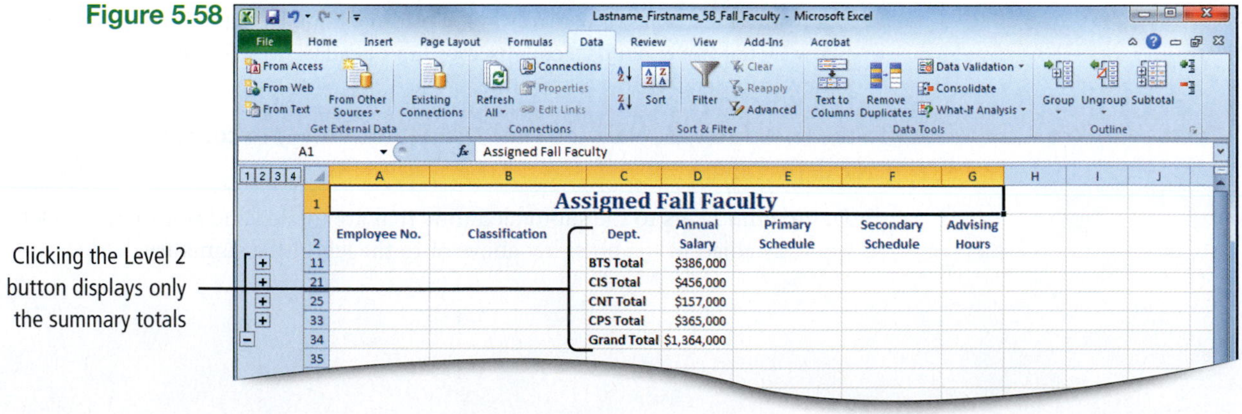

11 Group the two worksheets. Insert a footer in the **left section** that includes the file name, and in the **right section**, insert the **Sheet Name**. Click any cell to exit the footer area, and then on the status bar, click the **Normal** button. On the **Page Layout tab**, set the **Width** to **1 page** and set the **Height** to **1 page**—this will scale each worksheet to fit on a single page. You may hear a double chime. Press Ctrl + Home to move to cell **A1**.

12 Display the **Document Panel**, and in the **Author** box, type your firstname and lastname, in the **Subject** box, type your course name and section number, and in the **Keywords** box, type **faculty, schedule, salaries Close** the **Document Properties**.

13 Display the **Print Preview**, redisplay the workbook, and then make any necessary corrections or adjustments.

14 **Save** your workbook. Along with your other two workbooks from this project, print or submit electronically as directed. If required, print or create an electronic version of your worksheets with formulas displayed, using the instructions in Activity 1.16 in Project 1A. **Close** Excel.

More Knowledge | Outlining a Worksheet

A horizontal outline bar can be created for data that is summarized by row, rather than summarized by column as it was in this activity. In addition, if the data is not organized so that Excel can outline it automatically, you can create an outline manually. To do so, on the Data tab, in the Outline group, click the Group button, and then click Auto Outline.

End **You have completed Project 5B**

Content-Based Assessments

Summary

In this chapter, you navigated and managed a large worksheet to locate, insert, and delete information. You also used two of Excel's formatting tools—Themes and Table Styles—to create custom enhanced results for an attractive worksheet. You saved Excel data in several file formats—Web page, CSV, PDF, and XPS. Finally, you used advanced sort and filter techniques along with subtotaling, outlining, and grouping for data analysis.

Key Terms

Matching

Match each term in the second column with its correct definition in the first column by writing the letter of the term on the blank line in front of the correct definition.

____ 1. The command to set the column and row headings so that they remain on the screen while you scroll to other parts of the worksheet.

____ 2. The command that tiles all open program windows on the screen.

____ 3. A set of formatting characteristics that you can apply to a cell.

____ 4. Colored and underlined text that, when clicked, takes you to another location in the worksheet, to another file, to a Web page on the Internet, or on your organization's intranet.

____ 5. The file type that saves an Excel file so that there is a comma between each cell and a paragraph return at the end of each row.

____ 6. The file type that saves an Excel file with tabs between each cell in a row and a paragraph return at the end of each row.

____ 7. An organized collection of facts related to a specific topic.

____ 8. All of the categories of data pertaining to one person, place, thing, event, or idea.

____ 9. A single piece of information that is stored in every record.

A Arrange All
B AutoFilter menu
C Cell styles
D Comparison operators
E Criteria
F CSV file (comma separated values)
G Database
H Extract area
I Field
J Freeze Panes
K Hyperlink
L Query
M Record
N Tab delimited text file
O Wildcard

_____ 10. The term that refers to asking a question of the data in a database.

_____ 11. The term used for conditions that you specify that must be matched for the record to be included in the search results.

_____ 12. A menu of filtering commands that displays when you click one of the filter arrows in an Excel table.

_____ 13. The Equal sign (=), Greater Than sign (>), or Less Than sign (<) used singly or in combinations to compare two values.

_____ 14. A character such as the asterisk (*) used to search a field when you are uncertain of the exact value or when you want to widen the search to include more records.

_____ 15. The area where you place the results when copying the results of a filter to another location in the worksheet.

Multiple Choice

Circle the correct answer.

1. The command to find and select specific text, formatting, or type of information within a workbook quickly is:
A. match **B.** sort **C.** find

2. A portion of a worksheet window bounded by and separated from other portions by vertical or horizontal bars is a:
A. border **B.** pane **C.** window

3. A predesigned set of colors, fonts, lines, and fill effects that look good together is a:
A. list **B.** theme **C.** text file

4. The page formatting that reduces the horizontal and vertical size of the printed data by a percentage or by the number of pages that you specify is:
A. extracting **B.** arranging **C.** scaling

5. The file type developed by Adobe Systems that is a visual representation of a document is:
A. PDF **B.** XPS **C.** CSV

6. The file type developed by Microsoft that is a visual representation of a document is:
A. PDF **B.** XPS **C.** CSV

7. To organize data in a particular order is to:
A. filter **B.** sort **C.** query

8. Numbers sorted from highest to lowest are sorted in:
A. descending order **B.** ascending order **C.** major order

9. The term that describes filtering actions in which each additional filter that you apply is based on the current filter is:
A. extracted **B.** scaled **C.** additive

10. The operator that requires each and every one of the comparison criteria that you specify must be true is the:
A. Or operator **B.** And operator **C.** detail operator

Content-Based Assessments

Apply 5A skills from these Objectives:

1. Navigate and Manage Large Worksheets
2. Enhance Worksheets with Themes and Styles
3. Format a Worksheet to Share with Others
4. Save Excel Data in Other File Formats

Skills Review | Project 5C Science Schedule

In the following Skills Review, you will assist Jack Littlefield, Program Chair for Science, in formatting and navigating a large worksheet that lists the class schedule for the Science departments at Capital Cities Community College. You will also save Excel data in other file formats. Your completed workbooks will look similar to Figure 5.59.

Project Files

For Project 5C, you will need the following files:

e05C_Science_Faculty
e05C_Science_Requests
e05C_Science_Schedule

You will save your workbooks as:

Lastname_Firstname_5C_Science_CSV
Lastname_Firstname_5C_Science_Faculty
Lastname_Firstname_5C_Science_Schedule
Lastname_Firstname_5C_Science_Webpage

Project Results

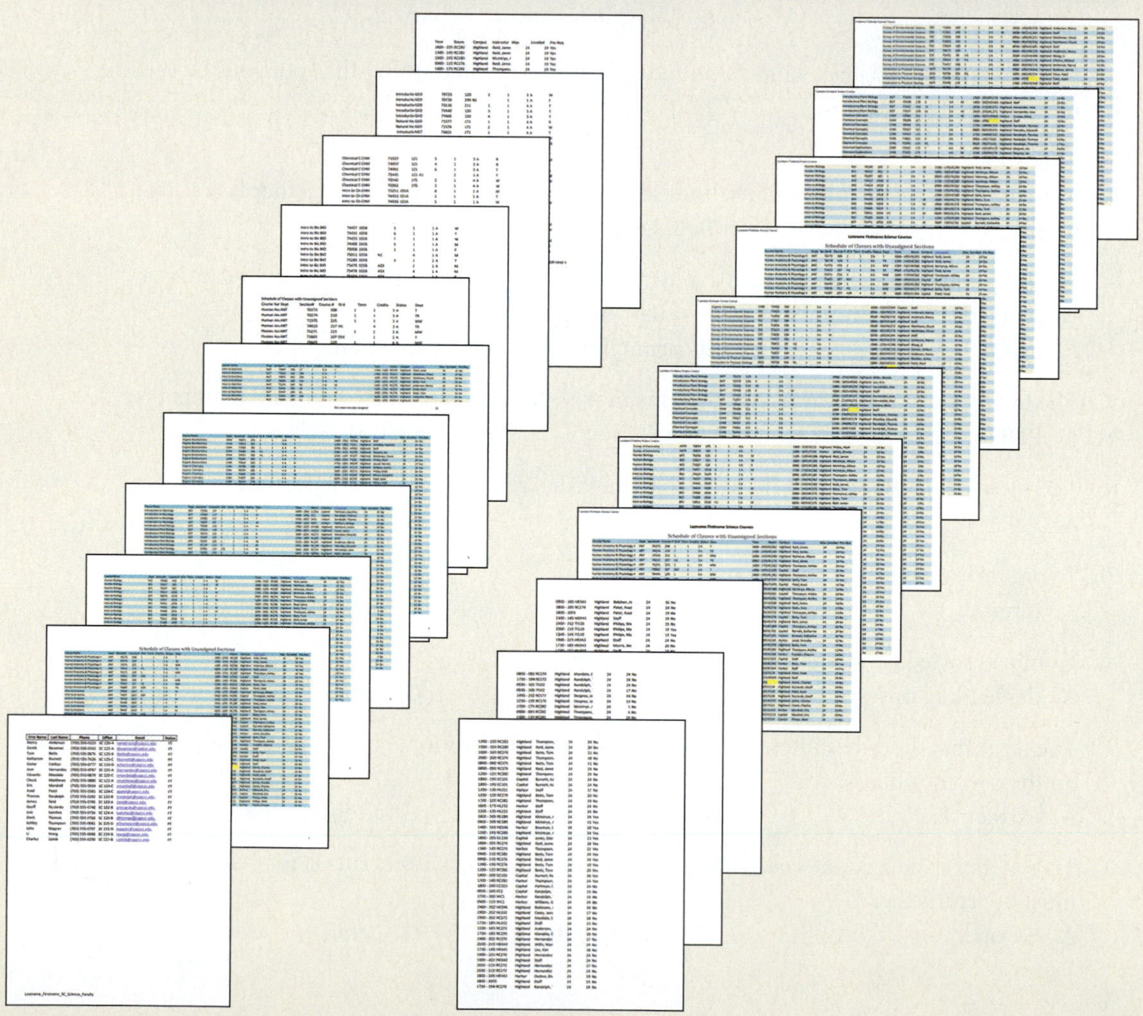

Figure 5.59

(Project 5C Science Schedule continues on the next page)

Skills Review | Project 5C Science Schedule (continued)

1 **Start** Excel. From your student files, open the file **e05C_Science_Schedule**. Display the **Save As** dialog box, navigate to your **Excel Chapter 5** folder, and then save the workbook as **Lastname_Firstname_5C_Science_Schedule**

a. On the **Home tab**, in the **Editing group**, click the **Find & Select** button, and then click **Go To Special**. In the first column, click the **Blanks** option button, and then click **OK** to select all blank cells in the worksheet's active area. Point to the selected cell **K31** and right-click. On the Mini toolbar, click the **Fill Color button arrow**, and then under **Standard Colors**, click the fourth color—**Yellow**—to fill all the selected blank cells. These cells still require Room assignments.

b. Press Ctrl + Home. From the column heading area, select **columns E:H**. Right-click over the selected area, and then click **Hide**.

c. On the **Home tab**, in the **Editing group**, click the **Find & Select** button, and then click **Go To**. In the **Go To** dialog box, in the **Reference** box, type **m172** and then click **OK**. With cell **M172** active, on the **Formulas tab**, click the **More Functions** button, point to **Statistical**, and then click **COUNTIF**. As the **Range**, type **m2:m170** and as the **Criteria**, type **Staff** Click **OK**. Your result is 27, indicating that 27 courses still indicate *Staff* and need an instructor assigned. In cell **I172**, type **Still need instructor assigned** and press Enter. Press Ctrl + Home and click **Save**.

2 From your student files, open **e05C_Science_Requests**. On the **View tab**, in the **Window group**, click the **Switch Windows** button, and then at the bottom of the list, click your **Lastname_Firstname_5C_Science_Schedule** file to make it the active worksheet. In the **Window group**, click the **Arrange All** button. Click **Horizontal**, and then click **OK**. If necessary, click the title bar of your **5C_Science_Schedule** worksheet to make it the active worksheet. Press Ctrl + End to move to cell **P172**.

a. Click cell **A172**. In the **Window group**, click **Split**. Above the split bar, click any cell in **column C**. Press Ctrl + F to display the **Find and Replace** dialog box. Locate the first request in the **e05C_Science_Requests** worksheet, which is from *Eric Marshall* to teach *Survey of Astronomy Section # 76822*. In the **Find what** box, type **76822** so that you can locate the course in the worksheet.

b. Click **Find Next**. Drag the title bar of the dialog box into the upper right area of your screen so that you can see the **Name Box**, which indicates *C38*. In your **5C_Science_Schedule** worksheet, click in cell **M38**, type **Marshall, Eric** to delete *Staff* and assign the class to Mr. Marshall. Press Enter.

c. Continue to use the **Find and Replace** dialog box to locate the remaining three **Section #s** listed in the **e05C_Science_Requests** worksheet, and enter the appropriate instructor name for each class in **column M** of your **5C_Science_Schedule** worksheet. **Close** the **Find and Replace** dialog box. In cell **M172**, notice that *23* classes remain unassigned.

d. Click any cell in the **e05C_Science_Requests** worksheet, and then on this worksheet's title bar, click the **Close** button. Then, on the title bar of your **5C_Science_Schedule** worksheet, click the **Maximize** button to restore the size of the worksheet to its full size. On the **View tab**, in the **Window group**, click **Split** to remove the split.

e. Press Ctrl + Home. From the **column heading area**, select **columns D:I**. Right-click over the selected area, and then click **Unhide**. Press Ctrl + Home, and then **Save** your workbook.

3 Point to the **row 1 heading** to display the → pointer, right-click, and then click **Insert**. In cell **A1**, type **Schedule of Classes with Unassigned Sections** **Merge & Center** this title across the range **A1:P1**, and then apply the **Title** cell style.

a. On the **Page Layout tab**, in the **Themes group**, click the **Themes** button, and then, click the **Apex** theme. In the **Themes group**, click the **Fonts** button. Scroll to the top and click the **Office** fonts.

b. On the **Home tab**, in the **Styles group**, click the **Format as Table** button. At the bottom, click **New Table Style**. In the **New Table Quick Style** dialog box, in the **Name** box, replace the existing text by typing **Science Schedule** In the list under **Table Element**, click **First Row Stripe**, and then click the **Format** button. In the **Format Cells** dialog box, click the **Fill tab**. In the fifth column of colors, click the second color. In the lower right corner, click **OK**.

(Project 5C Science Schedule continues on the next page)

Skills Review | Project 5C Science Schedule (continued)

c. In the list of table elements, click **Second Row Stripe**, click the **Format** button, and then in the third row of colors, click the seventh color. Click **OK**. In the list of table elements, click **Header Row**, click the **Format** button, and then in the seventh column, click the fourth color. Click **OK**, in the lower left corner of the dialog box, click to select the check box **Set as default table quick style for this document**, and then click **OK**.

d. Select the range **A2:P171**, and then in the **Styles group**, click **Format as Table**. At the top of the gallery, under **Custom**, locate and click your custom **Science Schedule** table style. In the **Format As Table** dialog box, click **OK**. Then, because you do not need to filter the table, in the **Tools group**, click **Convert to Range**, and then click **Yes**. Press Ctrl + Home to deselect and move to cell **A1**. Click **Save**.

4 Select **columns A:P**, in the **Cells group**, click the **Format** button, and then click **AutoFit Column Width**. On the **Page Layout tab**, in the **Page Setup group**, set the **Orientation** to **Landscape**. Then, in the **Scale to Fit group**, click the **Width arrow**, and then click **1 page**. Click the **Height arrow** and click **4 pages**.

a. From the **Insert tab**, insert a footer in the **left section** that includes the file name. Click in the right section, and then in the **Header & Footer Elements group**, click the **Page Number** button. Click in a cell just above the footer to exit the Footer area.

b. On the **View tab**, in the **Workbook Views group**, click **Page Break Preview**, and close the dialog box if necessary. Point to the horizontal page break line between **Page 1** and **Page 2** to display the pointer, and then drag the line up between **row 42** and **row 43**. Position the break between **Page 2** and **Page 3** between **row 74** and **row 75**. Position the break between **Page 3** and **Page 4** between **row 116** and **row 117**. Position the break between **Page 4** and **Page 5** between **row 152** and **row 153**.

c. On the **View tab**, in the **Workbook Views group**, click the **Normal** button to redisplay the worksheet in **Normal** view, and then press Ctrl + Home.

d. Display the **Print Preview**, scroll through the pages, and notice that the column titles display only on the first page. Click the **Page Layout tab**, in the **Page Setup group**, click the **Print Titles** button to display the **Sheet tab** of the **Page Setup** dialog box.

e. Under **Print titles**, click in the **Rows to repeat at top** box, and then in the worksheet, select **row 2**. Click **OK**. Click **Save**.

5 From **Backstage** view, display the **Open** dialog box, and then from your student files, open the file **e05C_Science_Faculty**. Display the **Save As** dialog box, navigate to your **Excel Chapter 5** folder, and then save the file as **Lastname_Firstname_5C_Science_Faculty** Insert a footer in the **left section** with the file name, click outside the footer area, press Ctrl + Home and return to **Normal** view. Click **Save**, and then close this workbook to redisplay your **5C_Science_Schedule** workbook.

a. Click cell **M2**. On the **Insert tab**, in the **Links group**, click the **Hyperlink** button. Under **Link to**, click **Existing File or Web Page**. Click the **Look in arrow**, navigate to your **Excel Chapter 5** folder, and then select your **Lastname_Firstname_5C_Science_Faculty** workbook. Click **OK**.

b. Point to cell **M2** to display the pointer, and then click to confirm that the link opens the workbook containing the contact information. Close the workbook with the faculty contacts.

c. Point to cell **M2**, right-click, and then click **Edit Hyperlink**. In the upper right corner of the **Insert Hyperlink** dialog box, click the **ScreenTip** button. In the **ScreenTip text** box, type **Click here for contact information** Click **OK** two times. Point to cell **M2** and confirm that your ScreenTip displays.

d. Display the **Document Panel** and in the **Author** box, type your firstname and lastname, in the **Subject** box, type your course name and section number, and in the **Keywords** box, type **science schedule** **Close** the Document Panel and click **Save**. Leave the workbook open.

6 Display the **Save As** dialog box, in the lower portion, click the **Save as type arrow**, and then click **Web Page**.

a. Click the **Change Title** button. In the **Enter Text** dialog box, in the **Page title** box, using your own name, type **Lastname Firstname Science Courses** Click **OK**, and notice that in the **Page title** box, your typed text displays. In the **Save As** dialog box, click the **Publish** button.

b. In the **Publish as Web Page** dialog box, click the **Choose arrow**, and then click **Items on Science Classes**—recall that the worksheet name is *Science*

(Project 5C Science Schedule continues on the next page)

Skills Review | Project 5C Science Schedule (continued)

Classes. In the lower left corner, if necessary, click to select (place a check mark in) the **Open published web page in browser** check box.

c. Click the **Browse** button to display the **Publish As** dialog box. If necessary, navigate to your **Excel Chapter 5** folder. In the **File name** box, type **Lastname_Firstname_5C_Science_Webpage** Click **OK**, and then in the displayed **Publish as Web Page** dialog box, click **Publish**.

d. If you are instructed to print your Web page on paper, consult the instructions to print from your specific browser software. On the browser title bar, click the **Close** button. Leave your **Lastname_Firstname_5C_Science_Schedule** workbook open for the next step.

e. Display the **Save As** dialog box, be sure you are saving in your **Excel Chapter 5** folder, set the **Save as type** to **CSV (Comma delimited)**, and as the **File name**, type **Lastname_Firstname_5C_Science_CSV** Click **Save**, and then click **Yes**.

f. **Close** your **5C_Science_CSV** file, click **Save**, and then click **Yes**. **Close** Excel. As directed by your instructor, submit the four files that comprise the results of this project.

End **You have completed Project 5C**

Content-Based Assessments

Apply 5B skills from these Objectives:

- 5 Use Advanced Sort Techniques
- 6 Use Custom and Advanced Filters
- 7 Subtotal, Outline, and Group a List of Data

Skills Review | Project 5D Spring Sections

In the following Skills Review, you will use advanced table features to provide Dr. Paula Marshall, the Dean of the Arts Division, information about the Spring course sections and assigned faculty in the Division. Your completed worksheets will look similar to Figure 5.60.

Project Files

For Project 5D, you will need the following files:

e05D_Spring_Faculty
e05D_Spring_Sections

You will save your workbooks as:

Lastname_Firstname_5D_Spring_Faculty
Lastname_Firstname_5D_Spring_Sections

Project Results

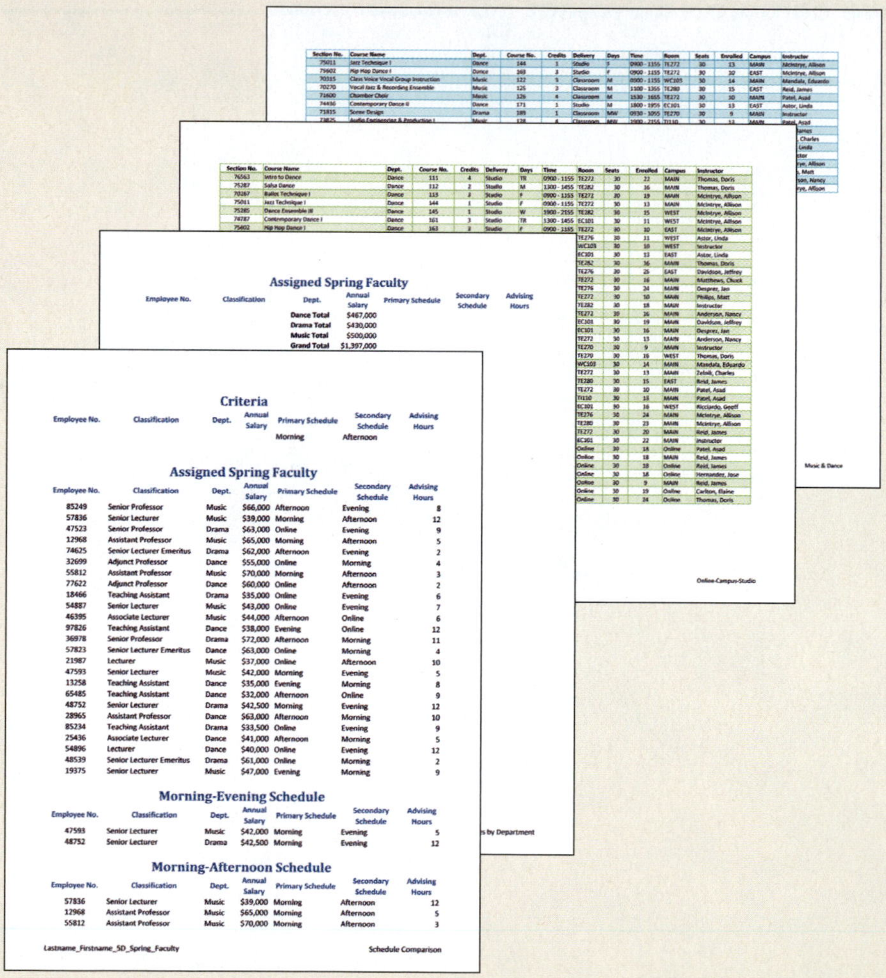

Figure 5.60

(Project 5D Spring Sections continues on the next page)

Skills Review | Project 5D Spring Sections (continued)

1 **Start** Excel. From your student files, open the file **e05D_Spring_Sections**, and then **Save** the file in your **Excel Chapter 5** folder as **Lastname_Firstname_5D_Spring_Sections** Be sure the first worksheet, **Online-Campus-Studio** displays.

a. On the **Data tab**, in the **Sort & Filter group**, click **Sort**. In the **Sort** dialog box, under **Column**, click the **Sort by arrow**, and then click **Delivery**. Under **Sort On**, click the **arrow**, and then click **Values**. Under **Order**, click the **Order arrow** for this sort level, and then click **Custom List**. In the dialog box, under **Custom lists**, be sure **NEW LIST** is selected. Then, under **List entries**, click in the empty box and type **Studio** Press Enter, type **Classroom** Press Enter, and then type **Online**

b. In the **Custom Lists** dialog box, click the **Add** button, and then click **OK**. If necessary, in the **Sort** dialog box, click the **Order arrow**, and then click your **Studio, Classroom, Online** custom list so that it displays in the **Order** box. Click the **Add Level** button, and then as the second level sort, click **Dept**. Click the **Add Level** button again, and as the third level sort, click **Course Name**. Click **OK**.

2 Click the **Music & Dance sheet tab** to display the *second* worksheet. In cell **C1**, click the **Dept. filter arrow**. On the displayed list, click the **(Select All)** check box to clear all the check boxes, and then select the **Music** and **Drama** check boxes. Click **OK**.

a. In cell **E1**, click the **Credits filter arrow**, and then filter the list further by **3**. In cell **F1**, click the **Delivery filter arrow**, and filter the list further by **Online**. The status bar information reveals that *4* of the *39* course sections that are either in the Music or Drama departments and that are 3-credit courses offered online.

b. On the **Data tab**, in the **Sort & Filter group**, **Clear** all filters. In cell **K1**, click the **Enrolled filter arrow**, point to **Number Filters**, and then click **Less Than Or Equal To**. In the first box, be sure that *is less than or equal to* displays, and then in the second box type **15** Click **OK** to display *16* records.

c. Right-click over either of the two sheet tabs, and then click **Select All Sheets**. With the sheets grouped, insert a footer in the **left section** that includes the file name. Click in the **center section** of the footer, and then on the **Design tab**, in the **Header & Footer Elements group**, click the **Page Number** button. Press Spacebar one time, type **of** and press Spacebar again, and then click the **Number of Pages** button. Click in the **right section** of the footer, and then on the **Design tab**, in the **Header & Footer Elements group**, click the **Sheet Name** button.

d. Click a cell outside of the footer, and then on the **Page Layout tab**, set the orientation to **Landscape**, and set the **Width** to **1 page**. Click the **Normal** button, and then press Ctrl + Home to move to cell **A1**.

e. Display the **Document Panel** and in the **Author** box, type your firstname and lastname, in the **Subject** box, type your course name and section number, and in the **Keywords** box, type **sort, filter, sections** **Close** the **Document Properties**, and then display **Print Preview**. Make any necessary corrections or adjustments.

f. **Save** your workbook. Hold this workbook until the end of this project, and then print or submit the two worksheets in this workbook electronically as directed by your instructor. **Close** this workbook, but leave Excel open.

3 From your student files, open **e05D_Spring_Faculty**. Display the **Save As** dialog box, navigate to your **Excel Chapter 5** folder, and then **Save** the workbook as **Lastname_Firstname_5D_Spring_Faculty** Be sure the **Schedule Comparison** worksheet is active. **Copy** the range **A6:G7**, **Paste** it in cell **A1**, and then change the title in cell **A1** to **Criteria**

a. Select the range **A2:G3**, and then in the **Name Box**, name this range **Criteria** **Copy** the range **A1:G2**, scroll down to view **row 34**, point to cell **A34**, right-click, and then click **Paste**. Click cell **A34**, and then change the title to **Morning-Evening Schedule** and then press Enter. Select the range **A35:G35** and then in the **Name Box**, name this range **Extract** Select the range **A7:G32** and then in the **Name Box**, name this range **Database**

b. At the top of your worksheet, in cell **E3**, type **Morning** and in cell **F3**, type **Evening** On the **Data tab**, in the **Sort & Filter group**, click the **Advanced** button. Under **Action**, click the **Copy to another location** option button. Verify that in the **Copy to** box—*$A$35:$G$35*—displays. Click **OK**, and then scroll to view the lower portion of your worksheet. Two records meet the criteria.

(Project 5D Spring Sections continues on the next page)

Skills Review | Project **5D** Spring Sections (continued)

c. Copy the range **A34:G35**, and then **Paste** it in cell **A39**. In cell **A39**, change the word *Evening* to **Afternoon** In cell **F3**, change the criteria to **Afternoon** Display the **Advanced Filter** dialog box, and then click the **Copy to another location** option button.

d. In the **Copy to** box, click the **Collapse Dialog** button, and then select the range **A40:G40**. Click the **Expand Dialog** button and then click **OK**. *Three* records meet the criteria and are copied to the extract area on your worksheet. **Save** the workbook.

4 Display the **Salaries by Department** worksheet. Select the range **A2:G30**. On the **Data tab**, in the **Sort & Filter group**, click the **Sort** button. In the **Sort** dialog box, sort by the **Dept.** column, and then by the **Annual Salary** column. Click **OK**.

a. With the range still selected, on the **Data tab**, in the **Outline group**, click the **Subtotal** button. In the **Subtotal** dialog box, in the **At each change in** box, display the list, and then click **Dept**. In the **Use function** box, display the list and click **Sum**. In the **Add subtotal to** list, select the **Annual Salary** check box, and then deselect any other check boxes. Click **OK**.

b. Click any cell to deselect, and then along the left edge of your workbook, locate the outline. To the left of **row 22**, click the **Hide Detail** button (-) to collapse the detail for the **Drama** department.

c. Select **rows 25:28**, and then on the **Data tab**, in the **Outline group**, click the **Group** button. To the left of **row 29**, click the **Hide Detail** button. At the top of the outline area, click the **Level 2** button to hide all Level 3 and 4 details, and display only the Level 2 summary information, and the Level 1 Grand Total. Press Ctrl + Home.

d. Group the two worksheets. Insert a footer in the **left section** that includes the file name, and in the **right section**, insert the **Sheet Name**. Click any cell to exit the footer area. On the **Page Layout tab**, set the **Width** to **1 page** and set the **Height** to **1 page**—this will scale each worksheet to fit on a single page. On the status bar, click the **Normal** button. Press Ctrl + Home to move to cell **A1**.

e. Display the **Document Panel**, and in the **Author** box, type your firstname and lastname, in the **Subject** box, type your course name and section number, and in the **Keywords** box, type **faculty, schedule, salaries** **Close** the **Document Properties** and display the **Print Preview**. Make any necessary corrections or adjustments.

f. **Save** your workbook, and then close it. Along with your other workbook from this project, print or submit electronically as directed If required, print or create an electronic version of your worksheets with formulas displayed, using the instructions in Activity 1.16 in Project 1A. **Close** Excel.

End **You have completed Project 5D**

Content-Based Assessments

Apply 5A skills from these Objectives:

1. Navigate and Manage Large Worksheets
2. Enhance Worksheets with Themes and Styles
3. Format a Worksheet to Share with Others
4. Save Excel Data in Other File Formats

Mastering Excel | Project 5E Sports Schedule

In the following Mastering Excel project, you will assist Tom Bloomington, Athletic Director at Capital Cities Community College, in formatting and navigating a large worksheet that lists the sports events schedule for spring sports. You will also save Excel data in other file formats. Your completed workbooks will look similar to Figure 5.61.

Project Files

For Project 5E, you will need the following files:

e05E_Sports_Coaches
e05E_Referee_Requests
e05E_Sports_Schedule

You will save your workbooks as:

Lastname_Firstname_5E_Sports_Coaches
Lastname_Firstname_5E_Sports_PDF
Lastname_Firstname_5E_Sports_Schedule
Lastname_Firstname_5E_Sports_Webpage

Project Results

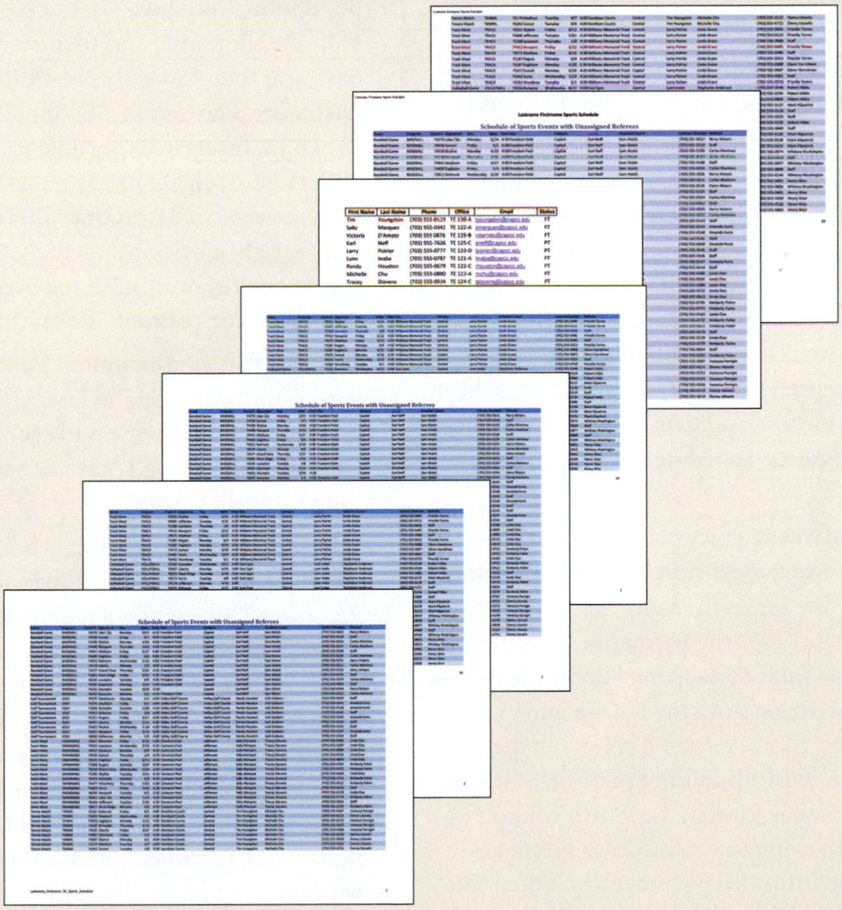

Figure 5.61

(Project 5E Sports Schedule continues on the next page)

Mastering Excel | Project 5E Sports Schedule (continued)

1 Start **Excel**. Open the file **e05E_Sports_Schedule** and **Save** it in your **Excel Chapter 5** folder as **Lastname_Firstname_5E_Sports_Schedule Go To** cell **M82**, and then insert the **COUNTIF** function. Set the **Range** as **m2:m80** and the **Criteria** as **Staff** resulting in *23* sporting events that still require a Referee assigned. In cell **K82**, type **Events with Unassigned Referees** Press Ctrl + Home. Open the file **e05E_Referee_Requests**. Switch windows, and then click your **Lastname_Firstname_5E_Sports_Schedule** file. Click **Arrange All** so the files are **Horizontal** with your **Lastname_Firstname_5E_Sports_Schedule** as the active worksheet in the top window.

2 Go to cell **A82**, **Split** the window horizontally, and then above the split bar, click in any cell in **column C**. Display the **Find and Replace** dialog box. Locate the first request in the **e05E_Referee_Requests** worksheet, which is from *Danny Litowitz* to referee *Tennis Match Event # 76243*. In the **Find what** box, type **76243** and then click **Find Next**, which indicates cell *C48*. In the **Lastname_Firstname_5E_Sports_Schedule** worksheet, click in cell **M48**, and then type **Danny Litowitz** to assign him as the *Referee*.

3 Use the **Find** command to locate the remaining three **Event #s** listed in the **e05E_Referee_Requests** worksheet, and then enter the appropriate referee for each sports event in **column M** of your **5E_Sports_Schedule** worksheet. **Close** the **Find and Replace** dialog box. In cell **M82**, notice that *19* sports events still need a referee assigned. Click in the **e05E_Referee_Requests** worksheet to display the Close button, and then **Close** the workbook. **Maximize** your **5E_Sports_Schedule** worksheet, and then remove the **Split**.

4 Select **row 1** and **insert** a new blank row. In cell **A1**, type **Schedule of Sports Events with Unassigned Referees Merge & Center** the title across the range **A1:M1**, and then apply the **Title** cell style. Click the **Format as Table** button, and then create a **New Table Style** named **Sports Schedule** Format the **First Row Stripe** from the **Fill tab** and in the fifth column of colors, click the second color. For the **Second Row Stripe**, in the fifth column of colors, click the third color. For the **Header Row**, in the fourth column of colors click the fourth color. Select the check box **Set as default table quick style for this document**, and then click **OK**. Select the range **A2:M81**, click **Format as Table**, and then select the **Custom** table style, *Sports Schedule*. In the **Tools group**, click **Convert to Range**, and then click **Yes**. Press Ctrl + Home to deselect and move to cell **A1**.

5 Select **columns A:M** and then apply **AutoFit Column Width**. Set the **Orientation** to **Landscape**, and then in the **Scale to Fit group**, set the **Width** to **1 page** and the **Height** to **4 pages**. Insert a footer in the **left section** that includes the file name, and in the **right section**, insert a page number. Apply **Page Break Preview**, and then drag the line to break **Page 1** after **row 49**—this will end the page with *TENNIS* and begin **Page 2** with *TRACK*. Return to **Normal** view. On the **Page Layout tab**, set **Print Titles** to repeat **row 2** at the top of each page. Display **Print Preview** and examine the pages. Redisplay the workbook, make any necessary adjustments, and then **Save**. Leave this workbook displayed.

6 Open the file **e05E_Sports_Coaches** and **Save** it in your **Excel Chapter 5** folder as **Lastname_Firstname_5E_Sports_Coaches** Insert a footer in the **left section** with the file name, and then return to **Normal** view. **Save** and then **Close** this workbook to redisplay your **Lastname_Firstname_5E_Sports_Schedule** workbook. In cell **J2**, **Insert** a **Hyperlink** to link to an **Existing File or Web Page,** navigate to your **Excel Chapter 5** folder, and then select your **5E_Sports_Coaches** workbook. Point to cell **J2**, right-click, and then click **Edit Hyperlink**. Click the **ScreenTip** button. In the **ScreenTip text** box, type **Click here for contact information** Click **OK** two times.

7 Display the **Document Panel** and in the **Author** box, type your firstname and lastname, in the **Subject** box, type your course name and section number, and in the **Keywords** box, type **sports schedule Close** the **Document Panel** and click **Save**.

8 **Save** your **5E_Sports_Schedule** workbook as a **Web Page** with the name **Lastname_Firstname_Sports_Webpage** Change the **Page title** to **Lastname Firstname Sports Schedule** and then **Publish**. If necessary, place a check mark in the **Open published web page in browser** check box, select **Items on Sporting Events**, and then **Publish**. If you are instructed to print your Web page on paper, consult the instructions to print from your specific browser software. **Close** your browser. Leave your **Lastname_Firstname_5E_Sports_Schedule** workbook open.

(Project 5E Sports Schedule continues on the next page)

Mastering Excel | Project 5E Sports Schedule (continued)

9 Display the **Save As** dialog box, navigate to your **Excel Chapter 5** folder, set the **Save as type** to **PDF (Portable Document Format)**, and as the **File name** type **Lastname_Firstname_5E_Sports_PDF** Click **Save**. **Close** all files.

As directed by your instructor, print or submit electronically the four files that comprise the results of this project—two Excel files, a PDF file, and an HTML file.

End You have completed Project 5E

Apply **5B** skills from these Objectives:

- **5** Use Advanced Sort Techniques
- **6** Use Custom and Advanced Filters
- **7** Subtotal, Outline, and Group a List of Data

Mastering Excel | Project 5F Vocational Programs

In the following Mastering Excel project, you will edit a worksheet for Ron Lattimer, Vice President of Instruction, with data that has been sorted, filtered, and grouped that analyzes vocational programs at Capital Cities Community College. The worksheets of your workbook will look similar to Figure 5.62.

Project Files

For Project 5F, you will need the following file:

e05F_Vocational_Programs

You will save your workbook as:

Lastname_Firstname_5F_Vocational_Programs

Project Results

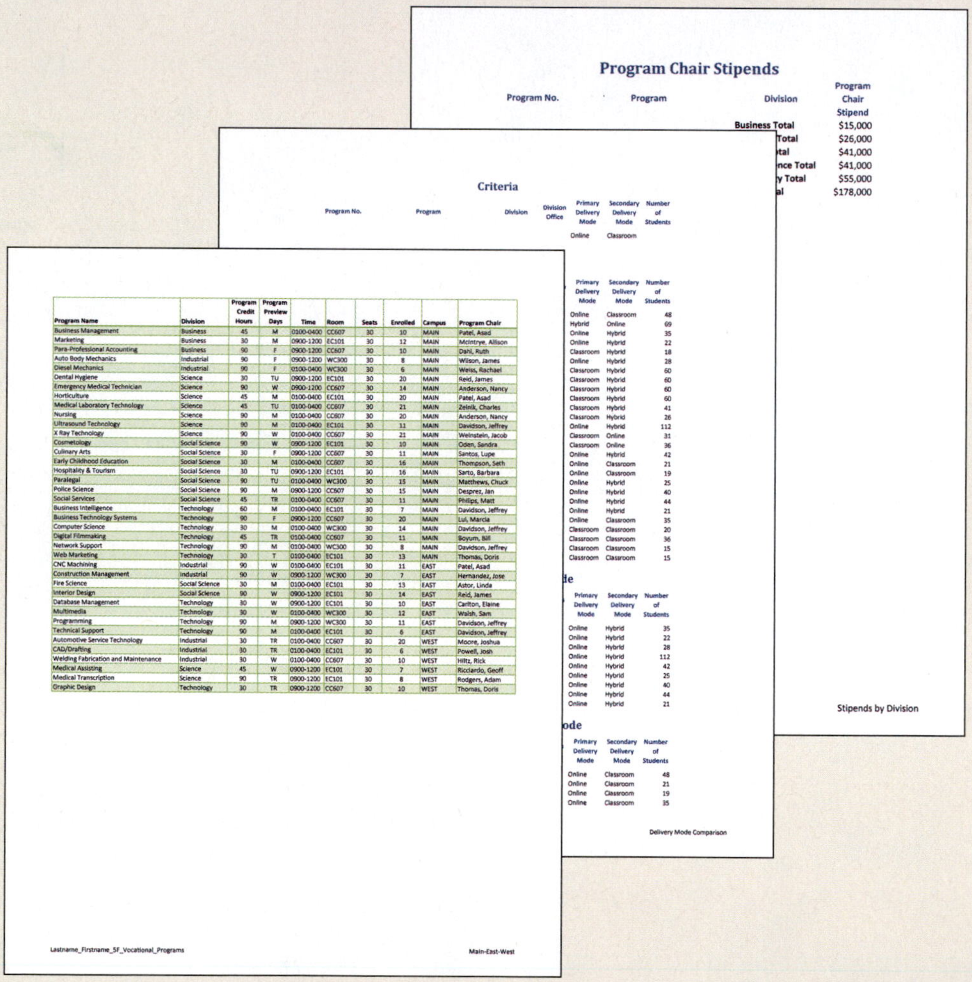

Figure 5.62

(Project 5F Vocational Programs continues on the next page)

Mastering Excel | Project 5F Vocational Programs (continued)

1 **Start** Excel. **Open** the file **e05F_Vocational_Programs**. **Save** the file in your **Excel Chapter 5** folder as **Lastname_Firstname_5F_Vocational_Programs** Display the *first* worksheet, **Main-East-West**. Select the range **A1:J40**, insert a table, and then apply **Table Style Light 18**. Click anywhere to deselect, on the **Data tab**, from the **Sort & Filter group**, display the **Sort** dialog box.

For the first sort level, sort by **Campus**, sort on **Values**, and then under **Order**, click the **arrow** and click **Custom List**. With **NEW LIST** selected, under **List entries**, type **Main** Press Enter, type **East** Press Enter, and then type **West** Click the **Add** button, and then click **OK**. In the **Order** box, click your **Main, East, West** custom list and click **OK**. Add a second level, sort by **Division** in alphabetical order on **Values**. Add a third level, sort by **Program Name** in alphabetical order on **Values**. Click **OK**.

2 On the **Design tab**, convert the data to a range. Display the *second* worksheet, **Delivery Mode Comparison**. **Copy** the range **A6:G7**. **Paste** it in cell **A1**, and then change the title in cell **A1** to **Criteria** Select the range **A2:G3**, and then in the **Name Box**, name this range **Criteria**

Copy the range **A1:G2**, scroll down to view **row 36**, point to cell **A36**, right-click, and then click **Paste**. Click cell **A36**, and then change the title to **Online-Hybrid Delivery Mode** and then press Enter. Select the range **A37:G37** and then in the **Name Box**, name this range **Extract** Select the range **A7:G34** and then in the **Name Box**, name this range **Database**

3 At the top of your worksheet, in cell **E3**, type **Online** and in cell **F3**, type **Hybrid** and then press Enter. On the **Data tab**, in the **Sort & Filter group**, click the **Advanced** button. Under **Action**, click the **Copy to another location** option button. Verify that in the **Copy to** box, the absolute reference to the Extract area—*$A$37:$G$37*—displays. Click **OK**. **Copy** the range **A36:G37**, and then **Paste** it in cell **A48**. In cell **A48** change the word *Hybrid* to **Classroom** In cell **F3**, change the criteria to **Classroom**

Display the **Advanced Filter** dialog box, and then click the **Copy to another location** option button. In the **Copy to** box, click the **Collapse Dialog** button, scroll down as necessary, and then select the range **A49:G49**. Click the **Expand Dialog** button, and then click **OK**.

4 Display the *third* worksheet—**Stipends by Division**. Select the range **A2:D41**. Display the **Sort** dialog box, **Sort** first by the **Division**, then by the **Program Chair Stipend**. Click **OK**. **Subtotal** at each change in **Division**, select the **Sum** function, add the subtotal to the **Program Chair Stipend**, and then click **OK**. **Group** the data so each **Division** is collapsed and a break in the row numbers indicates that some rows are hidden from view. Apply **AutoFit** to **column D** to display the **Grand Total**.

5 Select all three worksheets. Insert a footer in the **left section** that includes the file name, and in the **right section**, insert the **Sheet Name**. On the **Page Layout tab**, set the **Width** to **1 page** and set the **Height** to **1 page**. Click the **Margins** button, click **Custom Margins**, and then center horizontally. Return to **Normal** view, and then press Ctrl + Home to move to cell **A1**.

6 Display the **Document Panel**, and in the **Author** box, type your firstname and lastname, in the **Subject** box, type your course name and section number, and in the **Keywords** box, type **vocational programs** Examine the **Print Preview**, make any necessary corrections or adjustments, and then **Save** and **Close** the workbook. Print or submit your workbook electronically as directed. If required, print or create an electronic version of your worksheets with formulas displayed, using the instructions in Activity 1.16 in Project 1A. **Close** Excel.

End **You have completed Project 5F**

Apply 5A and 5B skills from these Objectives:

1. Navigate and Manage Large Worksheets
2. Enhance Worksheets with Themes and Styles
3. Format a Worksheet to Share with Others
4. Save Excel Data in Other File Formats
5. Use Advanced Sort Techniques
6. Use Custom and Advanced Filters
7. Subtotal, Outline, and Group a List of Data

myitlab grader

Mastering Excel | Project 5G Sports Programs

In the following Mastering Excel project, you will create a worksheet for Ron Latham, Assistant Director of Athletics, with data that has been sorted, filtered, and grouped and that analyzes sports programs at Capital Cities Community College. Assistant Director Latham will use this information to make decisions for these sports programs for the upcoming academic year. The worksheets of your workbook will look similar to Figure 5.63.

Project Files

For Project 5G, you will need the following files:

e05G_Sports_Programs
e05G_Coach_Information

You will save your workbook as:

Lastname_Firstname_5G_Sports_Programs

Project Results

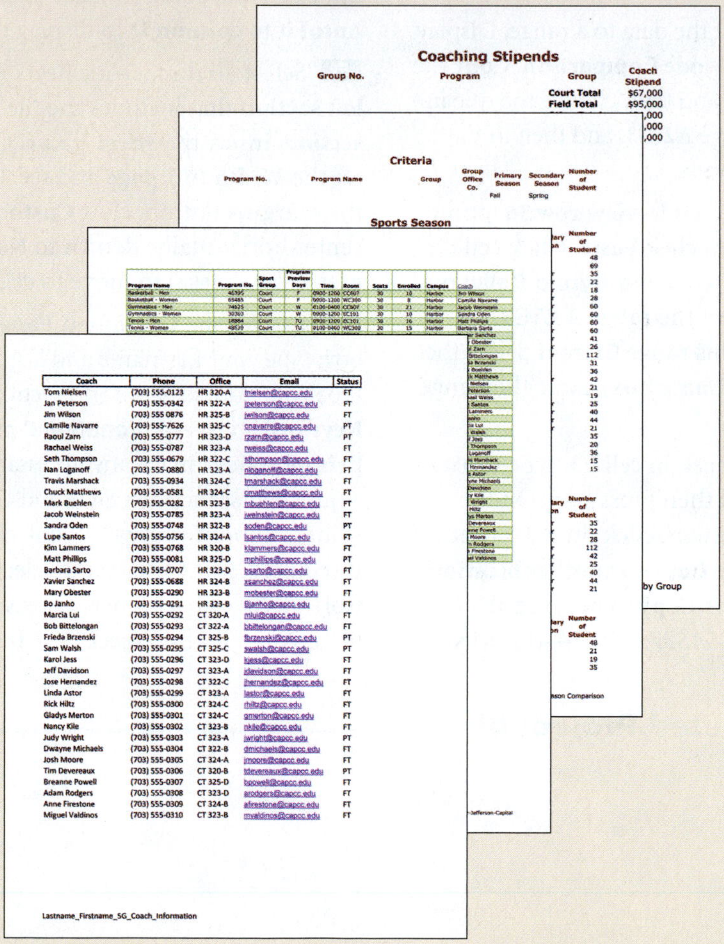

Figure 5.63

(Project 5G Sports Programs continues on the next page)

Mastering Excel | Project 5G Sports Programs (continued)

1 **Start** Excel. From your student files, locate and open **e05G_Sports_Programs**. **Save** the file in your **Excel Chapter 5** folder as **Lastname_Firstname_5G_Sports_Programs** Display the *first* worksheet, **Harbor-Jefferson-Capital**. Select the range **A1:J40**, insert a table, and then apply **Table Style Light 19**. In the **Sort** dialog box, **Sort** by **Campus**, sort on **Values**, and then click **Custom List**. With **NEW LIST** selected, under **List entries**, create entries for **Harbor** and **Jefferson** and **Capital** Click the **Add** button, and then click **OK**. If necessary, in the **Order** box, click your **Harbor, Jefferson, Capital** custom list so that it displays.

As the second level, sort the **Sport Group** column alphabetically on **Values**. As the third level, sort the **Program Name** column alphabetically on **Values**. Click **OK**, and then click anywhere to deselect. Convert the table to a range.

2 Display the *second* worksheet, **Sports Season Comparison**. **Copy** the range **A6:G7**, **Paste** it in cell **A1**, and then change the title in cell **A1** to **Criteria** Select the range **A2:G3**, and then in the **Name Box**, name this range **Criteria**

Copy the range **A1:G2**, scroll down, right-click cell **A36**, and then **Paste** the copied range. Change the title in cell **A36** to **Fall-Summer Sports Season** Name the range **A37:G37** **Extract** and then name the range **A7:G34 Database**

3 At the top of your worksheet, in cell **E3**, type **Fall** and in cell **F3**, type **Summer** On the **Data tab**, in the **Sort & Filter group**, click the **Advanced** button. Under **Action**, click the **Copy to another location** option button. Verify that in the **Copy to** box, the absolute reference to the Extract area—*$A$37:$G$37*—displays. Click **OK**.

4 Scroll to view the lower portion of your worksheet. **Copy** the range **A36:G37**, and then **Paste** it in cell **A48**. In cell **A48**, change the word *Summer* to **Spring** In cell **F3**, change the criteria to **Spring**

Display the **Advanced Filter** dialog box, and then click the **Copy to another location** option button. In the **Copy to** box, click the **Collapse Dialog** button, scroll down as necessary, and then select the range **A49:G49**. Click the **Expand Dialog** button, and then click **OK**. Scroll to view the lower portion of the worksheet.

5 Display the *third* worksheet—**Stipends by Group**. Select the range **A2:D41**. **Sort** by **Group**, then by the **Coach Stipend**. **Subtotal** at each change in **Group**, select the **Sum** function, select the **Add subtotal to** the **Coach Stipend** check box, and then click **OK**. **Group** the data so each **Group** venue is collapsed and a break in the row numbers indicates that some rows are hidden from view. Display the **Level 2** summary information, and the **Level 1** Grand Total. AutoFit columns as necessary. Press Ctrl + Home.

6 Select all three worksheets. Insert a footer in the **left section** that includes the file name, and in the **right section**, insert the **Sheet Name**. On the **Page Layout tab**, set the **Width** to **1 page** and set the **Height** to **1 page**. Display **Custom Margins** and **Center** the worksheets horizontally.

Return to **Normal** view, and then press Ctrl + Home to move to cell **A1**. Change the theme to **Solstice**, and then change the **Fonts** to **Aspect**. Display the **Document Panel**, and in the **Author** box, type your firstname and lastname, in the **Subject** box, type your course name and section number, and in the **Keywords** box, type **sports programs, campus, sports season, stipends** Display the worksheet in **Print Preview**, and then make any necessary corrections or adjustments.

7 Open the file **e05G_Coach_Information** and **Save** it in your **Excel Chapter 5** folder as **Lastname_Firstname_5G_Coach_Information** Insert a footer in the **left section** with the file name, and then return to **Normal** view. **Save** and then close this workbook to redisplay your **Lastname_Firstname_5G_Sports_Programs** workbook.

8 On the **Harbor-Jefferson-Capital** worksheet, in cell **J1**, **Insert** a **Hyperlink** to link to an **Existing File or Web Page,** navigate to your **Excel Chapter 5** folder, and then select your **Lastname_Firstname_5G_Coach_Information** workbook. Point to cell **J1**, right-click, and then click **Edit Hyperlink**. Click the **ScreenTip** button. In the **ScreenTip text** box, type **Click here for contact information** Click **OK** two times. Change the **Font Color** in cell **J1** to **Indigo, Accent 6, Darker 50%**. **Save** the workbook.

9 Display the **Save As** dialog box, navigate to your **Excel Chapter 5** folder, set the **Save as type** to **XPS Document,** and as the **File name**, type **Lastname_Firstname_5G_Sports_XPS** Click **Save**. **Close** all files. As directed by your instructor, print or submit electronically the three files that comprise the results of this project—two Excel files and one XPS file. There are no formulas in this workbook. **Close** Excel.

End **You have completed Project 5G**

Apply a combination of the **5A** and **5B** skills.

GO! Fix It | Project **5H** Programs

Project Files

For Project 5H, you will need the following file:

e05H_Programs

You will save your workbook as:

Lastname_Firstname_5H_Programs

Open the file **e05H_Programs**, and then save the file in your Excel Chapter 5 folder as **Lastname_Firstname_5H_Programs** In row 36, notice that the extract area is supposed to show programs offered in both an Online mode and a Classroom mode. Edit this worksheet and use the Advanced Filter dialog box to filter and then display the correct data in the extract area. Add your name and course name, and section number to the document properties, and include **vocational programs** as the keywords.

Insert the file name in the footer, save your file, and then print or submit your worksheet electronically as directed by your instructor.

End **You have completed Project 5H**

Apply a combination of the **5A** and **5B** skills.

GO! Make It | Project 5I Arts Faculty

Project Files

For Project 5I, you will need the following file:

e05I_Arts_Faculty

You will save your workbook as:

Lastname_Firstname_5I_Arts_Faculty

From your student files, open the file **e05I_Arts_Faculty**, and then save it in your chapter folder as **Lastname_Firstname_5I_Arts_Faculty** By using the skills you have practiced, format the worksheet as shown in Figure 5.64 by adding Subtotals using the Subtotal feature. Apply the Waveform theme. Insert the file name in the footer. Add your name, course name, and section number to the document properties, and include **arts faculty** as the keywords Submit as directed by your instructor.

Project Results

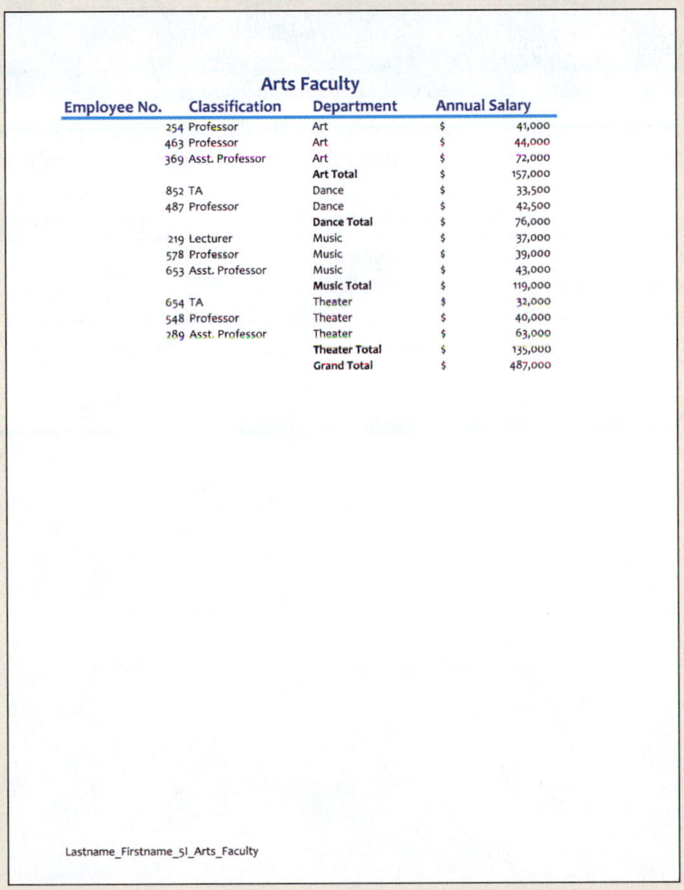

Arts Faculty

Employee No.	Classification	Department	Annual Salary	
254	Professor	Art	$	41,000
463	Professor	Art	$	44,000
369	Asst. Professor	Art	$	72,000
		Art Total	$	157,000
852	TA	Dance	$	33,500
487	Professor	Dance	$	42,500
		Dance Total	$	76,000
219	Lecturer	Music	$	37,000
578	Professor	Music	$	39,000
653	Asst. Professor	Music	$	43,000
		Music Total	$	119,000
654	TA	Theater	$	32,000
548	Professor	Theater	$	40,000
289	Asst. Professor	Theater	$	63,000
		Theater Total	$	135,000
		Grand Total	$	487,000

Lastname_Firstname_5I_Arts_Faculty

Figure 5.64

End **You have completed Project 5I**

Apply a combination of the 5A and 5B skills.

GO! Solve It | Project 5J Dept Tutors

Project Files

For Project 5J, you will need the following file:

e05J_Dept_Tutors

You will save your workbook as:

Lastname_Firstname_5J_Dept_Tutors

Open the file e05J_Dept_Tutors and save it in your chapter folder as **Lastname_Firstname_5J_Dept_Tutors**

The Director of the Tutoring Center wants to know which tutors who are classified as grad student tutors are available in the afternoons from the CNT and CPS departments. By using the table feature and filtering, filter the data to present the information requested. Include the file name in the footer, add appropriate properties, and then save your workbook. Submit as directed.

		Performance Level		
		Exemplary: You consistently applied the relevant skills	Proficient: You sometimes, but not always, applied the relevant skills	Developing: You rarely or never applied the relevant skills
Performance Criteria	Convert Data to a Table	The data is properly converted to a table.	Only part of the data is in the form of a table.	The data is not properly converted to a table.
	Filter on Multiple Columns	The Filter Function is properly applied using supplied criteria.	The Filter Function is properly applied to some but not all supplied criteria.	The Filter Function is not properly applied and did not meet the supplied criteria.

End You have completed Project 5J

Apply a combination of the **5A** and **5B** skills.

GO! Solve It | Project 5K Organizations

Project Files

For Project 5K, you will need the following file:

e05K_Organizations

You will save your workbook as:

Lastname_Firstname_5K_Organizations

Open the file e05K_Organizations and save it in your chapter file as **Lastname_Firstname_5K_Organizations**

To update the worksheet, sort the data by the organization name. Then, filter to display only those records that are missing a Contact Number. Format to print on one sheet in landscape. Include the file name in the footer, add appropriate properties, the keywords **student organizations**, save the file, and then submit as directed.

Performance Criteria	Performance Level: Exemplary: You consistently applied the relevant skills	Proficient: You sometimes, but not always, applied the relevant skills	Developing: You rarely or never applied the relevant skills
Use Sort Function	The Sort function sorts the organization data in ascending order.	The organization data is sorted in the wrong order.	The organization data is not sorted.
Filter for blank cells	Seven filtered records missing a contact number display.	The filter was applied incorrectly.	The list was not filtered.
Page Layout	The page layout displays in landscape orientation on one page.	The page is missing either the landscape orientation or the scaling.	Neither landscape nor scaling applied to the page layout.

End **You have completed Project 5K**

Rubric

The following outcomes-based assessments are *open-ended assessments*. That is, there is no specific correct result; your result will depend on your approach to the information provided. Make *Professional Quality* your goal. Use the following scoring rubric to guide you in *how* to approach the problem and then to evaluate *how well* your approach solves the problem.

The *criteria*—Software Mastery, Content, Format and Layout, and Process—represent the knowledge and skills you have gained that you can apply to solving the problem. The *levels of performance*—Professional Quality, Approaching Professional Quality, or Needs Quality Improvements—help you and your instructor evaluate your result.

	Your completed project is of Professional Quality if you:	**Your completed project is Approaching Professional Quality if you:**	**Your completed project Needs Quality Improvements if you:**
1-Software Mastery	Choose and apply the most appropriate skills, tools, and features and identify efficient methods to solve the problem.	Choose and apply some appropriate skills, tools, and features, but not in the most efficient manner.	Choose inappropriate skills, tools, or features, or are inefficient in solving the problem.
2-Content	Construct a solution that is clear and well organized, contains content that is accurate, appropriate to the audience and purpose, and is complete. Provide a solution that contains no errors in spelling, grammar, or style.	Construct a solution in which some components are unclear, poorly organized, inconsistent, or incomplete. Misjudge the needs of the audience. Have some errors in spelling, grammar, or style, but the errors do not detract from comprehension.	Construct a solution that is unclear, incomplete, or poorly organized; contains some inaccurate or inappropriate content; and contains many errors in spelling, grammar, or style. Do not solve the problem.
3-Format and Layout	Format and arrange all elements to communicate information and ideas, clarify function, illustrate relationships, and indicate relative importance.	Apply appropriate format and layout features to some elements, but not others. Overuse features, causing minor distraction.	Apply format and layout that does not communicate information or ideas clearly. Do not use format and layout features to clarify function, illustrate relationships, or indicate relative importance. Use available features excessively, causing distraction.
4-Process	Use an organized approach that integrates planning, development, self-assessment, revision, and reflection.	Demonstrate an organized approach in some areas, but not others; or, use an insufficient process of organization throughout.	Do not use an organized approach to solve the problem.

Outcomes-Based Assessments

Apply a combination of the **5A** and **5B** skills.

GO! Think | Project 5L Summer Sections

Project Files

For Project 5L, you will need the following file:

e05L_Summer_Sections

You will save your workbook as:

Lastname_Firstname_5L_Summer_Sections

From your student files, open the file e05L_Summer_Sections, and then save it in your chapter folder as **Lastname_Firstname_5L_Summer_Sections** Select the entire range and insert a table with headers. Create a custom table style, name it **Summer Sections**, and then apply it to the table. Create a custom sort, and then custom sort the Campus information in Online, Jefferson, Harbor, Capital order. Include the file name in the footer, add appropriate properties, the keywords **summer sections**, save the file as a PDF, and then submit as directed.

End You have completed Project 5L

Apply a combination of the **5A** and **5B** skills.

GO! Think | Project 5M Social Science

Project Files

For Project 5M, you will need the following file:

e05M_Social_Science

You will save your workbook as:

Lastname_Firstname_5M_Social_Science

From your student files, open the file e05M_Social_Science, and then save it in your chapter folder as **Lastname_Firstname_5M_Social_Science** Select the entire range and insert a table with headers. Create a custom sort, and then custom sort the Delivery information in Online, Classroom order. Within each delivery type—Online and Classroom—sort the data further by Dept. and then by Course Name. Hide column M, Status. Change the Theme to Opulent and the Font to Concourse. Include the file name in the footer, add appropriate properties, the keywords, **social science**, save the file, and then submit as directed.

End You have completed Project 5M

Outcomes-Based Assessments

Apply a combination of the **5A** and **5B** skills.

You and GO! | Project 5N Personal Expenses

Project Files

For Project 5N, you will need the following file:

e05N_Personal_Expenses

You will save your workbook as:

Lastname_Firstname_5N_Personal_Expenses

In this chapter, you practiced using Excel to subtotal, outline, and group a list of data. You also practiced changing and customizing a workbook theme. From your student files, open **e05N_Personal_Expenses**, and then save it in your **Excel Chapter 5** folder as **Lastname_Firstname_5N_Personal_Expenses**

By using the skills you practiced in this chapter, modify the **Lastname_Firstname_5N_Personal_Expenses** worksheet by adding and deleting your personal expenses, as applicable. Sort the data by the Category column, and then by the Amount. Subtotal the data by Category, and Sum the Amount. Change and customize a table with your preferences and apply it to the worksheet. Title it **Personal Expenses**. Insert a footer with the file name. Add appropriate document properties and include the keywords **personal expenses**. Save your file as **Lastname_Firstname_5N_Personal_Expenses** and then print or submit electronically as directed.

End You have completed Project 5N

Creating Charts, Diagrams, and Templates

OUTCOMES

At the end of this chapter you will be able to:

OBJECTIVES

Mastering these objectives will enable you to:

PROJECT 6A

Create 3-D column charts, line charts, process diagrams, and organization charts.

1. Create and Format Sparklines and a 3-D Column Chart (p. 353)
2. Create and Format a Line Chart (p. 362)
3. Create and Modify a SmartArt Graphic (p. 367)
4. Create and Modify an Organization Chart (p. 370)

PROJECT 6B

Create and use an Excel template and protect worksheets to ensure consistency in formulas and data.

5. Create an Excel Template (p. 374)
6. Protect a Worksheet (p. 381)
7. Create a Worksheet Based on a Template (p. 384)

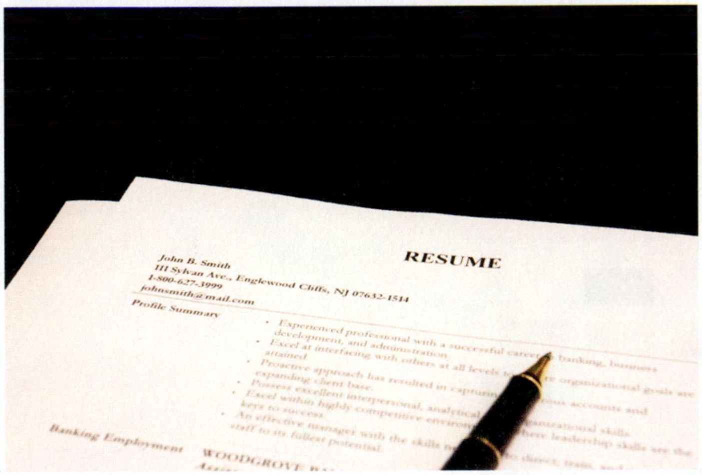

javarman/Shutterstock

In This Chapter

In this chapter, you will create charts and diagrams to communicate data visually. Charts make a set of numbers easier to understand by displaying numerical data in a graphical format. Excel's SmartArt illustrations make diagrams, like an organizational chart or process cycle, easy to comprehend.

In this chapter, you will also use several predefined templates that can be used for common financial reports such as an expense report, sales invoice, or purchase order. Templates have built-in formulas for performing calculations based on the data that you enter. Templates are commonly used in organizations for standardization and protection of data. You will create and protect a template for an order form.

The **New York-New Jersey Job Fair** is a nonprofit organization that brings together employers and job seekers in the New York and New Jersey metropolitan areas. Each year the organization holds a number of targeted job fairs and the annual New York-New Jersey Job Fair draws over 900 employers in more than 75 industries and registers more than 30,000 candidates. Candidate registration is free; employers pay a nominal fee to display and present at the fairs. Candidate resumes and employer postings are managed by a state-of-the-art database system, allowing participants quick and accurate access to job data and candidate qualifications.

Project 6A Attendance Charts and Diagrams

myitlab
Project 6A Training

Project Activities

In Activities 6.01 through 6.17, you will create and format 3-D column and line charts for the New York-New Jersey Job Fair that display attendance patterns at the fairs over a five-year period. You will also create a process diagram and an organization chart. Your completed worksheets will look similar to Figure 6.1.

Project Files

For Project 6A, you will need the following file:

e06A_Attendance

You will save your workbook as:

Lastname_Firstname_6A_Attendance

Project Results

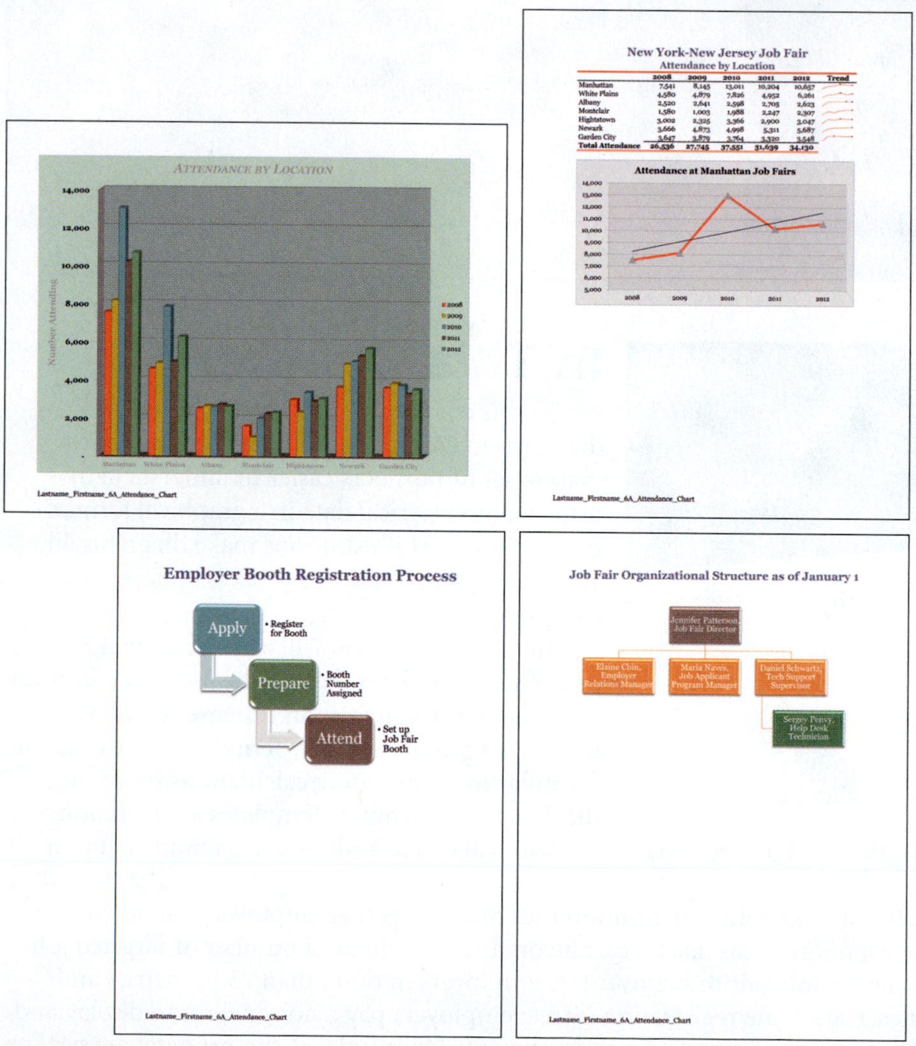

Figure 6.1
Project 6A Attendance Charts and Diagrams

Objective 1 | Create and Format Sparklines and a 3-D Column Chart

Recall that ***sparklines*** are tiny charts that fit within a cell and give a visual trend summary alongside your data. Recall also that a ***column chart***, which presents data graphically in vertical columns, is useful to make comparisons among related data.

Activity 6.01 | Creating and Formatting Sparklines

To create sparklines, first select the data you want to plot—represent graphically—and then select the range of cells alongside each row of data where you want to display the sparklines.

1 **Start** Excel. From your student files, open the file **e06A_Attendance**. Display the **Save As** dialog box, navigate to the location where you will store your workbooks for this chapter, and then create a new folder named **Excel Chapter 6** Open your new folder, and then **Save** the workbook as **Lastname_Firstname_6A_Attendance**

This data shows the number of applicants who have attended job fairs held over a five-year period at various locations in the greater New York-New Jersey area.

2 Select the range **A4:F10**. On the **Insert tab**, in the **Sparklines group**, click the **Line** button. Compare your screen with Figure 6.2.

The Create Sparklines dialog box displays with the Data Range indicated as *A4:F10*.

Figure 6.2

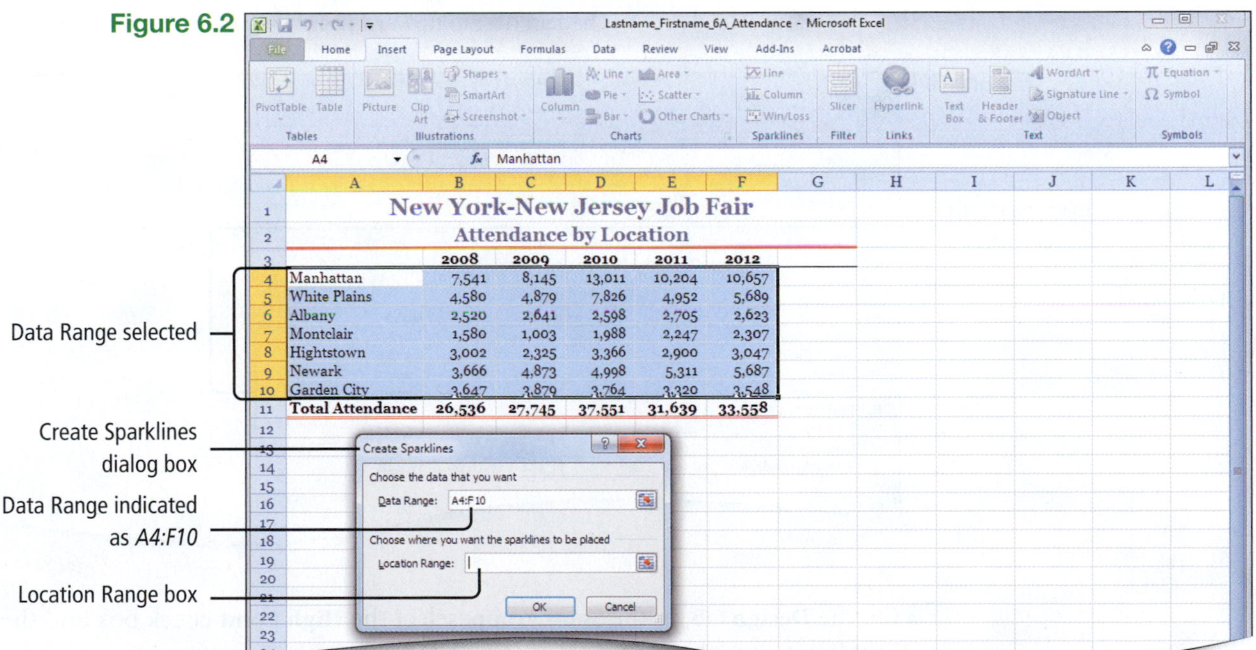

3 If necessary, drag the Create Sparklines dialog box so you can see column G. With the insertion point blinking in the **Location Range** box, select the range **G4:G10**. Compare your screen with Figure 6.3.

Figure 6.3

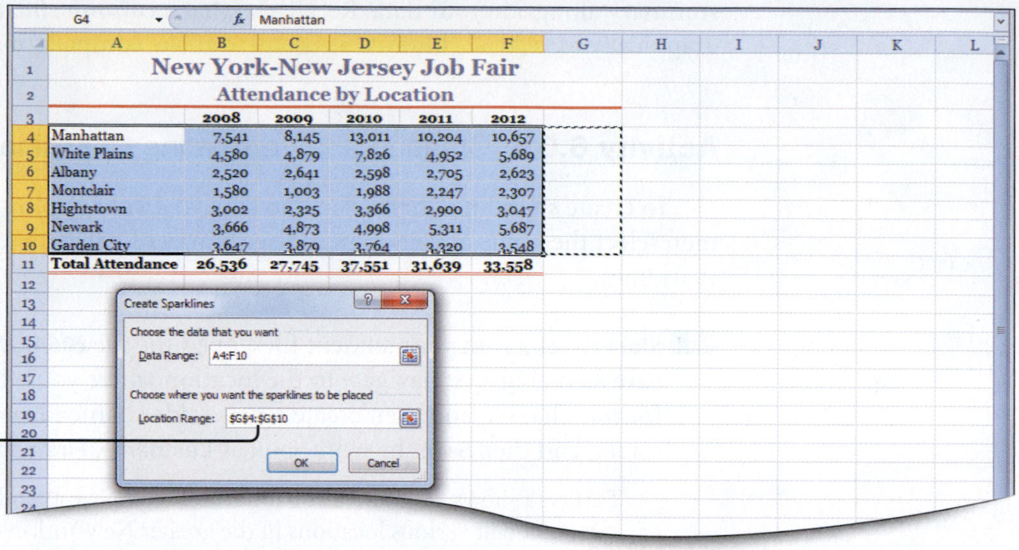

4 Click **OK**, and then compare your screen with Figure 6.4.

Sparklines display alongside each row of data and provide a quick visual trend summary for each city's job fair attendance. The sparklines provide a quick indication that for each location, attendance has had an overall upward trend over the five-year period.

Figure 6.4

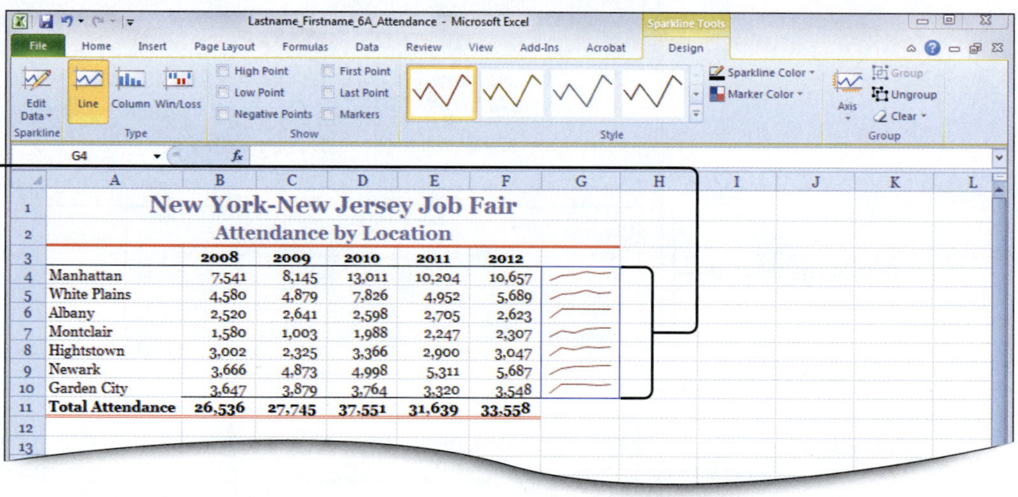

5 On the **Design tab**, in the **Show group**, select the **High Point** check box and the **Last Point** check box.

By adding the High Point and Last Point markers, you further emphasize the visual story that sparklines depict.

6 On the **Design tab**, in the **Style group**, click the **More** button, and then in the third row, click the first style—**Sparkline Style Accent 1, (no dark or light)**.

7 In cell **G3**, type **Trend** and press Enter. Press Ctrl + Home, and then compare your screen with Figure 6.5.

Use styles in this manner to further enhance your sparklines.

Figure 6.5

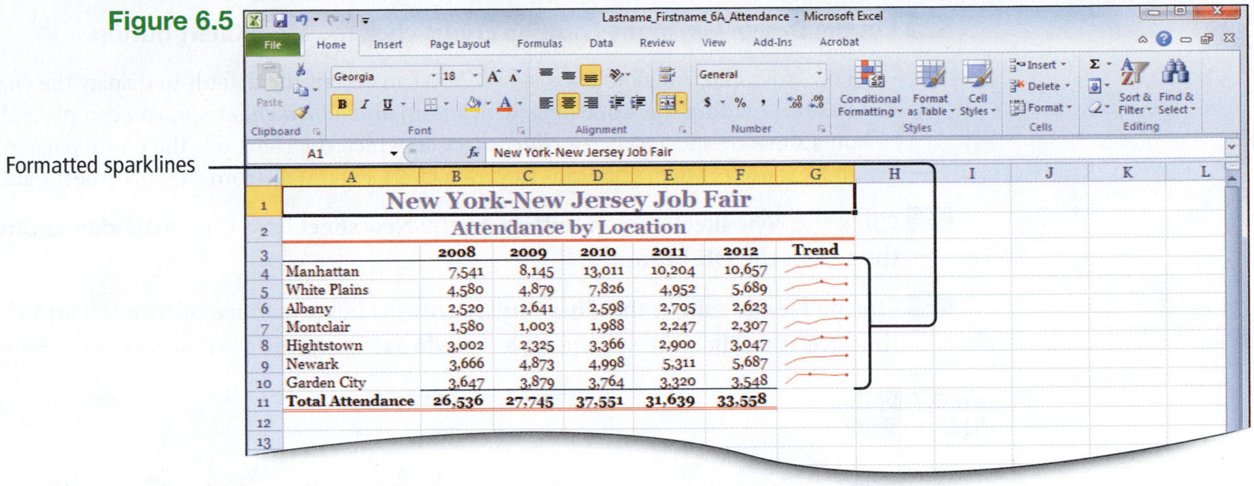

8 **Save** your workbook.

Activity 6.02 | Creating a 3-D Column Chart

A chart is a graphic representation of data. When you create a chart, first decide whether you are going to plot the values representing totals or the values representing details—you cannot plot both in the same chart. In this activity, you will select the details—the number of attendees at each location each year. To help the reader understand the chart, you will also select the ***labels*** for the data—the column and row headings that describe the values. Here, the labels are the location names and the years.

1 Take a moment to study the data elements shown in Figure 6.6.

Figure 6.6

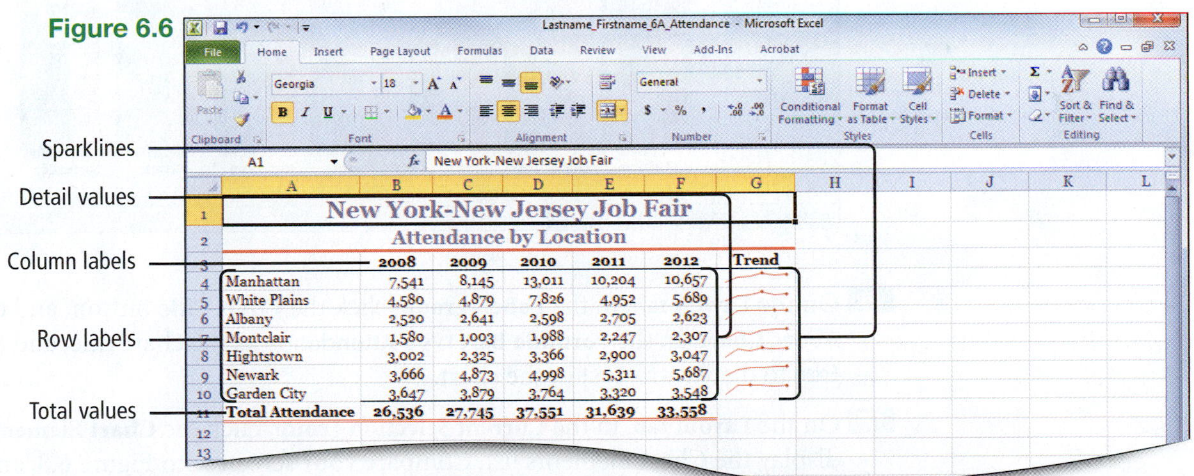

2 Select the range **A3:F10**. On the **Insert tab**, in the **Charts group**, click the **Column** button. Under **3-D Column**, click the first chart—**3-D Clustered Column**.

The 3-D Clustered Column chart displays on the worksheet.

3 On the **Design tab**, in the **Location group**, click the **Move Chart** button.

The Move Chart dialog box displays. You can accept the default to display the chart as an object within the worksheet, which is an ***embedded chart***. Or, you can place the chart on a separate sheet, called a ***chart sheet***, in which the chart fills the entire page. A chart sheet is useful when you want to view a chart separately from the worksheet data.

4 Click the **New sheet** option button. In the **New sheet** box, type **Attendance Chart** and then click the **OK** button.

5 On the **Design tab**, in the **Chart Styles** group, click the **More** button [▾], and then in the fifth row, click the second style—**Style 34**. Compare your screen with Figure 6.7.

Figure 6.7

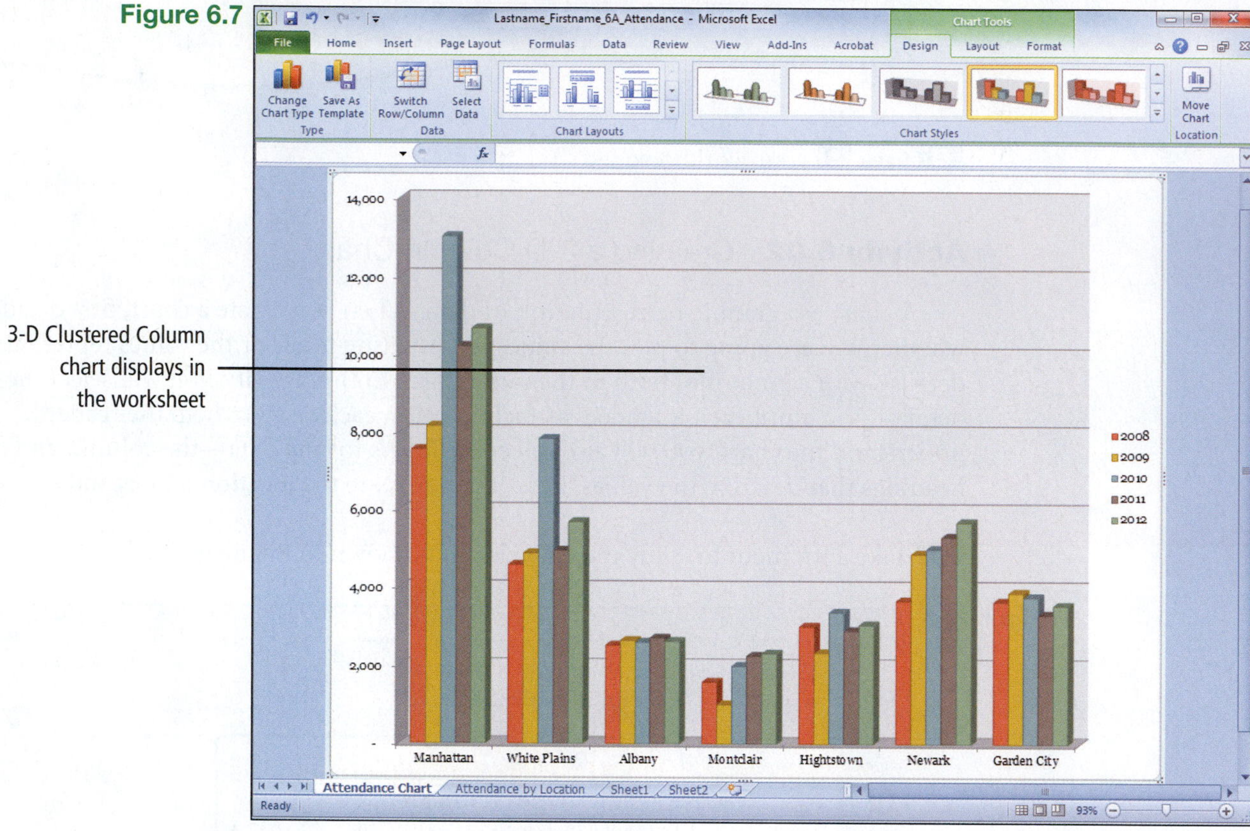

6 On the **Layout tab**, in the **Labels group**, click the **Chart Title** button, and then click **Above Chart**. In the **Formula Bar**, type **Attendance** as the chart title, and then press Enter to display the text in the chart.

7 On the **Layout tab**, in the **Current Selection group**, click the **Chart Elements arrow** to display the Chart Elements list. Compare your screen with Figure 6.8, and then take a moment to study the table in Figure 6.9, which lists the elements that are typically found in a chart.

The Chart Elements list displays. ***Chart elements*** are the objects that make up a chart. The entire chart and all of its elements comprise the ***chart area***. From the Chart Elements list, you can select a chart element to format it.

Figure 6.8

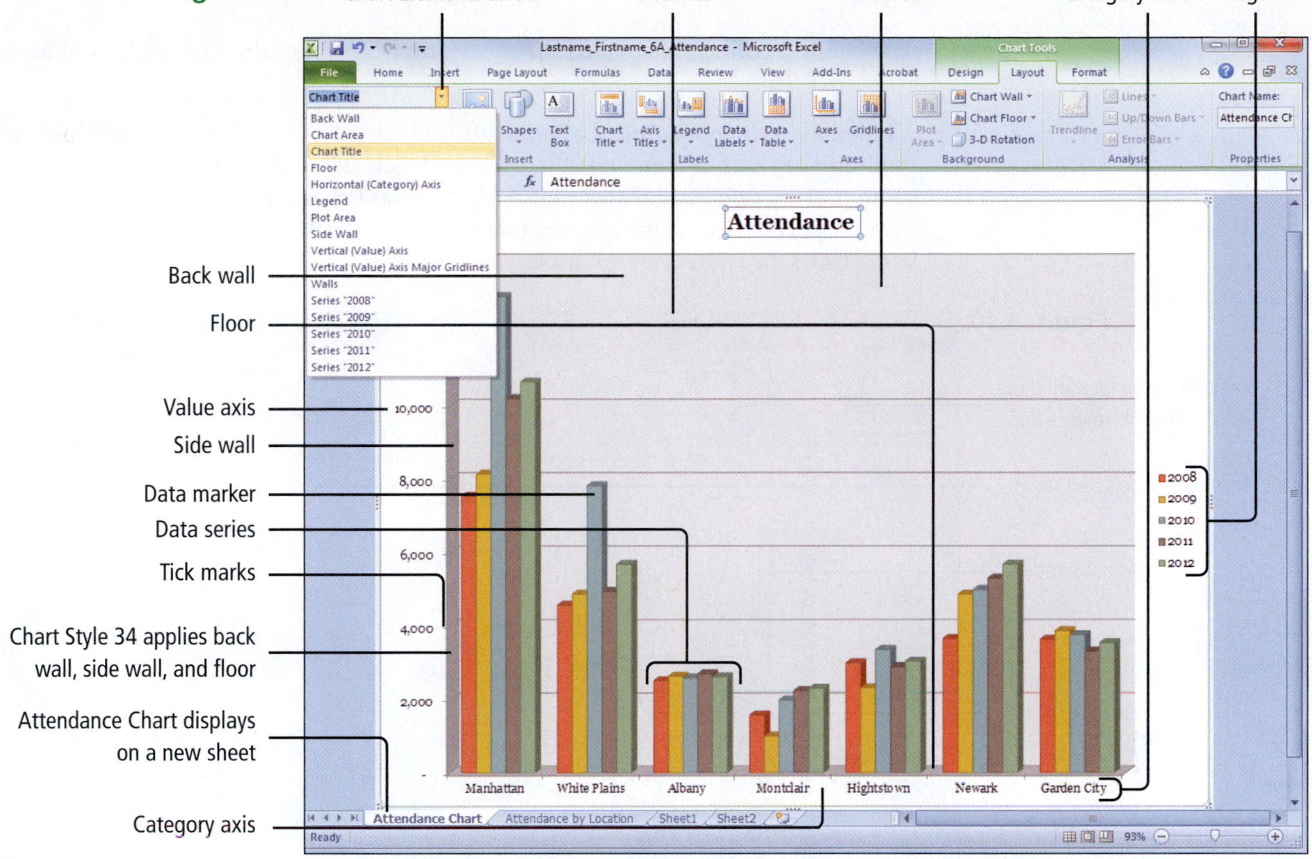

Excel Chart Elements

Object	Description
Axis	A line that serves as a frame of reference for measurement and that borders the chart plot area.
Category labels	The labels that display along the bottom of the chart to identify the category of data.
Chart Area	The entire chart and all its elements.
Data labels	Labels that display the value, percentage, and/or category of each particular data point and can contain one or more of the choices listed—Series name, Category name, Value, or Percentage.
Data marker	A column, bar, area, dot, pie slice, or other symbol in a chart that represents a single data point.
Data points	The numeric values of the selected worksheet.
Data series	A group of related data points that are plotted in a chart.
Gridlines	Lines in the plot area that aid the eye in determining the plotted values.
Horizontal Category axis (x-axis)	The axis that displays along the bottom of the chart to identify the category of data. Excel uses the row titles as the category names.
Legend	A key that identifies patterns or colors that are assigned to the categories in the chart.
Major unit value	The value that determines the spacing between tick marks and between the gridlines in the plot area.
Plot area	The area bounded by the axes, including all the data series.
Tick mark labels	Identifying information for a tick mark generated from the cells on the worksheet used to create the chart.
Tick marks	The short lines that display on an axis at regular intervals.
Vertical Value axis (y-axis)	The axis that displays along the left side of the chart to identify the numerical scale on which the charted data is based.
Walls and floor	The areas surrounding a 3-D chart that give dimension and boundaries to the chart. Two walls and one floor display within the plot area.

Figure 6.9

8 Click the tallest column displayed for the Manhattan category. Compare your screen with Figure 6.10.

All the columns representing the Series *2010* are selected—selection handles display at the corners of each column in the series—and a ScreenTip displays the value for the column you are pointing to. Recall that a data series is a group of related data—in this case, the attendees to all the job fairs that were held in 2010. Also notice that the Formula Bar displays the address for the selected data series.

Figure 6.10

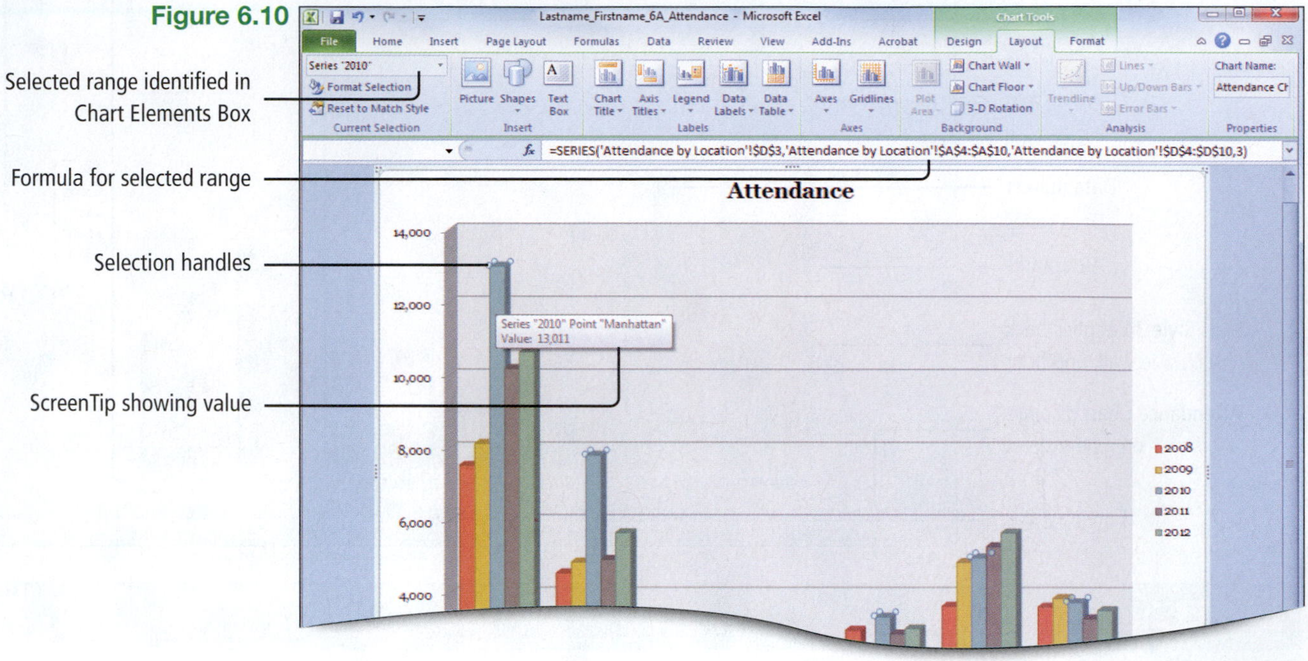

9 Locate the **Montclair** category, and then click the shortest column in that group.

The selected series changes to those columns that represent the attendees at the job fairs in 2009. The Formula Bar and Chart Elements box change and a new ScreenTip displays.

10 Click outside the chart area to deselect the series.

> **More Knowledge | Sizing Handles and Selection Handles**
>
> Sizing handles and selection handles look the same, and the terms are often used interchangeably. If a two-headed resize arrow—[↕], [↔], [↘], [↗]—displays when you point to boxes surrounding an object, it is a sizing handle; otherwise, it is a selection handle. Some objects in a chart cannot be resized, such as the category axis or the value axis, but they can be selected and then reformatted.

Activity 6.03 | Changing the Display of Chart Data

As you create a chart, you make choices about the data to include, the chart type, chart titles, and location. You can change the chart type, change the way the data displays, add or change titles, select different colors, and modify the background, scale, or chart location.

In the column chart you created, the attendance numbers are displayed along the value axis—the vertical axis—and the locations for each job fair are displayed along the category axis—the horizontal axis. The cells you select for a chart include the row and column labels from your worksheet. In a column or line chart, Excel selects whichever has *more* items—either the rows or the columns—and uses those labels to plot the data series, in this case, the locations.

After plotting the data series, Excel uses the remaining labels—in this example, the years identified in the row headings—to create the data series labels on the ***legend***. The legend is the key that defines the colors used in the chart; here it identifies the data series for the years. A different color is used for each year in the data series. The chart, as currently displayed, compares the change in attendance year to year grouped by category location. You can change the chart to display the years on the category axis and the locations as the data series identified in the legend.

1 In the **Manhattan** category, click the second column.

All columns with the same color are selected. The ScreenTip displays *Series "2009" Point "Manhattan" Value: 8,145.*

2 Point to each of the other gold columns that are selected and notice that the ScreenTip that displays identifies each gold column as being in the *Series "2009."*

3 On the **Design tab**, in the **Data group,** click the **Switch Row/Column** button, and then compare your screen with Figure 6.11.

The chart changes to display the locations as the data series. The locations are the row headings in the worksheet and are now identified in the legend. The years display as the category labels.

Figure 6.11

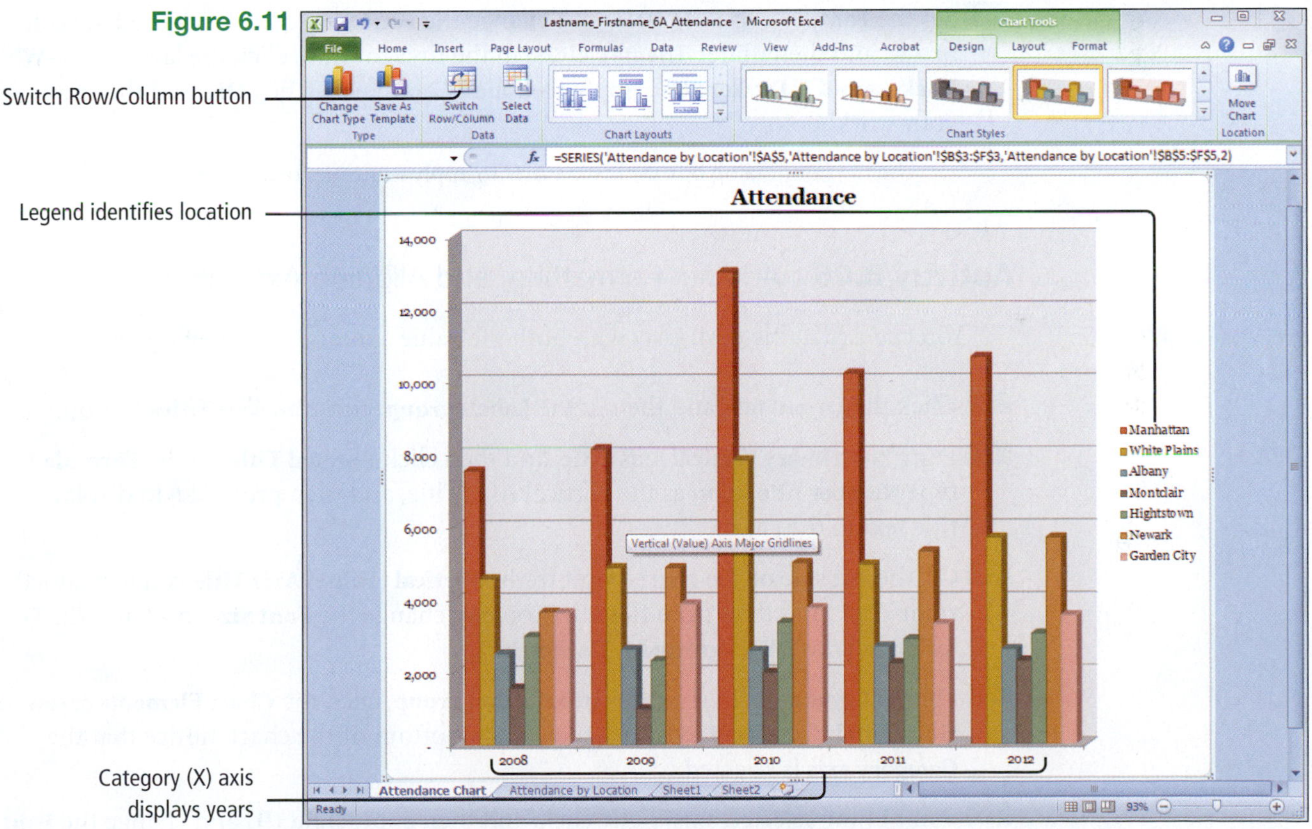

4 If necessary, click one of the gold columns. Point to each gold column and read the ScreenTip.

The ScreenTips for the gold columns now identify this as the White Plains series.

5 On the **Design tab**, in the **Data group**, click the **Switch Row/Column** button again, and then **Save** your workbook.

The chart changes back to the more useful arrangement with the years identified in the legend and the locations displayed as the category labels.

More Knowledge | Changing the Range of Data in a Chart

After you have created a chart, you can adjust the range of data that is displayed in the chart. To do so, on the Design tab, in the Data group, click the Select Data button. Edit the source address displayed in the Chart data range box, or drag the data in the worksheet to adjust the range as needed.

Activity 6.04 | Editing and Formatting the Chart Title

The data displayed in the chart focuses on the *attendance by location*. It is good practice to create a chart title to reflect your charted data.

1. Click the **Chart Title**—*Attendance*—to select it, and then click to position the mouse pointer to the right of *Attendance*.

   To edit a title, click once to select the chart object, and then click a second time to position the insertion point in the title and change to editing mode.

2. Press Spacebar one time, and then type **by Location**
3. Point to the **Chart Title**—*Attendance by Location*—right-click the border of the chart title, and then on the shortcut menu, click **Font** to display the **Font** dialog box.
4. Set the **Font style** to **Bold Italic** and change the **Font Size** to **20**. Click the **Font color arrow**, and then under **Theme Colors**, in the first column, click the last color—**White, Background 1, Darker 50%**. Apply the **Small Caps** effect. Click **OK**, and then **Save** your workbook.

   Use the Font dialog box in this manner to apply multiple formats to a chart title.

Activity 6.05 | Adding, Formatting, and Aligning Axis Titles

You can add a title to display with both the value axis and the category axis.

1. Click the **Layout tab**, and then in the **Labels group**, click the **Axis Titles** button.
2. Point to **Primary Vertical Axis Title**, and then click **Rotated Title**. In the **Formula Bar**, type **Number Attending** as the Vertical Axis Title, and then press Enter to display the title text in the chart.
3. On the left side of the chart, point to the **Vertical (Value) Axis Title** you just added, right-click, and then from the Mini toolbar, change the **Font Size** to **14** and the **Font Color** to **White, Background 1, Darker 50%**.
4. On the **Layout tab**, in the **Current Selection group**, click the **Chart Elements arrow**, click **Horizontal (Category) Axis**, and then at the bottom of the chart, notice that the **Category axis** is selected.
5. Point to the selected axis, right-click, and then apply **Bold** B and change the **Font Color** to **White, Background 1, Darker 50%**.
6. On the left side of the chart, point to any value in the **Value Axis**, and then right-click to select the **Vertical (Value) Axis**. On the Mini toolbar, change the **Font Size** to **12**.
7. **Save** your workbook, and then compare your screen with Figure 6.12.

Figure 6.12

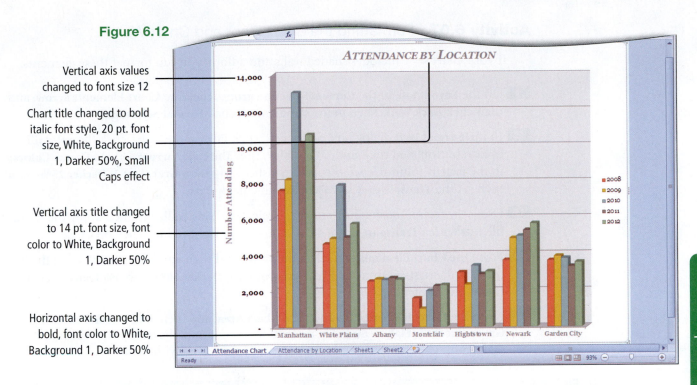

Vertical axis values changed to font size 12

Chart title changed to bold italic font style, 20 pt. font size, White, Background 1, Darker 50%, Small Caps effect

Vertical axis title changed to 14 pt. font size, font color to White, Background 1, Darker 50%

Horizontal axis changed to bold, font color to White, Background 1, Darker 50%

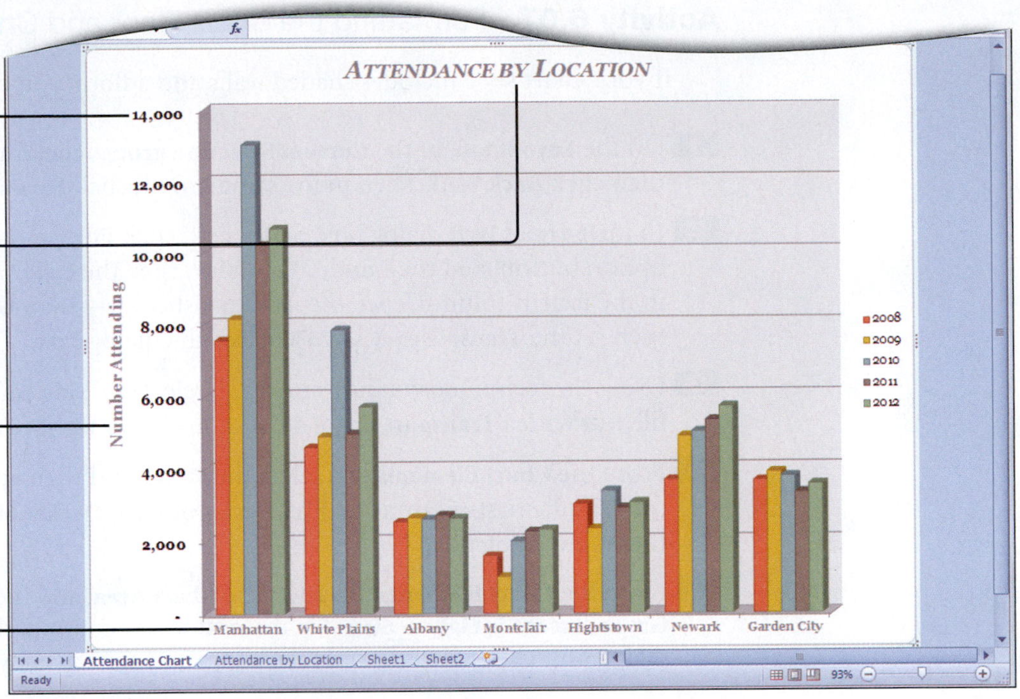

Activity 6.06 | Editing Source Data

One of the characteristics of an Excel chart is that it reflects changes made to the underlying data.

1 In the **White Plains** column cluster, point to the last column—**2012**. Notice that the *Value* for this column is *5,689*.

2 Display the **Attendance by Location** worksheet, and then in cell **F5**, type **6261** and press Enter.

3 Redisplay the **Attendance Chart** worksheet, and then point to the **White Plains** column for 2012. **Save** your workbook, and then compare your screen with Figure 6.13.

Figure 6.13

ScreenTip reflects the change in data

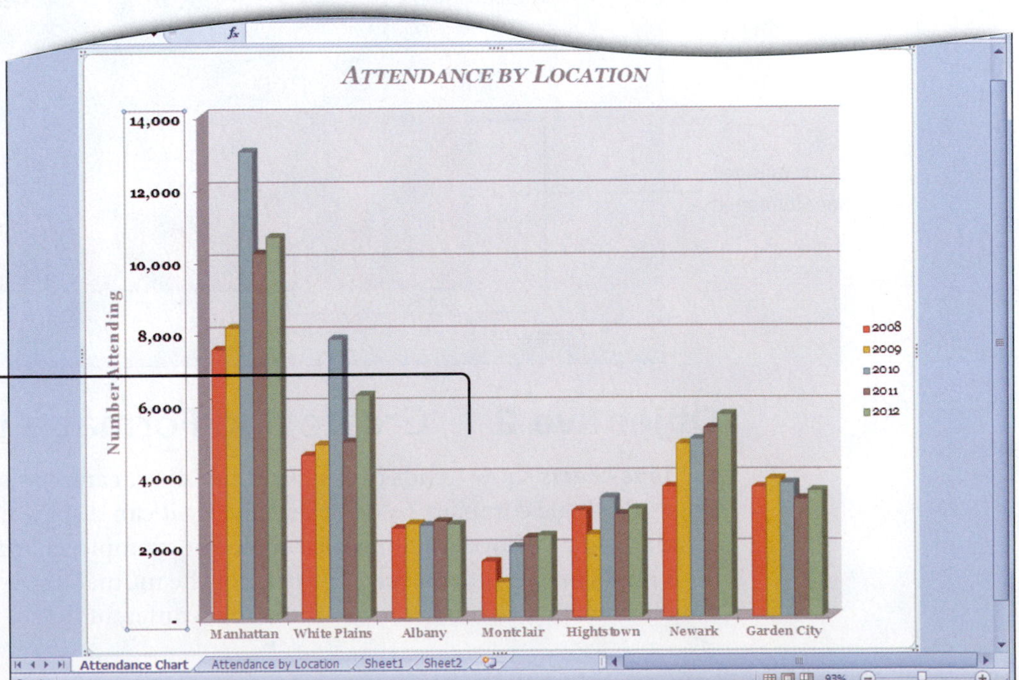

Activity 6.07 | Formatting the Chart Floor and Chart Walls

If your chart style includes shaded walls and a floor, you can format these elements.

1. On the **Layout tab**, in the **Current Selection group**, click the **Chart Elements arrow**, and then click **Back Wall**. Then in the same group, click **Format Selection**.

2. In the **Format Wall** dialog box, on the left, click **Fill**, on the right, click the **Solid fill** option button, and then under **Fill Color**, click the **Color arrow**. Under **Theme Colors**, in the fourth column, click the next to last color—**Blue-Gray, Text 2, Darker 25%**—and then set the **Transparency** to **75%**. **Close** the dialog box.

3. Using the technique you just practiced, select the **Side Wall**, and then apply the same fill, but with a **Transparency** of **60%**. In the lower right corner, click on **Close**.

4. From the **Chart Elements** list, select the **Floor**, and then apply a **Solid fill** using the last color in the first column—**White, Background 1, Darker 50%** with **0% Transparency**. **Close** the dialog box.

5. From the **Chart Elements** list, select the **Chart Area**, and then apply a **Solid fill** using **Green, Accent 5, Lighter 60%**—in the next to last column, the third color. **Close** the dialog box, click **Save**, and then compare your screen with Figure 6.14.

Figure 6.14

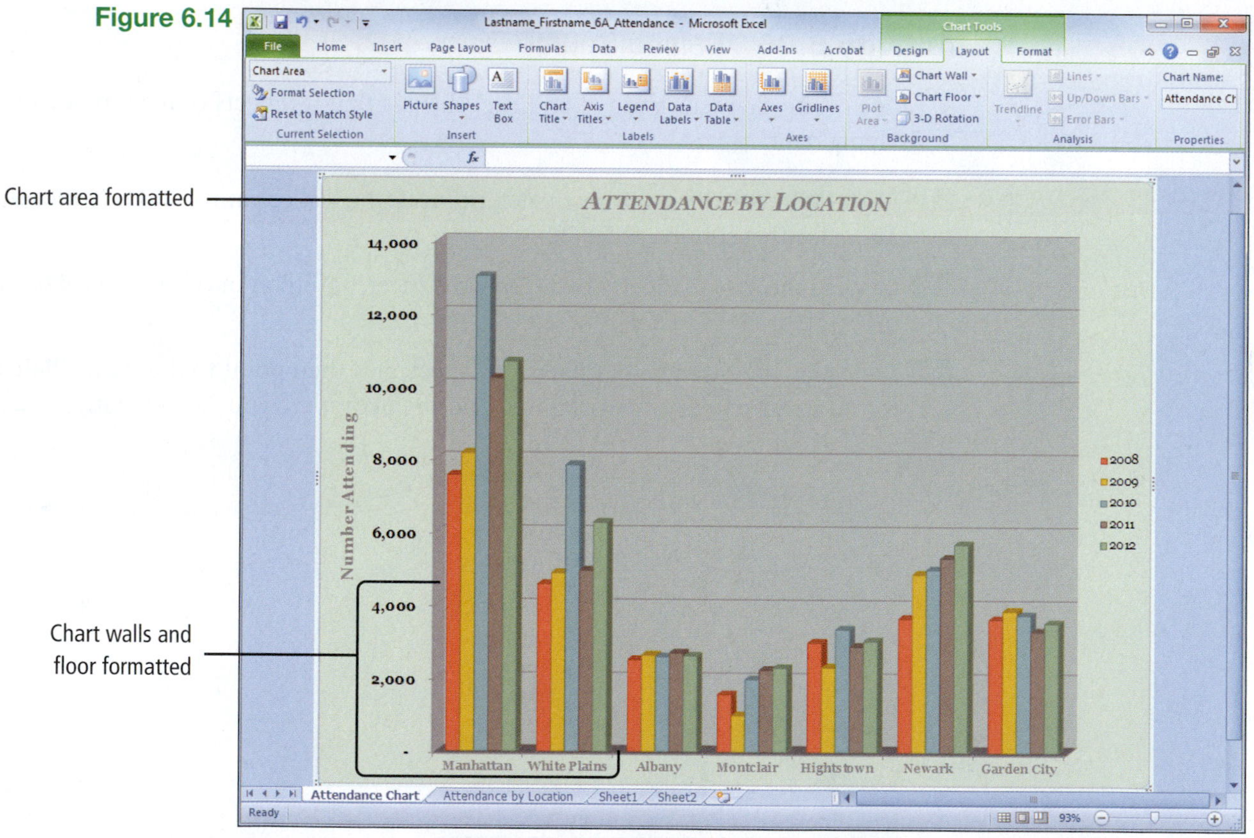

Objective 2 | Create and Format a Line Chart

Line charts show trends over time. A line chart can consist of one line, such as the price of a single company's stock over time, or it can display more than one line to show a comparison of related numbers over time. For example, charts tracking stock or mutual fund performance often display the price of the mutual fund on one line and an industry standard for that particular type of fund on a different line.

Activity 6.08 | Creating a Line Chart

In this activity, you will create a line chart showing the change in attendance at the New York-New Jersey Job Fair over a five-year period.

1 Display the **Attendance by Location** worksheet.

2 Select the range **A3:F4**, and then, on the **Insert tab**, in the **Charts group**, click the **Line** button. In the second row, click the first chart type—**Line with Markers**. Compare your screen with Figure 6.15.

Cell A3 must be included in the selection, despite being empty, because the same number of cells must be in each selected row. Excel identifies the first row as a category because of the empty first cell.

Figure 6.15

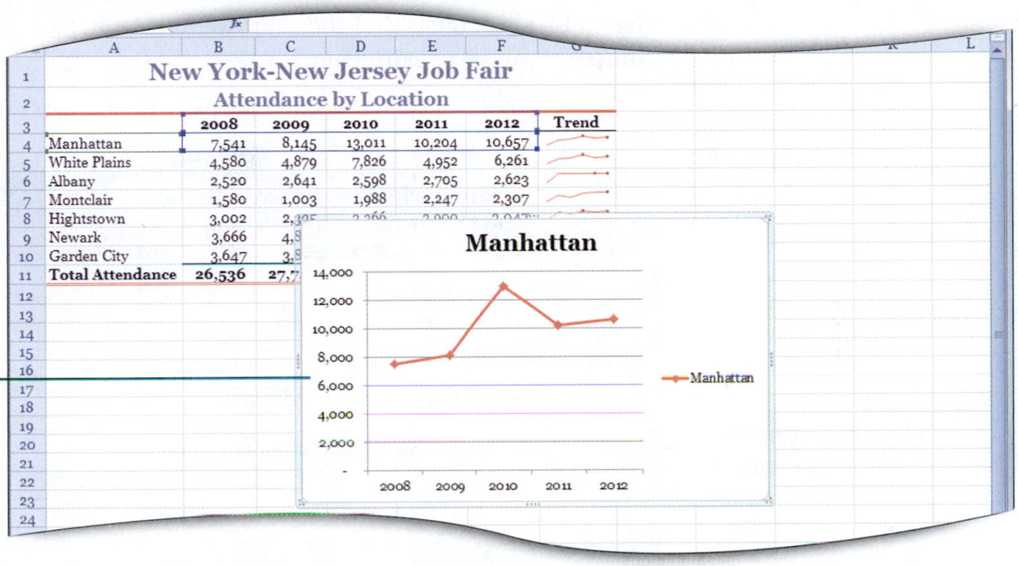

Line chart embedded in the worksheet

3 Point to the chart border to display the pointer, and then drag the upper left corner of the chart inside the upper left corner of cell **A13**.

4 Scroll down as necessary to view **row 30**. Point to the lower right corner of the chart to display the pointer, and then drag the lower right corner of the chart inside the lower right corner of cell **G29**. **Save** your workbook. Compare your screen with Figure 6.16.

When you use the corner sizing handles to resize an object, the proportional dimensions—the relative height and width—are retained.

Figure 6.16

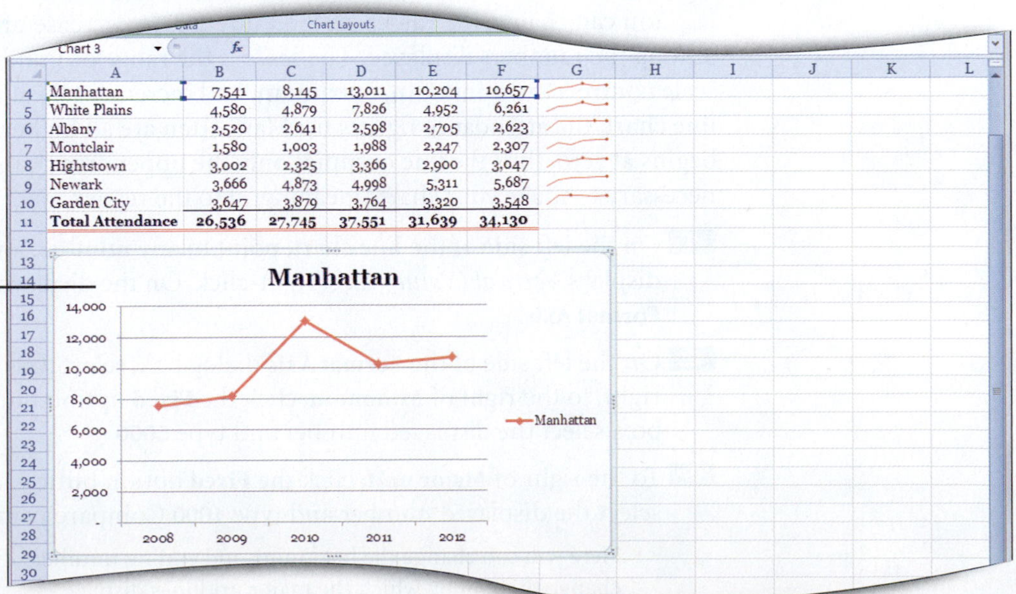

Chart repositioned

Activity 6.09 | Deleting a Legend and Changing a Chart Title

When you select the chart type, the resulting chart might contain elements that you want to delete or change. In the line chart, the title is *Manhattan*, and there is a legend that also indicates *Manhattan*. Because there is only one line of data, a legend is unnecessary, and the chart title can be more specific.

1 In the embedded chart, click the **Legend**—*Manhattan*—to select it. Press Del.

The legend is removed from the chart, and the chart plot area expands.

2 Click the **Chart Title**—*Manhattan*. In the **Formula Bar**, type **Attendance at Manhattan Job Fairs** as the chart title, and then press Enter to display the title text in the chart.

3 Point to the **Chart Title**, right-click, and then from the Mini toolbar, change the **Font Size** to **14**. Click outside of the chart to deselect it, **Save** your workbook, and then compare your chart with Figure 6.17.

The size of the title increases, and the plot area decreases slightly.

Figure 6.17

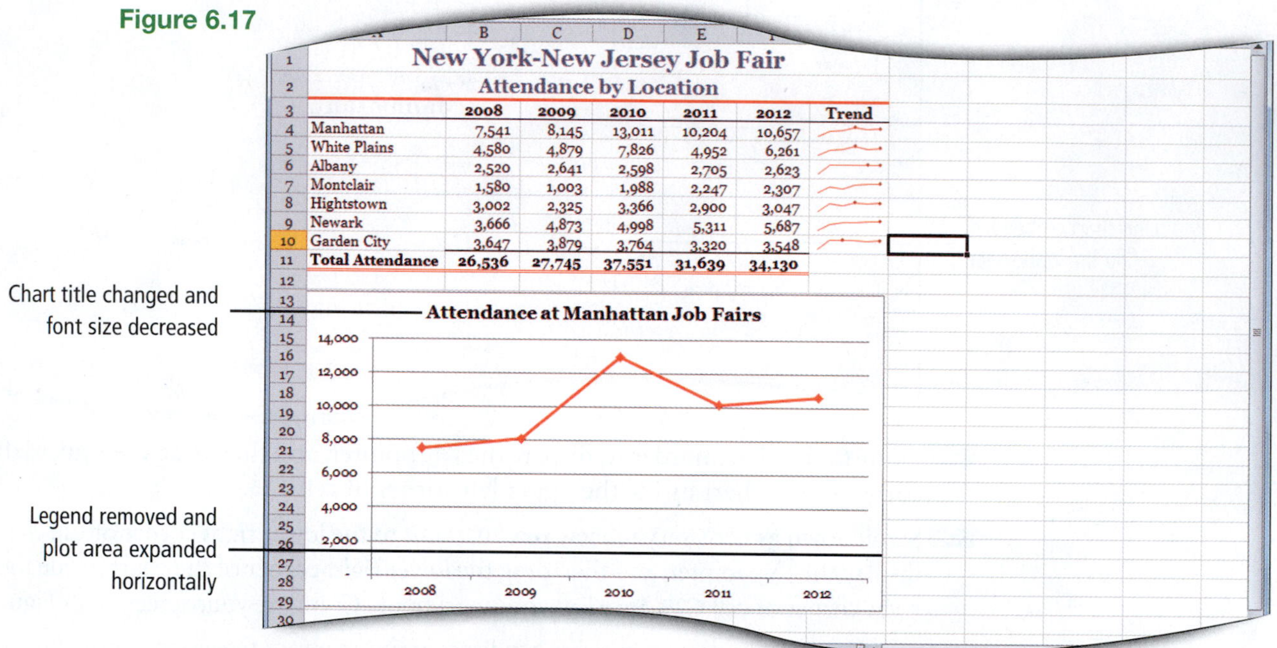

Activity 6.10 | Changing the Values on the Value Axis

You can change the values on the value axis to increase or decrease the variation among the numbers displayed. The ***scale*** is the range of numbers in the data series; the scale controls the minimum, maximum, and incremental values on the value axis. In the line chart, the attendance figures for Manhattan are all higher than 7,000, but the scale begins at zero, thus the line occupies only the upper area of the chart. Adjust the scale as necessary to make your charts meaningful to the reader.

1 On the left side of the line chart, point to any number, and then when the ScreenTip displays *Vertical (Value) Axis*, right-click. On the displayed shortcut menu, click **Format Axis**.

2 On the left side of the **Format Axis** dialog box, select **Axis Options**, if necessary. On the right, to the right of **Minimum**, click the **Fixed** option button, and then in the **Fixed** box, select the displayed number and type **5000**

3 To the right of **Major unit**, click the **Fixed** option button, and then in the **Fixed** box, select the displayed number and type **1000** Compare your screen with Figure 6.18.

Here you can change the beginning and ending numbers displayed on the chart and also change the unit by which the major gridlines display.

Figure 6.18

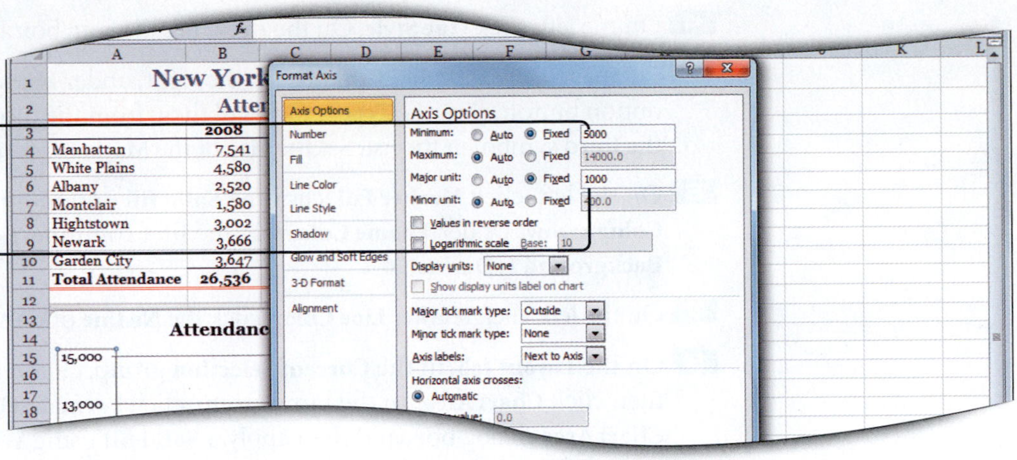

4 In the lower right corner, click **Close**. Click **Save**. Compare your screen with Figure 6.19.

The Value Axis begins at 5000 with major gridlines at intervals of 1000. This will emphasize the change in attendance over the five years by starting the chart at a higher number and decreasing the interval for gridlines.

Figure 6.19

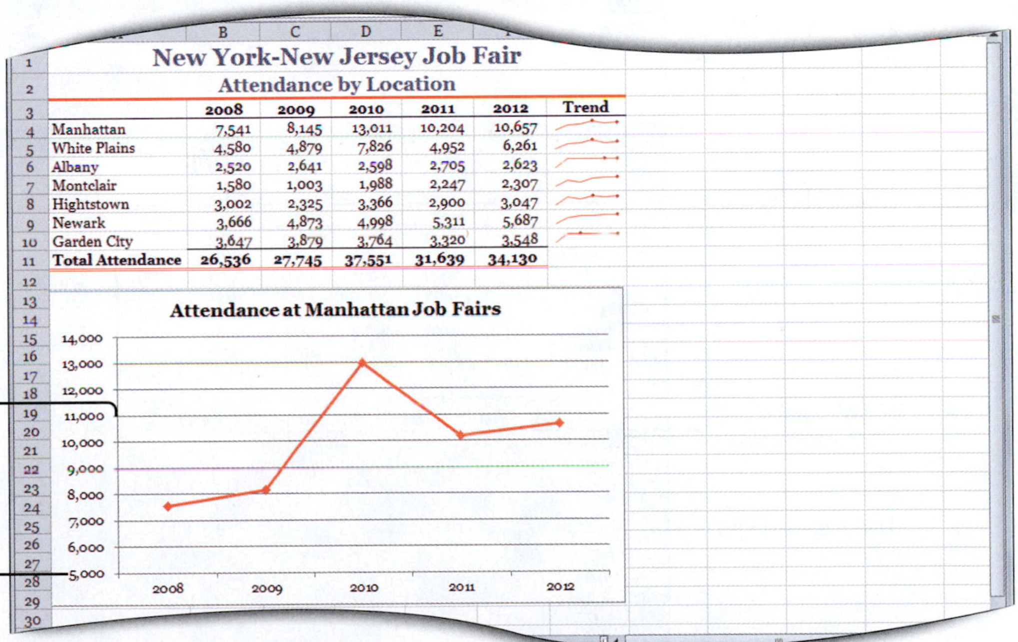

Activity 6.11 | Formatting the Plot Area and the Data Series

1 Right-click anywhere within the gray lined **Plot Area**, and then from the displayed shortcut menu, click **Format Plot Area**.

The Format Plot Area dialog box displays. Here you can change the border of the plot area or the background color.

2 On the left, select **Fill**, if necessary. On the right, click the **Solid fill** option button. Under **Fill Color**, click the **Color arrow**, and then under **Theme Colors**, in the first column, click the fourth color—**White, Background 1, Darker 25%. Close** the dialog box.

3 Point to the orange chart line, right-click, and then click **Format Data Series**.

In the Format Data Series dialog box, you can change the ***data markers***—the indicators for a data point value, which on the line chart is represented by a diamond shape. Here you can also change the line connecting the data markers.

4 On the left, click **Line Style.** On the right, use the spin box arrows to set the **Width** to **4 pt.**

5 On the left, click **Marker Options.** On the right, under **Marker Type**, click the **Built-in** option button, click the **Type arrow**, and then, from the displayed list, click the **triangle**—the third symbol in the list. Set the **Size** of the **Marker Type** to **12.**

6 On the left, click **Marker Fill**, click the **Solid fill** option button, and then click the **Color arrow**. Under **Theme Colors**, in the first column, click the last color—**White, Background 1, Darker 50%.**

7 On the left, click **Marker Line Color**, click the **No line** option button, and then click **Close.**

8 On the **Layout tab**, in the **Current Selection** group, click the **Chart Elements arrow**, and then click **Chart Area**. In the same group, click **Format Selection** to display the **Format Chart Area** dialog box, and then apply a **Solid fill** using **White, Background 1, Darker 15%**—in the first column, the third color. Click **Close.**

9 Click in any cell outside of the chart, Save your workbook, and then compare your screen with Figure 6.20.

The dialog box closes, and the data line and series markers change.

Figure 6.20

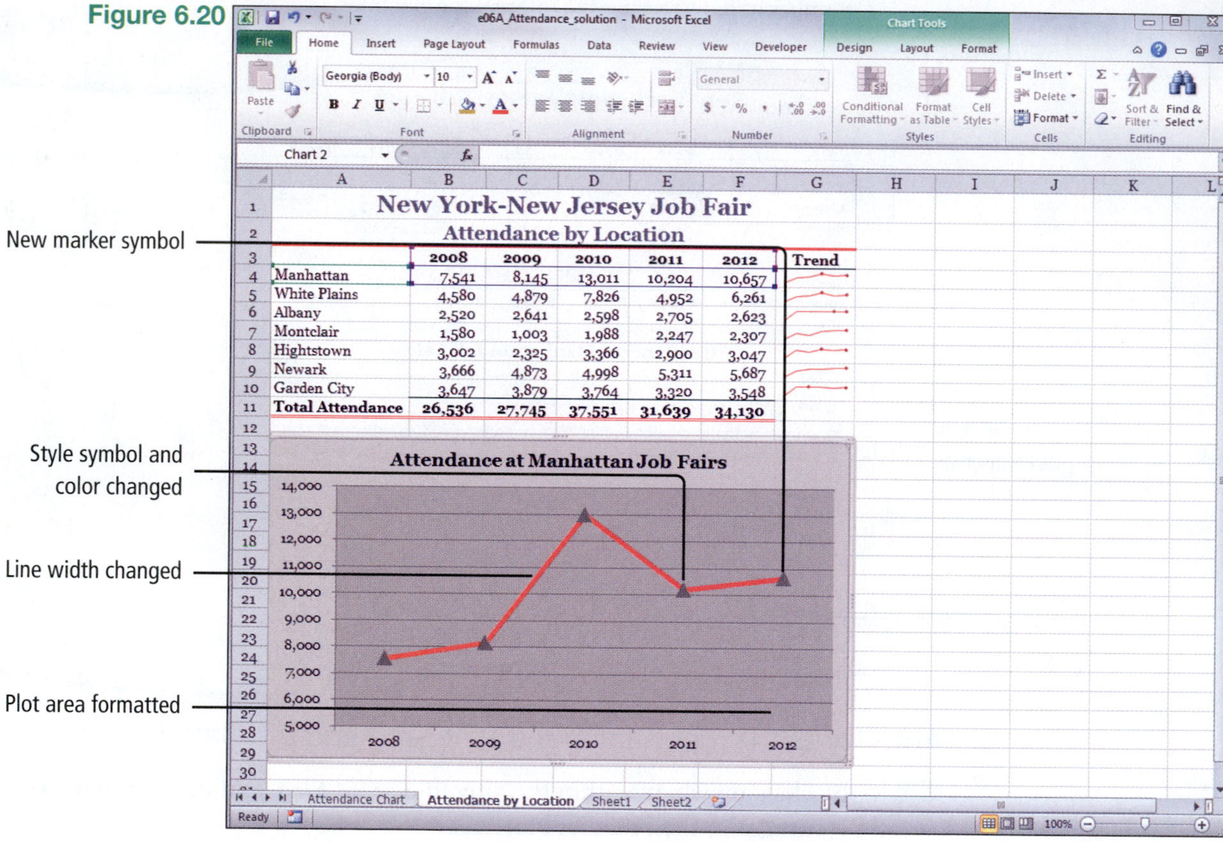

Activity 6.12 | Inserting a Trendline

A ***trendline*** is a graphic representation of trends in a data series, such as a line sloping upward to represent increased sales over a period of months. A trendline is always associated with a data series, but it does not represent the data of that data series. Rather, a trendline depicts trends in the existing data.

1 Click slightly inside the chart border to select the entire chart. On the **Layout tab**, in the **Analysis group**, click the **Trendline** button, and then click **Linear Trendline**. **Save** your workbook, and then compare your screen with Figure 6.21.

A linear trendline displays in the chart. The chart shows a significant increase in attendance for 2010, a drop in attendance in 2011, but the trendline indicates an overall increasing trend in attendance over the past five years.

Figure 6.21

Linear trendline added

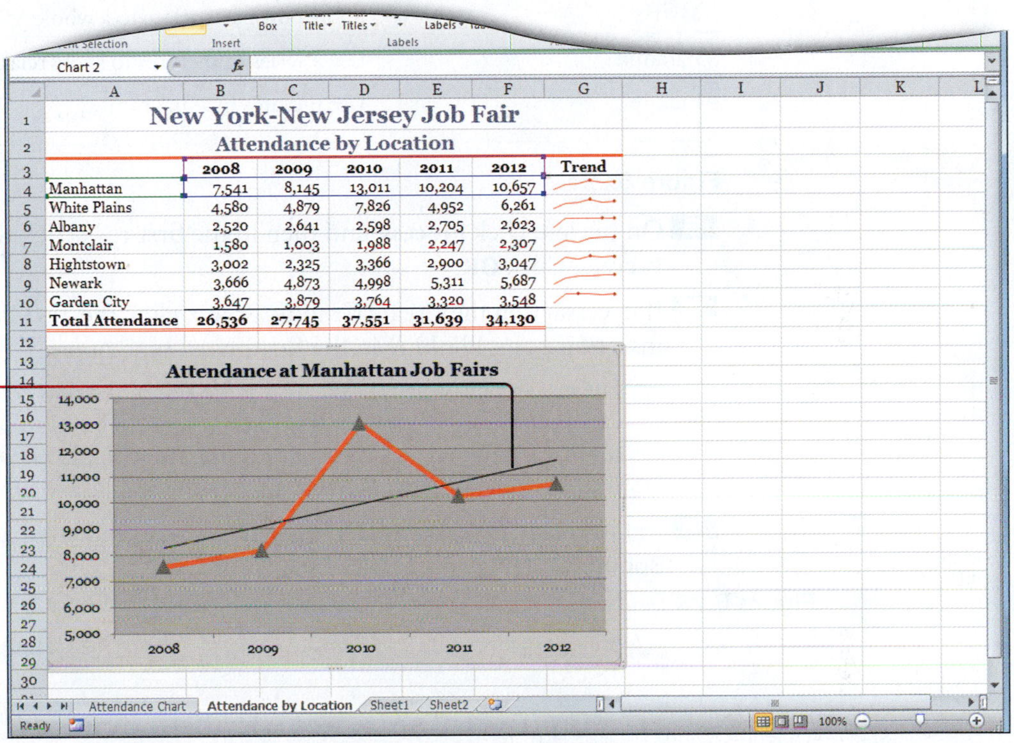

Objective 3 | Create and Modify a SmartArt Graphic

A ***SmartArt graphic*** is a visual representation of your information and ideas. You can create SmartArt graphics by choosing from among many different layouts to communicate complex messages and relationships easily and effectively.

Unlike charts, a SmartArt graphic does not depend on any underlying data in a worksheet; rather, it is a graphical tool that depicts ideas or associations. In the following activities, you will create a process diagram to illustrate how to register for an employer booth at the job fair.

Activity 6.13 | Creating a Process SmartArt Graphic

In this activity, you will use a Process SmartArt graphic, which shows steps in a process or timeline.

1 Click the **Sheet1 tab**, and rename the sheet tab **Process Chart** Click cell **A1** and type **Employer Booth Registration Process** and then press Enter.

2 Merge and center the text you just typed across **A1:H1**, apply the **Title** cell style, and change the **Font Size** to **24**.

3 On the **Insert tab**, in the **Illustrations group**, click the **SmartArt** button.

4 On the left, notice the types of SmartArt graphics that are available, and then take a moment to examine the table in Figure 6.22.

SmartArt

Use this SmartArt type:	To do this:
List	Show nonsequential information
Process	Show steps in a process or timeline
Cycle	Show a continual process
Hierarchy	Create an organization chart or show a decision tree
Relationship	Illustrate connections
Matrix	Show how parts relate to a whole
Pyramid	Use a series of pictures to show relationships
Picture	Use pictures in a diagram

Figure 6.22

5 On the left, click **Process**, and then in the first row, click the third option—**Step Down Process**. Click **OK**.

6 If necessary, in the Create Graphic group, click the Text Pane button. With your insertion point blinking in the first bullet, type **Apply**

The text *Apply* displays in the ***Text Pane*** and in the first box in the diagram. Use the Text Pane, which displays to the left of the graphic, to build your graphic by entering and editing your text. The Text Pane is populated with placeholder text that you replace with your information. If you prefer, close the Text Pane and type directly into the graphic.

7 In the **Text Pane**, click the next bullet, which is indented, and then type **Register for Booth** Compare your screen with Figure 6.23.

Figure 6.23

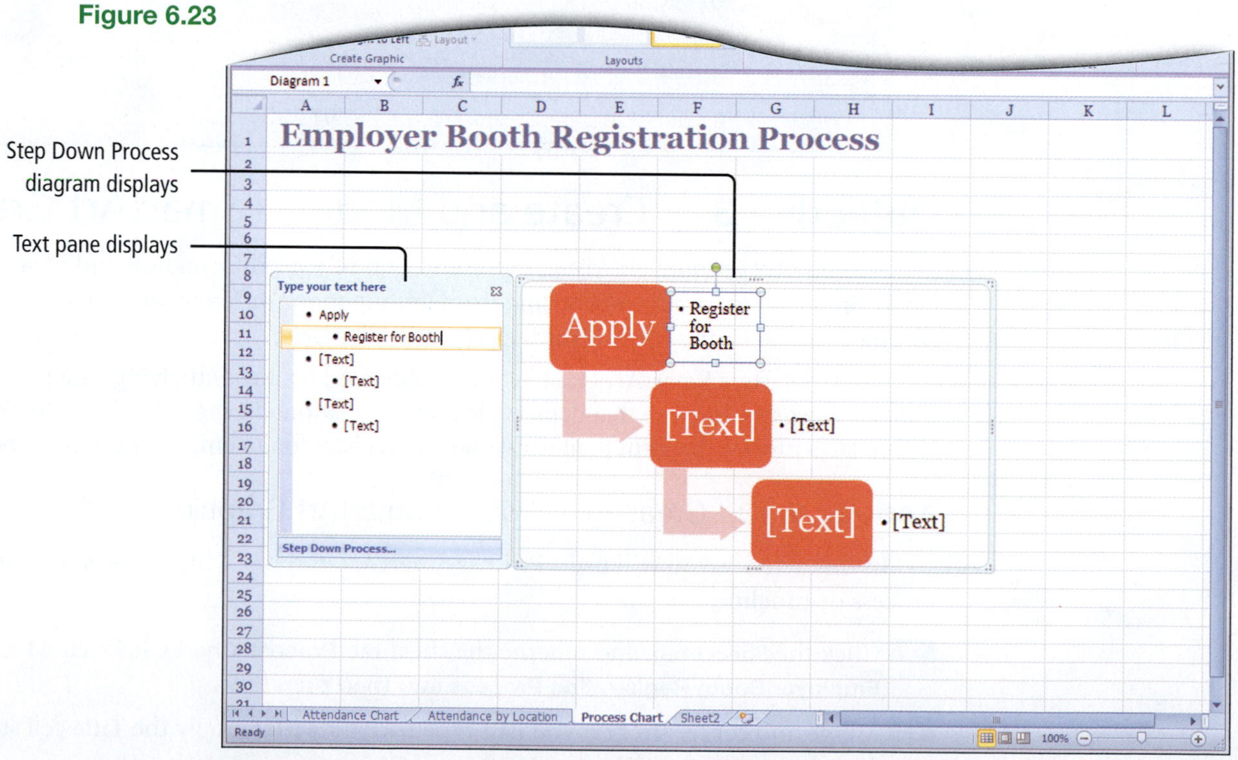

8 In the **Text Pane**, click the next bullet, and then type **Prepare** Under *Prepare* click the indented bullet and type **Booth Number Assigned**

9 Click the next bullet and type **Attend** Click the next bullet, and then type **Set up Job Fair Booth** Compare your diagram with Figure 6.24.

The Text Pane entries display on the left in the Text Pane, and the process diagram with entries displays on the right in the process diagram.

Figure 6.24

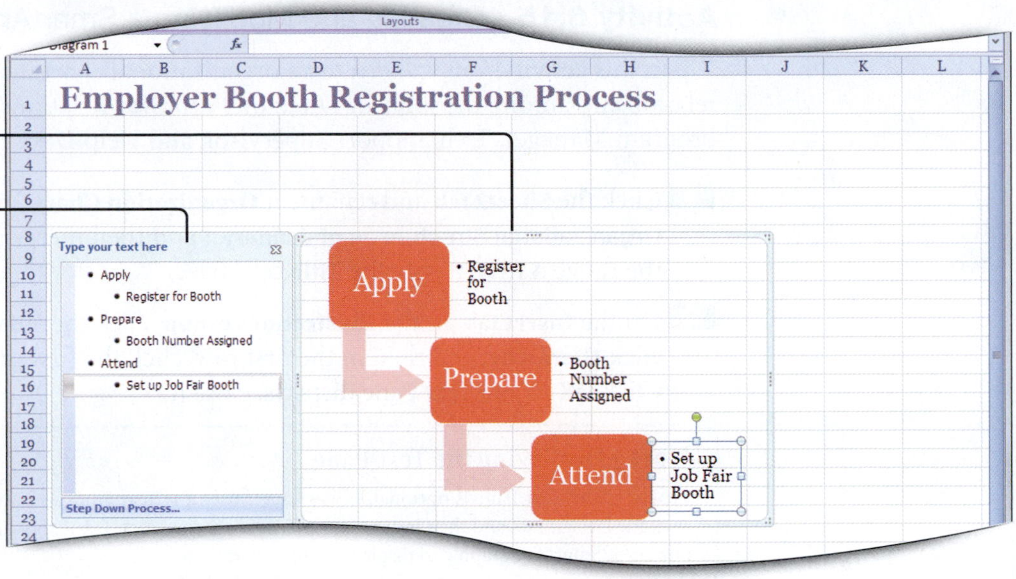

10 **Close** the **Text Pane**, and then **Save** your workbook.

Activity 6.14 | Modifying the Diagram Style

Excel offers preformatted SmartArt styles that can be applied to a diagram.

1 With the SmartArt still selected, in the **SmartArt Styles group**, click the **More** button. Under **3-D**, click the first style—**Polished**.

2 In the **SmartArt Styles group**, click the **Change Colors** button, and then under **Colorful**, click the third option—**Colorful Range – Accent Colors 3 to 4**.

3 By using the pointer, drag the upper left corner of the graphic border inside the upper left corner of cell **A4**. Point to the lower right corner of the graphic's border to display the pointer, and then drag to position the lower right corner inside the lower right corner of cell **H22**. **Save** your workbook, and then compare your screen with Figure 6.25.

Figure 6.25

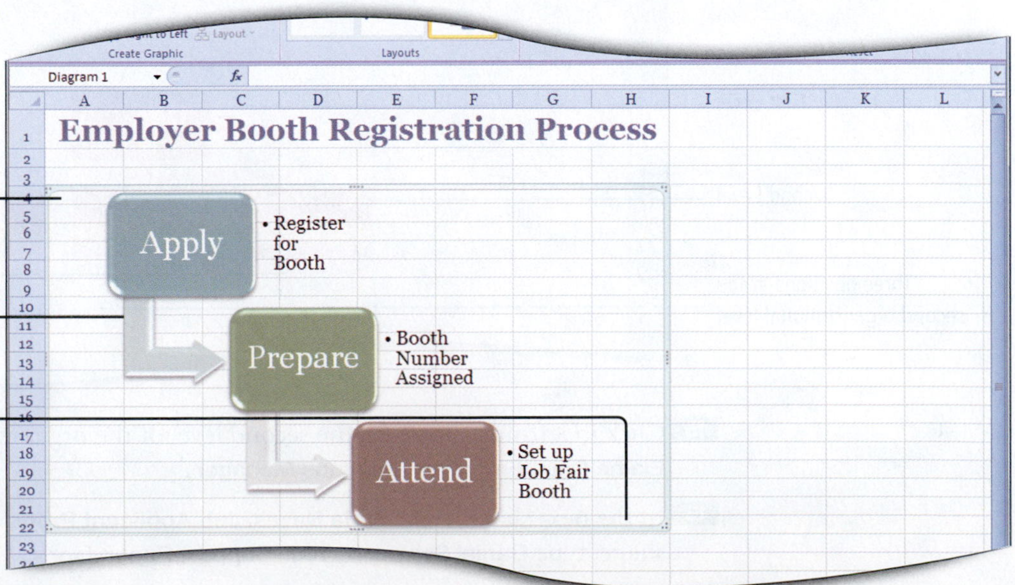

Objective 4 | Create and Modify an Organization Chart

An ***organization chart*** depicts reporting relationships within an organization.

Activity 6.15 | Creating and Modifying a SmartArt Organization Chart

In this activity, you will create an organizational chart that shows the reporting relationship among the Job Fair Director, Employer Relations Manager, Job Applicant Program Manager, Tech Support Supervisor, and Help Desk Technician.

1 Click the **Sheet2 tab** and rename it **Organization Chart**. In cell **A1**, type **Job Fair Organizational Structure as of January 1** and then merge and center this title across the range **A1:H1**. Apply the **Title** cell style.

2 On the **Insert tab**, in the **Illustrations group**, click the **SmartArt** button. On the left, click **Hierarchy**, and then in the first row, click the first graphic—**Organization Chart**. Click **OK**. If the Text Pane displays, close it.

> **Note | Displaying the Text Pane**
>
> Typing in the Text Pane is optional. If you have closed the Text Pane and want to reopen it, select the graphic, click the Design tab, and then in the Create Graphic group, click Text Pane. Alternatively, click the arrows on left border of SmartArt graphic to display the Text Pane.

3 In the graphic, click in the first **[Text]** box, and then type **Jennifer Patterson, Job Fair Director**

4 In the box below the *Job Fair Director*, click on the *edge* of the box to display a solid line border—if a dashed border displays, click the edge of the box again. With the box bordered with a solid line, press Del. Compare your screen with Figure 6.26.

Three shapes comprise the second level of the organization chart.

Figure 6.26

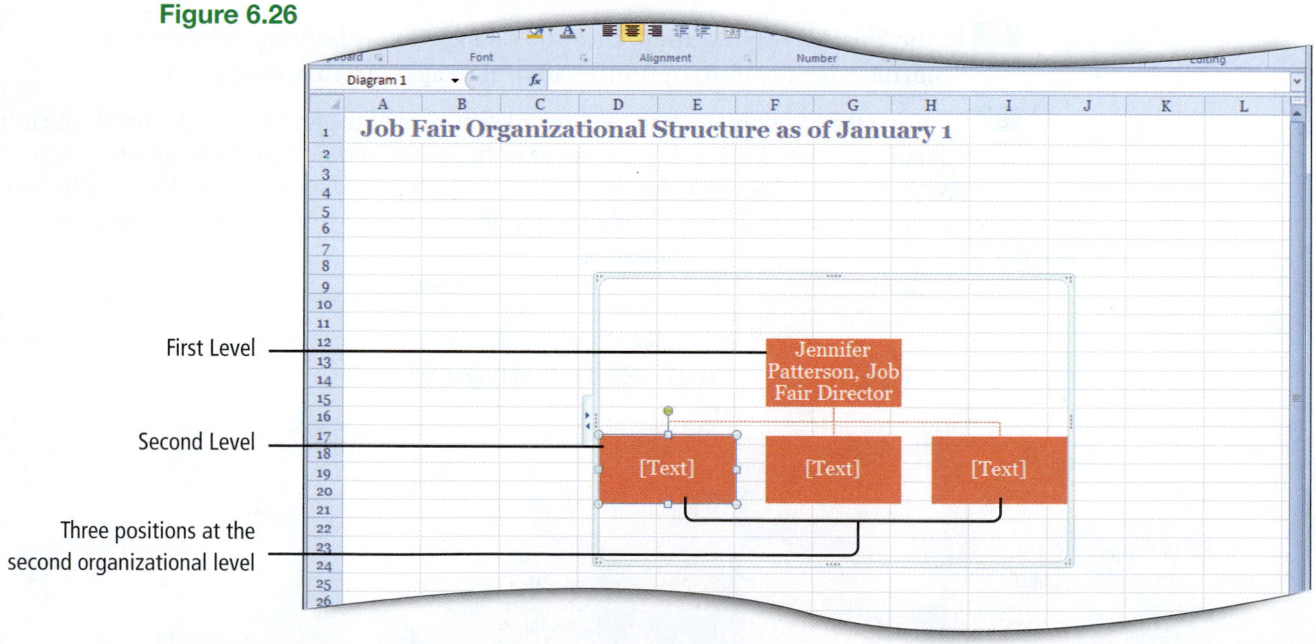

5 Click in leftmost shape on the second level of the organization chart, and then type **Elaine Chin, Employer Relations Manager**

6 In the next shape, type **Maria Naves, Job Applicant Program Manager** In the rightmost shape, type **Daniel Schwartz, Tech Support Supervisor**

> **Another Way**
>
> Alternatively, right-click the shape, click Add Shape, and then click Add Shape Below.

7 If necessary, click in the *Daniel Schwartz* shape. On the **Design tab**, in the **Create Graphic group**, click the **Add Shape arrow**, and then click **Add Shape Below**.

A new shape displays below the Tech Support Supervisor shape.

8 Type **Sergey Penvy, Help Desk Technician**

9 In the **SmartArt Styles group**, click the **More** button, and then under **3-D**, click the first style—**Polished**. Click the **Change Colors** button, and then under **Colorful**, click the fifth color arrangement—**Colorful Range – Accent Colors 5 to 6**. Click **Save** and then compare your screen with Figure 6.27.

Figure 6.27

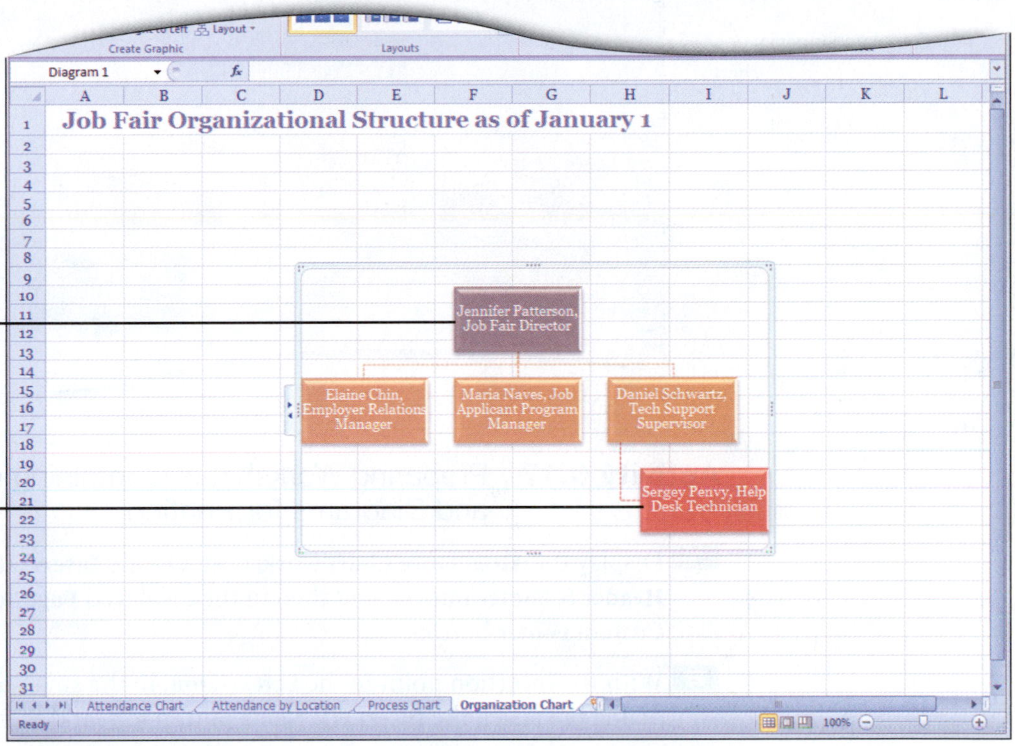

Activity 6.16 | Adding Effects to a SmartArt Graphic

In this activity, you will change the formatting and layout of the graphic.

1 Click in the *Sergey Penvy* shape.

2 On the **Format tab**, in the **Shape Styles group**, click **Shape Fill**, and then under **Theme Colors**, in the next to last column, click the fifth color—**Green, Accent 5, Darker 25%.**

3 Click the edge of the *Sergey Penvy* shape so that it is surrounded by a solid line and sizing handles and the polished shape displays. Then, hold down Ctrl, and click each of the other shapes until all five are selected.

4 With all five shapes selected, in the **Shape Styles group**, click the **Shape Effects** button, point to **Bevel**, and then under **Bevel**, in the third row, click the second bevel shape—**Riblet.**

5 By using the pointer, drag the upper left corner of the graphic inside the upper left corner of cell **A4**. By using the pointer, drag the lower right corner of the chart inside the lower right corner of cell **H20**.

6. In the second level, in the shape for *Maria Naves*, click to position the insertion point after the comma, hold down Shift, and then press Enter to insert a line break. Press Del to delete the extra space.

7. Click cell **A1**, and then **Save** your workbook. Compare your screen with Figure 6.28.

Figure 6.28

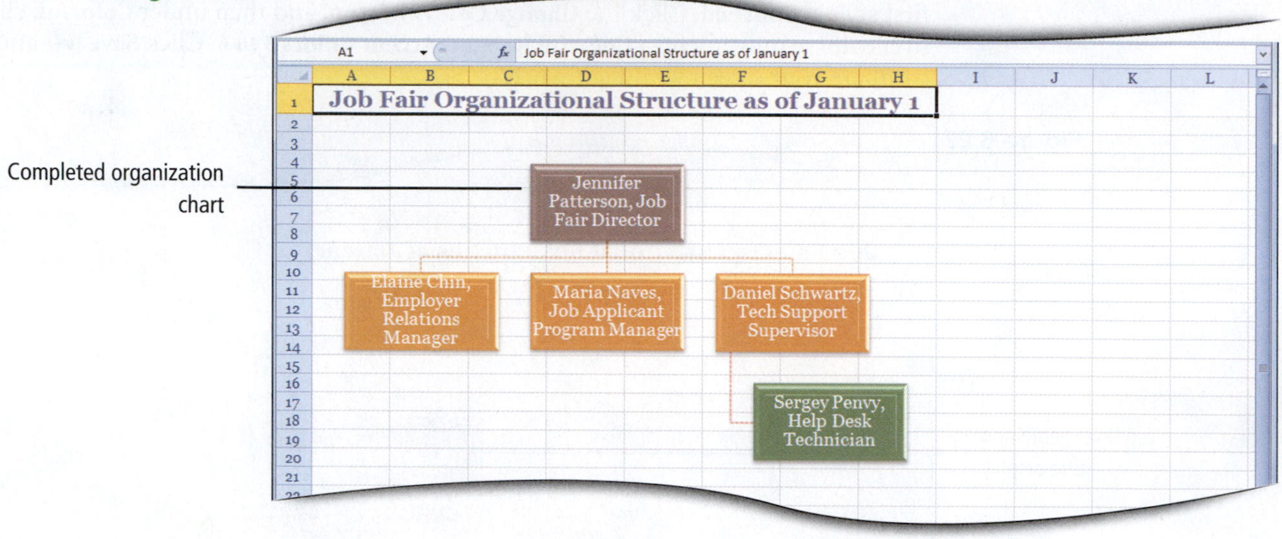

Activity 6.17 | Preparing Worksheets Containing Charts and Diagrams for Printing

1. Display the **Attendance Chart** worksheet. On the **Insert tab**, in the **Text group**, click the **Header & Footer** button, and then in the displayed **Page Setup** dialog box, click the **Custom Footer** button.

2. With the insertion point in the **Left section**, in the small toolbar in the center of the dialog box, click the **Insert File Name** button, and then click **OK** two times.

3. Click the **Attendance by Location sheet tab**, hold down Ctrl, and then click the **Process Chart sheet tab** and the **Organization Chart sheet tab** to select the remaining three worksheets and group them.

4. With the three sheets grouped, insert a footer in the **left section** that includes the file name. Click outside the footer area, and then on the **Page Layout tab**, click the **Margins** button, click **Custom Margins**, and then center the sheets horizontally. Press Ctrl + Home and return to **Normal** view.

5. Right-click any of the four sheet tabs, and then click **Select All Sheets**. From **Backstage** view, display the **Document Panel**. In the **Author** box, delete any text, and then type your firstname and lastname. In the **Subject** box, type your course name and section number, and in the **Keywords** box, type **attendance statistics, organization charts** **Close** the **Document Panel**.

6. Press Ctrl + F2, examine the **Print Preview**, make any necessary adjustments, and then **Save** your workbook.

7. Print or submit your workbook electronically as directed by your instructor. **Close** Excel.

End You have completed Project 6A

Project 6B Order Form Template

myitlab Project 6B Training

Project Activities

In Activities 6.18 through 6.25, you will create, format, and edit a booth registration order form template for use by Job Fair staff to ensure that totals for items ordered are calculated accurately. You will also protect the template. Your completed worksheets will look similar to Figure 6.29.

Project Files

For Project 6B, you will need the following files:

New blank Excel workbook
e06B_Logo

You will save your workbooks as:

Lastname_Firstname_6B_Booth_Order
Lastname_Firstname_6B_Order_Template
Lastname_Firstname_6B_Topaz_Order

Project Results

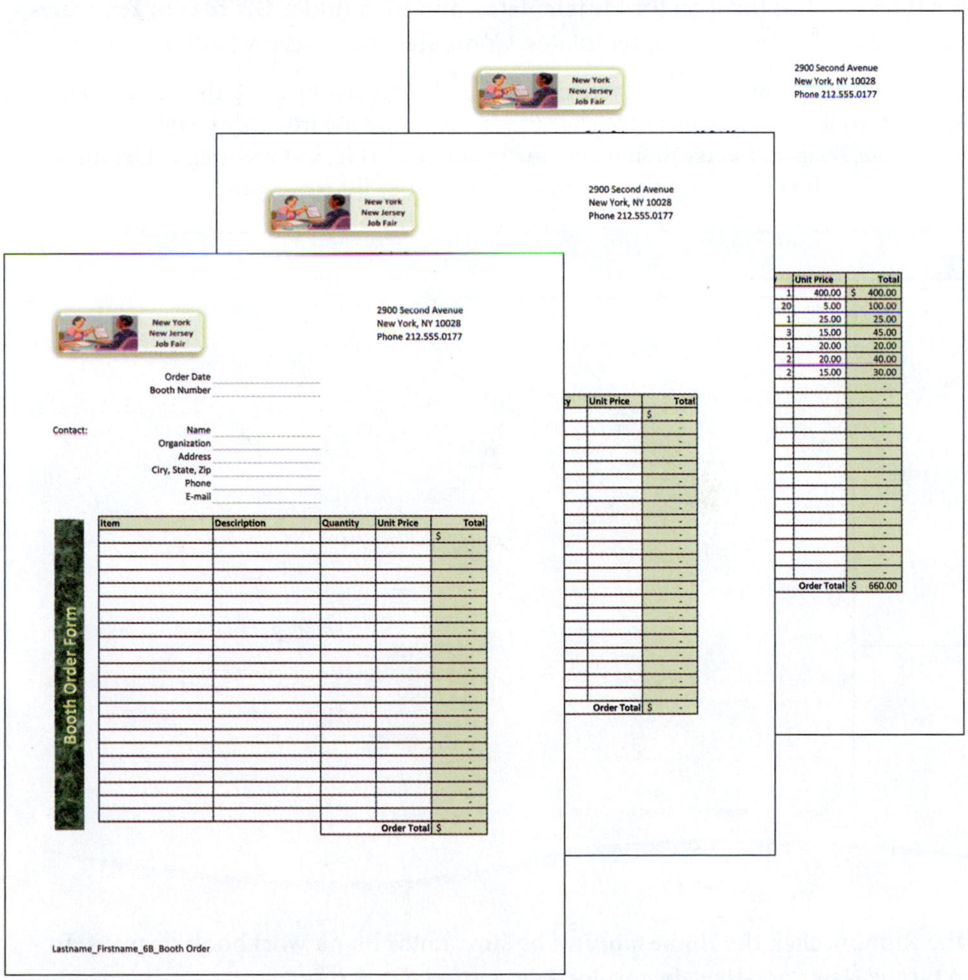

Figure 6.29
Project 6B Order Form Template

Objective 5 | Create an Excel Template

A ***template*** is a workbook that you create and use as the basis for other similar workbooks. Excel also has predesigned templates that include, among others, financial forms to record expenses, time worked, balance sheet items, and other common financial reports.

Standardization and ***protection*** are the two main reasons for creating templates for commonly used forms in an organization. Standardization means that all forms created within the organization will have a uniform appearance; the data will always be organized in the same manner. Protection means that individuals entering data cannot change areas of the worksheet that are protected, and thus, cannot alter important formulas and formats built in to the template.

Activity 6.18 | Entering Template Text

To create a template, start with a blank worksheet; enter the text, formatting, and formulas needed for the specific worksheet purpose, and then save the file as a template. Saving a workbook as a template adds the extension *.xltx* to the file name. In this activity, you will start a workbook for the purpose of creating a purchase order template.

1 **Start** Excel and display a new blank workbook. Click the **File tab**, and then in **Backstage** view, click the **New tab**.

2 Under **Home**, notice the icon for **My templates**, and then under **Office.com Templates**, notice the various categories of templates. Compare your screen with Figure 6.30.

When you create and save a template on your own computer by using the default save location, your template will be available to you for future use from *My templates*. From *Office.com Templates*, you can find and download many different predesigned templates from Microsoft's Office.com site. Microsoft updates this list frequently.

Figure 6.30

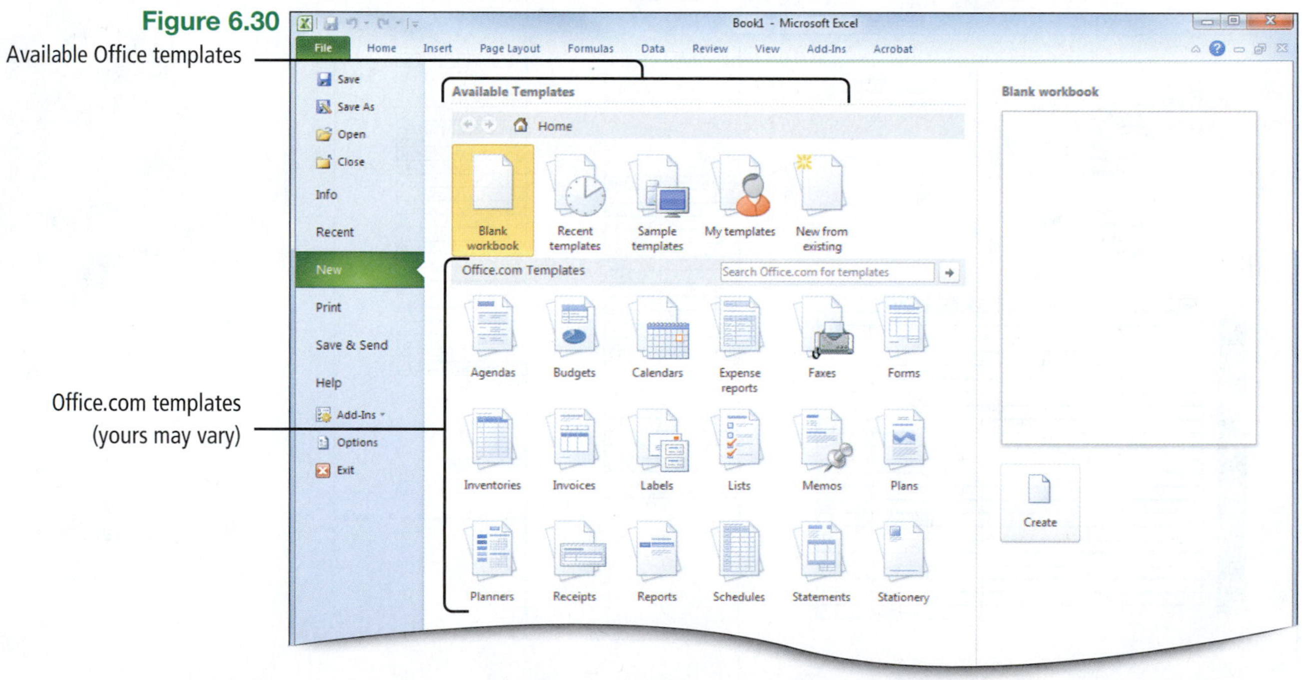

3 On the Ribbon, click the **Home tab**, and be sure a new blank workbook displays. In cell **A1**, type **New York-New Jersey Job Fair**

4 Click in cell **E1**, type **2900 Second Avenue** and then press Enter. In cell **E2**, type **New York, NY 10028** and press Enter. In cell **E3** type **Phone 212.555.0177** and press Enter. Click cell **B6**, type **Order Date** and press Enter. In cell **B7**, type **Booth Number** press Enter.

5 Click cell **B10**. Type **Name** and press Enter. In cell **B11**, type **Organization** and press Enter. In cell **B12**, type **Address** and press Enter. In cell **B13**, type **City, State, Zip** and press Enter. In cell **B14**, type **Phone** and press Enter. In cell **B15**, type **E-mail** and press Enter. Click cell **A10**. Type **Contact:** and press Enter. Press Ctrl + Home.

These labels will comprise the form headings.

6 Click cell **B17**. Type **Item** and press Tab to move to cell **C17**. Continuing across **row 17**, in cell **C17**, type **Description** and press Tab, in cell **D17**, type **Quantity** and press Tab, in cell **E17**, type **Unit Price** and press Tab, and in cell **F17**, type **Total** and press Enter. Select the range **B17:F17**, and then in the **Font** group, click the **Bold** button **B**. Compare your screen with Figure 6.31, and then make any necessary corrections.

The column headings are added to the order form.

Figure 6.31

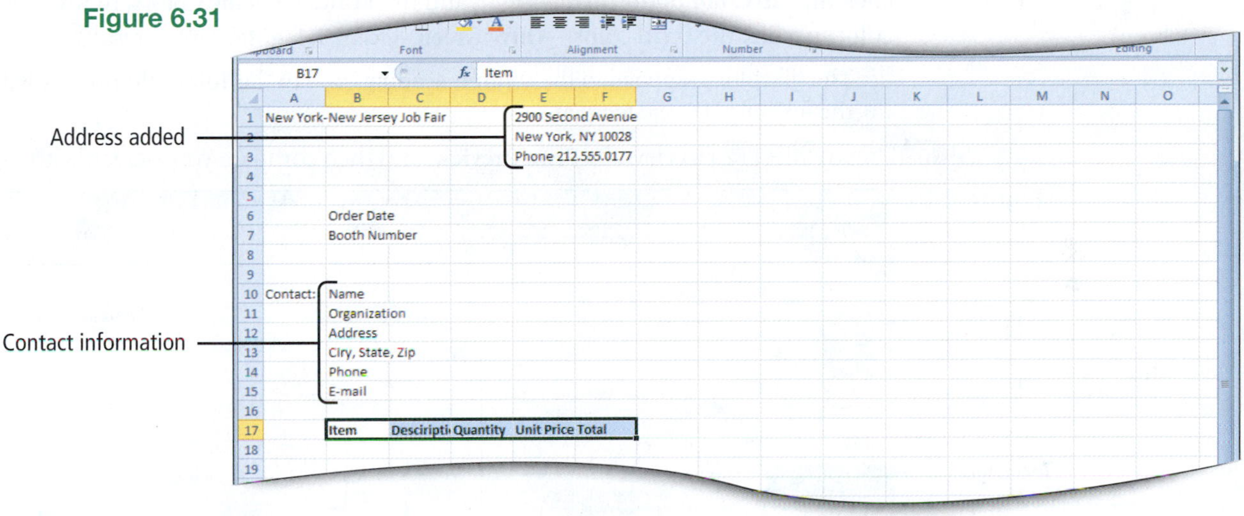

7 **Save** the file in your **Excel Chapter 6** folder as **Lastname_Firstname_6B_Booth_Order**

Until the format and design of the order form is complete, you will save your work as a normal workbook.

Activity 6.19 | Formatting a Template

One of the goals in designing a template is to make it easy for others to complete. It should be obvious to the person completing the form what information is necessary and where to place the information.

1 Widen **column B** to **155 pixels**. Widen **column C** to **145 pixels**. Select **columns D:F** and widen to **75 pixels**.

2 Select the range **B6:B15**, hold down Ctrl and select the range **C10:C15**, and then on the **Home tab**, in the **Alignment group**, click the **Align Text Right** button.

3 Click cell **F17**, and then in the **Alignment group**, click the **Align Text Right** button.

4 Select the range **C6:C7**. In the **Alignment group**, click the **Dialog Box Launcher** button. In the **Format Cells** dialog box, click the **Border tab**. Under **Line**, in the **Style** list, click the first line in the first column—**the dotted line**.

5 Click the **Color arrow**, and then under **Theme Colors**, in the third column, click the fourth color—**Tan, Background 2, Darker 50%**. Under **Border**, click the **Middle Border** button, and the **Bottom Border** button. Click **OK**.

6 With the range **C6:C7** still selected, in the **Alignment group**, click the **Align Text Right** button. Then, with the range still selected, right-click, and on the Mini toolbar, click **Format Painter**, and then select the range **C10:C15** to copy the format.

Inserting borders on cells in a template creates lines as a place to record information when the form is filled out. This provides a good visual cue to the person filling out the form as to where information should be placed.

7 Select the range **B17:F40**. Right-click the selected area and click **Format Cells**. From the displayed **Format Cells** dialog box, if necessary, click the **Border tab.** Under **Presets**, click the **Outline** button and the **Inside** button, and then click **OK**.

This action applies a grid of columns and rows, which is helpful to those individuals completing the form.

8 Select the range **B17:F17**, hold down Ctrl and select the range **F18:F40**. In the **Font group**, click the **Fill Color button arrow**, and then under **Theme Colors**, in the seventh column, click the third color—**Olive Green, Accent 3, Lighter 60%**. Press Ctrl + Home.

The fill color is applied to the column headings and to the Total column that will contain the formulas for the template.

9 Press Ctrl + F2 to view the **Print Preview**, and then compare your screen with Figure 6.32.

Figure 6.32

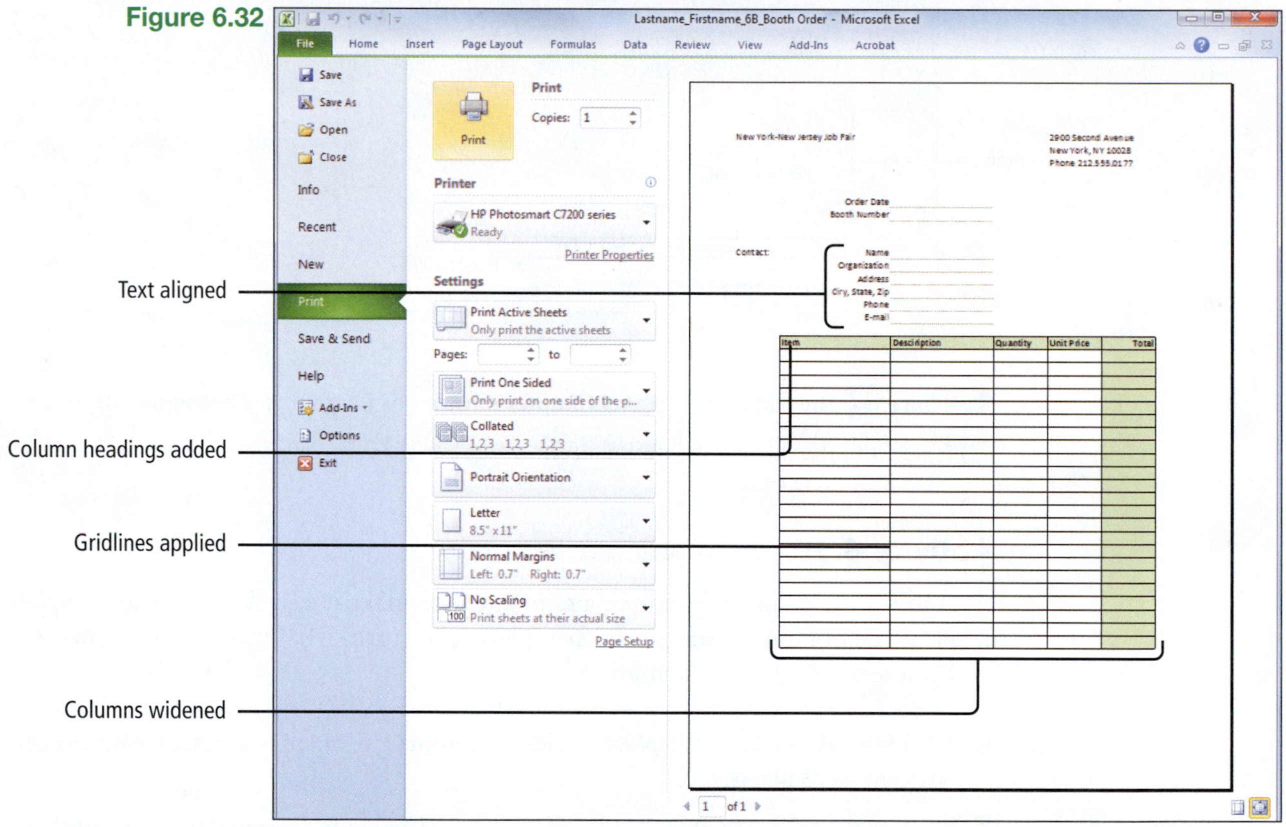

10 At the top of the navigation bar, click **Save** to save and return to your workbook.

A dotted line on the worksheet indicates where the first page would end if the worksheet were printed as it is currently set up. As you develop your template, use the Print Preview to check your progress.

Activity 6.20 | Entering Template Formulas

After the text is entered and formatted in your template, add formulas to the cells where you want the result of the calculations to display. In this activity, you will create a formula in the Total column to determine the dollar value for the quantity of each item ordered, and then create another formula to sum the Total column.

1 In cell **F18**, type **=d18*e18** and press Enter.

A value of 0 displays in cell F18. However, when the person entering information into the worksheet types the Quantity in cell D18 and the Unit Price in cell E18, the formula will multiply the two values to calculate a total for the item.

2 Use the fill handle to copy the formula in cell **F18** down through cell **F39**.

3 Click cell **F40**. On the **Home tab**, in the **Editing group**, click the **AutoSum** button Σ. Be sure the range displays as *F18:F39*, and then press Enter.

4 Select the range **E18:E39**. On the **Home tab**, in the **Number group**, click the **Comma Style** button ,.

The Comma Style is applied; thus, when values are typed into the form, they will display with two decimals and commas in the appropriate locations.

5 Click cell **F18**, hold down Ctrl, and then click cell **F40**. In the **Number group**, click the **Accounting Number Format** button $. Select the range **F19:F39**, and then click the **Comma Style** button ,.

Formats are applied to the Total column, and the zero in each cell displays as a hyphen.

6 Select the range **D40:E40**. In the **Alignment group**, click the **Merge and Center** button. Type **Order Total** and press Enter. Click cell **D40** again, and then in the **Alignment group**, click the **Align Text Right** button. In the **Font** group, click the **Bold** button **B**.

A label is added and formatted to identify the total for the entire order.

7 Select the range **B40:C40**, right-click, and then from the displayed list, click **Format Cells**. In the **Format Cells** dialog box, if necessary, click the **Border tab**, and then in the **Border preview** area, click the **Left Border** button, the **Middle Border** button and the **Bottom Border** button to *remove* these borders from the preview—be sure the right and top lines remain in the preview area. Compare your dialog box with Figure 6.33.

Figure 6.33

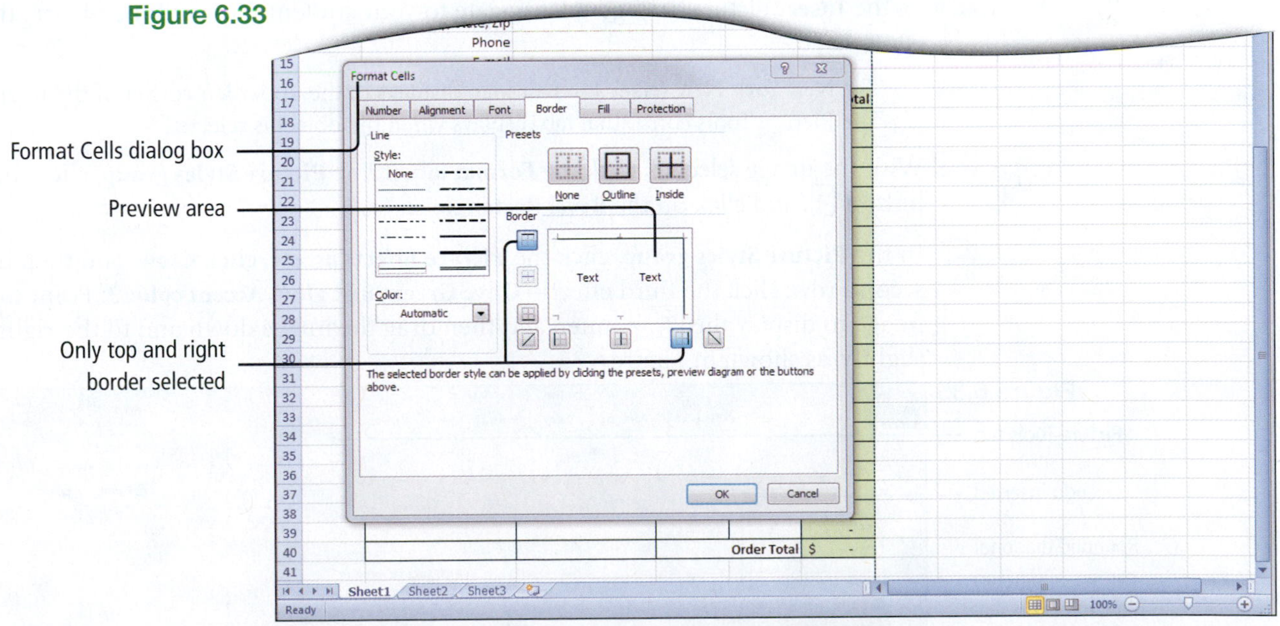

8 Click **OK**. Press Ctrl + F2 to view the **Print Preview**. Compare your screen with Figure 6.34.

Figure 6.34

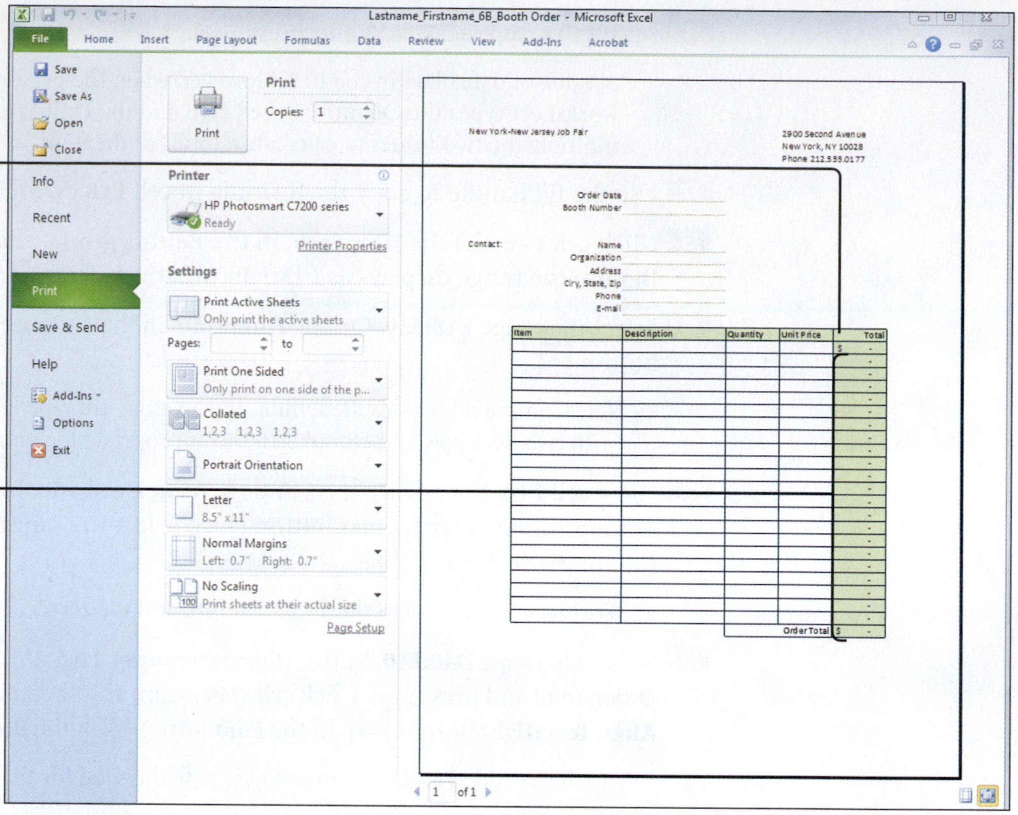

9 In the **Backstage** view, click **Save** to save and return to your workbook.

Activity 6.21 | Inserting and Modifying an Image

In the following activity, you will add a logo image to the form.

1 Click cell **A1** and press Del to remove the company name. On the **Insert tab**, in the **Illustrations group**, click the **Picture** button.

2 In the **Insert Picture** dialog box, navigate to your student files, and then insert the file **e06B_Logo**.

The New York-New Jersey Job Fair logo displays in the upper left corner of the worksheet. The Picture Tools contextual tab displays when the object is selected.

3 With the image selected, click the **Format tab**, in the **Picture Styles group**, click the **More** button, and click on the **Bevel Rectangle style**.

4 In the **Picture Styles group**, click the **Picture Effects arrow**, click **Glow**, and then in second row, click the third effect—**Olive Green, 8 pt glow, Accent color 3**. Point to the image to display the pointer, and then drag the image down and to the right slightly, as shown in Figure 6.35.

Figure 6.35

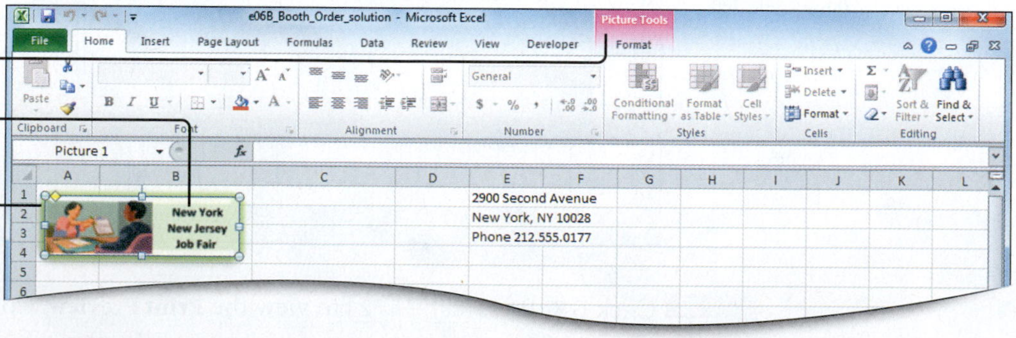

5 **Save** your workbook.

Activity 6.22 | Inserting and Modifying a WordArt Image

WordArt is a feature with which you can insert decorative text in your document, for example to create a stylized image for a heading or logo. Because WordArt is a graphical object, it can be moved and resized. In addition, you can change its shape and color. In this activity, you will create and modify a vertical WordArt heading and place it at the left side of the order form grid.

1 Scroll so that **row 16** is at the top of the Excel window. Then, click cell **A17**. On the **Insert tab**, in the **Text group**, click the **WordArt** button, and then in the fifth row, click the fourth WordArt—**Fill – Olive Green, Accent 3, Powder Bevel**. Type **Booth Order Form** and then compare your screen with Figure 6.36.

Figure 6.36

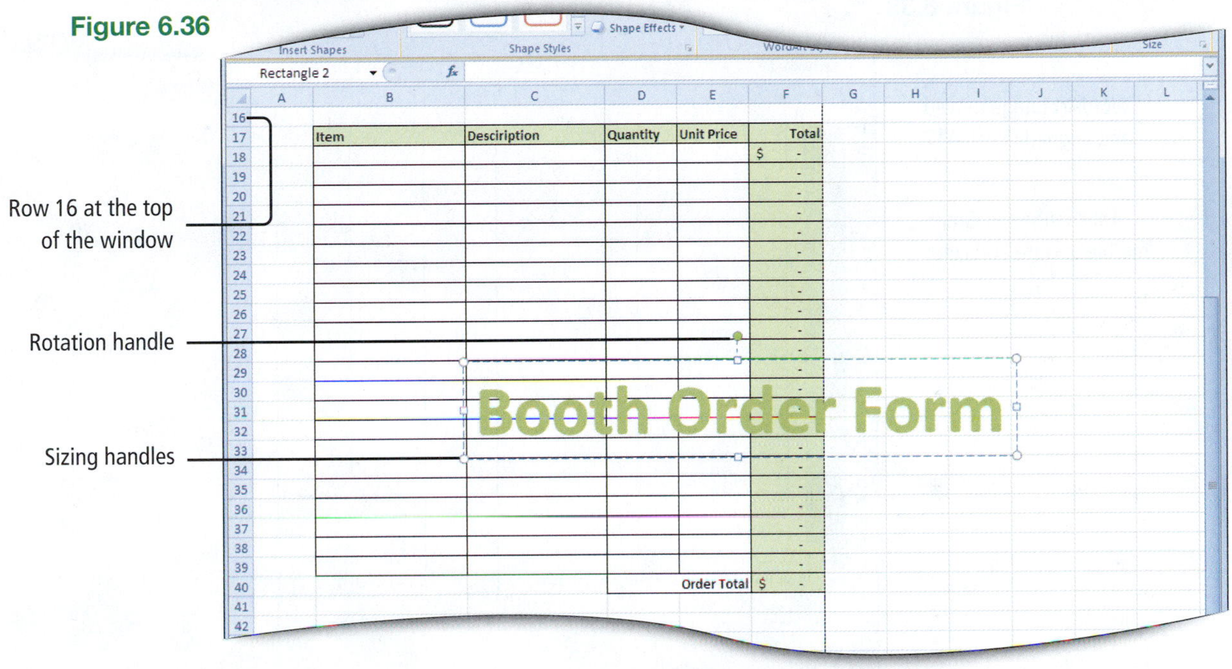

2 Select the text you just typed, right-click, and then from the Mini toolbar, set the **Font Size arrow** to **20**.

The WordArt image floats on your screen. Sizing handles display around the outside of the WordArt, and a green ***rotation handle*** displays on the top side of the image. Use the rotation handle to rotate an image to any angle.

3 Point to the green **rotation handle** until the pointer displays, drag to the left until the WordArt is vertical, as shown in Figure 6.37, and then release the mouse button.

As you rotate the image, lines display to show the position where the image will be placed when you release the mouse button. You can use the rotation handle to revolve the image 360 degrees.

Figure 6.37

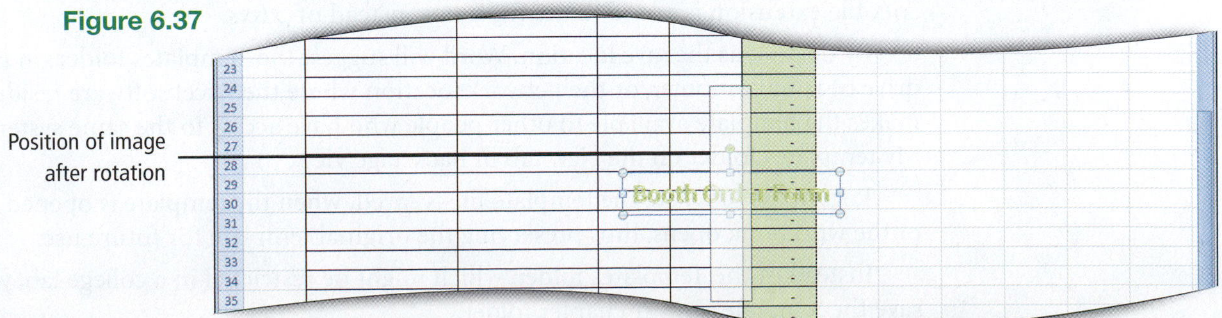

4 Point to the edge of the **WordArt** image to display the [pointer icon] pointer. Drag the WordArt image to **column A** and align the top of the image with the top of cell **A17**—centered in the column.

5 At the lower edge of the WordArt image, point to the center resize handle and drag down so the end of the image aligns at the lower edge of cell **A39**.

6 With the WordArt still selected, on the **Format tab**, in the **Shape Styles group**, click the **Shape Fill arrow**, click **Texture**, and then in the third row, click the first texture—**Green Marble.** Compare your screen with Figure 6.38.

The WordArt text box fills with Green Marble texture and color.

Figure 6.38

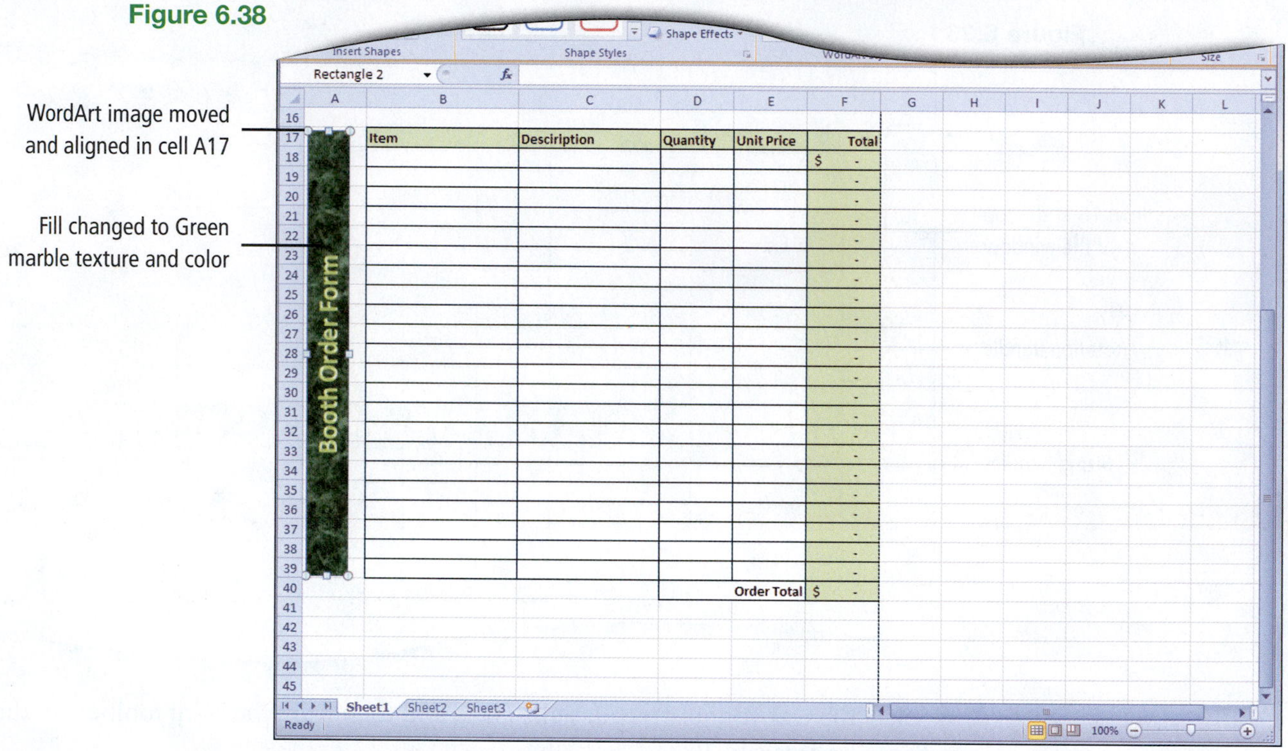

7 Delete any unused sheets. Press Ctrl + Home. Insert a footer in the **left section** that includes the file name. Click any cell outside the footer to deselect. On the status bar, click the **Normal** button [Normal button icon]. Press Ctrl + Home to move to the top of the worksheet. Click in any empty cell. **Save** [Save icon] your workbook.

Activity 6.23 | Saving a File as a Template

After you complete the formatting and design of a worksheet that you would like to use over and over again, save it as a template file. When saved as a template file, the *.xltx* file extension is added to the file name instead of *.xlsx*.

By default, as the save location, Word will suggest the Templates folder on the hard drive of your computer, or the network location where the Excel software resides. This makes the template available to other people who have access to the same system from the My templates folder on the New tab in Backstage view.

Regardless of where the template file is saved, when the template is opened, a new *copy* of the workbook opens, thus preserving the original template for future use.

Instead of the Templates folder, which might be restricted in a college lab, you will save the template in your chapter folder.

1 From **Backstage** view, display the **Save As** dialog box, and then click the **Save as type arrow**. On the list, click **Excel Template**.

2 In the **address bar** at the top of the dialog box, notice that Excel suggests the **Templates** folder on your system as the default save location.

3 Navigate to your **Excel Chapter 6 folder**.

> **Alert! | Saving a Template**
>
> If you are working in a college computer lab, your college may have placed restrictions on saving files to the Templates folder. Saving to the Templates folder makes the template available to anyone at this computer when they click the File tab, and then click New. For this project, you will save the template in your chapter folder. The difference is that the template will be available to you only.

4 In the **File name** box, change the **File name** to **Lastname_Firstname_6B_Order_Template** and then click **Save**.

A copy of the template is saved with your other files.

5 From **Backstage** view, click **Close** to close the file but leave Excel open.

6 From the **Start** menu, click **Computer**, navigate to your **Excel Chapter 6** folder, and then notice that the template file icon displays with a small gold bar at the top. This indicates that the file is a template, and not a workbook. Compare your screen with Figure 6.39.

Figure 6.39

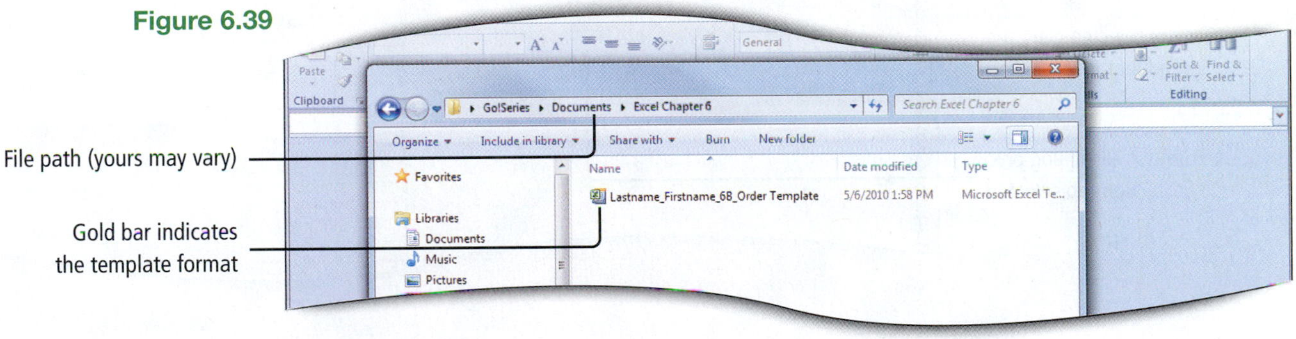

7 **Close** the Windows Explorer window.

Objective 6 | Protect a Worksheet

When the template design is complete, you can enable the protection of the worksheet. Protection prevents anyone from changing the worksheet—they cannot insert, modify, delete, or format data in a locked cell.

For purposes of creating a form that you want someone to complete, you can protect the worksheet, and then unlock specific areas where you do want the person completing the form to enter data.

By default, all cells in Excel are ***locked***—data cannot be typed into them. However, the locked feature is disabled until you protect the worksheet. After protection is enabled, the locked cells cannot be changed. Of course, you will want to designate some cells to be ***unlocked***, so that individuals completing your form can type in their data.

Thus, the basic process is to determine the cells that you will allow people to change or unlock, and then protect the entire worksheet. Then, only the cells that you designated as unlocked will be available to any person using the worksheet. You may add an optional ***password*** to prevent someone from disabling the worksheet protection. The password can be any combination of numbers, letters, or symbols up to 15 characters long. The password should be shared only with people who have permission to change the template.

Activity 6.24 | Protecting a Worksheet

1. From your **Excel Chapter 6** folder, open your template file **Lastname_Firstname_6B_Order_Template.** Select the range **C6:C7**, hold down Ctrl, select the range **C10:C15** and the range **B18:E39**.

   The selected cells are the ones that you want individuals placing booth orders to be able to fill in—they should *not* be locked when protection is applied.

2. With the three ranges selected, on the **Home tab**, in the **Cells group**, click **Format**, and then click **Format Cells**. In the displayed **Format Cells** dialog box, click the **Protection tab**.

3. Click to *clear* the check mark from the **Locked** check box, and then compare your screen with Figure 6.40.

   Recall that all cells are locked by default, but the locking feature is only enabled when protection is applied. Therefore, you must *unlock* the cells you want to have available for use in this manner *before* you protect the worksheet.

Figure 6.40

For the selected cells, the Locked feature is cleared

Format Cells dialog box, Protection tab selected

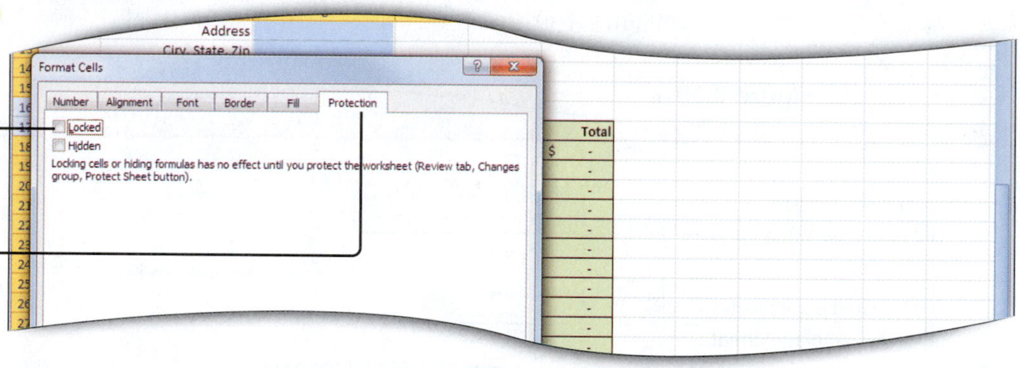

4. Click **OK** to close the **Format Cells** dialog box.

5. In the **Cells group**, click the **Format** button, and then under **Protection**, click **Protect Sheet.**

   The Protect Sheet dialog box displays. Under *Allow all users of this worksheet to*, the *Select locked cells* and *Select unlocked cells* check boxes are selected by default. The *Select locked cells* option allows the user to click the locked cells and *view* the formulas, but because the cells are locked, they cannot *change* the content or format of the locked cells. If you deselect this option, the user cannot view or even click in a locked cell.

   For the remaining check boxes, you can see that, because they are not selected, are restricted from performing all other actions on the worksheet.

6. Leave the first two check boxes selected. At the top of the dialog box, be sure the **Protect worksheet and contents of locked cells** check box is selected. In the **Password to unprotect sheet** box type **goseries** Compare your screen with Figure 6.41.

   The password does not display—rather bullets display as placeholders for each letter or character that is typed. Passwords are case sensitive, therefore, *GOSeries* is different from *goseries.*

Figure 6.41

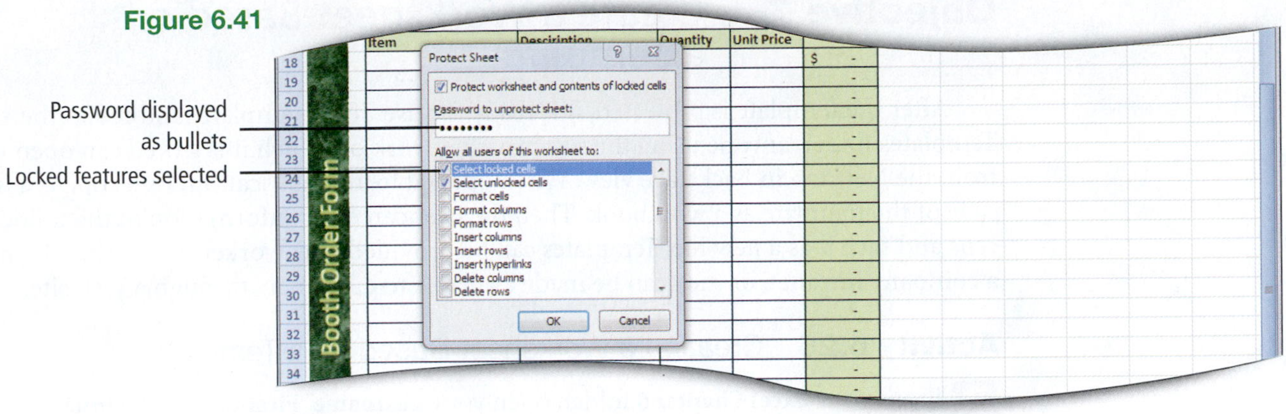

7 Click **OK**. In the displayed **Confirm Password** dialog box, type **goseries** to confirm the password, and then click **OK** to close both dialog boxes.

8 Click in any cell in the **Total** column, type **123** and observe what happens.

The number is not entered; instead a message informs you that the cell you are trying to change is protected and therefore, read-only.

9 Click **OK** to acknowledge the message. Click cell **D18**, type **2** and press Tab, type **150** and press Enter.

The numbers are recorded and the formulas in cell F18 and F40 calculate and display the results—$300.00.

10 On the **Quick Access Toolbar**, click the **Undo** button two times to remove the two numbers that you typed, and then click the **Save** button.

You have tested your template, and it is protected and saved.

> **Note** | Footer Updates Automatically
>
> The footer will update automatically when you save with a new name, so there is no need to change the footer.

11 Display the **Document Panel** and in the **Author** box, type your firstname and lastname, in the **Subject** box, type your course name and section number, and in the **Keywords** box, type **booth order form, template Close** the **Document Panel**.

12 Display the **Print Preview**, redisplay the workbook, and then make any necessary corrections or adjustments.

13 **Save** your workbook, and then print or submit electronically as directed by your instructor. If required, print or create an electronic version of your worksheet with formulas displayed using the instructions in Activity 1.16 in Project 1A. **Close** the workbook, but leave Excel open.

> **More Knowledge** | Modifying a Template
>
> If you need to make changes to a template after it is protected, you must first remove the protection.

Objective 7 | Create a Worksheet Based on a Template

After the template is protected, it is ready for use. If the template is stored in the Templates folder, anyone using the system or network on which it is stored can open it from the New tab in Backstage view. When opened from this location, Excel opens a *new copy* of the template as a workbook. Then the user can enter information in the unlocked cells and save it as a new file. Templates can be provided to coworkers by storing them on a company intranet, or they can be made available to customers through a Web site.

Activity 6.25 | Creating a Worksheet Based on a Template

1. From your **Excel Chapter 6** folder, open your **Lastname_Firstname_6B_Order_Template** file.

2. From **Backstage** view, display the **Save As** dialog box, and then set the **Save as type** box to **Excel Workbook**—the first choice at the top of the list. Navigate to your **Excel Chapter 6** folder, and then in the **File name** box type **Lastname_Firstname_6B_Topaz_Order** Compare your screen with Figure 6.42.

> **Note | Creating a Workbook from a Template in the My Templates Folder in Backstage View**
>
> When you are able to open a template from the Templates folder in Backstage view, a new copy of the template opens as a workbook, not as a template, and displays a *1* at the end of the file name in the title bar. The *1* indicates a new workbook. Thus, if you are able to work from the Templates folder, the Save operation would automatically set the file type to Excel Workbook.

Figure 6.42

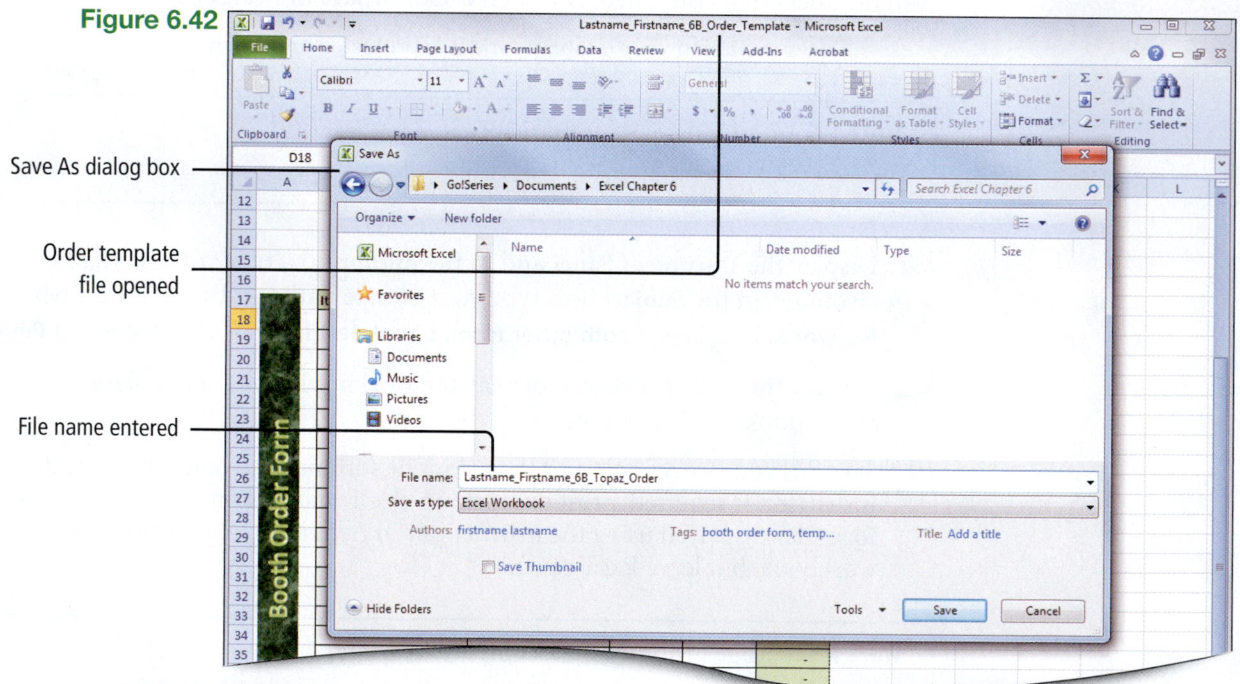

3. Press Enter. Click cell **C6,** type **October 13, 2016** press Enter, and notice that Excel applies the default date format. As the booth number, type **A-3421** and then press Enter three times to move to cell **C10**.

4 Starting in cell **C10**, enter the company information as follows:

Name	**McKenzie Peterson**
Company	**Topaz Business, Inc.**
Address	**653 Riverside Drive**
City, State, Postal code	**New York, NY 10025**
Phone	**212.555.0230**
E-mail	**mpeterson@topaz.net**

5 In cell **B18** type **Booth space** and press Tab, type **10 feet by 10 feet** and press Tab, type **1** and press Tab, type **400.00** and then press Tab.

6 Complete the order by entering the following items, pressing Tab to move from cell to cell. When you are finished, compare your screen with Figure 6.43.

Item	Description	Quantity	Unit Price
Booth Space	**10 feet by 10 feet**	**1**	**400.00**
Flooring	**Carpet Squares**	**20**	**5.00**
Table	**6 feet, skirted**	**1**	**25.00**
Chairs	**Guest chair**	**3**	**15.00**
Projector screen	**Standard**	**1**	**20.00**
Sign	**Standard**	**2**	**20.00**
Curtain	**Back wall**	**2**	**15.00**

Figure 6.43

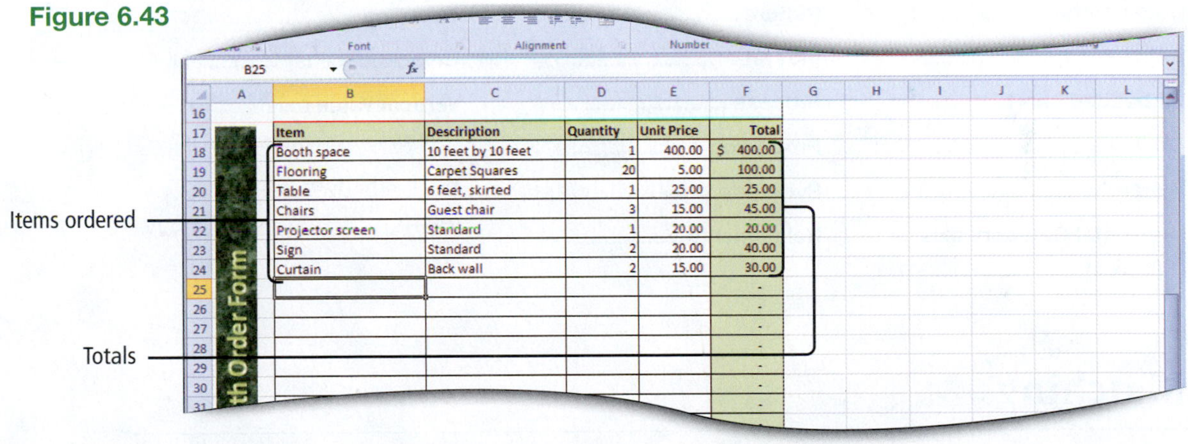

7 Display the **Document Panel**. Be sure your name displays in the **Author** box and your course name and section number displays in the **Subject** box. Change the **Keywords** box to **Topaz booth order** Be sure the file name displays in the left section of the footer and that the worksheet is horizontally centered.

8 Return to **Normal** view and make cell **A1** active, display the **Print Preview**, redisplay the workbook, and then make any necessary corrections or adjustments.

9 **Save** your workbook, and then print or submit electronically as directed by your instructor. If required, print or create an electronic version of your worksheet with formulas displayed using the instructions in Activity 1.16 in Project 1A. **Close** Excel.

End **You have completed Project 6B**

Content-Based Assessments

Summary

You created and modified a column chart to show a comparison among related numbers and a line chart to display a trend over time. Within each chart type, you identified and modified various chart objects and created and formatted titles and labels.

You created and modified a Process SmartArt graphic. You also created and modified a SmartArt organizational chart to practice building a hierarchy diagram.

You created and modified a template using text, formatting, formulas, locked and unlocked cells, and password protection for improved accuracy and record keeping.

Key Terms

Matching

Match each term in the second column with its correct definition in the first column by writing the letter of the term on the blank line in front of the correct definition.

____ 1. Tiny charts that fit within a cell and give a visual trend summary alongside your data.
____ 2. A type of chart that shows comparisons among related data.
____ 3. Lines in the plot area of a chart that aid the eye in determining plotted values.
____ 4. A chart that is inserted into the same worksheet that contains the data used to create the chart.
____ 5. A separate worksheet used to display an entire chart.
____ 6. A single value in a worksheet represented by a data marker in a chart.
____ 7. A group of related data points.

A Chart area
B Chart elements
C Chart sheet
D Column chart
E Data point
F Data series
G Embedded chart
H Gridlines
I Legend
J Line chart
K Scale

____ 8. A chart element that identifies the patterns or colors that are assigned to the categories in the chart.

____ 9. Objects that make up a chart.

____ 10. The entire chart and all of its elements.

____ 11. A type of chart that uses lines to show a trend over time.

____ 12. The range of numbers in the data series that controls the minimum, maximum, and incremental values on the value axis.

____ 13. A graphic representation of trends in a data series, such as a line sloping upward to represent increased sales over a period of months.

____ 14. An Excel feature that provides a visual representation of your information and ideas.

____ 15. An optional area in which you can type the text for a SmartArt graphic in a list format.

L SmartArt graphic
M Sparklines
N Text pane
O Trendline

Multiple Choice

Circle the correct answer.

1. A visual representation of numeric data in a worksheet is a:
A. diagram **B.** graphic **C.** chart

2. The graphic element that represents a single data point is a:
A. data marker **B.** data element **C.** data series

3. The data along the bottom of a chart displays on the:
A. category axis **B.** value axis **C.** legend

4. The numbers along the left side of a chart display on the:
A. category axis **B.** value axis **C.** legend

5. A diagram that shows hierarchical relationships is a:
A. cycle chart **B.** list **C.** organization chart

6. When you create a template, Excel adds the file extension:
A. .xlsx **B.** .xltx **C.** .xmlx

7. The process of locking cells in a workbook so that users cannot make any changes is:
A. protection **B.** standardization **C.** passwording

8. Cells in a worksheet that cannot be edited are:
A. merged cells **B.** blocked cells **C.** locked cells

9. A feature with which you can insert decorative text into your worksheet is:
A. SmartArt **B.** WordArt **C.** GraphicArt

10. An optional element added to a template to prevent someone from disabling a worksheet's protection is:
A. a password **B.** a security key **C.** a trendline

Content-Based Assessments

Apply **6A** skills from these Objectives:

1. Create and Format Sparklines and a 3-D Column Chart
2. Create and Format a Line Chart
3. Create and Modify a SmartArt Graphic
4. Create and Modify an Organization Chart

Skills Review | Project 6C Employer Attendance

In the following Skills Review, you will assist Elaine Chin, Employer Relations Manager, in displaying the employer participation for the New York-New Jersey Job Fair in charts and diagrams. Your completed workbook will look similar to Figure 6.44.

Project Files

For Project 6C, you will need the following file:

e06C_Employer_Participation

You will save your workbook as:

Lastname_Firstname_6C_Employer_Participation

Project Results

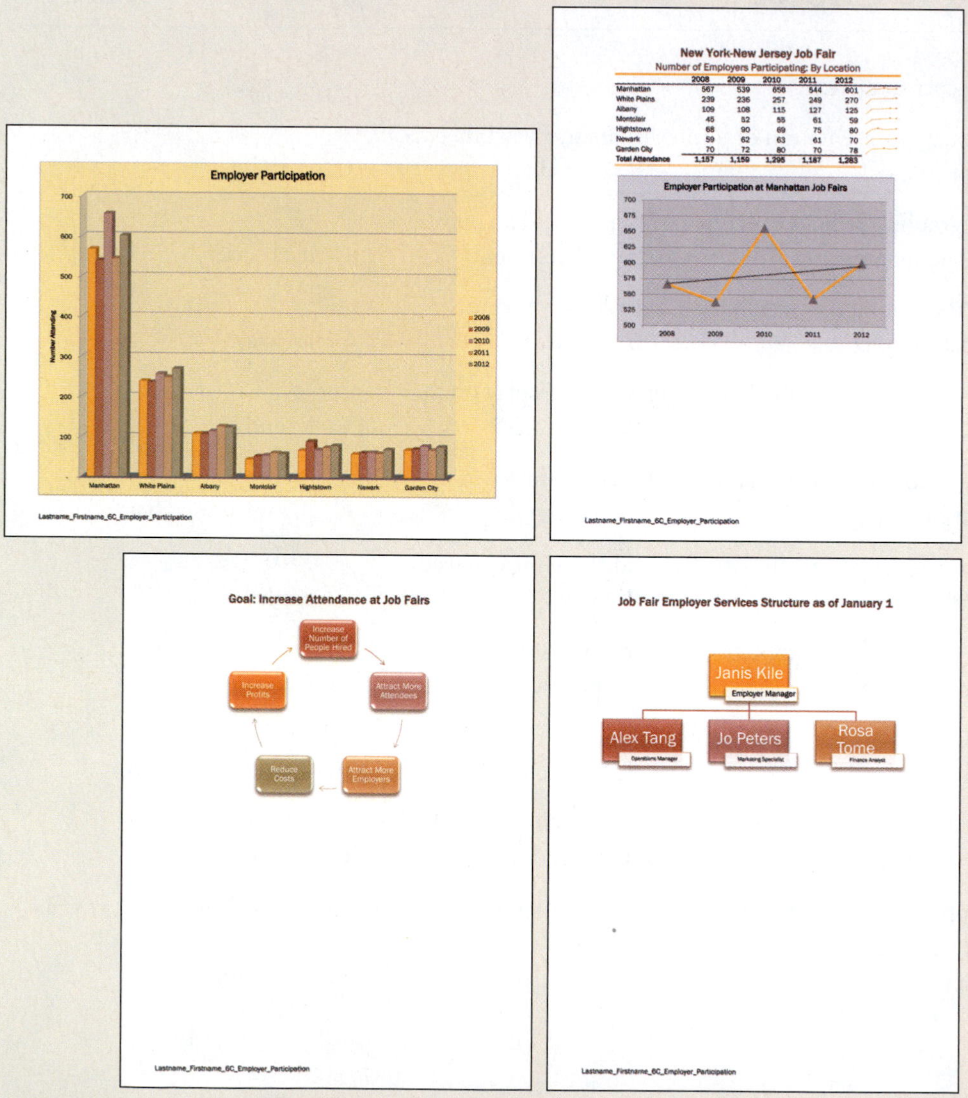

Figure 6.44

(Project 6C Employer Attendance continues on the next page)

Skills Review | Project 6C Employer Attendance (continued)

1 **Start** Excel. From your student files, open **e06C_Employer_Participation**. **Save** the file in your **Excel Chapter 6** folder as **Lastname_Firstname_6C_Employer_Participation**

a. Select the range **A4:F10**. On the **Insert tab**, in the **Sparklines group**, click the **Line** button. With the insertion point in the **Location Range**, select the range **G4:G10**, and then click **OK**. On the **Design tab**, in the **Show group,** select the **High Point** check box and the **Last Point** check box. On the **Design tab**, in the **Style group**, click the **More** button, and then in the third row, click the first style—Sparkline Style Accent 1, (no dark or light). In cell **G3**, type **Trend**

b. Select the range **A3:F10**. On the **Insert tab**, in the **Charts group**, click the **Column** button. Under **3-D Column**, click the first chart—**3-D Clustered Column**. On the **Design tab**, in the **Location group**, click the **Move Chart** button. Click the **New sheet** option button, name the new sheet **Participation Chart** and then click **OK**. On the **Design tab**, in the **Chart Styles** group, click the **More** button, and then in the fifth row, click the second style—**Style 34**. On the **Layout tab**, in the **Labels group**, click the **Chart Title** button, and then click **Above Chart**. In the **Formula Bar**, type **Employer Participation** as the chart title, and then press Enter.

c. On the **Layout tab**, in the **Labels group**, click the **Axis Titles** button. Point to **Primary Vertical Axis Title**, and then click **Rotated Title**. In the **Formula Bar**, type **Number Attending** and then press Enter. **Save** your workbook.

d. In the **White Plains** column cluster, point to the last column—**2012**. Notice that the Value for this column is *255*. Display the **Participation by Location** worksheet, and then in cell **F5**, type **270** and press Enter.

e. Display the **Participation Chart**. On the **Layout tab**, in the **Current Selection group**, click the **Chart Elements arrow**, and then click **Back Wall**. Then in the same group, click **Format Selection**. In the **Format Wall** dialog box, on the left, click **Fill**, on the right, click the **Solid fill** option button, and then under **Fill Color**, click the **Color arrow**. Under **Theme Colors**, in the first column, click the third color—**White, Background 1, Darker 15%**—and then set the **Transparency** to **75%**. **Close** the dialog box.

f. Using the same technique, select the **Side Wall**, and then apply the same fill, but with a **Transparency** of **60%**. To the **Floor**, apply a **Solid fill** using the last color in the first column—**White, Background 1, Darker 50%** with **0% Transparency**. To the **Chart Area**, apply a **Solid fill** using **Light Yellow, Background 2, Darker 10%**—in the third column, the second color. **Close** the dialog box.

2 Display the **Participation by Location** worksheet. Select the range **A3:F4**, and then on the **Insert tab**, in the **Charts group**, click the **Line** button. In the second row, click the first chart type—**Line with Markers**. Drag the upper left corner of the chart inside the upper left corner of cell **A13**. Drag the lower right corner of the chart inside the lower right corner of cell **G29**.

a. In the embedded chart, click the **Legend** *Manhattan* to select it. Press Del. Click the **Chart Title** *Manhattan*, type **Employer Participation at Manhattan Job Fairs** and press Enter. Point to the **Chart Title**, right-click, and then change the font size to **14**.

b. On the left side of the line chart, point to the **Vertical (Value) Axis**, right-click, and then click **Format Axis**. On the left, click **Axis Options**. Under **Axis Options**, to the right of **Minimum**, click the **Fixed** option button, and then in the **Fixed** box, select the displayed number and type **500** To the right of **Major unit**, click the **Fixed** option button, and then in the **Fixed** box, select the displayed number and type **25** **Close** the dialog box.

c. Right-click anywhere within the **Plot Area**, click **Format Plot Area**, and then on the left, click **Fill**. Under **Fill**, click the **Solid fill** option button. Under **Fill Color**, click the **Color arrow**, and then under **Theme Colors**, in the first column, click the fourth color—**White, Background 1, Darker 25%**. **Close** the dialog box.

d. Point to the chart line, right-click, and then click **Format Data Series**. On the left, click **Line Style**. Set the **Width** to **4 pt**. On the left, click **Marker Options**. Under **Marker Type**, click the **Built-in** option button, click the **Type arrow**, and then click the **triangle**—the third symbol in the list. Set the **Size** to **14**.

e. On the left, click **Marker Fill**. Click the **Solid fill** option button, and then click the **Color arrow**. Under **Theme Colors**, in the first column, click the sixth color—**White, Background 1, Darker 50%**.

(Project 6C Employer Attendance continues on the next page)

Skills Review | Project 6C Employer Attendance (continued)

f. On the left, select **Marker Line Color**, click the **No line** option button, and then click **Close**. Using any of the techniques you have practiced to select a chart element, select the **Chart Area**, display the **Format Chart Area** dialog box, and then apply a **Solid fill** using **White, Background 1, Darker 15%**—in the first column, the third color. Close the dialog box. Click in any cell outside of the chart.

g. Click the edge of the chart border to select the entire chart. On the **Layout tab**, in the **Analysis group**, click the **Trendline** button, and then click **Linear Trendline**. **Save** your workbook.

3 Click the **Sheet1 tab**, and then rename the sheet **Process Chart** In cell **A1**, type **Goal: Increase Attendance at Job Fairs** and then press Enter. Merge and center the text across the range **A1:H1** and apply the **Title** cell style. On the **Insert tab**, in the **Illustrations group**, click the **SmartArt** button. On the left, click **Cycle**, and then in the first row, click the third option—**Block Cycle**. Click **OK**.

a. On the **Design tab**, in the **Create Graphic group**, if necessary, click **Text Pane**. As the first bullet, type **Increase Number of People Hired** Click the next bullet, and then type **Attract More Attendees** As the third bullet, type **Attract More Employers** As the fourth bullet, type **Reduce Costs** As the last bullet, type **Increase Profits Close** the **Text Pane**.

b. Click the edge of the graphic to select it. On the **Design tab**, in the **SmartArt Styles group**, click the **More** button. Under **3-D**, click the first style—**Polished**. Click the **Change Colors** button, and then under **Colorful**, click the first option—**Colorful – Accent Colors**. Drag the upper left corner of the graphic into the left corner of cell **A3**. Drag the lower right corner inside the lower right corner of cell **H20**. Click cell **A1**, and then click **Save**.

4 Display **Sheet2** and rename the sheet tab **Organization Chart** In cell **A1**, type **Job Fair Employer Services Structure as of January 1** and then merge and center this title across the range **A1:H1**. Apply the **Title** cell style. On the **Insert tab**, in the **Illustrations group**, click the **SmartArt** button. On the left, click **Hierarchy**, and then in the first row, click the third graphic—**Name and Title Organization Chart**. Click **OK**.

a. If the Text Pane displays, close it. In the graphic, click in the first **[Text]** box, and then type **Janis Kile** Click the edge of the small white box below *Janis Kile* to select it and type **Employer Manager** In the **[Text]** box below *Employer Manager*, click on the *edge* of the box to display a solid line border—if a dashed border displays, click the edge of the box again. With the box bordered with a solid line, press Del.

b. On the second level, click in the leftmost shape, and then using the technique you just practiced, type **Alex Tang** and **Operations Manager** In the next shape, type **Jo Peters** and **Marketing Specialist** In the rightmost shape, type **Rosa Tome** and **Finance Analyst** Hold down Ctrl, and then click the edge of each of the smaller title boxes to select all four. Then, right-click over any of the selected boxes, change the font size to **8**, and click **Center**.

c. Drag the upper left corner of the graphic into cell **A3** and the lower right corner into cell **H20**. On the **Design tab**, in the **SmartArt Styles group**, click the **More** button, and then apply **Intense Effect**. Change the colors to **Colorful – Accent Colors**.

d. Display the **Participation Chart** sheet. On the **Insert tab**, click **Header & Footer**, and then click **Custom Footer**. With the insertion point in the **left section**, from the small toolbar in the dialog box, click the **Insert File Name** button. Click **OK** two times.

e. Display the **Participation by Location** sheet. Hold down Ctrl and select the remaining two worksheets to group the three sheets. Insert a footer with the file name in the **left section**. Click outside the footer area to deselect. On the **Page Layout tab**, click the **Margins** button, click **Custom Margins**, and then center the sheets horizontally. Click **OK**. Return to **Normal** view and press Ctrl + Home to move to cell **A1**.

f. Right-click any of the sheet tabs and click **Select All Sheets** to select all four worksheets. From **Backstage** view, display the **Document Panel**, type your firstname and lastname as the author, type your course name and section in the **Subject** box, and as the **Keywords** type **employer participation, organization chart Close** the Document Information Panel.

g. Click **Save**. Display and examine the **Print Preview**, make any necessary corrections, **Save**, and then print or submit electronically as directed by your instructor. If you are directed to do so, print the formulas on the Participation by Location worksheet.

End **You have completed Project 6C**

Apply **6B** skills from these Objectives:

- **5** Create an Excel Template
- **6** Protect a Worksheet
- **7** Create a Worksheet Based on a Template

Skills Review | Project 6D Purchase Order

In the following Skills Review, you will assist Job Fair Director, Jennifer Patterson, in creating a template for a Purchase Order, and then a Purchase Order for items with a logo and name imprint of the New York-New Jersey Job Fair. Your completed worksheets will look similar to Figure 6.45.

Project Files

For Project 6D, you will need the following file:

New blank Excel workbook

You will save your workbooks as:

Lastname_Firstname_6D_Purchase_Order
Lastname_Firstname_6D_PO_Template
Lastname_Firstname_6D_Hancock_PO

Project Results

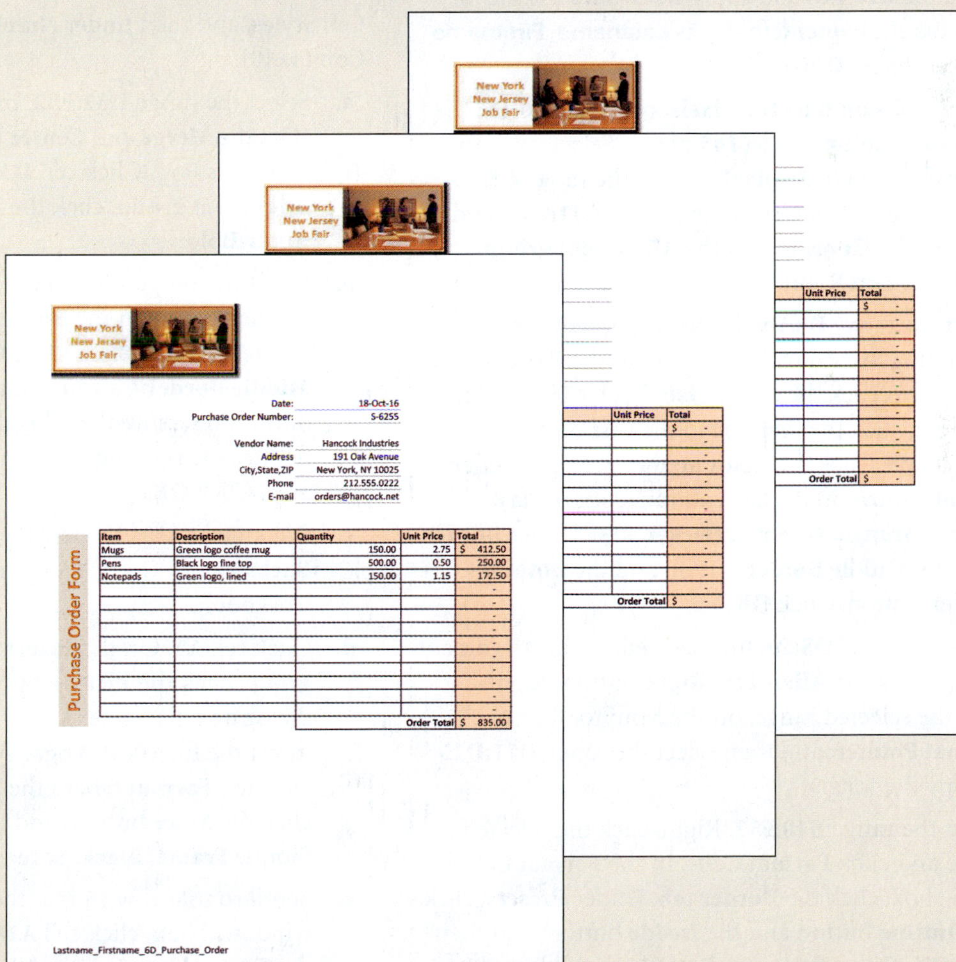

Figure 6.45

(Project 6D Purchase Order continues on the next page)

Skills Review | Project 6D Purchase Order (continued)

1 **Start** Excel and display a new blank workbook. Beginning in cell **E1**, type **2900 Second Avenue** and press Enter. In cell **E2**, type **New York, NY 10028** and in cell **E3**, type **Phone 212.555.0177** and press Enter.

a. Click cell **C8**, type **Date:** and press Enter. In cell **C9**, type **Purchase Order Number:** Click cell **C11**. Type **Vendor Name:** and press Enter. In cell **C12**, type **Address** In cell **C13**, type **City, State, ZIP** In cell **C14**, type **Phone** In cell **C15**, type **E-mail**

b. Click cell **B18**. Type **Item** and press Tab to move to cell **C18**. Continuing across **row 18**, in cell **C18**, type **Description** and press Tab, in cell **D18**, type **Quantity** and press Tab, in cell **E18**, type **Unit Price** and press Tab, and in cell **F18**, type **Total** and press Enter. Select the range **B18:F18** and apply **Bold**. **Save** the file in your **Excel Chapter 6** folder as **Lastname_Firstname_6D_Purchase_Order**

c. Widen **column B** to **100 pixels, column C** to **165 pixels** and **column D** to **145 pixels**. Select **columns E:F** and widen to **75 pixels**. Select the range **C8:C9**, hold down Ctrl and select the range **C11:C15**, and then on the **Home tab**, in the **Alignment group**, click the **Align Text Right** button.

d. Select the range **D8:D9**. In the **Alignment group**, click the **Dialog Box Launcher** button. In the **Format Cells** dialog box, click the **Border tab**. Under **Line**, in the **Style** list, click the first line in the first column—a dotted line. Click the **Color arrow**, and then under **Theme Colors**, in the last column, click the last color—**Orange, Accent 6, Darker 50%**. Under **Border**, click the **Middle Border** button and the **Bottom Border** button. Click **OK**.

e. With the range **D8:D9** still selected, in the **Alignment group**, click the **Align Text Right** button. Right-click over the selected range, on the Mini toolbar, click **Format Painter**, and then select the range **D11:D15** to copy the format.

f. Select the range **B18:F32**. Right-click the selected range and click **Format Cells**. In the **Format Cells** dialog box, click the **Border tab**. Under **Presets**, click the **Outline** button and the **Inside** button, and then click **OK.** Select the range **B18:F18**, hold down Ctrl and select the range **F19:F32**. In the **Font group,** click the **Fill Color button arrow**, and then under **Theme Colors**, in the last column, click the third color—**Orange, Accent 6, Lighter 60%**.

g. Press Ctrl + Home. Press Ctrl + F2 to examine the **Print Preview**. In **Backstage** view, click **Save** to save and return to your workbook.

2 To construct a formula to multiply the Quantity times the Unit Price, in cell **F19**, type **=d19*e19** and press Enter. Use the fill handle to copy the formula in cell **F18** down through cell **F31**. Click cell **F32**. On the **Home tab**, in the **Editing group**, click the **AutoSum** button. Be sure the range displays as *F19:F31*, and then press Enter. Select the range **E19:E31**. In the **Number group**, click the **Comma Style** button. Click cell **F19**, hold down Ctrl, and then click cell **F32**. In the **Number group**, click the **Accounting Number Format** button. Select the range **F20:F31**, and then click the **Comma Style** button. Select the range **D19:D31**, and then in the **Styles group**, click **Cell Styles**, and then under **Number Format**, click **Comma [0]**.

a. Select the range **D32:E32**. In the **Alignment group**, click the **Merge and Center** button. Type **Order Total** and press Enter. Click cell **D32** again, and then in the **Alignment group**, click the **Align Text Right** button. Apply **Bold**.

b. Select the range **B32:C32**, right-click, and then click **Format Cells**. On the **Border tab**, in the **Border** preview area, click the **Left Border** button, the **Middle Border** button and the **Bottom Border** button to *remove* these borders from the preview—be sure the right and top lines remain in the preview area. Click **OK**.

c. Press Ctrl + F2 to view the **Print Preview**. In the **Backstage** view, click **Save** to save and return to your workbook.

d. Click cell **A1**. On the **Insert tab**, in the **Illustrations group**, click the **Picture** button. In the **Insert Picture** dialog box, navigate to your student files, and then insert the file **e06D_Logo**. With the image selected, click the **Format tab**, in the **Picture Styles group**, click the **More** button, and then locate and click the **Simple Frame, Black**. **Save** your workbook.

e. Scroll so that **row 16** is at the top of the Excel window. Then, click cell **A18**. On the **Insert tab**, in the **Text group**, click the **WordArt** button, and then in the fourth row, click the second WordArt—**Gradient Fill – Orange, Accent 6, Inner Shadow**. Type **Purchase Order Form** Select the text you just typed, right-click, and then from the Mini toolbar,

(Project 6D Purchase Order continues on the next page)

Skills Review | Project 6D Purchase Order (continued)

set the **Font Size** to **20**. Drag the green rotation handle to the left until the WordArt is vertical. Then, drag the WordArt image to **column A** and align the top of the image with the top of cell **A18**—centered in the column. At the lower edge of the WordArt image, point to the center resize handle and drag down so the end of the image aligns at the lower edge of cell **A32**.

f. With the WordArt still selected, on the **Format tab**, in the **Shape Styles group**, click the **Shape Fill arrow**, click **Texture**, and then in the fourth row, click the second texture—**Recycled Paper**. Delete the unused sheets. Click to deselect the WordArt, and then press Ctrl + Home. Insert a footer in the **left section** that includes the file name. Click any cell outside the footer to deselect. On the status bar, click the **Normal** button. Press Ctrl + Home to move to the top of the worksheet. From **Backstage** view, display the **Document Panel**, type your firstname and lastname as the **Author**, your course name and section as the **Subject**, and **purchase order** as the **Keywords**. **Close** the Document Information Panel, and then **Save** your workbook.

g. From **Backstage** view, display the **Save As** dialog box, and then click the **Save as type arrow**. On the list, click **Excel Template**. In the **address bar** at the top of the dialog box, notice that Excel suggests the **Templates** folder on your system as the default save location. Navigate to your **Excel Chapter 6 folder**. In the **File name** box, change the **File name** to **Lastname_Firstname_6D_PO_Template** and then click **Save**.

3 Select the range **D8:D9**, hold down Ctrl, select the range **D11:D15** and the range **B19:E31**. With the three ranges selected, on the **Home tab**, in the **Cells group**, click **Format**, and then click **Format Cells**. In the displayed **Format Cells** dialog box, click the **Protection tab**. Click to *clear* the check mark from the **Locked** check box. Click **OK**.

a. In the **Cells group**, click the **Format** button, and then under **Protection**, click **Protect Sheet**. Under **Allow all users of this worksheet to:** leave the first two check boxes selected. At the top of the dialog box, be sure the **Protect worksheet and contents of locked cells** check box is selected. In the **Password to unprotect sheet** box, type **goseries** Click **OK**. In the displayed **Confirm Password** dialog box, type **goseries** to confirm the password, and then click **OK** to close both dialog boxes. Click **Save**.

b. Display the **Document Panel**. The **Author** and **Subject** boxes contain your previous information. As the **Keywords**, type **purchase order form, template** **Close** the Document Panel.

c. Check the **Print Preview**, and then **Save** your template.

4 To create a purchase order from your template, from **Backstage** view, display the **Save As** dialog box, and then set the **Save as type** box to **Excel Workbook**—the first choice at the top of the list. Navigate to your **Excel Chapter 6** folder, and then in the **File name** box, type **Lastname_Firstname_6D_Hancock_PO** Click **Save**.

a. Click cell **D8**, type **October 18, 2016** and press Enter—Excel applies the default date format. As the Purchase Order Number, type **S-6255** and then press Enter two times to move to cell **D11**. Beginning in cell **D11**, enter the vendor information as follows:

Vendor Name:	**Hancock Industries**
Address	**191 Oak Avenue**
City, State, ZIP	**New York, NY 10025**
Phone	**212.555.0222**
E-mail	**orders@hancock.net**

b. Click cell **B19**, and then complete the order by entering the following items as shown in Table 1, pressing Tab to move from cell to cell.

Table 1

Item	Description	Quantity	Unit Price
Mugs	**Green logo coffee mug**	**150**	**2.75**
Pens	**Black logo fine tip**	**500**	**0.50**
Notepads	**Green logo, lined**	**150**	**1.15**

(Return to Step 4b)

(Project 6D Purchase Order continues on the next page)

Skills Review | Project 6D Purchase Order (continued)

c. Display the **Document Panel**. Be sure your name displays in the **Author** box and your course name and section number displays in the **Subject** box. Change the **Keywords** to **Hancock, promotional items** Check the **Print Preview** to be sure the file name updated and displays in the left section of the footer.

d. **Save** your workbook. As directed by your instructor, print or submit electronically the three workbooks you created in this project. If required to do so, print or create an electronic version of your worksheets that contain formulas by following the instructions in Activity 1.16 in Project 1A. **Close** Excel.

End **You have completed Project 6D**

Apply **6A** skills from these Objectives:

1. Create and Format Sparklines and a 3-D Column Chart
2. Create and Format a Line Chart
3. Create and Modify a SmartArt Graphic
4. Create and Modify an Organization Chart

Mastering Excel | Project 6E Hires

In the following project, you will assist Elaine Chin, Employer Relations Manager, in tracking the number of people who get hired by an employer at each fair. You will create and modify a chart to display the number of people hired at the fairs in the past five years, create a diagram of the communities served, and create an organizational chart for staff at the Job Fair. Your completed worksheets will look similar to Figure 6.46.

Project Files

For Project 6E, you will need the following file:

e06E_Hires

You will save your workbook as:

Lastname_Firstname_6E_Hires

Project Results

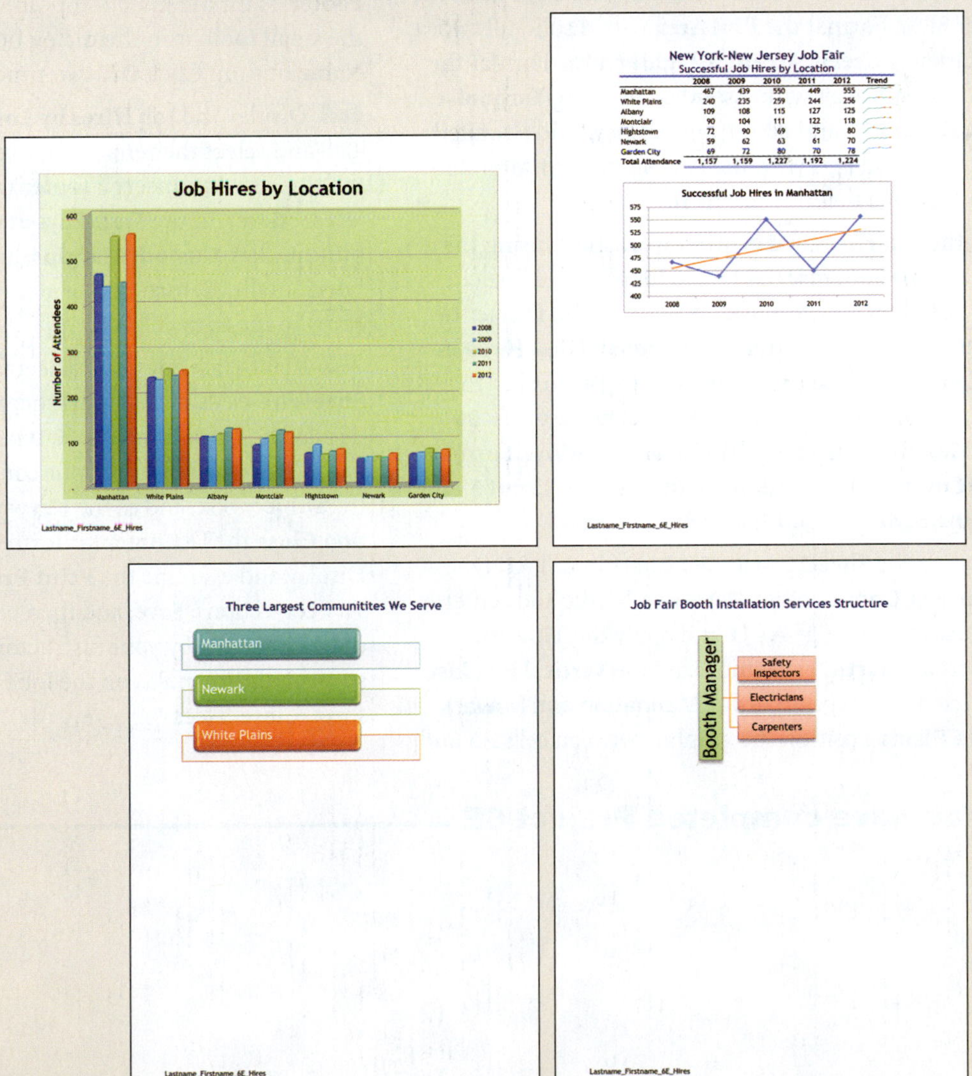

Figure 6.46

(Project 6E Hires continues on the next page)

Mastering Excel | Project 6E Hires (continued)

1 **Start** Excel. From your student files, open **e06E_Hires** and **Save** the file in your **Excel Chapter 6** folder as **Lastname_Firstname_6E_Hires** Using the data in the range **A4:F10**, insert **Sparklines** using the **Line** format. Place the sparklines in the range adjacent to the **2012** column, show the **High Point** and **Last Point**, and then apply Sparkline Style Accent 4- Darker 25%. Type **Trend** in the cell above the sparklines, and then use **Format Painter** to apply the format in cell **F3** to cell **G3**.

2 Using the data for the years and for each location (not the totals), create a 3-D Clustered Column chart on a separate chart sheet named **Hires by Location Chart** Apply **Style 18**, and add a **Chart Title** above the chart with the text **Job Hires by Location** Set the title's font size to **28**. Format the **Chart Area** with a solid fill using **Green, Accent 3, Lighter 80%**. Format the **Plot Area** with a solid fill two shades darker—**Green, Accent 3, Lighter 40%**. Format the floor and the side wall with a solid color using **Turquoise, Accent 2, Darker 50** and **80%** transparency. Add a rotated title to the vertical axis with the text **Number of Attendees Hired** and change the font size to **16**.

3 On the **Job Hires by Location** worksheet, using the data for Manhattan, insert a **Line with Markers** line chart. Position the chart between cells **A13** and **G26**. Delete the legend, change the chart title to **Successful Job Hires in Manhattan** and set the title's font size to **14**. Format the **Vertical (Value) Axis** so that the **Minimum** value is **400** and the **Major unit** is **25** Add a **Linear Trendline**. Format the **Line Color** of the trendline with **Orange, Accent 5** and set the **Line Style** to a width of **2 pt**.

4 Rename the **Sheet2** tab as **List Chart** In cell **A1**, type **Three Largest Communities We Serve** Merge and center this title across the range **A1:I1** and apply the **Title** cell style. Insert a **SmartArt** graphic using the **Vertical Box List**. In the three boxes, type, in order, **Manhattan** and **Newark** and **White Plains** Position the graphic between cells **A3** and **G16**. Apply the **Inset** style and change the colors to **Colorful Range – Accent Colors 4 to 5**. Click cell **A1**.

5 Rename the **Sheet3 tab** as **Organization Chart** In cell **A1**, type **Job Fair Booth Installation Services Structure** Merge and center this title across the range **A1:H1** and apply the **Title** cell style. Insert a **SmartArt** graphic using **Horizontal Multi-Level Hierarchy**. In the vertical box, type **Booth Manager** and in the three remaining boxes, type **Safety Inspectors** and **Electricians** and **Carpenters** Position the graphic between cells **A4** and **H16**. Apply the **Subtle Effect** style and change the colors to **Colorful Range – Accent Colors 4 to 5**. Click cell **A1** to deselect.

6 Display the **Hires by Location Chart** sheet. On the **Insert tab**, click **Header & Footer**, and then click **Custom Footer**. With the insertion point in the **left section**, from the small toolbar in the dialog box, click the **Insert File Name** button. Click **OK** two times.

7 Display the **Job Hires by Location** sheet. Hold down Ctrl and select the remaining two worksheets to group the three sheets. Insert a footer with the file name in the **left section**. On the **Page Layout tab**, click the **Margins** button, click **Custom Margins**, and then center the sheets horizontally. Return to **Normal** view and press Ctrl + Home to move to cell **A1**.

8 Right-click any of the sheet tabs and click **Select All Sheets** to select all four worksheets. From **Backstage** view, display the **Document Panel**, type your firstname and lastname as the author, type your course name and section in the **Subject** box, and as the **Keywords**, type **hires by location** **Close** the Document Information Panel and **Save**. Display and examine the **Print Preview**, make any necessary corrections, **Save**, and then print or submit electronically as directed by your instructor. If you are directed to do so, print the formulas on the Job Hires by Location worksheet. **Close** Excel.

End **You have completed Project 6E**

Apply **6B** skills from these Objectives:

- **5** Create an Excel Template
- **6** Protect a Worksheet
- **7** Create a Worksheet Based on a Template

Mastering Excel | Project 6F Event Budget

In the following Mastering Excel project, you will create a budget template for the Manhattan location of the New York-New Jersey Job Fair. You will also create a worksheet based on the budget template for review by Louis Goldstein, Manhattan Job Fair Director. Your completed worksheets will look similar to Figure 6.47.

Project Files

For Project 6F, you will need the following files:

New blank Excel workbook
e06F_Logo

You will save your workbooks as:

Lastname_Firstname_6F_Budget_Template
Lastname_Firstname_6F_Manhattan_Budget

Project Results

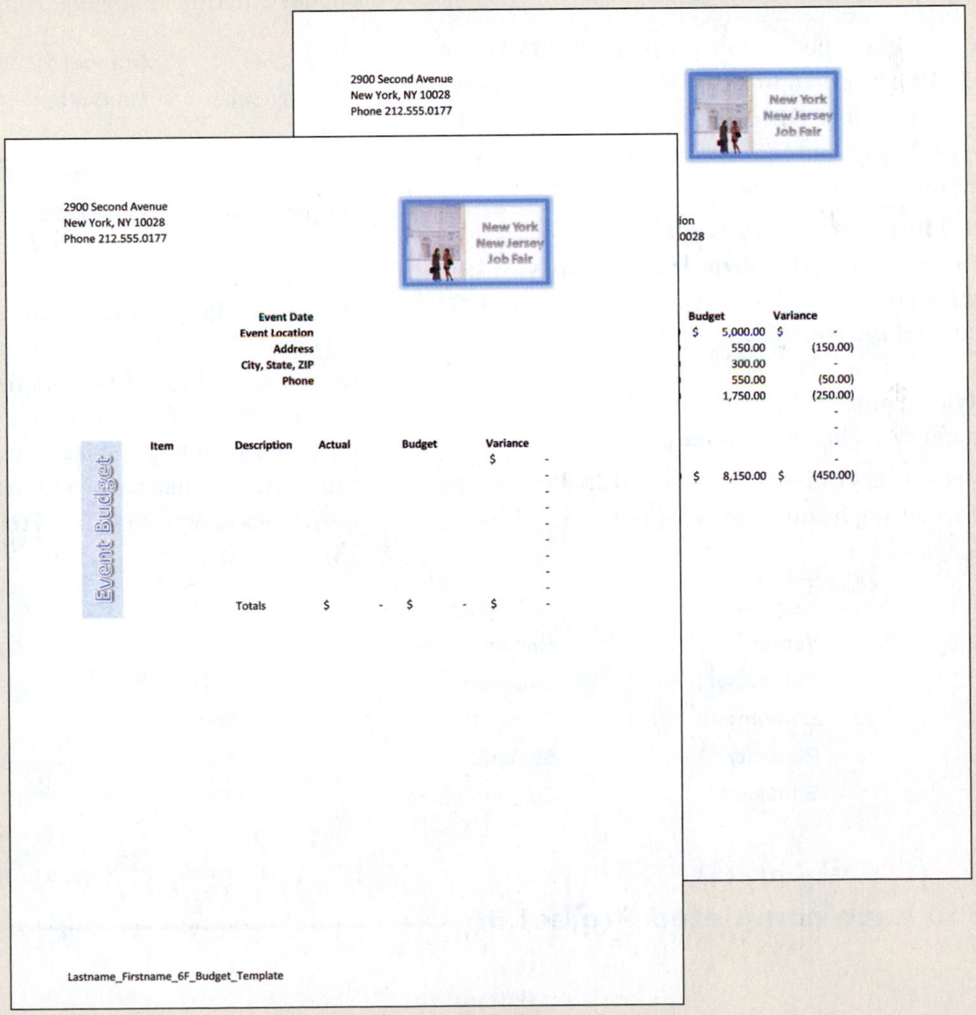

Figure 6.47

(Project 6F Event Budget continues on the next page)

Mastering Excel | Project 6F Event Budget (continued)

1 **Start** Excel and display a new blank workbook. In cell **A1**, type **2900 Second Avenue** In cell **A2**, type **New York, NY 10028** In cell **A3**, type **Phone 212.555.0177**

In cell **C8**, type **Event Date** In cell **C9**, type **Event Location** In cell **C10**, type **Address** In cell **C11**, type **City, State, ZIP** In cell **C12**, type **Phone**

In cell **B16**, type **Item** and press Tab. In cell **C16**, type **Description** In cell **D16**, type **Actual** In cell **E16**, type **Budget** In cell **F16**, type **Variance** Click cell **C26** and type **Totals**

2 To the ranges **C8:C12** and **B16:F16**, apply **Bold**. To the range **C8:C12**, apply **Align Text Right**. To the range **D8:D12**, apply **Align Text Left**. Widen **columns A:F** to **95 pixels**.

To construct a formula to compute the Variance (Variance = Actual – Budget) for each budget item, in cell **F17**, type **=d17-e17** and copy the formula through cell **F25**. In the range **D26:F26**, insert appropriate formulas to sum these columns. To the range **D18:F25**, apply **Comma Style**. To the ranges **D17:F17** and **D26:F26**, apply Accounting Number Format.

3 In cell **E1**, insert the picture **e06F_Logo**. Click cell **A16**, insert a **WordArt** using **Gradient Fill – Blue, Accent 1**—in the third row, the fourth WordArt. As the text, type **Event Budget** and set the **Font Size** to **24**. Rotate the WordArt vertically, and align it between cells **A16** and **A26**. In the **Shape Styles group**, click the **Shape Fill arrow**, click **Texture**, and then click **Blue tissue paper**.

4 Select the ranges **D8:D12** and **B17:E25**. Remove the **Locked** formatting from the selected cells, and then protect the worksheet. Be sure the check box at the top and the first two check boxes in the list are selected, and as the password type **goseries** Complete the order by entering the following items as shown in **Table 1**.

Delete the unused worksheets. Insert a footer in the **left section** with the file name. Add your name, course information, and the keywords **budget template** to the **Document Information Panel**, and then check the **Print Preview**. **Save** your workbook as an **Excel Template** in your **Excel Chapter 6** folder as **Lastname_Firstname_6F_Budget_Template**

5 To create a new budget report using the template as your model, display the **Save As** dialog box again, and then **Save** the template as an **Excel Workbook** in your chapter folder as **Lastname_Firstname_6F_Manhattan_Budget** Enter the following data:

Event Date	**October 22, 2016**
Event Location	**Manhattan**
Address	**2885 Third Station**
City, State, ZIP	**New York, NY 10028**
Phone	**212.555.6575**

6 Change the **Keywords** to **Manhattan event budget** Examine the **Print Preview**; notice the file name is updated and displays in the left section of the footer. **Save** your workbook. As directed by your instructor, print or submit electronically the two workbooks you created in this project. If required to do so, print or create an electronic version of your worksheets that contain formulas by following the instructions in Activity 1.16 in Project 1A. **Close** Excel.

Table 1

Item	Description	Actual	Budget
Venue	**Hall rental fee**	**5000**	**5000**
Personnel	**Site staff**	**400**	**550**
Equipment	**Computers**	**300**	**300**
Publicity	**Signage**	**500**	**550**
Speakers	**Speaking fees**	**1500**	**1750**

(Return to Step 4)

End **You have completed Project 6F**

Content-Based Assessments

Apply **6A** and **6B** skills from these Objectives:

1. Create and Format Sparklines and a 3-D Column Chart
2. Create and Format a Line Chart
3. Create and Modify a SmartArt Graphic
4. Create and Modify an Organization Chart
5. Create an Excel Template
6. Protect a Worksheet
7. Create a Worksheet Based on a Template

myitlab grader

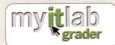

Mastering Excel | Project 6G Internships and Travel Template

In the following project, you will assist Jan Stewart, Internship Coordinator, in tracking the number of internships by industry at each job fair and in creating a template to use for travel expenses. Your completed worksheets will look similar to Figure 6.48.

Project Files

For Project 6G, you will need the following files:

e06G_Internships
e06G_Travel_Expense

You will save your workbooks as:

Lastname_Firstname_6G_Internships
Lastname_Firstname_6G_Travel_Template
Lastname_Firstname_6G_Silverton_Report

Project Results

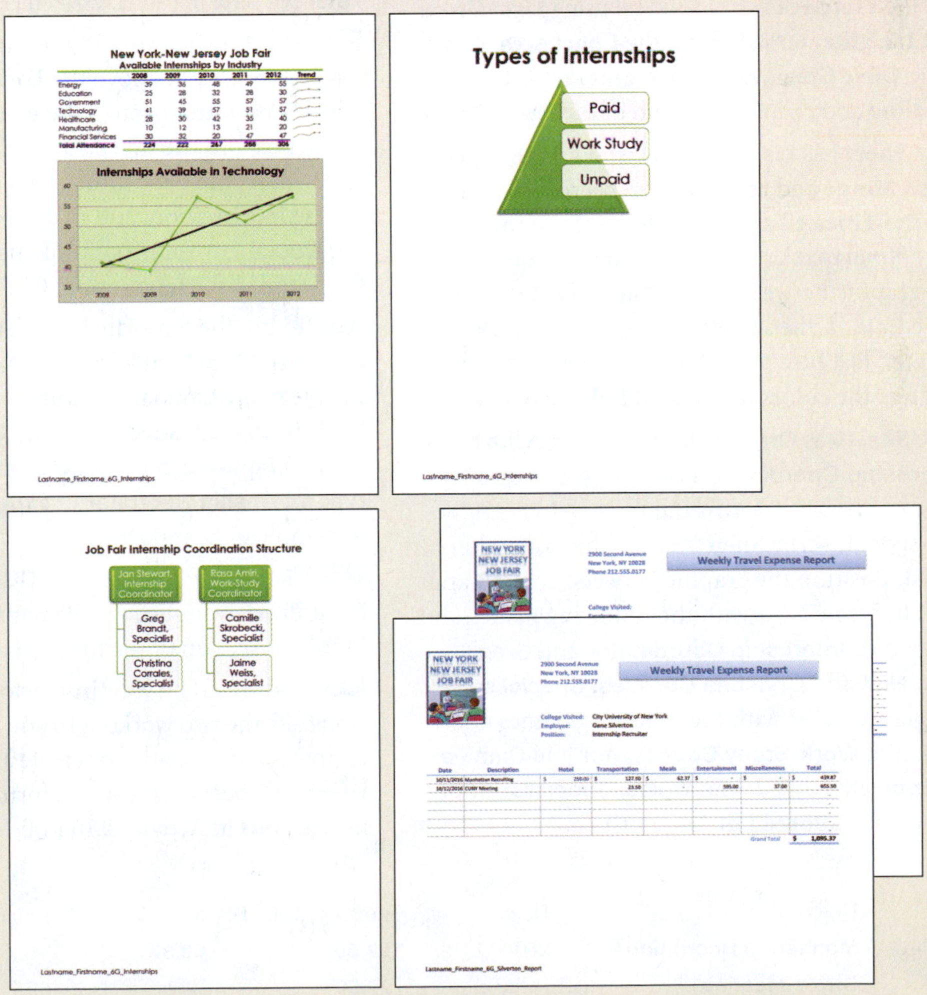

Figure 6.48

(Project 6G Internships and Travel Template continues on the next page)

Mastering Excel | Project 6G Internships and Travel Template (continued)

1 Start **Excel**. From your student files, locate and open **e06G_Internships**. **Save** the file in your **Excel Chapter 6** folder as **Lastname_Firstname_6G_Internships** Using the range **A4:F10**, insert **Sparklines** in the **Line** format in the range adjacent to the last year of data. Show the **High Point** and **Last Point** and apply Sparkline Style Accent 4 - (no dark or light). In cell **G3**, type **Trend** and apply the format from cell **F3**.

2 Select the ranges representing the years (including the blank cell **A3**) and the data for **Technology** internships. Insert a line chart using the **Line with Markers** chart style. Reposition the chart between cells **A13** and **G29**. Delete the **Legend**. Change the **Chart Title** to **Internships Available in Technology** Edit the **Vertical (Value) Axis** to set the **Minimum** to **35** and the **Major unit** to **5**

3 Format the **Plot Area** with a solid fill using **Light Green, Background 2, Lighter 60%**. Format the **Chart Area** with a solid fill using **Olive Green, Accent 4, Lighter 60%**. Insert a **Linear Trendline** and change the width of the line to **2.5 pt**.

4 Rename **Sheet2** as **List Chart** In cell **A1**, type **Types of Internships** Merge and center the text across the range **A1:I1**, apply the **Title** cell style, and then set the **Font Size** to **36**. Insert a **SmartArt** graphic using the **Pyramid List**. Position the graphic between cells **A3** and **I18**. In the top text box, type **Paid** In the second text box, type **Work Study** and in the last box, type **Unpaid** Apply the **Inset** style and change the colors to **Colored Fill – Accent 1**.

5 Rename **Sheet3** as **Organization Chart** In cell **A1** type **Job Fair Internship Coordination Structure** and then merge and center this title across the range **A1:I1**. Apply the **Title** cell style. Insert a **SmartArt** graphic using the **Hierarchy List**. Position the graphic between cells **A3** and **I17**. On the left, create a list with the following names and titles: **Jan Stewart, Internship Coordinator** and **Greg Brandt, Specialist** and **Christina Corrales, Specialist** On the right, create a list with the following names and titles: **Rasa Amiri, Work-Study Coordinator** and **Camille Skrobecki, Specialist** and **Jaime Weiss, Specialist** Apply the **Inset** style and **Colored Fill – Accent 1**.

6 Group the three sheets, insert a footer with the file name in the **left section**, and then center the sheets horizontally. Display the **Document Panel**. Add your name, your course name and section, and the keywords **internship organization** Examine the **Print Preview**, **Save** and **Close** this workbook, but leave Excel open.

7 From your student files, open the file **e06G_Travel_Expense**. Display the **Save As** dialog box, and then **Save** the workbook as an **Excel Template** in your **Excel Chapter 6** folder with the name **Lastname_Firstname_6G_Travel_Template** In the range **H15:H21**, create formulas to sum the data in each row—do not include the *Date* or *Description* columns. In cell **H22**, create a formula to create a grand total of expenses for each date. Apply appropriate financial formatting to all the cells that will contain expenses, including the **Total** cell style in cell **H22**—refer to Figure 6.48.

8 Select the ranges **D8:D10**, hold down Ctrl, and select **A15:G21**. Remove the **Locked** formatting from the selected cells and protect the worksheet. Be sure the top check box and the first two check boxes in the list are selected. As the password, type **goseries** Add your name, course information, and the **Keywords travel template** to the Document Information Panel. Insert a footer with the file name in the **left section**. Click **Save**.

9 To use the template for an employee's report, **Save** it as an **Excel Workbook** in your **Excel Chapter 6** folder with the file name **Lastname_Firstname_6G_Silverton_Report** As the **College Visited**, type **City University of New York** As the **Employee**, type **Gene Silverton** and as the **Position**, type **Internship Recruiter** Use the following data in Table 1 to complete the report:

10 Change the **Keywords** to **CUNY meeting** Examine the **Print Preview**; notice the file name is updated and displays in the left section of the footer. **Save** your workbook.

11 As directed by your instructor, print or submit electronically the two workbooks you created in this project. If required to do so, print or create an electronic version of your worksheets that contain formulas by following the instructions in Activity 1.16 in Project 1A. **Close** Excel.

Table 1

Date	Description	Hotel	Transport	Meals	Entertainment	Misc.
11-Oct-16	Manhattan Recruiting	250	127.50	62.37		
12-Oct-16	CUNY Meeting		23.50		595	37

(Return to Step 9)

End **You have completed Project 6G**

Apply a combination of the **6A** and **6B** skills.

GO! Fix It | Project 6H Operations Chart

Project Files

For Project 6H, you will need the following file:

e06H_Operations_Chart

You will save your workbook as:

Lastname_Firstname_6H_Operations_Chart

Open the file e06H_Operations_Chart, and then save the file in your Excel Chapter 6 folder as **Lastname_Firstname_6H_Operations_Chart** Edit the diagram so that employees whose job titles relate to College Recruiting and Internships fall under their respective areas. You might find it useful to open the Text Pane. Add your name and course information to the document properties, and include **recruiting operations, internship operations** as the keywords. Insert the file name in the footer, save your file, and then print or submit your worksheet electronically as directed by your instructor.

End **You have completed Project 6H**

Content-Based Assessments

Apply a combination of the **6A** and **6B** skills.

GO! Make It | Project 6I Advertisers

Project Files

For Project 6I, you will need the following file:

e06I_Advertisers

You will save your workbook as:

Lastname_Firstname_6I_Advertisers

Each Job Fair event attracts numerous advertisers who place ads inside the event venue and on the various forms and handouts used by both the employers with booth space and the attendees. From your student files, open the file e06I_Advertisers, and then save it in your chapter folder as **Lastname_Firstname_6I_Advertisers** By using the skills you have practiced, create the worksheet shown in Figure 6.49. Include sparklines showing the high point, a line chart with a trendline to track the advertisers at the White Plains location, and format the chart as shown. Insert the file name in the footer, add appropriate information to the document properties including the keyword **advertisers** and submit as directed by your instructor.

Project Results

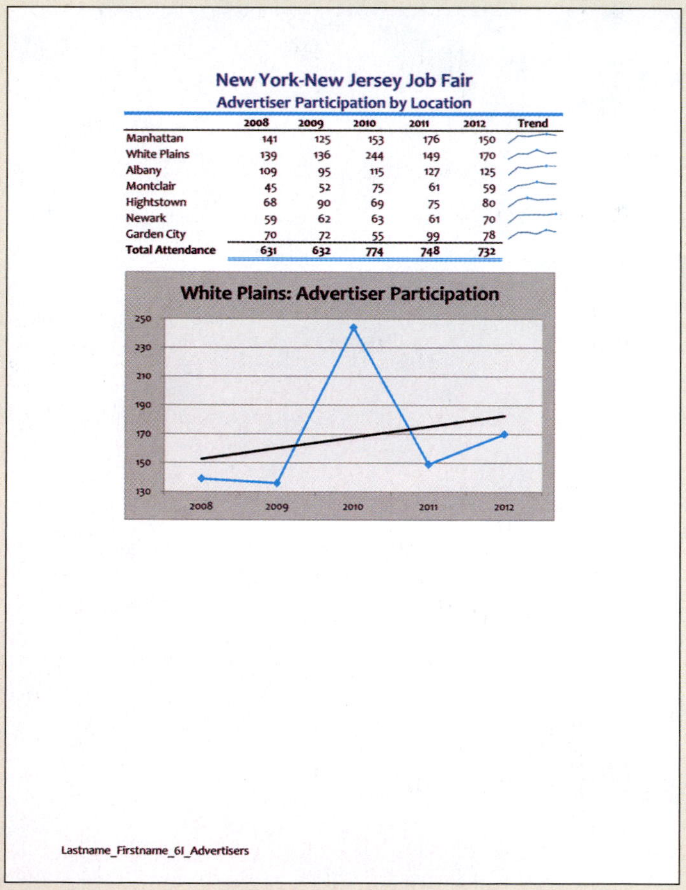
New York-New Jersey Job Fair
Advertiser Participation by Location

	2008	2009	2010	2011	2012	Trend
Manhattan	141	125	153	176	150	
White Plains	139	136	244	149	170	
Albany	109	95	115	127	125	
Montclair	45	52	75	61	59	
Hightstown	68	90	69	75	80	
Newark	59	62	63	61	70	
Garden City	70	72	55	99	78	
Total Attendance	631	632	774	748	732	

Figure 6.49

End **You have completed Project 6I**

Apply a combination of the **6A** and **6B** skills.

GO! Solve It | Project 6J Sponsors

Project Files

For Project 6J, you will need the following file:

e06J_Sponsors

You will save your workbook as:

Lastname_Firstname_6J_Sponsors

Open the file e06J_Sponsors and save it as **Lastname_Firstname_6J_Sponsors** Using the data for all locations, create a 3-D column chart to show sponsors by location. Format the chart attractively by applying varying colors of solid fill to the chart area, the plot area, and the floors and walls of the chart. Include a rotated vertical axis title and a chart title. Insert the file name in the footer of both sheets, add appropriate information to the document properties including the keyword **sponsors** and submit as directed by your instructor.

	Performance Level		
	Exemplary: You consistently applied the relevant skills.	Proficient: You sometimes, but not always, applied the relevant skills.	Developing: You rarely or never applied the relevant skills.
Performance Criteria — Create a 3-D Column Chart	Location and year data is appropriately used to create a 3-D column chart.	Partial location and year data is used to create a 3-D column chart.	Location and year data is not used appropriately to create a 3-D column chart.
Performance Criteria — Format a 3-D Column Chart	The chart is attractively formatted with a variety of colors for the chart elements. The chart contains a chart title and a rotated vertical axis title.	The chart is attractively formatted with a variety of colors for some of the chart elements. The chart contains some but not all of the correct information for a chart title and a rotated vertical axis.	The chart is not attractively formatted with a variety of colors for the chart elements. The chart does not contain a chart title or a rotated vertical axis title.

End **You have completed Project 6J**

Apply a combination of the **6A** and **6B** skills.

GO! Solve It | Project 6K Time Card

Project Files

For Project 6K, you will need the following file:

e06K_Time_Card

You will save your workbook as:

Lastname_Firstname_6K_Time_Template

Open the file e06K_Time_Card and save it as a template in your chapter file with the name **Lastname_Firstname_6K_Time_Template** Insert formulas to total the hours for the week, and a formula to calculate the total pay (Total Pay = Total Hours X Rate Per Hour). Apply appropriate number and financial formatting. Reposition the WordArt above the Time Card chart. Unlock the cells in which an individual would enter variable data, and then protect the sheet with the password **goseries** Insert the file name in the footer, add appropriate information to the document properties including the keywords **time card, payroll** and submit as directed by your instructor.

		Performance Level		
		Exemplary: You consistently applied the relevant skills.	Proficient: You sometimes, but not always, applied the relevant skills.	Developing: You rarely or never applied the relevant skills.
Performance Criteria	Place WordArt Object and Apply Financial Formatting	Appropriate formulas, cell formatting, and WordArt placement are applied.	Appropriate formulas, cell formatting, and WordArt placement are partially applied.	Appropriate formulas, cell formatting, and WordArt placement are not applied.
	Lock Formulas	Formula cells are locked and variable data cells are unlocked.	Only one of the formula cells or variable data cells has the locked or unlocked feature applied appropriately.	Formula cells are unlocked and variable data cells are locked.
	Protect Worksheet	The worksheet is protected with the password **goseries**.	The worksheet is protected but not with the password **goseries**.	The worksheet is not protected with the password **goseries**.

End **You have completed Project 6K**

Rubric

The following outcomes-based assessments are *open-ended assessments*. That is, there is no specific correct result; your result will depend on your approach to the information provided. Make *Professional Quality* your goal. Use the following scoring rubric to guide you in *how* to approach the problem and then to evaluate *how well* your approach solves the problem.

The *criteria*—Software Mastery, Content, Format and Layout, and Process—represent the knowledge and skills you have gained that you can apply to solving the problem. The *levels of performance*—Professional Quality, Approaching Professional Quality, or Needs Quality Improvements—help you and your instructor evaluate your result.

	Your completed project is of Professional Quality if you:	**Your completed project is Approaching Professional Quality if you:**	**Your completed project Needs Quality Improvements if you:**
1-Software Mastery	Choose and apply the most appropriate skills, tools, and features and identify efficient methods to solve the problem.	Choose and apply some appropriate skills, tools, and features, but not in the most efficient manner.	Choose inappropriate skills, tools, or features, or are inefficient in solving the problem.
2-Content	Construct a solution that is clear and well organized, contains content that is accurate, appropriate to the audience and purpose, and is complete. Provide a solution that contains no errors in spelling, grammar, or style.	Construct a solution in which some components are unclear, poorly organized, inconsistent, or incomplete. Misjudge the needs of the audience. Have some errors in spelling, grammar, or style, but the errors do not detract from comprehension.	Construct a solution that is unclear, incomplete, or poorly organized; contains some inaccurate or inappropriate content; and contains many errors in spelling, grammar, or style. Do not solve the problem.
3-Format and Layout	Format and arrange all elements to communicate information and ideas, clarify function, illustrate relationships, and indicate relative importance.	Apply appropriate format and layout features to some elements, but not others. Overuse features, causing minor distraction.	Apply format and layout that does not communicate information or ideas clearly. Do not use format and layout features to clarify function, illustrate relationships, or indicate relative importance. Use available features excessively, causing distraction.
4-Process	Use an organized approach that integrates planning, development, self-assessment, revision, and reflection.	Demonstrate an organized approach in some areas, but not others; or, use an insufficient process of organization throughout.	Do not use an organized approach to solve the problem.

Outcomes-Based Assessments

Apply a combination of the **6A** and **6B** skills.

GO! Think | Project 6L Tech Industry

Project Files

For Project 6L, you will need the following file:

e06L_Tech_Industry

You will save your workbook as:

Lastname_Firstname_6L_Tech_Industry

From your student files, open the file e06L_Tech_Industry, and then save it in your chapter folder as **Lastname_Firstname_6L_Tech_Industry** Format the data attractively, add appropriate formulas, add sparklines, and insert a line chart in the sheet that tracks the data for the White Plains location. Create a 3-D chart on a separate page based on the data in the worksheet, and format it attractively. Change the White Plains 2012 data point from 70 to 85. Insert the file name in the footer on each page, format each sheet for printing, add appropriate information to the document properties including the keywords **technology employers** and submit as directed by your instructor.

End You have completed Project 6L

Apply a combination of the **6A** and **6B** skills.

GO! Think | Project 6M Location List

Project Files

For Project 6M, you will need the following file:

e06M_Locations

You will save your workbook as:

Lastname_Firstname_6M_Locations

From your student files, open the file e06M_Locations, and then save it in your chapter folder as **Lastname_Firstname_6M_Locations** Select an appropriate SmartArt graphic to visually indicate the cities where Job Fairs will be held, which include Manhattan, White Plains, Albany, Montclair, Hightstown, Newark, Upper Saddle River, and Garden City. Arrange the cities in alphabetic order. Insert the file name in the footer, add appropriate information to the document properties including the keywords **fair locations** and submit as directed by your instructor.

End You have completed Project 6M

Outcomes-Based Assessments

Apply a combination of the **6A** and **6B** skills.

You and GO! | Project 6N Job Finding

Project Files

For Project 6N, you will need the following file:

New blank Excel workbook

You will save your workbook as:

Lastname_Firstname_6N_Job_Finding

In this chapter, you practiced using Excel to create SmartArt graphics. Think about the steps involved in searching for a job. If necessary, research some Internet sites for assistance. For example, go to *www.bls.gov* and type **Job Search Methods** in the search box. Then, create a visual guide to the job search steps or methods using one of the SmartArt graphics. Save the file in your chapter folder as **Lastname_Firstname_6N_Job_Finding** Format the worksheet attractively for printing, insert the file name in the footer, add appropriate information to the document properties including the keywords **job finding** and submit as directed by your instructor.

End You have completed Project 6N

Business Running Case

Razvan CHIRNOAGA/Shutterstock

In this project, you will apply the Excel skills you practiced in Chapters 4 through 6. This project relates to **Front Range Action Sports**, which is one of the country's largest retailers of sports gear and outdoor recreation merchandise. The company has large retail stores in Colorado, Washington, Oregon, Idaho, California, and New Mexico, in addition to a growing online business. Major merchandise categories include fishing, camping, rock climbing, winter sports, action sports, water sports, team sports, racquet sports, fitness, golf, apparel, and footwear.

In this project, you will apply skills you practiced from the Objectives in Excel Chapters 4 through 6. You will develop two workbooks for Frank Osei, the Vice President of Finance. You will create a loan payment table and an organization chart for the new Idaho store, develop a phone order form for the newest lines of apparel, create a chart displaying skier attendance, and standardize an expense report template to ensure accurate data entry for winter carnival expenses. Your completed worksheets will look similar to Figure 2.1.

Project Files

For Project BRC2, you will need the following files:

eBRC2_Expense_Report
eBRC2_Financial_Report
eBRC2_Erica
eBRC2_Kate
eBRC2_Laura
eBRC2_Sean
eBRC2_Tyler

You will save your workbooks as:

Lastname_Firstname_BRC2_Expense_Template
Lastname_Firstname_BRC2_Financial_Report

Project Results

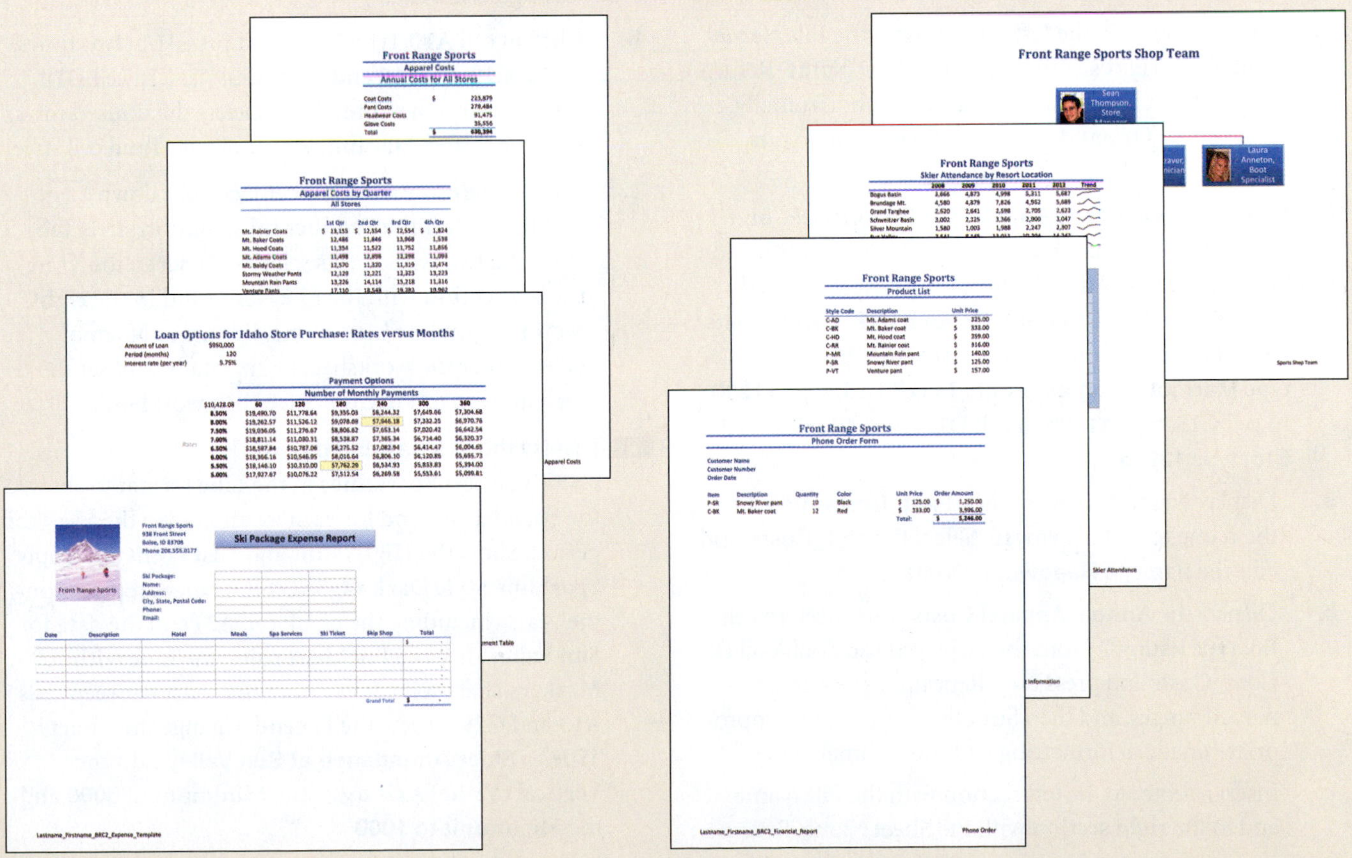

Figure 2.1

Business Running Case

Front Range Action Sports

1 **Start** Excel. From the student files that accompany this textbook, locate and open **eBRC2_Financial_Report**. In the location where you are storing your projects, create a new folder named **Front Range Action Sports** or navigate to this folder if you have already created it. **Save** the workbook as **Lastname_Firstname_BRC2_Financial_Report**

a. Display the **Idaho Store Payment Table** worksheet. In the range **B9:B16**, enter interest rates in increments of .5% beginning with **8.50%** and ending with **5.00%** Format rates with two decimal places, bold and centered. In cell **B8**, enter a **PMT** function using the information in the range **B2:B4**; be sure to divide the rate by 12 and insert a minus sign to enter the amount of the loan (Pv) as a negative number.

b. Create a **Data Table** in the range **B8:H16** using the information in cells **B2:B4** in which the **Row input cell** is the **Period** and the **Column input cell** is the **Interest rate**. Apply the format from **B8** to the results in the data table. Select the two payment options closest to and less than $8,000 per month and format the two options with the **Note** cell style.

c. Insert a footer in the **left section** with the **File Name** and in the **right section** with the **Sheet Name**. Return to **Normal** view, center the worksheet horizontally, and set the **Orientation** to **Landscape**. **Save** your workbook.

2 Display the **Quarterly Apparel Costs** worksheet, and then apply appropriate **Currency [0]**, **Comma [0]**, and **Total** cell styles. Name the following ranges: **B6:E10 Coat_Costs** B11:E14 **Pant_Costs** B15:E16 **Hat_Costs** B17:E17 **Glove_Costs** **Insert** a new row **15**. In cell **A15**, type **Marmot Mountain Pants** In cell **B15**, type **11200** In cell **C15**, type **11695** In cell **D15**, type **12315** In cell **E15**, type **13275**

a. Display **Name Manager**, click **Pant_Costs** and edit the name to include **row15**. Select the **Hat_Costs**, and edit the name to **Headwear_Costs**

b. Display the **Annual Apparel Costs** worksheet. In cell **B5**, type **=sum(C** From the displayed list, double-click **Coat_Costs** and press Enter. Repeat for the remaining named ranges, and then **Sum** the values. Apply appropriate financial formatting with no decimal places.

c. Insert a footer in the **left section** with the **File Name** and in the **right section** with the **Sheet Name**. Return to **Normal** view, center the worksheet horizontally, and set the **Orientation** to **Portrait**. **Save** your workbook.

3 Display the **Product Information** worksheet. Select the range **A4:C11**, and then **Sort** by **Style Code**. Display the **Phone Order** worksheet. In cell **A9**, type **P-SR** and then press Tab. With cell **B9** as the active cell, insert the **VLOOKUP** function. As the **Lookup_value** box, click cell **A9**. Click in the **Table_array** box, display the **Product Information** worksheet, select the range **A4:C11**, and then press F4 to make the cell reference absolute. In the **Col_index_num** box, type **2** and then click **OK**.

a. With cell **B9** as the active cell, fill the VLOOKUP formula through cell **B18**. In cell **C9**, type **10** as the *Quantity ordered*. Press Tab. In cell **D9**, type **Black** and press Tab. With cell **E9** as the active cell, insert the **VLOOKUP** function. As the **Lookup_value** box, click cell **A9**, and then click in the **Table_array** box. Display the **Product Information** worksheet, select the range **A4:C11**. Press F4. In the **Col_index_num** box, type **3** Click **OK**. Copy the VLOOKUP formula through cell **E18**.

b. Click in cell **A10**, type **C-BK** and press Tab two times. In cell **C10**, type **12** and then press Tab. In cell **D10**, type **Red** and then press Enter. Delete the unused rows, sum the **Order Amount**, and apply the **Total** cell style.

c. Select the **Phone Order sheet tab**, hold down Ctrl, and then select the **Product Information sheet tab**. With the two worksheets selected, **Insert** a footer in the **left section** with the **File Name** and in the **right section** with the **Sheet Name**. Return to **Normal** view, center the worksheet horizontally, and set the **Orientation** to **Portrait**. **Save** your workbook.

4 Display the **Skier Attendance** worksheet. In the range **G4:G10**, insert **Sparklines** in the **Line** format to show the attendance trend for each location over the five-year period. Show the **High Point** and **Last Point** and apply **Sparkline Style Dark #4**. Select the ranges representing the years (including the blank cell A3) and the data for **Sun Valley**. Insert a line chart using the **Line with Markers** chart style. Reposition the chart between cells **A13** and **G29**. Delete the **Legend**. Change the **Chart Title** to **Skier Attendance at Sun Valley** Edit the **Vertical (Value) Axis** to set the **Minimum** to **5000** and the **Major unit** to **1000**

(Business Running Case: Front Range Action Sports continues on the next page)

Front Range Action Sports (continued)

a. Format the **Plot Area** with a solid fill using **Blue, Accent 1, Lighter 80%**. Format the **Chart Area** with a solid fill using **Blue, Accent 1, Lighter 60%**. Change the width of the line to **4.0 pt.** and insert a **Linear Trendline**. Deselect the chart. Insert a footer in the **left section** with the **File Name** and in the **right section** with the **Sheet Name**. Return to **Normal** view, center the worksheet horizontally, and set the **Orientation** to **Portrait**. **Save** your workbook.

5 Display the **Sports Shop Team** worksheet. Insert a SmartArt graphic from the **Hierarchy** for a **Picture Organization Chart**. Position the graphic between cells **A3** and **O21**.

a. Delete the Assistant position box. Beginning at the top of the chart, insert a name, title, and picture for **Sean Thompson, Store Manager eBRC2_Sean**. Insert four staff members, all at the same level, from left to right as follows: **Kate Wallace, Customer Service eBRC2_Kate**; **Erica Wilson, Customer Service eBRC2_Erica**; **Tyler Weaver, Ski Technician eBRC2_Tyler**; and **Laura Anneton, Boot Specialist eBRC2_Laura**. Apply SmartArt style, **3-D Polished**.

b. Insert a footer in the **left section** with the **File Name** and in the **right section** with the **Sheet Name**. Return to **Normal** view, center the worksheet horizontally, scale the **Width** to **1 page**, and set the **Orientation** to **Landscape**. **Save** your workbook. Add your name, course information, and the **Keywords financial report** to the Document Panel. **Save** your workbook, and then print or submit electronically as directed. If required, print or create an electronic version of your worksheets with formulas displayed using the instructions in Activity 1.16 in Project 1A. If you printed your formulas, be sure to redisplay the worksheet by pressing Ctrl + `. **Close** the workbook.

6 Open the file **eBRC2_Expense_Report**. Display the **Save As** dialog box, set **Save as type** to **Excel Template**, navigate to your **Front Range Action Sports** folder, and then **Save** the file as **Lastname_Firstname_BRC2_Expense_Template** In the range **H15:H21**, create formulas to sum the data in each row—do not include *Date* or *Description*. In cell **H22**, create a formula to create a grand total of expenses for each date. Apply appropriate financial formatting to cells that contain expenses. Apply the **Total** cell style to cell **H22**. Select the ranges **D7:F12** and **A15:G21**. Remove the Locked formatting from the selected cells and protect the worksheet. Be sure the top check box and the first two check boxes in the list are selected. As the password, type **goseries** Insert a footer with the **file name** in the **left section**, and then center horizontally. Add your name, course information, and the **Keywords expense report template** **Save** your template file, and then print or submit electronically as directed. If required, print or create an electronic version of your worksheets with formulas displayed using the instructions in Activity 1.16 in Project 1A. If you printed your formulas, be sure to redisplay the worksheet by pressing Ctrl + `.

End **You have completed Business Running Case 2**

Enhancing Tables

OUTCOMES

At the end of this chapter you will be able to:

OBJECTIVES

Mastering these objectives will enable you to:

PROJECT 4A
Maneuver data and enforce data integrity.

PROJECT 4B
Format tables and validate data entry.

TebNad/Shutterstock

In This Chapter

In this chapter, you will enhance tables and improve data accuracy and data entry. You will begin by identifying secure locations where databases will be stored and by backing up existing databases to protect the data. You will edit existing tables and copy data and table design across tables. You will create a new table in Design view and determine the best data type for each field based on its characteristics. You will use the field properties to enhance the table and to improve data accuracy and data entry, including looking up data in another table and attaching an existing document to a record.

Westland Plains, Texas, is a city of approximately 800,000 people in the western portion of the second-most populous state in the United States. The city's economy is built around the oil industry, a regional airport serving western Texas and eastern New Mexico, a multi-location medical center, and a growing high-tech manufacturing industry. Westland Plains has a rich cultural history that is kept alive by a number of civic organizations and museums; new culture and traditions are encouraged through the city's arts council. City residents of all ages enjoy some of the finest parks, recreation areas, and sports leagues in the state.

Project 4A City Directory

myitlab
Project 4A Training

Project Activities

In Activities 4.01 through 4.12, you will redesign the tables and edit and proofread data, taking advantage of table relationships to avoid entering and storing redundant data. Joaquin Alonzo, the new City Manager of Westland Plains, has a database of city directory information. This database has three tables that have duplicate information in them. Your completed tables and relationships will look similar to Figure 4.1.

Project Files

For Project 4A, you will need the following files:

a04A_City_Directory
a04A_City_Employees

You will save your files as:

Lastname_Firstname_4A_City_Directory
Lastname_Firstname_4A_City_Directory_2015-10-30 (date will vary)
Lastname_Firstname_4A_City_Employees

Project Results

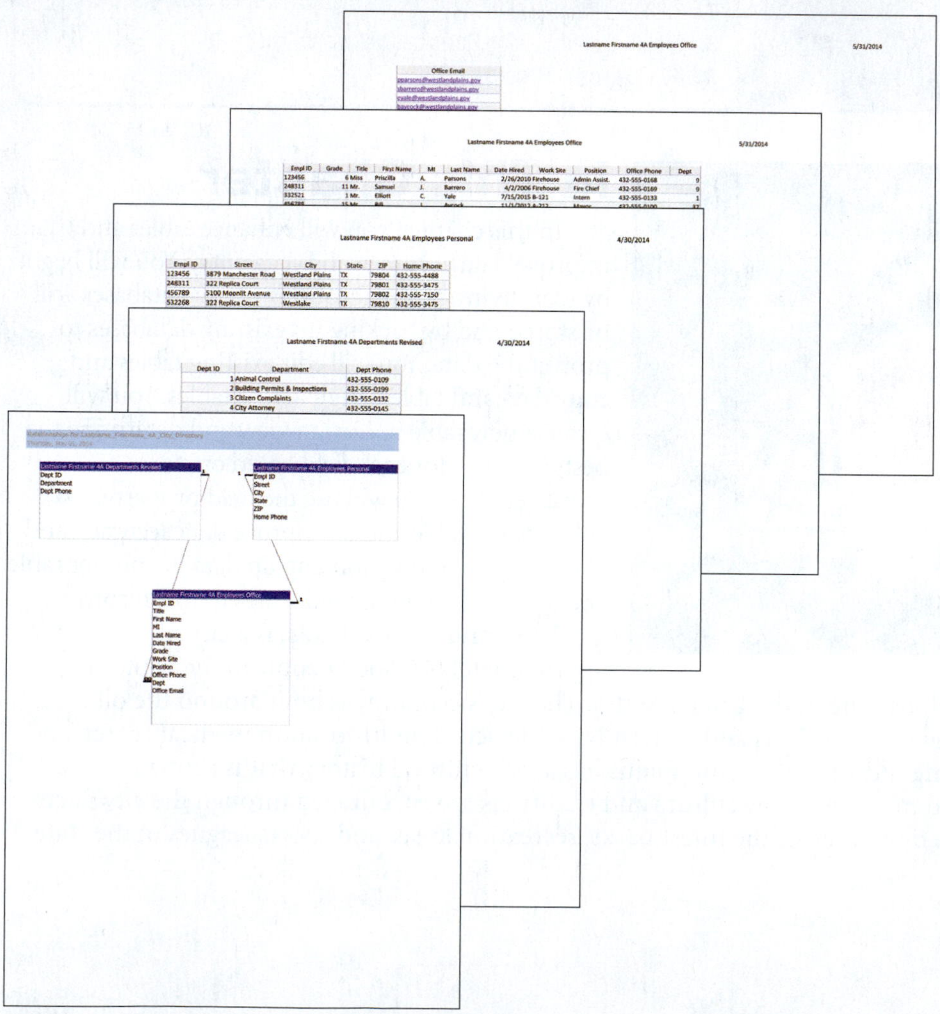

Figure 4.1
Project 4A City Directory

Objective 1 | Manage Existing Tables

A database is most effective when the data is maintained accurately and efficiently. It is important to back up your database often to be sure you can always obtain a clean copy if the data is corrupted or lost. Maintaining the accuracy of the field design and data is also critical to have a useful database; regular reviews and updates of design and data are necessary. It is also helpful to avoid rekeying data that already exists in a database; using copy/paste or appending records reduces the chances for additional errors as long as the source data is accurate.

Activity 4.01 | Backing Up a Database

Before modifying the structure of an existing database, it is important to ***back up*** the database so that a copy of the original database will be available if you need it. It is also important to back up databases regularly to avoid losing data.

1 **Start** Access. Navigate to the student data files for this textbook. Locate and open the **a04A_City_Directory** file and enable the content.

2 Display **Backstage** view, click **Save & Publish**, and then, under **Save Database As**, double-click **Back Up Database**. In the **Save As** dialog box, navigate to the drive on which you will be saving your folders and projects for this chapter. Create a new folder named **Access Chapter 4** and then compare your screen with Figure 4.2.

Access appends the date to the file name as a suggested name for the backed-up database. Having the date as part of the file name assists you in determining the copy that is the most current.

Figure 4.2

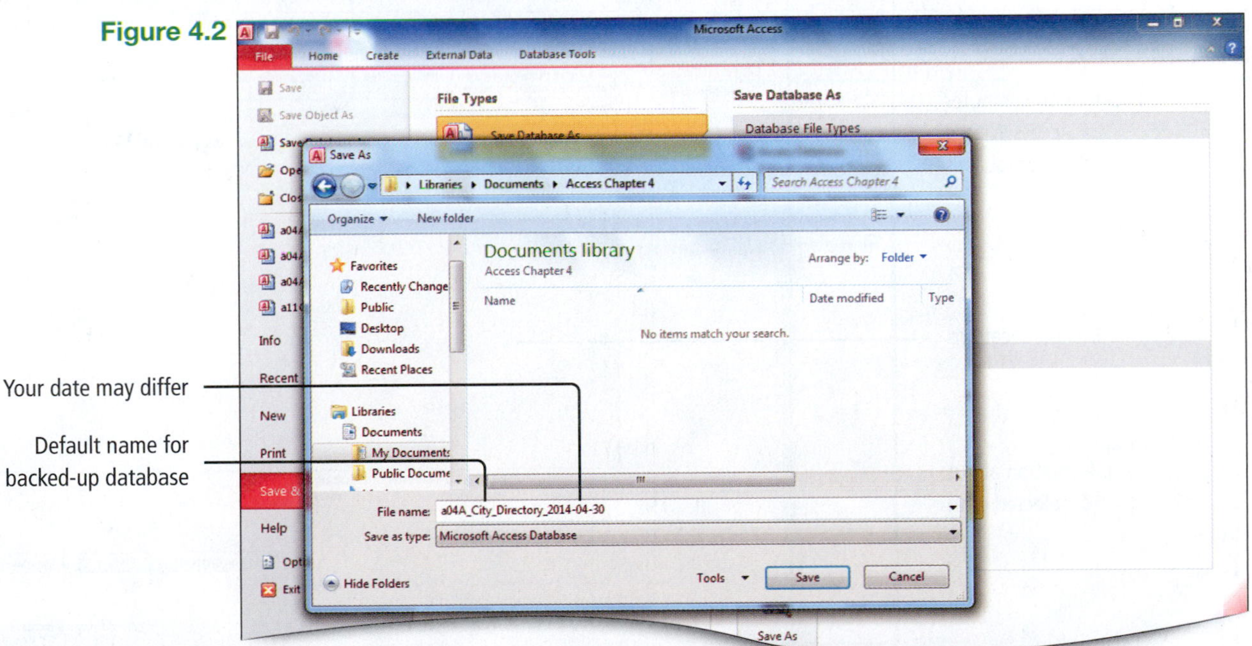

3 In the **File name** box, before the file name, type **Lastname_Firstname_** and remove **a0** from the name. In the **Save As** dialog box, click **Save**. In the title bar, notice that the original database file—not the backed-up file—is open.

4 Click the **Start** button, click **Computer**, and then navigate to the location of your **Access Chapter 4** folder. Open the folder to verify that the backed-up database exists, but do not open the file. **Close** [X] Windows Explorer.

5 **Save** the database as **Lastname_Firstname_4A_City_Directory** in your **Access Chapter 4** folder.

This is another method of making a copy of a database. The original file exists with the original name—the date is not appended to the database name, and the newly saved file is open.

Activity 4.02 | Adding File Locations to Trusted Locations

In this activity, you will add the location of your database files for this chapter and the location of the student data files to the ***Trust Center***—a security feature that checks documents for macros and digital signatures. When you open any database from a location displayed in the Trust Center, no security warning will display. You should not designate the My Documents folder as a trusted location because others may try to gain access to this known folder.

1 Display **Backstage** view, and click the **Enable Content** button. Click **Advanced Options** to display the **Microsoft Office Security Options** dialog box. In the lower left corner, click **Open the Trust Center**.

2 In the **Trust Center** window, in the left pane, click **Trusted Locations**. Compare your screen with Figure 4.3.

The right pane displays the locations that are trusted sources. A ***trusted source*** is a person or organization that you know will not send you databases with malicious code. Under Path and User Locations, there is already an entry. A ***path*** is the location of a folder or file on your computer or storage device.

Figure 4.3

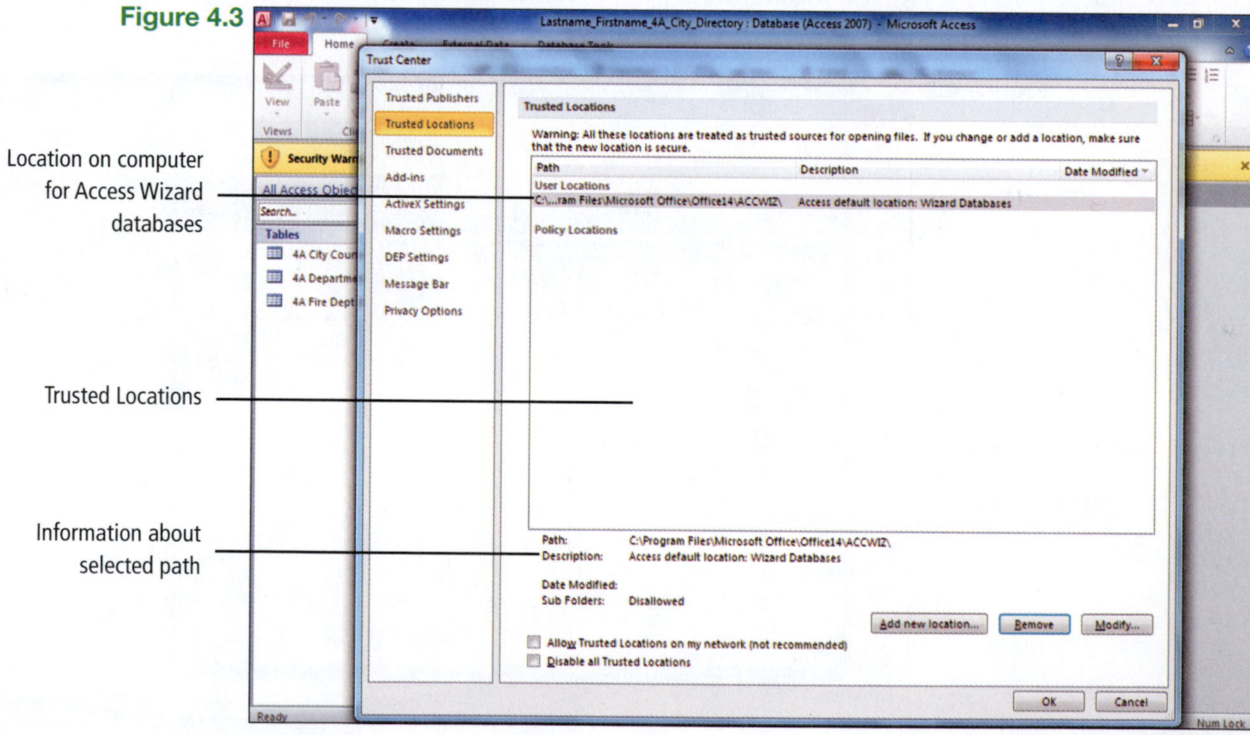

3 In the **Trusted Locations** pane, at the lower right, click **Add new location**. In the **Microsoft Office Trusted Location** dialog box, click **Browse**. In the **Browse** dialog box, navigate to where you saved your *Access Chapter 4* folder, double-click **Access Chapter 4**, and then click **OK**. Compare your screen with Figure 4.4.

The Microsoft Office Trusted Location dialog box displays the path to a trusted source of databases. Notice that you can trust any subfolders in the *Access Chapter 4* folder by checking that option.

Figure 4.4

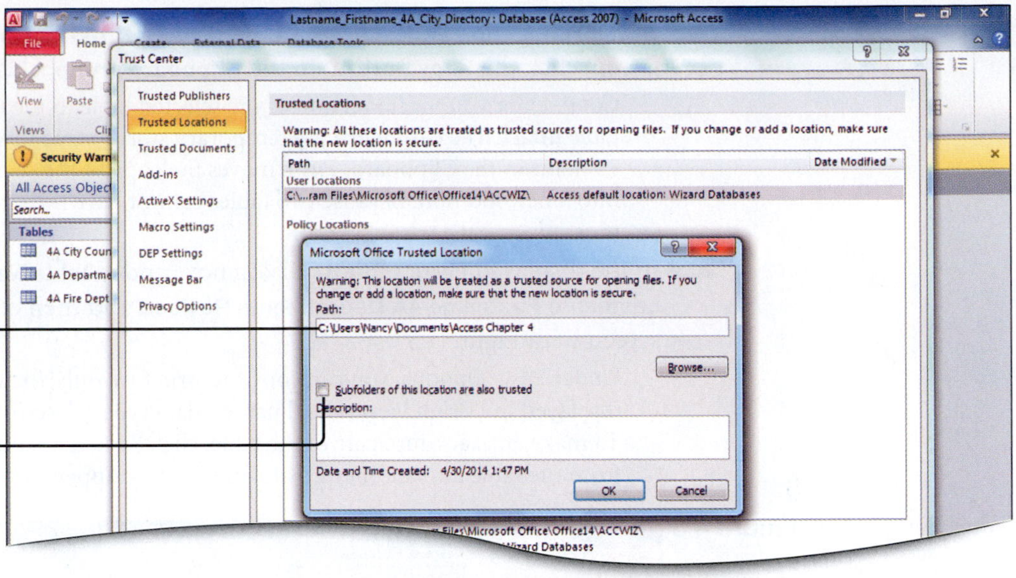

Path to Access Chapter 4 folder—yours may differ

Check box to trust subfolders within this folder

4 In the **Microsoft Office Trusted Location** dialog box, under **Description**, using your own first and last name, type **Databases created by Firstname Lastname** and then click **OK**.

The Trusted Locations pane displays the path of the *Access Chapter 4* folder. You will no longer receive a security warning when you open databases from this location.

5 Using the technique you just practiced, add the location of your student data files to the Trust Center. For the description, type **Student data files created for GO! Series**

Only locations that you know are secure should be added to the Trust Center. If other people have access to the databases and can change the information in the database, the location is not secure.

6 At the lower right corner of the **Trust Center** dialog box, click **OK**. In the displayed **Microsoft Office Security Options** dialog box, click **OK**.

The message bar no longer displays—you opened the database from a trusted location.

7 Display **Backstage** view, and then click **Close Database**. Open **Lastname_Firstname_4A_City_Directory**.

The database opens, and the message bar with the Security Alert does not display. Using the Trust Center button is an efficient way to open databases that are saved in a safe location.

More Knowledge | Remove a Trusted Location

Display Backstage view, and then click the Options button. In the Access Options dialog box, in the left pane, click Trust Center. In the right pane, click the Trust Center Settings button, and then click Trusted Locations. Under Path, click the trusted location that you want to remove, and then click the Remove button. Click OK to close the dialog box.

Activity 4.03 | Copying a Table and Modifying the Structure

In this activity, you will copy the *4A Departments* table, modify the structure by deleting fields and data that are duplicated in other tables, and then designate a primary key field.

1 In the Navigation Pane, click **4A Departments**. On the **Home tab**, in the **Clipboard group**, click the **Copy** button. In the **Clipboard group**, click the **Paste** button.

Copy sends a duplicate version of the selected table to the Clipboard, leaving the original table intact. The ***Clipboard*** is a temporary storage area in Windows. Office can store up to 24 items in the Clipboard. ***Paste*** moves the copy of the selected table from the Clipboard into a new location. Because two tables cannot have the same name in a database, you must rename the pasted version.

2 In the displayed **Paste Table As** dialog box, under **Table Name**, type **Lastname Firstname 4A Departments Revised** and then compare your screen with Figure 4.5.

Under Paste Options, you can copy the structure only, including all the items that are displayed in Design view—field names, data types, descriptions, and field properties. To make an exact duplicate of the table, click Structure and Data. To copy the data from the table into another existing table, click Append Data to Existing Table.

Figure 4.5

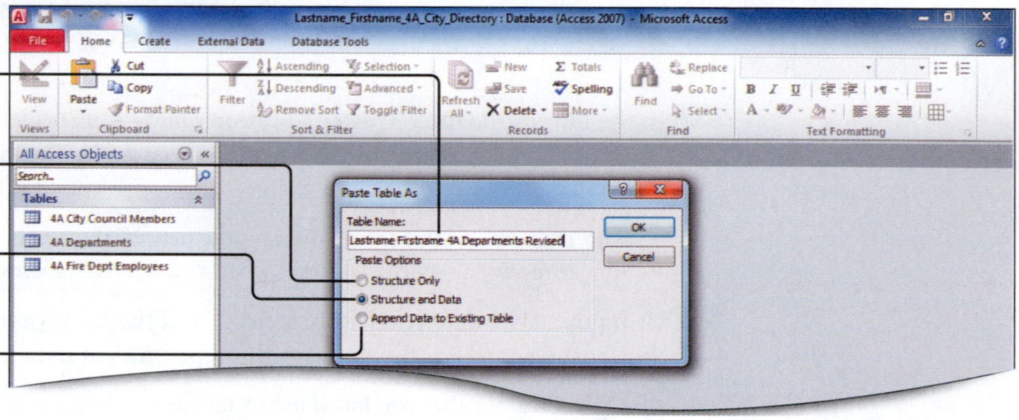

Another Way

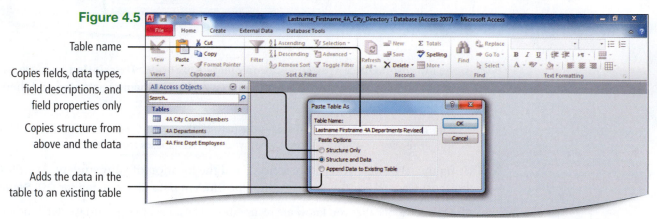

There are two other methods to copy and paste selected tables:

- In the Navigation Pane, right-click the table, and from the displayed list, click Copy. To paste the table, right-click the Navigation Pane, and click Paste from the options listed.
- In the Navigation Pane, click the table, hold down Ctrl, and then press C. To paste the table, point to the Navigation Pane, hold down Ctrl, and then press V.

3 Under **Paste Options**, be sure that the **Structure and Data** option button is selected, and then click **OK**. Notice that the copied table displays in the **Navigation Pane**. Open the **4A Departments Revised** table in **Datasheet** view. **Close** « the **Navigation Pane**.

The *4A Departments Revised* table is an exact duplicate of the *4A Departments* table. Working with a duplicate table ensures that the original table will be available if needed.

4 Point to the **Dept Head** field name until the ⬇ pointer displays. Drag to the right to the **Admin Asst** field name to select both fields. On the **Home tab**, in the **Records group**, click the **Delete** button. In the displayed message box, click **Yes** to permanently delete the fields and the data.

The names of the employees are deleted from this table to avoid having employee data in more than one table. Recall that a table should store data about one subject—this table now stores only departmental data. In addition to removing duplicate data, the fields that you deleted were also poorly designed. They combined both the first and last names in the same field, limiting the use of the data to entire names only.

5 Switch to **Design** view. To the left of **Department**, click the row selector box. On the **Design tab**, in the **Tools group**, click the **Insert Rows** button to insert a blank row (field) above the *Department* field.

6 Under **Field Name**, click in the blank field name box, type **Dept ID** and then press Tab. In the **Data Type** box, type **a** and then press Tab. Alternatively, click the Data Type arrow, and then select the AutoNumber data type. In the **Tools group**, click the **Primary Key** button, and then compare your screen with Figure 4.6.

Recall that a primary key field is used to ensure that each record is unique. Because each department has a unique name, you might question why the Department field is not the primary key field. Primary key fields should be data that does not change often. When companies are reorganized, department names are often changed.

Figure 4.6

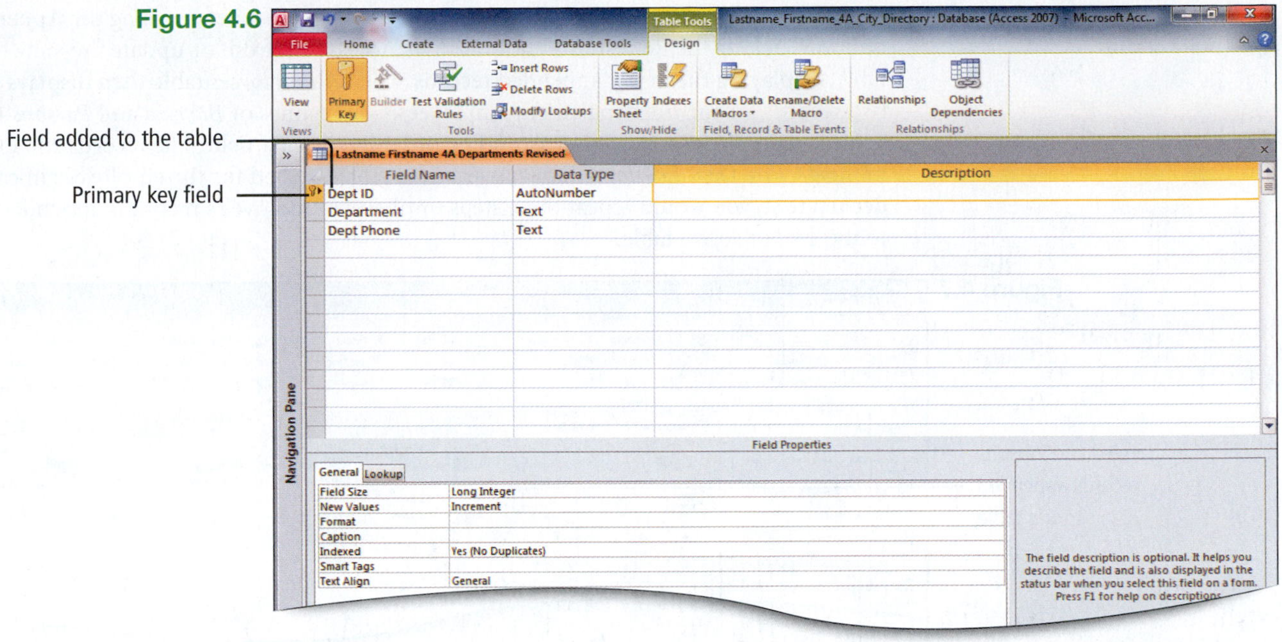

7 Switch to **Datasheet** view, and in the displayed message box, click **Yes** to save the table.

Because the *Dept ID* field has a data type of AutoNumber, each record is sequentially numbered. The data in this field cannot be changed because it is generated by Access.

8 In the datasheet, next to **Department**, click the **Sort and Filter arrow**, and then click **Sort A to Z**.

Sorting the records by the department name makes it easier to locate a department.

9 **Save** the table. **Close** the table. **Open** the **Navigation Pane**.

> **More Knowledge** | Clipboard Size Limitations
>
> Access tables can be very large, depending on the number of fields and records in the table. Although the Office Clipboard can store up to 24 selected items, you might find that you cannot add more items to the Clipboard even if there are fewer than 24 stored items. Access will prompt you to clear items from the Clipboard if there is not enough storage space.

Activity 4.04 | Appending Records to a Table

In this activity, you will copy the *4A City Council Members* table to use as the basis for a single employees table. You will then copy the data in the *4A Fire Dept Employees* table and ***append***—add on—the data to the new employees table.

1 Using the technique you practiced in Activity 4.03, copy and paste the structure and data of the **4A City Council Members** table, and then **Save** the pasted table as **Lastname Firstname 4A Employees**

An exact duplicate of the *4A City Council Members* table is created. The *4A Employees* table will be used to build a table of all employees.

2 Open the **4A Employees** table, and notice the records that were copied from the *4A City Council Members* table.

3 **Copy** the **4A Fire Dept Employees** table, and then click the **Paste** button. In the **Paste Table As** dialog box, under **Table Name**, type **Lastname Firstname 4A Employees** Under **Paste Options**, click the **Append Data to Existing Table** option button, and then click **OK**. With the **4A Employees table** active, in the **Records group**, click the **Refresh All** button, and then compare your screen with Figure 4.7.

The table to which you are appending the records must exist before using the Append option. Clicking the Refresh All button causes Access to refresh or update the view of the table, displaying the newly appended records. The *4A Employees* table then displays the two records for the fire department employees—last names of *Barrero* and *Parsons*—and the records are arranged in ascending order by the first field. The records still exist in the *4A Fire Dept Employees* table. If separate tables existed for the employees in each department, you would repeat these steps until every employee's record is appended to the *4A Employees* table.

Figure 4.7

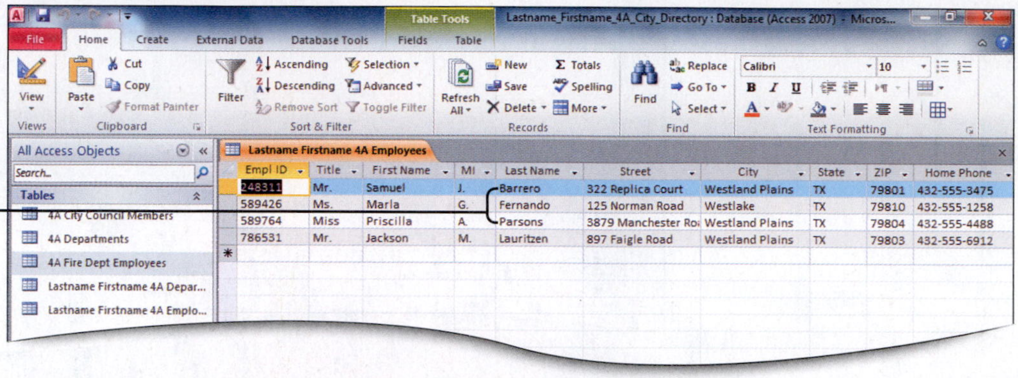

Alert! | Does a Message Box Display?

If a message box displays stating that the Microsoft Office Access database engine could not find the object, you probably mistyped the name of the table in the Paste Table As dialog box. In the Navigation Pane, note the spelling of the table name to which you are copying the records. In the message box, click OK, and then in the Paste Table As dialog box, under Table Name, correctly type the table name.

4 **Close** the table.

More Knowledge | Appending Records

Access appends all records from the ***source table***—the table from which you are copying records—into the ***destination table***—the table to which the records are appended—as long as the field names and data types are the same in both tables. Exceptions include:

- If the source table does not have all of the fields that the destination table has, Access will still append the records, leaving the data in the missing fields empty in the destination table.
- If the source table has a field name that does not exist in the destination table or the data type is incompatible, the append procedure will fail.

Before performing an append procedure, carefully analyze the structure of both the source table and the destination table.

Activity 4.05 | Splitting a Table into Two Tables

The *4A Employees* table stores personal data and office data about the employees. Although the table contains data about one subject—employees—you will split the table into two separate tables to keep the personal information separate from the office information.

1 Using the technique you practiced, copy and paste the structure and data of the **4A Employees** table, naming the pasted table **Lastname Firstname 4A Employees Personal** Repeat the procedure for the **4A Employees** table, naming the pasted table **Lastname Firstname 4A Employees Office**

Access creates two exact duplicates of the *4A Employees* table. These tables will be used to split the *4A Employees* table into two separate tables, one storing personal data and the other storing office data.

2 Open the **4A Employees Personal** table, widening the navigation pane as necessary. **Close** [«] the **Navigation Pane**. Scroll to the right, if needed, to display the **Date Hired**, **Office Phone**, **Position**, and **Office Email** fields. Select all four fields. On the **Home tab**, in the **Records group**, click the **Delete** button. In the displayed message box, click **Yes** to permanently delete the fields and data.

Because these fields contain office data, they are deleted from the *4A Employees Personal* table. These fields will be stored in the *4A Employees Office* table.

3 Select the **Title**, **First Name**, **MI**, and **Last Name** fields, and then delete the fields. **Save** the table.

These fields you deleted are stored in the *4A Employees Office* table. You have deleted redundant data from the *4A Employees Personal* table.

4 **Open** [»] the **Navigation Pane**. Open the **4A Employees Office** table. **Close** [«] the **Navigation Pane**. Point to the **Street** field name until the [↓] pointer displays. Click and drag to the right to the **Home Phone** field name, and then compare your screen with Figure 4.8.

Five fields are selected and will be deleted from this table. This is duplicate data that exists in the *4A Employees Personal* table. The *Empl ID* field will be the common field between the two tables.

Figure 4.8

Duplicate data—stored in 4A Employees Personal table

Common field—4A Employees Office table and 4A Employees Personal table

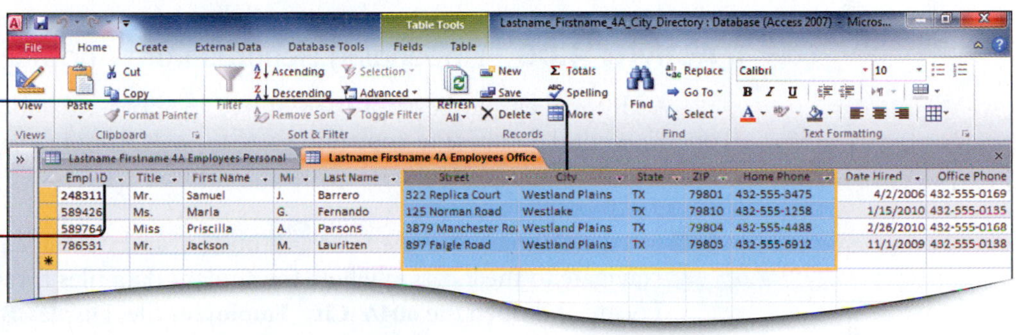

5 **Delete** the selected fields and data from the table.

The *4A Employees Office* table now stores only office data about the employees and can be linked to the *4A Employees Personal* table through the common field, *Empl ID*.

6 Click the **Position** field name. Under **Table Tools**, click the **Fields tab**. In the **Add & Delete group**, click the **Number** button.

A blank field is inserted between the *Position* field and the *Office Email* field, and it holds numeric data. Because this field will be used to link to the *4A Departments Revised* Dept ID field, which has a data type of AutoNumber, this field must use a data type of Number, even though it will not be used in a calculation.

7 The default name *Field1* is currently selected; type **Dept** to replace it and name the new field. Press [Enter].

8 **Open** [»] the **Navigation Pane**. Open the **4A Departments Revised** table.

The *4A Departments Revised* table opens in Datasheet view, and the records are sorted in ascending order by the *Department* field.

9 Locate the **Dept ID** for the **Fire Administration** department. On the **tab row**, click the **4A Employees Office tab** to make the table active. In the record for Samuel Barrero, enter the Fire Administration Dept ID, **9**, in the **Dept** field. Press [↓] two times. In the third record for **Empl ID—Priscilla Parsons**—type **9**

Access | Chapter 4

10 Using the techniques you just practiced, find the **Dept ID** for the **City Council** department, and then enter that number in the **Dept** field for the second and fourth records in the **4A Employees Office** table. Compare your screen with Figure 4.9.

The *Dept* field is a common field with the *Dept ID* field in the *4A Departments Revised* table and will be used to link or join the two tables.

Figure 4.9

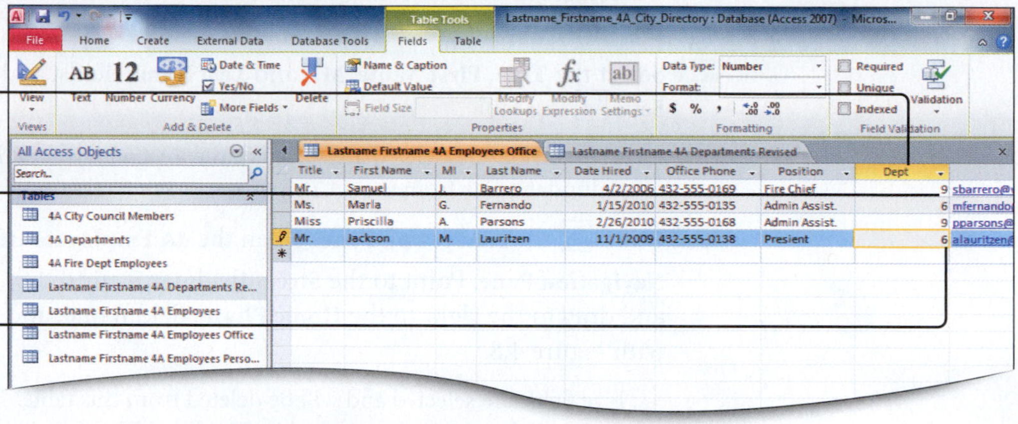

11 On the **tab row**, right-click any table tab, and then click **Close All**.

Activity 4.06 | Appending Records from Another Database

Additional employee records are stored in another database. In this activity, you will open a second database to copy and paste records from tables in the second database to tables in the *4A_City_Directory* database.

1 On the taskbar, click the **Start** button, and then **open** a second instance of **Access**. Navigate to the location where the student data files for this textbook are saved. Locate and open the **a04A_City_Employees** file. Display **Backstage view**, click **Save Database As**, and save the database as **Lastname_Firstname_4A_City_Employees** in your **Access Chapter 4** folder.

2 In the **4A_City_Employees** database window, in the **Navigation Pane**, right-click **4A Office**, and then click **Copy**. Click the Access icon in the taskbar to see two instances of Access open. Compare your screen with Figure 4.10.

Each time you start Access, you open an ***instance*** of it. Two instances of Access are open, and each instance displays in the taskbar.

You cannot open multiple databases in one instance of Access. If you open a second database in the same instance, Access closes the first database. You can, however, open multiple instances of Access that display different databases. The number of times you can start Access at the same time is limited by the amount of your computer's available RAM.

Figure 4.10

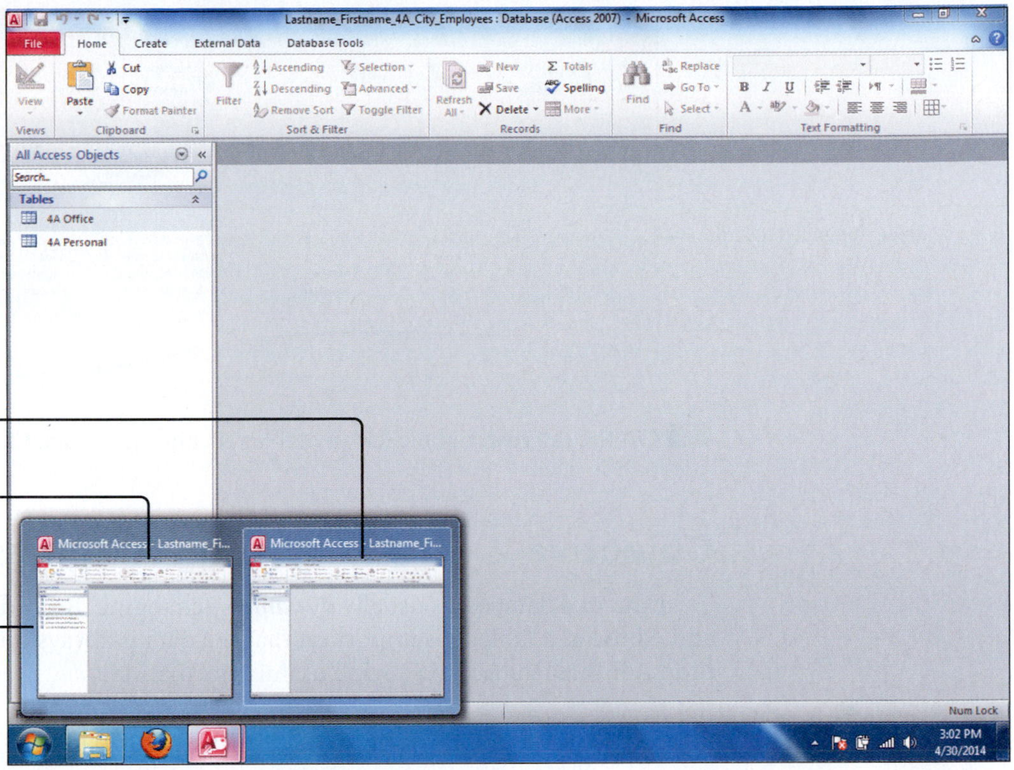

3 Point to each thumbnail to display the ScreenTip, and then click the button for the **4A_City_Directory** database. In the **4A_City_Directory** database window, right-click the **Navigation Pane**, and then click **Paste**—recall that you copied the *4A Office* table. In the **Paste Table As** dialog box, under **Table Name**, type **Lastname Firstname 4A Employees Office** being careful to type the table name exactly as it displays in the Navigation Pane. Under **Paste Options**, click the **Append Data to Existing Table** option button, and then click **OK**.

The records from the *4A Office* table in the source database—*4A_City_Employees*—are copied and pasted into the *4A Employees Office* table in the destination database—*4A_City_Directory*.

4 Using the techniques you just practiced, append the records from the **4A Personal** table in the **4A_City_Employees** database to the **Lastname Firstname 4A Employees Personal** table in the **4A_City_Directory** database.

5 Make the **4A_City_Employees** database active, and on the title bar for the **4A_City_Employees** database window, click the **Close** button.

6 If the **4A_City_Directory** database is not active, on the taskbar, click the **Microsoft Access** button. Open the **4A Employees Personal** table, and then open the **4A Employees Office** table. **Close** [«] the **Navigation Pane**.

7 If necessary, on the tab row, click the **4A Employees Office tab** to make the table active, and then compare your screen with Figure 4.11.

In addition to appending records, you can copy a single record or data in a field from a table in the source database file to a table in the destination database file. Now that you have finished restructuring the database, you can see that it is wise to plan your database before creating the tables and entering data.

Figure 4.11

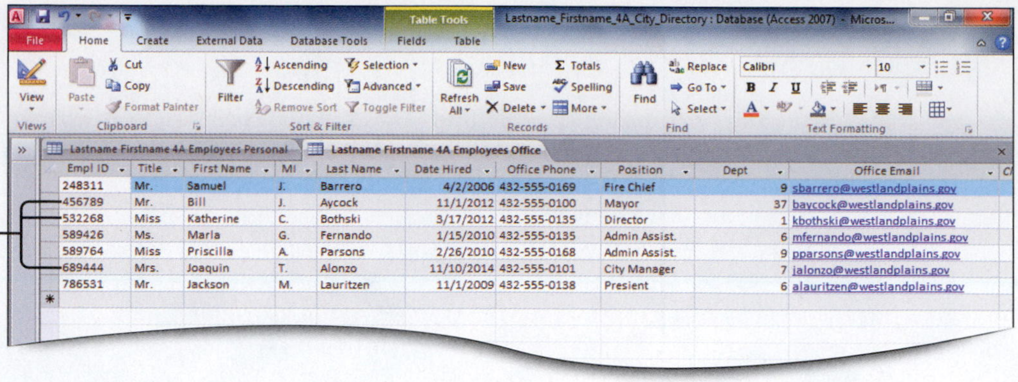

8 On the **tab row**, right-click any table tab, and then click **Close All**.

Objective 2 | Modify Existing Tables

Data in a database is usually ***dynamic***—changing. Records can be created, deleted, and edited in a table. It is important that the data is always up-to-date and accurate in order for the database to provide useful information.

Activity 4.07 | Finding and Deleting Records

1 **Open** [»] the **Navigation Pane**. Open the **4A Departments Revised** table. **Close** [«] the **Navigation Pane**. In the datasheet, next to Dept ID, click the **Sort and Filter arrow**, and then click **Sort Smallest to Largest**.

Sorting the records by the department ID returns the data to its primary key order.

2 In the table, in the **Department** field, click in the record containing the City Teasurer—Record 8. On the **Home tab**, in the **Find group**, click the **Find** button. Alternatively, hold down Ctrl, and then press F. The Find and Replace dialog box displays with the Find tab active.

3 In the **Find and Replace** dialog box, in the **Find What** box, type **City Assessor**

The Look In box displays *Current field,* which refers to the Department field because you clicked in that field before you clicked the Find button.

4 In the **Find and Replace** dialog box, click the **Look in box arrow**. Notice that Access can search for the data in the entire Departments table instead of only the Department field. Leaving the entry as **Current field**, click the **Look in box arrow** one time to close the list, and then click the **Find Next** button. Compare your screen with Figure 4.12.

If Access did not locate Record 5, ensure that you typed *City Assessor* correctly in the Find What box. If you misspelled *City Assessor* in the table, type the misspelled version in the Find What box. This is an example of how important accuracy is when entering data in your tables.

Figure 4.12

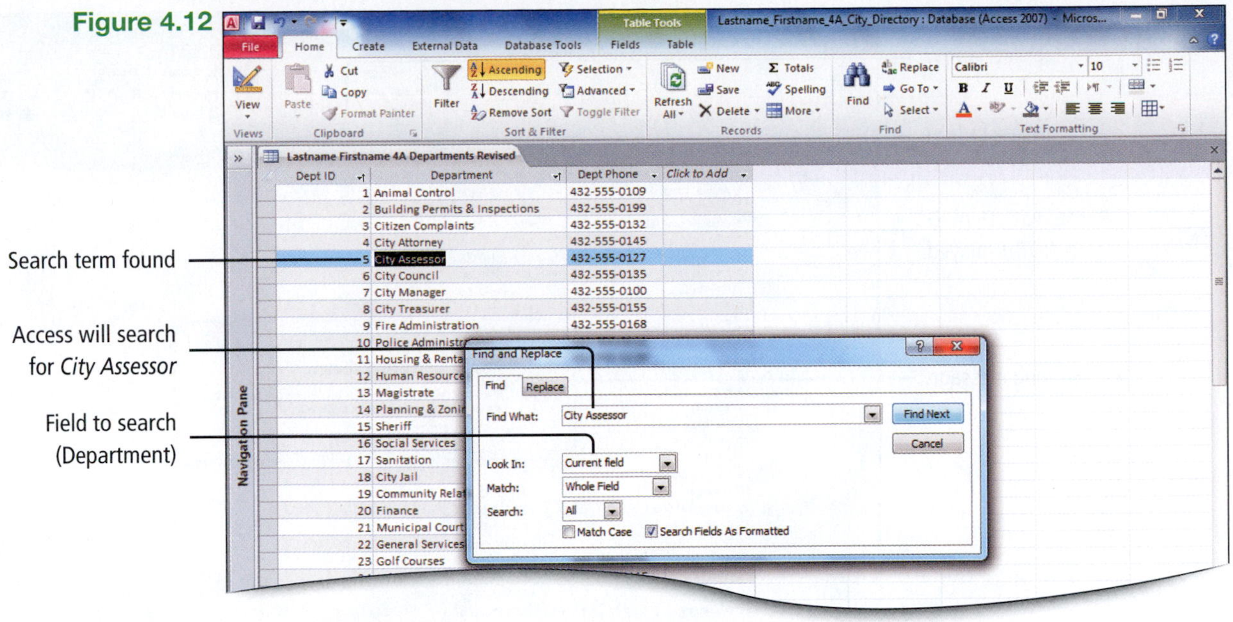

5 In the **Find and Replace** dialog box, click **Cancel** to close the dialog box.

The table displays with *City Assessor* selected in Record 5. Even though you can locate this record easily in the table because there are a limited number of records, keep in mind that most database tables contain many more records. Using the Find button is an efficient way to locate a record in the table.

6 Point to the **Record Selector** box for the *City Assessor* record until the [→] pointer displays. Click one time to ensure that the entire record is selected, and then compare your screen with Figure 4.13.

Figure 4.13

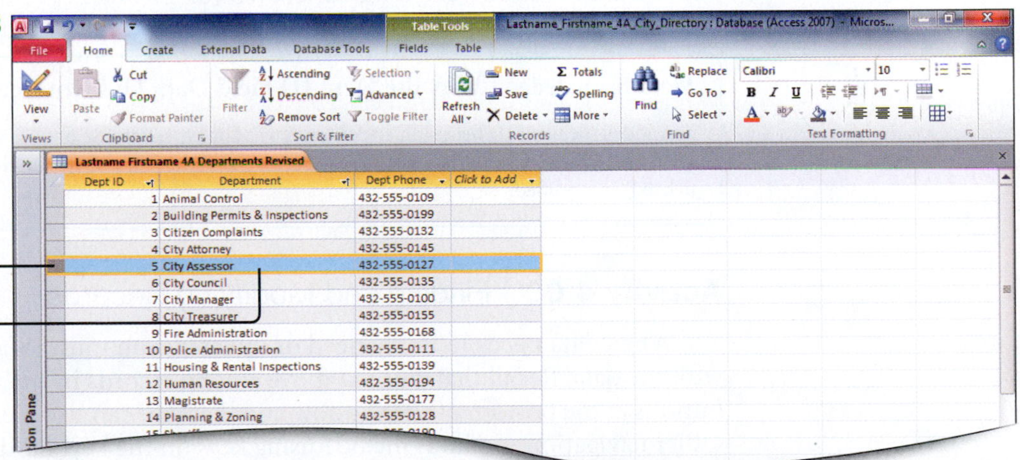

Another Way

There are three other methods to delete selected records in a table:

- On the Home tab, in the Records group, click the Delete button arrow, and then click Delete Record.
- On the selected record, right-click, and then click Delete Record.
- From the keyboard, press [Del].

7 On the **Home tab**, in the **Records group**, click the **Delete** button, and then compare your screen with Figure 4.14. Notice that Access displays a message stating that you are about to delete one record and will be unable to undo the Delete operation.

Figure 4.14

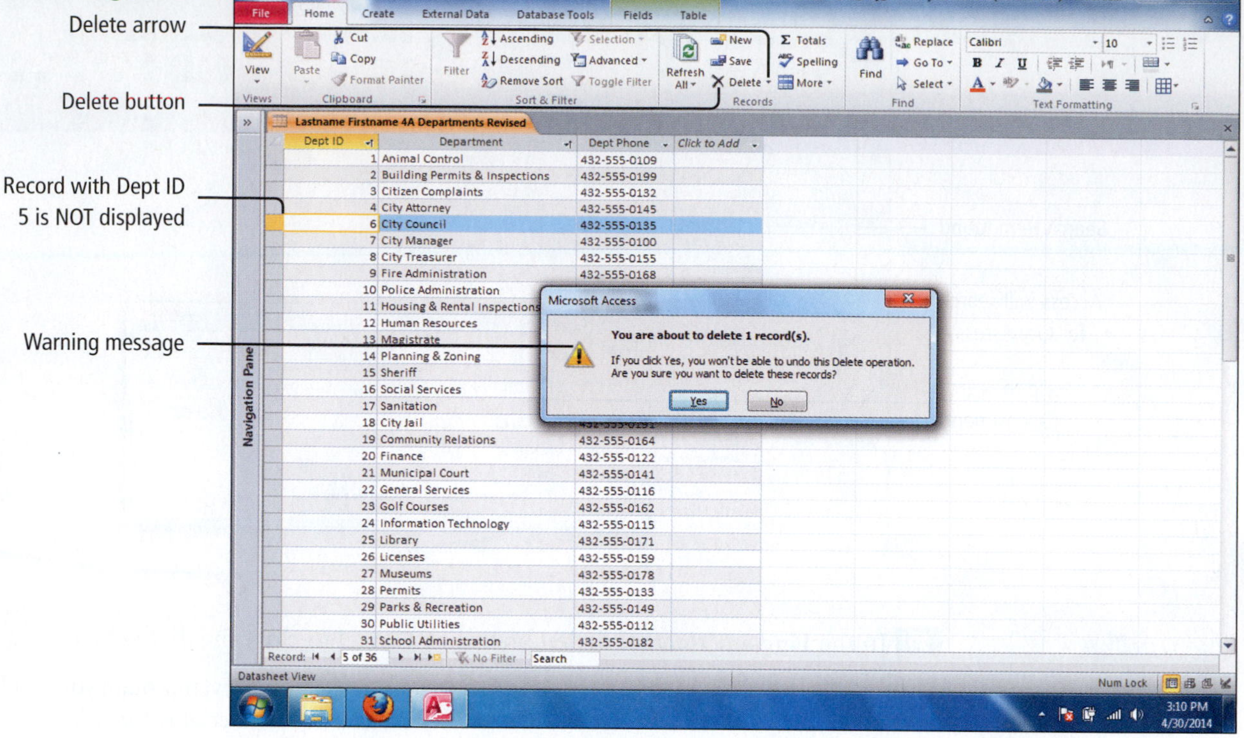

8 In the message box, click **Yes** to confirm the deletion.

The record holding information for *City Assessor* no longer displays in the table, has been permanently deleted from the table, and will no longer display in any other objects that were created using the Contacts table. The record number of Dept ID 6—City Council—is now record 5 and is the current record.

> **More Knowledge | Why the Dept ID Field Data Did Not Renumber Sequentially**
>
> You added the Dept ID field with an Autonumber data type. Because of this, when data is entered into the table, Dept ID is automatically numbered sequentially, and those numbers are not changed as records are added, deleted, or modified.

Activity 4.08 | Finding and Modifying Records

When data needs to be changed or updated, you must locate and modify the record with the data. Recall that you can move among records in a table using the navigation buttons at the bottom of the window and that you can use Find to locate specific data. Other navigation methods include using keys on the keyboard and using the Search box in the navigation area.

1 Take a moment to review the table in Figure 4.15, which lists the key combinations you can use to navigate within an Access table.

Key Combinations for Navigating a Table

Keystroke	Movement
[↑]	Moves the selection up one record at a time.
[↓]	Moves the selection down one record at a time.
[Page Up]	Moves the selection up one screen at a time.
[PageDown]	Moves the selection down one screen at a time.
[Ctrl] + [Home]	Moves the selection to the first field in the table or the beginning of the selected field.
[Ctrl] + [End]	Moves the selection to the last field in the table or the end of the selected field.
[Tab]	Moves the selection to the next field in the table.
[Shift] + [Tab]	Moves the selection to the previous field in the table.
[Enter]	Moves the selection to the next field in the table.

Figure 4.15

2 On the keyboard, press [↓] to move the selection down one record. Record 6—*City Manager*—is now the current record.

3 On the keyboard, hold down [Ctrl], and then press [Home] to move to the first field of the first record in the table—Dept ID *1*.

4 In the navigation area, click the **Next record** button five times to navigate to Record 6—Dept ID *7*.

5 On the keyboard, hold down [Ctrl], and then press [End] to move to the last field in the last record in the table—Dept Phone *432-555-0162*.

6 On the keyboard, hold down [Shift], and then press [Tab] to move to the previous field in the same record in the table—*City Mayor* in the Department field.

7 In the navigation area at the bottom of the screen, click in the **Search** box, and type **b**

Record 2 is selected, and the letter *B* in *Building Permits & Inspections* is highlighted. Search found the first occurrence of the letter *b*. It is not necessary to type capital letters in the Search box; Access will locate the words regardless of capitalization.

8 In the **Search** box, replace the b with **sa**

Record 16 is selected, and the letters *Sa* in *Sanitation* are highlighted. Search found the first occurrence of the letters *sa*. This is the record that needs to be modified. It is not necessary to type an entire word in the Search box to locate a record containing that word.

9 In the field box, double-click the word *Sanitation* to select it. Type **Trash Pickup** to replace the current entry. The Small Pencil icon in the Record Selector box means that the record is being edited and has not yet been saved. Press [↓] to move to the next record and save the change.

If you must edit part of a name, drag through letters or words to select them. You can then type the new letters or words over the selection to replace the text without having to press [Del] or [Backspace].

10 **Save** and **Close** the table. **Open** [»] the **Navigation Pane**.

Activity 4.09 | Adding and Moving Fields in Design View and Datasheet View

In this activity, you will add and move fields in Design view and in Datasheet view.

1 Right-click the **4A Employees Office** table to display a shortcut menu, and click **Design View** to open the table in Design view. Alternatively, double-click the table name in the **Navigation Pane** to open the table in Datasheet view, and click the **View** button to switch to Design view. **Close** « the **Navigation Pane**.

2 In the **Field Name** column, locate the **Office Phone** field name, and then click anywhere in the box.

3 On the **Design tab**, in the **Tools group**, click the **Insert Rows** button. Alternatively, right-click, and then from the shortcut menu, click Insert Rows.

A new row is inserted above the *Office Phone* field. Recall that a row in Design view is a field.

4 In the empty **Field Name** box, type **Grade** and then press Tab to move to the **Data Type** column. Click the **Data Type arrow** to display the list of data types, and then click **Number** to set the data type for this field. Compare your screen with Figure 4.16.

A new field has been created in the *Lastname Firstname_4A Employees Office* table. An advantage of adding a field in the Design view is that you name the field and set the data type when you insert the field.

Figure 4.16

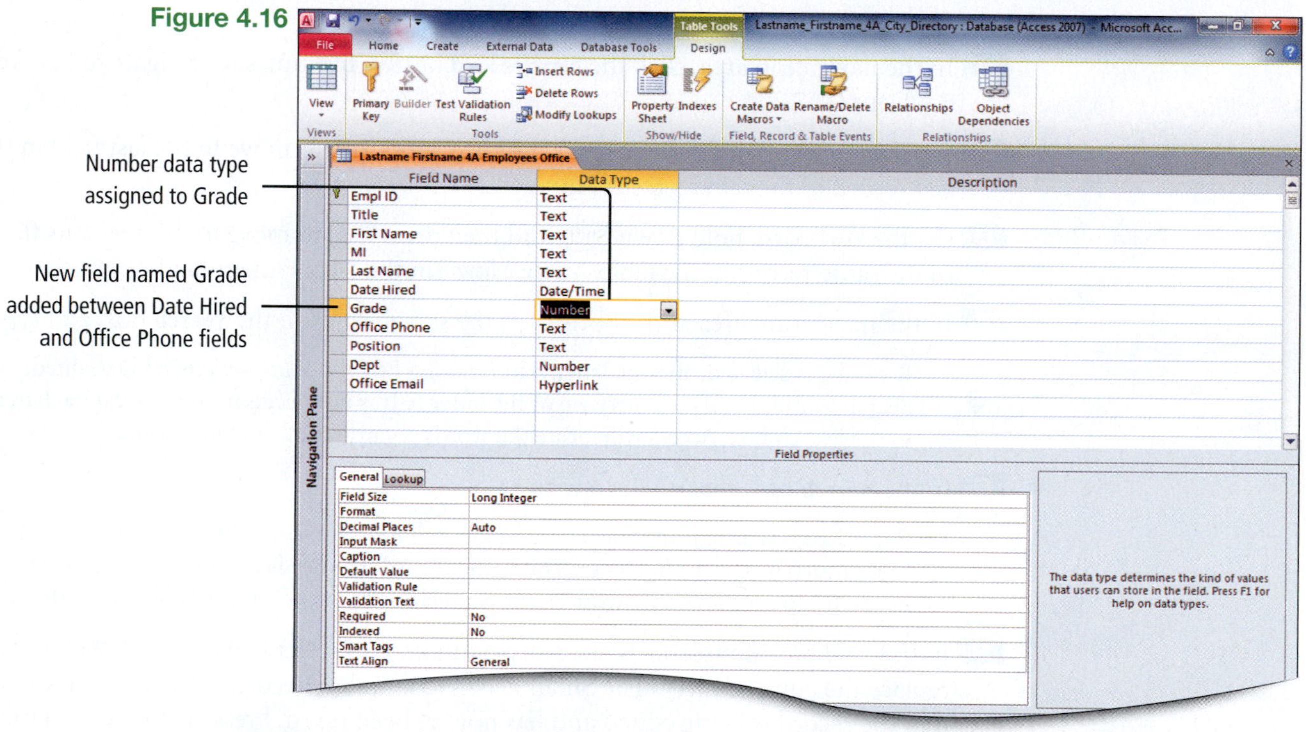

5 Switch the **4A Employees Office** table to **Datasheet** view. In the displayed message box, click **Yes** to save the design change.

The *Grade* field displays to the left of the *Office Phone* field.

6 Point to **Grade** until the ⬇ pointer displays, and click one time to select the column. Drag the field left until you see a dark horizontal line between *Empl ID* and *Title*, and then release the mouse button. Compare your screen with Figure 4.17.

The *Grade* field is moved after the *Empl ID* field and before the *Title* field. If you move a field to the wrong position, select the field again, and then drag it to the correct position. Alternatively, on the Quick Access Toolbar, click the Undo button to place the field back in its previous position.

Figure 4.17

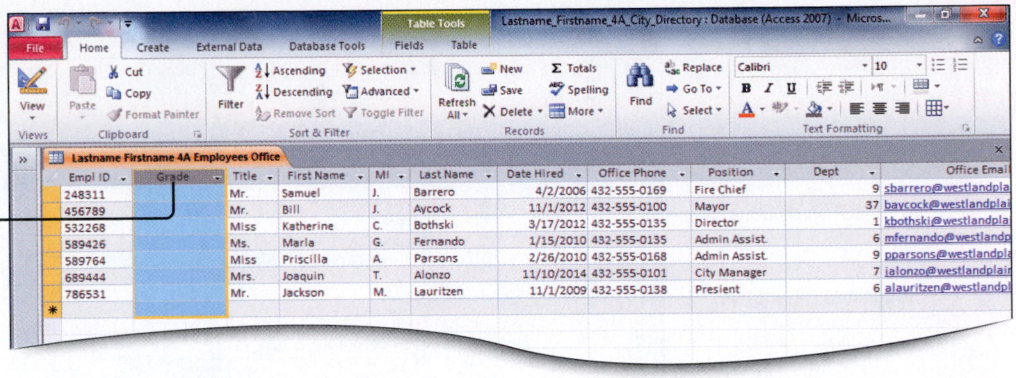

Lastname_Firstname_4A_City_Directory : Database (Access 2007) - Micros...
Table Tools
File
Home
Create
External Data
Database Tools
Fields
Table
Lastname Firstname 4A Employees Office
Empl ID
Grade
Title
First Name
MI
Last Name
Date Hired
Office Phone
Position
Dept
Office Email
248311 Mr. Samuel J. Barrero 4/2/2006 432-555-0169 Fire Chief 9
456789 Mr. Bill J. Aycock 11/1/2012 432-555-0100 Mayor 37
532268 Miss Katherine C. Bothski 3/17/2012 432-555-0135 Director 1
589426 Ms. Maria G. Fernando 1/15/2010 432-555-0135 Admin Assist. 6
589764 Miss Priscilla A. Parsons 2/26/2010 432-555-0168 Admin Assist. 9
689444 Mrs. Joaquin T. Alonzo 11/10/2014 432-555-0101 City Manager 7
786531 Mr. Jackson M. Lauritzen 11/1/2009 432-555-0138 Presient 6

Grade field moved between Empl ID and Title fields

7 Select the **Office Phone** column. On the **Fields** tab, in the **Add & Delete** group, click **Text**. Alternatively, right-click the selected field and, from the shortcut menu, click **Insert Column**. A new column is inserted to the right of *Office Phone*.

8 If necessary, double-click **Field1**—the name of your field may differ if you have been experimenting with adding fields—to select the field name. Type **Work Site** and press Enter to save the field name. On the first record, click in the first empty **Work Site** field box. On the **Fields** tab, in the **Formatting group**, verify that the **Data Type** is **Text**.

9 In the first record—248311—click in the **Grade** field. Using the techniques you have practiced, enter the grade for each record shown in the following list, pressing ↓ after each entry to move to the next record. Repeat the process for the **Work Site** field.

Empl ID	Grade	Work Site
248311	**11**	**Firehouse**
456789	**15**	**A-212**
532268	**8**	**B-121**
589426	**6**	**A-214**
589764	**6**	**Firehouse**
689444	**8**	**A-210**
786531	**12**	**A-214**

10 Switch to **Design** view. Scroll the field list until the **Office Phone** and **Dept** fields both display, if necessary. In the **Field Name** column, locate **Office Phone**, and then click the **Row Selector** box to select the field. Point to the **Row Selector** box to display the ➡ pointer. Drag the field down until you see a dark horizontal line following *Position*, and then release the mouse button. **Save** the table.

11 Switch to **Datasheet** view. Notice that the **Office Phone** field is moved to the right of **Position**.

Activity 4.10 | Checking Spelling

In this exercise, you will use the spelling checker to find spelling errors in your data. It is important to realize that this will not find all data entry mistakes, so you will need to use additional proofreading methods to ensure the accuracy of the data.

1 In the first record—248311—click in the **Empl ID** field. On the **Home tab**, in the **Records group**, click the **Spelling** button. Alternatively, press F7. Compare your screen with Figure 4.18.

The Spelling dialog box displays, and *Barrero* is highlighted because it is not in the Office dictionary. Many proper names will be ***flagged***—highlighted—by the spelling checker. Take a moment to review the options in the Spelling dialog box; these are described in the table in Figure 4.19.

Figure 4.18

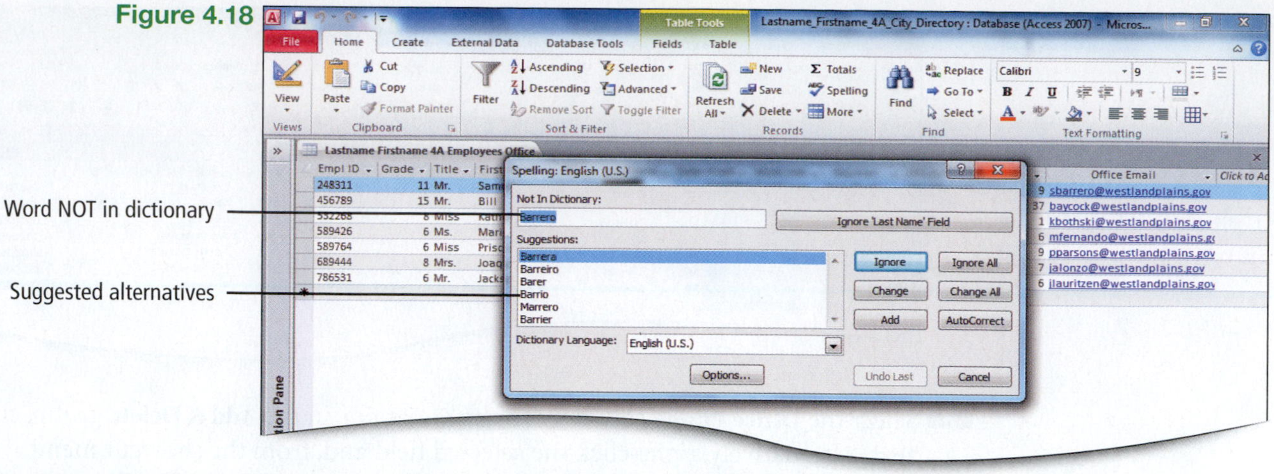

Spelling Dialog Box Buttons

Button	Action
Ignore 'Last Name' Field	Ignores any words in the selected field.
Ignore	Ignores this one occurrence of the word but continues to flag other instances of the word.
Ignore All	Discontinues flagging any instance of the word anywhere in the table.
Change	Changes the identified word to the word highlighted under Suggestions.
Change All	Changes every instance of the word in the table to the word highlighted under Suggestions.
Add	Adds the word to a custom dictionary, which can be edited. This option does not change the built-in Office dictionary.
AutoCorrect	Adds the flagged word to the AutoCorrect list, which will subsequently correct the word automatically if misspelled in any objects typed in the future.
Options	Displays the Access Options dialog box.
Undo Last	Undoes the last change.

Figure 4.19

2 In the **Spelling** dialog box, click the **Ignore 'Last Name' Field** button.

Presient, which displays in the Position field, is flagged by the spelling checker. In the Spelling dialog box under Suggestions, *President* is highlighted.

3 In the **Spelling** dialog box, click the **Change** button to change the word from *Presient* to *President*.

When the spelling checker has completed checking the table and has found no other words missing from its dictionary, a message displays stating *The spelling check is complete*.

4 In the message box, click **OK**.

5 **Close** the table.

Objective 3 | Create and Modify Table Relationships

Recall that Access databases are ***relational databases***—the tables a database can relate to or connect to other tables through common fields. A relational database avoids redundant data, helps to reduce errors, and saves space. To create a relationship, the common fields must have the same data type and same field size, but they do not need to have the same field name. Table relationships work by matching data using the common fields in the tables. For example, you could have four tables relating to employees—one table for personal data, one table for office data, one table for benefits data, and one table for training data. All of these tables are connected to one another through a common field—the employee ID.

Activity 4.11 | Creating Table Relationships and Testing Referential Integrity

You should create relationships before creating other database objects, such as queries, forms, and reports, because when you create another object, Access displays all of the available tables and fields. For example, if you create a query on a stand-alone table—one that is not related to other tables—you cannot access relevant information in other tables. You must add the tables to the query and then establish a relationship. In this activity, you will create relationships between the tables in the *4A City Directory* database.

1 On the Ribbon, click the **Database Tools tab**. In the **Relationships group**, click the **Relationships** button. If the Show Table dialog box does not display, on the **Relationship Tools Design tab**, in the **Relationships** group, click the **Show Table** button or right-click an empty area in the **Relationships** window and then click **Show Table**.

The Show Table dialog box displays, and the Tables tab is active. The Tables tab displays all of the tables in the database, including the hidden tables.

2 In the **Show Table** dialog box, click **4A Departments Revised**. Holding down Ctrl, click **4A Employees Office**, and then click **4A Employees Personal**. Notice that three tables are selected. Click **Add**, and then click **Close**.

The three tables are added to the Relationships window. If you have any extra tables in the Relationship window, right-click the *title bar* of the table, and select *Hide Table* from the list. Three field lists display all of the field names. The *4A Employees Office* field list displays a vertical scroll bar, indicating that there are more fields than those displayed.

3 Expand the field list box for the **4A Employees Office** table by dragging the bottom border downward and to the right until the table name and all of the field names display fully. Expand the field list box for the other two tables so the table names display fully. Point to the title bar of the middle field list box, and drag down to move the field list below the other two.

4 In the **4A Departments Revised** field list, click **Dept ID**, and then drag it on top of **Dept** in the **4A Employees Office** field list. Release the mouse button.

> **Alert!** | **Are the Wrong Field Names Displayed in the Edit Relationships Dialog Box?**
>
> If you released the mouse button on a field other than Dept in the 4A Employees Office field list, that field name will be displayed in the Edit Relationships dialog box. To correct this, in the Edit Relationships dialog box, click Cancel, and then re-create the relationship.

5 In the displayed **Edit Relationships** dialog box, select the **Enforce Referential Integrity** check box, and then click **Create**.

Recall that ***referential integrity*** is a set of rules Access uses to ensure that the data between related tables is valid. Enforcing referential integrity prevents ***orphan records***—records that reference deleted records in a related table.

6 In the **4A Employees Office** field list, click **Empl ID**, drag it on top of **Empl ID** in the **4A Employees Personal** field list, and then release the mouse button. In the displayed **Edit Relationships** dialog box, verify that **4A Employees Office** appears on the left side of the box, and then select the **Enforce Referential Integrity** check box. Notice the Relationship Type—One-to-One—and then click **Create**.

A join line displays between the two field lists, indicating a one-to-one relationship between the two tables. By enforcing referential integrity in a ***one-to-one relationship***, each record in the first table—*4A Employees Office*—can have only one matching record in the second table—*4A Employees Personal*—and each record in the second table can have only one matching record in the first table. A one-to-one relationship can be used to divide a table with many fields, to isolate part of the table for security reasons, or to store a part of the main table.

7 Close the Relationships tab. Click **Yes** to save changes to the layout of Relationships. On the **Design tab**, in the **Tools group**, click the **Relationship Report** button. If you are instructed to submit this result, create a paper or electronic printout. On the **Print Preview** tab, in the **Close Preview** group, click **Close Print Preview**. Close the Design view, saving changes.

8 **Open** [»] the **Navigation Pane**. Open the **4A Departments Revised** table, and then open the **4A Employees Office** table. **Close** [«] the **Navigation Pane**.

Both tables open in Datasheet view. Make the *4A Employees Office* table the active table if it is not already. Recall that enforcing referential integrity in a one-to-many table relationship ensures that a department for an employee cannot be added to the *4A Employees Office* table if that department does not exist in the *4A Departments Revised* table. Also, you will be unable to delete a department from the *4A Departments Revised* table if an employee who works in that department is stored in the *4A Employees Office* table. In this activity, you will test these two integrity protection features.

> **Note | Check the Order of the Fields**
>
> If the fields are not in the order displayed, return to Design view to reorder them. Save the changes before moving to Step 9.

9 In the **4A Employees Office** table, add a new record by using the following information.

Empl ID	Grade	Title	First Name	MI	Last Name	Date Hired	Work Site	Position	Office Phone	Dept	Office Email
332521	**1**	**Mr.**	**Elliott**	**C.**	**Yale**	**7/15/15**	**B-121**	**Intern**	**432-555-0133**	**50**	**eyale@westlandplains.gov**

10 Press [Tab] to move to the next record, and then compare your screen with Figure 4.20.

A message box displays indicating that you cannot add or change this record because a related record—a record for Dept 50—is required in the *4A Departments Revised* table. Enforcing referential integrity prevents you from creating this record because there is no related record for the department.

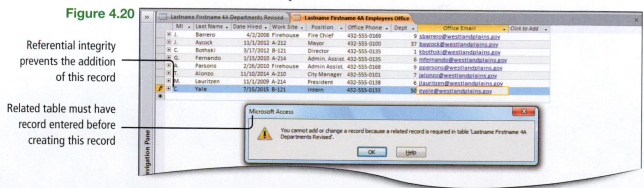

Figure 4.20

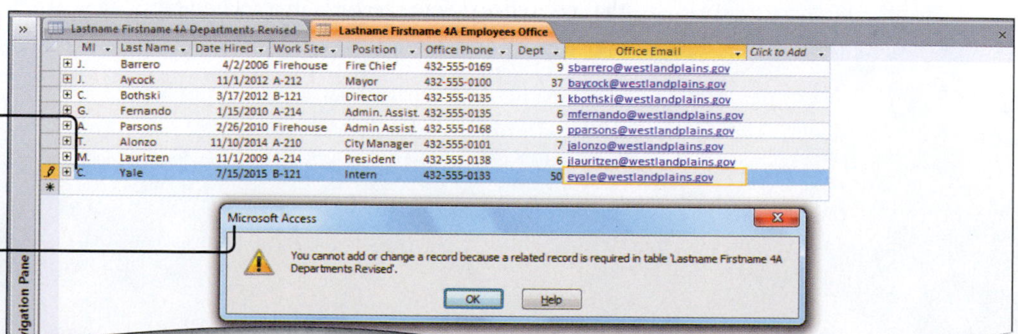

11 In the displayed message box, click **OK**. In the new record, under Dept, select **50** and then type **1**—the Department ID for Animal Control. **Close** the table.

The *4A Employees Office* table closes, and the *4A Departments Revised* table is active.

12 In the **4A Departments Revised** table, point to the record selector box for the fifth record—**City Council**—and then click to select the record. On the **Home tab**, in the **Records group**, click the **Delete** button.

A message displays stating that the record cannot be deleted or changed because of related records in the *4A Employees Office* table. Referential integrity protects an individual from deleting a record in one table that has related records in another table.

13 In the displayed message box, click **OK**. View the table in **Print Preview**. If you are instructed to submit this result, create a paper or electronic printout. **Close** the **4A Departments Revised** table.

Activity 4.12 | Setting and Testing Cascade Options

There might be a time that you need to make a change to the primary key field in a table on the *one* side of a relationship. For example, the employee ID may have been incorrectly entered into the database, and it needs to be changed for all records. You also may need to delete a record that has a related record in another table. When referential integrity is enforced, you cannot make these changes. For that reason, Access provides ***cascade options***—options that update records in related tables when referential integrity is enforced. This enables you to complete these tasks even when referential integrity is enforced. To use Cascade Options, referential integrity must be enforced.

1 On the Ribbon, click the **Database Tools tab**. In the **Relationships group**, click the **Relationships** button. Click the **join line** between the **4A Employees Office** field list and the **4A Employees Personal** field list. On the **Design tab**, in the **Tools group**, click the **Edit Relationships** button. Alternatively, right-click the join line, and then click Edit Relationships; or double-click the join line.

2 In the displayed **Edit Relationships** dialog box, select the **Cascade Update Related Fields** check box, and then click **OK**. **Close** the Relationships object, saving changes, and then **Open** [»] the **Navigation Pane**.

3 **Open** the **4A Employees Office** table. Recall that this table has a one-to-one relationship with the *4A Employees Personal* table. **Close** [«] the **Navigation Pane**.

4 Locate the record for **Empl ID 589764**. Between the record selector box and the Empl ID field, click the plus sign (+), and then compare your screen with Figure 4.21.

After you create a relationship between two tables, in Datasheet view, plus signs display next to every record of the table that is the one side of the relationship. Clicking the plus sign displays the ***subdatasheet***—record or records from the related table—and changes the plus sign to a minus sign (–). Clicking the minus sign collapses the subdatasheet.

Access | Chapter 4

Figure 4.21

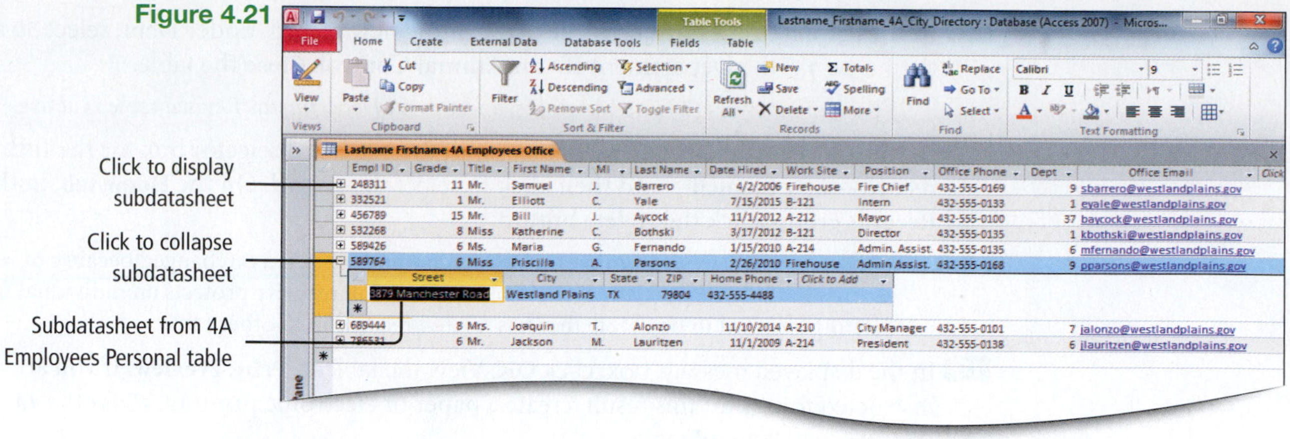

5 Click the minus sign (–) to collapse the related record. In the **Empl ID** field, select **589764**, type **123456** and then press [↓].

6 **Open** [»] the **Navigation Pane**. Open the **4A Employees Personal** table. Notice that the first record—the **Empl ID**—is now **123456**.

The ***Cascade Update*** option enables an individual to change a primary key field, and updates automatically follow in the records in the related tables.

7 **Close** [«] the **Navigation Pane**. In the **4A Employees Personal** table, click the plus sign (+) for the first record.

Because this table and the *4A Employees Office* table are joined with a one-to-one relationship, each table displays the subdatasheet for the other table. If tables are joined with a one-to-many relationship, the subdatasheet can be displayed only in the table on the *one* side of the relationship.

8 Collapse the subdatasheet for the first record, and then close the open tables. Click the **Database Tools tab**, and then in the **Relationships group**, click the **Relationships** button. Double-click the **join line** between the **4A Employees Office** field list and the **4A Employees Personal** field list to display the **Edit Relationships** dialog box.

To edit relationships, the tables must be closed.

Alert! | Is the Edit Relationships Dialog Box Empty?

If the names of the tables and fields do not display in the Edit Relationships dialog box, you may not have clicked the join line—instead, you probably clicked near the join line. Click Cancel and then begin again.

9 In the displayed **Edit Relationships** dialog box, select the **Cascade Delete Related Records** check box, and then click **OK. Close** the **Relationships tab. Open** [»] the **Navigation Pane.** Open the **4A Employees Personal** table, and then open the **4A Employees Office** table. **Close** [«] the **Navigation Pane.**

10 In the **4A Employees Office** table, locate the record for the **Empl ID** of **589426**, and then select the record. Delete the record—do not click a button in the displayed message box. Compare your screen with Figure 4.22.

A message displays stating that deleting this record in this table will cause records in the related tables to also be deleted.

Figure 4.22

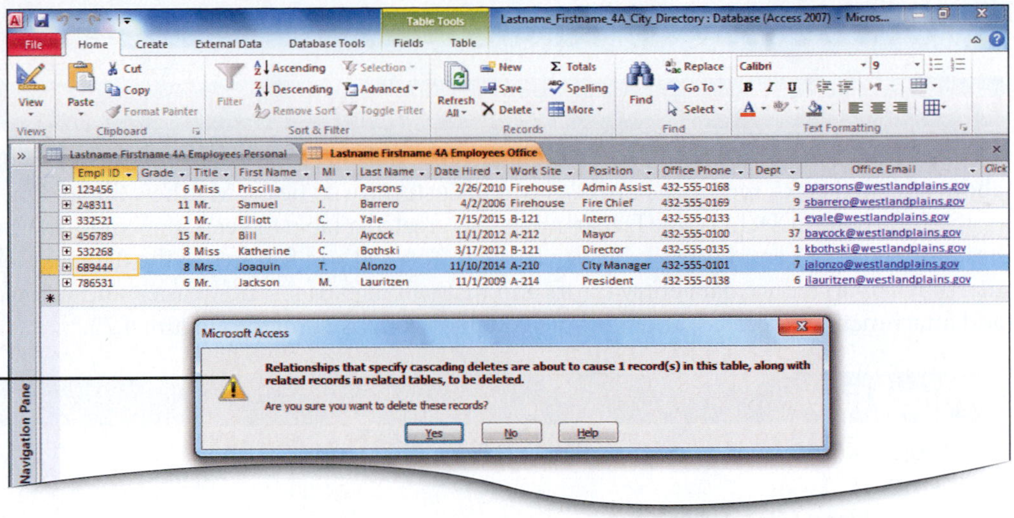

Cascade Delete Records causes this message to display

Note | Record Must Be Deleted in Correct Table for Cascade Update or Delete to Work

When the Cascade Delete option is selected, the record must be deleted from the table that is listed on the one side of the Edit Relationships dialog box. Deleting the record from the table listed on the many side of the Edit Relationships dialog box deletes the record from that table only. If the tables are joined in a one-to-one relationship, the record must be deleted from the table listed on the left primary key side in the Edit Relationships dialog box.

11 In the displayed message box, click **Yes**. Click the **4A Employees Personal** table to make it active. On the **Home tab**, in the **Records group**, click the **Refresh All** button.

Recall that if a table is open and changes are made to fields or records in a related object, the changes are not immediately displayed. Clicking the Refresh All button updates the view of the table, removing the deleted record—the record for Marla Fernando.

The ***Cascade Delete*** option enables you to delete a record in a table and delete all of the related records in related tables.

12 For the **4A Employees Personal** and **4A Employees Office** tables, adjust all column widths, ensuring that all of the field names and all of the data displays. View each table in **Print Preview**, and then change the orientation to **Landscape**. As necessary, adjust the margins to display each table on one page. If you are instructed to submit this result, create a paper or electronic printout.

13 **Close** all open objects. Display **Backstage** view, **Close** the database, and then **Exit** [X] Access.

More Knowledge | Delete a Table Relationship

To remove a table relationship, you must delete the join line in the Relationships window. Right-click the join line, and from the shortcut menu, click Delete. Alternatively, click the join line to select it, and then press Del. When you delete a relationship, you also delete referential integrity between the tables.

End You have completed Project 4A

Project 4B IT Tasks

myitlab
Project 4B Training

Project Activities

In Activities 4.13 through 4.24, you will create a table in Design view that stores records about assigned tasks, modify its properties, and customize its fields. Matthew Shoaf, Director of the Information Technology Department, has created a table to keep track of tasks that he has assigned to the employees in his department. You will add features to the database table that will help to reduce data entry errors and that will make data entry easier, and you will add attachments to records. Your completed table will look similar to Figure 4.23.

Project Files

For Project 4B, you will need the following files:

a04B_IT_Tasks
a04B_WorkOrder_1.docx
a04B_WorkOrder_2.docx

You will save your database as:

Lastname_Firstname_4B_IT_Tasks

Project Results

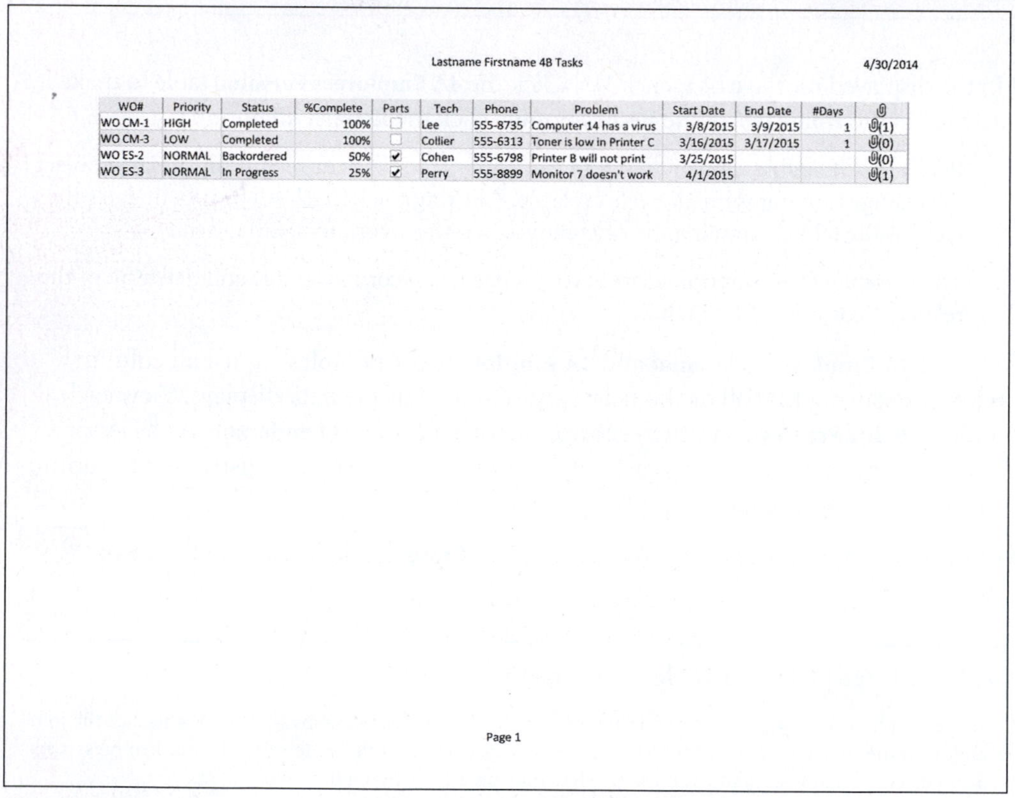
Lastname Firstname 4B Tasks 4/30/2014

WO#	Priority	Status	%Complete	Parts	Tech	Phone	Problem	Start Date	End Date	#Days	📎
WO CM-1	HIGH	Completed	100%	☐	Lee	555-8735	Computer 14 has a virus	3/8/2015	3/9/2015	1	📎(1)
WO CM-3	LOW	Completed	100%	☐	Collier	555-6313	Toner is low in Printer C	3/16/2015	3/17/2015	1	📎(0)
WO ES-2	NORMAL	Backordered	50%	✔	Cohen	555-6798	Printer B will not print	3/25/2015			📎(0)
WO ES-3	NORMAL	In Progress	25%	✔	Perry	555-8899	Monitor 7 doesn't work	4/1/2015			📎(1)

Page 1

Figure 4.23
Project 4B IT Tasks

Objective 4 | Create a Table in Design View

In this activity, you will create a second table in a database using Design view.

Activity 4.13 | Creating a Table in Design View

In this activity, you will create a table to keep track of the tasks that the IT department will be completing. Creating a table in Design view gives you the most control over the characteristics of the table and the fields. Most database designers use Design view to create tables, setting the data types and formats before entering any records. Design view is a good way to create a table when you know exactly how you want to set up your fields.

1 **Start** Access. Navigate to the location where the student data files for this textbook are saved. Locate and open the **a04B_IT_Tasks** file. **Save** the database in your **Access Chapter 4** folder as **Lastname_Firstname_4B_IT_Tasks**

2 If you did not add the Access Chapter 4 folder to the Trust Center, enable the content. In the **Navigation Pane**, under **Tables**, rename **4B Employees** by adding **Lastname Firstname** to the beginning of the table name. **Close** « the **Navigation Pane**.

3 On the Ribbon, click the **Create tab**. In the **Tables group**, click the **Table Design** button to open an empty table in Design view, and then compare your screen with Figure 4.24.

Figure 4.24

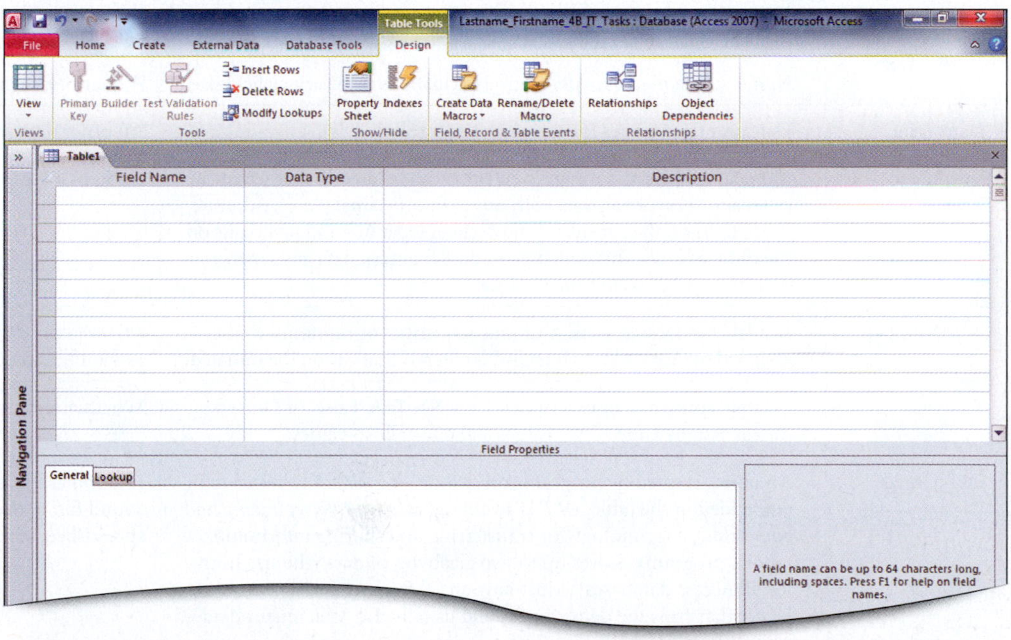

4 In the first **Field Name box**, type **WO#,** press Tab, and then on the **Design tab**, in the **Tools** group, click the **Primary Key** button. Press Tab.

5 Click the **Data Type arrow** to display a list of data types, as shown in Figure 4.25. Take a moment to study the table in Figure 4.26 that describes all 12 possible data types.

In Design view, all the data types are displayed. In Datasheet view, the list depends on the data entered in the field and does not display Lookup Wizard.

Access | Chapter 4

Figure 4.25

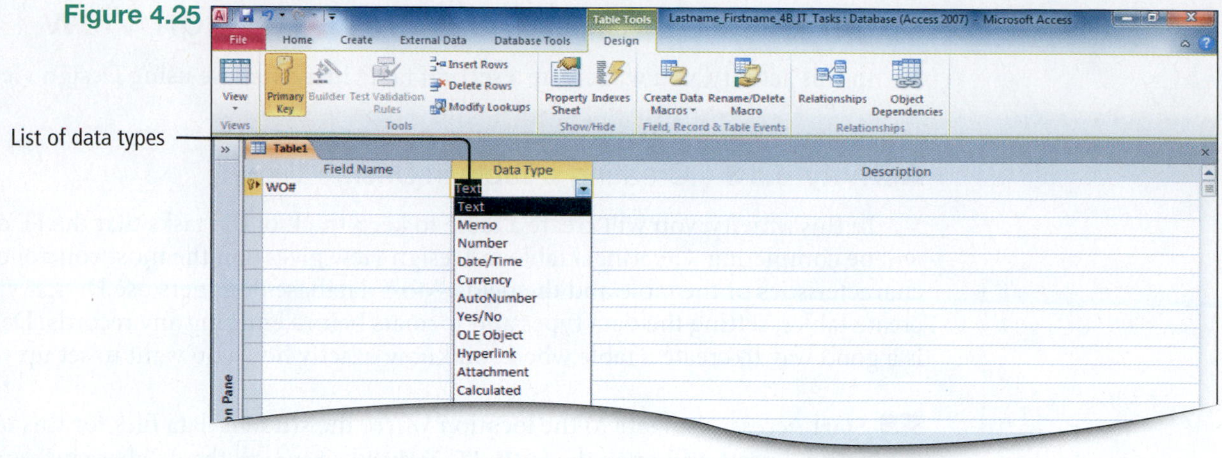

Data Types

Data Type	Description	Example
Text	Text or combinations of text and numbers; also, numbers that are not used in calculations. Limited to 255 characters or length set on field, whichever is less. Access does not reserve space for unused portions of the text field. This is the default data type.	An inventory item, such as towels, or a phone number or postal code that is not used in calculations and that may contain characters other than numbers.
Memo	Lengthy text or combinations of text and numbers that can hold up to 65,535 characters depending on the size of the database.	A description of a product.
Number	Numeric data used in mathematical calculations with varying field sizes.	A quantity, such as 500.
Date/Time	Date and time values for the years 100 through 9999.	An order date, such as 11/10/2012 3:30 p.m.
Currency	Monetary values and numeric data that can be used in mathematical calculations involving data with one to four decimal places. Accurate to 15 digits on the left side of the decimal separator and to 4 digits on the right side. Use this data type to store financial data and when you do not want Access to round values.	An item price, such as $8.50.
AutoNumber	Available in Design view. A unique sequential or random number assigned by Access as each record is entered that cannot be updated.	An inventory item number, such as 1, 2, 3, or a randomly assigned employee number, such as 3852788.
Yes/No	Contains only one of two values—Yes/No, True/False, or On/Off. Access assigns 1 for all Yes values and 0 for all No values.	Whether an item was ordered—Yes or No.
OLE Object	An object created by programs other than Access that is linked to or embedded in the table. *OLE* is an abbreviation for *object linking and embedding*, a technology for transferring and sharing information among programs. Stores up to two gigabytes of data (the size limit for all Access databases). Must have an OLE server registered on the server that runs the database. Should usually use Attachment data type instead.	A graphics file, such as a picture of a product, a sound file, a Word document, or an Excel spreadsheet stored as a bitmap image.
Hyperlink	Web or e-mail addresses.	An e-mail address, such as dwalker@ityourway.com, or a Web page, such as http://www.ityourway.com.
Attachment	Any supported type of file—images, spreadsheet files, documents, or charts. Similar to e-mail attachments.	Same as OLE Object.
Calculated	Available in Design view. Opens the Expression Builder to create an expression based on existing fields or numbers. Field must be designated as a Calculated field when it is inserted into the table; the expression can be editing in the Field Properties.	Adding two existing fields such as [field1]+[field2], or performing a calculation with a field and a number such as [field3]*5.
Lookup Wizard	Available in Design view. Not really a data type, but will display in the list of data types. Links to fields in other tables to display a list of data instead of having to manually type the data.	Link to another field in the same or another table.

Figure 4.26

6 From the displayed list, click **Text**, and then press Tab to move to the **Description** box. In the **Description** box, type **Identification number assigned to task reported on work order form**

Field names should be short; use the description box to display more information about the contents of the field.

7 Press F6 to move to the **Field Properties** pane at the bottom of the screen. In the **Field Size** box, type **8** to replace the 255. Compare your screen with Figure 4.27.

Pressing F6 while in the Data Type column moves the insertion point to the first field property box in the Field Properties pane. Alternatively, click in the Field Size property box.

Recall that a field with a data type of Text can store up to 255 characters. You can change the field size to limit the number of characters that can be entered into the field to promote accuracy. For example, if you use the two-letter state abbreviations for a state field, limit the size of the field to two characters. When entering a state in the field, you will be unable to type more than two characters.

Figure 4.27

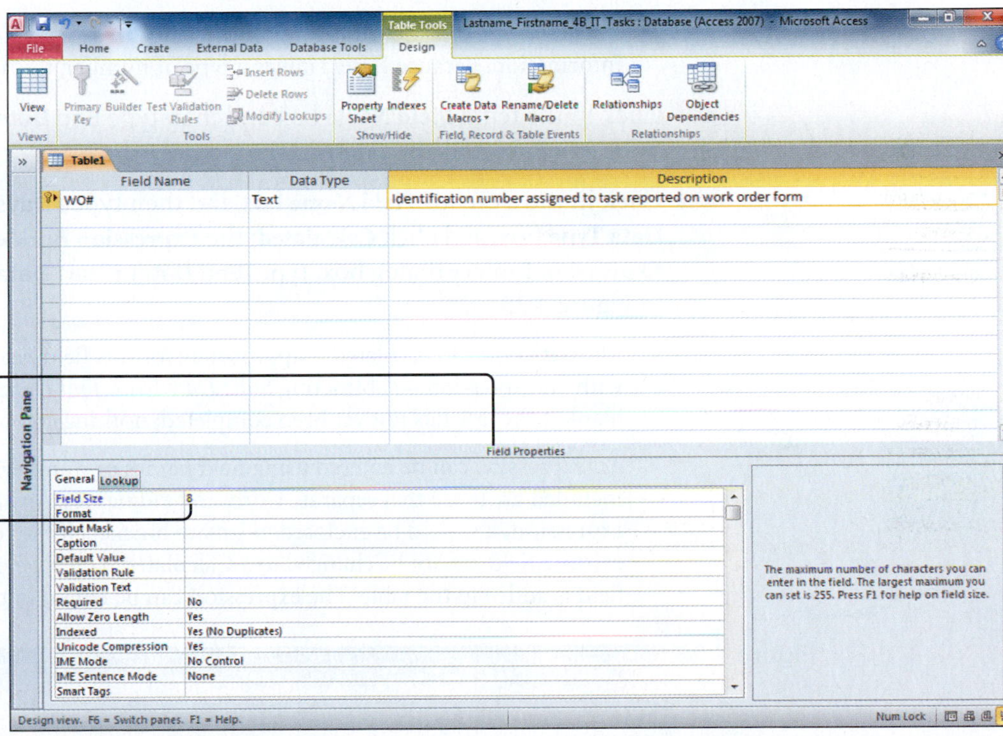

8 Click in the second **Field Name** box, type **Priority** and then press Tab twice to move to the **Description** box. Type **Indicate the priority level for this task** Press F6 to move to the **Field Properties** pane at the bottom of the screen. Click in the **Format** box and type **>**

Because Text is the default data type, you do not have to select it if it is the correct data type for the field.

A greater than symbol (>) in the Format property box in a Text field converts all entries in the field to uppercase. Using a less than symbol (<) would force all entries to be lowercase.

9 In the third **Field Name** box, type **Status** and then press Tab three times to move to the next Field Name box.

If the field name is descriptive enough, the Description box is optional.

10 In the fourth **Field Name** box, type **%Complete** Press Tab twice to move to the **Description** box, and type **Percentage of the task that has been completed**

Access | Chapter 4

11 In the fifth **Field Name** box, type **Parts** Press [Tab] to move to the **Data Type** box, and click **Yes/No**. Press [Tab] to move to the **Description** box. Type **Click the field to indicate parts have been ordered to complete the task**

The data type of Yes/No is appropriate for this field because there are only two choices, parts are on order (yes) or parts are not on order (no). In **Datasheet view,** click the check box to indicate yes with a checkmark.

12 In the sixth **Field Name** box, type **Tech** and then press [Tab] three times to move to the next Field Name box.

13 In the seventh **Field Name** box, type **Phone** Press [Tab] two times to move to the **Description** box, type **Enter as ###-####** and then change the **Field Size** property to **8**

14 Click in the eighth **Field Name** box, and then type **Problem** Press [Tab] twice to move to the **Description** box, and then type **Description of the IT problem**

15 Click in the ninth **Field Name** box, and then type **Start Date** Press [Tab] to move to the **Data Type** box, and click **Date/Time**.

The data type of Date/Time is appropriate for this field since it will only display date information. Because Date/Time is a type of number, this field can be used in calculations.

16 Click in the tenth **Field Name** box and then type **End Date** Press [Tab] to move to the **Data Type** box, and click **Date/Time**.

17 Click in the eleventh **Field Name** box and then type **#Days** Press [Tab] to move to the **Data Type** box, and click **Calculated**; the **Expression Builder** dialog box appears. In the **Expression Builder** dialog box, type **[End Date]-[Start Date]** and compare your screen to Figure 4.28.

The data type of Calculated is appropriate for this field because the entry is calculated with an expression—subtracting *Start Date* from *End Date*. The *# Days* field will remain blank if the task has not yet been completed; nothing can be entered in the field.

An expression can be entered using field names or numbers where the only spaces included are those that separate words in field names. Any time a field name is used in the expression, it should be enclosed in square brackets if the field name includes spaces. An existing field cannot be changed to a Calculated data type; it must be assigned when the field is added to the table. The expression can be edited in the Field Properties.

Figure 4.28

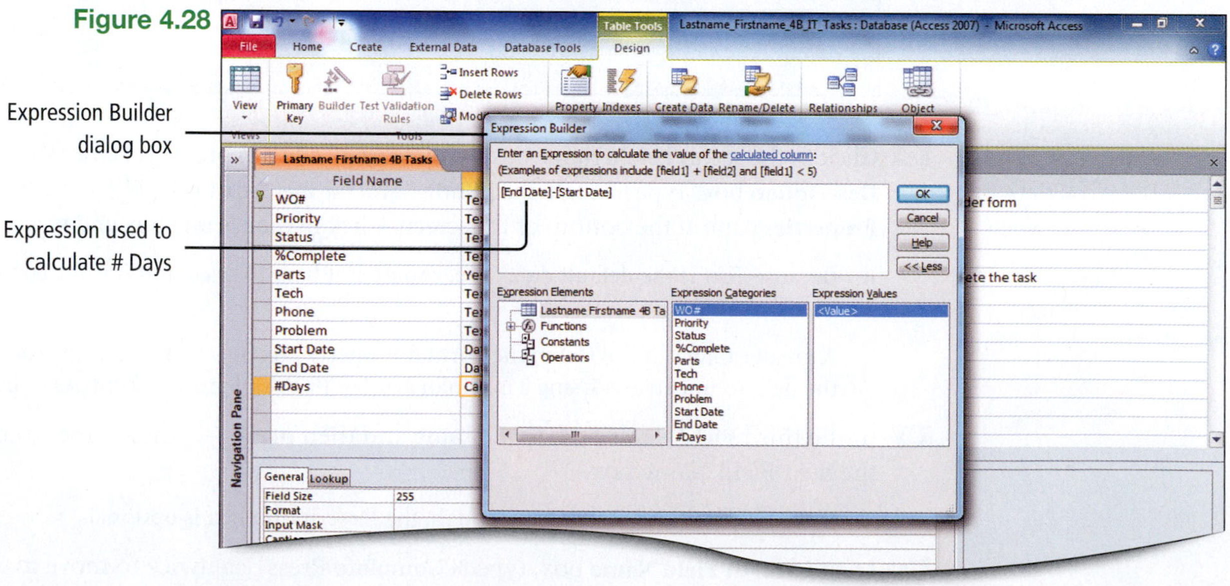

18 Click **OK.** In the **Description** box, type **Number of days necessary to complete the task** Press F6 to move to the **Field Properties** pane at the bottom of the screen. Click in the **Result Type** property, and select **Integer.** Click in the **Format** property, and select **Fixed.** Click in the **Decimal Places** property, and select **0.**

19 Display **Backstage** view, click **Save** to display the **Save As** dialog box. Under **Table Name**, type **Lastname Firstname 4B Tasks** and then click **OK**. Switch to **Datasheet** view to view the table you have just created; there are no records in the table yet.

Objective 5 | Change Data Types

Before creating a table, it is important to decide on the data types for the fields in the table. Setting a specific data type helps to ensure that the proper data will be entered into a field; for example, it is not possible to enter text into a field with a Currency data type. It is also important to choose a number data type when it is appropriate to avoid problems with calculations and sorting.

Activity 4.14 | Changing Data Types

Once data is entered into a field, caution must be exercised when changing the data type—existing data may not be completely visible or may be deleted. You can change the data type in either Datasheet view or Design view.

1 With the **4B Tasks** table open, switch to **Design** view. Change the **Data Type** for the **%Complete** field to **Number.** Press F6 to move to the **Field Properties** pane at the bottom of the screen. Click in the **Result Type**, and select **Single.** Click in the **Format** property and select **Percent.** Set the **Decimal Places** property to **0.**

The data type of Number is more appropriate for this field since it will display only the amount of a task that has been completed. Defining the number as a percent with zero decimal places further restricts the entries. This will allow the field to be accurately used in calculations, comparisons, and sorts.

2 Change the data type for the **Problem** field to **Memo.**

The data type of Memo is more appropriate for this field since it may require more than 255 characters and spaces to effectively describe the IT problem that needs attention.

3 **Save** the changes, and then compare your screen with Figure 4.29.

Figure 4.29

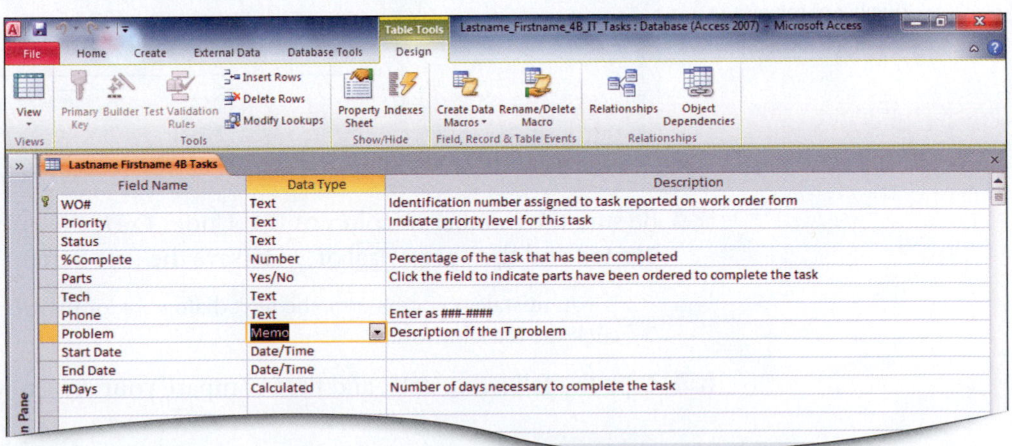

Objective 6 | Create a Lookup Field

Creating a ***lookup field*** can restrict the data entered in a field because the person entering data selects that data from a list retrieved from another table, query, or list of entered values. The choices can be displayed in a ***list box***—a box containing a list of choices—or a ***combo box***—a box that is a combination of a list box and a text box. You can create a lookup field by using the Lookup Wizard or manually by setting the field's lookup field properties. Whenever possible, use the Lookup Wizard because it simplifies the process, ensures consistent data entry, automatically populates the associated field properties, and creates the needed table relationships.

Activity 4.15 | Creating a Lookup Field Based on a List of Values

In this activity, you will create a lookup field for the Status field.

1 With the **4B Tasks** table open in **Design** view, in the **Status** field, click in the **Data Type** box, and then click the **arrow**. From the displayed list of data types, click **Lookup Wizard**. If a Windows Access Security Notice displays, click **Open**.

2 In the first **Lookup Wizard** dialog box, click the **I will type in the values that I want** option button, and then click **Next**. Compare your screen with Figure 4.30.

The first step of the Lookup Wizard enables you to choose whether you want Access to locate the information from another table or query or whether you would like to type the information to create a list.

The second step enables you to select the number of columns you want to include in the lookup field. The values are typed in the grid, and you can adjust the column width of the displayed list.

Figure 4.30

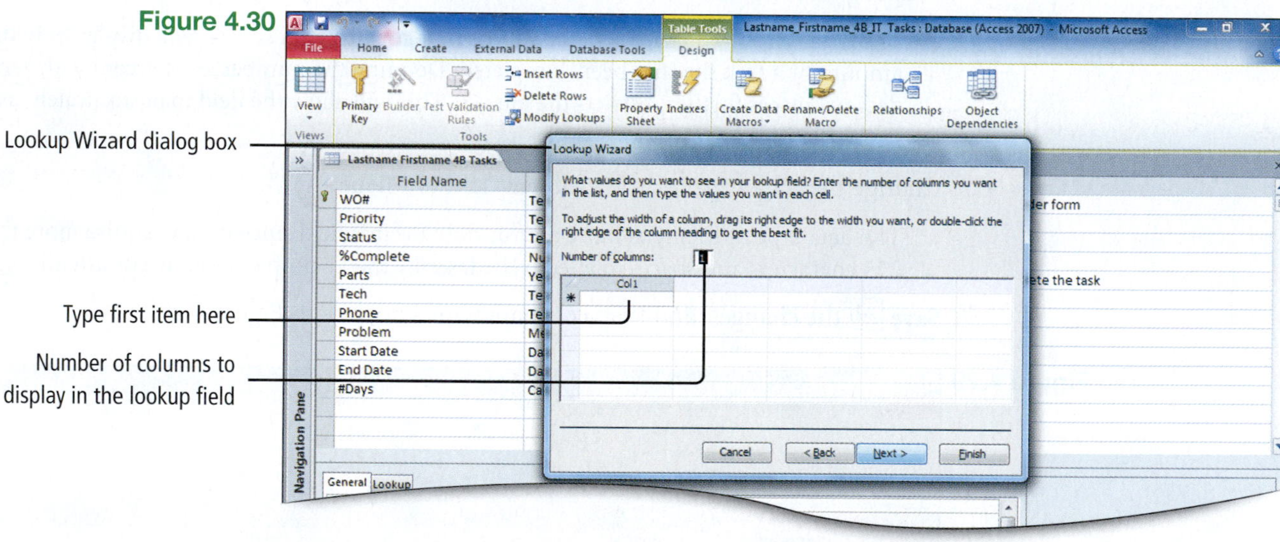

3 Be sure the number of columns is **1**. Under **Col1**, click in the first row, type **Not Started** and then press Tab or ↓ to save the first item.

If you mistakenly press Enter, the next dialog box of the wizard displays. If that happens, click the Back button.

4 Type the following data, and then compare your screen with Figure 4.31.

In Progress
Completed
Deferred to someone else

Figure 4.31

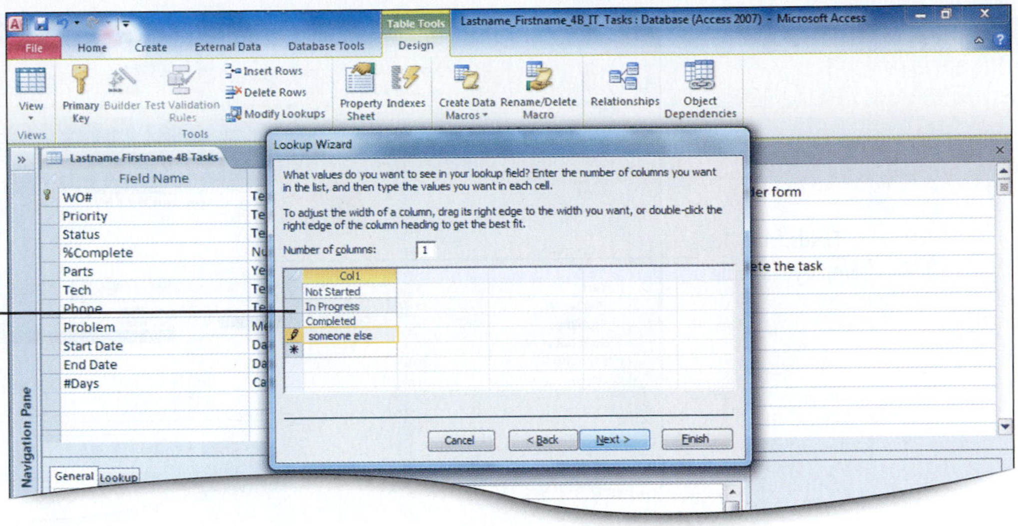

5 Double-click the right edge of **Col1** to adjust the column width so all entries display, and then click **Next**. In the final dialog box, click **Finish**. With the **Status** field selected, under **Field Properties**, click the **Lookup tab**.

The Lookup Wizard populates the Lookup property boxes. The *Row Source Type* property indicates that the data is retrieved from a Value List, a list that you created. The *Row Source* property displays the data you entered in the list. The *Limit to List* property displays No, so you can type alternative data in the field.

6 **Save** the changes, and switch to **Datasheet** view. Click the **Status** field in the first record, and then click the drop-down arrow to view the lookup list. Press Esc to return to a blank field.

> **Alert! | Is the Last Item in the List Truncated?**
>
> If the last item in the list—Deferred to someone else—is truncated, switch to Design view. Select the field. Under Field Properties, on the Lookup tab, click in the List Width box, and then increase the width of the list box by typing a larger number than the one displayed.

Activity 4.16 | Creating a Lookup Field Based on Data in Another Table

In this activity, you will create a lookup field for the Assigned to field.

1 In the **4B Tasks** table, switch to **Design** view. In the **Tech** field, click in the **Data Type** box, and then click the **Data Type arrow**. From the displayed list of data types, click **Lookup Wizard**.

2 In the first **Lookup Wizard** dialog box, be sure that the **I want the lookup field to get the values from another table or query** option button is selected.

3 Click **Next**. The **4B Employees table** is selected.

4 Click **Next** to display the third **Lookup Wizard** dialog box. Under **Available Fields**, click **Last Name**, and then click the **Add Field** (>) button to move the field to the **Selected Fields** box. Move the **First Name** and **Job Title** fields from the **Available Fields** box to the **Selected Fields** box. Compare your screen with Figure 4.32.

Because there might be several people with the same last name, the First Name field and the Job Title field are included.

Figure 4.32

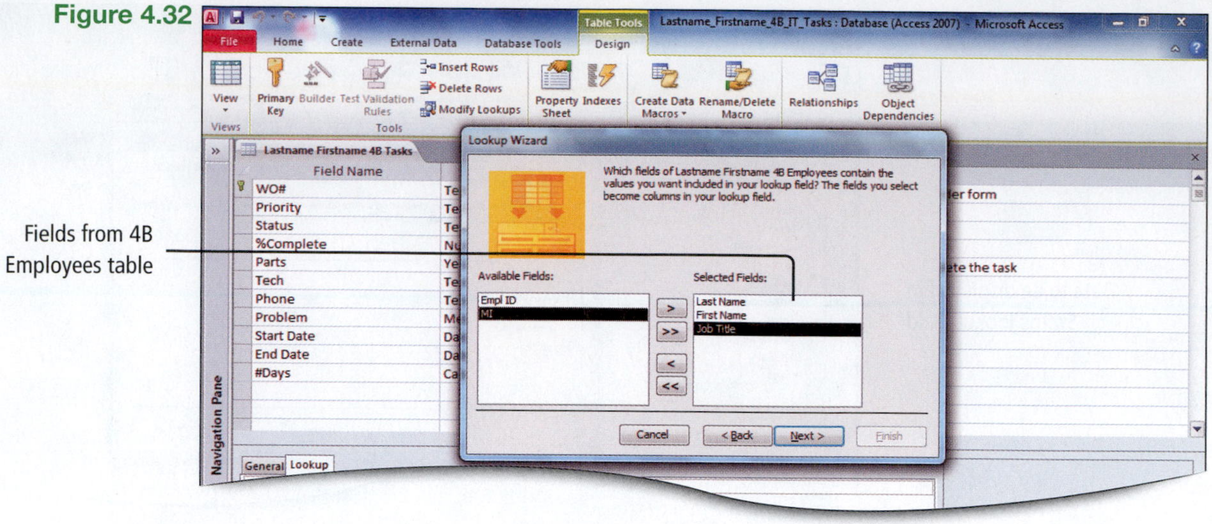

5 Click **Next** to display the fourth **Lookup Wizard** dialog box. In the **1** box, click the **arrow**, and then click **Last Name**. In the **2** box, click the **arrow**, and then click **First Name**. In the **3** box, click the **arrow**, and then click **Job Title**. Leave all three sort orders as **Ascending**.

The list will first display last names in ascending order. If there are duplicate last names, then the duplicate last names will then be sorted by the first name in ascending order. If there are duplicate last names and first names, then those names will be sorted in ascending order by the job title.

6 Click **Next** to display the fifth **Lookup Wizard** dialog box. This screen enables you to change the width of the lookup field and to display the primary key field. Be sure the **Hide key column (recommended)** check box is selected, and then click **Next** to display the sixth and final **Lookup Wizard** dialog box.

The actual data that is stored in the lookup field is the data in the primary key field.

7 Under **What label would you like for your lookup field?**, leave the default of **Tech** and be sure that **Allow Multiple Values** is *not* selected.

Because you have already named the field, the default name is appropriate. If you were creating a new field that had not yet been named, a label would be entered on this screen. If you want to allow the selection of more than one last name when the lookup field displays and then store the multiple values, select the Allow Multiple Values check box, which changes the lookup field to a multivalued field. A ***multivalued field*** holds multiple values, such as a list of people to whom you have assigned the same task.

8 Click **Finish**. A message displays stating that the table must be saved before Access can create the needed relationship between the *4B Tasks* table and the *4B Employees* table. Click **Yes**.

9 With the **Tech** field selected, under **Field Properties**, click the **Lookup tab**.

The Lookup Wizard populates the Lookup properties boxes. The *Row Source Type* property indicates that the data is retrieved from a Table or Query. The *Row Source* property displays the SQL statement that is used to retrieve the data from the fields in the *4B Employees* table. The *Limit to List* property displays Yes, which means you must select the data from the list and cannot type data in the field.

10 Click the **General tab** to display the list of general field properties.

Objective 7 | Set Field Properties

A ***field property*** is an attribute or characteristic of a field that controls the display and input of data. You previously used field properties to change the size of a field and to specify a specific format for data types. When you click in any of the property boxes, a description of the property displays to the right. Available field properties depend upon the data type of each field.

Activity 4.17 | Creating an Input Mask Using the Input Mask Wizard

An ***input mask*** is a field property that determines the data that can be entered, how the data displays, and how the data is stored. For example, an input mask can require individuals to enter telephone numbers in a specific format like (757) 555-1212. If you enter the telephone number without supplying an area code, you will be unable to save the record until the area code is entered. Input masks provide ***data validation***—rules that help prevent individuals from entering invalid data—and help ensure that individuals enter data in a consistent manner. By default, you can apply input masks to fields with a data type of Text, Number, Currency, and Date/Time. The Input Mask Wizard can be used to apply input masks to fields with a data type of Text or Date/Time only.

1 Under **Field Name**, click **Phone**. Under **Field Properties**, click in the **Input Mask** box. At the right side of the Field Properties, notice the description given for this property. In the **Input Mask** box, click the **Build** button. If a Windows Access Security Notice displays, click **Open**. Compare your screen with Figure 4.33.

The Build button displays after you click in a field property box so you can further define the property. The Input Mask Wizard starts, which enables you to create an input mask using one of several standard masks that Access has designed, such as Phone Number, Social Security Number, Zip Code, and so on. Clicking in the Try It box enables you to enter data to test the input mask.

Figure 4.33

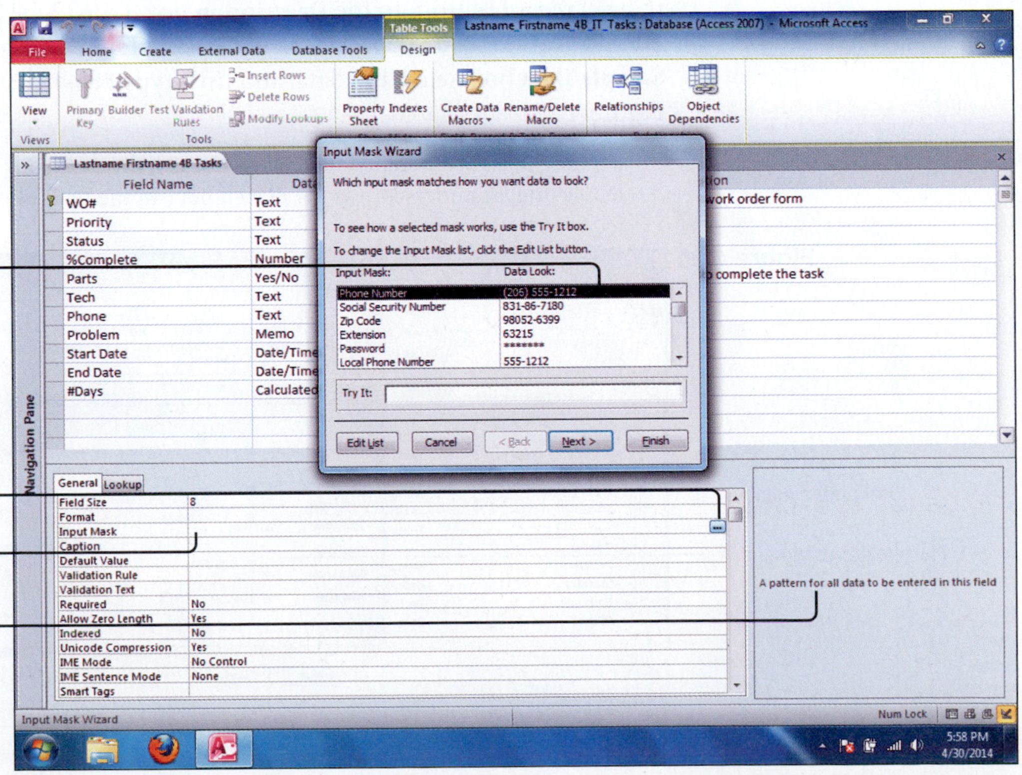

2 In the displayed **Input Mask Wizard** dialog box, with **Phone Number** selected, click **Next**, and then compare your screen with Figure 4.34. In the **Input Mask Wizard** dialog box, notice the entry in the **Input Mask** box.

A *0* indicates a required digit; a *9* indicates an optional digit or space. The area code is enclosed in parentheses, and a hyphen (-) separates the three-digit prefix from the four-digit number. The exclamation point (!) causes the input mask to fill in from left to right. The Placeholder character indicates that the field will display an underscore character (_) for each digit before data is entered in Datasheet view.

Figure 4.34

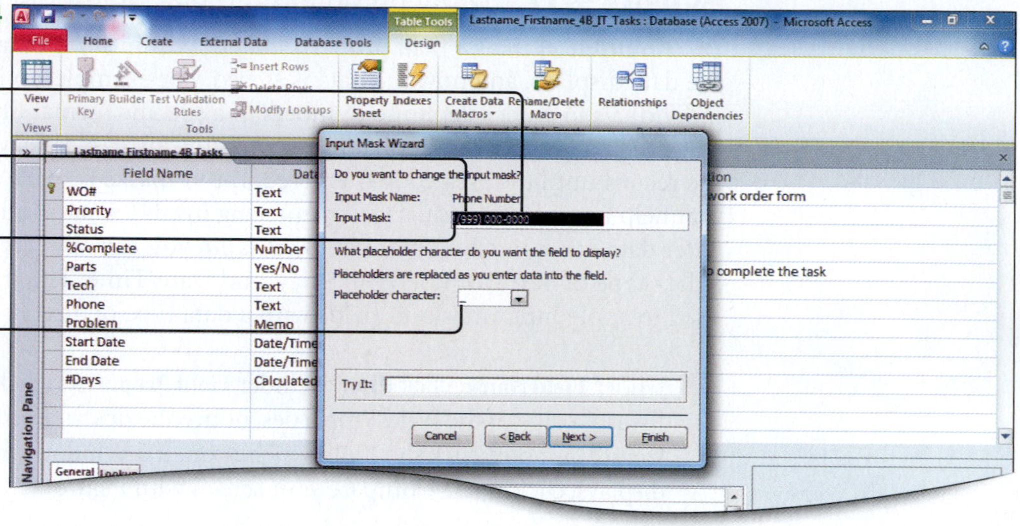

3 In the **Input Mask Wizard** dialog box, click **Back**, and then click **Edit List**.

The Customize Input Mask Wizard dialog box displays, which enables you to edit the default input mask or add an input mask.

4 In the **Customize Input Mask Wizard** dialog box, in the navigation area, click the **New (blank) record** button. In the **Description** box, type **Local Phone Number** In the **Input Mask** box, type **!000-0000** Click in the **Placeholder** box, and change _ to **#** Click in the **Sample Data** box, select the data, and then type **555-1212** Compare your screen with Figure 4.35.

Because tasks are assigned to local personnel, the area code is unnecessary. Instead of displaying an underscore as the placeholder in the field, the number sign (#) displays.

Figure 4.35

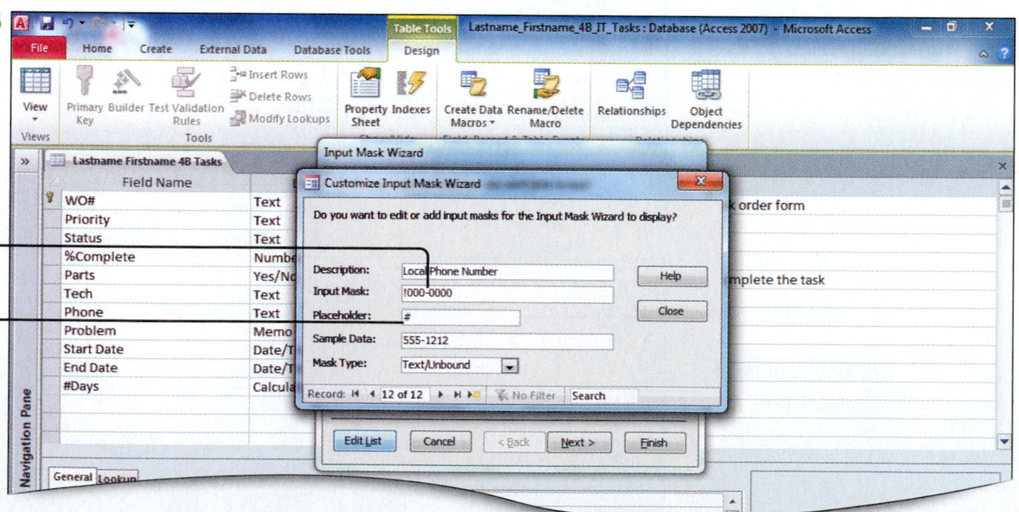

5 In the **Customize Input Mask Wizard** dialog box, click **Close**.

The newly created input mask for Local Phone Number displays below the input mask for Password.

6 Under **Input Mask**, click **Local Phone Number**, and then click **Next**. Click the **Placeholder character arrow** to display other symbols that can be used as placeholders. Be sure that # is displayed as the placeholder character, and then click **Next**.

After creating an input mask to be used with the Input Mask Wizard, you can change the placeholder character for individual fields.

7 The next wizard screen enables you to decide how you want to store the data. Be sure that the **Without the symbols in the mask, like this** option button is selected, as shown in Figure 4.36.

Saving the data without the symbols makes the database size smaller.

Figure 4.36

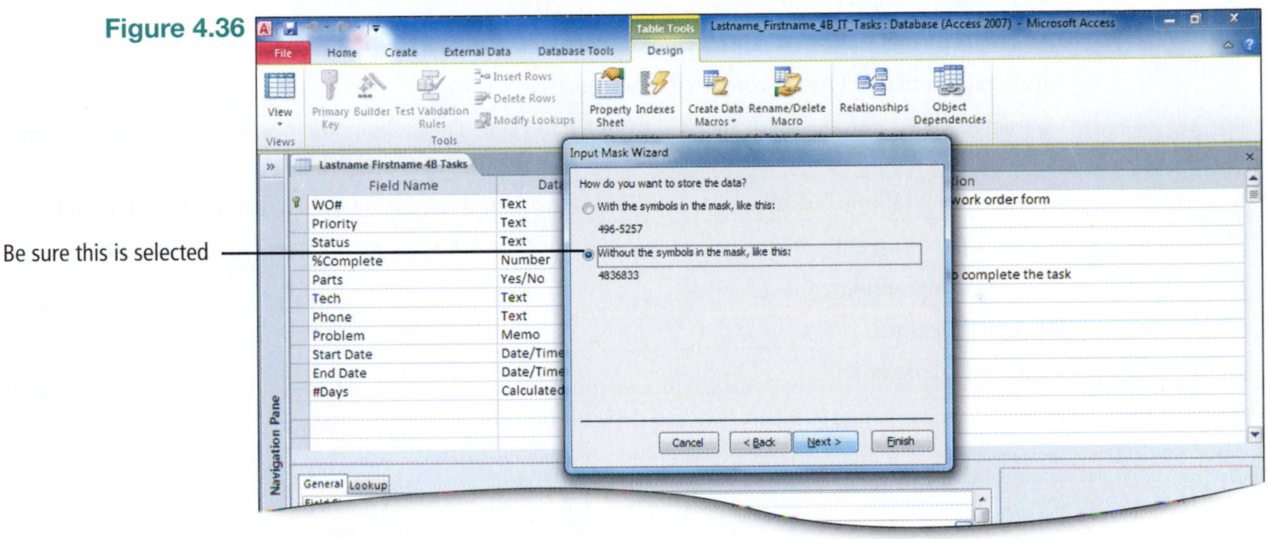

8 Click **Next**. In the final wizard screen, click **Finish**. Notice that the entry in the **Input Mask** box displays as **!000\-0000;;#**. **Save** the table.

Recall that the exclamation point (!) fills the input mask from left to right, and the 0s indicate required digits. The two semicolons (;) are used by Access to separate the input mask into three sections. This input mask has data in the first section—the 0s—and in the third section—the placeholder of #.

The second and third sections of an input mask are optional. The second section, which is not used in this input mask, determines whether the literal characters—in this case, the hyphen (-)—are stored with the data. A *0* in the second section will store the literal characters; a *1* or leaving it blank stores only the characters entered in the field. The third section of the input mask indicates the placeholder character—in this case, the # sign. If you want to leave the fill-in spaces blank instead of using a placeholder, type " "—there is a space between the quotation marks—in the third section.

9 Take a moment to study the table shown in Figure 4.37, which describes the characters that can be used to create a custom input mask.

Access | Chapter 4

Most Common Input Mask Characters

Character	Description
0	Required digit (0 through 9).
9	Optional digit or space.
#	Optional digit, space, plus sign, or minus sign; blank positions are converted to spaces.
L	Required letter (A through Z).
?	Optional letter.
A	Required digit or letter.
a	Optional digit or letter.
&	Any character or space; required.
C	Any character or space; optional.
<	All characters that follow are converted to lowercase.
>	All characters that follow are converted to uppercase.
!	Characters typed into the mask are filled from left to right. The exclamation point can be included anywhere in the input mask.
\	Character that follows is displayed as text. This is the same as enclosing a character in quotation marks.
Password	Creates a password entry box that displays asterisks (*) as you type. Access stores the characters.
“ ”	Used to enclose displayed text.
.	Decimal separator.
,	Thousands separator.
: ; - /	Date and time separators. Character used depends on your regional settings.

Figure 4.37

Activity 4.18 | Creating an Input Mask Using the Input Mask Properties Box

In addition to using the wizard, input masks can be created directly in the Input Mask Properties box. In this activity, you will use the Input Mask Properties box to create a mask that will ensure the Work Order # is entered according to departmental policy. An example of a work order number used by the Information Technology department is WO CM-46341. WO is an abbreviation for Work Order. CM represents the initials of the person entering the work order data. A hyphen separates the initials from a number assigned to the work order.

1 With the **4B Tasks** table displayed in **Design** view, click in the **WO#** field. Under **Field Properties**, click in the **Input Mask** box, type **WO**, press Spacebar, type **>LL-99** and then compare your screen with Figure 4.38.

The letters *WO* and a space will display at the beginning of every Work Order # (WO#). The greater than (>) sign converts any text following it to uppercase. Each *L* indicates that a letter (not a number) is required. A hyphen (-) follows the two letters, and the two 9s indicate optional numbers.

Take a moment to study the examples of input masks shown in Figure 4.39.

Figure 4.38

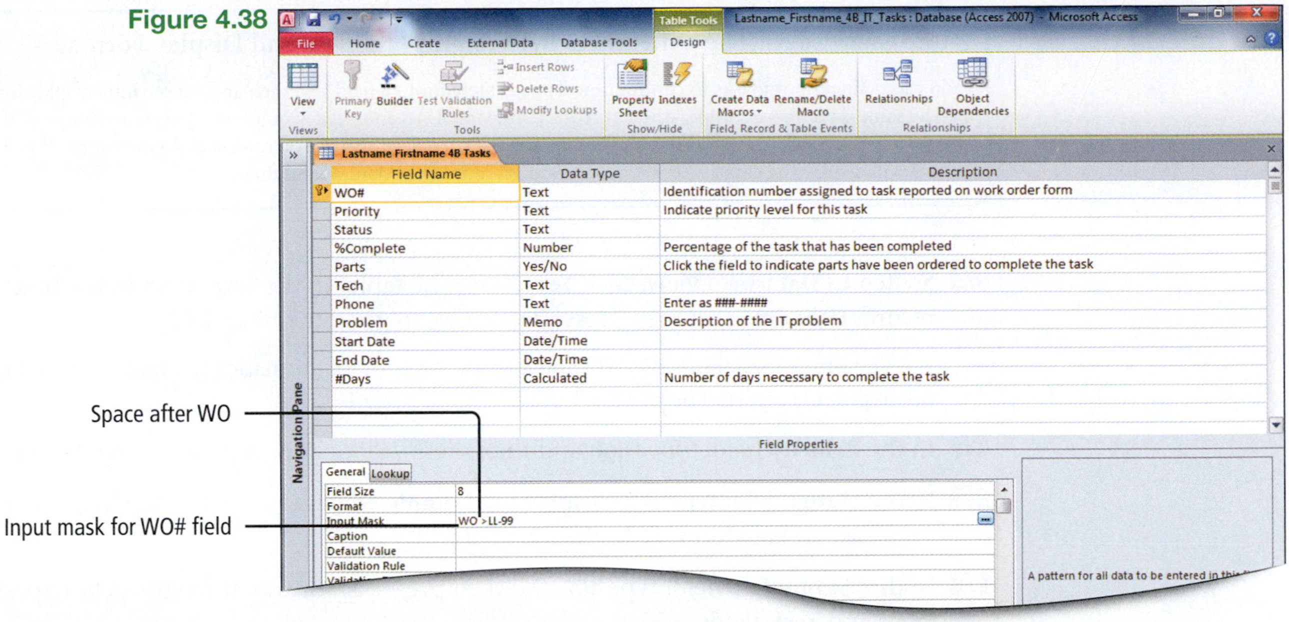

Examples of Input Masks

Input Mask	Sample Data	Description
(000) 000-0000	(206) 555-5011	Must enter an area code because of the 0s enclosed in parentheses.
(999) 000-0000!	(206) 555-6331 ( )555-6331	Area code is optional because of the 9s enclosed in parentheses. Exclamation point causes mask to fill in from left to right.
(000) AAA-AAAA	(206) 555-TELE	Enables you to substitute the last seven digits of a U.S.–style phone number with letters. Area code is required.
#999	-20 2009	Can accept any positive or negative number of no more than four characters and no thousands separator or decimal places.
>L????L?000L0	GREENGR339M3 MAY R 452B7	Allows a combination of required (L) and optional (?) letters and required numbers (0). The greater than (>) sign changes letters to uppercase.
00000-9999	23703- 23703-5100	Requires the five-digit postal code (0) and optional plus-four section (9).
>L<??????????????	Elizabeth Rose	Enables up to 15 letters in which the first letter is required and is capitalized; all other letters are lowercase.
ISBN 0-&&&&&&&&&-0	ISBN 0-13-232762-7	Allows a book number with text of ISBN, required first and last digits, and any combination of characters between those digits.
>LL00000-0000	AG23703-0323	Accepts a combination of two required letters, both uppercase, followed by five required numbers, a hyphen, and then four required numbers. Could be used with part or inventory numbers.

Figure 4.39

2 Click in the **Start Date** field to make the field active. Under **Field Properties**, click in the **Format** box, and then click the **arrow**. From the displayed list, click **Short Date**. Also set the format of **End Date** to **Short Date**.

Access | Chapter 4

More Knowledge | The Differences Between Input Masks and Display Formats

You can define input masks to control how data is entered into a field and then apply a separate display format to the same data. For example, you can require individuals to enter dates in a format such as 30 Dec. 2016 by using an input mask of DD MMM. YYYY. By using the Format property, you can specify a format of Short Date, which will display the data as 12/30/2016, regardless of how the data was entered.

3 Switch to **Datasheet** view, click **Yes** to save the table. In the **WO#** field in the first record, type **cm1** and then press Tab or Enter to go to the next field.

The input mask adds the WO and a space. The cm is automatically capitalized, and the hyphen is inserted before the 1.

4 In the **Priority** field, type **High** and then press Tab or Enter to go to the next field.

5 In the **Status** field, type **C** to display the **Completed** item in the lookup list, and then press Tab or Enter to move to the next field.

6 In the **%Complete** field, type **100** and then press Tab or Enter three times to bypass the **Parts** and **Tech** fields.

Leaving the Yes/No field blank assigns a No value in the Parts field, so parts are not on order for this task.

7 In the **Phone#** field, type 5558735 and then press Tab or Enter to move to the next field.

8 In the **Problem** field, type **Computer 14 has a virus** and then press Tab or Enter to move to the next field.

9 In the **Start Date** field, type **3/8/2015** and then press Tab or Enter to move to the next field.

10 In the **End Date** field, type **3/9/15** and then press Tab or Enter to move to the **#Days** field. Notice the calculated field now displays a 1.

11 Switch to **Design** view. The data entry is automatically saved when the record is complete.

Activity 4.19 | Specifying a Required Field

Recall that if a table has a field designated as the primary key field, an entry for the field is ***required***; it cannot be left empty. You can set this requirement on other fields in either Design view or Datasheet view. In this activity, you will require an entry in the Status and Tech fields. Use the Required field property to ensure that a field contains data and is not left blank.

1 Click in the **Status** field, and then under **Field Properties**, click in the **Required** box. Click the **Required arrow**, and then compare your screen with Figure 4.40.

Only Yes and No options display in the list.

Figure 4.40

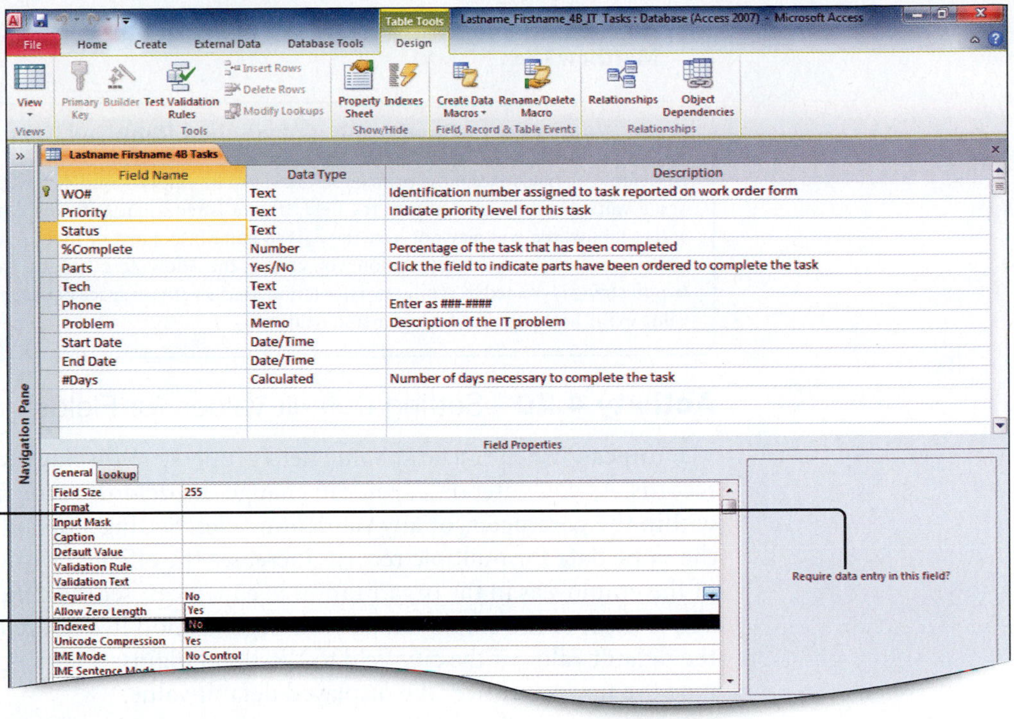

2 Click **Yes** to require an individual to enter the status for each record. **Save** the changes to the table.

A message displays stating that data integrity rules have been changed and that existing data may not be valid for the new rules. This message displays when you change field properties where data exists in the field. Clicking Yes requires Access to examine the field in every record to see if the existing data meets the new data validation rule. For each record Access finds where data does not meet the new validation rule, a new message displays that prompts you to keep testing with the new setting. You also can revert to the prior validation setting and continue testing or cancel testing of the data.

3 If the message is displayed, click **No**. Switch to **Datasheet** view. Click in the **Status** field. On the **Fields tab**, in the **Field Validation** group, notice that the **Required** check box is selected.

4 In the table, click in the **Tech** field, and then on the **Fields tab**. In the **Field Validation** group, click the **Required** check box. Compare your screen with Figure 4.41.

A message displays stating that the existing data violates the Required property for the Tech field because the field is currently blank.

Figure 4.41

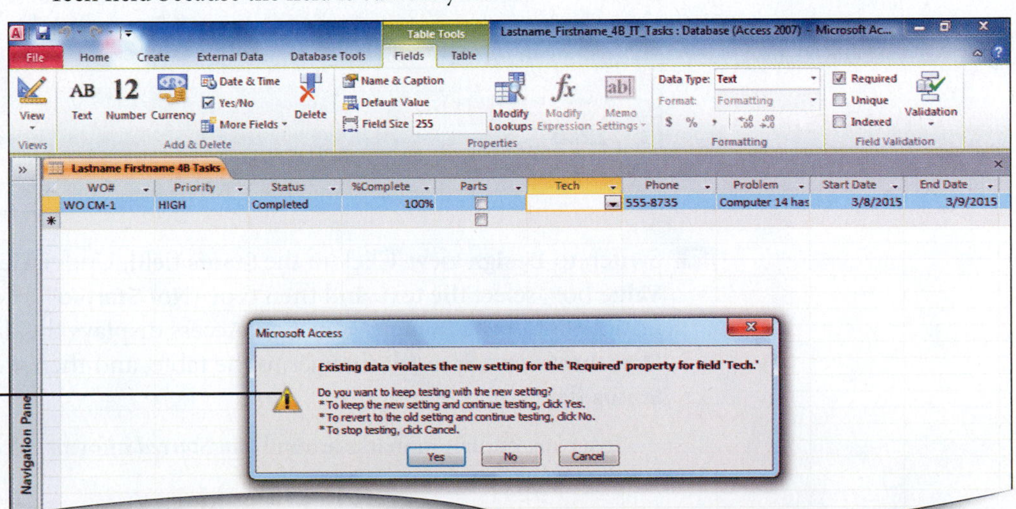

5 In the message box, click **Cancel**. Click the **arrow** at the right of the **Tech** field and select **Matthew Lee**.

> **More Knowledge | Allowing Blank Data in a Required Text or Memo Field**
>
> By default, all fields except the primary key field can be empty—null. If the Required property for a field is set to Yes, a value must be entered into the field. If data is required, Access will not save the record until a value is entered; however, you may not have the data to enter into a text or memo field where the Required property is set to Yes. To allow for this situation, you can set the Allow Zero Length property for the field to Yes. A ***zero-length string*** is created by typing two quotation marks with no space between them (""), which indicates that no value exists for a required text or memo field.

Activity 4.20 | Setting Default Values for Fields

You can use the Default Value field property to display a value in a field for new records. As you enter data, you can change the ***default value*** in the field to another value within the parameters of any validation rules. Setting a default value for fields that contain the same data for multiple records increases the efficiency of data entry. For example, if all of the employees in the organization live in Texas, set the default value of the state field to TX. If most of the employees in your organization live in the city of Westland Plains, set the default value of the city field to Westland Plains. If an employee lives in another city, type the new value over the displayed default value.

1 Switch to **Design** view. Under **Field Name**, click the **Priority** field. Under **Field Properties**, click in the **Default Value** box, and then type **Low** Switch to **Datasheet** view, and then **Save** changes to the table. Notice that the **Priority** field displays *LOW* in the New Record row.

Setting a default value does not change the data in saved records; the default value will display in new records and will be saved only if nothing else is typed in the field.

2 Switch back to **Design** view. Using the technique you just practiced, for the **Status** field, set the **Default Value** property to **Not Started** For the **%Complete** field, set the **Default Value** property to **0**

3 For the **Start Date** field, set the **Default Value** to **1/1/10** Switch to **Datasheet** view, and then **Save** changes to the table. Compare your screen with Figure 4.42.

The Status field shows a default value of *Not "Started"*. *Not* is an Access logical operator; therefore, Access excluded the word *Not* from the text expression.

Figure 4.42

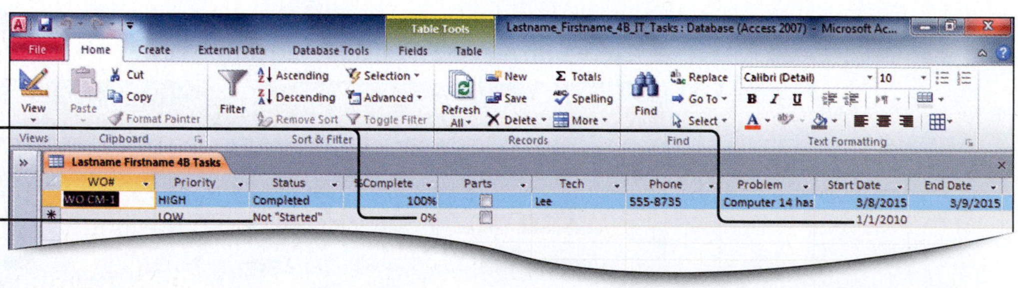

4 Switch to **Design** view. Click in the **Status** field. Under **Field Properties**, in the **Default Value** box, select the text, and then type **"Not Started"** Click in the **Start Date** field, and notice that in the **Default Value** box, Access displays the date as **#1/1/2010#**. Switch to **Datasheet** view, **Save** changes to the table, and then view the default value in the **Status** field.

Inserting quotation marks around *Not Started* informs Access that both words are part of the text expression.

> **More Knowledge** | **Using the Current Date as a Default Value**
>
> To use the current date as the default value for a Date/Time field, in the Default Value box, type date().

Activity 4.21 | Indexing Fields in a Table

An ***index*** is a special list created in Access to speed up searches and sorting—such as the index at the back of a book. The index is visible only to Access and not to you, but it helps Access find items much faster. You should index fields that you search frequently, fields that you sort, or fields used to join tables in relationships. Indexes, however, can slow down the creation and deletion of records because the data must be added to or deleted from the index.

1 Switch to **Design** view. Under **Field Name**, click **WO#**. Under **Field Properties**, locate the **Indexed** property box, and notice the entry of **Yes (No Duplicates)**.

By default, primary key fields are indexed. Because WO# is the primary key field, the field is automatically indexed, and no duplicate values are permitted in this field.

2 Under **Field Name**, click **Tech**. Under **Field Properties**, click in the **Indexed** property box, and then click the displayed **arrow**. Compare your screen with Figure 4.43.

Three options display for the Indexed property—No, Yes (Duplicates OK), and Yes (No Duplicates).

Figure 4.43

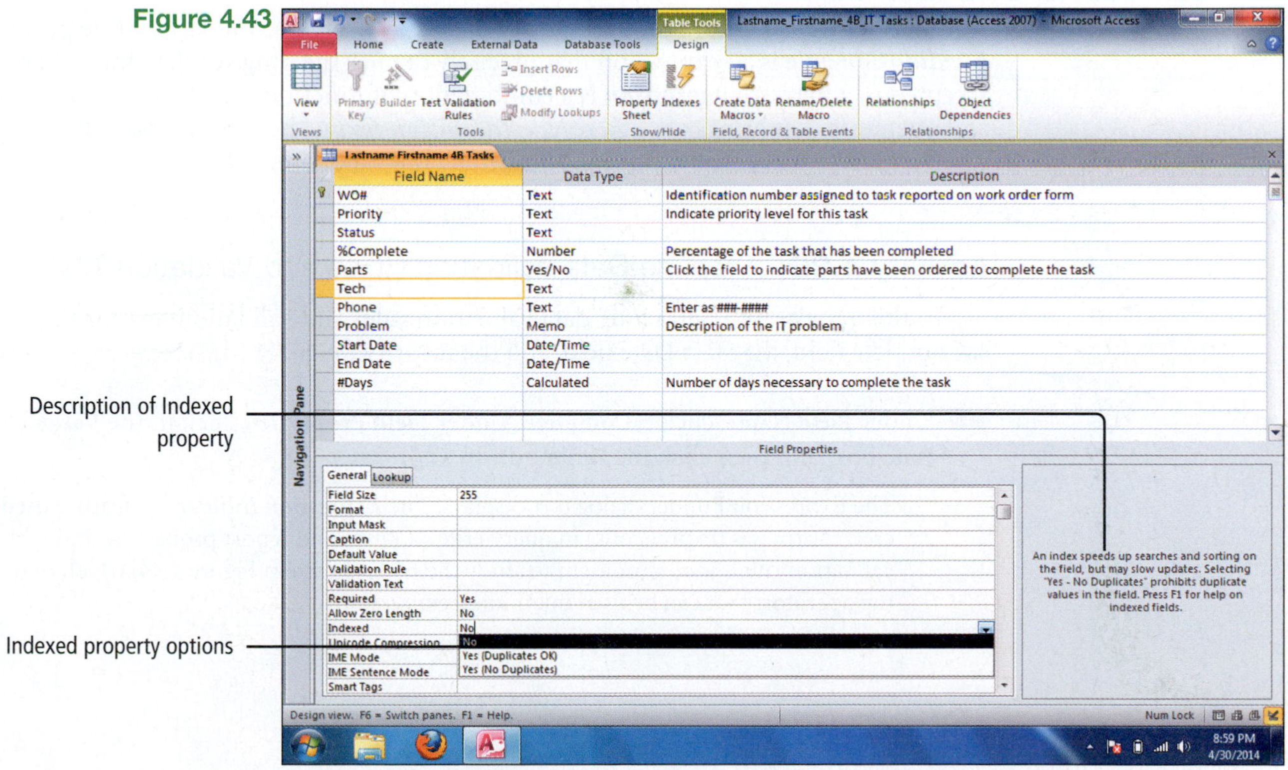

3 Click **Yes (Duplicates OK)**.

By adding an index to the field and allowing duplicates, you create faster searches and sorts on this field, while allowing duplicate data. Because a person may be assigned more than one task, allowing duplicate data is appropriate.

4 **Save** the table design.

5 On the **Design tab**, in the **Show/Hide group**, click the **Indexes** button.

An Indexes dialog box displays the indexes in the current table. Opening the Indexes dialog box is an efficient way to determine the fields that have been indexed in a table.

6 In the **Indexes: 4B Tasks** dialog box, click the **Close** button.

More Knowledge | About the Caption Property

The Caption property is used to give a name to fields used on forms and reports. Many database administrators create field names in tables that are short and abbreviated. In a form or report based on the table, a more descriptive name is desired. The value in the Caption property is used in label controls on forms and reports instead of the field name. If the Caption property is blank, the field name is used in the label control. A caption can contain up to 2,048 characters.

Objective 8 | Create Data Validation Rules and Validation Text

You have practiced different techniques to help ensure that data entered into a field is valid. Data types restrict the type of data that can be entered into a field. Field sizes control the number of characters that can be entered into a field. Field properties further control how data is entered into a field, including the use of input masks to require individuals to enter data in a specific way.

Another way to ensure the accuracy of data is by using the Validation Rule property. A ***validation rule*** is an expression that precisely defines the range of data that will be accepted in a field. An ***expression*** is a combination of functions, field values, constants, and operators that brings about a result. ***Validation text*** is the error message that displays when an individual enters a value prohibited by the validation rule.

Activity 4.22 | Creating Data Validation Rules and Validation Text

In this activity, you will create data validation rules and validation text for the %Complete field, the Start Date field, and the Priority field.

1 Under **Field Name**, click **%Complete**. Under **Field Properties**, click in the **Validation Rule** box, and then click the **Build** button.

The Expression Builder dialog box displays. The ***Expression Builder*** is a feature used to create formulas (expressions) in query criteria, form and report properties, and table validation rules. Take a moment to study the table shown in Figure 4.44, which describes the operators that can be used in building expressions.

Operators Used in Expressions

Operator	Function	Example
Not	Tests for values NOT meeting a condition.	**Not** > 10 (the same as <=10)
In	Tests for values equal to existing members in a list.	**In** ("High","Normal","Low")
Between...And	Tests for a range of values, including the vales on each end.	**Between** 0 **And** 100 (the same as >=0 **And** <=100)
Like	Matches pattern strings in Text and Memo fields.	**Like** "Car*"
Is Not Null	Requires individuals to enter values in the field. If used in place of the Required field, you can create Validation Text that better describes what should be entered in the field.	**Is Not Null** (the same as setting Required property to Yes)
And	Specifies that all of the entered data must fall within the specified limits.	>=#01/01/2014# **And** <=#03/01/2014# (Date must be between 01/01/2014 and 03/01/2014) Can use And to combine validation rules. For example, **Not** "USA" **And Like** "U*"
Or	Specifies that one of many entries can be accepted	"High" **Or** "Normal" **Or** "Low"
<	Less than.	<100
<=	Less than or equal to.	<=100
>	Greater than.	>0
>=	Greater than or equal to.	>=0
=	Equal to.	=Date()
<>	Not equal to.	<>#12/24/53#

Figure 4.44

Another Way

When using the Expression Builder to create an expression, you can either type the entire expression or, on the small toolbar in the dialog box, click an existing button, such as the > button, to insert operators in the expression.

2 In the upper box of the **Expression Builder** dialog box, type **>=0 and <=1** Alternatively, type the expression in the **Validation Rule** property box. In the **Expression Builder** dialog box, click **OK**.

The %Complete field has a data type of Number and is formatted as a percent. Recall that the Format property changes the way the stored data displays. To convert the display of a number to a percent, Access multiplies the value by 100 and appends the percent sign (%). Therefore, 100% is stored as 1—Access multiples 1 by 100, resulting in 100. A job that is halfway completed—50%—has the value stored as .5 because .5 times 100 equals 50.

3 Click in the **Validation Text** box, and then type **Enter a value between 0 and 100** so that the percentages are reflected accurately. Compare your screen with Figure 4.45.

Figure 4.45

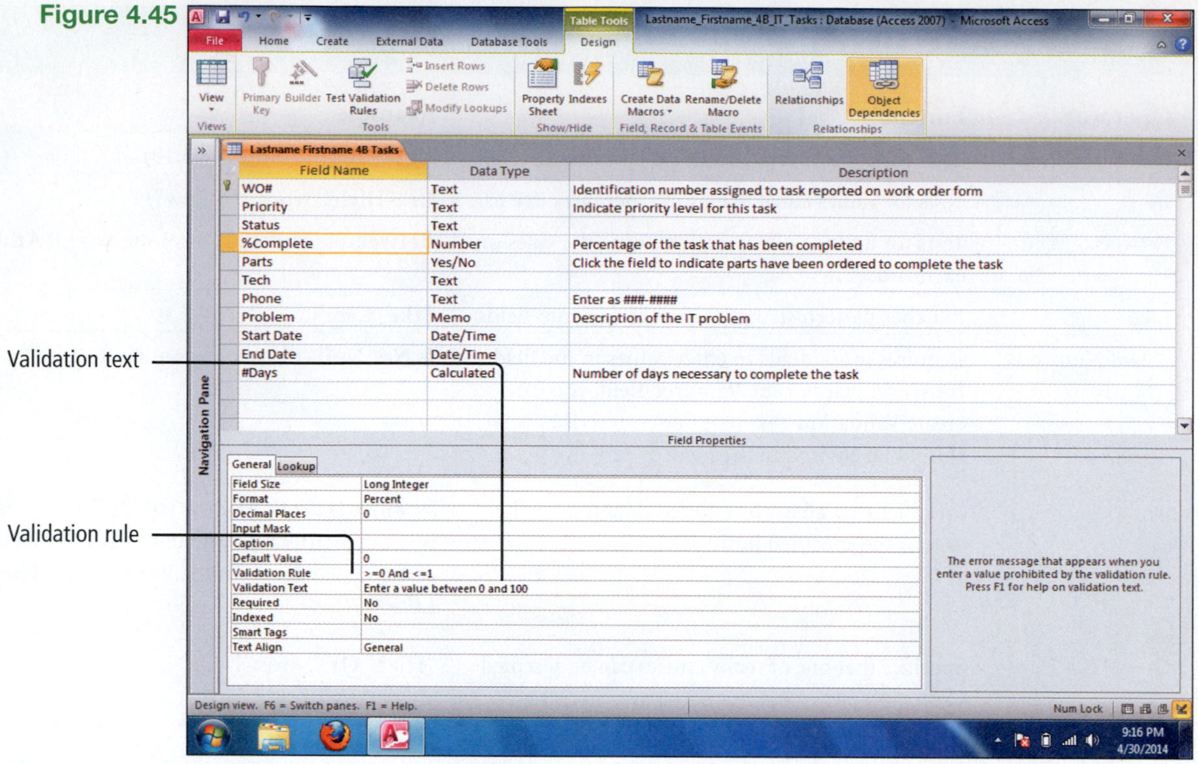

4 Under **Field Name**, click **Start Date** to make the field active. Under **Field Properties**, click in the **Validation Rule** box, and then type **>=1/1/2010** Click in the **Validation Text** box, and then type **Enter a date 1/1/2010 or after** Compare your screen with Figure 4.46.

In expressions, Access inserts a number or pound sign (#) before and after a date. This validation rule ensures that the person entering data cannot enter a date prior to 1/1/2010.

Figure 4.46

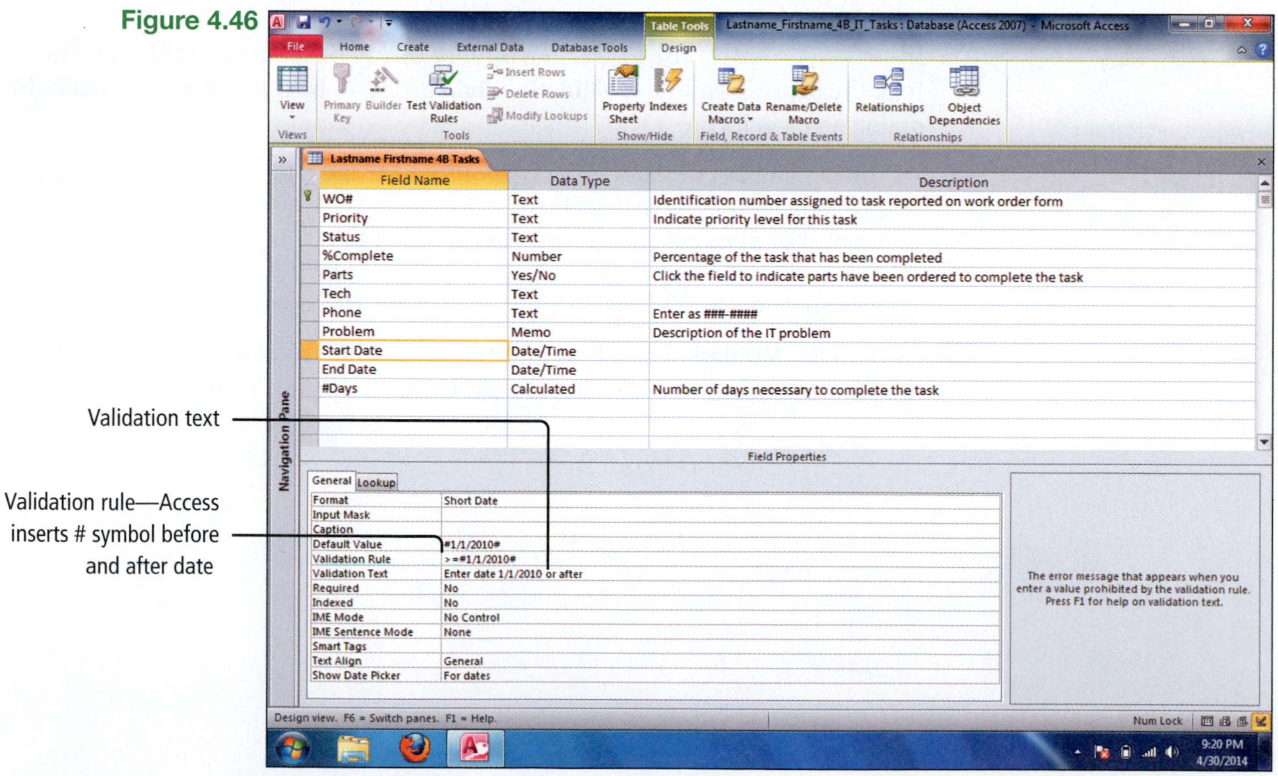

5 Under **Field Name**, click **Priority**. Under **Field Properties**, click in the **Validation Rule** box, and then type **in ("High","Normal","Low")** Click in the **Validation Text** box, and then type **You must enter High, Normal, or Low** Compare your screen with Figure 4.47.

The operators are not case sensitive; Access will capitalize the operators when you click in another property box. With the *In* operator, the members of the list must be enclosed in parentheses, and each member must be enclosed in quotation marks and separated from each other by commas. Another way to specify the same validation rule is: "High" Or "Normal" Or "Low".

Figure 4.47

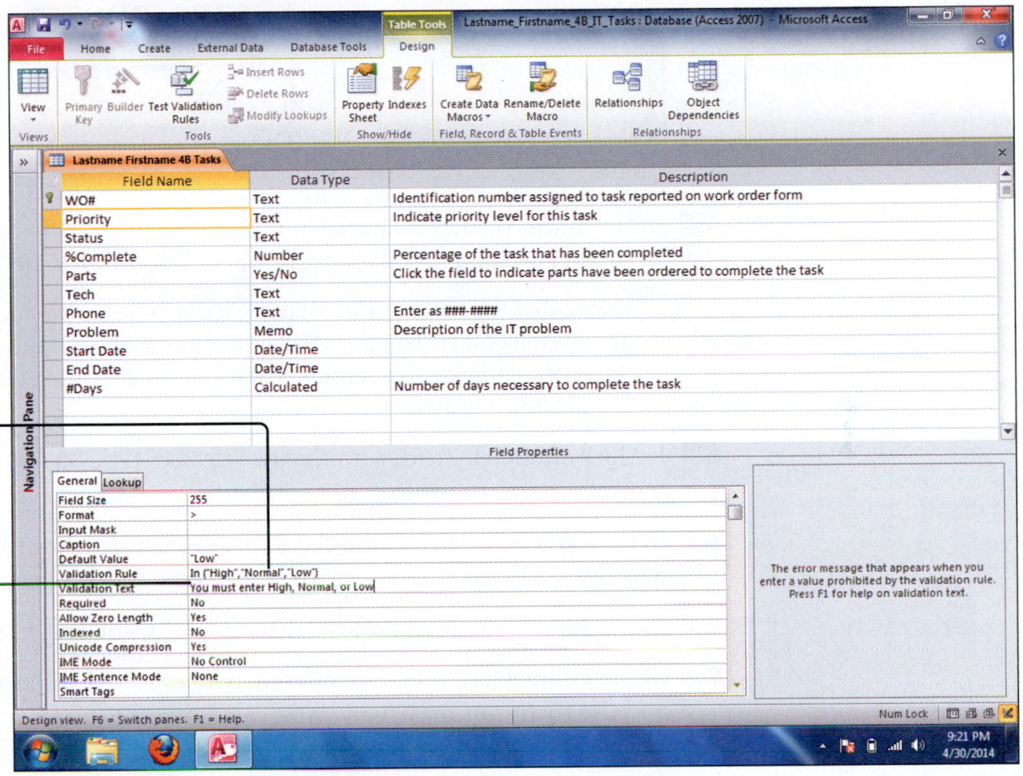

6 **Save** the changes to the table. Switch to **Datasheet** view.

A message displays stating that data integrity rules have changed. Even though you have clicked No in previous message boxes, click **Yes**. In a large database, you should click Yes to have Access check the data in all of the records before moving on.

Activity 4.23 | Testing Table Design and Field Properties

In this activity, you will add additional records to the *4B Tasks* table to test the design and field properties.

1 With the **4B Tasks** table open in **Datasheet** view, in the second record in the **WO#** field, type **es2** and then press Tab or Enter to go to the next field.

2 In the **Priority** field, type **Medium** to replace the default entry *Low*, and then press Tab or Enter to go to the next field. The message *You must enter High, Normal, or Low* appears on your screen because the validation rule limits the entry in this field. Compare your screen with Figure 4.48. Click OK and type **Normal** in the **Priority** field to replace *Medium*. Press Tab or Enter to go to the next field.

Figure 4.48

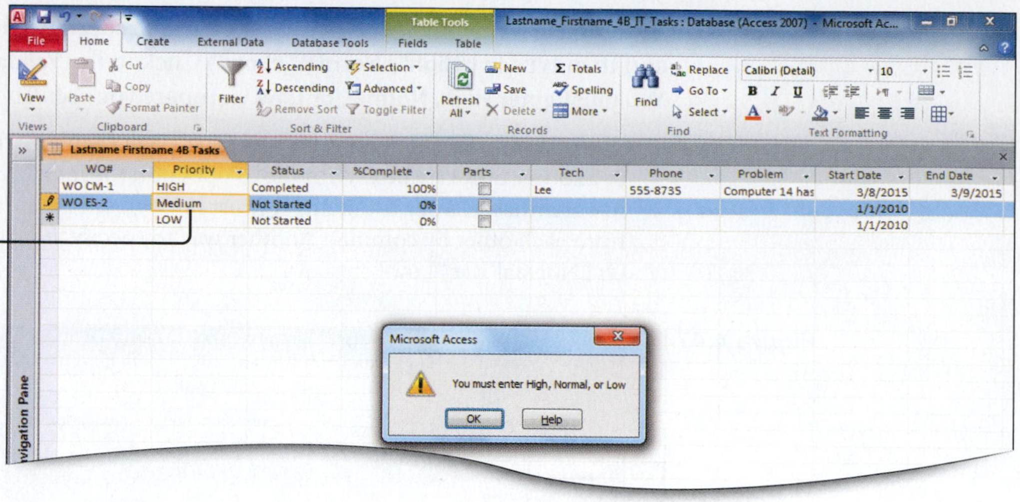

Validation rule prohibits entry of medium

3 In the **Status** field, **Not Started** automatically appears because it is the default entry. Type **Backordered** and then press Tab or Enter to move to the next field.

Recall that the Limit to List property setting is set to No for the lookup field, enabling you to type data other than that displayed in the list box. If the purpose of the lookup field is to restrict individuals to entering only certain data, then the Limit to List property setting should be set to Yes.

4 In the **%Complete** field, with the **0%** selected, type **50** and then press Tab or Enter to move to the next field

5 In the **Parts** field, click in the check box or press Spacebar to add a checkmark to indicate parts are on order to complete the task. Press Tab or Enter to move to the next field.

Another Way

You can locate an entry in a long list faster if you type the first letter of the data for which you are searching. For example, if you are searching for a last name that begins with the letter *M*, when the list displays, type *m* or *M*. The selection will move down to the first entry that begins with the letter.

6 In the **Tech** field, select **Susan Cohen**. Press Tab or Enter to move to the next field.

7 In the **Phone** field, type **aaa** and notice that Access will not allow a letter entry because the input mask you just created requires numbers in this field. Type **5556798** and then press Tab or Enter to move to the next field.

8 In the **Problem** field, type **Printer B will not print** Press Tab or Enter to move to the next field.

9 In the **Start Date** field, type **3/25/2015** Press Tab or Enter three times to move past **#Days** and move to the next record.

Notice the calendar icon that appears to the right of the date fields. Clicking the icon enables you to choose a date from a calendar.

End Date is not a required field, so it accepts a blank entry. Because End Date is blank, there is nothing to calculate in the Task Duration field.

10 In the third record, in the **WO#** field, type **cm3** and then press Tab or Enter twice to move to the **Status** field.

11 In the **Status** field, select **Completed**. Press Tab or Enter to move to the next field.

12 In the **%Complete** field, with the *0%* selected, type **110** and then press Tab or Enter to move to the next field.

A message, *Enter a value between 0 and 100*, appears on your screen because the validation rule limits the entry in this field.

13 Select the *110%* and type **100** Press Tab or Enter twice move to the **Tech** field.

14 In the **Tech** field, type **Rukstad** Press Tab or Enter to move to the next field. Compare your screen with Figure 4.49.

A message *The text you entered isn't an item in the list* appears on your screen. Recall that the Limit to List property setting is set to Yes for the lookup field, which restricts you from entering anything that is not on the list.

Figure 4.49

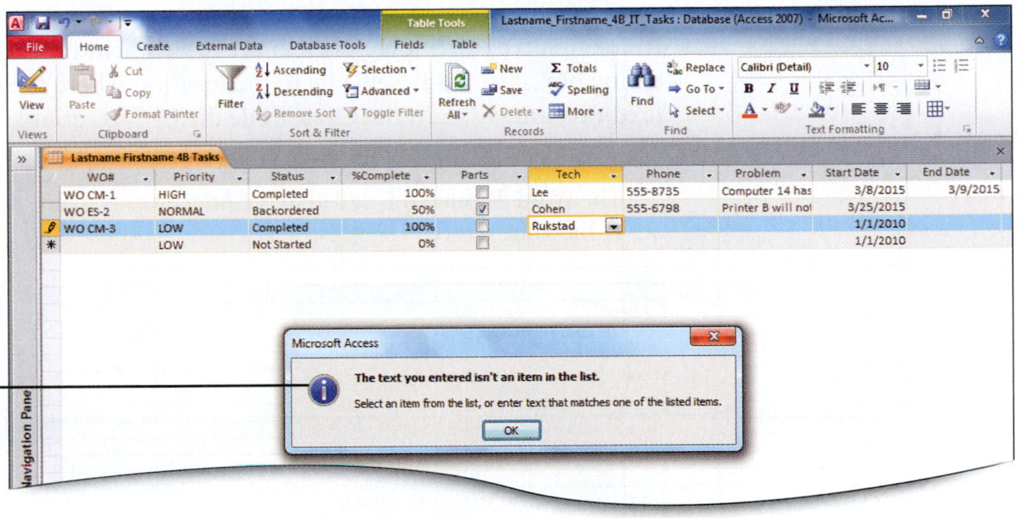

Lookup list prohibits entries not on the list

15 Click **OK** and select **Roberta Collier** from the lookup list. Press Tab or Enter to move to the next field.

16 In the **Phone#** field, type **5556313** Press Tab or Enter to move to the next field. In the **Problem** field, type **Toner is low in Printer C** Press Tab or Enter to move to the next field.

17 In the **Start Date** field, type **3/16/2015** Press Tab or Enter to move to the next field. In the **End Date** field, type **3/17/2015** Press Tab or Enter to move to the next field.

Objective 9 | Attach Files to Records

The attachment data type can be used to add one or more files to the records in a database. For example, if you have a database for an antique collection, you can attach a picture of each antique and a Word document that contains a description of the item. Access stores the attached files in their native formats—if you attach a Word document, it is saved as a Word document. By default, fields contain only one piece of data; however, you can attach more than one file by using the attachment data type. As you attach files to a record, Access creates one or more ***system tables*** to keep track of the multiple entries in the field. You cannot view or work with these system tables.

Activity 4.24 | Attaching a Word Document to a Record

In this activity, you will attach a Work Order Report that was created in Word to records in the *4B Tasks* table.

1 Switch to **Design** view, click in the empty field name box under **#Days**, type **Work Order** and then press Tab to move to the **Data Type** box. Click the **Data Type arrow**, click **Attachment**, and then press F6. Under **Field Properties**, on the **General tab**, and notice that only two field properties—**Caption** and **Required**—are displayed for an Attachment field.

2 Switch to **Datasheet** view, saving changes to the table. If necessary, scroll to the right to display the newly created Attachment field. Notice that the field name of *Work Order* does not display; instead, a paper clip symbol displays. In the first record, *(0)* displays after the paper clip symbol, indicating that there are no attachments for this record.

Because multiple files can be attached to a record, the name of the field displays the paper clip symbol.

3 In the first record, double-click in the **Attachment** field. In the displayed **Attachments** dialog box, click **Add**. Navigate to the location where the student data files for this textbook are saved. In the **Choose File** dialog box, double-click **a04B_WorkOrder_1**, and then compare your screen with Figure 4.50.

The Word document is added to the Attachments dialog box. You can attach multiple files to the same record.

Figure 4.50

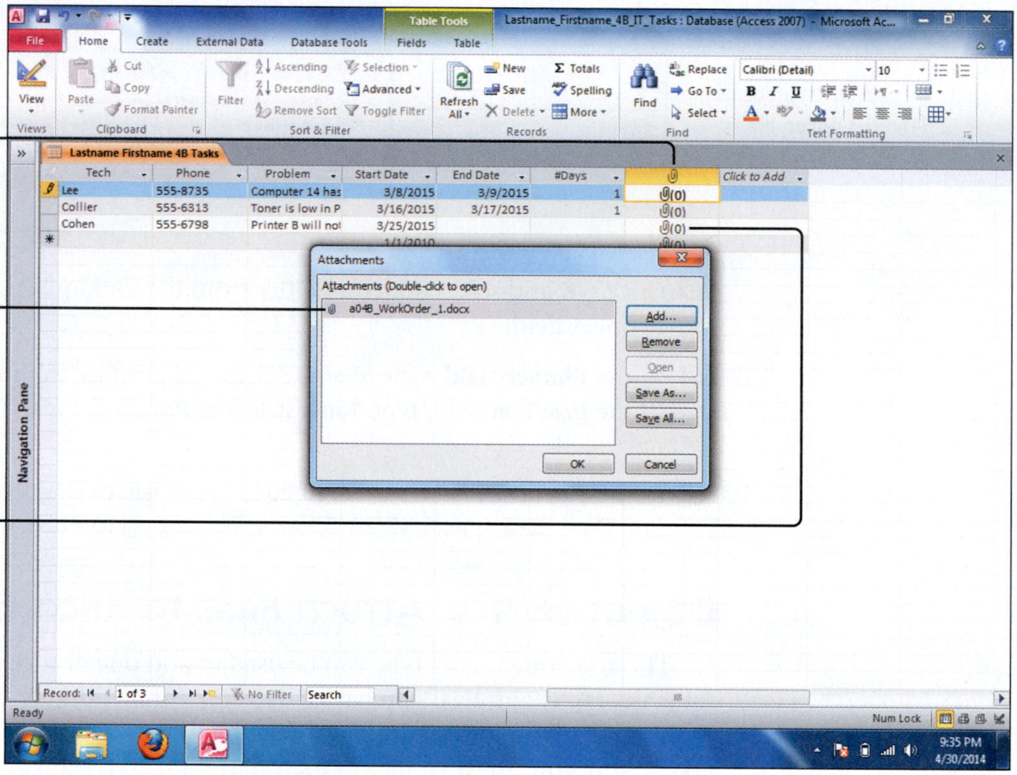

4 In the **Attachments** dialog box, click **OK**. Notice that the **Attachment** field now indicates there is **1** attachment for the first record.

5 In the first record, double-click in the **Attachment** field. In the **Attachments** dialog box, click **a04B_WorkOrder_1.docx**, and then click **Open**.

Word opens, and the document displays. You can make changes to the document, and then save it in the database.

6 **Close**  Word. In the **Attachments** dialog box, click **OK**.

Note | Saving Changes to an Attached File

When you open an attached file in the program that was used to create it, Access places a temporary copy of the file in a temporary folder on the hard drive of your computer. If you change the file and save changes, Access saves the changes in the temporary copy. Closing the program used to view the attachment returns you to Access. When you click OK to close the Attachments dialog box, Access prompts you to save the attached file again. Click Yes to save the changes to the attached file in the database, or click No to keep the original, unedited version in the database.

To find the location of your temporary folder, start Internet Explorer. On the Tools menu, click Internet Options. On the General tab, in the Browsing History section, click Settings. In the Settings dialog box, the temporary folder path displays in the Current location section.

7 Enter the following data for **Record 4**—a new record. Do not enter any data in the **End Date** field. The attachment is located in the student data files.

WO#	Priority	Status	%Complete	Parts	Tech	Phone#	Problem	Start Date	End Date	Attachment
es3	**Normal**	**In Progress**	**25**	**Yes**	**Jennifer Perry**	**5558899**	**Monitor 7 doesn't work**	**4/1/15**		**a04B_ WorkOrder_2**

8 Adjust all column widths, ensuring that all of the field names and all of the field data display. View the table in **Print Preview**, and then change the orientation to **Landscape**. Adjust the margins to display the table on one page, and be sure that the table name, date, and page number display. If you are instructed to submit this result, create a paper or electronic printout.

9 **Close** the table, saving changes. **Open** » the **Navigation Pane**. **Close** the database, and **Exit** X Access.

End You have completed Project 4B

Content-Based Assessments

Summary

Database security is in important part of database maintenance. Create regular back-up files and add secure locations to the Trust Center to protect a database. Using existing tables as the basis to create new ones eliminates the chances of mistakes in table design. Use the Find feature to efficiently locate data in a table to edit or modify records. Establishing relationships between the database tables along with setting referential integrity and cascade options reduce data redundancy and increase data entry accuracy.

Create a table in Design view to control the field characteristics. Choose the best data type for each field based on the information it tracks, and set the appropriate field properties to minimize the chance for errors in data entry.

Key Terms

Append 419
Back up 415
Cascade Delete 436
Cascade options 433
Cascade Update 434
Combo box 442
Clipboard 418
Copy 418
Data validation 445
Default value 452
Destination table 420
Dynamic 424
Expression 454
Expression Builder 454
Field property 445
Flagged 429
Index 453
Input mask 445
Instance 422
List box 442
Lookup field 442
Multivalued field 444
One-to-one relationship 432
Orphan record 431
Paste 418
Path 416
Referential integrity 431
Relational databases 430
Required 450
Source table 420
Subdatasheet 433
System tables 459
Trust Center 416
Trusted source 416
Validation rule 454
Validation text 454
Zero-length string 452

Matching

Match each term in the second column with its correct definition in the first column by writing the letter of the term on the blank line in front of the correct definition.

____ 1. To make a copy of the original database for use if data is lost or becomes corrupt.
____ 2. A security feature that checks documents for macros and digital signatures.
____ 3. A temporary storage area in Windows.
____ 4. A record that references a deleted record in a related table.
____ 5. Options that update records in related tables when referential integrity is enforced.
____ 6. A good way to create a table when you know exactly how fields will be set up.
____ 7. An attribute or characteristic of a field that controls the display and input of data.
____ 8. Determines the data that can be entered and how the data displays.
____ 9. Rules that help prevent individuals from entering invalid data and help ensure that individuals enter data in a consistent manner.
____ 10. A special list created in Access to speed up searches and sorting.
____ 11. An expression that precisely defines a range of data that will be accepted in a field.
____ 12. The error message that displays when an individual enters a value prohibited by the validation rule.

A Back up
B Cascade options
C Clipboard
D Data validation
E Design view
F Expression Builder
G Field property
H Index
I Input mask
J Multivalued field
K Orphan records
L System tables
M Trust Center
N Validation rule
O Validation text

_____ 13. A feature used to create formulas in query criteria, form and report properties, and table validation rules.

_____ 14. A field that holds multiple values, such as a list of people to whom you have assigned the same task.

_____ 15. A table that is used to keep track of the multiple entries in a field but cannot be viewed or worked with.

Multiple Choice

Circle the correct answer.

1. Opening a database from a location in the Trust Center avoids the appearance of a(n):
   A. security warning **B.** error message **C.** error warning
2. Which option sends a duplicate version of the selected table to the Clipboard, leaving the original table intact?
   A. Cut **B.** Paste **C.** Copy
3. To add one or more records from a source table to a destination table is to:
   A. attach records **B.** erase records **C.** append records
4. The tables in a database can relate to or connect to other tables through common fields because Access databases are:
   A. dynamic **B.** relational **C.** linked
5. Which option should be used to ensure that orphan records are not left in the database?
   A. Cascade Update **B.** Cascade Join **C.** Cascade Delete
6. To apply an attribute or characteristic to a field that controls the display and input of data, use:
   A. Field Description **B.** Field Properties **C.** Data Properties
7. Which data type should be used to enter an expression that will compute the entry displayed?
   A. Expression **B.** Calculated **C.** Equation
8. Which field property is used to ensure that a field contains data and is not left empty?
   A. Default value **B.** Required **C.** Validated
9. Which field property is used to display a value in a field for all new records?
   A. Default value **B.** Required **C.** Validated
10. Which data type should be used to add one or more files to the records in a database?
    A. Document **B.** Attachment **C.** Add-on

Content-Based Assessments

Apply 4A skills from these Objectives:

1. Manage Existing Tables
2. Modify Existing Tables
3. Create and Modify Table Relationships

Skills Review | Project 4C Industries

Joaquin Alonzo, the City Manager of Westland Plains, has a database of the city's industry information. This database has five tables. The Industries table contains summary information from the other four tables. Each update to an individual industry table would require updates to the summary table. In the following Skills Review, you will redesign the tables, taking advantage of table relationships to avoid entering and storing redundant data. Your completed tables and relationships will look similar to Figure 4.51.

Project Files

For Project 4C, you will need the following file:

a04C_Industries

You will save your files as:

Lastname_Firstname_4C_Industries
Lastname_Firstname_a04C_Industries_2016-10-30 (date will vary)

Project Results

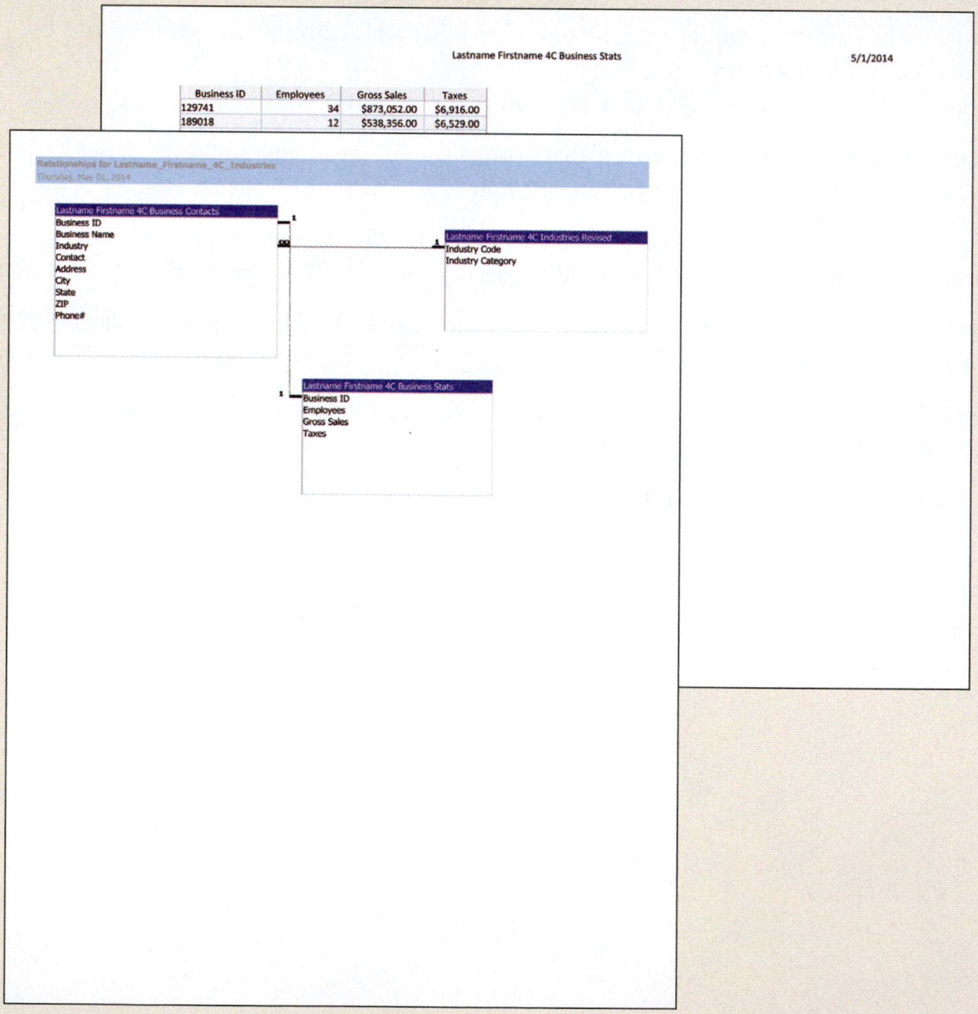

Figure 4.51

(Project 4C Industries continues on the next page)

Skills Review | Project 4C Industries (continued)

1 **Start** Access. Locate and open the **a04C_Industries** file.

a. Display **Backstage** view, click on **Save & Publish**, and then double-click **Back Up Database**. In the **Save As** dialog box, navigate to your Access Chapter 4 folder, and then click **Save** to accept the default name.

b. **Save** the database in your **Access Chapter 4** folder as **Lastname_Firstname_4C_Industries**

2 In the **Navigation Pane**, double-click **4C Industries**. Take a moment to review the contents of the table, and then **Close** the table.

a. On the **Home tab**, in the **Clipboard group**, click the **Copy** button.

b. In the **Clipboard group**, click the **Paste** button.

c. In the displayed **Paste Table As** dialog box, under **Table Name**, type **Lastname Firstname 4C Industries Revised** Under **Paste Options**, be sure that the **Structure and Data** option button is selected, and then click **OK**.

3 Double-click **4C Industries Revised** to open the table in **Datasheet** view. Close the **Navigation Pane**.

a. Point to the **Business #5** field name until the pointer displays. Drag to the left to the **Business #1** field name to select the five fields. On the **Home tab**, in the **Records group**, click the **Delete** button. In the displayed message box, click **Yes** to permanently delete the fields and the data.

b. Switch to **Design** view. To the left of **Industry Code**, click the **row selector** box, and then in the **Tools group**, click the **Primary Key** button. **Close** the table, saving any changes. Open the **Navigation Pane**.

c. Using the technique you just practiced, copy and paste the structure and data of the **4C Airports** table, and then **Save** the pasted table as **Lastname Firstname 4C Business Contacts.**

4 In the Navigation Pane, click **4C High-Tech Manufacturing**.

a. On the **Home tab**, in the **Clipboard group**, click the **Copy** button, and then click the **Paste** button.

b. In the **Paste Table As** dialog box, under **Table Name**, type **Lastname Firstname 4C Business Contacts** Under **Paste Options**, click the **Append Data to Existing Table** option button, and then click **OK**.

c. Using the same procedure, append the **4C Medical Centers** table and the **4C Oil Companies** table to the **Lastname Firstname 4C Business Contacts** table.

5 Repeat the procedure, copying and pasting the structure and data of the **4C Business Contacts** table, and then naming the pasted table **Lastname Firstname 4C Business Stats** One table will contain only contact information, and the other table will contain only statistical information.

6 Open the **4C Business Contacts** table, and then close the **Navigation Pane**.

a. Select the **Employees**, **Gross Sales**, and **Taxes** fields. On the **Home tab**, in the **Records group**, click the **Delete** button. In the displayed message box, click **Yes** to permanently delete the fields and data.

b. Click the **Business Name** field name. On the Ribbon, click the **Fields tab**. In the **Add & Delete group**, click the **Text** button. Type **Industry** to replace **Field1,** and then press Enter. **Save** your work.

c. Open the **Navigation Pane**, and then open the **4C Industries Revised** table. Under **Industry Category**, locate the record for the **Airports**, and notice the **Industry Code** of **AIR**.

d. On the **tab row**, click the **4C Business Contacts tab** to make the table active. In the **Business ID** of **189018**, in the **Industry** field, type **AIR** Locate the **Business ID** of **675234**, and then in the **Industry Code** field, type **AIR** Locate the **Business ID** of **234155**, and then type **AIR**

e. Using the techniques you just practiced, locate the **Industry** for the **High-Tech Manufacturing**, **Medical Center**, and **Oil Company** Industry Categories. In Business IDs **258679**, **399740**, **479728**, **927685**, and **966657**, type **HTM** In Business IDs **252479**, **295738**, **362149**, and **420879**, type **MED** and then in Business IDs **129741**, **329718**, **420943**, and **462296**, type **OIL**

f. Switch the **4C Business Contacts** table to **Design** view. With the insertion point in the **Business ID** field, in the **Tools group**, click the **Primary Key** button. **Save** the changes.

7 Open the **4C Business Stats** table, and then close the **Navigation Pane**.

a. Select the **Business Name** field, and then press Del. Click **Yes** to delete the field and data. Scroll to the

(Project 4C Industries continues on the next page)

Skills Review | Project 4C Industries (continued)

right to display the **Address**, **City**, **State**, **ZIP**, **Contact**, and **Phone#** fields. Select all six fields, and then press Del Click **Yes** to delete the fields and data.

b. Switch the **4C Business Stats** table to **Design** view, set the **Business ID** field as the primary key field, and then **Save** the changes. Switch to **Datasheet** view.

c. In the **4C Business Stats** table, click in the **Employees** field in the first record. On the **Home tab**, in the **Find group**, click the **Find** button. In the **Find What** box, type **17** Click **Find Next** to select the next occurrence in the table. Click **Cancel** in the **Find and Replace** dialog box.

d. Click the **Record Selector** box to select the record containing *17*. On the **Home tab**, in the **Records group**, click the **Delete** button. In the displayed message box, click **Yes** to permanently delete the record.

8 Click on the **4C Business Contacts** tab to make it active. Switch to the **Datasheet** view. In the **Search** box in the navigation area at the bottom of the window, type **adv** Click at the end of AdventuCom. Press the Spacebar and type **Resources**

a. Switch to **Design** view. To the left of **Contact**, click the **row selector** box. Drag the field up until you see a dark horizontal line between *Industry Code* and *Business Name*, and then release the mouse button. **Save** the changes.

b. Switch to **Datasheet** view. On the **Home tab**, in the **Records group**, click the **Spelling** button. When it selects *Airpot*, **Change** the spelling to *Airport*. Ignore the other names selected. On the **tab row**, right-click any tab, and then click **Close All**.

9 On the Ribbon, click the **Database Tools tab**. In the **Relationships group**, click the **Relationships** button. If the Show Table dialog box does not display, on the **Design tab**, in the **Relationships** group, click the **Show Table** button. From the **Show Table** dialog box, add the **4C Industries Revised**, **4C Business Contacts**, and the **4C Business Stats** tables, and then click **Close**.

a. Expand the field lists to fully display the table name and field names, moving the center table down as necessary. In the **4C Industries Revised** field list, drag the **Industry Code** field to the **4C Business Contacts** field list until the pointer points to **Industry**, and then release the mouse button.

b. In the **Edit Relationships** dialog box, select the **Enforce Referential Integrity**, **Cascade Update Related Fields**, and **Cascade Delete Related Records** check boxes. In the **Edit Relationships** dialog box, click **Create**.

c. In the **4C Business Contacts** field list, drag the **Business ID** field to the **4C Business Stats** field list until the pointer points to **Business ID**, and then release the mouse button.

d. In the displayed **Edit Relationships** dialog box, select the **Enforce Referential Integrity** check box. Click **Create**.

e. On the **Design tab**, in the **Tools group**, click the **Relationship Report** button. If you are instructed to submit this result, create a paper or electronic printout. On the **Close Preview** group of the **Print Preview** tab, click **Close Print Preview**. The report is displayed in **Design** view. Close the relationships report, and then click **Yes** to save the design of Report 1. In the displayed **Save As** dialog box, click **OK** to accept the default report name.

f. Click the **join line** between the **4C Business Contacts** field list and the **4C Business Stats** field list. On the **Design tab**, in the **Tools group**, click the **Edit Relationships** button. In the **Edit Relationships** dialog box, select the **Cascade Update Related Fields** and **Cascade Delete Related Records** check boxes, and then click **OK**. **Close** the Relationships window. **Open** the **Navigation Pane**.

10 Open the **4C Business Contacts** table. Locate the record for **Business ID 927685**. In the **Business ID** field, select **927685**, type **987654** Locate the record for the **Business ID** of **420943**. Click in the record selector box to select the record. On the **Home tab**, in the **Records group**, click the **Delete** button. In the displayed message box, click **Yes**.

11 Open the **4C Business Stats** table to view the changes. For each table, adjust all column widths to view the field names and data. View the table in **Print Preview**, and then change the orientation to **Landscape**. If you are instructed to submit the results, create a paper or electronic printout.

12 **Close** the tables, **Close** the database, and then **Exit** Access.

End You have completed Project 4C

Content-Based Assessments

Apply 4B skills from these Objectives:

- 4 Create a Table in Design View
- 5 Change Data Types
- 6 Create a Lookup Field
- 7 Set Field Properties
- 8 Create Data Validation Rules and Validation Text
- 9 Attach Files to Records

Skills Review | Project 4D Airport Employees

Joaquin Alonzo, City Manager of Westland Plains, Texas, has created a table to keep track of airport personnel. In the following Skills Review, you will add a table that stores records about the employees and modify the properties and customize the fields in the table. You will add features to the database table that will help to reduce data entry errors and that will make data entry easier. You will add attachments to records. Your completed table will look similar to Figure 4.52.

Project Files

For Project 4D, you will need the following files:

a04D_Airport_Employees
a04D_Service_Award
A new blank Word document

You will save your files as:

Lastname_Firstname_4D_Airport_Employees
Lastname_Firstname_4D_Screens

Project Results

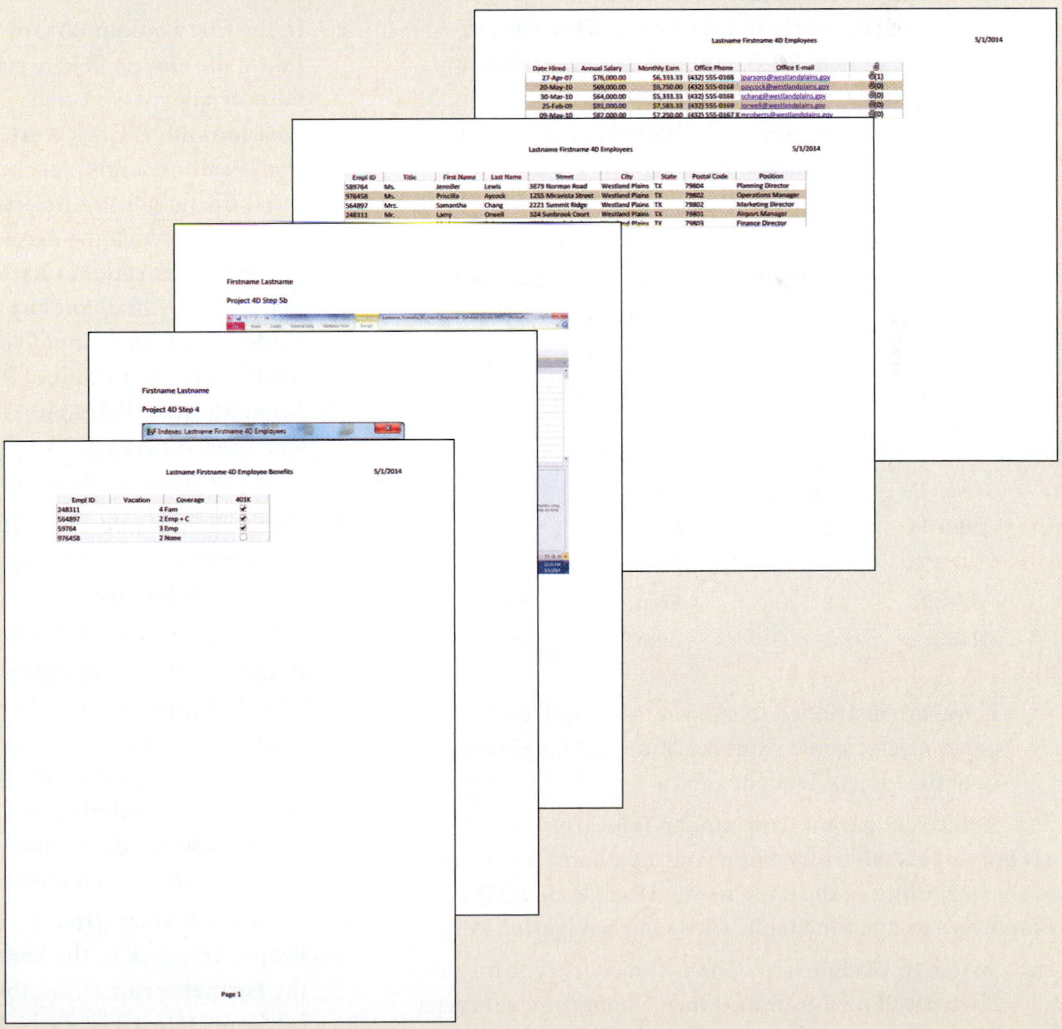

Figure 4.52

(Project 4D Airport Employees continues on the next page)

Skills Review | Project 4D Airport Employees (continued)

1 **Start** Access. Locate and open the **a04D_Airport_Employees** file. **Save** the database in your **Access Chapter 4** folder as **Lastname_Firstname_4D_Airport_Employees**

2 Close the **Navigation Pane**. On the Ribbon, click the **Create tab**. In the **Tables group**, click the **Table Design** button to open an empty table in Design view.

a. In the first **Field Name** box, type **Empl ID** and press Tab. On the **Design tab** in the **Tools group**, click the **Primary Key** button. Press Tab three times to move to the next field.

b. In the second **Field Name** box, type **Vacation** Press Tab to move to the **Data Type** box, and click **Number**. Press Tab to move to the **Description** box. Type **Indicate how many weeks of vacation the employee receives per year** Press Tab or Enter to move to the next field.

c. In the third **Field Name** box, type **Coverage** and then press Tab twice to move to the **Description** box. Type **Indicate the type of insurance coverage the employee has selected** Press F6 to move to the **Field Properties** pane at the bottom of the screen. In the **Field Size** box, type **10** to replace the 255.

d. Click in the fourth **Field Name** box, type **401K** Press Tab, and select a **Yes/No** data type. Press Tab to move to the **Description** box. Type **Indicate whether or not the employee participates in the 401K plan**

e. Save the table as **Lastname Firstname 4D Employee Benefits** Switch to **Datasheet** view and enter these records:

Empl ID	Vacation	Coverage	401K
589764	3	Emp	Yes
976458	2	None	No
564897	2	Emp + C	Yes
248311	4	Fam	Yes

If you are instructed to submit this result, create a paper or electronic printout of the **4D Employee Benefits** table. **Close** the table.

3 In the **Navigation Pane**, under **Tables**, rename the **4D Employees** table by adding your **Lastname Firstname** to the beginning of the table name. Double-click **4D Employees** to open the table. Close the **Navigation Pane**.

a. Switch to **Design** view. Change the data type for the **Date Hired** field to **Date/Time**. Change the data type for the **Annual Salary** field to **Currency**. Change the data type for the **Office E-mail** field to **Hyperlink**. **Save** your work. You will see message boxes warning that some data may be lost. Click **Yes** to continue.

b. In the **Title** field, click in the **Data Type** box, and then click the **arrow**. From the displayed list of data types, click **Lookup Wizard**.

c. In the first **Lookup Wizard** dialog box, click **I will type in the values that I want** option button, and then click **Next**. Be sure the number of columns is **1**. Click in the first row under **Col1**, type **Mr.** and then press Tab or ↓ to save the first item. Type the following data: **Mrs.** and **Miss** and **Ms.** and then click **Next**. In the final dialog box, click **Finish**.

d. In the **Position** field, click in the **Data Type** box, and then click the **arrow**. From the displayed list of data types, click **Lookup Wizard**.

e. In the first **Lookup Wizard** dialog box, be sure that **I want the lookup field to get the values from another table or query** is selected. Click **Next**. Select the **4D Positions** table. Click **Next**. Under **Available Fields**, click **Position**, and then click the **Add Field** button to move the field to the **Selected Fields** box. Click **Next**. In the **1** box, click the **arrow**, and then click **Position**. Leave the sort order as **Ascending**. Click **Next** twice to display the final **Lookup Wizard** dialog box. Under **What label would you like for your lookup field?**, leave the default of **Position** and be sure that **Allow Multiple Values** is *not* selected. Click **Finish**. Click **Yes**. If necessary, in the message box, click **Yes** to test the existing data with the new rules.

f. Under **Field Name**, click **Office Phone**. Under **Field Properties**, click in the **Input Mask** box and then click the **Build** button.

g. In the **Input Mask** dialog box, scroll down, click **Phone Number with Extension**, and then click **Next**. Change the placeholder from # to _ and then click **Next**. The next wizard screen enables you to decide how you want to store the data. Be sure that the **Without the symbols in the mask, like this** option button is selected, and then click **Next**. In the final wizard screen, click **Finish**.

h. Click in the **Date Hired** field. Under **Field Properties**, click in the **Format** box, and then click the **Format arrow**. From the displayed list, click **Medium Date**. Click in the **Required** box. Click the

(Project 4D Airport Employees continues on the next page)

Skills Review | Project 4D Airport Employees (continued)

Required arrow, and then click **Yes**. Click in the **Monthly Earn** field. Under **Field Properties**, click in the **Expression** box, and edit the expression to read **[Annual Salary]/12** Click the **Format arrow**, and select **Currency** from the displayed list.

i. Under **Field Name**, click **State**. Under **Field Properties**, click in the **Format** box, and then type **>** Click in the **Default Value** box, and then type **tx**

j. Using the same technique, set the **Default Value** of the **City** field to **Westland Plains**

k. Under **Field Name**, click **Last Name**. Under **Field Properties**, click in the **Indexed** property box, and then click the displayed **arrow**. Click **Yes (Duplicates OK)**. **Save** your work. In the message box, click **Yes** to test the existing data with the new rules.

4 On the **Design tab**, in the **Show/Hide group**, click the **Indexes** button. Hold down Alt, and then press PrtScr. Start **Word 2010**. Type your first and last names, and press Enter. Type **Project 4D Step 4** and press Enter. Press Ctrl + V. **Save** the document in your **Access Chapter 4** folder as **Lastname_Firstname_4D_Screens**. Leave the Word document open. Return to Access. **Close** Indexes.

5 Under **Field Name**, click **Date Hired**. Under **Field Properties**, click in the **Validation Rule** box, and then click the **Build** button.

a. In the upper box of the **Expression Builder** dialog box, type **<=now( )** and then click OK. Click in the **Validation Text** box, and then type **You cannot enter a date later than today** Hold down Alt, and then press PrtScr.

b. In the Word document, press Enter, and then press Ctrl + Enter to insert a page break. Type your first and last names, press Enter, and then type **Project 4D Step 5b** Press Enter. Press Ctrl + V and **Save** the document. If you are instructed to submit this result, create a paper or electronic printout. **Exit** Word.

6 With the **4D Employees** table open in **Design** view, click in the first blank field name box type **Service Award** Press Tab to move to the **Data Type** box, and click **Attachment**.

a. Switch to **Datasheet** view, saving changes to the table. In the message box, click **No** to test the existing data with the new rules.

b. In the first record, double-click in the **Attachment** field. In the **Attachments** dialog box, click **Add**. Navigate to the location where the student data files for this textbook are stored, and double-click **a04D_Service_Award**. Click **OK**.

c. Click the **New (blank) record** button. Type the following data:
Empl ID: **543655**
Title: **Mr.**
First Name: **Mark**
Last Name: **Roberts**
Street: **1320 Woodbriar Ln.**
City: **Westland Plains**
State: **tx**
Postal Code: **79803**
Position: **Finance Director**
Date Hired: **5/09/10**
Salary: **87000**
Office Phone: **(432) 555-0167 X101**
Office E-mail: **mroberts@westlandplains.gov**

d. If you are instructed to submit this result, create a paper or electronic printout of the **4D Employees** table in **Landscape** orientation. This table will print on two pages. **Close 4D Employees**. If you are to submit your work electronically, follow your instructor's directions.

7 Open the **Navigation Pane**. **Close** the **Object Definition** window. **Close** the database, and **Exit** Access.

End **You have completed Project 4D**

Apply **4A** skills from these Objectives:

1. Manage Existing Tables
2. Modify Existing Tables
3. Create and Modify Table Relationships

Mastering Access | Project 4E Arts Council

In the following Mastering Access project, you will manage and modify tables and create relationships for the database that contains cultural information about the city of Westland Plains. The database will be used by the arts council. Your completed tables and report will look similar to Figure 4.53.

Project Files

For Project 4E, you will need the following file:

a04E_Arts_Council

You will save your database as:

Lastname_Firstname_4E_Arts_Council

Project Results

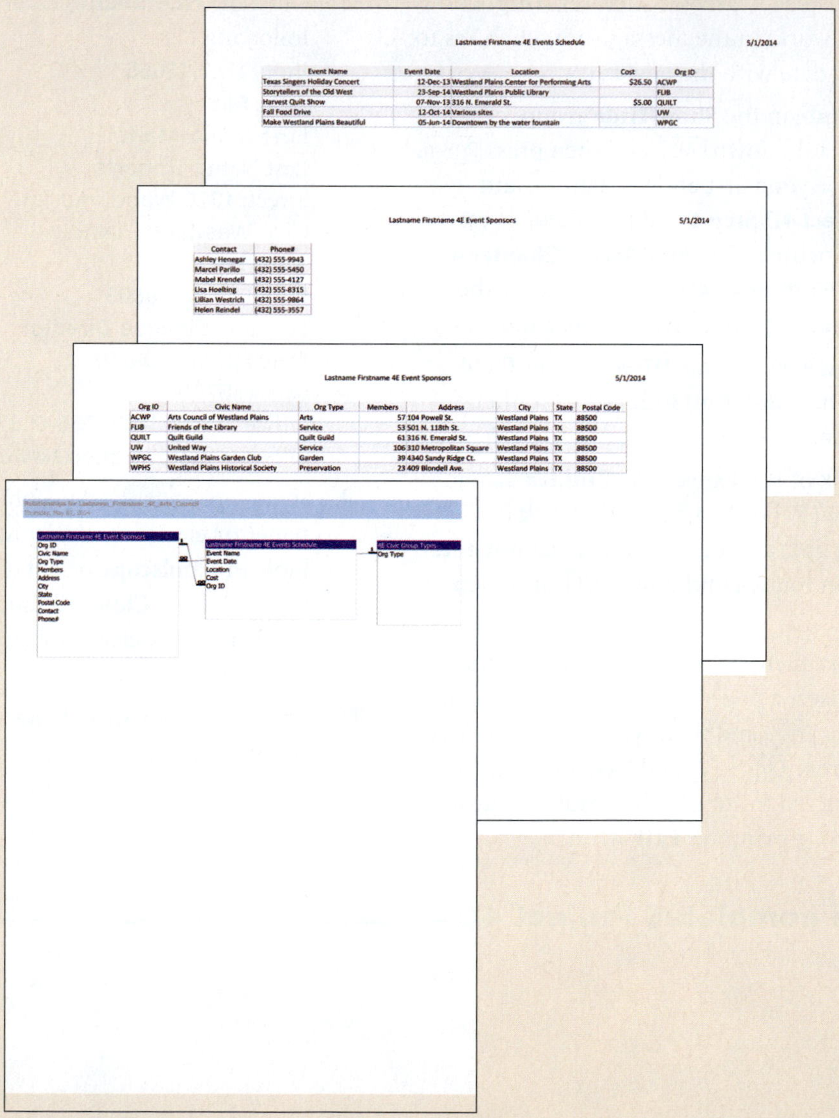

Lastname Firstname 4E Events Schedule 5/1/2014

Event Name	Event Date	Location	Cost	Org ID
Texas Singers Holiday Concert	12-Dec-13	Westland Plains Center for Performing Arts	$26.50	ACWP
Storytellers of the Old West	23-Sep-14	Westland Plains Public Library		FLIB
Harvest Quilt Show	07-Nov-13	316 N. Emerald St.	$5.00	QUILT
Fall Food Drive	12-Oct-14	Various sites		UW
Make Westland Plains Beautiful	05-Jun-14	Downtown by the water fountain		WPGC

Lastname Firstname 4E Event Sponsors 5/1/2014

Contact	Phone#
Ashley Henegar	(432) 555-9943
Marcel Parillo	(432) 555-5450
Mabel Krendell	(432) 555-4127
Lisa Hoelting	(432) 555-8315
Lillian Westrich	(432) 555-9864
Helen Reindel	(432) 555-3557

Lastname Firstname 4E Event Sponsors 5/1/2014

Org ID	Civic Name	Org Type	Members	Address	City	State	Postal Code
ACWP	Arts Council of Westland Plains	Arts	57	104 Powell St.	Westland Plains	TX	88500
FLIB	Friends of the Library	Service	53	501 N. 118th St.	Westland Plains	TX	88500
QUILT	Quilt Guild	Quilt Guild	61	316 N. Emerald St.	Westland Plains	TX	88500
UW	United Way	Service	106	310 Metropolitan Square	Westland Plains	TX	88500
WPGC	Westland Plains Garden Club	Garden	39	4340 Sandy Ridge Ct.	Westland Plains	TX	88500
WPHS	Westland Plains Historical Society	Preservation	23	409 Blondell Ave.	Westland Plains	TX	88500

Figure 4.53

(Project 4E Arts Council continues on the next page)

Mastering Access | Project **4E** Arts Council (continued)

1 **Start** Access. Locate and open the **a04E_Arts_Council** file. **Save** the database in your **Access Chapter 4** folder as **Lastname_Firstname_4E_Arts_Council**

2 Right-click the **4E Cultural Events** table. Select **Copy**, and then in the clear area of the **Navigation Pane**, right-click and select **Paste**. In the **Paste Table As** dialog box, in the **Table Name** box, type **Lastname Firstname 4E Events Schedule** The **Paste Options** should include **Structure and Data**. Click **OK**.

3 Make a second copy of the **4E Cultural Events** table. Name the table **Lastname Firstname 4E Event Sponsors** and paste the **Structure and Data** from the source table.

4 Open the **4E Event Sponsors** table in **Datasheet** view. Select the first four columns beginning with the **Event Name** field through the **Cost** field. Press Del, and then click **Yes** to delete the fields and data. Switch to **Design** view, and then make the **Org ID** field the **Primary Key** field. Switch to **Datasheet** view, saving the changes. If you are instructed to submit this result, create a paper or electronic printout of the **4E Event Sponsors** table in **Landscape** orientation. It will print on two pages. **Close** the table.

5 Open the **4E Events Schedule** table in **Datasheet** view. Close the **Navigation Pane**. Select and delete the following fields: **Civic Name**, **Org Type**, **Members**, **Address**, **City**, **State**, **Postal Code**, **Contact**, and **Phone#**. **Save** the table.

6 Using **Find**, find **1876** in the **Event Name** field; in the **Match** field, select **Any Part of Field**. Select and delete the record.

7 In the navigation area at the bottom of the window, search for *v* in the records. When it stops at *Harvest Time Quilt Show*, delete the word **Time** and the space following the word from the Event Name.

8 Switch to **Design** view. Select the **Event Date** field, and drag it up until it is between **Event Name** and **Location**. Release the mouse button. Switch to **Datasheet** view, saving the changes.

9 On the **Home tab**, click **Spelling** in the **Records** group. Make any spelling corrections necessary in the table. If you are instructed to submit this result, create a paper or electronic printout of the **4E Events Schedule** table in **Landscape** orientation. **Close** the table.

10 Create a relationship between the **4E Event Sponsors** and the **4E Events Schedule** tables using **Org ID** as the common field. Select **Enforce Referential Integrity**, **Cascade Update Related Fields**, and **Cascade Delete Related Records**.

11 Create a relationship between the **4E Civic Group Types** table and the **4E Event Sponsors** table using **Org Type** as the common field. Check **Enforce Referential Integrity**, **Cascade Update Related Fields**, and **Cascade Delete Related Records**. Adjust all field lists so that all table names and field names display.

12 Create a **Relationship Report**. Accept the default name for the report. If you are instructed to submit this result, create a paper or electronic printout. **Close** the **Relationships** window.

13 **Close** the database, and **Exit** Access.

End **You have completed Project 4E**

Content-Based Assessments

Apply 4B skills from these Objectives:

- 4 Create a Table in Design View
- 5 Change Data Types
- 6 Create a Lookup Field
- 7 Set Field Properties
- 8 Create Data Validation Rules and Validation Text
- 9 Attach Files to Records

Mastering Access | Project 4F Library Programs

Joaquin Alonzo, City Manager, has asked Ron Singer, Database Manager for the city, to improve the library database. In the following Mastering Access project, you will create a table that stores records about the Westland Plains Library in Design view and then modify the properties and customize the fields in the table. You will add features to the database table that will help to reduce data entry errors and that will make data entry easier. You will add attachments to records. Your completed table will look similar to Figure 4.54.

Project Files

For Project 4F, you will need the following files:

a04F_Library_Programs
a04F_Photo_1.jpg
a04F_Photo_2.jpg
a04F_Photo_3.jpg

You will save your database as:

Lastname_Firstname_4F_Library_Programs

Project Results

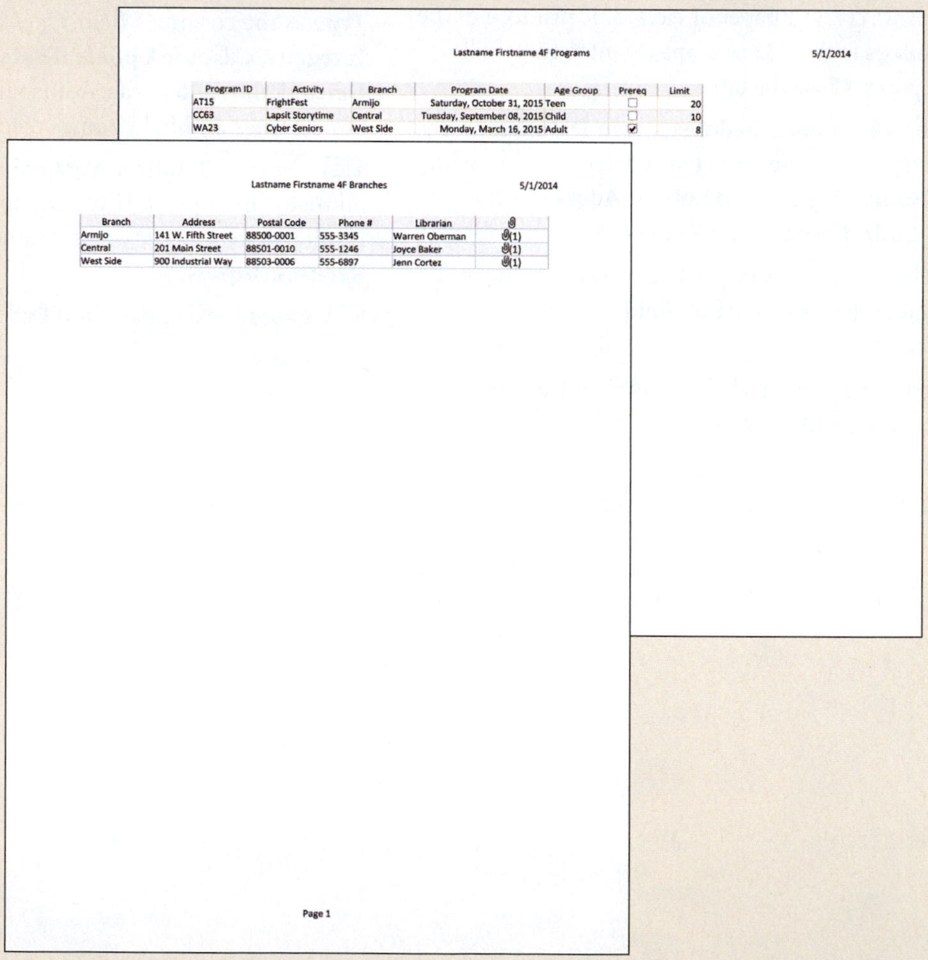

Lastname Firstname 4F Programs 5/1/2014

Program ID	Activity	Branch	Program Date	Age Group	Prereq	Limit
AT15	FrightFest	Armijo	Saturday, October 31, 2015	Teen	☐	20
CC63	Lapsit Storytime	Central	Tuesday, September 08, 2015	Child	☐	10
WA23	Cyber Seniors	West Side	Monday, March 16, 2015	Adult	☑	8

Lastname Firstname 4F Branches 5/1/2014

Branch	Address	Postal Code	Phone #	Librarian	📎
Armijo	141 W. Fifth Street	88500-0001	555-3345	Warren Oberman	📎(1)
Central	201 Main Street	88501-0010	555-1246	Joyce Baker	📎(1)
West Side	900 Industrial Way	88503-0006	555-6897	Jenn Cortez	📎(1)

Page 1

Figure 4.54

(Project 4F Library Programs continues on the next page)

Mastering Access | Project 4F Library Programs (continued)

1 **Start** Access. Locate and open the **a04F_Library_Programs** file. **Save** the database in your **Access Chapter 4** folder as **Lastname_Firstname_4F_Library_Programs** Rename the table by adding your **Lastname Firstname** to the beginning of the table name. Close the **Navigation Pane**.

2 Create a table in **Design** view. In the first **Field Name** box, type **Program ID** and press Tab twice. Make it the Primary Key field. Change the **Field size** to **5** and the format to all caps.

3 In the second **Field Name** box, type **Activity** and press Tab twice. In the **Field Properties**, click the **Indexed down arrow**, and then select **Yes (Duplicates OK)**. Make it a **Required** field.

4 In the third **Field Name** box, type **Branch** and press Tab to move to the **Data Type** box. Select **Lookup Wizard**. Be sure that **I want the lookup field to get the values from another table or query** is selected. Click **Next**. There is only one other table in this database from which to choose—*4F Branches*—and it is selected. Click **Next**. Under **Available Fields**, click **Branch**, and then click the **Add Field** button. Click **Next**. In the **1** box, click the **arrow**, and then click **Branch**. Leave the sort order as **Ascending**. Click **Next** two times. Under **What label would you like for your lookup field?**, accept the default of **Branch**, and then be sure that **Allow Multiple Values** is *not* selected. Click **Finish**.

5 **Save** the table as **Lastname Firstname 4F Programs**

6 In the fourth **Field Name** box, type **Program Date**, and press Tab to move to the **Data Type** box. Select **Date/Time**. Click in the **Format** box, and select **Long Date**.

7 In the fifth **Field Name** box, type **Age Group** and press Tab twice. In the **Validation Rule** box, type **"Child" OR "Teen" OR "Adult"** For the **Validation Text**, type **Entry must be Child, Teen, or Adult**

8 Click in the sixth **Field Name** box, and type **Prereq** Press Tab to move to the **Data Type** box. Click **Yes/No**. Press Tab to move to the **Description** box, and then type **Click if there is a prerequisite required before enrolling in this activity**

9 Click in the seventh **Field Name** box, type **Limit** and press Tab to move to the **Data Type** box. Click **Number** and change the **Field Size** to **Integer**. In the **Validation Rule** box, type **<=20** In the **Validation Text** box, type **Participation is limited to a maximum of 20**

10 Switch to **Datasheet** view, saving the changes to the design. Populate the table with the data in **Table 1**.

11 Adjust the column widths so all data is visible. **Close** the table, saving the changes.

12 Open the **Navigation Pane**, and then open the **4F Branches** table in **Design** view. Add a **Photo ID** field at the bottom of the field list using an **Attachment** data type.

13 In the **Postal Code** field, under **Input Mask**, click the **Build** button. **Save** the table. From the **Input Mask Wizard**, under **Input Mask**, select **Zip Code**, and then click **Next**. Accept the default "_" as the placeholder character. Click **Next**. Store the data without the symbols in the mask, click **Next**, and then click **Finish**.

14 Switch to **Datasheet** view, saving the changes to the table design. Update the data for each branch.

Branch	Postal Code	Attachment
Armijo	**88500-0001**	**a04F_Photo_1.jpg**
Westside	**88501-0010**	**a04F_Photo_2.jpg**
Central	**88503-0006**	**a04F_Photo_3.jpg**

15 Adjust column widths as needed to display all of the data and field names in each table. **Save** the tables. If you are instructed to submit this result, create a paper or electronic printout of both tables. **Close** the tables.

16 **Close** the database, and **Exit** Access.

Table 1

Program ID	Activity	Branch	Program Date	Age Group	Prereq	Limit
WA23	**Cyber Seniors**	**West Side**	**3/16/15**	**Adult**	**Yes**	**8**
AT15	**FrightFest**	**Armijo**	**10/31/15**	**Teen**	**No**	**20**
CC63	**Lapsit Storytime**	**Central**	**9/8/15**	**Child**	**No**	**10**

(Return to Step 11)

End **You have completed Project 4F**

Apply **4A** and **4B** skills from these Objectives:

- **1** Manage Existing Tables
- **3** Create and Modify Table Relationships
- **5** Change Data Types
- **7** Set Field Properties
- **9** Attach Files to Records

myitlab grader

Mastering Access | Project 4G Parks and Recreation

Yvonne Guillen is the Chair of the Parks & Recreation Commission for Westland Plains, Texas. The database she is using has separate tables that should be combined. In the following Mastering Access project, you will combine these tables into a facilities table. You will modify the existing tables, set field properties to ensure more accurate data entry, and add driving directions to the facilities as an attached document. Your completed work will look similar to Figure 4.55.

Project Files

For Project 4G, you will need the following files:

A new blank Word document
a04G_Parks_and_Recreation.docx
a04G_Harris_Park.docx
a04G_Northwest_Rec.docx

You will save your files as:

Lastname_Firstname_4G_Parks_and_Recreation
Lastname_Firstname_4G_Screen

Project Results

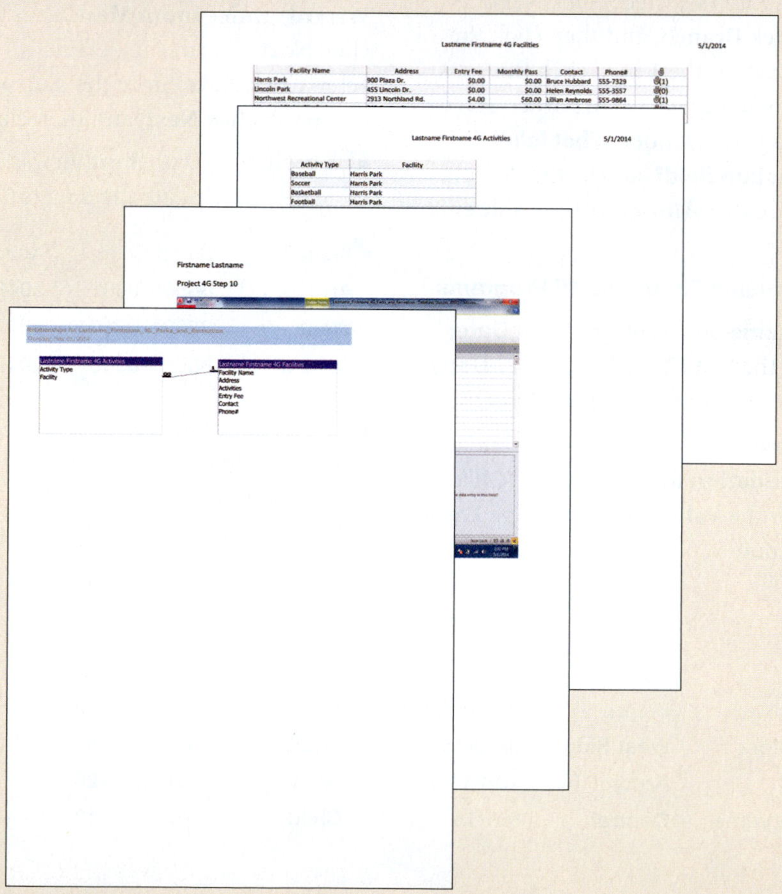

Figure 4.55

(Project 4G Parks and Recreation continues on the next page)

Content-Based Assessments

Mastering Access | Project 4G Parks and Recreation (continued)

1 **Start** Access. Locate and open the **a04G_Parks_and_Recreation** file. **Save** the database in your **Access Chapter 4** folder as **Lastname_Firstname_4G_Parks_and_Recreation** Rename all tables by adding your **Lastname Firstname** to the beginning of each table name.

2 Select the **4G Community Centers** table. **Copy** and **Paste** the table. Name the table **Lastname Firstname 4G Facilities** In the **Paste Table As** dialog box, be sure the **Structure and Data** option is selected. Click **OK**.

3 Select the **4G Parks** table, click the **Copy** button, and then click **Paste**. In the **Table Name** box, type **Lastname Firstname 4G Facilities** Under **Paste Options**, select **Append Data to Existing Table**, and then click **OK** to create one table that contains all of the facility information for the Parks & Recreation Department.

4 From the **Database Tools tab**, in the **Relationships group**, click **Relationships**. Select the **4G Facilities** and **4G Activities** tables. Create a one-to-many relationship between the **4G Facilities** table **Facility Name** field and the **4G Activities** table **Facility** field. Be sure to check **Enforce Referential Integrity**, **Cascade Update Related Fields**, and **Cascade Delete Related Records**. Adjust the size and position of the field lists so the full table names are visible.

5 Create a **Relationship Report**. If you are instructed to submit this result, create a paper or electronic printout. **Save** the report using the default name. **Close** the report, and then **Close** the Relationships window.

6 Open the **4G Facilities** table in **Design** view. Delete the **Activities** field. This field is no longer needed in this table because the relationship is established.

7 Change the data type for the **Entry Fee** field to **Currency**. In the **Contact** field, change the field size to **20**.

8 Below the **Phone#** field add a new **Directions** field to the table and use a data type of **Attachment**. In the description box, type **How to get there**

9 Add a new **Monthly Pass** field between the **Entry Fee** and **Contacts** fields, and use a data type of **Calculated.** In the **Expression Builder** dialog box, type **[Entry Fee]*15** Change the **Result Type** to **Currency**.

10 Select the **Phone#** field. In the **Input Mask** box, type **!000-0000** Change the field size to **8** Set the **Field Property** of **Required** to **Yes**. Using the Clipboard and Word, submit a printed copy of the **Phone#** Field Properties if you are requested to do so. **Save** the document as **Lastname_Firstname_4G_Screen** Switch to **Datasheet** view. Save your changes. You will see a message box warning that some data may be lost. Click **Yes** to continue. You will also see a message explaining that data integrity rules have changed; click **No** to testing the data with the new rules.

11 In the **Harris Park** record, in the **Attachment** field, double-click, and then from the student data files, attach **a04G_Harris_Park**. Click **OK**.

12 Using the same technique, for the **Northwest Recreational Center**, add the directions that are in the **a04G_Northwest_Rec** file.

13 If you are instructed to submit this result, create a paper or electronic printout of the **4G Activities** table and the **4G Facilities** table. Be sure that all field names and data display.

14 **Close** the tables, **Close** the database, and **Exit** Access.

End **You have completed Project 4G**

Apply a combination of the **4A** and **4B** skills.

GO! Fix It | Project 4H Application Tracking

Project Files

For Project 4H, you will need the following file:

a04H_Application_Tracking

You will save your database as:

Lastname_Firstname_4H_Application Tracking

In this project, you will correct table design errors in a database used by the City Manager to track the application and permit process for the citizens of Westland Plains. From the student files that accompany this textbook, open the file a04H_Application_Tracking, and then save the database in your Access Chapter 4 folder as **Lastname_Firstname_4H_Application_Tracking** Rename all tables by adding your Lastname Firstname to the beginning of each table name.

To complete the project, you must find and correct errors in table design. In addition to the errors that you find, you should know:

- There are several spelling mistakes in the Application Types table. Make the necessary corrections.
- In the Applicants table, the order in which the fields are presented is disorganized. Reorder the fields so they display information about the file and the application in an orderly fashion. Add fields to hold the city and state for each applicant. Position the fields in an orderly fashion within the list. The state field should always be represented in all capital letters and allow for only two characters. Do not populate the fields.
- In the Applications table, many fields are not assigned accurate data types. Review the field names and descriptions to make appropriate changes. Change the field size for the Reviewer field to 3.
- Be sure that all applications are reviewed by an authorized reviewer; those are currently ROD, JDD, and NDH.
- All applications must include a submitted date.
- All relationships should be edited to enforce referential integrity and both cascade options.

Create a paper or electronic printout, as directed, of your updated Application Types table, Applicants table design, and relationship report.

End **You have completed Project 4H**

Apply a combination of the **4A** and **4B** skills.

GO! Make It | Project 4I Health Services

Project Files

For Project 4I, you will need the following files:

a04I_Health_Services
a04I_Badge

You will save your database as:

Lastname_Firstname_4I_Health_Services

From the student files that accompany this textbook, open the a04I_Health_Services database file, and then save the database in your Access Chapter 4 folder as **Lastname_Firstname_4I_Health_Services** Copy the Services table and paste it as **Lastname Firstname 4I Directors Personal** Modify the table design for the new table so the table appears as shown in Figure 4.56. Create a paper or electronic printout as directed.

Project Results

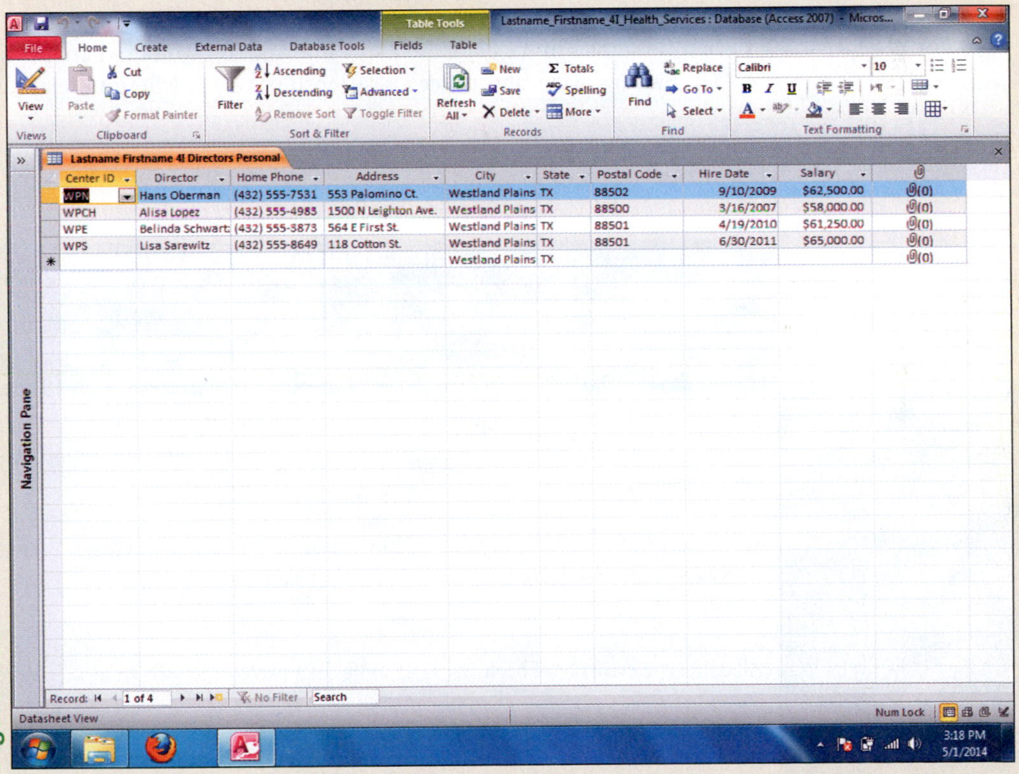

Figure 4.56

End **You have completed Project 4I**

Apply a combination of the **4A** and **4B** skills.

GO! Solve It | Project 4J Fire Department

Project Files

For Project 4J, you will need the following file:

a04J_Fire_Department

You will save your files as:

Lastname_Firstname_4J_Fire_Department
Lastname_Firstname_4J_Fire_Department_2015-10-30 (date will vary)

Samuel Barrero, the Fire Chief for Westland Plains, Texas, realizes that the Fire Department database is not designed efficiently. From the student files that accompany this textbook, open the a04J_Fire_Department database file, and then save the database in your Access Chapter 4 folder as **Lastname_Firstname_4J_Fire_Department** Make a backup copy of the original file before you make any changes.

Mr. Barrero has noticed that the 4J Administration Staff Directory, 4J Aircraft Rescue Staff Directory, and 4J Fire Prevention Staff Directory all contain the same fields. Use the copy and append techniques to create a combined table called **Lastname Firstname 4J Fire Department Directory**

Mr. Barrero sees some data type errors in the directory that need correcting. Change data types to match the data and descriptions, set field sizes, and apply input masks to assist with data entry. Utilize other tables in the database as the information source where possible.

Mr. Barrero also wants to see a relationships report where all relationships enforce referential integrity.

If you are instructed to submit this result, create a paper or electronic printout of your table design and relationship report.

Performance Elements	Performance Level: Exemplary: You consistently applied the relevant skills	Proficient: You sometimes, but not always, applied the relevant skills	Developing: You rarely or never applied the relevant skills
Create backup copy of database	Entire database was backed up correctly with a file name that describes it as a backup.	Database was backed up with no more than two missing elements.	Database was not backed up correctly.
Create 4J Fire Department Directory	Table was created with correct fields and appended records in easy-to-follow format.	Table was created with no more than two missing elements.	Table was created with more than two missing elements.
Edit data types in 4J Fire Department Directory	All data type errors have been corrected, field sizes set, and input masks and lookup fields have been used where possible.	No more than two corrections were missed.	More than two corrections were not made.
Create 4J relationship report	Report was created with correct tables and fields; referential integrity options are all selected.	Report was created with no more than two missing elements.	Report was created with more than two missing elements.

End **You have completed Project 4J**

Apply a combination of the **4A** and **4B** skills.

GO! Solve It | Project 4K City Zoo

Project Files

For Project 4K, you will need the following files:

a04K_City_Zoo
a04K_Butterfly.jpg

You will save your database as:

Lastname_Firstname_4K_City_Zoo

Amanda Hartigan, Deputy City Manager for the Quality of Life Division of Westland Plains, Texas, and City Manager Joaquin Alonzo are meeting with the Mayor, Bill J. Aycock, to discuss the funding for the city zoo. The Corporate and Foundation Council provides citizens and corporations with a partnering opportunity to support the city zoo. Amanda has outlined a database to organize the sponsorships.

From the student files that accompany this textbook, open the a04K_City_Zoo database file, and then save the database in your Access Chapter 4 folder as **Lastname_Firstname_4K_City_Zoo**

In this project, you will open the a04K_City_Zoo database and examine the tables. Rename the tables by adding your **Lastname Firstname** to the beginning of each table name. Modify the 4K Sponsored Events table to eliminate redundancy between it and the 4K Sponsors table. Also, change data types and adjust field sizes to match the data. In the 4K Sponsors table, create data validation for sponsor type; it must be Individual, Family, or Corporate. In the 4K Sponsors table, use the 4K Sponsor Levels table as a lookup field. Apply an input mask to the Phone# field. To the 4K Sponsor Levels table, add **Logo** as an attachment field. Add the a04K_Butterfly file from the student data files to the appropriate record. Create a relationship between the 4K Sponsors table and the 4K Sponsored Events table, enforcing referential integrity. Create a relationship report. If you are instructed to submit this result, create a paper or electronic printout of the tables, and the relationship report.

Performance Elements	Performance Level: Exemplary: You consistently applied the relevant skills	Proficient: You sometimes, but not always, applied the relevant skills	Developing: You rarely or never applied the relevant skills
Modify the 4K Sponsored Events table to eliminate redundancy	Table was modified with correct fields in easy-to-follow format.	Table was modified with no more than two missing elements.	Table was modified with more than two missing elements.
Change data types and field properties in the 4K Sponsors table	Data types and field properties were assigned effectively for the data that each field will hold.	Data types and field properties were assigned with no more than two missing or incorrect elements.	Data types and field properties were assigned with more than two missing or incorrect elements.
Add field to 4K Sponsor Levels and populate field	Field was added with correct data type and correct data was added to the table.	Field was added with no more than two missing or incorrect elements.	Field was added with more than two missing or incorrect elements.
Create relationships and relationship report	Report was created with correct tables and fields; referential integrity options are all selected.	Report was created with no more than two missing elements.	Report was created with more than two missing elements.

End **You have completed Project 4K**

Outcomes-Based Assessments

Rubric

The following outcomes-based assessments are *open-ended assessments*. That is, there is no specific correct result; your result will depend on your approach to the information provided. Make *Professional Quality* your goal. Use the following scoring rubric to guide you in *how* to approach the problem and then to evaluate *how well* your approach solves the problem.

The *criteria*—Software Mastery, Content, Format and Layout, and Process—represent the knowledge and skills you have gained that you can apply to solving the problem. The *levels of performance*—Professional Quality, Approaching Professional Quality, or Needs Quality Improvements—help you and your instructor evaluate your result

	Your completed project is of Professional Quality if you:	**Your completed project is Approaching Professional Quality if you:**	**Your completed project Needs Quality Improvements if you:**
1-Software Mastery	Choose and apply the most appropriate skills, tools, and features and identify efficient methods to solve the problem.	Choose and apply some appropriate skills, tools, and features, but not in the most efficient manner.	Choose inappropriate skills, tools, or features, or are inefficient in solving the problem.
2-Content	Construct a solution that is clear and well organized, contains content that is accurate, appropriate to the audience and purpose, and is complete. Provide a solution that contains no errors in spelling, grammar, or style.	Construct a solution in which some components are unclear, poorly organized, inconsistent, or incomplete. Misjudge the needs of the audience. Have some errors in spelling, grammar, or style, but the errors do not detract from comprehension.	Construct a solution that is unclear, incomplete, or poorly organized; contains some inaccurate or inappropriate content; and contains many errors in spelling, grammar, or style. Do not solve the problem.
3-Format and Layout	Format and arrange all elements to communicate information and ideas, clarify function, illustrate relationships, and indicate relative importance.	Apply appropriate format and layout features to some elements, but not others. Overuse features, causing minor distraction.	Apply format and layout that does not communicate information or ideas clearly. Do not use format and layout features to clarify function, illustrate relationships, or indicate relative importance. Use available features excessively, causing distraction.
4-Process	Use an organized approach that integrates planning, development, self-assessment, revision, and reflection.	Demonstrate an organized approach in some areas, but not others; or, use an insufficient process of organization throughout.	Do not use an organized approach to solve the problem.

Outcomes-Based Assessments

Apply a combination of the **4A** and **4B** skills.

GO! Think | Project **4L** Street Repairs

Project Files

For Project 4L, you will need the following files:

a04L_Street_Repairs
a04L_Request_Form.docx

You will save your database as:

Lastname_Firstname_4L_Street_Repairs

In this project, you will examine the database that has been created to help the Deputy City Manager of Infrastructure Services organize and track the constituent work requests for the city street repairs. Rename all of the tables by adding your **Lastname Firstname** to the beginning of each table name. Modify the design of the 4L Work Requests table. Set the Work Order # field as the primary key field, and then create an input mask to match the data for that field in the first record. For the Type field, create a lookup table using the 4L Repair Types table. In the Repair Team field, create a Lookup Wizard data type using the 4L Repair Teams table. In the Priority field, set the Required property to Yes, and then create a validation rule requiring an entry of 1, 2, or 3. Explain this rule with appropriate validation text. Open a04L_Request_Form, and then use the data to add information to the first record in the table. Use today's date as the start date. Add an attachment field to the table, and then add a04L_Request_Form as the attachment. Save the database as **Lastname_Firstname_4L_Street_Repairs** If you are instructed to submit this result, create a paper or electronic printout of the 4L Work Requests table.

End **You have completed Project 4L**

Apply a combination of the **4A** and **4B** skills.

GO! Think | Project **4M** Police Department

Project Files

For Project 4M, you will need the following file:

a04M_Police_Department

You will save your files as:

Lastname_Firstname_4M_Police_Department
Lastname_Firstname_4M_Police_Department_2015_05_01 (your date will vary)

The City Manager of Westland Plains City, Texas, Joaquin Alonzo, is the governing official over the police department. He has reviewed the database that contains the information about the force and the individual officers. In this project, you will update the database to be more efficient. Before you begin this project, back up the original database. The database contains one table of many fields. Your job is to separate the table into two smaller tables that can be related—personal and professional information joined by the Badge ID. The first and last name fields should appear only in the 4M Police Force Professional table.

Change the field sizes and set data types as appropriate. Create validation rules, and then select field properties that will decrease the number of data entry errors. Enter your own information as the first record in each table. All Badge IDs will follow the same format as yours: **WP-321** You may choose a Regional Command from the following: Central, Northeast, Southside, or Westside. Choices for Precinct include First, Second, Third, or Fourth. The rank must be Commander, Sergeant, or Lieutenant. You were hired the second Monday of last month. Save the modified database as **Lastname_Firstname_4M_Police_Department** If you are instructed to submit this result, create a paper or electronic printout of the tables and the relationship report.

End **You have completed Project 4M**

Outcomes-Based Assessments

Apply a combination of the **4A** and **4B** skills.

You and GO! | Project 4N Club Directory

Project Files

For Project 4N, you will need the following file:

New blank Database

You will save your database as:

Lastname_Firstname_4N_Club_Directory

Create a database that stores information about a club or group with which you are involved. It might be through your school, community, or employer. Name the database **Lastname_Firstname_4N_Club_Directory** The database should include two related tables. The 4N Activities table will list the activities your organization has planned for the rest of the school year, and the 4N Directory table will be a directory of the members of the group.

The 4N Activities table should include the activity name, date, cost, location, and attached directions to each event. Be sure to assign a primary key, choose correct data types, and apply field properties for effective management of data. The 4N Directory table should include each member's name, address, phone number, e-mail, and an activity that they are planning. Be sure to assign a primary key, choose correct data types, and apply field properties for effective management of data. Every member should be planning one event. You should include at least five data types across the two tables. Enter at least six records in the 4N Activities table and twelve in the 4N Directory table. Establish a relationship between the two tables enforcing referential integrity. Create a backup copy of this database. If you are instructed to submit this result, create a paper or electronic printout of the tables and the relationship report.

You will be using this database in future chapters. Be sure to make corrections to your tables as necessary to prepare for the next chapter.

End You have completed Project 4N

Enhancing Queries

OUTCOMES

At the end of this chapter you will be able to:

OBJECTIVES

Mastering these objectives will enable you to:

PROJECT 5A

Create special-purpose queries.

PROJECT 5B

Create action queries and modify join types.

Nikolay Okhitin/Shutterstock

In This Chapter

Queries can do more than extract data from tables and other queries. You can create queries to perform special functions, such as calculate numeric fields and summarize numeric data. Queries can also be used to find duplicate and unmatched records in tables, which is useful for maintaining data integrity. If you want more flexibility in the data that the query extracts from underlying tables, you can create a parameter query, where an individual is prompted for the criteria. Queries can create additional tables in the database, append records to an existing table, delete records from a table, and modify data in a table. This is useful when you do not want to directly modify the data in the tables.

College classmates Mary Connolly and J.D. Golden grew up in the sun of Orange County, California, but they also spent time in the mountain snow. After graduating with business degrees, they combined their business expertise and their favorite sports to open **4Ever Boarding**, a snowboard and surf shop. The store carries top brands of men's and women's apparel, goggles and sunglasses, and boards and gear. The surfboard selection includes both classic boards and the latest high-tech boards. Snowboarding gear can be purchased in packages or customized for the most experienced boarders. Connolly and Golden are proud to count many of Southern California's extreme sports games participants among their customers.

Project 5A Inventory

myitlab
Project 5A Training

Project Activities

In Activities 5.01 through 5.10, you will help Ally Mason, Purchasing Manager of 4Ever Boarding Surf and Snowboard Shop, create special-purpose queries to calculate data, summarize and group data, display data in a spreadsheet-like format, and find duplicate and unmatched records. You will also create a query that prompts individuals to enter the criteria. Your completed queries will look similar to Figure 5.1.

Project Files

For Project 5A, you will need the following file:

a05A_Inventory

You will save your database as:

Lastname_Firstname_5A_Inventory

Project Results

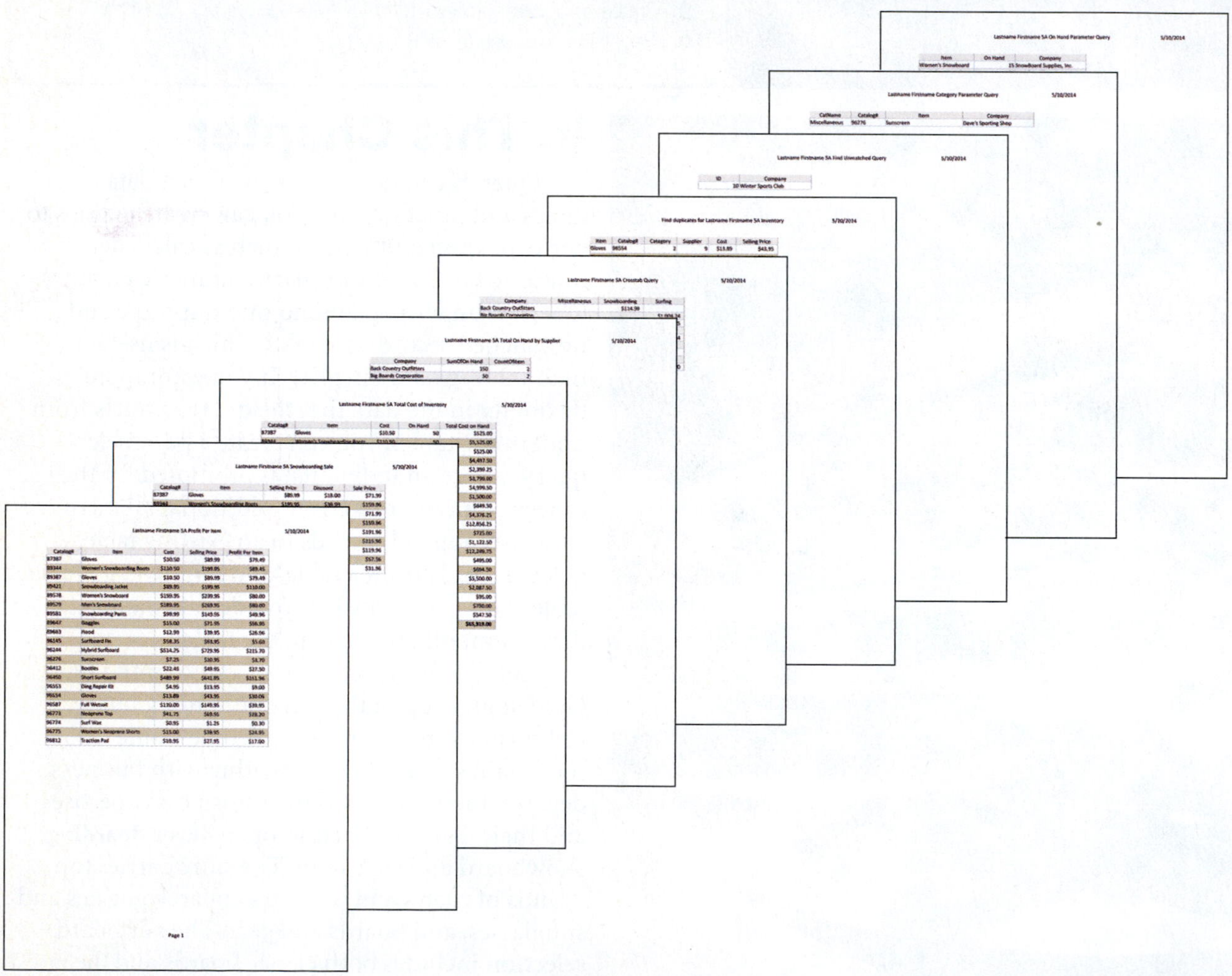

Figure 5.1
Project 5A Inventory

Objective 1 | Create Calculated Fields in a Query

Queries can be used to create a ***calculated field***—a field that obtains its data by performing a calculation or computation, using a formula. For example, to determine the profit that will be made from the sale of an item, subtract the cost of the item from the sale price of the item. Another example is to create a calculated field that computes the gross pay for an employee. There are two steps needed to produce a calculated field in a query. First, in the design grid of the query, in a blank column, type the name of the field that will store the results of the calculated field—the name must be followed by a colon (:). Second, type the ***expression***—the formula—that will perform the calculation. *Each field name* used in the expression must be enclosed within *its own pair* of square brackets, [ ]. If you are using a number in the expression—for example, a percentage—type only the percentage; do not enclose it in brackets.

Activity 5.01 | Creating a Calculated Field Based on Two Existing Fields

In this activity, you will create a calculated field to determine the profit for each item in the inventory database.

1 **Start** Access. Navigate to the location where the student data files for this textbook are saved. Locate and open the **a05A_Inventory** file. Display **Backstage** view, and click **Save Database As**. In the **Save As** dialog box, navigate to the drive on which you will be saving your folders and projects for this chapter. Create a new folder named **Access Chapter 5** and then save the file as **Lastname_Firstname_5A_Inventory** in the folder.

2 If necessary, enable the content or add the Access Chapter 5 folder to the Trust Center. In the **Navigation Pane**, rename each table by adding **Lastname Firstname** to the beginning of each table name.

3 In the **Navigation Pane**, double-click **5A Inventory**. If the Field List pane opens, close it. Take a moment to study the fields in the table.

Snowboarding items have a catalog number beginning with *8*; surfing items have a catalog number beginning with *9*. The *Category* field is a Lookup column. If you click in the Category field, and then click the arrow, a list of category numbers and their descriptions display. The *Supplier* field identifies the supplier numbers with descriptions. *Cost* is the price the company pays to a supplier for each item. *Selling Price* is what the company will charge its customers for each item. *On Hand* refers to the current inventory for each item.

4 Switch to **Design** view, and then take a moment to study the data structure. Notice the Category field has a data type of Number; this reflects the autonumber field (ID field) in the Category table used in the Lookup field. When you are finished, **Close** [X] the table, and then **Close** [«] the **Navigation Pane**.

5 On the Ribbon, click the **Create tab**. In the **Queries group**, click the **Query Design** button. In the **Show Table** dialog box, double-click **5A Inventory** to add the table to the Query design workspace, and then click **Close**. Expand the list so the table name and all fields are visible.

If you add the wrong table to the workspace or have two copies of the same table, right-click the extra table, and click Remove Table.

6 From the **5A Inventory** field list, add the following fields, in the order specified, to the design grid: **Catalog#**, **Item**, **Cost**, and **Selling Price**. Recall that you can double-click a field name to add it to the design grid, or you can drag the field name to the field box on the design grid. You can also click in the field box, click the arrow, and click the field name from the displayed list.

7 On the **Design tab**, in the **Results group**, click the **Run** button to display the four fields used in the query, and then compare your screen with Figure 5.2.

Figure 5.2

Four fields extracted from the table

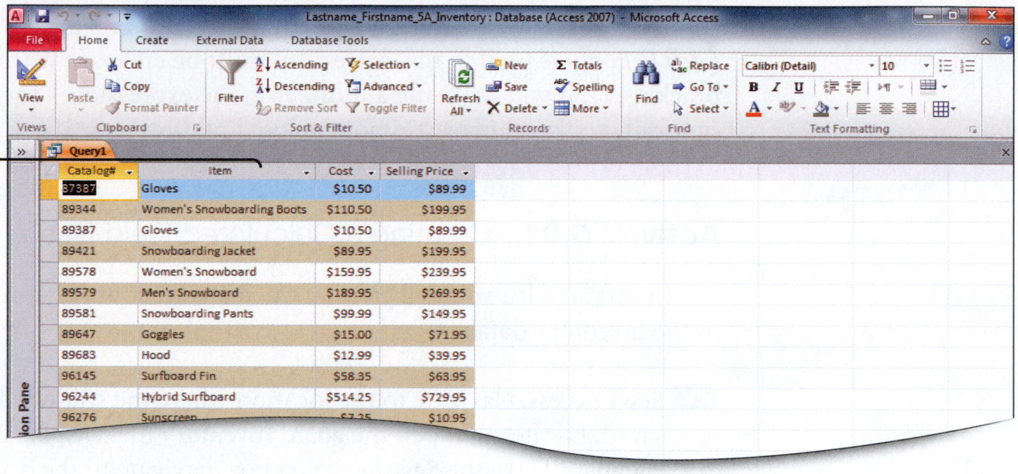

8 Switch to **Design** view. In the **Field row**, right-click in the field cell in the first empty column—the fifth column—to display a shortcut menu, and then click **Zoom**. ***Arithmetic operators*** are mathematical symbols used to build expressions in calculated fields. Take a moment to study the arithmetic operators as described in Figure 5.3.

The Zoom dialog box gives you working space so that you can see the expression—formula—as you enter it. The expression can also be entered directly in the empty Field box.

Operator	Description	Example	Result
+	Addition	Cost:[Price]+[Tax]	Adds the value in the Price field to the value in the Tax field and displays the result in the Cost field.
–	Subtraction	Cost:[Price]– [Markdown]	Subtracts the value in the Markdown field from the value in the Price field and displays the result in the Cost field.
*	Multiplication	Tax:[Price]*.05	Multiplies the value in the Price field by .05 (5%) and displays the result in the Tax field. (Note: This is an asterisk, not an *x*.)
/	Division	Average:[Total]/3	Divides the value in the Total field by 3 and displays the result in the Average field.
^	Exponentiation	Required:2^[Bits]	Raises 2 to the power of the value in the Bits field and stores the result in the Required field.
\	Integer division	Average:[Children]\ [Families]	Divides the value in the Children field by the value in the Families field and displays the integer portion—the digits to the left of the decimal point—in the Average field.

Figure 5.3

9 In the **Zoom** dialog box, type **Profit Per Item:[Selling Price]-[Cost]** and then compare your screen with Figure 5.4.

The first element of the calculated field—*Profit Per Item*—is the new field name that will display the calculated value. The field name must be unique for the table being used in the query. Following the new field name is a colon (:). A colon in a calculated field separates the new field name from the expression. *Selling Price* is enclosed in square brackets because it is an existing field name from the *5A Inventory* table and contains data that will be used in the calculation. Following *[Selling Price]* is a hyphen (-), which, in math calculations, signifies subtraction. Finally, *Cost*, an existing field in the *5A Inventory* table, is enclosed in square brackets. This field also contains data that will be used in the calculation.

Figure 5.4

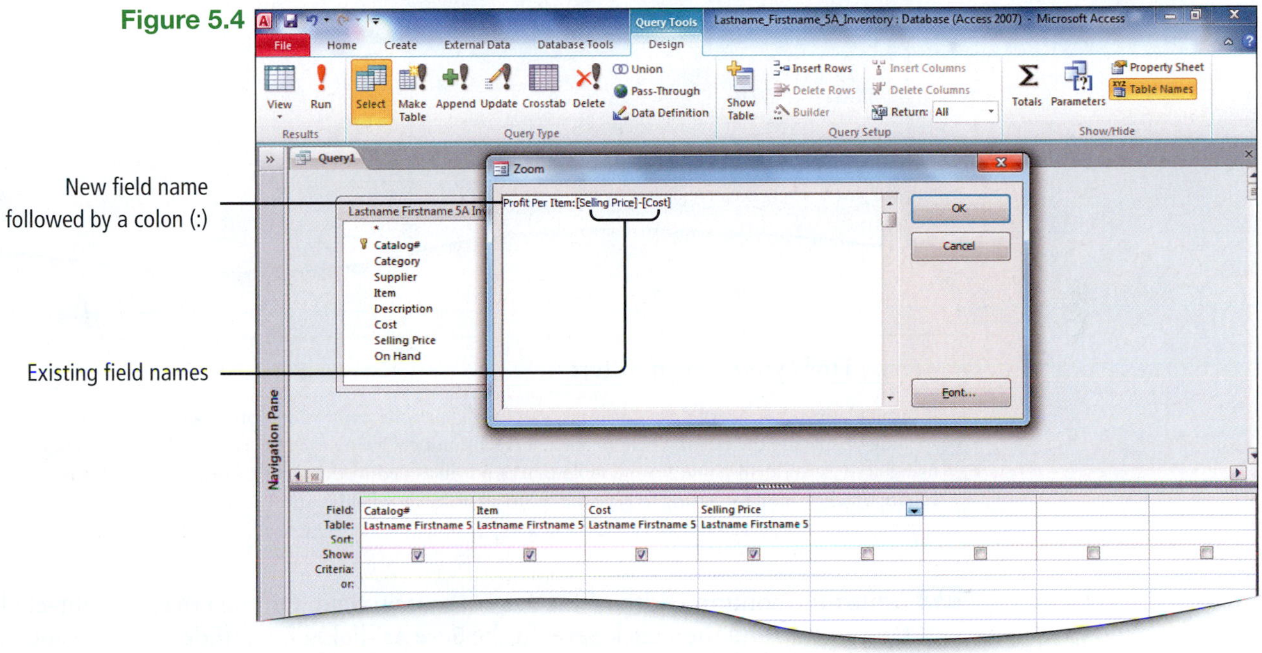

Note | Using Square Brackets Around Field Names in Expressions

Square brackets are not required around a field name in an expression if the field name is only one word. For example, if the field name is *Cost*, it is not necessary to type brackets around it—Access will automatically insert the square brackets. If a field name has a space in it, however, you must type the square brackets around the field name. Otherwise, Access will display a message stating that the expression you entered contains invalid syntax.

10 In the **Zoom** dialog box, click **OK**, and then **Run** the query. Compare your screen with Figure 5.5.

A fifth column—the calculated field—with a field name of *Profit Per Item* displays. For each record, the value in the *Profit Per Item* field is calculated by subtracting the value in the *Cost* field from the value in the *Selling Price* field.

Figure 5.5

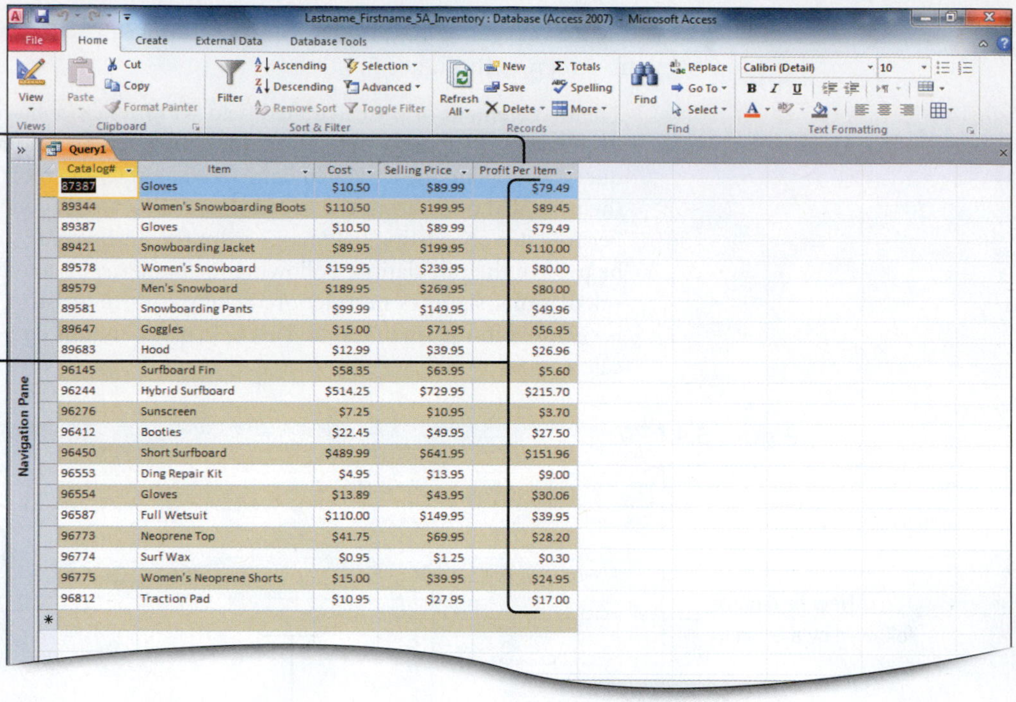

Catalog#	Item	Cost	Selling Price	Profit Per Item
87387	Gloves	$10.50	$89.99	$79.49
89344	Women's Snowboarding Boots	$110.50	$199.95	$89.45
89387	Gloves	$10.50	$89.99	$79.49
89421	Snowboarding Jacket	$89.95	$199.95	$110.00
89578	Women's Snowboard	$159.95	$239.95	$80.00
89579	Men's Snowboard	$189.95	$269.95	$80.00
89581	Snowboarding Pants	$99.99	$149.95	$49.96
89647	Goggles	$15.00	$71.95	$56.95
89683	Hood	$12.99	$39.95	$26.96
96145	Surfboard Fin	$58.35	$63.95	$5.60
96244	Hybrid Surfboard	$514.25	$729.95	$215.70
96276	Sunscreen	$7.25	$10.95	$3.70
96412	Booties	$22.45	$49.95	$27.50
96450	Short Surfboard	$489.99	$641.95	$151.96
96553	Ding Repair Kit	$4.95	$13.95	$9.00
96554	Gloves	$13.89	$43.95	$30.06
96587	Full Wetsuit	$110.00	$149.95	$39.95
96773	Neoprene Top	$41.75	$69.95	$28.20
96774	Surf Wax	$0.95	$1.25	$0.30
96775	Women's Neoprene Shorts	$15.00	$39.95	$24.95
96812	Traction Pad	$10.95	$27.95	$17.00

Alert! | Does your screen differ?

If a calculation in a query does not work, carefully check the expression you typed. Common errors include spelling or spacing the existing field name incorrectly, not enclosing each existing field name in square brackets, using an existing field name from a table that is not included in the Query workspace, enclosing numbers in square brackets, and forgetting to type the colon after the new field name.

11 Adjust the column width of the *Profit Per Item* field. On the **tab row**, right-click the **Query1 tab**, and then click **Save**. In the **Save As** dialog box, under **Query Name**, type **Lastname Firstname 5A Profit Per Item** and then click **OK**. View the query in **Print Preview**, ensuring that the query prints on one page; if you are instructed to submit this result, create a paper or electronic printout. **Close** [X] the query.

Activity 5.02 | Creating a Calculated Field Based on One Existing Field and a Number

In this activity, you will calculate the sale prices of each snowboarding item for the annual sale. During this event, all snowboarding supplies are discounted by 20 percent.

1 On the Ribbon, click the **Create tab**. In the **Queries group**, click the **Query Design** button. Add the **5A Inventory** table to the Query design workspace, and then **Close** the **Show Table** dialog box. Expand the field list.

2 From the **5A Inventory** field list, add the following fields, in the order specified, to the design grid: **Catalog#**, **Item**, and **Selling Price**.

3 In the **Field row**, right-click in the field cell in the first empty column—the fourth column—to display a shortcut menu, and then click **Zoom**. In the **Zoom** dialog box, type **Discount:[Selling Price]*.20** and then compare your screen with Figure 5.6.

The value in the *Discount* field is calculated by multiplying the value in the *Selling Price* field by .20—20%. Recall that only field names are enclosed in square brackets.

Figure 5.6

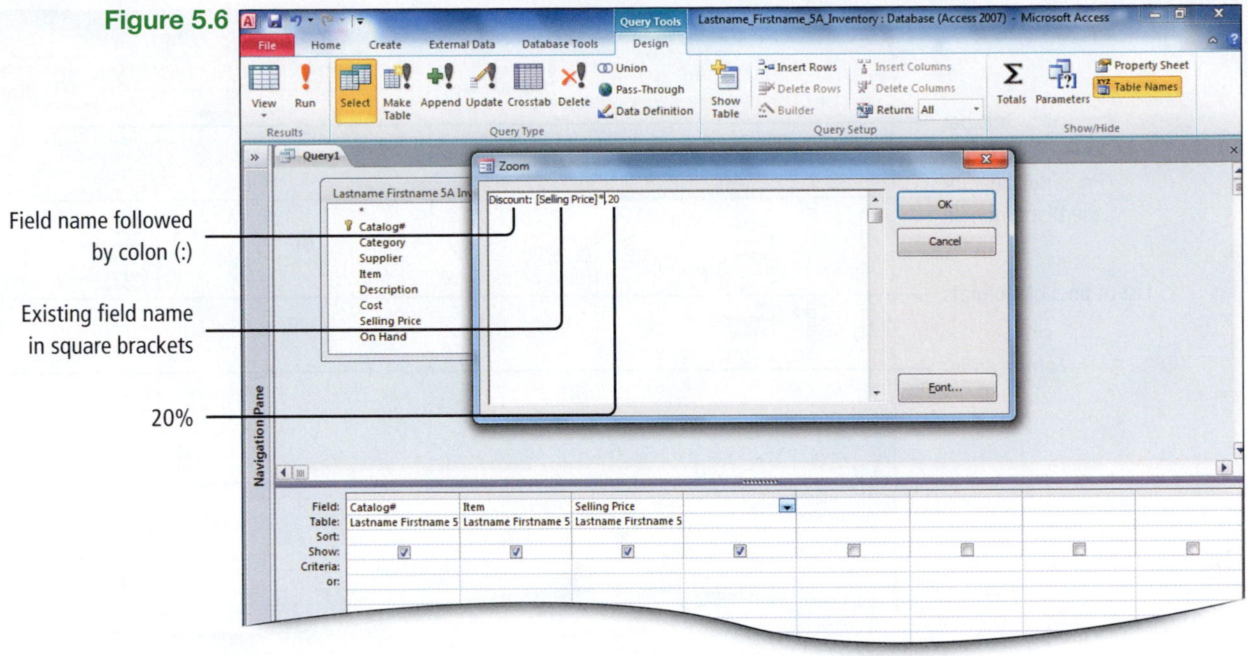

4 In the **Zoom** dialog box, click **OK**, and then **Run** the query.

The *Discount* field displays the results of the calculation. The data is not formatted with a dollar sign, and the first record displays a discount of 17.998. When using a number in an expression, the values in the calculated field may not be formatted the same as in the existing field.

5 Switch to **Design** view. On the **Design tab**, in the **Show/Hide group**, click the **Table Names** button.

In the design grid, the Table row no longer displays. If all of the fields in the design grid are from one table, you can hide the Table row. The Table Names button is a toggle button; if you click it again, the Table row displays in the design grid.

6 In the **Field row**, click in the **Discount** field box. On the **Design tab**, in the **Show/Hide group**, click the **Property Sheet** button. Alternatively, right-click in the field box and click Properties, or hold down Alt and press Enter.

The Property Sheet for the selected field—*Discount*—displays on the right side of the screen. In the Property Sheet, under the title of *Property Sheet*, is the subtitle—*Selection type: Field Properties*.

Alert! | Does the Property Sheet Display a Subtitle of Selection Type: Query Properties?

To display the Property Sheet for a field, you must first click in the field; otherwise, the Property Sheet for the query might display. If this occurs, in the Field row, click the Discount field box to change the Property Sheet to this field.

7 In the **Property Sheet**, on the **General tab**, click in the **Format** box, and then click the displayed **arrow**. Compare your screen with Figure 5.7.

Figure 5.7

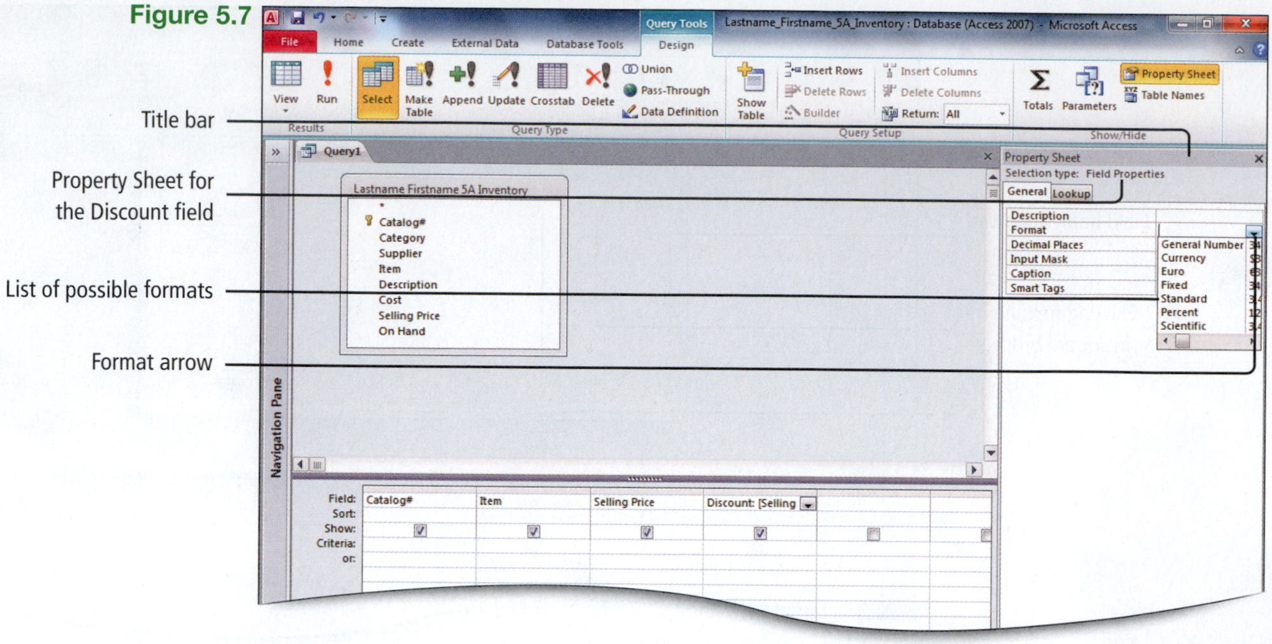

8 In the list of formats, click **Currency**. On the **Property Sheet** title bar, click the **Close** button. **Run** the query to display the results.

The values in the Discount field now display with a dollar sign, and the first record's discount—$18.00—displays with two decimal places.

9 Switch to **Design** view. In the **Field row**, right-click in the first empty column, and then click **Zoom**. In the **Zoom** dialog box, type **Sale Price:[Selling Price]-[Discount]** and then click **OK**. **Run** the query to display the results.

The *Sale Price* for Catalog #8737, Gloves, is *$71.99*. The value in the *Sale Price* field is calculated by subtracting the value in the *Discount* field from the value in the *Selling Price* field. The field names are not case sensitive—you can type a field name in lower case, such as *[selling price]*. Because you used only existing fields in the expression that were formatted as currency, the values in the *Sale Price* field are formatted as currency.

10 Switch to **Design** view. In the design grid, under **Catalog#**, click in the **Criteria** box, type **8*** and then press Enter.

Recall that the asterisk (*) is a wildcard. In this criteria, Access will extract those records where the catalog number begins with *8* followed by one or more characters. Also, recall that Access formats the criteria. For example, you typed *8**, and Access formatted the criteria as *Like "8*"*.

11 **Run** the query. Notice that only the records with a **Catalog#** beginning with an **8** display—snowboarding items.

12 **Save** the query as **Lastname Firstname 5A Snowboarding Sale** View the query in **Print Preview**, ensuring that the query prints on one page. If you are instructed to submit this result, create a paper or electronic printout. **Close** the query.

Objective 2 | Use Aggregate Functions in a Query

In Access queries, you can use ***aggregate functions*** to perform a calculation on a column of data and return a single value. Examples are the Sum function, which adds a column of numbers, and the Average function, which adds a column of numbers, ignoring null values, and divides by the number of records with values. Access provides two ways to use aggregate functions in a query—you can add a total row in Datasheet view or create a totals query in Design view.

Activity 5.03 | Adding a Total Row to a Query

In this activity, you will create and run a query. In Datasheet view, you will add a Total row to insert an aggregate function in one or more columns without having to change the design of the query.

1 Create a new query in **Query Design**. Add the **5A Inventory** table to the Query design workspace, and then **Close** the **Show Table** dialog box. Expand the field list. From the **5A Inventory** field list, add the following fields, in the order specified, to the design grid: **Catalog#**, **Item**, **Cost**, and **On Hand**.

2 In the **Field row**, right-click in the first empty column, and then click **Zoom**. In the **Zoom** dialog box, type **Total Cost On Hand:[Cost]*[On Hand]**

The value in the *Total Cost On Hand* field is calculated by multiplying the value in the *Cost* field by the value in the *On Hand* field. This field will display the cost of all of the inventory items, not just the cost per item.

3 In the **Zoom** dialog box, click **OK**, and then **Run** the query to display the results in Datasheet view. Adjust the column width of the newly calculated field to display the entire field name, and then compare your screen with Figure 5.8.

If the *Total Cost On Hand* for Catalog #8937, Gloves, is not *$525.00*, switch to **Design** view and edit the expression you entered for the calculated field.

Figure 5.8

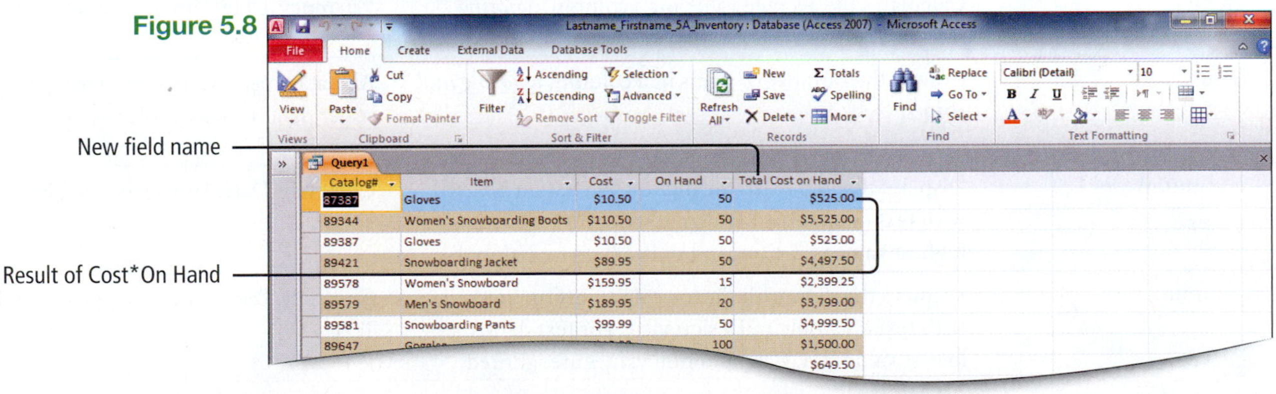

4 On the **Home tab**, in the **Records group**, click the **Totals** button. If necessary, scroll down until the newly created Total row displays. In the **Total row**, under **Total Cost On Hand**, click in the empty box to display an arrow at the left edge. Click the **arrow**, and then compare your screen with Figure 5.9. Take a moment to study the aggregate functions that can be used with both the Total row and the design grid as described in the table in Figure 5.10.

The Total row displays after the New record row. The first field in a Total row contains the word *Total*. The Total row is not a record. The list of aggregate functions displayed will vary depending on the data type for each field or column; for example, number types display a full list of functions, whereas a text field will display only the *Count* function.

Figure 5.9

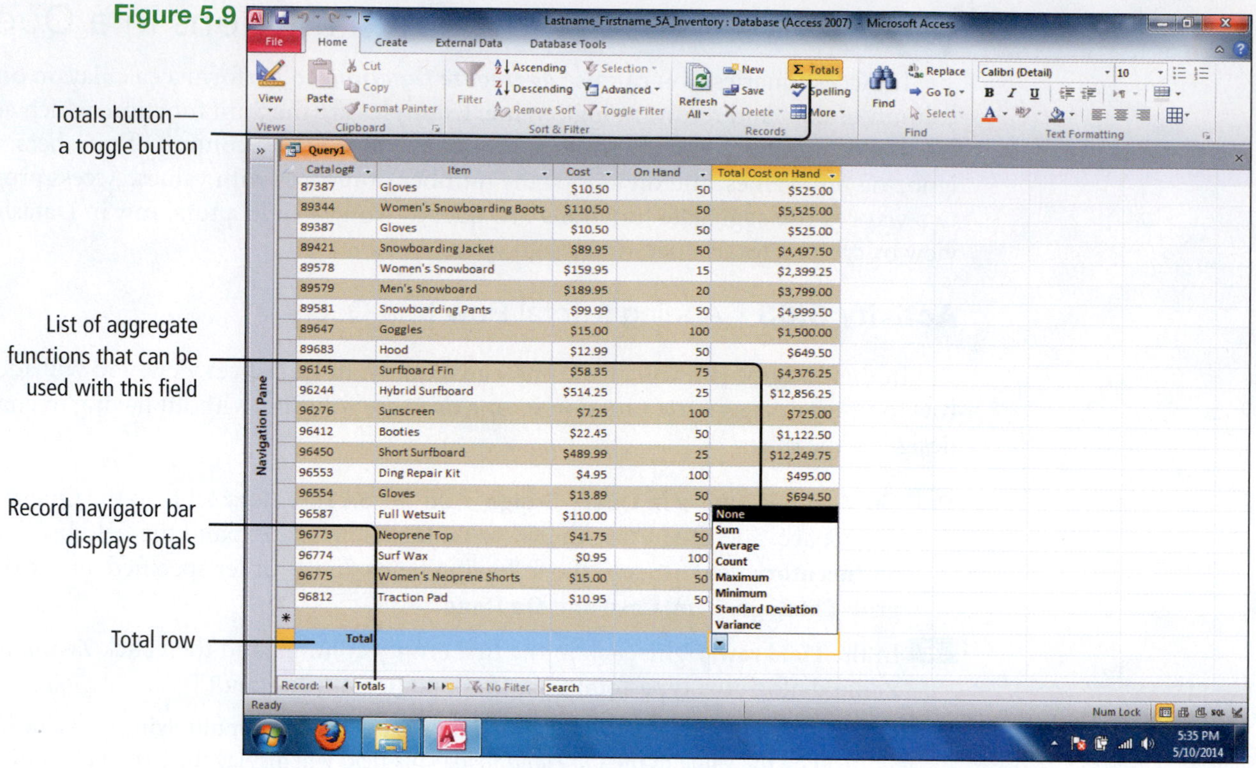

Function	Description	Can Be Used with Data Type(s)
Sum	Adds the values in a column.	Currency, Decimal, Number
Average	Calculates the average value for a column, *ignoring null values.*	Currency, Date/Time, Decimal, Number
Count	Counts the number of items in a column, *ignoring null values.*	All data types, except complex repeating scalar data, such as a column of multivalued lists
Maximum	Displays the item with the highest value. Can be used with text data only in Design view. With text data, the highest value is *Z*. Case and null values are ignored.	Currency, Date/Time, Decimal, Number, Text
Minimum	Displays the item with the lowest value. Can be used with text data only in Design view. For text data, the lowest value is *A*. Case and null values are ignored.	Currency, Date/Time, Decimal, Number, Text
Standard Deviation	Measures how widely values are dispersed from the mean value.	Currency, Decimal, Number
Variance	Measures the statistical variance of all values in the column. If the table has less than two rows, a null value is displayed.	Currency, Decimal, Number

Figure 5.10

5 From the displayed list, click **Sum**, and then compare your screen with Figure 5.11.

A sum of $65,919.00 displays, which is the total of all the data in the Total Cost On Hand field.

Figure 5.11

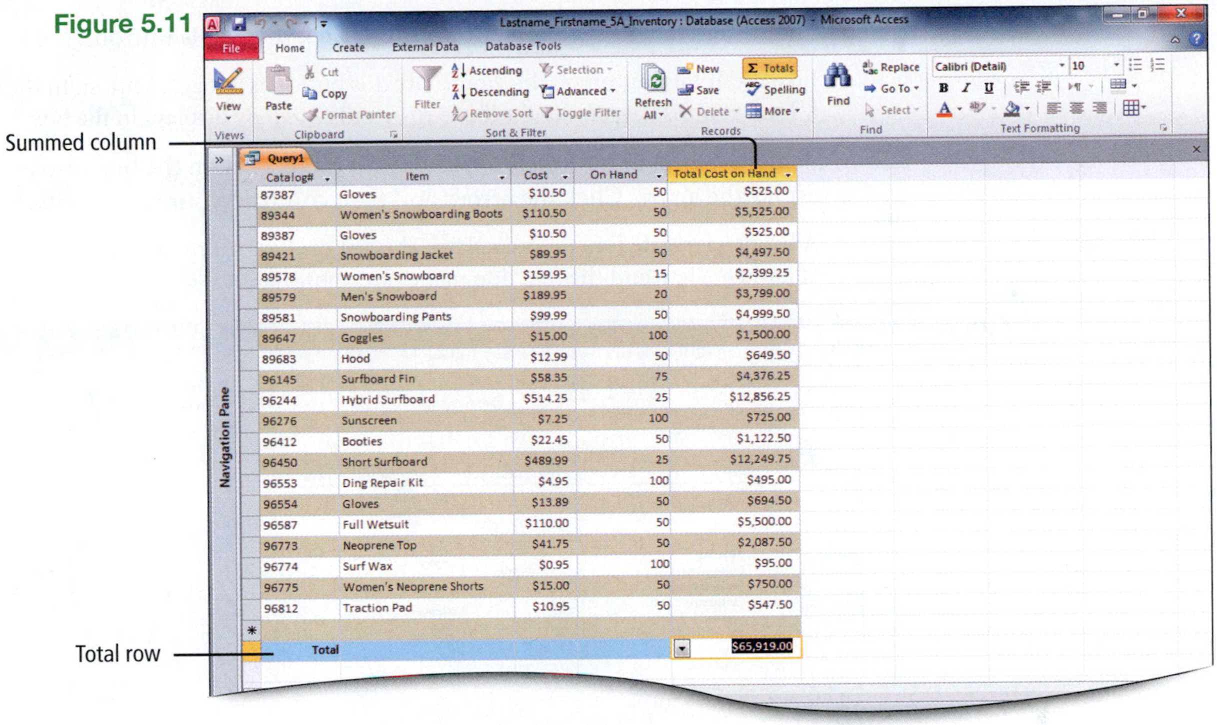

Note | Applying Aggregate Functions to Multiple Fields

You can apply aggregate functions to more than one field by clicking in the Total row for the field, clicking the arrow, and then clicking the function. The functions for multiple fields can be different functions.

6 **Save** the query as **Lastname Firstname 5A Total Cost of Inventory** View the query in **Print Preview**, ensuring that the query prints on one page; if you are instructed to submit this result, create a paper or electronic printout. **Close** the query.

More Knowledge | Removing the Aggregate Function and Removing the Total Row

To remove an aggregate function from a column, on the Total row under the field, click the arrow and then click None. To remove the Total row, on the Home tab, in the Records group, click the Totals button. You cannot cut or delete a Total row; you can only turn it on or off. You can copy a Total row and paste it into another file—for example, an Excel worksheet or a Word document.

Activity 5.04 | Creating a Totals Query

In this activity, you will create a ***totals query***—a query that calculates subtotals across groups of records. For example, to subtotal the number of inventory items by suppliers, use a totals query to group the records by the supplier and then apply an aggregate function to the On Hand field. In the previous activity, you created a Total row, which applied an aggregate function to one column—field—of data. A totals query is used when you need to apply an aggregate function to some or all of the records in a query. A totals query can then be used as a source for another database object, such as a report.

1 Create a new query in **Query Design**. Add the **5A Suppliers** table and the **5A Inventory** table to the Query design workspace, and then **Close** the **Show Table** dialog box. Expand both field lists. Notice that there is a one-to-many relationship between the tables—*one* supplier can supply *many* items. From the **5A Inventory** field list, add **On Hand** to the first field box in the design grid.

2 On the **Design tab**, in the **Show/Hide group**, click the **Totals** button.

Like the Totals button on the Home tab, this button is a toggle button. In the design grid, a Total row displays under the Table row; and *Group By* displays in the box.

3 In the design grid, in the **Total row**, under **On Hand**, click in the box displaying *Group By* to display the arrow. Click the **arrow**, and then compare your screen with Figure 5.12.

A list of aggregate functions displays. This list displays more functions than the list in Datasheet view, and the function names are abbreviated.

Figure 5.12

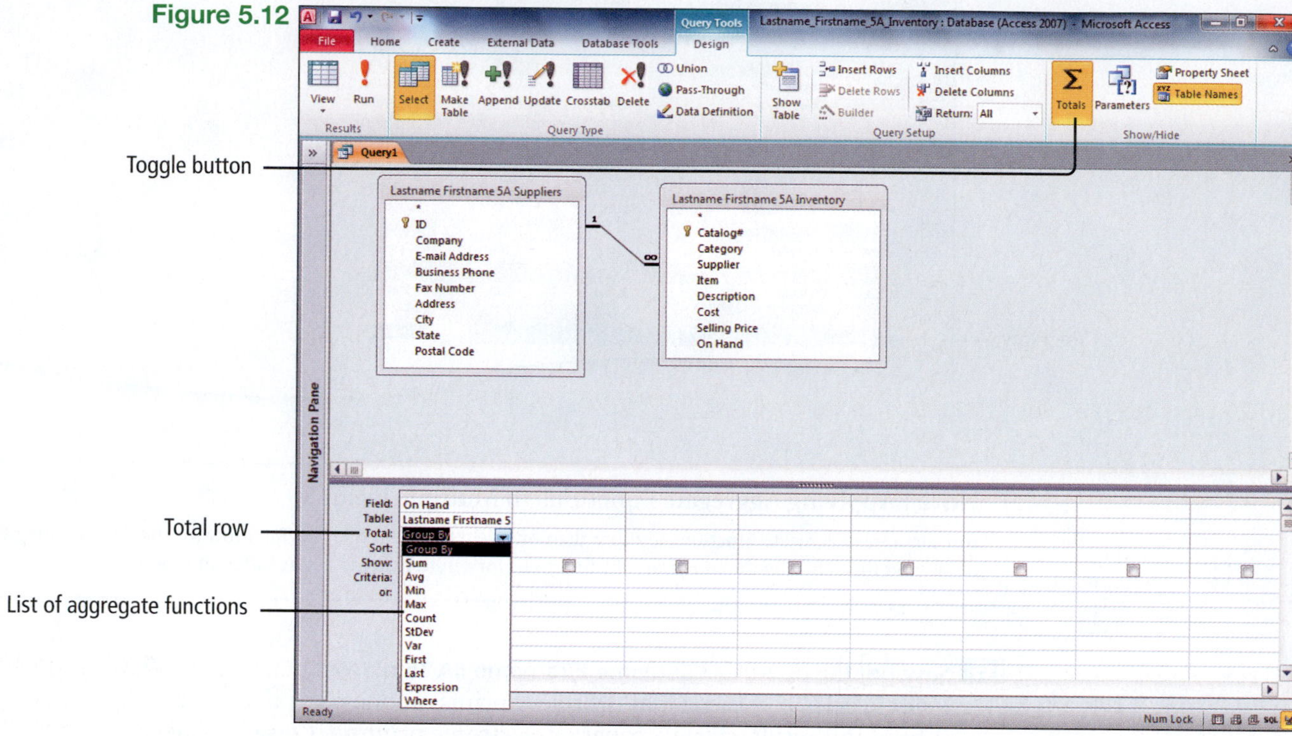

4 From the displayed list, click **Sum**. **Run** the query, and then compare your screen with Figure 5.13.

When you run a totals query, the result—*1160*—of the aggregate function is displayed; the records are not displayed. The name of the function and the field used are displayed in the column heading.

> **More Knowledge | Changing the Name of the Totals Query Result**
>
> To change the name from the combination aggregate function and field name to something more concise and descriptive, in Design view, in the Field row, click in the On Hand field box. On the Design tab, in the Show/Hide group, click the Property Sheet button. In the Property Sheet, on the General tab, click in the Caption box, and type the new name for the result.

Figure 5.13

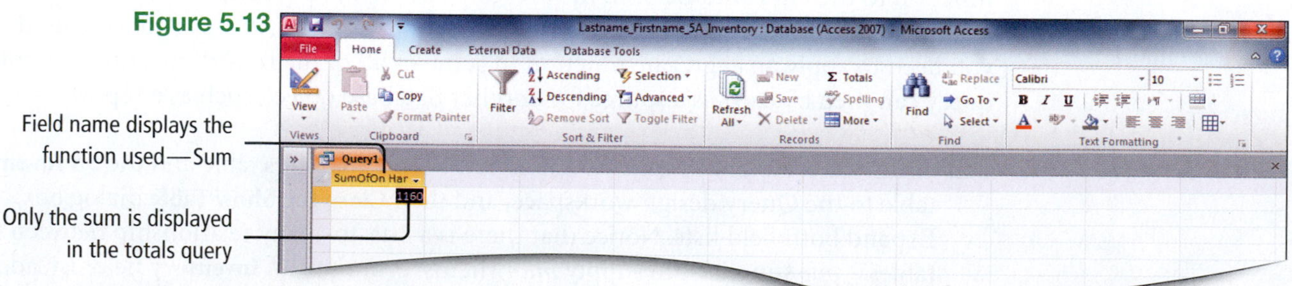

5 Adjust the width of the column to display the entire field name, and then switch to **Design** view. In the **5A Inventory** field list, double-click **Item** to insert the field in the second column in the design grid. In the design grid, under **Item**, click in the **Total row** box, click the displayed **arrow**, and then click **Count**. **Run** the query. Adjust the width of the second column to display the entire field name.

The number of records—*21*—displays. You can include multiple fields in a totals query, but each field in the query must have an aggregate function applied to it. If you include a field but do not apply an aggregate function, the query results will display every record and will not display a single value for the field or fields. The exception to this is when you group records by a category, such as supplier name.

6 Switch to **Design** view. From the **5A Suppliers** field list, drag **Company** to the design grid until the field is on top of **On Hand**.

Company is inserted as the first field, and the *On Hand* field moves to the right. In the *Total* row under *Company*, *Group By* displays.

7 **Run** the query. If necessary, adjust column widths to display all of the field names and all of the data under each field, and then compare your screen with Figure 5.14.

The results display the total number of inventory items on hand from each supplier and the number of individual items purchased from each supplier. By using this type of query, you can identify the supplier that provides the most individual items—Wetsuit Country—and the supplier from whom the company has the most on-hand inventory items—Dave's Sporting Shop.

Figure 5.14

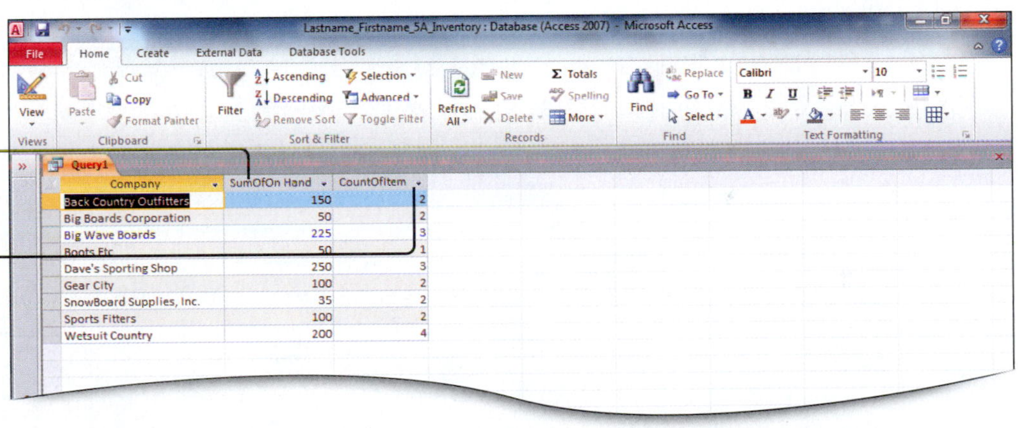

8 **Save** the query as **Lastname Firstname 5A Total On Hand By Supplier** View the query in **Print Preview**, ensuring that the query prints on one page. If you are instructed to submit this result, create a paper or electronic printout. **Close** the query.

Objective 3 | Create a Crosstab Query

A ***crosstab query*** uses an aggregate function for data that is grouped by two types of information and displays the data in a compact, spreadsheet-like format. A crosstab query always has at least one row heading, one column heading, and one summary field. Use a crosstab query to summarize a large amount of data in a small space that is easy to read.

Activity 5.05 | Creating a Select Query as the Source for the Crosstab Query

In this activity, you will create a select query displaying suppliers, the category of the inventory item, the inventory item, and the cost per item paid to the supplier. Recall that a select query is the most common type of query, and it extracts data from one or more tables or queries, displaying the results in a datasheet. After creating the select query, you will use it to create a crosstab query to display the data in a format that is easier to analyze. Because most crosstab queries extract data from more than one table or query, it is best to create a select query containing all of the fields necessary for the crosstab query.

1 Create a new query in **Query Design**. Add the following tables, in the order specified, to the Query design workspace: **5A Category**, **5A Inventory**, and **5A Suppliers**. In the **Show Table** dialog box, click **Close**. Expand the field lists.

2 In the **5A Suppliers** field list, double-click **Company** to add it to the first field box in the design grid. In the **5A Category** field list, double-click **CatName** to add it to the second field box in the design grid. In the **5A Inventory** field list, double-click **Cost** to add it to the third field box in the design grid. In the design grid, under **Company**, click in the **Sort** box. Click the **arrow**, and then click **Ascending**. Sort the **CatName** field in **Ascending** order.

3 On the **Design tab**, in the **Show/Hide group**, click the **Totals** button. In the design grid, notice a **Total row** displays under the **Table row**. Under **Cost**, click in the **Total** box, click the **arrow**, and then click **Sum**. Compare your screen with Figure 5.15.

Figure 5.15

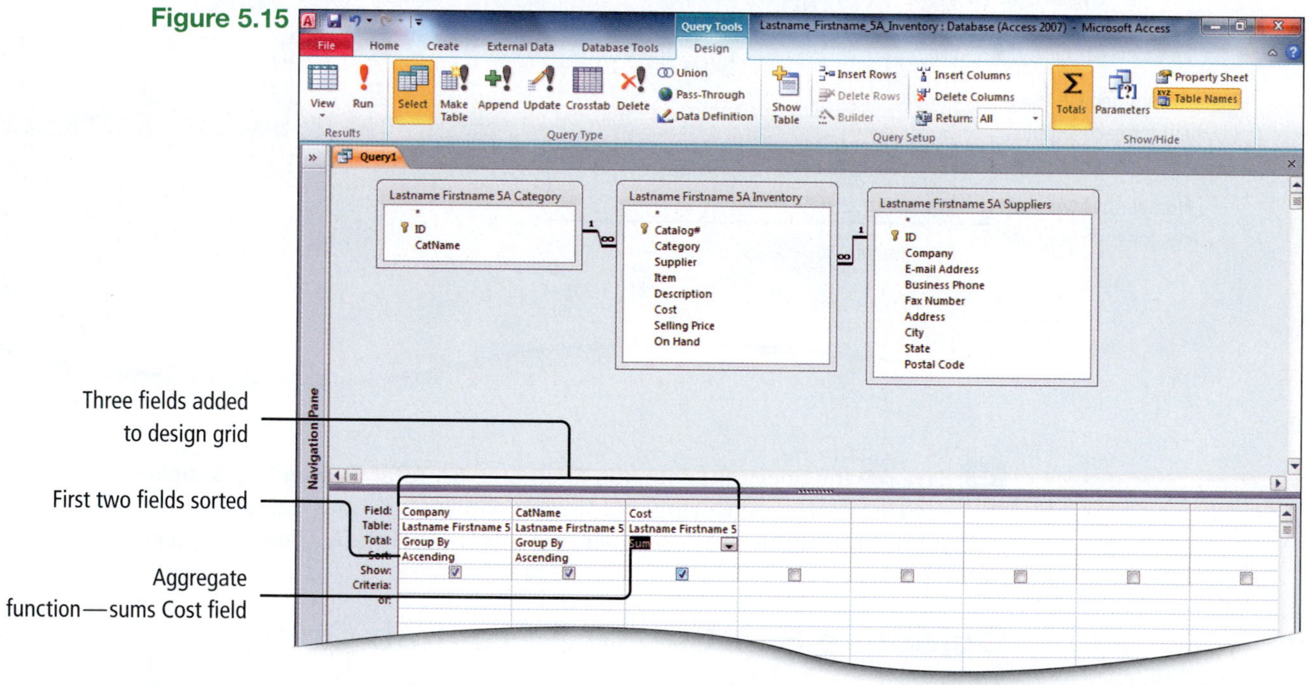

4 **Run** the query. In the datasheet, adjust all column widths to display the entire field name and the data for each record, and then compare your screen with Figure 5.16.

The select query groups the totals vertically by company and then by category.

Figure 5.16

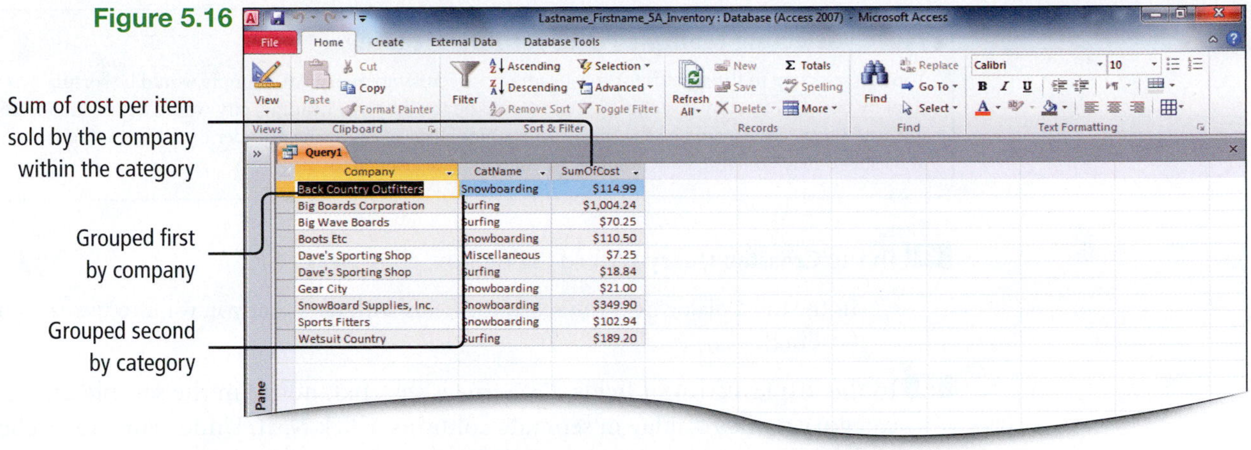

5 Switch to **Design** view. On the **Design tab**, in the **Show/Hide group**, click the **Totals** button to remove the **Total row** from the design grid.

This select query will be used to create the crosstab query. When you create a crosstab query, you will be prompted to use an aggregate function on a field, so it should not be summed prior to creating the query.

6 **Save** the query as **Lastname Firstname 5A Cost Per Company and Category** and then **Close** the query.

Activity 5.06 | Creating a Crosstab Query

In this activity, you will create a crosstab query using the 5A Cost Per Company and Category query as the source for the crosstab query.

1 On the Ribbon, click the **Create tab**. In the **Queries group**, click the **Query Wizard** button. In the **New Query** dialog box, click **Crosstab Query Wizard**, and then click **OK**.

In the first Crosstab Query Wizard dialog box, you select the table or query to be used as the source for the crosstab query.

2 In the middle of the dialog box, under **View**, click the **Queries** option button. In the list of queries, click **Query: 5A Cost Per Company and Category**, and then click **Next**.

In the second Crosstab Query Wizard dialog box, you select the fields with data that you want to use as the row headings.

3 Under **Available Fields**, double-click **Company**, and then compare your screen with Figure 5.17.

Company displays under Selected Fields. At the bottom of the dialog box, in the Sample area, a preview of the row headings displays. Each company name will be listed on a separate row in the first column.

Figure 5.17

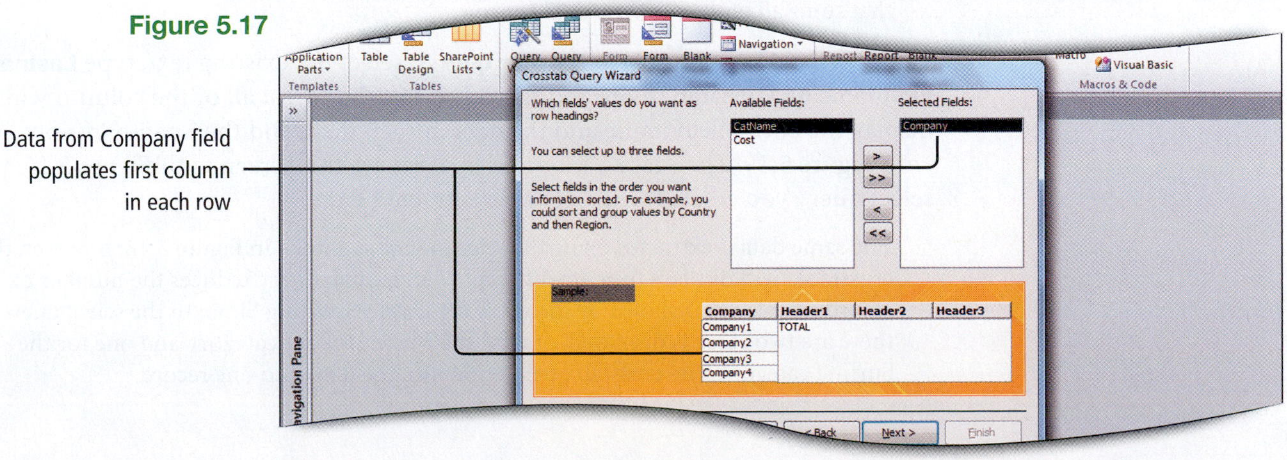

> **Note | Selecting Multiple Fields for Row Headings**
>
> You can select up to three fields for row headings in a crosstab query. An example would be sorting first by state, then by city, and then by Postal code. State would be the first row heading, city would be the second row heading, and Postal code would be the third row heading. Regardless of the number of fields used for row headings, at least two fields must remain available to complete the crosstab query.

4 In the **Crosstab Query Wizard** dialog box, click **Next**.

In the third dialog box, you select the fields with data that you want to use as column headings.

5 In the displayed list of fields, **CatName** is selected; notice in the sample area that the category names display in separate columns. Click **Next**. Under **Functions**, click **Sum**, and then compare your screen with Figure 5.18.

This dialog box enables you to apply an aggregate function to one or more fields. The function will add the cost of every item sold by each company for each category. Every row can also be summed.

Figure 5.18

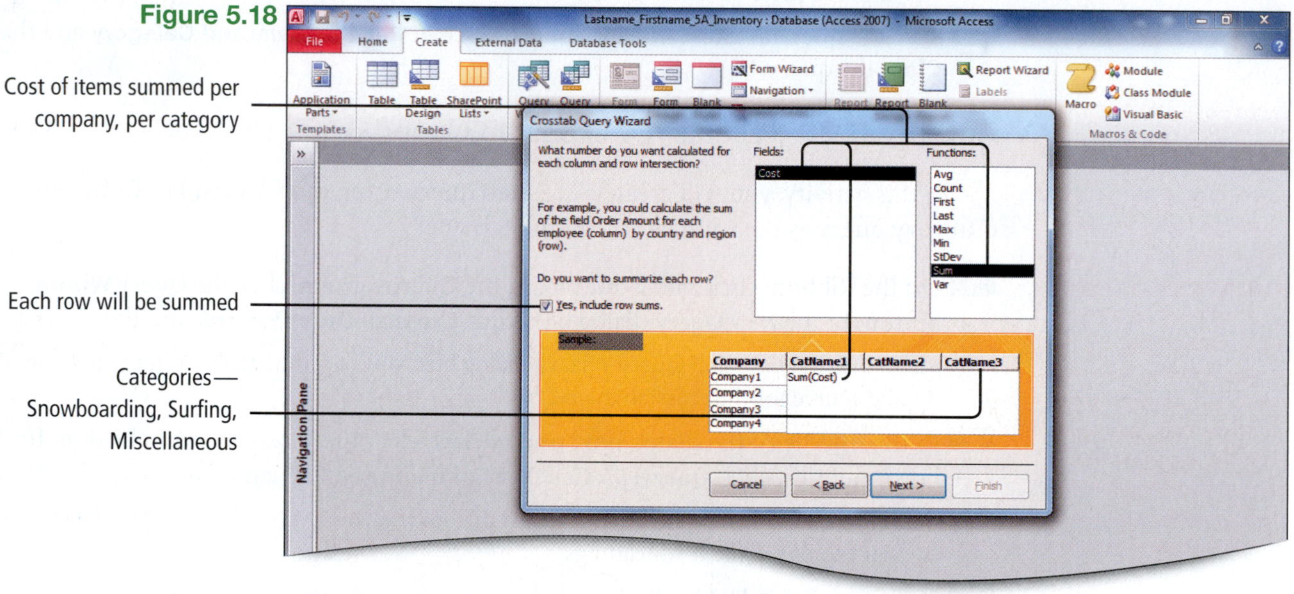

6 On the left side of the **Crosstab Query Wizard** dialog box, above the **Sample** area, clear the **Yes, include row sums** check box, and then click **Next**.

If the check box is selected, a column will be inserted between the first and second column that sums all of the numeric data per row.

7 Under **What do you want to name your query?**, select the existing text, type **Lastname Firstname 5A Crosstab Query** and then click **Finish**. Adjust all of the column widths to display the entire field name and the data in each field, and then compare your screen with Figure 5.19. Then take a moment to compare this screen with Figure 5.16, the select query you created with the same extracted data.

The same data is extracted using the select query as shown in Figure 5.16; however, the crosstab query displays the data differently. A crosstab query reduces the number of records displayed as shown by the entry for Dave's Sporting Shop. In the select query, there are two records displayed, one for the Miscellaneous category and one for the Surfing category. The crosstab query combines the data into one record.

Figure 5.19

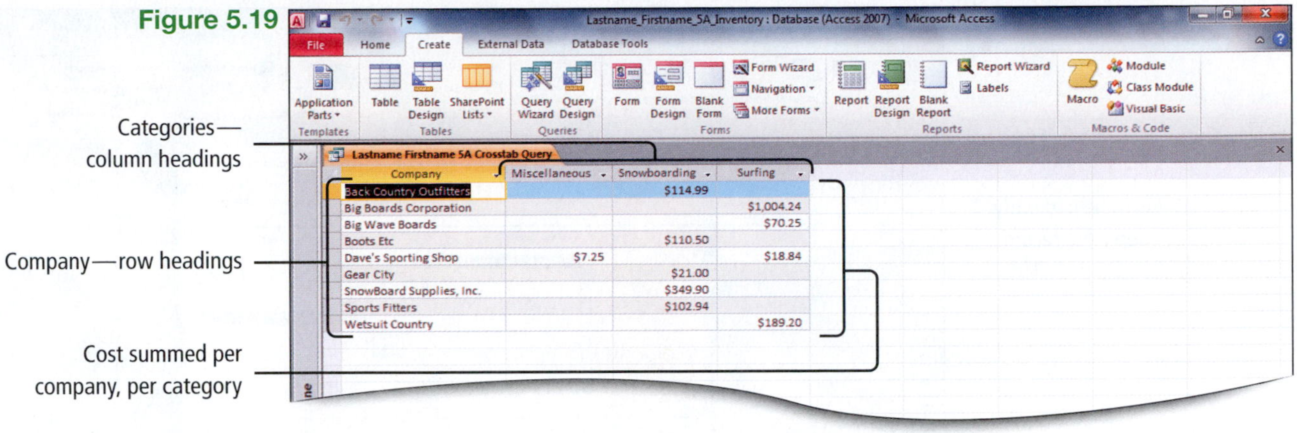

Note | Including Row Sums

If you include row sums in a crosstab query, the sum will display in a column following the column for the row headings. In this activity, the row sums column would display following the Company column. For Dave's Sporting Shop, the row sum would be $26.09—$7.25 plus $18.84.

8 View the query in **Print Preview**, ensuring that the query prints on one page. If you are instructed to submit this result, create a paper or electronic printout. **Close** the query, saving changes—you adjusted the column widths.

Objective 4 | Find Duplicate and Unmatched Records

Even when a table contains a primary key, it is still possible to have duplicate records in a table. For example, the same inventory item can be entered with different catalog numbers. You can use the ***Find Duplicates Query Wizard*** to locate duplicate records in a table. As databases grow, you may have records in one table that have no matching records in a related table; these are ***unmatched records***. For example, there may be a record for a supplier in the Suppliers table, but no inventory items are ordered from that supplier. You can use the ***Find Unmatched Query Wizard*** to locate unmatched records.

Activity 5.07 | Finding Duplicate Records

In this activity, you will find duplicate records in the *5A Inventory* table by using the Find Duplicates Query Wizard.

1 On the **Create tab**, in the **Queries group**, click the **Query Wizard** button. In the **New Query** dialog box, click **Find Duplicates Query Wizard**, and then click **OK**.

2 In the first **Find Duplicates Query Wizard** dialog box, in the list of tables, click **Table: 5A Inventory**, and then click **Next**.

The second dialog box displays, enabling you to select the field or fields that may contain duplicate data. If you select all of the fields, then every field must contain the same data, which cannot be the case for a primary key field.

3 Under **Available fields**, double-click **Item** to move it under **Duplicate-value fields**, and then click **Next**.

The third dialog box displays, enabling you to select one or more fields that will help you distinguish duplicate from nonduplicate records.

4 Under **Available fields**, add the following fields, in the order specified, to the **Additional query fields** box: **Catalog#**, **Category**, **Supplier**, **Cost**, and **Selling Price**. Compare your screen with Figure 5.20.

Figure 5.20

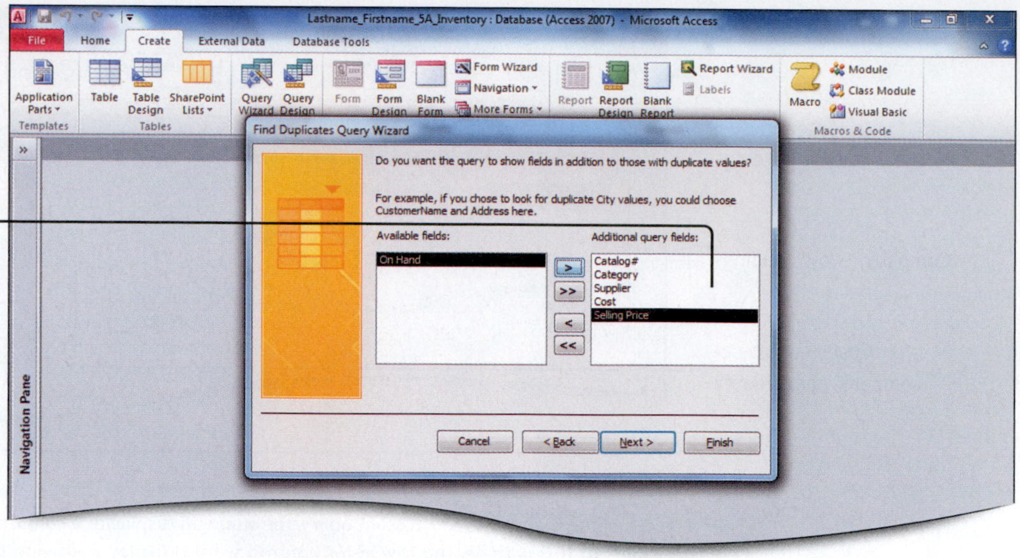

5 Click **Next**. Click **Finish** to accept the suggested query name—*Find duplicates for Lastname Firstname 5A Inventory*—and then compare your screen with Figure 5.21.

Three records display with a duplicate value in the *Item* field. Using the displayed fields, you can determine that the second and third records are duplicates; the *Catalog#* was entered incorrectly for one of the records. By examining the *5A Inventory* table, you can determine that Category 1 is Snowboarding and Category 2 is Surfing. You must exercise care when using the Find Duplicates Query Wizard. If you do not include additional fields to help determine whether the records are duplicates or nonduplicates, you might mistakenly determine that they are duplicates.

Figure 5.21

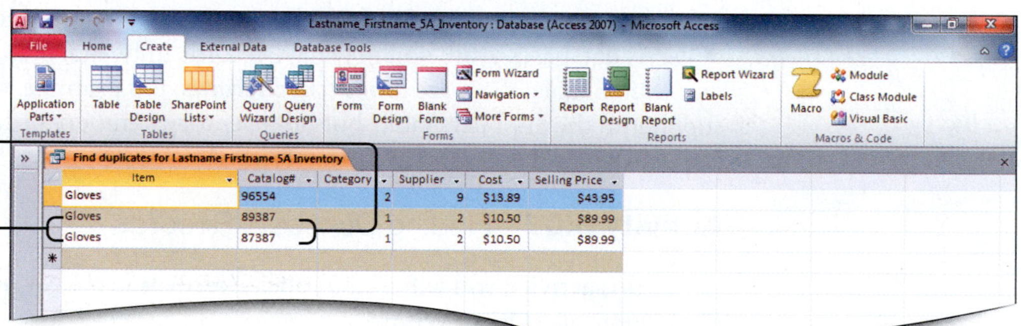

6 Adjust all column widths, as needed. View the query in **Print Preview**, ensuring that the query prints on one page. If you are instructed to submit this result, create a paper or electronic printout. **Close** the query, saving changes.

Normally, you would delete the duplicate record, but your instructor needs to verify that you have found the duplicate record by using a query.

More Knowledge | **Removing Duplicate Records**

If you choose to delete duplicate records, you must first deal with existing table relationships. If the record you want to delete exists in the table on the *many* side of the relationship, you can delete the record without taking additional steps. If the record exists in the table on the *one* side of the relationship, you must first delete the relationship, and then delete the record. You should then re-create the relationship between the tables. You can either manually delete the duplicate records or create a delete query to remove the duplicate records.

Activity 5.08 | Finding Unmatched Records

In this activity, you will find unmatched records in related tables—*5A Suppliers* and *5A Inventory*—by using the Find Unmatched Query Wizard.

1 On the **Create tab**, in the **Queries group**, click the **Query Wizard** button. In the **New Query** dialog box, click **Find Unmatched Query Wizard**, and then click **OK**.

2 In the first **Find Unmatched Query Wizard** dialog box, in the list of tables, click **Table: 5A Suppliers**, and then click **Next**.

The second dialog box displays, enabling you to select the related table or query that you would like Access to compare to the first table to find unmatched records.

3 In the list of tables, click **Table: 5A Inventory**, and then click **Next**.

The third dialog box displays, enabling you to select the matching fields in each table.

4 Under **Fields in '5A Suppliers'**, if necessary, click **ID**. Under **Fields in 5A Inventory**, if necessary, click **Supplier**. Between the two fields columns, click the button that displays <=>, and then compare your screen with Figure 5.22.

At the bottom of the dialog box, Access displays the matching fields of ID and Supplier.

Figure 5.22

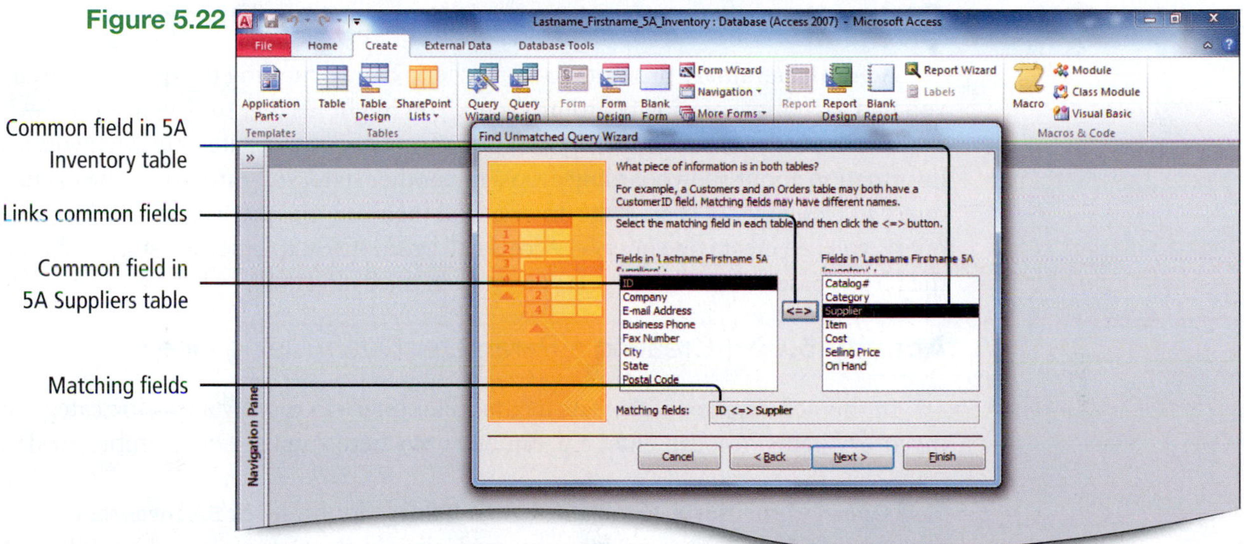

5 Click **Next**. Under **Available fields**, double-click **ID**, and then double-click **Company** to move the field names under **Selected fields.** Notice that these fields will display in the query results. Click **Next**.

6 In the last dialog box, under **What would you like to name your query?**, type **Lastname Firstname 5A Find Unmatched Query** and then click **Finish**. Compare your screen with Figure 5.23.

The query results display one company—*Winter Sports Club*—that has no inventory items in the *5A Inventory* table. Normally, you would either delete the Winter Sports Club record from the *5A Suppliers* table or add inventory items in the related *5A Inventory* for the Winter Sports Club, but your instructor needs to verify that you have located an unmatched record by using a query.

Figure 5.23

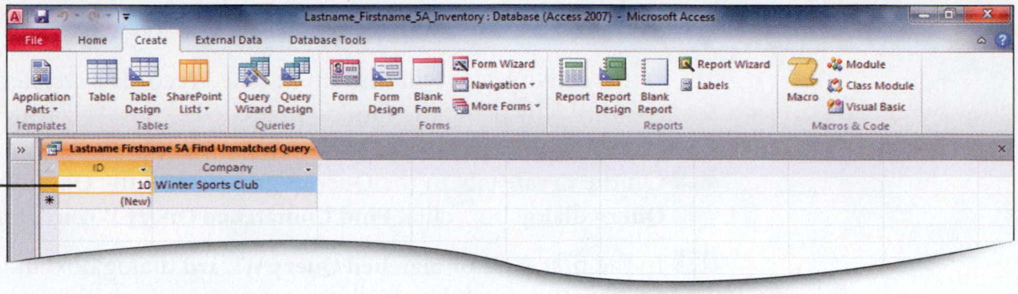

7 Adjust all column widths. View the query in **Print Preview**, ensuring that the query prints on one page. If you are instructed to submit this result, create a paper or electronic printout. **Close** the query, saving changes.

> **More Knowledge | Finding Unmatched Records in a Table with Multivalued Fields**
>
> You cannot use the Find Unmatched Query Wizard with a table that has ***multivalued fields***—fields that appear to hold multiple values. If your table contains multivalued fields, you must first create a query, extracting all of the fields except the multivalued fields, and then create the query to find unmatched records.

Objective 5 | Create a Parameter Query

A ***parameter query*** prompts you for criteria before running the query. For example, if you had a database of snowboarding events, you might need to find all of the snowboarding events in a particular state. You can create a select query for a state, but when you need to find information about snowboarding events in another state, you must open the original select query in Design view, change the criteria, and then run the query again. With a parameter query, you can create one query—Access will prompt you to enter the state and then display the results based upon the criteria you enter in the dialog box.

Activity 5.09 | Creating a Parameter Query Using One Criteria

In this activity, you will create a parameter query to display a specific category of inventory items. You can enter a parameter anywhere you use text, number, or date criteria.

1 **Open** [»] the **Navigation Pane**. Under **Tables**, double-click **5A Inventory** to open the table in **Datasheet** view. In any record, click in the **Category** field, and then click the **arrow** to display the list of categories. Take a moment to study the four categories used in this table. Be sure you do not change the category for the selected record. **Close** the table, and **Close** [«] the **Navigation Pane**.

2 Create a new query in **Query Design**. Add the **5A Category** table, the **5A Inventory** table, and the **5A Suppliers** table to the Query design workspace, and then **Close** the **Show Table** dialog box. Expand the field lists. From the **5A Category** field list, add **CatName** to the first column in the design grid. From the **5A Inventory** field list, add **Catalog#** and **Item** to the second and third columns in the design grid. From the **5A Suppliers** field list, add **Company** to the fourth column in the design grid.

3 In the **CatName** field, in the **Criteria row**, type **[Enter a Category]** and then compare your screen with Figure 5.24.

The brackets indicate a ***parameter***—a value that can be changed—rather than specific criteria. When you run the query, a dialog box will display, prompting you to Enter a Category. The category you type will be set as the criteria for the query. Because you are prompted for the criteria, you can reuse this query without resetting the criteria in Design view.

Figure 5.24

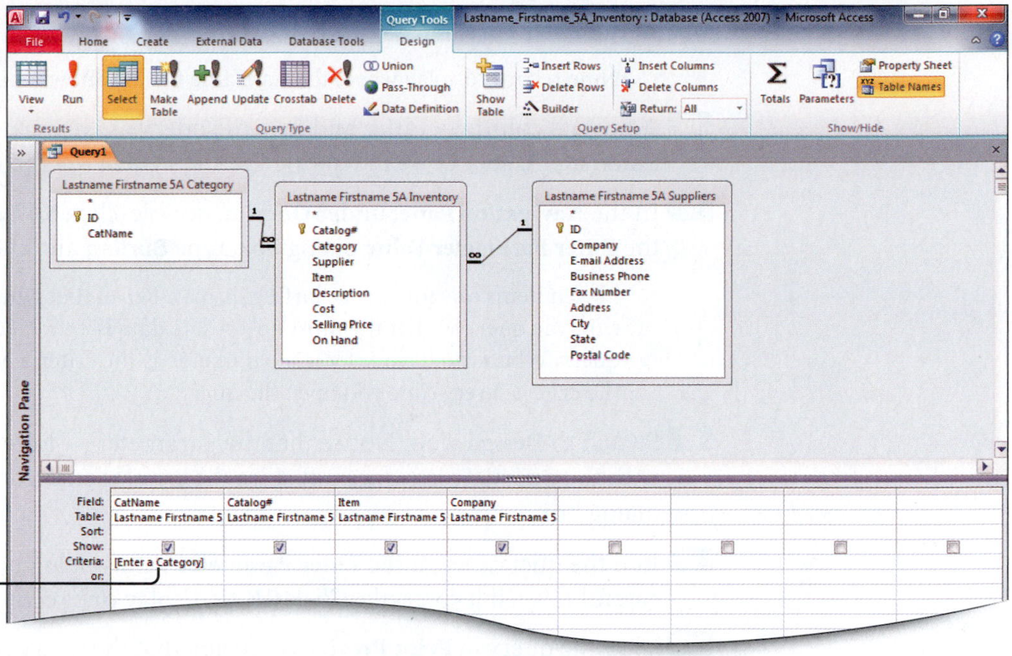

4 **Run** the query. In the **Enter Parameter Value** dialog box, type **Snowboarding** and then compare your screen with Figure 5.25.

Figure 5.25

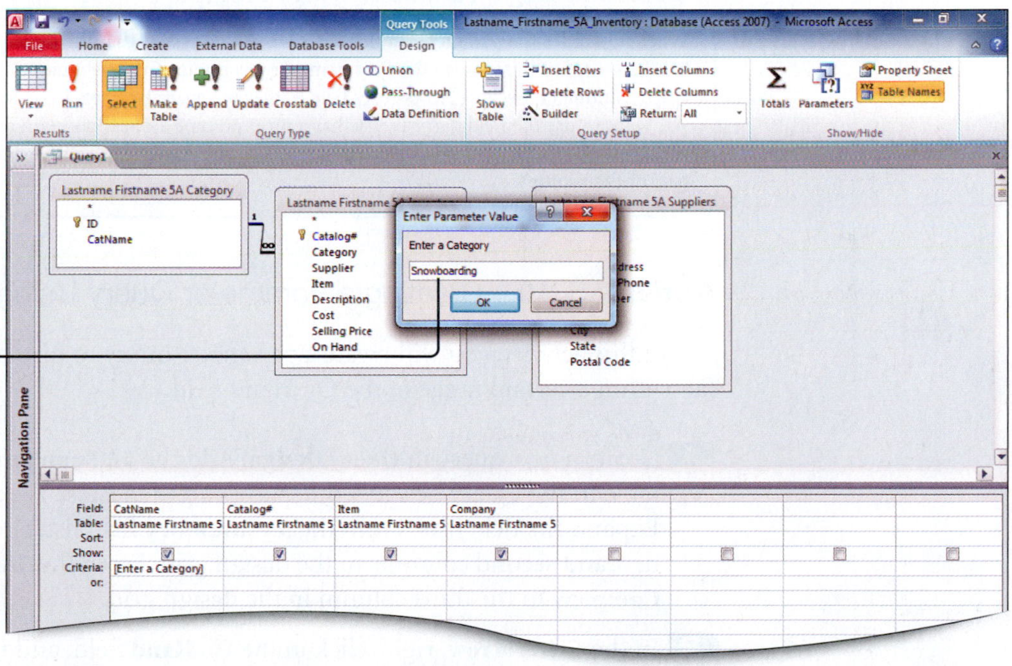

Alert! | Does Your Screen Differ?

If the Enter Parameter Value dialog box does not display, you may have typed the parameter incorrectly in the design grid. Common errors include using parentheses or curly braces instead of square brackets around the parameter text, causing Access to interpret the text as specific criteria. When you run the query, there are no records displayed. If you use curly braces, the query will not run. To correct, display the query in Design view, and then correct the parameter entered in the criteria row.

5. In the **Enter Parameter Value** dialog box, click **OK**.

   Nine records display where the CatName field is Snowboarding.

6. Adjust all column widths, and **Save** the query as **Lastname Firstname 5A Category Parameter Query Close** the query, and then **Open** [»] the **Navigation Pane**.

7. In the **Navigation Pane**, under **Queries**, double-click **5A Category Parameter Query**. In the **Enter Parameter Value** dialog box, type **Surfing** and then click **OK**.

   Eleven items categorized as Surfing display. Recall that when you open a query, Access runs the query so that the most up-to-date data is extracted from the underlying table or query. When you have entered a parameter as the criteria, you will be prompted to enter the criteria every time you open the query.

8. Switch to **Design** view. Notice that the parameter—[Enter a Category]—is stored with the query. Access does not store the criteria entered in the Enter Parameter Value dialog box.

9. **Run** the query, and in the **Enter Parameter Value** dialog box, type **Miscellaneous** being careful to spell it correctly. Click **OK** to display one record. Adjust all column widths.

10. View the query in **Print Preview**, ensuring that the query prints on one page. If you are instructed to submit this result, create a paper or electronic printout. **Close** the query, saving changes, and then **Close** [«] the **Navigation Pane**.

> **More Knowledge | Parameter Query Prompts**
>
> When you enter the parameter in the criteria row, make sure that the prompt—the text enclosed in the square brackets—is not the same as the field name. For example, if the field name is *Category*, do not enter *[Category]* as the parameter. Because Access uses field names in square brackets for calculations, no prompt will display. If you want to use the field name by itself as a prompt, type a question mark at the end of the prompt; for example, *[Category?]*. You cannot use a period, exclamation mark (!), square brackets ([]), or the ampersand (&) as part of the prompt.

Activity 5.10 | Creating a Parameter Query Using Multiple Criteria

In this activity, you will create a parameter query to display the inventory items that fall within a certain range in the On Hand field.

1. Create a new query in **Query Design**. Add the **5A Suppliers** table and the **5A Inventory** table to the Query design workspace, and then **Close** the **Show Table** dialog box. Expand the field lists. From the **5A Inventory** field list, add **Item** and **On Hand** to the first and second columns in the design grid. From the **5A Suppliers** field list box, add **Company** to the third column in the design grid.

2. In the **Criteria row**, right-click in the **On Hand** field, and then click **Zoom**. In the **Zoom** dialog box, type **Between [Enter the lower On Hand number] And [Enter the higher On Hand number]** and then compare your screen with Figure 5.26.

   The Zoom dialog box enables you to see the entire parameter. The parameter includes *Between* and *And*, which will display a range of data. Two dialog boxes will display when you run the query. You will be prompted first to enter the lower number and then the higher number.

Figure 5.26

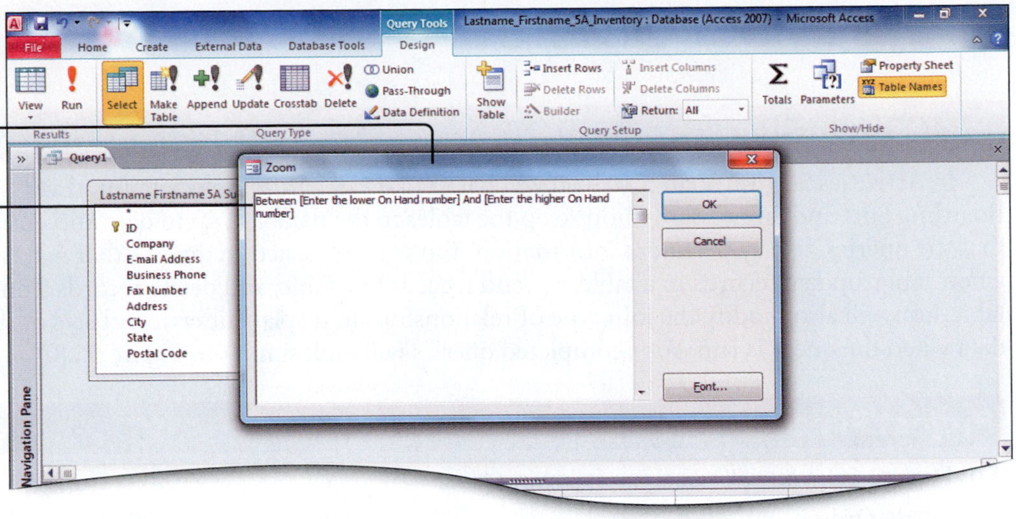

3 After verifying that you have entered the correct parameter, in the **Zoom** dialog box, click **OK**, and then **Run** the query. In the first **Enter Parameter Value** dialog box, type **10** and then click **OK**. In the second **Enter Parameter Value** dialog box, type **20** and then click **OK**. Compare your screen with Figure 5.27.

Two records have On Hand items in the range of 10 to 20. These might be inventory items that need to be ordered.

Figure 5.27

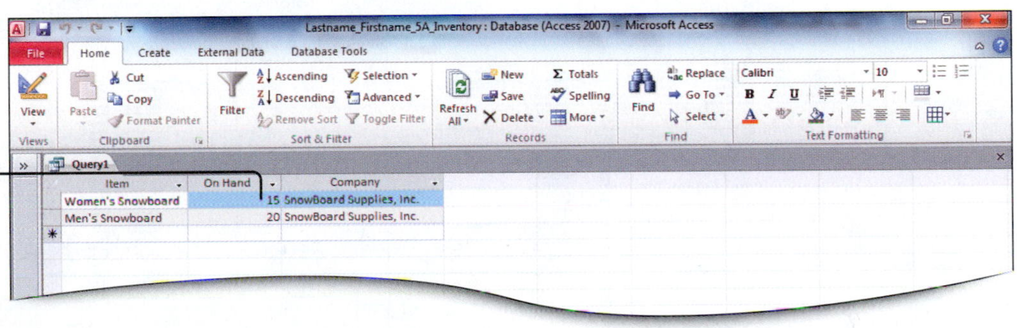

4 Adjust all column widths, and **Save** the query as **Lastname Firstname 5A On Hand Parameter Query**

5 View the query in **Print Preview**, ensuring that the query prints on one page. If you are instructed to submit this result, create a paper or electronic printout. **Close** the query.

6 **Open** the **Navigation Pane**. **Close** the database, and **Exit** Access.

More Knowledge | Creating a Parameter Query Using Multiple Criteria

When you create a query using more than one field with parameters, the individual sees the prompts in the order that the fields are arranged from left to right in the design grid. When you create a query using more than one parameter in a single field, the individual sees the prompts in the order displayed, from left to right, in the criteria box. If you want the prompts to display in a different order, on the Design tab, in the Show/Hide group, click the Parameters button.

In the Parameter column, type the prompt for each parameter exactly as it was typed in the design grid. Enter the parameters in the order you want the dialog boxes to display when the query is run. In the Data type column, next to each entered parameter, specify the data type by clicking the arrow and displaying the list of data types. Click OK, and then run the query.

End **You have completed Project 5A**

Project 5B Orders

myitlab
Project 5B Training

Project Activities

In Activities 5.11 through 5.19, you will help Miko Adai, Sales Associate for 4Ever Boarding Surf and Snowboard Shop, keep the tables in the database up to date and ensure that the queries display pertinent information. You will create action queries that will create a new table, update records in a table, append records to a table, and delete records from a table. You will also modify the join type of relationships to display different subsets of the data when the query is run. Your completed queries will look similar to Figure 5.28.

Project Files

For Project 5B, you will need the following files:

a05B_Orders
a05B_Potential_Customers

You will save your databases as:

Lastname_Firstname_5B_Orders
Lastname_Firstname_5B_Potential_Customers

Project Results

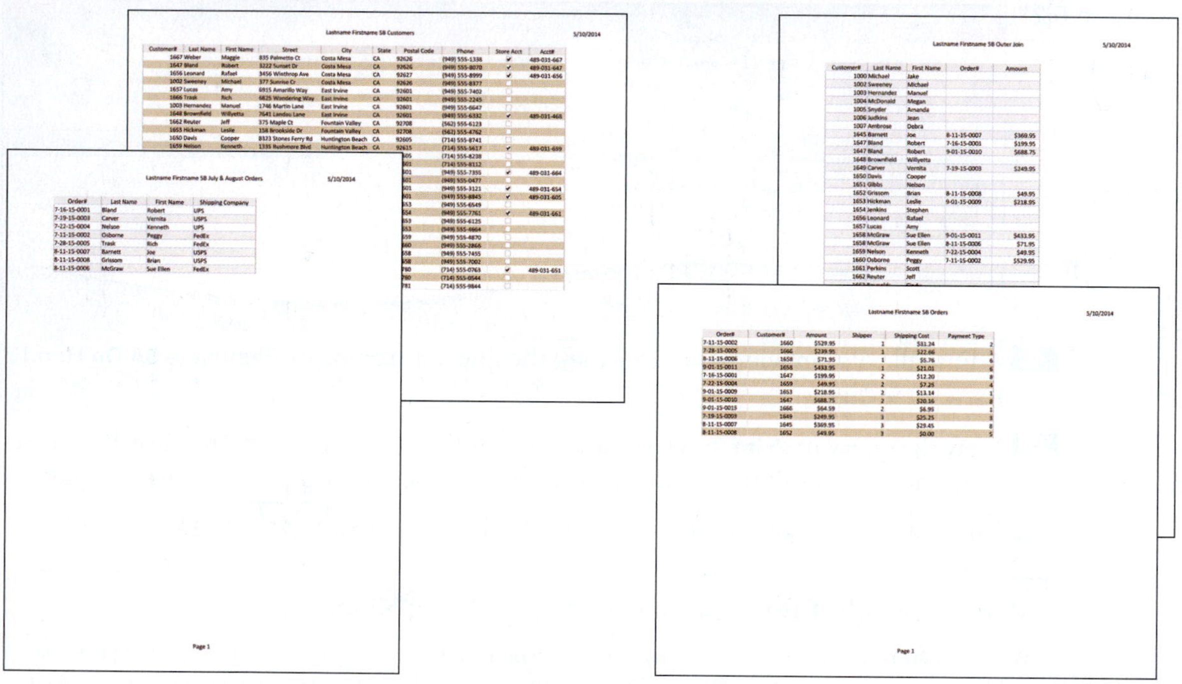

Figure 5.28
Project 5B Orders

Objective 6 | Create a Make Table Query

An ***action query*** enables you to create a new table or change data in an existing table. A ***make table query*** is an action query that creates a new table by extracting data from one or more tables. Creating a new table from existing tables is useful when you need to copy or back up data. For example, you may wish to create a table that displays the orders for the past month. You can extract that data and store it in another table, using the new table as a source for reports or queries. Extracting data and storing it in a new table reduces the time to retrieve ***static data***—data that does not change—and creates a convenient backup of the data.

Activity 5.11 | Creating a Select Query

In this activity, you will create a select query to extract the fields you wish to store in the new table.

1. **Start** Access. Navigate to the location where the student data files for this textbook are saved. Locate and open the **a05B_Orders** file. **Save** the database in your **Access Chapter 5** folder as **Lastname_Firstname_5B_Orders**

2. If you did not add the Access Chapter 5 folder to the Trust Center, enable the content. In the **Navigation Pane**, under **Tables**, rename the four tables by adding **Lastname Firstname** to the beginning of each table name. Take a moment to open each table and observe the data in each. In the **5B Orders** table, make a note of the data type for the **Order#** field and the pattern of data entered in the field. When you are finished, close all of the tables, and **Close** « the **Navigation Pane**.

   In the *5B Orders* table, the first record contains an Order# of 7-11-15-0002. The first section of the order number is the month of the order, the second section is the day of the month, and the third section is the year. The fourth section is a sequential number. Records with orders for July, August, and September are contained in this table.

> **Alert! | Action Queries and Trusted Databases**
>
> To run an action query, the database must reside in a trusted location, or you must enable the content. If you try running an action query and nothing happens, check the status bar for the following message: *This action or event has been blocked by Disabled Mode*. Either add the storage location to Trusted Locations or enable the content. Then, run the query again.

3. **Create** a new query in **Query Design**. From the **Show Table** dialog box, add the following tables to the Query design workspace: **5B Customers**, **5B Orders**, and **5B Shippers**. **Close** the **Show Table** dialog box, and then expand the field lists. Notice the relationships between the tables.

   The *5B Customers* table has a one-to-many relationship with the *5B Orders* table—*one* customer can have *many* orders. The *5B Shippers* table has a one-to-many relationship with the *5B Orders* table—*one* shipper can ship *more* than one order.

4. From the **5B Orders** field list, add **Order#** to the first column of the design grid. From the **5B Customers** field list, add **Last Name** and **First Name**, in the order specified, to the second and third columns of the design grid. From the **5B Shippers** field list, add **Shipping Company** to the fourth column of the design grid.

5 In the design grid, under **Order#**, click in the **Criteria row**, type **7*** and then compare your screen with Figure 5.29.

Recall that the asterisk is a wildcard that stands for one or more characters—Access will extract the records where the Order# starts with a 7, and it does not matter what the following characters are. The first section of the Order# contains the month the order was placed without any regard for the year; all July orders will display whether they were placed in 2014, 2015, or any other year. You do not need criteria in a select query to convert it to a make table query.

Figure 5.29

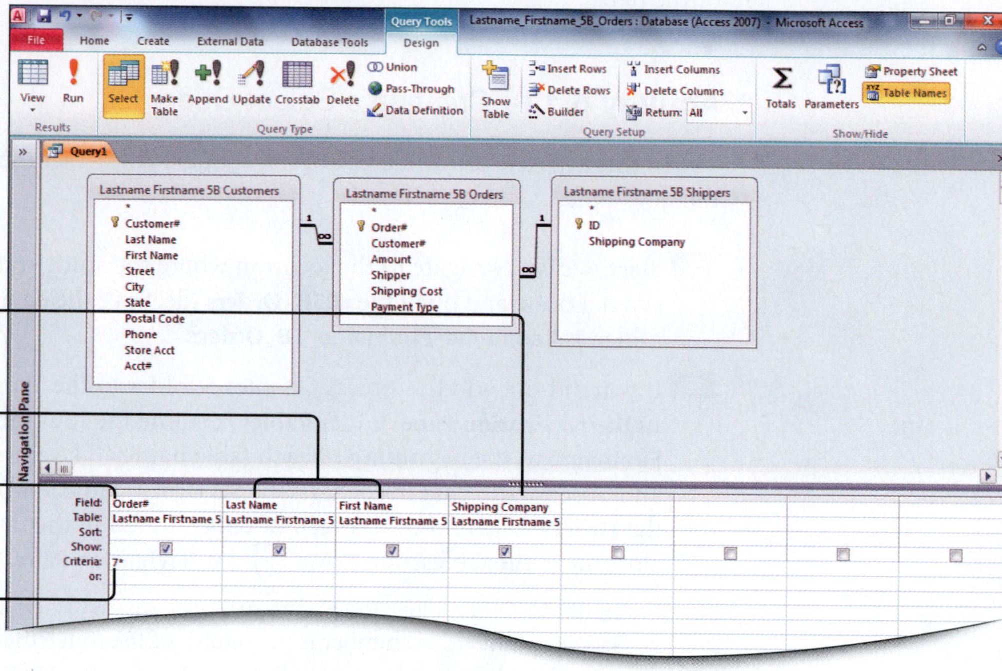

> **Note | Using Expressions and Aggregate Functions in a Make Table Query**
>
> In addition to using criteria in a select query upon which a make table query is based, you can use expressions to create a calculated field; for example, *Total Price:[Unit Price]*[On Hand]*. You can also use aggregate functions; for example, you may want to sum the *On Hand* field.

6 **Run** the query, and notice that five orders were placed in July.

The select query displays the records that will be stored in the new table.

Activity 5.12 | Converting a Select Query to a Make Table Query

In this activity, you will convert the select query you just created to a make table query.

1 Switch to **Design** view. On the **Design tab**, in the **Query Type group**, click the **Make Table** button. Notice the dark exclamation point (!) in several of the buttons in the Query Type group—these are action queries. In the **Make Table** dialog box, in the **Table Name** box, type **Lastname Firstname 5B July Orders** and then compare your screen with Figure 5.30.

The table name should be a unique table name for the database in which the table will be saved. If it is not, you will be prompted to delete the first table before the new table can be created. You can save a make table query in the current database or in another existing database.

Figure 5.30

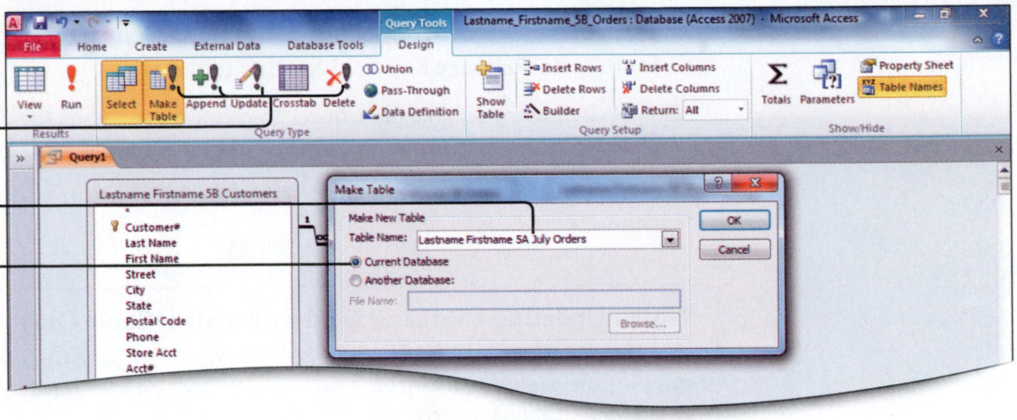

2 In the **Make Table** dialog box, be sure that **Current Database** is selected, and then click **OK**. **Run** the query.

A message displays indicating that *You are about to paste 5 row(s) into a new table* and that you cannot use the Undo command.

3 In the displayed message box, click **Yes**. **Close** the query, click **Yes** in the message box prompting you to save changes, and then name the query **Lastname Firstname 5B Make Table Query**

4 **Open** [»] the **Navigation Pane**. Notice that under **Tables**, the new table you created—**5B July Orders**—is displayed. Under **Queries**, the **5B Make Table Query** is displayed.

5 In the **Navigation Pane**, click the title—**All Access Objects**. Under **Navigate To Category**, click **Tables and Related Views**, widen the **Navigation Pane**, and then compare your screen with Figure 5.31.

The Navigation Pane is grouped by tables and related objects. Because the 5B Make Table Query extracted records from three tables—*5B Customers*, *5B Orders*, and *5B Shippers*—it is displayed under all three tables. Changing the grouping in the Navigation Pane to Tables and Related Views enables you to easily determine which objects are dependent upon other objects in the database.

Figure 5.31

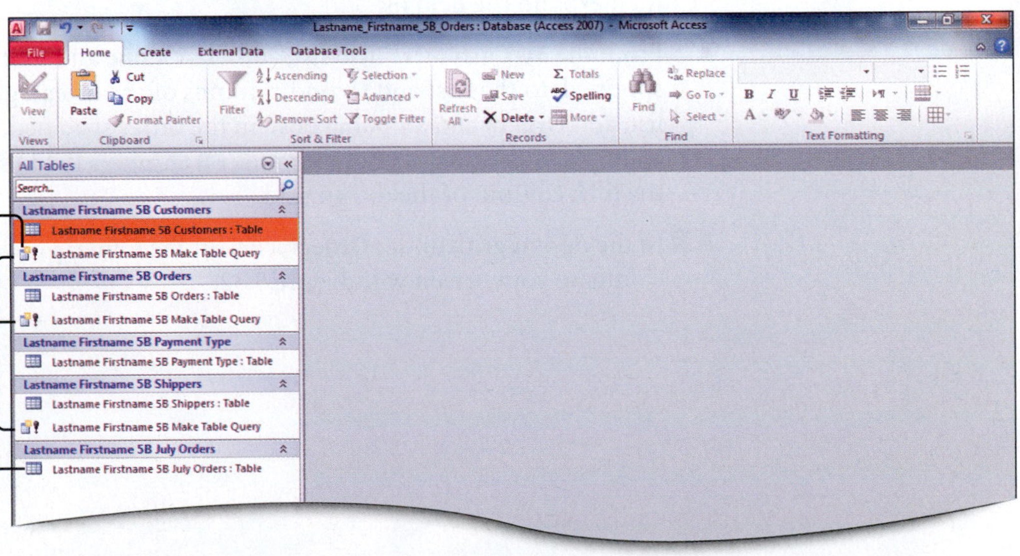

6 In the **Navigation Pane**, double-click **5B July Orders** to open the table in **Datasheet** view. Notice that the data in the **Order#** field does not display as it did in the **5B Orders** table. Switch to **Design** view.

If you click the category title instead of the table, the category will close—if that happens, double-click the category title to redisplay the table, and then double-click the table.

7 Notice that the **Order#** field does not have an input mask associated with it and that there is no **Primary Key** field for this table.

When using a make table query to create a new table, the data in the new table does not inherit the field properties or the Primary Key field setting from the original table.

8 Switch to **Datasheet** view, and then adjust all column widths. **Close** the table, saving changes.

> **Note | Updating a Table Created with a Make Table Query**
> The data stored in a table created with a make table query is not automatically updated when records in the original tables are modified. To keep the new table up to date, you must run the make table query periodically to be sure the information is current.

Objective 7 | Create an Append Query

An ***append query*** is an action query that adds new records to an existing table by adding data from another Access database or from a table in the same database. An append query can be limited by criteria. Use an append query when the data already exists and you do not want to manually enter it into an existing table. Like the make table query, you first create a select query and then convert it to an append query.

Activity 5.13 | Creating an Append Query for a Table in the Current Database

In this activity, you will create a select query to extract the records for customers who have placed orders in August and then append the records to the *5B July Orders* table.

1 **Close** [«] the **Navigation Pane**. Create a new query in **Query Design**. From the **Show Table** dialog box, add the following tables to the Query design workspace: **5B Customers**, **5B Orders**, and **5B Shippers**. **Close** the **Show Table** dialog box, and then expand the field lists.

2 From the **5B Customers** field list, add **First Name** and **Last Name**, in the order specified, to the first and second columns of the design grid. From the **5B Orders** field list, add **Order#** and **Shipping Cost**, in the order specified, to the third and fourth columns of the design grid. From the **5B Shippers** field list, add **Shipping Company** to the fifth column of the design grid.

3 In the design grid, under **Order#**, click in the **Criteria row**, type **8*** and then press [↓]. Compare your screen with Figure 5.32.

Figure 5.32

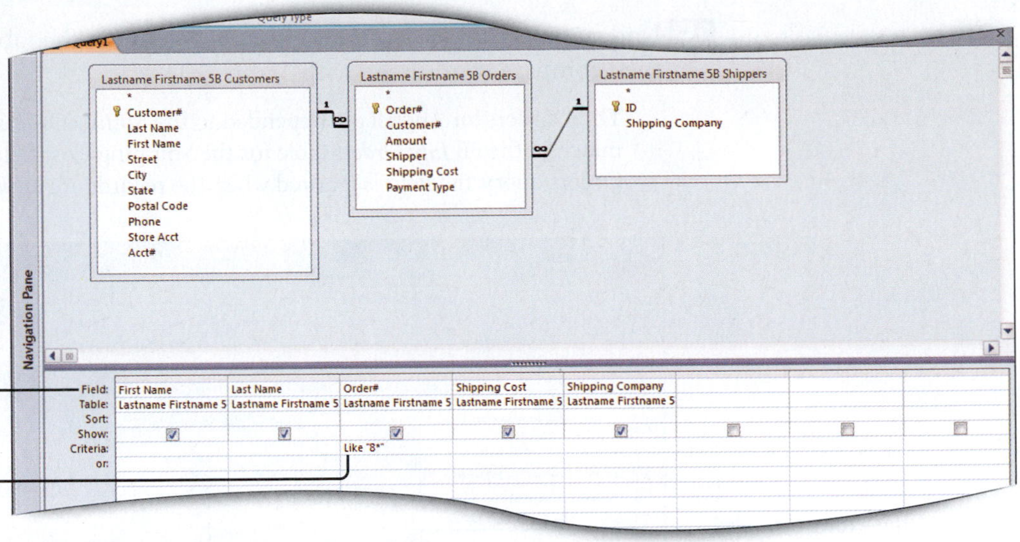

4 **Run** the query, and notice that three customers placed orders in August.

5 Switch to **Design** view. On the **Design tab**, in the **Query Type group**, click the **Append** button. In the **Append** dialog box, click the **Table Name arrow**, and from the displayed list, click **Lastname Firstname 5B July Orders**, and then click **OK**. Compare your screen with Figure 5.33.

In the design grid, Access inserts an *Append To* row above the Criteria row. Access compares the fields in the query with the fields in the ***destination table***—the table to which you are appending the fields—and attempts to match fields. If a match is found, Access adds the name of the destination field to the Append To row in the query. If no match is found, Access leaves the destination field blank. You can click the box in the Append To row and select a destination field.

Figure 5.33

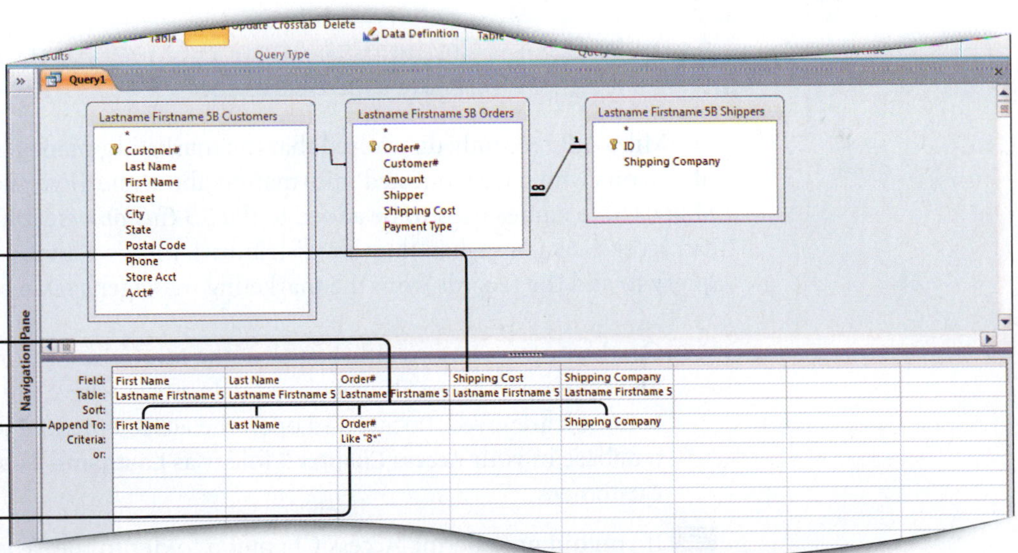

6 **Run** the query. In the displayed message box, click **Yes** to append the three rows to the *5B July Orders* table.

7 **Close** the query, and then save it as **Lastname Firstname 5B Append August Orders**

8 **Open** [»] the **Navigation Pane**. Notice that **5B Append August Orders** displays under the three tables from which data was extracted.

9 In the **Navigation Pane**, click the title—**All Tables**. Under **Navigate To Category**, click **Object Type** to group the Navigation Pane objects by type. Under **Queries**, notice the icon that displays for **5B Append August Orders**. Recall that this icon indicates the query is an action query.

10 Under **Tables**, double-click **5B July Orders** to open the table in **Datasheet** view, and then compare your screen with Figure 5.34.

Three orders for August are appended to the *5B July Orders* table. Because there is no match in the *5B July Orders* table for the Shipping Cost field in the 5B Append August Orders query, the field is ignored when the records are appended.

Figure 5.34

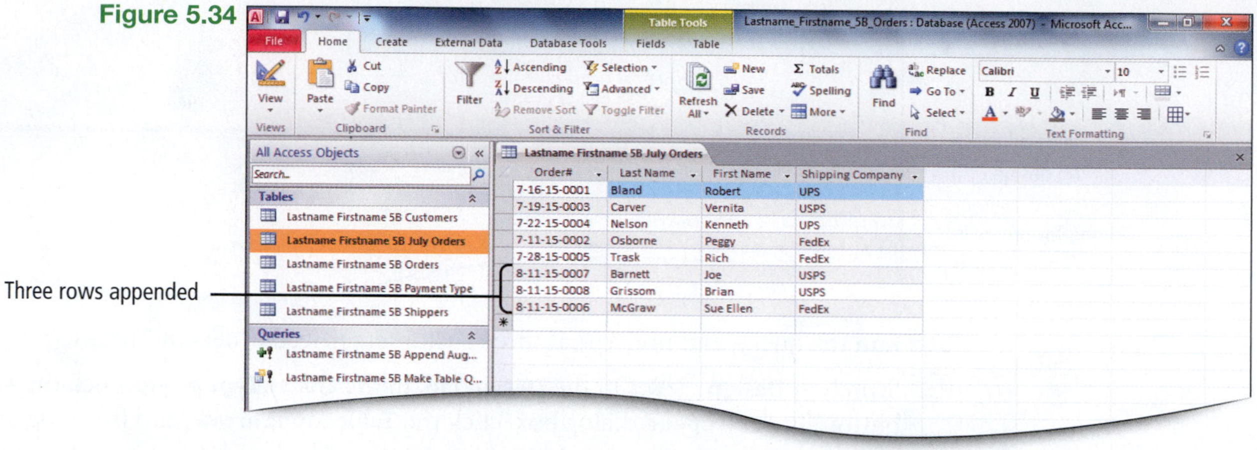

11 **Close** the table. In the **Navigation Pane**, under **Tables**, right-click **5B July Orders**, and then click **Rename**. **Rename** the table as **Lastname Firstname 5B July & August Orders**

12 With **5B July & August Orders** selected, display **Backstage** view and view the table in **Print Preview**. If you are instructed to submit this result, create a paper or electronic printout of the table, and then **Close** the Print Preview window.

Activity 5.14 | Creating an Append Query for a Table in Another Database

Miko Adai recently discovered that the marketing manager has been keeping a database of persons who have requested information about the 4Ever Boarding Surf and Snowboard Shop. These names need to be added to the *5B Customers* table so those potential clients can receive catalogs when they are distributed. In this activity, you will create an append query to add the records from the marketing manager's table to the *5B Customers* table.

1 On the Access window title bar, click the **Minimize** button. Click the **Start** button, and then open **Access**. Navigate to the location where the student data files for this textbook are saved. Locate and open the **a05B_Potential_Customers** file. **Save** the database in your **Access Chapter 5** folder as **Lastname_Firstname_5B_Potential_Customers**

2 If you did not add the Access Chapter 5 folder to the Trust Center, enable the content. In the **Navigation Pane**, under **Tables**, rename the table by adding **Lastname Firstname** to the beginning of **5B Potential Customers**. Take a moment to open the table, noticing the fields and field names. When you are finished, **Close** the table, and **Close** [«] the **Navigation Pane**.

The *5B Potential Customers* table in this database contains similar fields to the *5B Customers* table in the 5B_Orders database.

3 Create a new query in **Query Design**. From the **Show Table** dialog box, add the **5B Potential Customers** table to the Query design workspace, and then **Close** the **Show Table** dialog box. Expand the field list.

4 In the **5B Potential Customers** field list, click **Customer#**, hold down Shift, and then click **Phone** to select all of the fields. Drag the selection down into the first column of the design grid.

Although you could click the asterisk (*) in the field list to add all of the fields to the design grid, it is easier to detect which fields have no match in the destination table when the field names are listed individually in the design grid.

5 On the **Design tab**, in the **Query Type group**, click the **Append** button. In the **Append** dialog box, click the **Another Database** option button, and then click the **Browse** button. Navigate to your **Access Chapter 5** folder, and then double-click **5B Orders**.

The 5B Orders database contains the destination table.

6 In the **Append** dialog box, click the **Table Name arrow**, click **5B Customers**, and then compare your screen with Figure 5.35.

Once you select the name of another database, the tables contained in that database display.

Figure 5.35

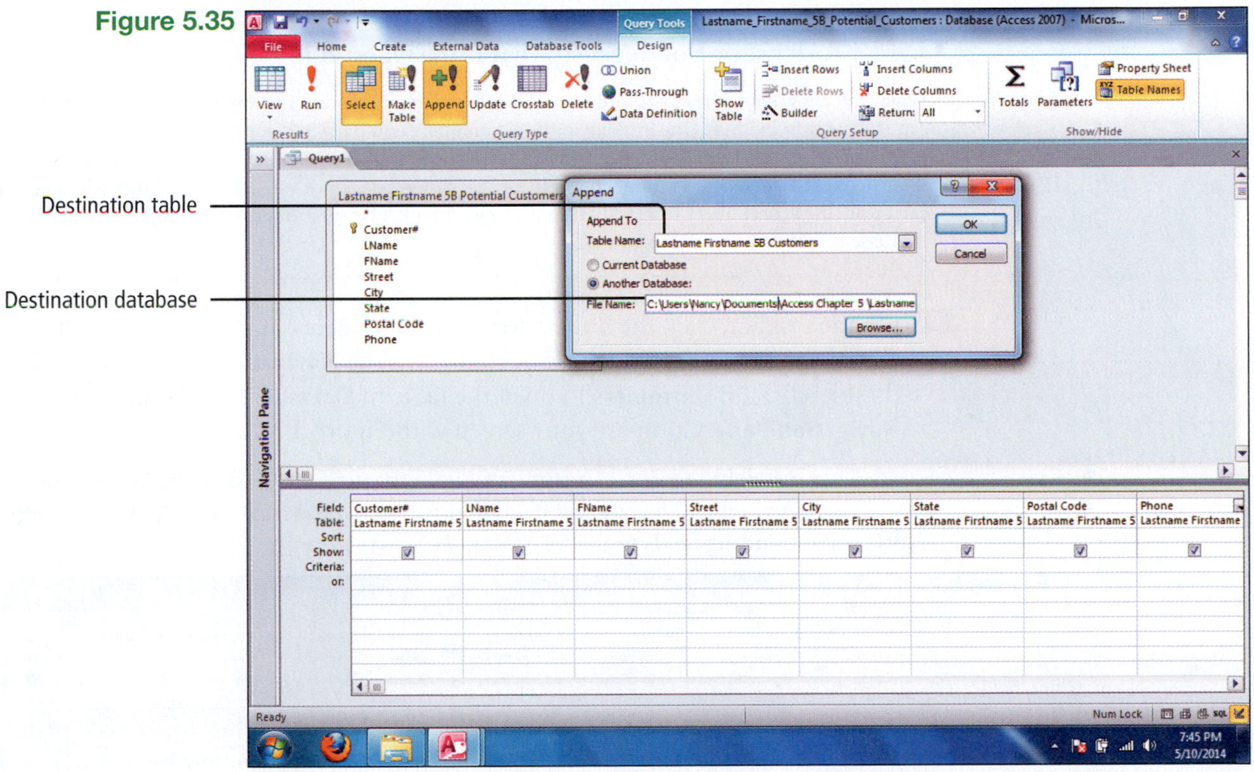

7 Click **OK**. In the design grid, notice that in the **Append To row**, Access found field name matches for all fields, except **LName** and **FName**.

8 In the design grid, under **LName**, click in the **Append To row**, click the **arrow**, and then compare your screen with Figure 5.36.

A list displays the field names contained in the *5B Customers* table. If the field names are not exactly the same in the source and destination tables, Access will not designate them as matched fields. A ***source table*** is the table from which records are being extracted.

Figure 5.36

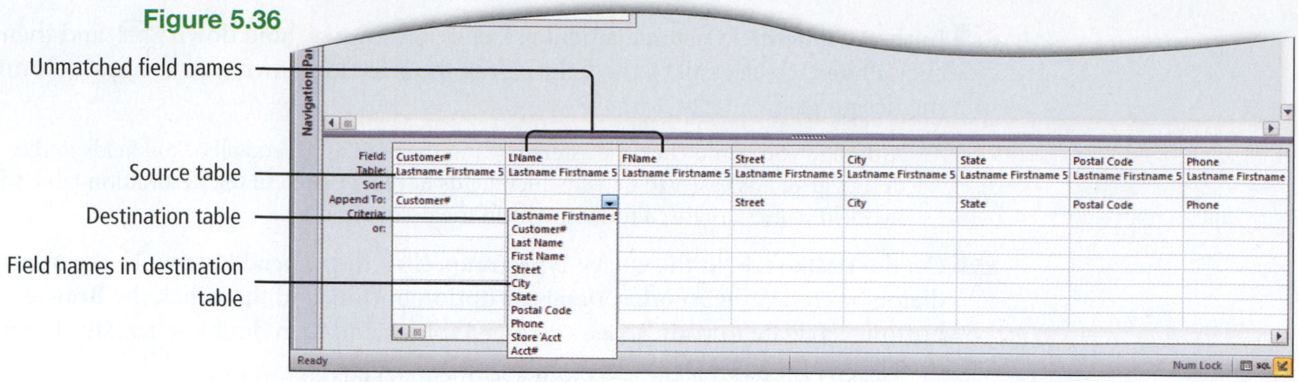

9 In the displayed list, click **Last Name**. Under **FName**, click in the **Append To row**, and then click the **arrow**. In the displayed list, click **First Name**.

10 **Save** the query as **Lastname Firstname 5B Append to 5B Customers** and then **Run** the query, clicking **Yes** to append 8 rows. **Close** the query, and then **Open** the **Navigation Pane. Close** the database, and then **Exit** this instance of Access.

> **Alert! | To Trust or Not to Trust? That Is the Question!**
>
> When you allow someone else to run an action query that will modify a table in your database, be sure that you can trust that individual. One mistake in the action query could destroy your table. A better way of running an action query that is dependent upon someone else's table is to obtain a copy of the table, place it in a database that you have created, and examine the table for malicious code. Once you are satisfied that the table is safe, you can create the action query to modify the data in your tables. Be sure to make a backup copy of the destination database before running action queries.

11 On the taskbar, click the button for your **5B_Orders** database. If you mistakenly closed the 5B_Orders database, reopen it. In the **Navigation Pane**, under **Tables**, double-click **5B Customers** to open the table in **Datasheet** view. **Close** the **Navigation Pane**. Compare your screen with Figure 5.37.

The first eight records—Customer#'s 1000 through 1007—have been appended to the *5B Customers* table. The last two fields—Store Acct and Acct#—are blank since there were no corresponding fields in the *5B Potential Customers* table.

Figure 5.37

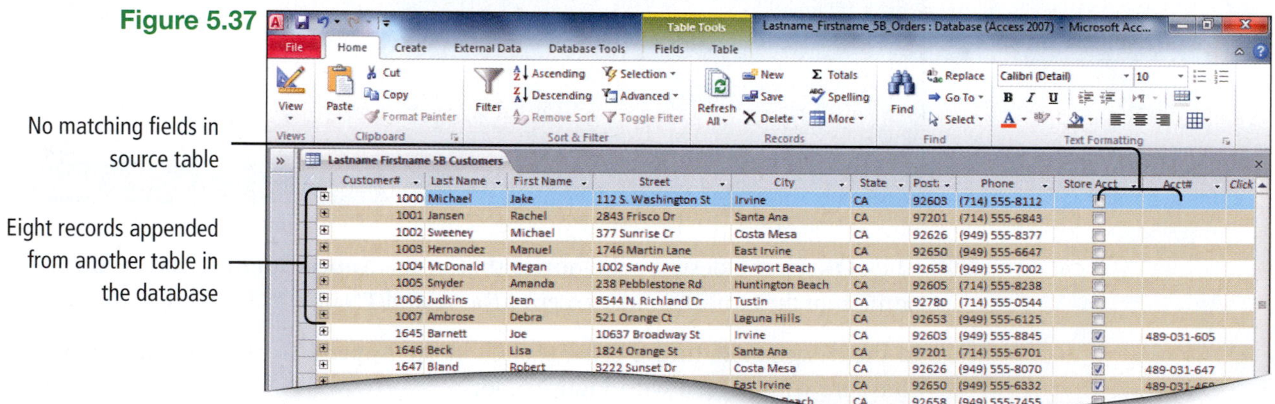

> **More Knowledge | Running the Same Append Query a Second Time**
>
> If you run the same append query a second time with the same records in the source table and no primary key field is involved in the appending of records, you will have duplicate records in the destination table. If a primary key field is part of the record being duplicated, a message will display stating that Access cannot append all of the records due to one of several rule violations. If new records were added to the source table that were not originally appended to the destination table, clicking Yes in the message dialog box will enable those records to be added without adding duplicate records.

Objective 8 | Create a Delete Query

A ***delete query*** is an action query that removes records from an existing table in the same database. When information becomes outdated or is no longer needed, the records should be deleted from your database. Recall that one method you can use to find unnecessary records is to create a Find Unmatched query. Assuming outdated records have a common criteria, you can create a select query, convert it to a delete query, and then delete all of the records at one time rather than deleting the records one by one. Use delete queries only when you need to remove many records quickly. Before running a delete query, you should back up the database.

Activity 5.15 | Creating a Delete Query

A competing store has opened in Santa Ana, and the former customers living in that city have decided to do business with that store. In this activity, you will create a select query and then convert it to a delete query to remove records for clients living in Santa Ana.

1 With the **5B Customers** table open in **Datasheet** view, under **City**, click in any row. On the **Home tab**, in the **Sort & Filter group**, click the **Descending** button to arrange the cities in descending alphabetical order.

2 At the top of the datasheet, in the record for **Customer# 1660**, click the **plus (+) sign** to display the subdatasheet. Notice that this customer has placed an order that has been shipped.

3 Display the subdatasheets for the four customers residing in **Santa Ana**, and then compare your screen with Figure 5.38.

The four customers residing in Santa Ana have not placed orders.

Figure 5.38

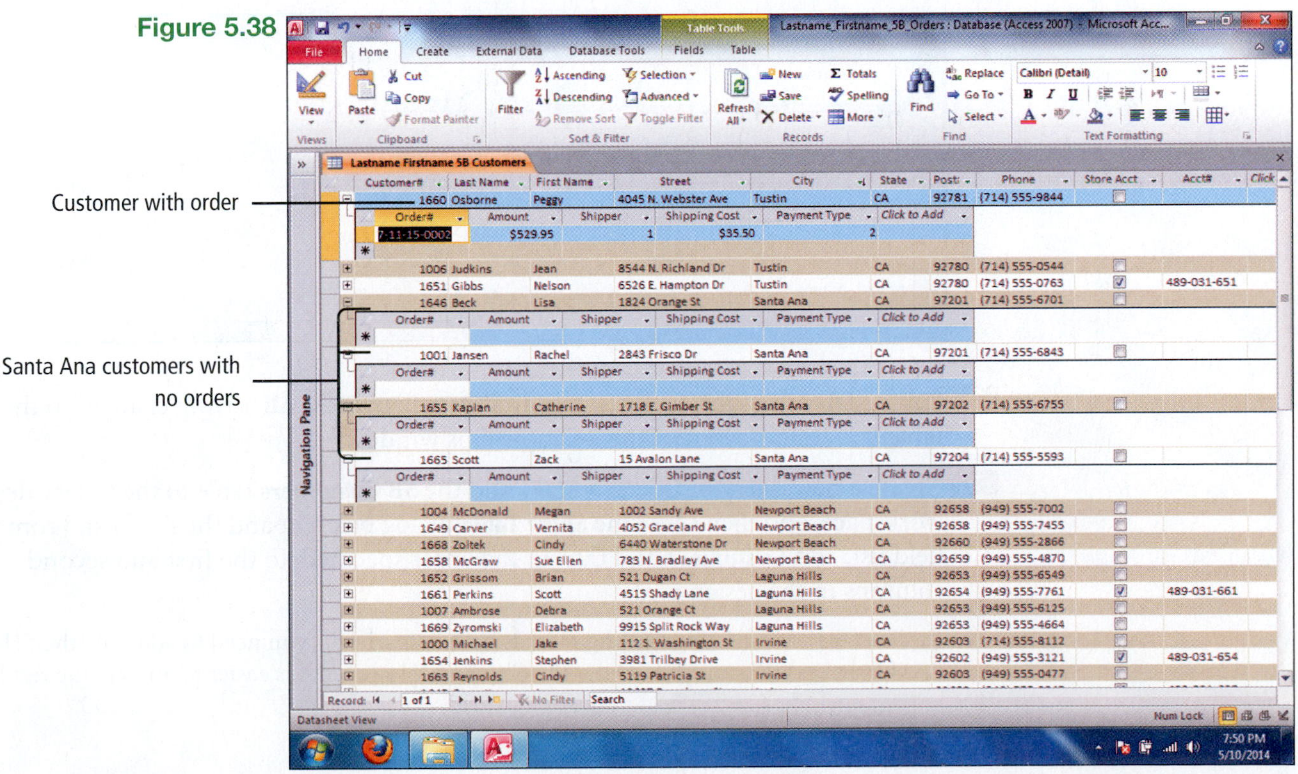

4 Collapse all of the subdatasheets by clicking each **minus (–) sign**.

5 On the Ribbon, click the **Database Tools tab**. In the **Relationships group**, click the **Relationships** button. On the **Design tab**, in the **Relationships group**, click the **All Relationships** button. Expand the field lists and rearrange the field lists to match the layout displayed in Figure 5.39.

The *5B Customers* table has a one-to-many relationship with the *5B Orders* table, and referential integrity has been enforced. By default, Access will prevent the deletion of records from the table on the *one* side of the relationship if related records are contained in the table on the *many* side of the relationship. Because the records for the Santa Ana customers do not have related records in the related table, you will be able to delete the records from the *5B Customers* table, which is on the *one* side of the relationship.

To delete records from the table on the *one* side of the relationship that have related records in the table on the *many* side of the relationship, you must either delete the relationship or enable Cascade Delete Related Records. If you need to delete records on the *many* side of the relationship, you can do so without changing or deleting the relationship.

Figure 5.39

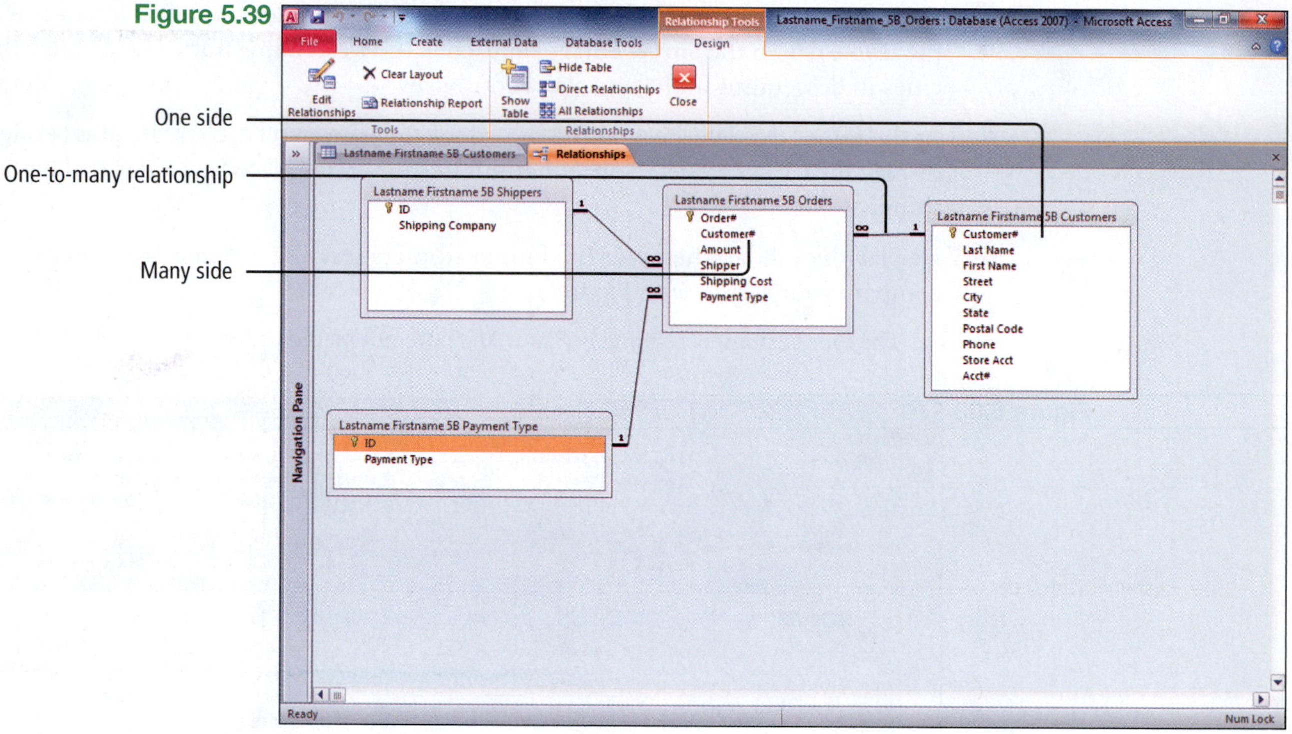

6 On the **tab row**, right-click any tab, and then click **Close All**, saving changes to the table and to the layout of the Relationships window.

7 Create a new query in **Query Design**. Add the **5B Customers** table to the Query design workspace, and then **Close** the **Show Table** dialog box. Expand the field list. From the field list, add **Customer#** and **City**, in the order specified, to the first and second columns in the design grid.

Since you are deleting existing records based on criteria, you need to add only the field that has criteria attached to it—the City field. However, it is easier to analyze the results if you include another field in the design grid.

8 In the design grid, under **City**, click in the **Criteria** row, type **Santa Ana** and then press [↓].

Access inserts the criteria in quotation marks because this is a Text field.

9 **Run** the query, and then compare your screen with Figure 5.40.

Four records for customers in Santa Ana are displayed. If your query results display an empty record, switch to Design view and be sure that you typed the criteria correctly.

Figure 5.40

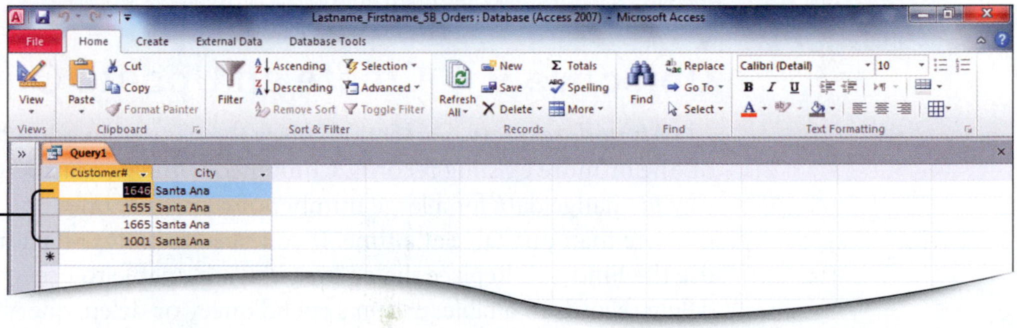

Customers living in Santa Ana

10 Switch to **Design** view. In the Query design workspace, to the right of the field list, right-click in the empty space. From the displayed shortcut menu, point to **Query Type**, and click **Delete Query**. Compare your screen with Figure 5.41. Alternatively, on the **Design** tab, in the **Query Type** group, click the **Delete** button.

In the design grid, a Delete row is inserted above the Criteria row with the word *Where* in both columns. Access will delete all records *Where* the City is Santa Ana. If you include all of the fields in the query using the asterisk (*), Access inserts the word *From* in the Delete row, and all of the records will be deleted.

Figure 5.41

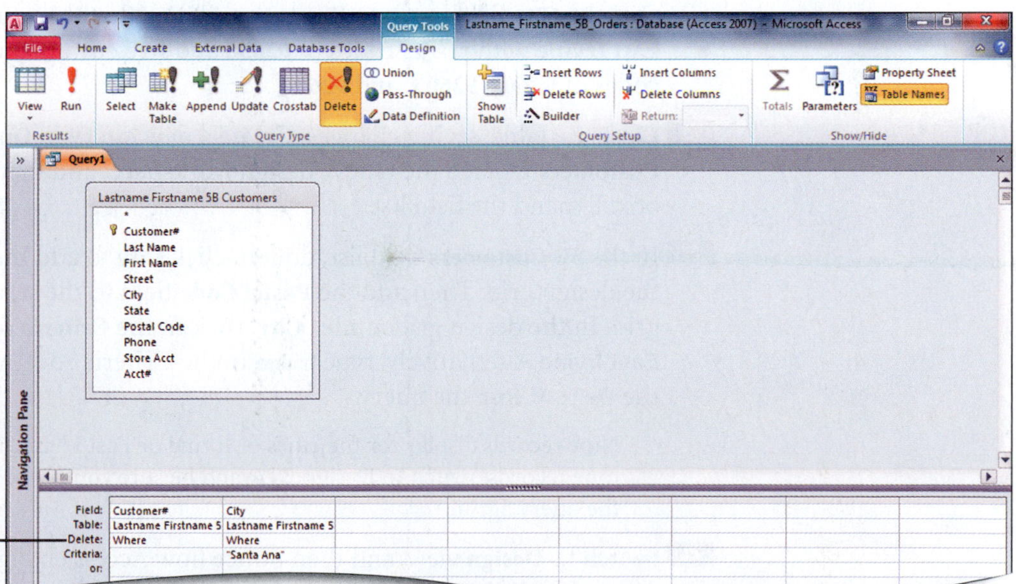

Delete query

11 **Save** the query as **Lastname Firstname 5B Delete Santa Ana Customers** and then **Run** the query. In the message box stating that *You are about to delete 4 row(s) from the specified table*, click **Yes**.

12 **Close** the query, and then **Open** [»] the **Navigation Pane**. Under **Queries**, notice the icon that is associated with a delete query—**5B Delete Santa Ana Customers**. Under **Tables**, open the **5B Customers** table in **Datasheet** view. Notice that the records are still in descending order by the **City** field, and notice that the four records for customers living in **Santa Ana** have been deleted from the table.

13 **Close** [«] the **Navigation Pane**, leaving the table open for the next activity. On the **Home tab**, in the **Sort & Filter group**, click the **Remove Sort** button to clear all sorts from the **City** field.

Objective 9 | Create an Update Query

An ***update query*** is an action query that is used to add, change, or delete data in fields of one or more existing records. Combined with criteria, an update query is an efficient way to change data for a large number of records at one time, and you can change records in more than one table at a time. If you need to change data in a few records, you can use the Find and Replace dialog box. You are unable to use update queries to add or delete records in a table; use an append query or delete query as needed. Because you are changing data with an update query, you should back up your database before running one.

Activity 5.16 | Creating an Update Query

The postal codes are changing for all of the customers living in Irvine or East Irvine to a consolidated postal code. In this activity, you will create a select query to extract the records from the *5B Customers* table for customers living in these cities and then convert the query to an update query so that you change the postal codes for all of the records at one time.

1 With the **5B Customers** table open in **Datasheet** view, click in the **City** field in any row. Sort the **City** field in **Ascending** order. Notice that there are four customers living in **East Irvine** with postal codes of **92650** and five customers living in **Irvine** with postal codes of **92602**, **92603**, and **92604**.

2 **Close** the table, saving changes. Create a new query in **Query Design**. Add the **5B Customers** table to the Query design workspace, and then close the **Show Table** dialog box. Expand the field list.

3 In the **5B Customers** field list, double-click **City** to add the field to the first column of the design grid. Then add the **Postal Code** field to the second column of the design grid. In the design grid, under **City**, click in the **Criteria row**, and then type **Irvine or East Irvine** Alternatively, type **Irvine** in the Criteria row, and then type **East Irvine** in the **Or** row. **Run** the query.

Nine records display for the cities of Irvine or East Irvine. If your screen does not display nine records, switch to Design view and be sure you typed the criteria correctly. Then run the query again.

4 Switch to **Design** view, and then notice how Access changed the criteria under the **City** field, placing quotation marks around the text and capitalizing *or*. On the **Design tab**, in the **Query Type group**, click the **Update** button.

In the design grid, an Update To row is inserted above the Criteria row.

5 In the design grid, under **Postal Code**, click in the **Update To** row, type **92601** and then compare your screen with Figure 5.42.

Figure 5.42

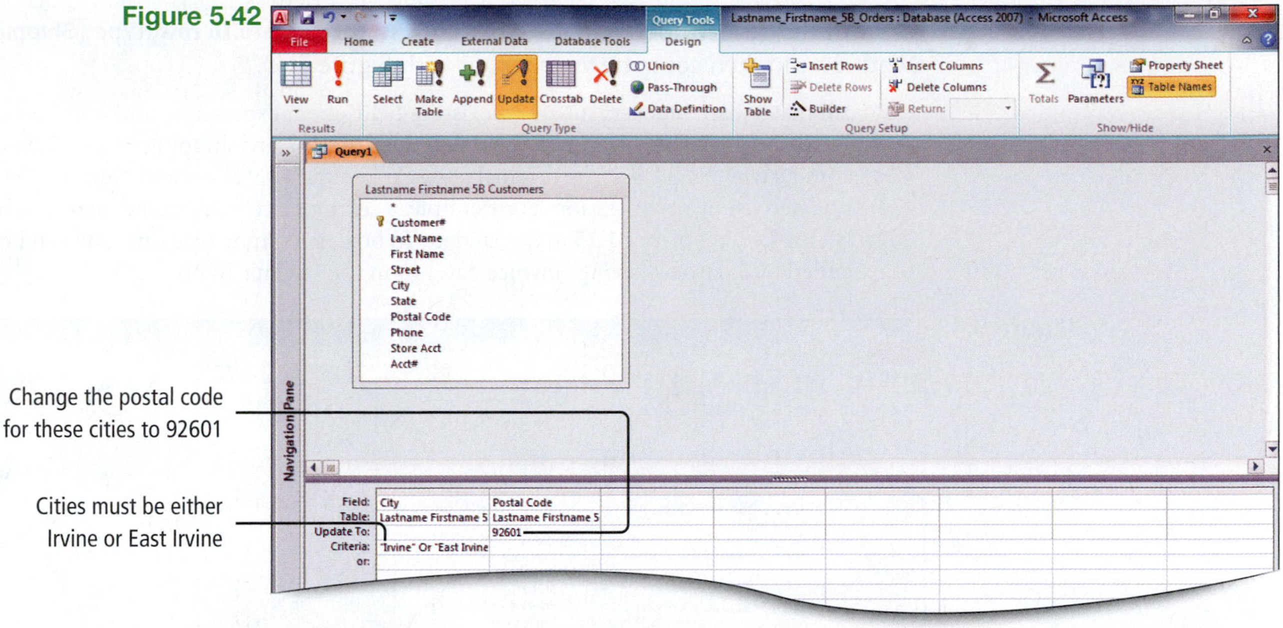

6 **Save** the query as **Lastname Firstname 5B Update Postal Codes** and then **Run** the query. In the message box stating that *You are about to update 9 row(s)*, click **Yes**.

7 **Close** the query, and then **Open** » the **Navigation Pane**. Under **Queries**, notice the icon that is associated with an update query—**5B Update Postal Codes**. Under **Tables**, open the **5B Customers** table in **Datasheet** view. Notice that the nine records for customers living in **East Irvine** and **Irvine** have **Postal** codes of **92601**.

8 View the table in **Print Preview**. Change the orientation to **Landscape**, and, if necessary, change the margins to ensure that the table prints on one page. If you are instructed to submit this result, create a paper or electronic printout, and then **Close** the Print Preview window. **Close** the table.

Activity 5.17 | Creating an Update Query with an Expression

There was a computer problem, and customers were overcharged for items shipped FedEx. In this activity, you will create an update query to correct the field to reflect an accurate shipping cost. Any item shipped FedEx will be discounted 12 percent.

1 Open the **5B Orders** table in **Datasheet** view, and **Close** « the **Navigation Pane**. Click the right side of the **Shipper** field to see the lookup list. Notice an entry of **1** means the order was shipped using FedEx. Press Esc to return to the field box. Sort the **Shipper** field from **Smallest to Largest**. Notice that there are four orders that were shipped using FedEx. Make note of the shipping cost for each of those items.

2 **Close** the table, saving changes. Create a new query in **Query Design**. From the **Show Table** dialog box, add the **5B Shippers** table and the **5B Orders** table to the Query design workspace, and then **Close** the **Show Table** dialog box. Expand the field lists.

3 From the **5B Shippers** field list, add **Shipping Company** to the design grid. From the **5B Orders** field list, add **Shipping Cost** to the design grid. In the **Criteria row,** under **Shipping Company**, type **FedEx Run** the query.

Four records display for FedEx. If your screen does not display four records, switch to Design view and be sure you typed the criteria correctly. Then run the query again.

4 Switch to **Design** view. On the **Design tab**, in the **Query Type group**, click the **Update** button.

In the design grid, an Update To row is inserted above the Criteria row.

5 In the design grid, under **Shipping Cost**, click in the **Update To row**, type **[Shipping Cost]*.88** and then compare your screen with Figure 5.43.

Recall that square brackets surround existing fields in an expression, and numbers do not include any brackets. This expression will reduce the current shipping cost by 12%, so the customers will pay 88% of the original cost. Currency, Date/Time, and Number fields can be updated using an expression. For example, a selling price field can be increased by 15% by keying [selling price]*1.15 in the Update To box , and an invoice due date can be extended by 3 days by keying [invoice date]+3 in the Update To box.

Figure 5.43

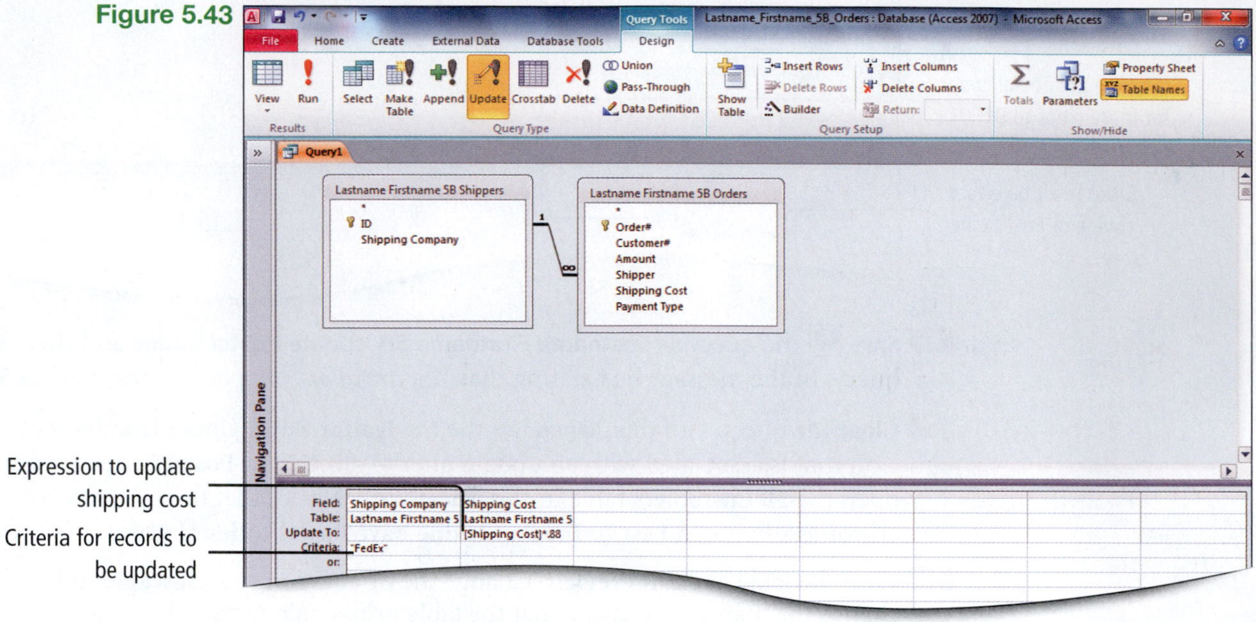

6 **Save** the query as **Lastname Firstname 5B Update FedEx Shipping Costs** and then **Run** the query. In the message box stating that *You are about to update 4 row(s)*, click **Yes**.

The update query runs every time the query is opened, unless it is opened directly in Design view. To review or modify the query, right-click the query name, and then click Design view.

7 **Close** the query, and then **Open** » the **Navigation Pane**. Under **Tables**, open the **5B Orders** table in **Datasheet** view. Notice that the four records for orders shipped FedEx have lower shipping costs than they did prior to running the query, 88 percent of the original cost.

8 View the table in **Print Preview**. Change the orientation to **Landscape**, and, if necessary, change the margins to ensure that the table prints on one page. If you are instructed to submit this result, create a paper or electronic printout and then **Close** the Print Preview window. **Close** the **5B Orders** table.

More Knowledge | Restrictions for Update Queries

It is not possible to run an update query with these types of table fields:

- Calculated fields, created in a table or in a query.
- Fields that use total queries or crosstab queries as their source.
- AutoNumber fields, which can change only when you add a record to a table.
- Fields in union queries.
- Fields in unique-values or unique-records queries.
- Primary key fields that are common fields in table relationships, unless you set Cascade Update Related Fields.

You cannot cascade updates for tables that use a data type of AutoNumber to generate the primary key field.

Objective 10 | Modify the Join Type

When multiple tables are included in a query, a ***join*** helps you extract the correct records from the related tables. The relationship between the tables, based upon common fields, is represented in a query by a join, which is displayed as the join line between the related tables. When you add tables to the Query design workspace, Access creates the joins based on the defined relationships. If you add queries to the Query design workspace or tables where the relationship has not been defined, you can manually create joins between the objects by dragging a common field from one object to the common field in the second. Joins establish rules about records to be included in the query results and combine the data from multiple sources on one record row in the query results.

Activity 5.18 | Viewing the Results of a Query Using an Inner Join

The default join type is the ***inner join***, which is the most common type of join. When a query with an inner join is run, only the records where the common field exists in both related tables are displayed in the query results. All of the queries you have previously run have used an inner join. In this activity, you will view the results of a query that uses an inner join.

1 **Close** « the **Navigation Pane**. On the Ribbon, click the **Database Tools tab**, and then in the **Relationships group** click the **Relationships** button. Notice the relationship between the **5B Customers** table and the **5B Orders** table.

Because referential integrity has been enforced, it is easy to determine that the *5B Customers* table is on the *one* side of the relationship, and the *5B Orders* table is on the *many* side of the relationship. *One* customer can have *many* orders. The common field is Customer#.

2 In the **Relationships** window, double-click the **join line** between the **5B Customers** table and the **5B Orders** table. Alternatively, right-click the join line, and then click **Edit Relationship**, or click the line, and then in the **Tools** group, click the **Edit Relationships** button. Compare your screen with Figure 5.44.

The Edit Relationships dialog box displays, indicating that referential integrity has been enforced and that the relationship type is *One-to-Many*. Because the relationship has been established for the tables, you can view relationship properties in the Relationships window.

Figure 5.44

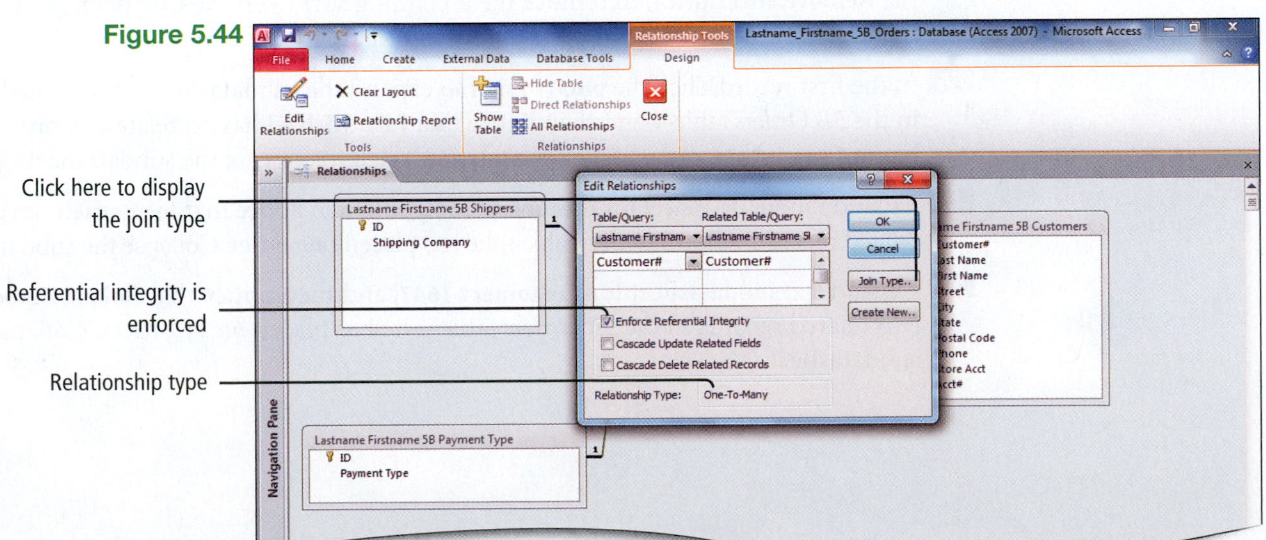

Alert! | Is Your Edit Relationships Dialog Box Empty?

If your Edit Relationships dialog box does not display as shown in Figure 5.44, you may have double-clicked near the join line and not on the join line. In the Edit Relationships dialog box, click Cancel, and then try again.

3. In the **Edit Relationships** dialog box, click **Join Type**, and then compare your screen with Figure 5.45. In the displayed **Join Properties** dialog box, notice that option **1** is selected—*Only include rows where the joined fields from both tables are equal.*

   Option 1 is the default join type, which is an inner join. Options 2 and 3 are outer join types.

Figure 5.45

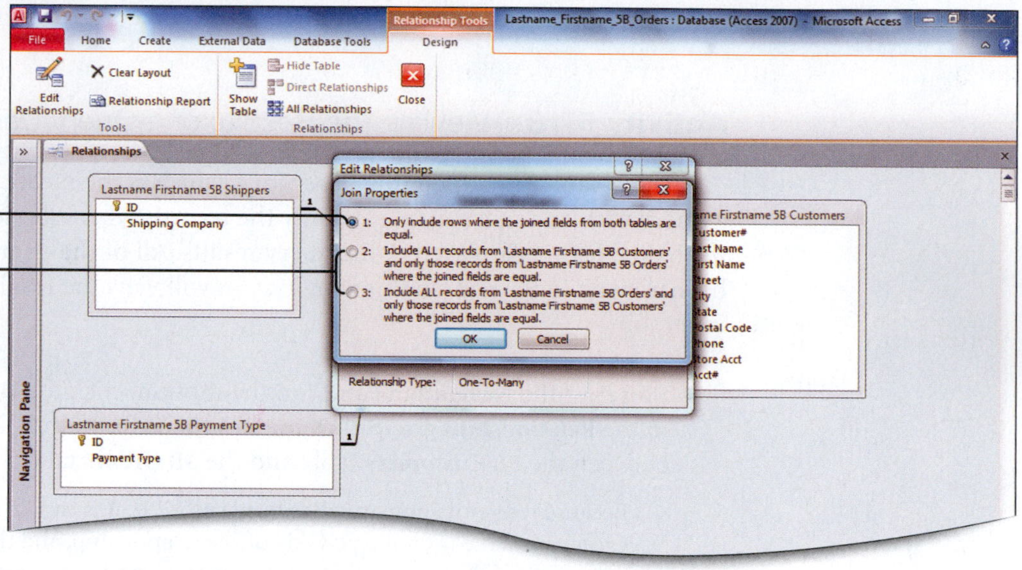

4. In the **Join Properties** dialog box, click **Cancel**. In the **Edit Relationships** dialog box, click **Cancel**. **Close** the Relationships window.

   Because the relationships have been established and saved in the database, you should not change the join properties in the Relationships window. You should only change join properties in the Query design workspace.

5. **Open** [»] the **Navigation Pane**. In the **Navigation Pane**, open the **5B Orders** table and the **5B Customers** table, in the order specified, and then **Close** [«] the **Navigation Pane**.

6. With the **5B Customers** table active, on the **Home tab**, in the **Sort & Filter group**, click the **Remove Sort** button to remove the ascending sort from the **City** field. Notice that the records are now sorted by the **Customer#** field—the primary key field.

7. In the first record, click the **plus (+) sign** to expand the subdatasheet—the related record in the *5B Orders* table—and then notice that **Jake Michael** has no related records—he has not placed any orders. Click the **minus (–) sign** to collapse the subdatasheet.

8. Expand the subdatasheet for **Customer# 1645**, and then notice that **Joe Barnett** has one related record in the *5B Orders* table—he has placed one order. Collapse the subdatasheet.

9. Expand the subdatasheet for **Customer# 1647**, and then notice that **Robert Bland** has two related records in the *5B Orders* table—he has placed *many* orders. Collapse the subdatasheet.

10 On the **tab row**, click the **5B Orders tab** to make the datasheet active, and then notice that **12** orders have been placed. On the **tab row**, right-click any tab, and then click **Close All**, saving changes, if prompted.

11 Create a new query in **Query Design**. From the **Show Table** dialog box, add the **5B Customers** table and the **5B Orders** table to the Query design workspace, and then close the **Show Table** dialog box. Expand both field lists.

12 From the **5B Customers** field list, add **Customer#**, **Last Name**, and **First Name**, in the order specified, to the design grid. In the design grid, under **Customer#**, click in the **Sort row**, click the **arrow**, and then click **Ascending**. **Run** the query, and then compare your screen with Figure 5.46. There is no record for **Jake Michael**, there is one record for **Customer# 1645**—Joe Barnett—and there are two records for **Customer# 1647**—Robert Bland.

Because the default join type is an inner join, the query results display records only where there is a matching Customer#—the common field—in both related tables, even though you did not add any fields from the *5B Orders* table to the design grid. All of the records display for the table on the *many* side of the relationship—*5B Orders*. For the table on the *one* side of the relationship—*5B Customers*—only those records that have matching records in the related table display. Recall that there were 29 records in the *5B Customers* table and 12 records in the *5B Orders* table.

Figure 5.46

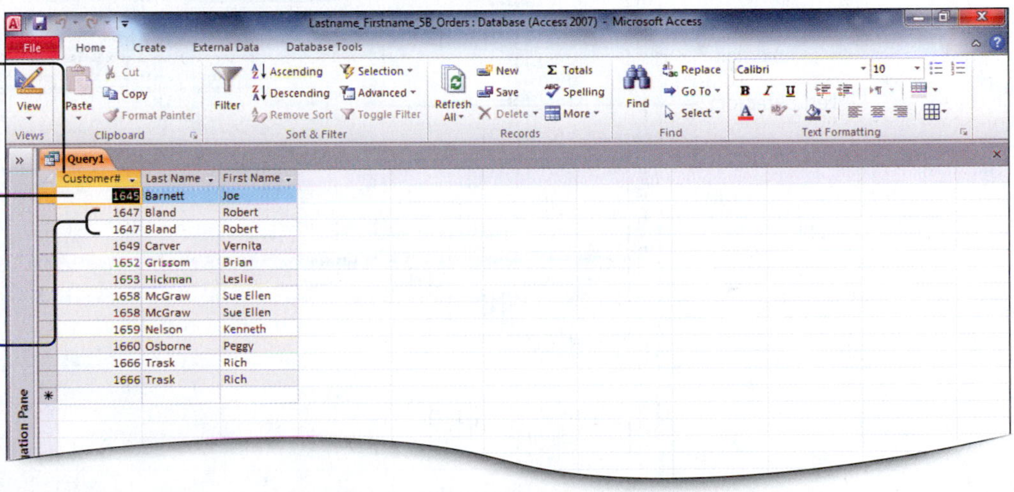

13 Switch to **Design** view. From the **5B Orders** field list, add **Order#** to the fourth column of the design grid, and then add **Amount** to the fifth column of the design grid. **Run** the query to display the results.

The same 12 records display but with two additional fields.

Activity 5.19 | Changing the Join Type to an Outer Join

An ***outer join*** is typically used to display records from both tables, regardless of whether there are matching records. In this activity, you will modify the join type to display all of the records from the *5B Customers* table, regardless of whether the customer has placed an order.

1 Switch to **Design** view. In the Query design workspace, double-click the **join line** to display the **Join Properties** dialog box. Alternatively, right-click the join line, and then click **Join Properties**. Compare your screen with Figure 5.47.

The Join Properties dialog box displays the tables used in the join and the common fields from both tables. Option 1—inner join type—is selected by default. Options 2 and 3 are two different types of outer joins.

Option 2 is a ***left outer join***. Select a left outer join when you want to display all of the records on the *one* side of the relationship, whether or not there are matching records in the table on the *many* side of the relationship. Option 3 is a ***right outer join***. Selecting a right outer join will display all of the records on the *many* side of the relationship, whether or not there are matching records in the table on the *one* side of the relationship. This should not occur if referential integrity has been enforced because all orders should have a related customer.

Figure 5.47

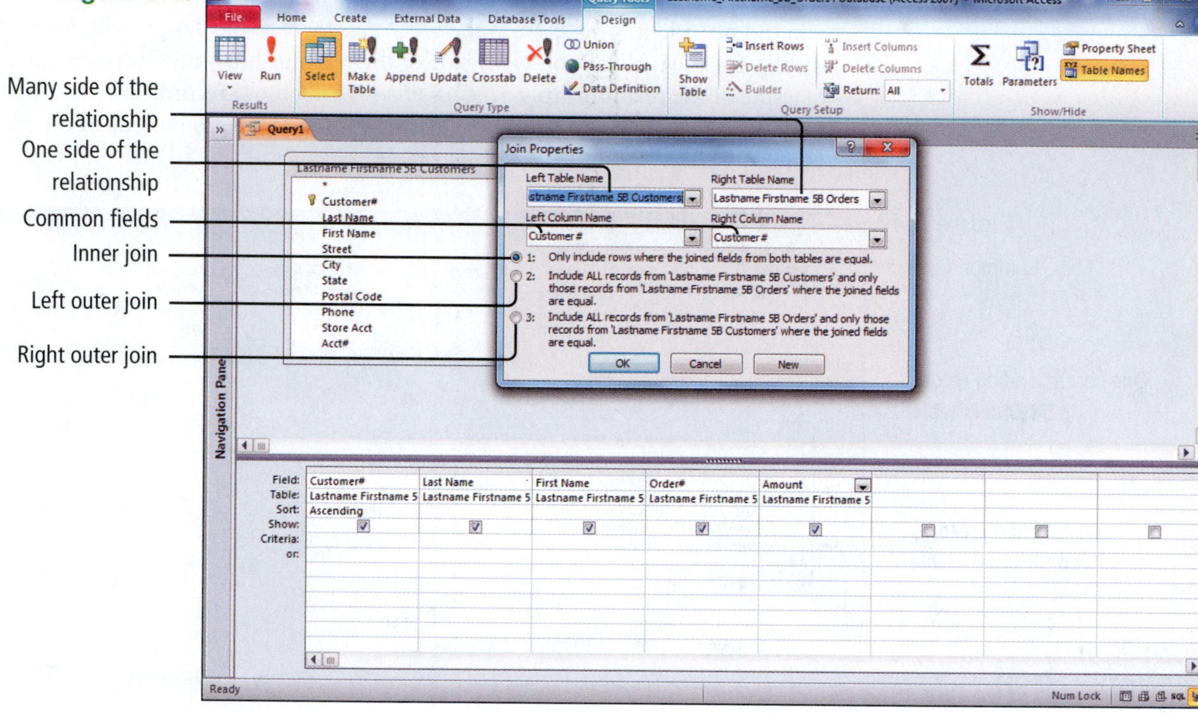

2 In the **Join Properties** dialog box, click the option button next to **2**, and then click **OK**. **Run** the query, and then compare your screen with Figure 5.48.

Thirty-two records display. There are 29 records in the *5B Customers* table; however, three customers have two orders, so there are two separate records for each of these customers. If a customer does not have a matching record in the *5B Orders* table, the Order# and Amount fields are left empty in the query results.

Figure 5.48

Fields blank because there are no matching records in 5B Orders table

Two orders for this customer

Number of records in query results

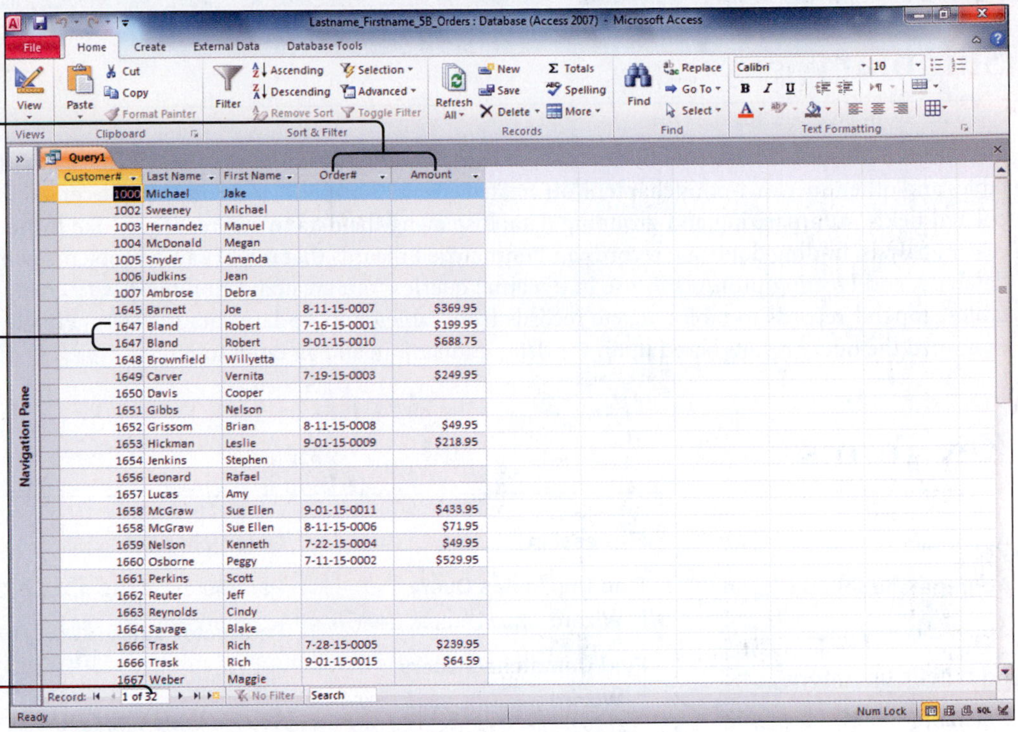

3 **Save** the query as **Lastname Firstname 5B Outer Join** View the query in **Print Preview**, ensuring that the table prints on one page. If you are instructed to submit this result, create a paper or electronic printout.

4 **Close** the query, and then **Open** the **Navigation Pane**. **Close** the database, and then **Exit** Access.

More Knowledge | Other Types of Joins

There are two other types of joins: ***cross joins*** and ***unequal joins***. A cross join is not explicitly set in Access 2010. In a cross join, each row from one table is combined with each row in a related table. Cross joins are usually created unintentionally when you do not create a join line between related tables. In fact, the results of the query will probably not make much sense. In the previous query, you would create a cross join by deleting the join line between the *5B Customers* table and the *5B Orders* table. A cross join produces many records; depending on the number of records in both tables, the cross join can take a long time to run. A cross join using the aforementioned tables would result in 348 displayed records when the query is run (29 customers × 12 orders = 348 records).

An unequal join is used to combine rows from two data sources based on field values that are not equal. The join can be based on any comparison operator, such as greater than (>), less than (<), or not equal to (<>). The results in an unequal join using the not equal to comparison operator are difficult to interpret and can display as many records as those displayed in a cross join. Unequal joins cannot be created in Design view; they can be created only in SQL view.

End **You have completed Project 5B**

Content-Based Assessments

Summary

Queries are powerful database objects that can be created to do more than just extract data from tables and other queries. In this chapter, you created queries for special purposes, such as creating calculated fields, summarizing and grouping data, displaying the data in a spreadsheet-like format for easier analysis, finding duplicate records and unmatched records that might cause problems with the database, and creating prompts to use in dynamic queries. You created action queries to create new tables, append records to tables, delete records from tables, and update data in tables. Finally, you examined the query results based upon the default inner join and an outer join.

Key Terms

Matching

Match each term in the second column with its correct definition in the first column by writing the letter of the term on the blank line in front of the correct definition.

_____ 1. A formula that performs a calculation.
_____ 2. Performs a calculation on a column of data to return a single value.
_____ 3. A query that calculates subtotals across groups of records.
_____ 4. A query that uses an aggregate function for data that is grouped by two types of information and then displays the data in a compact, spreadsheet-like format.
_____ 5. Used to perform a query that locates duplicate records in a table.
_____ 6. Records in one table that have no matching records in a related table.
_____ 7. A query that prompts you for criteria before running it.
_____ 8. A query that enables you to create a new table or change data in an existing table.
_____ 9. An action query that creates a new table by extracting data from one or more tables.
_____ 10. Data that does not change.
_____ 11. An action query that adds new records to an existing table by adding data from another Access database or from a table in the same database.
_____ 12. An action query that removes records from an existing table in the same database.

A Action query
B Aggregate function
C Append query
D Crosstab query
E Delete query
F Expression
G Find Duplicates Query Wizard
H Inner join
I Make table query
J Outer join
K Parameter query
L Static data
M Totals query
N Unmatched records
O Update query

_____ 13. An action query that is used to add, change, or delete data in fields of one or more existing records.

_____ 14. The type of join in which only the records where the common field exists in both related tables are displayed in the query results.

_____ 15. A join that is typically used to display records from both tables, regardless of whether there are matching records.

Multiple Choice

Circle the correct answer.

1. Symbols such as +, –, *, and / that are used to build expressions are known as:
   A. symbolic arguments **B.** arithmetic arguments **C.** arithmetic operators
2. In Access queries, you can use aggregate functions in the Datasheet view by adding a:
   A. Total row **B.** Group by row **C.** Zoom row
3. Which function should be used to add a column of numbers and return a single value?
   A. Sum **B.** Average **C.** Count
4. What type of query has to include at least one row heading, one column heading, and one summary field?
   A. Parameter query **B.** Totals query **C.** Crosstab query
5. Which Query Wizard is used to locate records in one table that do not have related records in a related table?
   A. Find Duplicates **B.** Find Unmatched **C.** Find Unrelated Records
6. A criteria value in a query that can be changed is called a:
   A. multivalue **B.** parameter **C.** duplicate
7. When creating an append query, the table to which you are appending the fields is called the:
   A. source table **B.** destination table **C.** navigation table
8. When creating an append query, the table from which records are being extracted is called the:
   A. source table **B.** destination table **C.** navigation table
9. Which expression would be used to update the current hourly wage by $.50?
   A. hourly wage+.5 **B.** [hourly wage]+[.5] **C.** [hourly wage]+.5
10. What is used to help a query return only the records from each table you want to see, based on how those tables are related to other tables in the query?
    A. Join **B.** Relationship **C.** Properties

Content-Based Assessments

Apply 5A skills from these Objectives:

1. Create Calculated Fields in a Query
2. Use Aggregate Functions in a Query
3. Create a Crosstab Query
4. Find Duplicate and Unmatched Records
5. Create a Parameter Query

Skills Review | Project 5C Payroll

Lee Kawano, Lead Sales Associate of 4Ever Boarding Surf and Snowboard Shop, has a database containing employee data and payroll data. In the following Skills Review, you will create special-purpose queries to calculate data, summarize and group data, display data in a spreadsheet-like format, and find duplicate and unmatched records. You will also create a query that prompts an individual to enter the criteria. Your completed queries will look similar to Figure 5.49.

Project Files

For Project 5C, you will need the following file:

a05C_Payroll

You will save your database as:

Lastname_Firstname_5C_Payroll

Project Results

Figure 5.49

(Project 5C Payroll continues on the next page)

Skills Review | Project 5C Payroll (continued)

1 **Start** Access. Locate and open the **a05C_Payroll** file. Display **Backstage** view. **Save** the database in your **Access Chapter 5** folder as **Lastname_Firstname_5C_Payroll**

- **a.** If necessary, enable the content or add the Access Chapter 5 folder to the Trust Center.
- **b.** Rename the tables by adding **Lastname Firstname** to the beginning of each table name. **Close** the **Navigation Pane**.

2 On the Ribbon, click the **Create tab**. In the **Queries group**, click the **Query Design** button. In the **Show Table** dialog box, select the following three tables—**5C Employees**, **5C Payroll**, and **5C Timecard**. **Add** the tables to the Query design workspace, and then click **Close**. Expand the field lists.

- **a.** From the **5C Employees** field list, add the following fields, in the order specified, to the design grid: **EmpID**, **Last Name**, and **First Name**.
- **b.** From the **5C Payroll** field list, add the **Pay Rate** field.
- **c.** From the **5C Timecard** field list, add the **Timecard Date** and the **Hours** field in this order. In the **Timecard Date** field **Criteria row**, type **6/29/2015**
- **d.** In the **Field row**, right-click in the first cell in the first empty column to display a shortcut menu, and then click **Zoom**. In the **Zoom** dialog box, type **Gross Pay:[Pay Rate]*[Hours]** and then click **OK**. Press Enter. Run the query. Return to **Design** view.
- **e.** If the **Gross Pay** does not show as currency, click in the **Gross Pay** field that you just added. On the **Design tab**, in the **Show/Hide group**, click the **Property Sheet** button. In the **Property Sheet**, on the **General tab**, click in the **Format** box, and then click the displayed **arrow**. In the list of formats, click **Currency**. On the **Property Sheet** title bar, click the **Close** button.
- **f.** In the **Field row**, right-click in the first cell in the first empty column to display a shortcut menu, and then click **Zoom**. In the **Zoom** dialog box, type **Social Security:[Gross Pay]*0.062** and then click **OK**. Using the technique you just practiced, set a **Currency** format for this field if necessary. **Close** the Property Sheet.
- **g.** In the **Field row**, right-click in the first cell in the first empty column to display a shortcut menu, and then click **Zoom**. In the **Zoom** dialog box, type **Net Pay:[Gross Pay]-[Social Security]** and then click **OK**. **Run** the query to display the payroll calculations.
- **h.** In the **Records group**, click the **Totals** button. In the **Total row**, under **Net Pay**, click in the empty box, and then click the **arrow** at the left edge. From the displayed list, click **Sum**.
- **i.** Adjust column widths to display all field names and all data under each field. On the **tab row**, right-click the **Query1 tab**, and then click **Save**. In the **Save As** dialog box, under **Query Name**, type **Lastname Firstname 5C Net Pay** and then click **OK**. View the query in **Print Preview**, ensuring that the query prints on one page. If you are instructed to submit this result, create a paper or electronic printout. **Close** the query.

3 Create a new query in **Query Design**. Add the **5C Employees** table and the **5C Sales** table to the Query design workspace, and then **Close** the **Show Table** dialog box. Expand both field lists.

- **a.** From the **5C Employees** field list, add **Last Name** to the first field box in the design grid. From the **5C Sales** table, add **Sales** to both the second and third field boxes.
- **b.** On the **Design tab**, in the **Show/Hide group**, click the **Totals** button. In the design grid, in the **Total row**, under the first **Sales** field, click in the box displaying *Group By* to display the arrow, and then click the **arrow**. From the displayed list, click **Count**.
- **c.** Under the second **Sales** field, click in the box displaying *Group By* to display the arrow, and then click the **arrow**. From the displayed list, click **Sum**.
- **d.** In the design grid, in the **Sort row**, under **Last Name**, click in the box to display the arrow, and then click the **arrow**. From the displayed list, click **Ascending**. **Run** the query to display the total number of sales and the total amount of the sales for each associate.
- **e.** If necessary, adjust column widths to display all field names and all data under each field. **Save** the query as **Lastname Firstname 5C Sales by Employee** View the query in **Print Preview**, ensuring that the query prints on one page. If you are instructed to submit this result, create a paper or electronic printout. **Close** the query.

(Project 5C Payroll continues on the next page)

Skills Review | Project 5C Payroll (continued)

4 **Create** a new query in **Query Design**. Add the following tables to the Query design workspace: **5C Employees** and **5C Sales**. In the **Show Table** dialog box, click **Close**. Expand the field lists.

a. From the **5C Employees** table, add the **Last Name** and **First Name** fields. From the **5C Sales** table, add the **Timecard Date** and **Sales** fields. **Run** the query to display the sales by date. **Save** the query as **Lastname Firstname 5C Sales by Date** and then **Close** the query.

b. On the Ribbon, click the **Create tab**. In the **Queries group**, click the **Query Wizard** button. In the **New Query** dialog box, click **Crosstab Query Wizard**, and then click **OK**. In the middle of the dialog box, under **View**, click the **Queries** option button. In the list of queries, click **Query: 5C Sales by Date**, and then click **Next**.

c. Under **Available Fields**, double-click **Last Name** and **First Name**, and then click **Next**. In the displayed list of fields, double-click **Timecard Date**. Select an interval of **Date**. Click **Next**. Under **Functions**, click **Sum**. On the left side of the **Crosstab Query Wizard** dialog box, above the **Sample** area, clear the **Yes, include row sums** check box, and then click **Next**.

d. Under **What do you want to name your query?**, select the existing text, type **Lastname Firstname 5C Crosstab** and then click **Finish**. Adjust all of the column widths to display the entire field name and the data in each field. The result is a spreadsheet view of total sales by employee by payroll date. View the query in **Print Preview**, ensuring that the query prints on one page. If you are instructed to submit this result, create a paper or electronic printout. **Close** the query, saving changes.

5 On the **Create tab**, in the **Queries group**, click the **Query Wizard** button. In the **New Query** dialog box, click **Find Duplicates Query Wizard**, and then click **OK**.

a. In the first **Find Duplicates Query Wizard** dialog box, in the list of tables, click **Table: 5C Payroll**, and then click **Next**. Under **Available fields**, double-click **EmpID** to move it under **Duplicate-value fields**, and then click **Next**.

b. Under **Available fields**, add all of the fields to the **Additional query fields** box. Click **Next**. Click **Finish** to accept the suggested query name—*Find duplicates for Lastname Firstname 5C Payroll*. Adjust all column widths. View the query in **Print Preview**, ensuring that the query prints on one page. If you are instructed to submit this result, create a paper or electronic printout. **Close** the query, saving changes.

c. Open the **5C Payroll** table. Locate the second record for **EmpID**, **13**. Click the row selector, and then press Del. Click **Yes** to confirm the deletion. The employee with *EmpID 13* is now in the *5C Payroll* table only one time. **Close** the table.

6 On the **Create tab**, in the **Queries group**, click the **Query Wizard** button. In the **New Query** dialog box, click **Find Unmatched Query Wizard**, and then click **OK**.

a. In the first **Find Unmatched Query Wizard** dialog box, in the list of tables, click **Table: 5C Employees**, and then click **Next**. In the list of tables, click **Table: 5C Payroll**, and then click **Next**. Under **Fields in '5C Employees'**, if necessary, click **EmpID**. Under **Fields in 5C Payroll**, if necessary, click **EmpID**. Click the <=> button. Click **Next**.

b. Under **Available fields**, double-click **EmpID**, **Last Name**, and **First Name** to move the field names under **Selected fields**. Click **Next**. In the last dialog box, under **What would you like to name your query?**, type **Lastname Firstname 5C Find Unmatched** and then click **Finish**. The query results display one employee—*Michael Gottschalk*—who took unpaid time off during this pay period.

c. Adjust all column widths. View the query in **Print Preview**, ensuring that the query prints on one page. If you are instructed to submit this result, create a paper or electronic printout. **Close** the query, saving changes if necessary.

7 **Create** a new query in **Query Design**. Add the **5C Employees** table and the **5C Timecard** table to the Query design workspace, and then **Close** the **Show Table** dialog box. Expand the field lists.

a. From the **5C Employees** field list, add **Last Name** and **First Name** to the first and second columns in the design grid. From the **5C Timecard** field list, add **Timecard Date** and **Hours** to the third and fourth columns in the design grid.

b. In the **Criteria row**, in the **Timecard Date** field, type **[Enter Date]**

(Project 5C Payroll continues on the next page)

Skills Review | Project 5C Payroll (continued)

c. In the **Criteria row**, right-click in the **Hours** field, and then click **Zoom**. In the **Zoom** dialog box, type **Between [Enter the minimum Hours] And [Enter the maximum Hours]** and then click **OK**.

d. **Run** the query. In the **Enter Parameter Value** dialog box, type **6/29/15** and then click **OK**. Type **60** and then click **OK**. Type **80** and then click **OK**. Three employees have worked between 60 and 80 hours during the pay period for 6/29/15. They have earned vacation hours.

e. Adjust all column widths, and **Save** the query as **Lastname Firstname 5C Parameter** View the query in **Print Preview**, ensuring that the query prints on one page. If you are instructed to submit this result, create a paper or electronic printout. **Close** the query.

8 Open the **Navigation Pane**, **Close** the database, and then **Exit** Access.

End **You have completed Project 5C**

Content-Based Assessments

Apply **5B** skills from these Objectives:

- **6** Create a Make Table Query
- **7** Create an Append Query
- **8** Create a Delete Query
- **9** Create an Update Query
- **10** Modify the Join Type

Skills Review | Project 5D Clearance Sale

Ally Mason, Purchasing Manager for 4Ever Boarding Surf and Snowboard Shop, must keep the tables in the database up to date and ensure that the queries display pertinent information. Two of the suppliers, Wetsuit Country and Boots Etc, will no longer provide merchandise for 4Ever Boarding Surf and Snowboard Shop. This merchandise must be moved to a new discontinued items table. In the following Skills Review, you will create action queries that will create a new table, update records in a table, append records to a table, and delete records from a table. You will also modify the join type of relationships to display different subsets of the data when the query is run. Your completed queries will look similar to Figure 5.50.

Project Files

For Project 5D, you will need the following files:

a05D_Clearance_Sale
a05D_Warehouse_Items

You will save your databases as:

Lastname_Firstname_5D_Clearance_Sale
Lastname_Firstname_5D_Warehouse_Items

Project Results

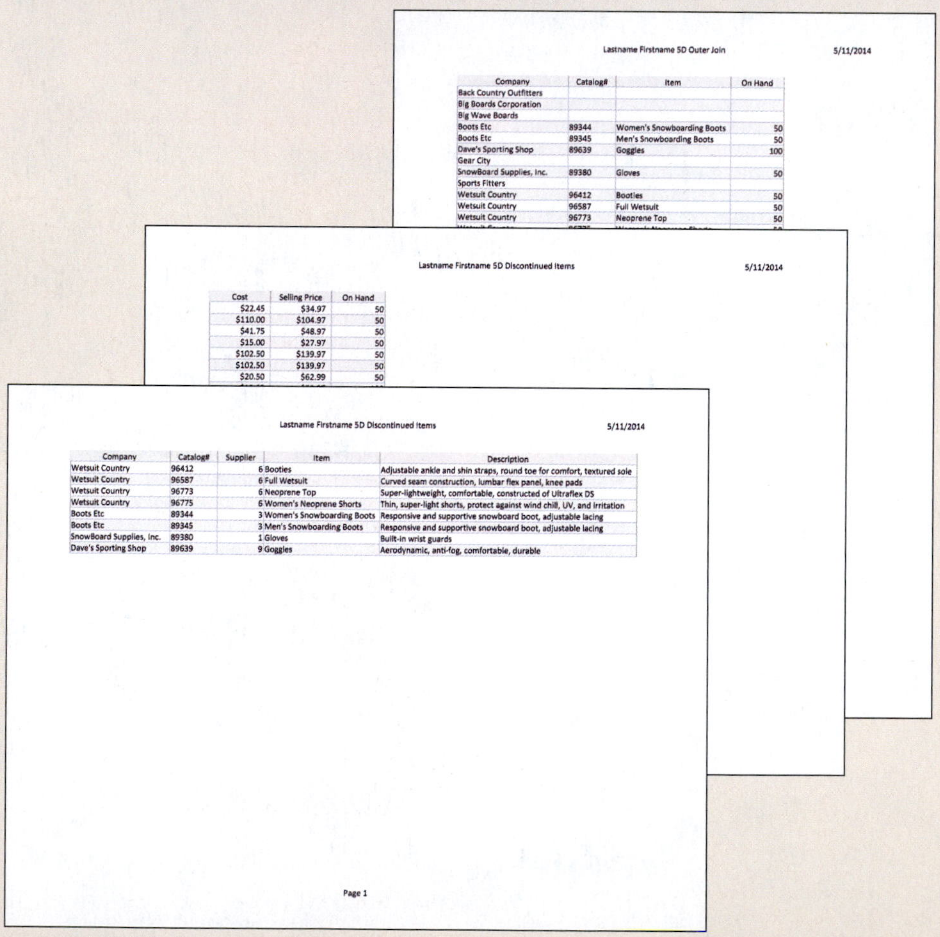

Lastname Firstname 5D Outer Join 5/11/2014

Company	Catalog#	Item	On Hand
Back Country Outfitters			
Big Boards Corporation			
Big Wave Boards			
Boots Etc	89344	Women's Snowboarding Boots	50
Boots Etc	89345	Men's Snowboarding Boots	50
Dave's Sporting Shop	89639	Goggles	100
Gear City			
SnowBoard Supplies, Inc.	89380	Gloves	50
Sports Fitters			
Wetsuit Country	96412	Booties	50
Wetsuit Country	96587	Full Wetsuit	50
Wetsuit Country	96773	Neoprene Top	50

Lastname Firstname 5D Discontinued Items 5/11/2014

Cost	Selling Price	On Hand
$22.45	$34.97	50
$110.00	$104.97	50
$41.75	$48.97	50
$15.00	$27.97	50
$102.50	$139.97	50
$102.50	$139.97	50
$20.50	$62.99	50

Lastname Firstname 5D Discontinued Items 5/11/2014

Company	Catalog#	Supplier	Item	Description
Wetsuit Country	96412	6	Booties	Adjustable ankle and shin straps, round toe for comfort, textured sole
Wetsuit Country	96587	6	Full Wetsuit	Curved seam construction, lumbar flex panel, knee pads
Wetsuit Country	96773	6	Neoprene Top	Super-lightweight, comfortable, constructed of Ultraflex DS
Wetsuit Country	96775	6	Women's Neoprene Shorts	Thin, super-light shorts, protect against wind chill, UV, and irritation
Boots Etc	89344	3	Women's Snowboarding Boots	Responsive and supportive snowboard boot, adjustable lacing
Boots Etc	89345	3	Men's Snowboarding Boots	Responsive and supportive snowboard boot, adjustable lacing
SnowBoard Supplies, Inc.	89380	1	Gloves	Built-in wrist guards
Dave's Sporting Shop	89639	9	Goggles	Aerodynamic, anti-fog, comfortable, durable

Page 1

Figure 5.50

(Project 5D Clearance Sale continues on the next page)

Skills Review | Project 5D Clearance Sale (continued)

1 **Start** Access. Locate and open the **a05D_Clearance_Sale** file. Display **Backstage** view. **Save** the database in your **Access Chapter 5** folder as **Lastname_Firstname_5D_Clearance_Sale**

a. If necessary, enable the content or add the Access Chapter 5 folder to the Trust Center.

b. Rename the tables by adding your **Lastname Firstname** to the beginning of each table name. **Close** the **Navigation Pane**.

2 Create a new query in **Query Design**. From the **Show Table** dialog box, add the following tables to the Query design workspace: **5D Suppliers** and **5D Inventory**. **Close** the **Show Table** dialog box, and then expand the field lists.

a. From the **5D Suppliers** field list, add **Company** to the first column of the design grid. From the **5D Inventory** field list, double-click each field to add them all to the design grid.

b. In the design grid, under **Supplier**, click in the **Criteria** row, type **6** and then **Run** the query. Notice that four items are supplied by *Wetsuit Country*.

c. Switch to **Design** view. On the **Design tab**, in the **Query Type group**, click the **Make Table** button. In the **Make Table** dialog box, in the **Table Name** box, type **Lastname Firstname 5D Discontinued Items** In the **Make Table** dialog box, be sure that **Current Database** is selected, and then click **OK**. **Run** the query. In the displayed message box, click **Yes** to paste the rows to the new table.

d. **Close** the query, click **Yes** in the message box asking if you want to save changes, and then name the query **Lastname Firstname 5D Wetsuit Country Items**

3 Create a new query in **Query Design**. From the **Show Table** dialog box, add the following tables, in the order specified, to the Query design workspace: **5D Suppliers** and **5D Inventory**. **Close** the **Show Table** dialog box, and then expand the field lists.

a. From the **5D Suppliers** field list, add **Company** to the first column of the design grid. From the **5D Inventory** field list, add all fields in the field list to the design grid.

b. In the design grid, under **Supplier**, click in the **Criteria row**, type **3** and then **Run** the query. Notice that one item is supplied by *Boots Etc*

c. Switch to **Design** view. On the **Design tab**, in the **Query Type group**, click the **Append** button. In the **Append** dialog box, click the **Table Name arrow**, and from the displayed list, click **Lastname Firstname 5D Discontinued Items**, and then click **OK**.

d. **Run** the query. In the displayed message box, click **Yes** to append one row. **Close** the query, and then save it as **Lastname Firstname 5D Append1**

4 On the Access window title bar, click the **Minimize** button. **Start** a second instance of Access. Navigate to the location where the student data files for this textbook are saved. Locate and open the **a05D_Warehouse_Items** file. Save the database in your **Access Chapter 5** folder as **Lastname_Firstname_5D_Warehouse_Items** If necessary, enable the content or add the Access Chapter 5 folder to the Trust Center.

5 Create a new query in **Query Design**. From the **Show Table** dialog box, add the **5D Suppliers** table and the **5D Discontinued Items** table to the Query design workspace, and then close the **Show Table** dialog box. Expand the field lists. From the **5D Suppliers** field list, add **Company** to the first column of the design grid. From the **5D Discontinued Items** field list, add all of the fields to the design grid in the order listed.

a. On the **Design tab**, in the **Query Type group**, click the **Append** button. In the **Append** dialog box, click the **Another Database** option button, and then click the **Browse** button. Navigate to your **Access Chapter 5** folder, and then double-click **Lastname_Firstname_5D_Clearance_Sale**.

b. In the **Append** dialog box, click the **Table Name arrow**, click **5D Discontinued Items**, and then click **OK**. **Save** the query as **Lastname Firstname 5D Append2** and then **Run** the query. In the displayed message box, click **Yes** to append 3 rows. **Close** the query. **Close** the database, and then **Exit** this instance of Access.

c. From the Windows taskbar, click the **5D_Clearance_Sale** database. Verify that the **5D Discontinued Items** table now contains 8 rows. Create a new query in **Query Design**. Add the **5D Inventory** table to the Query design workspace, and then **Close** the **Show Table** dialog box.

d. Expand the field list. From the field list, add **Catalog#** and **On Hand**, in this order, to the first and second columns in the design grid. In the design grid, under **On Hand**, click in the **Criteria row**, type **0** and then **Run** the query.

(Project 5D Clearance Sale continues on the next page)

Skills Review | Project 5D Clearance Sale (continued)

- **e.** Switch to **Design** view. In the Query design workspace, right-click in the empty space. From the displayed shortcut menu, point to **Query Type**, and then click **Delete Query**.
- **f.** **Save** the query as **Lastname Firstname 5D Delete Zero Inventory** and then **Run** the query. In the message box stating that *You are about to delete 1 row(s) from the specified table*, click **Yes**. **Close** the query. You have removed this item from the inventory.

6 Create a new query in **Query Design**. Add the **5D Discontinued Items** table to the Query design workspace, and then **Close** the **Show Table** dialog box. Expand the field list.

- **a.** In the **5D Discontinued Items** field list, double-click **Catalog#** to add the field to the first column of the design grid. Then add the **Selling Price** field to the second column of the design grid.
- **b.** On the **Design tab**, in the **Query Type group**, click the **Update** button. In the design grid, under **Selling Price**, click in the **Update To row**, and then type **[Selling Price]*0.7**
- **c.** **Save** the query as **Lastname Firstname 5D Discounted Selling Prices** and then **Run** the query. In the message box stating that *You are about to update 8 row(s)*, click **Yes**. **Close** the query.
- **d.** Open the **Navigation Pane**, and then double-click the **5D Discontinued Items** table to open it in **Datasheet** view. Close the **Navigation Pane**. Adjust all column widths. View the table in **Print Preview**. If you are instructed to submit this result, create a paper or electronic printout in **Landscape** orientation. **Close** the table, saving changes.

7 Create a new query in **Query Design**. From the **Show Table** dialog box, add the **5D Suppliers** table and the **5D Discontinued Items** table to the Query design workspace, and then **Close** the **Show Table** dialog box.

- **a.** Expand both field lists. From the **5D Suppliers** table, drag the **ID** field to the **5D Discontinued Items** table **Supplier** field to create a join between the tables.
- **b.** From the **5D Suppliers** field list, add **Company** to the first column in the design grid. From the **5D Discontinued Items** field list, add **Catalog#**, **Item**, and **On Hand**, in this order, to the design grid. In the design grid, under **Company**, click in the **Sort row**, click the **arrow**, and then click **Ascending**. **Run** the query.
- **c.** Switch to **Design** view. Verify that the **5D Suppliers** table appears on the left, and the **5D Discontinued Items** table is on the right. Correct as necessary. In the Query design workspace, double-click the **join line** to display the **Join Properties** dialog box. Click the option button next to **2**, and then click **OK**. **Run** the query. This query displays all of the supplier companies used by the shop, not just those with discontinued items.
- **d.** **Save** the query as **Lastname Firstname 5D Outer Join** View the query in **Print Preview**, ensuring that the table prints on one page. If you are instructed to submit this result, create a paper or electronic printout. **Close** the query.

8 Open the **Navigation Pane**, **Close** the database, and then **Exit** Access.

End **You have completed Project 5D**

Apply 5A skills from these Objectives:

1. Create Calculated Fields in a Query
2. Use Aggregate Functions in a Query
3. Create a Crosstab Query
4. Find Duplicate and Unmatched Records
5. Create a Parameter Query

Mastering Access | Project 5E Surfing Lessons

Mary Connolly, one of the owners of 4Ever Boarding Surf and Snowboard Shop, has a database containing student, instructor, and surfing lesson data. In the following Mastering Access project, you will create special-purpose queries to calculate data, summarize and group data, display data in a spreadsheet-like format, and find duplicate and unmatched records. You will also create a query that prompts an individual to enter the criteria. Your completed queries will look similar to Figure 5.51.

Project Files

For Project 5E, you will need the following file:

a05E_Surfing_Lessons

You will save your database as:

Lastname_Firstname_5E_Surfing_Lessons

Project Results

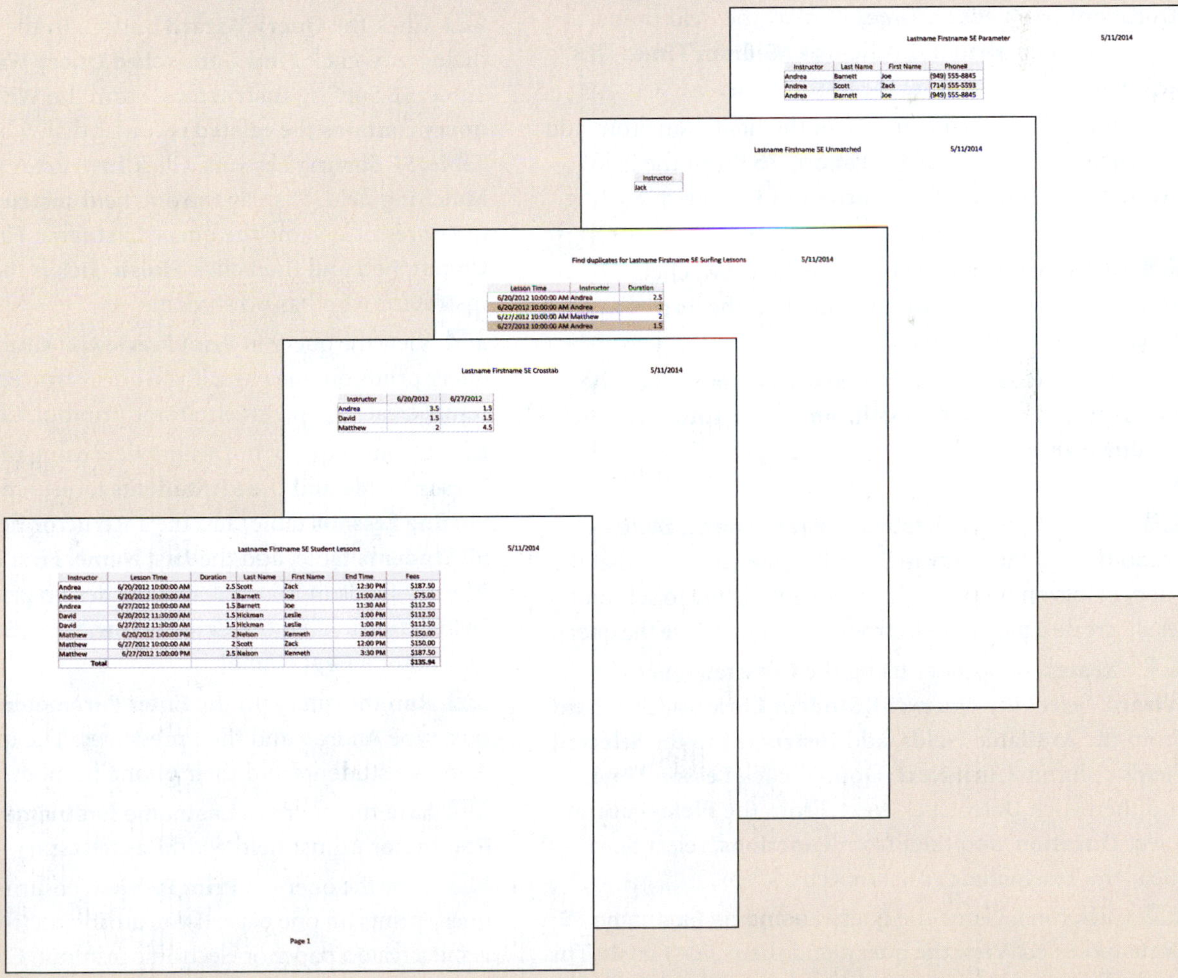

Lastname Firstname 5E Parameter 5/11/2014

Instructor	Last Name	First Name	Phone#
Andrea	Barnett	Joe	(949) 555-8845
Andrea	Scott	Zack	(714) 555-5593
Andrea	Barnett	Joe	(949) 555-8845

Lastname Firstname 5E Unmatched 5/11/2014

Instructor
Jack

Find duplicates for Lastname Firstname 5E Surfing Lessons 5/11/2014

Lesson Time	Instructor	Duration
6/20/2012 10:00:00 AM	Andrea	2.5
6/20/2012 10:00:00 AM	Andrea	1
6/27/2012 10:00:00 AM	Matthew	2
6/27/2012 10:00:00 AM	Andrea	1.5

Lastname Firstname 5E Crosstab 5/11/2014

Instructor	6/20/2012	6/27/2012
Andrea	3.5	1.5
David	1.5	1.5
Matthew	2	4.5

Lastname Firstname 5E Student Lessons 5/11/2014

Instructor	Lesson Time	Duration	Last Name	First Name	End Time	Fees
Andrea	6/20/2012 10:00:00 AM	2.5	Scott	Zack	12:30 PM	$187.50
Andrea	6/20/2012 10:00:00 AM	1	Barnett	Joe	11:00 AM	$75.00
Andrea	6/27/2012 10:00:00 AM	1.5	Barnett	Joe	11:30 AM	$112.50
David	6/20/2012 11:30:00 AM	1.5	Hickman	Leslie	1:00 PM	$112.50
David	6/27/2012 11:30:00 AM	1.5	Hickman	Leslie	1:00 PM	$112.50
Matthew	6/20/2012 1:00:00 PM	2	Nelson	Kenneth	3:00 PM	$150.00
Matthew	6/27/2012 10:00:00 AM	2	Scott	Zack	12:00 PM	$150.00
Matthew	6/27/2012 1:00:00 PM	2.5	Nelson	Kenneth	3:30 PM	$187.50
Total						$135.94

Page 1

Figure 5.51

(Project 5E Surfing Lessons continues on the next page)

Mastering Access | Project 5E Surfing Lessons (continued)

1 **Start** Access. Locate and open the **a05E_Surfing_Lessons** file. Display **Backstage** view. Save the database in in your **Access Chapter 5** folder as **Lastname_Firstname_5E_Surfing_Lessons** If necessary, enable the content or add the Access Chapter 5 folder to the Trust Center. Rename the tables by adding your **Lastname Firstname** to the beginning of each table name.

2 **Create** a query in **Query Design** using the **5E Surfing Lessons** table and the **5E Students** table. From the **5E Surfing Lessons** table, add the **Instructor** field, the **Lesson Time** field, and the **Duration** field to the first, second, and third columns of the design grid. From the **5E Students** table, add the **Last Name** and **First Name** fields to the fourth and fifth columns.

3 In the sixth column of the design grid, add a calculated field. In the field name row, type **End Time: [Duration]/24+[Lesson Time]** Display the field properties sheet, and then format this field as **Medium Time**. This field will display the time the lesson ends.

4 In the first blank column, in the field name row, add the calculated field **Fees:[Duration]*75** From the field properties sheet, select the **Format** of **Currency**. Surfing lessons cost $75.00 an hour.

5 In the **Instructor** field, in the **Sort row**, click **Ascending**. In the **Lesson Time** field, in the **Sort row**, click **Ascending**. **Run** the query.

6 On the **Home tab**, in the **Records group**, click the **Totals** button. In the **Fees column**, in the **Total row**, click the **down arrow**, and then click **Average**. Adjust field widths as necessary.

7 **Save** the query as **Lastname Firstname 5E Student Lessons** View the query in **Print Preview**, ensuring that the query prints on one page. If you are instructed to submit this result, create a paper or electronic printout. **Close** the query.

8 **Create** a new query using the **Crosstab Query Wizard**. Select the **Query: 5E Student Lessons**. Click **Next**. From the **Available Fields**, add **Instructor** to the **Selected Fields** column. Click **Next**. Double-click **Lesson Time**, and then click **Date**. Click **Next**. From the **Fields column**, select **Duration**, and then from **Functions**, select **Sum**. Clear the **Yes, include row sums** check box.

9 Click **Next**. Name the query **Lastname Firstname 5E Crosstab** Select **View the query**, and then click **Finish**. This query displays the instructor and the number of hours he or she taught by date. Adjust field widths as necessary.

10 View the query in **Print Preview**, ensuring that the query prints on one page. If you are instructed to submit this result, create a paper or electronic printout. **Close** the query, saving changes.

11 Click the **Query Wizard** button. In the **New Query** dialog box, click **Find Duplicates Query Wizard**. Search the **Table: 5E Surfing Lessons**, and select the **Lesson Time** field for duplicate information. Click **Next**. From **Available fields**, add the **Instructor** and **Duration** fields to the **Additional query fields** column. Accept the default name for the query. Click **Finish**. The query results show that there are duplicate lesson times. Adjust field widths as necessary.

12 View the query in **Print Preview**, ensuring that the query prints on one page. If you are instructed to submit this result, create a paper or electronic printout. **Close** and **Save** the query.

13 Click the **Query Wizard** button. In the **New Query** dialog box, click **Find Unmatched Query Wizard**. Select **Table: 5E Surfing Instructors**. From the **Which table or query contains the related records?** dialog box, click **Table: 5E Surfing Lessons**. Click **Instructor** as the **Matching** field. Display the one field **Instructor** in the query results. Name the query **Lastname Firstname 5E Unmatched** and then click **Finish**. Jack is the only instructor who has no students.

14 View the query in **Print Preview**, ensuring that the query prints on one page. If you are instructed to submit this result, create a paper or electronic printout. **Close** the query.

15 **Create** a query in **Design** view using the **5E Surfing Lessons** table and the **5E Students** table. From the **5E Surfing Lessons** table, add the **Instructor** field. From the **5E Students** table, add the **Last Name**, **First Name**, and **Phone#** fields in that order to the design grid. In the **Instructor** field, in the **Criteria row**, type **[Enter Instructor's First Name]**

16 **Run** the query. In the **Enter Parameter Value** dialog box, type **Andrea** and then press Enter. The query displays Andrea's students and their phone numbers.

17 **Save** the query as **Lastname Firstname 5E Parameter** Adjust field widths as necessary.

18 View the query in **Print Preview**, ensuring that the query prints on one page. If you are instructed to submit this result, create a paper or electronic printout. **Close** the query.

19 Open the **Navigation Pane**, **Close** the database, and then **Exit** Access.

End **You have completed Project 5E**

Apply **5B** skills from these Objectives:

6 Create a Make Table Query
7 Create an Append Query
8 Create a Delete Query
9 Create an Update Query
10 Modify the Join Type

Mastering Access | Project 5F Gift Cards

Karen Walker, Sales Associate for 4Ever Boarding Surf and Snowboard Shop, has decided to offer gift cards for purchase at the shop. She has a database of the employees and the details of the cards they have sold. In the following Mastering Access project, you will create action queries that will create a new table, update records in a table, append records to a table, and delete records from a table. You will also modify the join type of the relationship to display a different subset of the data when the query is run. Your completed queries will look similar to Figure 5.52.

Project Files

For Project 5F, you will need the following file:

a05F_Gift_Cards

You will save your database as:

Lastname_Firstname_5F_Gift_Cards

Project Results

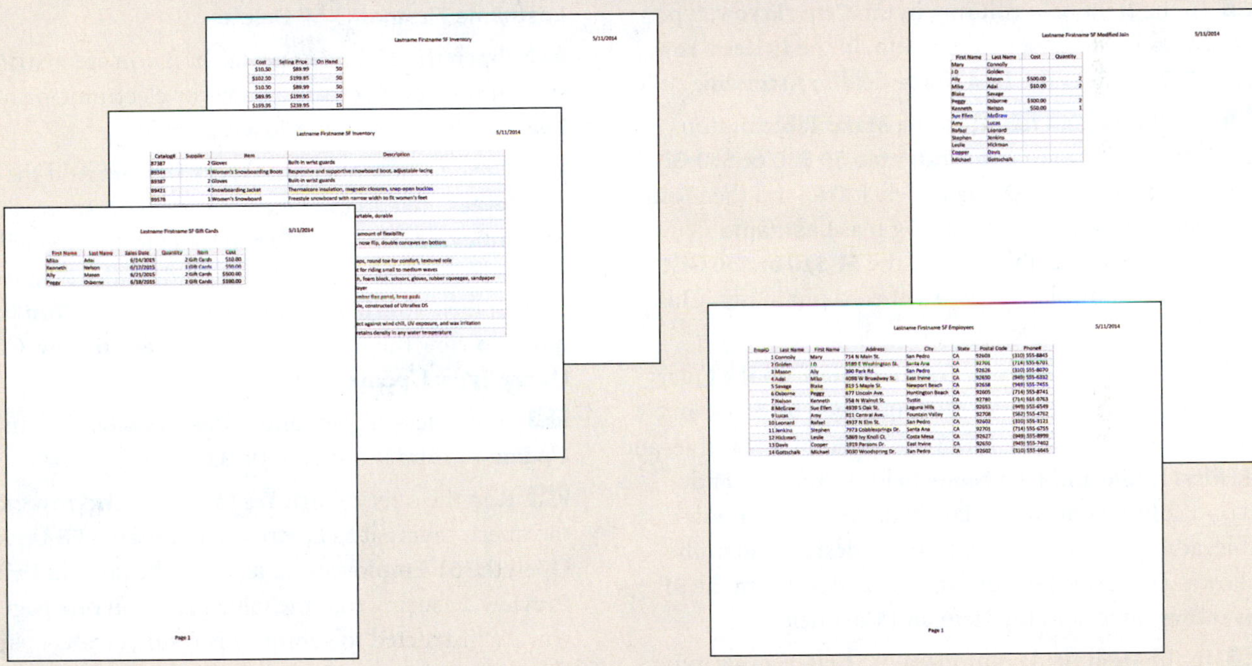

Figure 5.52

(Project 5F Gift Cards continues on the next page)

Mastering Access | Project 5F Gift Cards (continued)

1 **Start** Access. Locate and open the **a05F_Gift_Cards** file. Display **Backstage** view. Save the database in your **Access Chapter 5** folder as **Lastname_Firstname_5F_Gift_Cards** If necessary, enable the content or add the Access Chapter 5 folder to the Trust Center. Rename the tables by adding your **Lastname Firstname** to the beginning of each table name.

2 Create a new query in **Query Design**. To the Query design workspace, add the **5F Employees**, **5F Sales**, and the **5F Inventory** tables. From the **5F Employees** table, add the **First Name** and **Last Name** fields to the first and second columns of the design grid. From the **5F Sales** table, add the following fields to the design grid in the order specified: **Sales Date** and **Quantity**. From the **5F Inventory** table, add the **Item** and **Cost** fields.

3 In the **Item** field column, in the **Criteria row**, type **Gift Cards** In the **Cost** field column, in the **Criteria row**, type **10 Or 50** **Sort** the **Last Name** field in **Ascending** order.

4 On the **Design tab**, click the **Make Table** button. Name the table **Lastname Firstname 5F $10 or $50 Gift Cards** Select **Current Database**, click **OK**, and then **Run** the query. **Close** the query, saving it as **Lastname Firstname 5F Make Table** Open the **5F $10 or $50 Gift Cards** table to display the two gift card purchases. **Close** the table.

5 Create a new query in **Query Design**. To the Query design workspace, add the **5F Employees**, **5F Sales**, and the **5F Inventory** tables. From the **5F Employees** table, add the **First Name** and **Last Name** fields to the first and second columns of the design grid. From the **5F Sales** table, add the following fields to the design grid in the following order: **Sales Date** and **Quantity**. From the **5F Inventory** table, add the **Item** and **Cost** fields.

6 In the **Item** field column, in the **Criteria row**, type **Gift Cards** In the **Cost** field column, in the **Criteria row**, type **100 Or 500** **Sort** the **Last Name** field in **Ascending** order.

7 Click the **Append** button, and then append the records to the **5F $10 or $50 Gift Cards** table. Click **OK**. **Run** the query. Click **Yes** to append two rows. **Close** the query, saving it as **Lastname Firstname 5F Append** Open the **5F $10 or $50 Gift Cards** table to display all gift card purchases. **Close** the table, and then rename it **Lastname Firstname 5F Gift Cards**

8 View the table in **Print Preview**, ensuring that the table prints on one page. If you are instructed to submit this result, create a paper or electronic printout. **Close** the table.

9 Create a new query in **Query Design**. Add the **5F Inventory** table to the Query design workspace. From the **5F Inventory** table, add the **Catalog#** and **Item** fields to the first and second columns of the design grid. In the design grid, under **Item**, click in the **Criteria row**, and then type **Gift Cards**

10 **Run** the query to view the results. Switch to **Design** view, click the **Query Type: Delete** button, and then **Run** the query. Click **Yes** to delete the gift cards from the **5F Inventory** table. The gift cards are not to be counted as inventory items. **Close** and **Save** the query, naming it **Lastname Firstname 5F Delete**

11 Open the **5F Inventory** table. If you are instructed to submit this result, create a paper or electronic printout in **Landscape** orientation. **Close** the table.

12 Create a new query in **Query Design**. Add the **5F Employees** table to the Query design workspace. From the **5F Employees** table, add **Postal Code** to the first column of the design grid. In the design grid, under **Postal Code**, click in the **Criteria row**, and then type **972*** **Run** the query to view the results. Switch to **Design** view. Click the **Query Type: Update** button.

13 In the design grid, under **Postal Code**, click in the **Update To row**, and then type **92701**

14 **Run** the query. Click **Yes** to update two rows. **Close** the query, saving it as **Lastname Firstname 5F Update** Open the **5F Employees** table. View the table in **Print Preview**, ensuring that the table prints on one page. If you are instructed to submit this result, create a paper or electronic printout. **Close** the table.

15 Create a new query in **Query Design**. Add the **5F Employees** and **5F Gift Cards** tables to the Query design workspace. From the **5F Employees** field list, add **First Name** and **Last Name** to the first two columns of the design grid. From the **5F Gift Cards** field list, add **Cost** and **Quantity** field, in this order, to the design grid.

16 From the **5F Employees** field list, click **Last Name**, and then drag to the **5F Gift Cards Last Name** field. Double-click the **join line**, and then select option **2**. **Run**

(Project 5F Gift Cards continues on the next page)

Mastering Access | Project 5F Gift Cards (continued)

the query to display the results, which include all 14 employees and not just gift card sellers. **Save** the query as **Lastname Firstname 5F Modified Join**

17 View the table in **Print Preview**, ensuring that the table prints on one page. If you are instructed to submit this result, create a paper or electronic printout. **Close** the query.

18 **Close** the database, and then **Exit** Access.

End **You have completed Project 5F**

Content-Based Assessments

Apply **5A** and **5B** skills from these Objectives:

1. Create Calculated Fields in a Query
2. Use Aggregate Functions in a Query
3. Create a Crosstab Query
9. Create an Update Query

myitlab grader

Mastering Access | Project 5G Advertisements

J.D. Golden, one of the owners of 4Ever Boarding Surf and Snowboard Shop, is responsible for all of the advertising for the business. In the following Mastering Access project, you will create special-purpose queries to calculate data, and then summarize and group data for advertising cost analysis. You will also create a query that prompts an individual to enter the criteria for a specific type of advertisement media. Your completed queries will look similar to Figure 5.53.

Project Files

For Project 5G, you will need the following file:

a05G_Advertisements

You will save your database as:

Lastname_Firstname_5G_Advertisements

Project Results

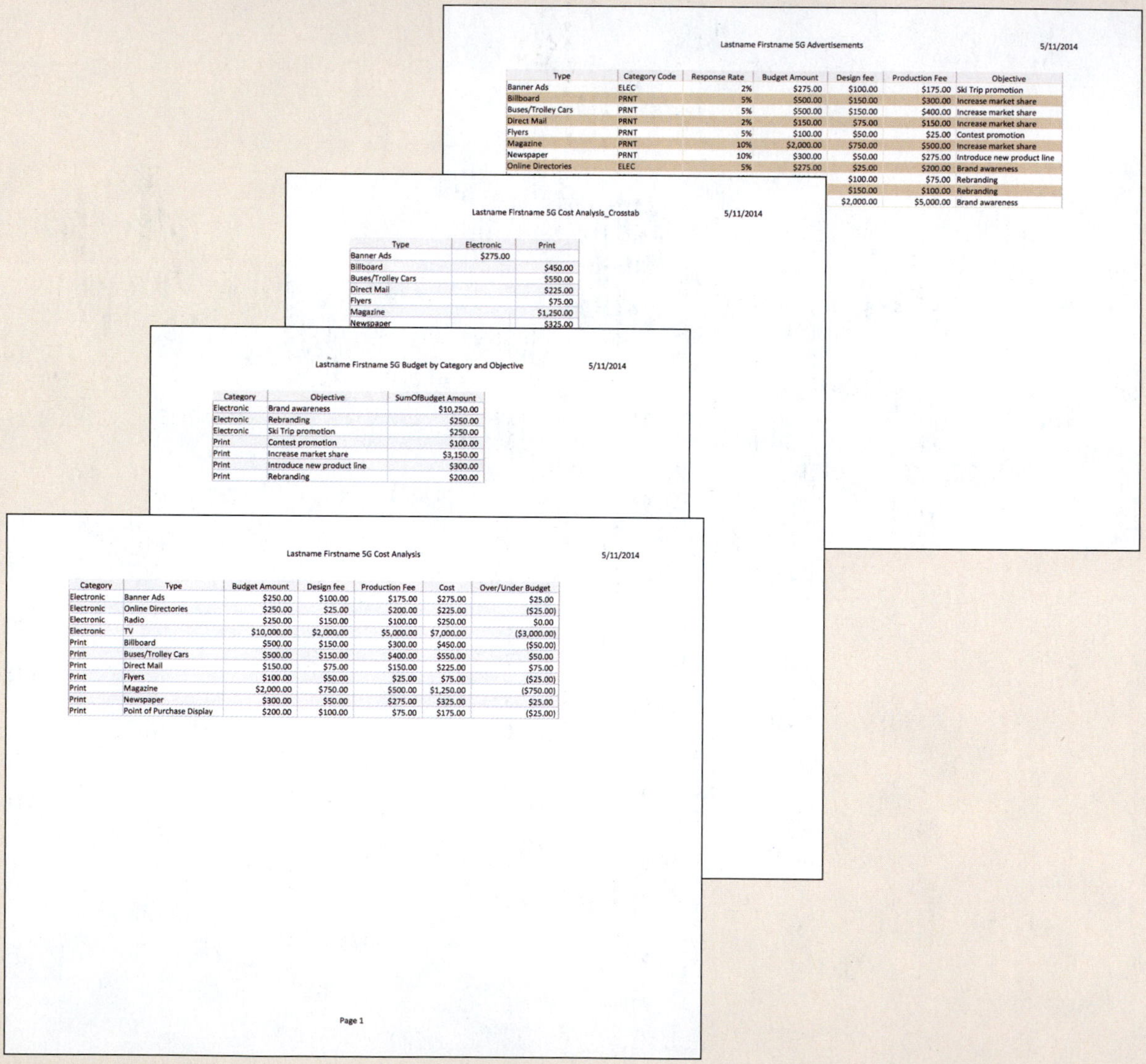

Lastname Firstname 5G Advertisements 5/11/2014

Type	Category Code	Response Rate	Budget Amount	Design fee	Production Fee	Objective
Banner Ads	ELEC	2%	$275.00	$100.00	$175.00	Ski Trip promotion
Billboard	PRNT	5%	$500.00	$150.00	$300.00	Increase market share
Buses/Trolley Cars	PRNT	5%	$500.00	$150.00	$400.00	Increase market share
Direct Mail	PRNT	2%	$150.00	$75.00	$150.00	Increase market share
Flyers	PRNT	5%	$100.00	$50.00	$25.00	Contest promotion
Magazine	PRNT	10%	$2,000.00	$750.00	$500.00	Increase market share
Newspaper	PRNT	10%	$300.00	$50.00	$275.00	Introduce new product line
Online Directories	ELEC	5%	$275.00	$25.00	$200.00	Brand awareness
				$100.00	$75.00	Rebranding
				$150.00	$100.00	Rebranding
				$2,000.00	$5,000.00	Brand awareness

Lastname Firstname 5G Cost Analysis_Crosstab 5/11/2014

Type	Electronic	Print
Banner Ads	$275.00	
Billboard		$450.00
Buses/Trolley Cars		$550.00
Direct Mail		$225.00
Flyers		$75.00
Magazine		$1,250.00
Newspaper		$325.00

Lastname Firstname 5G Budget by Category and Objective 5/11/2014

Category	Objective	SumOfBudget Amount
Electronic	Brand awareness	$10,250.00
Electronic	Rebranding	$250.00
Electronic	Ski Trip promotion	$250.00
Print	Contest promotion	$100.00
Print	Increase market share	$3,150.00
Print	Introduce new product line	$300.00
Print	Rebranding	$200.00

Lastname Firstname 5G Cost Analysis 5/11/2014

Category	Type	Budget Amount	Design fee	Production Fee	Cost	Over/Under Budget
Electronic	Banner Ads	$250.00	$100.00	$175.00	$275.00	$25.00
Electronic	Online Directories	$250.00	$25.00	$200.00	$225.00	($25.00)
Electronic	Radio	$250.00	$150.00	$100.00	$250.00	$0.00
Electronic	TV	$10,000.00	$2,000.00	$5,000.00	$7,000.00	($3,000.00)
Print	Billboard	$500.00	$150.00	$300.00	$450.00	($50.00)
Print	Buses/Trolley Cars	$500.00	$150.00	$400.00	$550.00	$50.00
Print	Direct Mail	$150.00	$75.00	$150.00	$225.00	$75.00
Print	Flyers	$100.00	$50.00	$25.00	$75.00	($25.00)
Print	Magazine	$2,000.00	$750.00	$500.00	$1,250.00	($750.00)
Print	Newspaper	$300.00	$50.00	$275.00	$325.00	$25.00
Print	Point of Purchase Display	$200.00	$100.00	$75.00	$175.00	($25.00)

Page 1

Figure 5.53

(Project 5G Advertisements continues on the next page)

Mastering Access | Project **5G** Advertisements (continued)

1 **Start** Access. Locate and open the **a05G_Advertisements** file. Display **Backstage** view. Save the database in your **Access Chapter 5** folder as **Lastname_Firstname_5G_ Advertisements** If necessary, enable the content or add the Access Chapter 5 folder to the Trust Center. Rename the table by adding your **Lastname Firstname** to the beginning of the table names. Close the **Navigation Pane**.

2 Create a new query in **Query Design**. From the **5G Categories** table, add the **Category** field to the design grid. From the **5G Advertisements** table, add the **Type**, **Budget Amount**, **Design Fee**, and **Production Fee** fields to the design grid in this order.

3 In the first blank field column, add a calculated field. Type **Cost:[Design Fee]+[Production Fee]** In the next blank field column, add a second calculated field: **Over/Under Budget: [Cost]-[Budget Amount]**

4 **Run** the query. Save it as **Lastname Firstname 5G Cost Analysis.** View the results in **Print Preview**, ensuring that it fits on one page. If you are instructed to submit this result, create a paper or electronic printout. **Close** the query.

5 Create a new query in **Query Design**. From the **5G Categories** table, add the **Category** field to the design grid. From the **5G Advertisements** table, add the **Objective** and **Budget Amount** fields to the design grid. On the **Design tab**, in the **Show/Hide group**, click the **Totals** button. In the design grid, in the **Total row**, under **Budget Amount**, click **Sum**.

6 **Run** the query. Save it as **Lastname Firstname 5G Budget by Category and Objective** View the results in **Print Preview**, ensuring that it on one page. If you are instructed to submit this result, create a paper or electronic printout. **Close** the query.

7 Create a new crosstab query using the Query Wizard. Select the **Query: 5G Cost Analysis**. For row headings, use **Type**, and for column headings, use **Category**. Select **Cost** for the calculated field, using the **Sum** function. Do not summarize each row. Accept the default name for this query.

8 Click **Finish** to view the cost in relation to the response rate for each type of advertisement.

9 View the query in **Print Preview**, ensuring that the query prints on one page. If you are instructed to submit this result, create a paper or electronic printout. **Close** the query.

10 Create a new query in **Query Design**. From the **5G Categories** table, add the **Category** field to the design grid. From the **5G Advertisements** table, add the **Budget Amount** field to the design grid. In the design grid, under **Category** field, click in the **Criteria row**, and then type **Electronic**

11 Click the **Query Type: Update** button. In the design grid, under **Budget Amount**, click in the **Update To row**, and then type **[Budget Amount]*1.10**

12 **Run** the query. Click **Yes** to update four rows. **Close** the query, saving it as **Lastname Firstname 5G Update** Open the **Navigation Pane**. Open the **5G Advertisements** table. View the table in **Print Preview**, ensuring that the table prints on one page. If you are instructed to submit this result, create a paper or electronic printout. **Close** the table.

13 **Close** the database, and then **Exit** Access.

End **You have completed Project 5G**

Apply a combination of the 5A and 5B skills.

GO! Fix It | Project 5H Contests

Project Files

For Project 5H, you will need the following files:

a05H_Snowboarding_Contests
a05H_Online_Registration

You will save your databases as:

Lastname_Firstname_5H_Snowboarding_Contests
Lastname_Firstname_5H_Online_Registration

In this project, you will correct query design errors in a database used to manage snowboarding contests for children, teenagers, and adults. To complete the project you must find and correct errors in relationships, query design, and column widths.

- In the **5H Snowboarding Contests** database, you should add your last name and first name to the beginning of each query name; do *not* rename the tables.
- All registration information should be kept in a table of its own. Use the 5H Contestants query to create the 5H Registration table. Append the customers that registered online; their information is found in the **5H Online Registration** database.
- Nelson Gibbs forgot to turn in his date of birth (DOB). Create a query to update his date of birth to 8/27/1990. He is registered for two contests.
- 5H Contestant Ages on Event Date only includes the customers that registered in the store. Update the design to reflect data from the correct table. Be sure that the contestant's full name, event date, and DOB are displayed in the results. The age is represented in days; update the expression to show the age in years only.
- Several queries do not accurately reflect the result implied in the query name. Open each query and examine and correct the design; modify them to accurately reflect the query name.

End **You have completed Project 5H**

Content-Based Assessments

Apply a combination of the **5A** and **5B** skills.

GO! Make It | Project 5I Ski Trips

Project Files

For Project 5I, you will need the following file:

a05I_Ski_Trips

You will save your database as:

Lastname_Firstname_5I_Ski_Trips

From the student files that accompany this textbook, open the **a05I_Ski_Trips** database file. Save the database in your Access Chapter 5 folder as **Lastname_Firstname_5I_Ski_Trips** In Query Design, create a query to display the following fields from existing tables: **Ski Trips**: **Depart Date, Return Date**, **Resort**, **Price**, **Rentals**, **Lift**; **Ski Trip Captains**: **First Name** and **Last Name** in **Ascending** order. Add a calculated field to display the **#Days** included in the trip and the **Total Cost** including **Price**, **Rentals**, and **Lift**. Compare your results to those shown in Figure 5.54. Create a paper or electronic printout as directed.

Project Results

Lastname Firstname 5I Trip Details

5/11/2014

Depart Date	Return Date	#Days	Resort	Price	Rentals	Lift	Total Cost	First name	Last Name
12/28/2015 10:00:00 AM	1/1/2016 10:00:00 PM	4.50	Timber Ridge	$619	$0.00	$0.00	$619.00	Ashley	Henegar
12/12/2015 6:00:00 AM	12/13/2015 6:00:00 PM	1.50	Valley Lodge	$300	$15.00	$20.00	$335.00	Ashley	Henegar
1/8/2016 5:00:00 AM	1/9/2016 5:00:00 PM	1.50	Snow Time	$250	$0.00	$0.00	$250.00	Ashley	Henegar
12/11/2015 6:00:00 AM	12/12/2015 6:00:00 AM	1.00	Valley Lodge	$200	$15.00	$20.00	$235.00	Kenneth	Pliecher
12/20/2015 4:00:00 AM	12/21/2015 4:00:00 AM	1.00	Winter Haven	$125	$20.00	$25.00	$170.00	Kenneth	Pliecher
11/25/2015 6:00:00 AM	11/26/2015 6:00:00 AM	1.00	Valley Lodge	$200	$15.00	$20.00	$235.00	Kenneth	Pliecher
12/30/2015 7:30:00 PM	1/1/2016 7:30:00 PM	2.00	Timber Ridge	$519	$0.00	$0.00	$519.00	Kenneth	Pliecher
2/1/2016 7:30:00 PM	2/5/2016 7:30:00 PM	4.00	Timber Ridge	$449	$0.00	$0.00	$449.00	Kenneth	Pliecher
1/22/2016 5:00:00 AM	1/24/2016 5:00:00 PM	2.50	Snow Time	$375	$0.00	$0.00	$375.00	Kenneth	Pliecher
1/3/2016 8:00:00 PM	1/5/2016 8:00:00 PM	2.00	Chile Andes	$1,849	$0.00	$0.00	$1,849.00	Helen	Reindel
12/19/2015 4:00:00 AM	12/20/2015 4:00:00 AM	1.00	Winter Haven	$125	$20.00	$25.00	$170.00	Helen	Reindel
1/27/2016 7:00:00 PM	2/3/2016 1:00:00 AM	6.25	Switzerland	$1,699	$0.00	$0.00	$1,699.00	Helen	Reindel
12/26/2015 7:00:00 PM	1/1/2016 7:00:00 PM	6.00	Italy	$1,689	$0.00	$0.00	$1,689.00	Helen	Reindel
12/29/2015 4:00:00 AM	12/30/2015 4:00:00 PM	1.50	Winter Haven	$185	$20.00	$25.00	$230.00	Mitch	Taccaro
1/6/2016 2:00:00 PM	1/13/2016 8:00:00 PM	7.25	Canada	$1,349	$0.00	$0.00	$1,349.00	Mitch	Taccaro
11/27/2015 6:00:00 AM	11/28/2015 6:00:00 PM	1.50	Valley Lodge	$300	$15.00	$20.00	$335.00	Mitch	Taccaro

Page 1

Figure 5.54

End **You have completed Project 5I**

Access | Chapter 5

Apply a combination of the **5A** and **5B** skills.

GO! Solve It | Project 5J Applicant

Project Files

For Project 5J, you will need the following file:

a05J_Job_Applicants

You will save your database as:

Lastname_Firstname_5J_Job_Applicants

The owners of 4Ever Boarding Surf and Snowboard Shop, Mary Connolly and J.D. Golden, will be hiring more employees for the busy season. In this project, you will create special function queries to assist with their selection process. From the student files that accompany this textbook, open the **a05J_Job_Applicants** database file, and then save the database in your Access Chapter 5 folder as **Lastname_Firstname_5J_Job_Applicants**

Create a find unmatched records query to show all fields for applicants that have not been scheduled for an interview. Create a parameter query to locate a particular applicant and display all of his or her data. Use an aggregate function in a query that will count the number of applicants grouped by position. Save your queries by using your last and first names followed by the query type. View the queries in Print Preview, ensuring that the queries each print on one page. If you are instructed to submit this result, create a paper or electronic printout. Close the queries. Save and close the database.

Performance Element	Performance Level: Exemplary: You consistently applied the relevant skills	Proficient: You sometimes, but not always, applied the relevant skills	Developing: You rarely or never applied the relevant skills
Create 5J Unmatched Records Query	Query created to identify applicants without an interview scheduled.	Query created with no more than two missing elements.	Query created with more than two missing elements.
Create 5J Parameter Query	Query created to display a particular applicant's data.	Query created with no more than two missing elements.	Query created with more than two missing elements.
Create 5J Totals Query	Query created to count the applicants for each position.	Query created with no more than two missing elements.	Query created with more than two missing elements.

End **You have completed Project 5J**

Apply a combination of the 5A and 5B skills.

GO! Solve It | Project 5K Ski Apparel

Project Files

For Project 5K, you will need the following file:

a05K_Ski_Apparel

You will save your database as:

Lastname_Firstname_5K_Ski_Apparel

Ally Mason is the Purchasing Manager for the 4Ever Boarding Surf and Snowboard Shop. It is her responsibility to keep the clothing inventory current and fashionable. You have been asked to help her with this task. From the student files that accompany this textbook, open the **a05K_Ski_Apparel** database file, and then save the database in your **Access Chapter 5** folder as **Lastname_Firstname_5K_Ski_Apparel**

The database consists of a table of ski apparel for youth, women, and men. Create a query to identify the inventory by status of the items (promotional, in stock, and discontinued clothing). Count how many items are in each category. Update the selling price of the discontinued items to 90 percent of the cost. Use a make table query to separate the promotional clothing into its own table and a delete query to remove those items from the 5K Ski Apparel table. Save your queries using your last and first names followed by the query type . View the queries in Print Preview, ensuring that the queries print on one page. If you are instructed to submit this result, create a paper or electronic printout. Close the queries, and then close the database.

Performance Element	Performance Level: Exemplary: You consistently applied the relevant skills	Proficient: You sometimes, but not always, applied the relevant skills	Developing: You rarely or never applied the relevant skills
Create 5K Totals Query	Query created to display the inventory by status.	Query created with no more than two missing elements.	Query created with more than two missing elements.
Create 5K Update Query	Query created to update clearance sale prices.	Query created with no more than two missing elements.	Query created with more than two missing elements.
Create 5K Make Table Query	Query created to make a table for promotional clothing.	Query created with no more than two missing elements.	Query created with more than two missing elements.
Create 5K Delete Query	Query created to delete promotional clothing from the Ski Apparel table.	Query created with no more than two missing elements.	Query created with more than two missing elements.

End You have completed Project 5K

Outcomes-Based Assessments

Rubric

The following outcomes-based assessments are *open-ended assessments.* That is, there is no specific correct result; your result will depend on your approach to the information provided. Make *Professional Quality* your goal. Use the following scoring rubric to guide you in *how* to approach the problem and then to evaluate *how well* your approach solves the problem.

The *criteria*—Software Mastery, Content, Format and Layout, and Process—represent the knowledge and skills you have gained that you can apply to solving the problem. The *levels of performance*—Professional Quality, Approaching Professional Quality, or Needs Quality Improvements—help you and your instructor evaluate your result.

	Your completed project is of Professional Quality if you:	**Your completed project is Approaching Professional Quality if you:**	**Your completed project Needs Quality Improvements if you:**
1-Software Mastery	Choose and apply the most appropriate skills, tools, and features and identify efficient methods to solve the problem.	Choose and apply some appropriate skills, tools, and features, but not in the most efficient manner.	Choose inappropriate skills, tools, or features, or are inefficient in solving the problem.
2-Content	Construct a solution that is clear and well organized, contains content that is accurate, appropriate to the audience and purpose, and is complete. Provide a solution that contains no errors in spelling, grammar, or style.	Construct a solution in which some components are unclear, poorly organized, inconsistent, or incomplete. Misjudge the needs of the audience. Have some errors in spelling, grammar, or style, but the errors do not detract from comprehension.	Construct a solution that is unclear, incomplete, or poorly organized; contains some inaccurate or inappropriate content; and contains many errors in spelling, grammar, or style. Do not solve the problem.
3-Format and Layout	Format and arrange all elements to communicate information and ideas, clarify function, illustrate relationships, and indicate relative importance.	Apply appropriate format and layout features to some elements, but not others. Overuse features, causing minor distraction.	Apply format and layout that does not communicate information or ideas clearly. Do not use format and layout features to clarify function, illustrate relationships, or indicate relative importance. Use available features excessively, causing distraction.
4-Process	Use an organized approach that integrates planning, development, self-assessment, revision, and reflection.	Demonstrate an organized approach in some areas, but not others; or, use an insufficient process of organization throughout.	Do not use an organized approach to solve the problem.

Outcomes-Based Assessments

Apply a combination of the **5A** and **5B** skills.

GO! Think | Project **5L** Surfboards

Project Files

For Project 5L, you will need the following file:

a05L_Surfboards

You will save your database as:

Lastname_Firstname_5L_Surfboards

Ally Mason, Purchasing Manager for 4Ever Boarding Surf and Snowboard Shop, is stocking the shop with a variety of surfboards and accessories for the upcoming season.In this project, you will open the **5L_Surfboards** database and create queries to perform special functions. Save the database as **Lastname_Firstname_5L_Surfboards** Create a query to display the item, cost, selling price, on hand, and two calculated fields: Profit Per Item by subtracting the cost from the selling price and Inventory Profit by multiplying Profit Per Item by the number on hand for each item. Include a sum for the Inventory Profit column at the bottom of the query results. Check the supplier against the inventory using a find unmatched records query. Create a query to show the company that supplies each item, their e-mail address, and then the item and on hand fields for each item in the inventory. Before running the query, create an outer join query using the *5L Suppliers* table and the *5L Inventory* table. Save your queries using your last and first names followed by the query type. View the queries in Print Preview, ensuring that the queries print on one page. If you are instructed to submit this result, create a paper or electronic printout. Close the queries.

End **You have completed Project 5L**

Apply a combination of the **5A** and **5B** skills.

GO! Think | Project **5M** Shop Promotions

Project Files

For Project 5M, you will need the following file:

a05M_Shop_Promotions

You will save your database as:

Lastname_Firstname_5M_Shop_Promotions

The owners of 4Ever Boarding Surf and Snowboard Shop have invited some of Southern California's best extreme sports game participants to the shop to promote certain lines of clothing and gear. These participants will be on hand to answer questions, give demonstrations, and distribute prizes to customers. In this project, you will enhance the database by creating queries to perform special functions.

Open the **5M_Shop_Promotions** database. Save the database as **Lastname_Firstname_5M_Shop_Promotions** Use the Find Duplicates Query Wizard to find any events that may have been scheduled at the same time for the same day. The shop must be closed for remodeling. Use an update query to select only those events that are scheduled between July 31, 2015, and August 30, 2015, and reschedule those events for 30 days later than each original date. Create a parameter query to display the events by activity; run the query to display giveway activities. Save your queries using your last and first names followed by the query type. View the queries in Print Preview, ensuring that the queries print on one page. If you are instructed to submit this result, create a paper or electronic printout. Close the queries.

End **You have completed Project 5M**

Outcomes-Based Assessments

Apply a combination of the 5A and 5B skills.

You and GO! | Project 5N Club Directory

Project Files

For Project 5N, you will need the following file:

Lastname_Firstname_4N_Club_Directory (your file from Chapter 4)

You will save your database as:

Lastname_Firstname_5N_Club_Directory

Create a personal database containing information about a club and its activities, if you do not already have one from Project 4N. Name the new database **Lastname_Firstname_5N_Club_Directory** If you do not have the database from Project 4N, create two related tables, one that lists the activities your organization has planned and the other to serve as the directory of the group. The Activities table should include information about the name (primary key field), date, cost, and location of the activity. The dates must all occur next year, and consider attaching directions to the event to the table. The Directory table should include full name, address, phone number, e-mail, and an activity they are planning. If you have the database from Project 4N, make any necessary corrections before saving it in your Access Chapter 5 folder.

Using the Activities table, create a query to determine the total and average cost of the activities they are planning. Also using the Activities table, create a list of all of the activities and the location for all activities that are free (you might not have any results). Create a query to display each activity along with how many students are working on the event. Create a query to display a list of events, along with the location and price; sort the query by date in ascending order. Create a parameter query to display all student information based on an activity. View the queries in Print Preview, ensuring that the queries print on one page. If you are instructed to submit this result, create a paper or electronic printout. Save the database as **Lastname_Firstname_5N_Club_Directory**

You will be using this database in future chapters. Be sure to make corrections to your tables as necessary to prepare for the next chapter.

End You have completed Project 5N

Customizing Forms and Reports

OUTCOMES
At the end of this chapter you will be able to:

OBJECTIVES
Mastering these objectives will enable you to:

PROJECT 6A
Customize forms.

PROJECT 6B
Customize reports.

Nayashkova Olga/Shutterstock

In This Chapter

Forms provide you with a way to enter, edit, and display data from underlying tables. You have created forms using the Form button and the Form Wizard. Forms can also be created in Design view. Access provides tools that can enhance the visual appearance of forms, for example, adding color, backgrounds, borders, or instructions to the person using the form. Forms can also be used to manipulate data from multiple tables if a relationship exists between the tables.

Reports display data in a professional-looking format. Like forms, reports can also be created using a wizard or in Design view, and they can all be enhanced using Access tools. Reports can be based on tables or queries

Sand Dollar Cafe is a "quick, casual" franchise restaurant chain with headquarters in Palm Harbor, Florida. The founders wanted to create a restaurant where the flavors of the Caribbean islands would be available at reasonable prices in a bright, comfortable atmosphere. The menu features fresh food and quality ingredients in offerings like grilled chicken skewers, wrap sandwiches, fruit salads, mango ice cream, smoothies, and coffee drinks. All 75 outlets offer wireless Internet connections, making Sand Dollar Cafe the perfect place for groups and people who want some quiet time.

Project 6A Franchises

myitlab
Project 6A Training

Project Activities

In Activities 6.01 through 6.10, you will help Linda Kay, President, and James Winchell, Vice President of Franchising, create robust forms to match the needs of Sand Dollar Cafe. For example, the forms can include color and different types of controls and can manipulate data from several tables. You will customize your forms to make them easier to use and more attractive. Your completed form will look similar to Figure 6.1.

Project Files

For Project 6A, you will need the following files:

a06A_Franchises
a06A_Logo
a06A_Background

You will save your database as:

Lastname_Firstname_6A_Franchises

Project Results

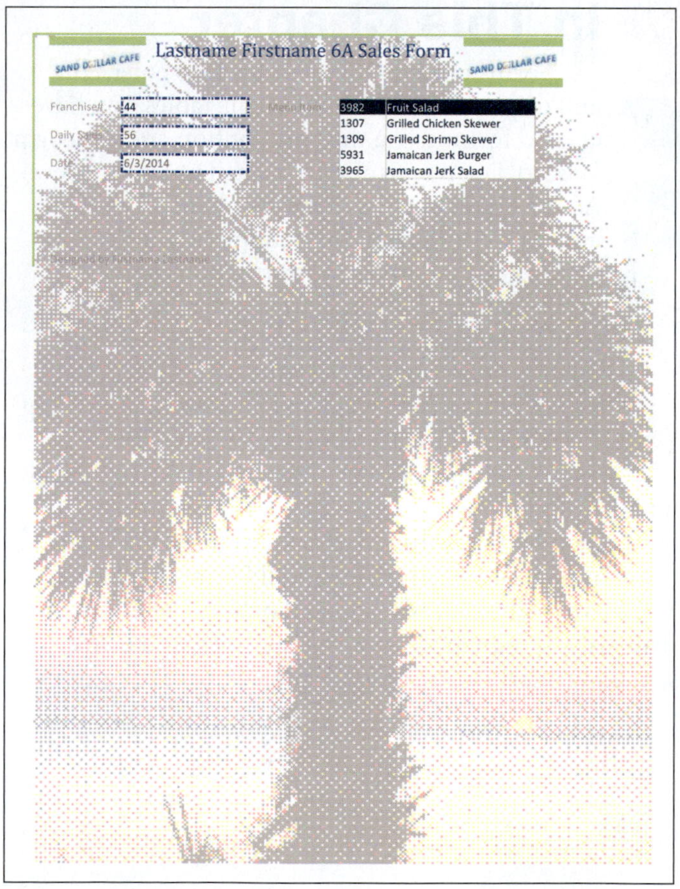

Figure 6.1
Project 6A Franchises

Objective 1 | Create a Form in Design View

You usually create a form using the Form tool or the Form Wizard and then modify the form in Design view to suit your needs. Use Design view to create a form when these tools do not meet your needs, or if you want more control in the creation of a form. Creating or modifying a form in Design view is a common technique when additional controls, such as combo boxes or images, need to be added to the form.

Activity 6.01 | Creating a Form in Design View

In this activity, you will create a form in Design view that will enable employees to enter the daily sales data for each franchise of Sand Dollar Cafe.

1. **Start** Access. Navigate to the location where the student data files for this textbook are saved. Locate and open the **a06A_Franchises** file. Display **Backstage** view, and click **Save Database As**. In the **Save As** dialog box, navigate to the drive on which you will be saving your folders and projects for this chapter. Create a new folder named **Access Chapter 6** and then save the database as **Lastname_Firstname_6A_Franchises** in the folder.

2. Enable the content or add the Access Chapter 6 folder to the Trust Center.

3. In the **Navigation Pane**, double-click **6A Sales** to open the table in **Datasheet** view. Take a moment to examine the fields in the table. In any record, click in the **Franchise#** field, and then click the **arrow**. This field is a Lookup field—the values are looked up in the *6A Franchises* table. The Menu Item field is also a Lookup field—the values are looked up in the *6A Menu Items* table.

4. **Close** [X] the table, and then **Close** [«] the **Navigation Pane**. On the Ribbon, click the **Create tab**. In the **Forms group**, click the **Form Design** button.

   The design grid for the Detail section displays.

5. On the **Design tab**, in the **Tools group**, click the **Property Sheet** button. Compare your screen with Figure 6.2. Notice that the *Selection type* box displays *Form*—this is the Property Sheet for the entire form.

   Every object on a form, including the form itself, has an associated ***Property Sheet*** that can be used to further enhance the object. ***Properties*** are characteristics that determine the appearance, structure, and behavior of an object. This Property Sheet displays the properties that affect the appearance and behavior of the form. The left column displays the property name, and the right column displays the property setting. Some of the text in the property setting boxes may be truncated.

Figure 6.2

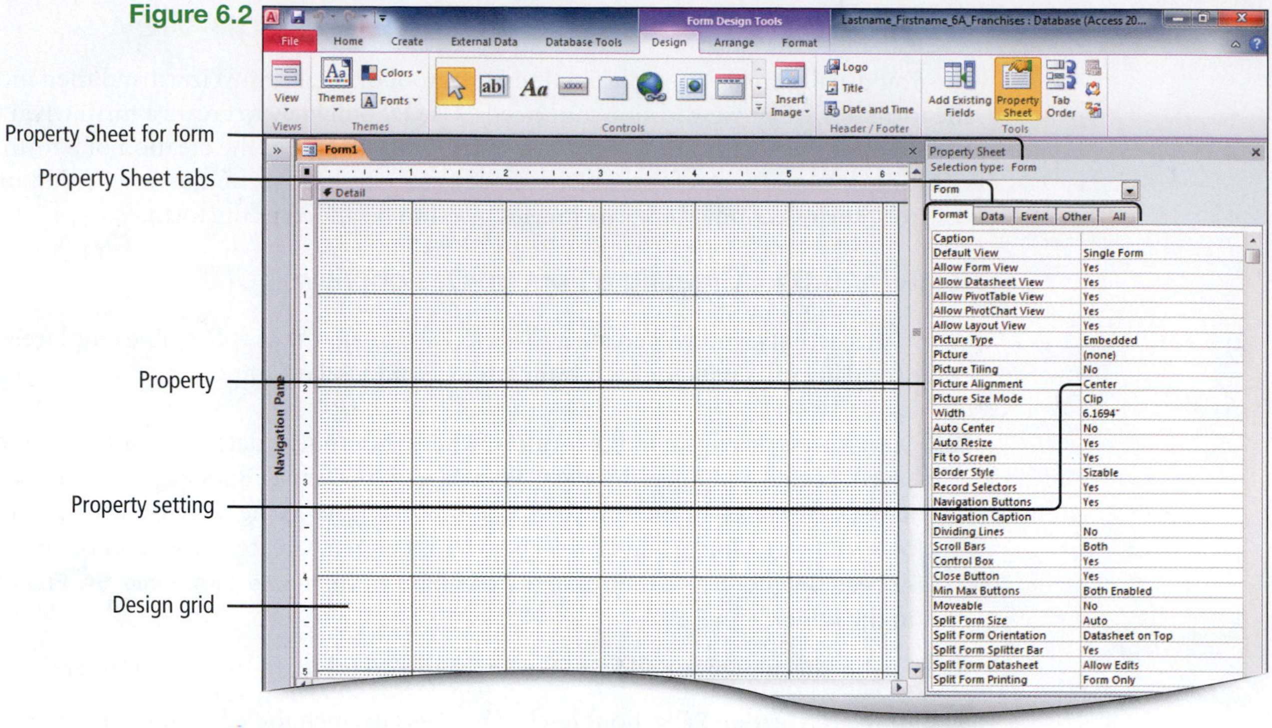

> **Another Way**
>
> On the Property Sheet for the form, click the Data tab. In the Record Source property setting box, click the Build button, which displays a Query Builder window and the Show Table dialog box. Add the objects from the Show Table dialog box, and then drag the appropriate fields down into the design grid. A query will be created that is used in the form.

6 If necessary, on the **Property Sheet**, click the **Format tab**, and then scroll down to display the **Split Form Orientation** property box. Point to the left edge of the **Property Sheet** until the pointer displays. Drag to the left until the setting in the **Split Form Orientation** property box—**Datasheet on Top**—displays entirely.

7 On the **Property Sheet**, click the **Data tab**. Click the **Record Source property setting box arrow**, and then click **6A Sales**.

The ***Record Source property*** enables you to specify the source of the data for a form or a report. The property setting can be a table name, a query name, or an SQL statement.

8 **Close** the **Property Sheet**. On the **Design tab**, in the **Tools group**, click the **Add Existing Fields** button, and then compare your screen with Figure 6.3.

The Field List for the record source—6A Sales—displays.

Figure 6.3

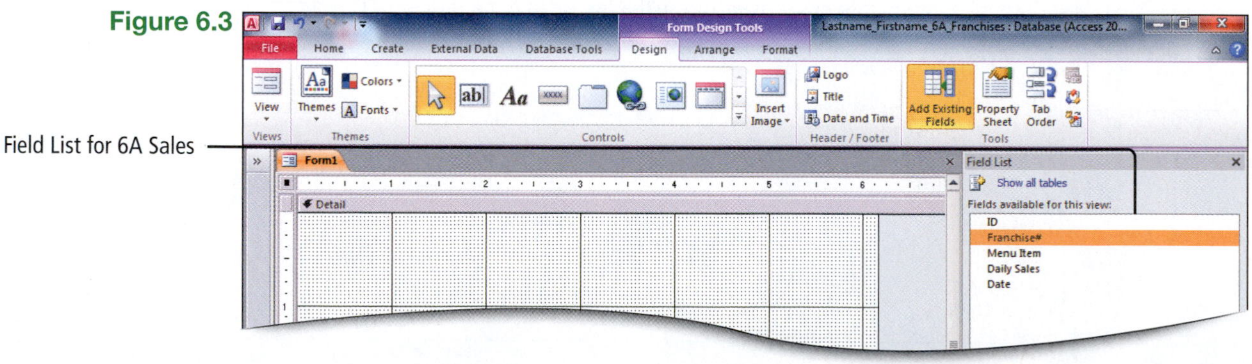

Another Way

In the Field List, double-click each field name to add the fields to the form. It is not possible to select all the fields and then double-click. Alternatively, in the Field List, right-click a field name, and then click Add Field to View.

9 In the **Field List**, click **Franchise#**. To select multiple fields, hold down Shift, and then click **Date**. Drag the selected fields onto the design grid until the top of the arrow of the pointer is **three dots** below the bottom edge of the **Detail section bar** and aligned with the **1.5-inch mark on the horizontal ruler** as shown in Figure 6.4, and then release the mouse button.

Drag the fields to where the text box controls should display. If you drag to where the label controls should display, the label controls and text box controls will overlap. If you move the controls to an incorrect position, click the Undo button before moving them again.

Figure 6.4

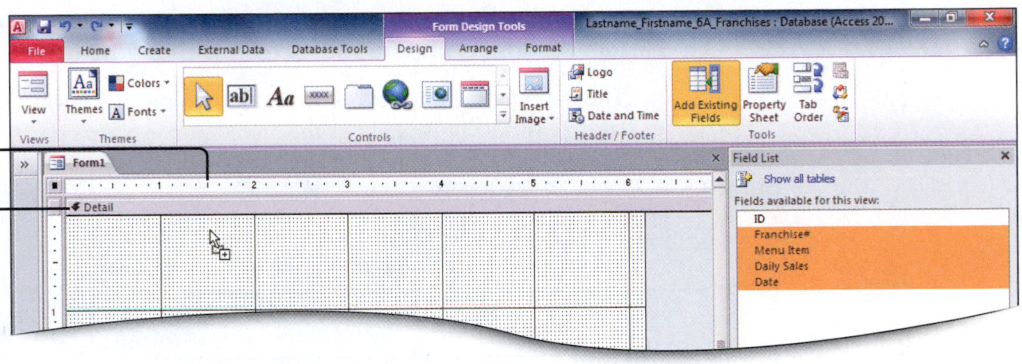

10 **Close** the **Field List**.

11 On the Ribbon, click the **Arrange tab**. With all controls selected, in the **Table group**, click the **Stacked** button.

When you create a form in Design view, the controls are not automatically grouped in a stacked or tabular layout. Grouping the controls makes it easier to format the controls and keeps the controls aligned.

12 **Save** the form as **Lastname Firstname 6A Sales Form**

More Knowledge | Horizontal and Vertical Spacing Between Controls

If the controls on a form are not grouped in a tabular or stacked layout, you can change the spacing between the controls. With the controls selected, click the Arrange tab. In the Sizing & Ordering group, click the Size/Space button, and then click the appropriate button to control spacing. Spacing options include Equal Horizontal, Increase Horizontal, Decrease Horizontal, Equal Vertical, Increase Vertical, and Decrease Vertical.

Activity 6.02 | Adding Sections to the Form

The only section that is automatically added to a form when it is created in Design view is the Detail section. In this activity, you will add a Form Header section and a Form Footer section.

1 Switch to **Form** view, and notice that the form displays only the data. There is no header section with a logo or name of the form.

2 Switch to **Design** view. Click the **Design tab.** In the **Header/Footer group**, click the **Logo** button. Navigate to the location where the student data files for this textbook are saved. Locate and double-click **a06A_Logo** to insert the logo in the Form Header section.

Two sections—the Form Header and the Form Footer—are added to the form along with the logo. Sections can be added only in Design view.

3 On the selected logo, point to the right middle sizing handle until the pointer ↔ displays. Drag to the right until the right edge of the logo is aligned with the **1.5-inch mark on the horizontal ruler.**

4 In the **Header/Footer group**, click the **Title** button to insert the title in the Form Header section. Compare your screen with Figure 6.5.

The name of the form is inserted as a title into the Form Header section, and the label control is the same height as the logo.

Figure 6.5

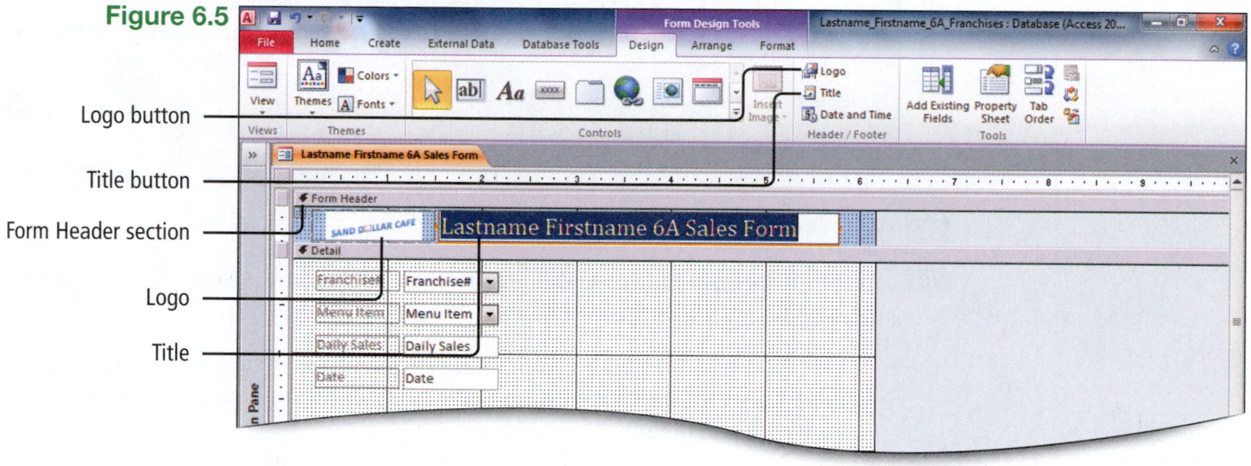

5 Scroll down until the **Form Footer** section bar displays. Point to the top of the **Form Footer** section bar until the pointer ↔ displays. Drag upward until the top of the Form Footer section bar aligns with the **2-inch mark on the vertical ruler.**

The height of the Detail section is decreased. Extra space at the bottom of the Detail section will cause blank space to display between records if the form is printed.

6 In the **Controls group**, click the **Label** button *Aa*. Point to the **Form Footer** section until the plus sign (+) of the pointer aligns with the bottom of the **Form Footer** section bar and with the left edge of the **Date label control** in the Detail section. Drag downward to the bottom of the **Form Footer** section and to the right to **3 inches on the horizontal ruler.** Using your own first name and last name, type **Designed by Firstname Lastname** Press Enter, and then compare your screen with Figure 6.6.

Figure 6.6

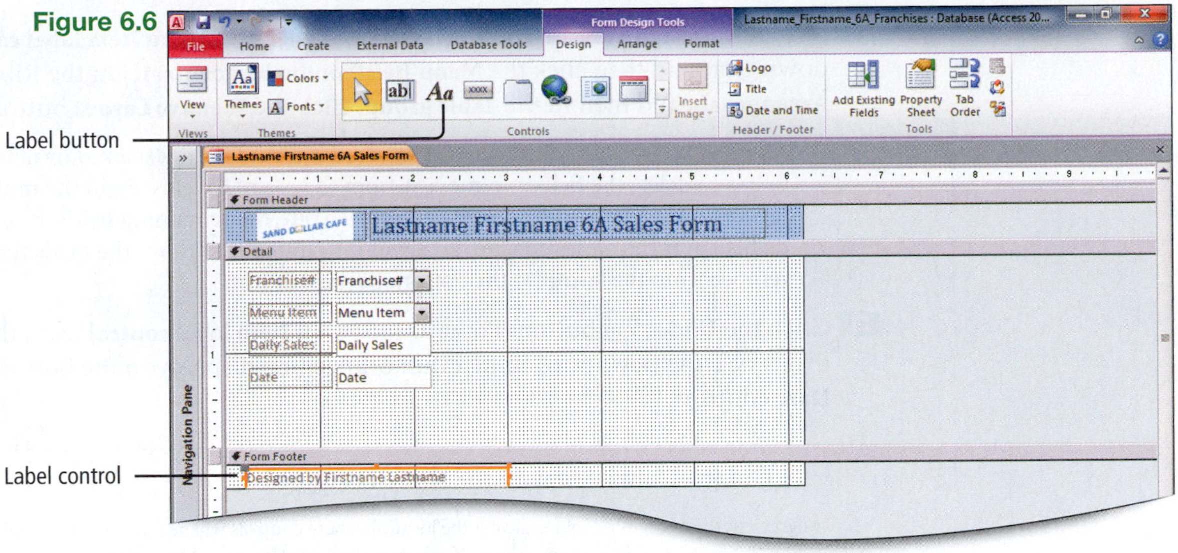

7 With the label control in the Form Footer section selected, hold down Shift, and then click each of the label controls in the Detail section. On the Ribbon, click the **Arrange tab**. In the **Sizing & Ordering group**, click the **Align** button, and then select **Left**. **Save** the form, and then switch to **Form** view.

The Form Header section displays the logo and the title of the form. The Form Footer section displays the label control that is aligned with the label controls in the Detail section. Both the Form Header and Form Footer sections display on every form page.

Objective 2 | Change and Add Controls

A ***control*** is an object, such as a label or text box, in a form or report that enables you to view or manipulate information stored in tables or queries. You have worked with label controls, text box controls, and, earlier in the chapter, logo controls, but there are more controls that can be added to a form. By default, when you create a form, Access uses the same field definitions as those in the underlying table or query. More controls are available in Design view than in Layout view.

Activity 6.03 | Changing Controls on a Form

In this activity, you will change a combo box control to a list box control.

1 Click the **Menu Item field arrow**.

Because the underlying table—*6A Sales*—designated this field as a lookup field, Access inserted a combo box control for this field instead of a text box control. The Franchise# field is also a combo box control. A ***combo box*** enables individuals to select from a list or to type a value.

2 Switch to **Design** view. In the **Detail** section, click the **Menu Item label control**, hold down [Shift], and then click the **Menu Item combo box control**. On the Ribbon, click the **Arrange tab**, and then in the **Table group**, click the **Remove Layout** button.

The Remove Layout button is used to remove a field from a stacked or tabular layout—it does not delete the field or remove it from the form. If fields are in the middle of a stacked layout column and are removed from the layout, the remaining fields in the column will display over the removed field. To avoid the clutter, first move the fields that you want to remove from the layout to the bottom of the column.

3 Click the **Undo** button. Point to the **Menu Item label control** until the pointer displays. Drag downward until a thin orange line displays on the bottom edges of the **Date** controls.

> **Alert! | Did the Control Stay in the Same Location?**
>
> In Design view, the orange line that indicates the location where controls will be moved is much thinner than—and not as noticeable as—the line in Layout view. If you drag downward too far, Access will not move the selected fields.

4 In the **Table group**, click the **Remove Layout** button to remove the Menu Item field from the stacked layout. Point to the selected controls, and then drag to the right and upward until the **Menu Item label control** is aligned with the **Franchise#** controls and with the **3-inch mark on the horizontal ruler**. Compare your screen with Figure 6.7.

Figure 6.7

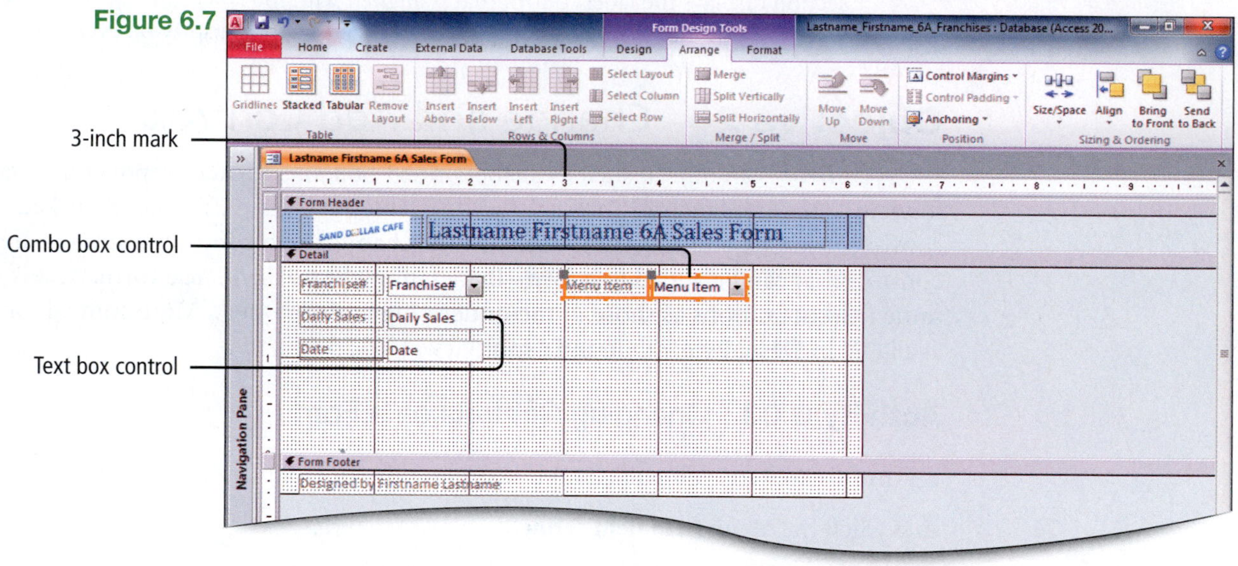

5 With the **Menu Item controls** selected, in the **Table group**, click the **Stacked** button. Click anywhere in the **Detail** section to deselect the second column.

The Menu Item controls display in the second column and are grouped in a stacked layout. Recall that a stacked layout keeps the controls aligned and makes it easier to edit and move the controls.

6 Right-click the **Menu Item combo box control**. From the shortcut menu, point to **Change To**, and then click **List Box**.

A ***list box*** enables individuals to select from a list but does not enable individuals to type anything that is not in the list. Based on the data in the underlying table or query, Access displays the control types to which you can change a field. The control type can be changed in Design view only.

7 **Save** the form, and then switch to **Form** view. Notice the **Menu Item list box control** is not wide enough to display both columns and that there are horizontal and vertical scroll bars to indicate there is more data. To display another problem, click the **Franchise# combo box arrow**, and then notice that some of the city names are truncated. Press Esc.

8 Switch to **Design** view. Click the **Franchise# combo box**, and then point to the right edge of the control until the pointer ↔ displays. Drag to the right until the right edge of the control aligns with the **2.75-inch mark on the horizontal ruler** to resize all three controls in the column. Switch to **Form** view, click the **Franchise# arrow**, and then be sure that all of the city names display—if they do not, return to Design view and increase the width of the combo box control.

9 Switch to **Layout** view. Click the **Menu Item list box control**. Point to the right edge of the control until the pointer ↔ displays. Drag to the right until all of the Menu Item *1307* displays. Release the mouse button to display the resized list box.

10 **Save** the form, and switch to **Design** view.

> **More Knowledge** | Validate or Restrict Data in Forms
>
> When you design tables, set field properties to ensure the entry of valid data by using input masks, validation rules, and default values. Any field in a form created with a table having these properties inherits the validation properties from the underlying table. Setting these properties in the table is the preferred method; however, you can also set the properties on controls in the form. If conflicting settings occur, the setting on the bound control in the form will override the field property setting in the table.

Activity 6.04 | Adding Controls to a Form

In this activity, you will add an image control and button controls to the form. An ***image control*** enables individuals to insert an image into any section of a form or report. A ***button control*** enables individuals to add a command button to a form or report that will perform an action when the button is clicked.

1 On the **Design tab**, in the **Controls group**, click the **Insert Image** button, and then click Browse. In the displayed **Insert Picture** dialog box, navigate to the location where the student data files for this textbook are saved and double-click **a06A_Logo**. Align the plus sign (+) of the pointer with the bottom of the **Form Header** section bar at **5.5-inches on the horizontal ruler**, as shown in Figure 6.8.

Figure 6.8

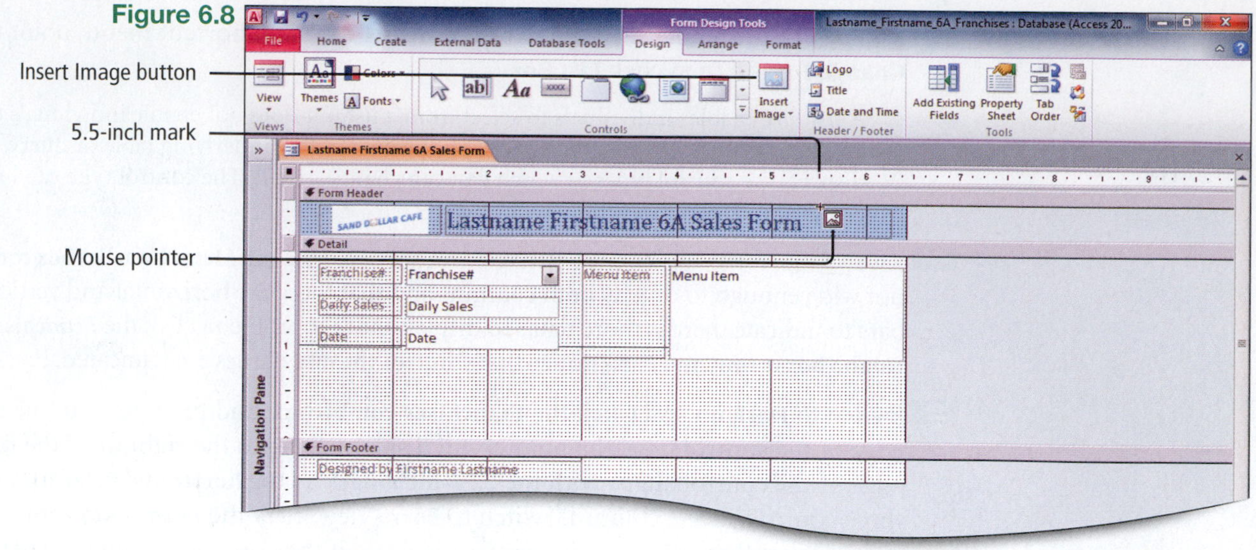

2 Drag the pointer downward to the bottom of the **Form Header** section and to the right to **6.5 inches on the horizontal ruler**. Release the mouse button to insert the picture in the Form Header section.

Using the logo control inserts a picture in a predetermined location—the left side—of the Form Header section. The image control is used to insert a picture anywhere in the form. There is a second image control in the Controls gallery on the Design tab.

3 Click the **title's label control**. Point to the right edge of the label control until the pointer [icon] displays. Drag to the left until there is **one dot** between the right edge of the label control and the left edge of the image control. On the **Format tab**, in the **Font group**, click the **Center** button [icon]. Switch to **Form** view, and then compare your screen with Figure 6.9.

The title is centered between the logo on the left and the image on the right, but the logo and the image are not the same size.

Figure 6.9

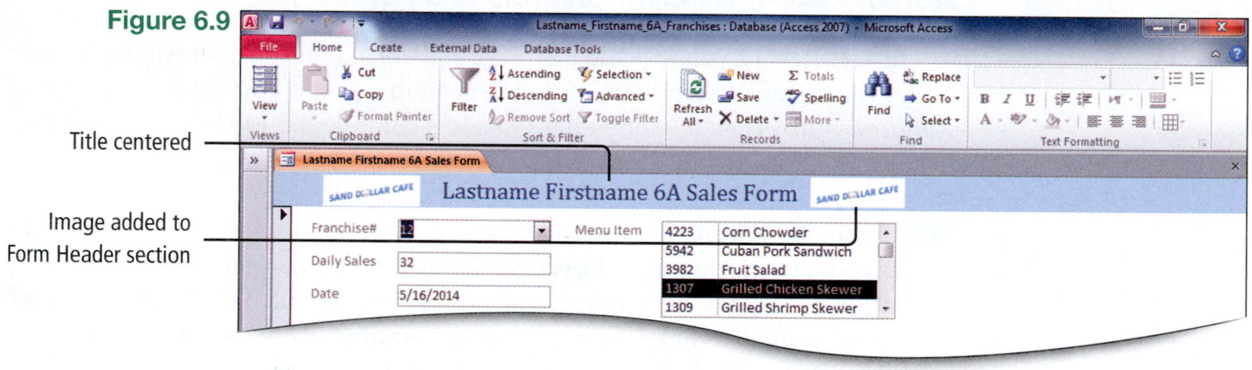

4 Switch to **Design** view, and then click the **image control**—the Sand Dollar Cafe image on the right side in the Form Header section. On the **Design tab**, in the **Tools group**, click the **Property Sheet** button. If necessary, on the **Property Sheet**, click the **Format tab**, and then compare your screen with Figure 6.10. Notice the **Width** and **Height** property settings.

The Width property setting is 1 inch—yours may differ. The Height property setting is 0.375 inches—yours may differ.

Figure 6.10

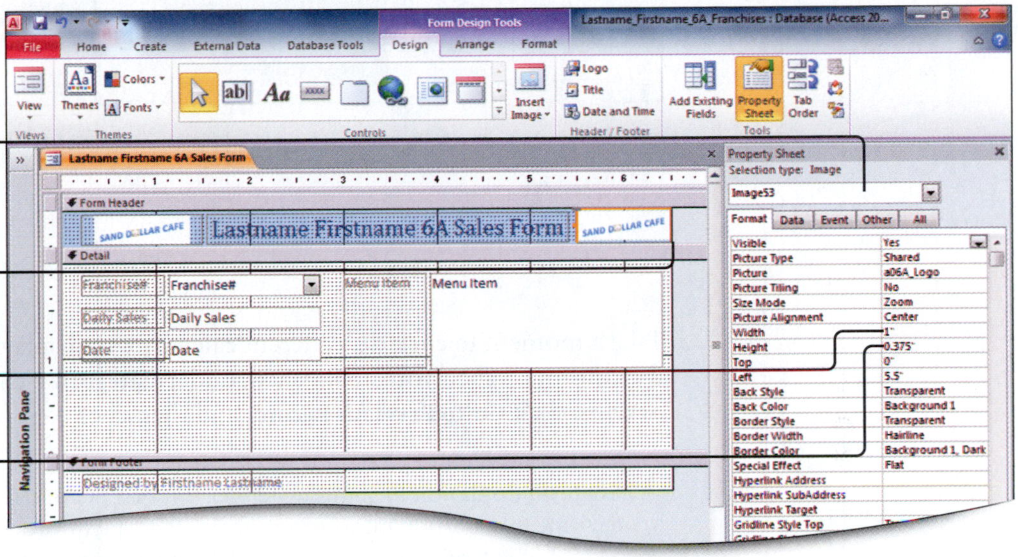

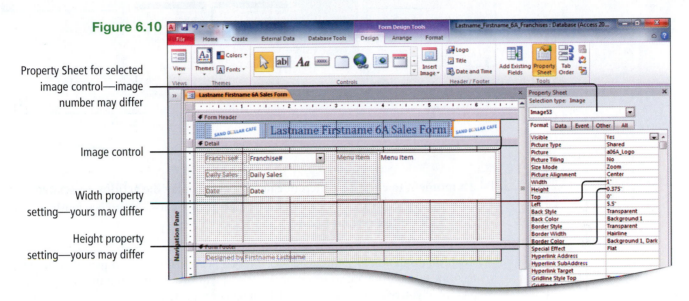

5 If necessary, change the **Width** property setting to **1.25** and then change the **Height** property setting to **0.625** In the **Form Header** section, on the left side, click the **logo control**, and then notice that the Property Sheet for the logo control displays. On the **Property Sheet**, change the **Width** property setting to **1.25** and then change the **Height** property setting to **0.625**

The width and height of the two controls are now the same.

6 On the Ribbon, click the **Arrange tab**. With the logo control selected, hold down Shift, and then click the **image control**. In the **Sizing & Ordering group**, click the **Align** button, click **Bottom**. Click the **title's label control**. In the **Table group**, click **Remove Layout**, and then point to the left middle sizing handle until the pointer ↔ displays. Drag to the right until there is **one dot** between the right edge of the logo control and the left edge of the title's label control.

The logo control and the image control are aligned at the bottom, and the title's label control is resized.

7 **Close** ☒ the **Property Sheet**. On the Ribbon, click the **Design tab**, click the **More** button at the right edge of the **Controls gallery**, and be sure that the **Use Control Wizards** option is active. Click the **Button** button. Move the mouse pointer down into the **Detail** section. Align the plus sign (+) of the pointer at **1.5 inches on the vertical ruler** and **1.5 inches on the horizontal ruler**, and then click. Compare your screen with Figure 6.11.

The Command Button Wizard dialog box displays. The first dialog box enables you to select an action for the button based on the selected category.

Figure 6.11

Button control button

Command Button Wizard dialog box

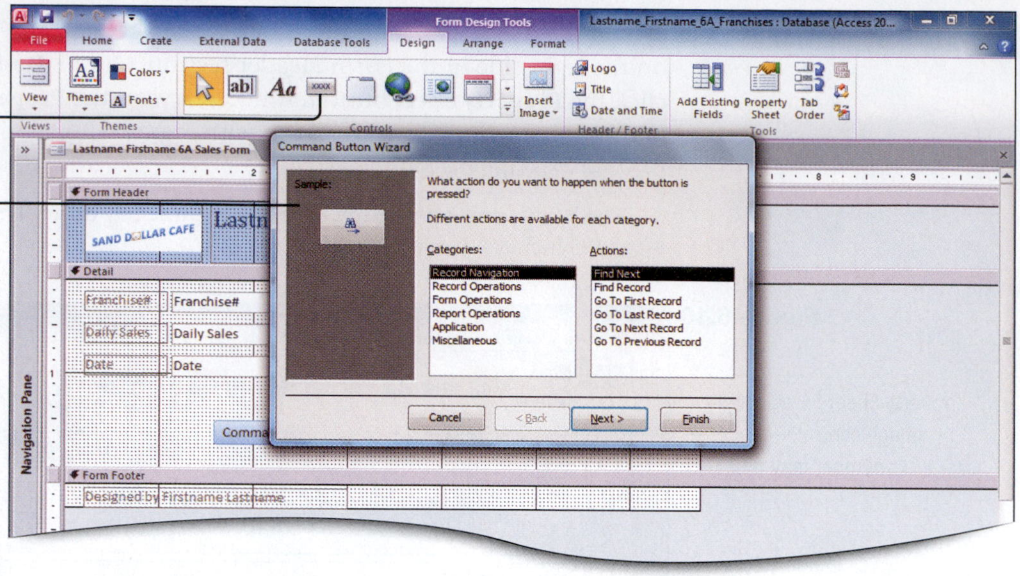

8 Take a moment to click the different categories to display the actions associated with the category. When you are finished, under **Categories**, click **Record Navigation**. Under **Actions**, click **Go To Previous Record**, and then click **Next**.

The second Command Button Wizard dialog box displays, which enables you to select what will display on the button—either text or a picture. If you select picture, you can navigate to a location on your computer where pictures are saved, and then select any picture. If you select text, accept the default text or type new text. A preview of the button displays on the left side of the dialog box.

9 Next to **Picture**, be sure **Go to Previous** is selected, and then click **Next**.

The third Command Button Wizard dialog box displays, which enables you to name the button. If you need to refer to the button later—usually in creating macros—a meaningful name is helpful. The buttons created with the Command Button Wizard are linked to macros—programs—that cannot be run or edited in previous versions of Access.

10 In the text box, type **btnPrevRecord** and then click **Finish**.

When creating controls that can later be used in programming, it is a good idea to start the name of the control with an abbreviation of the type of control—btn—and then a descriptive abbreviation of the purpose of the control.

11 Using the techniques you have just practiced, add a **button control** about **1 inch** to the right of the **Previous Record button control**. Under **Categories**, click **Record Navigation**. Under **Actions**, click **Go to Next Record**. For **Picture**, click **Go to Next**, and then name the button **btnNextRecord** Do not be concerned if the button controls are not exactly aligned.

12 With the **Next Record button control** selected, hold down Shift, and then click the **Previous Record button control**. Click the **Arrange tab**, and then in the **Sizing & Ordering group**, click the **Align** button, and then **Top**. Click the **Size/Space** button, and then click either **Increase Horizontal Spacing** button or **Decrease Horizontal Spacing** until there is approximately **1 inch** of space between the two controls. Compare your screen with Figure 6.12.

Figure 6.12

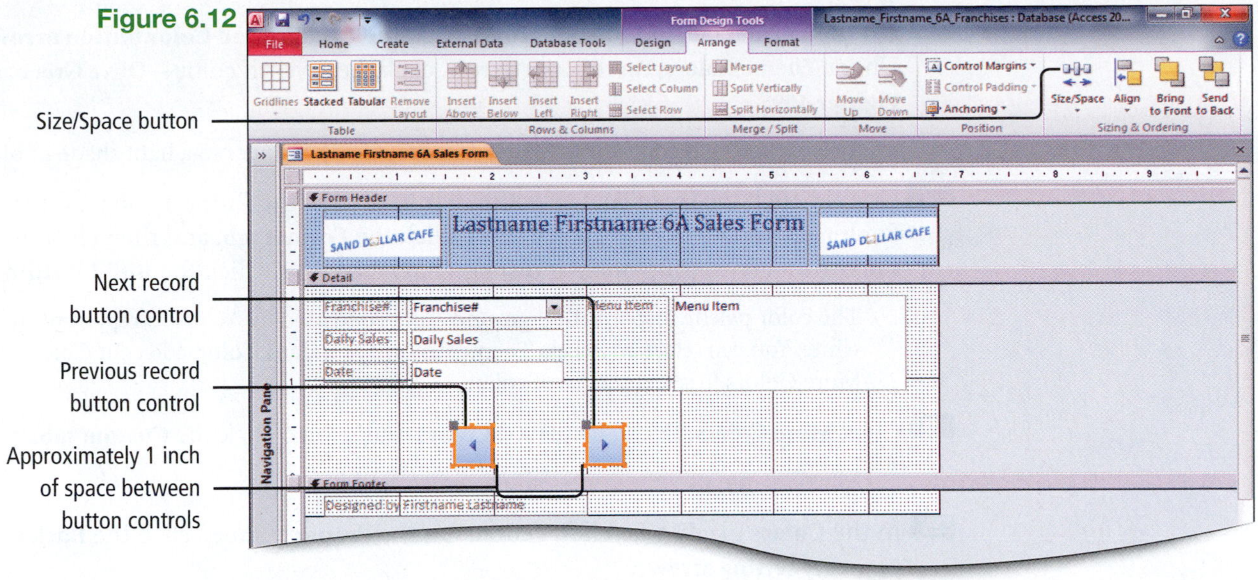

13 **Save** the form, and then switch to **Form** view. Experiment by clicking the **Next Record** button and the **Previous Record** button, and notice in the record navigator that you are displaying different records.

14 Switch to **Design** view. On the **Design tab**, in the **Controls group**, click the **Button** button. Align the plus sign (+) of the pointer at **1.5 inches on the vertical ruler** and at **5 inches on the horizontal ruler**, and then click.

15 In the **Command Button Wizard** dialog box, under **Categories**, click **Form Operations**. Under **Actions**, click **Print Current Form**, and then click **Next**. Click the **Text** option button to accept *Print Form*, and then click **Next**. Name the button **btnPrtForm** and then click **Finish**.

You will use this button to print one form when you are finished formatting the form.

16 **Save** the form.

Objective 3 | Format a Form

There are several methods you can use to modify the appearance of a form. Each section and control on a form has properties. Some properties can be modified by using buttons in the groups on a tab or by changing the property setting on the Property Sheet.

Activity 6.05 | Adding a Background Color

In this activity, you will modify the background color of the Form Header section, the Form Footer section, and the Detail section of the *6A Sales Form*. The background color is a property setting for each section; there is no background color property setting for the entire form. Property settings can also be changed in Layout view.

1 With **6A Sales Form** open in **Design** view, click the **Form Header** section bar.

The darkened bar indicates that the entire Form Header section of the form is selected.

2 On the **Format tab**, in the **Font group**, click the **Background Color button arrow**. Under **Theme Colors**, on the fourth row, click the seventh color—**Olive Green, Accent 3, Lighter 40%**.

The background color for the Form Header section changes to a light shade of olive green.

3 Double-click the **Form Footer** section bar to display the Property Sheet for the Form Footer section. On the **Property Sheet**, click the **Format tab**, and then click in the **Back Color** property setting box—it displays Background 1. Click the **Build** button.

The color palette displays. Background 1 is a code used by Access to represent the color white. You can select an Access Theme Color, a Standard Color, a Recent Color, or click More Colors to select shades of colors.

4 Click **More Colors**. In the displayed **Colors** dialog box, click the **Custom tab**.

All colors use varying shades of Red, Green, and Blue.

5 In the **Colors** dialog box, click **Cancel**. On the **Property Sheet**, click the **Back Color property setting arrow**.

A list of color schemes display. These colors also display on the color palette under Access Theme Colors.

> **Another Way**
>
> Open the form in Layout view. To select a section, click in an empty area of the section. On the Home tab, in the Text Formatting group, click the Background Color button.

6 From the displayed list, experiment by clicking on different color schemes and viewing the effects of the background color change. You will have to click the property setting arrow each time to select another color scheme. When you are finished, click the **Build** button. Under **Theme Colors**, on the fourth row, click the seventh color—**Olive Green, Accent 3, Lighter 40%**—and then press Enter.

You can change the background color either by using the Background Color button in the Font group or by changing the Back Color property setting on the Property Sheet.

7 Using one of the techniques you have just practiced, change the background color of the **Detail** section to **Olive Green, Accent 3, Lighter 40%**. Switch to **Form** view, and then compare your screen with Figure 6.13.

Figure 6.13

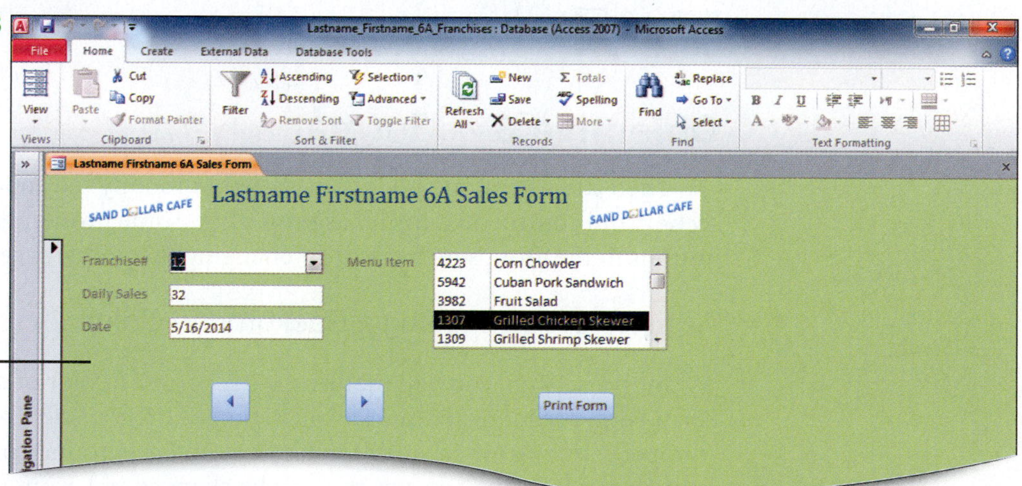

Background color set to Olive Green, Accent 3, Lighter 40%

8 **Save** the form, and then switch to **Design** view. **Close** the **Property Sheet**.

More Knowledge | **Adding a Background Color to Controls**

You can also add background colors to controls. First, click the control or controls to which you want to add a background color. If you want to use color schemes, open the Property Sheet, and then click the Back Color property setting arrow. If you want to use the color palette, in Design view, click the Format tab. In the Font group, click the Background Color button.

Activity 6.06 | Adding a Background Picture to a Form

In this activity, you will add a picture to the background of *6A Sales Form*.

1 With **6A Sales Form** open in **Design** view, locate the **Form selector**, as shown in Figure 6.14.

The ***Form selector*** is the box where the rulers meet, in the upper left corner of a form in Design view. Use the Form selector to select the entire form.

Figure 6.14

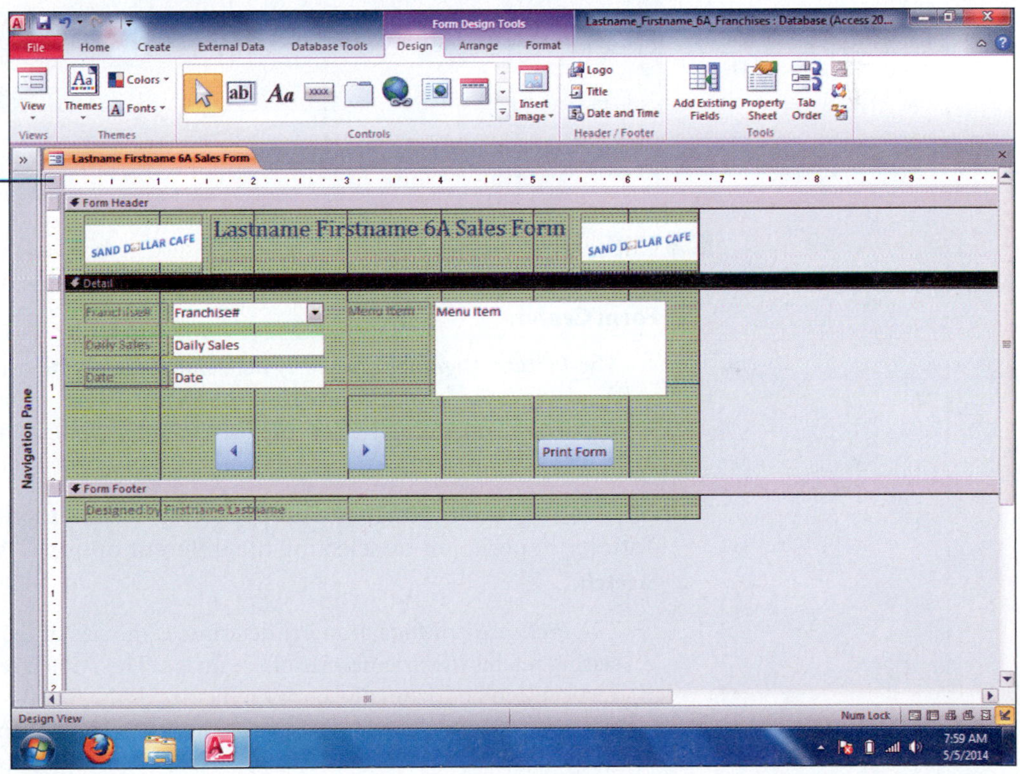

Access | Chapter 6

2 Double-click the **Form selector** to open the **Property Sheet** for the form.

3 On the **Property Sheet**, on the **Format tab**, click in the **Picture** property setting box. Click the **Build** button. Navigate to the location where the student data files for this textbook are saved. Locate and double-click **a06A_Background** to insert the picture in the form, and then compare your screen with Figure 6.15.

Figure 6.15

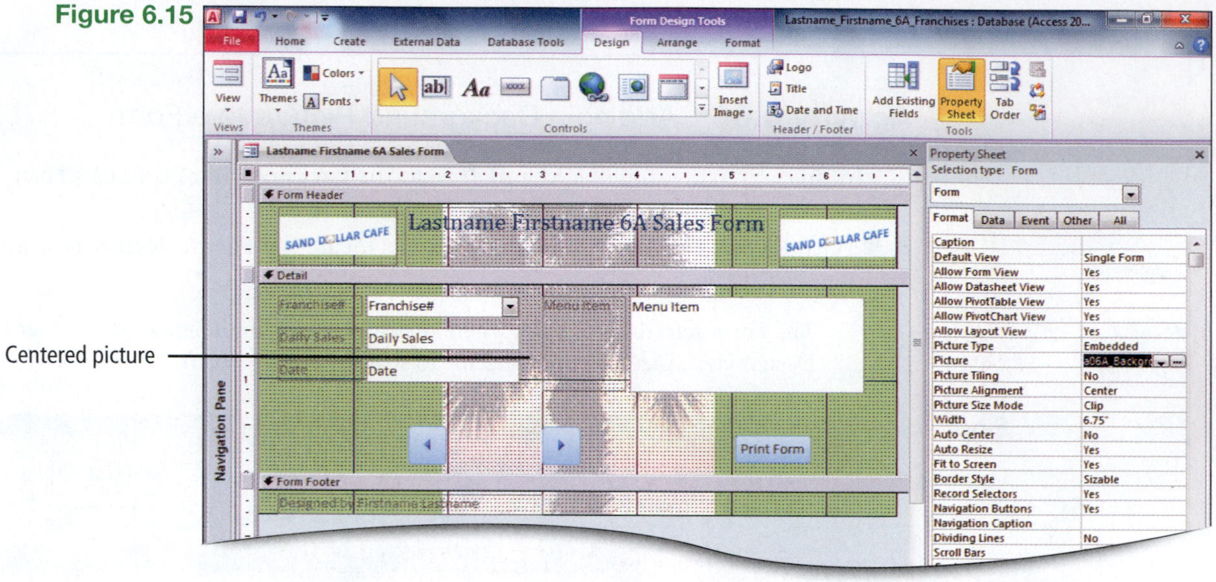

4 Click in the **Picture Alignment** property setting box, click the **arrow**, and then experiment by clicking the different alignment options. When you are finished, click **Form Center**.

The ***Picture Alignment property*** determines where the background picture for a form displays on the form. Center places the picture in the center of the page when the form is printed. Form Center places the picture in the center of the form data when the form is printed

5 Click in the **Picture Size Mode** property setting, and then click the **arrow** to display the options. Experiment by selecting the different options. When you are finished, click **Stretch**.

The ***Picture Size Mode property*** determines the size of the picture in the form. The Clip setting retains the original size of the image. The Stretch setting stretches the image both vertically and horizontally to match the size of the form—the image may be distorted. The Zoom setting adjusts the image to be as large as possible without distorting the image. Both Stretch Horizontal and Stretch Vertical can distort the image. If you have a background color and set the Picture Type property setting to Stretch, the background color will not display.

6 **Close** the **Property Sheet**, **Save** the form, and then switch to **Layout** view. Compare your screen with Figure 6.16.

Figure 6.16

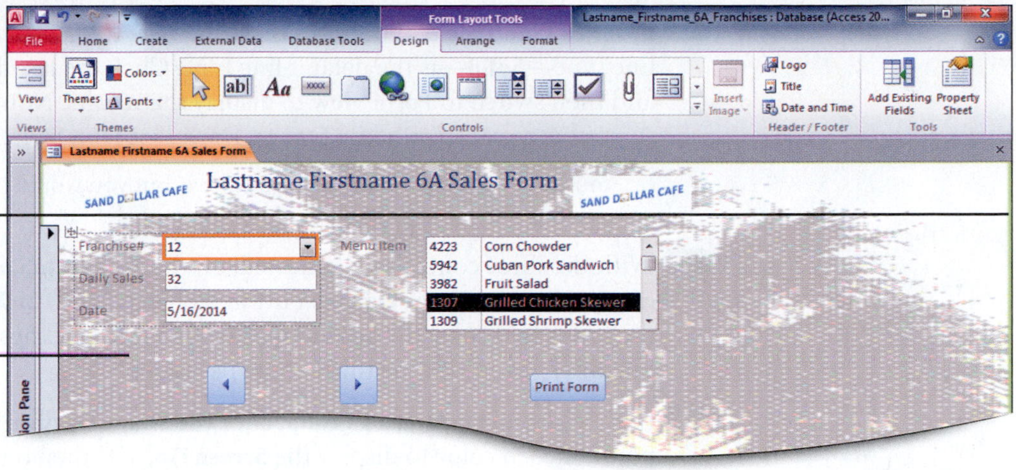

Activity 6.07 | Modifying the Borders of Controls

In this activity, you will modify the borders of some of the controls on *6A Sales Form*. There are related property settings on the Property Sheet.

1 With **6A Sales Form** open in **Layout** view, click the **Franchise#** combo box control. Holding down Shift, click the **Daily Sales** text box control, and then click the **Date** text box control. On the **Format tab**, in the **Control Formatting group**, click **Shape Outline**. Notice the options that are used to modify borders—Colors, Line Thickness, and Line Type. Compare your screen with Figure 6.17.

Figure 6.17

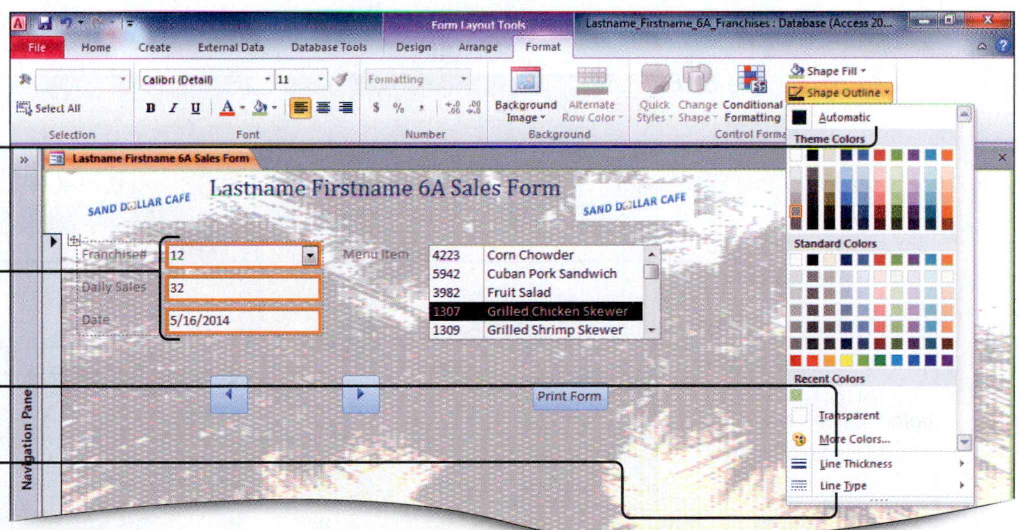

2 Point to **Line Type** and point to each line type to display the **ScreenTip**. The second line type—**Solid**—is the default line type. Click the last line type—**Dash Dot Dot**—and then switch to **Form** view to display the results. Notice that the borders of the three controls display a line type of Dash Dot Dot. Switch to **Layout** view.

You can review the results in Layout view, but you would have to deselect the three controls.

3 With the three controls still selected, on the **Format tab**, in the **Control Formatting group**, click the **Shape Outline** button. Point to **Line Thickness** and point to each line thickness to display the **ScreenTip**. The first line thickness—**Hairline**—is the default line thickness. Click the third line type—**2 pt**.

4 In the **Control Formatting group, click** the **Shape Outline** button. Under **Theme Colors**, point to each color to display the **ScreenTip**, and then on the first row, click the fourth color—**Dark Blue, Text 2**. Switch to **Form** view to display the results.

The borders of the three controls display a line thickness of 2 points, and the color of the borders is a darker shade. A ***point*** is 1/72 of an inch.

5 Switch to **Layout** view. With the three controls still selected, on the **Design tab**, in the **Tools group**, click the **Property Sheet** button, and then compare your screen with Figure 6.18. Notice the properties that are associated with the buttons on the Ribbon with which you changed the borders of the selected controls.

Because multiple items on the form are selected, the Property Sheet displays *Selection type: Multiple selection*. You changed the property settings of the controls by using buttons, and the Property Sheet displays the results of those changes. You can also select multiple controls, open the Property Sheet, and make the changes to the properties. The Property Sheet displays more settings than those available through the use of buttons.

Figure 6.18

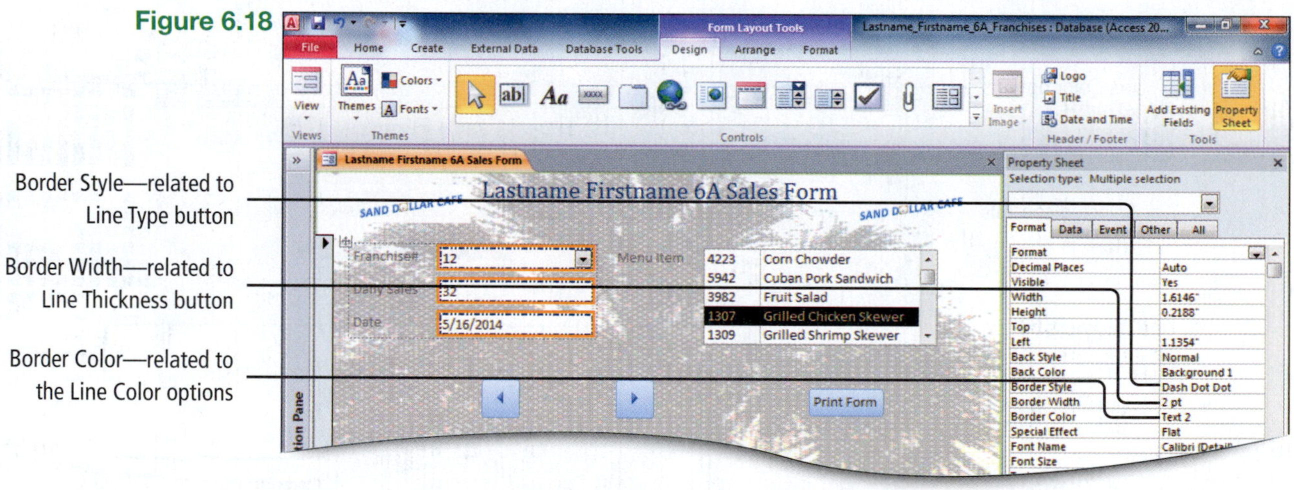

6 **Close** the **Property Sheet**, and then **Save** the form. Switch to **Form** view.

> **More Knowledge | Adding Borders to Label Controls**
>
> By default, the border style—line style—of a Label control is transparent, effectively hiding the border from the display. Because borders display around bound controls that contain data, it is recommended that you do not add borders to label controls so that individuals can easily distinguish the control that holds data.

Objective 4 | Make a Form User Friendly

To make forms easy to use, you can add instructions that display on the status bar while data is being entered and custom ***ControlTips*** that display when an individual pauses the mouse pointer over a control on a form. Additionally, you can change the tab order of the fields on a form. ***Tab order*** refers to the order in which the fields are selected when the Tab key is pressed. By default, the tab order is created based on the order in which the fields are added to the form.

Activity 6.08 | Adding a Message to the Status Bar

When you created tables, you may have added a description to the field, and the description displayed in the status bar of the Access window. If a description is included for a field in the underlying table of a form, the text of the description will also display in the status bar when an individual clicks in the field on the form. In this activity, you will add a description to the Daily Sales field in the *6A Sales* table, and then ***propagate***—disseminate or apply—the changes to *6A Sales Form*. You will also add status bar text to a field on a form using the Property Sheet of the control.

1 With **6A Sales Form** open in **Form** view, click in the **Daily Sales** field. On the left side of the status bar, *Form View* displays—there is no text that helps an individual enter data.

2 **Close** the form, and then **Open** [»] the **Navigation Pane**. Under **Tables**, right-click **6A Sales**, and then from the shortcut menu, click **Design View**. In the **Daily Sales** field, click in the **Description** box. Type **How many items were sold?** and then press Enter. Compare your screen with Figure 6.19.

A ***Property Update Options button*** displays in the Description box for the Date field. When you make changes to the design of a table, Access displays this button, which enables individuals to update the Property Sheet for this field in all objects that use this table as the record source.

Figure 6.19

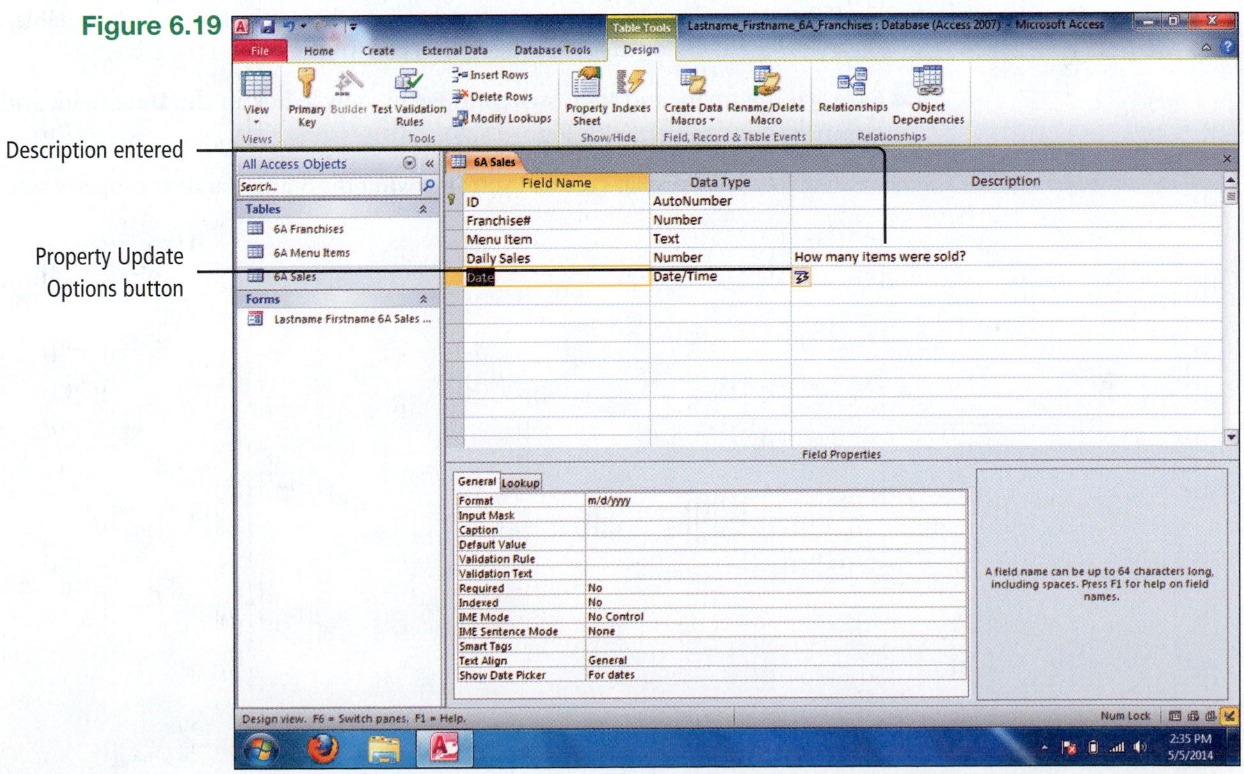

3. Click the **Property Update Options** button, and then click **Update Status Bar Text everywhere Daily Sales is used**. In the displayed **Update Properties** dialog box, under **Update the following objects?**, notice that only one object—*Form: 6A Sales Form*—displays, and it is selected. In the **Update Properties** dialog box, click **Yes**.

   The changes in the Description field in the table will be propagated to *6A Sales Form*. If multiple objects use the *6A Sales* table as the underlying object, you can propagate the change to all of the objects.

4. **Close** the table, saving changes, and then open the **6A Sales** table in **Datasheet** view. On any record, click in the **Daily Sales** field, and then notice the text—*How many items were sold?*—that displays on the left side of the status bar.

5. **Close** the table. In the **Navigation Pane**, under **Forms**, double-click **6A Sales Form** to open it in **Form** view. Close « the **Navigation Pane**. Click in the **Daily Sales** field, and then notice that on the left side of the status bar, *How many items were sold?* displays.

   Access propagated the change made in the underlying table to the form.

6. Switch to **Design** view. Click the **Daily Sales text box control**. On the **Design tab**, in the **Tools group**, click the **Property Sheet** button.

7. On the **Property Sheet**, click the **Other tab**. Locate the **Status Bar Text** property, and notice the setting *How many items were sold?*

   When Access propagated the change to the form, it populated the Status Bar Text property setting. The ***Status Bar Text property*** enables individuals to add descriptive text that will display in the status bar for a selected control.

8. In the **Detail** section, click the **Date text box control**, and then notice that the **Property Sheet** changes to display the properties for the **Date** text box control. Click in the **Status Bar Text** property setting box, type **Enter date of sales report** and then Press Enter.

   You do not have to enter a description for the field in the underlying table for text to display in the status bar when a field is selected in a form. Access does not display a Property Update Options button to propagate changes to the underlying table, and the text will not be added to the Description box for the field in the table.

9. **Save** the form, and then switch to **Form** view. Click in the **Date** field, and then compare your screen with Figure 6.20.

   The status bar displays the text you entered in the Status Bar Text property setting box.

Figure 6.20

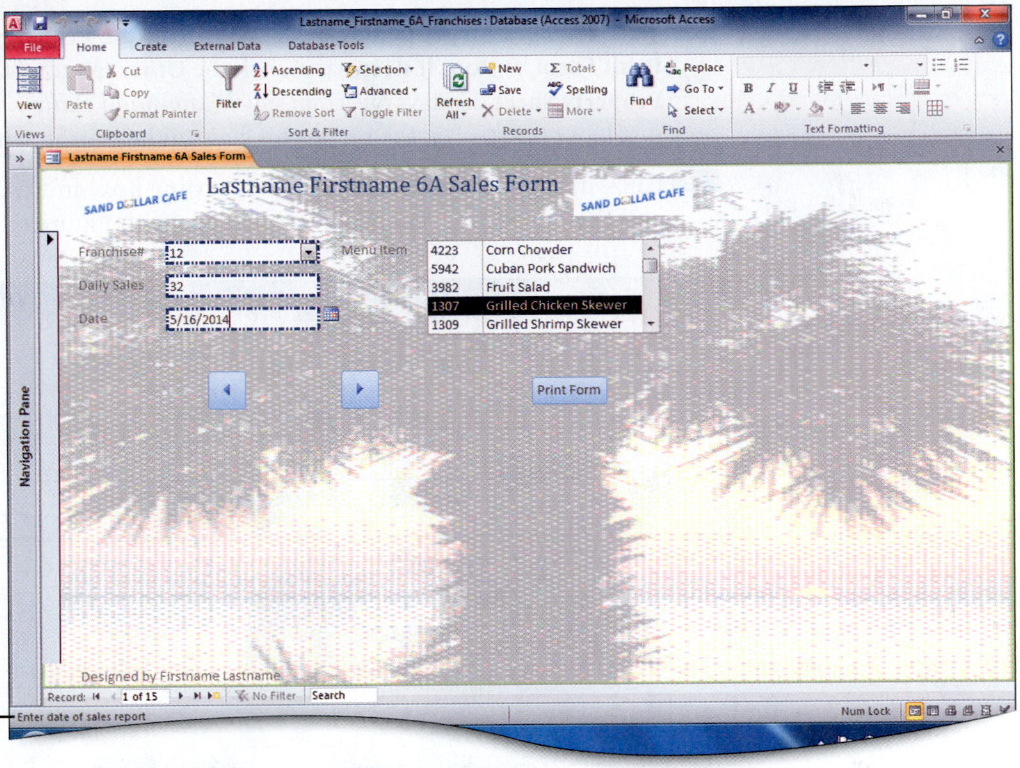

Entered in Status Bar Text property setting box

10 Switch to **Design** view.

> **More Knowledge** | **Conflicting Field Description and Status Bar Text Property Setting**
>
> When you create a form, the fields inherit the property settings from the underlying table. You can change the Status Bar Text property setting for the form, and it will override the setting that is inherited from the table. If you later change field properties in Table Design view, the Property Update Options button displays—you must manually propagate those changes to the table's related objects; propagation is not automatic. An exception to this is entering Validation Rules—changes are automatically propagated.

Activity 6.09 | Creating Custom ControlTips

Another way to make a form easier to use is to add custom ControlTips to objects on the form. A ControlTip is similar to a ScreenTip and temporarily displays descriptive text while the mouse pointer is paused over the control. This method is somewhat limited because most individuals press Tab or Enter to move from field to field and thus do not see the ControlTip. However, a ControlTip is a useful tool in a training situation when an individual is learning how to use the data entry form. In this activity, you will add a ControlTip to the Print Form button control.

1 With **6A Sales Form** open in **Design** view and the **Property Sheet** displayed, click the **Print Form** button. If necessary, click the **Other tab** to make it active. Notice the **Property Sheet** displays *Selection type: Command Button* and the Selection type box displays *btnPrtForm*, the name you gave to the button when you added it to the form.

2 Click in the **ControlTip Text** property setting box, and type **Prints the selected record** and then press Enter. Compare your screen with Figure 6.21.

Figure 6.21

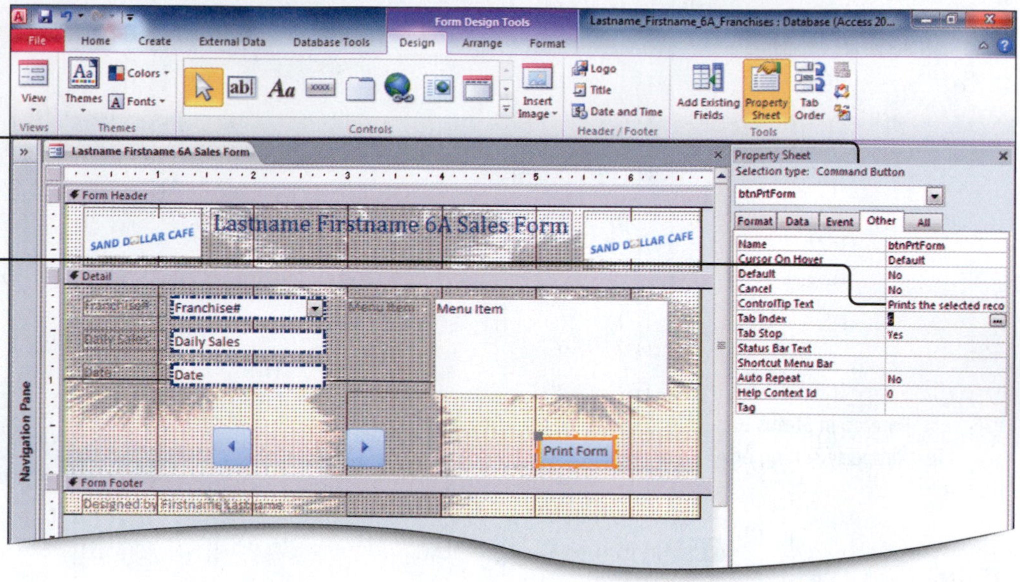

3 **Close** the **Property Sheet**, **Save** the form, and then switch to **Form** view. Point to the **Print Form** button, and then compare your screen with Figure 6.22.

A ControlTip displays the message you typed for the ControlTip Text property setting.

Figure 6.22

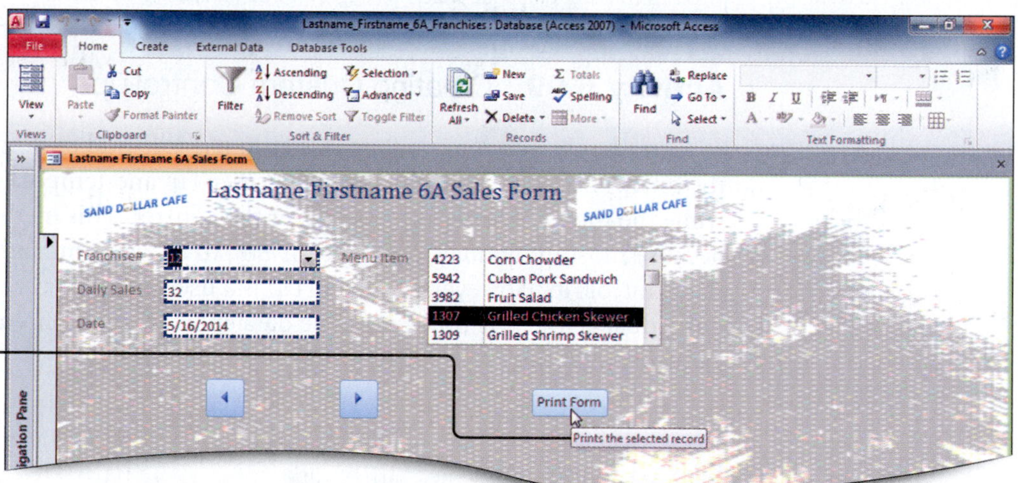

Activity 6.10 | Changing the Tab Order

You can customize the order in which you enter data on a form by changing the tab order. Recall that tab order refers to the order in which the fields are selected each time Tab is pressed. As you press Tab, the ***focus*** of the form changes from one control to another control. Focus refers to the object that is selected and currently being acted upon.

1 With **6A Sales Form** open in **Form** view, in the record navigator, click the **New (blank) record** button. If necessary, click in the **Franchise#** combo box. Press Tab three times, and then notice that the insertion point moves from field to field, ending with the **Date** text box. Press Tab three more times, and then notice the **Print form** button is the focus. The button displays with a darker border. Press Enter.

Because the focus is on the Print Form button, the Print dialog box displays.

2 In the **Print** dialog box, click **Cancel**. Switch to **Design** view.

3 On the Ribbon, click the **Design tab**. In the **Tools group**, click the **Tab Order** button, and then compare your screen with Figure 6.23.

The Tab Order dialog box displays. Under Section, Detail is selected. Under Custom Order, the fields and controls display in the order they were added to the form. To the left of each field name or button name is a row selector button.

As you rearrange fields on a form, the tab order does not change from the original tab order. This can make data entry chaotic because the focus is changed in what appears to be an illogical order. The Auto Order button will change the tab order based on the position of the controls in the form from left to right and top to bottom.

Figure 6.23

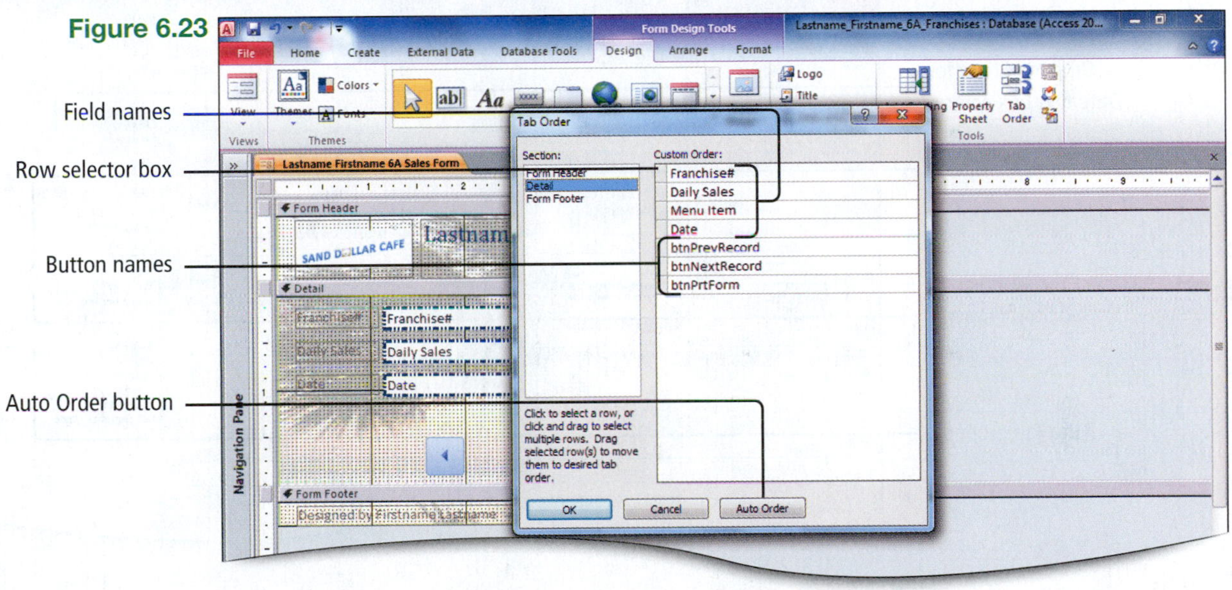

4 To the left of **Menu Item**, click the **row selector** box. Point to the **row selector** box, and then drag downward until a dark horizontal line displays between **Date** and **btnPrevRecord**.

The Menu Item field will now receive the focus after the Date field.

> **Alert! | Did the Field Stay in the Same Location?**
>
> You must point to the row selector box before dragging the field. If you point to the field name, the field will not be moved.

5 In the **Tab Order** dialog box, click **OK**. **Save** the form, and then switch to **Form** view. In the record navigator, click the **Last Record** button. When the Menu Item field has the focus, it is easier to see it on a blank record. In the record navigator, click the **New (blank) record** button.

The insertion point displays in the Franchise# field.

6 Press Tab three times. Even though it is difficult to see, the focus changes to the **Menu Item** list box. Press Tab again, and then notice that the focus changes to the **btnPrevRecord** button.

Before allowing individuals to enter data into a form, you should always test the tab order to ensure that the data will be easy to enter.

7 Switch to **Design** view. In the **Detail** section, right-click the **Date text box control**, click **Properties**. If necessary, click the **Other** tab, and then compare your screen with Figure 6.24.

Text box controls have three properties relating to tab order: Tab Index, Tab Stop, and Auto Tab. Combo box controls and list box controls do not have an Auto Tab property.

Figure 6.24

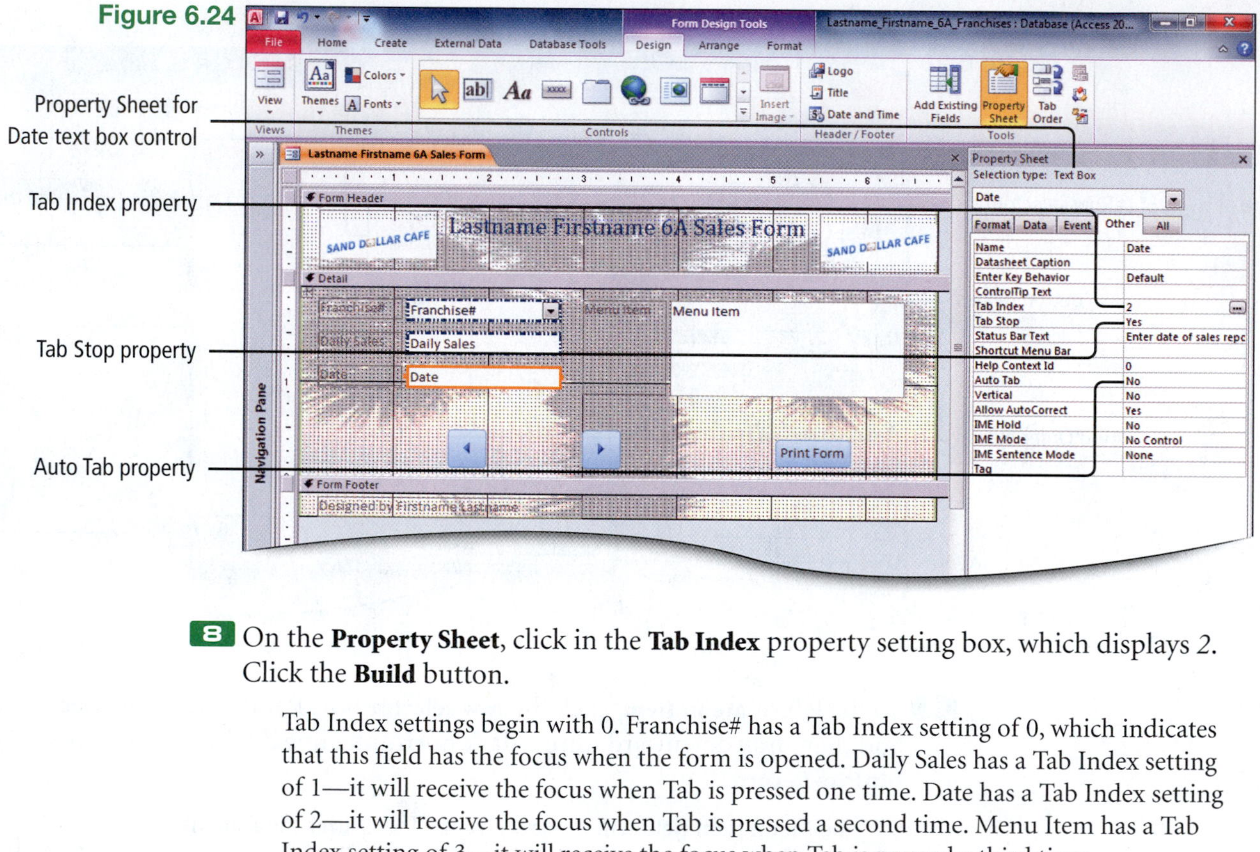

8 On the **Property Sheet**, click in the **Tab Index** property setting box, which displays *2*. Click the **Build** button.

Tab Index settings begin with 0. Franchise# has a Tab Index setting of 0, which indicates that this field has the focus when the form is opened. Daily Sales has a Tab Index setting of 1—it will receive the focus when Tab is pressed one time. Date has a Tab Index setting of 2—it will receive the focus when Tab is pressed a second time. Menu Item has a Tab Index setting of 3—it will receive the focus when Tab is pressed a third time.

9 In the **Tab Order** dialog box, click **Cancel**. On the **Property Sheet**, notice that the **Tab Stop** property setting is **Yes**, which means individuals can Press Tab to move to this field.

The Auto Tab property setting is No. It should be changed to Yes only when a text field has an input mask. Recall that an input mask controls how the data is entered into a field; for example, the formatting of a phone number.

10 In the **Detail** section, click the **Franchise# combo box control**, and then on the **Property Sheet**, notice the settings for the **Tab Index** and **Tab Stop** properties.

The Tab Index setting is 0, which means this field has the focus when the form page is displayed—it is first on the tab order list. The Tab Stop setting is Yes. Because an input mask cannot be applied to a combo box, there is no Auto Tab property. The Auto Tab property applies only to a text box control.

11 In the **Detail** section, click the **Previous Record** button control. On the **Property Sheet**, click in the **Tab Stop** property setting box, click the **arrow**, and then click **No**.

Changing the Tab Stop property setting to No means that the focus will not be changed to the button by pressing Tab.

12 **Save** the form, and then switch to **Form** view. In the record navigator, click the **Last record** button. Press Tab two times, watching the focus change from the **Franchise#** field to the **Date** field. Press Tab two more times, and then compare your screen with Figure 6.25.

Because the Tab Stop property setting for the Previous Record button control was changed to No, the button does not receive the focus by pressing the Tab key.

Figure 6.25

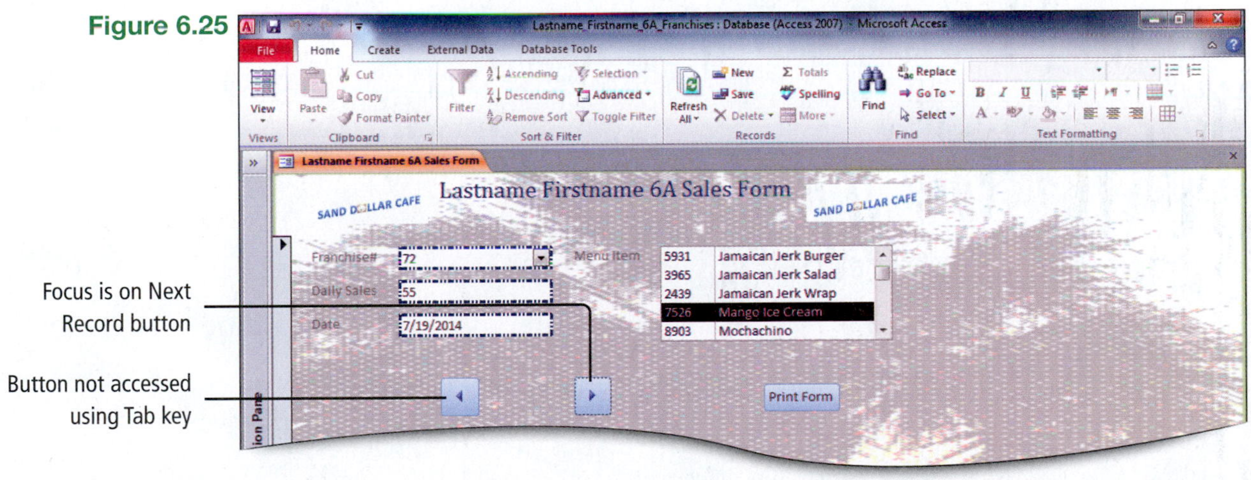

13 In the **Detail** section, click the **Previous Record** button.

The previous record displays—you can still use the button by clicking on it.

14 Switch to **Design** view. Using the techniques you have just practiced, for the **Next Record** button and the **Print Form** button, change the **Tab Stop** property setting to **No**.

15 **Close** the **Property Sheet**. **Save** the form, and then switch to **Form** view. Test the tab order by pressing Tab, making sure that the focus does not change to the **Next Record** button or the **Print Form** button.

When the focus is on the Date field, pressing the Tab key moves the focus to the Franchise# field in the next record.

16 Navigate to **Record 5**—Franchise# 44. Unless you are required to submit your database electronically, in the **Detail** section, click the **Print Form** button. In the **Print** dialog box under **Print Range**, click **Selected Record(s)**, and then click **OK**. If you are instructed to submit this result as an electronic printout, select the record using the selector bar, and then from **Backstage** view, click **Save & Publish**. Click the **Save Object As** button, and click **PDF or XPS**. Navigate to the folder where you store your electronic printouts. Click the **Options** button, click **Selected records**, and then click **OK**. Click **Publish**.

17 **Close** the form, and then **Open** the **Navigation Pane**. **Close** the database, and then **Exit** Access.

End **You have completed Project 6A**

Project 6B SDC

myitlab Project 6B Training

Project Activities

In Activities 6.11 through 6.18, you will create customized reports. The corporate office of Sand Dollar Cafe (SDC) maintains a database about the franchises, including daily sales of menu items per franchise, the franchise owners, and franchise fees and payments. Reports are often run to summarize data in the tables or queries. Creating customized reports will help the owners and officers of the company view the information in the database in a meaningful way. Your completed reports will look similar to Figure 6.26.

Project Files

For Project 6B, you will need the following files:

a06B_SDC
a06B_Logo

You will save your database as:

Lastname_Firstname_6B_SDC

Project Results

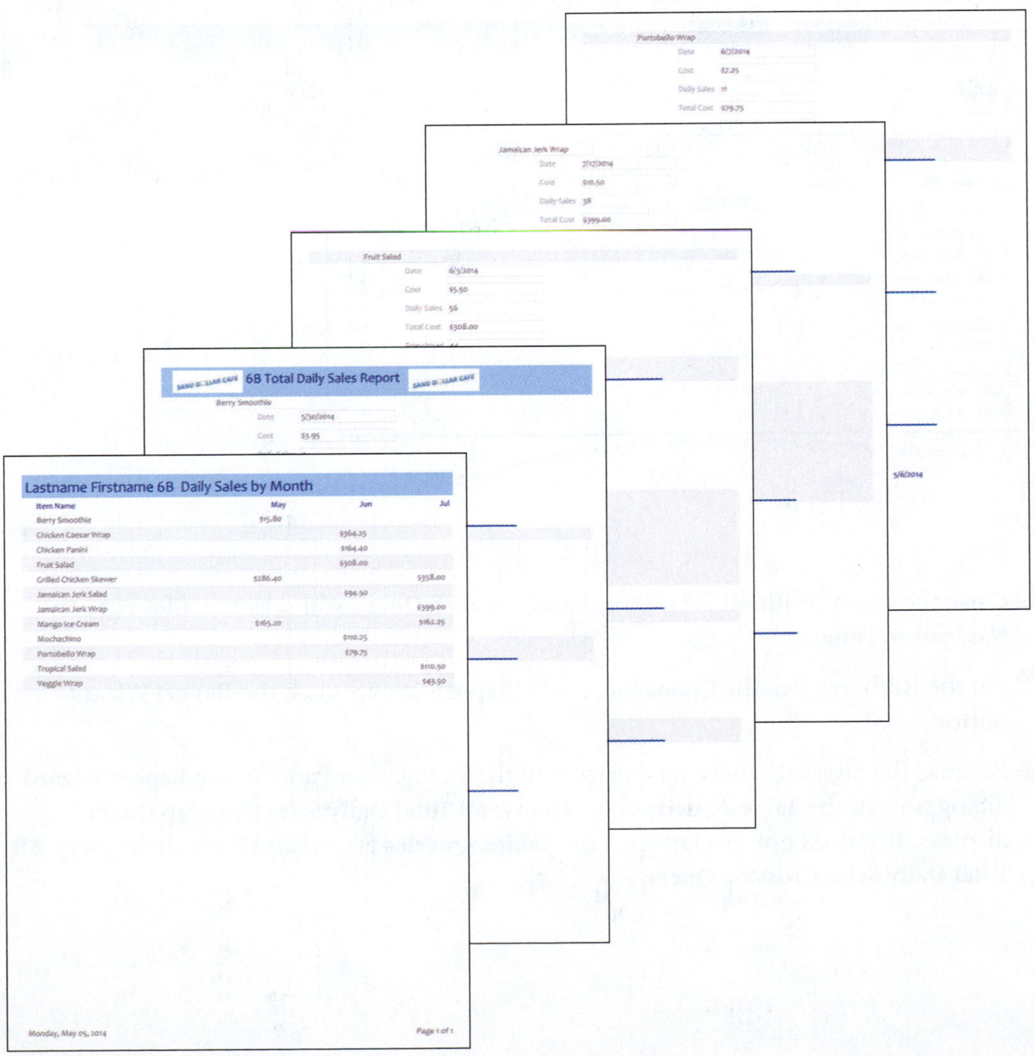

Figure 6.26
Project 6B SDC

Objective 5 | Create a Report Based on a Query Using a Wizard

A report wizard is a more efficient way to start a report, although Design view does offer you more control as you create your report. Once the report has been created, its appearance can be modified in Design or Layout view.

Activity 6.11 | Creating a Report Using a Wizard

In this activity, you will use a wizard to create a report for Sand Dollar Cafe that displays the data from the 6B Total Daily Sales Crosstab Query.

1 **Start** Access. Navigate to the location where the student data files for this textbook are saved. Locate and open the **a06B_SDC** file. Save the database in your **Access Chapter 6** folder as **Lastname_Firstname_6B_SDC**

2 If you did not add the Access Chapter 6 folder to the Trust Center, enable the content. In the **Navigation Pane**, under **Queries**, double-click **6B Total Daily Sales Crosstab Query**. Take a moment to study the data in the query, as shown in Figure 6.27.

The data is grouped by Item Name and Month. The sum function calculates the total daily sales for each item per month.

Figure 6.27

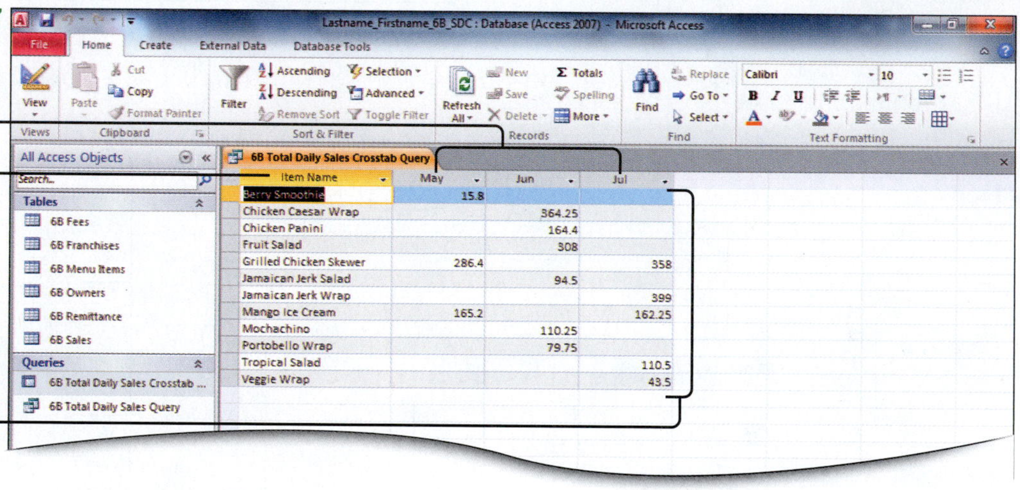

3 **Close** the query. With **6B Total Daily Sales Crosstab Query** still selected, **Close** « the **Navigation Pane**.

4 On the Ribbon, click the **Create tab**. In the **Reports group**, click the **Report Wizard** button.

5 Because the crosstab query was selected in the Navigation Pane, in the **Report Wizard** dialog box, in the **Tables/Queries** box, **Query: 6B Total Daily Sales Crosstab Query** displays. If it does not display, click the **Tables/Queries** arrow, and then click **Query: 6B Total Daily Sales Crosstab Query**.

6 Under **Available Fields**, notice there are more months than those that were displayed in 6B Total Daily Sales Crosstab Query.

Because there was data for the months of May, June, and July only, the other months were hidden from the display in the query. To hide a column in Datasheet view, right-click the column header, and then from the shortcut menu, click Hide Fields.

7 Under **Available Fields**, double-click each field name, in the order specified, to add the field names to the Selected Fields box: **Item Name**, **May**, **Jun**, and **Jul**.

8 In the **Report Wizard** dialog box, click **Next**. Because no grouping levels will be used, click **Next**.

9 To sort the records within the report by Item Name, click the **arrow** next to the **1** box. From the displayed list, click **Item Name**. Leave the sort order as **Ascending**, and then click **Next**.

10 Under **Layout**, be sure the **Tabular** option button is selected. Under **Orientation**, be sure the **Portrait** option button is selected, and then click **Next**.

11 For the title of the report, type **Lastname Firstname 6B Daily Sales by Month** and then click **Finish**.

The report displays in Print Preview. Because this report uses a crosstab query as the record source, it displays calculated data grouped by two different types of information.

Activity 6.12 | Modifying a Report Created Using a Wizard

In this activity, you will modify controls in the report to change its appearance. Although the report was created using a wizard, its appearance can be modified in Design view and Layout view.

1 On the **Print Preview tab**, in the **Close Preview group**, click the **Close Print Preview** button. If the **Field List** or **Property Sheet** displays, **Close** it.

2 On the Ribbon, click the **Design tab**. In the **Themes group**, click the **Themes** button to display a list of available themes. Under **Built-In**, on the tenth row, click the fourth theme—**Waveform**.

Themes simplify the process of creating professional-looking objects within one program or across multiple programs. A theme includes theme colors and theme fonts that will be applied consistently throughout the objects in the database. It is a simple way to provide professional, consistent formatting in a database.

3 If necessary, click anywhere in an empty area of the report to deselect the **Item Name** column. Click the **Report title text box control**. On the **Format tab**, in the **Font group**, click the **Font Color button arrow** [A ▾]. Under **Theme Colors**, on the first row, click the fourth color—**Dark Blue, Text 2**.

4 Select all of the controls in the **Page Header** section by pointing to the top left of the **Page Header** section, holding down your mouse button, dragging the mouse across the Page Header controls and to the bottom of the Page Header section, and then releasing the mouse button. Use the techniques you have practiced to change the font color to **Dark Blue, Text 2.**

Any group of controls can be selected using this lasso method. It can be more efficient than holding down [Shift] while clicking each control.

5 **Save** the report, and then switch to **Layout** view.

6 In the **Item Name** column, select any **text box control**. Point to the right edge of the control until the ↔ pointer displays. Drag to the left until the box is approximately **1.5 inches** wide; be sure none of the data in the column is cut off.

7 To select all of the text box controls, in the **May** column, click **15.8.** Holding down [Shift], in the **Jun** and **Jul** columns, click a **text box control**. Compare your screen with Figure 6.28.

Figure 6.28

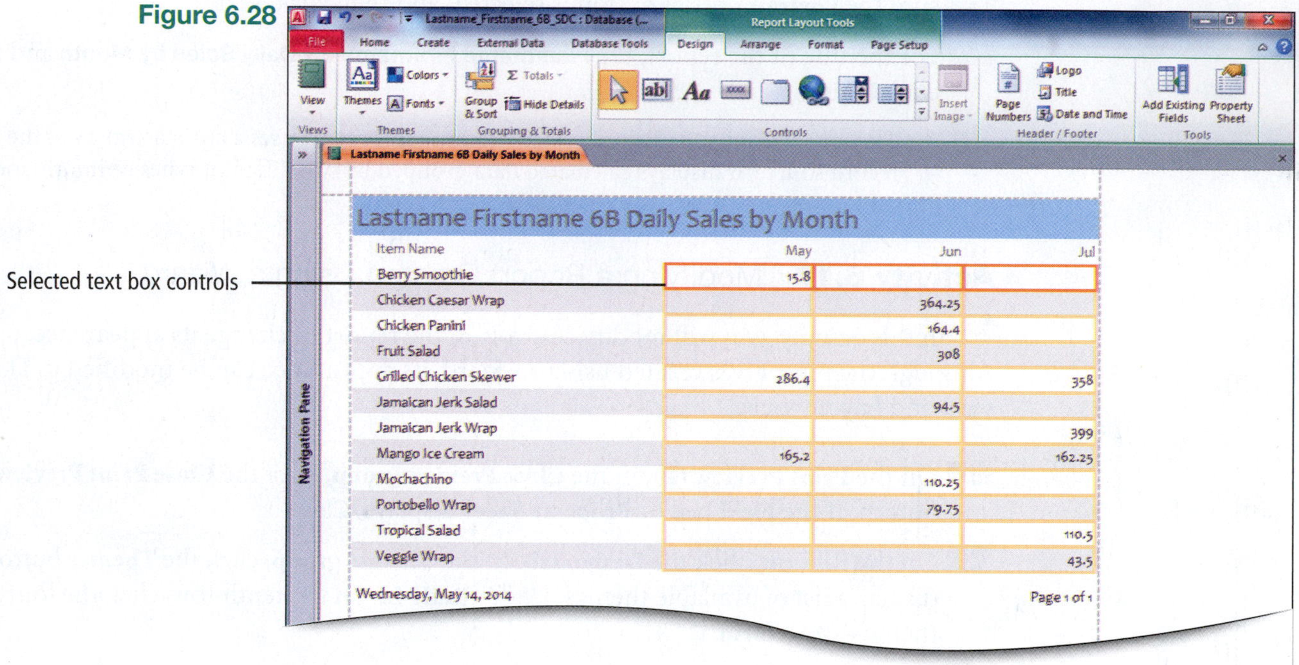

8 On the Ribbon, click the **Design tab**. In the **Tools group**, click the **Property Sheet** button. Notice that the selection type is *Multiple selection*.

9 On the **Property Sheet**, click the **Format tab**. Click the **Format property setting arrow**. From the displayed list, select **Currency**. Click the **Border Style property setting arrow**, and click **Sparse Dots**. **Close** the **Property Sheet**.

10 **Save** the report, and then switch to **Print Preview** view. If you are instructed to submit this result, create a paper or electronic printout. On the **Print Preview tab**, in the **Close Preview group**, click the **Close Print Preview** button.

11 **Close** the report, and then **Open** » the **Navigation Pane**.

Objective 6 | Create a Report in Design View

You usually create a report using the Report tool, the Blank Report tool, or the Report Wizard, and then modify the report in Design view to suit your needs. Use Design view to create a report when these tools do not meet your needs or if you want more control in the creation of a report. Creating or modifying a report in Design view is a common technique when additional controls, such as calculated controls, need to be added to the report or properties need to be changed.

Activity 6.13 | Creating a Report in Design View

Creating a report with the Report tool, the Blank Report tool, or the Report Wizard is the easiest way to start the creation of a customized report, but you can also create a report from scratch in Design view. Once you understand the sections of a report and how to manipulate the controls within the sections, it is easier to modify a report that has been created using the report tools.

1 In the **Navigation Pane**, open **6B Total Daily Sales Query**. Switch to **Design** view, and then notice the underlying tables that were used in the creation of the query. Notice the calculated field—*Total Cost*.

Recall that a calculated field contains the field name, followed by a colon, and then an expression. In the expression, the existing field names must be enclosed in square brackets. The Total Cost was calculated by multiplying the value in the Cost field by the value in the Daily Sales field.

2 When you are finished, **Close** the query, and **Close** « the **Navigation Pane**. On the Ribbon, click the **Create tab**. In the **Reports group**, click the **Report Design** button. When the design grid displays, scroll down to display all of the report sections.

Three sections are included in the blank design grid: the Page Header section, the Detail section, and the Page Footer section. A page header displays at the top of every printed page, and a page footer displays at the bottom of every printed page.

3 Select the report using the report selector. On the **Design tab**, in the **Tools group**, click the **Property Sheet** button. On the **Property Sheet**, click the **Data tab**. Click the **Record Source property setting box arrow**, and then compare your screen with Figure 6.29. If necessary, increase the width of the Property Sheet.

As with forms, the Record Source property setting is used to select the underlying table or query for the report.

Figure 6.29

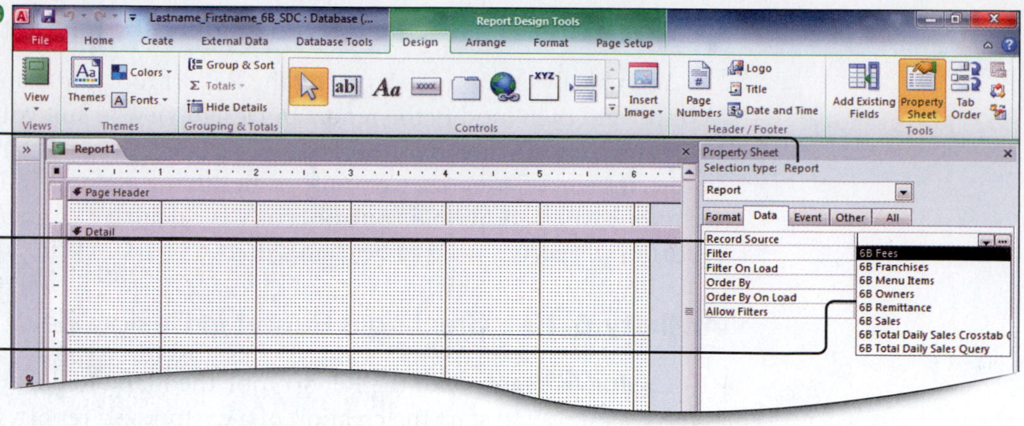

4 From the displayed list of tables and queries, click **6B Total Daily Sales Query**, and then **Close** the **Property Sheet**.

6B Total Daily Sales Query is the record source—underlying query—for this report.

5 On the **Design tab**, in the **Tools group**, click the **Add Existing Fields** button to display the fields in 6B Total Daily Sales Query.

6 If all tables display in the field list, click **Show only fields in the current record source** at the bottom of the Field List box. In the **Field List**, click **Date**. Hold down Shift, and then click **Franchise#** to select all of the fields.

7 Drag the selected fields into the **Detail** section of the design grid until the top of the arrow of the pointer is **one dot** below the bottom edge of the **Detail** section bar and aligned with the **3-inch mark on the horizontal ruler**, and then compare your screen with Figure 6.30.

As with forms, drag the fields to where the text box controls should display.

Figure 6.30

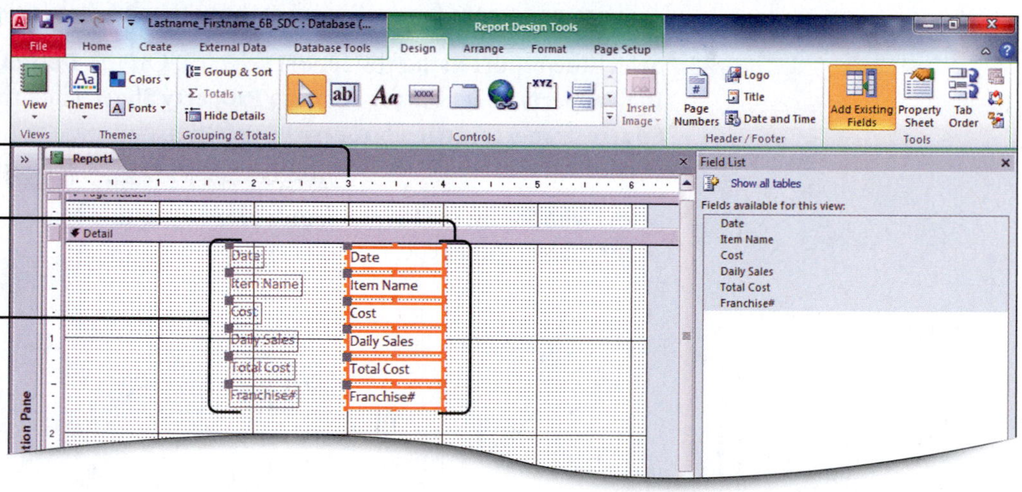

8 With the label controls and text box controls for the fields selected, on the Ribbon, click the **Arrange tab**. In the **Table group**, click the **Stacked** button to group the fields together for easier formatting.

> **More Knowledge | Using the Tabular Arrangement**
>
> When you want your data to display efficiently in a report, in the Table group, on the Arrange tab, click the Tabular button. This will place the labels in the Page Header and the data in the Detail section for a table-like appearance.

9 On the Ribbon, click the **Design tab**. In the **Themes group**, click the **Themes** button. Under **In This Database**, notice the theme used in this database—**Waveform**. Press Esc to close the gallery.

10 **Close** the **Field List**, and then **Save** the report as **Lastname Firstname 6B Total Daily Sales Report**

Activity 6.14 | Modifying the Sections of a Report

By default, a report created in Design view includes a Page Header section and a Page Footer section. Reports can also include a Report Header section and a Report Footer section. In this activity, you will add the Report Header and Report Footer sections and hide the Page Header section. Recall that a Report Header displays at the top of the first printed page of a report, and the Report Footer displays at the bottom of the last printed page of a report.

1 Right-click in the **Detail** section of the report, and click **Report Header/Footer**. Notice that the **Report Header** section displays at the top of the design grid. Scroll down to display the **Report Footer** section.

2 Scroll up to display the **Report Header** section. On the **Design tab**, in the **Header/Footer group**, click the **Logo** button. Locate and double-click **a06B_Logo** to insert the logo in the Report Header section. On the selected logo, point to the right middle sizing handle until the pointer ↔ displays. Drag to the right until the right edge of the logo is aligned with the **1.5-inch mark on the horizontal ruler**.

3 On the **Design tab**, in the **Header/Footer group**, click the **Title** button. In the **title's label control**, click to the left of your **Lastname**, delete your **Lastname Firstname** and the space, and then press Enter. On the **title's label control**, point to the right middle sizing handle until the pointer ↔ displays, and then double-click to adjust the size of the label control to fit the text. Alternatively, drag the right middle sizing handle to the left.

4 Scroll down until the **Page Footer** section bar displays. Point to the top edge of the **Page Footer** section bar until the pointer ╪ displays. Drag upward until the top of the **Page Footer** section bar aligns with the **2.25-inch mark on the vertical ruler**.

This prevents extra blank space from printing between the records.

5 Scroll up until the **Report Header** section displays. Point to the top edge of the **Detail** section bar until the pointer [+] displays. Drag upward until the top edge of the **Detail** section bar aligns with the bottom edge of the **Page Header** section bar, and then compare your screen with Figure 6.31.

The Page Header and Page Footer sections are paired together. Likewise, the Report Header and Report Footer sections are paired together. You cannot remove only one section of the pair. If you wish to remove one section of a paired header/footer, decrease the height of the section. Alternatively, set the Height property for the section to 0. Because there is no space in the Page Header section, nothing will print at the top of every page. To remove both of the paired header/footer sections, right click in the Detail section, and click the Page Header/Footer to deselect it.

Figure 6.31

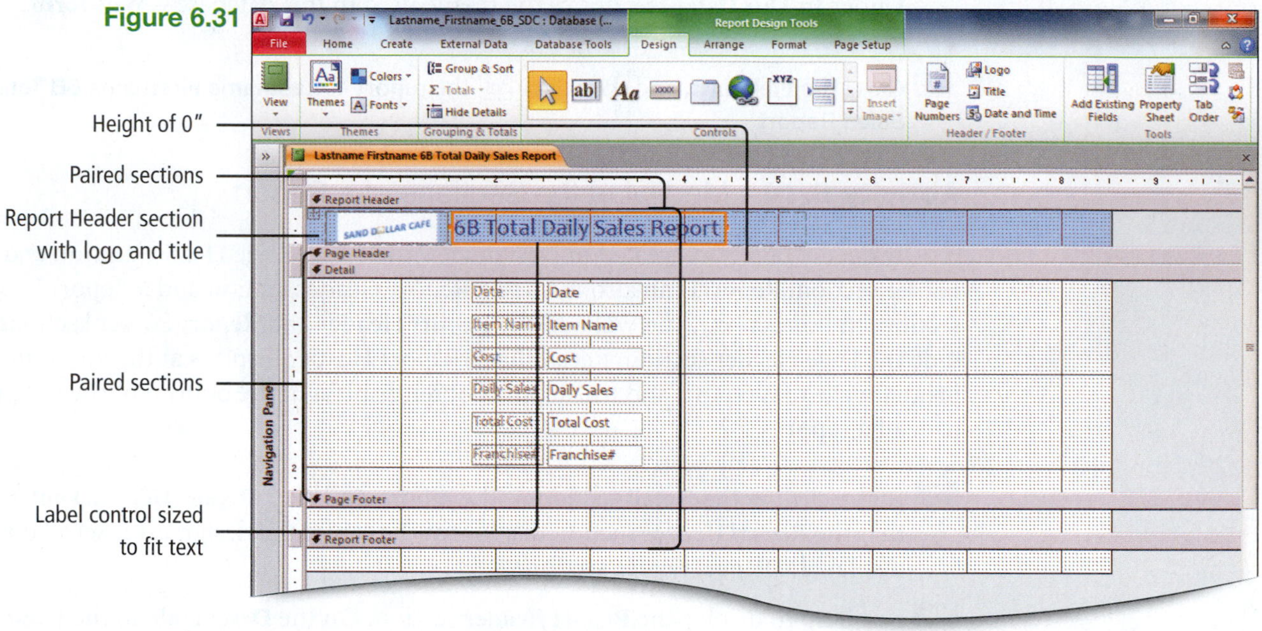

6 Drag the right edge of the design grid to the left until it aligns with the **6.5-inch mark on the horizontal ruler**. **Save** the report.

The width of the report page is decreased, which will enable the report to fit within the margins of paper in portrait orientation.

Objective 7 | Add Controls to a Report

Reports are not used to manipulate data in the underlying table or query, so they contain fewer types of controls. You can add label controls, text box controls, images, hyperlinks, or calculated controls to a report.

Activity 6.15 | Adding Label and Text Box Controls to a Report

In this activity, you will add controls to the report that will contain the page number, the date, and your first name and last name.

1 On the **Design tab**, in the **Header/Footer group**, click the **Page Numbers** button. In the displayed **Page Numbers** dialog box, under **Format**, click **Page N of M**. Under **Position**, click **Bottom of Page [Footer]**. Alignment should remain **Center**; click **OK**.

A text box control displays in the center of the Page Footer section. The control displays an expression that will display the page number. Every expression begins with an equal sign (=). "Page" is enclosed in quotation marks. Access interprets anything enclosed in quotation marks as text and will display it exactly as it is typed within the quotation marks, including the space. The & symbol is used for ***concatenation***—linking or joining—of strings. A ***string*** is a series of characters. The word *Page* followed by a space will be concatenated—joined—to the string that follows the & symbol. [Page] is a reserved name that retrieves the current page number. This is followed by another & symbol that concatenates the page number to the next string—" of ". The & symbol continues concatenation of [Pages], a reserved name that retrieves the total number of pages in the report.

2 **Save** the report. On the **Design tab**, in the **Views group**, click the **View button arrow**, and then click **Print Preview**. On the **Print Preview tab**, in the **Zoom group**, click the **Two Pages** button. Notice at the bottom of each page the format of the page number.

3 In the **Close Preview group**, click the **Close Print Preview** button.

4 On the **Design tab**, in the **Controls group**, click the **Label** button *Aa*. Point to the **Report Footer** section until the plus sign (+) of the pointer aligns with the bottom edge of the **Report Footer** section bar and with the left edge of the **Report Footer** section. Drag downward to the bottom of the **Report Footer** section and to the right to the **2.5-inch mark on the horizontal ruler**. Using your own first name and last name, type **Submitted by Firstname Lastname** and then compare your screen with Figure 6.32.

Figure 6.32

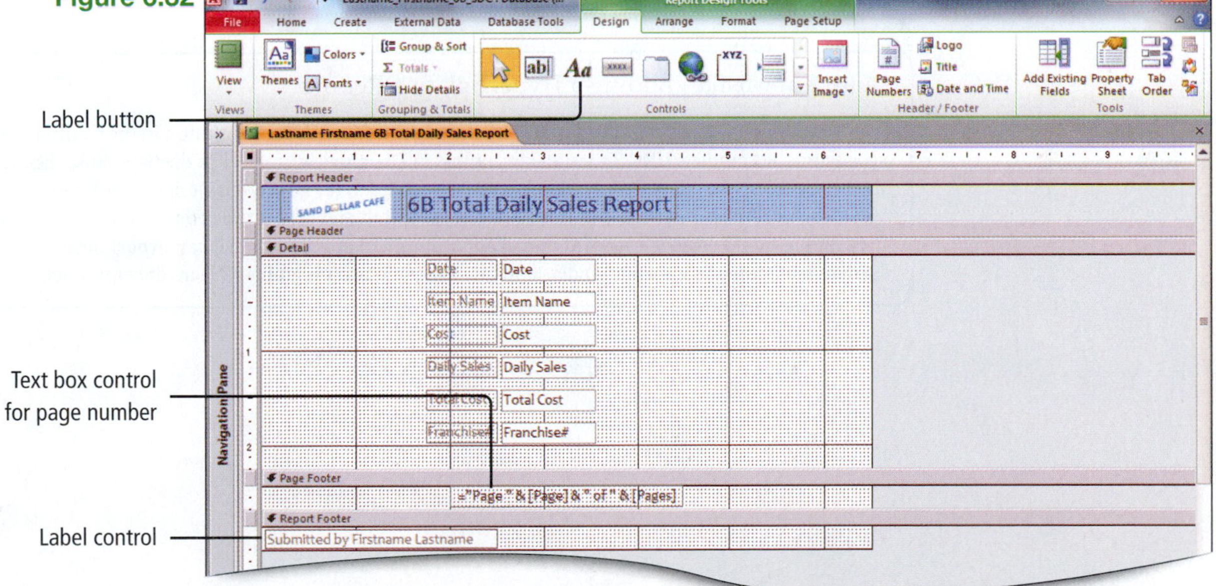

5 Click away from the label box, and then **Save** the report. On the **Design tab**, in the **Header/Footer group**, click the **Date and Time** button. In the **Date and Time** dialog box, under **Include Date**, click the third option button, which displays the date as mm/dd/yyyy. Clear the **Include Time** check box, and then click **OK**.

A text box control with an expression for the current date displays in the Report Header section. It may display over the Report title.

6 In the **Report Header**, click the **Date text box control** to select it. On the Ribbon, click the **Arrange tab**. In the **Table group**, click the **Remove Layout** button so the **Date text box control** can be moved. Right-click the selected control, and click **Cut**. Point to the **Report Footer** section bar, right-click, and then click **Paste**. Drag the text box control until the right edge of the text box control aligns with the **6.25-inch mark on the horizontal ruler**. Click the **Title label control** to select it, point to the right middle sizing handle until the pointer ↔ displays, and then drag to the right until the right edge of the text box control aligns with the **4.5-inch mark on the horizontal ruler**.

7 **Save** the report, and then switch to **Layout** view. Notice that, for the first record, the data for the **Item Name** field does not fully display. Click the **Item Name text box control**, which partially displays *Berry Smoothie*. Point to the right edge of the **Item Name text box control** until the pointer ✛ displays. Drag to the right approximately **1 inch.** Because no ruler displays in Layout view, you will have to estimate the distance to drag.

Because the controls are in a stacked layout, the widths of all of the text box controls are increased.

8 Scroll down, observing the data in the **Item Name** field. Ensure that all of the data displays. If the data is not all visible in a record, use the technique you just practiced to increase the width of the text box control until all of the data displays.

9 Switch to **Design** view. Point to the right edge of the design grid until the pointer ↔ displays. If necessary, drag to the left until the right edge of the design grid aligns with the **6.5-inch mark on the horizontal ruler**. **Save** the report.

The width of the report page will change with the addition of more text boxes, making it necessary to readjust the width so the report will fit within the margins of paper in portrait orientation.

More Knowledge | Adding a Hyperlink to a Report

Add a hyperlink to a report in Design view by clicking the Insert Hyperlink button in the Controls group and then specifying the complete URL. To test the hyperlink, in Design view, right-click the hyperlink, click Hyperlink, and then click Open Hyperlink. The hyperlink is active—jumps to the target—in Design view, Report view, and Layout view. The hyperlink is not active in Print Preview view. If the report is exported to another Office application, the hyperlink is active when it is opened in that application. An application that can ***export*** data can create a file in a format that another application understands, enabling the two programs to share the same data.

Activity 6.16 | Adding an Image Control and a Line Control to a Report

1 In **Design** view, in the **Report Header** section, right-click the **logo control**. From the displayed shortcut menu, click **Copy**. Right-click anywhere in the **Report Header** section, and then from the shortcut menu, click **Paste**.

A copy of the image displays on top and slightly to the left of the original logo control.

2 Point to the selected logo until the pointer displays. Drag to the right until the left edge of the outlined control is the same distance from the title as the logo control on the left. Point to the top edge of the **Page Header** section bar until the pointer displays. Drag upward until the top of the **Page Header** section bar aligns with the **0.5-inch mark on the vertical ruler.**

Recall that when you created a form in Design view, you clicked the Insert Image button and selected the location in the header section. You then had to change the properties of the image to match the size of the image in the logo control. Because you copied the original image from the logo, the images are the same size.

3 With the image control on the right selected, hold down Shift, and then click the **logo control**. On the Ribbon, click the **Arrange tab**. In the **Sizing & Ordering group**, click the **Align button**, and select **Bottom.** Compare your screen with Figure 6.33.

Both the logo control and the image control are aligned along the bottom edges.

Figure 6.33

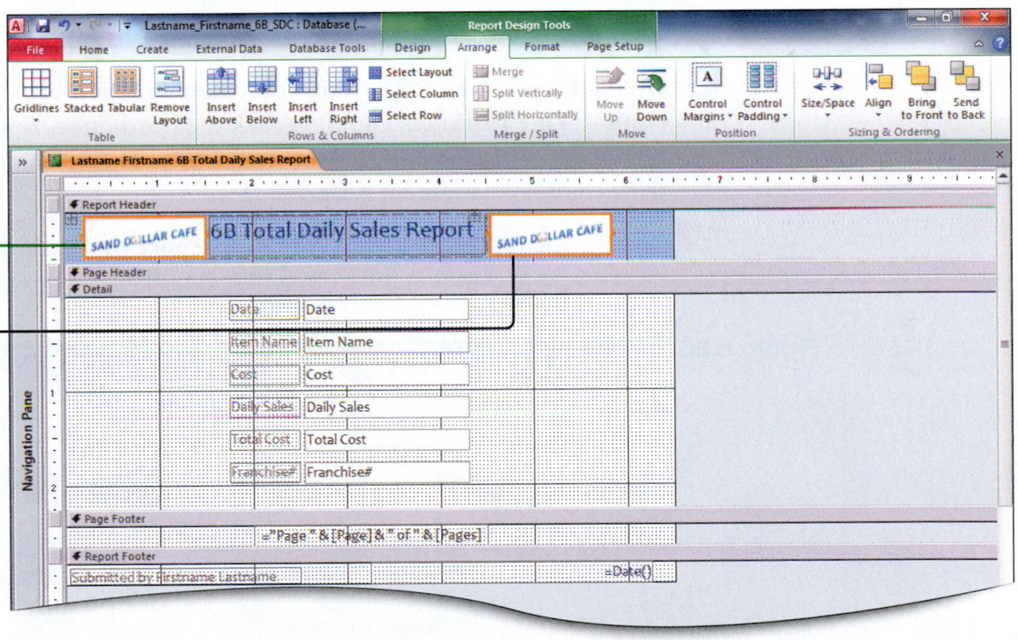

4 On the Ribbon, click the **Design tab**. In the **Controls group**, click the More button, and then click the **Line** button. Point to the **Detail** section until the middle of the plus sign (+) of the pointer aligns at **2 inches on the vertical ruler** and **0 inches on the horizontal ruler**, as shown in Figure 6.34.

A ***line control*** enables an individual to insert a line in a form or report.

Figure 6.34

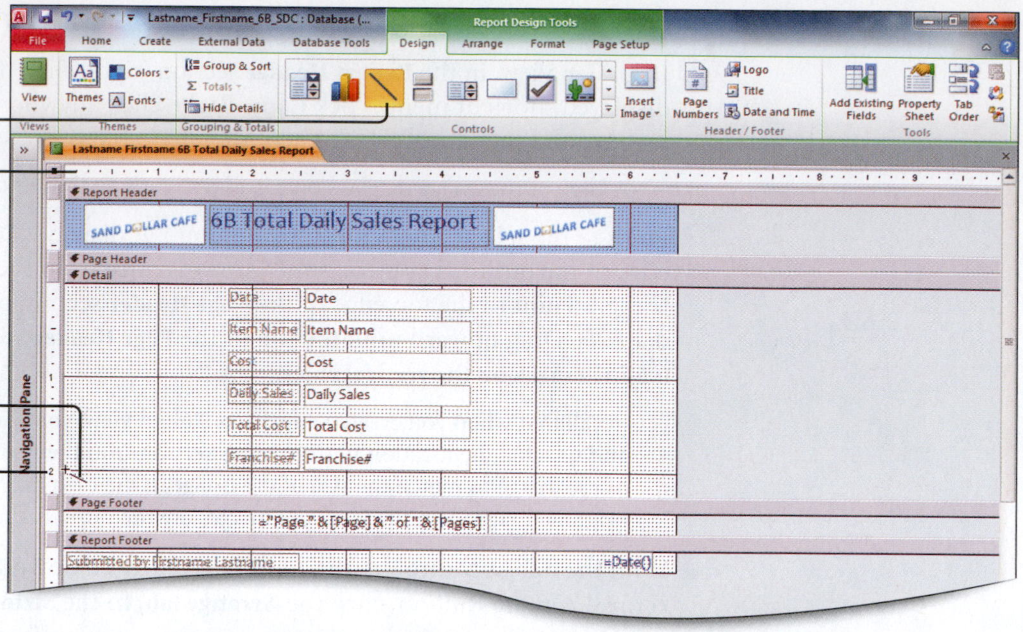

5 Hold down Shift, drag to the right to **6.5 inches on the horizontal ruler**, and then release the mouse button.

An orange line control displays. Holding down the Shift key ensures that the line will be straight.

6 On the **Format tab**, in the **Control Formatting group**, click the **Shape Outline** button. Point to **Line Thickness** and then click the third line—**2 pt**. In the **Control Formatting group**, click the **Shape Outline** button. Under **Theme Colors**, on the fifth row, click the sixth color—**Blue, Accent 2, Darker 25%**.

7 **Save** the report, and then switch to **Report** view. Compare your screen with Figure 6.35. Notice the horizontal line that displays between the records.

Figure 6.35

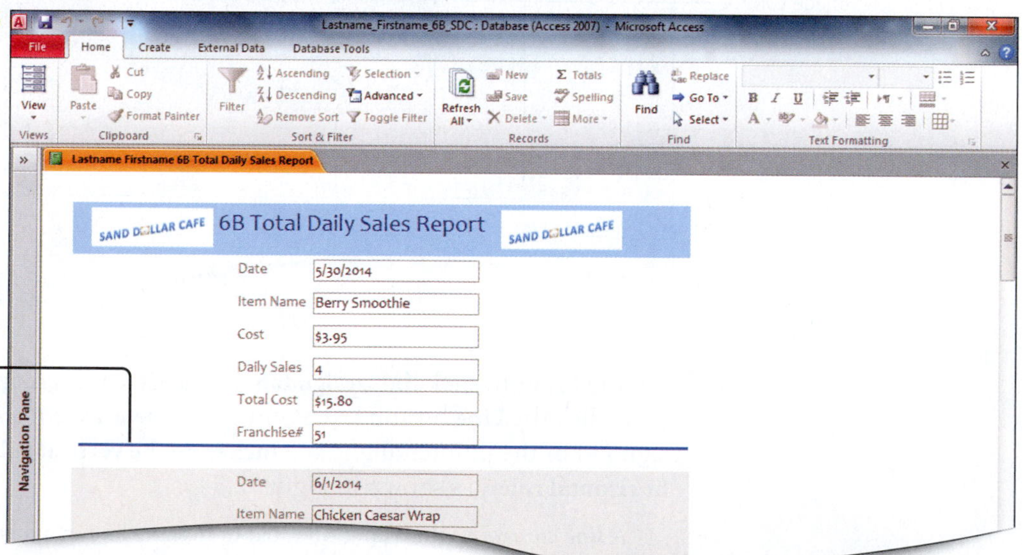

8 Switch to **Design** view.

Objective 8 | Group, Sort, and Total Records in Design View

Although it is much easier to create a report that is grouped and sorted using the Report Wizard, the same tasks can be completed in Design view. If a report has been created that was not grouped, you can modify the report in Design view to include grouping and summary data. Calculated controls are often added to reports to display summary information in reports with grouped records.

Activity 6.17 | Adding a Grouping and Sort Level to a Report

In this activity, you will add a grouping and sort order to the report, and then move a control from the Detail section to the Header section.

1 On the **Design tab**, in the **Grouping & Totals group**, click the **Group & Sort** button, and then compare your screen with Figure 6.36.

The Group, Sort, and Total Pane displays at the bottom of the screen. Because no grouping or sorting has been applied to the report, two buttons relating to these functions display in the Group, Sort, and Total Pane.

Figure 6.36

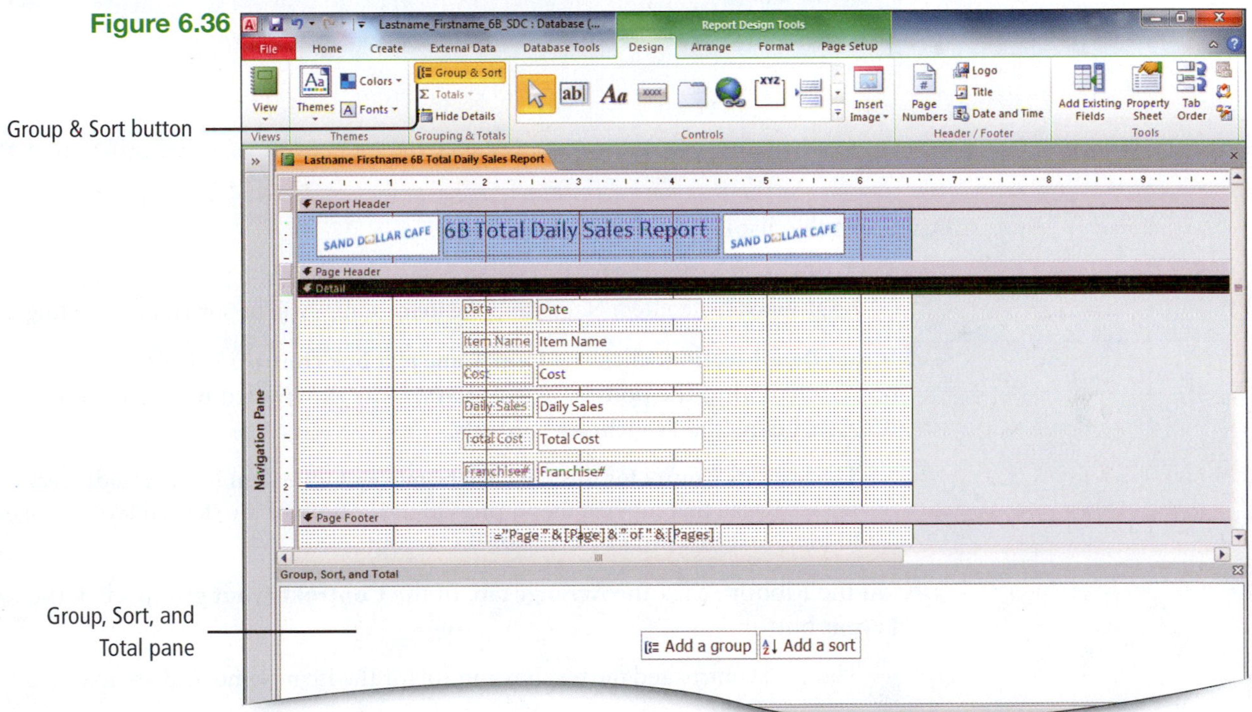

2 In the **Group, Sort, and Total Pane**, click the **Add a group** button. A list of fields that are used in the report displays as shown in Figure 6.37.

Figure 6.37

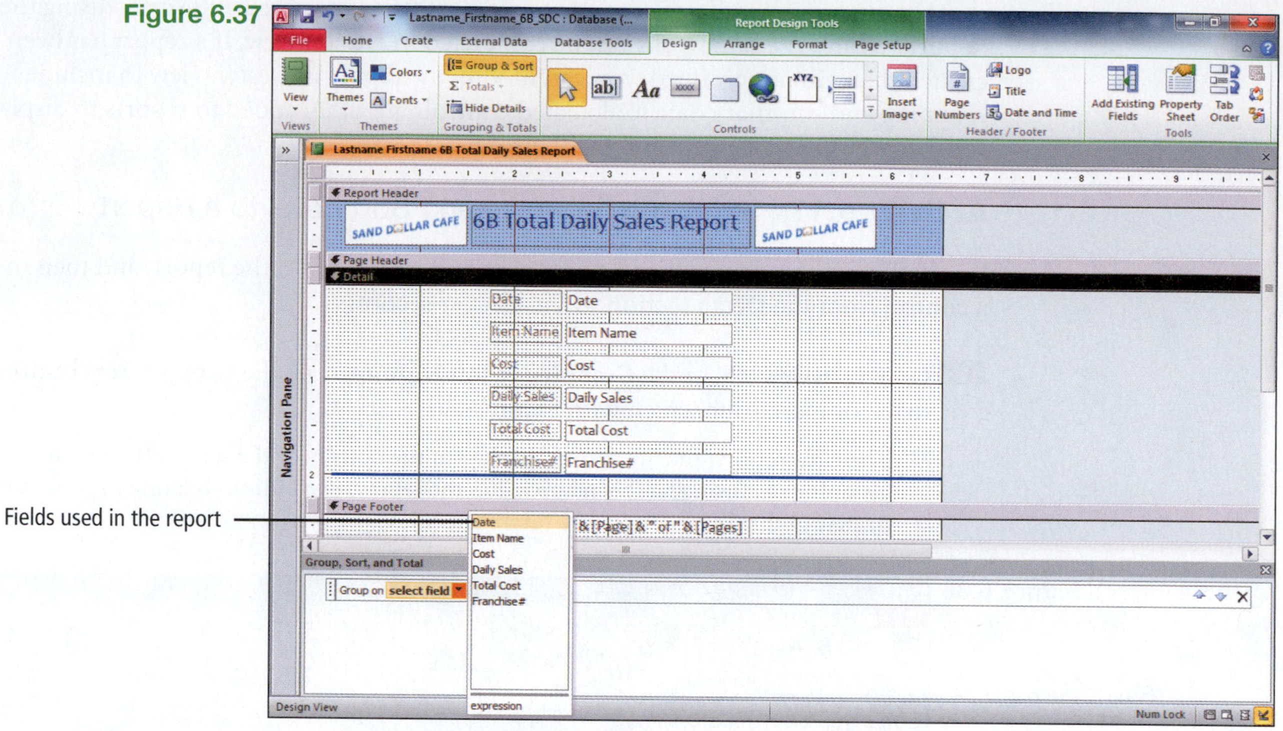

3 From the displayed list, click **Item Name**.

An empty Item Name Header section is inserted above the Detail section. The report will be grouped by the Item Name, and the Item Names will be sorted in ascending order.

4 In the **Detail** section, click the **Item Name text box control**. Point to the selected text box control until the pointer displays. Drag downward until a thin orange line displays below the **Franchise#** controls.

The text box control for this field will be moved to the Item Name Header section in the report. Recall that moving the controls to the bottom of the stacked layout makes it easier to remove the controls from the stacked layout.

5 On the Ribbon, click the **Arrange tab**. In the **Control Layout group**, click the **Remove Layout** button.

The label control and the text box control for the Item Name field are removed from the stacked layout.

6 Right-click the selected **Item Name text box control** to display the shortcut menu, and click **Cut**. Click the **Item Name Header** section bar to select it, right click to display the shortcut menu, and click **Paste**.

The controls for the Item Name are moved from the Detail section to the Item Name Header section. Because the report is being grouped by this field, the controls should be moved out of the Detail section.

7 In the **Item Name Header** section, click the **Item Name label control**, and then press Del. Click the **Item Name text box control** to select it, and then drag it to the right until the left edge of the control aligns with the **1-inch mark on the horizontal ruler.** Compare your screen with Figure 6.38.

Because the records are grouped by the data in the Item Name field, the name of the field is unnecessary.

Figure 6.38

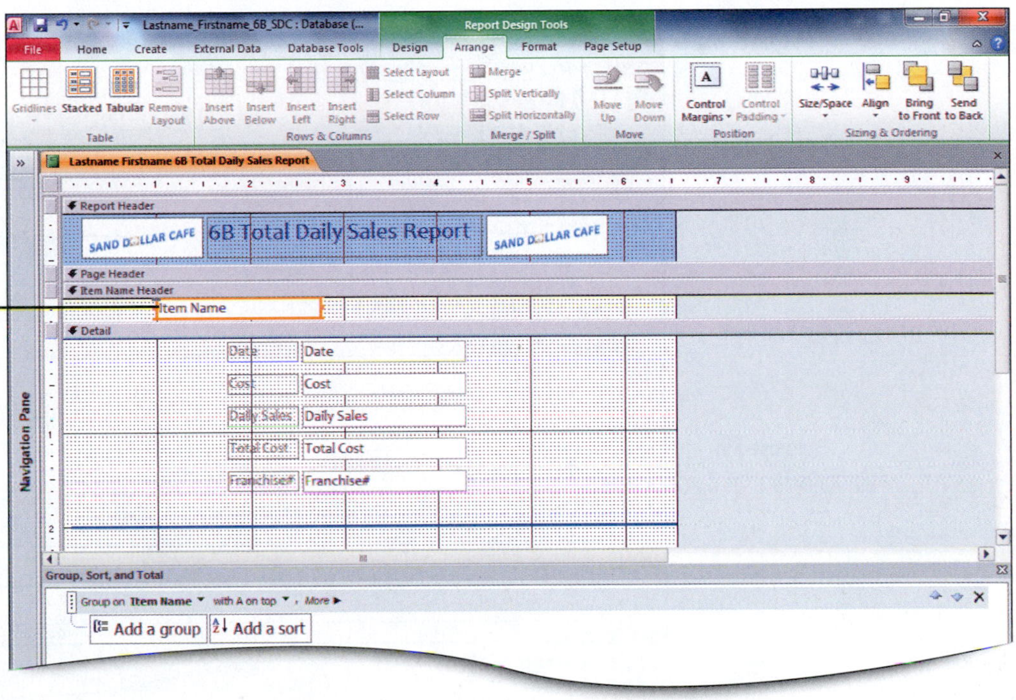

Item Name text box control moved from Detail section

8 **Save** the report, and then switch to **Report** view. Scroll down, noticing the grouping of records, until the grouping for **Grilled Chicken Skewer** displays. Notice that there are two records, one for Franchise# 12 and another for Franchise# 60. For these two records, notice the dates.

9 Switch back to **Design** view. In the **Group, Sort, and Total Pane**, click the **Add a sort** button, and then click **Date.** Notice that the Date will be sorted from oldest to newest.

10 **Save** the report, and then switch to **Report** view. Scroll down until the **Grilled Chicken Skewer** grouping displays. Within the grouping, the two records are arranged in order by the date with the oldest date listed first.

11 Switch to **Design** view, and then **Close** the **Group, Sort, and Total Pane**. Be sure to click the Close [X] button located in the title bar and not the Delete button that is inside the pane.

Activity 6.18 | Adding Calculated Controls to a Report

1 In the **Detail** section, click the **Total Cost text box control**. On the **Design tab**, in the **Grouping & Totals group**, click the **Totals** button, and then compare your screen with Figure 6.39.

A list of ***aggregate functions***—functions that group and perform calculations on multiple fields—displays. Before selecting the Totals button, the field that will be used in the aggregate function must be selected. If you wish to perform aggregate functions on multiple fields, you must select each field individually, and then select the aggregate function to apply to the field.

Figure 6.39

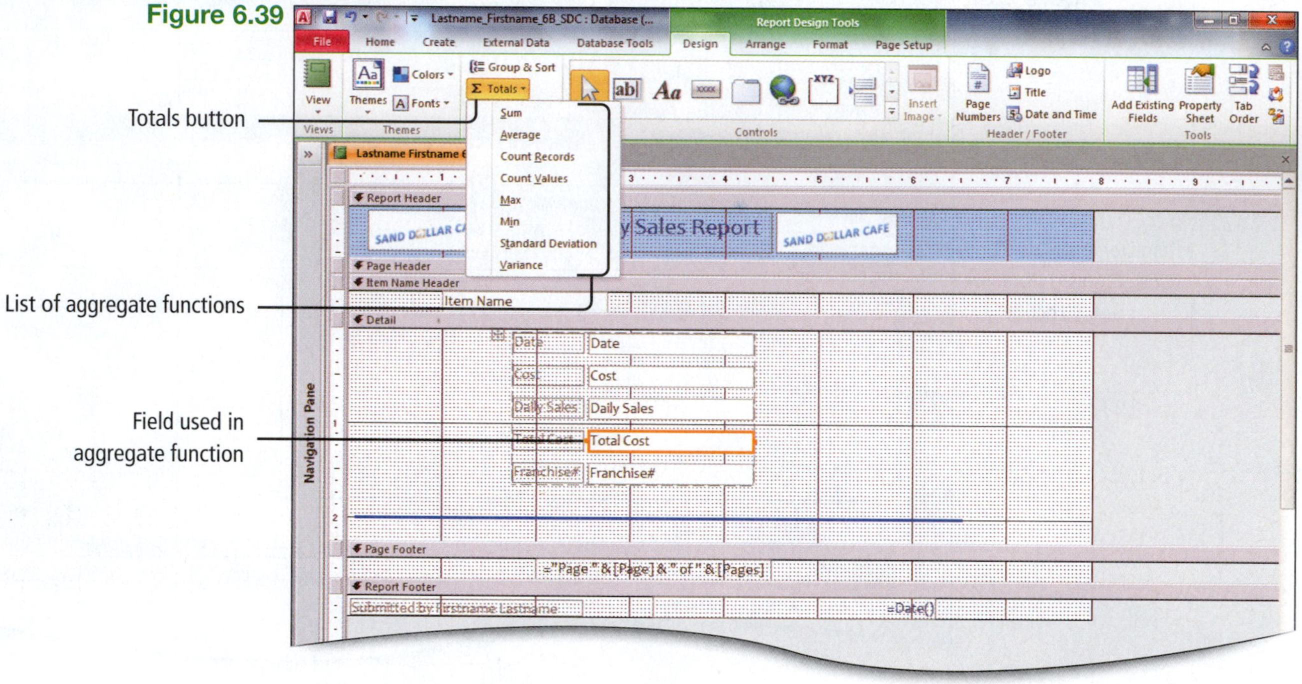

2 In the displayed list of aggregate functions, click **Sum**, and then compare your screen with Figure 6.40.

The Item Name Footer section is added to the report. A calculated control is added to the section that contains the expression that will display the sum of the Total Cost field for each grouping. A calculated control is also added to the Report Footer section that contains the expression that will display the grand total of the Total Cost field for the report. Recall that an expression begins with an equal sign (=). The Sum function adds or totals numeric data. Field names are included in square brackets.

Figure 6.40

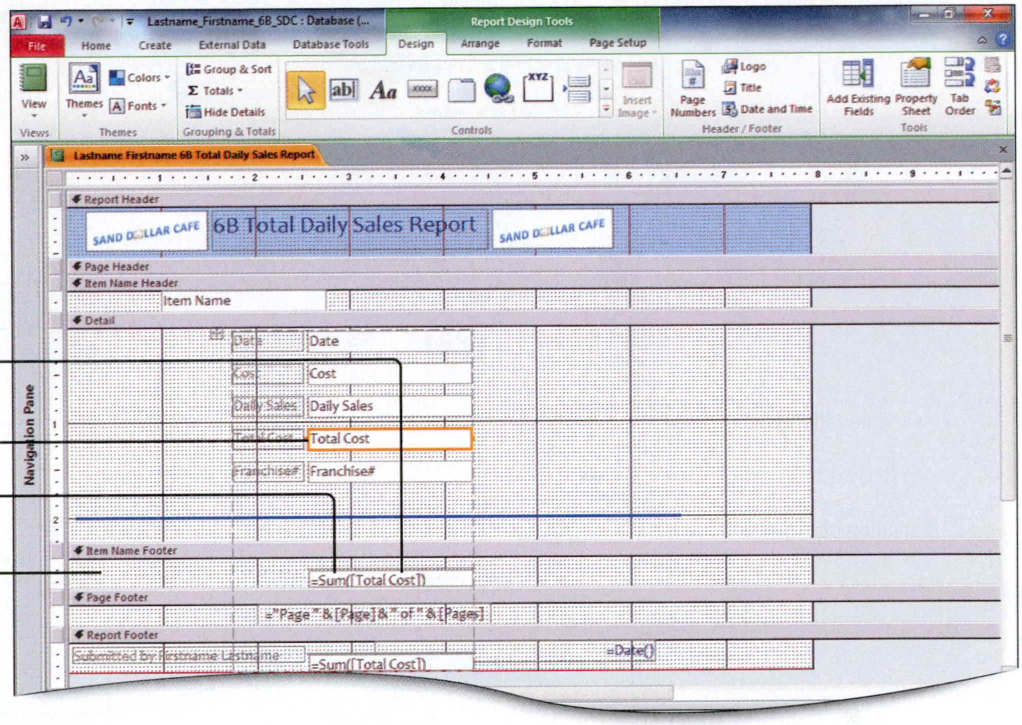

3 **Save** the report, and then switch to **Report** view. Notice that for the first grouping—Berry Smoothie—which only contains one record, the sum of the grouping displays below the horizontal line. Scroll down to the **Grilled Chicken Skewer** grouping, and then notice that the total for the grouping—**$644.40**—displays below the horizontal line for the second record in the grouping.

The placement of the horizontal line is distracting in the report, and there is no label attached to the grouping total.

4 Switch to **Design** view. On the **Design tab**, in the **Controls group**, click the **Text Box** button. Point to the **Item Name Footer** section until the plus sign (+) of the pointer aligns with the bottom edge of the **Item Name Footer** section bar and with the **0.5-inch mark on the horizontal ruler**. Drag downward to the bottom of the **Item Name Footer** section and to the right to the **2.5-inch mark on the horizontal ruler**.

5 Click inside the text box, and type **=[Item Name] & " Total Cost:"** ensuring that you include a space between the quotation mark and *Total* and that *Item Name* is enclosed in square brackets. Compare your screen with Figure 6.41.

Because a field name is included in the description of the total, a text box control must be used. This binds the control to the Item Name field in the underlying query, which makes this control a bound control. If you wish to insert only string characters as a description—for example, Total Cost—add a label control, which is an unbound control.

Figure 6.41

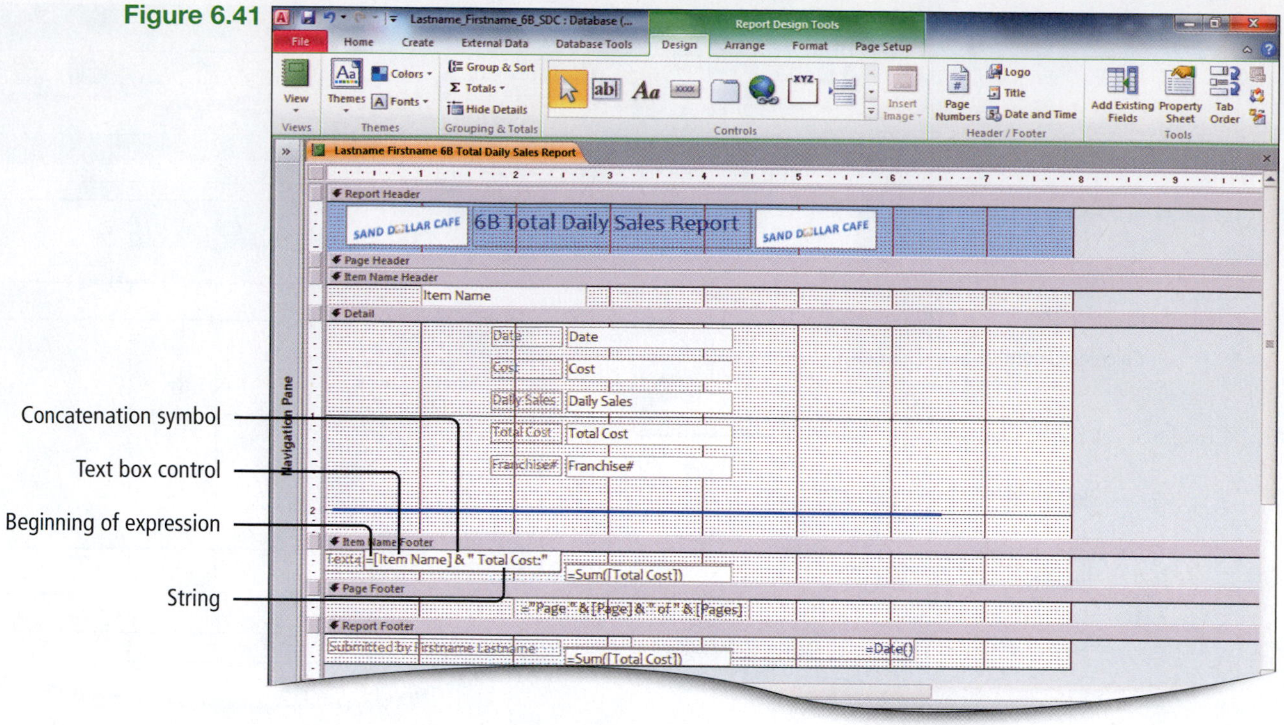

6 In the **Item Name Footer** section, click the **label control** that displays to the left of the text box control where you typed the expression. Press Del to delete the text box control's associated label control.

The data in the text box control is descriptive and does not require an additional label control.

7 In the **Item Name Footer** section, click the **text box control** that contains the expression you typed. Point to the left middle sizing handle until the pointer displays. Drag to the left until the left edge of the text box control aligns with the left edge of the design grid. With the text box control selected, hold down Shift. In the **Item Name Footer** section, click the **calculated control** for the sum. On the Ribbon, click the **Arrange tab**. In the **Sizing & Ordering group**, click the **Align** button, and then click **Bottom** to align both controls at the bottom.

8 Point to the top of the **Page Footer** section bar until the pointer displays. Drag downward to the top of the **Report Footer** section bar to increase the height of the Item Name Footer section so **three dots** display below the **Total Cost** controls.

9 In the **Detail** section, click the **line control**. Point to the line control until the pointer displays. Drag downward into the **Item Name Footer** section under the controls until there are approximately **two dots** between the text box controls and the line control, and then release the mouse button.

The line control is moved from the Detail section to the Item Name Footer section.

10 Point to the top of the **Item Name Footer** section bar until the pointer displays. Drag upward until approximately **two dots** display between the **Franchise#** controls and the top edge of the **Item Name Footer** section bar. Compare your screen with Figure 6.42.

The height of the Detail section is decreased.

Figure 6.42

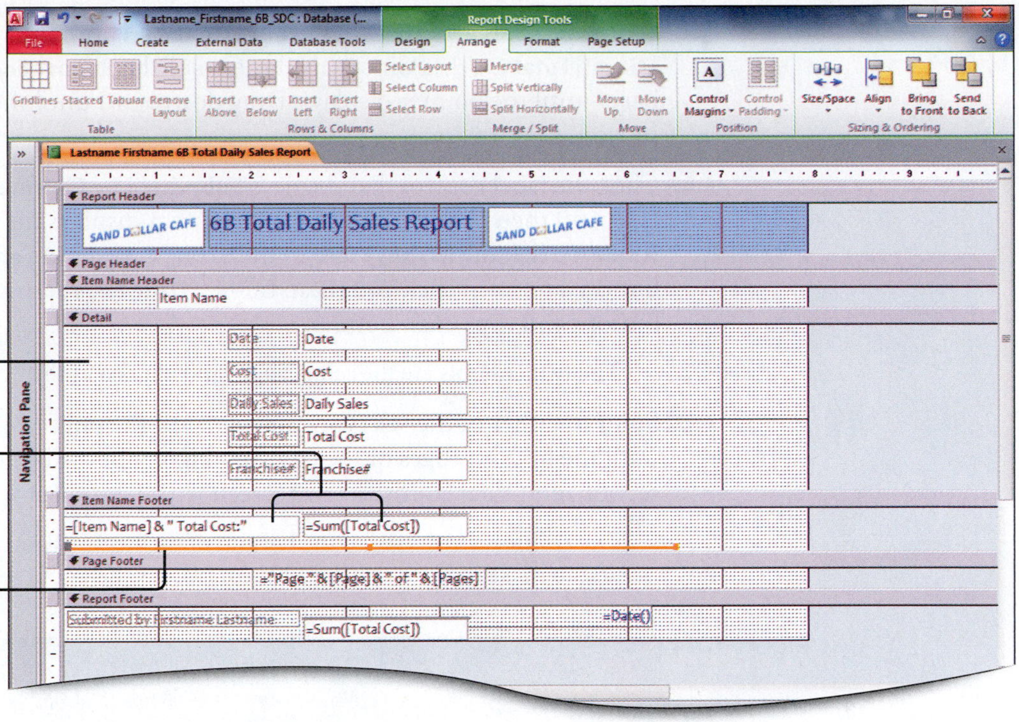

11 **Save** the report, and then switch to **Report** view. Scroll down until the **Grilled Chicken Skewer** grouping displays, and then compare your screen with Figure 6.43.

The report is easier to read with the horizontal line moved to the grouping footer section and with an explanation of the total for the grouping.

Figure 6.43

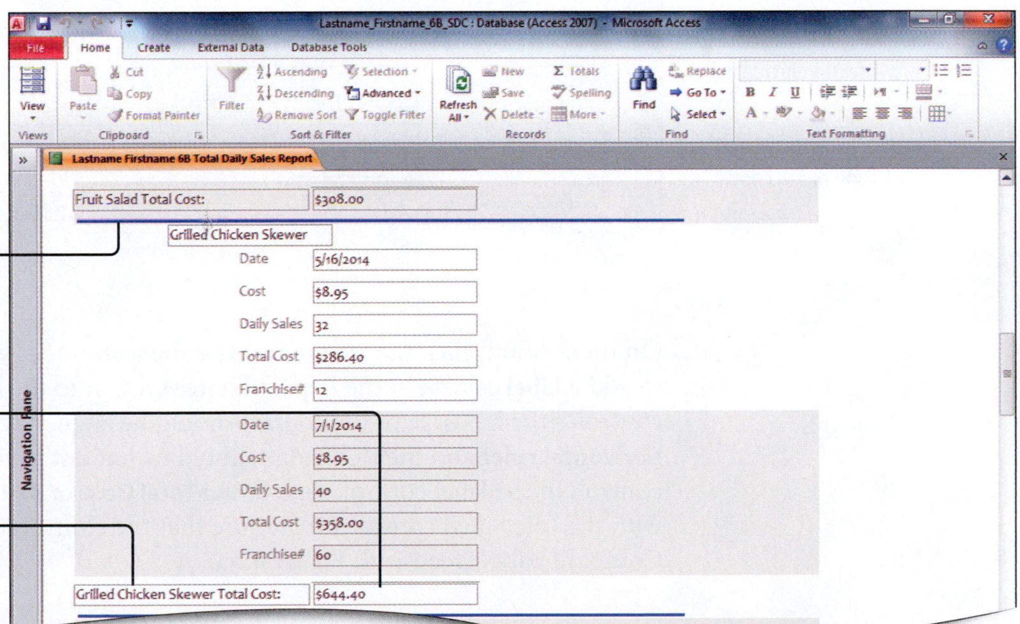

12 Hold down Ctrl, and then press End to move to the end of the report. Notice the sum of **$2,661.80**.

By default, when you insert an aggregate function into a report, a calculated control for the grand total is inserted in the Report Footer section. The control is aligned with the text box control that is being used in the aggregate function. If the Report Footer section is not tall enough and multiple aggregate functions are used, the controls will display on top of one another.

13 Switch to **Design** view. In the **Report Footer** section, the calculated control displays =**Sum**([**Total Cost**]). Point to the bottom of the **Report Footer** section—not the section bar—until the pointer displays. Drag downward until the height of the **Report Footer** section is approximately **1 inch**.

14 Click the label control that displays **Submitted by Firstname Lastname**. Hold down Shift, and then click the text box control that displays the **Date** expression. On the Ribbon, click the **Arrange tab**. In the **Sizing & Ordering group**, click the **Size/Space** button, and then click **To Tallest**. In the **Sizing & Ordering group**, click the **Align** button, and then click **Bottom**.

The two controls are the same height and aligned at the bottom edges of the controls.

15 Point to either of the selected controls until the pointer displays. Drag downward until the bottom edges of the controls align with the bottom edge of the Report Footer section, and then compare your screen with Figure 6.44.

The controls are moved to the bottom of the Report Footer section to increase readability and to make space to insert a label control for the grand total.

Figure 6.44

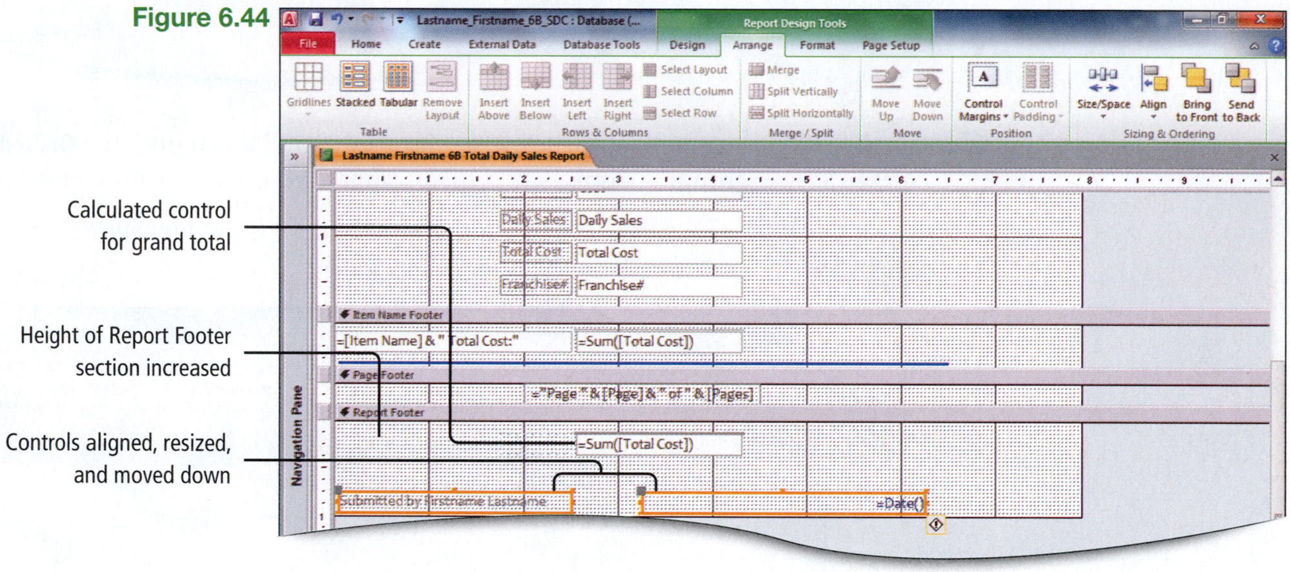

16 On the Ribbon, click the **Design tab**. Use the techniques you have practiced previously to add a **label control** in the Report Footer section to the left of the calculated control—the left edge of the control should be aligned with the **0-inch mark on the horizontal ruler** and the right edge should be **one dot** to the left of the calculated control. In the label control, type **Grand Total Cost of All Items:** Align the label control with the calculated control and be sure that the controls are the same height. Compare your screen with Figure 6.45.

Figure 6.45

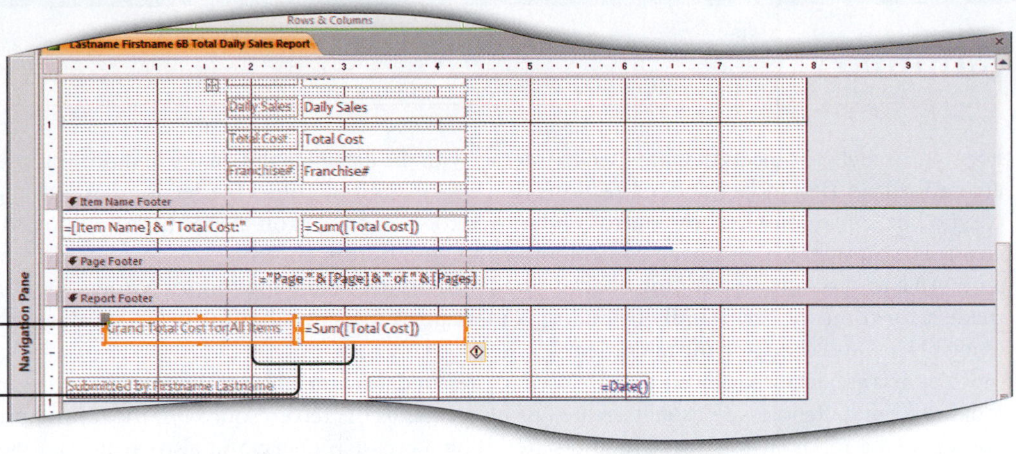

> **Alert! | Does Your Control Display with Two Boxes?**
>
> If your control displays with two boxes—one that displays text and a number; for example Text35, and one that displays Unbound—you selected the Text Box button instead of the Label button. If that happens, click the Undo button, and then begin again.

17 **Save** the report, and then switch to **Report** view. Hold down Ctrl, and then press End to move to the end of the report. Notice that the grand total is now easier to distinguish because a description of the control has been added and the other controls are moved down.

18 Switch to **Print Preview** view. If necessary, on the **Print Preview tab**, in the **Zoom group**, click the **Two Pages** button. Look at the bottom of Page 1 and the top of Page 2, and notice that the grouping breaks across two pages. In the navigation area, click the **Next Page** button to display Pages 3 and 4. Groupings are split between these pages.

For a more professional-looking report, avoid splitting groupings between pages.

19 In the **Close Preview group**, click the **Close Print Preview** button. Switch to **Design** view. On the **Design tab**, in the **Grouping & Totals group**, click the **Group & Sort** button.

20 In the displayed **Group, Sort, and Total Pane**, on the **Group on Item Name** bar, click **More**. Click the **do not keep group together on one page arrow**, and then click **keep whole group together on one page. Close** the **Group, Sort, and Total Pane**—do not click the Delete button.

21 **Save** the report, and then switch to **Print Preview** view. In the navigation area, click the buttons to display pages in the report, and then notice that groupings are no longer split between pages. Also notice that more blank space displays at the bottom of some pages.

22 If you are instructed to submit this result, create a paper or electronic printout. On the **Print Preview tab**, in the **Close Preview group**, click the **Close Print Preview** button. **Close** the report, and then **Open** the **Navigation Pane. Close** the database, and **Close** Access.

> **More Knowledge | Formatting a Report**
>
> You can add a background picture to a report or change the background color of a report using the same techniques you used in forms.

End **You have completed Project 6B**

Content-Based Assessments

Summary

Forms are database objects that are used to interact with the data in tables. In the first project, you created a form in Design view, added sections to the form, and modified the sections. You changed a combo box control to a list box control, and moved controls around on the form. In addition to label controls, you inserted an image control and command button controls. You formatted forms by adding a background color, adding a background picture, and modifying control borders. Finally, you made a form more user friendly by adding a message to the status bar for fields, creating custom ControlTips, and changing the tab order.

Reports are database objects that are used to present data from tables or queries in a professional-looking format. Reports are usually created using queries as the record source. In the second project, you created a report using a wizard and based it on a crosstab query. You also created a report in Design view and modified the sections of the report. You added text box controls to the report that contained expressions. You concatenated strings and field names to build expressions. You also added an image control and a line control to a report. In Design view, you added grouping and sorting levels to the report. You then added calculated controls that used aggregate functions.

Key Terms

Matching

Match each term in the second column with its correct definition in the first column by writing the letter of the term on the blank line in front of the correct definition.

____ 1. An Access object that provides you with a way to enter, edit, and display data from underlying tables.

____ 2. Characteristics that determine the appearance, structure, and behavior of an object.

____ 3. Displays the properties that affect the appearance and behavior of an object.

____ 4. An object in a form or report in Design view that enables individuals to perform actions or view/enhance data.

____ 5. Enables an individual to insert an image into any section of a form or report.

____ 6. Enables an individual to add a command button to a form or report that will perform an action when the button is clicked.

____ 7. The box where the rulers meet, in the upper left corner of a form in Design view.

A Button control
B Control
C ControlTip
D Focus
E Form
F Form selector
G Image control
H Line control
I Point
J Propagate
K Properties
L Property Sheet
M Property Update Options button
N Tab order
O Themes

_____ 8. The measurement equal to 1/72 of an inch.

_____ 9. Text that displays when an individual pauses the mouse pointer over a control on a form.

_____ 10. Refers to the order in which the fields are selected when the Tab key is pressed.

_____ 11. To spread, disseminate, or apply.

_____ 12. A button that enables an individual to update the Property Sheet for a field in all objects that use this table as the record source.

_____ 13. Refers to the object that is selected and currently being acted upon.

_____ 14. A design tool that simplifies the process of creating professional-looking objects.

_____ 15. A control that enables an individual to insert a line in a form or a report.

Multiple Choice

Circle the correct answer.

1. What can be used to further enhance every object on a form, including the form itself?
   A. Layout view **B.** Control sheet **C.** Property sheet

2. Which view should be used to create a form, if you want more control over the creation?
   A. Form view **B.** Design view **C.** Layout view

3. Which property enables you to specify the source of the data for a form or a report?
   A. Object source **B.** Record source **C.** Control source

4. An action is applied to a button control using the
   A. Combo Box Wizard **B.** Button Control Wizard **C.** Command Button Wizard

5. Which Form property is modified to apply color to the background of a form?
   A. Background **B.** Back color **C.** Wallpaper

6. What property determines where the background picture for a form displays on the form?
   A. Picture Alignment **B.** Picture Update **C.** Picture Size Mode

7. In the Picture Size Mode property, which setting stretches the image both vertically and horizontally to match the size of the form?
   A. Zoom **B.** Stretch **C.** Clip

8. Which form property enables an individual to add descriptive text that will display in the status bar for a selected control?
   A. Hint Text **B.** Description **C.** Status Bar Text

9. Which section of a report appears at the top of the first printed page?
   A. Report header **B.** Page header **C.** Detail header

10. Functions that group and perform calculations on multiple fields are
    A. aggregate functions **B.** arithmetic functions **C.** logical functions

Apply 6A skills from these Objectives:

1 Create a Form in Design View
2 Change and Add Controls
3 Format a Form
4 Make a Form User Friendly

Skills Review | Project 6C Party Orders

Marty Kress, Vice President of Marketing for the Sand Dollar Cafe franchise restaurant chain, wants to expand the chain's offerings to include party trays for advance order and delivery. In the following project, you will create a form to use for the data entry of these party order items. Your completed form, if printed, will look similar to Figure 6.46. An electronic version of the form will look slightly different.

Project Files

For Project 6C, you will need the following files:

a06C_Party_Orders
a06C_Logo
a06C_Sand_Dollar

You will save your database as:

Lastname_Firstname_6C_Party_Orders

Project Results

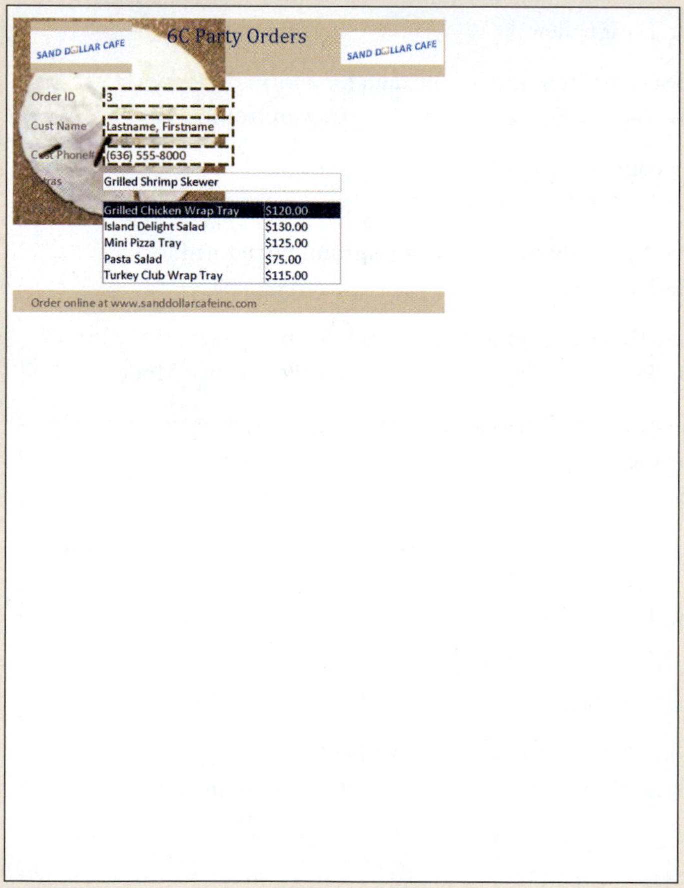

Figure 6.46

(Project 6C Party Orders continues on the next page)

Skills Review | Project **6C** Party Orders (continued)

1 **Start** Access. Locate and open the **a06C_Party_Orders** file. Save the database in your **Access Chapter 6** folder as **Lastname_Firstname_6C_Party_Orders** If necessary, click **Enable Content**.

2 Double-click **6C Party Orders** to open the table in **Datasheet** view. Take a moment to examine the fields in the table.

- **a.** In any record, click in the **Party Tray** field, and then click the **arrow**. This field is a Lookup field in the *6C Trays* table. In any record, click in the **Extras** field, and then click the **arrow**. This field is a Lookup field in the *6C Menu Items* table.
- **b.** **Close** the table, and then close the **Navigation Pane**.

3 On the Ribbon, click the **Create tab**. In the **Forms group**, click the **Form Design** button.

- **a.** If necessary, on the **Design tab**, in the **Tools group**, click the **Property Sheet** button. On the Property Sheet, click the **Data tab**. Click the **Record Source property setting box arrow**, and then click **6C Party Orders**. Close the **Property Sheet**.

4 On the **Design tab**, in the **Tools group**, click the **Add Existing Fields** button.

- **a.** In the **Field List**, click **Order ID**, hold down Shift, and then click **Extras**. Drag the selected fields onto the design grid until the top of the pointer arrow is aligned at **0.25 inch on the vertical ruler** and **2 inches on the horizontal ruler**, and then release the mouse button. **Close** the **Field List**.
- **b.** With all of the controls still selected, on the **Arrange tab**, in the **Table group**, click the **Stacked** button.
- **c.** Drag the left edge of the selected text box controls to the **0.5-inch mark on the horizontal ruler**. Increase the width of the text boxes by approximately **0.5 inch**. Save the form as **Lastname Firstname 6C Party Order Form**

5 On the **Design tab**, in the **Header/Footer group**, click the **Logo** button.

- **a.** Navigate to the location where the student data files for this textbook are saved. Locate and double-click **a06C_Logo** to insert the logo in the **Form Header**.
- **b.** On the selected logo, point to the right middle sizing handle until the pointer displays. Drag to the right until the right edge of the logo is aligned with the **1.5-inch mark on the horizontal ruler**.

6 In the **Header/Footer group**, click the **Title** button.

- **a.** In the **label control** for the title, replace the text with **6C Party Orders** and then press Enter.
- **b.** Drag the right edge of the title to align it with the **4-inch mark on the horizontal ruler**.
- **c.** With the title selected, on the **Format tab**, in the **Font group**, click the **Center** button.

7 Scroll down until the **Form Footer** section bar displays. Point to the top of the **Form Footer** section bar until the pointer displays. Drag upward until the top of the Form Footer section bar aligns with the **2.5-inch mark on the vertical ruler**.

- **a.** On the **Design tab**, in the **Controls group**, click the **Label** button. Point to the **Form Footer** section until the plus sign (+) of the pointer aligns with the bottom of the **Form Footer** section bar and the **0.25-inch mark on the horizontal ruler**. Drag downward to the bottom of the **Form Footer** section and to the right to the **3.25-inch mark on the horizontal ruler**.
- **b.** Type **Order online at www.sanddollarcafeinc.com** and then press Enter.
- **c.** With the **label control** in the **Form Footer** section selected, hold down Shift, and then click the **Logo control** and the **Extras label control**. On the Ribbon, click the **Arrange tab**. In the **Sizing & Ordering group**, click the **Align** button, and then click **Left**. **Save** the form.

8 Click and hold the **Party Tray text box control** until the pointer displays. Drag downward until a thin orange line displays on the bottom edges of the **Extras** controls and then release the mouse button.

- **a.** With the **Party Tray text box control** selected, hold down Shift, and then click the **Party Tray label control, Extras text box control**, and **Extras label control**.
- **b.** On the **Arrange tab**, in the **Table group**, click the **Remove Layout** button to remove the *Extras* field and the *Party Tray* field from the stacked layout.
- **c.** Click in the **Detail** section to deselect the controls. Right-click the **Party Tray combo box control**. From the shortcut menu, point to **Change To**, and then click **List Box**.

(Project 6C Party Orders continues on the next page)

Skills Review | Project 6C Party Orders (continued)

d. **Save** the form, and then switch to **Form** view. Notice that the **Party Tray list box control** is not wide enough to display all columns and that there are horizontal and vertical scroll bars to indicate there is more data.

e. Click the **Extras combo box arrow** to be sure that none of the menu item names and prices are cut off. Press Esc.

f. Switch to **Design** view, and click the **Party Tray list box control**. Point to the right edge of the control until the pointer displays. Drag to the right until the right edge of the control aligns with the **4-inch mark on the horizontal ruler**.

g. Switch to **Layout** view. Resize the **Extras combo box control** to be the same size as the **Party Tray list box control**. **Save** the form and switch to **Design** view. Click the **Form Header section bar**.

9 On the **Design tab**, in the **Controls group**, click the **Insert Image** button, and then click **Browse**. In the displayed **Insert Picture** dialog box, navigate to the location where the student data files for this textbook are saved.

a. Locate and double-click **a06C_Logo**.

b. Align the plus sign with the bottom of the **Form Header** section bar and with the **4-inch mark on the horizontal ruler**. Drag downward to the top of the **Detail** section bar and to the right to the **5.25-inch mark on the horizontal ruler**.

c. Click the **image control**—the Sand Dollar Cafe image on the right side in the **Form Header** section. On the **Design tab**, in the **Tools group**, click the **Property Sheet** button. If necessary, on the **Format tab**, change the **Width** property setting to **1.25** and then change the **Height** property setting to **0.625**.

d. In the **Form Header** section, click the **logo control**. On the **Property Sheet**, change the **Width** property setting to **1.25** and change the **Height** property setting to **0.625**.

e. With the logo control selected, hold down Shift, and then click the **image control**. On the **Arrange tab**, in the **Sizing & Ordering group**, click the **Align** button, and then click **Top**. **Close** the **Property Sheet**.

10 On the Ribbon, click the **Design tab**, and then in the **Controls group**, click the **Button** button.

a. Move the mouse pointer down into the **Detail** section. Align the plus sign (+) of the pointer at **0.25 inches on the vertical ruler** and **3 inches on the horizontal ruler**, and then click.

b. Under **Categories**, click **Record Navigation**. Under **Actions**, click **Find Record**, and then click **Next** two times. In the text box, type **btnFindRecord** and then click Finish.

c. Using the technique you just practiced, add a **button control** right next to the **Find Record button**. Under **Categories**, click **Form Operations**. Under **Actions**, click **Print Current Form**, and then click **Next** two times. Name the button **btnPrtForm** Click **Finish**.

d. With the **Print Current Form button control** selected, hold down Shift, and then click the **Find Record button control**. On the **Arrange tab**, in the **Sizing & Ordering group**, click the **Align** button, and then click **Top**.

11 Switch to **Layout** view. Click in the **Form Footer** section to the right of the label control.

a. On the **Format tab**, in the **Font group**, click the **Background Color** button. Under **Theme Colors**, in the second row, click the third color—**Tan, Background 2, Darker 10%**.

b. Using the technique you just practiced, change the color of the **Form Header** section to match the **Form Footer** section.

12 Switch to **Design** view, and then double-click the **Form selector** to open the Property Sheet for the form.

a. On the **Property Sheet**, on the **Format tab**, click in the **Picture** property setting box, and then click the **Build** button. Navigate to where the student data files for this textbook are saved. Locate and double-click **a06C_Sand_Dollar** to insert the picture in the form.

b. Click in the **Picture Alignment** property setting box, click the **arrow**, and then click **Form Center**. **Close** the **Property Sheet**, and then **save** the form.

13 Switch to **Layout** view, click the **Order ID text box control**, hold down Shift, and then click the **Cust Name text box control** and the **Cust Phone# text box control**.

(Project 6C Party Orders continues on the next page)

Skills Review | Project 6C Party Orders (continued)

a. On the **Format tab**, in the **Control Formatting group**, click the **Shape Outline** button. Point to **Line Type**, and click the third line type—**Dashes**.

b. On the **Format tab**, in the **Control Formatting group**, click the **Shape Outline** button. Point to **Line Thickness**, and then click the third line type—**2 pt**.

c. In the **Control Formatting group**, click the **Shape Outline button**. Under **Theme Colors**, in the fifth row, click the third color—**Tan, Background 2, Darker 75%**.

14 Switch to **Form** view, and then click in the **Cust Phone# text box control**. On the left side of the status bar, *Form View* displays—there is no text that helps an individual enter data. **Close** the form, **Save** your changes, and open the **Navigation Pane**.

a. Under **Tables**, right-click **6C Party Orders**; from the shortcut menu, click **Design View**. In the **Cust Phone#** field, click in the **Description** box. Type **Include area code for 10-digit dialing** and then press Enter.

b. Click the **Property Update Options** button, and then click **Update Status Bar Text everywhere Cust Phone# is used**. In the displayed **Update Properties** dialog box, click **Yes**. **Close** the table, saving changes.

15 Open **6C Party Order Form** in **Design** view. Close the **Navigation Pane**. If necessary, on the **Design** tab, in the **Tools** group, click the **Property Sheet** button.

a. Click the **Print Form** button in the **Detail** section. Notice that the **Property Sheet** is displayed for the button you selected.

b. On the **Other tab**, click in the ControlTip Text property setting box, type **Prints the Current Form** to replace the existing **Print Form** text, and then press Enter.

c. **Close** the **Property Sheet**, Save the form, and then switch to **Form** view. Point to the **Print Form** button to display the ControlTip.

16 Switch to **Design** view. In the **Detail** section, click the **Order ID text box control**, hold down Shift, and then click the **Find Record button control** and the **Print Current Form button control**.

a. On the **Design tab**, in the **Tools group**, click the **Property Sheet** button. If necessary, on the **Property Sheet**, click the **Other tab**. On the **Property Sheet**, click in the **Tab Stop** property setting box, click the **arrow**, and then click **No**.

b. Click the **Cust Name text box control**. Click in the **Tab Index** property setting box, and then type **0** **Close** the **Property Sheet**.

17 Switch to **Form** view. With the **Cust Name** control selected, click the **Find Record** button.

a. In the **Find and Replace** dialog box, in the **Find What** box, type **Gonzalez, Ricardo** Click **Find Next**. **Close** the Find and Replace dialog box.

b. In the Cust Name text box, type your **Lastname, Firstname** replacing Ricardo's name. Press Tab. In the **Cust Phone#** field, enter your phone number, and then press Enter. **Save** the form.

18 If you are instructed to submit this result, click the **Print Current Form** button to create a paper or electronic printout. If you are to submit your work electronically, follow your instructor's directions.

19 **Close** the form, open the **Navigation Pane**, **Close** the database, and then **Exit** Access.

End **You have completed Project 6C**

Apply 6B skills from these Objectives:

- 5 Create a Report Based on a Query Using a Wizard
- 6 Create a Report in Design View
- 7 Add Controls to a Report
- 8 Group, Sort, and Total Records in Design View

Skills Review | Project 6D Catering

The individual restaurants of Sand Dollar Cafe each maintain a database about the orders that are placed for the catering entity of the business. Reports are run to summarize data in the tables or queries. Creating customized reports will help the managers of each location view the information in the database in a meaningful way. In this project, you will create customized reports. Your completed reports will look similar to Figure 6.47.

Project Files

For Project 6D, you will need the following files:

a06D_Catering
a06D_Logo

You will save your database as:

Lastname_Firstname_6D_Catering

Project Results

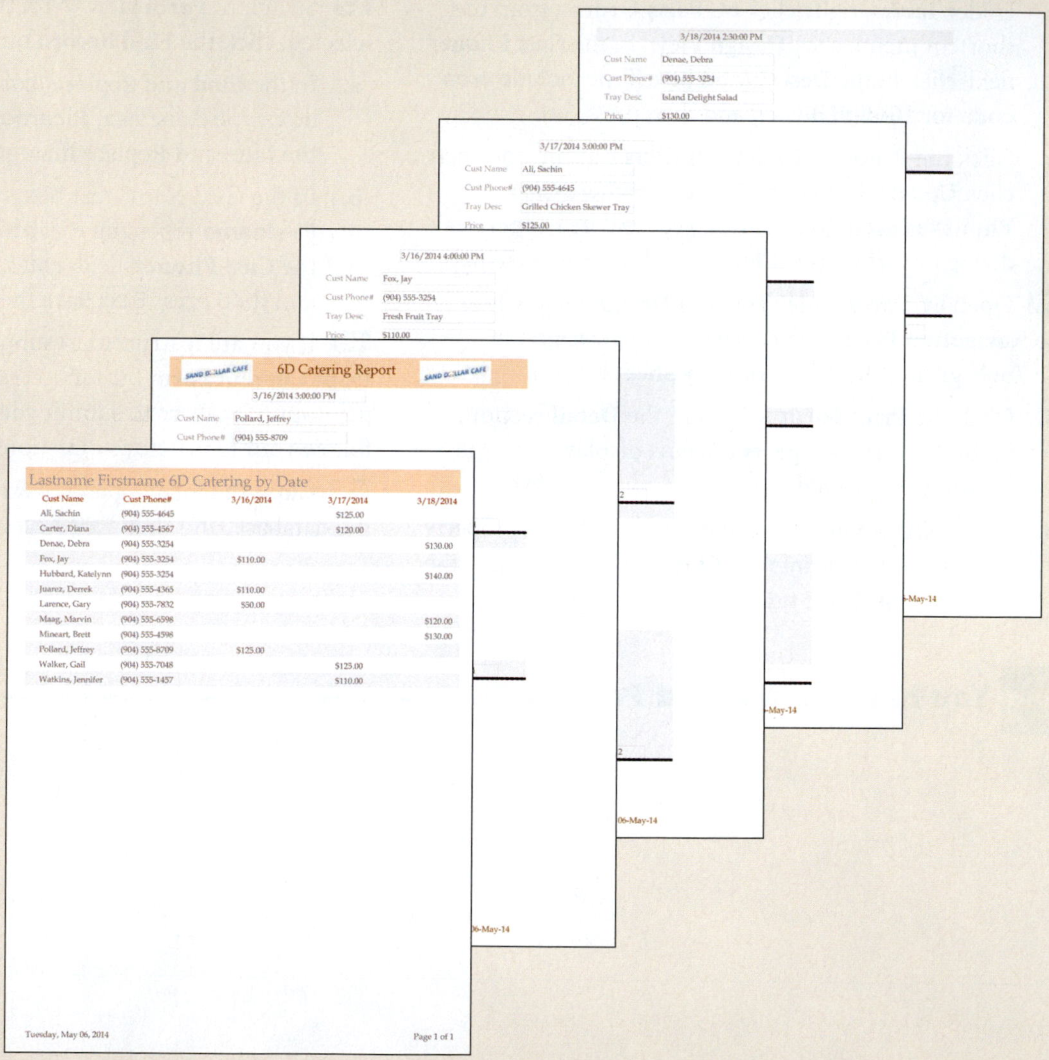

Figure 6.47

(Project 6D Catering continues on the next page)

Content-Based Assessments

Skills Review | Project 6D Catering (continued)

1 **Start** Access. Locate and open the **a06D_Catering** file. Save the database in your **Access Chapter 6** folder as **Lastname_Firstname_6D_Catering** If necessary, click **Enable Content**.

2 In the Navigation Pane, under **Queries**, double-click **6D Catering _ Crosstab Query**. Take a moment to study the data in the query. **Close** the query, and then close the **Navigation Pane**.

3 On the Ribbon, click the **Create tab**. In the **Reports group**, click the **Report Wizard** button.

a. Click the **Tables/Queries arrow**, and then click **Query: 6D Catering Crosstab Query**. Under **Available Fields**, click the **All Fields** button to add all of the field names to the **Selected Fields** box. Click **Next** twice.

b. Click the **arrow** next to the **1** box, and then click **Cust Name**. Leave the sort order as **Ascending**, and then click **Next**.

c. Under **Layout**, be sure the **Tabular** option button is selected. Under **Orientation**, be sure the **Portrait** option button is selected. Be sure the **Adjust the field width so all fields fit on a page** check box is selected. Click **Next**.

d. For the title of the report, type **Lastname Firstname 6D Catering by Date** Select **Modify the report's design**, and then click **Finish**.

4 On the Ribbon, click the **Design tab**. In the **Themes group**, click the **Themes** button, and then click the first theme on the sixth row—**Hardcover**.

5 Switch to **Layout** view. If necessary, in the **Cust Phone# column**, point to the right edge of any **text box control**, and then drag to the right until all of the data displays. Click in a blank area of the report to deselect the column. Switch to **Design** view. Drag the right edge of the report to the **7.75-inch mark on the horizontal ruler**.

6 Select all of the controls in the **Page Header** section, by pointing to the top left of the **Page Header** section, holding down your mouse button, and then dragging the mouse across the **Page Header controls** and to the bottom of the **Page Header** section. Release the mouse button.

a. On the **Format tab**, in the **Font group**, click the **Font color button arrow**. Under **Theme Colors**, on the first row, click the fifth color—**Dark Red, Accent 1**.

7 **Save** the report, and then switch to **Print Preview**. If you are instructed to submit this result, create a paper or electronic printout. **Close Print Preview**. **Close** the report.

8 On the Ribbon, click the **Create tab**. In the **Reports group**, click the **Report Design** button.

a. On the **Design tab**, in the **Tools group**, click the **Property Sheet** button. On the **Property Sheet**, click the **Data tab**. Click the **Record Source arrow**, click **6D Catering**, and then **Close** the **Property Sheet**.

b. On the **Design tab**, in the **Tools group**, click the **Add Existing Fields** button. If necessary, click **Show only fields in the current record source** at the bottom of the Field List box.

c. In the **Field List**, click **Pickup Time**. Hold down Shift, and then click **Price** to select all of the fields. Drag the selected fields into the **Detail** section until the top of the arrow of the pointer is aligned with the **0.25-inch mark on the vertical ruler** and with the **1.5-inch mark on the horizontal ruler**.

d. With the controls still selected, on the Ribbon, click the **Arrange tab**. In the **Table group**, click the **Stacked** button. **Close** the **Field List**, and then **Save** the report as **Lastname Firstname 6D Catering Report**

9 On the **Design tab**, in the **Header/Footer group**, click the **Logo** button.

a. Locate and double-click **a06D_Logo** to insert the logo in the Report Header section.

b. On the selected logo, point to the right middle sizing handle until the pointer displays. Drag to the right until the right edge of the logo is aligned with the **1.5-inch mark on the horizontal ruler**.

10 On the **Design tab**, in the **Header/Footer group**, click the **Title** button. In the **title's label control**, select **Lastname Firstname**, and then press Del.

11 Point to the top edge of the **Page Footer** section bar until the pointer displays. Drag upward until the top of the **Page Footer** section bar aligns with the **2-inch mark on the vertical ruler**.

12 Point to the top edge of the **Detail** section bar until the pointer displays. Drag upward until the top edge of the **Detail** section bar aligns with the bottom edge of the **Page Header** section bar. **Save** the report.

13 On the **Design tab**, in the **Header/Footer group**, click the **Page Numbers** button.

a. In the displayed **Page Numbers** dialog box, under **Format**, click **Page N**. Under **Position**, click **Bottom of Page [Footer]**, and then click **OK**.

(Project 6D Catering continues on the next page)

Skills Review | Project 6D Catering (continued)

b. Resize and move the **Page Number control box** until it fits between the **2-inch and 4-inch marks on the horizontal ruler**.

14 On the **Design tab**, in the **Controls group**, click the **Label** button.

a. Drag the plus sign (+) from the bottom edge of the **Report Footer** section bar at the **0.25-inch mark on the horizontal ruler** to the bottom of the **Report Footer** section at the **3-inch mark on the horizontal ruler**.

b. Using your own first and last names, type **Catering Manager: Firstname Lastname** Press Enter.

15 On the **Design tab**, in the **Header/Footer group**, click the **Date & Time** button. In the **Date and Time** dialog box, under **Include Date**, click the second option button. Under **Include Time**, remove the check mark, and then click **OK**. **Save** the report.

a. Click the **Date text box control**. On the Ribbon, click the **Arrange tab**. In the **Table group**, click the **Remove Layout** button.

b. Right-click the selected control, and click **Cut**. Right-click the **Page Footer** section, and click **Paste**.

c. Move the **Date text box control** until the right edge of the text box control aligns with the **6.25-inch mark on the horizontal ruler**.

d. Click the **Title text box control** to select it, point to the right middle sizing handle until the pointer displays, and then drag to the right until the right edge of the text box control aligns with the **4.75-inch mark on the horizontal ruler**.

16 Drag the right edge of the design grid to the left until it aligns with the **6.5-inch mark on the horizontal ruler**. **Save** the report.

a. Switch to **Layout** view. In the first record, click the **Tray Desc text box control**, and then point to the right edge of the control until the pointer displays. Drag to the right until all of the text displays in the **Tray Desc text box control**—*Grilled Chicken Skewer Tray*.

17 Switch to **Design** view. In the **Report Header** section, right-click the **logo control**. From the displayed shortcut menu, click **Copy**. Right-click anywhere in the **Report Header** section, and then from the shortcut menu, click **Paste**.

a. Point to the selected logo, and then drag to the right until the left edge of the outlined control aligns with the **4.75-inch mark on the horizontal ruler**.

b. With the image control on the right selected, hold down Shift, and then click the **logo control**. On the Ribbon, click the **Arrange tab**. In the **Sizing & Ordering group**, click the **Align** button, and then click **Bottom**.

c. Resize the **Title text box control** so the right edge is **one dot** away from the image on its right. **Center** the title in the control. Drag the **Page Header section bar** up to the **0.5-inch mark on the vertical ruler**.

18 On the **Design tab**, in the **Grouping & Totals group**, click the **Group & Sort** button.

a. In the **Group, Sort, and Total Pane**, click the **Add a group** button. From the displayed list, click **Pickup Time**.

b. Click the **by quarter arrow** that displays after **from oldest to newest**, and then click **by entire value**. Click the **More arrow**, click the **do not keep group together on one page arrow**, and then click **keep whole group together on one page**.

c. In the **Group, Sort, and Total Pane**, click the **Add a sort** button, and then click **Cust Name**. **Close** the **Group, Sort, and Total Pane**.

19 In the **Detail** section, click the **Pickup Time text box control**. Drag downward until a thin orange line displays at the bottom of the **Price** controls, and then release the mouse button.

a. On the Ribbon, click the **Arrange tab**. In the **Table group**, click the **Remove Layout** button.

b. Move the **Pickup Time text box control** into the **Pickup Time Header** section so the left edge of the text box control aligns with the **1.5-inch mark on the horizontal ruler**.

c. In the **Pickup Time Header** section, click the **Pickup Time label control**, and then press Del.

20 In the **Detail** section, click the **Tray Desc text box control**. On the **Design tab**, in the **Grouping & Totals group**, click the **Totals** button. In the displayed list of aggregate functions, click **Count Records**.

21 In the **Pickup Time Footer** section, select the **Count text box control**, and then holding down Shift, in the **Report Footer** select the **Count text box control**.

(Project 6D Catering continues on the next page)

Skills Review | Project 6D Catering (continued)

a. On the Ribbon, click the **Arrange tab**. In the **Table group**, click the **Remove Layout** button.

b. Align and resize the controls so the left edge of each control is even with the **5.5-inch marker on the horizontal ruler** and the right edge of each control is even with the **6-inch marker on the horizontal ruler**.

c. On the **Design tab**, in the **Controls group**, click the **Text Box** button. Drag the plus sign (+) from the bottom edge of the **Pickup Time Footer** section at the **2.75-inch mark on the horizontal ruler** to the bottom of the **Pickup Time Footer** section and to the right to the **5.5-inch mark on the horizontal ruler**.

d. Type **=[Pickup Time] & " # of Orders:"** In the **Pickup Time Footer** section, click the **label control** that displays to the left of the text box control, and then press Del.

e. In the **Pickup Time Footer** section, click the **text box control** that contains the expression you typed. Hold down Shift and click the **count calculated control** in the **Pickup Time Footer**. On the Ribbon, click the **Arrange tab**. In the **Sizing & Ordering group**, click **Size/Space**, and then click **To Tallest**. In the **Sizing & Ordering group**, click the **Align** button, and then click **Bottom**.

22 Drag the right edge of the design grid to the left until it aligns with the **6.5-inch mark on the horizontal ruler**. Switch to **Report** view. Hold down Ctrl, and then press End to move to the end of the report.

23 Switch to **Design** view. Point to the bottom of the **Report Footer** section, and then drag downward until it reaches the **0.5-inch mark on the vertical ruler**.

a. Click the **Count text box control** in the **Report Footer** section, and then drag downward until the bottom edge of the control aligns with the bottom edge of the **Report Footer** section.

b. Use the techniques you have practiced to add a label control in the **Report Footer** section to the left of the calculated control—the left edge of the control should be aligned with the **4-inch mark on the horizontal ruler**. In the **label control**, type **Total # of Orders:**

c. Align the label control with the calculated control and then be sure that the controls are the same height.

24 On the Ribbon, click the **Design tab**. In the **Controls group**, click the **Line** button. Point to the bottom of the **Pickup Time Footer** section until the middle of the plus sign (+) of the pointer aligns with the top of the **Page Footer** section bar and the **0-inch mark on the horizontal ruler**. Hold down Shift, drag to the right to the **6.5-inch mark on the horizontal ruler**, and then release the mouse button and Shift.

25 On the **Format tab**, in the **Control Formatting group**, click the **Shape Outline** button. Click **Line Thickness**, and then click the fourth line—**3 pt**. In the **Control Formatting group**, click the **Shape Outline** button. Under **Theme Colors**, on the first row, click the fifth color—**Dark Red, Accent 1**. **Save** the report.

26 Switch to **Print Preview**. Adjust the margins or report width as needed. If you are instructed to submit this result, create a paper or electronic printout. **Close Print Preview**.

Close the report, and then open the **Navigation Pane**. **Close** the database, and then **Exit** Access.

End **You have completed Project 6D**

Apply **6A** skills from these Objectives:

1. Create a Form in Design View
2. Change and Add Controls
3. Format a Form
4. Make a Form User Friendly

Mastering Access | Project 6E Monthly Promotions

In the following project, you will create a form that will be used to enter the data for the monthly promotions that are offered to guests of the Sand Dollar Cafe restaurant franchise. Your task includes designing a form that will be attractive and provide data entry ease for the staff. Your completed form will look similar to Figure 6.48.

Project Files

For Project 6E, you will need the following files:

a06E_Monthly_Promotions
a06E_Logo
a06E_Dollar

You will save your database as:

Lastname_Firstname_6E_Monthly_Promotions

Project Results

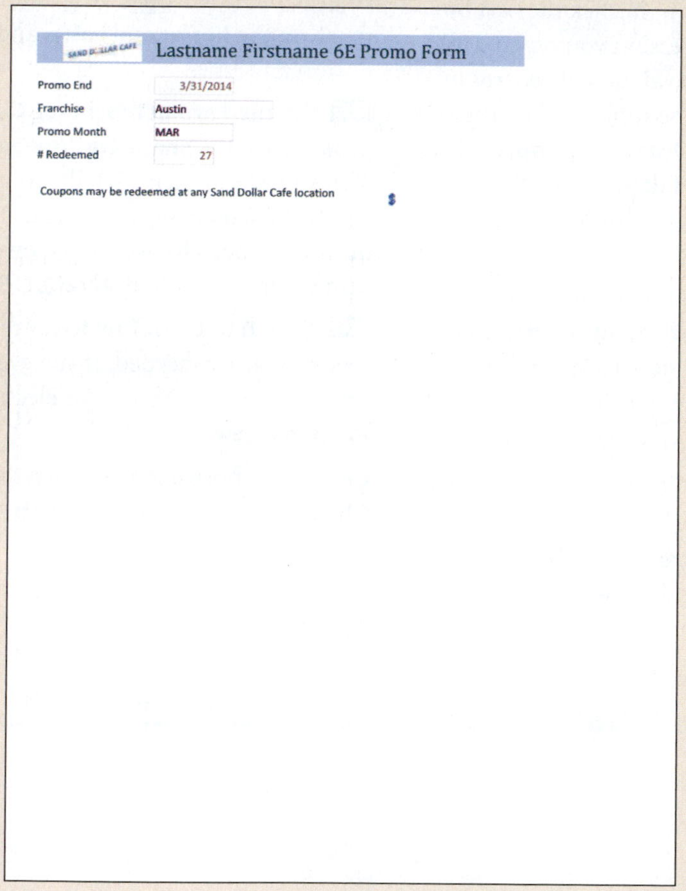

Figure 6.48

(Project 6E Monthly Promotions continues on the next page)

Mastering Access | Project 6E Monthly Promotions (continued)

1 **Start** Access. Locate and open the **a06E_Monthly_Promotions** file. Save the database in your **Access Chapter 6** folder as **Lastname_Firstname_6E_Monthly_Promotions** If necessary, click **Enable Content**.

2 On the **Create tab**, in the **Forms group**, click the **Form Design** button. Display the **Property Sheet**. On the **Data tab**, click the **Record Source property setting box arrow**, and then click **6E Monthly Results**. **Close** the **Property Sheet**.

3 On the **Design tab**, in the **Tools group**, click **Add Existing Fields**. In the **Field List**, display the fields for the *6E Monthly Results* table, and then select all of the fields. Drag the selected fields onto the design grid until the top of the arrow of the pointer is aligned with the **0.25-inch mark on the vertical ruler** and aligned with the **1-inch mark on the horizontal ruler**. **Close** the **Field List**.

4 With all of the text box controls selected, display the **Property Sheet**, and then click the **Format tab**. In the **Left** property box, type **1.5** and press Enter. Click anywhere in the **Detail** section to deselect the controls. Select the **Franchise text box control**, and then drag the right edge to the **3-inch mark on the horizontal ruler**. Select the **# Redeemed text box control**, and in the **Property Sheet**, on the **Format tab**, click in the **Width** property box, and then type **0.75** and press Enter. **Save** the form as **Lastname Firstname 6E Promo Form** Switch to **Form** view, and then click the **Promo Month** text box control to view the entries. Switch to **Design** view, and **Close** the Property Sheet.

5 On the **Design tab**, in the **Header/Footer group**, click the **Logo** button, and then insert the **a06E_Logo**. Widen the selected logo to the **1.5-inch mark on the horizontal ruler**.

6 In the **Header/Footer group**, add a **Title**, and then, if necessary, resize the **Title label control** so the entire title is visible. With the title selected, select all of the label controls. On the **Format tab**, in the **Font group**, change the font color to **Aqua, Accent 5, Darker 50%**—the ninth color in the sixth row under Theme colors.

7 Scroll down until the **Form Footer** section bar displays. Point to the top of the **Form Footer**; drag up until the top of the Form Footer section bar aligns with the **1.5-inch mark on the vertical ruler**.

8 On the **Design tab**, in the **Controls group**, click the **Label** button. Point to the **Form Footer** section until the plus sign (+) of the pointer aligns with the bottom of the **Form Footer** section bar and with the **0-inch mark on the horizontal ruler**. Drag downward to the bottom of the **Form Footer** section and to the right to the **4-inch mark on the horizontal ruler**. Type **Coupons may be redeemed at any Sand Dollar Cafe location** Press Enter. Use the techniques you have practiced previously to change the font color to **Aqua, Accent 5, Darker 50%**.

9 On the **Design tab**, in the **Controls group**, click the **Image** button. Move the mouse pointer down into the **Form Footer** section. Align the plus sign (+) of the pointer with the top of the **Form Footer** section and with the **4.25-inch mark on the horizontal ruler**.

10 Drag downward to the bottom of the **Form Footer** section and to the right to the **5-inch mark on the horizontal ruler**. Locate and insert the file **a06E_Dollar**. Display the Property Sheet, and change the **Width** and **Height** to **0.35**

11 On the **Design tab**, in the **Controls group**, click the **Button** button. Move the mouse pointer down into the **Detail** section. Align the plus sign (+) of the pointer with the **0.5-inch mark on the vertical ruler** and the **3.5-inch mark on the horizontal ruler**, and then click.

12 Under **Categories**, click **Form Operations**. Under **Actions**, click **Close Form**, and then click **Next**. Select the **Text** radio button, and then click **Next**. In the text box, type **btnCloseForm** and then click **Finish**. With the button selected, click the **Format tab**, and, in the **Font group**, change the **Font Color** to **Aqua, Accent 5, Darker 50%**.

13 With the **Close Form** button selected, click the **Property Sheet** button. Click the **Other tab**, click in the **Tab Stop** property setting box, click the **arrow**, and then click **No**. **Close** the **Property Sheet**.

14 If you are instructed to submit this result, create a paper or electronic printout of **record 8**. If you are to submit your work electronically, follow your instructor's directions.

15 Click the **Close Form** button, saving changes. Open the **Navigation Pane**. **Close** the database, and then **Exit** Access.

End **You have completed Project 6E**

Apply **6B** skills from these Objectives:

- **5** Create a Report Based on a Query Using a Wizard
- **6** Create a Report in Design View
- **7** Add Controls to a Report
- **8** Group, Sort, and Total Records in Design View

Mastering Access | Project 6F Promotional Results

In the following project, you will create a report that will display the promotions that are offered to guests of the Sand Dollar Cafe restaurant franchise. You will also create a crosstab report that will summarize the results of the promotions. Creating customized reports will help the managers of each location view the information in the database in a meaningful way. Your completed reports will look similar to Figure 6.49.

Project Files

For Project 6F, you will need the following files:

a06F_Promotional_Results
a06F_Logo

You will save your database as:

Lastname_Firstname_6F_Promotional_Results

Project Results

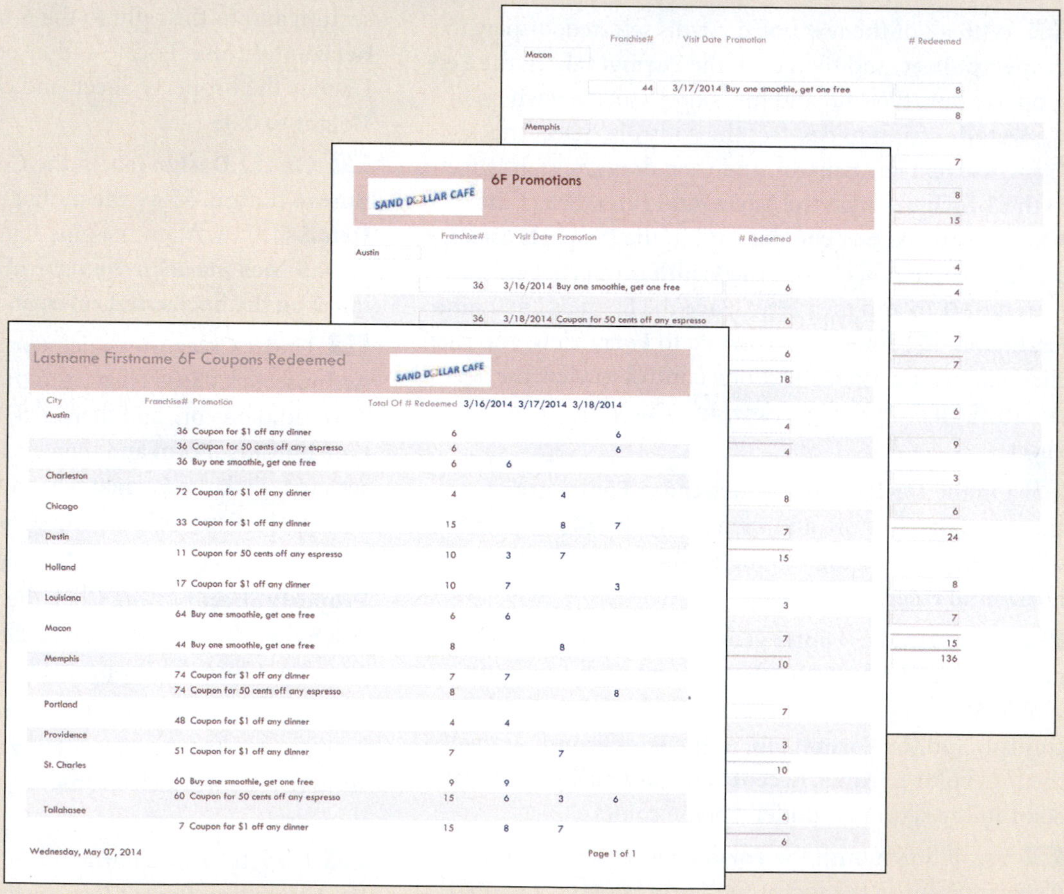

Figure 6.49

(Project 6F Promotional Results continues on the next page)

Mastering Access | Project 6F Promotional Results (continued)

1 **Start** Access. Locate and open the **a06F_Promotional Results** file. Save the database in your **Access Chapter 6** folder as **Lastname_Firstname_6F_Promotional_Results** If necessary, click **Enable Content**.

2 Under **Queries**, double-click the **6F Coupons Crosstab Query**. Take a moment to study the data in the query. **Close** the query, and then close the **Navigation Pane**.

3 **Create** a report using the **Report Wizard**. From the **Query: 6F Coupons Crosstab Query**, select all of the fields. Under **Do you want to add any grouping or levels?**, select **City**. **Sort** the records within the report by **Franchise#** in **Ascending** order. Under **Layout**, be sure the **Stepped** option button is selected. Under **Orientation**, click the **Landscape** option button. Be sure the **Adjust the field width so all fields fit on a page** check box is selected. For the title of the report, type **Lastname Firstname 6F Coupons Redeemed** Select **Modify the report's design**, and then click **Finish**.

4 Switch to **Layout** view. If any data is cut off, select the label control, and drag to the right to widen the column to display all data. Reduce the width of any columns that display a lot of blank space to allow for the widened columns. On the **Design tab**, click the **Themes** button, and then apply the **Median** theme.

5 Switch to **Design** view. Insert the **a06F_Logo** image so it appears from the **5.5-inch mark on the horizontal ruler** to the **7-inch mark**, and is the height of the Report Header section.

6 Select the three **Date label controls and textbox controls**. Change the width to **0.8** Change the **Font Color** to **Ice Blue, Accent 1, Darker 50%**—the fifth option in the sixth row under **Theme Colors**.

7 Resize and move controls so you can resize the report to **9.5 inches**, and it prints on one landscape page. **Save** the report. If you are instructed to submit this result, create a paper or electronic printout. **Close** the report.

8 Open the **6F Coupons** query. Switch to **Design** view, and then notice the underlying tables that were used in the creation of the query. **Close** the query, and then close the **Navigation Pane**.

9 On the **Create tab**, open a new report in **Report Design**. On the **Design tab**, display the **Property Sheet**. On the **Data tab**, click the **Record Source property setting box arrow**, and then click **6F Coupons**. **Close** the **Property Sheet**. Display the **Field List**.

10 From the **Field List**, select all fields included in the query. Drag the selected fields into the **Detail** section of the design grid until the top of the pointer is aligned with the **0.25-inch mark on the vertical ruler** and the **1-inch mark on the horizontal ruler**. With the controls selected, on the **Arrange tab**, in the **Table group**, click the **Tabular** button. **Close** the **Field List**. Drag the **Page Footer section bar** up to the **0.5-inch mark on the vertical ruler**.

11 **Save** the report as **Lastname Firstname 6F Promotions** Switch to **Layout** view to be sure all data is visible in the report. If necessary, adjust the width of any columns where data is cut off. Switch to **Design** view.

12 On the **Design tab**, click the **Group & Sort** button. Click the **Add a group** button, and then from the displayed list, click **City**. Apply **Keep whole group together on one page**. Click the **Add a sort** button, and then click **Visit Date**. **Close** the **Group, Sort, and Total Pane**.

13 In the **Page Header** section, click the **City** label control, and then press Del. In the **Detail** section, right-click the **City text box control** to display the shortcut menu, and click **Cut**. Click the **City Header** section bar to select it, right-click to display the shortcut menu, and click **Paste**

14 In the **Detail** section, click the **#Redeemed text box control**. On the **Design tab**, click the **Totals** button. From the list of aggregate functions, click **Sum**. Point to the top edge of the **Report Footer** section bar, and then drag up to the bottom of the **Page Footer** section bar.

15 On the **Design tab**, in the **Header/Footer group**, click the **Logo** button, and then insert the **a06F_Logo**. On the **Property Sheet**, increase the width to **1.75** inches and the height to **0.75** inches. In the **Header/Footer group**, click **Title**. Delete your Lastname Firstname from the beginning of the title.

16 Add a **label control** to the **Report Footer**. Position the plus sign of the pointer at the bottom of the **Report Footer** section bar and the **3.5-inch mark on the horizontal ruler**. Drag upward to the top of the **Report Footer** section and to the right to the left edge of the Sum control box. Type **Total # Redeemed Coupons**

(Project 6F Promotional Results continues on the next page)

Mastering Access | Project 6F Promotional Results (continued)

17 Click the **Date & Time** button. Under **Include Date**, click the second option button. Do not **Include Time**. Remove the **Date text box control** from the **Layout**.

18 Move the control to the left edge of the **Report Footer**. In the **Report Footer** section, click the **Date text box control** two times. Position the insertion point between the equal sign and the *D*. Type **"Prepared by Firstname Lastname on "&** and then Press Enter. Click the **Title label control**, and resize it so the right edge aligns with the **4-inch mark on the horizontal ruler**. Resize the report to **6.5 inches wide**.

19 Select all of the controls in the **Report Footer**. Be sure they are all the same height and aligned at the bottom.

20 Switch to **Layout** view, and then adjust all controls to fit the data without extending beyond the right margin. **Save** the report. If you are instructed to submit this result, create a paper or electronic printout in **Landscape** orientation. **Close** the report.

21 Open the **Navigation Pane**, **Close** the database, and then **Exit** Access.

End **You have completed Project 6F**

Content-Based Assessments

Apply 6A and 6B skills from these Objectives:

1. Create a Form in Design View
2. Change and Add Controls
3. Format a Form
4. Make a Form User Friendly
5. Create a Report Based on a Query Using a Wizard

Mastering Access | Project 6G Wireless

Marty Kress, Vice President of Marketing for Sand Dollar Cafe Franchises, keeps a database on the wireless usage per franchise on a monthly basis. The individual restaurants report the number of customers using the wireless connections and the average length of usage per customer. In this project, you will design a form for the data entry of this data and design a report that can be used by Mr. Kress to plan next year's marketing strategies. Your completed work will look similar to Figure 6.50.

Project Files

For Project 6G, you will need the following files:

a06G_Wireless
a06G_Logo

You will save your database as:

Lastname_Firstname_6G_Wireless

Project Results

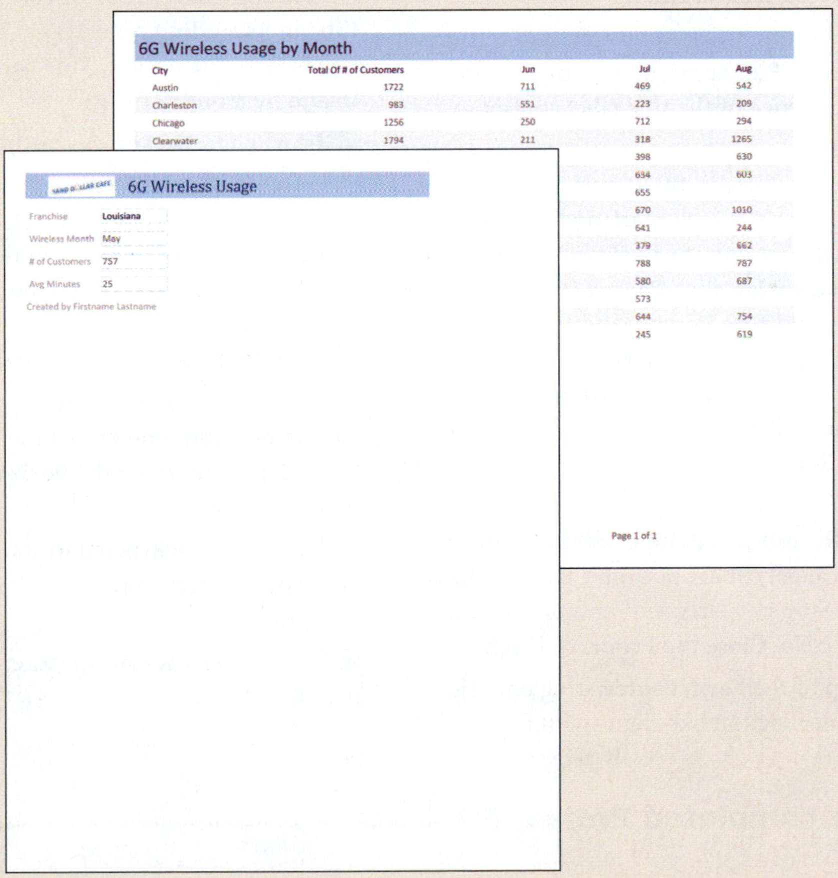

Figure 6.50

(Project 6G Wireless continues on the next page)

Mastering Access | Project 6G Wireless (continued)

1 **Start** Access. Locate and open the **a06G_ Wireless** file. Save the database in your **Access Chapter 6** folder as **Lastname_Firstname_6G_Wireless** If necessary, **Enable Content**. Close the **Navigation Pane**.

2 Create a form in **Form Design**. For the **Record Source**, use the **6G Wireless Usage** table. Select all of the fields, and then drag them onto the design grid until the top of the arrow is aligned with the **1-inch mark on the horizontal ruler** and the **0.25-inch mark on the vertical ruler**. **Save** the form as **Lastname Firstname 6G Wireless Usage**

3 With all controls still selected, on the **Arrange tab**, click the **Stacked** button. Add a light blue dashed outline to the text box controls in the **Detail** section.

4 On the **Design tab**, click the **Logo** button. Locate and double-click **a06G_Logo**. Widen the selected logo to the **1.5-inch mark on the horizontal ruler**.

5 Click the **Title** button. Click to the left of **6G**, delete the space and Lastname Firstname, and then press Enter. Double-click the right edge of the title label control to just fit the text.

6 Click the **Button** button. In the **Detail** section, align the plus sign (+) with the **0.5-inch mark on the vertical ruler** and the **2.5-inch mark on the horizontal ruler**, and then click. Under **Categories**, click **Record Operations**. Under **Actions**, click **Add New Record**, and then click **Next**. Next to **Picture**, be sure **Go to New** is selected, and then click **Next**. In the text box, type **btnNewRcrd** and then click **Finish**. Add a button to print the record below the **Add New Record** button. Place a picture on it, and name it **btnPrtRcrd**

7 With the **New Record** and **Print Record** buttons selected, click the **Property Sheet** button. Click the **Other tab**, click in the **Tab Stop** property setting box, click the **arrow**, and then click **No**. **Close** the **Property Sheet**.

8 Point to the top of the **Form Footer**; drag until the top of the Form Footer section bar aligns with the **1.5-inch mark on the vertical ruler**. Click the **Label** button. In the **Form Footer** section, align the plus sign (+) pointer with the bottom of the **Form Footer** section bar and the left edge of the form. Click and type **Created by Firstname Lastname** and then press Enter.

9 Switch to **Form** view. Click the **New Record** button. From the list of **Franchises**, select **Louisiana MO**. In the **Wireless Month text box control**, select the date on which this project is due. In the **# of Customers text box control**, type **757** In the **Avg Minutes text box control**, type 25.

10 If you are instructed to submit this result, create a paper or electronic printout of the new, selected record only. **Close** the form and **Save** changes.

11 **Create** a report using the **Report Wizard**. From the **Query: 6G Wireless Crosstab Query**, select the **City, Total Of # of Customers, Jun, Jul**, and **Aug** fields. Do not add any grouping levels. **Sort** records within the report by **City**, in **Ascending** order. Use a **Tabular** layout and a **Landscape** orientation. Title your report as **6G Wireless Usage by Month**

12 Switch to **Layout** view. Adjust control widths to display all field names and data to fit across the page.

13 Switch to **Design** view. Select the **Title** label controls and all of the label controls in the **Page Header** section. Change the font color to **Purple, Accent 4, Darker 50%**. Reduce the width of the **Page # control** so the right edge aligns with the **8-inch mark on the horizontal ruler**.

14 Modify the **Page Footer** by adding **Prepared by Firstname Lastname on** before **Now()**. Widen the control to the **5-inch mark on the horizontal ruler**. Switch to **Print Preview**.

15 If you are instructed to submit this result, create a paper or electronic printout. **Close** the report and **Save** changes.

16 Open the **Navigation Pane**, **Close** the database, and then **Exit** Access.

End **You have completed Project 6G**

Apply a combination of the **6A** and **6B** skills.

GO! Fix It | Project 6H Ads

Project Files

For Project 6H, you will need the following files:

a06H_Ads
a06H_Logo

You will save your database as:

Lastname_Firstname_6H_Ads

In the following project, you modify a form that will be used to enter the details of the advertising contracts for the Sand Dollar Cafe franchise restaurant chain. You will also modify a report to group, sort, and total this data.

Make the following modifications to the **6H Costs Form**:

- Apply a Theme. Arrange it in a Stacked Layout.
- The form needs to be identified with the logo and appropriate form title. Be sure to include your first and last names as part of the form title.
- Be sure all field names and data are visible in the form.
- Marty would like to have buttons on the form to add a new record and to print the current record. Use text to identify the buttons, align the buttons, and remove them as tab stops on the form. Change the font color to a Theme color to coordinate with the form.
- Add a solid outline to each of the textboxes on the form and a dotted/dashed outline to the buttons; choose a Theme color to coordinate with the form.
- Add text to appear in the status bar when entering data in the Frequency text box; it should read: *How many times per year?*
- View the form, saving the changes.
- If you are instructed to submit this result, create a paper or electronic printout.

Make the following modifications to the **6H Ad Costs Report**:

- Be sure all field names and data are visible on the report. Remove the colon following each of the Page Header label controls.
- Copy the logo to the right edge of the report. Center the title between the logos. Align the controls.
- Draw a line below the column headings (label boxes). Apply a Theme Color to coordinate with the form.
- Add a control to the left edge of the Report Footer. It should read **Prepared by Firstname Lastname on *date*** (use today's date). Add a text box control aligned at the right edge of the Report Footer. It should calculate the annual cost (Frequency x Cost Per Placement); be sure it displays as currency and includes a descriptive label. Format the font for the label controls to match the line drawn above. Apply a matching outline to the calculated control.
- View the report, saving the changes.
- If you are instructed to submit this result, create a paper or electronic printout.

End **You have completed Project 6H**

Content-Based Assessments

Apply a combination of the **6A** and **6B** skills.

GO! Make It | Project 6I Supply Orders

Project Files

For Project 6I, you will need the following files:

a06I_Supply_Orders
a06I_Logo
a06I_Sand_Dollar

You will save your database as:

Lastname_Firstname_6I_Supply_Orders

From the student files that accompany this textbook, open the **a06I_Supply_Orders** database file. Save the database in your Access Chapter 6 folder as **Lastname_Firstname_6I_Supply_Orders.** Modify the design of the **6I_Supply_Order** form by modifying and moving controls, modifying the header, and adding a background image. Modify the appearance of the **6I Orders by City** report. Your completed objects, if printed, will look similar to Figure 6.51. An electronic version of the form will look slightly different. Create a paper or electronic printout as directed.

Project Results

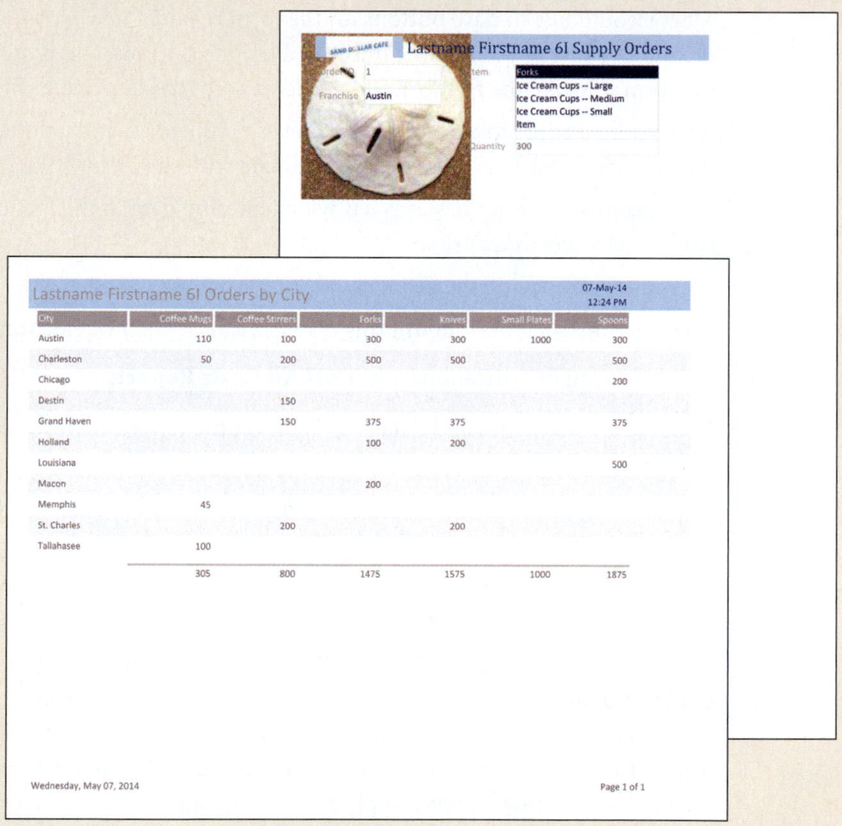

Figure 6.51

End **You have completed Project 6I**

Apply a combination of the **6A** and **6B** skills.

GO! Solve It | Project 6J Menu

Project Files

For Project 6J, you will need the following files:

a06J_Menu
a06J_Logo

You will save your database as:

Lastname_Firstname_6J_Menu

Brian Davidson, Executive Chef for the Sand Dollar Cafe restaurant chain, wants to know which menu items are most popular at the individual franchise locations. Open the **a06J_Menu** database and save it as **Lastname_Firstname_6J_Menu** In this project, you will create a form to be used by the managers of the different franchises to enter the most popular menu items. From the *6J Popular Items* table, use all fields except the ID field. Save the form as **Lastname Firstname 6J Popular Items** In the Detail and Header sections, add a background color and change the font and font color of the label controls. In Design view, resize the Detail section to reduce the blank space. Add **a06J_Logo** and title the form **6J Popular Menu Items** In the Form Footer section, insert a label control aligned with the right edge of the form; it should read **Designed by Firstname Lastname** Adjust the label controls and the text box controls to fit the data. If you are instructed to submit this result, create a paper or electronic printout of only the first record.

Use a wizard to create a report based on the *6J Popular Items Crosstab* query. Select all fields from the query. Sort by Franchise. Title the report **6J Popular Items by Franchise** Center the title across the report, and change the color of the background. In the Report Footer section, modify the date control to include your name. Change the background for the entire Report Footer section to match the Report Header. Adjust all label and text controls to display all data. Resize the report to 8 inches wide.

Modify the *6J Popular Menu Items* report. Add your Lastname Firstname to the title. Add **a06J_Logo** to the Report Header, resize it, and then move the title to the right of the logo. Group the report by Franchise and sort by Sales Month. Be sure the data for each franchise stays on the same page. Select the Sales Month label control and a text box control in the column; center align the column. Change the font color of the label controls for each column. Draw a line below the column headings; change the Outline Color. Add a Report Footer that reads **Report Modified by Firstname Lastname** Save the changes to the report. If you are instructed to submit this result, create a paper or electronic printout.

Performance Element	Performance Level: Exemplary: You consistently applied the relevant skills.	Proficient: You sometimes, but not always, applied the relevant skills.	Developing: You rarely or never applied the relevant skills.
Create 6J Popular Items Form	Form created with the correct controls and formatted as directed.	Form created with no more than two missing elements.	Form created with more than two missing elements.
Create 6J Popular Items by Franchise Report	Report created and formatted correctly.	Report created with no more than two missing elements.	Report created with more than two missing elements.
Modify 6J Popular Menu Items Report	Report modified to include the correct controls, grouping, sorting, and formatting.	Report modified with no more than two missing elements.	Report modified with more than two missing elements.

End You have completed Project 6J

Apply a combination of the 6A and 6B skills.

GO! Solve It | Project 6K Birthday Coupons

Project Files

For Project 6K, you will need the following files:

a06K_Birthday_Coupons
a06K_Sand_Dollar
a06K_Birthday

You will save your database as:

Lastname_Firstname_6K_Birthday_Coupons

The Vice President of Marketing, Marty Kress, encourages each of the individual restaurants of the Sand Dollar Cafe franchise to offer birthday coupons to its customers as a promotional venture. Open the **a06K_Birthday_Coupons** database, and then save it as **Lastname_Firstname_6K_Birthday_Coupons** Use the *6K Birthdates* table to create a form to enter the names, birthday months, and e-mail addresses of the customers visiting one of the restaurants. Save the form as **Lastname Firstname 6K Birthday Form** Add a button control to print the current form. Include the Sand Dollar image as the logo and title the form **6K Happy Birthday!** Be sure all data is visible on the form. Add a new record using the form and your own information.

Create a report to display the customers grouped by their birthday month using the months as a section header and sorted by customer name. Save the report as **Lastname Firstname 6K Birthdate Report** Add the **a06K_Birthday** image as the logo resized to 1 inch tall and wide. Add a title. Draw a line above the Birthday Month header control to separate the months; apply a Line Color and Line Style. Save the report as **Lastname Firstname 6K Birthdate Report** Save the report.

Create a report based on the 6K Second Quarter Birthdays query. Include both of the fields arranged in a tabular format. Save the report as **Lastname Firstname 6K Second Quarter Birthdays** Add a title to the report, **Lastname Firstname 6K Second Quarter Birthdays** Add the current date and time to the Report Header section, and then move them to the Report Footer section. Resize the Page Footer section to 0. Apply a dotted outline to the label controls in the Page Header section; choose a Line Color, Line Thickness, and Line Style. Add the **a06K_Birthday** image and place it in the bottom right of the report. Add a count of how many second quarter birthdays there are to the Report Footer; include a descriptive label to the right of the count. Save the report as **Lastname Firstname 6K Second Quarter Birthdays** Adjust the width of the report to fit on a landscape page. Save the changes. If you are instructed to submit the results, create a paper or electronic printout of the objects created.

Performance Element	Performance Level: Exemplary: You consistently applied the relevant skills	Proficient: You sometimes, but not always, applied the relevant skills.	Developing: You rarely or never applied the relevant skills
Create 6K Birthday Form	Form created with the correct fields and formatted as directed.	Form created with no more than two missing elements.	Form created with more than two missing elements.
Create 6K Birthdate Report	Report created with the correct fields and formatted as directed.	Report created with no more than two missing elements.	Report created with more than two missing elements.
Create 6K Second Quarter Birthdays Report	Report created with the correct fields and formatted as directed.	Report created with no more than two missing elements.	Report created with more than two missing elements.

End You have completed Project 6K

Outcomes-Based Assessments

Rubric

The following outcomes-based assessments are *open-ended assessments*. That is, there is no specific correct result; your result will depend on your approach to the information provided. Make *Professional Quality* your goal. Use the following scoring rubric to guide you in *how* to approach the problem, and then to evaluate *how well* your approach solves the problem.

The criteria—Software Mastery, Content, Format and Layout, and Process—represent the knowledge and skills you have gained that you can apply to solving the problem. The levels of performance—Professional Quality, Approaching Professional Quality, or Needs Quality Improvements—help you and your instructor evaluate your result.

	Your completed project is of Professional Quality if you:	**Your completed project is Approaching Professional Quality if you:**	**Your completed project Needs Quality Improvements if you:**
1-Software Mastery	Choose and apply the most appropriate skills, tools, and features and identify efficient methods to solve the problem.	Choose and apply some appropriate skills, tools, and features, but not in the most efficient manner.	Choose inappropriate skills, tools, or features, or are inefficient in solving the problem.
2-Content	Construct a solution that is clear and well organized, contains content that is accurate, appropriate to the audience and purpose, and is complete. Provide a solution that contains no errors in spelling, grammar, or style.	Construct a solution in which some components are unclear, poorly organized, inconsistent, or incomplete. Misjudge the needs of the audience. Have some errors in spelling, grammar, or style, but the errors do not detract from comprehension.	Construct a solution that is unclear, incomplete, or poorly organized; contains some inaccurate or inappropriate content; and contains many errors in spelling, grammar, or style. Do not solve the problem.
3-Format and Layout	Format and arrange all elements to communicate information and ideas, clarify function, illustrate relationships, and indicate relative importance.	Apply appropriate format and layout features to some elements, but not others. Overuse features, causing minor distraction.	Apply format and layout that does not communicate information or ideas clearly. Do not use format and layout features to clarify function, illustrate relationships, or indicate relative importance. Use available features excessively, causing distraction.
4-Process	Use an organized approach that integrates planning, development, self-assessment, revision, and reflection.	Demonstrate an organized approach in some areas, but not others; or, use an insufficient process of organization throughout.	Do not use an organized approach to solve the problem.

Apply a combination of the **6A** and **6B** skills.

GO! Think | Project **6L** Vacation Days

Project Files

For Project 6L, you will need the following files:

a06L_Vacation_Days
a06L_Logo

You will save your database as:

Lastname_Firstname_6L_Vacation_Days

In this project, you will create a report to display the information for the employees of the Sand Dollar Cafe related to their vacation days. Open the **a06L_Vacation_Days** database and save it as **Lastname_Firstname_6L_Vacation_Days** From the *6L Vacation Days* table, add the following fields to the report: Employee Name, Allotted Days, and Days Taken. Add a calculated text box control to display the number of vacation days each employee has remaining (Days Allotted-Days Taken) with a label control to describe the field, and format the result as a General Number. In the Report Header section, add the Sand Dollar Cafe logo and a descriptive title. Add a label control to the Report Footer section that reads **Report Designed by Firstname Lastname** Align the left edge with the label controls in the Detail section. Change the background color used in the Report Header and Report Footer sections, and change the font color so they are easy to read. Sort the report on Employee Name. Add a dotted line between employees to make it easier to read. Adjust all label and text controls to display all field names and data. Center page numbers in the report footer. Resize the Detail section to reduce the blank space. Close the space for the Page Header. Adjust the width of the report so it is 6 inches wide. Save the report as **Lastname Firstname 6L Vacation** If you are instructed to submit this result, create a paper or electronic printout.

End You have completed Project 6L

Apply a combination of the **6A** and **6B** skills.

GO! Think | Project **6M** Seasonal Items

Project Files

For Project 6M, you will need the following files:

a06M_Seasonal_Items
a06M_Logo

You will save your database as:

Lastname_Firstname_6M_Seasonal_Items

The Executive Chef of the Sand Dollar Cafe franchise restaurant chain, Brian Davidson, adds seasonal items to the menu. In this project, you will open the **a06M_Seasonal_Items** database and save it as **Lastname_Firstname_6M_Seasonal_Items** You will create a report using the 6M Seasonal Items table. The report should include all fields grouped by Season, and sorted on the Menu Item. Be sure to keep each group together on a page. Include Season in a section header and total cost in a section footer including descriptive labels. Draw and format a line to separate sections for readability. Apply a theme to the database. Add the Sand Dollar Cafe logo and a report title that includes your Lastname Firstname. Reduce the width of the report to fit on a portrait page with default margins. Reduce the blank space visible in the Page Header and Detail sections of the report. Add page numbering to the right side of the footer. Align all labels and text boxes that you added, and be sure they are the same height. Adjust all label and text controls to display all field names and data. If you are instructed to submit this result, create a paper or electronic printout.

End You have completed Project 6M

Outcomes-Based Assessments

Apply a combination of the **6A** and **6B** skills.

You and GO! | Project 6N Club Directory

Project Files

For Project 6N, you will need the following file:

Lastname_Firstname_5N_Club_Directory (your file from Chapter 5)

You will save your database as:

Lastname_Firstname_6N_Club_Directory

Create a personal database containing information about a club and its activities, if you do not already have one from Project 5N. Name the new database **Lastname_Firstname_6N_Club_Directory** If you do not have the database from Project 5N, create two related tables, one that lists the activities your organization has planned and the other to serve as the directory of the group. The Activities table should include information about the name (primary key field), date, cost, and location of the activity. The dates must all occur next year; consider attaching directions to the event to the table. The Directory table should include full name, address, phone number, email, and an activity they are planning. If you have the database from Project 5N, save as an Access 2007 Database in your Access Chapter 6 folder.

Use all of the fields in the Directory table in a form. Include a title and applicable image. Be sure all data is visible in the text boxes. Apply a theme to the database. Add a background color to the Report Header and Footer. Select a coordinating font color for the label controls in the Detail section of the form. Add a button to print the current form. Add a form footer that reads **Form created by Firstname Lastname**

Create a report to include all of the fields in the Activities table. Present it in tabular format, sorted by date, in ascending order. In the Report Footer, add a count of how many activities there are, with an appropriate label. Change background, outline, and font colors in the control label boxes to create a well-formatted report. Submit your database as instructed.

You will be using this database in future chapters. Be sure to make corrections to your tables as necessary to prepare for the next chapter.

End You have completed Project 6N

Business Running Case

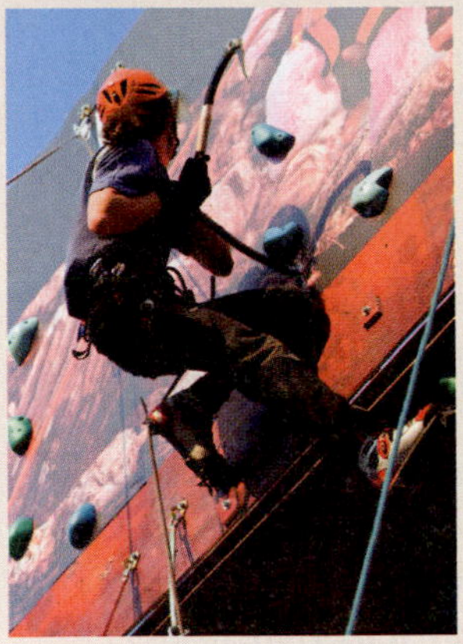

Razvan CHIRNOAGA/Shutterstock

Front Range Action Sports is one of the country's largest retailers of sports gear and outdoor recreation merchandise. The company has large retail stores in Colorado, Washington, Oregon, California, and New Mexico, in addition to a growing online business. Major merchandise categories include fishing, camping, rock climbing, winter sports, action sports, water sports, team sports, racquet sports, fitness, golf, apparel, and footwear.

In this project, you will apply skills you practiced from the Objectives in Access Chapters 4–6. You will update the current database for Frank Osei, the Vice President of Finance, as he manages the company's growth. You will modify existing tables and create a new one to track part-time employee information. In addition, you will create queries to assist Frank as he monitors the company's performance and requests that data be updated. You will also create forms and reports to display information from the current tables and queries. Your printed results will look similar to Figure 2.1.

Project Files

For Project BRC2, you will need the following files:

aBRC2_Company_Management
aBRC2_Logo
aBRC2_Snowboard

You will save your files as:

Lastname_Firstname_aBRC2_Company_Management
Lastname_Firstname_aBRC2_Company_Management_2014_05_12 (date may differ)

Project Results

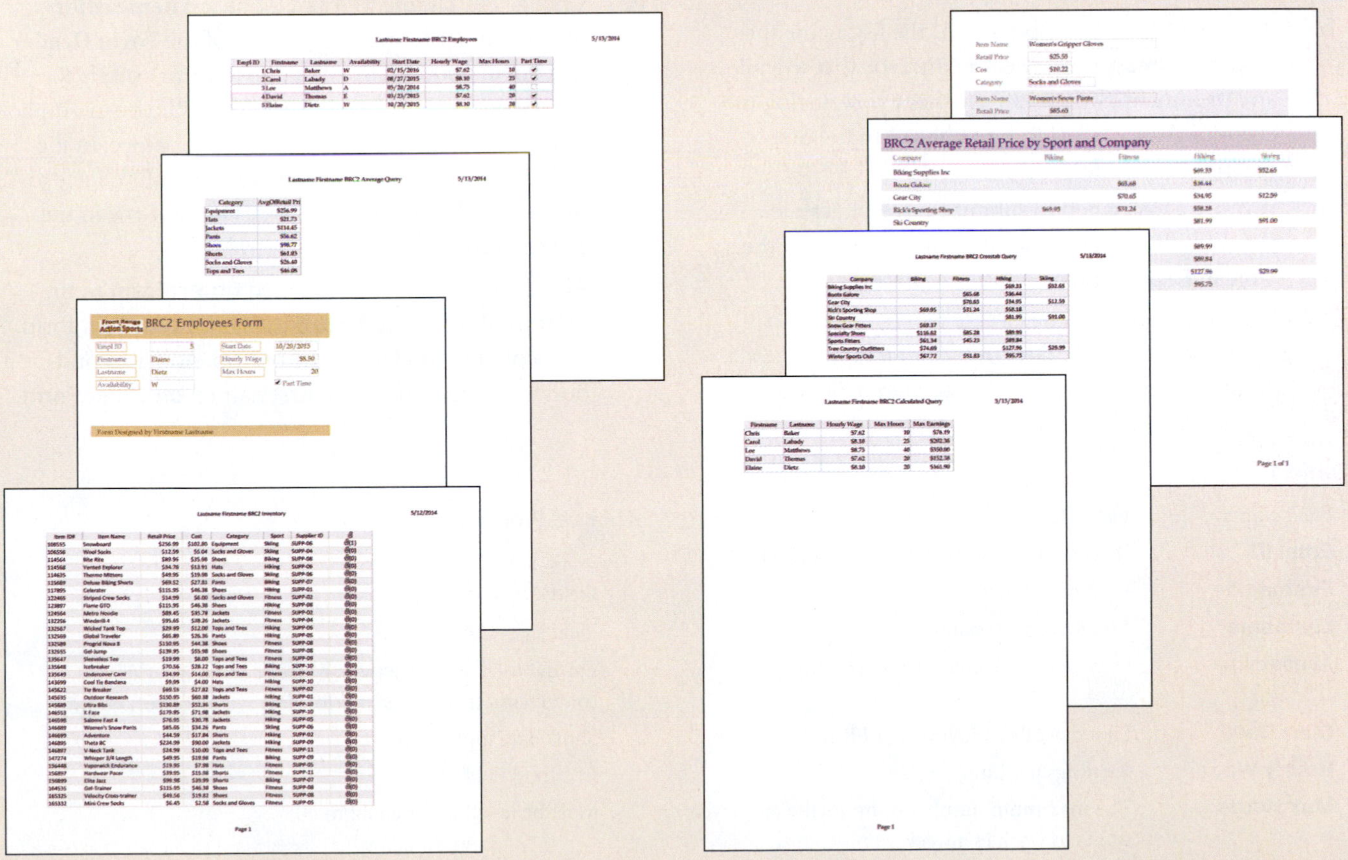

Figure 2.1

Business Running Case

Front Range Action Sports

1. **Start** Access. Navigate to the solution file for BRC1. Locate and open the **Lastname_Firstname_aBRC2_Company_Management** database. If you did not add the **Front Range Action Sports** folder to the **Trust Center**, enable the content.
2. Display **Backstage** view, click **Save & Publish**, and then click **Back Up Database**. Add **Lastname_Firstname** before the default name of the backup file. Click **Save**.
3. **Save** the database as **Lastname_Firstname_aBRC2_Company_Management** in your **Front Range Action Sports** folder.
4. Open the **Navigation Pane**, if necessary. **Rename** the tables to include your **Lastname Firstname** in front of the table name. Open the **BRC2 Inventory** table in **Design** view. Close the **Navigation Pane**.
   - **a.** Add a new field between **Retail Price** and **Category**. The field should be named **Cost** and it should be calculated as **[Retail Price]*0.40** Be sure to set the format as **Currency**.
   - **b.** Add a new field at the bottom of the list; name the field **Item Image** and select a data type that will allow an attachment. Switch to **Datasheet** view, saving the changes. Attach **aBRC2_Snowboard** to the first record in the table.
   - **c.** If you are instructed to submit this result, create a paper or electronic printout of the first page of the table in **Landscape** orientation. **Close** the table.
5. On the Ribbon, click the **Create** tab. In the **Tables** group, click the **Table Design** button to open a new table in **Design** view. Create the **Lastname Firstname BRC2 Employees** table using the information in **Table 1** for field design and properties. Determine the appropriate data type based on the field details.
6. Based on the **BRC2_Employees** table, use the **Form Design** tool to create a new form.
   - **a.** Add all fields from the table to the form design. Move **Start Date**, **Hourly Wage**, **Max Hours**, and **Part Time** to a second column with about 0.5 inch separating them. Align the **Empl ID** and **Start Date** fields at the top.
   - **b.** Add **aBRC2_Logo** to the **Form Header**. Resize the logo so it is **1.5 inches wide** and **0.5 inch tall**. Add a **title** to the **Form Header**; it should read **BRC2 Employees Form**
   - **c.** Drag the **Form Footer section bar** upward to the **2-inch mark on the vertical ruler**. Add a label in the form footer that reads **Form Designed by Firstname Lastname**
   - **d.** Change the **Theme** to **Apex**. Apply a **Theme color** of your choice to the background of the **Form Header** and **Form Footer**. Use the same color to outline the **label** controls in the **Detail** section of the form. Apply a **line thickness** and **line type** of your choice. In the Detail section, apply a **Theme color** of your choice to the font in the **text box** controls. Do the same in the **Footer** section to the **label** control.
   - **e.** Add a command button named **btnPrtForm** to the bottom of the **Form Detail** to print the current form. Use a picture to identify the button. Add a second button to the right of the first named **btnCloseForm**

Table 1

Field Name	Field Details	Field Properties
Empl ID	ID generated for each employee, primary key	
Firstname	Employee's first name	Field size = 18
Lastname	Employee's last name	Field size = 24
Availability	Preferred availability for scheduling	Format to all capital letters. Must be D, E, W, or A (one-character codes stand for day, evening, weekend, any)
Start Date	First day of employment at FRAS	Short date input mask
Hourly Wage	Earnings per hour	Required field
Max Hours	The maximum number of hours the employee wants to work in a week	Must be less than or equal to 40
Part Time	A box to check if the employee works part time	

Return to Step 5

(Business Running Case: Front Range Action Sports continues on the next page)

Front Range Action Sports (continued)

to close the form. Use the **Stop** picture to identify the button. Apply an outline that is the same color, type, and thickness as the label controls in the form. Align the buttons at the top.

f. Remove **btnPrtForm**, **btnCloseForm**, and the **Empl ID** field as tab stops on the form.

g. Save the form as **Lastname Firstname BRC2 Employees Form**

7 Switch to **Form** view. Add the records to the form as shown in **Table 2**.

8 Review the records to be sure all information is visible. Make adjustments to the width of label or text box controls as necessary. If you are instructed to submit this result, create a paper or electronic printout of **record 5**. **Close** the form, saving layout changes.

9 Based on the tables in the database, create the following queries to provide the information requested. Create paper or electronic printouts as directed.

a. Design a query to display the average retail price of the inventory by category. **Run** the query. **Save** the query as **Lastname Firstname BRC2 Average Query** If you are instructed to submit this result, create a paper or electronic printout of the query results. **Close** the query.

b. Design a query to update the **Hourly Wage** for all part-time employees to reflect a 5% increase. The new hourly wage will be 1.05 times the original wage. **Save** the query as **Lastname Firstname BRC2 Update Query** Be careful to **Run** the query only once. **Close** the query. If you are instructed to submit this result, open the **Employees** table, and then create a paper or electronic printout of the table.

c. Design a query to display each employee's **Firstname**, **Lastname**, **Hourly Wage**, **Max Hours**, and **Max Earnings**, which will be calculated by multiplying the hourly wage by the max hours. **Run** the query. **Autofit** all columns. **Save** the query as **Lastname Firstname BRC2 Calculated Query** If you are instructed to submit this result, create a paper or electronic printout of the query results. **Close** the query.

d. Design a query to display the **Company**, **Sport**, and **Retail Price** for all records. **Run** the query. **Save** the query as **Lastname Firstname BRC2 Crosstab Setup Query** **Close** the query.

e. Create a crosstab query using a **Query Wizard**; select the **BRC2 Crosstab Setup Query** for the basis of the crosstab query. Display **Company** as the row heading, **Sport** as the column heading, and an average of **Retail Price**. Do not display the row sums. **Save** the query as **Lastname Firstname BRC2 Crosstab Query** **View** the query results, and widen columns as necessary. If you are instructed to submit this result, create a paper or electronic printout of the query results. **Close** the query.

10 Select the **BRC2 Crosstab Query**, and using a **Report Wizard**, create a report.

a. Display all fields in the report. There will be no grouping.

b. Sort the report by **Company**, in ascending order.

c. Use a **tabular** format and **landscape** orientation.

d. Title the report **BRC2 Average Retail Price by Sport and Company**

Table 2

Empl ID	Firstname	Lastname	Availability	Start Date	Hourly Wage	Max Hours	Part Time
1	Chris	Baker	W	02/15/2016	8.00	10	Yes
2	Carol	Labady	D	08/27/2015	8.50	25	Yes
3	Lee	Matthews	A	05/20/2013	8.75	40	No
4	David	Thomas	E	03/23/2015	8.00	20	Yes
5	Elaine	Dietz	W	10/20/2015	8.50	20	Yes

(Return to Step 8)

(Business Running Case: Front Range Action Sports continues on the next page)

Front Range Action Sports (continued)

e. View the report's design. Adjust the width of the label boxes so the report fits across one page. Adjust the width of the report in Design view.

f. Modify the **Date Page Footer** so it says **Prepared by Firstname Lastname on Current Date** If necessary, adjust the width of the control so all information is visible.

g. Select the **title** and the **Page Footer controls**. Change the font to a **Theme color** of your choice.

h. Add a line below the column headings. Use the same color as you selected for the fonts above.

i. If you are instructed to submit this result, create a paper or electronic printout of the report on one landscape page. **Close** the report, saving changes.

11 Based on the **Inventory** table, create a report in **Design** view.

a. Display the following fields in the report: **Item Name**, **Retail Price**, **Cost, Category**, and **Sport** at the **1.5-inch mark on the horizontal ruler**. Save the report as **Lastname Firstname BRC2 Inventory by Sport Report**

b. Reduce the height of the **Detail** section to accommodate the data. Adjust the width of the label controls so all data is visible. Widen the **Item Name** text box until the right edge aligns with the **4-inch mark on the horizontal ruler**. Widen the **Category** text box until the right edge aligns with the **3-inch mark on the horizontal ruler**.

c. Group the report by **Sport**. Delete the **Sport label control**. Move the **Sport textbox control** to the left edge of the **Sport Header** section. Sort the report by **Item Name**, in ascending order.

d. Add the **BRC2_Logo** to the **Report Header**. Resize it to **1.5 inches wide** and **0.5 inch tall**.

e. Add the title **BRC2 Inventory by Sport Report** to the **Report Header**. Reduce the width of the **Title text box control** so the right edge aligns with the **6.5-inch mark on the horizontal ruler**. Center the title in the **label control**.

f. Add a count for the number of items per sport. Use an appropriate text box control to identify the calculation by sport in the **Sport Footer**. Use a label control to identify the calculation in the **Report Footer**. Be sure the label and text box controls are aligned in each section.

g. Add a line at the bottom of the **Sport Footer** to separate each sport section; choose an outline color and line thickness. Apply a **Theme Color** background to the label control and text box control in the **Sport Footer**.

h. Resize the width of the report to **7.5 inches**. In the **Report Footer**, add a label control aligned at the right edge of the report. It should read **Submitted by Firstname Lastname** using your full name.

i. If necessary, reduce the width of the report to fit across a portrait page with default margins.

j. **Save** the report. If you are instructed to submit this result, create a paper or electronic printout of the final page of the report. **Close** the report.

12 **Close** the database, and then **Exit** Access. If you are to submit your work electronically, follow your instructor's directions.

End **You have completed Business Running Case 2**

Creating Templates and Reviewing, Publishing, and Protecting Presentations

OUTCOMES

At the end of this chapter you will be able to:

OBJECTIVES

Mastering these objectives will enable you to:

PROJECT 4A

Create and apply a custom template.

1. Create a Custom Template by Modifying Slide Masters (p. 627)
2. Apply a Custom Template to a Presentation (p. 641)

PROJECT 4B

Review, publish, and protect presentations.

3. Create and Edit Comments (p. 650)
4. Prepare a Presentation for Distribution (p. 655)
5. Protect a Presentation (p. 662)

Kzenon\Shutterstock

In This Chapter

Microsoft Office PowerPoint provides built-in templates that contain layouts and formatting to use when creating a new presentation. You can create your own customized templates and reuse them. Tastefully designed templates ensure that presentations using the template maintain a consistent look.

PowerPoint also enables you to review and comment on the content of a presentation by inserting and editing comments in the file. It also provides a variety of ways to share presentations with others: converting to PDF or XPS format or printing handouts. PowerPoint also enables you to check a presentation for compatibility with other versions of PowerPoint and protect the presentation from further editing by marking it as Final.

Attorneys at **DeLong Grant Law Partners** counsel their clients on a wide variety of issues including contracts, licensing, intellectual property, and taxation, with emphasis on the unique needs of the entertainment and sports industries. Entertainment clients include production companies, publishers, talent agencies, actors, writers, artists—anyone involved in creating or doing business in the entertainment industry. Sports clients include colleges and universities, professional sports teams, athletes, and venue operators. Increasingly, amateur and community sports coaches and organizations with concerns about liability are also seeking the firm's specialized counsel.

Project 4A Instructional Presentation

Project Activities

In Activities 4.01 through 4.09, you will design a template for the DeLong Grant Law Partners to use to create presentations for meetings with the partners and clients. The template will contain formatting for the slide masters and shapes and images to add interest. Then you will use the template to create a presentation. You will also edit slide masters in an existing presentation in order to maintain uniformity in the slide designs. Your completed presentation will look similar to Figure 4.1.

Project Files

For Project 4A, you will need the following files:

New blank PowerPoint presentation
p04A_Law1.jpg

You will save your presentation as:

Lastname_Firstname_4A_Meeting_Template.potx
Lastname_Firstname_4A_Filing_Procedures.pptx

Project Results

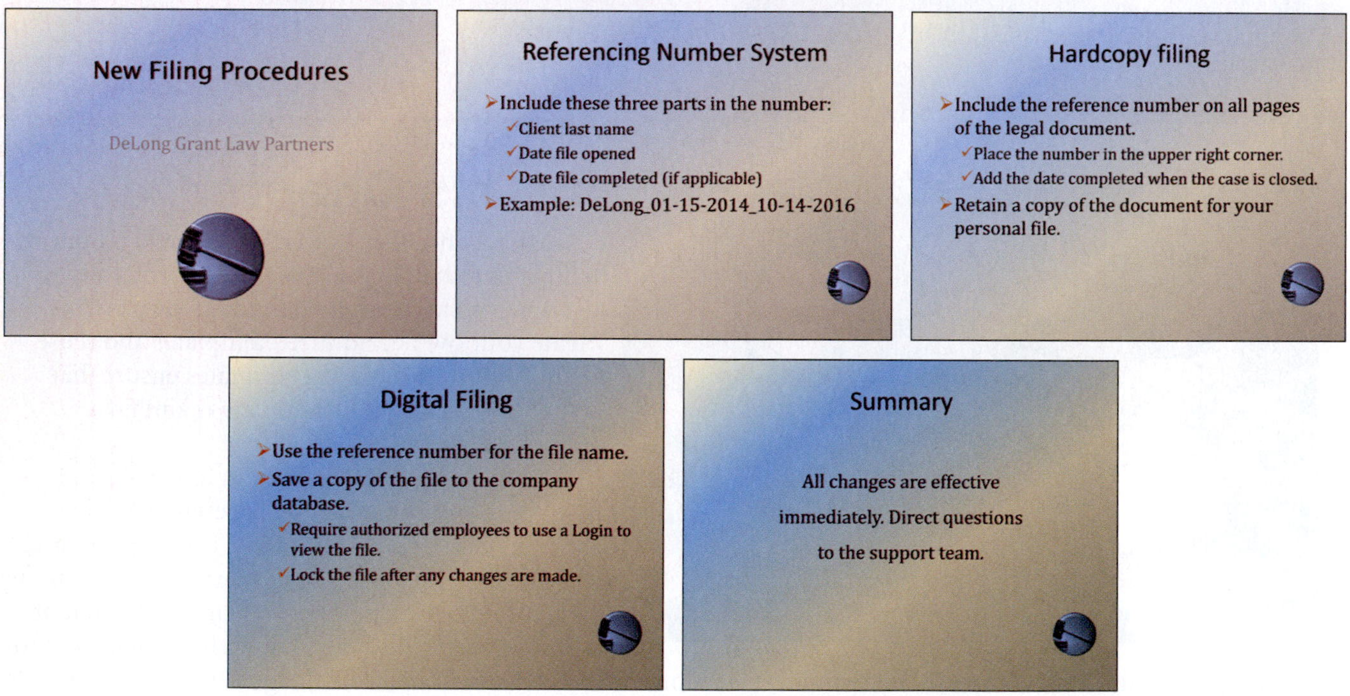

Figure 4.1
Project 4A Filing Procedures

Objective 1 | Create a Custom Template by Modifying Slide Masters

A PowerPoint ***template*** is a predefined layout for a group of slides and is saved as a .potx file. You use a template to standardize the design of the slides in a presentation. A ***slide master*** is part of a template that stores information about the formatting and text that displays on every slide in a presentation. The stored information includes such items as the placement and size of text and object placeholders.

For example, if your company or organization has a logo that should be displayed on all slides of a presentation, the logo can be inserted one time on the slide master. That logo will then display in the same location on all slides of the presentation.

There are several approaches to creating a template. You can create a template from a new blank presentation, modify an existing template, or modify master slides in an existing presentation.

Activity 4.01 | Displaying and Editing Slide Masters

In this activity, you will change the Office Theme Slide Master background and the Title Slide Layout font and font size. You will start with a blank PowerPoint file.

1 **Start** PowerPoint to display a new blank presentation. On the Ribbon, click the **View tab**. In the **Master Views group**, point to, but do not click, the **Slide Master** button. Read the ScreenTip: *Slide Master View Open Slide Master view to change the design and layout of the master slides.* Compare your screen with Figure 4.2.

In the Master Views group, notice the three views available—Slide Master, Handout Master, and Notes Master.

Figure 4.2

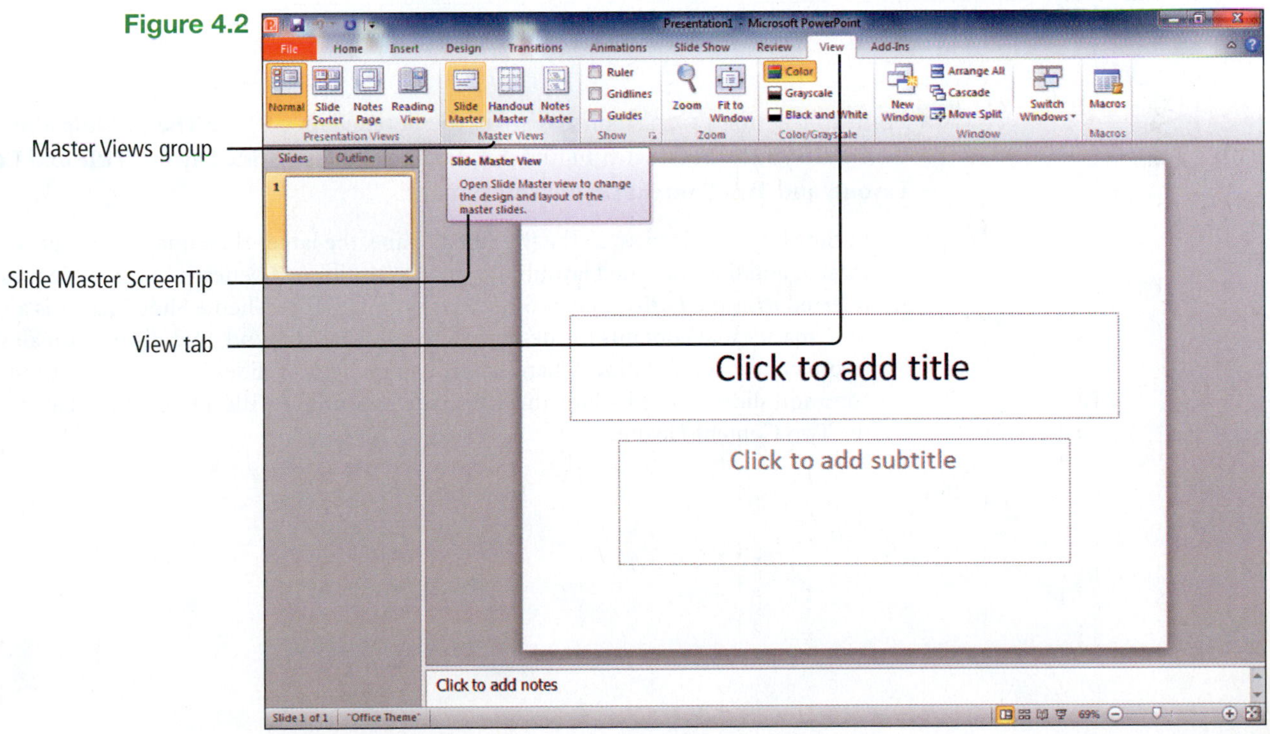

2 Click the **Slide Master** button. Take a moment to study the options associated with the Slide Master tab, as described in the table shown in Figure 4.3.

You are already familiar with editing themes, fonts, and colors by using the Edit Theme group, customizing a background by using the Background group, and modifying page setup and orientation by using the Page Setup group. From the Slide Master tab, you can apply these changes to certain layouts or to the entire theme.

Options on the Slide Master Tab

Screen Element	Description
Edit Master group	Enables you to:
Insert Slide Master	Add a new Slide Master to the presentation.
Insert Layout	Add a custom layout.
Delete	Delete a layout not in use by the presentation.
Rename	Rename a custom layout. This layout will become part of the layout gallery and will be visible when adding new slides to the presentation.
Preserve	Preserve the master slide so that it remains with the presentation, even if it is not used.
Master Layout group	Enables you to:
Master Layout	Choose which elements you want to include on the master layout.
Insert Placeholder	Add placeholders for content, text, pictures, charts, tables, SmartArt, media, and clip art.
Title	Show or hide the title placeholder.
Footers	Show or hide the placeholders for footers.

Figure 4.3

3 Point to the first thumbnail to display the ScreenTip—**Office Theme Slide Master**. Compare your screen with Figure 4.4. Locate the **Title Slide Layout**, **Title and Content Layout**, and **Two Content Layout** thumbnails.

In the Slide Master view, in the thumbnail pane, the larger slide image represents the slide master, and the associated layouts are smaller, positioned beneath it. The slide master is referred to as the ***Office Theme Slide Master***. The Office Theme Slide Master is a specific slide master that contains the design, such as the background, that displays on all slide layouts in the presentation. Changes made to it affect all slides in the presentation. Other common slide layouts include the Title Slide Layout, the Title and Content Layout, and the Two Content Layout.

Figure 4.4

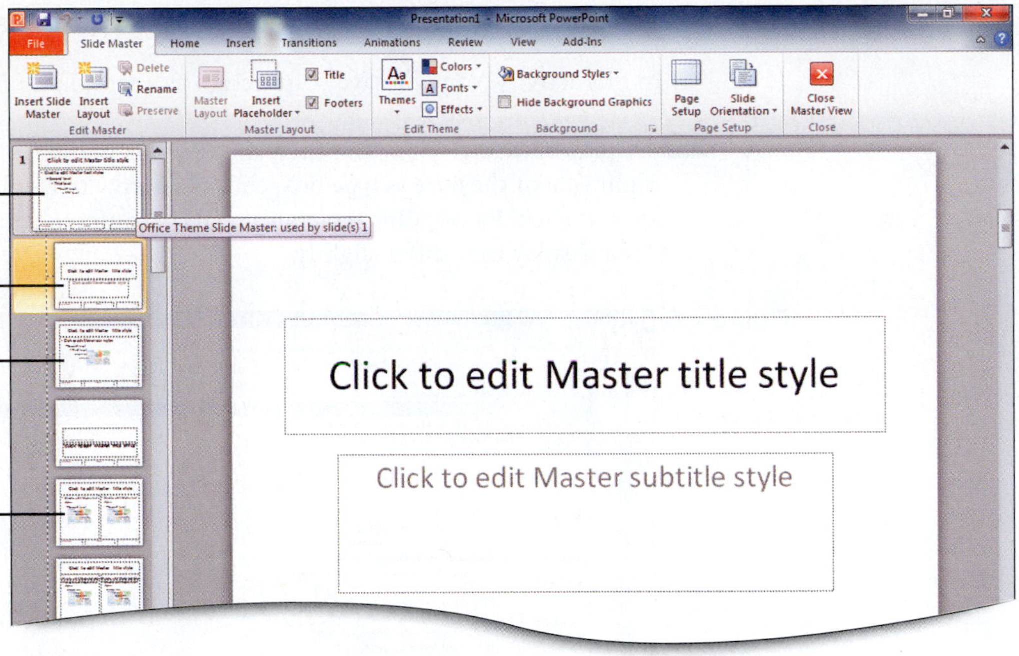

4. Click the first thumbnail—**Office Theme Slide Master**. In the **Background group**, click the **Background Styles** button. In the **Background Styles gallery**, scroll until you locate **Style 10**, and then click it.

   Notice that all slide layouts display with the same background style.

> **Another Way**
>
> You can also triple-click the text in the Master title style placeholder to select the text.

5. Click the second thumbnail—**Title Slide Layout**. On the slide, click anywhere on the dashed border on the Master title style placeholder to display the border as a solid line. Click the **Home tab**. In the **Font group**, change the font to **Lucida Sans Unicode**. Change the font size to **40**. Compare your screen with Figure 4.5.

   The font and font size change affects only the Title Slide.

Figure 4.5

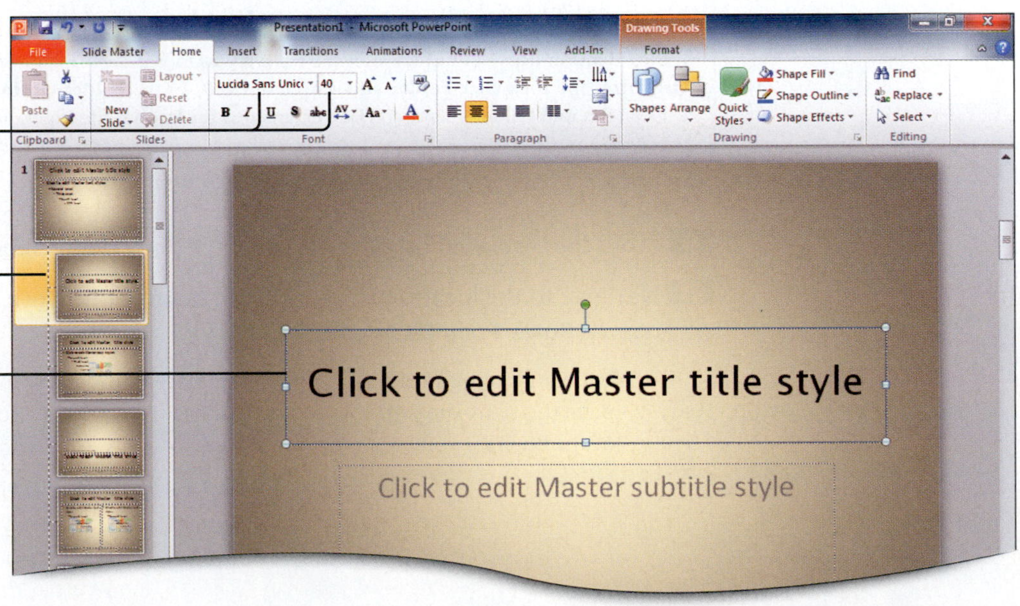

PowerPoint | Chapter 4

Activity 4.02 | Saving a Presentation as a Template

In this activity, you will save your design as a template.

1 Display **Backstage** view, and then click **Save As** to display the **Save As** dialog box. At the right side of the **Save as type** box, click the arrow to display the file types. Point to, but do not click, **PowerPoint Template (*.potx)**. Compare your screen with Figure 4.6. Your display may differ slightly.

Figure 4.6

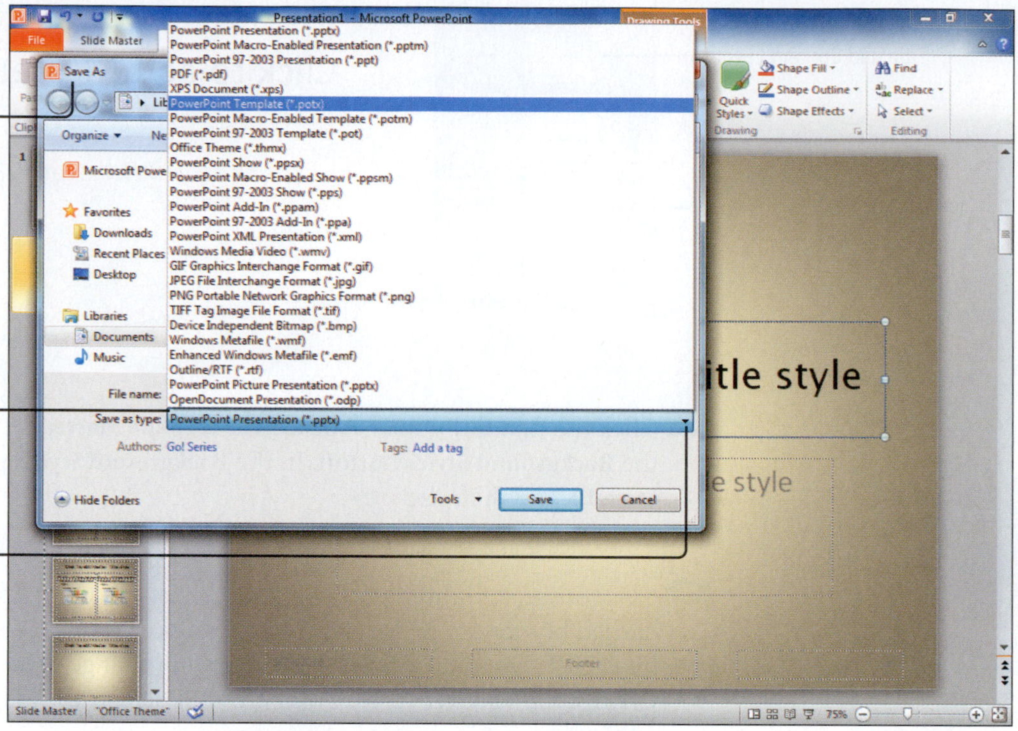

Save As dialog box

PowerPoint Template (*.potx)

Save as type box arrow

> **Note | Displaying File Extensions in Windows Explorer**
>
> If the extension does not display after the file type, go to Windows Explorer. On the Windows menu bar, click **Organize**, and then click **Folder and search options**. In the **Folder Options** dialog box, click the **View tab**. Under **Files and Folders**, scroll to **Hide extensions for known file types**, and then remove the check mark in the check box. Click **OK**.

2 From the displayed list of file types, click **PowerPoint Template (*.potx)**.

3 Navigate to the location where you are saving your work and create a new folder named **PowerPoint Chapter 4**

By default, templates are saved in a template folder on your computer's hard drive. To make the template portable so you can use it on another computer, change the drive to the location where you are saving your files.

4 Type the file name **Lastname_Firstname_4A_Meeting_Template** and then click **Save**. On the **Title bar**, look for ***.potx***, which is the file extension for templates.

The file extension .potx is automatically added to your file name. When working with templates, it is best to have the extensions displaying so you can tell the difference between a template and a presentation file.

> **More Knowledge | Modifying a Template**
>
> To make changes to a PowerPoint template, start PowerPoint, display Backstage view, click Open, navigate to the folder where the template is saved, click the file name, and then click Open.
>
> You can also open it from Windows Explorer. Navigate to the file, display Backstage view, and then click Open. Do not double-click on the file name because that action will display a copy of the template, not the template itself.

Activity 4.03 | Formatting a Slide Master with a Gradient Fill

In this activity, you will add a gradient fill to the slide master background. A ***gradient fill*** is a gradual progression of several colors blending into each other or shades of the same color blending into each other. A ***gradient stop*** allows you to apply different color combinations to selected areas of the background.

1 To the left of the Slide pane, click the **Office Theme Slide Master** thumbnail—the first thumbnail.

2 Click the **Slide Master tab**. In the **Background group**, click the **Background Styles** button to display the **Background Styles gallery**, and then click **Format Background**. In the **Format Background** dialog box, click **Fill**, if necessary. At the right, under **Fill**, click **Gradient fill**, if necessary. Click the **Type arrow** to display the list, and then click **Linear**.

> **Another Way**
>
> Instead of clicking the Add gradient stop button, you can click anywhere on the slider to add a gradient stop.

3 Under **Gradient stops**, at the right side, click the **Add gradient stop** button once. On the slider, drag the **gradient stop** to the left and then to the right and observe how the background changes on the slide and the percentage of gradation change in the Position box. Position the stop at **60%**.

> **Another Way**
>
> You can position the gradient stop by typing the value or using the spin arrows in the Position spin box.

4 Click the **Add gradient stop** button again to add another gradient stop, and then position it at **25%**. Click the **Color button arrow**, and then, click **Dark Blue, Text 2, Lighter 60%**, which is in the third row, fourth column. Compare your screen with Figure 4.7.

Applying a gradient stop to the background makes the color vary smoothly from a darker to a lighter shade. The additional stop with a different color provides more interest.

Figure 4.7

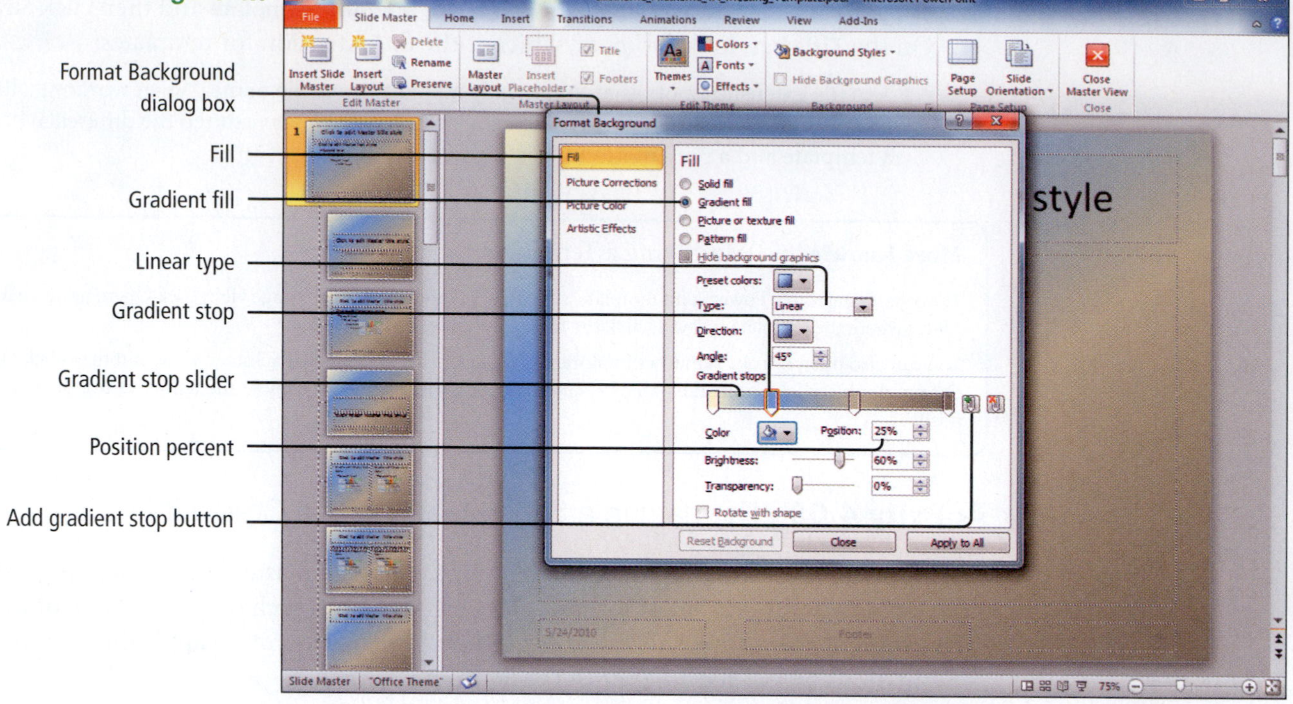

5 In the **Format Background** dialog box, click **Apply to All**. Click **Close**.

All slide layout thumbnails are displayed with the gradient fill.

6 **Save** the template.

Activity 4.04 | Formatting Slide Masters by Adding Pictures and Shapes

In this activity, you will add and format a shape and then insert a picture into the shape. Then you will duplicate the shape, move the copied shape to a different slide layout, and resize it.

1 Click the **Title Slide Layout** thumbnail—the second thumbnail—to make the **Title Slide Layout** master the active slide layout.

2 On the **View tab**, in the **Show group**, click the **Ruler** check box to display the horizontal and vertical rulers (if necessary). Click the **Insert tab**. In the **Illustrations group**, click the **Shapes** button. From the displayed list, under **Basic Shapes**, click the **Oval** shape. Position the pointer at **2 inches on the right side of the horizontal ruler** and **3 inches on the upper half of the vertical ruler**, and then click to insert the shape. It may look like a circle.

When you insert a shape, a Drawing Tools tab is displayed above the Ribbon tabs. A context-sensitive Format tab is displayed under the Drawing Tools tab. When you deselect the shape, the Drawing Tools and Format tabs disappear.

3 With the shape still selected, on the Ribbon, under **Drawing Tools**, click the **Format tab**. In the **Shapes Styles group**, click the **Shape Effects** button. From the displayed list, click **Bevel**. Point to some of the effects and note the changes made to the oval. In the first row, click the first effect— **Circle**. In the **Shapes Styles group**, click the **Shape Outline** button, and then click **No Outline**.

Removing the border softens the appearance of the shape.

4 With the oval still selected, in the **Size group**, change the **Shape Height** to **2"** and the **Shape Width** to **2"**. Compare your screen with Figure 4.8. If the placement of your oval does not match, click on the shape, and then move it to match the position shown in the figure.

Figure 4.8

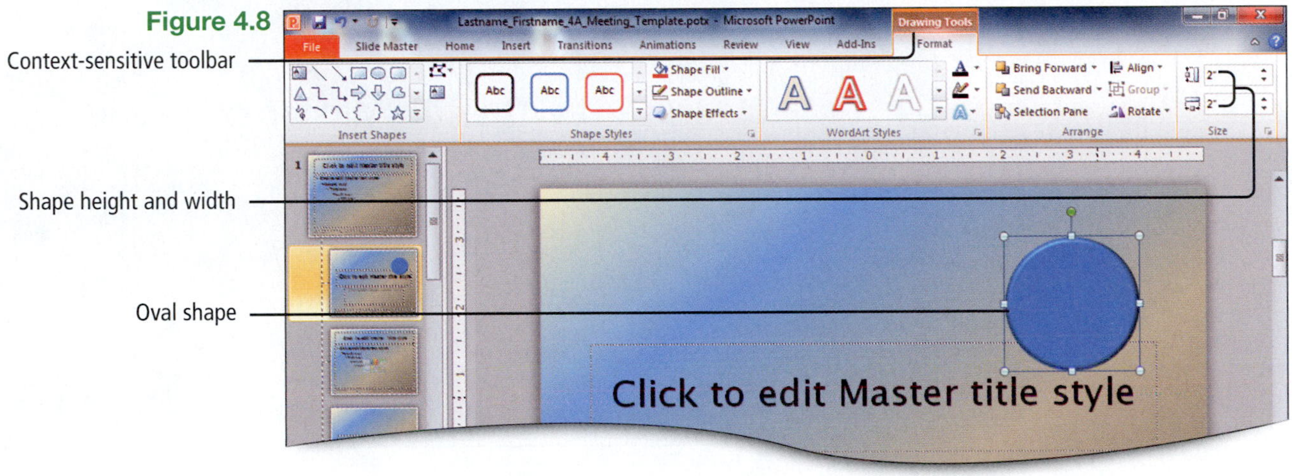

5 Click the **Format tab**. In the **Shape Styles group**, click the **Shape Fill** button, and then point to **Picture** to read the ScreenTip.

6 Click **Picture**. Navigate to the location where your data files are stored, and then click **p04A_Law1.jpg**. Click the **Insert** button.

The picture fills only the shape. When you add a picture inside the shape, a Picture Tools tab displays above the Ribbon tabs with a Format tab beneath it. One Format tab is for the Drawing Tools for the shape. The other Format tab is for the Picture Tools for the picture you inserted. When you deselect the shape, both the Drawing Tools and Picture Tools tabs disappear.

7 With the shape still selected, in the **Arrange group**, click the **Align** button to see the alignment options. Click **Align Center**. Click the **Align** button again, and then click **Align Bottom**. Deselect the shape to see it better. Click on the shape once again to select it.

The shape with the picture aligns in the horizontal center at the bottom of the slide.

8 On the Ribbon, under **Picture Tools**, click the **Format tab**. In the **Adjust Group**, click the **Color** button. Under **Recolor**, in the second row, click the second color—**Blue, Accent color 1 Dark**. Compare your screen with Figure 4.9.

Figure 4.9

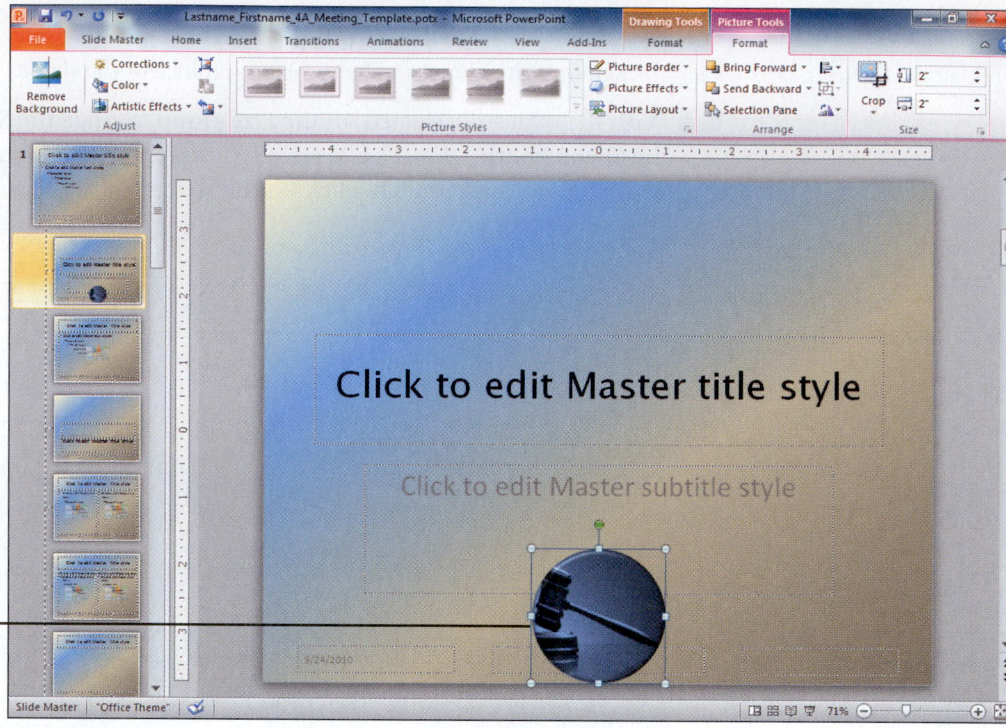

9 With the shape still selected, on the **Home tab**, in the **Clipboard group**, click the **Copy** button. Click the **Title and Content Layout** thumbnail, which is the third thumbnail. In the **Clipboard group**, click the **Paste** button.

The copied shape maintains the same format and position.

10 On the Ribbon, under **Drawing Tools**, click the **Format tab**. In the **Size group**, change the **Shape Height** to **1"** and the **Shape Width** to **1"**.

11 With the shape still selected, hold down the Shift key, and then click in the text placeholder. In the **Arrange group**, click the **Align** button, and then click **Align Right**. Click the **Align** button again, and then click **Align Bottom.** Compare your screen with Figure 4.10.

The logo now appears on the first slide of your presentation and then displays in a smaller format on slides using the title and content layout. If you wanted to have the logo on other slide layouts, you could copy the small logo to those layouts as well.

Figure 4.10

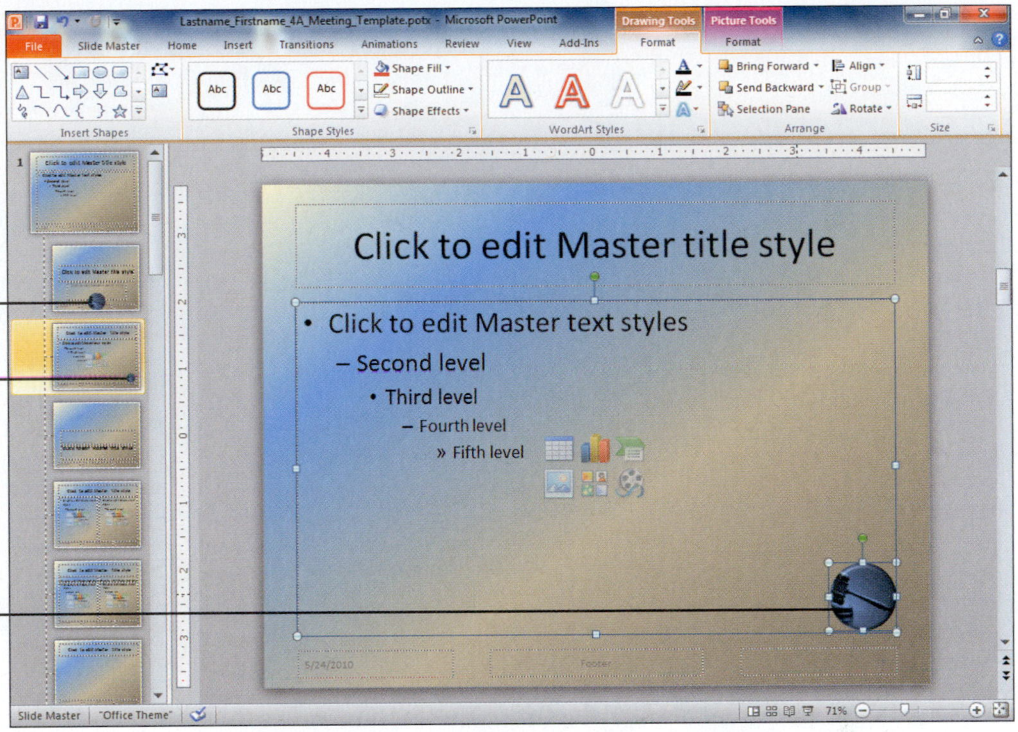

12 **Save** the template.

Activity 4.05 | Customizing Placeholders on a Slide Master

In this activity, you will change the size and position of the placeholders on the Title Slide master, format the Footer placeholder, and then change the bullet types on the Title and Content Slide master.

1 Click the **Title Slide Layout** thumbnail to make it the active slide. Click anywhere on the dashed border for the **title placeholder**, hold down the Shift key, and then drag the entire placeholder so the top border is at **3 inches on the upper half of the vertical ruler**. Release the Shift key. Click anywhere on the dashed border for the **subtitle placeholder**, hold down the Shift key, and then drag the entire placeholder so the top border is at **1 inch on the upper half of the vertical ruler**.

Moving a placeholder does not change the size of it. Using the Shift key while dragging the placeholder keeps the placeholder from moving to the left or right.

2 With the **subtitle placeholder** still selected, drag the **bottom middle sizing handle** to **.5 inches on the lower half of the vertical ruler** to decrease the size of the placeholder. Compare your screen with Figure 4.11.

Using the sizing handle changes the size of the placeholder.

Figure 4.11

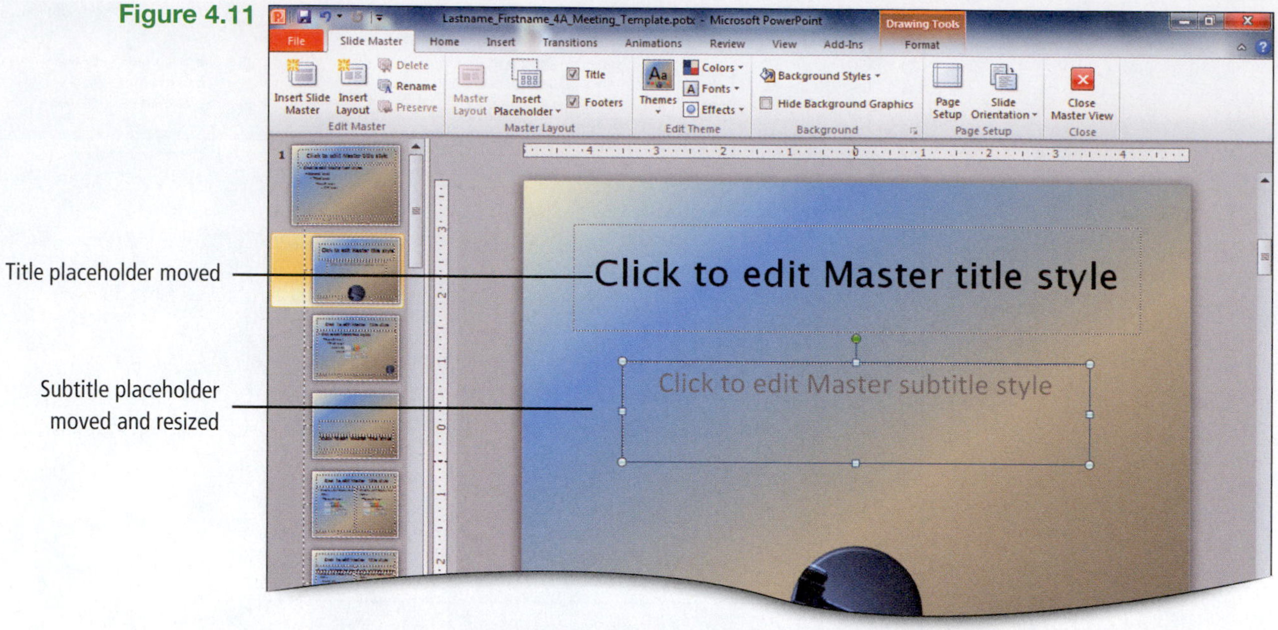

3 Click the **Office Theme Slide Master** thumbnail to make it the active slide. Click anywhere in the first bulleted line. On the **Home tab**, in the **Paragraph group**, click the **Bullets button arrow** [icon], and then click **Bullets and Numbering**. In the **Bullets and Numbering** dialog box, click the **Bulleted tab** if necessary. Click **Arrow Bullets**. At the bottom left, click the **Color button arrow**. Under **Theme Colors**, in the last column, click the last color—**Orange, Accent 6, Darker 50%**. Compare your screen with Figure 4.12. Click **OK**.

Figure 4.12

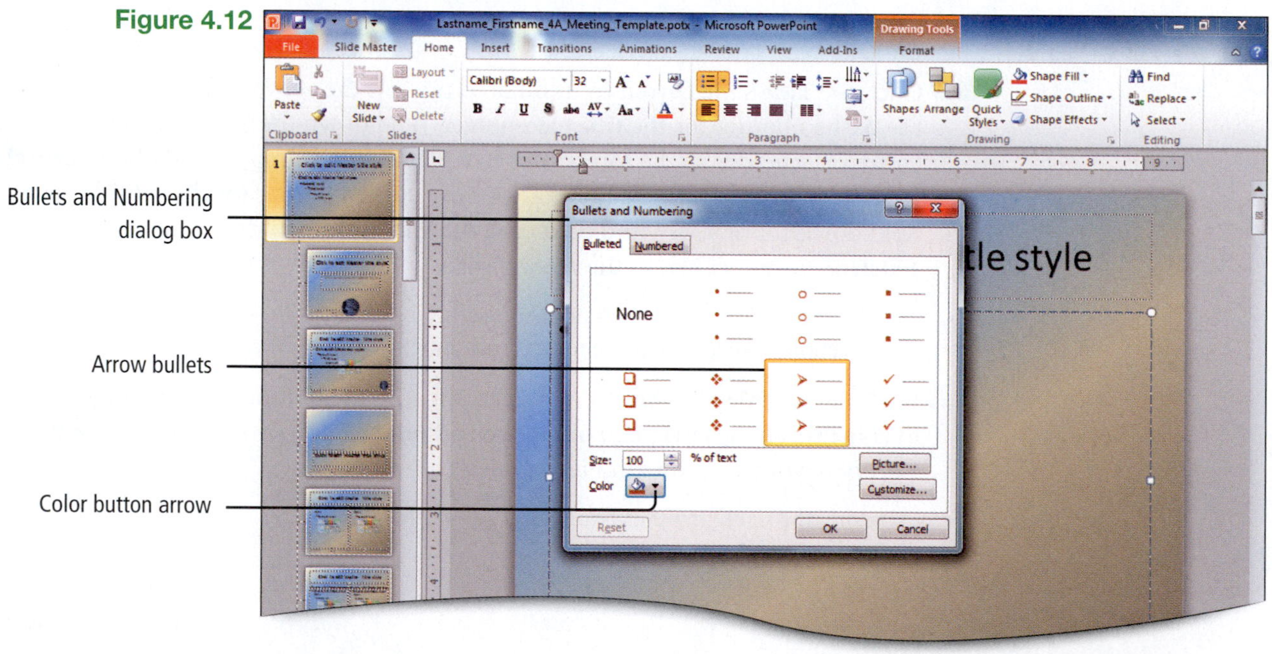

4 Click anywhere in the second bulleted line. Using the procedure that you used for the first bulleted line, display the **Bullets and Numbering** dialog box. Click the **Filled Square Bullets**. Click the **Color button arrow**, and then in the last row, last column, click **Orange, Accent 6, Darker 50%**. Click **OK**. Compare your screen with Figure 4.13.

All slides in the presentation will automatically display these custom bullets for the first two levels of the outline. If you intend to have more levels in your outline, you can continue customizing them.

Figure 4.13

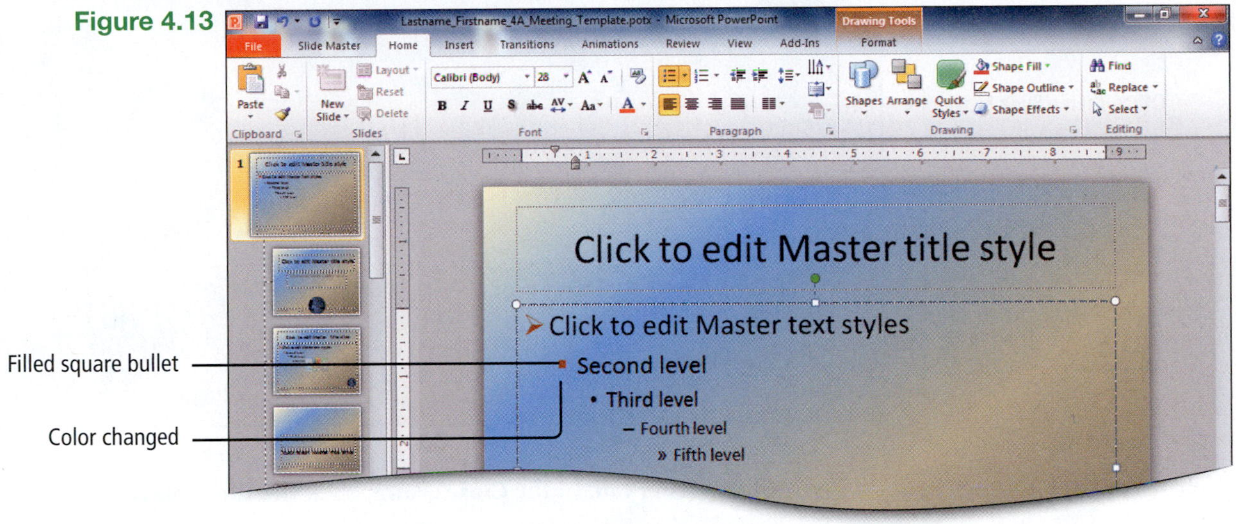

> **More Knowledge | Customizing Bullets on Different Slide Masters**
>
> When you customize the bullets on the Office Theme Slide Master, the customized bullets are available on all slides. If you want different bullets on some of the slide masters, customize the slide masters separately. For example, you could change the bullets on the Title and Content Layout and then change the bullets on the Two Content Layout.

> **Another Way**
>
> Highlight the date to select the date placeholder.

5 Click the first thumbnail, the **Office Theme Slide Master**. At the bottom left on the **Office Theme Master Slide**, click anywhere on the dashed border for the date placeholder to select the date. On the **Home tab**, change the **font size** to **10**.

Changing the font size on the Office Theme Slide Master will affect all slide layouts in the presentation.

6 Click the **Title Slide Layout** thumbnail. Select and drag the entire shape up so the top aligns at **1 inch on the lower half of the vertical ruler**. Under **Drawing Tools**, on the **Format tab**, in the **Arrange group**, click the **Align** button, and then select **Align Center**. Click outside to deselect the shape. Compare your screen with Figure 4.14.

When you drag a shape, you might change the alignment by accident, so set the alignment again. The shape now clears the area reserved for the footer.

Figure 4.14

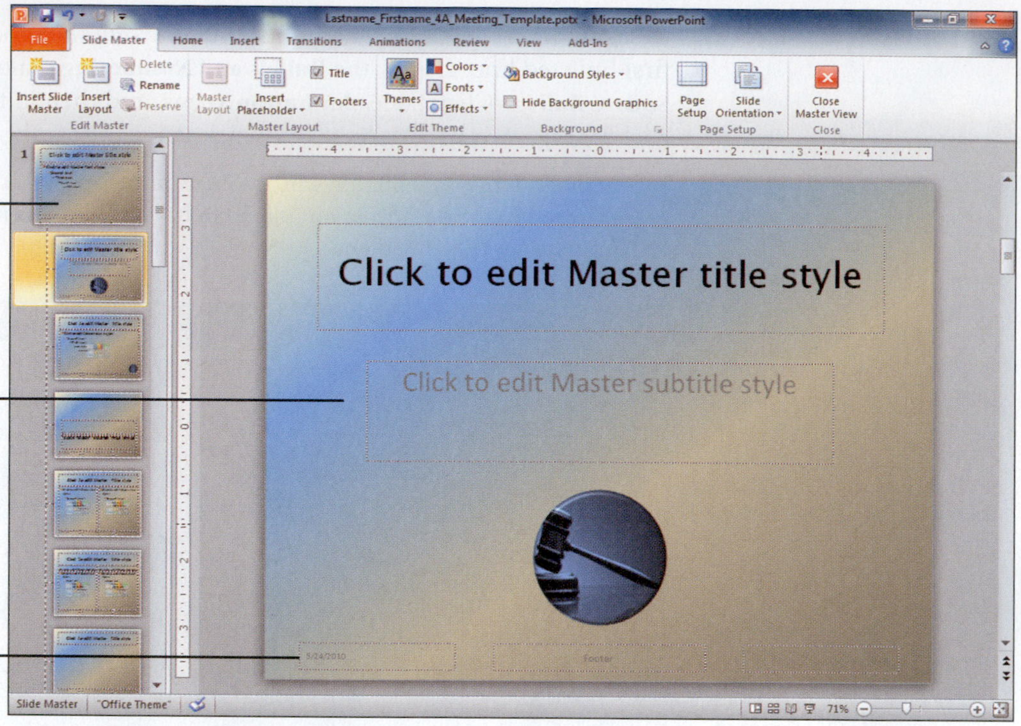

Office Theme Slide Master thumbnail

Office Theme Slide Master

Date placeholder

Another Way

On the status bar, click the Normal button to close the Master View.

7 Click the **Slide Master tab**. In the **Close group**, click the **Close Master View** button.

8 **Save** the template.

Activity 4.06 | Displaying and Editing the Handout Master

In this activity, you will edit the handout master for the meeting template you are building for the DeLong Grant Law Partners. You can print your presentation in the form of handouts that your audience can use to follow along as you give your presentation or keep for future reference. The ***Handout Master*** specifies the design of presentation handouts for an audience. You will learn how to change from landscape to portrait orientations, set the number of slides on a page, and specify whether you want to include the header, footer, date, and page number placeholders. Because you are working in a template file rather than a presentation file, the changes to the master affect presentations created from this template. You may change the settings in each presentation if you wish.

1 Open **Lastname_Firstname_4A_ Meeting_Template**, if necessary. Click the **View tab**. In the **Master View group**, click **Handout Master**. In the **Page Setup group**, click the **Handout Orientation** button, and then notice that the default orientation is **Portrait**. Click the **Slide Orientation** button, and then notice that the default orientation is **Landscape**. Leave the settings as they are. Compare your screen with Figure 4.15.

The Portrait handout orientation means that the slides will print on paper that is 8.5" wide by 11" long. The Landscape handout orientation means that the slides will print on paper that is 11" wide by 8.5" long.

Figure 4.15

Handout Master tab

Slide Orientation

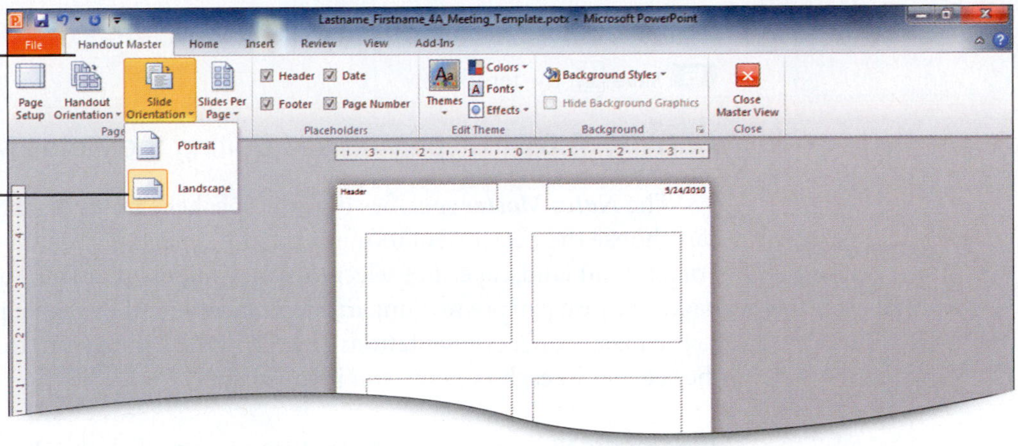

2 In the **Page Setup group**, click the **Slides Per Page** button. Click **3 Slides**. Compare your screen with Figure 4.16.

You can print the handouts with 1, 2, 3, 4, 6, or 9 slides per page.

Figure 4.16

Slides Per Page

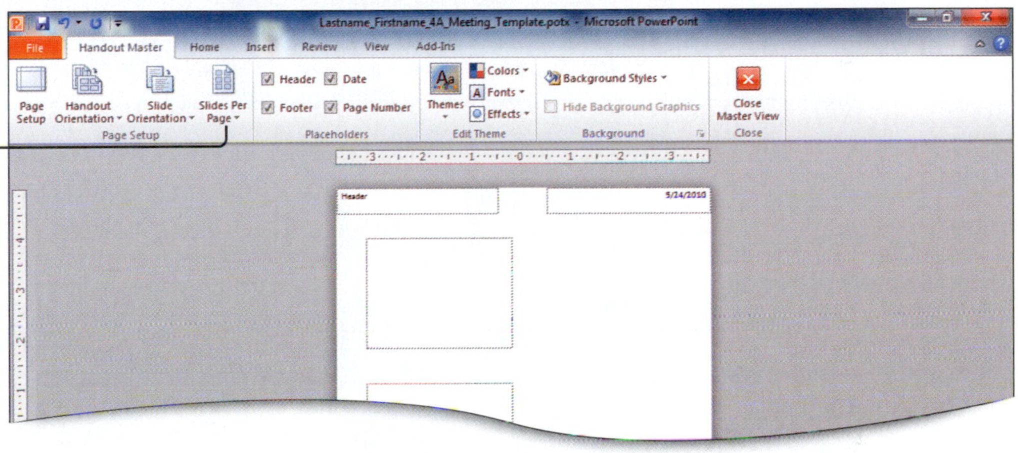

3 In the **Placeholders group**, click **Header** to remove the check mark. Compare your screen with Figure 4.17.

Notice that the Header placeholder disappeared. The placeholders for the notes master include Header, Footer, Date, and Page Number.

Figure 4.17

Header check box cleared

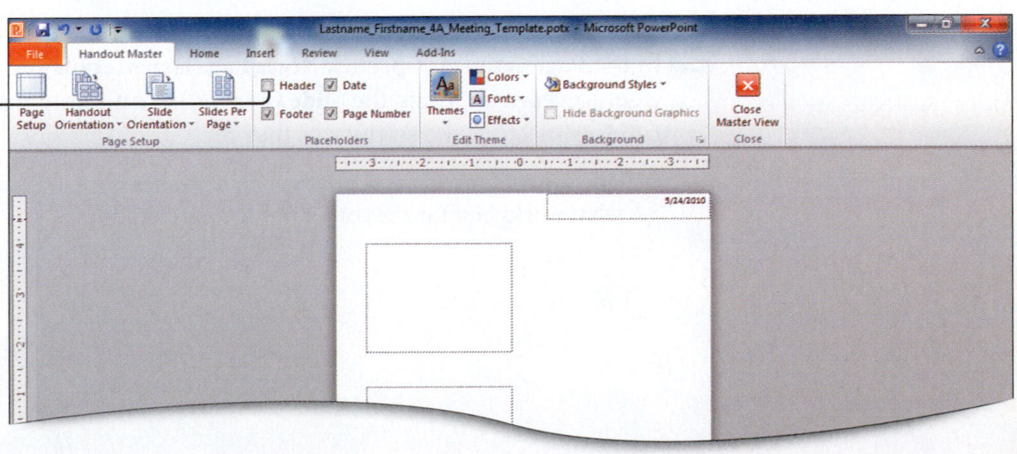

4 In the **Close group**, click **Close Master View**.

5 **Save** the template.

Activity 4.07 | Displaying and Editing the Notes Master

The ***Notes Master*** specifies how the speaker's notes display on the printed page. You can choose the page orientation for the notes page, switch the slide orientation between portrait and landscape, and select the placeholders that you want to display on the printed page. Because you are working in a template file rather than a presentation file, the changes to the master affect presentations created in the future from this template. You may change the settings in each presentation if you wish.

1 On the **View tab**, in the **Master Views group**, click the **Notes Master** button. Compare your screen with Figure 4.18.

Recall that the Notes page shows a picture of the slide as well as appropriate notes to assist the speaker when delivering the presentation to a group.

Figure 4.18

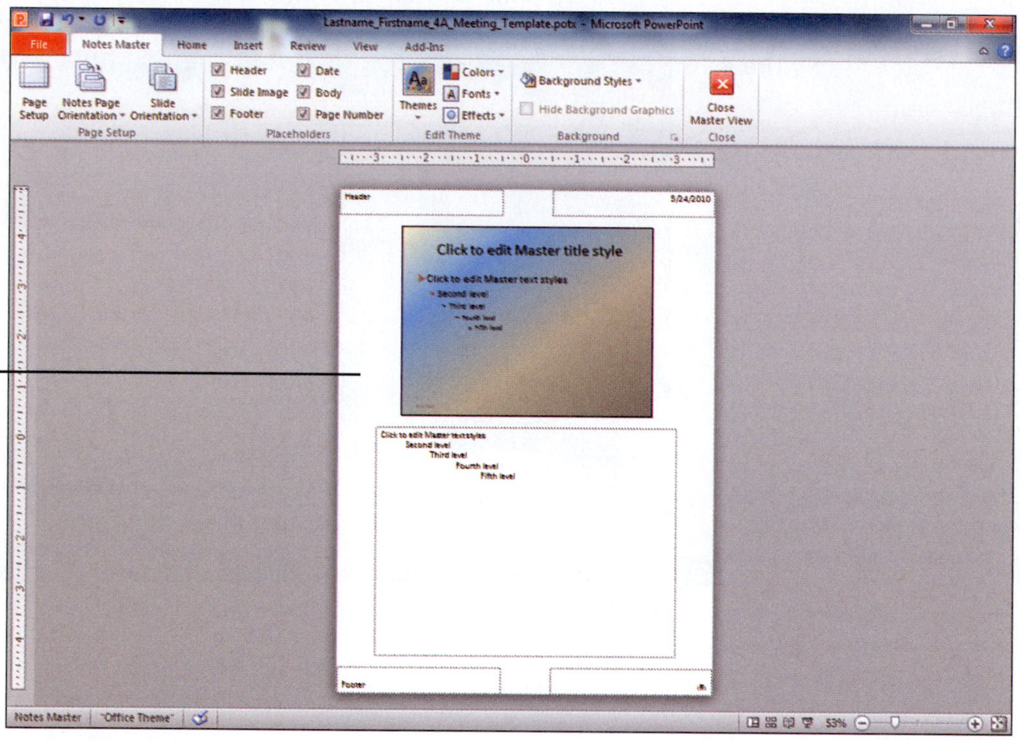

2 In the **Page Setup group**, click **Notes Page Orientation** and observe that the orientation is set for **Portrait**. Click the **Slide Orientation** and note that the orientation is set for **Landscape**. Leave the settings as they are.

The orientation that you use to print the notes page is a matter of personal preference and what works best for the content of the presentation.

3 In the **Placeholders group**, click **Header** to remove the Header placeholder. Compare your screen with Figure 4.19.

Notice that the Header placeholder disappears. The placeholders for the notes master include Header, Slide Image, Footer, Date, Body, and Page Number.

Figure 4.19

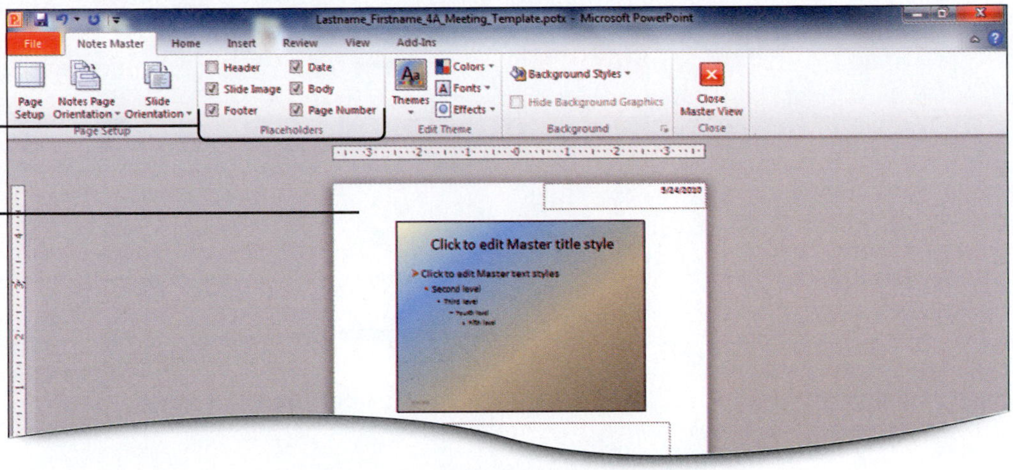

4 In the **Close group**, click **Close Master View**.

5 **Save** the presentation, and then close the template file.

Objective 2 | Apply a Custom Template to a Presentation

Activity 4.08 | Applying a Template to a Presentation

In this activity, you will use the meeting template to create a slide presentation that explains the new filing procedures to the law partners. Recall that templates you design are, by default, saved in a templates folder on the computer. You, however, are saving your template in your Chapter 4 folder.

1 **Start** PowerPoint if necessary. Display **Backstage** view, and then click **New**. Under **Available Templates and Themes**, you see several categories listed in the **Home group**. Compare your screen with Figure 4.20. For complete descriptions of the templates and themes, see Figure 4.21.

Recall that a PowerPoint template is a file that contains layouts, theme colors, theme fonts, theme effects, background styles, and content. It contains the complete blueprint for slides pertaining to a specific kind of presentations. A theme includes coordinated colors and matched backgrounds, fonts, and effects.

Figure 4.20

Available Templates and Themes

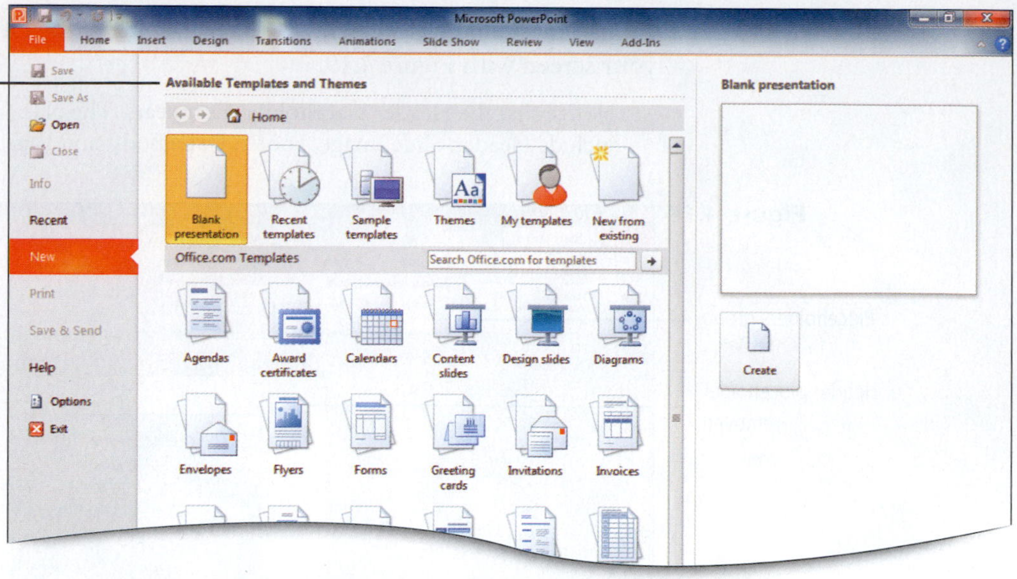

Available Templates and Themes

Available Templates and Themes	Description
Blank presentation	Default template that contains no content or design.
Recent templates	Templates that you have used recently.
Sample templates	Templates designed for specific uses, such as a photo album, quiz show, or training.
Themes	Templates with themes already added.
My templates	Templates that you have saved on your computer in the default template folder.
New from existing	Templates that you have created and saved.

Figure 4.21

2 Under **Available Templates and Themes**, click **New from existing**. Navigate to the location where you are saving your files. Locate **Lastname_Firstname_4A_Meeting Template.potx**. Click the file name one time, and then compare your screen with Figure 4.22.

Recall that the extension for a PowerPoint template is .potx and the extension for a PowerPoint file or presentation is ***.pptx***. The Open button changes to Create New.

Figure 4.22

Saved template file

Create New button

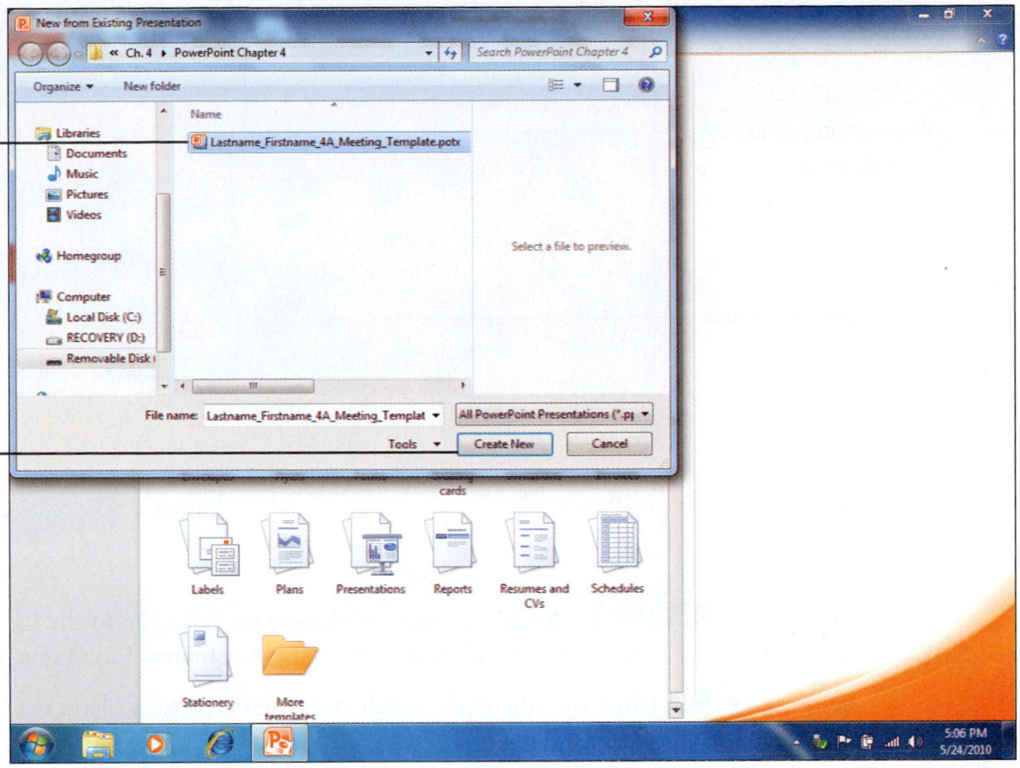

Alert! | **Did You Display the File Extensions?**

If the file extension does not display on the Title bar, go to Windows Explorer. On the Windows menu bar, click **Organize**, and then click **Folder and search options**. In the **Folder Options** dialog box, click the **View tab**. Under **Files and Folders**, scroll to **Hide extensions for known file types**, and then remove the check mark in the check box. Click **OK**.

3 At the lower right of the window, click the **Create New** button to display a copy of the template with the Title slide active. Compare your screen with Figure 4.23

The file name on the Title Bar displays as Presentation2 – Microsoft PowerPoint (the presentation number may vary).

More Knowledge | **Opening a Template**

If you need to edit a template, start PowerPoint. Display Backstage view, click Open, navigate to your storage location, and then open the file. You can also open a template by navigating to it in Windows Explorer, right-clicking the file name, and then clicking Open. Make sure that you see the .potx at the end of the file name in the Title bar. To open a template saved in the Template folder on your computer, you have to know the path to the template.

Figure 4.23

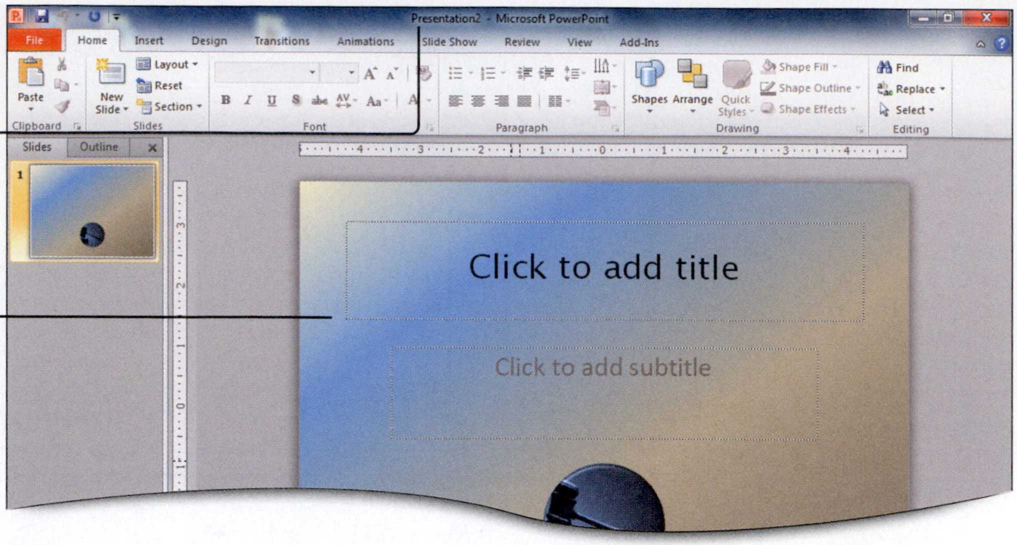

4 Display **Backstage** view, click **Save As**. Navigate to the location where you are saving your files, and then save the file as **Lastname_Firstname_4A_Filing_Procedures**

> **Another Way**
>
> Press the keyboard shortcut Ctrl + Enter to move to the subtitle placeholder.

5 Click the title placeholder, and then type **New Filing Procedures** Click the subtitle placeholder, and then type **DeLong Grant Law Partners**

6 On the **Home tab**, in the **Slides group**, click the **New Slide button arrow**. The displayed gallery shows the formatting you created for the slide layouts. Compare your screen with Figure 4.24.

Figure 4.24

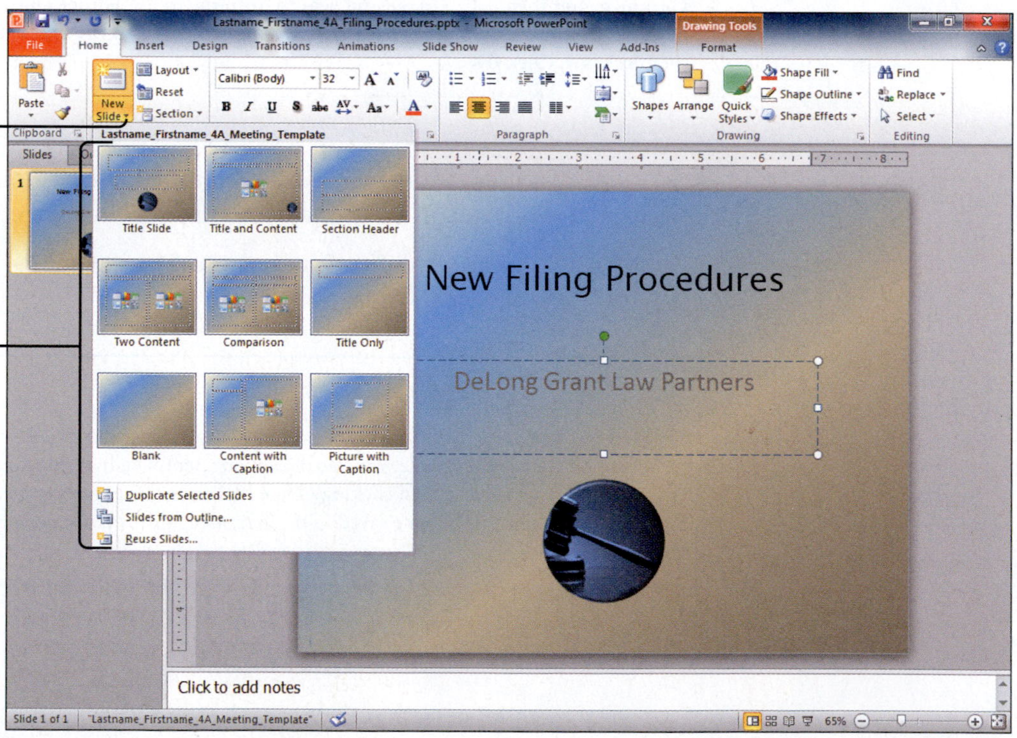

Another Way

Use the Tab to increase the outline level. Use the Shift + Tab key combination to decrease the outline level.

7 Click **Title and Content** to add the slide and make it the active slide. In the title placeholder, type **Referencing Number System** Press Ctrl + Enter. In the content placeholder, type **Include these three parts in the number:** and then press Enter. In the **Paragraph group**, click the **Increase List Level** button to increase the outline level. Type **Client last name** Press Enter, and then type **Date file opened** Press Enter, type **Date file completed (if applicable)** and then press Enter.

When you increase an outline level, the text moves to the right. When you press Enter, the same outline level continues.

8 In the **Paragraph group**, click the **Decrease List Level** button to decrease the outline level. Type **Example: DeLong_01-15-2014_10-14-2016**

To move the text to the left, you need to decrease the outline level.

Another Way

To add a slide with the same layout as the previous slide, you can click the New Slide Button without displaying the gallery.

9 In the **Slides group**, click the **New Slide button arrow**, and then click **Title and Content** to add a third slide. In the title placeholder, type **Hardcopy Filing** and then press Ctrl + Enter. Following the procedure explained for the previous slide, type the following bulleted items for the Hardcopy Filing slide in the content placeholder.

Include the reference number on all pages of the legal document.

- **Place the number in the upper right corner.**
- **Add the date completed when the case is closed.**

Retain a copy of the document for your personal file.

10 In the **Notes pane**, type **The ending date is the actual date that the case is closed. Until then, leave the ending date blank.** Compare your screen with Figure 4.25.

Figure 4.25

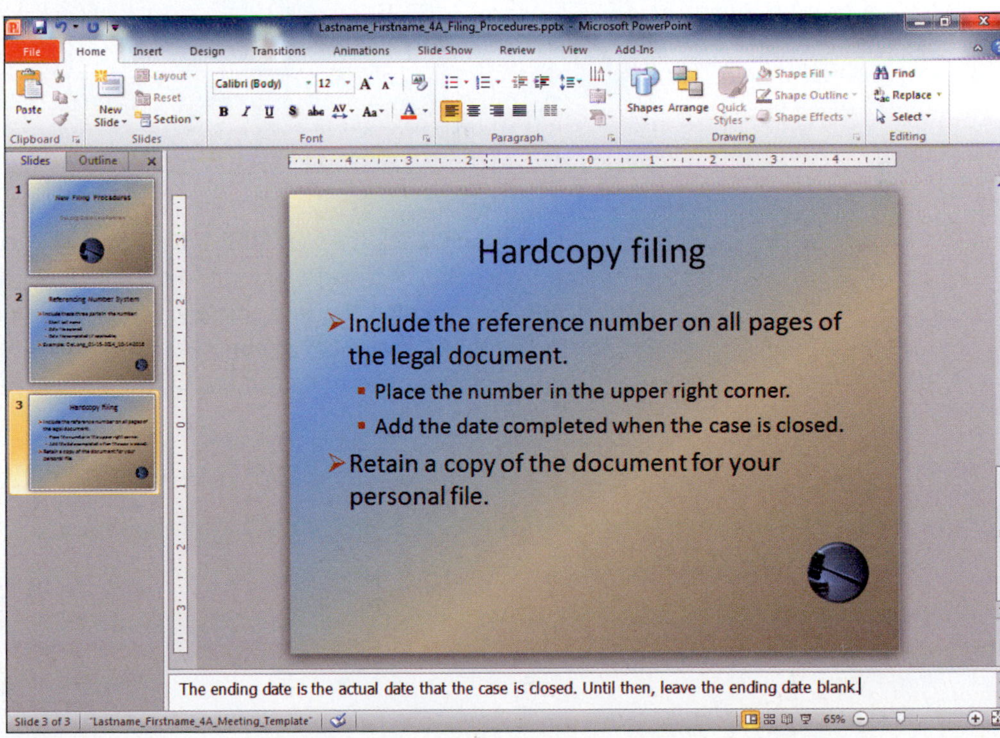

11 Add another **Title and Content** slide. In the title placeholder, type **Digital Filing** and then press Ctrl + Enter. In the content placeholder, type the following bulleted items. Compare your screen with Figure 4.26.

Use the reference number for the file name.

Save a copy of the file to the company database.

Require authorized employees to use a Login to view the file.

Lock the file after any changes are made.

Figure 4.26

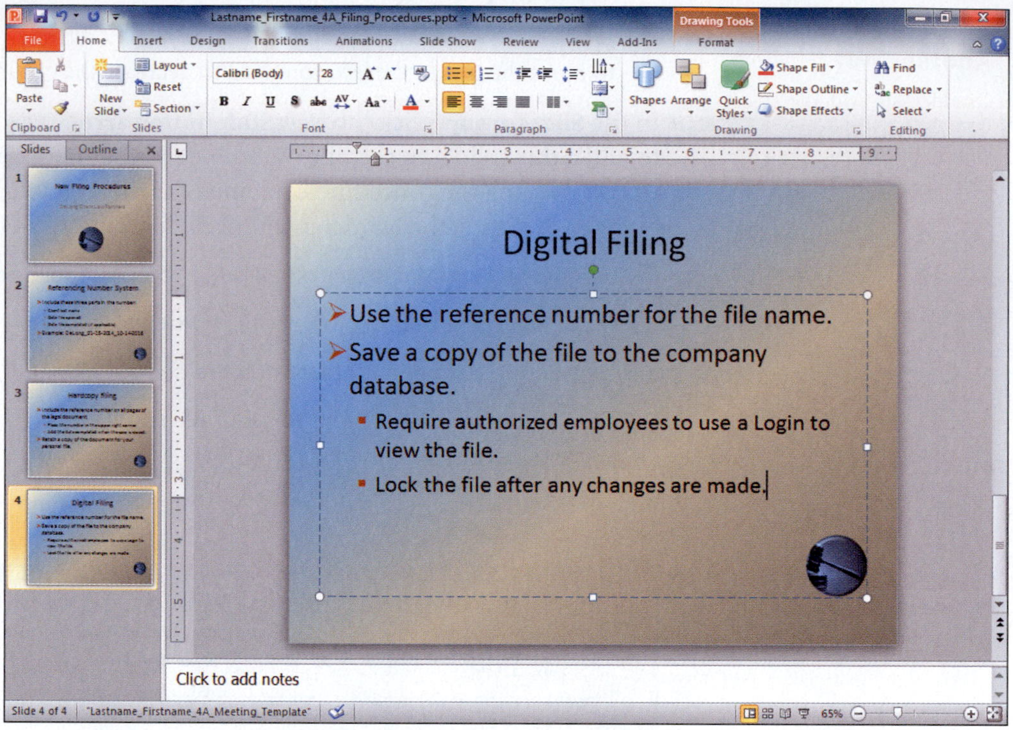

12 In the **Slides group**, click the **New Slide button arrow**, and then click **Title and Content** to add another slide. In the title placeholder, type **Summary** In the content placeholder, type **All changes are effective immediately. Direct questions to the support team.** On the **Home tab**, in the **Paragraph group**, click the **Bullets** button to remove the bullet. In the **Paragraph group**, click the **Center** button.

13 On the left side of the content placeholder, click the **middle sizing handle**, and then drag the sizing handle to **3 inches on the left side of the horizontal ruler**. On the right side of the content placeholder, drag the **middle sizing handle** to **3 inches on the right side of the horizontal ruler**. With the content placeholder still selected, at the bottom of the content placeholder, drag the **middle sizing handle** to **1.5 inches on the lower half of the vertical ruler** to reduce the size of the placeholder. Hold down the Shift key, and then click the top border of the content placeholder. Drag the entire placeholder down so the top is aligned at **1.5 inches on the upper half of the vertical ruler**. In the **Paragraph group**, click the **Line Spacing** button, and then click **1.5**. Compare your screen with Figure 4.27.

Figure 4.27

Bullet removed and text formatted

Placeholder positioned and resized

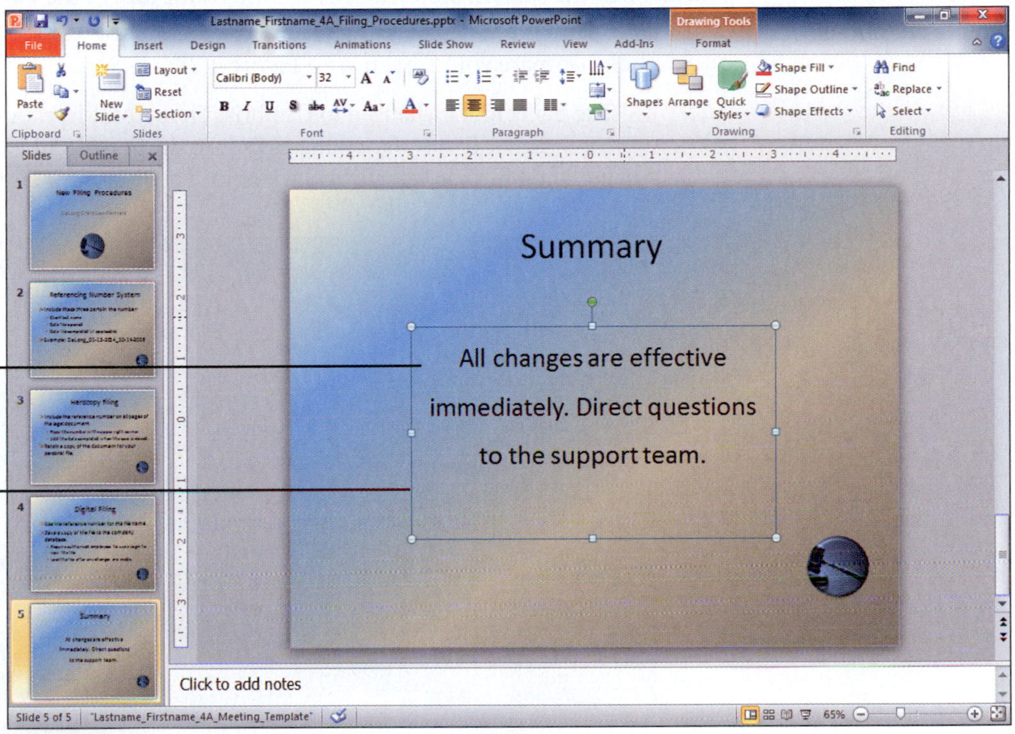

14 On the **Insert tab**, in the **Text group**, click the **Header & Footer** button to display the **Header and Footer** dialog box. Click the **Notes and Handouts tab**. Under **Include on page**, select the **Date and time** check box, and then select **Fixed**. If necessary, clear the **Header** check box, and then select the **Page number** and **Footer** check boxes. In the **Footer** box, using your own name, type **Lastname_Firstname_4A_Filing_Procedures** and then click **Apply to All**.

15 Display **Backstage** view, click **Properties**, and then click **Show Document Panel**. Replace the text in the **Author** box with your own first and last name. In the **Subject** box, type your course name and section number. In the **Keywords** box, type **filing, number, system Close** the **Document Information Panel**.

16 **Save** the presentation.

Activity 4.09 | Editing Slide Masters in an Existing Presentation

Occasionally, you might want to change the master design for a presentation created from your custom template. In this activity, you will change the bullet style on the Title and Content Layout slide master.

1 Open **Lastname_Firstname_4A_Filing_Procedures** if necessary. On the **View tab**, in the **Master View group**, click **Slide Master**.

2 Click the first thumbnail—**Lastname_Firstname_4A_Meeting...Slide Master**. On the **Slide Master tab**, in **Edit theme group**, click the **Fonts** button, and then click **Office 2**.

3 Click the second bulleted line. On the **Home tab**, in the **Paragraph group**, click the **Bullets button arrow**. Click **Checkmark Bullets**. Point to the Slide Master thumbnail, and then compare your screen with Figure 4.28.

The bullet font is changed to Cambria. The second-level bullets are now displayed as checkmarks. Recall, that changes made to the first thumbnail affect all slides. Notice that the first thumbnail, originally named Office Theme, is now displayed with the name of the file.

Figure 4.28

Font changed to Cambria

Slide Master

Bullets changed to check marks

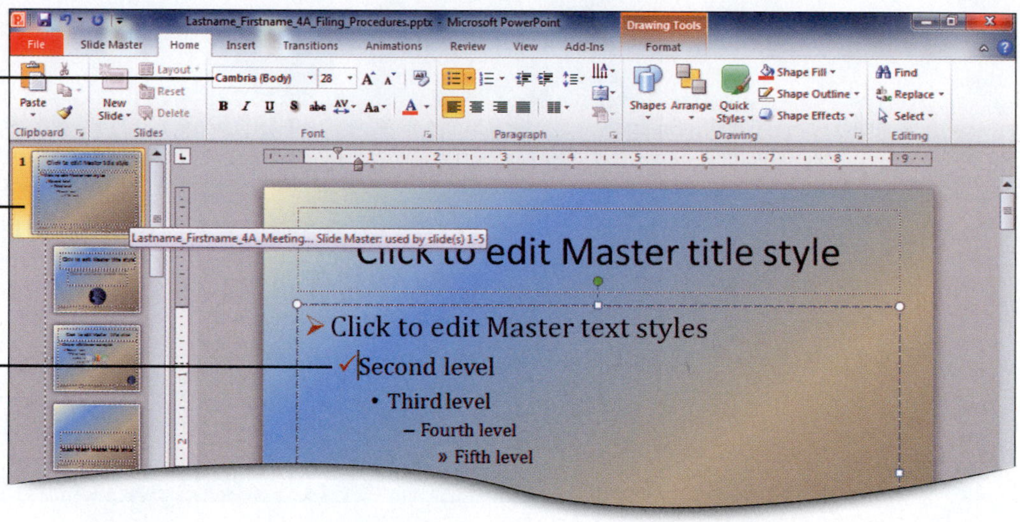

Another Way

Press F5 to start a slide show from the beginning.

4 On the **Slide Master tab**, in the **Close group**, click the **Close Master View** button. On the **Slide Show tab**, in the **Start Slide Show group**, click the **From Beginning** button. View the entire slide presentation.

Because you changed the second-level bullet to checkmarks on the slide master, all slides have checkmarks instead of square bullets. Changing the bullet style on the master slide saved you the time it would take to change the bullets on each slide.

5 **Save** your presentation. Print **Handouts 3 Slides**, or submit your presentation electronically as directed by your instructor.

The change that you made to the bullets affects only this presentation. The original meeting template still uses the square bullets. If you want the change to be permanent on the template, you should open the template and make the change in that file.

6 **Close** the presentation, and then **Exit** PowerPoint.

7 Submit **Lastname_Firstname_4A_Meeting_Template** and **Lastname_Firstname_4A_Filing_Procedures** as directed by your instructor.

End **You have completed Project 4A**

Project 4B Commented Presentation

myitlab
Project 4B Training

Project Activities

In Activities 4.10 through 4.16, you will use reviewing comments to provide feedback to a presentation created by a colleague at the DeLong Grant Law Partners firm. Then you will publish your presentation in both PDF and XPS formats. These formats preserve the document formatting and enable file sharing. You will save the presentation as Word handouts for the audience. Finally, you will check your presentation for compatibility with previous versions of PowerPoint and mark the presentation as final. Your completed presentation will look similar to Figure 4.29.

Project Files

For Project 4B, you will need the following file:

p04B_Entertainment_Basics.pptx

You will save your presentation as:

Lastname_Firstname_4B_Entertainment_Basics.pptx
Lastname_Firstname_4B_Entertainment_Basics.pdf
Lastname_Firstname_4B_Entertainment_Basics.xps
Lastname_Firstname_4B_Entertainment_Basics.docx

Project Results

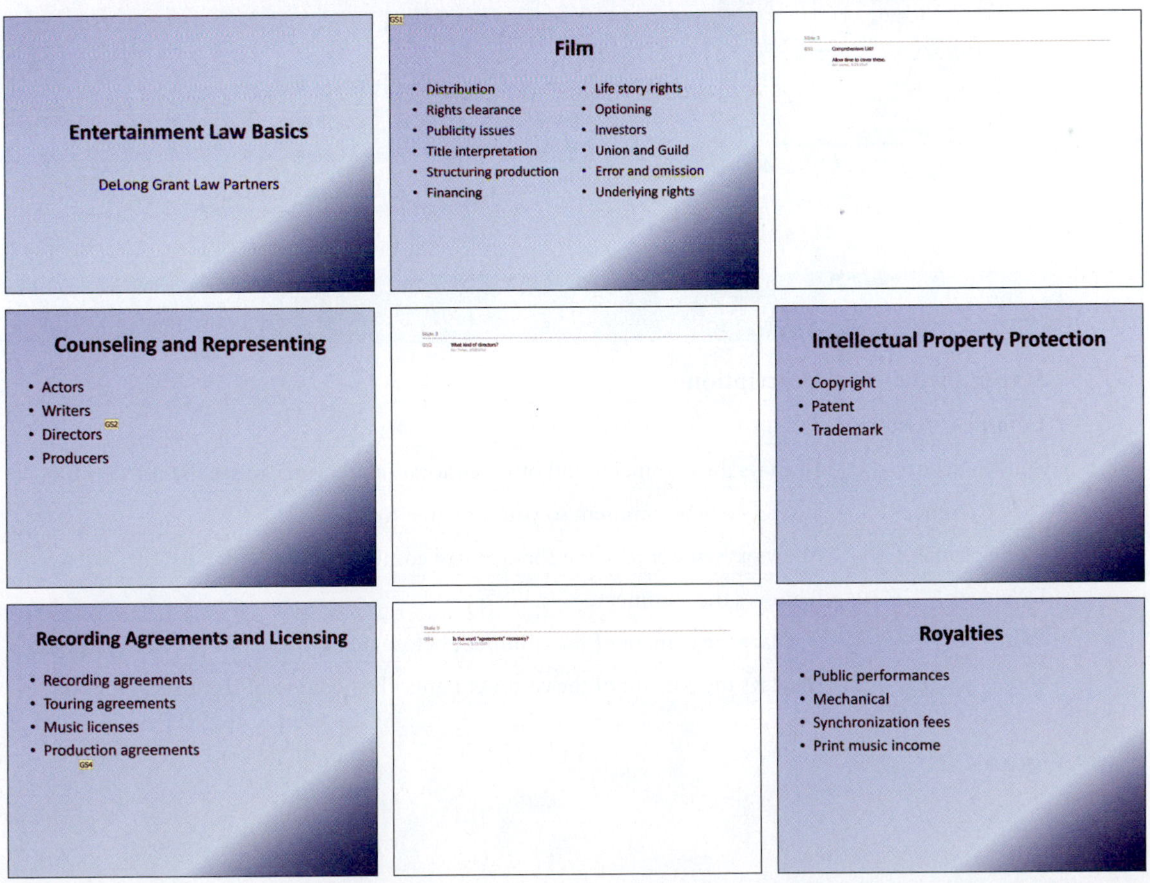

Figure 4.29
Project 4B Commented Presentation

Objective 3 | Create and Edit Comments

A ***comment*** is a note that you can attach to a letter or word on a slide or to an entire slide. People use comments to provide feedback on a presentation. A ***reviewer*** is someone who adds comments to the presentation to provide feedback.

Activity 4.10 | Adding Comments

In this activity, you will add comments to your meeting presentation. Comments may be added by the person who created the presentation or other persons who are invited to provide suggestions.

1 **Start** PowerPoint. Locate and open the file **p04B_Entertainment_Basics.pptx**. Navigate to the location where you are storing your folders and projects for this chapter, and then **Save** the file as **Lastname_Firstname_4B_Entertainment_Basics**

2 Make **Slide 2** the active slide. Click the **Review tab**. In the **Comments group**, point to each of the buttons and read the ScreenTips. Compare your screen with Figure 4.30. For a complete explanation of each of these buttons, see Figure 4.31.

Figure 4.30

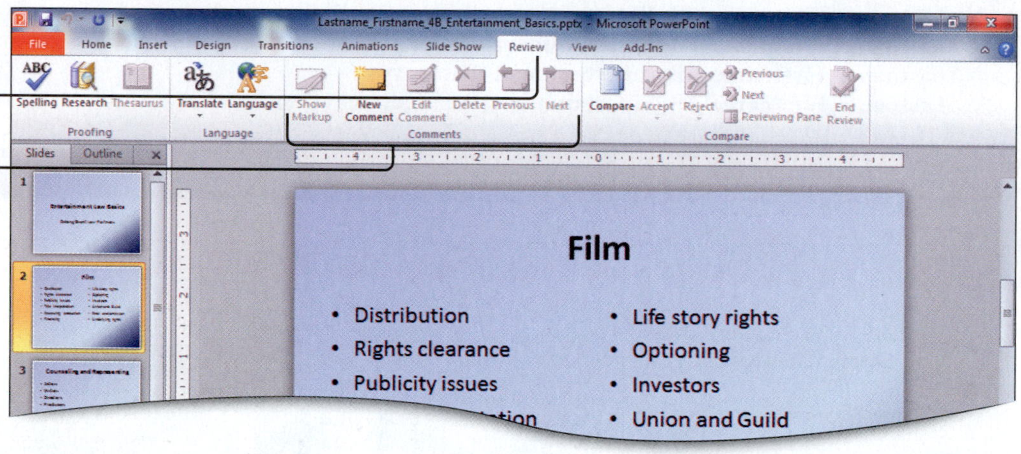

Reviewing Elements

Screen Element	Description
Comments Group	
Show Markup	Displays the comments and other annotations so you can see them.
New Comment	Displays a new comment so you can enter a note.
Edit Comment	Allows a reviewer to make changes to a comment.
Delete	Removes the comment.
Previous	Displays the content of the comment before the position of the insertion point.
Next	Displays the content of the comment after the position of the insertion point.

Figure 4.31

3 In the **Comments group**, click the **New Comment** button. In the space provided, type **Comprehensive List!** In the **Comments group**, all buttons in the Comments group become active. Compare your screen with Figure 4.32.

When there are no comments in the file, the only button in the Comments group that is active is the New Comment button. On other slides, the Edit button is active only when there is a comment on that slide. When a comment is added, the relevant buttons become active. When no placeholder or text is selected before adding a comment, by default the comment displays at the upper left corner of the slide. The person's name displays at the upper left and the date at the upper right in the comment.

Figure 4.32

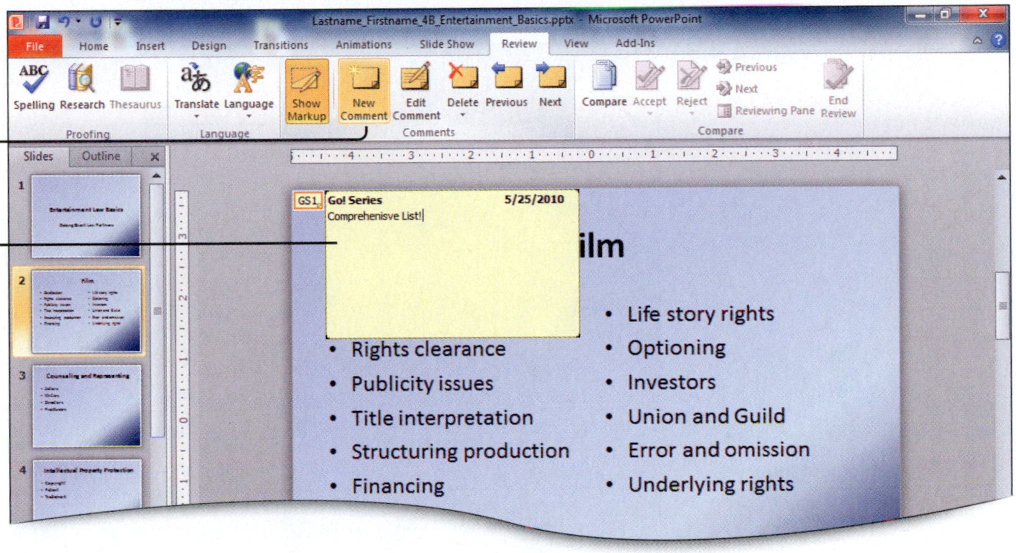

4 Make **Slide 3** the active slide. Click at the end of the third bulleted item, after *Directors*. In the **Comments group**, click **New Comment**. Type **What kind of directors?** Click outside the comment to close it. Compare your screen with Figure 4.33.

Placing the insertion point within a specific area of the slide will position the comment box at that place.

Figure 4.33

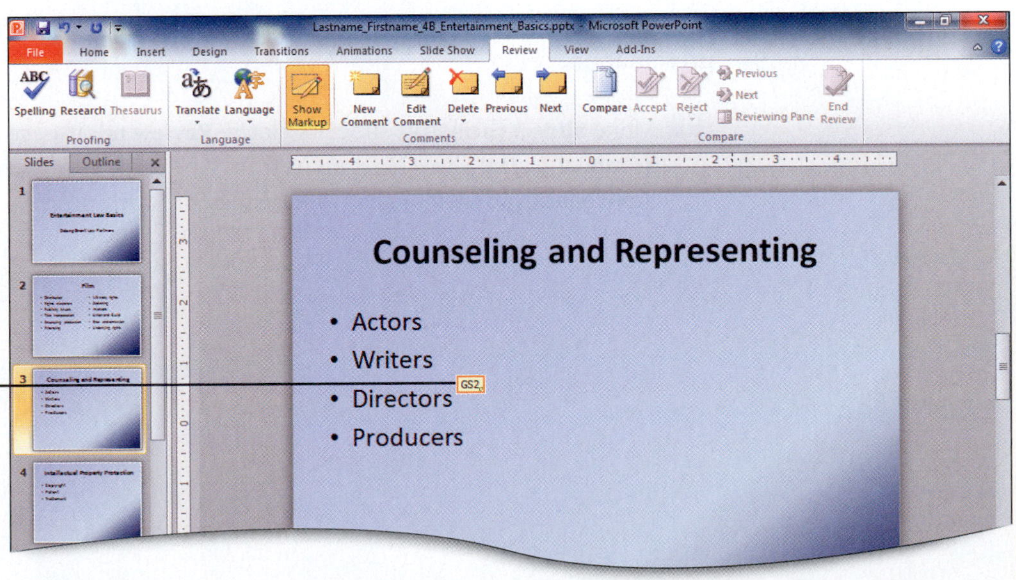

5 Make **Slide 4** the active slide. Select the word *Copyright*. Use the procedure explained in the previous steps to add this comment: **Add short definitions.** Click outside the comment to close it.

When you add a comment to selected text, the comment is displayed near the selected text.

6 Select **Slide 5**, and then enter this comment: **Is the word "agreements" necessary?** Click outside the comment. Drag the comment so it is positioned directly below the last bulleted line, under the word *Production*. Compare your screen with Figure 4.34.

You can drag a comment box to any position on the slide. Note that bold, underline, and italic are not available in the comment box.

Figure 4.34

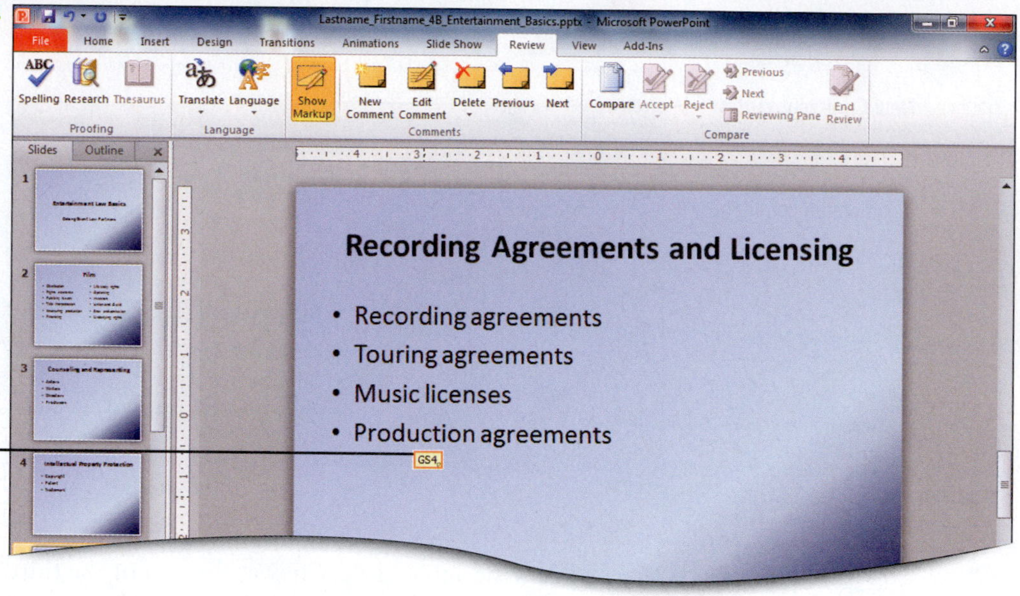

Comment moved to new location

7 **Save** the presentation.

Activity 4.11 | Reading Comments

In this activity, you will learn how to navigate among the comments entered in a presentation.

1 Make **Slide 2** the active slide. Click the **Review tab** if necessary. In the **Comments group**, click the **Show Markup** button. Notice that the comment disappears. Click the **Show Markup** button again to redisplay the comment.

Another Way

You can also point to a closed comment to reveal the message.

2 Make **Slide 1** the active slide. In the **Comments group**, click the **Next** button. The first comment displays so you can read it. Click the **Next** button again to read the second comment, which is on **Slide 3**. Continue clicking the **Next button** until you see the message *PowerPoint reached the end of all changes. Do you want to continue from the beginning of the change list?* Compare your screen with Figure 4.35. Click **Cancel**.

Comments are numbered consecutively in the order they were added.

Figure 4.35

3 In the **Comments group**, click the **Previous** button to read the previous comment. Continue clicking **Previous** until you receive this message: *PowerPoint reached the beginning of all changes. Do you want to continue from the end of the change list?* Click **Cancel**.

Use the Next and Previous buttons to read the comments in your presentation.

Activity 4.12 | Editing Comments

In this activity, you will learn how to edit a comment and how to delete a comment.

1 Make **Slide 2** the active slide, if necessary. At the upper left corner of the slide, click the comment. The text in the comment displays so you can read it, but you cannot edit it. See Figure 4.36.

Figure 4.36

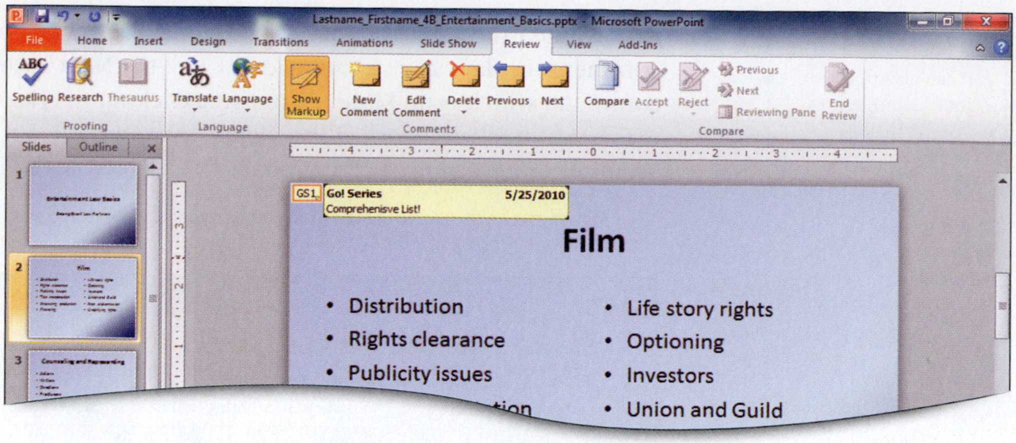

> **Another Way**
>
> You can double-click the comment box to edit the content. Also, you can right-click in the comment and click Edit Comment.

2 In the **Comments group**, click the **Edit Comment** button and notice the insertion point at the end of the text. Press Enter two times, and then type **Allow time to cover these.** Compare your screen with Figure 4.37.

When you point to or click on a comment, you can only read the message. To edit the comment, you need to click the Edit Comment button.

Figure 4.37

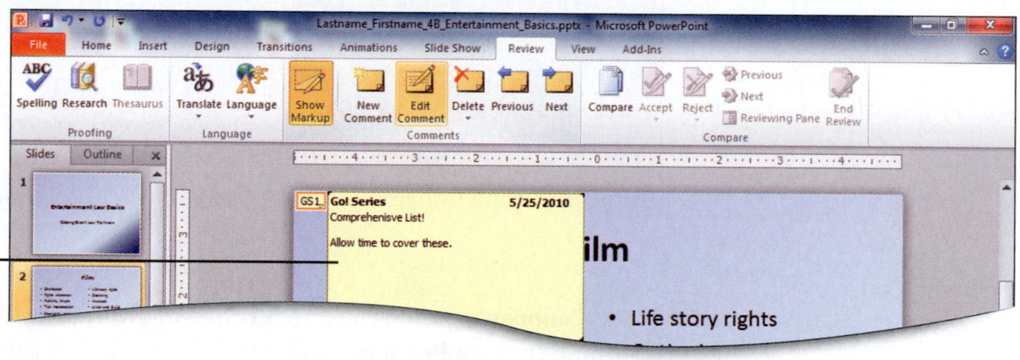

3 Click the **Next** button until you reach the comment on **Slide 4**. In the **Comments group**, click the **Delete button arrow**, and then read the three options: *Delete*, *Delete All Markup on the Current Slide*, and *Delete All Markup in this Presentation*. Compare your screen with Figure 4.38.

Figure 4.38

Another Way

To delete a comment, you can also right-click the comment and then click Delete Comment.

4 Click **Delete** to remove this comment. Click the **Next** and **Previous** buttons to see how comments are numbered.

Recall that comments are numbered consecutively in the order that they are inserted. When you delete a comment, the numbering of the rest of the comments does not change.

5 **Save** the presentation.

Objective 4 | Prepare a Presentation for Distribution

PowerPoint offers several ways to share, or distribute, a presentation. A common way is to create a PDF document that people who have Adobe Reader installed on their computers can read. You can also create an XPS document that people who have an XPS viewer can read. Another way to share a presentation is to create handouts in Microsoft Word.

Activity 4.13 | Publishing a Presentation in PDF and XPS Format

In this activity, you will save a presentation in PDF and XPS file formats. Adobe's ***Portable Document Format (PDF)*** preserves document formatting and enables file sharing. The PDF format is also useful if you intend to use commercial printing methods. ***XML Paper Specification (XPS)*** is Microsoft's electronic paper format, an alternative to the PDF format, that also preserves document formatting and enables file sharing. When an XPS or PDF file is viewed online or printed, it retains the format that you intended, and the data in the file cannot be easily changed.

1 Open **Lastname_Firstname_4B_Entertainment_Basics**, if necessary. On the **Insert tab**, in the **Text group**, click the **Header & Footer** button to display the **Header and Footer** dialog box. Click the **Notes and Handouts tab**. Under **Include on page**, select the **Date and time** check box, and then select **Fixed**. If necessary, clear the **Header** check box, and then select the **Page number** and **Footer** check boxes. In the **Footer** box, using your own name, type **Lastname_Firstname_4B_Entertainment_Basics** and then click **Apply to All**.

2 Make **Slide 1** active. Display **Backstage** view, and then click **Save & Send**. Under **File Types**, click **Create PDF/XPS Document**. At the right side of your screen, read the explanation of a PDF/XPS document. Compare your screen with Figure 4.39.

Presentations saved as a PDF/XPS document are saved in a fixed format. The document looks the same on most computers. Fonts, formatting, and images are preserved. Because content cannot be easily changed, your document is more secure. To view a PDF or XPS file, you must have a reader installed on your computer. Free viewers are available on the Web to view PDF and XPS documents.

Figure 4.39

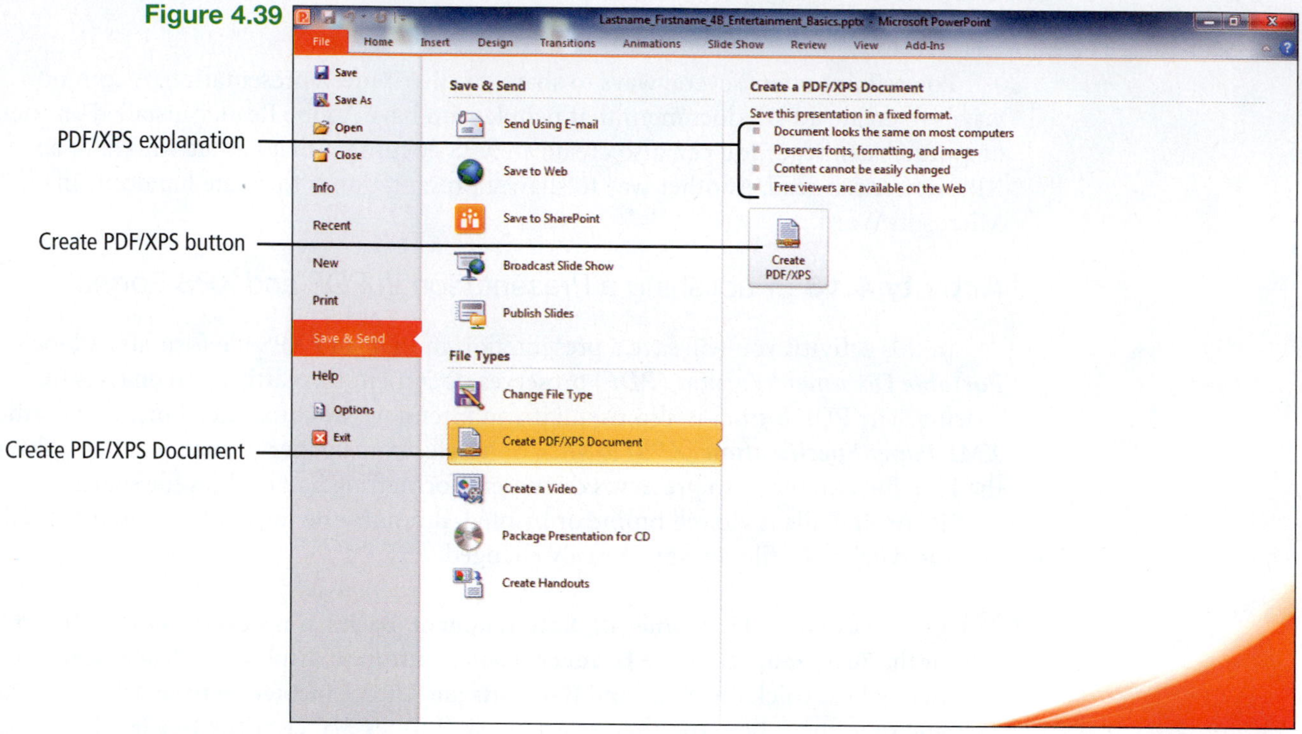

3 Click the **Create PDF/XPS** button. Click the **Save as type arrow** to see the two file formats—PDF (*.pdf) and XPS Document (*.xps). Click **PDF(*.pdf)**. If necessary, click the check boxes for **Open file after publishing** and **Standard (publishing online and printing)** to open the file after saving and to select the print quality. Compare your screen with Figure 4.40.

Opening a file after publishing allows you to see the document in the chosen format. Choose Standard (publishing online and printing) if the presentation requires high print quality. If the file size is more important than the print quality, click Minimum size (publishing online).

Figure 4.40

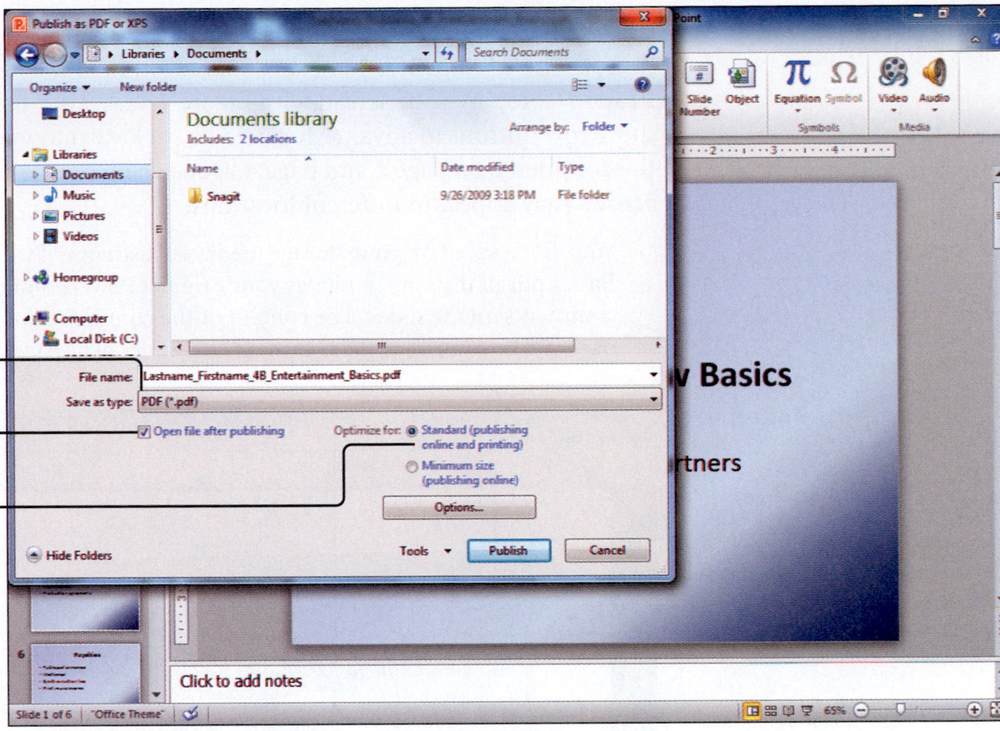

4 On the **Publish as PDF or XPS** window, click the **Options** button located just below the Standard and Minimum size choices. In the **Options** dialog box under **Publish options**, click **Include comments and ink markup**.

The options to publish a presentation to a PDF file are the same as the options to print the file.

> **Another Way**
> Enter the page number in the text box to change pages in the PDF.

5 Click the **Publish what arrow** to see the choices—Slides, Handouts, Notes pages, and Outline view. Click **Handouts**, and then click the **Slides per page arrow**. Click **3**, and then view the preview showing how the printed page will look. Compare your screen with Figure 4.41.

Figure 4.41

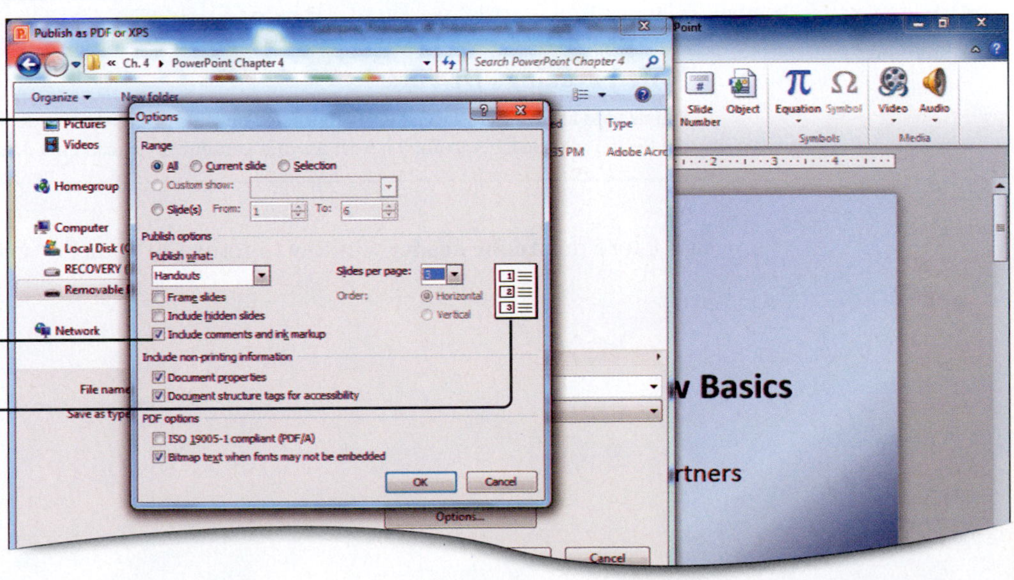

PowerPoint | Chapter 4

6 Click **OK**. Click **Publish**. If a license agreement message displays, read it, and then click **Accept**. The document is published (saved) in the PDF format and opens in Adobe Reader. Compare your screen with Figure 4.42. Under the **menu bar** at the top, click the arrow buttons to advance forward or backward to view the slides. Be sure to view the comments on page 2 and page 4. Depending on the version of Adobe Reader, the arrows may appear in different locations.

Your file is saved on your storage media as Lastname_Firstname_4B_Entertainment_Basics.pdf in the same folder as your original PowerPoint presentation file. Notice the comments on the slides. The content of the comments for Slides 1-3 (page 1) appear on page 2. The content of the comments for Slides 4-6 (page 3) appear on page 4.

Figure 4.42

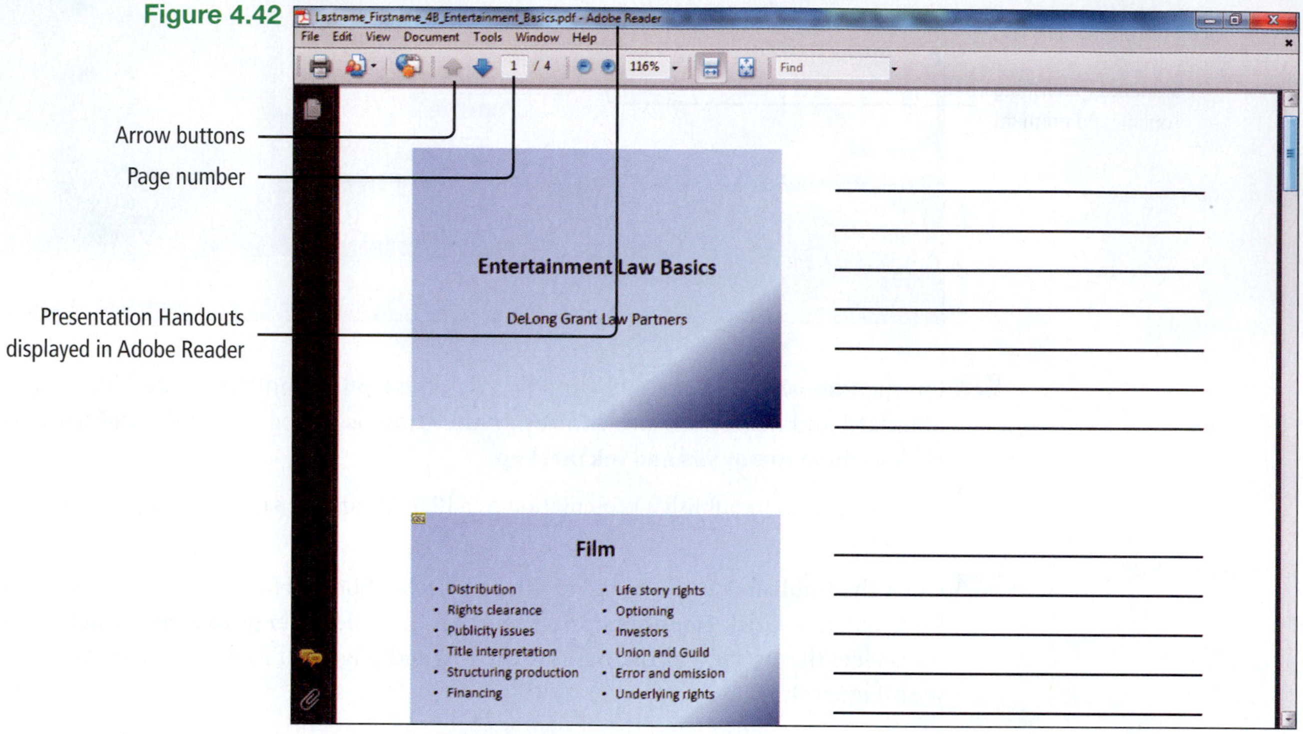

Note | Reading PDF Files

You need to have Adobe Acrobat Reader installed on your computer in order to read PDF files. Most people have the Reader installed. If you don't have it on your computer, you can download it free from www.adobe.com.

7 Close the **Adobe Reader** window to return to your PowerPoint presentation window.

8 Display **Backstage** view. Click **Save & Send**, and then click **Create PDF/XPS Document**. Click the **Create PDF/XPS** button. Change the file type to **XPS Document (*.xps)**. Click the **Options** button, and then click **Include comments and ink markup**. Click the **Publish what arrow**, and then click **Handouts**. Click **OK**, and then click **Publish**. The presentation is saved as an XPS document and opens in the XPS Viewer. Maximize your window if necessary. The menu bar on the XPS Viewer provides options to set permissions and digitally sign a document. Scroll to the bottom of page 1 so you can also see page 2. Compare your screen with Figure 4.43.

The handouts are displayed 6 slides per page. The comment numbers are displayed on the slides, and the comment content is displayed on the second page. Your file is saved on your storage media as Lastname_Firstname_4B_Entertainment_Basics.xps in the same folder as your original PowerPoint presentation file. You can only view XPS documents with an XPS Viewer, such as the one provided in Microsoft Windows. You can also download a free copy of the Viewer at www.microsoft.com. Only presentations formatted in PowerPoint 2000 or later versions can be saved and viewed in the Viewer.

Figure 4.43

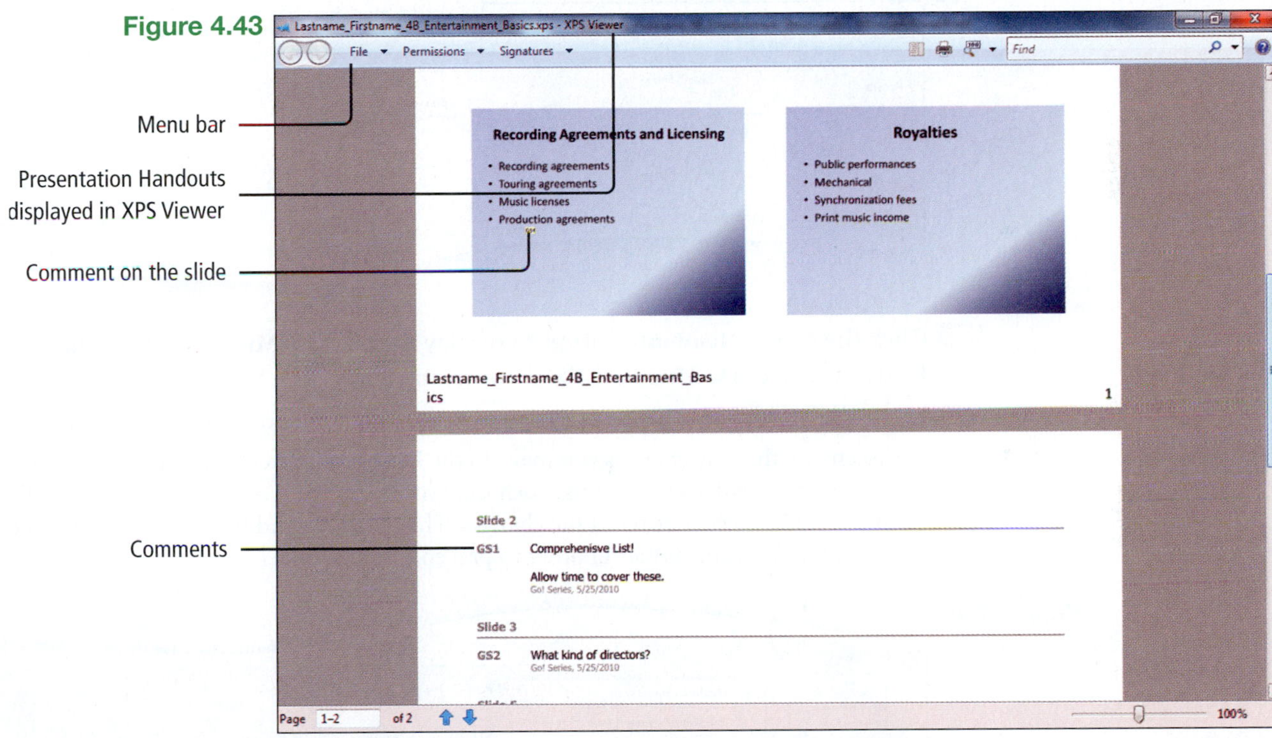

Another Way

To close the file and the viewer, press Alt + F4.

9 Click **File**, and then click **Exit** to close the XPS file and viewer.

Activity 4.14 | Creating Handouts in Microsoft Word

In this activity, you will create handouts that open in Microsoft Word.

1 Display **Backstage** view. Click **Save & Send**. Under **File Types**, click **Create Handouts**. At the right, under **Create Handouts in Microsoft Word**, read the explanation. Compare your screen with Figure 4.44.

The handouts are a document that contains the slides and notes from the presentation. You can use Word to change the layout and format and even add additional content to the handouts. If you link the handout file to your presentation, changes in your presentation will automatically update the handout content.

Figure 4.44

Create handouts explanation

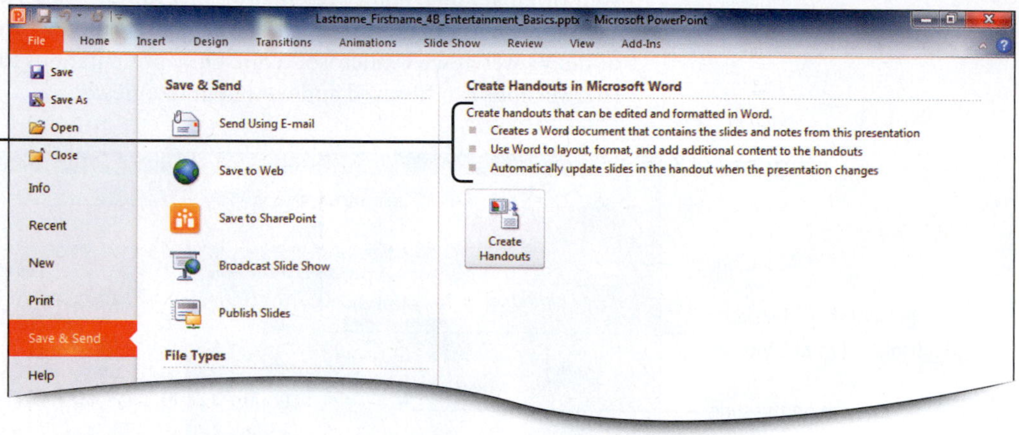

2 Click the **Create Handouts** button to display the **Send To Microsoft Word** dialog box. Under **Add slides to Microsoft Word document**, click **Paste link**. Compare your screen with Figure 4.45.

To ensure that any changes you make to the PowerPoint presentation are reflected in the Word document, use Paste link. Each time you open the Word document, you will be prompted to accept or reject the changes. The Word file and the PowerPoint file must remain in the same folder in order to prevent breaking the link.

Figure 4.45

Paste link

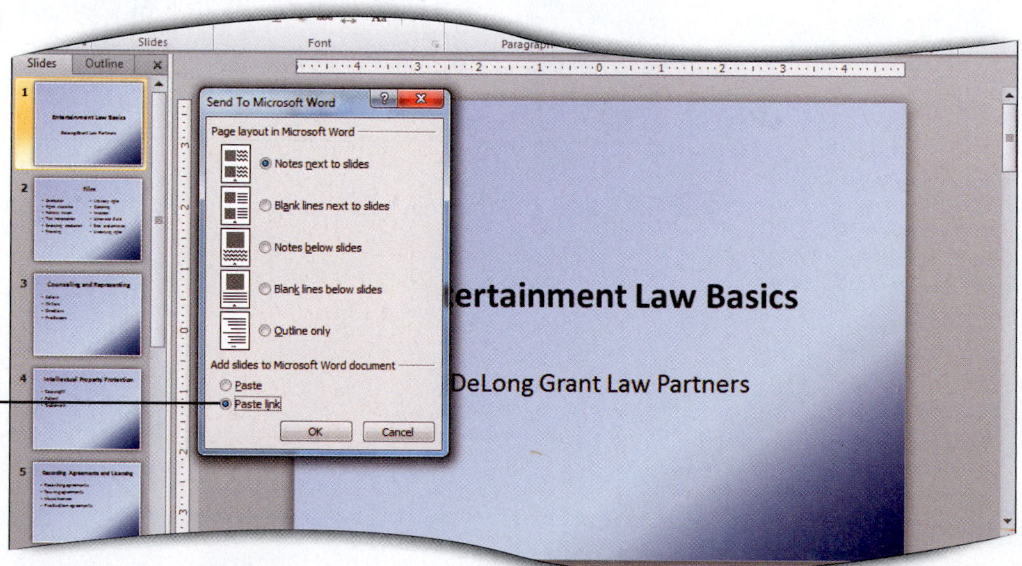

3 Click **OK**. Click **Word** on the taskbar to see the presentation slides displayed in a new Word document. Compare your screen with Figure 4.46.

Figure 4.46

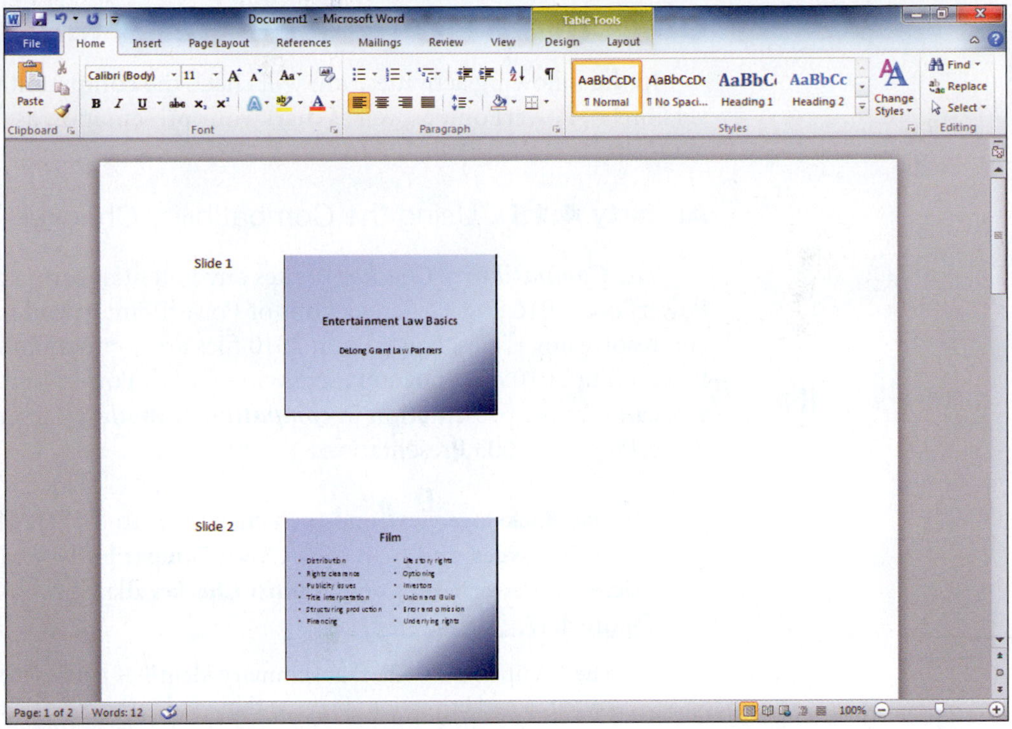

4 In the **Word document**, click the **Insert tab**. In the **Header & Footer group**, click the **Footer** button, and then click **Edit Footer**. At the left, type **Lastname_Firstname_4B_Entertainment_Basics** Press the Tab key two times, and then type the current date. On the **Design tab**, in the **Close group**, click **Close Header and Footer**.

5 Display **Backstage** view, and then click **Save As**. Navigate to the location where you are saving your work, and then save the Word file as **Lastname_Firstname_4B_Entertainment_Basics** **Close** the Word document and return to the presentation file.

6 Display **Backstage** view, click **Properties**, and then click **Show Document Panel**. Replace the text in the **Author** box with your own first and last name; in the **Subject** box, type your course name and section number; and then in the **Keywords** box, type **mission, agreements, licensing, film, royalties** **Close** the **Document Information Panel**.

7 **Save** the presentation.

Objective 5 | Protect a Presentation

In the following activities, you will check the compatibility of your file with previous versions of PowerPoint as well as mark your presentation as final and then save it as read-only.

Activity 4.15 | Using the Compatibility Checker

The ***Compatibility Checker*** locates any potential compatibility issues between PowerPoint 2010 and earlier versions of PowerPoint. It will prepare a report to help you resolve any issues. PowerPoint 2010 files are compatible with 2007 files; however, PowerPoint 2010 does not support saving files to PowerPoint 95 or earlier. If necessary, you can save the presentation in ***compatibility mode***, which means to save it as a PowerPoint 97-2003 Presentation.

1 Display **Backstage** view, and then click **Info**. To the left of **Prepare for Sharing**, click **Check for Issues**, and then click **Check Compatibility**. Read the report displayed in the **Microsoft PowerPoint Compatibility Checker** dialog box. Compare your screen with Figure 4.47.

The Compatibility Checker summary identifies parts of the presentation that cannot be edited in earlier versions because those features are not available.

Figure 4.47

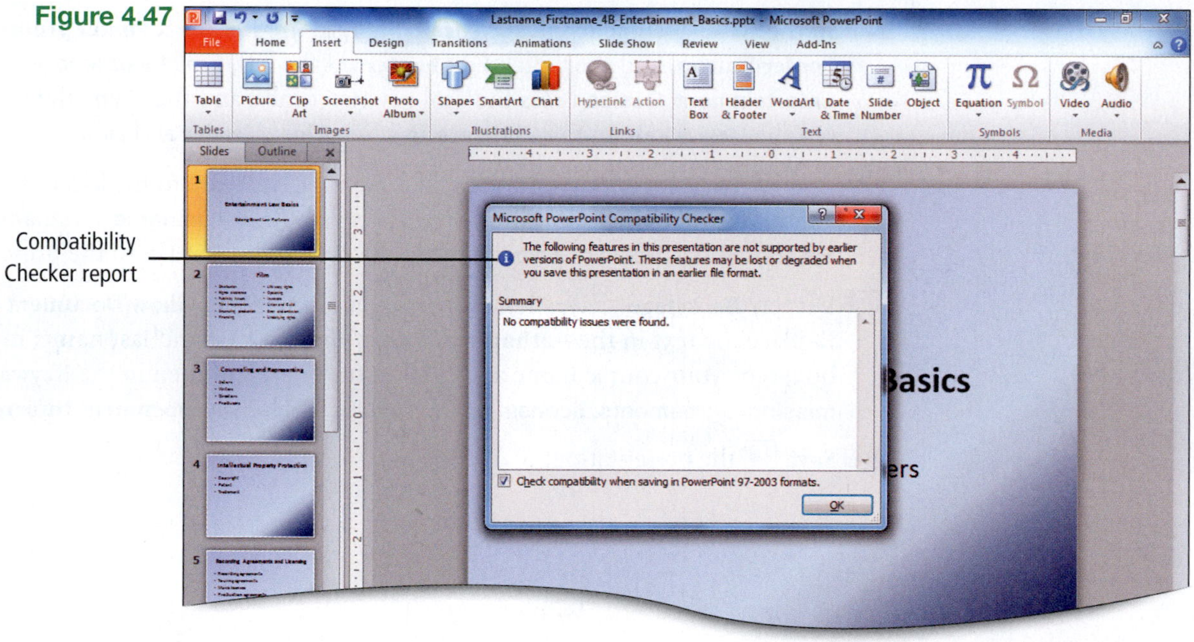

2 Click **OK**.

> **More Knowledge | Saving Presentations in Other File Formats**
>
> If you exchange PowerPoint presentations with other people, you may save the presentation in different formats. Display Backstage view, click Save & Send, click Change File Type, and then you may change the file type to PowerPoint 97-2003 Presentation. Other options include PowerPoint Show and PowerPoint Picture Presentation.

Activity 4.16 | Marking a Presentation as Final

In this activity, you will use the ***Mark as Final*** command to make your presentation document read-only in order to prevent changes to the document. Additionally, the Status property of the document is set to Final.

1 Display **Backstage** view, and then click **Info**. To the left of **Permissions**, click **Protect Presentation**. Notice that the current Permissions are: *Anyone can open, copy, and change any part of this presentation*. Examine the Protect Presentation options. Compare your screen with Figure 4.48.

The options to protect a presentation are Mark as Final, Encrypt with Password, Restrict Permission by People, and Add a Digital Signature.

Figure 4.48

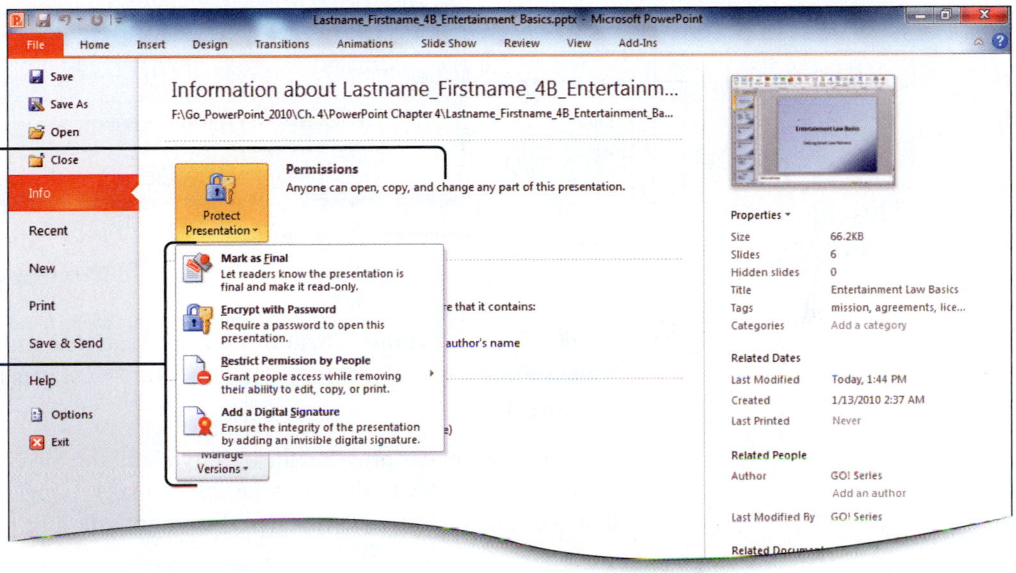

2 Click **Mark as Final**. Notice the message that the presentation will be marked as final and then saved. Compare your screen with Figure 4.49.

The Mark as Final command helps prevent reviewers or readers from accidentally making changes to the document. Because the Mark as Final command is not a security feature, anyone who receives an electronic copy of a document that has been marked as final can edit that document by removing Mark as Final status from the document.

Figure 4.49

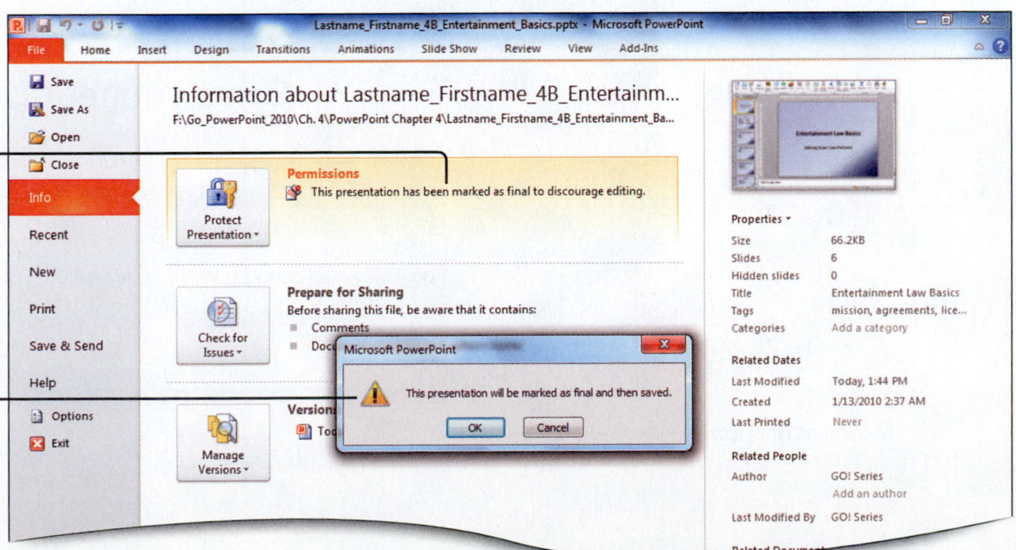

3 Click **OK**. A message displays that reminds you that the document will be saved as final. The message also tells you that a **Mark As Final** icon will display in the status bar. Compare your screen with Figure 4.50.

Figure 4.50

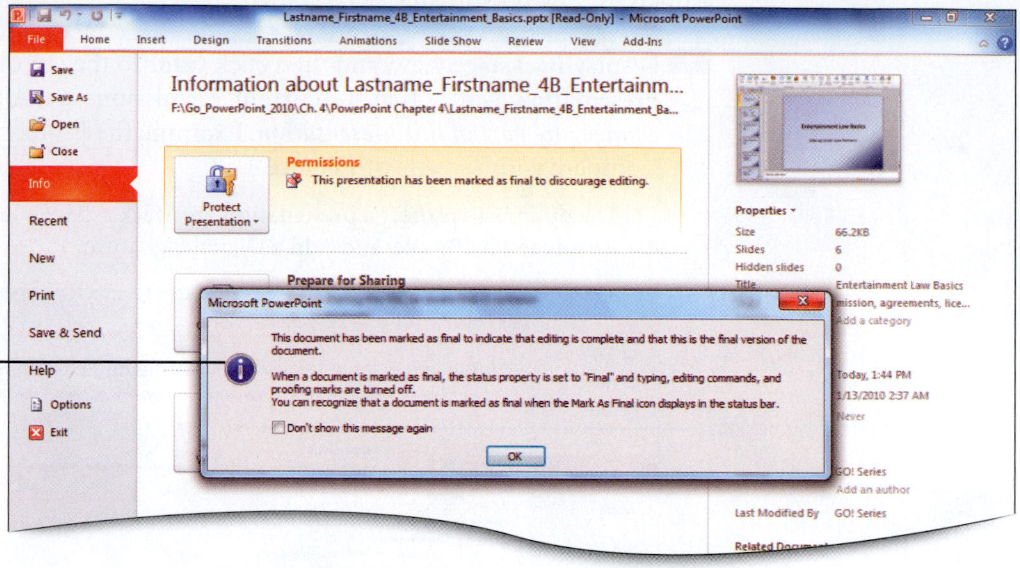

Marked as final message

4 Click **OK**. Click the **Home tab**, and then note the information bar at the top and the **Marked as Final** icon at the bottom left on the status bar. Compare your screen with Figure 4.51.

The information bar provides the option to edit the file even though you marked it as final, so be aware that others may be able to make changes. Marking the presentation as final tells others that you encourage them not to do this.

Figure 4.51

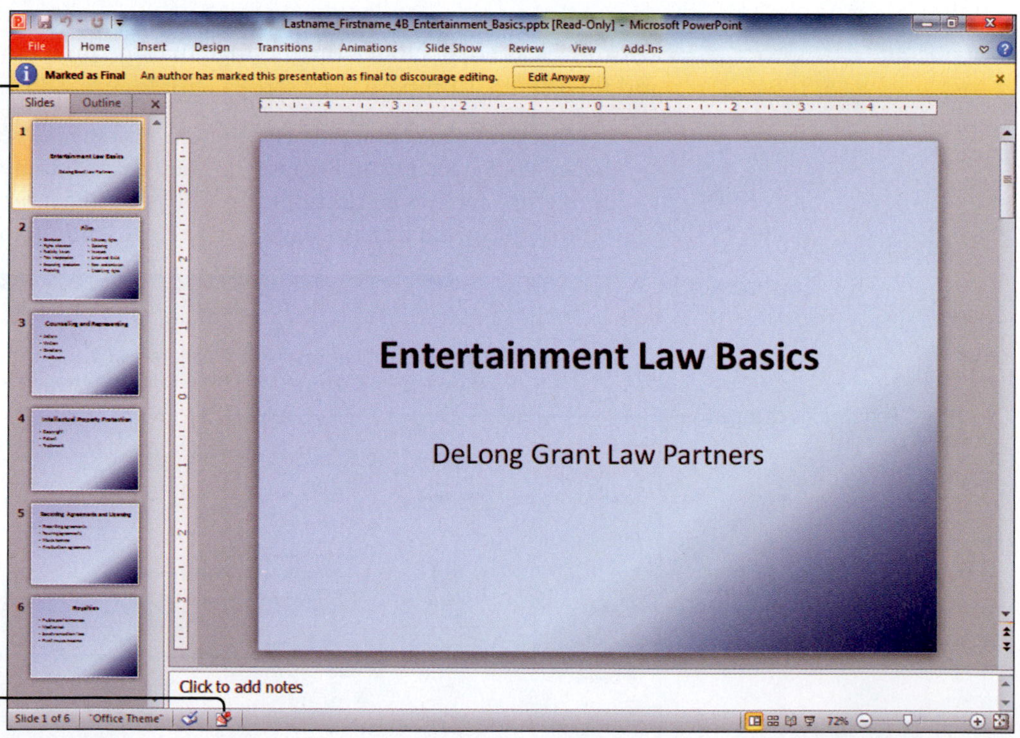

Information bar

Marked as Final icon

5 On the information bar, click the **Edit Anyway** button.

You are free to make changes to the document.

6 **Save** your presentation. Display **Backstage** view, click **Print**, and then under **Slides**, click the **Full Page Slides button arrow** to display the **Print Layout** dialog box. Click **Handouts 3 Slides.** Display the Print Layout dialog box again, if necessary, and then check **Print Comments and Ink Markup**. Print the slides. If requested, submit your presentation electronically as directed by your instructor instead of printing.

7 **Close** the presentation, and then **Exit** PowerPoint.

End **You have completed Project 4B**

Content-Based Assessments

Summary

In this chapter, you designed a PowerPoint template containing formats, shapes, and images on the master pages. You then created a presentation based on this template and entered the text for a meeting. You edited Handout and Notes Masters. You added comments into the presentation and practiced navigating through the presentation to read, edit, and delete comments. You prepared a presentation for distribution by publishing it in PDF and XPS formats. You created PowerPoint handouts in Microsoft Word and linked the Word content to the presentation file so any updates in the presentation file will be reflected in the Word file. You checked the compatibility of the file with other versions of PowerPoint and marked your presentation as Final to discourage anyone from changing your file.

Key Terms

Matching

Match each term in the second column with its correct definition in the first column by writing the letter of the term on the blank line in front of the correct definition.

_____ 1. A person who inserts comments into a presentation to provide feedback.
_____ 2. A predefined layout for a group of slides saved as a .potx file.
_____ 3. File extension for a PowerPoint presentation.
_____ 4. Includes the specifications for the design of presentation handouts.
_____ 5. A note that you can attach to a letter or word on a slide or to an entire slide.
_____ 6. File extension for a PowerPoint template.
_____ 7. Contains templates that you have saved on your computer in the default template folder.
_____ 8. A universal file format commonly associated with Microsoft Viewer.
_____ 9. Contains various slide master layouts.
_____ 10. A universal file format commonly associated with Adobe Reader.
_____ 11. A specific slide master that contains the design, such as the background, that displays on all slide layouts in the presentation.
_____ 12. Displays a logo on every slide that uses a title and only one column of bullet items.
_____ 13. Makes a presentation file read-only and discourages others from making changes to it.
_____ 14. Identifies features that potentially are not supported by earlier versions of PowerPoint.
_____ 15. Contains templates that you have saved in your chapter folder.

A Comment
B Compatibility Checker
C Handout Master
D Mark as Final
E My templates
F New from existing
G Office Theme Slide Master
H Portable Document Format (PDF)
I Reviewer
J Slide Master
K Template
L Title and Content Layout Slide Master
M XML Paper Specification (XPS)
N .potx
O .pptx

Content-Based Assessments

Multiple Choice

Circle the correct answer.

1. To ensure that a PowerPoint presentation can be viewed as a slide show on computers using earlier versions of PowerPoint, save the presentation in:
   A. compatibility mode **B.** Word handouts **C.** read-only format
2. To avoid having to use the same color and design of bullets on every slide in a presentation, make the changes on the:
   A. Handout Master **B.** Slide Master **C.** Title slide
3. Apply a Background Style for all slide layouts in a template on the:
   A. Office Theme Slide Master **B.** Title slide layout **C.** Title slide in normal view
4. The file extension for a PowerPoint 2010 template is:
   A. .pptx **B.** .pdf **C.** .potx
5. To make the background color vary smoothly from darker to lighter shades in more than one color combination, set a gradient:
   A. fill **B.** stop **C.** shape
6. Unless changed, the default location for saving templates is the:
   A. computer hard drive **B.** online server **C.** portable storage device
7. To change the content of a comment, click the ______ button.
   A. New Comment **B.** Review **C.** Edit Comment
8. To apply a template that is saved on your portable storage, in which location under Available Templates and Themes will you find it?
   A. New from existing **B.** My templates **C.** Sample templates
9. When dragging a placeholder up or down, what key should you use to prevent the placeholder from moving to the left or right?
   A. Ctrl **B.** Shift **C.** Alt
10. You can print the comments in a presentation by clicking which of these options?
    A. Print comments **B.** High quality **C.** Include comments and ink markup

Apply **4A** skills from these Objectives:

1. Create a Custom Template by Modifying Slide Masters
2. Apply a Custom Template to a Presentation

Skills Review | Project 4C Night Owls

In the following Skills Review, you will create a template that DeLong Grant Law Partners will use to prepare presentations for the initial meeting with a client. You will use the template to create a presentation for the musical group Billy and the Night Owls. Your completed presentation will look similar to Figure 4.52.

Project Files

For Project 4C, you will need the following files:

New blank PowerPoint presentation
p04C_Contract.jpg

You will save your presentation as:

Lastname_Firstname_4C_Contract_Template.potx
Lastname_Firstname_4C_Night_Owls.pptx

Project Results

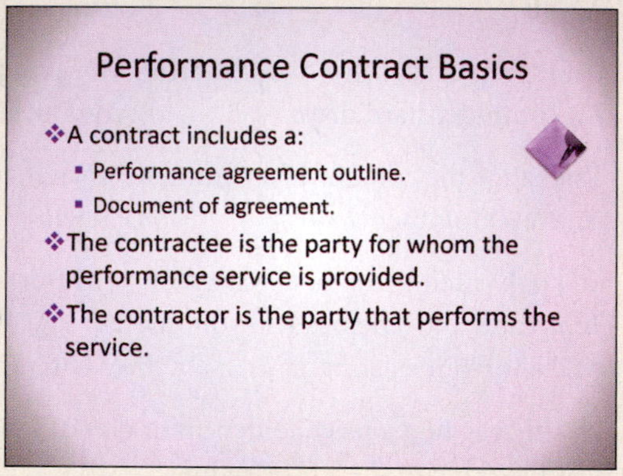

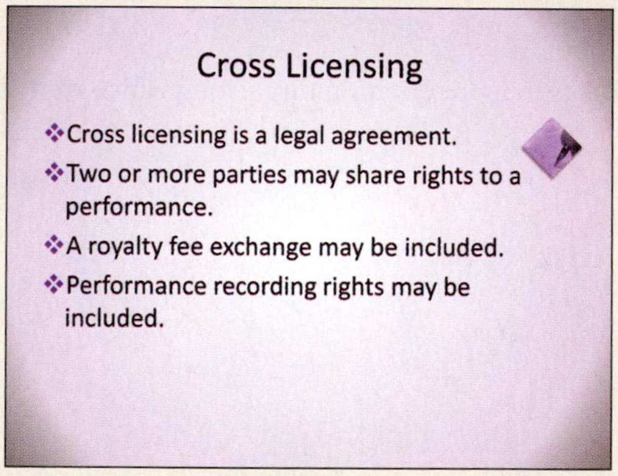

Figure 4.52

(Project 4C Night Owls continues on the next page)

Skills Review | Project 4C Night Owls (continued)

1 **Start** PowerPoint to display a new blank presentation. Display **Backstage** view, and then click **Save As**. Click the **Save as type box arrow**, and then click **PowerPoint Template (*.potx)**. Navigate to the location where you are saving your work, and then save your file as **Lastname_Firstname_4C_Contract_Template**

2 Click the **View tab**. In the **Master Views group**, click the **Slide Master** button.

a. Click the first thumbnail—**Office Theme Slide Master**. In the **Background group**, click the **Background Styles** button. In the **Background Styles gallery**, select **Style 9**.

b. Click the second thumbnail—**Title Slide Layout**. Click the dashed border on the Master title style placeholder, and then change the font size to **48 point**.

3 Click the **Office Theme Slide Master** thumbnail.

a. On the **Slide Master tab**, in the **Background group**, click the **Background Styles** button, and then click **Format Background**. Under **Fill**, click **Gradient fill**. Click the **Type arrow**, and then click **Radial**.

b. Click the **Add gradient stop** button once, and then position the stop at **80%**.

c. Click the **Color arrow**, and then in the eighth column in the second row, click **Purple, Accent 4, Lighter 80%**.

d. Click **Apply to All**. Click **Close**.

4 Click the **Title Slide Layout** thumbnail.

a. Click the **View tab**. In the **Show group**, click the **Ruler** checkbox to display the horizontal and vertical rulers (if necessary).

b. Click the **Insert tab**. In the **Illustrations group**, click the **Shapes** button. Under **Basic Shapes**, click the **Diamond** shape. At **2 inches on the right side of the horizontal ruler** and **3 inches on the upper half of the vertical ruler**, click to insert the shape.

c. On the Ribbon, under **Drawing Tools**, click the **Format tab**. In the **Shapes Styles group**, click the **Shape Effects** button, click **Preset**, and then click **Preset 2**. In the **Shapes Styles group**, click the **Shape Outline button arrow**, and then click **No Outline**.

d. With the diamond still selected, in the **Size group**, change the **Shape Height** to **1.5"** and the **Shape Width** to **1.5"**.

e. In the **Shape Styles group**, click the **Shape Fill** button, and then click **Picture**. Navigate to the location where your data files are stored and select **p04C_Contract.jpg**. Click the **Insert** button.

f. With the shape still selected, in the **Arrange group**, click the **Align** button. Click **Align Center**. Click the **Align button** again, and then click **Align Bottom**.

g. On the Ribbon, under **Picture Tools**, click the **Format tab**. In the **Adjust Group**, click the **Color** button. Under **Recolor**, click **Purple, Accent color 4 Dark**.

h. With the shape still selected, on the **Home tab**, in the **Clipboard group**, click the **Copy** button. Click the **Title and Content Layout** thumbnail. In the **Clipboard group**, click the **Paste** button.

i. Under the **Drawing Tools**, click the **Format tab**. In the **Size group**, change the **Shape Height** to **1"** and the **Shape Width** to **1"**.

j. With the shape still selected, press the Shift key, and then click the content placeholder. In the **Arrange group**, click the **Align** button, and then select **Align Right**. Click the **Align** button, and then select **Align Top**.

5 Click the **Title Slide** thumbnail.

a. Press the Shift key, and then drag the Master title placeholder up so the top aligns at **2.5 inches on the upper half of the vertical ruler**. Click outside the placeholder. Press the Shift key, and then drag the Master subtitle placeholder up so the top aligns with **.5 inch mark on the upper half of the vertical ruler**.

b. With the subtitle placeholder still selected, drag the bottom middle sizing handle to **1 inch on the lower half of the vertical ruler**.

c. Click the shape, and then drag the entire shape so the top aligns with **1.5 inches on the lower half of the vertical ruler**. Under **Drawing Tools**, on the **Format** tab, in the **Arrange group**, click the **Align** button, and then click **Align Center**.

6 Click the **Title and Content** thumbnail.

a. Click anywhere in the first bulleted line. Click the **Home tab**. In the **Paragraph group**, click the **Bullets button arrow**, and then click **Bullets and Numbering**. In the **Bullets and Numbering** dialog box, click the **Bulleted tab** if necessary. Click **Star Bullets**. Then click the **Color button arrow**. Under **Standard Colors**, click **Purple**. Click **OK**.

b. Click anywhere in the second bulleted line. Display the **Bullets and Numbering** dialog box. Click the

(Project 4C Night Owls continues on the next page)

Skills Review | Project 4C Night Owls (continued)

Filled Square Bullets. Click the **Color button arrow**. Under **Standard Colors**, click **Purple**. Click **OK**.

7 Click the first thumbnail, the **Office Theme Slide Master**.

a. At the bottom left on the **Office Theme Slide**, click anywhere on the dashed border of the date placeholder.

b. Click the **Home tab**, and then change the **font size** to **10**.

c. Click the **Slide Master tab**. In the **Close group**, click the **Close Master View** button.

8 On the **Insert tab**, in the **Text group**, click the **Header & Footer** button to display the **Header and Footer** dialog box. Click the **Notes and Handouts tab**. Under **Include on page**, select the **Date and time** check box, and then select **Fixed**. If necessary, clear the **Header** check box, and then select the **Page number** and **Footer** check boxes. In the **Footer** box, using your own name, type **Lastname_Firstname_4C_Contract_Template** and then click **Apply to All**.

9 Display **Backstage** view, click **Properties**, and then click **Show Document Panel**. Replace the text in the **Author** box with your own first and last name; in the **Subject** box, type your course name and section number; and then in the **Keywords** box, type **template Close** the **Document Information Panel**.

10 Print **Handouts 4 Slides Horizontal**, or submit your presentation electronically as directed by your instructor.

11 **Save** the template. **Close** the template.

12 Display **Backstage** view, click **New**, and then click **New from existing**.

a. Navigate to the location where you are saving your files. Click **Lastname_Firstname_4C_Contract_Template.potx** and then click **Create New**.

b. Save the file as **Lastname_Firstname_4C_Night_Owls** in your storage location.

13 Click **Slide 1**. In the title placeholder, type **Billy and the Night Owls** In the subtitle placeholder, type **DeLong Grant Law Partners**

a. On the **Home tab**, in the **Slides group**, click the **New Slide button arrow**, and then click **Title and Content**.

b. In the title placeholder, type **Performance Contract Basics**

c. In the content placeholder, type the following bulleted items, using the **Increase and Decrease List Level** buttons as needed:

A contract includes a:

Performance agreement outline.

Document of agreement.

The contractee is the party for whom the performance service is provided.

The contractor is the party that performs the service.

14 In the **Slides group**, click the **New Slide button arrow**, and then click **Title and Content** to add a third slide.

a. In the title placeholder, type **Cross Licensing** and then press Ctrl + Enter.

b. Type the following bulleted items in the content placeholder:

Cross licensing is a legal agreement.

Two or more parties may share rights to a performance.

A royalty fee exchange may be included.

Performance recording rights may be included.

15 **Save** your presentation.

16 Click the **View tab**. In the **Master Views group**, click **Handout Master**. In the **Page Setup group**, click the **Slides Per Page** button. Click **3 Slides**.

17 Click the **View tab**. In the **Master Views group**, click **Notes Master**. In the **Placeholders group**, remove the **Body**.

18 In the **Close group**, click **Close Master View**.

19 On the **Insert tab**, in the **Text group**, click the **Header & Footer** button to display the **Header and Footer** dialog box. Click the **Notes and Handouts tab**. In the **Footer** box, change the name to: **Lastname_Firstname_4C_Night_Owls** and then click **Apply to All**.

20 Display **Backstage** view, click **Properties**, and then click **Show Document Panel**. Replace the text in the **Author** box with your own first and last name. In the **Keywords** box, remove the existing content, and then type **cross licensing, royalty, rights Close** the **Document Information Panel**.

21 Print **Handouts 4 Slides Horizontal**, or submit your presentation electronically as directed by your instructor.

22 **Save** the presentation. **Exit** PowerPoint.

End **You have completed Project 4C**

Content-Based Assessments

Apply 4B skills from these Objectives:

- **3** Create and Edit Comments
- **4** Prepare a Presentation for Distribution
- **5** Protect a Presentation

Skills Review | Project 4D Nagursky Taxes

In the following Skills Review, you will modify a presentation created by DeLong Grant Law Partners as a brief overview of taxation issues to present to Finley Nagursky, who is a professional football player. You will add comments to the presentation, prepare the document for distribution, and then protect it. Your completed presentation will look similar to Figure 4.53.

Project Files

For Project 4D, you will need the following file:

p04D_Athlete_Taxes.pptx

You will save your presentation as:

Lastname_Firstname_4D_Nagursky_Taxes.pptx
Lastname_Firstname_4D_Nagursky_Taxes.pdf
Lastname_Firstname_4D_Nagursky_Taxes.xps

Project Results

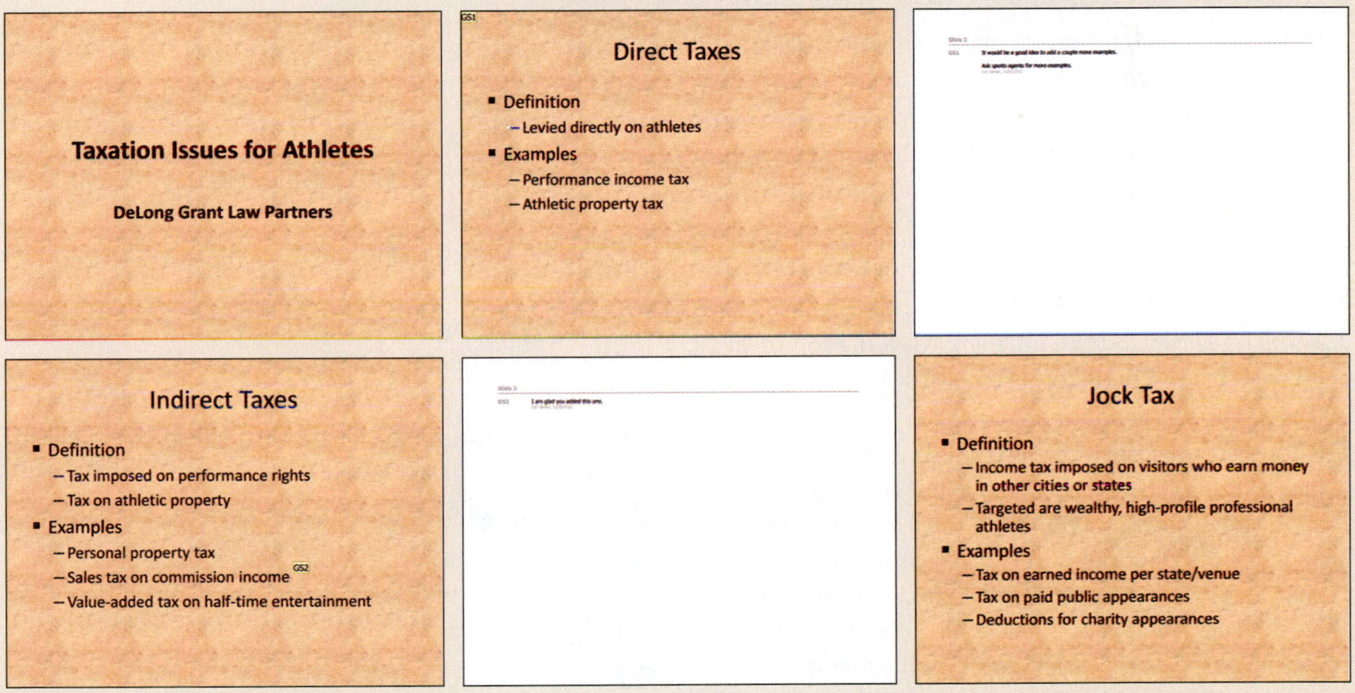

Figure 4.53

(Project 4D Nagursky Taxes continues on the next page)

Skills Review | Project 4D Nagursky Taxes (continued)

1 **Start** PowerPoint. Locate and open the file **p04D_Athlete_Taxes.pptx**. Navigate to the location where you are storing your folders and projects for this chapter, and then **Save** the file as **Lastname_Firstname_4D_Nagursky_Taxes**

2 Make **Slide 2** the active slide. Click the **Review tab**. In the **Comments group**, click the **New Comment** button. In the space provided, type **It would be a good idea to add a couple more examples.**

3 Make **Slide 3** the active slide. Click at the end of the bulleted item that ends with *commission income*. In the **Comments group**, click **New Comment**. Type **I am glad you added this one.** Click outside the comment to close it.

4 Make **Slide 4** the active slide. In the last bulleted item, select the word *Deductions*. Use the procedure explained in the previous steps to add this comment: **Is this clear enough for the client to understand?** Click outside the comment to close it.

5 Make **Slide 2** the active slide. At the upper left corner of the slide, click the **Comment**. In the **Comments group**, click the **Edit Comment** button and notice the insertion point at the end of the text.

6 Press Enter two times, and then type **Ask sports agents for more examples.**

7 Click the **Next** button until you reach the comment on **Slide 3**. In the **Comments group**, click **Delete** to remove this comment.

8 On the **Insert tab**, in the **Text group**, click the **Header & Footer** button to display the **Header and Footer** dialog box. Click the **Notes and Handouts tab**. Under **Include on page**, select the **Date and time** check box, and then select **Fixed**. If necessary, clear the **Header** check box, and then select the **Page number** and **Footer** check boxes. In the **Footer** box, using your own name, type **Lastname_Firstname_4D_Nagursky_Taxes** and then click **Apply to All**.

9 Display **Backstage** view, click **Properties**, and then click **Show Document Panel**. Replace the text in the **Author** box with your own first and last name. In the **Subject** box, type your course name and section number, and then in the **Keywords** box, type **direct taxes, jock tax, indirect taxes Close** the **Document Information Panel**.

10 Print **Handouts 4 Slides Horizontal**, or submit your presentation electronically as directed by your instructor.

11 Display **Backstage** view, and then click **Save & Send**. Under **File Types**, click **Create PDF/XPS Document**.

- **a.** Click **Create PDF/XPS**. Click the **Save as type**, and then click **PDF(*.pdf)**. If necessary, click the check boxes for **Open file after publishing** and **Standard (publishing online and printing)**.
- **b.** Click the **Options** button. Click the **Publish what arrow**, and then select **Handouts**. Click the **Slides per page arrow**, and then select **4**. Click the check box for **Include comments and ink markup**. Click **OK**.
- **c.** Click **Publish**. In Adobe Reader, scroll through the slides to see the comments on page 2.
- **d.** **Close** the Adobe Reader window to return to your PowerPoint presentation window.

12 Display **Backstage** view, Click **Save & Send**, and then click **Create PDF/XPS Document**.

- **a.** Click **Create PDF/XPS**. Change the file type to **XPS Document (*.xps)**.
- **b.** Click the **Options** button. Click the **Publish what arrow**, and then select **Handouts**. Click the **Slides per page arrow**, and then select **4**. Click the check box for **Include comments and ink markup**. Click **OK**.
- **c.** Click **Publish**. In the XPS Viewer, scroll through the slides to see the comments on page 2.
- **d.** Close the XPS file and viewer.

13 Display **Backstage** view, click **Info**. Click **Protect Presentation**, and then select **Mark as Final**.

14 **Exit** PowerPoint.

15 Submit the printed work for:

Lastname_Firstname_4D_Nagursky_Taxes.pptx
Lastname_Firstname_4D_Nagursky_Taxes.pdf
Lastname_Firstname_4D_Nagursky_Taxes.xps

or submit your presentations electronically as directed by your instructor.

End **You have completed Project 4D**

Apply **4A** skills from these Objectives:

1. Create a Custom Template by Modifying Slide Masters
2. Apply a Custom Template to a Presentation

Mastering PowerPoint | Project 4E Sports Law

In the following Mastering PowerPoint project, you will edit a presentation you already prepared to explain the aspects of Title IX in Collegiate Sports Law and then save it as a template. You will use the template to personalize it for a presentation to Hugh Appleton, who is a college athletic director. Your completed presentation will look similar to Figure 4.54.

Project Files

For Project 4E, you will need the following files:

p04E_Sports_Law.pptx
p04E_Sports1.jpg

You will save your presentation as:

Lastname_Firstname_4E_Sports_Template.potx
Lastname_Firstname_4E_Sports_Law.pptx

Project Results

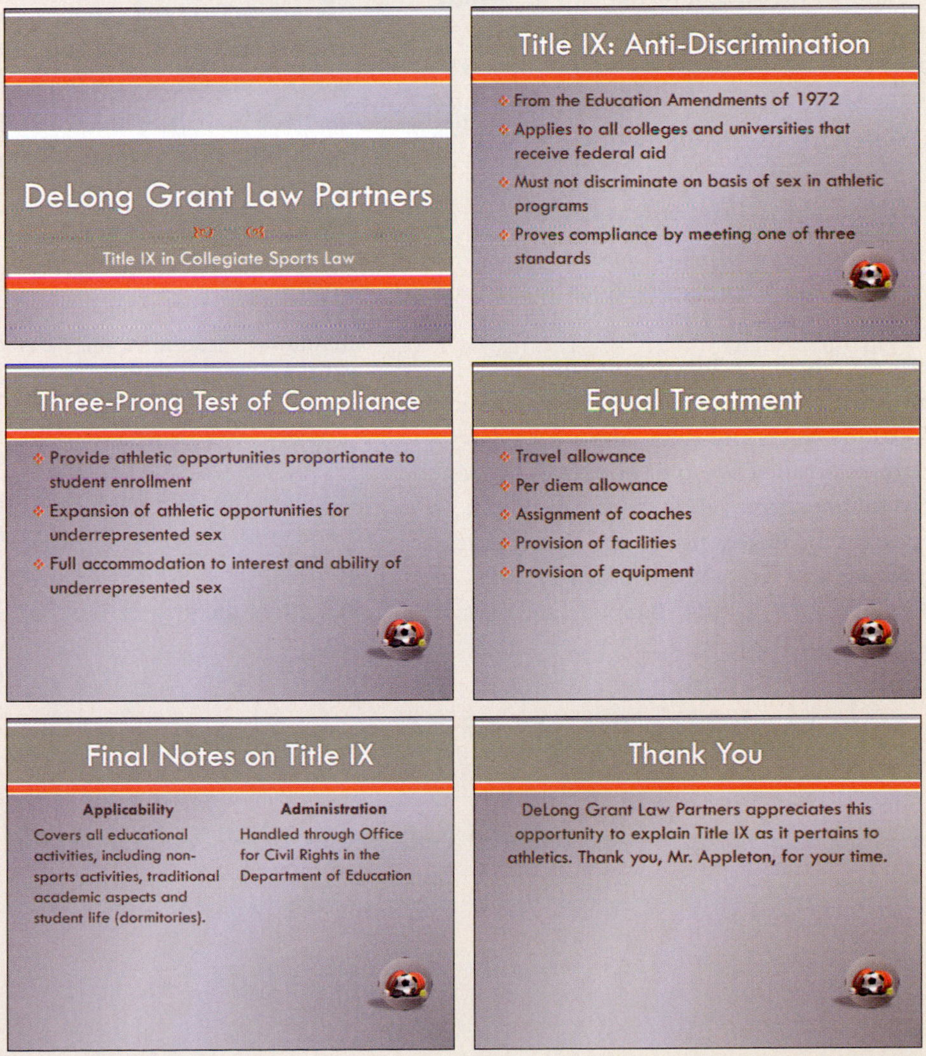

Figure 4.54

(Project 4E Sports Law continues on the next page)

PowerPoint | Chapter 4

Mastering PowerPoint | Project 4E Sports Law (continued)

1 **Start** PowerPoint. Locate and open the file **p04E_Sports_Law.pptx**. Save the file as a **PowerPoint Template** in your chapter folder, using the file name **Lastname_Firstname_4E_Sports_Template**

2 Edit the **Office Theme Slide Master**. In the **Edit Theme group**, in the **Themes group**, under **From Office.com**, use the **Decatur** theme. Within that theme, use the **Median** theme font. Apply Background **Style 6**. Format the background with a **Radial Gradient fill**, and then apply it to all slides. On the first bulleted item, change the font size to **32**.

3 On the **Title Slide Layout** thumbnail, change the Master title style placeholder **font size** to **60 pts**. Change the Master subtitle style placeholder **font size** to **32 pts**.

4 On the **Title and Content Layout** thumbnail, insert an **Oval** shape and set the **Height** to **1.2"** and the **Width** to **1.2"**. Apply a **Shadow Shape Effect** of **Perspective Diagonal Upper Left**. Fill the shape with **p04E_Sports1 .jpg**. Remove the **Shape Outline**, and then position the shape at the bottom right corner of the content placeholder.

5 Copy the shape to the **Two Content Layout** thumbnail.

6 Remove the Header from the **Handout Master**, and then close the Master View.

7 On the **Insert tab**, in the **Text group**, click the **Header & Footer** button to display the **Header and Footer** dialog box. Click the **Notes and Handouts tab**. Under **Include on page**, select the **Date and time** check box, and then select **Fixed**. If necessary, clear the **Header** check box, and then select the **Page number** and **Footer** check boxes. In the **Footer** box, using your own name, type **Lastname_ Firstname_4E_Sports_Template** and then click **Apply to All**.

8 Revise the document properties. Replace the text in the **Author** box with your own first and last name. In the **Subject** box, type your course name and section number, and then in the **Keywords** box, type **Title IX, discrimination**

9 **Save** the template. Print **Handouts 6 Slides Horizontal**, or submit your presentation electronically as directed by your instructor.

10 **Close** the template.

11 Create a **new presentation** using your template. Save the file as **Lastname_Firstname_4E_Sports_Law** in your storage location.

12 On **Slide 5**, in the left column, remove the bullet, center *Applicability*, and then add bold. Repeat the formatting for *Administration* in the second column.

13 Add a **Title and Content** slide. In the title placeholder, type **Thank You** In the content placeholder, type **DeLong Grant Law Partners appreciates this opportunity to explain Title IX as it pertains to athletics. Thank you, Mr. Appleton, for your time.** Remove the bullet and center the text.

14 On the **Slide Master**, change the first-level bullets to **Star Bullets**. Close the Master View.

15 Change the footer on the handouts to include **Lastname_Firstname_4E_Sports_Law** and then click **Apply to All**.

16 Edit the document properties. Replace the text in the **Author** box with your own first and last name.

17 **Save** the presentation. Print **Handouts 6 Slides Horizontal**, or submit your presentation electronically as directed by your instructor.

18 **Close** the presentation.

End **You have completed Project 4E**

Apply **4B** skills from these Objectives:

- **3** Create and Edit Comments
- **4** Prepare a Presentation for Distribution
- **5** Protect a Presentation

Mastering PowerPoint | Project 4F Contract Aspects

In the following Mastering PowerPoint project, you will complete a presentation that covers various aspects of contracts in the entertainment industry, including royalties, minors, and advances. You will review the presentation and add comments before preparing it for distribution. Your completed presentation will look similar to Figure 4.55.

Project Files

For Project 4F, you will need the following file:

p04F_Contract_Aspects.pptx

You will save your presentation as:

Lastname_Firstname_4F_Contract_Aspects.pptx
Lastname_Firstname_4F_Contract_Aspects.pdf
Lastname_Firstname_4F_Contract_Aspects.xps

Project Results

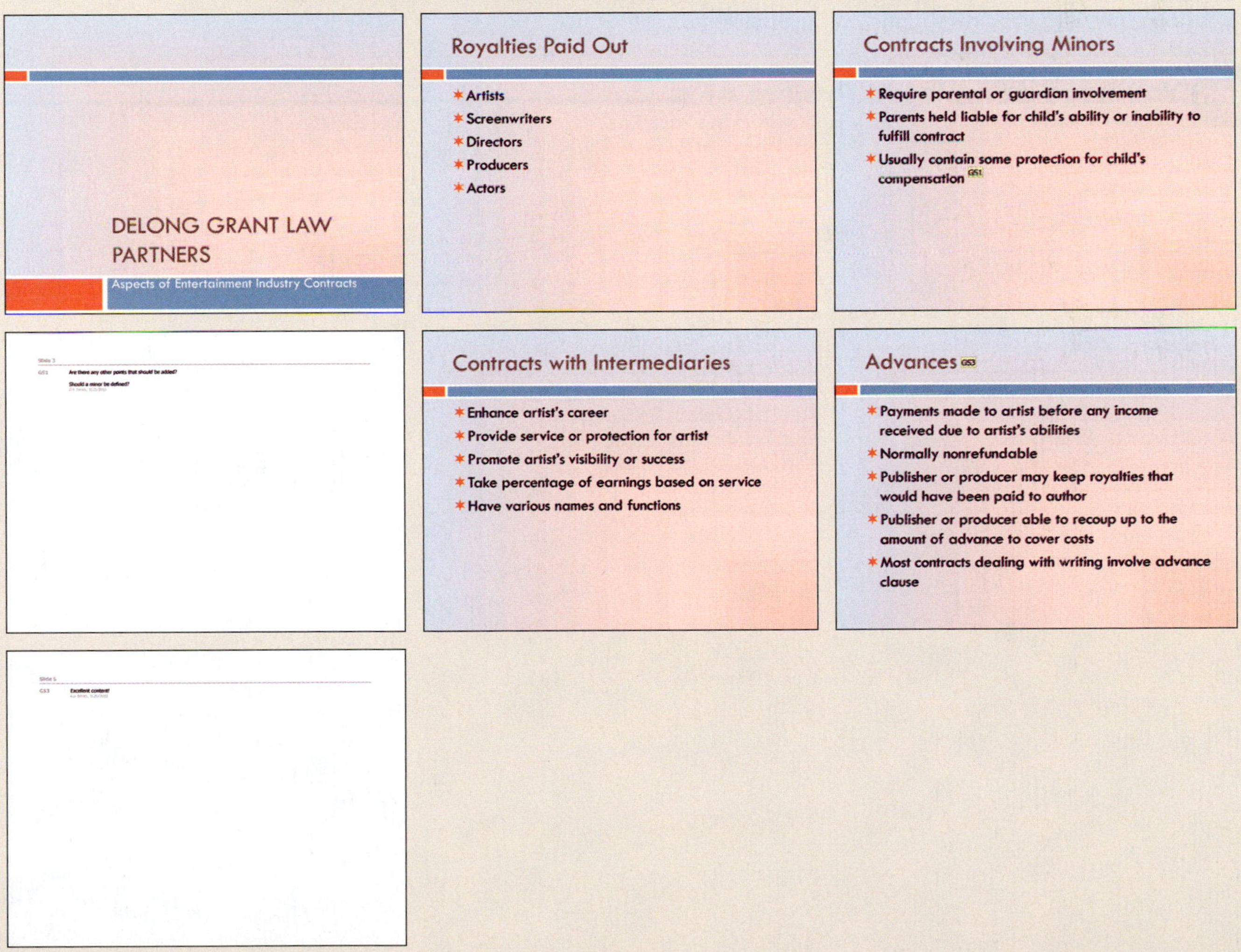

Figure 4.55

(Project 4F Contract Aspects continues on the next page)

Mastering PowerPoint | Project 4F Contract Aspects (continued)

1 **Start** PowerPoint. Locate and open the file **p04F_Contract_Aspects**. Save the file as **Lastname_Firstname_4F_Contract_Aspects**

2 Make **Slide 3** the active slide. At the end of the last bulleted item, insert a comment, and then type **Are there any other points that should be added?**

3 On **Slide 4**, select *Intermediaries*, and then add this comment: **I think this term needs to be defined.**

4 On **Slide 5**, add this comment: **Excellent content!** Drag the comment so it is positioned right after *Advances*.

5 Edit the comment on **Slide 3**. Press Enter two times, and then type **Should a minor be defined?**

6 Delete the comment on **Slide 4**.

7 Insert a footer on Notes and Handouts that includes the fixed date and time, page number, and file name.

8 Revise the document properties. Replace the text in the **Author** box with your own name. In the **Subject** box, type your course name and section number, and then in the **Keywords** box, type **entertainment, royalties, minors, advances**

9 **Save** the presentation.

10 **Save** the presentation as a **PDF** file. As you do, display the **Options** dialog box and specify **Include comments and ink markup**, **Handouts**, **6 slides per page**, and **Horizontal**.

11 **Print** the PDF file, or submit your presentation electronically as directed by your instructor

12 **Save** the presentation as an **XPS** file following the same instructions for saving the PDF file. **Print** the XPS file, or submit your presentation electronically as directed by your instructor.

13 Mark your presentation as **Final**, and then **Save**.

14 **Close** the presentation, and then **Exit** PowerPoint.

End **You have completed Project 4F**

Apply **4A** and **4B** skills from these Objectives:

1. Create a Custom Template by Modifying Slide Masters
2. Apply a Custom Template to a Presentation
3. Create and Edit Comments
4. Prepare a Presentation for Distribution
5. Protect a Presentation

Mastering PowerPoint | Project 4G Film Production

In the following Mastering PowerPoint project, you will open a presentation explaining the legal aspects of film production and modify the slide masters. Frequently, DeLong Grant Law Partners presents this information to college classes, so you will save the presentation as a template. Then you will create a presentation from the template and personalize it for the Film Production course at the local university. You will add some comments for other partners to see and save the presentation as a PDF file for the participants. Your completed presentation will look similar to Figure 4.56.

Project Files

For Project 4G, you will need the following file:

p04G_Film_Production.pptx

You will save your presentation as:

Lastname_Firstname_4G_Film_Template.potx
Lastname_Firstname_4G_Film_Production.pptx
Lastname_Firstname_4G_Film_Production.xps

Project Results

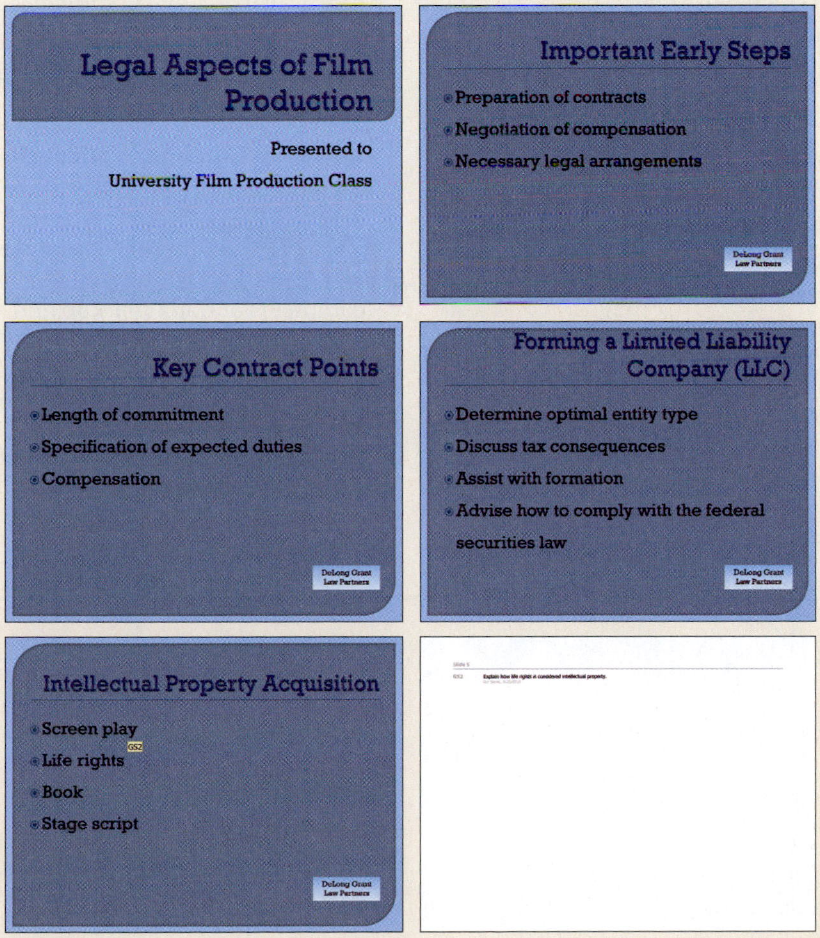

Figure 4.56

(Project 4G Film Production continues on the next page)

Mastering PowerPoint | Project **4G** Film Production (continued)

1 **Start** PowerPoint. Locate and open the file **p04G_Film_Production.pptx**, and then save it as a template with the name **Lastname_Firstname_4G_Film_Template**

2 In the **Slide Master View**, click the **Foundry Slide Master** thumbnail. Change the theme colors to **Elemental**, and then change the background to **Style 2**. Change the color of the first bulleted item to **Blue, Accent 1, Darker 50%**.

3 Click the **Title Slide Layout** thumbnail, and then change font size of the Master title style placeholder to **54**.

4 Click the **Title and Content Layout** thumbnail. Under **Basic Shapes**, insert a **Text Box** shape anywhere on the right side of the content placeholder. Inside the shape, type **DeLong Grant** Press Enter, and then type **Law Partners** Change the font size to **14 pt**, and then center the text. Select the text, and then change the **Height** to **.6"** and the **Width** to **1.6"**. Use **Shape Fill** to add a **Gradient** with a **Light Variation** of **Linear Down**. Then position the text box shape in the lower right corner of the content placeholder.

5 Remove the Header on the **Handout Master**, and then close the **Master View**.

6 Insert the **Header & Footer**. On the **Notes and Handouts tab**, include a **Fixed** date and the **Page number** and **Footer**. In the **Footer** box, using your own name, type **Lastname_Firstname_4G_Film_Template** and then click **Apply to All**.

7 Revise the document properties. Replace the text in the **Author** box with your own first and last name. In the **Subject** box, type your course name and section number, and then in the **Keywords** box, type **film production, LLC, intellectual property**

8 Print **Handouts 6 Slides Horizontal**, or submit your presentation electronically as directed by your instructor.

9 **Save** the template. **Close** the template.

10 Create a new document from existing template **Lastname_Firstname_4G_Film_Template.potx**, and then save it as **Lastname_Firstname_4G_Film_Production.pptx**

11 On **Slide 1**, after *Presented to*, press Enter, then and type **University Film Production Class**

12 On the **Foundry Slide Master**, select all of the text in the first bulleted item, change the line spacing to **1.5**, and then close the Master View.

13 On **Slide 4**, after the third bulleted item, add this comment: **Maybe clarify that you mean the formation of an LLC.**

14 On **Slide 5**, select *Life rights*, and then add this comment: **Explain how life rights is considered intellectual property.**

15 Delete the first comment.

16 Update the filename in the Notes and Handouts footer to **Lastname_Firstname_4G_Film_Production** and then update the Properties with your name as the Author.

17 Print **Handouts 6 Slides Horizontal**, or submit your presentation electronically as directed by your instructor.

18 **Save** the presentation.

19 **Save** the presentation as an **XPS file**, including the comments and ink markup and specifying handouts 6 slides per page. **Print** the XPS file, or submit the file electronically as directed by your instructor. **Close** the **XPS Viewer**.

20 Mark the presentation as **Final**, and then **Close** it. **Exit** PowerPoint.

End **You have completed Project 4G**

Apply a combination of the **4A** and **4B** skills.

GO! Fix It | Project 4H Labor Issues

Project Files

For Project 4H, you will need the following file:

p04H_Labor_Template.potx

You will save your presentation as:

Lastname_Firstname_4H_Labor_Template.potx
Lastname_Firstname_4H_Labor_Issues.pptx
Lastname_Firstname_4H_Labor_Issues.pdf

In this project, you will edit a template for the DeLong Grant Law Partners regarding labor issues in sports. From the student files that accompany this textbook, open the file **p04H_Labor_Template.potx**, and then save the file in your **PowerPoint Chapter 4** folder as **Lastname_Firstname_4H_Labor_Template.potx** After completing the template, you will create a presentation from the template and name it **Lastname_Firstname_4H_Labor_Issues.pptx** You will also save the presentation as PDF Handouts 6 slides per page including comments.

To complete the project, you must correct these errors:

In the master slide view:

- The Gradient type should be Linear and the Gradient stop positioned at 70%. The color should Aqua, Accent 5.
- First-level bullets on all slides should be Arrow Bullets.
- Line spacing for the first-level bullets on the Title and Content Layout should be changed to 1.5.
- The shape should be at the lower right of the Title and Content Layout content placeholder.
- Properties should include your name, course name and section, and the keywords **labor, sports, agent, bargaining**
- A header and footer should be inserted on the Notes and Handouts that includes a fixed date and time, the page number, and a footer with the text **Lastname_Firstname_4H_Labor_Template** applied to all slides.

In a new presentation named **Lastname_Firstname_4H_Labor_Issues** created from the template:

- The title slide should be personalized for the Association of Sports Agents.
- Slide 2 should have a comment after *Wages* with this text: **This is always a tough topic to cover.**
- The comment on Slide 4 should be deleted.
- The Notes and Handouts footer should include the file name.
- Your name should be the author in the properties.
- PDF Handouts 6 slides per page including comments should be prepared.

Submit your presentation files electronically, or print out the PDF file of handouts and submit it as directed by your instructor. Close the presentation and exit PowerPoint.

End You have completed Project 4H

Apply a combination of the **4A** and **4B** skills.

GO! Make It | Project 4I Consignment Contracts

Project Files

For Project 4I, you will need the following files:

p04I_Consignment_Contracts.pptx
p04I_Contract.jpg

You will save your presentation as:

Lastname_Firstname_4I_Consignment_Template.potx
Lastname_Firstname_4I_Consignment_Contracts.pptx
Lastname_Firstname_4I_Consignment_Contracts.pdf

Start PowerPoint, and then open p04I_Consignment_Contracts. Save the file in your PowerPoint Chapter 4 folder as **Lastname_Firstname_4I_Consignment_Template.potx** Modify the Slide Master in the template. Apply the Background Style 11, and then format the background with a Rectangular Gradient Fill and a Gradient Stop positioned at 90%. Add Bold to the Master title style, and then change the bullets as shown in Figure 4.57. Change the first-level bullet line spacing to 1.5. On the Title and Content Layout, insert and position the Plaque shape at the bottom right of the placeholder with p04I_Contract.jpg as the fill.

Insert a header on the notes and handouts that includes the page number and a fixed date and time and a footer with the text **Lastname_Firstname_4I_Consignment_Template** applied to all slides. Properties should include your name, the course name and section, and the keywords **financial, claim**

Create a new presentation from the template, and then save the file in your PowerPoint Chapter 4 folder as **Lastname_Firstname_4I_Consignment_Contracts** Refer to Figure 4.57 for the information for a new Slide 3. Add this comment to the right of . . . *each piece* on Slide 2: **How do you assess the market value?** Update the notes and handouts footer with the correct file name, and then change the author in Properties to your name.

Save the presentation as Handouts 3 slides per page in a PDF file, including the comments. Print the PDF file or submit electronically as directed by your instructor. Save the presentation, and then mark the presentation as final. Print the template file and the presentation file as Handouts 3 slides per page or submit electronically as directed by your instructor.

Project Results

Figure 4.57

End You have completed Project 4I

Apply a combination of the **4A** and **4B** skills.

GO! Solve It | Project 4J Legal Guide

Project Files

For Project 4J, you will need the following file:

p04J_Legal_Guide.pptx

You will save your presentation as:

Lastname_Firstname_4J_Legal_Template.potx
Lastname_Firstname_4J_Legal_Guide.pptx
Lastname_Firstname_4J_Legal_Guide.pdf

Open p04J_Legal_Guide, and then save it as **Lastname_Firstname_4J_Legal_Template.potx** Format the slide master with a Background Style, and then format the Background with two gradient stops applying a fill color at each gradient stop. Change the bullets on the appropriate slide master so they all display with a different bullet style. Change font formatting and bullet color to maintain good contrast with the background. Insert the fixed date and time, the page number, and the file name applied in the Notes and Handouts. Add your name, your course name and section number, and the keywords **athlete, legal, agent** to the Properties.

Create a new presentation from the template. Save the file in your PowerPoint Chapter 4 folder as **Lastname_Firstname_4J_Legal_Guide.pptx** On Slide 1, on the line below *Prepared for*, type **Association of Sports Agents** On Slide 4, insert a comment. Update the Notes and Handouts footer and the Properties. Save the presentation as Handouts 6 slides per page in a PDF file, including the comments. Mark the PowerPoint presentation as final, and then save the presentation.

Print the PDF or submit it electronically, and print the template file and the presentation file as Handouts 6 slides per page or submit electronically as directed by your instructor.

	Performance Level		
Performance Element	**Exemplary:** You consistently applied the relevant skills.	**Proficient:** You sometimes, but not always, applied the relevant skills.	**Developing:** You rarely or never applied the relevant skills.
Performance Criteria: Formatted Office Theme Slide Master with a background style and applied a fill color to two Gradient stops.	Slide background style was applied to the slide master and applied color to two Gradient stops.	Slide background style and added color to two Gradient stops, but did not apply them on the slide master.	Slide background style and color on two Gradient stops were not applied in the template.
Changed bullet style on the Office Theme Slide Master.	Bullet style changed for all bullets on the slide master. Good contrast with the background.	Bullet style was not changed on the template slide master. Contrast may not be appropriate.	Bullet style was not changed in the template.
Created and personalized a presentation based on the template.	Presentation file was created correctly; Subtitle and comment were inserted correctly.	Presentation file was created, but the subtitle information and/or the comment were entered in the template.	No presentation file was created from the template.
Saved presentation as PDF handouts with comments and marked as Final.	Presentation was saved correctly as PDF file and marked as Final.	Presentation was not saved correctly as PDF or not marked as Final.	Presentation was not saved as PDF and not marked as Final.

End You have completed Project 4J

Apply a combination of the **4A** and **4B** skills.

GO! Solve It | Project **4K** Actor Advice

Project Files

For Project 4K, you will need the following files:

p04K_Actor_Advice.pptx
p04K_Cinema.jpg

You will save your presentation as:

Lastname_Firstname_4K_Actor_Template.potx
Lastname_Firstname_4K_Actor_Advice.pptx
Lastname_Firstname_4K_Actor_Advice.pdf

Open p04K_Actor_Advice and save it as a template **Lastname_Firstname_4K_Actor_Template** Examine the slide content, and then modify the appropriate slide master with a background style or a theme. Adjust colors and fonts as needed. Change the bullet style for levels of bullets that are used. Insert a shape on the appropriate slide master so the shape displays only on Slide 1. Insert p04K_Cinema.jpg in the shape. On the Notes and Handouts, insert the fixed date and time, page number, and a footer with the file name. Add your name, your course name and section number, and the keywords **contracts, paparazzi, media** to the Properties.

Create a new presentation based on the template. Personalize the presentation for Julia Simpson. Save the presentation as **Lastname_Firstname_4K_Actor_Advice.pptx** On Slide 2, insert a comment. Update the Notes and Handouts footer with the correct file name, and then change the author in the Properties. Save the presentation in a PDF file as handouts, including the comments. Mark the presentation as final and save it. Print or submit electronically as directed by your instructor.

	Performance Level		
	Exemplary: You consistently applied the relevant skills	**Proficient:** You sometimes, but not always, applied the relevant skills	**Developing:** You rarely or never applied the relevant skills
Performance Criteria: Customized Office Theme Slide Master with a background/ theme and bullet styles.	Slide master was customized correctly with a background or theme and with bullet styles. Maintained good contrast.	Slide master was not customized with a background or theme and with bullet styles. Customization done on other slide masters.	No slide master customization was completed.
Inserted a shape with the picture on the Title Slide Layout master.	Shape was inserted on the slide master and was sized and placed in an appropriate position.	The shape was not inserted on the appropriate slide master.	The shape was not inserted.
Created and personalized a presentation. Saved presentation as PDF with comments and marked as Final.	Presentation file was created, personalized, and included comments. Saved as PDF handouts with comments and marked as Final.	Presentation file was created, but was not personalized. Presentation may or may not have been saved as PDF and marked as Final.	A presentation file was not created from the template.

End You have completed Project 4K

Outcomes-Based Assessments

Rubric

The following outcomes-based assessments are *open-ended assessments.* That is, there is no specific correct result; your result will depend on your approach to the information provided. Make *Professional Quality* your goal. Use the following scoring rubric to guide you in *how* to approach the problem and then to evaluate *how well* your approach solves the problem.

The *criteria*—Software Mastery, Content, Format and Layout, and Process—represent the knowledge and skills you have gained that you can apply to solving the problem. The *levels of performance*—Professional Quality, Approaching Professional Quality, or Needs Quality Improvements—help you and your instructor evaluate your result.

	Your completed project is of Professional Quality if you:	**Your completed project is Approaching Professional Quality if you:**	**Your completed project Needs Quality Improvements if you:**
1-Software Mastery	Choose and apply the most appropriate skills, tools, and features and identify efficient methods to solve the problem.	Choose and apply some appropriate skills, tools, and features, but not in the most efficient manner.	Choose inappropriate skills, tools, or features, or are inefficient in solving the problem.
2-Content	Construct a solution that is clear and well organized, contains content that is accurate, appropriate to the audience and purpose, and is complete. Provide a solution that contains no errors in spelling, grammar, or style.	Construct a solution in which some components are unclear, poorly organized, inconsistent, or incomplete. Misjudge the needs of the audience. Have some errors in spelling, grammar, or style, but the errors do not detract from comprehension.	Construct a solution that is unclear, incomplete, or poorly organized; contains some inaccurate or inappropriate content; and contains many errors in spelling, grammar, or style. Do not solve the problem.
3-Format and Layout	Format and arrange all elements to communicate information and ideas, clarify function, illustrate relationships, and indicate relative importance.	Apply appropriate format and layout features to some elements, but not others. Overuse features, causing minor distraction.	Apply format and layout that does not communicate information or ideas clearly. Do not use format and layout features to clarify function, illustrate relationships, or indicate relative importance. Use available features excessively, causing distraction.
4-Process	Use an organized approach that integrates planning, development, self-assessment, revision, and reflection.	Demonstrate an organized approach in some areas, but not others; or, use an insufficient process of organization throughout.	Do not use an organized approach to solve the problem.

Apply a combination of the **4A** and **4B** skills.

GO! Think | Project 4L Venue Risks

Project Files

For Project 4L, you will need the following file:

New blank PowerPoint presentation

You will save your presentation as:

Lastname_Firstname_4L_Venue_Template.potx
Lastname_Firstname_4L_Venue_Risks.pptx
Lastname_Firstname_4L_Venue_Risks.pdf

In this project, you will create a PowerPoint template for DeLong Grant Law Partners to educate colleges, universities, and other sports venues about safety and security.

Create a template named **Lastname_Firstname_4L_Venue_Template.potx** Customize the slide masters, applying formatting as needed. In the Notes and Handouts, include the fixed date and time, page number, and file name in the footer. Add your name, course name and section number, and the keywords **venue, sports, risk** to the Properties.

Create a new presentation based on the template that addresses safety and security concerns. Save the presentation as **Lastname_Firstname_4L_Venue_Risks.pptx**. Create three slides, each using a different layout. Add two comments. Update the Notes and Handouts footer with the new file name and the author name in the Properties. Save the presentation as Handouts 6 slides per page in a PDF file, including the comments. Mark the PowerPoint presentation as final. Print or submit electronically as directed by your instructor.

End You have completed Project 4L

Apply a combination of the **4A** and **4B** skills.

GO! Think | Project 4M Intellectual Property

Project Files

For Project 4M, you will need the following files:

New blank PowerPoint presentation
p04M_Intellectual_Property.jpg

You will save your presentation as:

Lastname_Firstname_4M_Property_Template.potx
Lastname_Firstname_4M_Intellectual_Property.pptx
Lastname_Firstname_4M_Intellectual_Property.xps

In this project, you will create a PowerPoint presentation for DeLong Grant Law Partners that provides an overview of intellectual property concepts.

Create a template and customize the appropriate slide masters. Insert a shape on the slides and fill it with p04M_Intellectual_Property.jpg. Design the appropriate master slides for an effective template. In the Notes and Handouts, include the date and time fixed, the page number, and the file name in the footer. Add your name, course name and section number, and the keywords **intellectual, property** to the Properties area.

Create a four-slide presentation based on your template. Update the Notes and Handouts footer and the Document Properties. Prepare XPS handouts with four slides per page, including the comments. Print or submit electronically as directed by your instructor.

End You have completed Project 4M

Apply a combination of the **4A** and **4B** skills.

You and GO! | Project 4N Copyright

Project Files

For Project 4N, you will need the following files:

New blank PowerPoint presentation
p04N_Copyright.jpg

You will save your presentation as:

Lastname_Firstname_4N_Copyright_Template.potx
Lastname_Firstname_4N_Copyright.pptx
Lastname_Firstname_4N_Copyright.pdf

Research the copyright law as it pertains to the exclusive right to copy literary, musical, artistic, or other original creations. Create a PowerPoint template, and then name it **Lastname_Firstname_4N_Copyright_Template** Customize the slide master, title slide, title and content, and two content layouts. Select an appropriate theme or background, and then customize the bullets. Insert a shape, and then fill it with p04N_Copyright.jpg. Apply appropriate formats.

In the Notes and Handouts, include the date and time fixed, the page number, and the template file name in the footer. Add your name, your course name and section number, and the keywords **copyright, art, music** to the Properties.

Then create a presentation that explains copyright and what it protects based on the template. Include four slides—one title slide, two title and content slides, and one two-content slide. Name the presentation **Lastname_Firstname_4N_Copyright** Focus on one area, such as literary or music copyrights.

Include comments on two slides in the presentation. Update the footer and properties as needed. Prepare PDF handouts with four slides per page, including comments. Mark the presentation as Final. Print or submit electronically as directed by your instructor.

End You have completed Project 4N

Applying Advanced Graphic Techniques and Inserting Audio and Video

OUTCOMES

At the end of this chapter you will be able to:

OBJECTIVES

Mastering these objectives will enable you to:

PROJECT 5A

Edit and format pictures and add sound to a presentation.

1. Use Picture Corrections (p. 689)
2. Add a Border to a Picture (p. 696)
3. Change the Shape of a Picture (p. 700)
4. Add a Picture to a WordArt Object (p. 701)
5. Enhance a Presentation with Audio and Video (p. 704)

PROJECT 5B

Create and edit a photo album and crop pictures.

6. Create a Photo Album (p. 716)
7. Edit a Photo Album and Add a Caption (p. 718)
8. Crop a Picture (p. 722)

Dudarev Mikhail/Shutterstock

In This Chapter

Microsoft Office PowerPoint provides a variety of methods for formatting and enhancing graphic elements. You have practiced using some of the tools that change the style and add an effect to a picture or a graphic. PowerPoint also provides sophisticated tools for changing the brightness, contrast, and shape of a picture; adding a border; and cropping a picture to remove unwanted areas. These tools eliminate the need to use a separate program to format a picture.

PowerPoint also allows you to include audio and video effects in presentations, although the resulting files are quite large. For example, you might want to introduce a slide with an audio effect or music, or have an audio effect or music play when the slide or a component on the slide, such as text or a graphic, is clicked. The inclusion of audio and video can significantly enhance the overall presentation when used properly.

Cross Oceans Music produces and distributes recordings of innovative musicians from every continent in genres that include Celtic, jazz, New Age, reggae, flamenco, calypso, and unique blends of all styles. Company scouts travel the world attending world music festivals, concerts, and small local venues to find their talented roster of musicians. These artists create new music using traditional and modern instruments and technologies. Cross Oceans' customers are knowledgeable about music and demand the highest quality digital recordings provided in state-of-the-art formats.

Project 5A Overview Presentation

myitlab
Project 5A Training

Project Activities

In Activities 5.01 through 5.10, you will change the sharpness or softness and the brightness and contrast of pictures. You will also add borders and change the outline shape of pictures. You will insert linked video files and add a trigger to the audio and video. Your completed presentation will look similar to Figure 5.1.

Project Files

For Project 5A, you will need the following files:

p05A_Cross_Oceans.pptx
p05A_Building.jpg
p05A_Island2.jpg
p05A_MP3.jpg
p05A_Smooth_Jazz.wav
p05A_NewAge.wav

You will save your presentation as:

Lastname_Firstname_5A_Cross_Oceans.pptx

Project Results

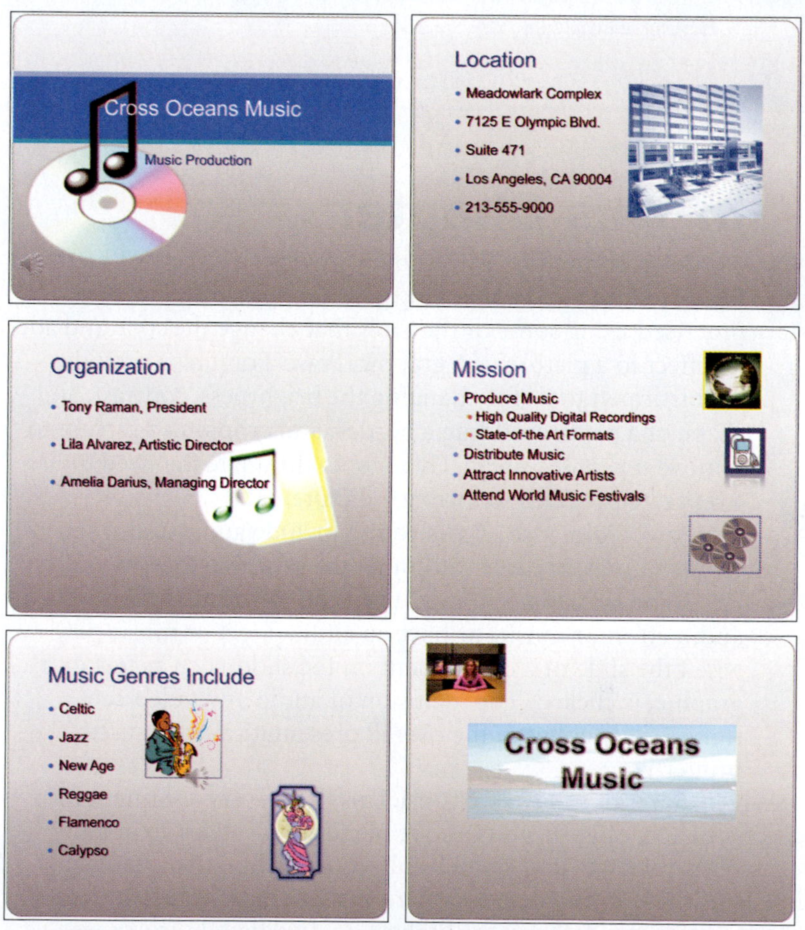

Figure 5.1
Project 5A Cross Oceans Music

Objective 1 | Use Picture Corrections

Pictures can be corrected to improve the brightness, contrast, or sharpness. For example, you can use Sharpen and Soften to enhance picture details or make a picture more appealing by removing unwanted blemishes. When you ***sharpen*** an image, the clarity of an image increases. When you ***soften*** an image, the picture becomes fuzzier. You can use Presets to choose common, built-in blurriness adjustments from a gallery. You can also use a slider to adjust the amount of blurriness, or you can enter a number in the box next to the slider.

Another way to correct pictures is to use Brightness and Contrast. ***Brightness*** is the relative lightness of a picture, and ***contrast*** is the difference between the darkest and lightest area of a picture. You can use **Presets** to choose common, built-in brightness and contrast combinations from a gallery, or you can use a slider to adjust the amount of brightness and contrast separately.

When you change the overall lightening and darkening of the image, you change the individual pixels in an image. ***Pixel*** is short for *picture element* and represents a single point in a graphic image. To increase brightness, more light or white is added to the picture by selecting positive percentages. To decrease brightness, more darkness or black is added to the image by selecting negative percentages.

Changing the contrast of a picture changes the amount of gray in the image. Positive percentages increase the intensity of a picture by removing gray; negative percentages decrease intensity by adding more gray.

When you ***recolor*** a picture, you change all colors in the image into shades of one color. This effect is often used to stylize a picture or make the colors match a background.

Activity 5.01 | Using Sharpen and Soften on a Picture

In this activity, you will change the sharpness of a picture so the text on the slide will have greater emphasis. You will also use the Presets, which allows you to apply one of five standard settings.

1 **Start** PowerPoint. Locate and open the file **p05A_Cross_Oceans** Display **Backstage** view, click **Save As**, and then navigate to the location where you are storing your projects for this chapter. Create a new folder named **PowerPoint Chapter 5** and then in the File name box and using your own name, save the file as **Lastname_Firstname_5A_Cross_Oceans** Click **Save** or press Enter.

2 Make **Slide 1** the active slide, if necessary, and then click to select the image.

3 Under **Picture Tools**, click the **Format tab**. In the **Arrange group**, click the **Send Backward button arrow**, and then click **Send to Back**.

> **Another Way**
>
> To move a picture behind all components on the slide, right-click the picture, click Send to Back.

The slide title and subtitle words are now displayed in front of the picture so you can read the words. When you click the Send Backward button, there are two options. Send Backward moves the image behind the title text. Send to Back moves the image behind both the title and subtitle text.

> **Alert! | Is the Text Visible?**
>
> If you cannot read the text in front of a picture that has been sent to the back, move the picture or change the text color.

4 Compare your screen with Figure 5.2, and then take a moment to study the descriptions of the picture adjustment settings, as shown in the table in Figure 5.3.

Figure 5.2

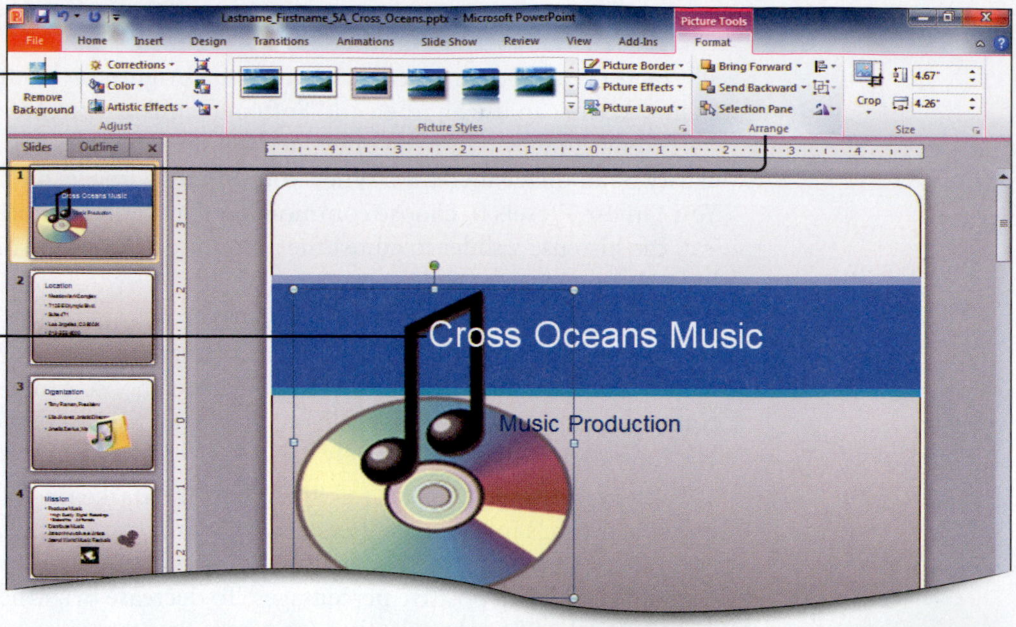

Picture Adjustment Options

Screen Element	Description
Remove Background	Removes unwanted portions of a picture. If needed, use marks to indicate areas to keep or remove from the picture.
Corrections	Improves the appearance of a picture by adjusting the: Brightness of the picture. Contrast between the darkest and lightest areas of a picture. Sharpness, or blurriness, of a picture.
Color	Adjusts the color intensity, color dominance, and color effects of a picture through the use of: Color saturation (intensity): A higher saturation makes a picture look more vivid. A lower saturation turns the colors toward gray. Color tone (temperature): The higher the temperature, the more orange is added to the picture. The lower the number, the more blue is added to the picture. These changes improve the appearance of a picture taken by a camera that did not measure the color temperature correctly. Recolor: A built-in stylized effect, such as grayscale or a color combination compatible with your picture, may be applied.
Artistic Effects	Adds an artistic effect to a picture to make it look like a sketch or painting. You can access the Artistic Effects Options from this menu.
Compress Pictures	Reduces the color format of the image to make the file size smaller. Compressing a picture makes the color take up fewer bits per pixel with no loss of quality. There are two compression options: The default is to compress the selected picture, but you can uncheck this option to compress all pictures in the document. If you have cropped a picture, you can delete the cropped area to reduce the file size. However, if you want to undo the cropping, you have to insert the picture again. Provides four target output methods: Print (220 ppi): Excellent quality on most printers and screens (selected by default). Screen (150 ppi): Good for Web pages and projectors. E-mail (96 ppi): Minimizes the document size for use when sharing the document through an e-mail attachment. Use document resolution: This option uses the resolution set on the File tab. By default this is set to Print or 220 ppi (pixels per inch), but you can change this default picture resolution.
Change Picture button	Allows you to select and insert a different picture to replace the current picture. The new picture maintains the formatting and size of the original picture.
Reset Picture button	Discards all formatting changes made to the picture.

Figure 5.3

5 In the **Adjust group**, click the **Corrections** button, and then click **Picture Corrections Options** to display the **Format Picture** dialog box. Drag the **Format Picture** dialog box to the side to make the picture visible, if necessary. Under **Sharpen and Soften**, drag the slider to the left to **-100%** and observe the fuzzy effect on the picture. Drag the slider to the right to **100%** and notice the sharpness of the picture.

6 Under **Sharpen and Soften**, click the **Presets** button. Compare your screen with Figure 5.4.

The ScreenTip for the Sharpen and Soften Presets button is Sharpen & Soften.

Figure 5.4

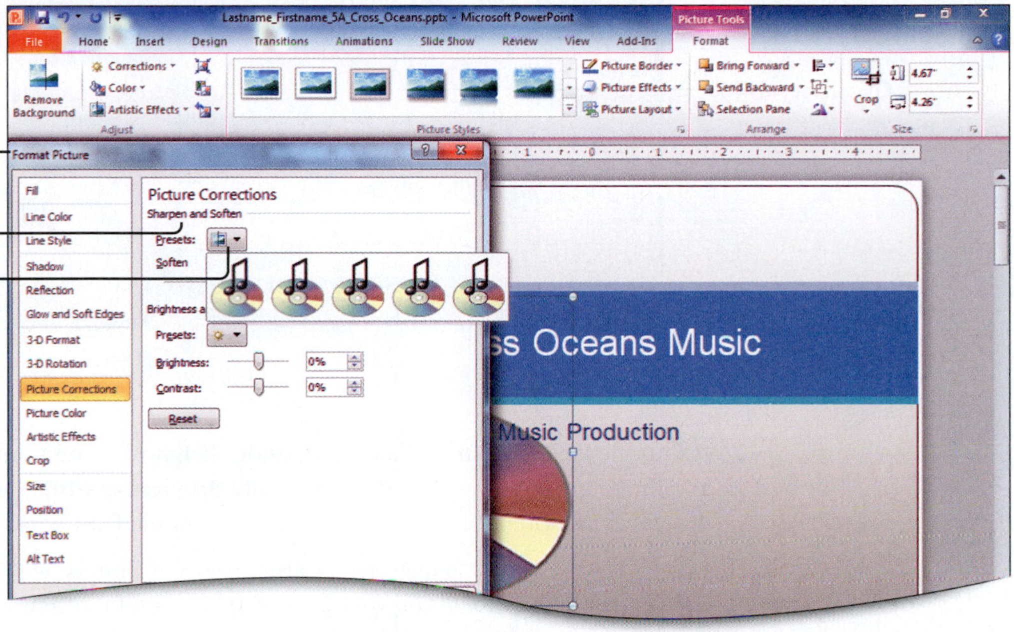

7 Click the first option—**Soften: 50%**.

The slider is now set at -50%, meaning that the picture is fuzzier than the text.

> **More Knowledge** | Using Picture Presets
>
> The default for Sharpen and Soften is 0%. The Presets range from Soften: 50% to Sharpen: 50%. The slider settings range from -100% to +100%. Soften: 50% in Presets is the same as -50% on the slider.

8 Click **Close** to close the **Format Picture** dialog box. **Save** the presentation.

Activity 5.02 | Changing the Brightness and Contrast of a Picture

In this activity, you will change the brightness and the contrast of a picture. You will also use the Presets, which allows you to select a combination of brightness and contrast settings.

1 With the image still selected, on the **Format tab**, in the **Adjust group**, click the **Corrections** button, and then click **Picture Corrections Options** to display the **Format Picture** dialog box again. Under **Brightness and Contrast**, drag the **Brightness** slider to the left and then to the right. Watch how the picture brightness changes. Type **20%** in the **Brightness** box.

2 Under **Brightness and Contrast**, drag the **Contrast** slider to the left and then to the right. Watch how the picture contrast changes. Type **40%** in the **Contrast** box. Compare your screen with Figure 5.5.

The picture is enhanced so the slide title displays with more prominence than the picture.

Figure 5.5

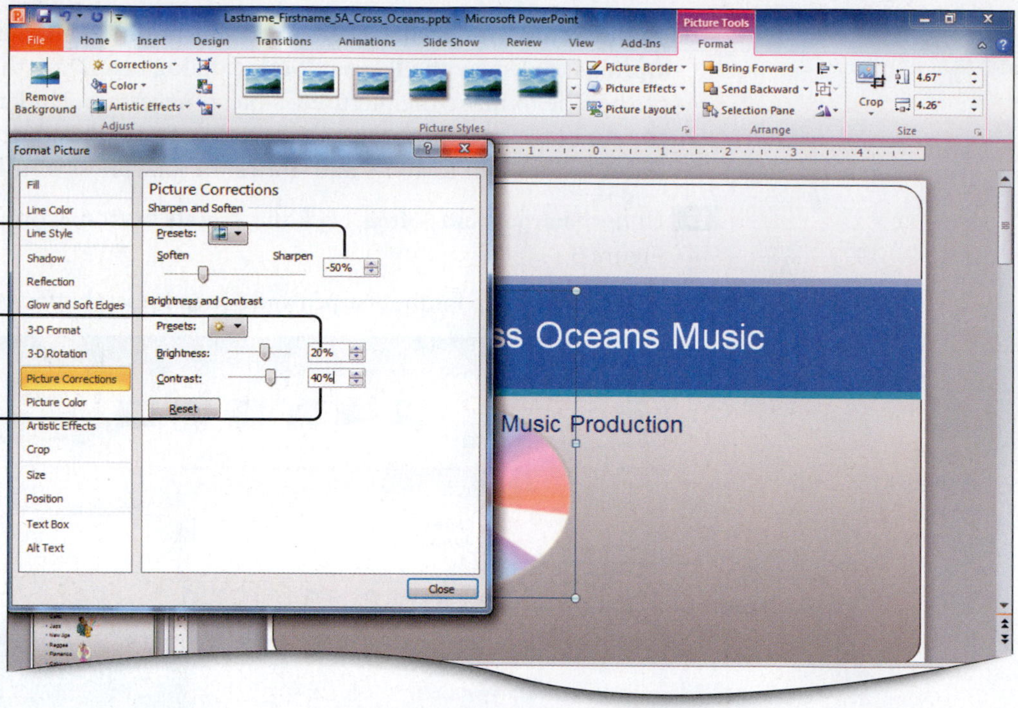

Sharpen and Soften set at –50%

Brightness set at 20%

Contrast set at 40%

3 In the **Format Picture** dialog box, under **Brightness and Contrast**, click the **Presets** button. In the gallery, in the bottom row locate **Brightness: +20% Contrast: +40%**, which is the combination of brightness and contrast you set. Compare your screen with Figure 5.6.

If you prefer, you may change brightness and contrast with one of the presets. The gallery displays the results on your picture to help you make a decision.

Figure 5.6

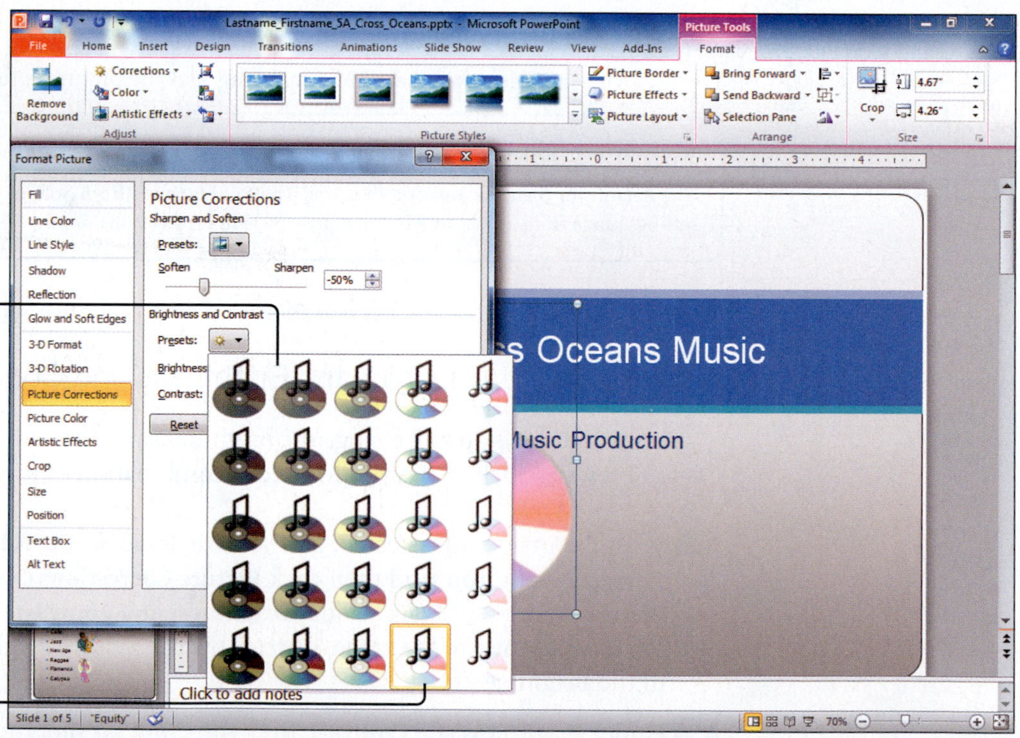

Brightness and Contrast Presets gallery

Selected Brightness and Contrast preset

4 Click outside the **Brightness and Contrast** gallery to collapse it. Click **Close**.

5 **Save** your changes.

Activity 5.03 | Recoloring a Picture

In this activity, you will recolor a picture.

> **Another Way**
> To display the gridlines, on the View tab, in the Show group, click a check mark in the Gridlines check box.

1 With the picture on **Slide 1** selected, under **Picture Tools**, click the **Format tab** if necessary. In the **Arrange group**, click the **Align** button, and then click **View Gridlines**. Click outside the picture to deselect it. Compare your screen with Figure 5.7.

The gridlines help you align objects at specific locations on the ruler.

Figure 5.7

Gridlines

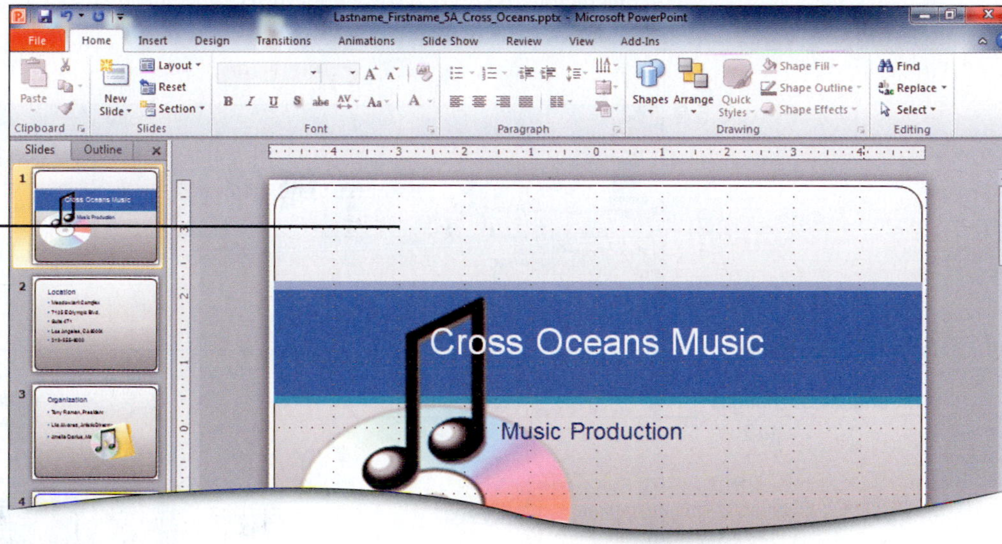

2 Make **Slide 2** the active slide. Click the **Insert tab**. In the **Images group**, click the **Picture** button. Navigate to the location where your student files are stored, and then insert the picture **p05A_Building.jpg**.

3 Move the entire picture so that the right edge aligns with the **4 inches on the right side of the horizontal ruler** and the **2 inches on the upper half of the vertical ruler**. Compare your screen with Figure 5.8.

Figure 5.8

Aligned at 4 inches on the right side of the horizontal ruler and 2 inches on the upper half of the vertical ruler

Another Way

To display the Format Picture dialog box, right-click the picture, and then click Format Picture.

4 With the picture still selected, on the **Format tab**, in the **Adjust group**, click the **Color** button. Click **Picture Color Options** to display the **Format Picture** dialog box. At the right, under **Recolor**, click the **Presets** button. In the third row, second column, locate **Blue, Accent color 1 Light**, and then click it. Do not close the **Format Picture** dialog box yet.

5 On the left side of the **Format Picture** dialog box, click **Picture Corrections**. Change the **Brightness** to **20%**. Compare your screen with Figure 5.9.

This effect increases the brightness of the picture and adds visual interest. Notice that you were able to access both the Picture Color and Picture Corrections without closing the Format Picture dialog box.

Figure 5.9

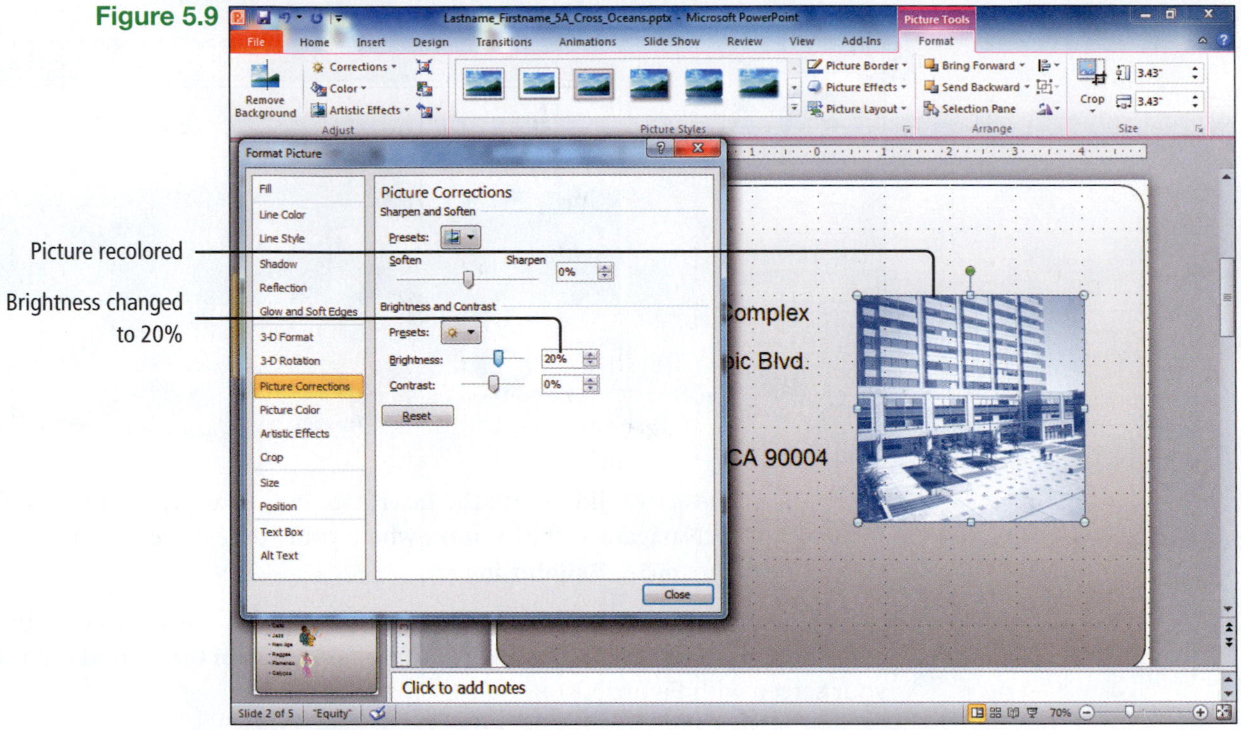

6 Click **Close**.

7 Make **Slide 3** the active slide, and then click to select the image. On the **Format tab**, in the **Arrange group**, click the **Send Backward button arrow**, and then click **Send to Back**.

8 With the image selected, in the **Adjust group**, click the **Corrections** button, and then click **Picture Corrections Options**. Under **Brightness and Contrast**, in the box next to **Contrast**, type **30%** and then press Tab. If necessary, drag the dialog box to the side so you can better see the picture effect.

This amount of contrast adds glare to the picture and makes the bulleted items difficult to read.

9 With the image still selected and the **Format Picture** window still displaying, use the method you prefer to change the **Brightness** to **+40**% and the **Contrast** to **+40**%. Change the softness to **-100%.** Click **Close**.

10 In the **Arrange group**, click the **Selection Pane** button to display the **Selection and Visibility pane**. Compare your screen with Figure 5.10. Click **Content Placeholder 2** to select the content placeholder including the three names. Click **Title 1** to select the title placeholder—*Organization*. Click **Picture 4** to select the picture on the slide.

The Selection and Visibility pane displays the shapes on the slide, making it easy to select the desired shape.

Figure 5.10

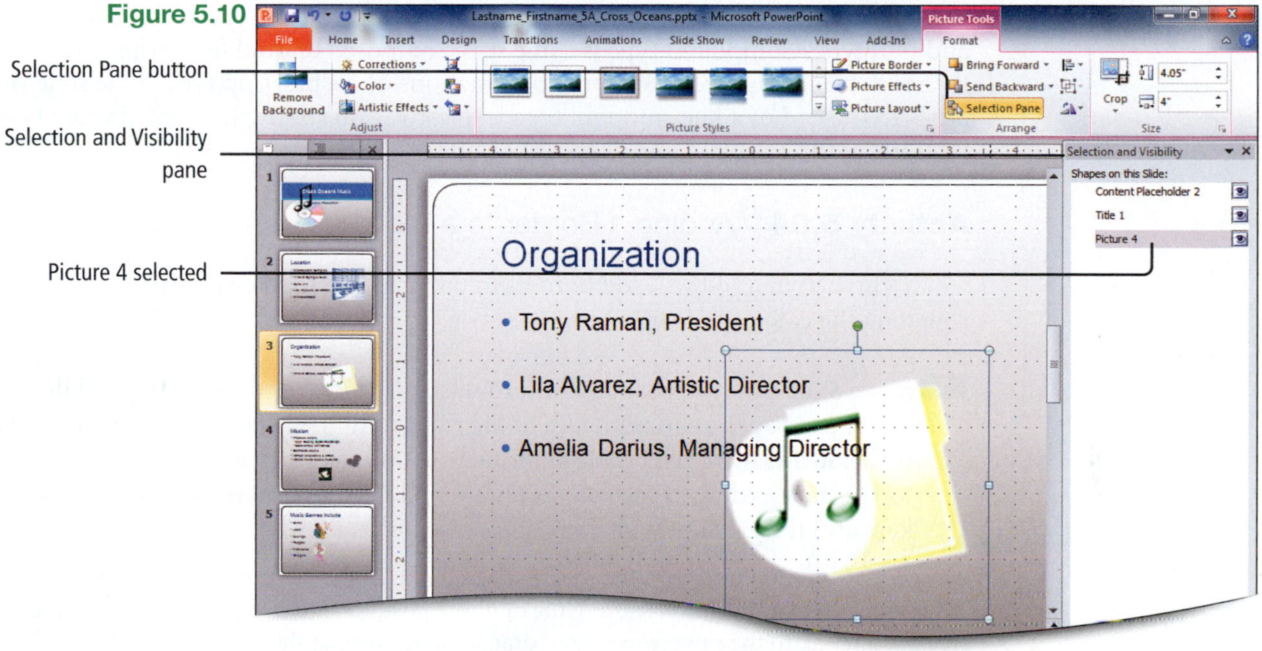

> **Another Way**
>
> On the Selection and Visibility pane, click the Close button ☒ to close the Selection Pane.

11 With the picture selected, drag it so the left side is aligned at **0 on the horizontal ruler** and the top edge of the picture aligns with **1.5 on the upper half of the vertical ruler**. On the **Format tab**, in the **Arrange group**, click the **Selection Pane** to close it. Click to the left of *Organization* to deselect the picture, and then compare your screen with Figure 5.11.

Reducing the contrast and softness of the picture makes the picture fade into the background, allowing the content of the bulleted items to appear more prominently. Repositioning the picture makes the words easier to read.

Figure 5.11

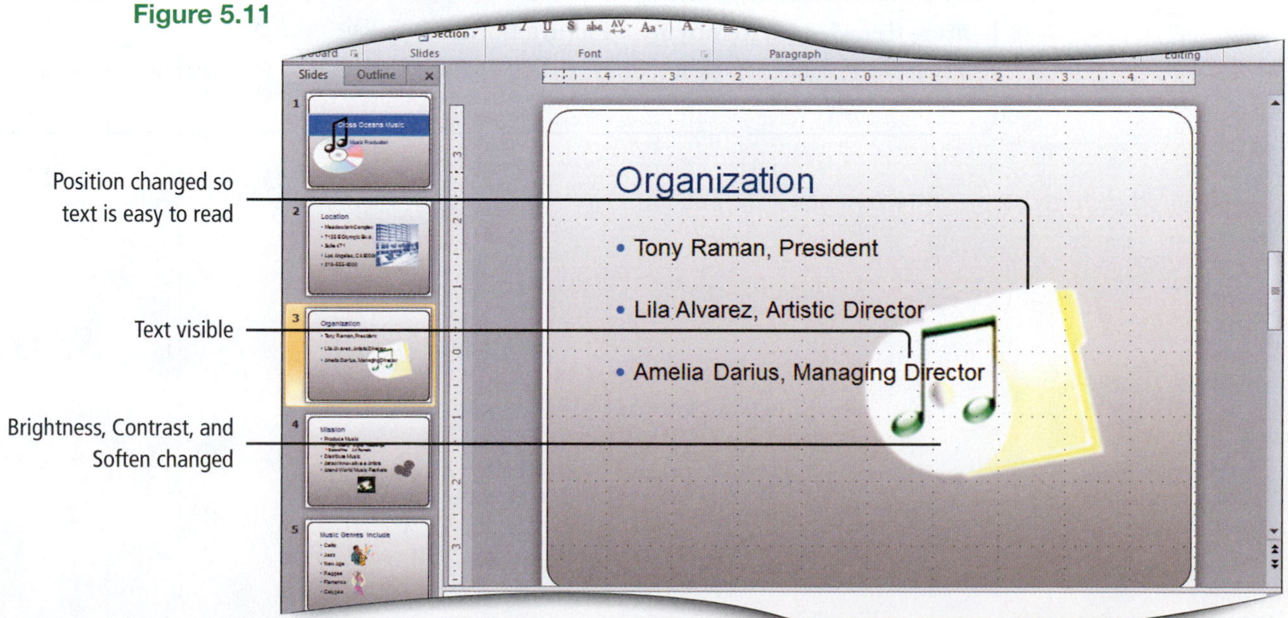

12 **Save** your changes.

Objective 2 | Add a Border to a Picture

After you have inserted a picture into a slide, you can add a ***border***, which is actually a frame, around the picture. It is possible to edit the color of the border and the line weight. The ***line weight*** is the thickness of the line measured in points (abbreviated as pt), similar to font sizes. It is sometimes also called line width.

You can also select the ***line style***, which is how the line displays, such as a solid line, dots, or dashes. You can also change Line Width, Compound type, Dash type, Cap type, and Join type. Compound type is a line style composed of double or triple lines. Dash type is a style composed of various combinations of dashes. Cap type is the style you apply to the end of a line, and Join type is the style you specify to be used when two lines intersect at the corner.

Activity 5.04 | Adding a Border to a Picture

In this activity, you will add borders to pictures and then customize those borders by changing the color, line weight, and line style.

1 Make **Slide 4** the active slide. Click to select the picture of the CDs. Hold down Shift, and then drag the entire picture to the right until the right edge of the picture aligns with **4 inches on the right side of the horizontal ruler**. Repeat the procedure to align the top of the picture at **1 inch on the lower half of the vertical ruler**. Use the Ctrl + arrow keys and the gridlines to help position the picture.

When you hold down the Shift key before dragging a picture, you can move the picture without accidentally shifting the opposite position. For example, if you start moving the picture to the right, you cannot drag it up or down at the same time.

2 With the picture still selected, click the **Format tab**. In the **Picture Styles group**, click the **Picture Border** button, and then in the first row, click the fourth color—**Dark Blue, Text 2**. Click **Picture Border**, click **Weight**, and then click **2 1/4 pt**. Click **Picture Border**, click **Dashes**, and then click **Round Dot**. Deselect the picture, and then compare your screen with Figure 5.12.

The picture displays with a border. The color, style, and weight have all been set.

More Knowledge | **Removing a Picture Border**

To remove the border on a picture, click to select the picture. Under Picture Tools, click the Format tab. In the Picture Styles group, click Picture Border, and then click No Outline.

Figure 5.12

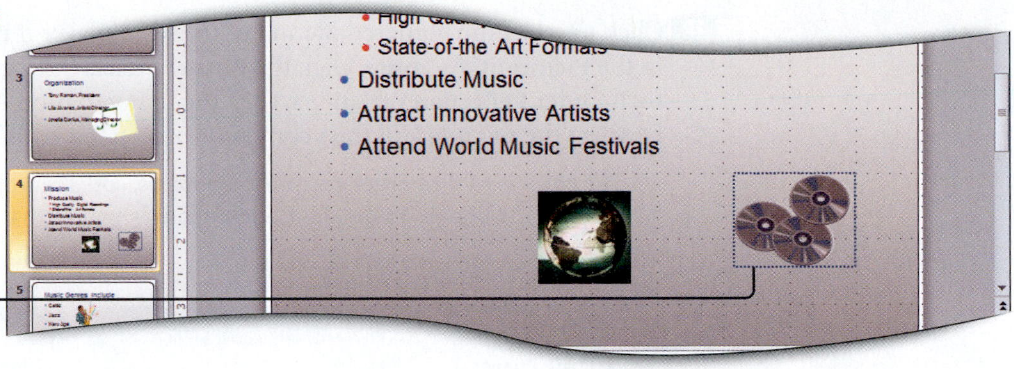

Picture moved and border added

> **Another Way**
>
> To size a picture proportionately, select the picture, and then drag a corner diagonally to the desired height or width.

3 Click the **Insert tab**. In the **Images group**, click the **Picture** button. Navigate to the location where your student files are stored, and then insert the picture **p05A_MP3.jpg**. On the **Format tab**, in the **Size group**, click the **Shape Height** box, type **1** and then press Enter.

The picture is sized proportionately.

4 Drag the entire picture so the top edge aligns at **1 inch on the upper half of the vertical ruler** and the right edge of the picture aligns at **4 inches on the right side of the horizontal ruler**.

5 With the picture still selected, on the **Format tab**, in the **Picture Styles group**, click the **Picture Border** button, and then in the last row, click the fifth color—**Blue, Accent 1, Darker 50%**. Click **Picture Border**. Point to **Weight**, and then click **More Lines** to display the **Format Picture** dialog box.

Recall that the Format Picture dialog box displays the picture formatting types. The Line Style option is selected because you displayed the Picture Border first and then clicked More Lines.

6 In the **Width** spin box, increase the line width to **9 pt**. In the **Join type** box, click the **down arrow**, and then click **Miter**. Compare your screen with Figure 5.13.

A ***mitered*** border has corners that are square. The default is rounded corners. The Format Picture dialog box allows you to enter borders wider than the maximum 6 pt listed when you click the Picture Border button and select Weight.

Figure 5.13

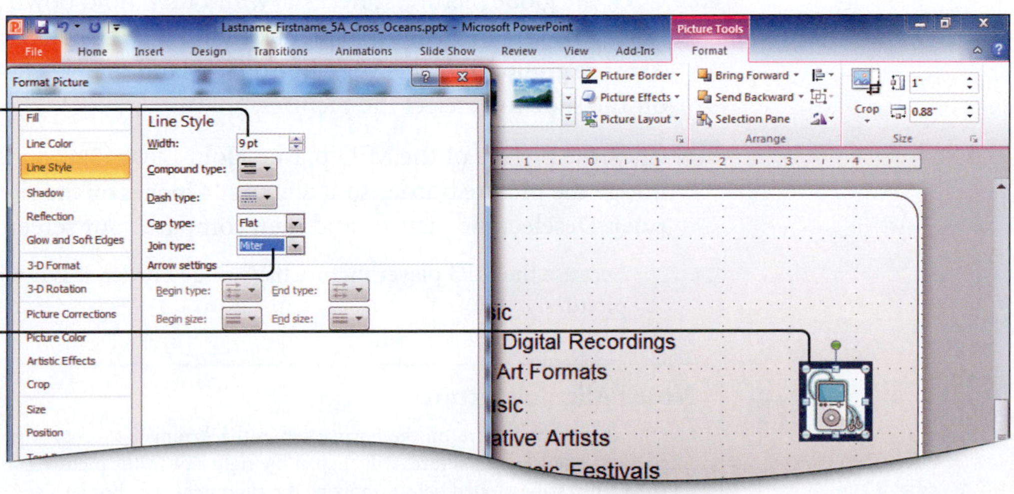

Line width set at 9 pt

Join type set as Miter

Picture added and positioned

7 Click **Close**.

8 Click to select the bordered picture of the MP3 player if necessary. On the **Format tab**, in the **Picture Styles group**, click the **Picture Effects** button, point to **Reflection**, and then under **Reflection Variations**, click the first variation—**Tight Reflection, touching**. Deselect the picture, and then compare your screen with Figure 5.14

The corners of the border are mitered borders, and a reflection is displayed below the picture. The border on the right side extends beyond the 4-inch mark on the horizontal ruler.

Figure 5.14

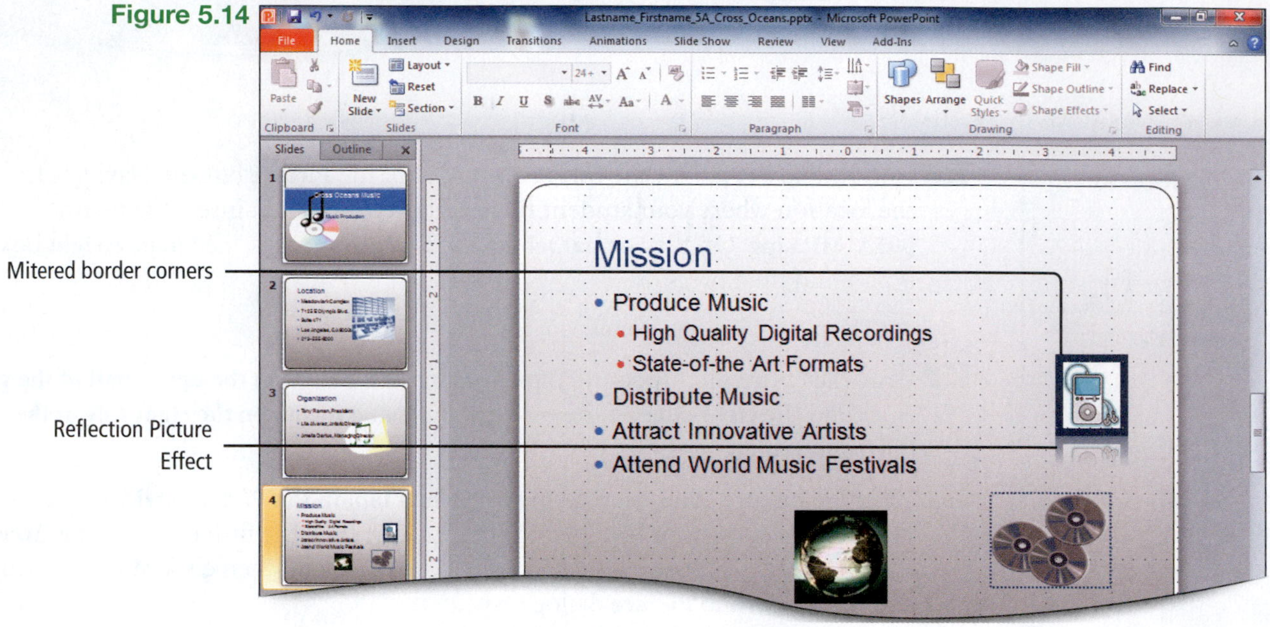

9 Click to select the picture of the globe. Drag the entire picture so the top edge aligns at **3 inches on the upper half of the vertical ruler** and the right edge aligns at **4 inches on the right side of the horizontal ruler.**

10 With the globe picture still selected, on the **Format tab**, in the **Picture Styles group**, click the **Picture Border** button, and then under **Standard Colors**, click **Yellow**. Click the **Picture Border** button, point to **Weight**, and then click **3 pt**.

11 Click the globe picture, if necessary, and then hold down Shift, and then click the other two pictures. All three pictures should be selected. On the **Format tab**, in the **Arrange group**, click the **Align** button, and then click **Align Right**. Click anywhere off the slide to deselect the pictures.

12 Click the picture of the MP3 player. Hold down Ctrl, and then press ← a few times to nudge the picture border so it aligns at **4 inches on the right side of the horizontal ruler**. Deselect the picture, and then compare your screen with Figure 5.15.

Because the MP3 player picture has a wide border, it is now aligned better with the other pictures.

Note | Aligning Pictures

Use the alignment options on the Format tab in the Arrange group to align pictures evenly. When you select Align Right, the selected pictures will align at the right side of the picture that is farthest to the right. Make sure that all pictures are selected before applying the alignment. The border size is not included in the alignment.

Figure 5.15

Globe repositioned and border added

Picture border nudged for better alignment

All three pictures aligned at the right

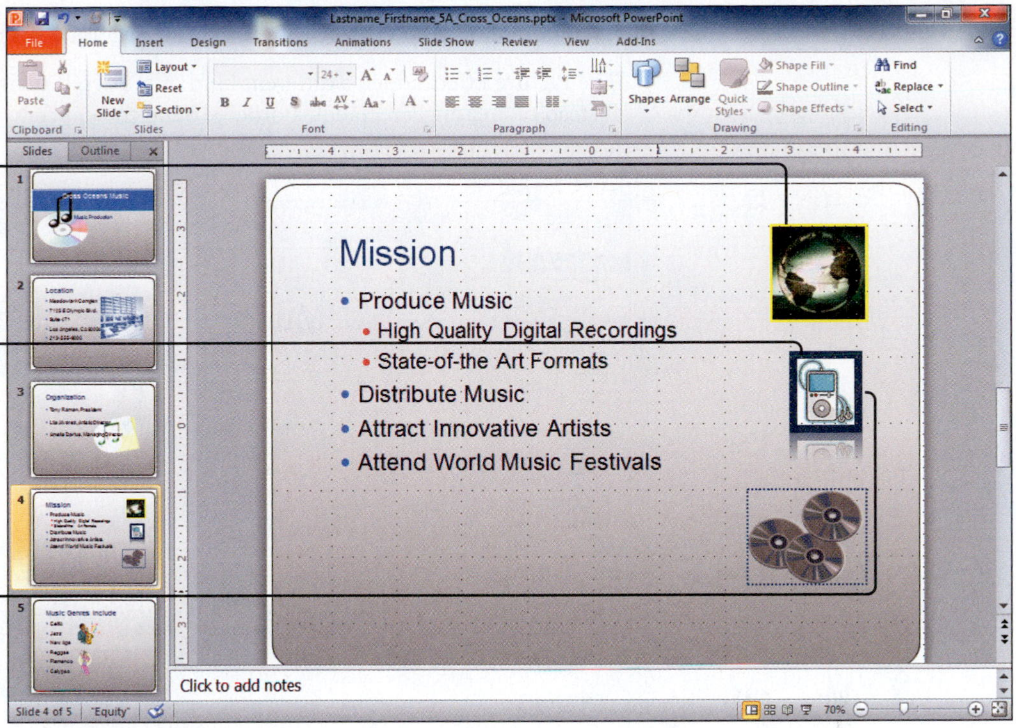

13 Make **Slide 5** the active slide, and then click to select the picture of the saxophone musician. Click the **Format tab**. In the **Picture Styles group**, click the **Picture Border** button. Under **Theme Colors**, in the last row, click the fifth color—**Blue, Accent 1, Darker 50%**.

14 Click the **Picture Border** button, point to **Weight**, and then click **1 pt**. Click outside the picture to deselect it, and then compare your screen with Figure 5.16.

Figure 5.16

Border added and weight changed

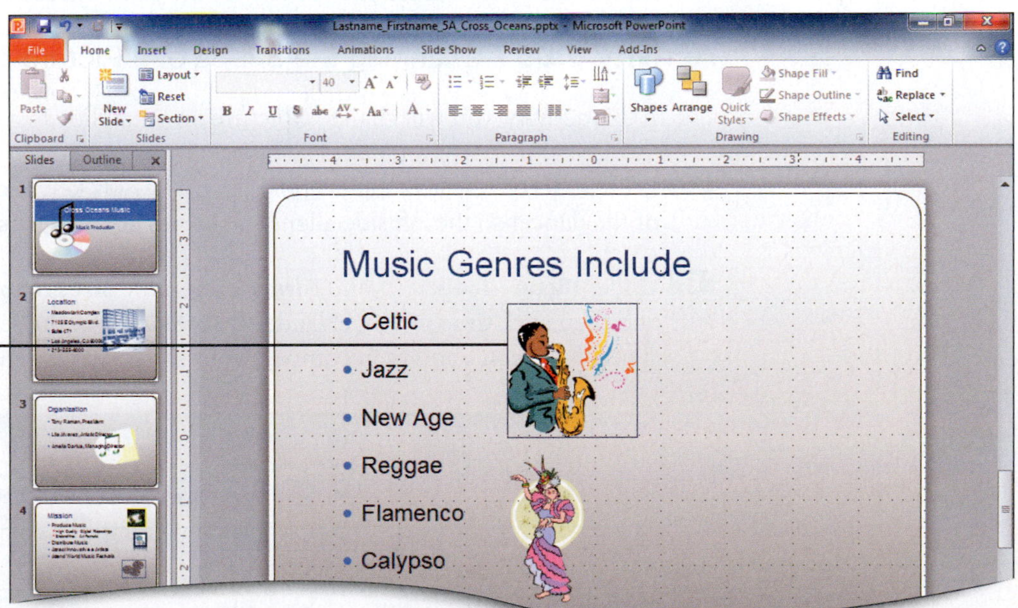

15 Click to select the picture of the Calypso dancer. On the **Format tab**, In the **Picture Styles group**, click the **Picture Effects** button, point to **Glow**, and then under **Glow Variations**, in the second row, click the first selection—**Blue, 8 pt glow, Accent color 1**.

16 Click to deselect the picture, and then compare your screen with Figure 5.17.

The Picture Effect added a different kind of border. It defined the shape of the picture instead of creating a rectangle border around the dancer.

Figure 5.17

17 **Save** your changes.

Objective 3 | Change the Shape of a Picture

After you have inserted a picture, you can change the outline shape of the image. This is possible with or without the addition of a border. A large selection of shapes is available in PowerPoint. We apply several formatting techniques in this project so you can experiment with different options. Keep in mind, however, that applying too many formatting techniques can distract from the content of the presentation.

Activity 5.05 | Changing the Shape of a Picture

In this activity, you will change a picture on your slide to a shape and then add a border.

1 With **Slide 5** as the active slide, hold down the Shift key, and then drag the entire picture of the dancer so the left side aligns at **2 inches on the right side of the horizontal ruler**.

2 Under **Picture Tools**, click the **Format tab**. In the **Size group**, click the **Crop button arrow**, and then click **Crop to Shape**. Under **Basic Shapes**, in the second row, locate the ninth symbol—**Plaque**, and then compare your screen with Figure 5.18.

Figure 5.18

3 Click the **Plaque** shape. Click the **Picture Border** button, and then in the sixth row, click the fifth color—**Blue, Accent 1, Darker 50%**. Click **Picture Border**, point to **Weight**, and then click **3 pt**. Click to deselect the picture, and then compare your screen with Figure 5.19.

Without the border, applying the shape is confusing. Adding the border emphasized the shape.

Figure 5.19

4 Click the **View tab**. In the **Show group**, deselect the **Gridlines** check box.

5 **Save** your changes.

Objective 4 | Add a Picture to a WordArt Object

A WordArt object may have a picture fill to add interest to a presentation. After adding the WordArt text, insert a picture fill that complements the WordArt message.

Activity 5.06 | Adding a WordArt Object and Embedding a Picture

In this activity, you will insert a new blank slide and add a WordArt object containing text. Then you will insert a picture as a fill for the object. You will also recolor the picture.

1 Click **Slide 5**. On the **Home tab**, in the **Slides group**, click the **New Slide button arrow**, and then click **Blank** to add a new slide.

2 On **Slide 6**, click the **Insert tab**. In the **Text group**, click the **WordArt** button. In the fourth row, in the third column, locate **Gradient Fill – Black, Outline – White, Outer Shadow**, and then compare your screen with Figure 5.20.

Figure 5.20

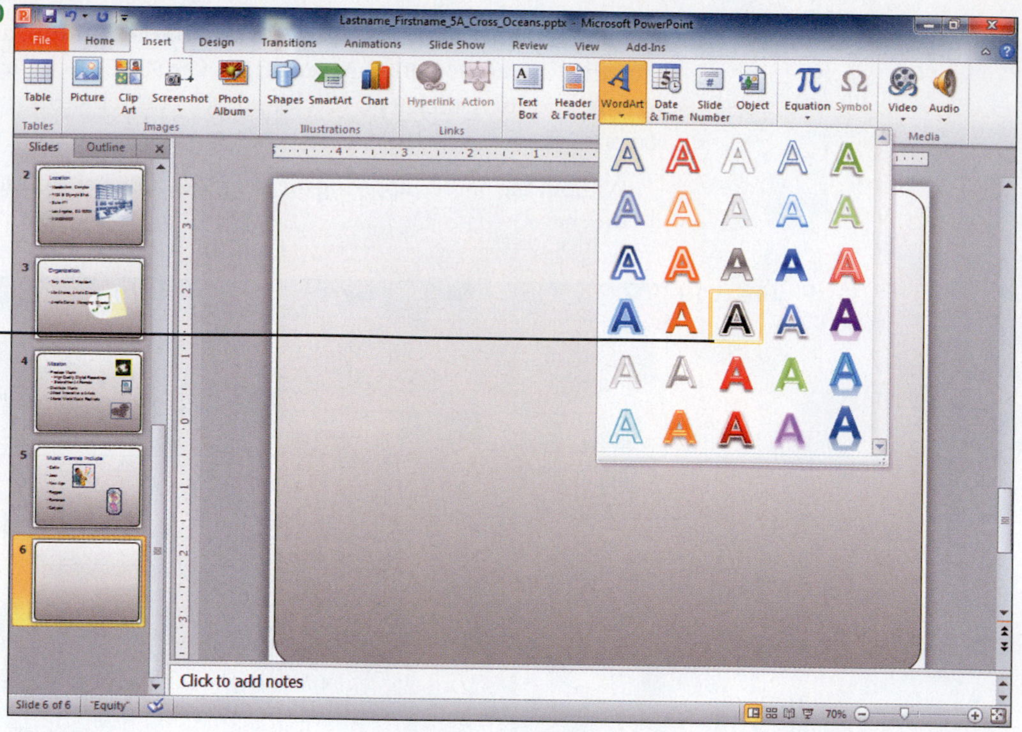

WordArt Gradient Fill – Black, Outline – White, Outer Shadow

3 Click **Gradient Fill – Black, Outline – White, Outer Shadow**. In the **WordArt** object, type **Cross Oceans** and then press Enter. Type **Music** on the second line.

4 Hold down the Shift key, and then drag the entire WordArt up so the top edge of the picture is aligned at **1.5 inches on the upper half of the vertical ruler**. Compare your screen with Figure 5.21.

Figure 5.21

5 With the **WordArt** object still selected, click the **Format tab**. In the **Shape Styles group**, click the **Shape Fill** button, and then click **Picture**. In the location where you are storing your files, click **p05A_Island2.jpg**, and then click **Insert**. Compare your screen with Figure 5.22.

Figure 5.22

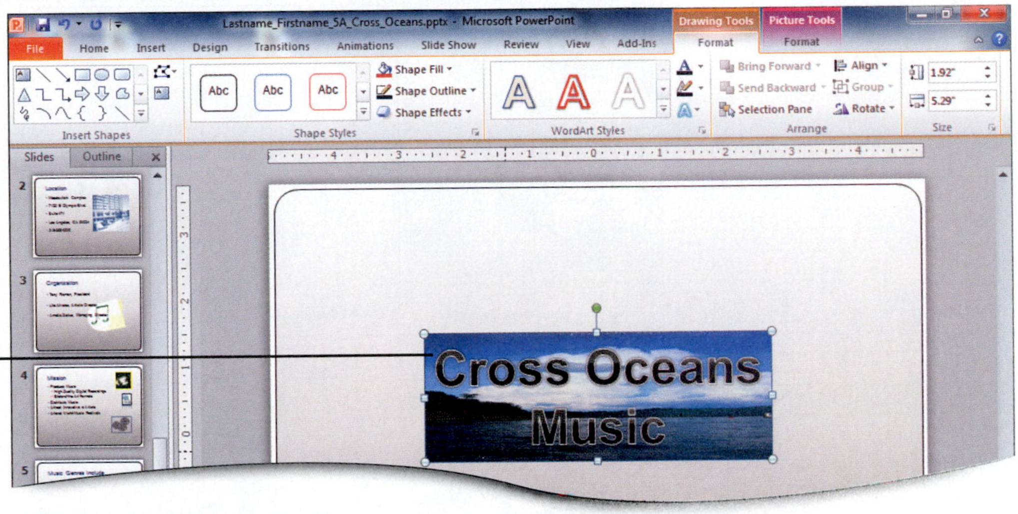

Picture file inserted as Shape Fill

6 With the **WordArt** object still selected, under **Picture Tools**, click the **Format tab**. In the **Adjust group**, click the **Color** button. Under **Recolor**, in the first row, in the fourth column, click **Washout**.

7 In the **Size group**, click the **Size & Position** button. Under **Scale**, click the **Lock aspect ratio** check box to select it. Under **Size and rotate**, change the **Height** to **2.5″**. Compare your screen with Figure 5.23.

When ***Lock aspect ratio*** is selected, you can change one dimension (height or width) of an object, such as a picture, and the other dimension will automatically be changed to maintain the proportion.

Figure 5.23

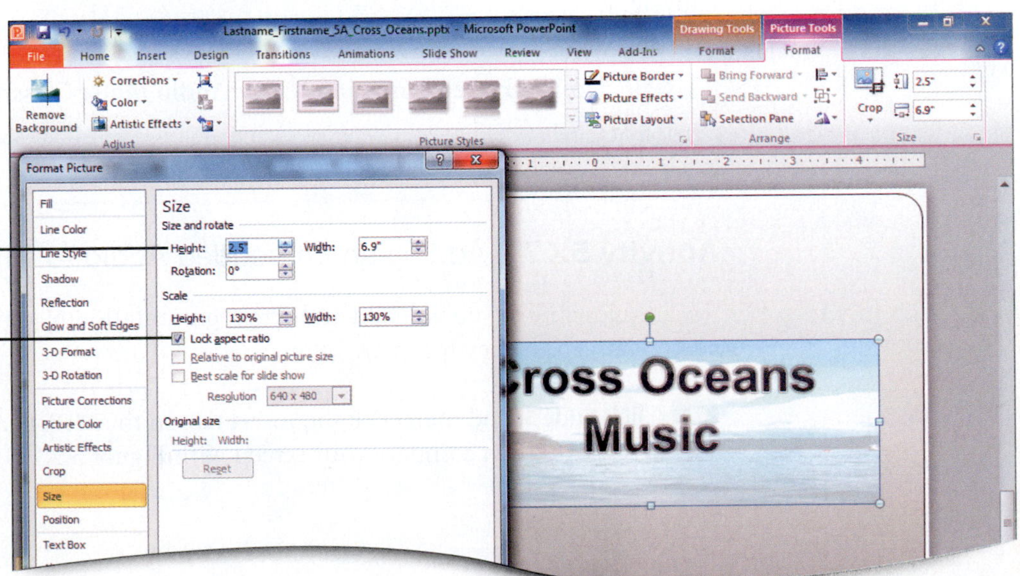

Height changed to 2.5″

Lock aspect ratio checked

8 Click **Close**. In the **Arrange group**, click the **Align** button, and then select **Align Center**. Deselect the WordArt, and then compare your screen with Figure 5.24

Figure 5.24

9 **Save** your changes.

Objective 5 | Enhance a Presentation with Audio and Video

To further enhance a presentation, you can add audio and video to the presentation. After you have applied audio and/or video to a presentation, you can control how you would like the files to play. A file can be set to play one time and then stop, or to ***loop***, meaning the audio or video file will play repeatedly from start to finish until it is stopped manually. A ***track***, or song, from a CD can also play during a slide show. Audio and video can be embedded or linked to the presentation. To ***embed*** is to save a presentation so that the audio or video file becomes part of the presentation file. To ***link*** is to save a presentation so that the audio or video file is saved separately from the presentation. Be sure to obtain permission to link or embed audio and video to a presentation to avoid violating the copyright.

Alert! | **Do You Have Permission to Use Audio in the Classroom?**

If you are not allowed to play audio in your classroom or lab, use a headset for these activities. If you do not have a headset, ask your instructor how to proceed.

Activity 5.07 | Adding an Embedded Audio to a Presentation

In this activity, you will add audio to a presentation by embedding audio files and customizing how they will play.

1 Click **Slide 5**, and then click the **Insert tab**. In the **Media group**, click the **Audio button arrow**, and then compare your screen with Figure 5.25

Figure 5.25

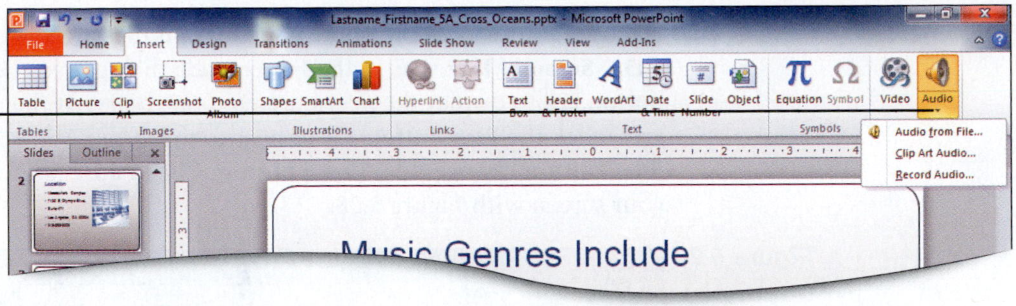

2 Take a moment to study the options available for inserting audio into a presentation, as shown in the table in Figure 5.26.

Sound Options

Screen Element	Description
Audio from File	Enables you to insert audio clips such as music, narration, or audio bites. Compatible audio file formats include .mid or .midi, .mp3, and .wav.
Clip Art Audio	Displays the Clip Art pane so that you can search for audio files in the Microsoft Office collection, both locally and online.
Record Audio	Enables you to insert audio by recording the audio through a microphone and then naming and inserting the recorded audio.

Figure 5.26

3 From the displayed menu, click **Audio from File** to display the **Insert Audio** dialog box.

4 Above the **Cancel** button, click the **Audio Files down arrow** to display the audio files supported by PowerPoint, and then compare your screen with Figure 5.27. Click the **Show preview pane** button if necessary.

The preview pane button in Windows Explorer is a toggle button. If the preview pane is not displaying, the button ScreenTip is *Show preview pane.* If the preview pane is displaying, the button ScreenTip is *Hide preview pane.*

Figure 5.27

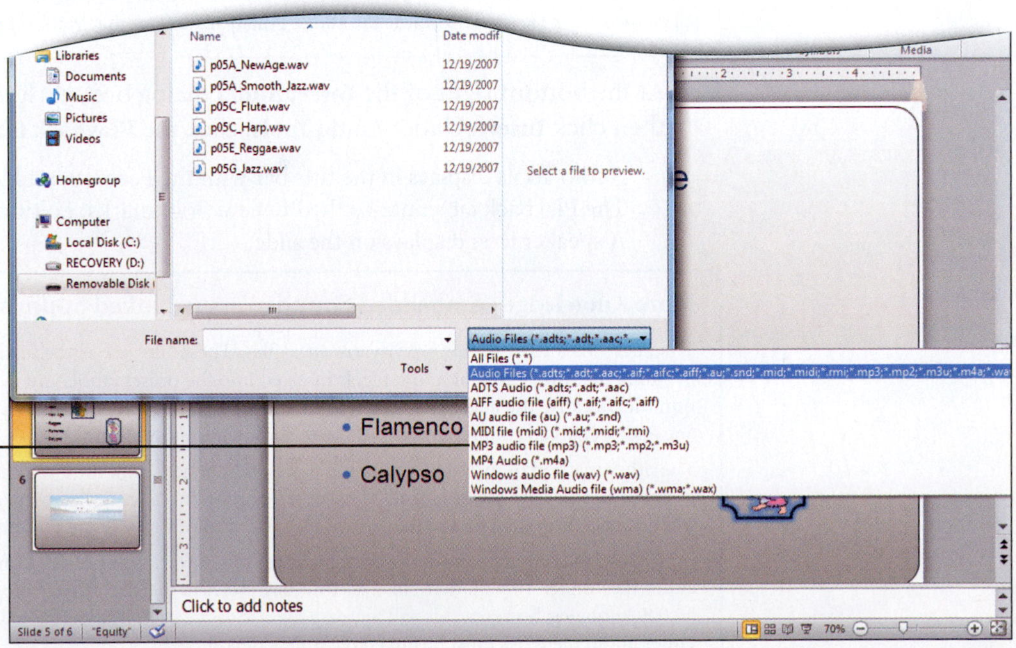

5 Navigate to the location where your student files are stored, click once on **p05A_Smooth_Jazz.wav**. In the **Insert Audio** dialog box, click the **Show the preview pane** button to display the preview area if necessary. At the right side, in the preview area, click the **Play** button to hear to the audio. While the audio is playing, the **Play** button changes to a **Pause** button. Click **Pause** to stop the audio. Compare your screen with Figure 5.28.

Figure 5.28

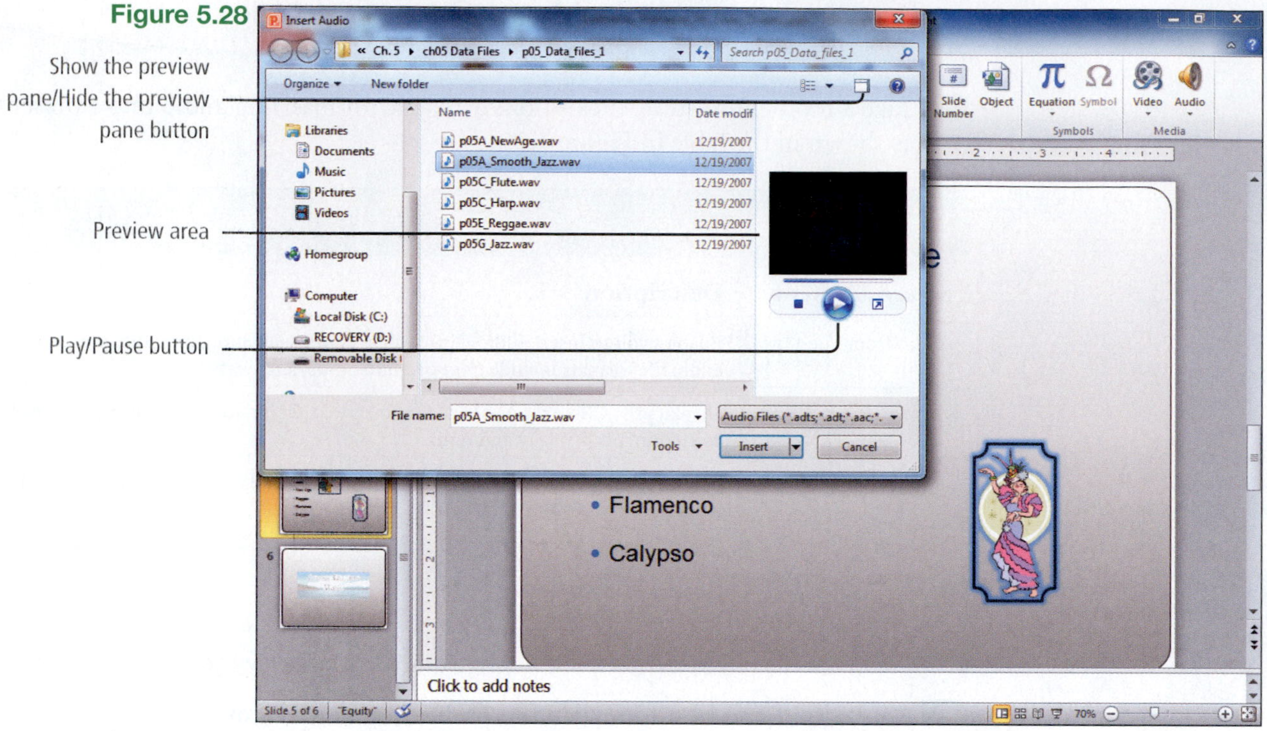

Alert! | Is the Audio Not Audible?

Your PC may not have audio capability. If you know for a fact that your PC has audio capability, open the Control Panel by clicking the Start button and then click Control Panel. In Control Panel, click Hardware and Sound. Under Sound, click Adjust system volume, and then drag the Speakers slider up to increase the volume. Make sure that the audio has not been muted. If the audio is muted, there will be a red stop symbol beside the speaker icon. Click the speaker icon and unmute the audio. Finally make sure that you have your speakers turned on.

6 At the bottom right of the **Insert Audio** dialog box, click the **Insert button arrow**, and then click **Insert**. Under **Audio Tools**, click the **Playback tab**.

Audio Tools displays in the title bar with the Format and Playback tabs located under it. The Playback tab contains the Preview, Bookmarks, Editing, and Audio Options groups. A speaker icon displays on the slide.

More Knowledge | Embedded Sounds Versus Linked Sounds

The audio files used in this activity are .wav files. These files are embedded in the PowerPoint presentation, meaning that the object, or audio file, is inserted into the presentation and becomes part of the saved presentation file. Because the audio is stored within the presentation file, this guarantees that the audio will play from any audio-enabled computer that you use to show the presentation.

The other method of inserting audio into a presentation is to link the audio file. When you link the audio file, it is stored outside the presentation. If your presentation includes linked files, you must copy both the presentation file and the linked files to the same folder if you want to show the presentation on another computer.

By default, the only files that may be embedded in a PowerPoint presentation are **.wav** *(waveform audio data)* audio files under 100 kilobytes in size. You may increase the size of the embedded .wav file to a maximum of 50,000 kilobytes; however, this will increase the size of the presentation file and may slow down its performance. Other audio file types must be linked regardless of size.

Another Way

To adjust the audio volume, on the taskbar, on the right side, click the Speakers icon, and then adjust the volume.

7 In the **Audio Options group**, click the **Hide During Show** check box. Click the **Volume button arrow**, and then click **Medium**. Click the **Start arrow**, and then click **Automatically**. Compare your screen with Figure 5.29.

Figure 5.29

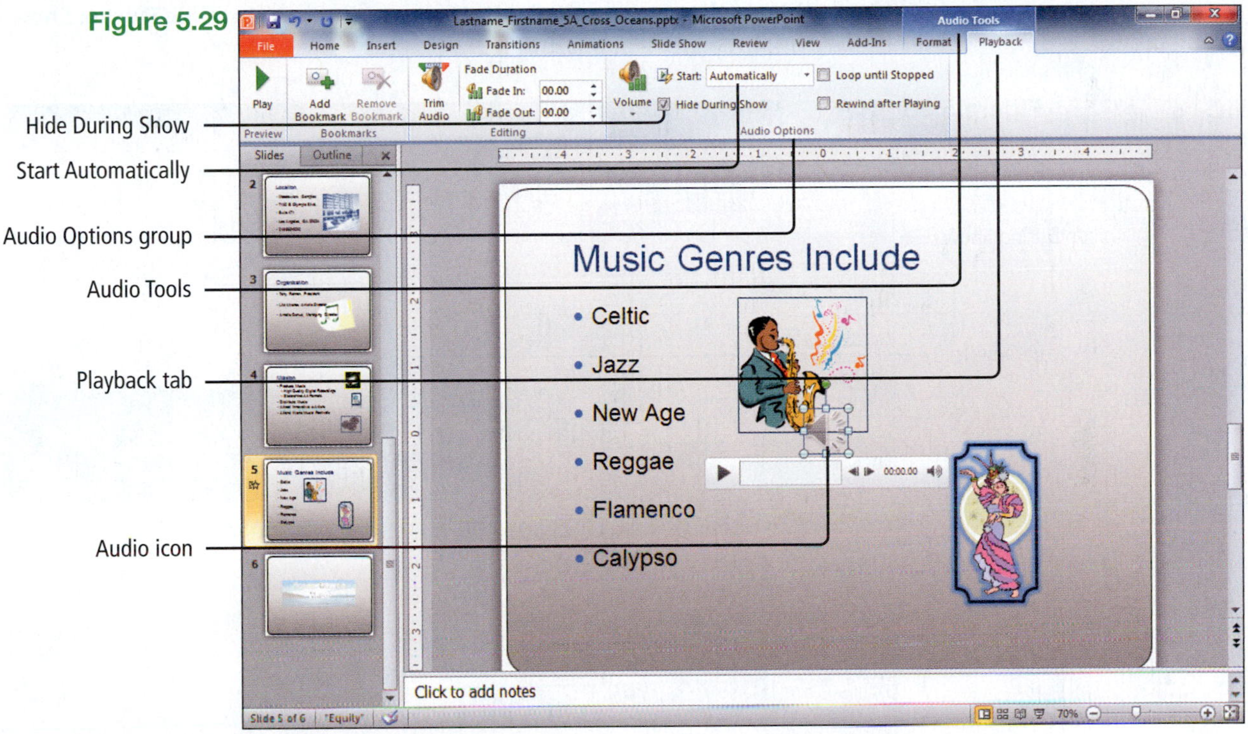

8 With **Slide 5** as the active slide, click the **Slide Show tab**. In the **Start Slide Show group**, click **From Current Slide**.

During a slide show presentation, the audio starts automatically when the slide displays. The audio plays one time and then stops. Because the audio icon is hidden, it does not display on the slide during the presentation of a slide show.

You can stop the audio by clicking the slide, by pressing Enter to advance to the next slide, or by pressing Esc.

9 Press Esc to end the slide show and return to **Normal** view.

It is possible to play sounds in Normal view. In the Slides pane, a small star-shaped icon displays to the left of the slide thumbnail. This is the ***Play Animations button***. Click this small button to play the sound.

10 Make **Slide 1**, the title slide, the active slide. Click the **Insert tab**, and then in the **Media group**, click the **Audio button arrow**. Click **Audio from File**. Navigate to the location where your student files are stored, click **p05A_NewAge.wav**, and then click **Insert**. Drag the audio icon to the lower left corner so the top edge aligns at **2.5 inches on the lower half of the vertical ruler** and the left edge aligns at **4.5 inches on the left side of the horizontal ruler**.

Note | Moving the Audio Icon

You can move the audio icon away from the main content of the slide so that the icon is easier for the presenter to locate. Avoid placing the icon where it interferes with the text the audience is viewing.

11 Under **Audio Tools**, click the **Playback tab**. Click the **Start arrow**, and then click **On Click**. On the slide, on the **Sound Control Panel**, click **Play** to listen to the audio clip.

> **Alert!** | **Is the Sound Control Panel Missing?**
>
> If you cannot see the Sound Control Panel, click the audio icon.

12 On the **Playback tab**, in the **Audio Options group**, click the **Hide During Show** box, and then compare your screen with Figure 5.30.

Figure 5.30

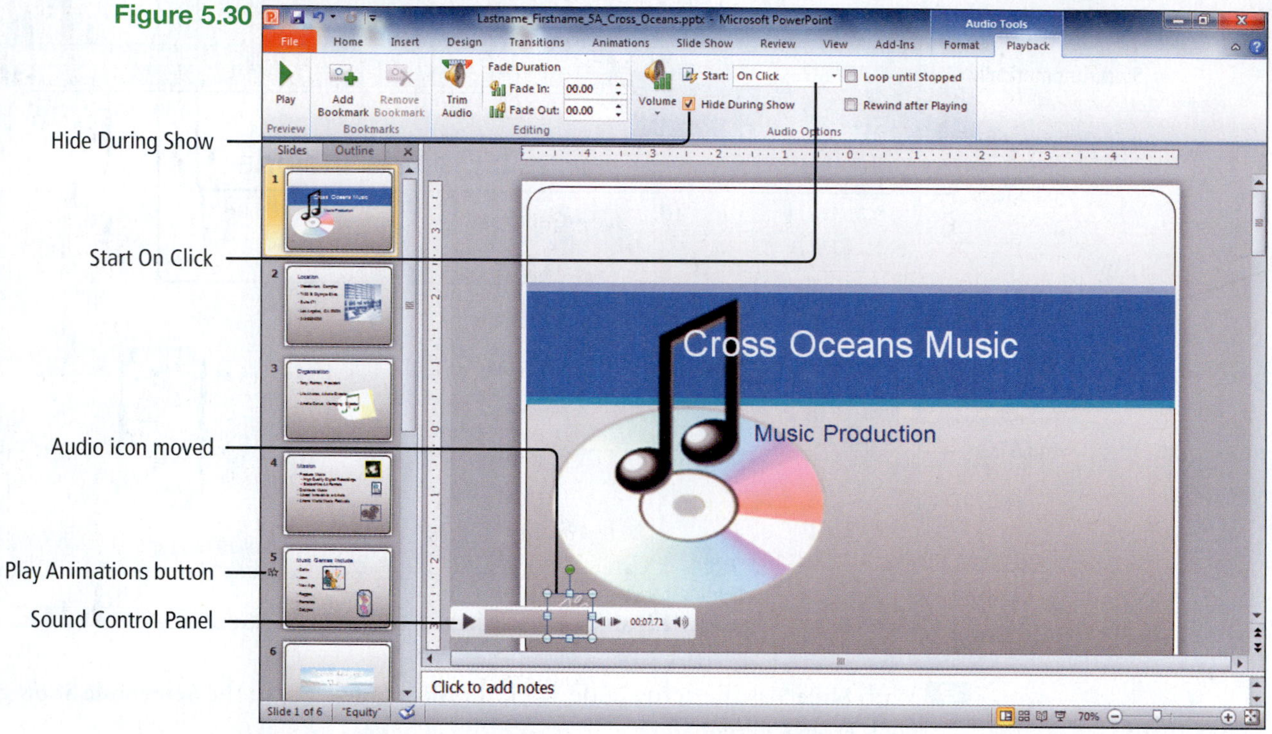

13 Click the **Slide Show tab**. In the **Start Slide Show group**, click **From Beginning**. Click the slide, and notice that no audio plays. Instead, it takes you to the next slide.

> **Note** | **Hiding the Audio Icon During a Slide Show**
>
> Hiding the audio icon during the slide show works only when the audio is set to play Automatically. If you select When Clicked, the icon must display. If you select Hide During Show, the audio will not play when you click the slide, unless you create a specific trigger.

14 Press Esc to end the slide show and return to **Normal** view.

15 Click **Slide 1**. Click to select the speaker icon. Under **Audio Tools**, click the **Playback tab**.

16 In the **Audio Options group**, deselect the **Hide During Show** check box. Click the **Slide Show tab**. In the **Start Slide Show group**, click the **From Current Slide** button. Point to the **Audio** icon. On the control panel, click the **Play** button. Alternatively, you can click the top part of the speaker icon to hear the sound.

After the slide show is started, there may be a delay before the mouse pointer becomes active.

17 Press Esc.

18 **Save** your changes.

Activity 5.08 | Setting a Trigger for an Embedded Audio in a Presentation

In this activity, you will set a trigger for an embedded audio. A ***trigger*** is a portion of text, a graphic, or a picture that, when clicked, causes the audio or video to play. You will display the Animation Pane to help you locate the trigger. The ***Animation Pane*** is an area used for adding and removing effects.

1 With **Slide 1** as the active slide, click to select the audio icon.

2 Click the **Animations tab**. In the **Advanced Animations group**, click **Animation Pane** to display the Animation Pane on the right side of the window. In the Animation Pane, the audio filename is displayed in the list.

> **Alert! | Did the Audio Filename Not Display in the Animation Pane?**
>
> If the name of the audio file does not display in the Animation Pane, click the audio icon on the slide, and then under Audio Tools, click the Playback button. In the Audio Options group, make sure that the Start is set for On Click.

3 Click the **Trigger button arrow**, and then point to **On Click of**. Compare your screen with Figure 5.31.

Notice the options to select for the trigger—Subtitle, Picture, Title, or the file name.

Figure 5.31

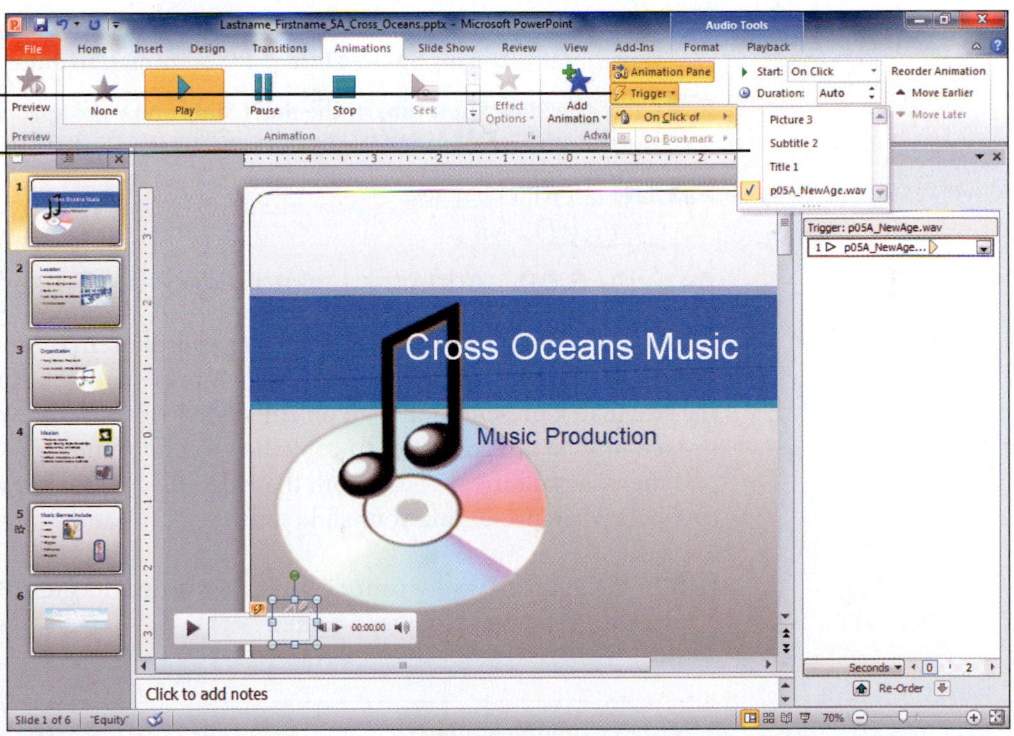

4 Click **Title 1**. Compare your screen with Figure 5.32.

At the right, in the Animation Pane, *Trigger: Title 1: Cross Oceans Music* is displayed at the top of the list. Notice that it is identified as the trigger.

Figure 5.32

Trigger identified in the Animation Pane

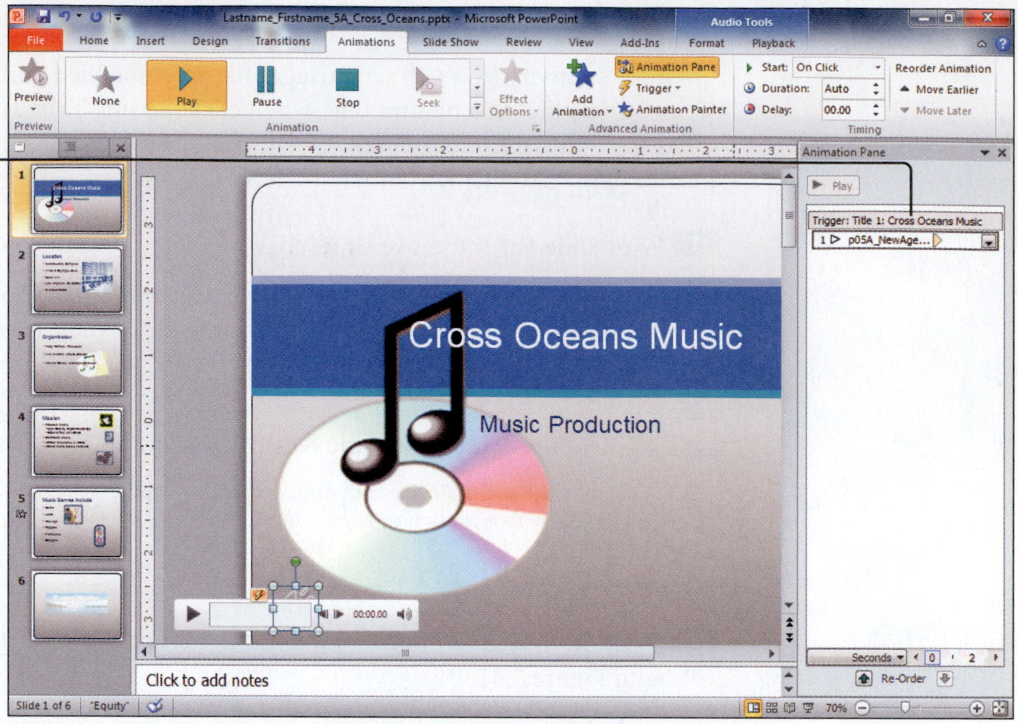

5 Under **Audio Tools**, click the **Playback tab**. In the **Audio Options group**, click the check box for **Hide During Show**. **Close** [×] the **Animation Pane**.

6 Click the **Slide Show tab**. In the **Start Slide Show group**, click **From Current Slide**. Click the title *Cross Oceans Music* to start the audio. Press Esc.

7 **Save** your changes.

Activity 5.09 | Adding a Linked Video to a Presentation

In this activity, you will link a video to your presentation. Recall that you have previously learned how to embed a video. A presentation with a linked video is smaller in file size than a presentation with an embedded video. To prevent possible problems with broken links, it is a good idea to copy the video into the same folder as your presentation and then link to it from there. Both the video file and the presentation file must be available when presenting your slide show.

1 In the location where your data files are stored, locate **p05_Music_Video.avi**, and then copy it into your Chapter 5 folder.

> **Note | Copying a File**
>
> To copy a file on your storage device, display the Documents library, locate the file you want, right-click the file name, and then click Copy. Next, open the folder where you are saving your completed files, right-click, and then and click Paste.

2 Click **Slide 6**. Click the **Insert tab**. In the **Media group**, click the **Video button arrow**, and then click **Video from File**. Navigate to your data files, and then click **p05_Music_Video.avi**. In the preview area on the right, click **Play** to view the video. Click **Pause** to stop the video. In the lower right corner of the **Insert Video** dialog box, click the **Insert button arrow**. Compare your screen with Figure 5.33.

The options on the Insert list are Insert and Link to File.

Figure 5.33

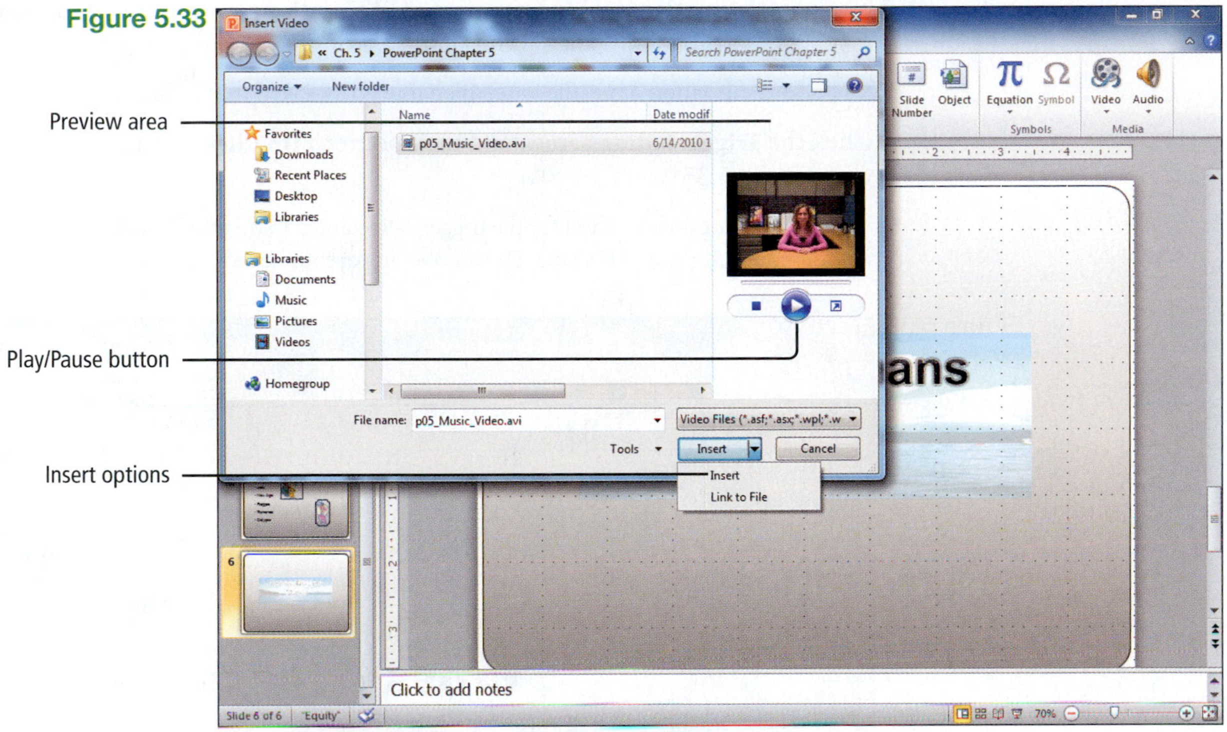

3 Click **Link to File**. In the **Size group**, change the **Video Height** to **1.5″**. Drag the entire video so the top aligns at **3.5 inches on the upper half of the vertical ruler** and the left side aligns at **4.5 inches on the left side of the horizontal ruler**. Compare your screen with Figure 5.34.

Moving the video allows you to see the content of the slide better. You can even resize the video if you wish.

Figure 5.34

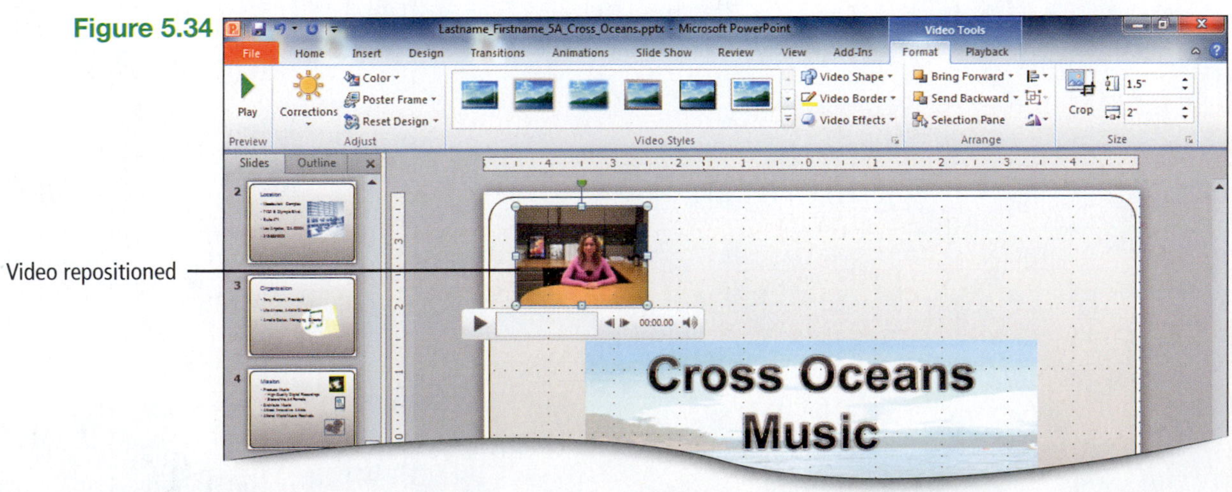

4 **Save** your changes.

Activity 5.10 | Changing the Trigger for a Linked Video in a Presentation

In this activity, you will use the Animation Pane to change the trigger that will play the video file from the video image to the WordArt shape. You will also set the video so it plays in full screen.

1 With **Slide 6** as the active slide, click to select the video, if necessary.

2 Click the **Animations tab**. In the **Advanced Animations group**, click **Animation Pane** to display the **Animation Pane** on the right side of the window.

In the Animation Pane, the video filename is displayed in the list.

3 Click the **Trigger button arrow**, and then point to **On Click of**. Compare your screen with Figure 5.35.

Notice the options to select for the trigger—Rectangle 1 and **p05_Music_Video.avi**. Rectangle represents the WordArt shape. The number in parentheses after Rectangle may vary.

Figure 5.35

Trigger options

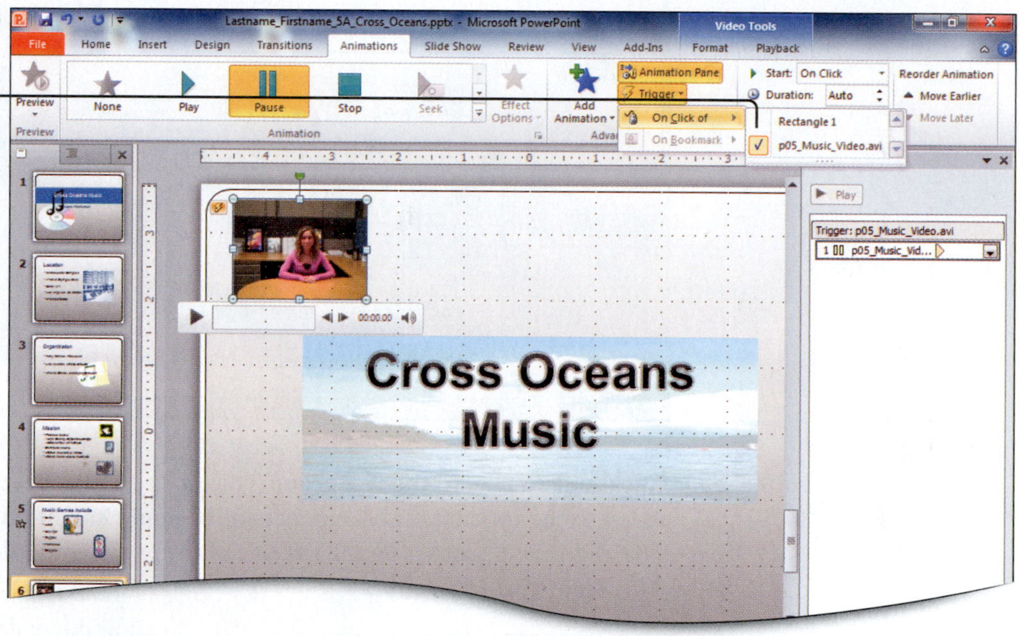

4 Click **Rectangle 1**. Compare your screen with Figure 5.36.

Rectangle refers to the WordArt.

Figure 5.36

Trigger identified in Animation Pane

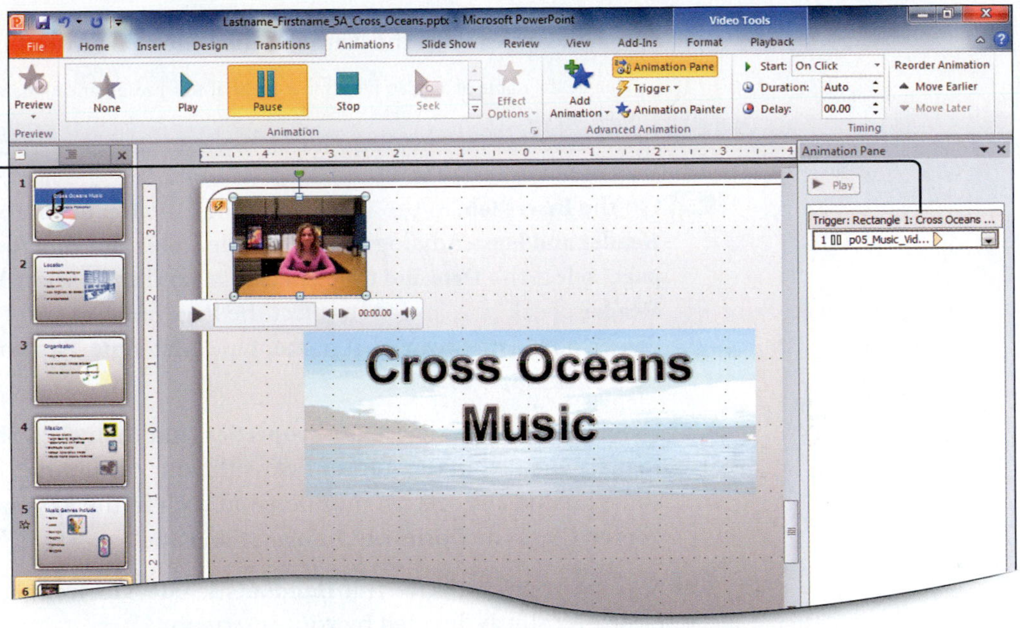

5 In the **Advanced Animation group**, click the **Animation Pane** button to close the **Animation Pane**. Under **Video Tools**, click the **Playback tab**. In the **Video Options group**, click the check box for **Hide While Not Playing**. Click check box for **Play Full Screen**. Compare your screen with Figure 5.37.

Figure 5.37

Play Full Screen checked

Hide While Not Playing checked

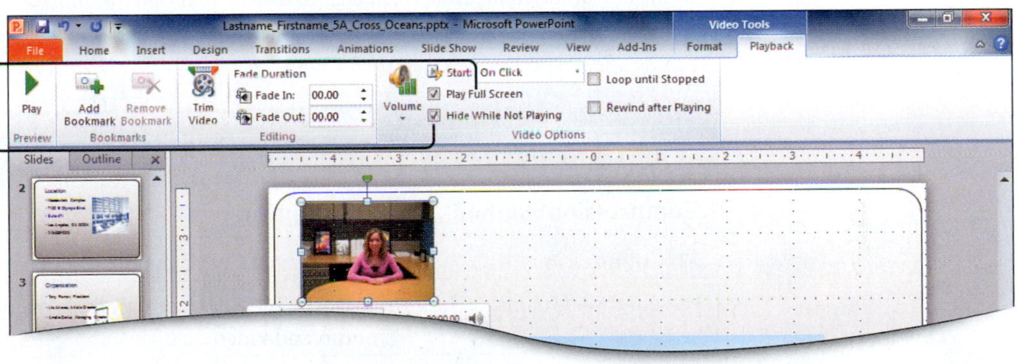

6 Click the **Slide Show tab**. In the **Start Slide Show group**, click **From Current Slide**. Click the *Cross Oceans Music* WordArt to start the audio. After the video plays, press Esc.

The video plays in full screen. Allow the video to play completely. If you stop the video, the video will display on the slide. For that reason, you might want to resize the video to a smaller size.

7 Press Esc. In the **Start Slide Show group**, click the **From Beginning** button to view the entire presentation. Click the trigger on **Slide 1** to hear the audio. Click the trigger on **Slide 6** to view the video. Press Esc.

8 In the **Documents library**, display the contents of your Chapter 5 folder. Observe that the size of the presentation file is much smaller than the size of the video file.

Because the presentation file contains a link to the video file, the actual video file is not a part of the presentation file size. For example, the video for this presentation is about 16,000 KB and the presentation file is about 2,000 KB. If you send this presentation electronically or transfer it to another location such as a USB drive, be sure to place both files in the same folder before sending or moving them.

Alert! | **Did You Change the Name of the Video File After Linking It to a Presentation?**

If you change the name of a video file after you link it to a presentation, the video will not play. You will have to link the file again.

9. On the **Insert tab**, in the **Text group**, click the **Header & Footer** button to display the **Header and Footer** dialog box. Click the **Notes and Handouts tab**. Under **Include on page**, select the **Date and time** check box, and then select **Fixed**. If necessary, clear the **Header** check box, and then select the **Page number** and **Footer** check boxes. In the **Footer** box, using your own name, type **Lastname_Firstname_5A_Cross_Oceans** and then click **Apply to All**.

10. Display **Backstage** view, click **Properties**, and then click **Show Document Panel**. Replace the text in the **Author** box with your own name; in the **Subject** box, type your course name and section number; and then in the **Keywords** box, type **mission, genres Close** the **Document Information Panel**.

11. **Save** your changes. Print **Handouts 4 Slides Horizontal**, or submit your presentation electronically as directed by your instructor.

12. **Close** the presentation, and then **Exit** PowerPoint.

More Knowledge | **Compressing Your Presentation Files**

If you are concerned about the size of your files or need to transmit them electronically, you may wish to consider using one of the compression methods. To display your options, in Backstage view, click Info, and then click Compress Media. Refer to Figure 5.38 for an explanation of compression qualities and the possible file sizes.

Compression File Size Comparison

Compression Method	Description	File Size Example
No Compression	The original size of the presentation.	18,010 KB
Presentation Quality	Reduced file size that maintains overall audio and video quality.	17,497 KB
Internet Quality	Quality comparable to media that is streamed over the Internet.	9,431 KB
Low Quality	Reduced file size sufficient for file sharing, such as sending as an e-mail attachment. Quality is not appropriate for a formal presentation.	2,766 KB

Figure 5.38

End **You have completed Project 5A**

Project 5B Business Photo Album

Project Activities

In Activities 5.11 through 5.13, you will create a PowerPoint photo album to display business photos of jazz musicians promoted and recorded by Cross Oceans Music. You will insert photos, add an attention-getting theme, and select a layout. You will also add frames to the photos and provide captions. You will experiment with tools that allow you to enter and format text in a text box and crop a photo to emphasize a key area of the photo. Your completed presentation will look similar to Figure 5.39.

Project Files

For Project 5B, you will need the following files:

New blank PowerPoint presentation
p05B_Jazz1.jpg
p05B_Jazz2.jpg
p05B_Jazz3.jpg
p05B_Jazz4.jpg
p05B_Jazz5.jpg
p05B_Jazz6.jpg
p05B_Jazz7.jpg

You will save your presentation as:

Lastname_Firstname_5B_Jazz_Album.pptx

Project Results

Figure 5.39
Project 5B Jazz Album

Objective 6 | Create a Photo Album

In the following activity, you will create a PowerPoint photo album. In PowerPoint, a ***photo album*** is a stylized presentation format to display pictures; you can display 1, 2, or 4 photos on a slide. The format may include a title or caption for the photo(s). A placeholder is inserted with each photo when the photo is added to the album. PowerPoint provides an easy and powerful tool to aid you in creating an exciting photo album.

Activity 5.11 | Creating a Photo Album

In this activity, you will create a photo album by inserting and customizing photos and selecting a theme. Each picture will be placed on its own slide.

1 **Start** PowerPoint. Click the **Insert tab**. In the **Images group**, click the **Photo Album button arrow**, and then click **New Photo Album**. Compare your screen with Figure 5.40.

The Photo Album dialog box provides an easy and convenient way to insert and remove pictures; rearrange and rotate pictures; apply brightness and contrast; insert captions; and select a layout, theme, and frame shape.

Figure 5.40

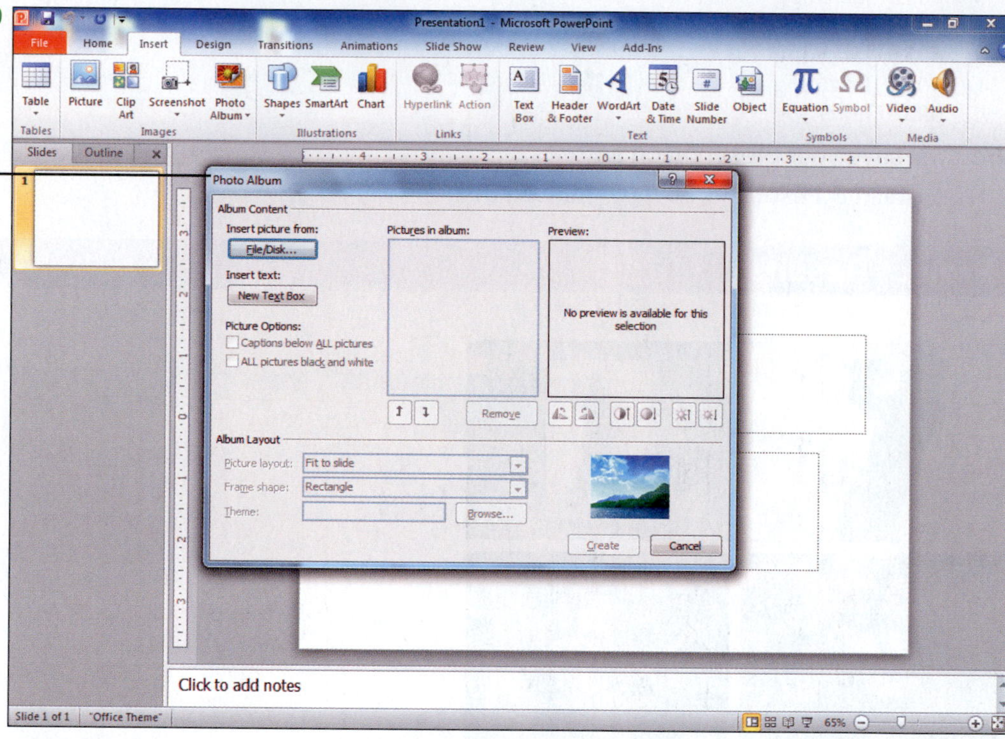

Another Way

When inserting pictures in the Photo Album dialog box, you can double-click the picture file name to insert it.

2 Under **Insert picture from**, click the **File/Disk** button to display the **Insert New Pictures** dialog box. Navigate to the location where your student files are stored, click **p05B_Jazz1.jpg**, and then click the **Insert** button. Compare your screen with Figure 5.41.

The file name displays as the first picture in the album, under Pictures in album, with a preview of the photograph.

Figure 5.41

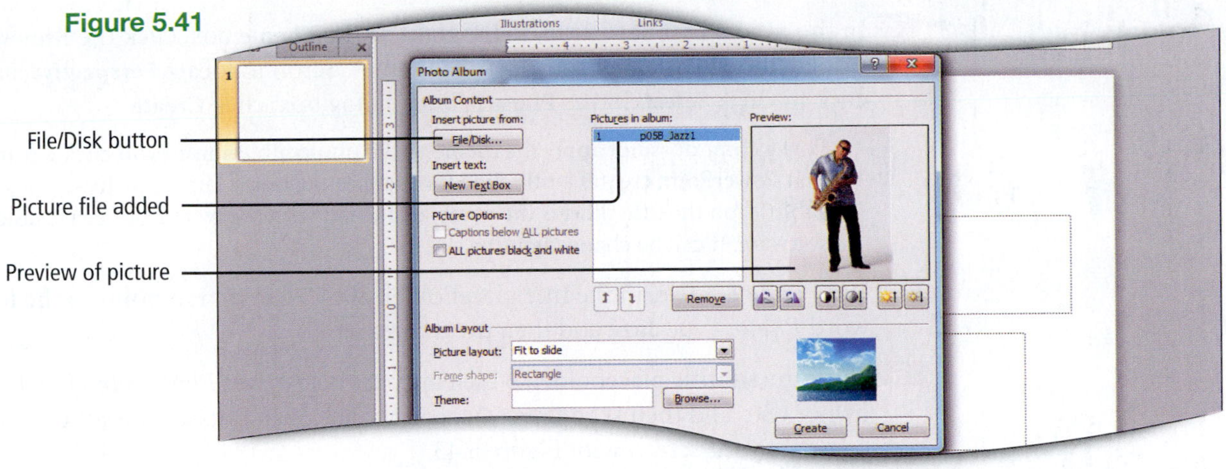

3 Using the technique you practiced, insert p05B_Jazz2.jpg, p05B_Jazz3.jpg, p05B_Jazz4.jpg, p05B_Jazz5.jpg, p05B_Jazz6.jpg, and p05B_Jazz7.jpg. Compare your screen with Figure 5.42:

Figure 5.42

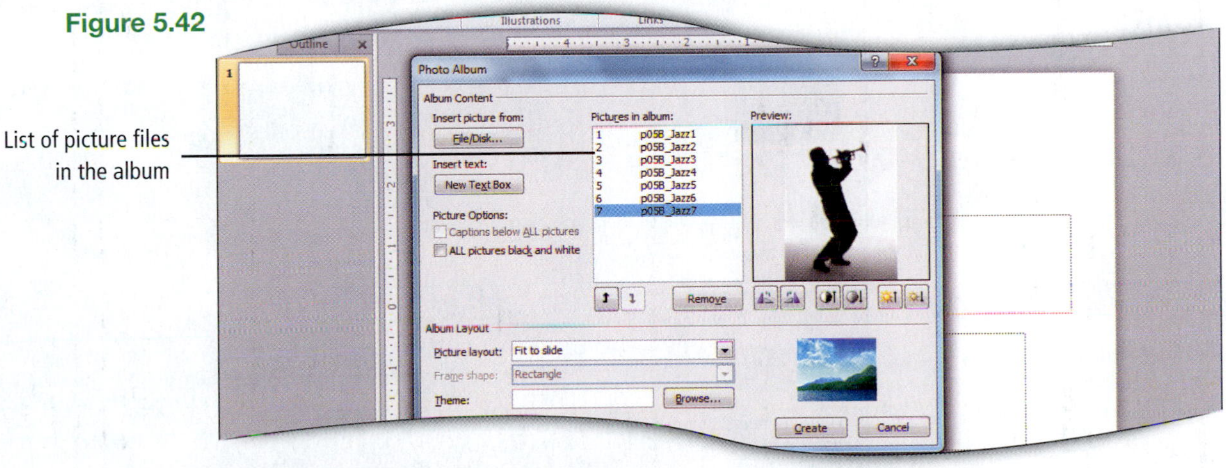

Note | Inserting a Picture in the Photo Album Dialog Box

If the pictures you want to insert into your photo album are listed in a sequence on your storage location, you can click on the first filename in the list, hold down the Shift key and click on the last picture in the list, and then click Insert. If the pictures are not in a sequence, you can hold down the Ctrl key while clicking the pictures individually, and then click Insert.

4 With **p05B_Jazz7.jpg** selected, under **Pictures in album**, click **Remove**.

The photo album now contains six pictures.

5 In the **Album Layout** section, click the **Picture layout arrow** to display the options.

You can choose to insert 1, 2, or 4 pictures on a slide, with or without a title, or you can choose Fit to slide.

6 Click **Fit to Slide** if necessary.

The Captions below ALL pictures check box is dimmed and therefore unavailable. Also, the Frame shape box is unavailable. In a photo album, the border around a picture is known as a ***frame***, and a limited number of styles are available. When you select ***Fit to slide***, the picture occupies all available space on the slide with no room for a frame or a caption.

Another Way

You can also double-click a document theme to select it.

7 In the **Album Layout** section, to the right of the **Theme** box, click the **Browse** button to display the **Choose Theme** dialog box themes. Scroll to locate **Perspective**, and then click it. Click **Select**. In the **Photo Album** dialog box, click **Create**.

PowerPoint does not apply the theme to the photo album until you click Create. Notice that PowerPoint creates a title slide for the photo album. The name inserted in the subtitle, on the title slide, is the name associated with the owner or license holder of the software. It can be changed on the slide.

8 With **Slide 1** active, in the title placeholder, click an insertion point to the left of the word *Photo*. Type **Jazz** and then press Spacebar.

9 Click the subtitle placeholder, which appears below *Jazz Photo Album*, delete the owner text, and then type **Cross Oceans Music**. Click outside the subtitle, and then compare your screen with Figure 5.43.

Cross Oceans Music now replaces the default owner or license holder of your software.

Figure 5.43

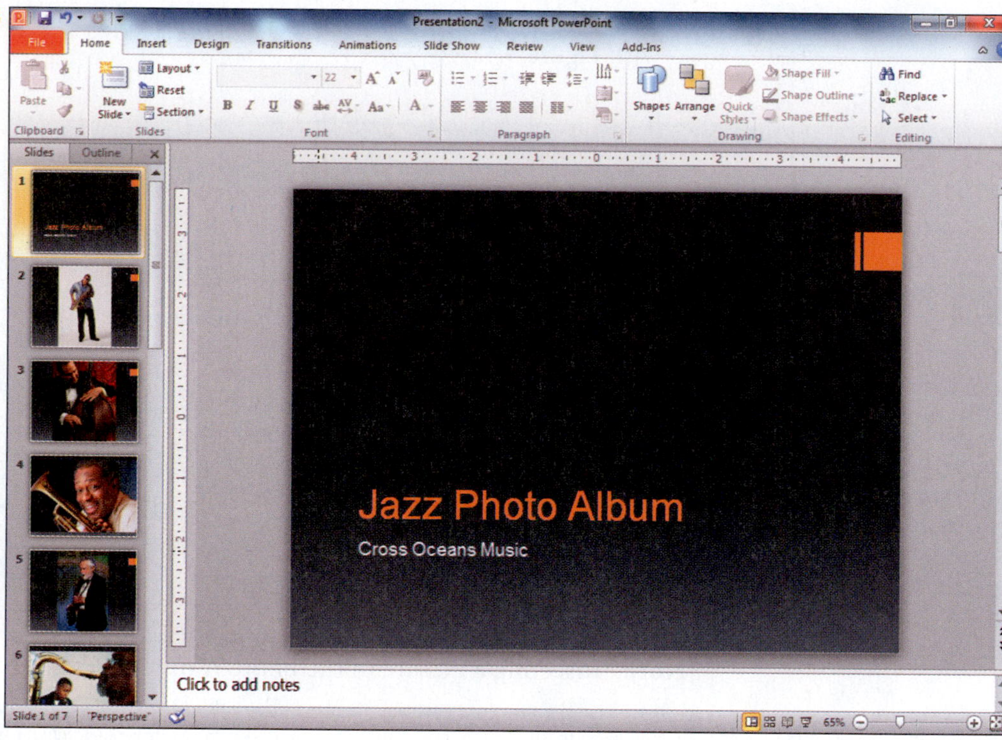

10 Display **Backstage** view, click **Save As**, and then navigate to the location where you are storing your projects for this chapter. Using your own name, save the file as **Lastname_Firstname_5B_Jazz_Album**

Because PowerPoint creates the photo album in a new presentation, you should wait until you click the Create button before saving the photo album. The original blank presentation that you started with is empty.

Objective 7 | Edit a Photo Album and Add a Caption

After you create a PowerPoint photo album, it is possible to format the background of the title slide by adding and customizing a caption for each photo. A ***caption*** is text that helps to identify or explain a picture or graphic.

Activity 5.12 | Editing a Photo Album and Adding a Caption

In this activity, you will edit a photo album, change the picture layout, and add captions.

1 With **Slide 1** as the active slide, right-click in the Slide pane to display the shortcut menu, and then click **Format Background**. In the **Format Background** dialog box, under the **Fill** options, select the **Picture or texture fill** option button.

2 Under **Insert from**, click **File**. Navigate to the location where your student files are stored, click **p05B_Jazz7.jpg**, and then click **Insert**. In the **Format Background** dialog box, click **Close**. Compare your screen with Figure 5.44.

This applies the background picture to the title slide only. Notice that the top of the picture is off the slide and the subtitle *Cross Oceans Music* is too light to read.

Figure 5.44

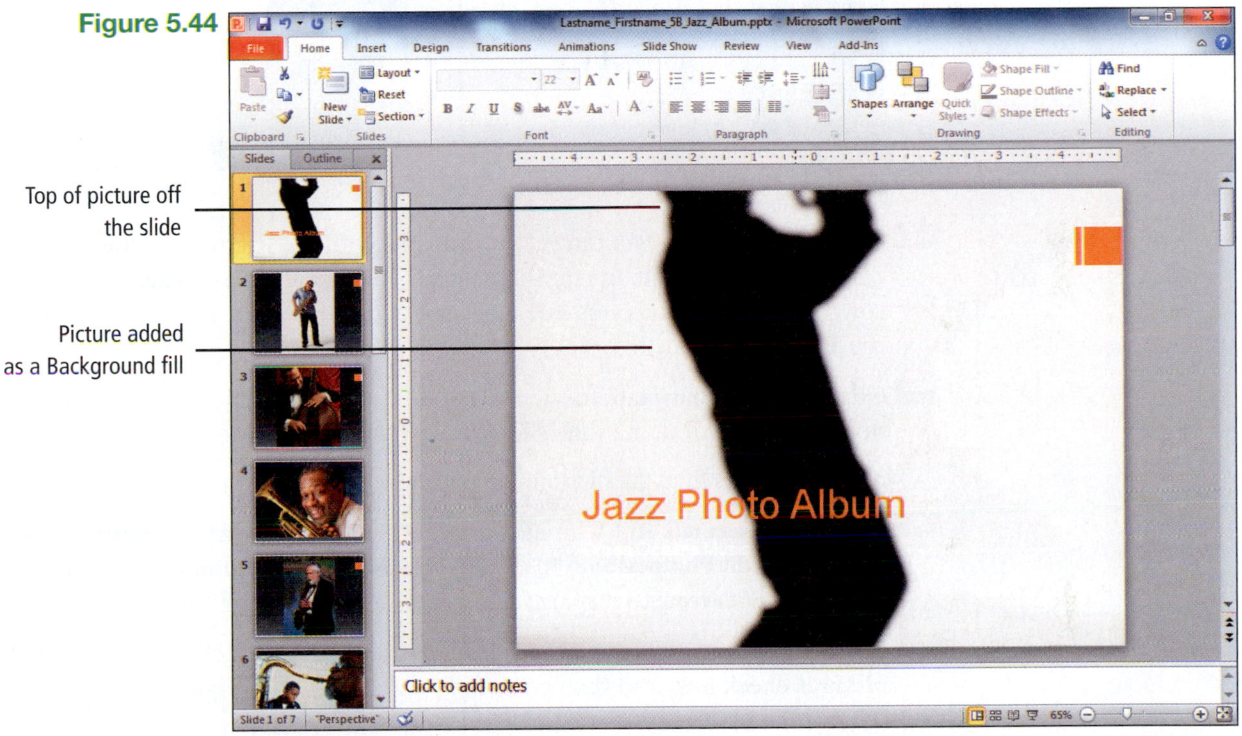

3 In the upper right corner of the slide, right-click, and then click **Format Background**. In the **Format Background** dialog box, under **Stretch options**, under **Offsets**, in the **Top** box, type **-20%**, and then click **Close**. Compare your screen with Figure 5.45.

This lowers the background silhouette to make the top visible on the slide. Because only the top was changed, the picture is a little distorted.

> **Alert! | Did Format Background Appear on the Context-Sensitive Menu?**
>
> If you did not see Format Background as a choice when you right-clicked the slide, you probably clicked on the Title or Subtitle placeholder. Right-click in another place on the slide, and you should see the appropriate options.

Figure 5.45

Slide with modified picture

4 On **Slide 1**, select the text in the subtitle placeholder. Right-click the selected text to display the Mini toolbar, and then click the **Font Color button arrow** [A ▾]. In the first row, click the fourth color—**Orange, Text 2**. On the **Home tab**, in the **Font group**, click the **Text Shadow** button [S].

5 Click the **Slide Show tab**. In the **Start Slide Show group**, click the **From Beginning** button. Click through all the slides. Press Esc to return to Normal view.

The pictures fit to the slide and do not allow room for a caption.

6 Click the **Insert tab**. In the **Images group**, click the **Photo Album button arrow**, and then click **Edit Photo Album** to display the **Edit Photo Album** dialog box. Click the **Picture layout arrow** to display the options, and then click **1 picture**.

7 In the **Album Content** section, under **Picture Options**, select the **Captions below ALL pictures** check box, and then compare your screen with Figure 5.46.

Figure 5.46

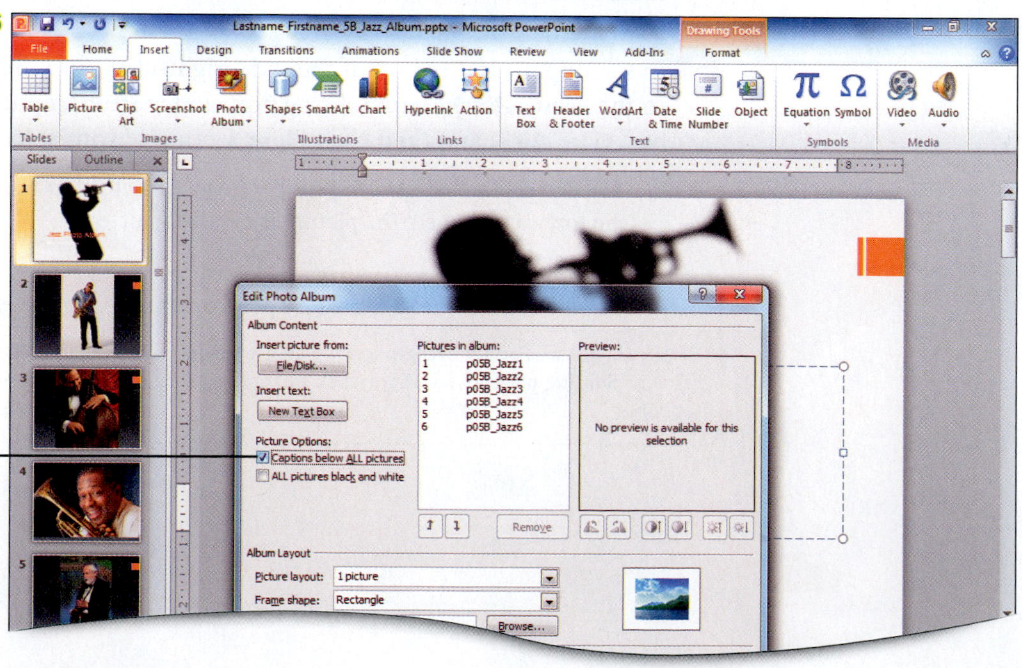

Captions below ALL pictures checked

8 Click **Update**, and then make **Slide 2** the active slide. Compare your screen with Figure 5.47.

Notice that, by default, the file name displays as the caption.

Figure 5.47

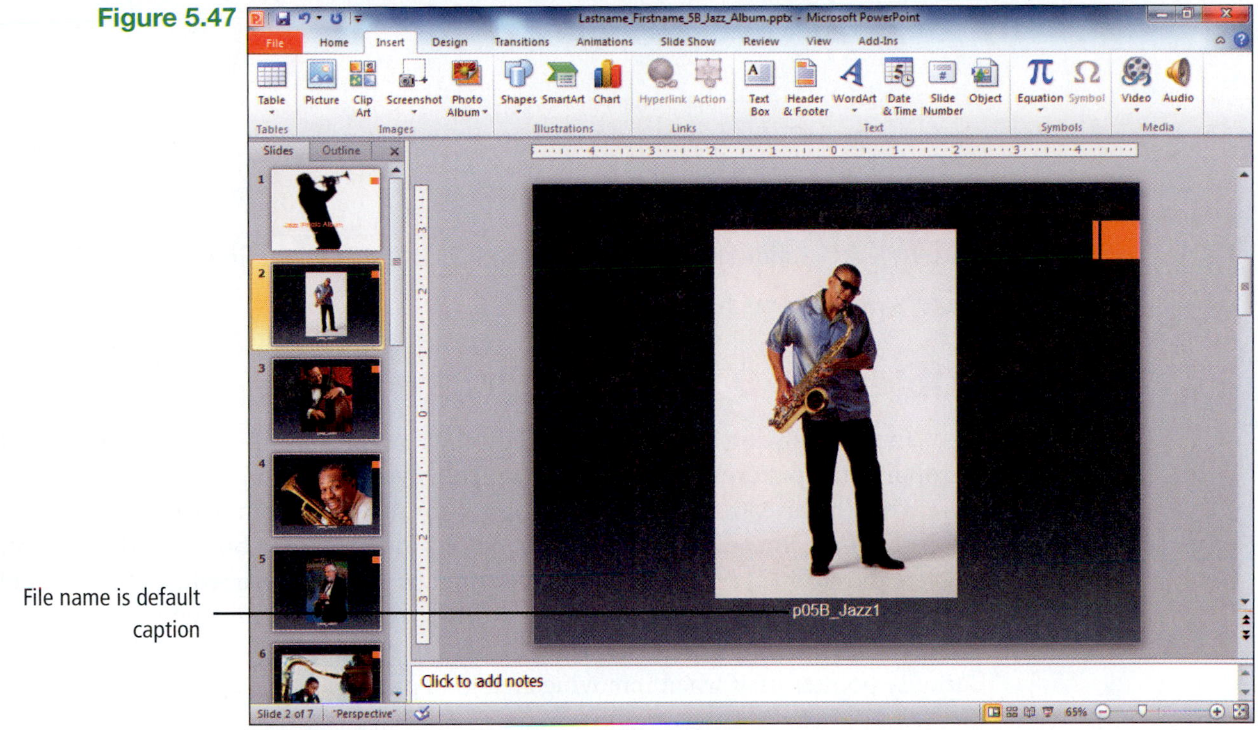

9 With **Slide 2** as the active slide, click to select the picture caption placeholder. Reposition the caption by dragging the entire placeholder down until the bottom edge of the placeholder aligns with the bottom edge of the slide.

10 Double-click to select the caption, and then press Del. Type **Tenor Saxophone** Compare your screen with Figure 5.48.

Figure 5.48

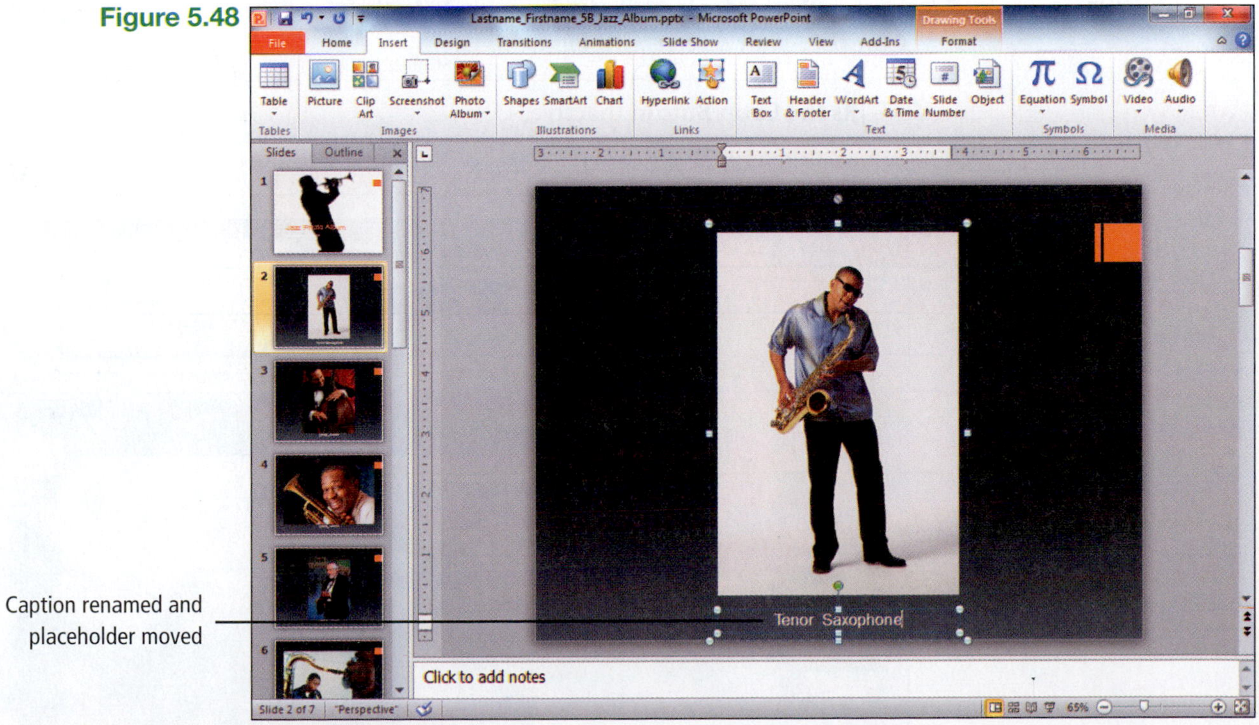

PowerPoint | Chapter 5

11 Using the technique you practiced, add the following captions to **Slides 3**, **4**, **5**, **6**, and **7**, and then reposition the captions to align with the bottom edge of the slide:

Slide 3	Bass
Slide 4	Trumpet
Slide 5	Alto Saxophone
Slide 6	Tenor Saxophone
Slide 7	Alto Saxophone

12 View the slide show **From beginning**. Click **Slide 1** when finished.

13 **Save** your changes.

Objective 8 | Crop a Picture

In the following activity, you will edit the PowerPoint photo album you created by cropping the picture. When you ***crop*** a picture, you remove unwanted or unnecessary areas of a picture. Images are often cropped to create more emphasis on the primary subject of the image. Recall that the Compress Picture dialog box provides the option to delete the cropped area of a picture. Deleting the cropped area reduces file size and also prevents people from being able to view the parts of the picture that you have removed. The ***crop handles*** are used like sizing handles to crop a picture, and the ***Crop tool*** is the mouse pointer used when removing areas of a picture.

Activity 5.13 | Cropping a Picture

1 Make **Slide 7** the active slide. Click the picture once to select the placeholder, and then click again to select the picture.

Because the placeholder is inserted at the time the picture is inserted, you must click the picture two times in order to gain access to the crop feature.

2 Under **Picture Tools**, click the **Format tab**. In the **Size group**, click the **Crop** button. Compare your screen with Figure 5.49.

> **Alert!** | **Is the Crop Button Inactive?**
>
> If you cannot display the Crop tool and crop lines, click the picture two times.

Figure 5.49

Format tab
Picture Tools
Crop button
Size group
Cropping handles

3 Position the Crop pointer just inside the middle cropping handle on the right edge of the picture.

The mouse pointer assumes the shape of the crop line, in this case a straight vertical line with a short horizontal line attached.

4 Drag the pointer to the left until the right edge of the picture aligns with approximately the **0-inch mark** on the **horizontal ruler**, and then release the mouse button. Compare your screen with Figure 5.50.

The dark area to the right represents the area that will be removed.

Figure 5.50

> **Another Way**
>
> You can also turn off the cropping button by pressing Esc or by clicking the Crop button.

5 Click outside the picture to turn off cropping.

6 Click the **Insert tab**. In the **Text group**, click **Text Box**, and then click one time to the right of the picture. Compare your screen with Figure 5.51.

Figure 5.51

PowerPoint | Chapter 5

7 In the text box, type **Meet the newest addition to our jazz musicians.**

8 Position the insertion point to the left of *to*, and then press Enter to break the text to a second line. Select both lines of text in the text box, and then increase the font size to **24. Center** the text.

> **Note | Selecting Text in Placeholders**
>
> Recall that you can click the border of a placeholder to select text. When the border is displayed as a solid border, you know the text is selected.

9 Position the text box so that the top edge is at **1.5 inches on the upper half of the vertical ruler** and the left edge is at **.5 inches on the right side of the horizontal ruler.** Click to deselect the text box. Compare your screen with Figure 5.52

Figure 5.52

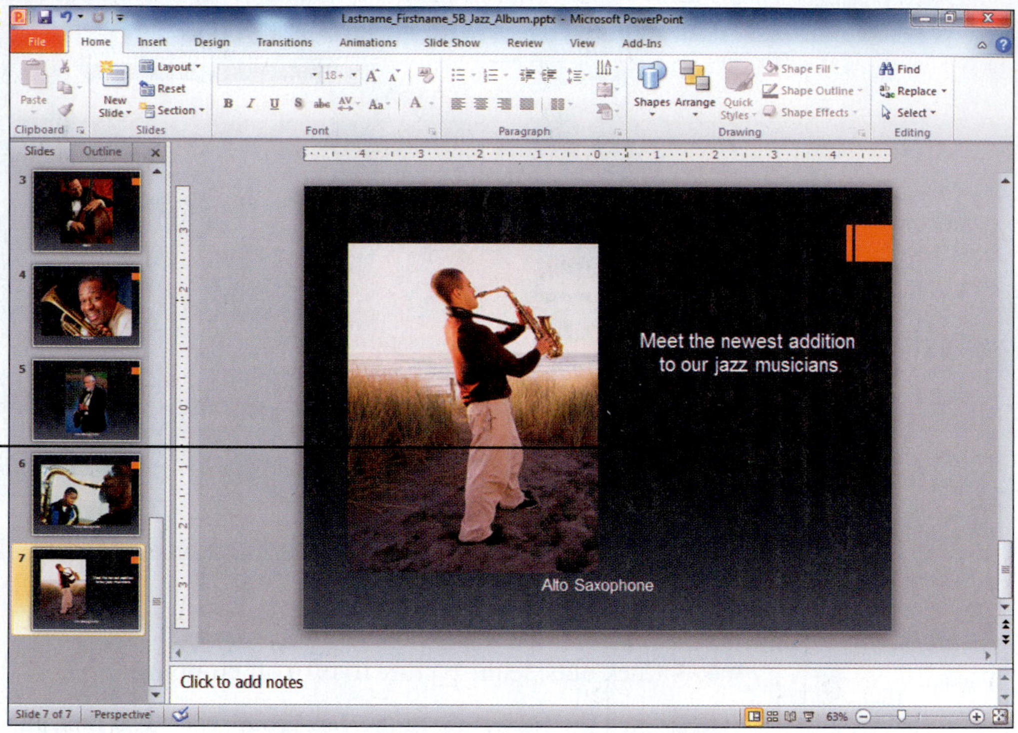

Text added and text box formatted

> **Another Way**
>
> To start the slide show from the beginning, make Slide 1 the active slide, and then press the F5 key or the Slide Show icon on the status bar.

10 Click the **Slide Show tab**. In the **Start Slide Show group**, click the **From Beginning** button, and then view the presentation. Press Esc to return to Normal view.

11 On the **Insert tab**, in the **Text group**, click the **Header & Footer** button to display the **Header and Footer** dialog box. Click the **Notes and Handouts tab**. Under **Include on page**, select the **Date and time** check box, and then select **Fixed**. If necessary, clear the **Header** check box, and then select the **Page number** and **Footer** check boxes. In the **Footer** box, using your own name, type **Lastname_Firstname_5B_Jazz_Album** and then click **Apply to All**.

12 Display **Backstage** view, click **Properties**, and then click **Show Document Panel**. Replace the text in the **Author** box with your own name; in the **Subject** box, type your course name and section number; and in the **Keywords** box, type **jazz, photo, album** **Close** the **Document Information Panel**.

13 **Save** your changes. Print **Handouts 4 Slides Horizontal**, or submit your presentation electronically as directed by your instructor.

14 **Close** the presentation, and then **Exit** PowerPoint.

End **You have completed Project 5B**

Content-Based Assessments

Summary

In this chapter, you practiced completing a PowerPoint presentation by inserting and modifying pictures and images, and by changing the sharpness and softness and also the brightness and contrast. Next, you added borders to images. You recolored pictures and added audio and video to a slide show. You changed the method by which audio and video play in a slide show and created triggers for starting them. You created and edited a photo album and you practiced cropping a picture and added captions to photos.

Key Terms

Matching

Match each term in the second column with its correct definition in the first column by writing the letter of the term on the blank line in front of the correct definition.

____ 1. The term used to describe the amount of light or white in a picture.
____ 2. The mouse pointer used when removing areas of a picture.
____ 3. The process of applying a stylized effect or hue to a picture.
____ 4. The pane used for adding and removing effects.
____ 5. The thickness of a line, measured in points.
____ 6. The term used to describe corners of a border that are angled to form a square.
____ 7. The term used to describe playing an audio file repeatedly until it is stopped manually.
____ 8. The term used to describe audio or video files that are saved as part of the PowerPoint presentation.
____ 9. The button that displays next to the slide thumbnail in the Slide/Outline pane that, when clicked, will play an audio file or an animation.
____ 10. A portion of text, a graphic, or a picture on a slide that, when clicked, will play an audio or video file.
____ 11. A frame or outline added to a picture or clip art.
____ 12. The text that displays beneath a picture in a photo album and, by default, is the file name.

A Animation
B Border
C Brightness
D Caption
E Crop handles
F Crop tool
G Embedded
H Line weight
I Loop
J Mitered
K Play Animations
L Recoloring
M Soften
N Track
O Trigger

_____ 13. The marks on a selected picture used to remove unwanted parts of a picture.

_____ 14. A feature that decreases the clarity of an image, making it look fuzzy.

_____ 15. A song from a CD.

Multiple Choice

Circle the correct answer.

1. The term for an .avi video file that is saved separately from a PowerPoint presentation is:
   A. embedded **B.** surrounded **C.** linked
2. In a photo album, which is the term used to describe a picture that occupies all available space on a slide, leaving no room for a caption?
   A. Unbordered **B.** Fit to slide **C.** Full screen
3. The term that describes a border around a picture in a photo album is:
   A. edging **B.** handle **C.** frame
4. The lines used to crop a picture are known as:
   A. crop handles **B.** sizing handles **C.** mitered corners
5. How lines display, such as a solid line, dots, or dashes, is referred to as:
   A. line weight **B.** line style **C.** line gradient
6. A single point in an image is called a(n):
   A. element **B.** pixel **C.** grid
7. The file size of a presentation with a linked video file, compared with a presentation with an embedded video file, is:
   A. larger **B.** the same **C.** smaller
8. A picture that has been formatted to look fuzzy is:
   A. cropped **B.** softened **C.** sharpened
9. The amount of difference between the light and dark extremes of color in an image is called the:
   A. contrast **B.** disparity **C.** brightness
10. A portion of text that, when clicked, causes an audio or video to play is called the:
    A. activator **B.** trigger **C.** frame

Apply **5A** skills from these Objectives:

1. Use Picture Corrections
2. Add a Border to a Picture
3. Change the Shape of a Picture
4. Add a Picture to a WordArt Object
5. Enhance a Presentation with Audio and Video

Skills Review | Project 5C Celtic Instruments

In the following Skills Review, you will modify pictures in a presentation about the instruments used in the Celtic music genre for the Cross Oceans Music company. You will change the brightness, contrast, and shapes of pictures and add borders to some pictures for emphasis. You will also add audio files that demonstrate the various instruments used in this type of music and a video file. Your completed presentation will look similar to Figure 5.53.

Project Files

For Project 5C, you will need the following files:

p05C_Celtic_Instruments.pptx
p05C_Flute.wav
p05C_Harp.wav
p05_Music_Video.avi
p05C_Sheet_Music.jpg

You will save your presentation as:

Lastname_Firstname_5C_Celtic_Instruments.pptx

Project Results

Figure 5.53

(Project 5C Celtic Instruments continues on the next page)

Skills Review | Project 5C Celtic Instruments (continued)

1 **Start** PowerPoint. Locate and open the file **p05C_ Celtic_Instruments**. Using your own first and last name, save the file as **Lastname_Firstname_5C_Celtic_ Instruments** in your PowerPoint Chapter 5 folder.

2 Click **Slide 1**, if necessary, and then click to select the image.

- **a.** Under **Picture Tools**, click the **Format tab**. In the **Size group**, click the **Crop button arrow**, and then point to **Crop to Shape**. Under **Flowchart**, locate and click **Flowchart: Punched Tape**, which is in the second row, fourth from the left.
- **b.** In the **Adjust group**, click the **Corrections** button, and then click **Picture Corrections Options** to display the **Format Picture** dialog box. Under **Sharpen and Soften**, drag the slider to the left to **-100%**. Under **Brightness and Contrast**, click the **Presets** button, and then in the first row, third column, click **Brightness: 0% (Normal) Contrast: -40%**. Click **Close**.
- **c.** Drag the entire image so the top edge is at **3 inches on the upper half of the horizontal ruler**. In the **Arrange group**, click the **Align** button, and then click **Align Center**.
- **d.** In the **Arrange group**, click the **Send Backward button arrow**, and then click **Send to Back**.

3 Make **Slide 3** the active slide, and then select the picture.

- **a.** Under **Picture Tools**, click the **Format tab**, and then click **Selection Pane**. In the **Selection and Visibility pane**, click **Picture 3**. Close the **Selection and Visibility pane**. In the **Adjust group**, click the **Corrections** button. Under **Brightness and Contrast**, locate and click **Brightness: 0% (Normal) Contrast: +20%**, which is in the fourth row, third column.
- **b.** In the **Arrange group**, click the **Send Backward button arrow**, and then click **Send to Back**.

4 Make **Slide 4** the active slide.

- **a.** Click the **picture of the musician playing bagpipes**. On the **Format tab**, in the **Size group**, click the **Crop button arrow**, and then point to **Crop to Shape**. Under **Basic Shapes**, locate and click **Hexagon**.
- **b.** In the **Picture Styles group**, click **Picture Border button arrow**, point to **Weight**, and then click **1 pt**.
- **c.** Click the **picture of the sheet music with the flute**. On the **Format tab**, in the **Size group**, click the **Crop button arrow**, and then point to **Crop to Shape**. Under **Basic Shapes**, locate and click **Oval**.

5 Make **Slide 5** the active slide.

- **a.** Click the **picture of the accordion**. On the **Format tab**, in the **Picture Styles group**, click the **More arrow**. Locate and click **Reflected Bevel, Black**, which is in the last row, first column.
- **b.** In the **Picture Styles group**, click the **Picture Border** button, and then click **No Outline**.

6 Make **Slide 6** the active slide.

- **a.** Click the **picture of the banjo**.
- **b.** In the **Adjust group**, click the **Corrections** button. Under **Brightness and Contrast**, locate and click **Brightness: +20% Contrast: -20%**.

7 Make **Slide 4** the active slide.

- **a.** Click the **Insert tab**. In the **Media group**, click the **Audio button arrow**, and then click **Audio from File**.
- **b.** Navigate to the location where your student files are stored. Locate and insert **p05C_Flute.wav**.
- **c.** Under **Audio Tools**, click the **Playback tab**. Click the **Start button arrow**, and then click **Automatically**. Click the **Hide During Show** check box.
- **d.** Move the speaker icon to the left side of the picture of the tin whistle so it is under the word *Tin* in the last bullet.

8 Make **Slide 6** the active slide.

- **a.** Click the **Insert tab**. In the **Media group**, click the **Audio button arrow**, and then click **Audio from File**.
- **b.** Navigate to the location where your student files are stored. Locate and insert **p05C_Harp.wav**.
- **c.** Under **Audio Tools**, click the **Playback tab**. Click the **Start button arrow**, and then click **Automatically**. Click the **Hide During Show** check box.
- **d.** Move the audio icon close to the left side of the picture of the harp.

9 On the **Home tab**, in the **Slides group**, click the **New Slide button arrow**, and then click **Blank** to insert a new blank **Slide 7**.

- **a.** On the **Insert tab**, in the **Text group**, click the **WordArt** button. In the third row, third column, locate and click **Gradient Fill – Gray, Outline – Gray**.
- **b.** Type **Celtic Instruments** Press Enter, and then type **Presented by** Press Enter, and then type **Cross Oceans Music**

(Project 5C Celtic Instruments continues on the next page)

Skills Review | Project 5C Celtic Instruments (continued)

c. Select the lines of text. On the **Home tab**, in the **Paragraph group**, click the **Line Spacing button arrow**, and then click **1.5**. In the **Font group**, click the **Font Color button arrow**. Locate and click **Dark Green, Accent 5, Darker 50%**.

d. Drag the **WordArt** so the top edge is at **2.5 inches on the upper half of the vertical ruler**. Under **Drawing Tools**, click the **Format tab**. In the **Arrange group**, click the **Align button arrow**, and then click **Align Center**.

e. On the **Format tab**, in the **Shape Styles group**, click **Shape Fill**, and then click **Picture**. Navigate to the location where your student files are stored. Locate and click **p05C_Sheet_Music.jpg**, and then click **Insert**.

f. Under **Picture Tools**, click the **Format tab**. In the **Adjust group**, click **Color**. Under **Recolor**, locate and click **Dark Green, Accent Color 5 Light**. Right-click the **WordArt shape**, and then click **Format Picture**. Under **Sharpen and Soften**, drag the slider to **-100%**. Click **Close**.

10 In the location where your data files are stored, locate **p05_Music_Video.avi**, and then copy it into your **Chapter 5 folder**.

11 Click **Slide 7**, and then click the **Insert tab**. In the **Media group**, click the **Video button arrow**, and then click **Video from File**.

a. Navigate to the location where your student files are stored, click **p05_Music_Video.avi**, and then click the **Insert button arrow**. Click **Link to File**.

b. Under **Video Tools**, click the **Playback tab**. Click the check boxes for **Play Full Screen** and **Hide While Not Playing**.

c. Click the **Animations tab**. In the **Advanced Animation group**, click the **Trigger** button, point to **On Click of**, and then click **Rectangle**.

d. Click the **Format tab**. In the **Size group**, change the **Video Height** to **1.5"**. Move the entire video to the upper left corner of the slide, at **3.5 inches on the upper half of the vertical ruler** and **4.5 inches on the left side of the horizontal ruler**.

12 Click the **Slide Show tab**. In the **Start Slide Show group**, click **From Beginning**. Listen for the two audio files, and then click the **WordArt** on **Slide 7** to view the video.

13 On the **Insert tab**, in the **Text group**, click the **Header & Footer** button to display the **Header and Footer** dialog box. Click the **Notes and Handouts tab**. Under **Include on page**, select the **Date and time** check box, and then select **Fixed**. If necessary, clear the **Header** check box, and then select the **Page number** and **Footer** check boxes. In the **Footer** box, using your own name, type **Lastname_Firstname_5C_Celtic_Instruments** and then click **Apply to All**.

14 Display **Backstage** view, Click **Properties**, and then click **Show Document Panel**. Replace the text in the **Author** box with your own name; in the **Subject** box, type your course name and section number; and in the **Keywords** box, type **Celtic, instruments, Ireland, Scotland** Close the **Document Information Panel**.

15 **Save** the presentation. Print **Handouts 4 Slides Horizontal**, or submit your presentation electronically as directed by your instructor. **Exit** PowerPoint.

End **You have completed Project 5C**

Content-Based Assessments

Apply 5B skills from these Objectives:

- 6 Create a Photo Album
- 7 Edit a Photo Album and Add a Caption
- 8 Crop a Picture

Skills Review | Project 5D Celtic Album

In the following Skills Review, you will create a photo album for the Cross Oceans Music company. You will insert photos of musicians who record Celtic music and are represented by Cross Oceans. You will also include photos of some of the unusual instruments used to create this type of music. You will add captions and crop unwanted areas of photos. Your completed presentation will look similar to Figure 5.54.

Project Files

For Project 5D, you will need the following files:

New blank PowerPoint presentation
p05D_Mandolin.jpg
p05D_Flautist.jpg
p05D_Banjo.jpg
p05D_Violinist.jpg
p05D_Bagpipes.jpg

You will save your presentation as:

Lastname_Firstname_5D_Celtic_Album.pptx

Project Results

Figure 5.54

(Project 5D Celtic Album continues on the next page)

Skills Review | Project **5D** Celtic Album (continued)

1 **Start** PowerPoint. Click the **Insert tab**. In the **Images group**, click the **Photo Album button arrow**, and then click **New Photo Album**.

2 Under **Insert picture from**, click **File/Disk** to display the **Insert New Pictures** dialog box. Navigate to the location where your student files are stored, click **p05D_Mandolin.jpg**, and then, if necessary, click the **Insert** button.

3 Using the technique you practiced, insert the following pictures into the photo album in this order: **p05D_Flautist.jpg**, **p05D_Banjo.jpg**, **p05D_Violinist.jpg**, and **p05D_Bagpipes.jpg**.

4 Under **Album Layout**, click the **Picture layout arrow** to display the selections. Click **1 picture**.

5 Click the **Frame shape arrow** to display the frame shape selections, and then click **Rounded Rectangle**.

6 To the right of the **Theme** box, click the **Browse** button to display the **Choose Theme** dialog box. Click **Clarity**, and then click **Select**. In the **Photo Album** dialog box, click **Create**.

7 Display **Backstage** view, click **Save As**, and then navigate to the location where you are storing your projects for this chapter and save the file as **Lastname_Firstname_5D_Celtic_Album**

8 Click **Slide 1**. Right-click to display the shortcut menu.

a. Click **Format Background**, and then click the **Hide background graphics** check box.

b. Select the **Gradient Fill** option, and then click the **Type arrow** and select **Rectangular**.

c. Click the **Color** button. In the first row, ninth column, click **Blue-Gray, Accent 5**.

d. Click the **Direction** button. Locate and click **From Bottom Left Corner**.

e. Drag the **Stop 2 position** slider to **75%**. Click **Apply to All**, and then **Close** the dialog box.

9 Position the insertion point to the left of *Photo Album*.

a. Type **Celtic Music** and then press **Enter**. The text will be in all capital letters.

b. Select both lines of the title—*CELTIC MUSIC PHOTO ALBUM*. Click the **Format tab**. In the **WordArt Styles group**, click the **Text Effects button arrow**, point to **Glow**, and then click **Gray-50%, 5 pt glow, Accent color 1**.

c. Click the **Text Outline button arrow**, and then in the second row, click **White, Background 1, Darker 5%**.

d. Increase the size of the title to **66 pts**, add **Bold**, and **Shadow**.

10 Delete the subtitle, and then type **Cross Oceans Music**

11 Click the **Insert tab**. In the **Images group**, click the **Photo Album button arrow**, and then click **Edit Photo Album**. In the **Edit Photo Album** dialog box, under **Picture Options**, select the **Captions below ALL pictures** check box, and then click **Update**.

12 Make **Slide 2** the active slide, and then click to select the caption. Select *p05D_*, and then press **Delete**. The caption should now read *Mandolin*.

13 Using the technique you practiced, edit the captions for **Slides 3**, **4**, **5**, and **6** as follows:

Flautist

Banjo

Violinist

Bagpipes

14 On **Slide 6**, click the **picture of the bagpipes**. Under **Picture Tools**, click the **Format tab**. In the **Size group**, click the **Crop** button.

a. Drag the right middle cropping handle left to **2.5 inches on the right side of the horizontal ruler**.

b. Repeat the procedure to crop the left side to **2.5 inches on the left side of the horizontal ruler**.

c. Click the **Crop** button to turn off cropping.

15 Click the **Slide Show tab**. In the **Start Slide Show group**, click **From Beginning**.

16 On the **Insert tab**, in the **Text group**, click the **Header & Footer** button to display the **Header and Footer** dialog box. Click the **Notes and Handouts tab**. Under **Include on page**, select the **Date and time** check box, and then select **Fixed**. If necessary, clear the **Header** check box, and then select the **Page number** and **Footer** check boxes. In the **Footer** box, using your own name, type **Lastname_Firstname_5D_Celtic_Album** and then click **Apply to All**.

17 Display **Backstage** view, click **Properties**, and then click **Show Document Panel**. Replace the text in the **Author** box with your own name; in the **Subject** box, type your course name and section number; and in the **Keywords** box, type **Celtic, music, album** **Close** the **Document Information Panel**.

18 **Save** the presentation. Print **Handouts 4 Slides Horizontal**, or submit your presentation electronically as directed by your instructor. Then **Close** your presentation and **Exit** PowerPoint.

End **You have completed Project 5D**

Content-Based Assessments

Apply 5A skills from these Objectives:

1. Use Picture Corrections
2. Add a Border to a Picture
3. Change the Shape of a Picture
4. Add a Picture to a WordArt Object
5. Enhance a Presentation with Audio and Video

Mastering PowerPoint | Project 5E Reggae Music

In the following Mastering PowerPoint project, you will modify pictures in a presentation used in educational seminars hosted by Cross Oceans Music. The presentation highlights Reggae music and its roots in jazz and rhythm and blues. You will also add an audio file that represents this genre of music and format it to play across the slides in the slide show. You will also add a video file. Your completed presentation will look similar to Figure 5.55.

Project Files

For Project 5E, you will need the following files:

p05E_Reggae_Music.pptx
p05E_Reggae.wav
p05E_Music.jpg
p05_Music_Video.avi

You will save your presentation as:

Lastname_Firstname_5E_Reggae_Music.pptx

Project Results

Figure 5.55

(Project 5E Reggae Music continues on the next page)

Mastering PowerPoint | Project 5E Reggae Music (continued)

1 **Start** PowerPoint. Locate and open the file **p05E_Reggae_Music**. Save the file in your chapter folder, using the file name **Lastname_Firstname_5E_Reggae_Music**

2 On the **title slide**, click to select the picture, click the **Format tab**, and then set the **Sharpen and Soften** to **0%**. Set the **Brightness** to **-15%**.

3 Make **Slide 2** the active slide, and then click to select the **picture of the Jamaican flag**. On the **Format tab**, click the **Crop button arrow**, and then crop the picture to the **Wave** shape, which is under **Stars and Banners**, in the second row, the seventh shape.

4 Make **Slide 3** the active slide. Click the **map and globe picture**, and the send the picture to the back. In the **Adjust group**, click **Color**, and then under **Recolor**, in the first row, fourth column, click **Washout**.

5 Make **Slide 4** the active slide, and then click the picture. Set the **Brightness** to **+20%** and the **Contrast** to **+20%**. Change the picture border to **Teal, Accent 2, Darker 50%**. Crop the picture to an **Oval** shape.

6 Make **Slide 5** the active slide, and then click to select the **picture of the flag of Trinidad**. Use **Crop to Shape**, and then under **Stars and Banners**, change the picture shape to **Double Wave**, which is in the second row, the last shape.

7 Make **Slide 6** the active slide, and then click to select the picture. Set the **Brightness** to **+40%**, and then **Send to Back**.

8 Make the **title slide** the active slide. Display the **Insert Audio** dialog box. From your student files, insert the audio file **p05E_Reggae.wav**. On the **Playback tab**, set the audio to **Hide During Show** and to start **Automatically**.

9 Click **Slide 6**, and then insert a **Blank** slide as **Slide 7**.

10 Make **Slide 7** the active slide, if necessary. On the **Insert tab**, click the **WordArt** button, and then click **Fill – Teal, Accent 2, Warm Matte Bevel**. Type **Reggae Music** on one line, type **Presented by** on the next line, and then type **Cross Oceans Music** on the third line. Change the **Font Color**

to **Teal, Accent 2, Darker 25%**. Drag the **WordArt** so the top edge is at **1.5 inches on the upper half of the vertical ruler**. On the **Format tab**, **Align Center** the WordArt shape.

11 With **Slide 7** as the active slide, use **Shape Fill** to insert from your data files the picture **p05E_Music.jpg**. Under **Picture Tools**, click the **Format tab**. Recolor the picture to **Teal, Accent color 2 Light**. Set the **Sharpen and Soften** at **-100%**.

12 In the location where your data files are stored, locate **p05_Music_Video.avi**, and then copy it into your Chapter 5 folder.

13 With **Slide 7** as the active slide. From your data files, insert **p05_Music_Video.avi** as a linked video. On the **Playback tab**, click the check boxes for **Play Full Screen** and **Hide While Not Playing**. On the **Animations tab**, set a trigger for the video to play **On click of** the WordArt rectangle. Change the **Video Height** to **1.5"**. Move the video to the upper left, at **3.0″ above 0 on the vertical ruler** and **4.5″ to the left of 0 on the horizontal ruler**.

14 Start the slide show from the beginning. Listen for the audio file, and then click the **WordArt** on **Slide 7** to view the video.

15 Insert a footer on the notes and handouts that includes a fixed date and time, the page number, and the file name.

16 Modify the **Properties** in the **Show Document Panel**. Replace the text in the **Author** box with your own name; in the **Subject** box, type your course name and section number; and in the **Keywords** box, type **Reggae, music** **Close** the **Document Information Panel**.

17 **Save** the presentation. Print **Handouts 4 Slides Horizontal**, or submit your presentation electronically as directed by your instructor. **Close** your presentation and **Exit** PowerPoint.

End **You have completed Project 5E**

Apply 5B skills from these Objectives:

- 6 Create a Photo Album
- 7 Edit a Photo Album and Add a Caption
- 8 Crop a Picture

Mastering PowerPoint | Project 5F CD Cover

In the following Mastering PowerPoint project, you will create a photo album of pictures of island settings for a CD entitled *Reggae Revisited*. One of these cover designs will be chosen by Cross Oceans Music to be the cover of the soon-to-be-released CD of reggae and Jamaican music. Your completed presentation will look similar to Figure 5.56.

Project Files

For Project 5F, you will need the following files:

New blank PowerPoint presentation
p05F_Island1.jpg
p05F_Island2.jpg
p05F_Island3.jpg
p05F_Island4.jpg
p05F_Island5.jpg

You will save your presentation as:

Lastname_Firstname_5F_CD_Cover.pptx

Project Results

Figure 5.56

(Project 5F CD Cover continues on the next page)

Mastering PowerPoint | Project 5F CD Cover (continued)

1 **Start** PowerPoint. Click the **Insert tab**. In the **Images group**, click the **Photo Album button arrow**, and then click **New Photo Album**.

2 From the student data files, insert the following pictures into the photo album: **p05F_Island1.jpg**, **p05F_Island2.jpg**, **p05F_Island3.jpg**, **p05F_Island4.jpg**, and **p05F_Island5.jpg**. In the **Picture layout** list, click **1 picture**. Select the **Module** theme. Click the **Create** button.

3 Edit the **Photo Album**, and remove the last two pictures—**p05F_Island4** and **p05F_Island5** from the album. Change the **Picture layout** to **1 picture with title** and the **Frame shape** to **Compound Frame, Black**.

4 Save the file in your chapter folder, using the file name **Lastname_Firstname_5F_CD_Cover**

5 Make the **title slide** the active slide. Change the subtitle text, the first placeholder, to **Cross Oceans Music** Apply **Bold**, and then change the font size to **28**.

6 Delete the title text, *Photo Album*, and then type **Design Entries for CD Cover** Press **Enter**, and then type **Reggae & Jamaican Music** Select both lines of the title. On the **Format tab**, in the **WordArt Styles group**, click the **More** button. Under **Applies to All Text in the Shape**, in the first row, click the third style—**Fill – Aqua, Accent 2, Warm Matte Bevel**.

7 Make **Slide 2** active. Change the title to **Design 1** Drag the picture so the left side aligns at **4.5 inches on the left side of the horizontal ruler**.

8 Insert a text box in the blank area to the right of the picture. In the text box, type **Reggae** press **Enter**, and then type **Revisited** Change the font to **Bauhaus 93** and the font size to **72**. Position the text box so that the left edge aligns with **0 on the horizontal ruler** and the top edge aligns with **1 inch on the upper half of the vertical ruler**.

9 Make **Slide 3** active. Change the title to **Design 2** Drag the picture so the right side aligns at **4.5 inches on the right side of the horizontal ruler.**

10 Insert a text box in the blank area to the left of the picture. In the text box, type **Reggae** press **Enter**, and then type **Revisited** Change the font to **Brush Script MT** and the font size to **88**. Apply **Bold** and **Text Shadow**. Position the text box so that the left edge aligns with at **4 inches on the left side of the horizontal ruler** and the top edge aligns at **1 inch on the upper half of the vertical ruler**.

11 Make **Slide 4** active, and then change the title to **Design 3** Drag the picture so the right side aligns at **4 inches on the right side of the horizontal ruler**.

12 Insert a text box in the middle of the slide, to the left of the picture. In the text box, type **Reggae** press **Enter**, and then type **Revisited** Change the font to **Algerian** and the font size to **60**. Apply **Bold**, **Italic**, and **Text Shadow**. With the text box selected, on the **Format tab**, in the **WordArt Styles group**, click the **More** button, and then under **Applies to Selected Text**, in the third row, click the fifth style—**Fill-Aqua 2, Double Outline - Accent 2**. Position the text box so that the top edge aligns at **1 inch on the bottom half of the vertical ruler** and the left edge aligns at **4.5 inches on the left side of the horizontal ruler**.

13 Make **Slide 2** the active slide. Select the picture. On the **Format tab**, click the **Crop** button, and then drag the left middle cropping handle to at **4 inches on the left side of the horizontal ruler**. Click outside to deselect the picture.

14 Review your presentation from the beginning.

15 Insert a footer on the notes and handouts that includes a fixed date and time, the page number, and the file name.

16 Modify the **Properties** on the **Show Document Panel**. Replace the text in the **Author** box with your own name; in the **Subject** box, type your course name and section number; and in the **Keywords** box, type **design, CD, entries** **Close** the **Document Information Panel**.

17 **Save** the presentation. Print **Handouts 4 Slides Horizontal**, or submit your presentation electronically as directed by your instructor. **Close** your presentation and **Exit** PowerPoint.

End **You have completed Project 5F**

Apply 5A and 5B skills from these Objectives:

1. Use Picture Corrections
2. Add a Border to a Picture
3. Change the Shape of a Picture
4. Add a Picture to a WordArt Object
5. Enhance a Presentation with Audio and Video
6. Create a Photo Album
7. Edit a Photo Album and Add a Caption
8. Crop a Picture

myitlab grader

Mastering PowerPoint | Project 5G Jazz Origins and Percussion Album

In the following Mastering PowerPoint project, you will edit a short presentation about the origins and elements of jazz by changing the brightness, contrast, and shape of pictures and adding a border. You will also format the presentation to play a short jazz video across slides during the slide show. Finally, you will create a photo album showing some of the percussion instruments used in Cross Oceans Music jazz recordings. The album will contain an audio clip of music. Your completed presentations will look similar to Figure 5.57

Project Files

For Project 5G, you will need the following files:

Presentation:
p05G_Jazz_Origins.pptx
p05_Music_Video.avi

Photo Album:
New blank PowerPoint presentation
p05G_Drums1.jpg
p05G_Drums2.jpg
p05G_Drums3.jpg
p05G_Drums4.jpg
p05G_Jazz.wav

You will save your presentations as:

Lastname_Firstname_5G_Jazz_Origins.pptx
Lastname_Firstname_5G_Percussion_.pptx

Project Results

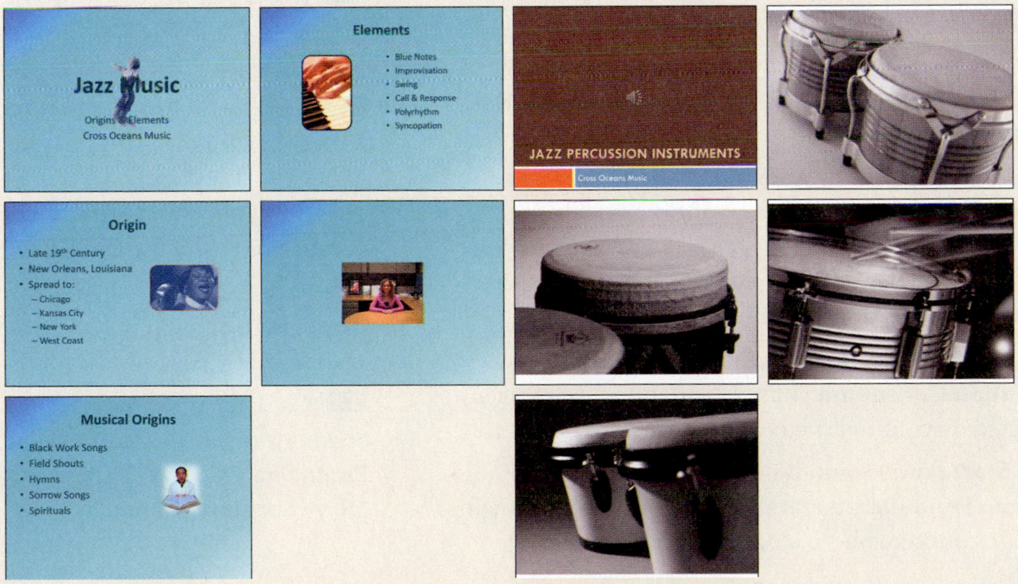

Figure 5.57

(Project 5G Jazz Origins and Percussion Album continues on the next page)

Mastering PowerPoint | Project 5G Jazz Origins and Percussion Album (continued)

1 **Start** PowerPoint. Locate and open the file **p05G_Jazz_Origins**, and then save the file as **Lastname_Firstname_5G_Jazz_Origins**

2 On **Slide 2**, change the picture **Color** to **Blue, Accent color 1 Light**, found under **Recolor** in the third row. **Crop** the picture to a **Rounded Rectangle** shape, found under **Rectangles**. Apply a **Picture Border—Orange, Accent 6, Darker 25%**, found in the last column.

3 On **Slide 3**, change the picture **Color** to **Temperature: 4700 K**, found under **Color Tone**. Change the **Picture Effects** to **Soft Edges, 25 Point**.

4 Display **Slide 4**. On the **picture of the hands on the piano keyboard**, apply **+20% Brightness**. Change the picture shape to **Flowchart: Alternate Process**, found under **Flowchart**, in the first row. Add a picture border that is **Dark Blue, Background 2, Darker 50%**, found in the last row, third column of the gallery. Set the border weight (also known as width) to **2¼ pt**.

5 Insert a new blank slide after **Slide 4**. In **Slide 5**, insert as a linked video **p05Music_Video.avi**. Set it to play **Automatically**, **Hide While Not Playing**, and **Play Full Screen**. View your presentation from the beginning.

6 Insert a footer on the notes and handouts that includes a fixed date and time, the page number, and the file name.

7 Modify the **Properties** on the **Show Document Panel**. Replace the text in the **Author** box with your own name; in the **Subject** box, type your course name and section number; and in the **Keywords** box, type **jazz, origin** **Close** the **Document Information Panel**.

8 **Save** the presentation. Print **Handouts 6 Slides Horizontal**, or submit your presentation electronically as directed by your instructor. **Close** your presentation.

9 **Start** PowerPoint, if necessary. Insert a **New Photo Album**. From the student data files, insert the following pictures into the photo album: **p05G_Drums1.jpg**, **p05G_Drums2.jpg**, **p05G_Drums3.jpg**, and **p05G_Drums4.jpg**.

10 Set the **Picture layout** to **Fit to slide**. Use the **Median** theme. Click to select the box **ALL pictures black and white**, and then create the photo album. In the location where you are storing your projects, save the file as **Lastname_Firstname_5G_Percussion_Album**

11 Make **Slide 1** the active slide. Replace the title—*Photo Album*—with **Jazz Percussion Instruments** It will be in all capital letters. Drag the middle sizing handle on each side of the title placeholder so the placeholder occupies the entire width of the slide and the entire title fits on one line. **Center** the text horizontally. Select the **title**, and then apply **Bold** and **Text Shadow**.

12 Click to select the **subtitle**. Delete the subtitle, and then type **Cross Oceans Music**

13 On **Slide 1**, insert the audio file **p05G_Jazz.wav**. On the **Playback tab**, click the **Start** option **Play across slides**. Click the check box for **Hide During Show**. View the slide show **From Beginning** and test the sound.

14 Insert a footer on the notes and handouts that includes a fixed date and time, the page number, and the file name.

15 Modify the **Properties** on the **Show Document Panel**. Replace the text in the **Author** box with your own name; in the **Subject** box, type your course name and section number; and in the **Keywords** box, type **jazz, percussion** **Close** the **Document Information Panel**.

16 **Save** the presentation. Print **Handouts 6 Slides Horizontal**, or submit your presentation electronically as directed by your instructor.

17 **Close** the presentation, and then **Exit** PowerPoint. Submit your work as directed for both **Lastname_Firstname_5G_Jazz_Origins** and **Lastname_Firstname_5B_Percussion_Album**.

End **You have completed Project 5G**

Apply a combination of the **5A** and **5B** skills.

GO! Fix It | Project 5H Caribbean Music and Strings Album

Project Files

For Project 5H, you will need the following files:

Presentation:
p05H_Caribbean_Music.pptx
p05H_Caribbean.wav

Photo Album:
p05H_Strings_Album.pptx
p05H_Harp.jpg
p05_Music_Video.avi

You will save your presentations as:

Lastname_Firstname_5H_Caribbean_Music.pptx
Lastname_Firstname_5H_Strings_Album.pptx

In this project, you will edit slides in a presentation that describes the soca genre of Caribbean music. Modify the color and shape of the images and add audio. Next, edit a photo album depicting instruments used in the production of Cross Oceans Music recordings.

Open **p05H_Caribbean_Music**, and then save the file in your chapter folder as **Lastname_Firstname_5H_Caribbean_Music** Correct these errors:

- On Slide 3, the picture of the two drums should have the color changed to Tan, Accent color 2 Light, one of the Recolor choices. The picture should be Sent to Back.
- On Slide 4, the flag should be cropped to a Wave shape. The Picture Effects should be set for Reflection, Tight Reflection, touching. The picture border should be Black, Text 1, Lighter 5%.
- On Slide 1, the audio file p05H_Caribbean.wav should be inserted and set to start Automatically. The audio icon should be set to Hide During Show. The speaker icon should be at the lower right corner.
- Insert a Header & Footer on the Notes and Handouts that includes the Date and time Fixed, the Page number, and a Footer with the text **Lastname_Firstname_5H_Caribbean_Music** Document Properties should include your name, course name and section, and the keywords **Caribbean, instruments**

Open the file **p05H_Strings_Album**, and then save the file in your chapter folder as **Lastname_Firstname_5H_Strings_Album** Correct these errors:

- Edit the Photo Album. The theme should be Apothecary, and the picture p05H_Harp.jpg should be added as the last slide in the album.
- On Slide 1, the title should be **String Instruments**. Titles for the remaining slides should be: **Bass, Classical Guitar, Mandolin, Violin, and Harp**.
- On Slide 1, p05_Music_Video.avi should be inserted as a linked video, resized to a height of 1.5 inches, and positioned in the upper left corner with a Trigger set to the slide title. The video should play Full Screen and Hide While Not Playing.
- A Header & Footer should be inserted on the Notes and Handouts that includes the Date and time Fixed, the Page number, and a Footer with the text **Lastname_Firstname_5H_Strings_Album** Document Properties should include your name, course name and section, and the keywords **strings, instruments**

Submit your presentations electronically or print Handouts 6 slides per page as directed by your instructor. Close the presentations.

End **You have completed Project 5H**

Apply a combination of the **5A** and **5B** skills.

GO! Make It | Project 5I Salsa Music and Latin Album

Project Files

For Project 5I, you will need the following files:

Presentation:
p05I_Salsa_Music.pptx
p05I_Marimba.jpg
p05I_Dancer1.jpg
p05I_Salsa.wav
p05_Music_Video.avi

Photo Album:
New blank PowerPoint presentation
p05I_Exotic1.jpg
p05I_Exotic2.jpg
p05I_Music.jpg

You will save your presentations as:

Lastname_Firstname_5I_Salsa_Music.pptx
Lastname_Firstname_5I_Latin_Album.pptx

Start PowerPoint and open p05I_Salsa_Music. Save the file in your PowerPoint Chapter 5 folder as **Lastname_Firstname_5I_Salsa_Music**

By using the skills you practiced in this chapter, create the first two slides of the presentation shown in Figure 5.58. On the first slide, insert the picture p05I_Marimba.jpg. Recolor the picture to Brown, Accent color 4 Light, and then add a picture effect of Soft Edges at 50 Point. Position the picture so the text can be read. Insert p05I_Salsa.wav with a trigger on the title—*Salsa Music*. Move the audio icon to the bottom left corner. On the second slide, insert p05I_Dancer1.jpg, and then apply a hexagon shape to the picture and add a border—Gray-50%, Accent 1, Darker 25%. Insert p05_Music_Video.avi as a linked video with a trigger on the dancer picture. Resize video height to 1.5" and position it at the bottom left corner of the screen. Set the playback so the video will play full screen.

Insert a Header & Footer on the Notes and Handouts that includes the Date and time Fixed, the Page number, and a Footer with the text **Lastname_Firstname_5I_Salsa_Music** In the Document Properties, include your name, course name and section, and the keywords **Salsa, Latin** Save, and then print Handouts 4 slides per page or submit the presentation electronically as directed by your instructor.

Create a new Photo Album and create the first three slides as shown in Figure 5.58. Insert p05I_Exotic1.jpg and p05I_Exotic2.jpg, then apply the Opulent theme. Save the file in your PowerPoint Chapter 5 folder as **Lastname_Firstname_5I_Latin_Album** Insert p05I_Music.jpg on Slide 1, crop and position it as shown. The picture will be distorted. Crop the picture on Slide 2.

Insert a Header & Footer on the Notes and Handouts that includes the Date and time Fixed, the Page number, and a Footer with the text **Lastname_Firstname_5I_Latin_Album**. In the Document Properties, add your name and course information and the keywords **exotic, music** Save, and then print Handouts 4 slides per page or submit the photo album electronically as directed by your instructor.

(Project 5I Salsa Music and Latin Album continues on the next page)

GO! Make It | Project 5I Salsa Music and Latin Album (continued)

Project Results

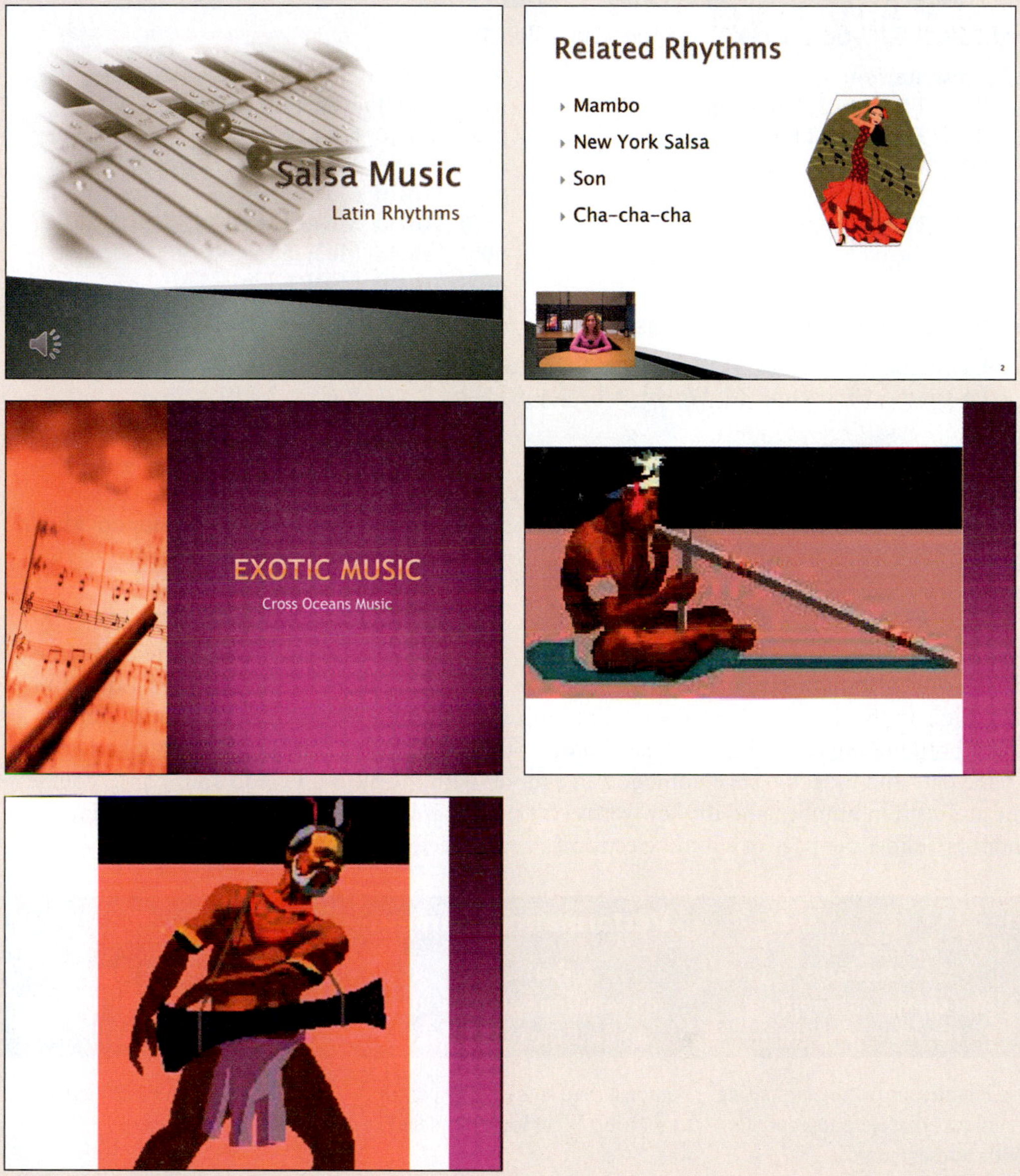

Figure 5.58

End **You have completed Project 5I**

Apply a combination of the **5A** and **5B** skills.

GO! Solve It | Project 5J Flamenco Music and World Album

Project Files

For Project 5J, you will need the following files:

Presentation:
P05J_Flamenco_Music.pptx
p05J_Flamenco2.jpg
p05J_Guitar1.jpg
p05J_Guitar2.jpg
p05J_Flamenco.wav
p05_Music_Video.avi

Photo Album:
New blank PowerPoint presentation
p05J_World_Music1.jpg
p05J_World_Music2.jpg
p05J_World_Music3.jpg
p05J_World_Music4.jpg
p05J_World_Music5.jpg
p05J_World_Music6.jpg

You will save your presentations as:

Lastname_Firstname_5J_Flamenco_Music.pptx
Lastname_Firstname_5J_World_Album.pptx

In this project, you will modify a presentation on the elements of Flamenco music and then create a photo album on World music. Demonstrate the skills you have covered in this chapter.

Open p05J_Flamenco_Music, and then save it as **Lastname_Firstname_5J_Flamenco_Music** Use the provided picture files or insert pictures of your own choosing. Add the provided audio and video files. Format the pictures and apply audio and video playback options.

Create a photo album to highlight other forms of World Music produced and distributed by Cross Oceans Music. Use the provided picture files or ones of your own choosing. Select a theme, and then place the photos on the slides in a manner that will highlight the performers. Add a title and subtitle on the title slide. Save the presentation as **Lastname_Firstname_5J_World_Album**

For both presentations, insert a header and footer on the Notes and Handouts that includes the fixed date and time, the page number, and a footer with the file name. Add your name, course name and section number, and the key words you feel are appropriate to the Properties. Print Handouts 6 slides per page or submit electronically as directed by your instructor.

Performance Element	Exemplary: You consistently applied the relevant skills.	Proficient: You sometimes, but not always, applied, the relevant skills.	Developing: You rarely or never applied the relevant skills.
Added and formatted pictures in the presentation.	Used numerous picture formatting techniques that were appropriate for the presentation.	Demonstrated some of the picture formatting. What was completed was correct.	Little or no picture formatting was demonstrated.
Inserted audio and video files and applied playback settings.	Inserted audio and video files in appropriate places and applied playback options. Both played correctly. May have used a trigger.	Inserted the audio, but either the playback options were not set or the audio did not play back correctly. May have used a trigger.	Inserted the audio, but either the playback options were not set or the audio did not play back correctly. May have used a trigger.
Created a photo album, selected a theme, and inserted pictures.	The photo album had a theme, and the pictures were inserted.	The pictures were inserted, but there was no theme. Presentation lacked consistency.	The photo album was not created.

End You have completed Project 5J

Apply a combination of the **5A** and **5B** skills.

GO! Solve It | Project **5K** New Age Music and Asian Album

Project Files

For Project 5K, you will need the following files:

Presentation:
p05K_NewAge_Music.pptx
p05K_Piano.wav
p05_Music_Video.avi

Photo Album:
New blank PowerPoint presentation
p05K_Asian_Music1.jpg
p05K_Asian_Music2.jpg
p05K_Asian_Music3.jpg
p05K_Asian_Music4.jpg
p05K_Asian_Music5.jpg
p05K_Asian_Music6.jpg

You will save your presentations as:

Lastname_Firstname_5K_NewAge_Music.pptx
Lastname_Firstname_5K_Asian_Album.pptx

In this presentation project, you will modify a short presentation that describes the elements of New Age music and create a photo album on Asian music. Demonstrate your knowledge of the skills you have covered in this chapter.

Open p05K_NewAge_Music, and then save it as **Lastname_Firstname_5K_NewAge_Music** Improve the presentation by including a title and subtitle, applying a theme, and modifying the photos in the slides. Add the provided audio and video files and set the playback options.

Using the graphic files provided, create a photo album to highlight Asian musical instruments, and add captions or titles, if necessary. Save the album as **Lastname_Firstname_5K_Asian_Music**

For both presentations, insert a header and footer on the Notes and Handouts that includes the fixed date and time, the page number, and a footer with the file name. Add your name, course name and section number, and appropriate key words to the Properties. Print Handouts 6 slides per page or submit electronically as directed by your instructor.

Performance Element	Exemplary: You consistently applied the relevant skills.	Proficient: You sometimes, but not always, applied, the relevant skills.	Developing: You rarely or never applied the relevant skills.
Modified photos in NewAge_Music.	Used a variety of picture corrections, shapes, and borders that enhanced the presentation.	Used some picture corrections, shapes, and borders to enhance the presentation.	Used few or no picture corrections, shapes, and borders to enhance the presentation.
Added audio and video files and applied playback options.	Inserted audio and video files in appropriate places and applied playback options. Both played correctly. May have used a trigger.	Inserted the audio, but either the playback options were not set or the audio did not play back correctly. May have used a trigger.	Inserted the audio, but either the playback options were not set or the audio did not play back correctly. May have used a trigger.
Created a photo album, inserted pictures, an added appropriate captions or titles.	The photo album had a theme, and the pictures were inserted. Used captions and titles as necessary and completed title slide.	The pictures were inserted, but there was no theme. Presentation and captions lacked consistency.	The photo album was not created.

End **You have completed Project 5K**

Outcomes-Based Assessments

Rubric

The following outcomes-based assessments are *open-ended assessments*. That is, there is no specific correct result; your result will depend on your approach to the information provided. Make *Professional Quality* your goal. Use the following scoring rubric to guide you in *how* to approach the problem and then to evaluate *how well* your approach solves the problem.

The *criteria*—Software Mastery, Content, Format and Layout, and Process—represent the knowledge and skills you have gained that you can apply to solving the problem. The *levels of performance*—Professional Quality, Approaching Professional Quality, or Needs Quality Improvements—help you and your instructor evaluate your result.

	Your completed project is of Professional Quality if you:	**Your completed project is Approaching Professional Quality if you:**	**Your completed project Needs Quality Improvements if you:**
1-Software Mastery	Choose and apply the most appropriate skills, tools, and features and identify efficient methods to solve the problem.	Choose and apply some appropriate skills, tools, and features, but not in the most efficient manner.	Choose inappropriate skills, tools, or features, or are inefficient in solving the problem.
2-Content	Construct a solution that is clear and well organized, contains content that is accurate, appropriate to the audience and purpose, and is complete. Provide a solution that contains no errors in spelling, grammar, or style.	Construct a solution in which some components are unclear, poorly organized, inconsistent, or incomplete. Misjudge the needs of the audience. Have some errors in spelling, grammar, or style, but the errors do not detract from comprehension.	Construct a solution that is unclear, incomplete, or poorly organized; contains some inaccurate or inappropriate content; and contains many errors in spelling, grammar, or style. Do not solve the problem.
3-Format and Layout	Format and arrange all elements to communicate information and ideas, clarify function, illustrate relationships, and indicate relative importance.	Apply appropriate format and layout features to some elements, but not others. Overuse features, causing minor distraction.	Apply format and layout that does not communicate information or ideas clearly. Do not use format and layout features to clarify function, illustrate relationships, or indicate relative importance. Use available features excessively, causing distraction.
4-Process	Use an organized approach that integrates planning, development, self-assessment, revision, and reflection.	Demonstrate an organized approach in some areas, but not others; or, use an insufficient process of organization throughout.	Do not use an organized approach to solve the problem.

Outcomes-Based Assessments

Apply a combination of the 5A and 5B skills.

GO! Think | Project 5L Ragtime and African Music

Project Files

For Project 5L, you will need the following files:

Presentation:
p05L_Ragtime_Music.pptx
p05_Music_Video.avi
p05L_Entertainer.wav

Photo Album:
New blank PowerPoint presentation

You will save your presentations as:

Lastname_Firstname_5L_Ragtime_Music.pptx
Lastname_Firstname_5L_African_Album.pptx

In this project, you will edit a presentation about the history and makeup of Ragtime music. Open p05L_Ragtime_Music and save it as **Lastname_Firstname_5L_Ragtime_Music** Modify the images on the slides. Add audio and video to the presentation. Set the audio file to start automatically and play across slides. Create a photo album using the provided pictures. Insert p05L_Africa.jpg on the title slide. Save it as **Lastname_Firstname_5L_African_Album** Insert appropriate headers and footers, and then update the Properties on both files. Submit your files as directed.

End You have completed Project 5L

Apply a combination of the 5A and 5B skills.

GO! Think | Project 5M Indian Music and Indian Instruments

Project Files

For Project 5M, you will need the following files:

Presentation:
p05M_Indian_Music.pptx
p05M_Indian_Music.wav
p05_Music_Video.avi

Photo Album:
New blank PowerPoint presentation
p05M_Bagilu.jpg
p05M_Ghantis.jpg
p05M_Indian_Dancer.jpg
p05M_Khangling.jpg
p05M_Nagphani.jpg

You will save your presentations as:

Lastname_Firstname_5M_Indian_Music.pptx
Lastname_Firstname_5M_Indian_Album.pptx

In this project, you will modify a short presentation about the basic tenets of Indian music and prepare a photo album. Open p05M_Indian_Music, modify the photos and graphics and add the provided audio and video files. Save as **Lastname_Firstname_5M_Indian_Music**. Create a photo album using the provided pictures. Save the album as **Lastname_Firstname_5M_Indian_Album** Insert appropriate headers and footers, and then update the Properties on both files. Submit your files as directed.

End You have completed Project 5M

Outcomes-Based Assessments

Apply a combination of the **5A** and **5B** skills.

You and GO! | Project 5N Swing Origins

Project Files

For Project 5N, you will need the following files:

Presentation:
p05N_Swing_Origins.pptx
p05N_Cakewalk.wav
p05N_Lindy_Hop.wav
p05N_Swing.wav
p05_Music_Video.avi

Photo Album:
New blank PowerPoint presentation
p05N_Violinist.jpg
p05N_Conductor.jpg
p05N_Strings.jpg
p05N_Horns.jpg
p05N_Orchestra.jpg
p05N_Orchestra2.jpg
p05N_Conducting.jpg

You will save your presentations as:

Lastname_Firstname_5N_Swing_Origins.pptx
Lastname_Firstname_5N_Orchestra_Album.pptx

In this project, you will modify a presentation about the origins and history of Swing music. Open p05N_Swing_Origins.You will improve the presentation by modifying and formatting the photos and graphics. Change the size and position of the images, where necessary, and adjust the transparency of the background graphic on Slide 5. Change the brightness and contrast, and recolor the images to emphasize the slide content. Where appropriate, add audio to the presentation by inserting the .wav files provided, and adjust how they will play in the presentation. If it is a lengthy audio clip, set it to Play Across Slides. On an appropriate slide, insert a linked video of your choice, or use p05_Music_Video.avi. Include a trigger for the video and set it to Play Full Screen. Save the presentation as **Lastname_Firstname_5N_Swing_Origins**

Insert a Header & Footer on the Notes and Handouts that includes the Date and time Fixed, the Page number, and a Footer with the text **Lastname_Firstname_5N_Swing_Origins** In the Document Properties, add your name and course information and the keywords **Swing, music** Save, and then print Handouts 4 slides per page or submit electronically as directed by your instructor.

In a new blank PowerPoint presentation, using the graphic files provided, create a photo album showing candid photos of one of the orchestras that appeared at a Music Festival sponsored by Cross Oceans Music. Save p05N_Conducting.jpg to use in the title slide.

Select a theme, and then place the photos on the slides with captions. Add frames to the photos and crop unwanted areas of pictures. Insert the image p05N_Conducting.jpg on the title slide. Add an informative title and subtitle. Save the album as **Lastname_Firstname_5N_Orchestra_Album**

Insert a Header & Footer on the Notes and Handouts that includes the Date and time Fixed, the Page number, and a Footer with the text **Lastname_Firstname_5N_Orchestra_Album** In the Document Properties, add your name and course information and the keywords **orchestra, instruments** Save, and then print Handouts 4 slides per page or submit electronically as directed by your instructor.

End **You have completed Project 5N**

Delivering a Presentation

OUTCOMES

At the end of this chapter you will be able to:

OBJECTIVES

Mastering these objectives will enable you to:

PROJECT 6A

Apply slide transitions and custom animation effects.

PROJECT 6B

Insert hyperlinks, create custom slide shows, and view presentations.

Monkey Business Images/Shutterstock

In This Chapter

Microsoft Office PowerPoint provides a wide range of tools that can turn a lackluster presentation into one that captivates the attention of the audience. Recall that SmartArt graphics can be used to add visual effects to text. SmartArt can also be animated. You can apply slide transitions, which are animation effects that occur as slides move from one to another when a slide show is played. Transitions and other animation effects can be applied to all slides or to selected slides. Animation can be applied to individual slides, a slide master, or a custom slide layout.

In addition, you can insert hyperlinks into a presentation to quickly link to a Web page, another slide, or a document. By inserting ready-made action buttons or creating your own action buttons, you can also link to a specific document or action. You may also want to create a custom show composed of selected slides. PowerPoint includes an annotation tool that enables you to write or draw on slides during a presentation.

Penn Liberty Motors has one of eastern Pennsylvania's largest inventories of popular new car brands, sport utility vehicles, hybrid cars, and motorcycles. Their sales, service, and finance staff are all highly trained and knowledgeable about their products, and the company takes pride in its consistently high customer satisfaction ratings. Penn Liberty also offers extensive customization options for all types of vehicles through its accessories division. Custom wheels, bike and ski racks, car covers, and chrome accessories are just a few of the ways Penn Liberty customers make personal statements with their cars.

Project 6A Informational Presentation

myitlab
Project 6A Training

Project Activities

In Activities 6.01 through 6.08, you will add slide transitions and animation effects to a presentation that outlines the organizational structure and location of Penn Liberty Motors. Your completed presentation will look similar to Figure 6.1.

Project Files

For Project 6A, you will need the following files:

p06A_Penn_Liberty.pptx
p06A_Tada.wav

You will save your presentation as:

Lastname_Firstname_6A_Penn_Liberty.pptx

Project Results

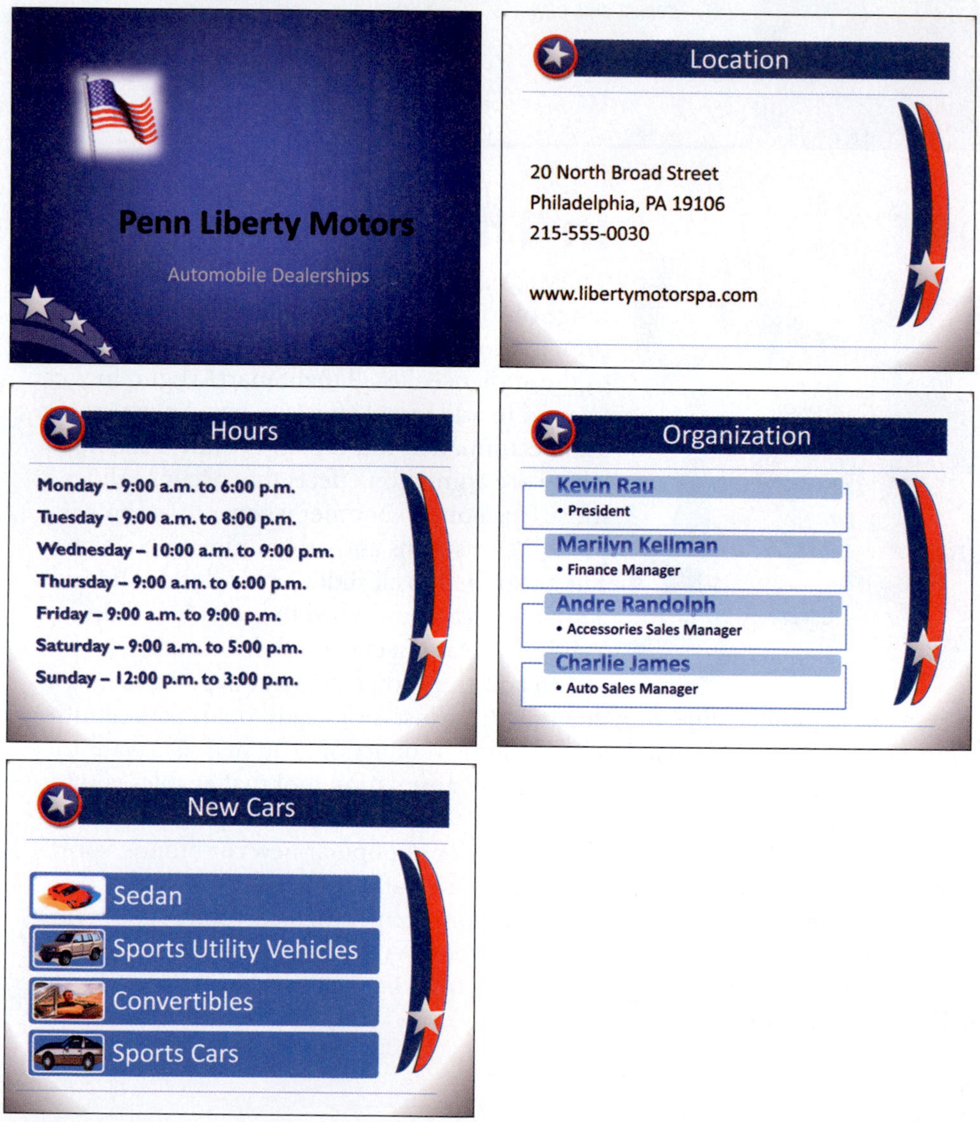

Figure 6.1
Project 6A Penn Liberty

Objective 1 | Apply and Modify Slide Transitions

Transitions are motion effects that occur when a presentation moves from slide to slide in Slide Show view and affect how the content is revealed. When referring to transitions, ***animation*** is any type of motion or movement that occurs as the presentation moves from slide to slide. Different transitions can be applied to selected slides or the same transition can be applied to all slides. Animation is also used in a second context in this chapter, meaning a special visual effect or sound effect that is added to text or an object.

You can modify the transitions by changing the ***transition speed***, which is the timing of the transition between all slides or between the previous slide and the current slide. It is also possible to apply a ***transition sound*** that will play as slides change from one to the next. Transition sounds are prerecorded sounds that can be applied and will play as the transition occurs.

Setting up a slide show also includes determining how you will advance the slide show from one slide to the next. You can set up the presentation to display each slide in response to the viewer clicking the mouse button or pressing the Enter key. You can also design the slide show so that the slides advance automatically after a set amount of time.

Note | Applying Transitions

In this project, you will learn how to apply and modify several kinds of transitions so that you are aware of how they work. When creating a presentation for an audience, however, you do not want to use too many transitions because they can be distracting and may destroy the professional appearance of your slide show. Remember, apply transitions in moderation.

Activity 6.01 | Applying and Modifying Slide Transitions

Slide transitions can be applied to all slides or to specific slides, and different transitions can be applied in one slide show. In this activity, you will modify slide transitions. In this case, modifications include changing the transition speed and sounds to be played during transitions.

1 **Start** PowerPoint. Locate and open the file **p06A_Penn_Liberty**. In the location where you are saving your work, create a new folder named **PowerPoint Chapter 6** and then save the file as **Lastname_Firstname_6A_Penn_Liberty**

2 Make the **title slide** the active slide. Click the **Transitions tab**. In the **Transition to This Slide group**, click the **More** button [icon] to display the **Transitions** gallery, and then compare your screen with Figure 6.2.

The Transitions gallery includes the following types of slide transitions: Subtle, Exciting, and Dynamic Content.

Figure 6.2

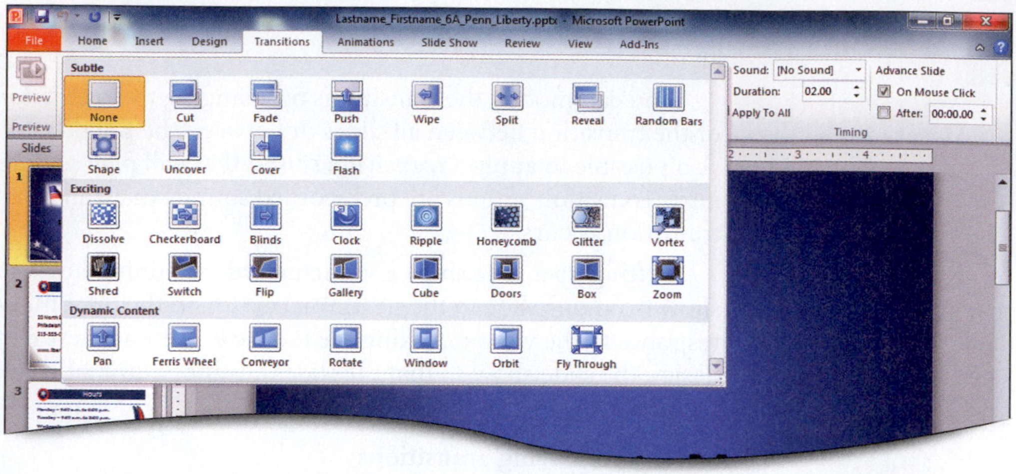

3 Under **Subtle**, point to the fifth selection—**Wipe**. As you point, notice that **Live Preview** displays how the transition will display.

If you were unable to see the transition, move the [pointer icon] pointer away, point to a different selection, and then point again to *Wipe*.

> **Another Way**
>
> To preview a slide transition, in the Slide pane, click the Play Animations icon that displays to the left of the slide thumbnail.

4 Click **Wipe**, and then in the **Timing group**, click the **Apply to All** button. On the **Transitions tab**, in the **Preview group**, click the **Preview** button. Compare your screen with Figure 6.3.

The Wipe transition played on Slide 1. In the Slides/Outline pane, a Play Animations icon displays next to every slide.

Figure 6.3

5 Click the **Slide Show tab**. In the **Start Slide Show group**, click the **From Beginning** button. Press Enter five times to view the entire slide show, and then press Enter or Esc to return to **Normal** view.

Because you selected Apply to All, the transition occurred between each slide.

6 Make **Slide 2** the active slide. Click the **Transitions tab**. In the **Transition to This Slide group**, click the **More** button .

7 In the **Transitions** gallery, under **Exciting**, take a moment to experiment with the different effects by pointing to—but not clicking—various thumbnails. When you are finished experimenting, in the first row, click the fourth column—**Clock**.

By not clicking the Apply to All button, the Clock transition will apply to Slide 2 only.

8 Using the technique you practiced, view the slide show **From Beginning**. When you are finished viewing the slide show, press Enter or Esc to return to **Normal** view.

The Clock transition occurs between Slide 1 and Slide 2. The transition between all the other slides remains set to Wipe.

More Knowledge | Animated GIFs and JPGs

Many images are ***GIF*** (Graphics Interchange Format) or ***JPG*** (Joint Photographic Experts Group, also JPEG) files. GIFs are usually drawings, and JPGs are typically photos. GIF files are smaller in size and display faster than JPGs. Because of this, GIFs are frequently used on Web pages. The image of the waving flag on the title slide is known as an ***animated GIF***. An animated GIF is a file format made up of a series of frames within a single file. Animated GIFs create the illusion of movement by displaying the frames one after the other in quick succession. They can loop endlessly or present one or more sequences of animation and then stop. The animation plays only when the the slide show runs.

9 If necessary, make Slide 2 the active slide. Click the **Transitions tab**. In the **Timing group**, click in the **Duration** box, type **3** press Enter, and then compare your screen with Figure 6.4.

The number of seconds it takes to reveal the slide content is now three seconds, which is longer than the default value of one second.

Figure 6.4

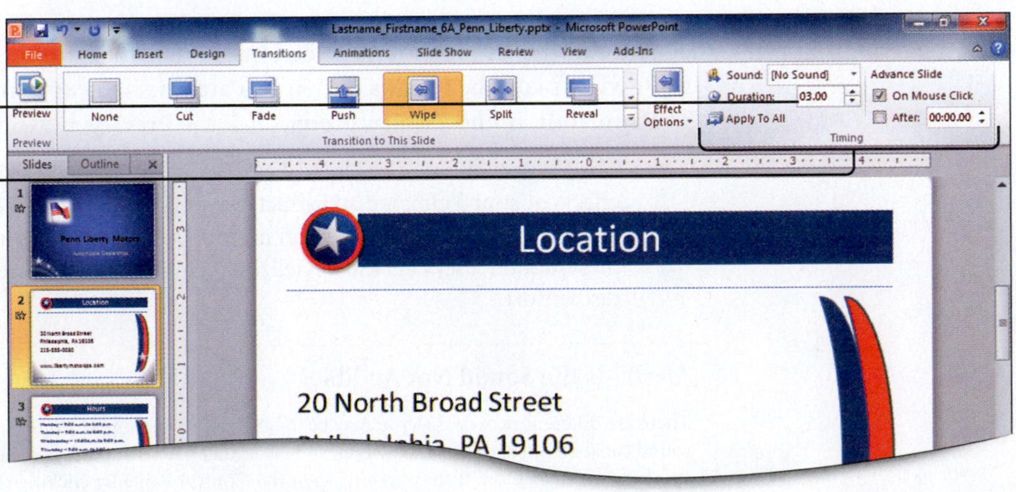

10 In the **Preview group**, click the **Preview** button.

The transition is displayed one time with the new speed setting. Slide 1 is displayed first and then three seconds later, slide 2 appears.

11 Make **Slide 5** the active slide. In the **Timing group**, click the **Duration spin box up arrow** to display **05.00**. On the **Slide Show tab**, in the **Start Slide Show group**, click **From Beginning**. Click or press Enter to view the slides. Click or press Esc when finished.

Notice that when you clicked slide 4 to advance to slide 5, the time delay was five seconds. Choose a speed that best displays the content.

12 If necessary, make **Slide 5** the active slide. On the **Transitions tab**, in the **Timing group**, click the **Sound button arrow**, and then compare your screen with Figure 6.5.

From the displayed list, you can choose from various prerecorded sound effects, choose your own sound effect by clicking Other Sound, or choose [No Sound] to remove a sound effect that was applied.

Figure 6.5

Sound button arrow

Sound selections

13 Point to the various sound selections. Notice that, without clicking the mouse, Live Preview plays the sounds. When you are finished experimenting, click to select **Drum Roll**. In the **Preview group**, click the **Preview** button.

The Drum Roll plays on Slide 4 before Slide 5 is displayed. The overuse of any animation effects or sound effects can distract the audience from the content of the presentation. Keep your audience and your intent in mind. Whereas animations may enhance a light-hearted presentation, they can also trivialize a serious business presentation or cause viewer discomfort.

Alert! | Is the Sound Not Audible?

There are different reasons that you may be unable to hear the sound. For example, your computer may not have sound capability or speakers. If, however, you know that your computer has sound capability, first check that your speakers are turned on. If they are on, open the Control Panel by clicking the Start button, and then clicking Control Panel. In the Control Panel window, click Hardware and Sound. Under Sound, click Adjust system volume. In the Volume Mixer – Speakers dialog box, click the Unmute Speakers button if necessary. If the device is not muted, use the slider to set the volume. The procedure used to adjust sound varies with different operating systems.

14 Make the **title slide** the active slide. On the **Transitions tab**, in the **Timing group**, click the **Sound arrow**, and then from the displayed list, click **Other Sound**.

15 In the displayed **Add Audio** dialog box, navigate to the location where your student files are stored, click **p06A_Tada.wav**, and then click **OK**. View the slide show **From Beginning**. Press Enter or click to advance each slide. Click or press Esc when finished.

The Wipe transition played on all slides except Slide 2. The Clock transition played on Slide 2. Sound occurred on Slides 1 and 5. The timing on Slide 2 was three seconds, and the timing on Slide five was five seconds. Transitions affect how the slide is revealed on the screen.

16 **Save** your changes.

Activity 6.02 | Advancing Slides Automatically

In this activity, you will customize a slide show by changing the Advance Slide method to advance slides automatically after a specified number of seconds.

1 Make **Slide 2** the active slide. Click the **Transitions tab**. In the **Timing group**, under **Advance Slide**, clear the **On Mouse Click** check box.

By clearing the On Mouse Click check box, viewers will no longer need to press Enter or click to advance the slide show. The slide show will advance automatically.

> **Another Way**
>
> To enter the time in the After box, click once in the box to select the current time, type 15, and then press Enter.

2 In the **Timing group**, under **Advance Slide**, click the **After spin box up arrow** to display **00:10.00**. Compare your screen with Figure 6.6.

The time is entered in number of seconds. This automatic switching of slides is only effective if no one is providing an oral presentation along with the slides.

Figure 6.6

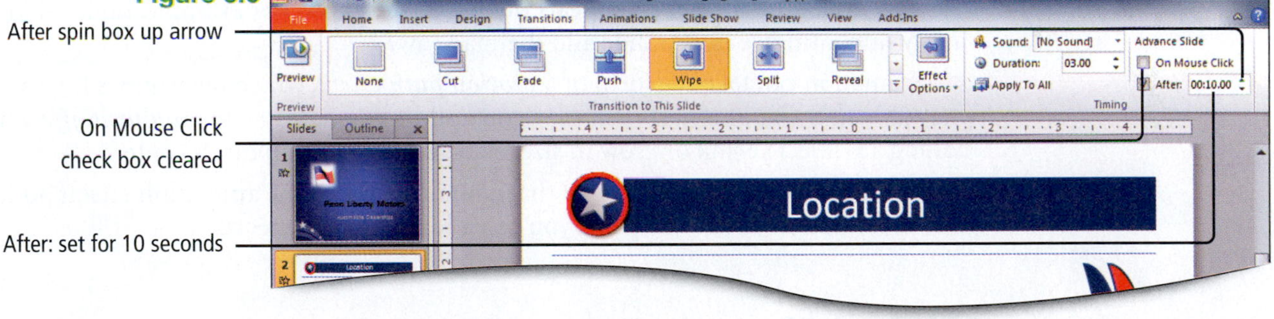

3 On the **Slide Show tab**, in **Start Slide Show group**, click **From Beginning**. Press Enter one time to advance the slide show to Slide 2. Wait 10 seconds for the third slide to display. When **Slide 3** displays, press Esc.

> **Note | Previewing Slides**
>
> Previewing a slide will not advance to the next slide. Play the Slide Show From Beginning or From Current Slide in order to verify the time it takes to display the next slide.

4 Make **Slide 2** the active slide. On the **Transitions tab**, in the **Timing group**, change number in the **After** box to **5**. Compare your screen with Figure 6.7.

If no person is speaking, set the number of seconds to allow people sufficient time to read the content. However, you may need to consider adding time to allow a speaker to make key points.

Figure 6.7

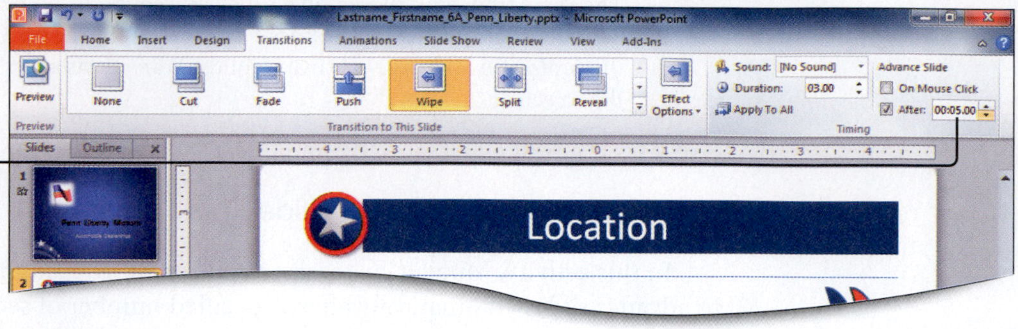

After: timing changed to 5 seconds

5 **Save** your changes.

Objective 2 | Apply Custom Animation Effects

Like other effects that you can customize in PowerPoint, you can customize animation effects. In this context, animation refers to a special visual effect or sound effect added to text or an object. You can add animation to bulleted items, text, or other objects such as charts, graphics, or SmartArt graphics.

Animation can be applied as an ***entrance effect***, which occurs as the text or object is introduced into the slide during a slide show, or as an ***exit effect***, which occurs as the text or object leaves the slide or disappears during a slide show. For example, bulleted items can fly into, or move into, a slide and then fade away.

Animation can take the form of a ***motion path effect***, which determines how and in what direction text or objects will move on a slide. Examples of an ***emphasis effect*** include making an object shrink or grow in size, change color, or spin on its center.

The ***Animation Pane*** is the area that contains a list of the animation effects added to your presentation. From this pane, you can add or modify effects.

Activity 6.03 | Adding Entrance Effects

In this activity, you will add entrance effects to text and objects by making them move in a specific manner as the text or graphic enters the slide.

1 Make **Slide 3** the active slide, and then click to select the body text placeholder. Click the **Animations tab**. In the **Advanced Animation group**, click the **Add Animation** button, and then compare your screen with Figure 6.8. Scroll the list to see all of the animation effects. Refer to Figure 6.9 for more information.

There are four groups of animations—Entrance, Emphasis, Exit, and Motion Paths. You have to scroll the list to see the Motion Paths animations.

Figure 6.8

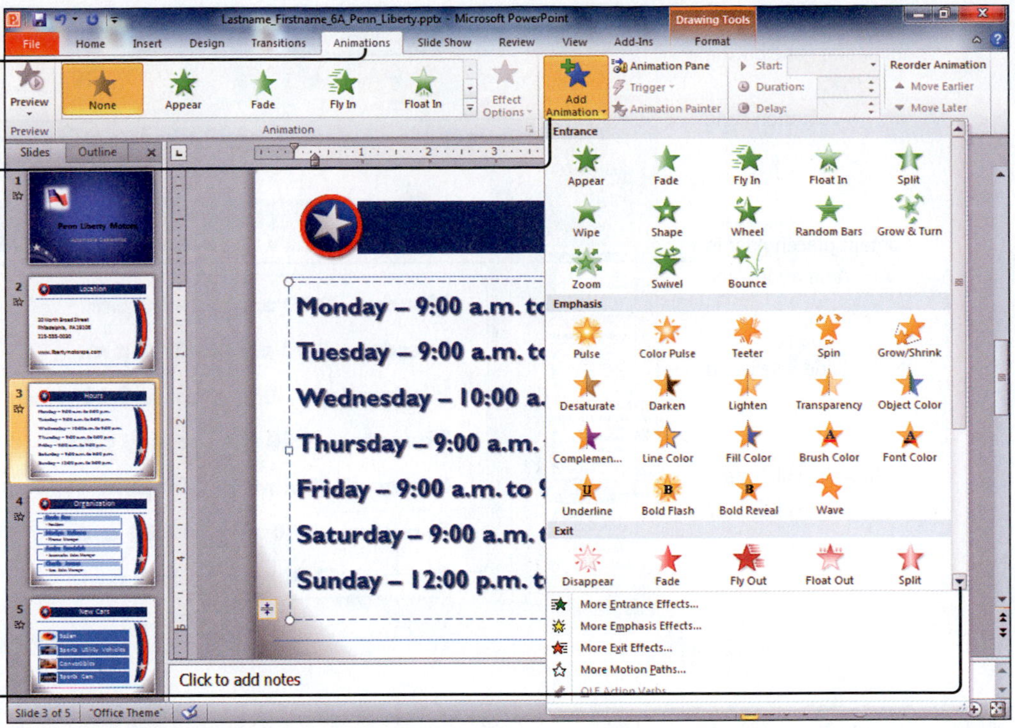

Animation Effects

Animation Effects	Examples
Entrance	Fade gradually into focus, fly onto the slide from an edge, or bounce into view.
Emphasis	Shrink or grow in size, change color, or spin on its center.
Exit	Fly off the slide, disappear from view, or spiral off the slide.
Motion Paths	Move up or down, left or right, or in a star or circular pattern.

Figure 6.9

2 From the displayed list, under **Entrance**, point to **Fade**—but do not click—and watch the Live Preview. Experiment with some of the other Entrance effects, and then click **Fade**.

Clicking Fade sets the text on the slide to display the various bulleted items one after the other, in order from top to bottom. Choose an animation that enhances the content of the slide.

3 In the **Advanced Animation group**, click the **Animation Pane** button, and then compare your screen with Figure 6.10.

The Animation Pane displays with the results of the animation you applied on Slide 3. In this case, the Animation Pane displays with the effect applied to the content placeholder selected. Each item on the slide content placeholder displays with a number next to it to indicate the order in which the items will display.

Figure 6.10

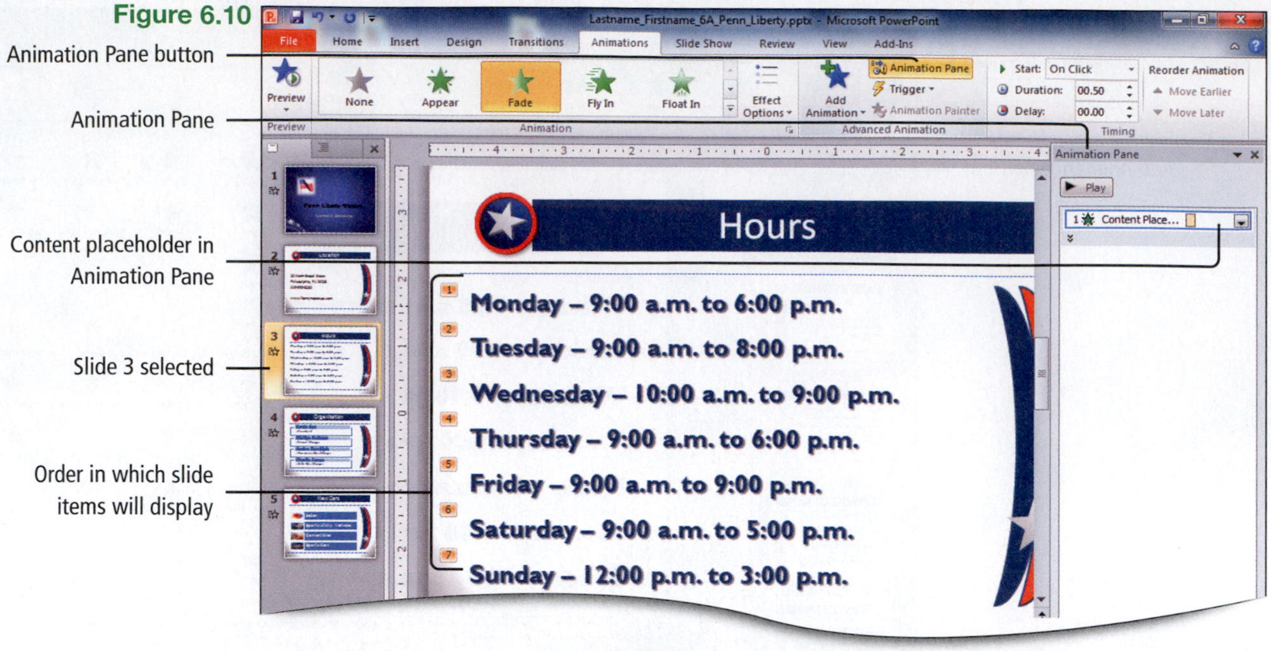

Alert! | **Do You Have Extra Items Displayed in the Animation Pane?**

If you clicked on an effect instead of pointing at it, you will have an extra item in the Animation Pane. Click the unwanted item in the Animation Pane, and then click the arrow and select Remove. If the item arrow does not display, click the correct placeholder on the slide or the item in the Animation Pane to make the item active.

Another Way

To remove an effect in the Animation Pane, right-click the effect to display the options, and then select Remove. You can also just click on the effect and press the Delete key.

4 In the **Animation Pane**, below *Content Placeholder*, point to the expand chevron to display the ScreenTip *Click to expand contents*. Compare your screen with Figure 6.11.

The ***chevron*** is a V-shaped pattern that indicates more information or options are available.

Figure 6.11

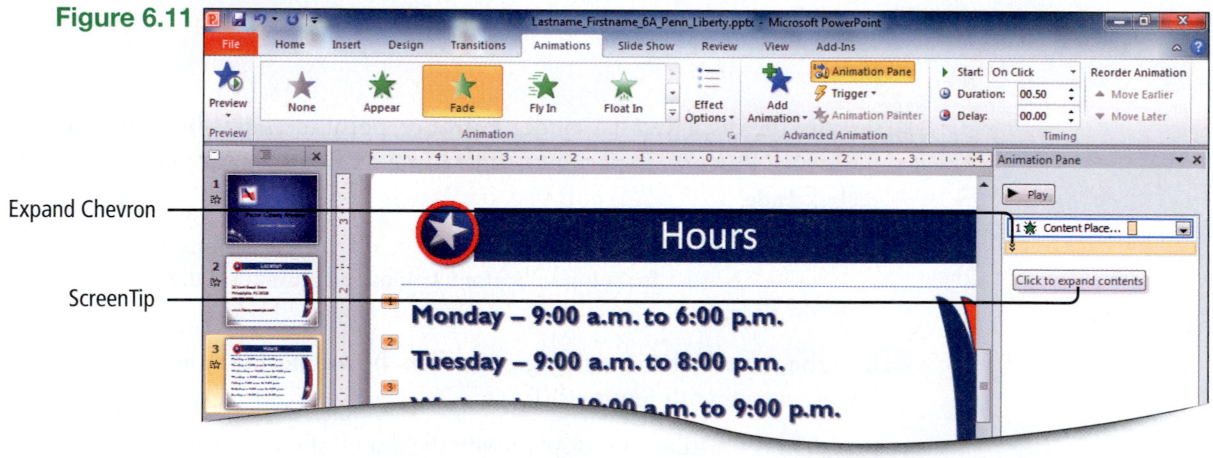

5 Click the chevron one time to expand the contents, and then compare your screen with Figure 6.12.

The numbers to the left of the items on the slide correspond with the numbers of the items in the Animation Pane.

Figure 6.12

Numbers in Animation Pane

Contents expanded

Corresponding numbers on slide

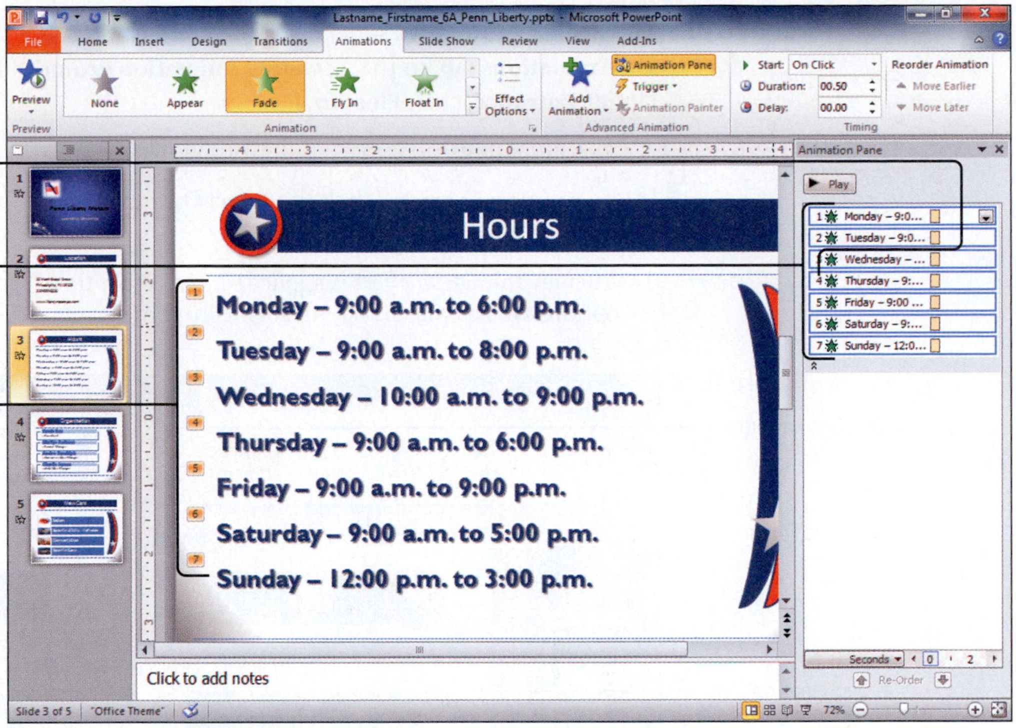

6 Right-click the entrance effect for the content placeholder, and then if necessary, click Show Advanced Timeline. In the **Animation Pane**, click the **Play** button to test the animation.

At the bottom right side of the Animation Pane, a ***timeline*** displays the number of seconds the animation takes to complete.

> **Alert! | Did the Timeline Display?**
>
> If you cannot see the timeline at the bottom of the Animation Pane, right-click the entrance effect for the content placeholder, and then click Show Advanced Timeline. If the timeline is visible, the option is displayed as Hide Advanced Timeline.

7 Click the hide chevron to hide the contents. Under the **Play** button, point to *Content Place …*, read the ScreenTip, *On Click Fade: Content Placeholder …*, and then compare your screen with Figure 6.13.

The ScreenTip identifies the start setting, which is On Click, and the Effect, which is Fade.

Figure 6.13

Screen Tip showing Fade animation and On Click

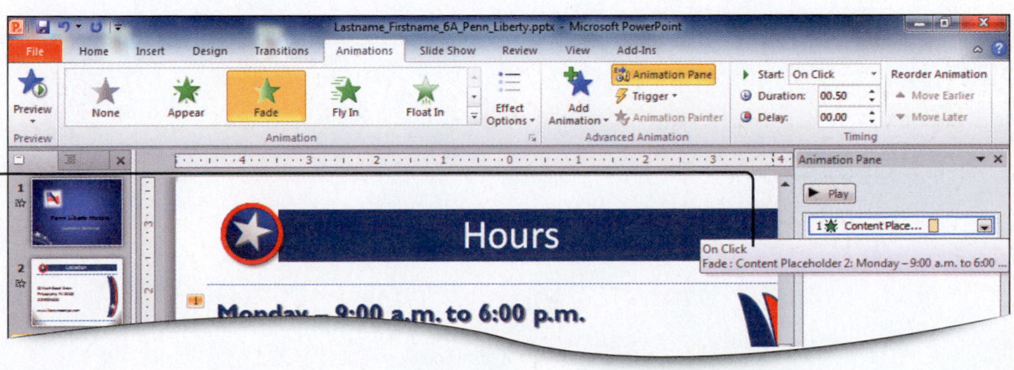

8 Make **Slide 5** the active slide. Click the content placeholder containing the cars. On the **Animations tab**, in the **Advanced Animation group**, click **Add Animation** button. Under **Entrance**, click **Float In**.

The animations tab is inactive until a slide element is selected.

9 In the **Animation group**, click the **Effect Options** button, and then compare your screen with Figure 6.14.

After an animation effect is applied, the Effect Options becomes active. The Sequence options are As One Object, All at Once, or One by One.

Figure 6.14

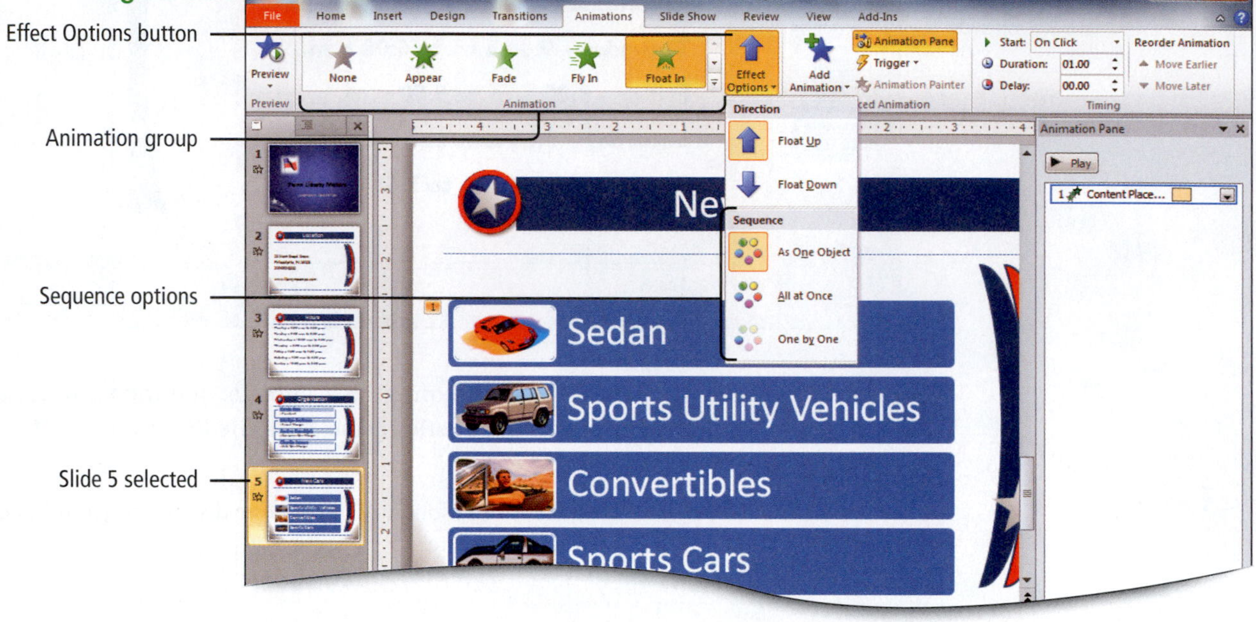

10 Under **Sequence**, click **One by One**. In the **Preview group**, click the **Preview** button.

Clicking One by One sets the shapes in the SmartArt graphic on Slide 5 as individual objects that display one at a time.

11 Make the **title slide** the active slide, and then click to select the title placeholder—*Penn Liberty Motors*. In the **Advanced Animation group**, click the **Add Animation** button, and then click **More Entrance Effects**. In the **Add Entrance Effect** dialog box, under **Moderate**, scroll the list, click **Rise Up**, and then compare your screen with Figure 6.15.

The Add Entrance Effect dialog box provides additional effects.

Figure 6.15

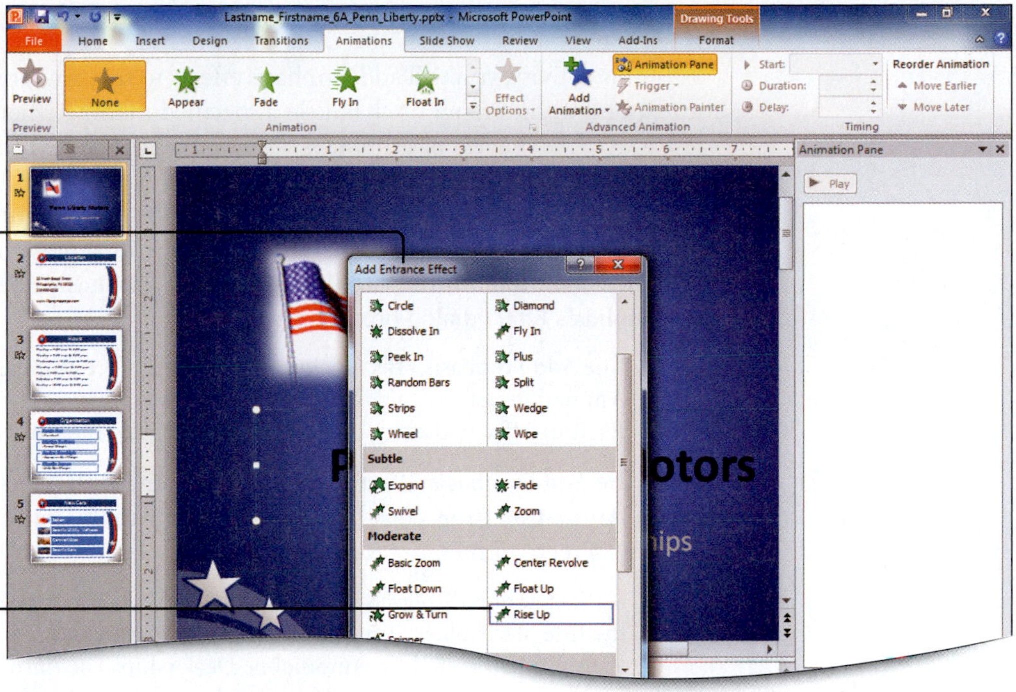

12 Click **OK**.

13 Click the subtitle placeholder. In the **Advanced Animation group**, click the **Add Animation** button, and then click **More Entrance Effects**. In the **Add Entrance Effect** dialog box, under **Moderate**, scroll the list, if necessary, and then click **Rise Up**. Click **OK**. Compare your screen with Figure 6.16. In the **Animation Pane**, click the **Play** button to test the animation.

The entrance effect for Slide 1 displays in the Animation Pane. The number 1 corresponds with the title placeholder. The number 2 corresponds with the subtitle placeholder. The numbers that appear on the slide in Normal view do not appear when you play the presentation.

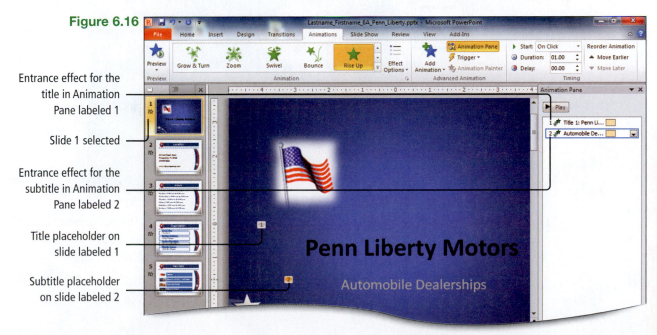

Figure 6.16

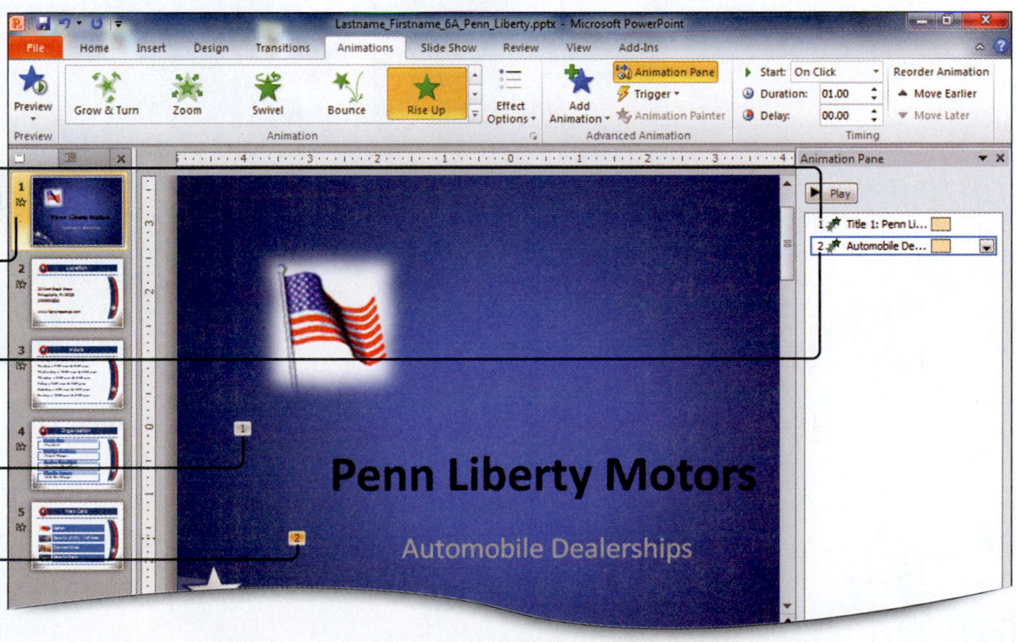

14 **Save** your changes.

Activity 6.04 | Adding Emphasis Effects

In this activity, you will add emphasis effects to text and graphics. These effects make the text or graphics move or change in a specified manner when you click the mouse or press Enter while the text or graphic is displayed on the slide. You will also reorder the effects.

1 With the **title slide** as the active slide, click to select the title placeholder—*Penn Liberty Motors*. On the **Animations tab**, in the **Advanced Animation group**, click the **Add Animation** button, and then click **More Emphasis Effects** to display the **Add Emphasis Effect** dialog box.

The Add Emphasis Effect dialog box includes more emphasis effects than the Add Animations gallery and organizes them into groups—Basic, Subtle, Moderate, and Exciting effects. Use this dialog box if you do not find the effect you want in the gallery.

2 In the **Add Emphasis Effect** dialog box. Under **Subtle**, click **Pulse**, and then click **OK**. In the **Animation Pane**, click the **Play** button to see the Pulse effect on the title. Compare your screen with Figure 6.17.

A third item is displayed in the Animation Pane. The first one is for the entrance effect for the title placeholder, Penn Liberty Motors. The second one is for the entrance effect for the subtitle placeholder, Automobile Dealership. The third one is for the emphasis effect for the title. The Pulse effect for the title is set to occur when the presenter clicks the mouse button. To make an item in the Animation Pane active, click the item or click on the placeholder on the slide. Notice that the numbers to the left of the title and subtitle on the slide correspond with the numbers for the effects in the Animation Pane.

Figure 6.17

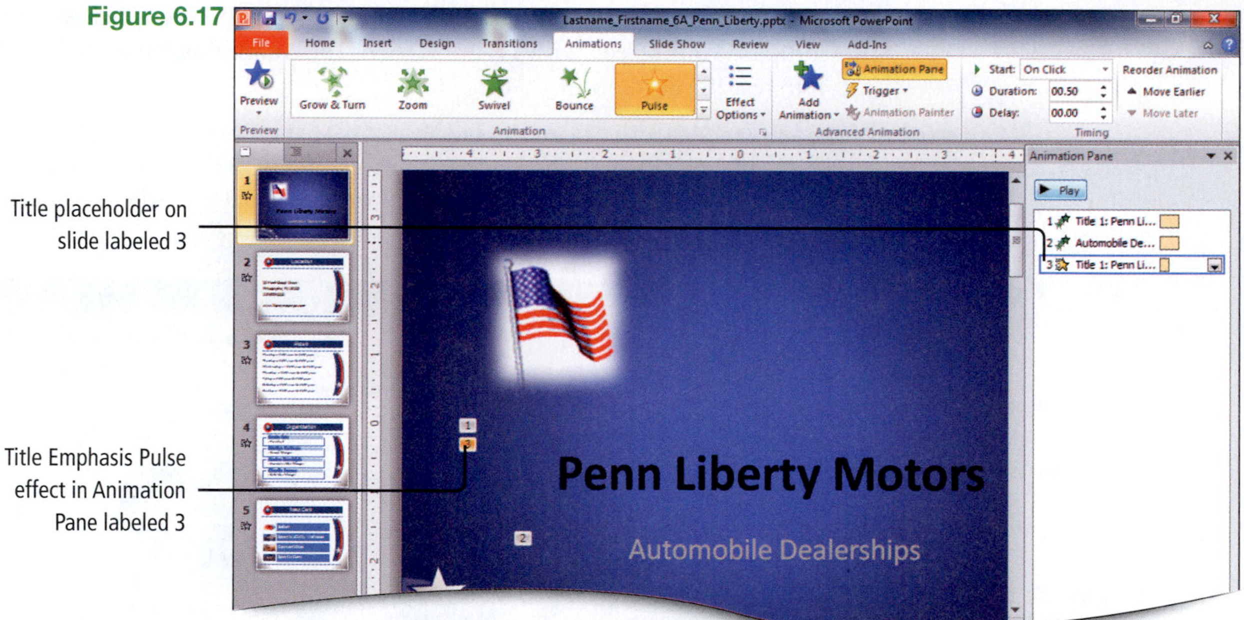

3 On the **Slide Show tab**, in the **Start Slide Show group**, click **From Current Slide**. Click to see the title entrance effect, click to see the subtitle entrance effect, and then click to see the title emphasis effect. Press Esc.

The sound effect played, the title moved up, the subtitle moved up, and then the title displayed the Pulse emphasis.

4 In the **Animation Pane**, click the third effect, the emphasis effect for the title—*3 Title1: Penn Li....* At the bottom of the **Animation Pane**, to the left of *Re-Order*, click the **move up arrow**. Compare your screen with Figure 6.18

Figure 6.18

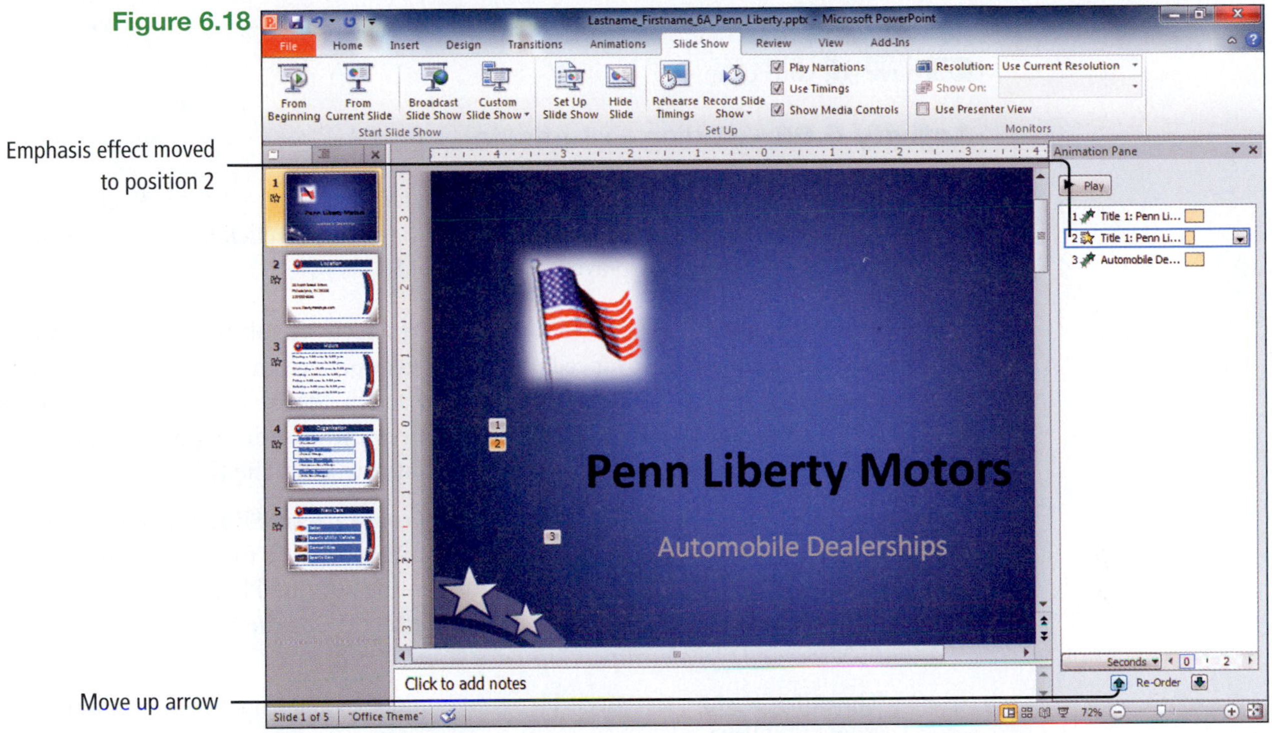

5 In the **Animation Pane**, click the **Play** button.

The order that the effects play is changed. The title moved up and displayed with the Pulse emphasis, and then the subtitle displayed. The sound effect does not play in the preview.

6 Make **Slide 4** the active slide, and then click to select the title placeholder—*Organization*. Using the technique you practiced, display the **Add Emphasis Effect** dialog box. Under **Subtle**, click **Bold Flash**, and then click **OK**. In the **Animation Pane**, point to the animation to display the ScreenTip—*On Click Bold Flash: Title 1: Organization*. Compare your screen with Figure 6.19.

Figure 6.19

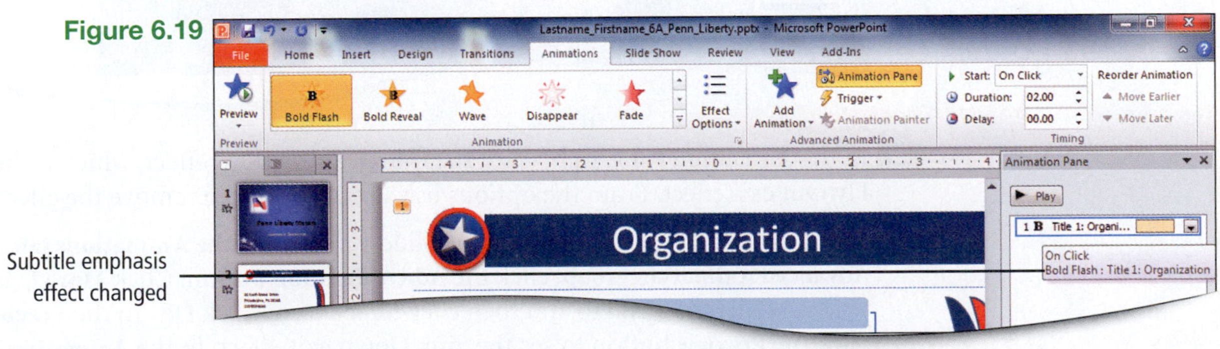

7 On the **Slide Show tab**, in the **Start Slide Show group**, click **From Current Slide**. Click to test the title emphasis effect. Click again to display Slide 5. When it appears, press Esc.

The title is displayed immediately. After the mouse click, the title blinks once and then returns to normal.

> **Alert!** | **Did the Title Blink More Than Once?**
>
> If the title blinked again on the second mouse click instead of advancing to Slide 5, you have applied the blink emphasis effect more than once. In the Animation Pane, right-click the extra effect, and then select Remove. Test the animation again.

8 **Save** your changes.

Activity 6.05 | Adding Exit Effects

In this activity, you will add exit effects to text and graphics. These effects make the text or graphics move or change in a specified manner when you click the mouse or press Enter while the text or graphic is displayed on the slide.

1 With the **title slide** as the active slide, click to select the subtitle placeholder. On the **Animations tab**, in the **Advanced Animation group**, click the **Add Animation** button. From the displayed list, under **Exit**, scroll to see the entire list. Point to—but do not click—**Disappear**, and then watch the Live Preview. Continue pointing at several of the effects. When you are finished, in the first row, click the third effect—**Fly Out**.

2 On the **Slide Show tab**, view the slide show **From Current Slide**. Click to display the title Rise Up entrance effect. Continue clicking to see the title Pulse emphasis effect, the subtitle Rise Up entrance effect, and then the subtitle Fly Out exit effect. Press Esc. In the **Animation Pane**, point to the fourth effect to see the ScreenTip *On Click Fly Out: Automobile Dealerships*. Compare your screen with Figure 6.20.

The order in which the effects play is determined by the sequence shown in the Animation Pane.

Figure 6.20

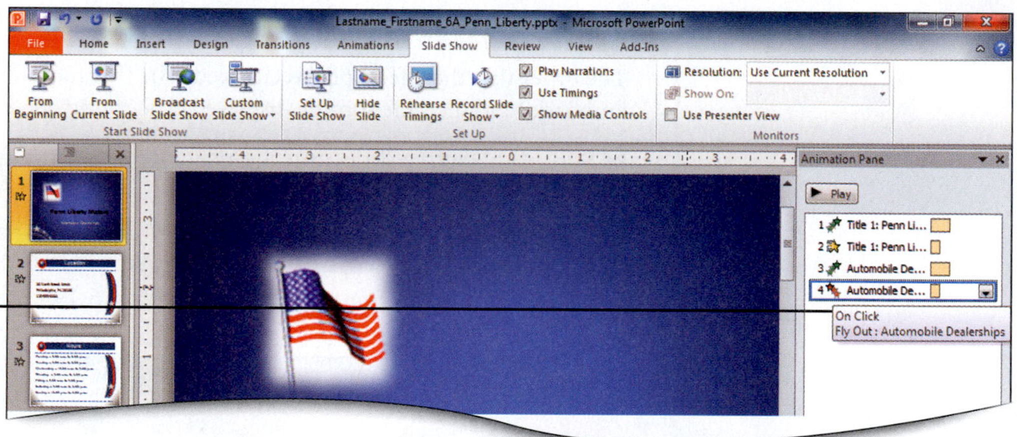

3 In the **Animation Pane**, right-click the fourth animations effect, which is the subtitle Fly Out exit effect. From the options list, select **Remove** to remove the effect.

4 Select the subtitle placeholder on the Slide 1 again. On the **Animations tab**, in the **Advanced Animation group**, click the **Add Animation** button. Click **More Exit Effects**. Under **Moderate**, scroll to and then click **Sink Down**. Click **OK**. In the **Preview group**, click the **Preview** button to see the Sink Down exit effect. In the **Animation Pane**, point to the fourth effect to see the ScreenTip—*On Click Sink Down: Automobile Dealerships*. Compare your screen with Figure 6.21.

In the Animation Pane, the entrance effect for the title is marked with a green star, the emphasis effect for the title is marked with a gold star, the entrance effect for the subtitle is marked with a green star, and the exit effect for the subtitle is marked with a red star. The stars are displayed with different actions to help define the pattern selected. The ScreenTip clarifies what specific effect was applied.

Figure 6.21

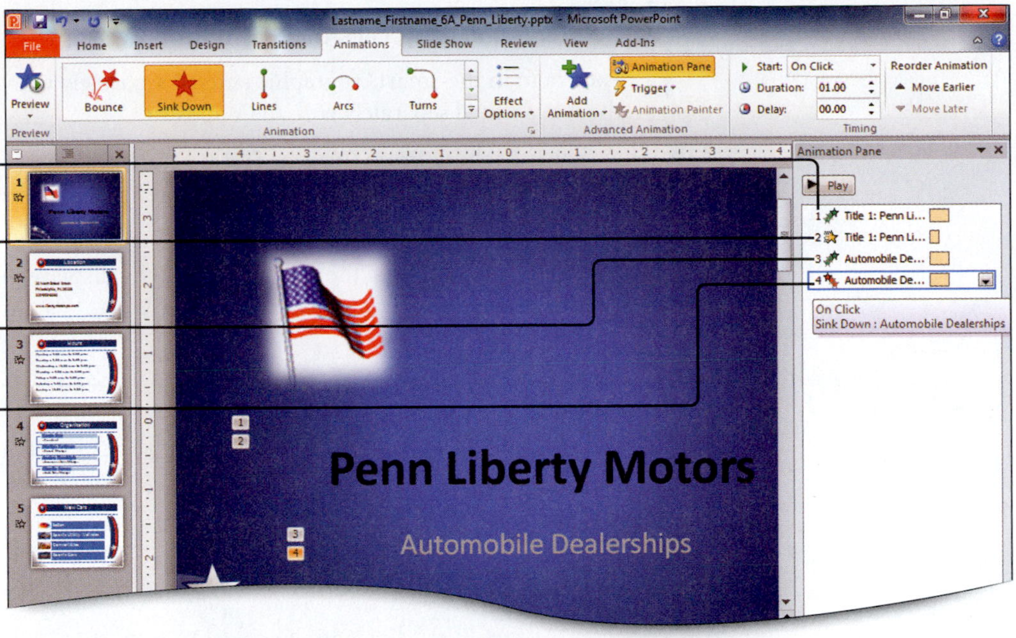

5 View the slide show **From Current Slide**. Click four times to activate the title entrance, the title emphasis, the subtitle entrance, and the subtitle exit effects. When Slide 2 displays, press Esc.

Slide 1 is displayed with the sound effect. With each click, the title enters in an upward direction, the title blinks, the subtitle enters, and finally the subtitle exits.

6 With **Slide 5** as the active slide, click the content placeholder to select the **SmartArt** graphic. On the **Animations tab**, in the **Advanced Animation group**, click the **Add Animation** button, and then click **More Exit Effects**. Under **Basic**, click **Wipe**, and then click **OK**. Compare your screen with Figure 6.22.

The first effect in the Animation Pane identifies the entrance effect for the SmartArt. Because there are four items in the SmartArt, the items are numbered 1 through 4 on the slide. The second effect in the Animation Pane identifies the exit effect for the SmartArt. The corresponding numbers on the slide are 5 through 8.

Figure 6.22

7 In the **Animation pane**, click the **Play** button to see the entrance and exit effects.

Each item in the SmartArt graphic entered separately with the Float In entrance, and then the items exited separately with the Wipe exit.

8 View the slide show **From Current Slide**. After the sound effect, click four times to see the cars enter, and then click four more times to see them exit. Click two more times to return to Normal view.

Because you are viewing the slide as it would be displayed in a slide show, you needed to click or press Enter in order to see the results.

9 **Save** your changes.

> **Note | Selecting Effects**
>
> Entrance, emphasis, exit, and motion effects may be selected from the Add Animation gallery or from the Add Effect dialog boxes. The Add Effect dialog box specific to each type of effect contains additional effects, which are categorized as Basic, Subtle, Moderate, and Exciting.

Activity 6.06 | Adding Motion Paths

Motion paths can also be applied to graphics. Built-in motion paths enable you to make text or a graphic move in a particular pattern, or you can design your own pattern of movement.

1 Make **Slide 2** the active slide. Click to select the title placeholder—*Location*. On the **Animations tab**, in the **Advanced Animation group**, click the **Add Animation** button, and then click **More Motion Paths**. In the **Add Motion Path** dialog box, scroll down, and then under **Lines & Curves**, click **Right**. Compare your screen with Figure 6.23.

Figure 6.23

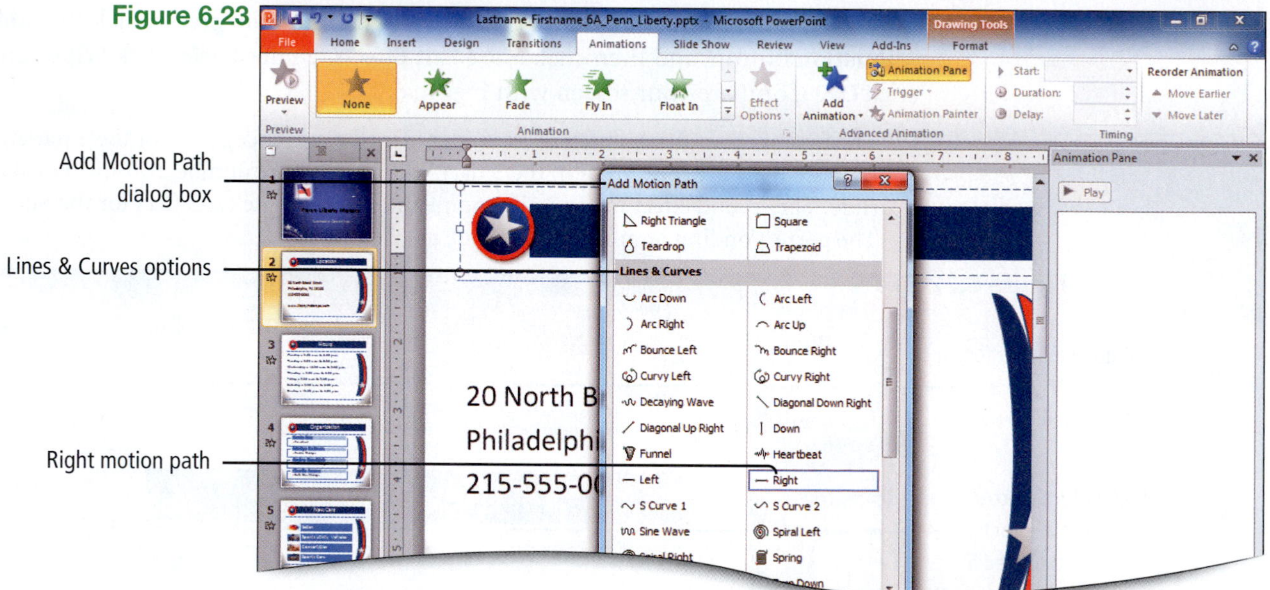

2 Click **OK**. View the slide show **From Current Slide**. Wait for the title to move to the right. When Slide 3 displays, press Esc.

The transition on Slide 2 displayed first, and then the title moved to the right. Use motion paths very sparingly. They can be very distracting, and the audience may watch the path of the text or graphic instead of listening to the presenter.

3 Make **Slide 2** the active slide. In the **Animation Pane**, click the motion path effect. Compare your screen with Figure 6.24.

The ScreenTip displays *On Click Right: Title 1: Location*. On the slide, the title placeholder displays a motion path graphic showing the direction of the movement.

Figure 6.24

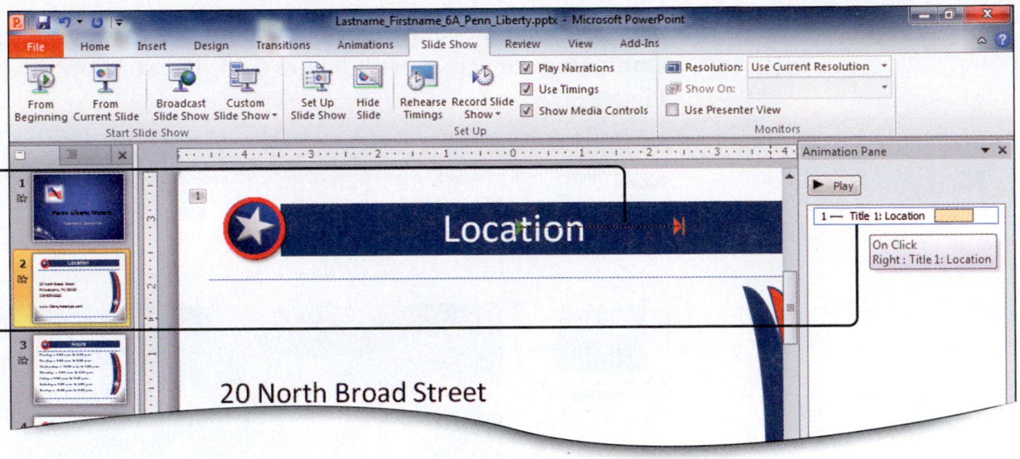

Direction of motion displayed on slide title

Title Motion Path effect on Slide 2

4 **Save** your changes.

Objective 3 | Modify Animation Effects

Entrance, emphasis, and exit effects as well as motion paths can be modified or customized by changing how they start, the speed at which they occur, and their direction. Effect settings such as timing delays and the number of times an effect is repeated can also be added. Effects can be set to start after a previous effect or simultaneously.

On Click allows you to start the animation effect when you click the slide or a trigger on the slide. On Click also allows you to display animation such as a motion path because the animation is triggered by the mouse click or, in some instances, by pressing Enter. Changing an animation start method to ***After Previous*** allows the animation effect to start immediately after the previous effect in the list finishes playing. Changing the start method to ***With Previous*** starts the animation effect at the same time as the previous effect in the list.

Activity 6.07 | Modifying Animation Effects

In this activity, you will modify the start method of some of the animation effects you added. You will also modify their speed and timing.

1 Click the **Slide Show tab**. In the **Start Slide Show group**, click **From Beginning**. Return to **Normal** view when finished.

On the title slide, you had to click for the title to enter, click for the title to blink, click for the subtitle to enter, and then click for the subtitle to exit. After clicking Slide 1, Slide 2 displayed after three seconds. Slide 3 advanced automatically after 5 seconds. On Slide 3, the hours of each day of the week displayed one by one as you clicked the mouse or pressed Enter. On Slide 4, the title effect occurred when you clicked the mouse. On Slide 5, each type of vehicle displayed with separate mouse clicks, and each one exited with separate mouse clicks.

Another Way

If animation has been applied to a placeholder or to an object such as a picture or graphic, you can select the object or placeholder by clicking the small number that displays on the slide. This number corresponds with the list of objects in the Animation Pane.

2 In **Normal** view, make the **title slide** the active slide, and then click to select the subtitle placeholder.

The title slide subtitle is displayed with two numbers. Number 3 represents the entrance effect, and number 4 represents the exit effect. Numbers 1 and 2 are for the title placeholder.

3 In the **Animation Pane**, right-click the subtitle exit effect, the fourth effect in the list. Compare your screen with Figure 6.25. The start options are defined in the table in Figure 6.26.

Figure 6.25

Start Options	
Screen Element	**Description**
Start On Click	Animation begins when the slide is clicked. Displays with a mouse icon in the option list.
Start With Previous	Animation begins at the same time as the previous effect. One click executes all animation effects applied to the object. Displays with no icon in the option list.
Start After Previous	Animation begins after the previous effect in the list finishes. No additional click is needed. One click executes all animation effects applied to the object. Displays with a clock icon in the option list.

Figure 6.26

Another Way

To select a start method, on the Animations tab, in the Timing group, click the Start arrow, and then select the method.

4 Click **Start After Previous**. View the slide show **From Current Slide**. Click three times to display the title entrance, the title emphasis, and then the subtitle entrance and effects. Press Esc.

By changing On Click to After Previous, it was not necessary to click the mouse to initiate the subtitle entrance and exit effects. On the Animations tab, in the Timing group, the Start box now displays After Previous. Both the emphasis effect and exit effect applied to the subtitle displayed automatically. Notice that numbers 3 and 4 disappeared from the exit effect in the Animation Pane.

5 Make **Slide 3** the active slide. In the **Animation Pane**, right-click the entrance effect for the content placeholder, and then click **Effect Options**. In the **Fade** dialog box, click the **Timing tab**, and then click the **Start arrow**. Click **After Previous**.

6 Click the **Duration arrow**, and then select **1 seconds (Fast)**. Compare your screen with Figure 6.27.

The Fade dialog box is a context-sensitive dialog box for the entrance effect applied to the title. The name of the dialog box reflects which effect you are modifying. In this dialog box, you can modify more than one setting.

Figure 6.27

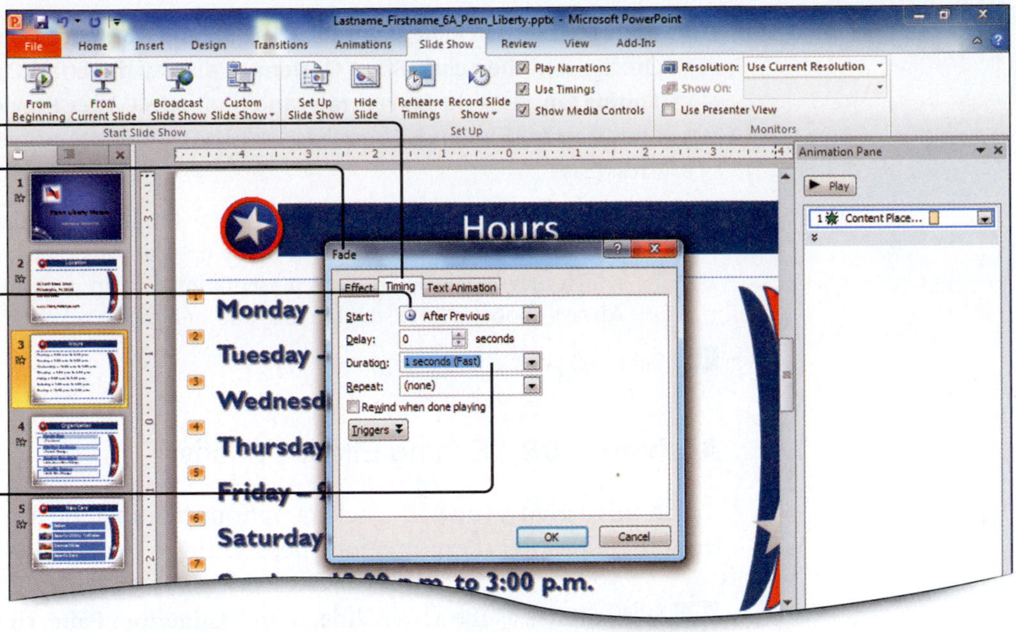

7 Click **OK**. On the **Slide Show tab**, in the **Start Slide Show group**, view the slide show **From Current Slide**. After the last day displays, press Esc.

Each day displayed automatically without any mouse clicks.

8 Make **Slide 2** the active slide, and then click to select the body text placeholder. On the **Animations tab**, click the **Add Animation** button, and then click **More Entrance Effects**. Under **Basic**, click **Fly In**, and then click **OK**. View the slide show **From Current Slide**. When **Slide 3** displays, press Esc to return to **Normal** view.

The title is displayed and then moved to the right. The items in the content placeholder fly in from the bottom one after the other. No mouse clicks were required.

9 Make **Slide 5** the active slide. In the **Animation Pane**, click the **Play** button, and then view the slide show **From Current Slide**. Press Esc.

The Play button displays all animations associated with the slide, in Normal view, regardless of how the animation is set to start. However, the From Beginning or From Current Slide button plays all animations applied to the slide in Slide Show view, and it displays them the way they will display in a slide show. If you are testing the effects with the Slide Show button and the animation is set to start On Click, you must click the mouse or press Enter to begin the animation.

10 In the **Animation Pane**, right-click the entrance effect for the SmartArt—the first effect. Click **Effect Options** to display the **Float Up** dialog box. On the **Timing tab**, click the **Start arrow**, and then select **After Previous**. Change the **Duration** to **.5 seconds (Very Fast)**. Click **OK**. View the slide show **From Current Slide**. Press Esc to return to **Normal** view.

The SmartArt items entered without mouse clicks. To view the exit effect, you had to click the mouse for each one. The Duration speed for the entrance effect was .5 seconds, which may be a little fast for a presentation, but appropriate for you to see the effect. Always choose a time suitable for your audience.

11 In the **Animation Pane**, right-click the second **Content Placeholder arrow**—the exit effect—and then click **Effect Options** to display the **Effect Options** dialog box. On the **Timing tab**, click the **Start arrow**, and then select **After Previous**. If necessary, change the Duration to .5 seconds (Very Fast). Click **OK**. View the slide show **From Current Slide**. Press Esc.

The SmartArt items entered and exited without mouse clicks. Notice that the pictures entered and exited separately from the descriptions. The Duration speed was .5 seconds, which may be a little fast for a presentation, but appropriate for you to see the effect. Always choose a time suitable for your audience.

12 **Save** your changes.

Activity 6.08 | Setting Effect Options

In this activity, you will set effect options that include having an animation disappear from the slide after the animation effect, setting a time delay, and animating text.

1 With **Slide 2** as the active slide, in the **Animation Pane**, right-click the second effect, the entrance effect for the content placeholder, and then click **Effect Options** to display the **Fly In** dialog box.

The Fly In dialog box has three tabs—Effect, Timing, and Text Animation. On the Effect tab, you can change the Settings and the Enhancements. You can change the direction of the Fly In, add sound, and change the way text is animated.

2 On the **Effect tab**, under **Settings**, click the **Direction arrow**, and then click **From Left**.

3 Under **Enhancements**, click the **After animation arrow**. Compare your screen with Figure 6.28.

You can apply a color change to the animated text or object. You can also automatically hide the animated object after the animation takes place or hide the animated object on the next mouse click. Don't Dim is selected by default.

Figure 6.28

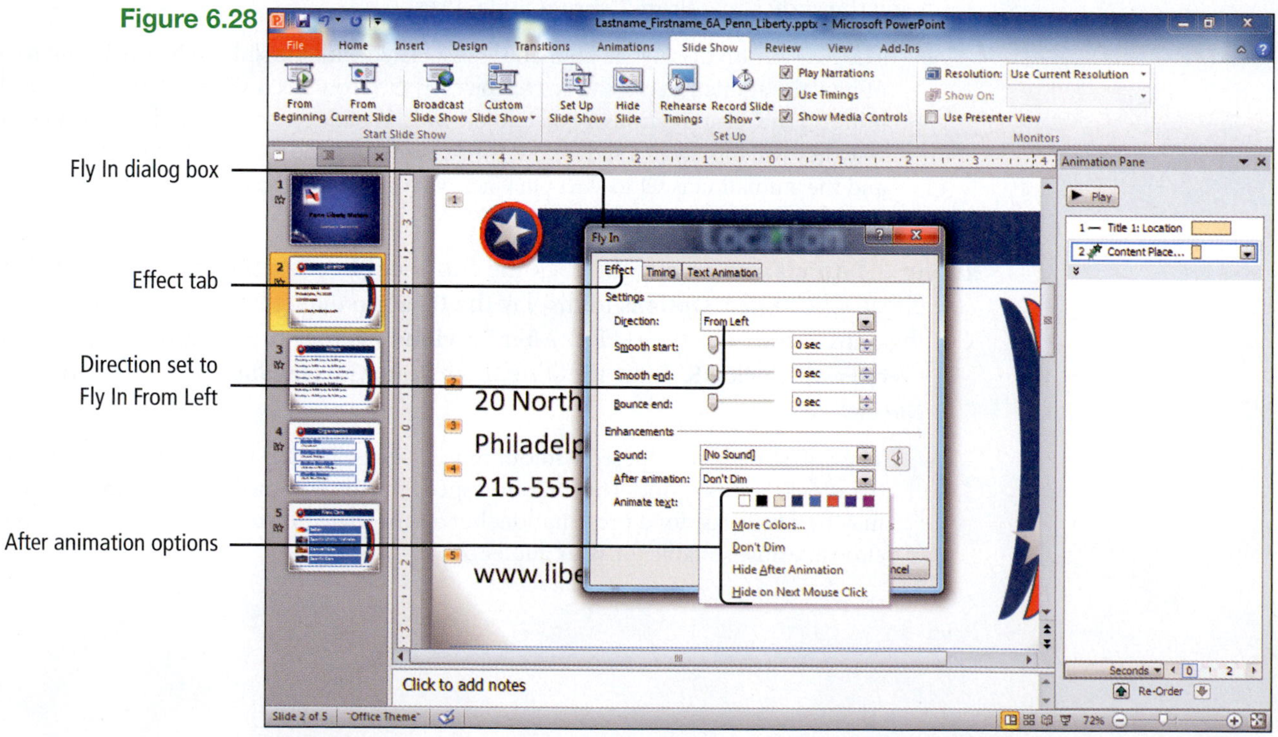

4 In the row of colors, click the second color—**Black**. Click **OK**. On the **Slide Show tab**, in the **Start Slide Show group**, view the slide show **From Current Slide**. When Slide 3 displays, press Esc.

The animation changes display automatically one at a time.

5 With **Slide 2** selected, in the **Animation Pane**, right-click the effect for the content placeholder, and then click **Effect Options**. In the **Fly In** dialog box, click the **Timing tab**. Click the **Duration arrow**, and then click **2 seconds (Medium)**. Compare your screen with Figure 6.29.

By using the Timing tab, you can change how the animation will start. You can also set a delay, in seconds, from when the slide displays until the text displays. You can select the speed and how many times you would like the animation to repeat. Selecting the *Rewind when done playing* check box will cause the animated text or object to disappear from the slide after the animation is completed, as opposed to remaining on the slide. From this tab you can also set a ***trigger***, which is a portion of text, a graphic, or a picture that, when clicked, produces a result. Recall that in the previous chapter you practiced inserting sounds into slides and selecting a placeholder or object that would start the sound when clicked. Triggers are created for animation purposes using the same technique.

Figure 6.29

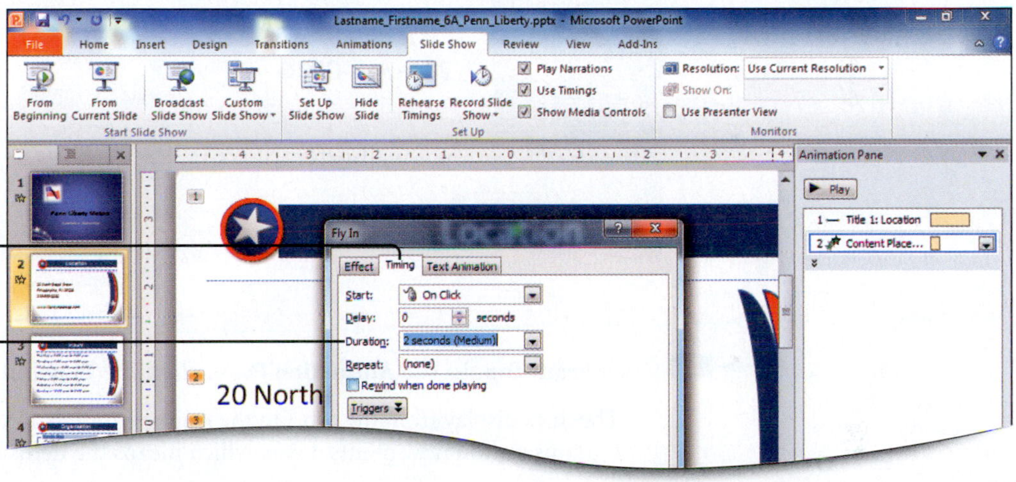

> **Note | Repeating an Animated List of Items**
>
> In the Fly In dialog box, on the Timing tab, if you elect to repeat a list of items that have animation applied to them, typing a number in the Repeat box will cause each line of text or each bulleted item to repeat before the next item displays. Repeating a list of two or three bulleted items might be used in a presentation as a special effect to emphasize the points but may produce unexpected and unwanted results, so be very cautious about using this option.

6 In the **Fly In** dialog box, click the **Text Animation tab**. Click the **Group text arrow**.

You can treat a list as one object and animate all paragraphs of text simultaneously. If your bulleted list has several levels of bulleted items, you can select how you want to animate the items. Use the Text Animation tab to set a delay in seconds, animate an attached shape, or reverse the order of the items.

7 If necessary, click By 1st Level Paragraphs, and then click **OK**.

Another Way

To set the direction and sequence of bullet points, use the Effect Options button in the Animation group.

8 With **Slide 2** active, click the content placeholder. On the **Animations tab**, in the **Animation group**, click the **Effect Options** button, and then compare your screen with Figure 6.30.

Figure 6.30

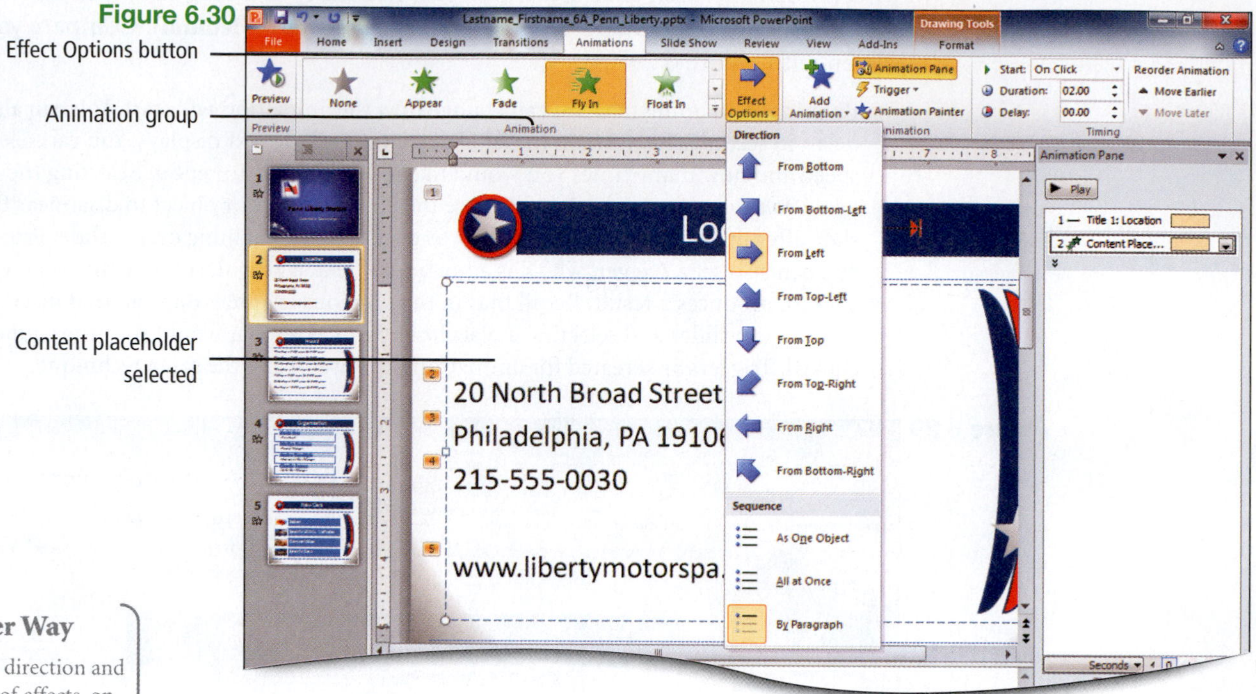

Another Way

To set the direction and sequence of effects, on the Animations tab, in the Animation group, click the Effect Options button, and then make your selection.

9 Click **From Top**. In the **Animation Pane**, click the **Play** button.

The lines display from the top. On the Animations tab, in the Animation group, the Effect Options button now points down, which means the items are coming from the top.

Another Way

To reorder effects in the Animation Pane, you can click on the effect, and then drag it to the new position.

10 With **Slide 2** active, click the title placeholder—*Location*. At the bottom of the **Animation Pane**, to the right of *Re-Order*, click the **down-pointing arrow**. Click the **Play** button. Compare your screen with Figure 6.31.

The order of the effects is changed. The address and Web site displayed first. The motion effect on the title is displayed last because the order of the effects was changed in the Animation Pane. You can easily reorder the list of animation sequences by selecting a placeholder and then clicking the Re-Order arrows at the bottom of the Animation Pane.

Figure 6.31

11 Under the **Content Placeholder**, click the chevron, and then click the **Play** button and watch the timeline. Click to hide the contents.

12 View the slide show **From Beginning**. Click when necessary to advance the slides.

13 On the **Animations tab**, in the **Advanced Animation group**, click the **Animation Pane** to close the pane.

14 On the **Insert tab**, in the **Text group**, click the **Header & Footer** button to display the **Header and Footer** dialog box. Click the **Notes and Handouts tab**. Under **Include on page**, select the **Date and time** check box, and then select **Fixed**. If necessary, clear the Header check box, and then select the **Page number** and **Footer** check boxes. In the **Footer** box, using your own name, type **Lastname_Firstname_6A_Penn_Liberty** and then click **Apply to All**.

15 Display **Backstage** view, click **Properties**, and then click **Show Document Panel**. Replace the text in the **Author** box with your own name; in the **Subject** box, type your course name and section number; and in the **Keywords** box, type **hours, cars** **Close** the **Document Information Panel**.

16 **Save** your changes. **Close** the presentation, and then **Exit** PowerPoint. Submit your work as directed.

End **You have completed Project 6A**

Project 6B Advertisement Presentation

myitlab
Project 6B Training

Project Activities

In Activities 6.09 through 6.19, you will insert various types of hyperlinks into a presentation created by Penn Liberty Motors as an advertisement for the company. The focus of the ad is the location of Penn Liberty Motors in Philadelphia. You will create two custom slide shows from a single presentation to appeal to two different audiences. You will also annotate the presentation. Finally, you will organize your slides into sections. Your completed presentation will look similar to Figure 6.32.

Project Files

For Project 6B, you will need the following file:

p06B_Advertisement.pptx

You will save your presentation as:

Lastname_Firstname_6B_Advertisement.pptx
Lastname_Firstname_6B_History.docx

Project Results

Figure 6.32
Project 6B Advertisement

Objective 4 | Insert Hyperlinks

In the following activities, you will insert hyperlinks into a PowerPoint presentation. Recall that ***hyperlinks*** are text or objects such as clip art, graphics, WordArt, or pictures that, when clicked, will move you to a Web page, an e-mail address, another document or file, or another area of the same document. In a PowerPoint presentation, hyperlinks can also be used to link to a slide in the presentation, to a slide in a different presentation, or to a custom slide show.

Activity 6.09 | Inserting a Hyperlink to Web Page

In this activity, you will insert a hyperlink into a slide that will connect to the Penn Liberty Motors Web page.

1 **Start** PowerPoint. Locate and open the file **p06B_Advertisement**. Navigate to the **PowerPoint Chapter 6** folder you created, and then save the file as **Lastname_Firstname_6B_Advertisement**

2 Make the **title slide** the active slide. Click to select the text box containing the Web page address *www.libertymotorspa.com*. Then click and drag to select the text.

3 Click the **Insert tab**. In the **Links group**, click the **Hyperlink** button to display the **Insert Hyperlink** dialog box. If necessary, under Link to, click Existing File or Web Page. Compare your screen with Figure 6.33.

The Insert Hyperlink dialog box provides an easy and convenient way to insert hyperlinks. You can link to an Existing File or Web Page (the default setting), a Place in This Document, Create New Document, or an E-Mail Address. You can also browse the Web, browse for a file, or change the text that displays in the ScreenTip.

Figure 6.33

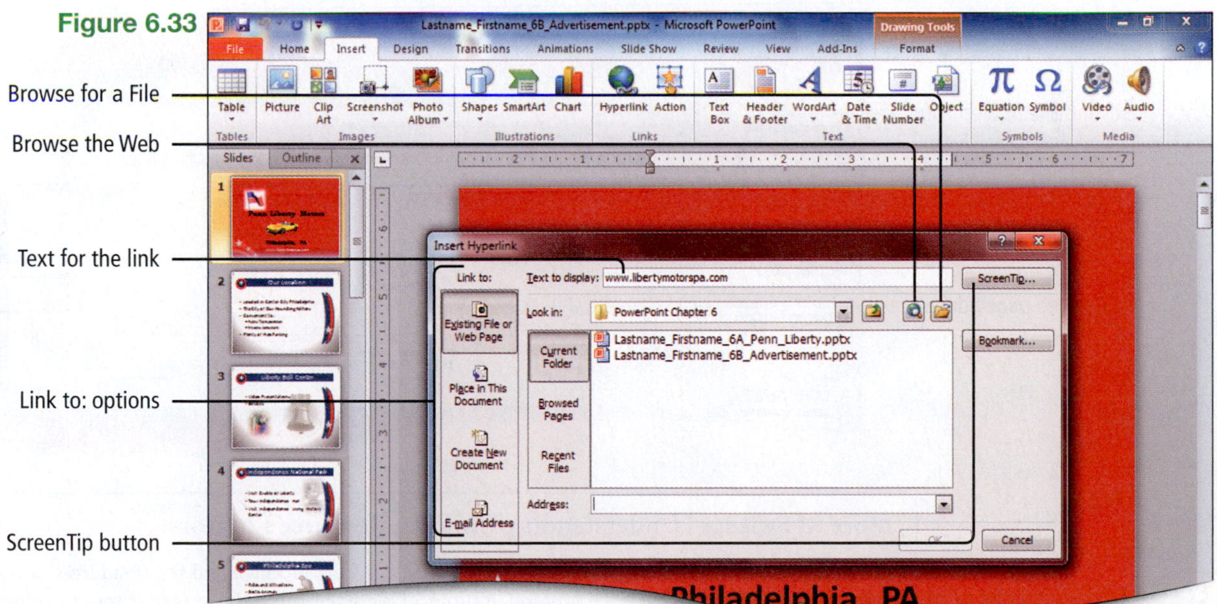

4 Click the **ScreenTip** button. In the **Set Hyperlink ScreenTip** dialog box, type **Penn Liberty Motors** Compare your screen with Figure 6.34.

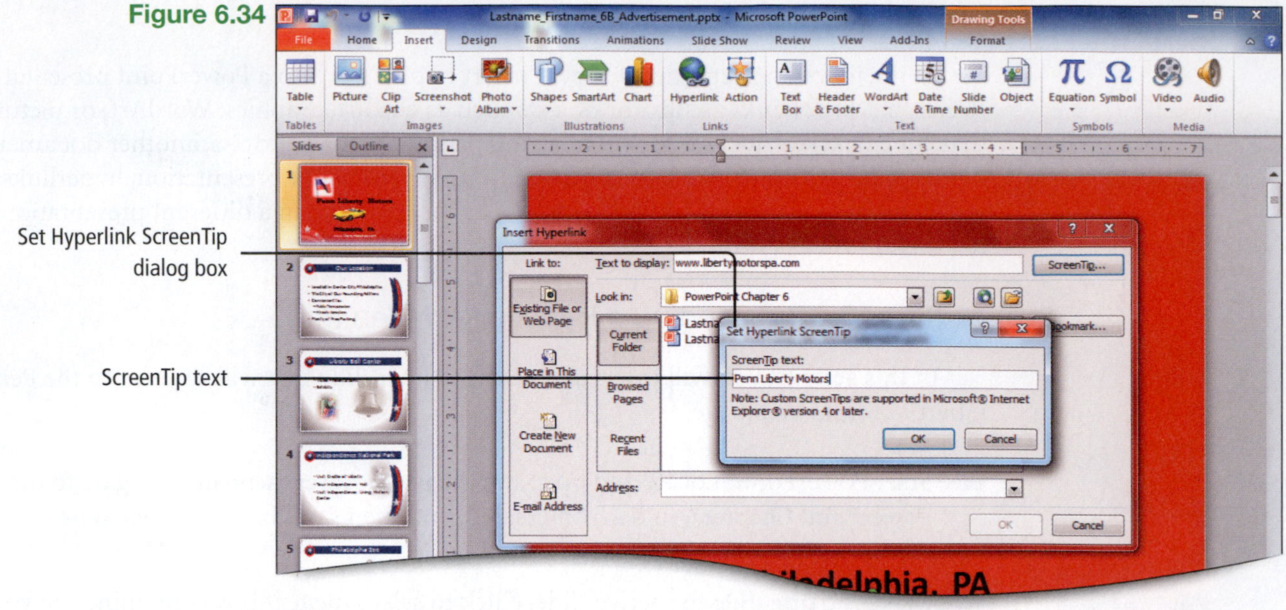

Figure 6.34

5 Click **OK**. In the **Address** box, delete the existing text, if any, and then type http://www.libertymotorspa.com Compare your screen with Figure 6.35.

The text you typed is a ***URL***, or ***Uniform Resource Locator***. A URL defines the address of documents and resources on the Web.

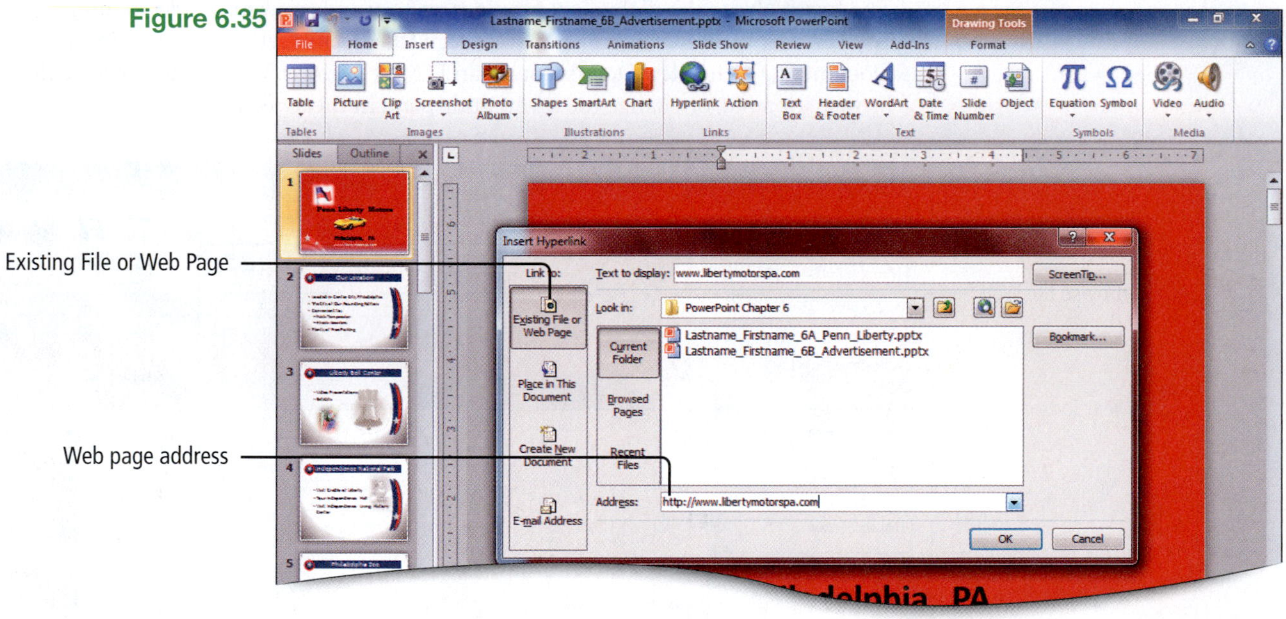

Figure 6.35

More Knowledge | Understanding Uniform Resource Locators

A Uniform Resource Locator, or URL, generally consists of the protocol and the IP address or domain name. The first part of the address is the ***protocol***. A protocol is a set of rules. ***HyperText Transfer Protocol (HTTP)*** is the protocol used on the World Wide Web to define how messages are formatted and transmitted. It also instructs the ***Web browser*** software how to display Web pages. Web browsers, such as Internet Explorer, format Web pages so that they display properly. The protocol is followed by a colon (:) and two forward slashes (//). The *www* stands for *World Wide Web*. The World Wide Web is a collection of Web sites. This is followed by the *domain name*. The domain name is a user friendly name that represents an *IP address*. An IP address, or Internet Protocol address, is a unique set of numbers, composed of a network ID and a machine ID, that identifies the Web server where the Web page resides. The *suffix* part of the domain name, the portion after the dot (.), is the *high level domain name (HLDN)* or top level domain name, such as *.com*, *.org*, or *.gov*. This is the upper level domain to which the lower level domain belongs.

6 Click **OK**.

The Web page address now displays with an underline and takes on the appearance of a hyperlink.

7 Start the slide show **From Current Slide**. On the **title slide**, without clicking, point to the address www.libertymotorspa.com, and then compare your screen with Figure 6.36.

The Link Select pointer displays. A ScreenTip displays with the text you typed.

Figure 6.36

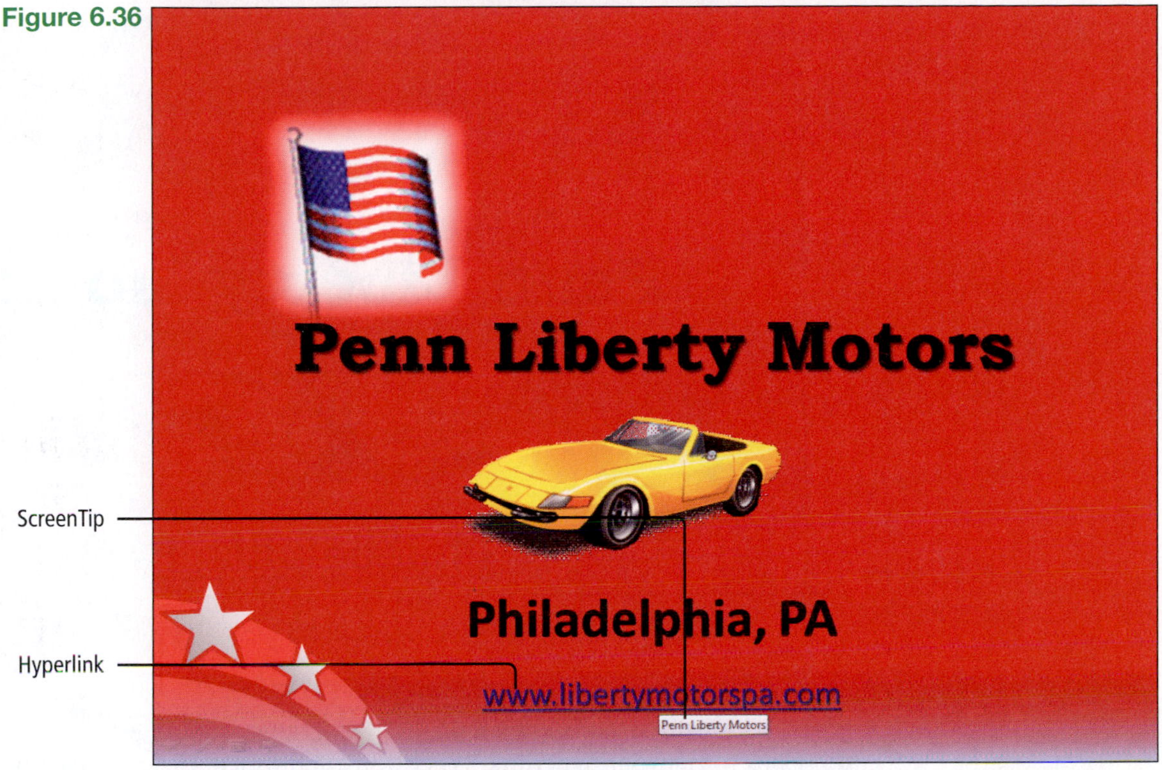

8 With the Link Select pointer, click the hyperlink.

The Web page is displayed if you are connected to the Internet.

> **Alert!** | **Did the www.libertymotorspa.com Web Site Not Appear?**
>
> As of this writing, the www.libertymotorspa.com Web site was active. You might receive an error message stating that the Internet server could not be located.

9 Close the Web page, return to PowerPoint, and then press Esc.

10 Right-click anywhere on the URL **www.libertymotorspa.com**, and then from the displayed shortcut menu, click **Remove Hyperlink**.

11 With the **title slide** still the active slide, drag to select the subtitle *Philadelphia, PA*. Click the **Insert tab**. In the **Links group**, click **Hyperlink**.

12 To the right of the **Look in** box, click the **Browse the Web** button.

If you are connected to the Internet, your selected home page will display. From there, you can browse for a particular page.

13 In the **Internet Explorer** address bar, type **www.google.com** and then press Enter.

14 In the **Google** search box, type **Philadelphia** and then press Enter. Click to display a Web page of your choosing.

15 On the status bar at the bottom of your screen, click the **PowerPoint** button. Click **OK**.

The Web site address is automatically displayed in the Insert Hyperlink dialog box Address box.

16 Start the slide show **From Current Slide**. Point to *Philadelphia, PA*, and then compare your screen with Figure 6.37.

It is not necessary to format the Web page hyperlink text in URL format as long as it is linked correctly to the Web page address. Any text or object can serve as a hyperlink.

Figure 6.37

17 Click to test your hyperlink. When you are finished, close the Web page and return to PowerPoint. Press Esc to return to your presentation screen.

18 **Save** your changes. Close any other Web page that may have opened during this activity.

Activity 6.10 | Inserting a Hyperlink to a Slide in Another Presentation

In this activity, you will insert a hyperlink into a presentation that will link to the Location slide in a previously created presentation.

1 In **Normal** view, make **Slide 12** the active slide. Drag to select the title—*Treat Yourself to a New Car*. Click the **Insert tab**. In the **Links group**, click the **Hyperlink** button to display the **Insert Hyperlink** dialog box.

2 If necessary, under **Link to**, click to select **Existing File or Web Page**, and then using the technique you practiced, navigate to the **PowerPoint Chapter 6** folder and click **Lastname_Firstname_6A_Penn_Liberty**. Compare your screen with Figure 6.38.

Figure 6.38

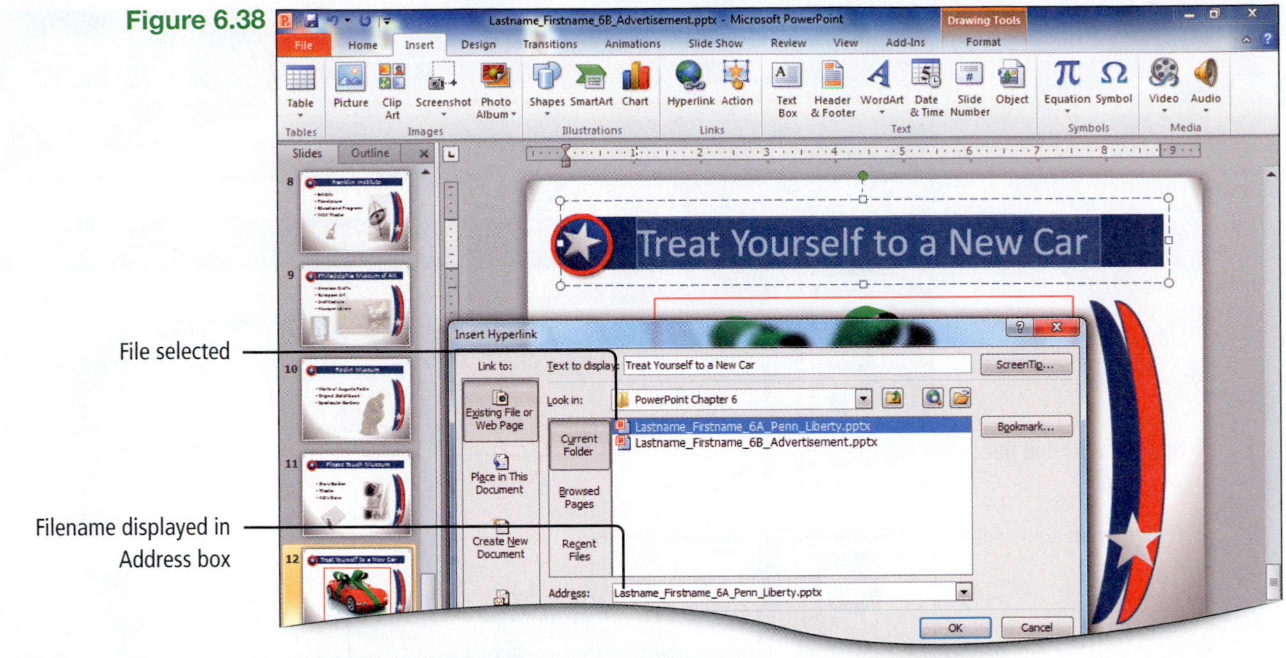

3 In the **Insert hyperlink** dialog box, click the **Bookmark** button to display the **Select Place in Document** dialog box. Compare your screen with Figure 6.39.

Notice that the slides from Lastname_Firstname_6A_Penn_Liberty are listed.

Figure 6.39

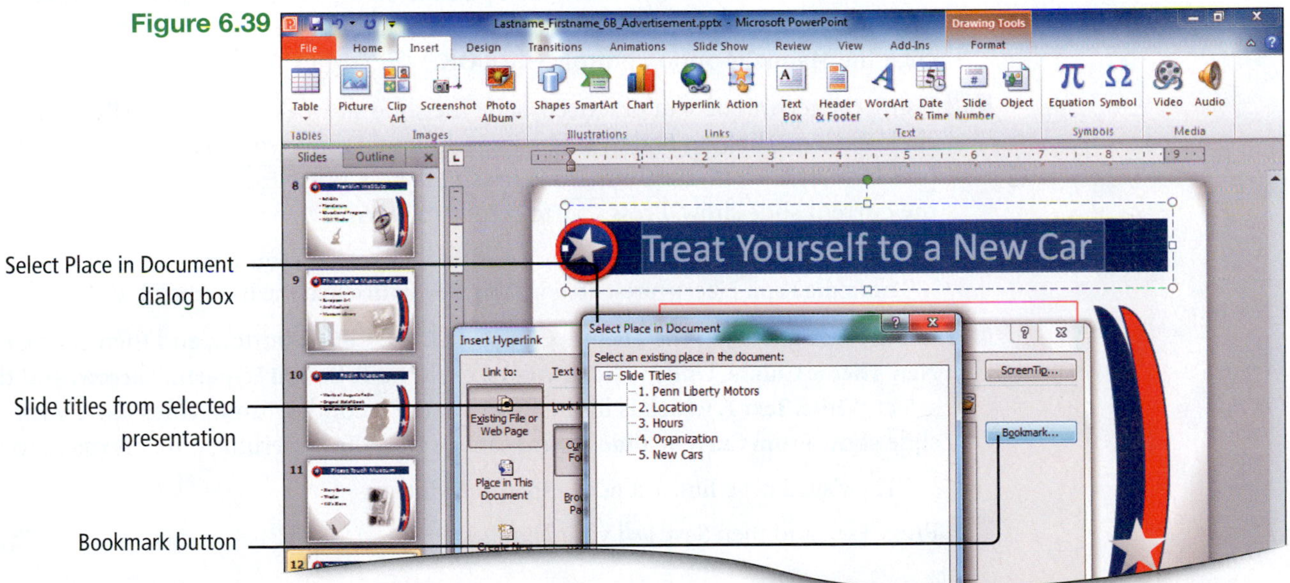

4 In the **Select Place in Document** dialog box, click the fifth slide—*New Cars*—and then click **OK**. Compare your screen with Figure 6.40.

The Address box contains the name of the presentation and the number and title of the slide.

Figure 6.40

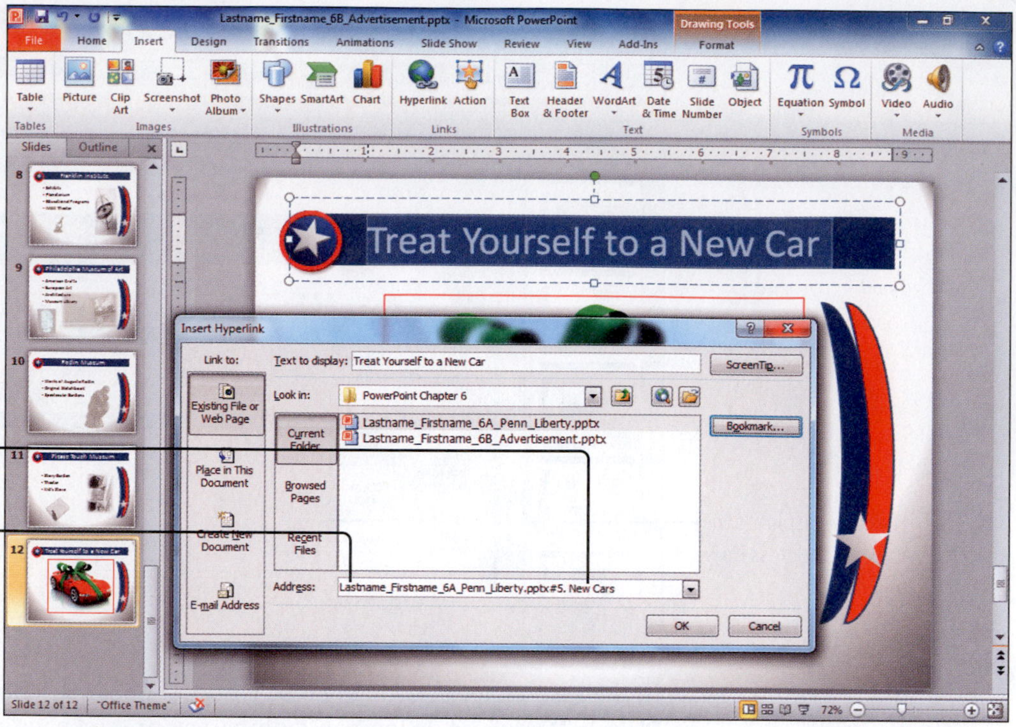

5 Click **OK**. Click the **Slide Show tab**, and then in the **Set Up group**, click the **Set Up Slide Show** button. If necessary, in the Set Up Show dialog box, under Show type, select the **Presented by a speaker (full screen)** option button. If necessary, under Advance slides, click the **Manually** option button. Click **OK**.

6 Using the technique you practiced, start the slide show **From Current Slide**, and then click the hyperlink on Slide 12. The hyperlink will move you to Slide 5 of the other presentation. When the animations finish playing, press Esc to return to Slide 12 of the current slide show. Press Esc to return to **Normal** view.

Because you selected Presented by a speaker (full screen), you were able to view Slide 5 from the Penn Liberty presentation. You may notice that the hyperlink is difficult to see.

7 On the **Design tab**, in the **Themes group**, click the **Colors** button, and then click **Create New Theme Colors**. Under **Theme colors**, click the **Followed Hyperlink arrow**, and then select **White, Text 1**, which is in the first row, the second column. Click **Save**. View the slide show **From Current Slide** so you can see that the hyperlinked text is easier to read.

The visited hyperlink text now displays in white.

8 Press Esc, and then **Save** your changes.

Activity 6.11 | Inserting a Hyperlink to an E-mail Address

In this activity, you will insert a hyperlink that will open an e-mail client and insert the recipient's e-mail address and subject.

1 In **Normal** view, make **Slide 6** the active slide. Drag to select the text *Contact Us*. Click the **Insert tab**. In the **Links group**, click the **Hyperlink** button.

2 In the **Insert Hyperlink** dialog box, under **Link to**, click to select **E-Mail Address**.

3 In the **E-mail address** box, type **kevin@libertymotors.com**

4 In the **Subject** box, type **Discount Tickets** and then compare your screen with Figure 6.41.

The word *mailto:* displays before the e-mail address. This is an *HTML* attribute instructing the Web browser software that this is an e-mail address. HTML stands for ***HyperText Markup Language*** and is the language used to code Web pages. The recently used e-mail addresses with the associated subject also display for easy selection. You may not have any in your list.

Figure 6.41

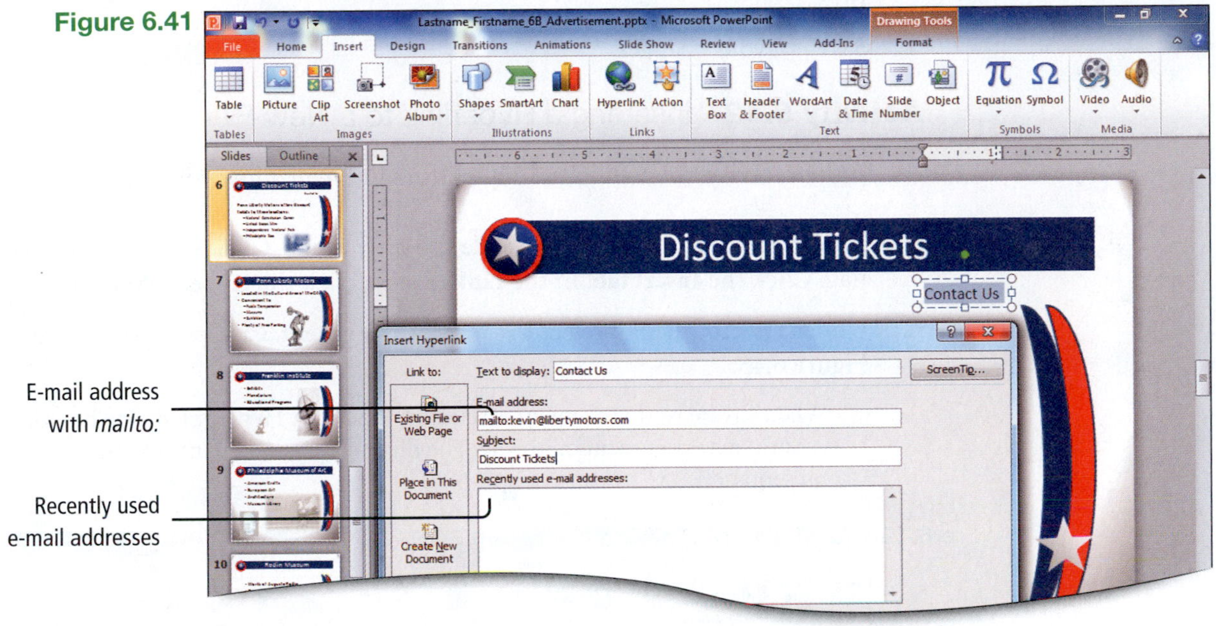

5 Click **OK**.

> **Alert!** | **Do You Have An E-mail Client to Use?**
>
> If you do not have an e-mail client that is configured to a mail service, skip the following steps in this activity. Instead, save your changes and proceed to the next activity.

6 Start the slide show **From Current Slide**, and when the slide show displays, click the hyperlink. Compare your screen with Figure 6.42.

An e-mail program opens with the e-mail address you typed in the To box. In this case, ***Microsoft Outlook*** opens. Microsoft Outlook is the program, or ***e-mail client***, that facilitates the sending and receiving of electronic messages. This enables you to type an e-mail message and click Send from within the PowerPoint presentation. An e-mail client is a software program that enables you to compose and send e-mail.

Figure 6.42

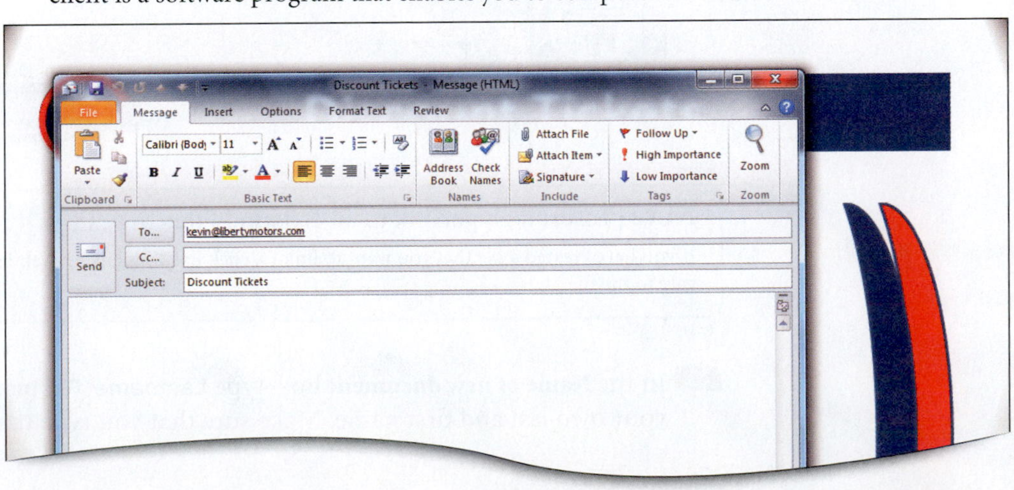

PowerPoint | Chapter 6

> **Alert! | Does Your Screen Differ?**
>
> If the e-mail client on the computer you are using is not Microsoft Outlook, the Discount Tickets window that displays will differ from the one shown in Figure 6.42. If you do not have an e-mail client, you will not be able to do this. If you get a startup screen when you click on the e-mail link, that means your client has not been configured.

7 **Close** the e-mail program without saving changes to the e-mail message, and then press Esc.

8 **Save** your changes.

Activity 6.12 | Inserting a Hyperlink to a New File

In this activity, you will insert a hyperlink that will allow you to create a new file.

1 In **Normal** view, make the **title slide** the active slide. Click to select the image of the flag. Click the **Insert tab**. In the **Links group**, click the **Hyperlink** button.

2 Under **Link to**, click to select **Create New Document**. Compare your screen with Figure 6.43.

When Create New Document is selected, the Insert Hyperlink dialog box allows you to create a new document on the fly. The file can be a document, a spreadsheet, or a presentation.

Figure 6.43

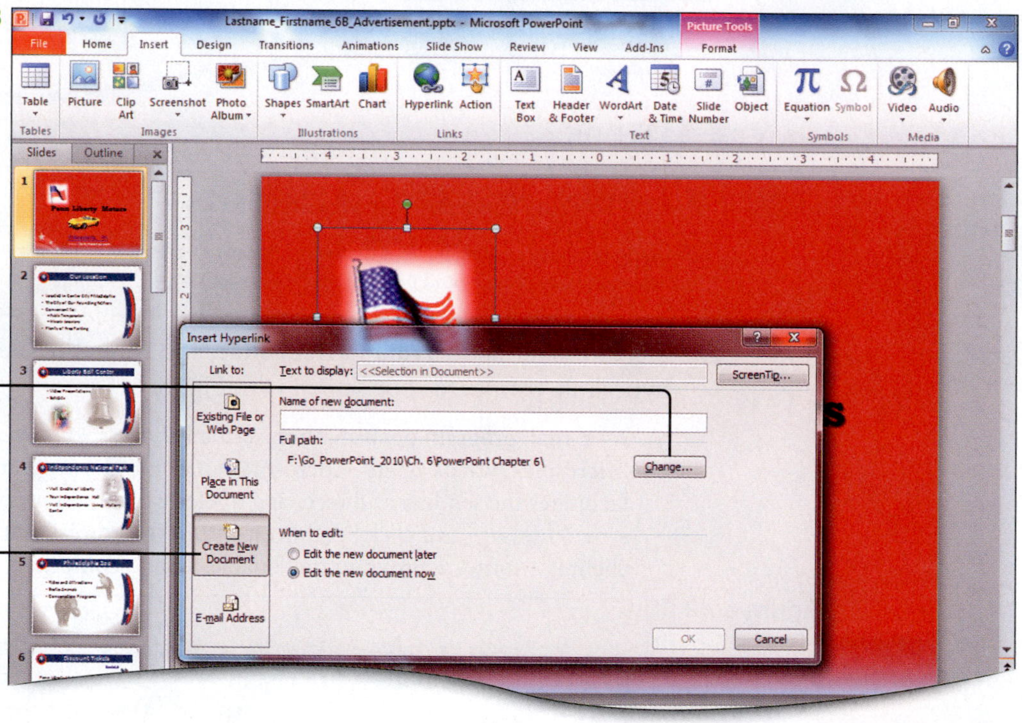

> **Note | Insert a Hyperlink to an Existing File**
>
> If you have created a file that you want to link to, click Existing File or Web Page (the default setting) and navigate to the file.

3 In the **Name of new document** box, type **Lastname_Firstname_6B_History.docx** using your own last and first name. Make sure that you type the file extension—.docx.

4 Click the **Change** button, and then navigate to your Chapter 6 folder if necessary. Click **OK**.

In this case, you are creating a Microsoft Word document. The ***file extension*** or file type identifies the format of the file or the application that was used to create it. If the ***full path*** listed is incorrect, click the Change button, and then navigate to the PowerPoint Chapter 6 folder you created. The full path includes the location of the drive, the folder, and any subfolders in which the file is contained.

> **Note | File Name and File Extension**
>
> Typing the file extension with the file name in the Name of new document box is the only way that Windows recognizes which application to start. If you do not type a file extension, Windows will assume you are creating a presentation and will start PowerPoint because you are currently using PowerPoint.

5 Under **When to edit**, make sure the **Edit the new document now** option button is selected, and then compare your screen with Figure 6.44.

Figure 6.44

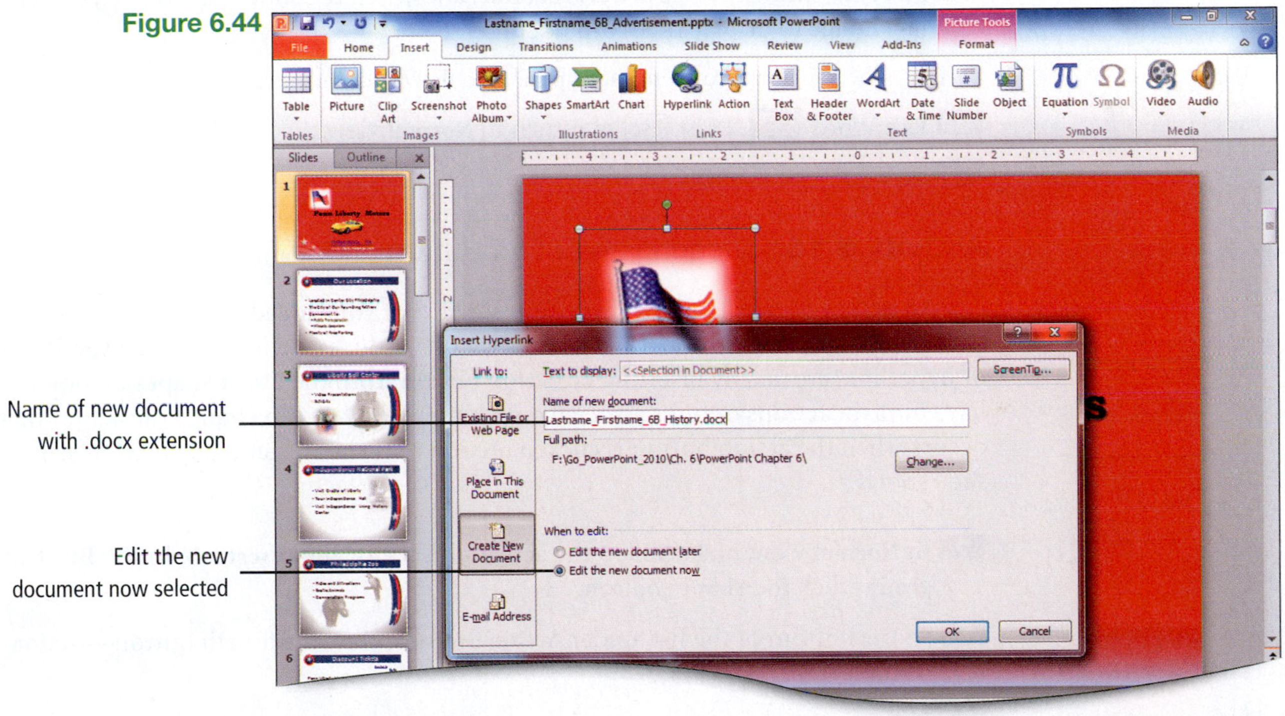

6 Click **OK** to open a new Microsoft Word file named Lastname_Firstname_6B_History.docx.

> **Alert! | Did You Have Trouble Displaying the Word Document?**
>
> If you made an error in the process of creating the hyperlink to create a new document and tried to do it again, you may find that the Word document does not display. If that happens, look in your chapter folder. If a file named Lastname_Firstname_6B_History.docx displays, delete the file. Return to PowerPoint, and then enter the hyperlink again.

7 At the top of the new Word document, type **Penn Liberty Motors was founded in 1903 by Martin Rau.** Press Enter two times, and then type **Lastname_Firstname_6B_History.docx** Compare your screen with Figure 6.45.

Figure 6.45

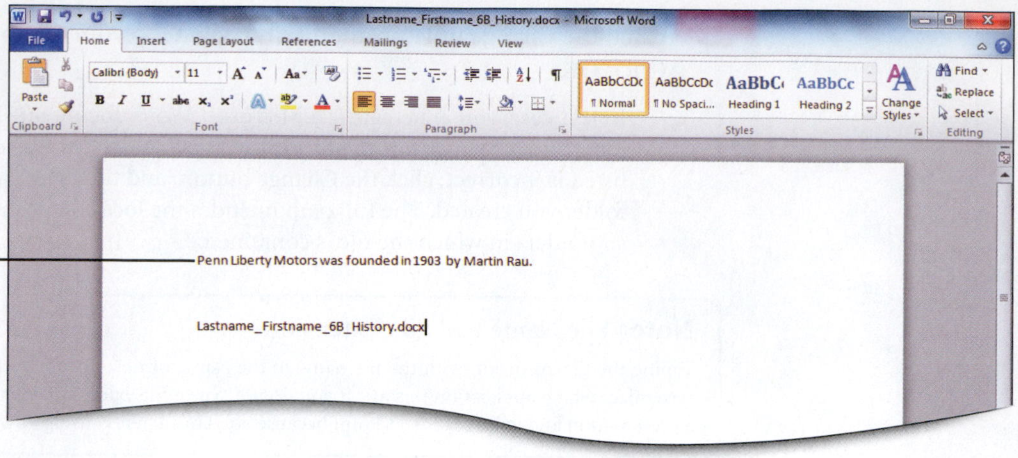

8 **Save** the document, and then **Exit** Microsoft Word.

9 Start the slide show **From Current Slide**, and when the slide show displays, click the flag image to display the Word document.

The flag image contains the hyperlink to the Word document.

10 **Exit** Word. Press Esc to return to **Normal** view.

11 **Save** your changes.

Activity 6.13 | Creating an Action Button

An ***action button*** is a built-in button shape that you can add to your presentation and then assign an action to occur upon the click of a mouse or with a mouse over. It is a type of hyperlink, created by inserting an action button from the list of shapes. Action buttons have built-in actions or links associated with them, or you can change the action that occurs when the action button is clicked. Action buttons are generally used in self-running slide shows.

1 In **Normal** view, make **Slide 5** the active slide. Click the **Insert tab**. In the **Illustration group**, click the **Shapes** button.

2 At the bottom of the list, under **Action Buttons**, click the fourth button—**Action Button: End.**

3 Position the pointer at the lower right corner—at **4 inches on the right side of the horizontal ruler** and **3 inches on the lower half of the vertical ruler**. Click once to display the **Action Settings** dialog box.

The Action Settings dialog box displays. Because the action associated with the End button is to link to the last slide in the presentation, *Last Slide* displays in the Hyperlink to box. The action button on the slide is too large, but you will resize it later.

4 Click the **Hyperlink to arrow**, and then scroll to review the list of options, which includes other slides in the presentation, a custom show, a URL, a file, and another PowerPoint presentation. Click **Last Slide** to close the list, and then compare your screen with Figure 6.46.

There are two tabs in the Action Settings dialog box. You can set the action to occur on a Mouse Click or ***Mouse Over***. Mouse Over means that the action will occur when the presenter points to (hovers over) the action button. It is not necessary to click.

Figure 6.46

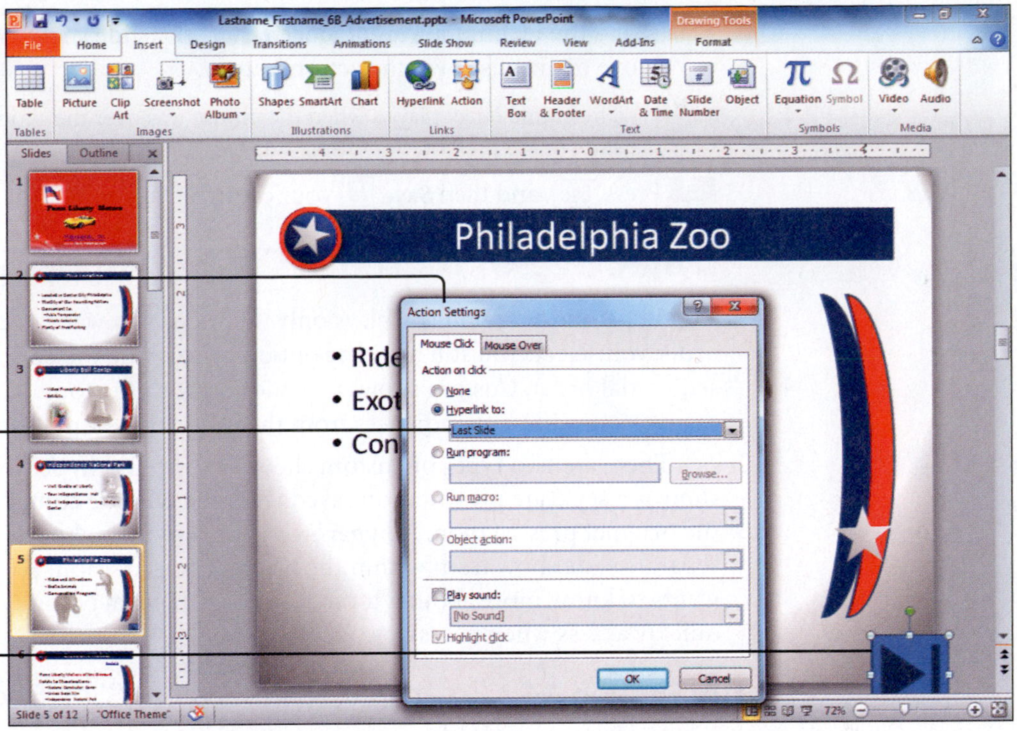

5 Click the **Mouse Over tab**. Click the **Hyperlink to** option, click the **Hyperlink to arrow**, and then select **Last Slide**. Click the **Play sound** check box, click the **Play sound check box arrow**, scroll down, and then click **Chime**. Click **OK**.

6 With the action button still selected, under **Drawing Tools**, click the **Format tab**. In the **Size group**, change the **Shape Height** to **.5"**. Change the **Shape Width** to **.5"**. Compare your screen with Figure 6.47.

The action button is displayed at the bottom right of the slide.

Figure 6.47

7 Using the technique you practiced, start the slide show **From Current Slide**, and then move the mouse over the action button.

The chime effect played when the mouse was over the action button, and then the last slide in the presentation displayed.

8 Press Esc, and then **Save** your changes.

Objective 5 | Create Custom Slide Shows

A ***custom slide show*** displays only the slides you want to display to an audience in the order you select. You still have the option of running the entire presentation in its sequential order. Custom shows provide you with the tools to create different slide shows to appeal to different audiences from the original presentation.

There are two types of custom shows—basic and hyperlinked. A ***basic custom slide show*** is a separate presentation saved with its own title containing some of the slides from the original presentation. A ***hyperlinked custom slide show*** is a quick way to navigate to a separate slide show from within the original presentation. For example, if your audience wants to know more about a topic, you could have hyperlinks to slides that you could quickly access when necessary.

Activity 6.14 | Creating a Basic Custom Slide Show

In this activity, you will create basic custom slide shows from an existing presentation. You will then save them as separate custom shows that can be run from the Slide Show tab.

1 Make the **title slide** the active slide. Click the **Slide Show tab**. In the **Start Slide Show group**, click the **Custom Slide Show** button, and then click **Custom Shows** to display the **Custom Shows** dialog box.

2 Click **New** to display the **Define Custom Show** dialog box, In the **Slide show name** box, type **Historic** and then compare your screen with Figure 6.48.

From the Define Custom Show dialog box, you can name a custom slide show and select the slides that will be included in the slide show. All the slides in the current presentation are displayed in the Slides in presentation box. The slides you want to include in the custom show will display in the Slides in custom show box.

Figure 6.48

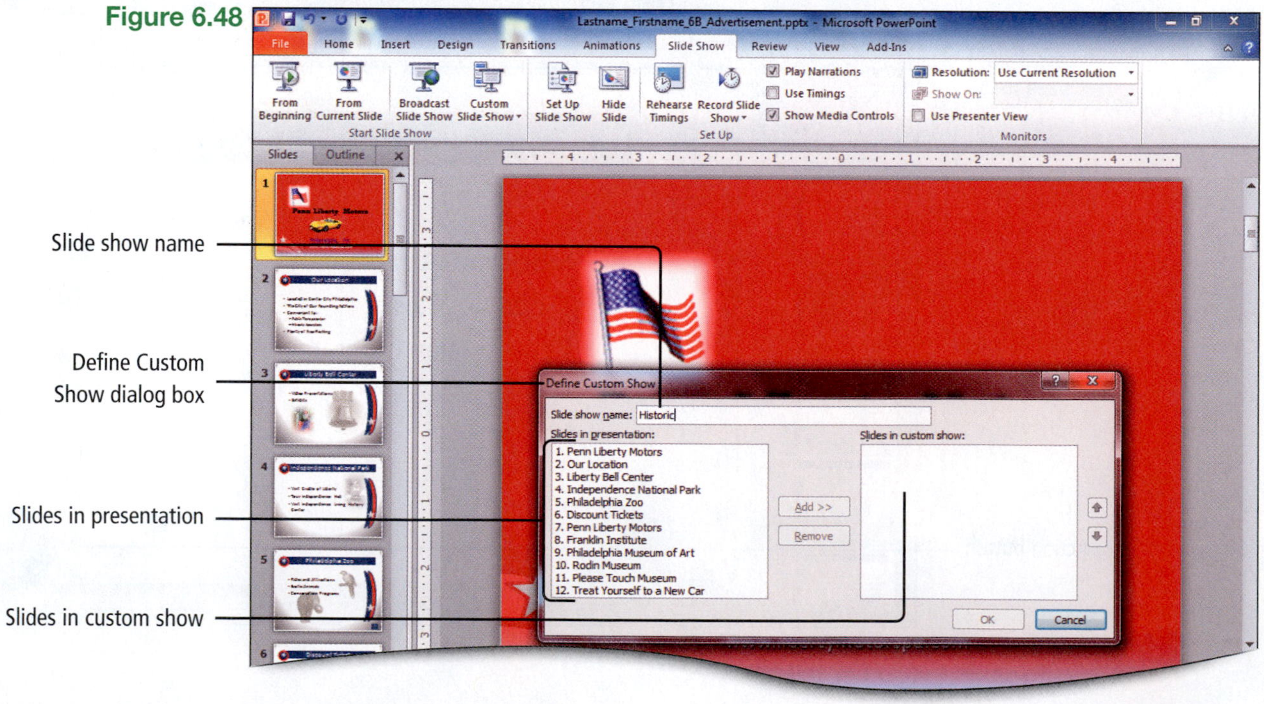

3 Under **Slides in presentation**, click **Slide 1**. Hold down [⇧ Shift], and then click **Slide 6** to select the six adjacent slides. Compare your screen with Figure 6.49

Figure 6.49

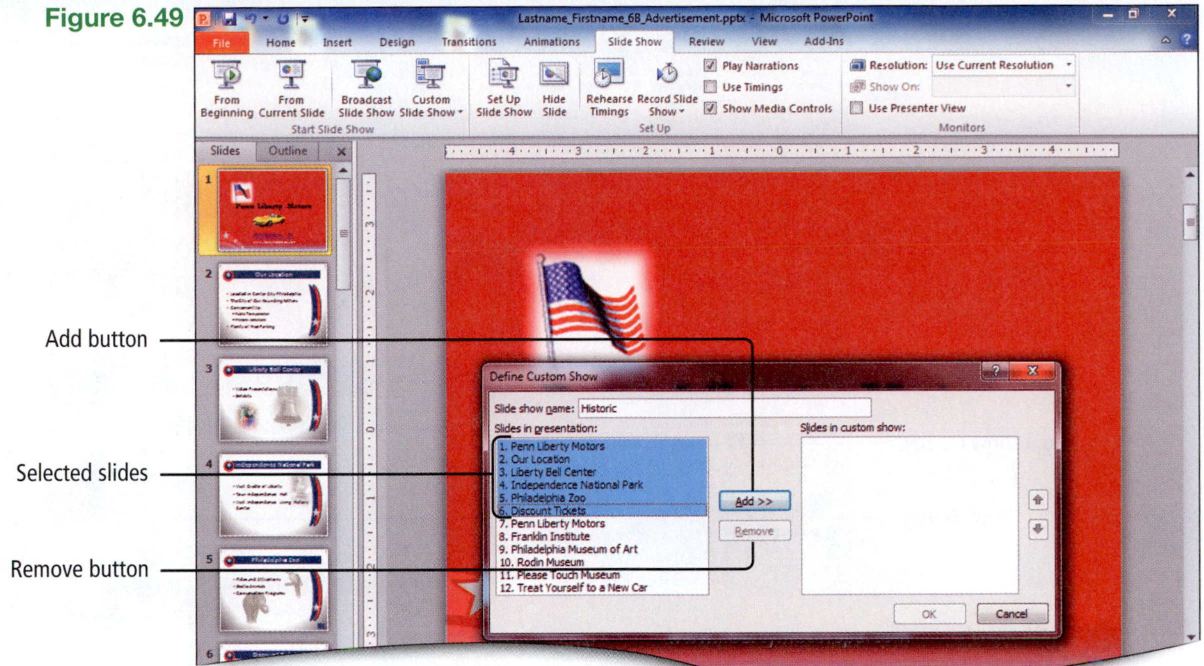

4 Click the **Add** button. Under **Slides in presentation**, double-click **Slide 12** to add it to the custom show. Compare your screen with Figure 6.50.

Slide 12 is renumbered as Slide 7 in the custom show.

Figure 6.50

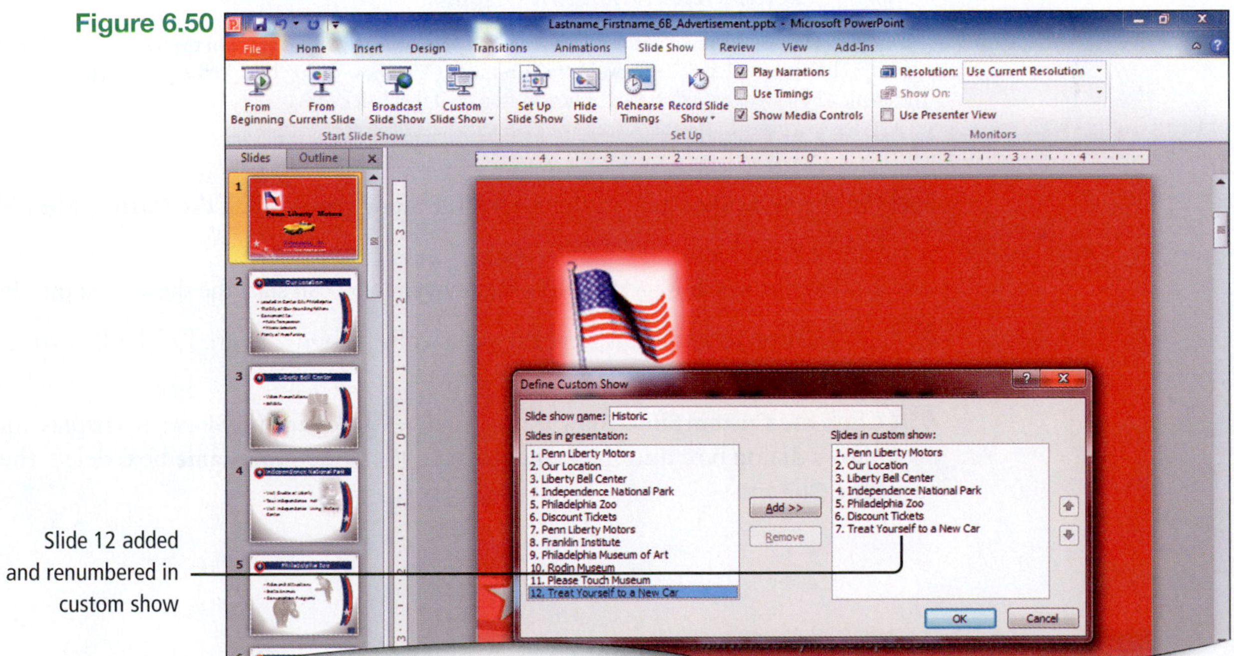

5 Click **OK**. Compare your screen with Figure 6.51.

Figure 6.51

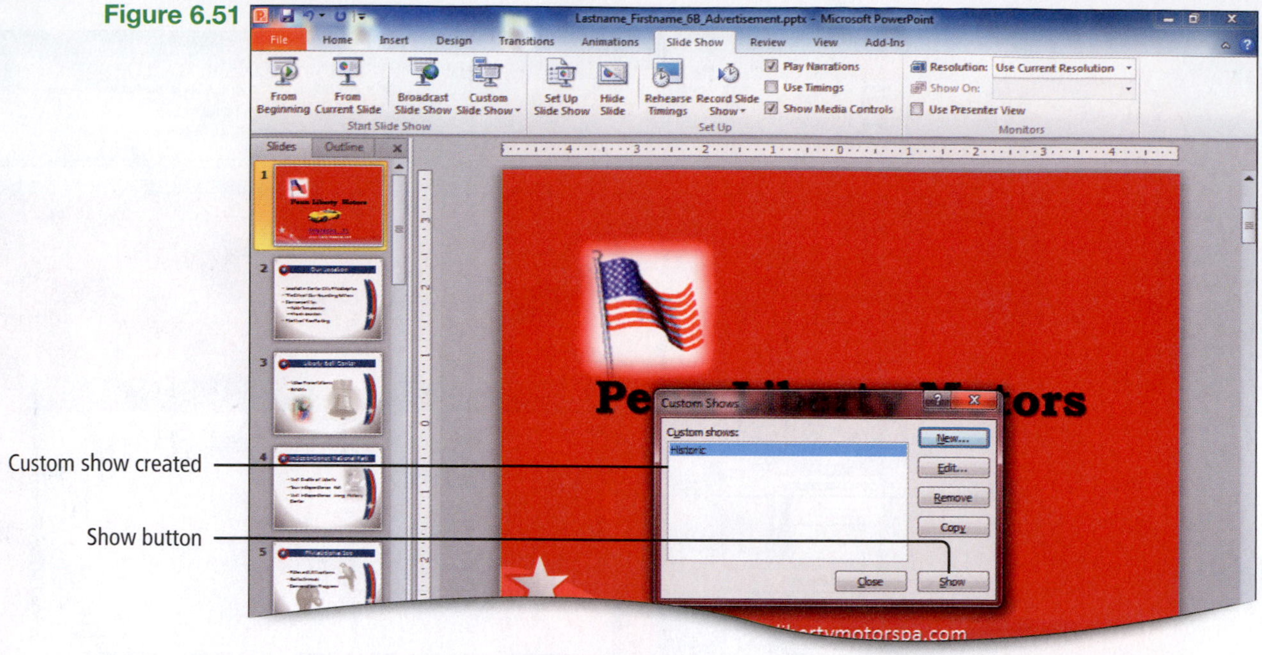

6 In the **Custom Shows** dialog box, click the **Show** button to preview your custom show. Click through the slides. When you are finished viewing the slide show, press Esc.

The custom slide show included only seven slides.

Alert! | **Did the Presentation Not Display?**

If the first slide of the presentation did not display automatically, press Esc. On the Slide Show tab, in the Set Up group, click the Set Up Slide Show button. In the Set Up Show dialog box, in the Show Type section, select the *Presented by a speaker (full screen)* option button, and then click OK.

7 On the **Slide Show tab**, in the **Start Slide Show group**, click the **Custom Slide Show** button.

The custom show—Historic—displays, and you can start the show from this list also.

8 Click **Historic**, and then view the slide show. When you are finished viewing the slide show, press Enter or Esc.

9 Click the **Custom Slide Show** button again. Click **Custom Shows** to display the **Custom Shows** dialog box, and then click **New**. In the **Slide show name** box, delete the text, and type **Cultural**

10 Under **Slides in presentation**, click to select **Slide 6**, hold down [⇧ Shift], and then click **Slide 12**. Click the **Add** button. Under **Slides in presentation**, double-click **Slide 1**.

Slide 1 is now Slide 8 in the custom show.

11 Under **Slides in custom show**, click **Slide 8**. Click the **Up arrow** seven times to move **Slide 8** so it is in the **Slide 1** position in the custom show, and then compare your screen with Figure 6.52.

Figure 6.52

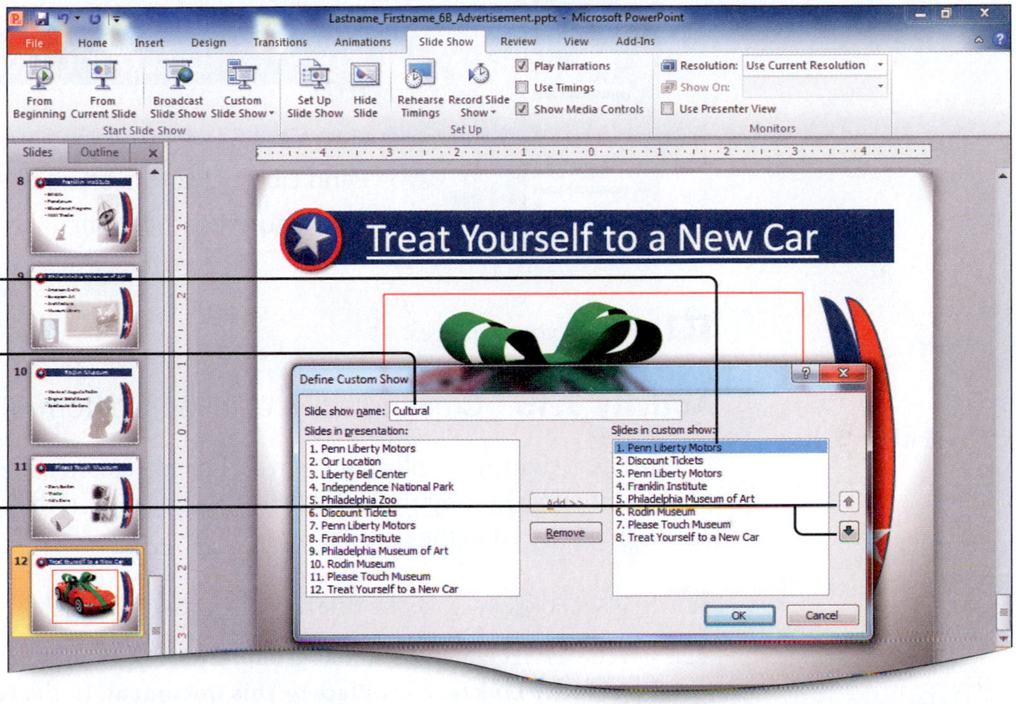

12 Click **OK**. In the **Custom Shows** dialog box, click **Show** to preview your custom show. When you are finished viewing the slide show, press [Enter] or [Esc].

Eight slides displayed.

13 In the **Start Slide Show group**, click the **Custom Slide Show** button. Click **Custom Shows** to display the **Custom Shows** dialog box. Click **Cultural**, and then click **Edit**. In the **Slides in custom show** list, click **2. Discount Tickets**, and then click the **Remove** button. Click **OK**. In the **Custom Shows** dialog box, click the **Show** button. Press [Enter] or [Esc] when you are done.

Seven slides displayed.

> **Alert! | Did You Click the Name of a Custom Show Instead of Custom Shows?**
>
> To edit a specific custom show, when you click the Custom Slide Show button, make sure you click Custom Shows to allow you to select the show and edit it. If you clicked a custom show by accident, press [Esc] and try again.

14 Click the **Custom Slide Show** button, and then click **Custom Shows** to display the **Custom Shows** dialog box. Click **New**. In the **Slide show name** box, delete the text, and then type **Location**

15 In the **Slides in presentation** box, click to select **Slide 2**, hold down [⇧ Shift], and then click **Slide 6**. Click the **Add** button. Click **OK**.

16 In the **Custom Shows** dialog box, click **Show** to preview your custom show. When you are finished viewing the slide show, press [Enter] or [Esc].

17 In the **Start Slide Show group**, click the **Custom Slide Show** button. Compare your screen with Figure 6.53.

Figure 6.53

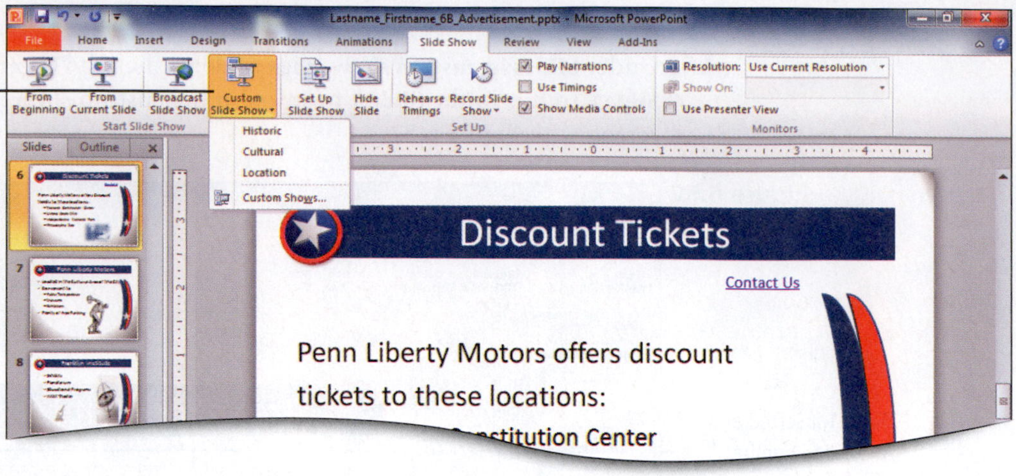

18 **Save** your changes.

Activity 6.15 | Creating a Hyperlinked Custom Slide Show

In this activity, you will create a hyperlinked custom slide show from an existing presentation by selecting the slides that will be shown in the custom show. These slides can be hyperlinked to the original presentation.

1 In **Normal** view, make the **title slide** the active slide. Click to select the picture of the car.

2 On the **Insert tab**, in the **Links group**, click **Hyperlink**. In the **Insert Hyperlink** dialog box, under **Link to**, click **Place in This Document**. In the **Insert Hyperlink** dialog box, scroll down to display the **Custom Shows**.

3 Under **Select a place in this document**, click **Location**, and then select the **Show and return** check box. Compare your screen with Figure 6.54.

Figure 6.54

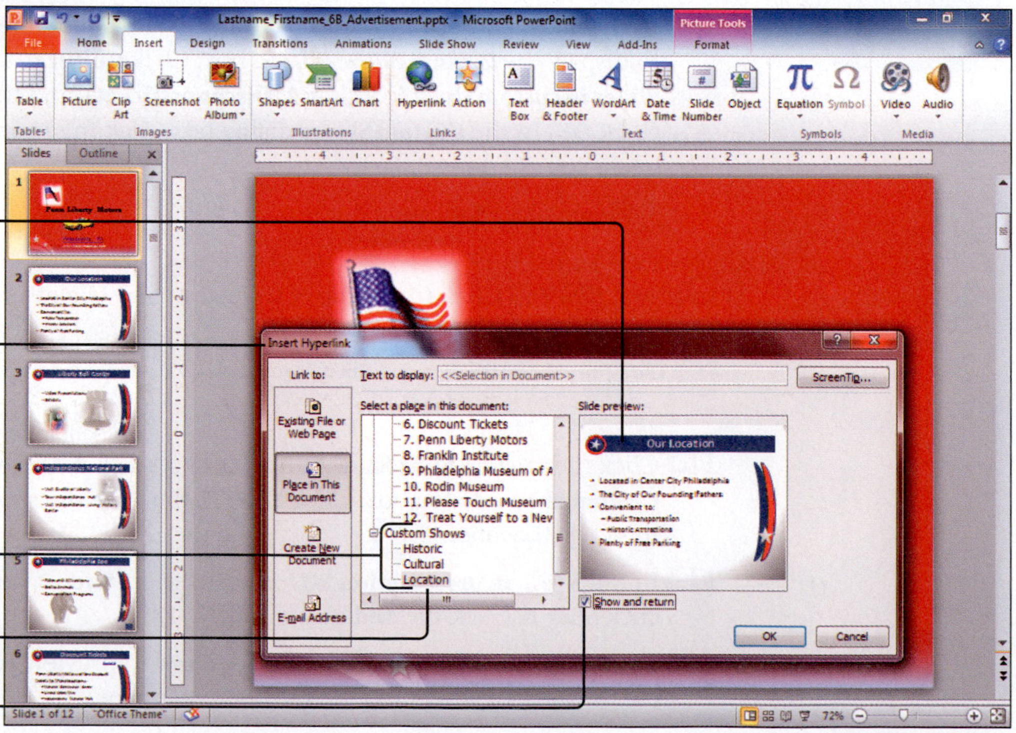

4 Click **OK**. Start the slide show **From Beginning**, and then click the picture of the car. When the title slide displays, press Esc.

The slides in the custom show—Location—will display, and after the last slide, the presentation will return to the title slide.

5 **Save** your changes.

Objective 6 | Present and View a Slide Presentation

In the following activities, you will use the navigation tools included with PowerPoint to view slide shows. You can start a slide show from the beginning or from any slide you choose. The ***navigation tools*** include buttons that display on the slides during a slide show that enable you to perform actions such as move to the next slide, the previous slide, the last viewed slide, or the end of the slide show. Additionally, you can add an ***annotation***, which is a note or a highlight that can be saved or discarded.

Activity 6.16 | Hiding a Slide

In this activity, you will hide the two slides so that they do not display during the slide show and unhide one slide.

1 Make **Slide 6** the active slide. If necessary, click the **Slide Show tab**. In the **Set Up group**, click the **Hide Slide** button. Scroll the thumbnail slides, and then compare your screen with Figure 6.55.

In the Slides/Outline pane, a hidden slide icon is displayed to the left of the slide thumbnail. The number inside the icon has a diagonal line through it.

Figure 6.55

Hide Slide button

Hidden slide icon

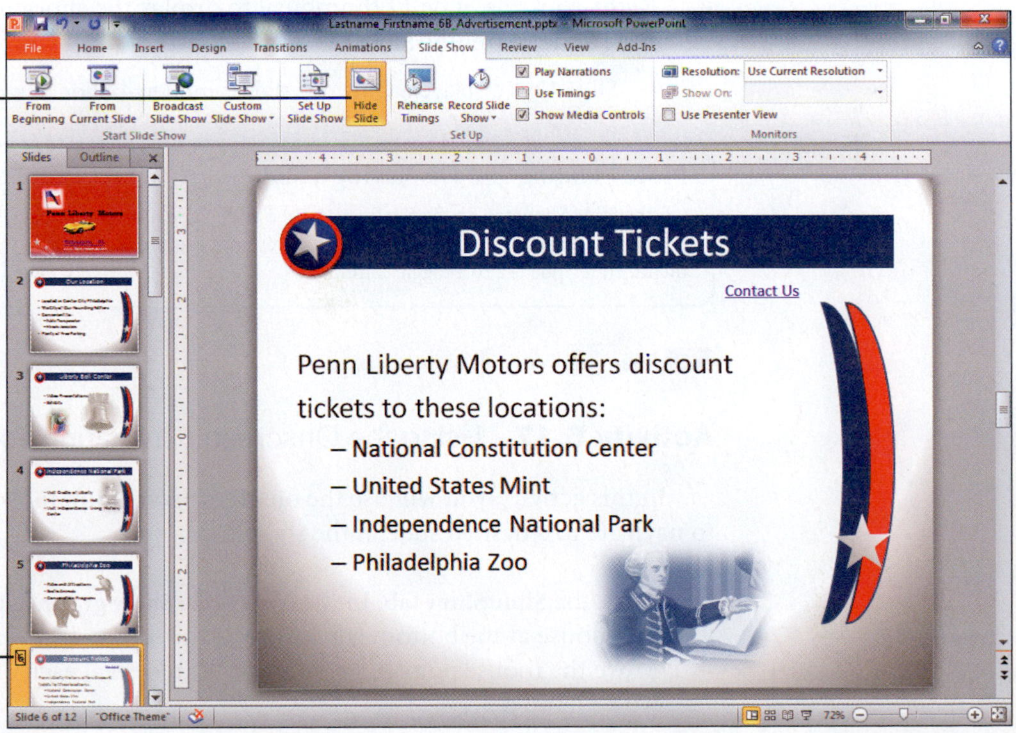

2 In the **Slides/Outline pane**, scroll to **Slide 12**. Right-click the thumbnail for **Slide 12** to display the shortcut menu, and then compare your screen with Figure 6.56.

You can hide a slide from the shortcut menu. Make sure you right-click the thumbnail.

Figure 6.56

3 Click **Hide Slide**.

4 Right-click the Slide 12 thumbnail to display the shortcut menu again, and then click **Hide Slide** to unhide **Slide 12**.

Slide 12 is displayed. Only one slide is hidden—Slide 6.

Note | Hiding and Displaying a Slide

On the Slide Show tab, in the Setup group, the Hide Slide button is a toggle button. Recall that a toggle button performs an action when clicked and then reverses the previous action when clicked again. In the shortcut menu, Hide Slide is also a toggle command.

5 **Save** your changes.

Activity 6.17 | Using the Onscreen Navigation Tools

In this activity, you will use the onscreen navigation tools and the slide shortcut menu to navigate to a desired slide in the slide show.

1 Click the **Slide Show tab**. In the **Start Slide Show group**, click **From Beginning**. Point the mouse at the bottom left corner of the screen to reveal the navigation buttons. Move the mouse pointer to the right to reveal each one. Compare your screen with Figure 6.57.

Notice that four semi-transparent buttons display for a few seconds and then disappear. If you move the mouse pointer, they display again for a few seconds. The buttons display as long as you are moving the mouse pointer or when you point to them.

Figure 6.57

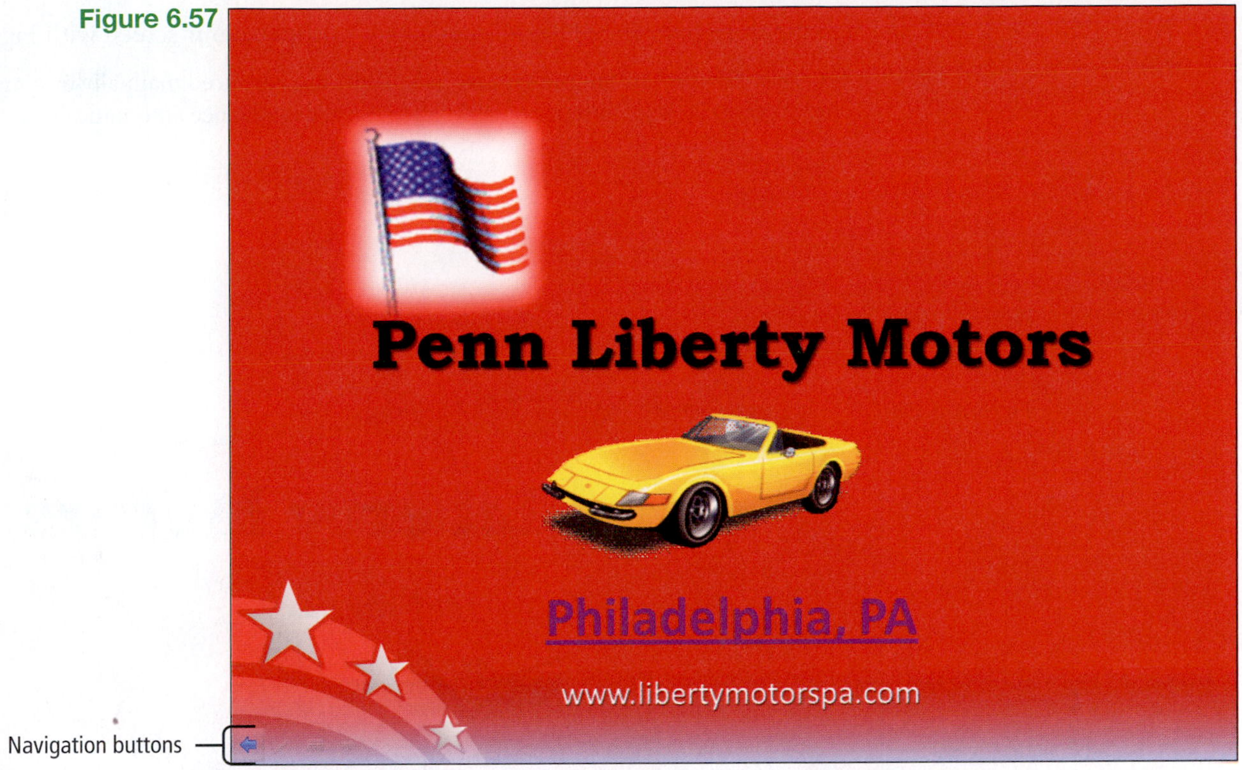

2 Point to the second button—the **Annotation pointer** button. Compare your screen with Figure 6.58.

The Previous slide button displays as a blue arrow. The other buttons are Annotation pointer, Slide shortcut menu, and Next slide button. As you move the mouse over them, they can be seen.

Figure 6.58

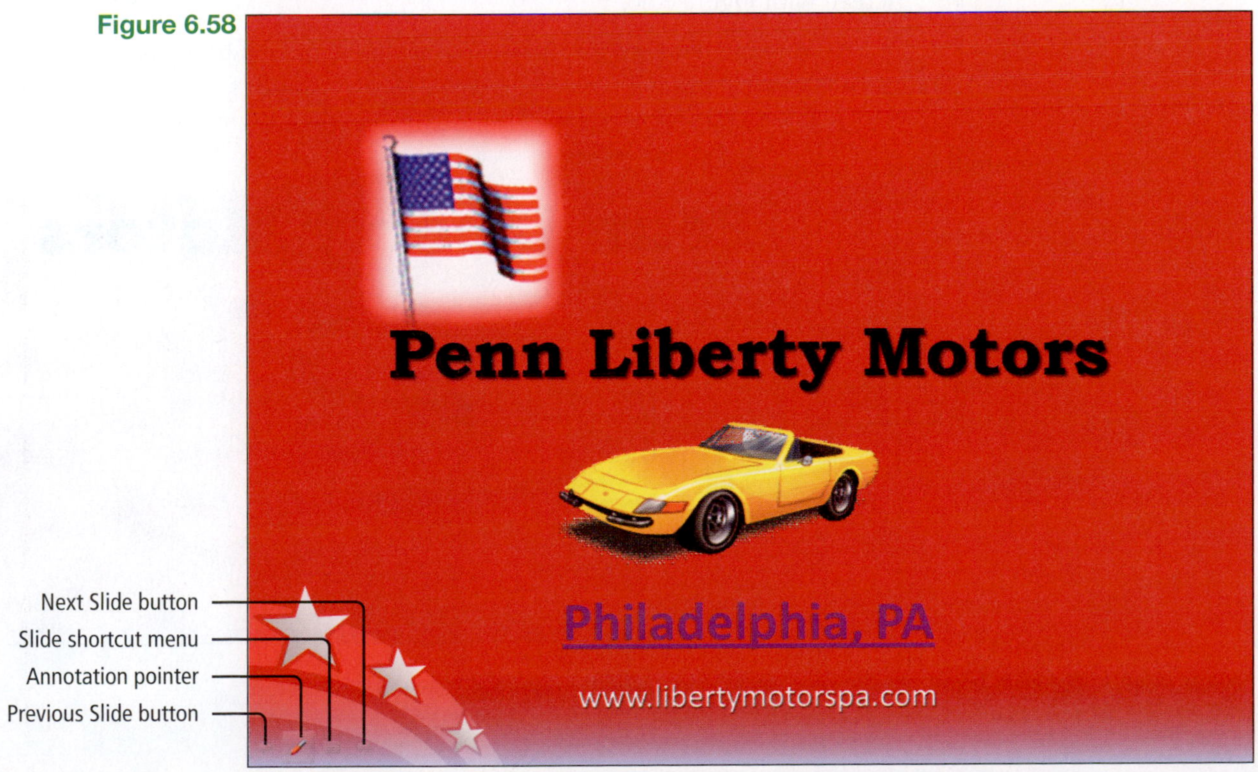

> **Another Way**
>
> To display the Slide shortcut menu, you can display the shortcut menu by right-clicking anywhere on a slide during a slide show. This shortcut menu also displays Pointer Options for the Annotation tool.

3 Click the third button—**Slide shortcut menu**. Compare your screen with Figure 6.59.

Pause is dimmed. In this presentation, the slides are advanced manually by a mouse click or by pressing Enter. Pause is available when the slides advance automatically.

Figure 6.59

4 From the shortcut menu, click **Go to Slide**. Point to **Slide 7**, and then compare your screen with Figure 6.60.

The currently displayed slide has a check mark, and the number of the hidden slide (Slide 6) is in parentheses.

Figure 6.60

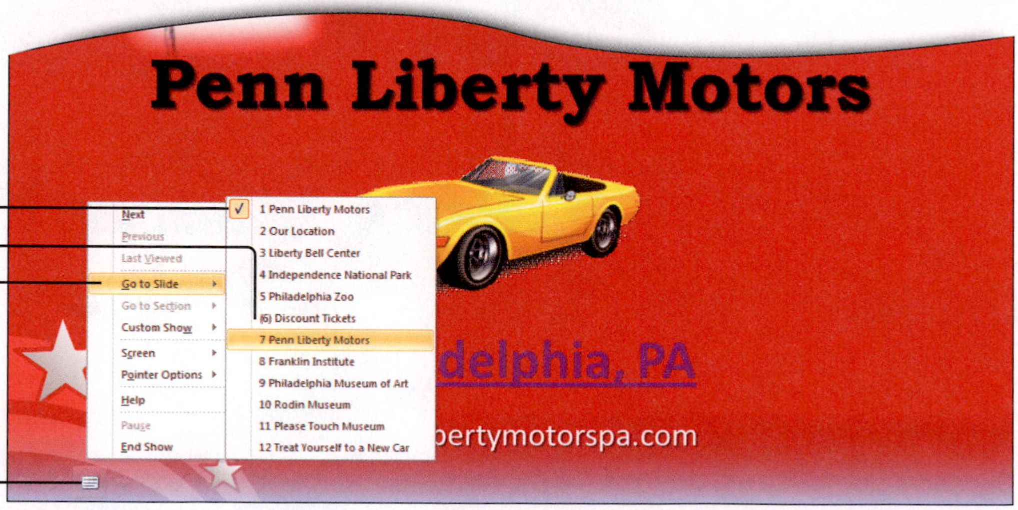

5 Click **Slide 7** to display Slide 7. Right-click anywhere on the slide, click **Custom Show**, and then click **Historic**. Click to view each of the slides in the custom show. When the slide show is finished, press Esc.

Slide 7 displayed. You also right-clicked Slide 7 to display the shortcut menu, and then you viewed the Historic custom show.

6 **Save** your changes.

Activity 6.18 | Using the Annotation Tool

In this activity, you will use the Annotation tool to highlight and annotate information on a slide.

1 Using the technique you practiced, start the slide show from the beginning. Right-click anywhere on the slide to display the **Slide shortcut menu**, click **Go to Slide**, and then click **Slide 7**.

2 At the lower left corner of the slide, click the second navigation button—**Annotation pointer**. Compare your screen with Figure 6.61. Take a moment to review the annotation options, as described in the table shown in Figure 6.62.

Figure 6.61

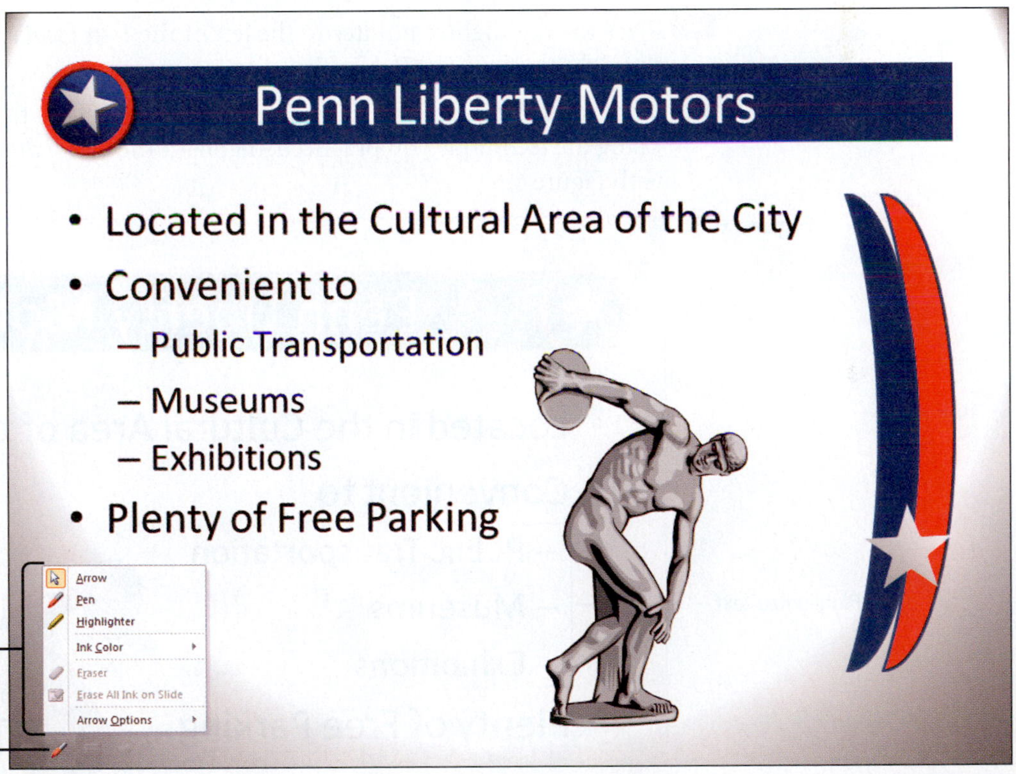

Menu options

Annotation pointer

Annotation Pointer Menu

Screen Element	Description
Arrow	Denotes that the mouse pointer displays when the Arrow Options is set for Visible. When the Arrow Options is set for Hidden, the mouse pointer does not display.
Pen	Allows you to write or circle items on the slide.
Highlighter	Allows you to emphasize parts of the slide.
Ink Color	Displays a selection of colors for highlighting or writing with the pen.
Eraser	Removes areas of an annotation.
Erase All Ink on Slide	Removes all annotations on a slide.
Arrow Options	Enables you to hide the mouse pointer or to allow it to remain visible during a slide show. The default is Visible.

Figure 6.62

3 From the shortcut menu, click **Highlighter**.

The mouse pointer displays as a yellow rectangle.

4 Place the highlighter pointer to the left of the *P* in *Public*, and then click and drag to the right to highlight *Public Transportation*.

5 Point to the left of *Museums*, and then click and drag to the right to highlight *Museums*. Using the technique you practiced, highlight the text *Exhibitions*. Compare your screen with Figure 6.63.

Figure 6.63

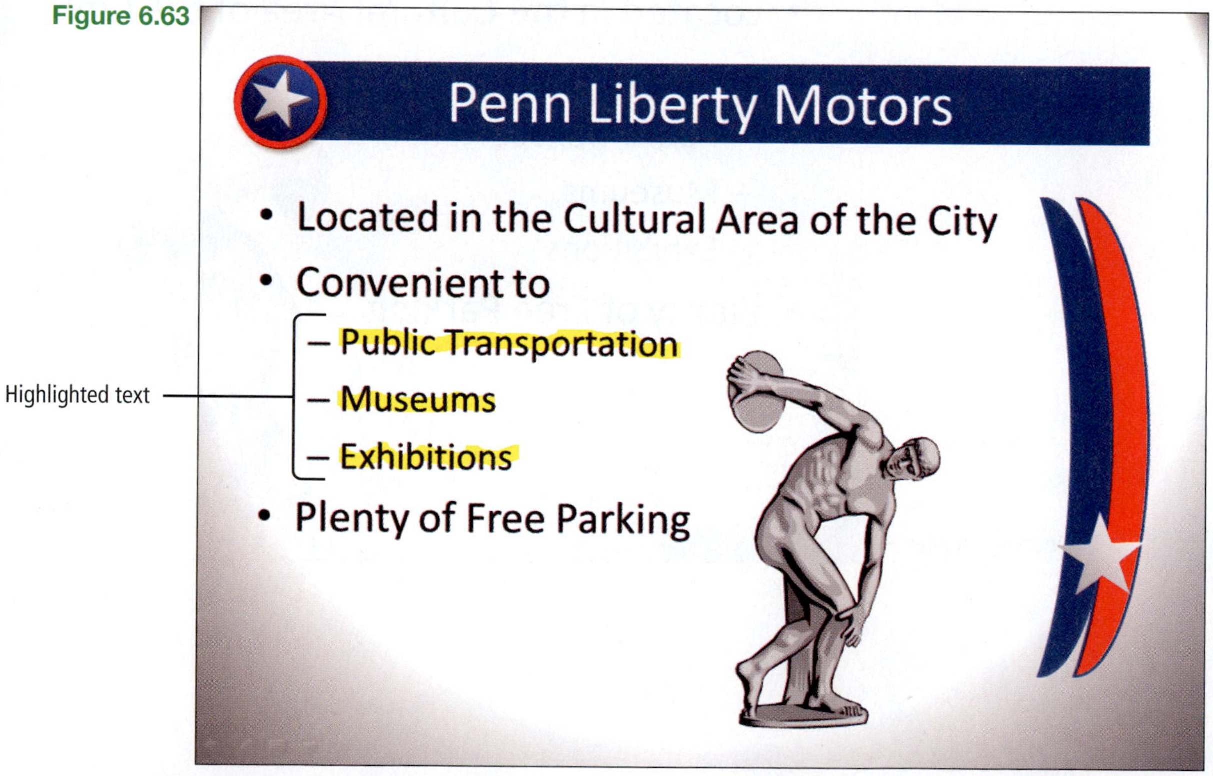

6 Click the **Annotation pointer** button. Click **Ink Color**, and then under **Standard Colors**, click the first color—**Dark Red**.

7 Click the **Annotation pointer** button, and then click **Pen**.

The annotation pointer displays as a small red circle or dot.

8 Point above the word *Parking*, and then click and drag to draw a circle around the word *Parking*. Compare your screen with Figure 6.64.

Figure 6.64

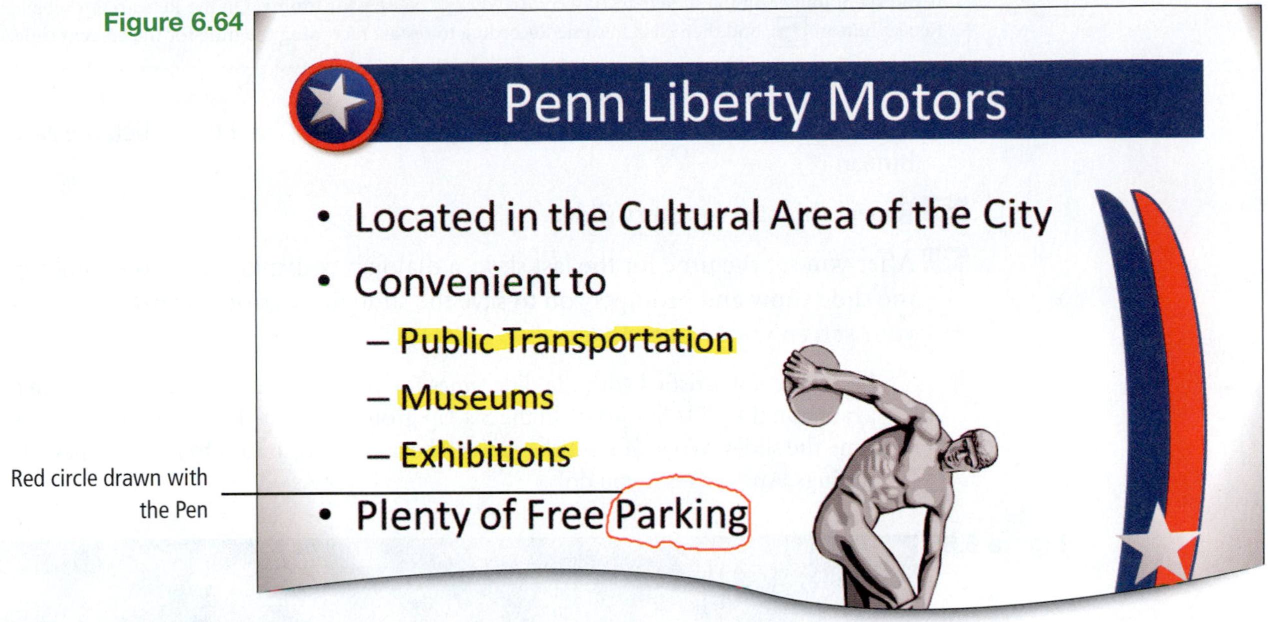

9 Click the **Annotation pointer** button, and then click **Eraser**. Click one time on the circle to remove the circle. It is not necessary to drag the eraser.

10 Click the **Annotation pointer** button, and then click **Pen**. Using the technique you practiced, draw a circle around the word *Free*.

11 Press Esc two times. In the displayed dialog box, which prompts you to keep your annotations, click the **Keep** button.

12 **Save** your changes.

Activity 6.19 | Creating a Self-Running Presentation

In this activity, you will set up a presentation to run without an individual present to run the slide show. Normally, self-running presentations run on a ***kiosk***. A kiosk is a booth that includes a computer and a monitor that may have a touch screen. Usually, kiosks are located in an area such as a mall, a trade show, or a convention—places that are frequented by many people.

1 With the **title slide** as the active slide, click the **Slide Show tab**. In the **Set Up group**, click **Rehearse Timings**. Compare your screen with Figure 6.65.

The Recording toolbar displays, and the Slide Time box begins timing the presentation.

Figure 6.65

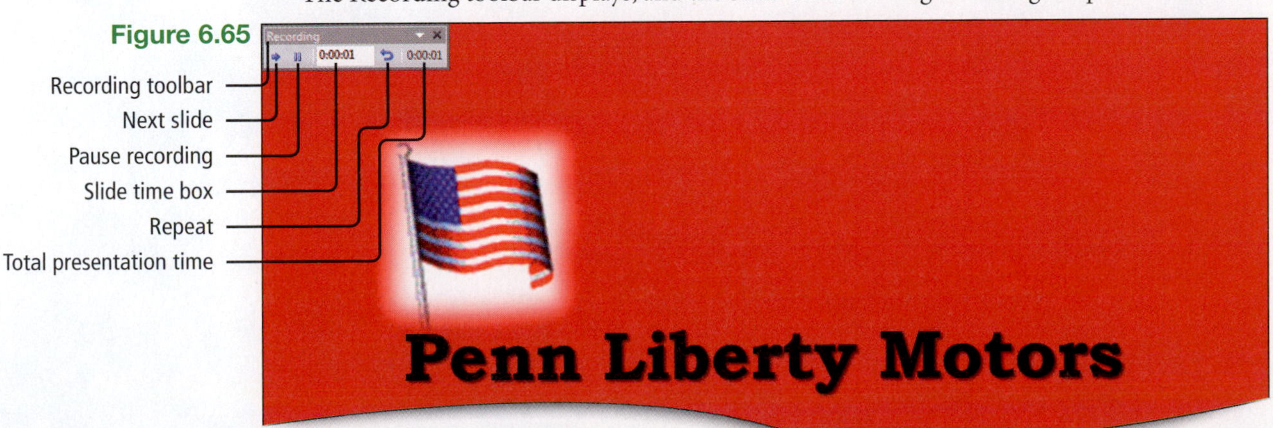

Alert | Did Your Time Get Past 10 Seconds?

If you spent longer on the slide than 10 seconds, you can revise your timing. On the Rehearsal toolbar, click the Repeat button, and then click Resume Recording to restart recording the time for the current slide.

2 Wait until the **Slide Time** box displays **10 (seconds)**, and then click the **Next** button.

3 Repeat this step for every slide.

4 After you set the time for the last slide, a dialog box displays with the total time for the slide show and prompts you to save the slide timings or discard them. Compare your screen with Figure 6.66.

If you are not satisfied with the slide times for your slide show, you can rehearse the times again. On the Slide Show tab, in the Set Up group, click the Rehearse Timings button, and time the slides. When you finish, you will be asked if you want to keep the new slide timings. Answer Yes if you do.

Figure 6.66

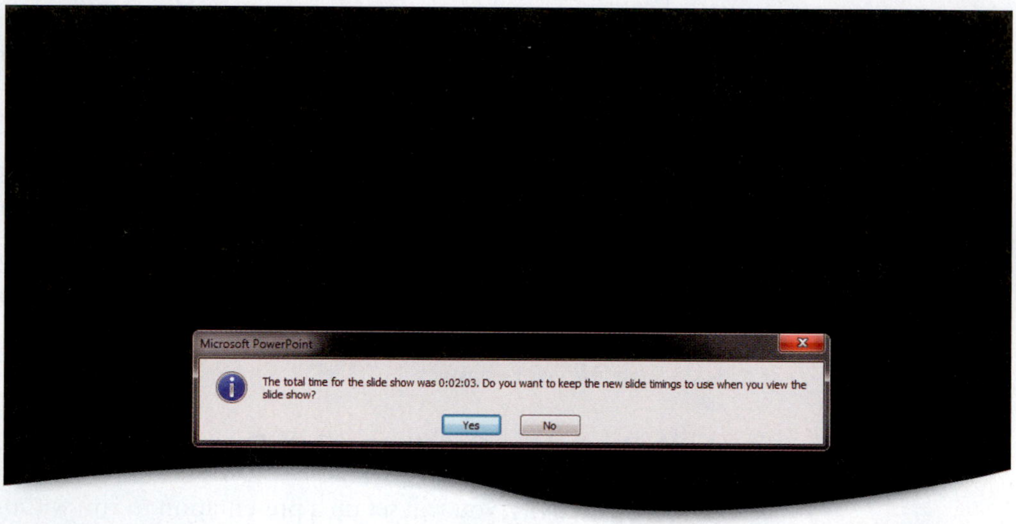

5 Click **Yes**. At the bottom right corner of the window, drag the Zoom slider to 70%. Compare your screen with Figure 6.67.

Slide Sorter view displays with the time of each slide in the presentation. Your slide times may not be timed at exactly 10 seconds. There is a delay between the click and the actual time, but that is not critical.

Figure 6.67

Slide Sorter view

Slide time

Hidden slide

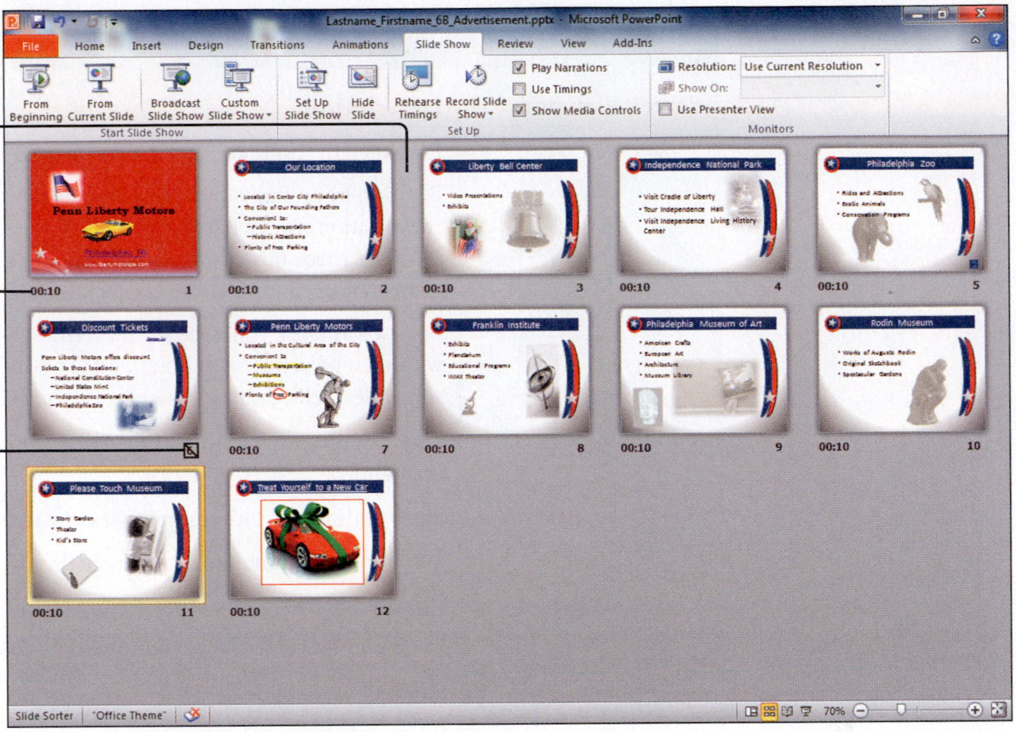

Alert! | **Are Your Slide Times Longer Than the Time You Expected?**

If you want your slide times to be an exact number of seconds, click the Next button early. For example, if you want each slide to be 10 seconds, click the Next button when you see 9 in the Slide Time box.

6 On the **Slide Show tab**, in the **Set Up group**, click the **Set Up Slide Show** button. Compare your screen with Figure 6.68.

The Set Up Show dialog box displays. The options in the Set Up Show dialog box are described in the table shown in Figure 6.69.

Figure 6.68

Set Up Show dialog box

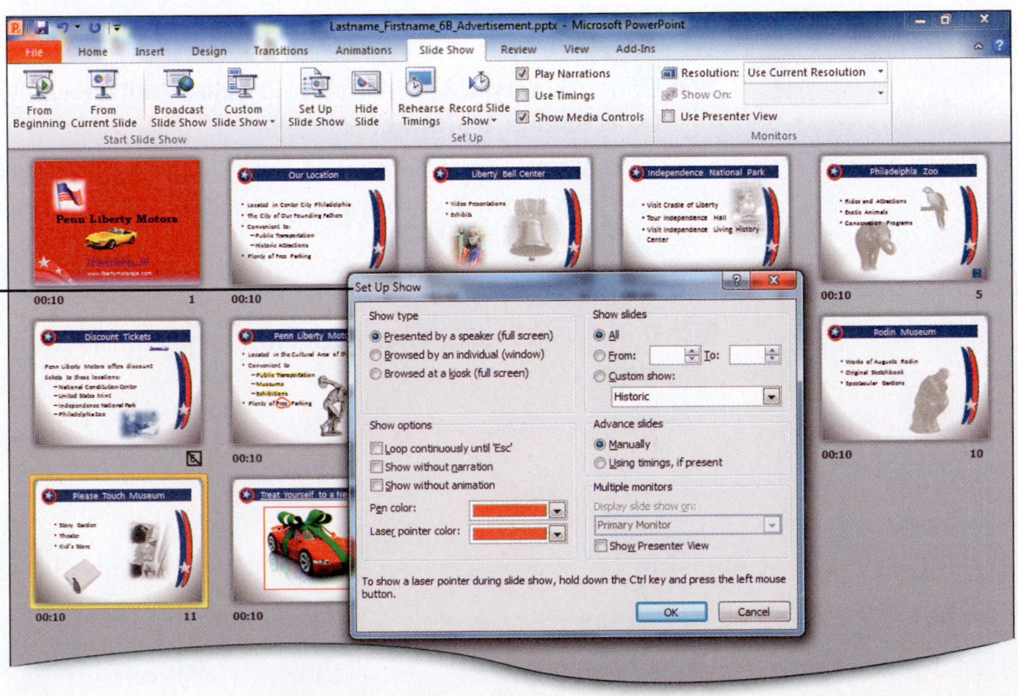

PowerPoint | Chapter 6

Set Up Show Options

Screen Element	Description
Show type	Presented by a speaker (full screen) is used to present to a live audience. Browsed by an individual (window) enables your audience to view the presentation from a hard drive, CD, or the Internet. Selecting the Show scrollbar check box allows the audience to scroll through a self-running presentation running on an unattended computer. Browsed at kiosk (full screen) delivers a self-running show that can run without a presenter in an unattended booth or kiosk. You can also send someone a self-running presentation on a CD.
Show options	Loop continuously until the Esc key is pressed is used when the show is unattended. Show without narration suppresses any recorded audio in the presentation. Show without animation suppresses the animation in the presentation. Pen color allows you to select a color for the slide show. Laser pointer color allows you to select a color for the slide show.
Show slides	Show all of the slides. Select a range of slides to view. Show a custom show.
Advance slides	Manually lets you advance the slides yourself. Using timings, if present, activates the timings you set for each slide.
Multiple monitors	If your computer supports using multiple monitors, a PowerPoint presentation can be delivered on two monitors. Show Presenter View allows you to run the PowerPoint presentation from one monitor while the audience views it on a second monitor. This enables you to run other programs that will not be visible to your audience.

Figure 6.69

7 Under **Show type**, select **Browsed at a kiosk (full screen)**. Under **Advance slides**, click **Using timings, if present**.

Under Show options, the Loop continuously until "Esc" check box is selected by default. This option refers to playing a sound file or animation continuously. It is also unavailable for you to change.

8 Click **OK**.

9 Start the slide show **From Beginning**. View a few slides, and then press Esc to end the show.

Note | To Change the Slide Show Timings

If you want new timings for your slides, you can rehearse the timings again. On the Slide Show tab, in the Set Up group, click the Rehearse Timings button, and then set new timings for each slide in the presentation. When all slides have been timed, you will be asked whether you want to keep the new timings or to cancel them and keep the old timings.

10 On the **Slide Show tab**, in the **Set Up group**, click **Set Up Slide Show** button. Under **Show type**, select **Presented by a speaker (full screen)**. Under **Advance slides**, click **Manually**. Click **OK**.

The timings are saved with the presentation. When you want to use them for a kiosk, click the Set Up Slide Show button, select Browsed at a kiosk (full screen) and Use timings, if present.

11 On the **View tab**, in the **Presentation Views group**, click the **Normal** button.

12 On the **Insert tab**, in the **Text group**, click the **Header & Footer** button to display the **Header and Footer** dialog box. Click the **Notes and Handouts tab**. Under **Include on page**, select the **Date and time** check box, and then select **Fixed**. If necessary, clear the Header check box, and then select the **Page number** and **Footer** check boxes. In the **Footer** box, using your own name, type **Lastname_Firstname_6B_Advertisement** and then click **Apply to All**.

13 Display **Backstage** view, click **Properties**, and then click **Show Document Panel**. Replace the text in the **Author** box with your own first name and last name; in the **Subject** box, type your course name and section number; and in the **Keywords** box, type **discount, tourist, attractions** **Close** the **Document Information Panel**.

14 **Save** your changes. **Close** your presentation, and then **Exit** PowerPoint. Submit your work as directed.

End You have completed Project 6B

Content-Based Assessments

Summary

In this chapter, you practiced various techniques related to viewing and presenting a slide show by adding and modifying slide transitions and various animation effects, including entrance, exit, and emphasis effects and motion paths. Within a slide show, you also inserted hyperlinks to link to a Web page, an e-mail address, other files, and other slides within a slide show. You practiced hiding slides and creating a basic custom slide show and a hyperlinked custom slide show. You created action buttons and used the onscreen navigation tools. You practiced annotating slides and created a self-running slide show.

Key Terms

Matching

Match each term in the second column with its correct definition in the first column by writing the letter of the term on the blank line in front of the correct definition.

____ 1. Term used to describe any type of movement or motion.

____ 2. File format used for graphic images.

____ 3. A quick way to navigate to a separate slide show from within the original presentation.

____ 4. File format used for photos.

____ 5. The term applied to how and in what direction text or objects move on a slide.

____ 6. An animation effect that, for example, makes an object shrink, grow in size, or change color.

____ 7. A V-shaped symbol that indicates more information or options are available.

____ 8. A graphical representation that counts the number of seconds the animation takes to complete.

____ 9. The term that identifies the application used to create a file.

____ 10. A portion of text, a graphic, or a placeholder on a slide that, when clicked, produces a result.

A Action button
B Animation
C Annotation
D Basic custom slide show
E Chevron
F Emphasis effect
G File extension
H GIF
I Hyperlinked custom slide show
J JPG (JPEG)
K Motion path effect
L Timeline
M Trigger
N URL
O With Previous

_____ 11. A separate presentation saved with its own title that contains some of the slides from the original presentation.

_____ 12. The term applied to describe a custom animation effect that starts at the same time as the preceding effect in the list.

_____ 13. The term that defines the address of documents and resources on the Web.

_____ 14. A built-in shape that you can add to your presentation and then assign an action to occur upon the click of a mouse.

_____ 15. A note or highlight on a slide that can be saved or discarded.

Multiple Choice

Circle the correct answer.

1. Animation effects that occur when a presentation moves from slide to slide are known as:
   A. transitions **B.** entrances **C.** protocol
2. The animation effect that occurs when the text or object is introduced into a slide is called the:
   A. beginning effect **B.** With Previous effect **C.** entrance effect
3. The animation effect that occurs when the text or object leaves the slide or disappears is called the:
   A. exit effect **B.** emphasis effect **C.** chevron
4. The start method of an animation that allows the animation to occur after preceding animations on the slide is:
   A. On Click **B.** After Previous **C.** With Previous
5. Text or objects that, when clicked, will transport you to a Web page, another document, or another area of the same document are:
   A. animated GIFs **B.** hyperlinks **C.** kiosks
6. The term that refers to an action that will occur when the mouse pointer is placed on an action button is:
   A. protocol **B.** resolution **C.** Mouse Over
7. A booth that includes a computer and a monitor that can include a touch screen is a:
   A. custom slide show **B.** URL **C.** kiosk
8. Buttons that display on the slides during a slide show and that allow you to perform actions such as move to the next slide, the previous slide, the last viewed slide, or the end of the slide show are:
   A. GIF buttons **B.** navigation tools **C.** motion path effects
9. Another name for the file type that defines the format of the file or the application that created it is:
   A. file extension **B.** timeline **C.** trigger
10. The protocol used on the World Wide Web to define how messages are formatted and transmitted is:
    A. URL **B.** HTTP **C.** HTML

Apply 6A skills from these Objectives:

1. Apply and Modify Slide Transitions
2. Apply Custom Animation Effects
3. Modify Animation Effects

Skills Review | Project 6C Vintage Car

In the following Skills Review, you will modify a PowerPoint presentation advertising the annual Vintage Car Event hosted by Penn Liberty Motors. You will apply slide transitions and custom animation effects to the slide show to generate interest in the event. Your completed presentation will look similar to Figure 6.70.

Project Files

For Project 6C, you will need the following file:

p06C_Vintage_Cars.pptx

You will save your presentation as:

Lastname_Firstname_6C_Vintage_Cars.pptx

Project Results

Figure 6.70

(Project 6C Vintage Car continues on the next page)

Skills Review | Project 6C Vintage Car (continued)

1 **Start** PowerPoint. Locate and open the file **p06C_Vintage_Cars**. Using your own first and last name, save the file as **Lastname_Firstname_6C_Vintage_Cars** in your **PowerPoint Chapter 6** folder.

2 Make the **title slide** the active slide.

a. Click the **Transitions tab**. In the **Transition to This Slide group**, click the **More** button. In the **Transitions** gallery, under **Subtle**, in the last row, click the first transition—**Shape**.

b. In the **Timing group**, click the **Apply to All**.

3 Make **Slide 2** the active slide.

a. In the **Transition to This Slide group**, click the **More** button. In the **Transitions** gallery, under **Subtle**, in the first row, click the fourth transition—**Push**.

b. Click the **Transitions tab**. In the **Timing group**, in the **Duration** box, click **spin box up arrow** to **02.00**, and then click the **Preview** button.

c. In the **Timing group**, click the **Sound arrow**, and then select **Click**. Click the **Preview** button.

d. In the **Timing group**, under **Advance Slide**, clear the **On Mouse Click** check box. Click once in the **After spin box**, type **3** and then press Enter.

4 Make **Slide 3** the active slide.

a. Apply the same transition, sound, and duration slide settings and advance slide mouse settings that you applied to **Slide 2**.

b. Click the **Slide Show tab**, and then view the slide show **From Beginning**. Wait for Slides 2 and 3 to advance after 3 seconds, and then press Esc.

c. On **Slide 3**, click the body text placeholder. On the **Animations tab**, in the **Advanced Animation group**, click the **Add Animation** button, and then under **Entrance**, click on **Fly In**.

d. In the **Advanced Animation group**, click the **Animation Pane** button. In the **Animation Pane**, below *Content Placeholder*, click the chevron to expand the contents. In the **Animation Pane**, click the **Play** button.

5 Make **Slide 4** the active slide.

a. Select the body text placeholder. On the **Animations tab**, in the **Advanced Animation group**, click the **Add Animation** button. Under **Entrance**, click **Wipe**.

b. In the **Animation group**, click the **Effect Options** button, and then select **All at Once**.

c. In the **Animation Pane**, click the **Play** button.

(Project 6C Vintage Car continues on the next page)

6 Make **Slide 1** the active slide.

a. Click to select the subtitle placeholder—*Penn Liberty Motors*. On the **Animations tab**, in the **Advanced Animation group**, click the **Add Animation** button. Under **Emphasis**, in the first row, click **Grow/Shrink**. In the **Animation Pane**, click the **Play** button.

b. Click the subtitle placeholder. In the **Advanced Animation group**, click the **Add Animation** button, and then click **More Exit Effects**. Under **Basic**, select **Disappear**. Click **OK**.

c. In the **Animation Pane**, right-click the second effect, which is the exit effect for the subtitle, and then click **Start After Previous**. In the **Preview group**, click the **Preview** button to view the effect.

7 Make **Slide 4** the active slide.

a. Click to select the text body placeholder. On the **Animations tab**, in the **Animation group**, click the **Effect Options** button, and then click **By Paragraph**.

b. In the **Animation Pane**, click the chevron to expand all effects. Right-click the first effect—**Model A Cars**, and then click **Effect Options** to display the **Wipe** dialog box. On the **Timing tab**, click the **Start arrow**, and then select **After Previous**. Change the **Duration** to **1 seconds (Fast)**. Click **OK**.

c. Click to select the title placeholder. Click the **Add Animation** button. Under **Motion Paths**, click **Shapes**.

8 Make **Slide 3** the active slide.

a. Click to select the **text body placeholder**. In the **Animation Pane**, right-click the first entrance effect—*Luxury Cars,* and then select **Effect Options** to display the **Fly In** dialog box. On the **Effect tab**, under the **Settings**, click the **Direction arrow**, and then click **From Bottom - Left**.

b. Under **Enhancements**, click the **After animation arrow**. In the row of colors, click the fifth color—**Teal**. Click the **Animate text arrow**, and then click **All at Once**.

c. On the **Timing tab**, click the **Duration arrow**, and then click **1 seconds (Fast)**.

d. On the **Text Animation tab**, click the **Group text arrow**, select **All Paragraphs at Once**, and then click **OK**.

e. Click to select the title placeholder. On the **Animations tab**, in the **Advanced Animation group**, click the **Add Animation** button. Under **Emphasis**, select **Pulse**. In the **Animation Pane**, click the **Play** button.

Skills Review | Project 6C Vintage Car (continued)

f. At the bottom of the **Animation Pane**, to the left of *Re-Order*, click the **up arrow** to move the title—*Title 1: Exotic Cars*—to the top of the list. Click **Play** in the **Animation Pane**.

g. Click on **Slide Show tab**, and then view the slide show **From Beginning**.

9 **Close** the **Animation Pane**.

10 On the **Insert tab**, in the **Text group**:

a. Click the **Header & Footer** button to display the **Header and Footer** dialog box.

b. Click the **Notes and Handouts tab**. Under **Include on page**, select the **Date and time** check box, and then select **Fixed**. If necessary, clear the Header check box, and then select the Page number and Footer check boxes. In the **Footer** box, using your own name, type **Lastname_Firstname_6C_Vintage_Cars** and then click **Apply to All**.

11 Display **Backstage** view, click **Properties**.

a. Click **Show Document Panel**. Replace the text in the **Author** box with your own first and last name; in the **Subject** box, type your course name and section number.

b. In the **Keywords** box, type **vintage cars, Penn Liberty**

c. **Close** the **Document Information Panel**.

12 Print **Handouts 4 Slides Horizontal**, or submit your presentation electronically as directed by your instructor.

13 **Save** the presentation. **Exit** PowerPoint.

End **You have completed Project 6C**

Apply 6B skills from these Objectives:

- 4 Insert Hyperlinks
- 5 Create Custom Slide Shows
- 6 Present and View a Slide Presentation

Skills Review | Project 6D Safety

In the following Skills Review, you will modify a PowerPoint presentation showcasing safety features of the cars sold by Penn Liberty Motors. You will insert hyperlinks to a Web page and the e-mail address of the company's safety director. You will also create custom slide shows of standard safety features available on all vehicles and custom safety features available on select vehicles. You will annotate the slide show and then create a self-running version of the presentation for use in a kiosk. Your completed presentation will look similar to Figure 6.71.

Project Files

For Project 6D, you will need the following files:

p06D_Safety.pptx
p06D_ESC.docx

You will save your presentation as:

Lastname_Firstname_6D_Safety.pptx
Lastname_Firstname_6D_ESC_Benefits.docx

Project Results

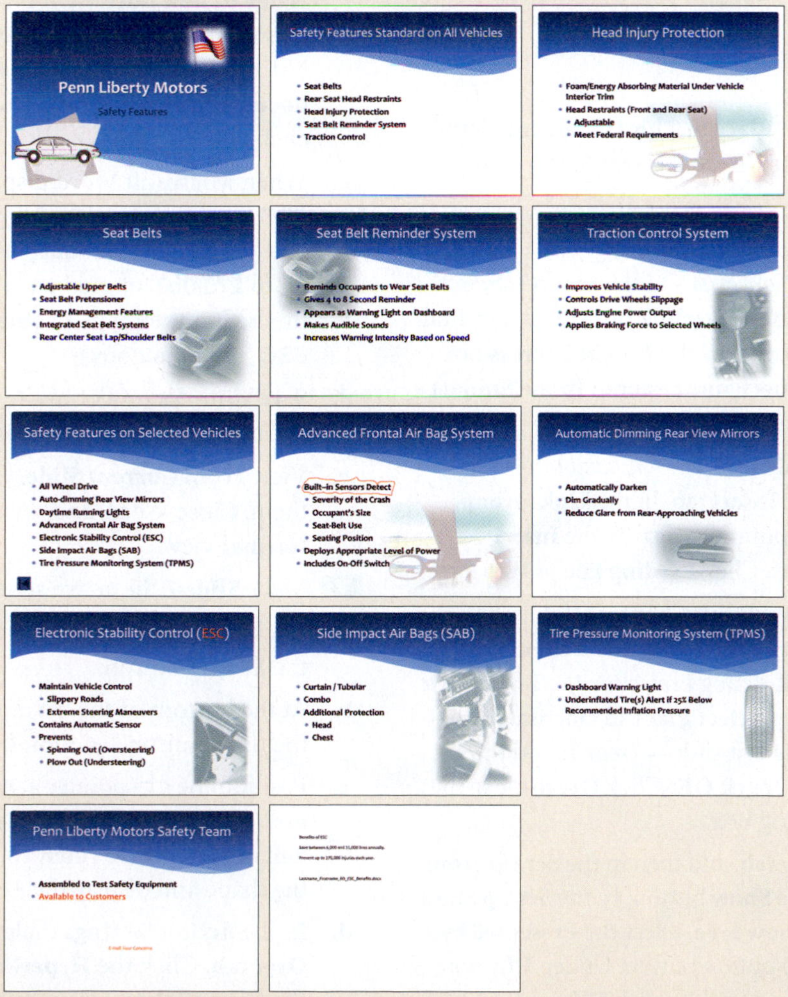

Figure 6.71

(Project 6D Safety continues on the next page)

Skills Review | Project **6D** Safety (continued)

1 **Start** PowerPoint. Locate and open the file **p06D_Safety**. Save the file as **Lastname_Firstname 6D_Safety** in your **PowerPoint Chapter 6** folder.

2 Make the **title slide** the active slide.

a. Click to select the graphic of the car.

b. Click the **Insert tab**. In the **Links group**, click the **Hyperlink** button. In the **Insert Hyperlink** dialog box, under **Link to**, click **Existing File or Web Page**.

c. In the **Address** box, type **http://www.nhtsa.dot.gov** This is the Web site for the National Highway Traffic Safety Administration.

d. Click the **ScreenTip** button. In the **Set Hyperlink ScreenTip** dialog box, type **National Highway Traffic Safety Administration** Click **OK**. Click **OK** again.

3 Confirm that the **title slide** is the active slide.

a. In the subtitle, click and drag to select *Safety Features*.

b. On the **Insert tab**, in the **Links group**, click the **Hyperlink** button.

c. Under **Link to**, click **Place in This Document**. Scroll down, click **13. Penn Liberty Motors Safety Team**, and then click **OK**.

4 Make **Slide 13** the active slide.

a. Select *E-mail Your Concerns*. On the **Insert tab**, in the **Links group**, click the **Hyperlink** button. Under **Link to**, click **E-mail Address**. In the **E-mail address** box, type **safetyteam@libertymotors.com** In the **Subject** box, type **Safety First** Click **OK**.

b. Select the second bulleted item—*Available to Customers*. Click the **Insert tab**. In the **Links group**, click the **Hyperlink** button to display the **Insert Hyperlink** dialog box. Click **Existing File or Web Page**.

c. Navigate to the **PowerPoint Chapter 6** folder and select **Lastname_Firstname_6B_Advertisement**. In the **Insert hyperlink** dialog box, click the **Bookmark** button to display the **Select Place in Document** dialog box. Click the last slide—*Treat Yourself to a New Car*—and then click **OK**. Click **OK** to close the Edit **Hyperlink** dialog box.

d. Click the **Slide Show tab**, and then in the **Set Up group**, click the **Set Up Slide Show** button. In the **Set Up Show** dialog box, under **Show type**, select the **Presented by a speaker (full screen)** option button. Under *Advance slides*, click **Manually**, and then click **OK**.

e. View **From Current Slide**. Click the hyperlinks to test them.

5 Make **Slide 10** the active slide.

a. Click to select the photo of the dashboard. Click the **Insert tab**. In the **Links group**, click the **Hyperlink** button. In the **Insert Hyperlink** dialog box, under **Link to**, click **Existing File or Web Page**.

b. Click the **Browse for File** button, navigate to the location where your student files are stored, and then double-click **p06D_ESC.docx**. Click **OK**.

6 **Slide 10** should be the active slide.

a. In the title, select *ESC*. On the **Insert tab**, in the **Links group**, click the **Hyperlink** button. In the **Insert Hyperlink** dialog box, click the **ScreenTip** button. Type **Benefits** Click **OK**.

b. Under **Link to**, click **Create New Document**. In the **Name of new document** box, type **Lastname_Firstname_6D_ESC_Benefits.docx** using your own last and first name. Make sure the **Edit the new document now** option button is selected, and then click **OK**.

c. When Microsoft Word displays, type **Benefits of ESC** and then press Enter. Type **Save between 6,000 and 11,000 lives annually.** Press Enter. Type **Prevent up to 275,000 injuries each year.** Press Enter two times, and then type **Lastname_Firstname_6D_ESC_Benefits.docx**

d. **Save** your document in the **PowerPoint Chapter 6** folder, and then **Exit** Microsoft Word.

e. View **From Current Slide**. Click the hyperlinks to test them. **Close** Word, and then press Esc to return to **Normal** view.

7 Make **Slide 7** the active slide.

a. Click the **Insert tab**. In the **Illustrations group**, click the **Shapes** button.

b. At the bottom of the list, under **Action Buttons**, click the third button—**Action Button: Beginning**.

c. Position the + pointer at **4.5 inches on the left side of the horizontal ruler** and at **3 inches on the lower half of the vertical ruler,** and then click once to insert the shape and display the **Action Settings** dialog box.

d. In the **Action Settings** dialog box, click the **Mouse Over tab**. Click the **Hyperlink to** option button, click the **Hyperlink to** arrow, and select **First Slide**. Click

(Project 6D Safety continues on the next page)

Skills Review | Project 6D Safety (continued)

the **Play sound** check box, click the **Play sound check box** arrow, and then select **Chime**. Click **OK**.

e. On the **Format tab**, in the **Size group**, change the **Height** to **.5"** and the **Width** to **.5"**.

f. View the slide show **From Current Slide**, click the action button to test it. Press Esc.

8 If necessary, make the title slide the active slide.

a. Click the **Slide Show tab**. In the **Start Slide Show group**, click the **Custom Slide Show** button, and then click **Custom Shows**. In the **Custom Shows** dialog box, click the **New** button. In the **Slide show name** box, type **Standard Safety Features**

b. In the **Slides in presentation** box, click to select **Slide 1**, hold down Shift, and then click **Slide 5**. Click **Add**. Scroll to and then double-click **Slide 13** to add it to the slides in the custom show. Click **OK**.

c. Click the **Edit** button. Under **Slides in presentation**, double-click **Slide 6** to add it to the custom show. Under **Slides in custom show**, click **Slide 7**, and then click the **up arrow** so the new slide is before the *Penn Liberty Motors Safety Team* slide. Click **OK**.

d. In the **Custom Shows** dialog box, click the **New** button. In the **Slide show name** box, type **Optional Safety Features**

e. In the **Slides in presentation** box, click to select **Slide 7**, hold down Shift, and then click **Slide 13**. Click **Add**. Click **OK**, and then **Close** the **Custom Shows** dialog box.

f. In the **Start Slide Show group**, click the **Custom Slide Show** button. Click **Standard Safety Features**, and then view the slides. Repeat the procedure to view **Optional Safety Features**.

9 Make the **title slide** the active slide.

a. Click to select the picture of the flag. On the **Insert tab**, in the **Links group**, click **Hyperlink**. In the **Insert Hyperlink** dialog box, under **Link to**, click **Place in This Document**.

b. Under **Select a place in this document**, scroll down to display the **Custom Shows**. Select **Optional Safety Features**, and then click the **Show and return** check box. Click **OK**.

c. View the slide show **From Beginning**, and then click the flag. When the title slide displays, press Esc.

10 Make **Slide 7** the active slide. Click the **Slide Show tab**. In the **Set Up group**, click the **Hide Slide** button.

(Project 6D Safety continues on the next page)

11 Make **Slide 8** the active slide.

a. In the **Start Slide Show group**, click **From Current Slide.**

b. At the bottom left corner of the screen, click the second navigation button—**Annotation pointer**.

c. From the shortcut menu, click **Pen**. Circle the first bulleted item—*Built-in Sensors Detect.*

d. Click the **Annotation pointer** button. Click **Ink Color**, and then under **Standard Colors**, click the sixth color—**Green**. Circle the last bullet—*Includes On-Off Switch.*

e. Click the **Annotation pointer** button, click **Eraser**, and then click to delete the green annotation on the last bulleted item.

f. Press Esc two times. In the displayed dialog box, which prompts you to keep your annotations, click the **Keep** button.

12 Make the **title slide** the active slide.

a. Click the **Slide Show tab**. In the **Set Up group**, click **Rehearse Timings**.

b. In the **Slide Time** display, wait for **4** seconds, and then click **Next Slide arrow**. Repeat for all slides. When prompted, click **Yes** to save the timings.

c. In the **Set Up group**, click the **Set Up Slide Show** button. In the **Set Up Show** dialog box, under **Show type**, select the **Browsed at a kiosk (full screen)** option button. Click **OK**.

d. View the slide show **From Beginning** and view all slides. When Slide 1 appears, press Esc.

e. On the **Slide Show tab**, in the **Set Up group**, click the **Set Up Slide Show** button. Under **Show type**, select **Presented by a speaker (full screen)**. Under **Advance slides**, select **Manually**. Click **OK**.

f. On the **View tab**, in the **Presentation Views**, click **Normal** to return to **Normal** view.

13 On the **Insert tab**, in the **Text group**:

a. Click the **Header & Footer** button to display the **Header and Footer** dialog box.

b. Click the **Notes and Handouts tab**. Under **Include on page**, select the **Date and time** check box, and then select **Fixed**. If necessary, clear the Header check box, and then select the Page number and Footer check boxes. In the **Footer** box, using your own name, type **Lastname_Firstname_6D_Safety** and then click **Apply to All**.

Skills Review | Project **6D** Safety (continued)

14 Display **Backstage** view, click **Properties**.

a. Click **Show Document Panel**. Replace the text in the **Author** box with your own first and last name; in the **Subject** box, type your course name and section number.

b. In the **Keywords** box, type **safety, seat belts, Penn Liberty**

c. **Close** the **Document Information Panel**.

15 Print **Handouts 9 Slides Horizontal**, or submit your presentation electronically as directed by your instructor.

16 **Save** the presentation. **Exit** PowerPoint.

End **You have completed Project 6D**

Apply 6A skills from these Objectives:

1. Apply and Modify Slide Transitions
2. Apply Custom Animation Effects
3. Modify Animation Effects

Mastering PowerPoint | Project 6E Race Car

In the following Mastering PowerPoint project, you will modify a PowerPoint presentation advertising the Annual Race Car Rally hosted by Penn Liberty Motors. You will apply slide transitions and custom animation effects to the slide show to make the slide show more dynamic. The purpose is to appeal to race car enthusiasts. Your completed presentation will look similar to Figure 6.72.

Project Files

For Project 6E, you will need the following files:

p06E_Race_Car.pptx
p06E_Fast_Car.wav
p06E_Car_Horn.wav
p06E_Tires1.wav
p06E_Drag_Race.wav

You will save your presentation as:

Lastname_Firstname_6E_Race_Car.pptx

Project Results

Figure 6.72

(Project 6E Race Car continues on the next page)

Mastering PowerPoint | Project 6E Race Car (continued)

1 **Start** PowerPoint. Locate and open the file **p06E_Race_Car**. Save the file in your chapter folder using the file name **Lastname_Firstname_6E_Race_Car**

2 Make the **title slide** the active slide. Display the **Transitions** gallery, and then under **Subtle**, in the first row, click the third transition—**Fade**. Set the **Duration** to **1.50**, and then click **Apply to All**.

3 Make **Slide 2** the active slide. Click the content placeholder to select the **SmartArt** graphic. In the **Add Animation** gallery, under **Entrance**, click **Fly In**. Click the **Effect Options** button. Under **Sequence**, choose **Level at Once**.

4 Open the **Animation Pane**, right-click the entrance effect for content placeholder, and then click **Effect Options**. Change the **Direction** to **From Left**. On the **Timing tab**, set the **Duration** to **1 seconds (Fast)**.

5 On **Slide 2**, click to select the car graphic, and then apply the **Fly In** entrance effect. Change **Direction** to **From Top-Left**, set the **Duration** to **2 seconds (Medium)**, and then set the **Start** to **After Previous**.

6 On **Slide 2**, click the **Transition tab**. In the **Timing group**, insert the sound file **p06E_Fast_Car.wav** from the student data files.

7 Make **Slide 3** the active slide. Select the **SmartArt** graphic, and then apply the **Fly In** entrance animation effect. Click the **Effect Options** button, and then select **One by one**. Click the **Effect Options** button again, and then select **From Top**. Change the **Duration** to **1 seconds (Fast)**. From the student data files, add the sound file **p06E_Car_Horn.wav**.

8 On **Slide 3**, click to select the car graphic, and then add the **Fly In** entrance effect. In the **Animation Pane**, right-click the entrance effect for the picture, select **Effect Options**, and then change the **Direction** to **From Top-Right**. Under **Enhancements**, add the sound **p06E_Car_Horn.wav**. Change the **Start** to **After Previous** and the **Duration** to **2 seconds (Medium)**.

9 View the slide show **From Current Slide** to test the transition and animation entrance effects on **Slide 3**.

10 Make **Slide 4** the active slide. Insert the sound **p06E_Tires1.wav**. Click to select the car graphic. Click the **Add Animation** button, and then click **More Exit Effects**. Under **Moderate**, click **Basic Zoom**.

11 View the slide show **From Current Slide** to test the transition and animation entrance effects on **Slide 4**.

12 Make **Slide 5** the active slide. Select the title placeholder. Click the **Add Animation** button. Select **More Motion Paths**, and then under **Lines & Curves**, select **Arc Up**.

13 On **Slide 5**, select the **SmartArt** graphic. Display the **Animations** gallery. Under **Exit**, click **Fade**. In the **Animation group**, click **Effect Options**, and then select **One by One**. Click to select the car graphic, and then apply the **Grow/Shrink** emphasis effect. Click the **Effect Options** button, and then select **Smaller**. Select the car graphic if necessary, and then insert the sound **p06E_Drag_Race.wav**.

14 View the slide show **From Current Slide** to test the transition and animation entrance effects on **Slide 5**.

15 Make the **title slide** the active slide. Click to select the title placeholder. Display the **Add Animation** gallery, and then click **More Entrance Effects**. Under **Basic**, select **Blinds**. In the **Animation Pane**, right-click the entrance effect for the title, and then click **Effect Options**. On the **Timing tab**, set the **Start** to **With Previous** and the **Duration** to **1 seconds (Fast)**. On the **Transitions tab**, in the **Timing group**, apply the **Whoosh** sound.

16 Start the slide show **From Beginning**, and then view the animation effects. When you are finished, return to **Normal** view.

17 Insert a footer on the notes and handouts that includes a fixed date and time, the page number, and the file name.

18 Modify the **Properties** in the **Show Document Panel**. Replace the text in the **Author** box with your own name; in the **Subject** box, type your course name and section number; and in the **Keywords** box, type **race, exhibition, events** **Close** the **Document Information Panel**.

19 Print **Handouts 6 Slides Horizontal**, or submit your presentation electronically as directed by your instructor

20 **Save** the presentation. **Exit** PowerPoint.

End **You have completed Project 6E**

Apply **6B** skills from these Objectives:

- 4 Insert Hyperlinks
- 5 Create Custom Slide Shows
- 6 Present and View a Slide Presentation

Mastering PowerPoint | Project 6F Custom Detail

In the following Mastering PowerPoint project, you will modify a PowerPoint presentation listing many of the customization services available at Penn Liberty Motors to give a vehicle a unique appearance. You will insert hyperlinks and create custom slide shows of interior and exterior detailing. You will annotate the slide show and create a self-running version of the presentation for use in the automobile dealership. Your completed presentation will look similar to Figure 6.73.

Project Files

For Project 6F, you will need the following file:

p06F_Custom_Detail.pptx

You will save your presentation as:

Lastname_Firstname_6F_Custom_Detail.pptx
Lastname_Firstname_6F_Dashboard.docx

Project Results

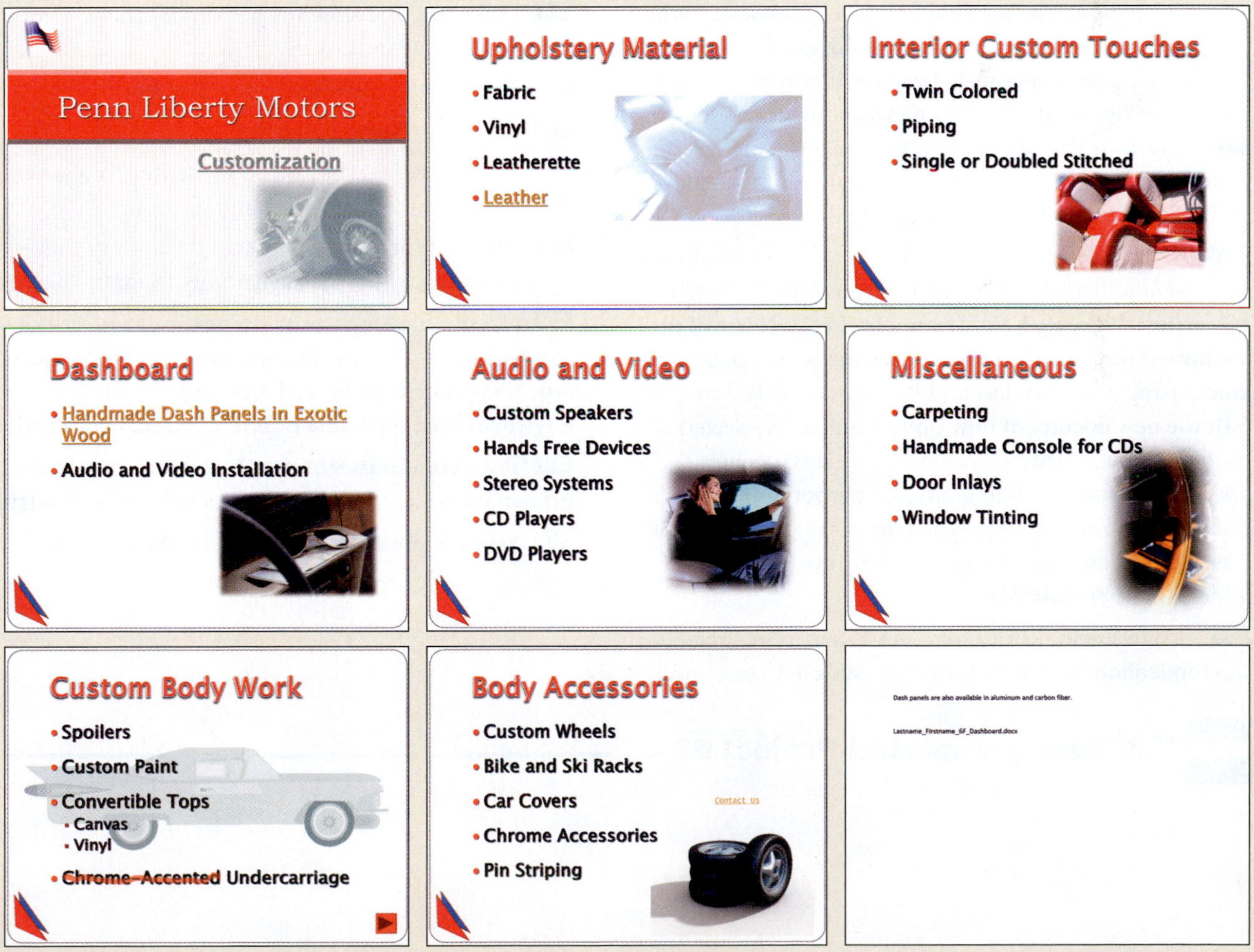

Figure 6.73

(Project 6F Custom Detail continues on the next page)

Mastering PowerPoint | Project 6F Custom Detail (continued)

1 **Start** PowerPoint. Locate and open the file **p06F_Custom_Detail**. Save the file in your chapter folder using the file name **Lastname_Firstname_6F_Custom_Detail**

2 Make the **title slide** the active slide. Click to select the graphic of the car. Display the **Insert Hyperlink** dialog box, and then type the **Address www.libertymotorspa.com** Include the ScreenTip **Liberty Motors Web site** View **From Current Slide** and test the link.

3 Make **Slide 7** the active slide. At the bottom right corner of the slide, insert an **Action Button: Forward or Next**, which is found in the last row of the **Shapes** gallery. Size the button about .5" wide and high. View **From Current Slide** and test the link.

4 Make **Slide 2** the active slide. Select *Leather*. Insert a hyperlink to **Place in This Document**, and then click **3. Interior Custom Touches**. Test the link.

5 Make **Slide 8** the active slide. Select *Contact Us*, and then add a **Hyperlink** to an **E-mail Address**. For the e-mail address, type **customteam@libertymotors.com** Include the **ScreenTip**, **Contact us for all your customization needs.** Test the link, and then close the e-mail program. Note: If you are using a campus computer, the actual e-mail may not work as it would at home.

6 Make **Slide 4** the active slide. Select the first bulleted item—*Handmade Dash Panels in Exotic Wood*. Set up a **Hyperlink** to **Create New Document**. In the **Name of new document** box, type **Lastname_Firstname_6F_Dashboard.docx** using your own last and first name. Make sure the **Edit the new document now** option button is selected. In the displayed Word document, type **Dash panels are also available in aluminum and carbon fiber.** Press Enter two times, and then type **Lastname_Firstname_6F_Dashboard.docx** **Save** the document in your chapter folder, and then **Exit** Word.

7 Create a new custom slide show named **Interior Customization** Add **Slide 1** through **Slide 6**. Create another custom slide show named **Body Customization** Add **Slide 1**, **Slide 7**, and **Slide 8**. Move the *Body Accessories* slide so it is number 2 in the list. Remove **Slide 1**.

8 Make the **title slide** the active slide. Double-click to select the subtitle *Customization*. Insert a hyperlink to **Place in This Document**. Scroll down to custom shows, and then click **Body Customization**. Select the **Show and return** check box, and then click **OK**. View **From Current Slide** and test the link to view the 2 slides, and then return to the title slide.

9 Hide **Slide 5**.

10 Use the onscreen navigation tools to go to **Slide 7**. Click the **Annotation pointer**, and then click **Highlighter**. Change the **Ink Color** to **Red**. In the last bulleted item, highlight *Chrome-Accented*. Highlight the first bulleted item—*Spoilers*. When prompted, keep your annotations.

11 Make the **title slide** the active slide. Set each slide to display for 4 seconds.

12 Remove the highlighting on *Spoilers*

13 Return to **Normal** view.

14 Set the presentation to be **Presented by a speaker (full screen)** and advanced manually.

15 Insert a footer on the notes and handouts that includes a fixed date and time, the page number, and the file name.

16 Modify the **Document Properties**. Replace the text in the **Author** box with your own name; in the **Subject** box, type your course name and section number; and in the **Keywords** box, type **dashboard, custom, accessories**

17 Print **Handouts 9 Slides Horizontal**, or submit your presentation electronically as directed by your instructor

18 **Save** the presentation. **Exit** PowerPoint.

End **You have completed Project 6F**

Apply **6A** and **6B** skills from these Objectives:

1. Apply and Modify Slide Transitions
2. Apply Custom Animation Effects
3. Modify Animation Effects
4. Insert Hyperlinks
5. Create Custom Slide Shows
6. Present and View a Slide Presentation

Mastering PowerPoint | Project 6G Repairs

In the following Mastering PowerPoint project, you will modify a PowerPoint presentation advertising Penn Liberty Motors' Repair Department, listing the types of repairs performed and the goodwill customer services available. You will apply slide transitions and custom animation effects, insert hyperlinks, and create custom slide shows. You will annotate the slide show and create a self-running version of the presentation. Your completed presentation will look similar to Figure 6.74.

Project Files

For Project 6G, you will need the following files:

p06G_Repairs.pptx
p06G_Emergency.docx

You will save your presentation as:

Lastname_Firstname_6G_Repairs.pptx

Project Results

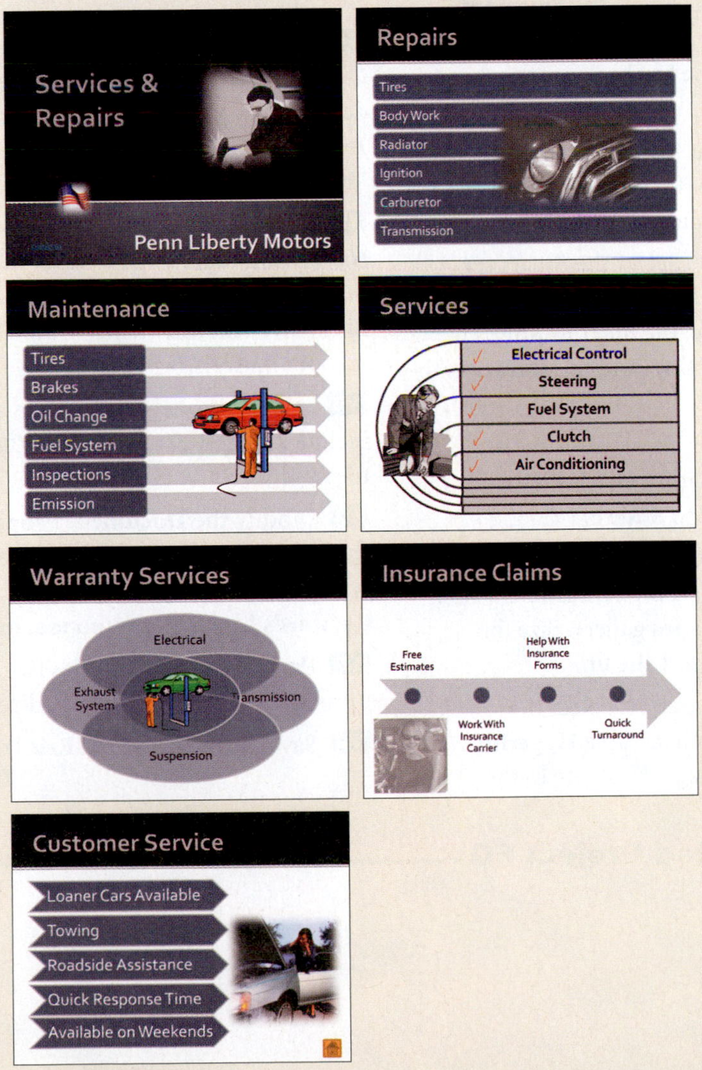

Figure 6.74

(Project 6G Repairs continues on the next page)

Mastering PowerPoint | Project 6G Repairs (continued)

1 **Start** PowerPoint. Locate and open the file **p06G_Repairs**, and then save the file as **Lastname_Firstname_6G_Repairs**

2 Make the **title slide** the active slide. Apply a **Wipe** transition to all slides.

3 Make **Slide 2** the active slide. Select the **SmartArt** graphic. Add the **Fly In** entrance effect, set the **Effect Options** to **One by One**, and then set the **Start** to **After Previous**. In the **Animation Pane**. select **Effect Options**. Set the **Direction** to **From Left**, and then change the **Duration** to **2 seconds (Medium)**.

4 Make **Slide 3** the active slide. Select the **SmartArt** graphic. Apply the **Fly In** entrance effect, set the **Effect Options** to **As One Object**, and then change the **Direction** to **From Left** and the **Duration** to **2 seconds**.

5 Make **Slide 4** the active slide. Select the **SmartArt** graphic, and then add the **Fade** entrance animation effect. Change the **Effect Options** to **One by One**. Change the **Start** to **After Previous**.

6 Make **Slide 5** the active slide. Using the same techniques, apply the same animation entrance effects to the **SmartArt** graphic as you applied to **Slide 4**.

7 Make **Slide 6** the active slide. Select the **SmartArt** graphic. Apply the **Wipe** entrance animation effect. Set the **Effect Options** to **One by One**, the **Start** to **After Previous**, the **Direction** to **From Left**, and the **Duration** to **1 seconds (Fast)**.

8 Make **Slide 7** the active slide. Using the same techniques, apply the same animation effects to the **SmartArt** graphic as you applied to **Slide 6**.

9 Make **Slide 7** the active slide. At the bottom right corner of the slide, insert an **Action Button: Home**, which is found in the last row of the **Shapes** gallery. Size the button about .5" wide and high. Test the link.

10 Make the **title slide** the active slide. Select the graphic of the repairman, and then set up a **Hyperlink** to **Link to** an **Existing File or Web Page**. Navigate to the location where your student files are stored, and then click **p06G_Emergency.docx**. For the **ScreenTip**, type **24-Hour Phone Number** Test the link.

11 Make **Slide 6** the active slide. Select the picture of the mother and child in the car, and then set up a **Hyperlink** to **Place in This Document**. Select *7. Customer Service.* Test the link.

12 Make **Slide 1** the active slide. Select *Contact Us*, and then set up a **Hyperlink** to an **E-mail Address**. For the **E-mail address**, type **repairs@libertymotors.com** Test the link.

13 Set up a new custom slide show named **Warranty and Maintenance** Add **Slides 1**, **3**, **4**, and **5** to the custom slide show. Set up a second custom slide show named **Insurance Claims** Add **Slide 6** and **Slide 7** to the custom slide show.

14 Make **Slide 2** the active slide. Select the picture of the car. Set up a **Hyperlink** to a **Place in This document**. Scroll down to the custom shows, and then click **Insurance Claims**. Click the **Show and return** check box. Test the link.

15 View the slide show **From Beginning**. Use the **Navigation tools** to go to **Slide 4**. Click the **Annotation pointer**, and then click **Pen**. In the gray area before each of the five text line items, draw a check mark. **Keep** the ink annotations.

16 Insert a footer on the notes and handouts that includes a fixed date and time, the page number, and the file name.

17 Modify the **Document Properties**. Replace the text in the **Author** box with your own name; in the **Subject** box, type your course name and section number; and in the **Keywords** box, type **insurance, maintenance, warranty**

18 Print **Handouts 9 Slides Horizontal**, or submit your presentation electronically as directed by your instructor

19 **Save** the presentation. **Exit** PowerPoint.

End **You have completed Project 6G**

Apply a combination of the **6A** and **6B** skills.

GO! Fix It | Project 6H Staff

Project Files

For Project 6H, you will need the following file:

p06H_Staff.pptx

You will save your presentation as:

Lastname_Firstname_6H_Staff.pptx
Lastname_Firstname_6H_Banks.docx

In this project, you will modify a PowerPoint presentation highlighting the employees of Penn Liberty Motors. Slide transitions and custom animation effects will add life to the slide show. You will also insert hyperlinks and create custom slide shows. You will annotate the slide show and create a self-running presentation.

Open **p06H_Staff**, and then save the file in your chapter folder as **Lastname_Firstname_6H_Staff** To complete the project, you will create a slideshow to do the following:

- Apply a Wipe transition and .5 Timing to all slides.
- On Slide 2, Slide 3, and Slide 6, apply the Wipe entrance animation to the SmartArt placeholder. Set the effect options to One by One, Start After Previous, Direction From Left, and Speed of Fast. Animate the salesman graphic on each slide with the Fade entrance effect starting after the previous effect.
- On Slide 4, animate the SmartArt placeholder with the Wipe entrance effect with the following options: One by One, Start After Previous, and Speed of Fast. Set the car graphic animation for an entrance effect of Fly In, From Left, Start After Previous, and Medium speed.
- On Slide 5, animate the SmartArt placeholder with a Fade entrance effect with the following options: One by One and Start After Previous. Add a Circle Motion path to the dollar sign graphic, and then apply Start After Previous. Use the dollar sign graphic to set up a hyperlink to Create New Document. Name the new document **Lastname_Firstname_6H_Banks.docx** In the Word document, type **We are committed to working with your bank, credit union, or other financial institution.** Press Enter two times, and then type **Lastname_Firstname_6H_Banks.docx** Save your document, and then exit Microsoft Word.
- Create a custom slide show named **Sales** that includes Slides 1, 2, and 3. Create a second custom slide show named **Service** that includes Slides 4, 5, and 6 to the show. On Slide 1, add a hyperlink to the flag graphic that takes you to the Service custom show. Set it to return to the title slide after showing.
- On Slide 4, highlight the bulleted item *Trained* and keep your annotation.
- Rehearse the slide show with timings of about 6 seconds for each slide. Set the slide show to advance the slide manually.
- Insert a Header & Footer on the Notes and Handouts that includes the date and time fixed, the page number, and a footer with the text **Lastname_Firstname_6H_Staff** Document Properties should include your name, course name and section, and the keywords **customer, quality, trainer**
- Save your presentation. Print Handouts 6 slides per page, or submit electronically as directed by your instructor.

End **You have completed Project 6H**

Content-Based Assessments

Apply a combination of the **6A** and **6B** skills.

GO! Make It | Project 6I Auto Show

Project Files

For Project 6I, you will need the following files:

p06I_Auto_Show.pptx
p06I_Registration.docx

You will save your presentation as:

Lastname_Firstname_6I_Auto_Show.pptx

By using the skills you practiced in this chapter, you will modify a presentation. Your presentation should look similar to Figure 6.75.

Start PowerPoint, open p06I_Auto_Show, and then save it in your chapter folder as **Lastname_Firstname_6I_Auto_Show** On the title slide, apply a transition to all slides and set a timing duration. On all slides, add an entrance effect for the content placeholder, and then apply effect options for direction, timing, and starting sequence.

On Slide 7, select the bell, and then add a hyperlink to the file p06I_Registration.docx, located in the student data files. Add an appropriate ScreenTip. On Slide 4, click the top auto, and then add an entrance animation with effect options for speed and starting sequence. On Slide 8, format the SmartArt placeholder for entrance and effect options. Link the last slide to the first slide using an action button.

On the title slide, format the text *Philadelphia International Auto Show* for exit animation and effect options. Hyperlink the text *Contact Us* to the e-mail address sponsor@libertymotors.com

Set up a new custom slide show. For the first show, use the name **Auto_Show** and add Slides 1, 2, 3, 4, and 5. For the second show, use the name **Convention_Center** and add Slides 6, 7, and 8. Hide Slide 4. On Slide 2, hyperlink the text *Pennsylvania Convention Center* to the custom show Convention_Center. Set up a slide show to be viewed on a kiosk with rehearsed timings for the presentation.

Insert a Header & Footer on the Notes and Handouts that includes the date and time fixed, the page number, and a footer with the text **Lastname_Firstname_6I_Auto_Show** In the Document Properties, add your name, course name and section, and the keywords **Pennsylvania, convention, trade** Save your file. Print Handouts 4 slides per page, or submit electronically as directed by your instructor.

(Project 6I Auto Show continues on the next page)

GO! Make It | Project 6I Auto Show (continued)

Figure 6.75

End **You have completed Project 6I**

Apply a combination of the **6A** and **6B** skills.

GO! Solve It | Project 6J Leasing

Project Files

For Project 6J, you will need the following files:

p06J_Leasing.pptx
p06J_Terms_ Conditions.docx

You will save your presentation as:

Lastname_Firstname_6J_Leasing.pptx

Open the file p06J_Leasing, and then save it as **Lastname_Firstname_6J_Leasing** Apply transitions and add entrance, emphasis, exit, and motion path animation effects. Modify and set effect options to the animation effects.

Add an action button on one slide. Create a hyperlink to the following e-mail address: **leasing @libertymotors.com** Insert a hyperlink to the Word document p06J_Terms_Conditions.docx. Create one custom show, and then hyperlink it on one of the slides. Use the animation pen tool to annotate one of the slides and keep the ink annotations. Rehearse the timings, and then set up the show for a kiosk.

Insert a Header & Footer on the Notes and Handouts that includes the date and time fixed, the page number, and a footer with the text **Lastname_Firstname_6J_Leasing** In the Document Properties, add your name, course information, and the keywords **lease, value** Save your presentation. Print Handouts 4 slides per page, or submit electronically as directed by your instructor.

	Performance Level		
Performance Element	**Exemplary:** You consistently applied the relevant skills.	**Proficient:** You sometimes, but not always, applied the relevant skills.	**Developing:** You rarely or never applied the relevant skills.
Formatted slides with a variety of transitions and effects.	Slide show included relevant transitions and effects.	Slide show included a variety of transitions and effects, but they were not appropriate for the presentation.	Slide show did not include transitions and effects.
Added action button and hyperlinks as instructed.	Action button and requested hyperlinks were present and completely functioning.	Action button and some hyperlinks were present, but not all functioned correctly.	There is little evidence that action button and hyperlinks are present.
Created a custom slide show and linked it on one slide.	Custom slide show was created and linked properly.	Custom slide show was created but not linked.	The custom slide show was not created.
Set up slide show for a kiosk.	The kiosk worked correctly.	The slide show timings were rehearsed, but the show was not set up as a kiosk.	The slide show timings were not rehearsed.

End **You have completed Project 6J**

Apply a combination of the 6A and 6B skills.

GO! Solve It | Project 6K Special Orders

Project Files

For Project 6K, you will need the following file:

p06K_Special_Orders.pptx

You will save your presentation as:

Lastname_Firstname_6K_Special_Orders.pptx

In this project, you will customize a slide show showcasing special-order vehicles, such as limousines, motorcycles, and race cars, available at Penn Liberty Motors. You will apply innovative transitions and customized entrance and exit animation effects.

Open p06K_Special_Orders, and then save it as **Lastname_Firstname_6K_Special_Orders** Insert a hyperlink to the Penn Liberty Motors Web site: **www.libertymotorspa.com** Insert a hyperlink to the Special Order Department's e-mail address: **custom@libertymotors.com** Use hyperlinks to link the picture of a vehicle to its features. Create at least two basic custom shows to appeal to two different vehicle enthusiasts, and then insert a hyperlink to one of the custom shows. Create an action button.

Insert a Header & Footer on the Notes and Handouts that includes the date and time fixed, the page number, and a footer with the text **Lastname_Firstname_6K_Special_Orders** In the Document Properties, add your name, course information, and the keywords **classic, limousines** Save your presentation. Print Handouts 4 slides per page, or submit electronically as directed by your instructor.

Performance Element	Performance Level: Exemplary: You consistently applied the relevant skills.	Proficient: You sometimes, but not always, applied the relevant skills.	Developing: You rarely or never applied the relevant skills.
Formatted slide show with a variety of transitions and effects.	Slide show included relevant transitions and effects.	Slide show included a variety of transitions and effects, but they were not appropriate for the presentation.	Slide show contained no transitions and effects.
Inserted hyperlinks to Web site, to e-mail address, and to place in the slide show.	All hyperlinks worked correctly.	One of the hyperlinks did not work correctly.	Hyperlinks were not created, or they did not work correctly.
Created two custom slide shows and linked one of them.	Created two custom shows and one was linked correctly.	Created one custom show and may not have linked it.	No custom slide shows were created.
Created an action button.	The action button produced the intended result.	Action button was created but did not work properly.	No action button was inserted.

End **You have completed Project 6K**

Outcomes-Based Assessments

Rubric

The following outcomes-based assessments are *open-ended assessments*. That is, there is no specific correct result; your result will depend on your approach to the information provided. Make *Professional Quality* your goal. Use the following scoring rubric to guide you in *how* to approach the problem and then to evaluate *how well* your approach solves the problem.

The *criteria*—Software Mastery, Content, Format and Layout, and Process—represent the knowledge and skills you have gained that you can apply to solving the problem. The *levels of performance*—Professional Quality, Approaching Professional Quality, or Needs Quality Improvements—help you and your instructor evaluate your result.

	Your completed project is of Professional Quality if you:	**Your completed project is Approaching Professional Quality if you:**	**Your completed project Needs Quality Improvements if you:**
1-Software Mastery	Choose and apply the most appropriate skills, tools, and features and identify efficient methods to solve the problem.	Choose and apply some appropriate skills, tools, and features, but not in the most efficient manner.	Choose inappropriate skills, tools, or features, or are inefficient in solving the problem.
2-Content	Construct a solution that is clear and well organized, contains content that is accurate, appropriate to the audience and purpose, and is complete. Provide a solution that contains no errors in spelling, grammar, or style.	Construct a solution in which some components are unclear, poorly organized, inconsistent, or incomplete. Misjudge the needs of the audience. Have some errors in spelling, grammar, or style, but the errors do not detract from comprehension.	Construct a solution that is unclear, incomplete, or poorly organized; contains some inaccurate or inappropriate content; and contains many errors in spelling, grammar, or style. Do not solve the problem.
3-Format and Layout	Format and arrange all elements to communicate information and ideas, clarify function, illustrate relationships, and indicate relative importance.	Apply appropriate format and layout features to some elements, but not others. Overuse features, causing minor distraction.	Apply format and layout that does not communicate information or ideas clearly. Do not use format and layout features to clarify function, illustrate relationships, or indicate relative importance. Use available features excessively, causing distraction.
4-Process	Use an organized approach that integrates planning, development, self-assessment, revision, and reflection.	Demonstrate an organized approach in some areas, but not others; or, use an insufficient process of organization throughout.	Do not use an organized approach to solve the problem.

Apply a combination of the **6A** and **6B** skills.

GO! Think | Project 6L Car Purchase

Project Files

For Project 6L, you will need the following files:

New blank PowerPoint presentation
p06L_Off_Lease.docx

You will save your presentation as:

Lastname_Firstname_6L_Car_Purchase.pptx

Penn Liberty Motors has launched a new sales initiative to sell used cars. In this project, you will create a presentation with a minimum of six slides comparing the benefits of buying a new car versus buying a used car. In addition, certified lease cars should be part of the presentation. Insert a hyperlink on one slide to link to the **p06L_Off_Lease.docx** file provided in the student files Include transitions and custom animation effects in the presentation. Create a self-running slide show.

Insert a Header & Footer on the Notes and Handouts that includes the date and time fixed, the page number, and a footer with the text **Lastname_Firstname_6L_Car Purchase** In the Document Properties, add your name and course information and the keywords **certification, lease** Save your presentation. Print Handouts 6 slides per page, or submit electronically as directed by your instructor.

End You have completed Project 6L

Apply a combination of the **6A** and **6B** skills.

GO! Think | Project 6M Security

Project Files

For Project 6M, you will need the following files:

p06M_Security.pptx
p06M_Silent_Alarms.docx
p06M_Brakes.wav
p06M_Car_Alarm.wav
p06M_Siren.wav

You will save your presentation as:

Lastname_Firstname_6M_Security.pptx

In this project, you will transform the existing presentation regarding security and anti-theft devices for automobiles into a dynamic slide show. Open **p06M_Security**, and then apply transitions, customized animation effects, and sound effects—use **p06M_Car_Alarm.wav**, **p06M_Brakes.wav**, and **p06M_Siren.wav**. Add a hyperlink to the Microsoft Word document **p06M_Silent_Alarms.docx**. The sound files and the Microsoft Word document are provided. Keep in mind that the animation effects should enhance and not overwhelm the content of the slides. Create a custom show from the original presentation, and then create a self-running show for Penn Liberty Motors to present at the upcoming Annual Auto Show.

Insert a Header & Footer on the Notes and Handouts that includes the date and time fixed, the page number, and a footer with the text **Lastname_Firstname_6M_Security** In the Document Properties, add your name and course information and the keywords **alarms, keyless** Save your presentation. Print Handouts 6 slides per page, or submit electronically as directed by your instructor.

End You have completed Project 6M

Apply a combination of the 6A and 6B skills.

You and GO! | Project 6N Digital Sound

Project Files

For Project 6N, you will need the following file:

p06N_Digital_Sound.pptx

You will save your presentations as:

Lastname_Firstname_6N_Digital_Sound.pptx
Lastname_Firstname_6N_Pricing.docx

In this project, you will create a slide show for Penn Liberty Motors to showcase their new and innovative digital stereo systems to be offered on select automobiles.

Include transitions, sounds, and animation effects to spark interest in this new technology. Insert a hyperlink to the Web page www.digital.libertymotorspa.com Include a hyperlink to a new document you create named **Lastname_Firstname_6N_Pricing.docx** In the document, type: **Pricing is not yet available for our integrated digital stereo system. However, we are now taking orders. Please e-mail Penn Liberty Motors at orders@libertymotors.com.**

Create a custom slide show and annotate at least one slide.

Insert a Header & Footer on the Notes and Handouts that includes the date and time fixed, the page number, and a footer with the text **Lastname_Firstname_6N_Digital_Sound** In the Document Properties, add your name and course information and the keywords **pricing, digital** Save your presentation. Print Handouts 6 slides per page, or submit electronically as directed by your instructor.

End You have completed Project 6N

Business Running Case

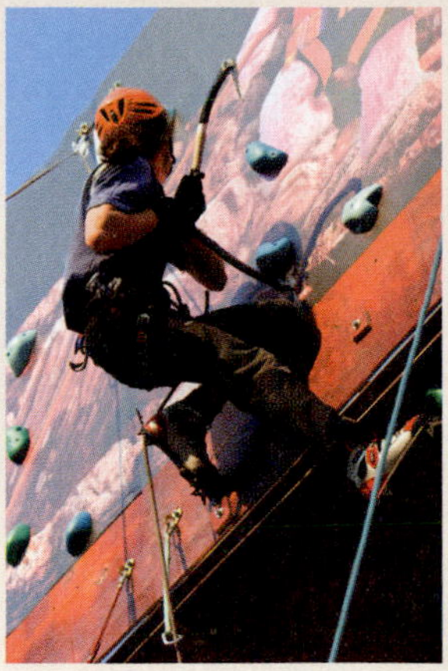

Razvan CHIRNOAGA/Shutterstock

In this project, you will apply the PowerPoint skills you practiced in Chapters 4 through 6. This project relates to **Front Range Action Sports**, which is one of the country's largest retailers of sports gear and outdoor recreation merchandise. The company has large retail stores in Colorado, Washington, Oregon, California, and New Mexico, in addition to a growing online business. Major merchandise categories include fishing, camping, rock climbing, winter sports, action sports, water sports, team sports, racquet sports, fitness, golf, apparel, and footwear. The company plans for expansion in other states in the west and into Vancouver, British Columbia.

You will develop a presentation that Irene Shviktar, Vice President of Marketing, will show at a corporate marketing retreat that summarizes the company's marketing and implementation plan to expand the footwear product lines. Your completed presentation will look similar to the one shown in Figure 2.1.

Project Files

For Project BRC2, you will need the following files:

- pBRC2_Goals.pptx
- pBRC2_Lake.jpg
- pBRC2_SkateSet.jpg
- pBRC2_Hiking.png
- pBRC2_Skating.jpg
- pBRC2_Sports.mid
- pBRC2_Target.wmf
- pBRC2_Athletic.jpg
- pBRC2_Sales.jpg

You will save your presentations as:

- Lastname_Firstname_BRC2_Goals_Template.potx
- Lastname_Firstname_BRC2_Goals.pptx
- Lastname_Firstname_BRC2_Goals.pdf
- Lastname_Firstname_BRC2_Album.pptx

Project Results

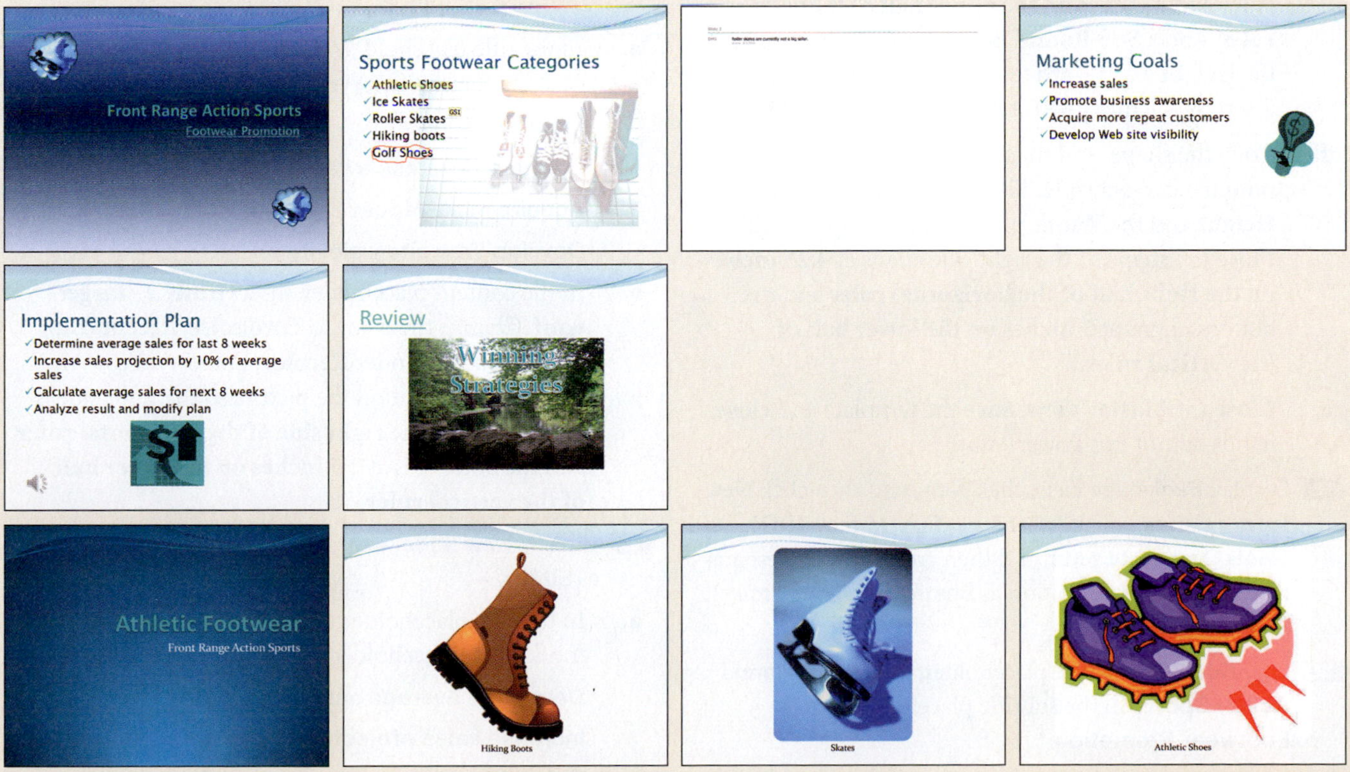

Figure 2.1

Business Running Case

Front Range Action Sports

1 **Start** PowerPoint. From the student files that accompany this textbook, locate and open **pBRC2_Goals.pptx**. Navigate to the folder you created for **Front Range Action Sports**, or create one if necessary, and then save the presentation as a **template** named **Lastname_Firstname_BRC2_Goals_Template.potx**

a. Display the **Slide Master** view. The Flow theme has already been applied. On the **Flow Slide Master**, change the **Master title style** font to **Lucida Sans** and the **Font size** to **40**. Change the content placeholder font to **Lucida Sans**. Change the bullets on the first line to **Arrow Bullets**.

b. On the **Title Slide Layout**, change the **Background Style** to **Style 11**. Format the **Background** with a **Gradient fill** set with a **Linear** type. Position the **middle gradient stop** at **45%** with the color **Blue, Accent 1, Darker 50%**, and then close the dialog box, without applying to all. Change the **Font size** of the Master title placeholder to **40**.

c. On the **Title Slide Layout**, from **Basic Shapes**, insert the **Cloud** shape—the eleventh shape in the third row—at **4.25 inches on the left half of the horizontal ruler** and **3 inches on the upper half of the vertical ruler**. Add a **Soft Round Bevel** shape effect. Change the **Height** and **Width** to **1.5"**. From your data files, insert the picture **pBRC2_Skating** as a **Shape Fill**.

d. Copy the shape, and then paste a second copy of it onto the current slide, **Title Slide Layout**. Change the **Height** and the **Width** of the copied shape to **1.2"**. Move the shape so the right side aligns at **4.25 inches on the right half of the horizontal ruler** and the bottom aligns at **3 inches on the lower half of the vertical ruler**.

e. **Close** the **Master View**. **Save** the template and **close** it, but do not exit PowerPoint.

2 Display **Backstage** view, click **New**, and then click **New from existing**. Click **Lastname_Firstname_BRC2_Goals_Template.potx**, and then create a new presentation. Save the presentation as **Lastname_Firstname_BRC2_Goals.pptx**

3 On **Slide 1**, in the title placeholder, type **Front Range Action Sports** In the subtitle placeholder, type **Footwear Promotion**

4 Insert a **New Slide** with the **Title and Content** layout as **Slide 2**.

a. In the title placeholder, type **Sports Footwear Categories** In the content placeholder, type the following bulleted items:

Athletic Shoes

Ice Skates

Roller Skates

Hiking Boots

Golf Shoes

b. Display the **Slide Master**. On the first thumbnail at the left, change the first-level bullets to **Checkmark Bullets**. Close the **Master View**.

c. On **Slide 2**, insert the picture **pBRC2_SkateSet.jpg**. Change the height to **4.5"**. Position the picture so the top is at **1.5 inches on the upper half of the vertical ruler** and the right side is at **4 inches on the right side of the horizontal ruler**. Apply **Send to Back**. Set the color to **Washout**, which is under **Recolor**, the first row, fourth color.

d. Insert the following comment after *Roller Skates*: **Roller skates are currently not a big seller.**

5 Insert a **New Slide** with the **Title and Content** layout as **Slide 3**.

a. In the title placeholder, type **Marketing Goals** In the content placeholder, type the following:

Increase sales

Promote business awareness

Acquire more repeat customers

Develop Web site visibility

b. In the content placeholder, insert **pBRC2_Target.wmf**. Change the color to **Turquoise, Accent color 3 Dark**, which is under **Recolor**, the second row, the fourth color. Position the picture so the right side is at **4 inches on the right side of the horizontal ruler** and the bottom is at **2.5 inches on the lower half of the vertical ruler**.

6 Insert a **New Slide** with the **Title and Content** layout as **Slide 4**.

a. In the title placeholder, type **Implementation Plan** In the content placeholder, type the following:

Determine average sales for last 8 weeks

Increase sales projection by 10% of average sales

Calculate average sales for next 8 weeks

Analyze result and modify plan

(Business Running Case: Front Range Action Sports continues on the next page)

Front Range Action Sports (continued)

b. Insert **pBRC2_Sales.jpg**. Set the **Brightness** to **-20%** and the **Contrast** to **40%**. Change the color to **Turquoise, Accent color 3 Dark**. Change the **Height** to **2"**, and then position the picture so that the bottom aligns at **3 inches on the lower half of the vertical ruler. Align Center.**

7 Insert a **New Slide** with the **Title Only** layout as **Slide 5**.

a. In the title placeholder, type **Review**

b. In the blank content area, insert a **WordArt** with a **Fill – Turquoise, Accent 3, Outline – Text 2**. In the text box, type **Winning** Press Enter, and then type **Strategies** Insert the picture **pBRC2_Lake.jpg** as a **Shape Fill**. Change the **Height** to **4"** and the **Width** to **6"**. Position the top edge at **1.5 inches on the upper half of the vertical ruler**, and then **Align Center**.

8 Make **Slide 4** the active slide. Insert the audio file **pBRC2_Sports.mid**. Set the **Volume** to **Medium**, and then check **Hide During Show**. Add a trigger to activate the audio **On Click of** the **Picture**. Position the speaker at the lower left corner of the slide.

9 Make **Slide 2** the active slide. View your slide show **From Current slide**. Use the **Highlighter** annotation tool to highlight *Athletic Shoes*. Use the **Pen** annotation tool to circle *Golf Shoes*. Make sure you **Keep** the annotations.

10 Insert a **Header & Footer** for the **Notes and Handouts**. Include the **Date and time fixed**, the **Page number**, and a **Footer** with the file name **Lastname_Firstname_BRC2_Goals** In the **Properties**, add your first and last name, course name and section number, and the **Keywords marketing, goals**

11 **Save** and **Close** the presentation, but do not exit PowerPoint.

12 Display a new blank presentation, and then insert a new **Photo Album**.

a. Insert the following pictures in this order: **pBRC2_Hiking**, **pBRC2_Skating**, and **pBRC2_Athletic**.

b. Set the picture layout to **1 picture**, the Frame shape to **Rounded Rectangle**, and then select the **Flow** theme. Include **Captions below ALL pictures**.

c. On **Slide 1**, replace the title text with **Athletic Footwear** and the subtitle text with **Front Range Action Sports**

d. For the pictures, use these captions:

Slide 2: **Hiking Boots**

Slide 3: **Skates**

Slide 3: **Athletic Shoes**

e. Save the album as **Lastname_Firstname_BRC2_Album**

f. Insert a **Header & Footer** for the **Notes and Handouts**. Include the **Date and time fixed**, the **Page number**, and a **Footer** with the file name **Lastname_Firstname_BRC2_Album** In the **Properties**, add your first and last name, course name and section number, and the **Keywords album, footwear**

g. Print **Handouts 4 Slides horizontal** showing all comments, or submit your presentation electronically as directed by your instructor. **Save** and **Close** the presentation.

13 Open Lastname_Firstname_BRC2_Goals.pptx.

a. Apply a **Fade** transition to all slides.

b. On **Slide 2**, set **Advance Slide** to **After 3** seconds, and then uncheck **On Mouse Click**.

c. On **Slide 3,** add a **Fade Entrance** animation effect to the Title to start **After Previous**.

d. On **Slide 4**, add a **Fade Entrance** animation effect to the Title to start **After Previous**.

e. On **Slide 1**, on *Footwear Promotion*, insert a hyperlink to the **Existing File** *Lastname_Firstname_Album_pptx*.

f. Create a **Custom Slide Show** named **Goals** and include **Slides 3 and 4**.

g. On **Slide 5**, on *Review*, insert a hyperlink to the **Goals** custom show. Click **Show and return** before clicking **OK**.

14 View the slide show from the beginning and check your links and the audio.

15 Create a PDF Document with the options to publish **Handouts** with **6 Slides per page** and **Include comments**.

16 **Save** your presentation. Print **Handouts, 6 Slides Horizontal**, or submit your presentation electronically as directed by your instructor.

17 Mark the presentation as **Final**, and then **Close**.

End **You have completed Business Running Case 2**

Glossary

.potx File extension for a PowerPoint template.

.pptx File extension for a PowerPoint presentation.

.wav (waveform audio data) A sound file that may be embedded in a presentation.

.xlsx file name extension The default file format used by Excel 2010 to save an Excel workbook.

Action button A built-in button shape that you can add to your presentation and then assign an action to occur upon the click of a mouse or with a mouse over.

Action query A query that creates a new table or changes data in an existing table.

Active area The area of the worksheet that contains data or has contained data—it does not include any empty cells that have not been used in the worksheet.

Additive The term that describes the behavior of a filter when each additional filter that you apply is based on the current filter, and which further reduces the number of records displayed.

Address bar The bar at the top of a folder window with which you can navigate to a different folder or library, or go back to a previous one.

Advanced Filter A filter that can specify three or more criteria for a particular column, apply complex criteria to two or more columns, or specify computed criteria.

After Previous A custom animation that starts the animation effect immediately after the previous effect in the list finishes playing.

Aggregate function Performs a calculation on a column of data and returns a single value.

Alignment The placement of text or objects relative to the left and right margins.

All Programs An area of the Start menu that displays all the available programs on your computer system.

AND comparison operator The comparison operator that requires each and every one of the comparison criteria to be true.

Animated GIF A file format made up of a series of frames within a single file that creates the illusion of animation by displaying the frames one after the other in quick succession.

Animation 1. Any type of motion or movement that occurs as the presentation moves from slide to slide. 2. A special visual effect or sound effect added to text or an object.

Animation Pane The area that contains a list of the animation effects added to your presentation. From this pane, you can add or modify effects.

Annotation A note or highlight on a slide that can be saved or discarded.

Append A feature that allows you to add data onto an existing table.

Append query An action query that adds new records to an existing table by adding data from another Access database or from a table in the same database.

Application Another term for a program.

Area chart A chart type that shows trends over time.

Arithmetic operators Mathematical symbols used in building expressions.

Arrange All The command that tiles all open program windows on the screen.

Ascending The order of text sorted alphabetically from A to Z, numbers sorted from lowest to highest, or dates and times sorted from earliest to latest.

Author The owner, or creator, of the original document.

AutoFilter menu A drop-down menu from which you can filter a column by a list of values, by a format, or by criteria.

AutoPlay A Windows feature that displays when you insert a CD, a DVD, or other removable device, and which lets you choose which program to use to start different kinds of media, such as music CDs, or CDs and DVDs containing photos.

Back and Forward buttons Buttons at the top of a folder window that work in conjunction with the address bar to change folders by going backward or forward one folder at a time.

Back up A feature that creates a copy of the original database to protect against lost data.

Backstage tabs The area along the left side of Backstage view with tabs to display various pages of commands.

Backstage view A centralized space for file management tasks; for example, opening, saving, printing, publishing, or sharing a file. A navigation pane displays along the left side with tabs that group file-related tasks together.

Balloon The outline shape in which a comment or formatting change displays.

Bar chart A chart type that shows a comparison among related data.

Basic custom slide show A separate presentation saved with its own title and that contains some of the slides from the original presentation.

Blog A Web site that displays dated entries, short for *Web log*.

Blog post An individual article entered in a blog with a time and date stamp.

Border A frame around a picture.

Brightness The relative lightness of an image.

Browser Software that interprets HTML files, formats them into Web pages, and then displays them. Also referred to as *Web browser*.

Building Blocks Reusable pieces of content or other document parts—for example, headers, footers, and page number formats—that are stored in galleries.

Building Blocks Organizer Provides a view of all available building blocks from all the different galleries in one location.

Caption Text that helps to identify or explain a picture or a graphic.

Cascade Delete An option that deletes all of the related records in related tables when a record in a table is deleted.

Cascade options Options that update records in related tables when referential integrity is enforced.

Cascade Update An option that updates records in related tables when the primary key field is changed.

Center alignment The alignment of text or objects that is centered horizontally between the left and right margin.

Character style A style, indicated by the symbol a, that contains formatting characteristics that you apply to text, such as font name, font size, font color, bold emphasis, and so on.

Chart A visual representation of numerical data.

Chart area The entire chart and all its elements.

Chart data range The group of cells surrounded by a blue border that Excel will use to create a chart.

Chart elements Objects that make up a chart.

Chart style The overall visual look of a chart in terms of its graphic effects, colors, and backgrounds.

Chevron A V-shaped symbol that indicates more information or options are available.

Click The action of pressing the left button on your mouse pointing device one time.

Click and type pointer The text select—I-beam—pointer with various attached shapes that indicate which formatting—left-aligned, centered, or right-aligned—will be applied when you double-click in a blank area of a document.

Clipboard A temporary storage area in Windows that can hold up to 24 items.

Column chart A chart type that shows a comparison among related data.

Combine A Track Changes feature that allows you to review two different documents containing revisions, both based on an original document.

Combo box A box that is a combination of a list box and text box in a lookup field.

Comma delimited file A file type that saves the contents of the cells by placing commas between them and an end-of-paragraph mark at the end of each row; also referred to as a *CSV (comma separated values) file*.

Command An instruction to a computer program that causes an action to be carried out.

Comment A note that an author or reviewer adds to a document.

Common dialog boxes The set of dialog boxes that includes Open, Save, and Save As, which are provided by the Windows programming interface, and which display and operate in all of the Office programs in the same manner.

Compare A Track Changes feature that enables you to review differences between an original document and the latest version of the document.

Compatibility Checker A feature that locates potential compatibility issues between PowerPoint 2010 and earlier versions of PowerPoint.

Compatibility mode Saves a presentation as PowerPoint 97-2003 Presentation.

Compound criteria The use of two or more criteria on the same row—all conditions must be met for the records to be included in the results.

Compound filter A filter that uses more than one condition—and one that uses comparison operators.

Compressed file A file that has been reduced in size and thus takes up less storage space and can be transferred to other computers quickly.

Context sensitive command A command associated with activities in which you are engaged.

Contextual tabs Tabs that are added to the Ribbon automatically when a specific object, such as a picture, is selected, and that contain commands relevant to the selected object.

Contiguous Items that are adjacent to one another.

Contrast The amount of difference between the light and dark extremes of color in an image.

Copy A command that duplicates a selection and places it on the Clipboard.

Criteria range An area on your worksheet where you define the criteria for the filter, and which indicates how the displayed records are filtered.

Crop Remove unwanted or unnecessary areas of a picture.

Crop handles Used like sizing handles to crop a picture.

Crop tool The mouse pointer used when removing areas of a picture.

Cross join A join that displays when each row from one table is combined with each row in a related table, usually created unintentionally when you do not create a join line between related tables.

CSV (comma separated values) file A file type in which the cells in each row are separated by commas; also referred to as a *comma delimited file*.

Custom Filter A filter with which you can apply complex criteria to a single column.

Custom list A sort order that you can define.

Custom slide show Displays only the slides you want to display to an audience in the order you select.

Cut A command that removes a selection and places it on the Clipboard.

Cycle A continual process diagram.

Data labels Labels that display the value, percentage, and/or category of each particular data point and can contain one or more of the choices listed—Series name, Category name, Value, or Percentage.

Data markers The shapes in a chart representing each of the cells that contain data.

Data points The cells that contain numerical data used in a chart.

Data range border The blue line that surrounds the cells that display in the chart.

Data series In a chart, related data points represented by a unique color.

Data table (Excel) A range of cells that shows how changing certain values in your formulas affect the results of those formulas and that makes it easy to calculate multiple versions in one operation.

Data validation Rules that help prevent invalid data entries and ensure data is entered consistently.

Data validation (Excel) A technique by which you can control the type of data or the values that are entered into a cell by limiting the acceptable values to a defined list.

Database An organized collection of facts related to a specific topic.

Default The term that refers to the current selection or setting that is automatically used by a computer program unless you specify otherwise.

Default value A value displayed for new records.

Defined name A word or string of characters in Excel that represents a cell, a range of cells, a formula, or a constant value; also referred to as simply a *name*.

Delete query An action query that removes records from an existing table in the same database.

Descending The order of text that is sorted alphabetically from Z to A, numbers sorted from highest to lowest, or dates and times sorted from latest to earliest.

Deselect The action of canceling the selection of an object or block of text by clicking outside of the selection.

Desktop In Windows, the opening screen that simulates your work area.

Detail data The subtotaled rows that are totaled and summarized; typically adjacent to and either above or to the left of the summary data.

Details pane The area at the bottom of a folder window that displays the most common file properties.

Dialog Box A small window that contains options for completing a task.

Dialog Box Launcher A small icon that displays to the right of some group names on the Ribbon, and which opens a related dialog box or task pane providing additional options and commands related to that group.

Direct formatting The process of applying each format separately, for example, bold, then font size, then font color, and so on.

Document properties Details about a file that describe or identify it, including the title, author name, subject, and keywords that identify the document's topic or contents; also known as *metadata*.

Double-click The action of clicking the left mouse button two times in rapid succession.

Drag The action of holding down the left mouse button while moving your mouse.

Drop cap A large capital letter at the beginning of a paragraph that formats text in a visually distinctive manner.

Dropped The position of a drop cap when it is within the text of the paragraph.

Dynamic An attribute applied to data in a database that changes.

Edit The actions of making changes to text or graphics in an Office file.

Ellipsis A set of three dots indicating incompleteness; when following a command name, indicates that a dialog box will display.

E-mail address link A hyperlink that opens a new message window so that an individual viewing a Web site can send an e-mail message.

E-mail client A software program that enables you to compose and send e-mail.

Embed Save a file so that the audio or video file becomes part of the presentation file.

Embedded chart A chart that is inserted into the same worksheet that contains the data used to create the chart.

Embedding The process of inserting an object, such as a chart, into a Word document so that it becomes part of the document.

Enhanced ScreenTip A ScreenTip that displays more descriptive text than a normal ScreenTip.

Expression 1. A combination of functions, field values, constants, and operators that produce a result. 2. The formula that will perform a calculation.

Expression Builder A feature used to create formulas (expressions) in query criteria, form and report properties, and table validation rules.

Extract To decompress, or pull out, files from a compressed form.

Extract area The location to which you copy records when extracting filtered rows.

Extracting The process of pulling out multiple sets of data for comparison purposes.

Field A single piece of information that is stored in a record.

File A collection of information stored on a computer under a single name, for example a Word document or a PowerPoint presentation.

File extension Also called the file type, it identifies the format of the file or the application used to create it.

File list In a folder window, the area on the right that displays the contents of the current folder or library.

Fill The inside color of an object.

Filtering A process in which only the rows that meet the criteria display; rows that do not meet the criteria are hidden.

Final A Track Changes view that displays the document with all proposed changes included and comments hidden.

Final: Show Markup The default Track Changes view that displays the final document with all revisions and comments visible.

Financial functions Pre-built formulas that perform common business calculations such as calculating a loan payment on a vehicle or calculating how much to save each month to buy something; financial functions commonly involve a period of time such as months or years.

Find A command that finds and selects specific text or formatting.

Find Duplicates Query A query that is used to locate duplicate records in a table.

Find Unmatched Query A query used to locate unmatched records so they can be deleted from the table.

Fit to slide The photo album option that allows the picture to occupy all available space on a slide with no room for a frame or caption.

Flagged A highlighted word that the spelling checker does not recognize from the Office dictionary.

Folder A container in which you store files.

Folder window In Windows, a window that displays the contents of the current folder, library, or device, and contains helpful parts so that you can navigate.

Font A set of characters with the same design and shape.

Font styles Formatting emphasis such as bold, italic, and underline.

Footer A reserved area for text or graphics that displays at the bottom of each page in a document.

Format Painter An Office feature that copies formatting from one selection of text to another.

Formatting The process of establishing the overall appearance of text, graphics, and pages in an Office file—for example, in a Word document.

Formatting marks Characters that display on the screen, but do not print, indicating where the Enter key, the Spacebar, and the Tab key were pressed; also called *nonprinting characters.*

Frame The border around a picture in a photo album.

Full path Includes the drive, the folder, and any subfolders in which a file is contained.

Future value (Fv) The value at the end of the time periods in an Excel function; the cash balance you want to attain after the last payment is made—usually zero for loans.

Gallery An Office feature that displays a list of potential results instead of just the command name.

GIF Stands for *Graphics Interchange Format.* It is a file format used for graphic images.

Go To A command that moves to a specific cell or range of cells that you specify.

Go To Special A command that moves to cells that have special characteristics, for example, to cells that are blank or to cells that contain constants, as opposed to formulas.

Gradient fill A gradual progression of several colors blending into each other or shades of the same color blending into each other.

Gradient stop Allows you to apply different color combinations to selected areas of the background.

Gridlines Lines in the plot area that aid the eye in determining the plotted values.

Groups On the Office Ribbon, the sets of related commands that you might need for a specific type of task.

Handout Master Includes the specifications for the design of presentation handouts for an audience.

Header A reserved area for text or graphics that displays at the top of each page in a document.

Hierarchy A category of SmartArt graphics used to create an organization chart or show a decision tree.

HLOOKUP An Excel function that looks up values that are displayed horizontally in a row.

Horizontal axis The axis that displays along the lower edge of a chart, also referred to as the *X-axis*.

Horizontal Category axis (x-axis) This displays along the bottom of the chart to identify the category of data.

HTML (HyperText Markup Language) The language used to code Web pages.

HTTP (HyperText Transfer Protocol) The protocol used on the World Wide Web to define how messages are formatted and transmitted.

Hyperlinked custom slide show A quick way to navigate to a separate slide show from within the original presentation.

Hyperlinks Text, buttons, pictures, graphics, or other objects that, when clicked, will take you to another location, such as a Web page, an e-mail address, another document, or a place within the same document.

Icons Pictures that represent a program, a file, a folder, or some other object.

In margin The position of a drop cap when it is in the left margin of a paragraph.

Index A special list created in Access to speed up searches and sorting.

Info tab The tab in Backstage view that displays information about the current file.

Ink Revision marks made directly on a document by using a stylus on a Tablet PC.

Inner join A join that allows only the records where the common field exists in both related tables to be displayed in query results.

Input mask A field property that determines the data that can be entered and how the data displays.

Insertion point A blinking vertical line that indicates where text or graphics will be inserted.

Instance Each simultaneously running Access session.

Interest The amount charged for the use of borrowed money.

Internal link A hyperlink that connects to another page in the same Web site.

Internet Explorer A Web browser developed by Microsoft.

Join A relationship that helps a query return only the records from each table you want to see, based on how those tables are related to other tables in the query.

JPEG (JPG) Stands for Joint Photographic Experts Group. It is a file format used for photos.

Keep lines together A formatting feature that prevents a single line from displaying by itself at the bottom of a page or at the top of a page.

Keep with next A formatting feature that keeps a heading with its first paragraph of text on the same page.

Keyboard shortcut A combination of two or more keyboard keys, used to perform a task that would otherwise require a mouse.

KeyTips The letter that displays on a command in the Ribbon and that indicates the key you can press to activate the command when keyboard control of the Ribbon is activated.

Kiosk A booth that includes a computer and a monitor that may have a touch screen.

Landscape orientation A page orientation in which the paper is wider than it is tall.

Left outer join A join used when you want to display all of the records on the *one* side of a one-to-many relationship, whether or not there are matching records in the table on the *many* side of the relationship.

Legend The part of a chart that identifies the colors assigned to each data series or category.

Library In Windows, a collection of items, such as files and folders, assembled from various locations that might be on your computer, an external hard drive, removable media, or someone else's computer.

Line chart A chart type that shows trends over time.

Line style How the line displays, such as a solid line, dots, or dashes.

Line weight The thickness of a line measured in points.

Link Saves a presentation so that the audio or video file is saved separately from the presentation.

Linked style A style, indicated by the symbol ¶a, that behaves as either a character style or a paragraph style, depending on what you select.

List 1. A series of rows that contains related data that you can group by adding subtotals. 2. A category of SmartArt graphics used to show non-sequential information.

List box A box containing a list of choices for a lookup field.

List style A style that applies a format to a list.

Live Preview A technology that shows the result of applying an editing or formatting change as you point to possible results—*before* you actually apply it.

Location Any disk drive, folder, or other place in which you can store files and folders.

Lock aspect ratio When this option is selected, you can change one dimension (height or width) of an object, such as a picture, and the other dimension will automatically be changed to maintain the proportion.

Locked [cells] Formula cells that prevent others from changing the formulas in the template.

Lookup field A way to restrict data entered in a field.

Lookup functions A group of Excel functions that look up a value in a defined range of cells located in another part of the workbook to find a corresponding value.

Loop When an audio or video file plays repeatedly from start to finish until it is stopped manually.

Major sort A term sometimes used to refer to the first sort level in the Sort dialog box.

Major unit value A number that determines the spacing between tick marks and between the gridlines in the plot area.

Make table query An action query that creates a new table by extracting data from one or more tables.

Mark as Final Makes a presentation file read-only in order to prevent changes to the document. Adds a Marked as Final icon to the Status bar.

Markup The formatting Word uses to denote a document's revisions visually.

Markup area The space to the right or left of a document where comments and formatting changes display in balloons.

Matrix A category of SmartArt graphics used to show how parts relate to a whole.

Memo A written message sent to someone working in the same organization; also referred to as a *memorandum*.

Memorandum *See* Memo.

Metadata Details about a file that describe or identify it, including the title, author name, subject, and keywords that identify the document's topic or contents; also known as *document properties*.

Microsoft Access A database program, with which you can collect, track, and report data.

Microsoft Communicator An Office program that brings together multiple modes of communication, including instant messaging, video conferencing, telephony, application sharing, and file transfer.

Microsoft Excel A spreadsheet program, with which you calculate and analyze numbers and create charts.

Microsoft InfoPath An Office program that enables you to create forms and gather data.

Microsoft Office 2010 A Microsoft suite of products that includes programs, servers, and services for individuals, small organizations, and large enterprises to perform specific tasks.

Microsoft OneNote An Office program with which you can manage notes that you make at meetings or in classes.

Microsoft Outlook An Office program with which you can manage e-mail and organizational activities.

Microsoft PowerPoint A presentation program, with which you can communicate information with high-impact graphics.

Microsoft Publisher An Office program with which you can create desktop publishing documents such as brochures.

Microsoft SharePoint Workspace An Office program that enables you to share information with others in a team environment.

Microsoft Word A word processing program, also referred to as an authoring program, with which you create and share documents by using its writing tools.

Mini toolbar A small toolbar containing frequently used formatting commands that displays as a result of selecting text or objects.

Mitered A border corner that has been angled to fit precisely in a square.

Motion path effect An animation effect that determines how and in what direction text or objects will move on a slide.

Mouse Over Refers to an action that will occur when the mouse pointer is placed on (over) an Action button. No mouse click is required.

Multilevel list A list in which the items display in a visual hierarchical structure.

Multivalued fields Fields that hold multiple values.

Name A word or string of characters in Excel that represents a cell, a range of cells, a formula, or a constant value; also referred to as a *defined name*.

Navigate The process of exploring within the organizing structure of Windows.

Navigation bar A series of text links across the top or bottom of a Web page that, when clicked, will link to another Web page on the same site.

Navigation pane In a folder window, the area on the left in which you can navigate to, open, and display favorites, libraries, folders, saved searches, and an expandable list of drives.

Navigation tools Buttons that display on the slides during a slide show that allow you to perform actions such as move to the next slide, the previous slide, the last viewed slide, or the end of the slide show.

Noncontiguous Items that are not adjacent to one another.

Nonprinting characters Characters that display on the screen, but do not print, indicating where the Enter key, the Spacebar, and the Tab key were pressed; also called *formatting marks*.

Normal Quick Style The default style in Word for new documents and which includes default styles and customizations that determine the basic look of a document; for example, it includes the Calibri font, 11 point font size, multiple line spacing at 1.15, and 10 pt. spacing after a paragraph.

Notes Master Includes the specifications for the design of speaker's notes.

Nper The abbreviation for *number of time periods* in various Excel functions.

Numerical data Numbers that represent facts.

Office Clipboard A temporary storage area that holds text or graphics that you select and then cut or copy.

Office Theme Slide Master A specific slide master that contains the design, such as the background, that displays on all slide layouts in the presentation.

One-to-one relationship A relationship between tables where a record in one table has only one matching record in another table.

One-variable data table A data table that changes the value in only one cell.

Open dialog box A dialog box from which you can navigate to, and then open on your screen, an existing file that was created in that same program.

Option button A round button that allows you to make one choice among two or more options.

Options dialog box A dialog box within each Office application where you can select program settings and other options and preferences.

OR comparison operator The comparison operator that requires only one of the two comparison criteria that you specify to be true.

Organization chart A type of graphic that is useful to depict reporting relationships within an organization.

Original A Track Changes view that hides the tracked changes and shows the original, unchanged document with comments hidden.

Original: Show Markup A Track Changes view that displays the original document with all revisions and comments visible.

Orphan record A record that references deleted records in a related table.

Outer join A join that is typically used to display records from both tables, regardless of whether there are matching records.

Paragraph style A style, indicated by the symbol ¶, that includes everything that a character style contains, plus all aspects of a paragraph's appearance; for example, text alignment, tab stops, line spacing, and borders.

Paragraph symbol The symbol ¶ that represents a paragraph.

Parameter A value that can be changed.

Parameter query A query that prompts you for criteria before running the query.

Password An optional element of a template added to prevent someone from disabling a worksheet's protection.

Paste The action of placing text or objects that have been copied or moved from one location to another location.

Paste Options Icons that provide a Live Preview of the various options for changing the format of a pasted item with a single click.

Path The location of a folder or file on your computer or storage device.

PDF (Portable Document Format) file A file format that creates an image that preserves the look of your file, but that cannot be easily changed; a popular format for sending documents electronically, because the document will display on most computers.

Photo album A stylized presentation format to display pictures.

Picture A type of graphic that is useful to display pictures in a diagram.

Pie chart A chart type that shows the proportion of parts to a whole.

Pixel The term, short for picture element, represents a single point in a graphic image.

Play Animations button The small star-shaped icon displaying to the left of a slide thumbnail that, when clicked, plays the sound or animation.

PMT function An Excel function that calculates the payment for a loan based on constant payments and at a constant interest rate.

Point The action of moving your mouse pointer over something on your screen.

Pointer Any symbol that displays on your screen in response to moving your mouse.

Points A measurement of the size of a font; there are 72 points in an inch, with 10-12 points being the most commonly used font size.

Portrait orientation A page orientation in which the paper is taller than it is wide.

Present value (Pv) The total amount that a series of future payments is worth now; also known as the *principal*.

Preview pane button In a folder window, the button on the toolbar with which you can display a preview of the contents of a file without opening it in a program.

Principal Another term for present value.

Print Preview A view of a document as it will appear when you print it.

Process A category of SmartArt graphics that is used to show steps in a process or timeline.

Program A set of instructions that a computer uses to perform a specific task, such as word processing, accounting, or data management; also called an *application*.

Program-level control buttons In an Office program, the buttons on the right edge of the title bar that minimize, restore, or close the program.

Protected view A security feature in Office 2010 that protects your computer from malicious files by opening them in a restricted environment until you enable them; you might encounter this feature if you open a file from an e-mail or download files from the Internet.

Protection This prevents anyone from altering the formulas or changing other template components.

Protocol A set of rules.

Pt. The abbreviation for *point*; for example when referring to a font size.

Pyramid A category of SmartArt graphics that uses a series of pictures to show relationships.

Query The process used to ask a question of the data in a database.

Quick Access Toolbar In an Office program, the small row of buttons in the upper left corner of the screen from which you can perform frequently used commands.

Quick Commands The commands Save, Save As, Open, and Close that display at the top of the navigation pane in Backstage view.

Quick Parts All of the reusable pieces of content that are available to insert into a document, including building blocks, document properties, and fields.

Quick Styles Combinations of formatting options that work together and look attractive together.

Quick Tables Tables that are stored as building blocks.

Rate In the Excel PMT function, the term used to indicate the interest rate for a loan.

Read-Only A property assigned to a file that prevents the file from being modified or deleted; it indicates that you cannot save any changes to the displayed document unless you first save it with a new name.

Recolor The term used to change all the colors in an image to shades of one color, often used to make the colors match a background or apply a stylized effect or hue to a picture.

Record All the categories of data pertaining to one person, place, thing, event, or idea.

Relationship A category of SmartArt graphics that is used to illustrate connections.

Required A field property that ensures a field cannot be left empty.

Reviewer An individual who reviews and inserts comments into a document.

Reviewing Pane A separate scrollable window that displays all of the current changes and comments in a document.

Revisions Changes made to a document.

Ribbon The user interface in Office 2010 that groups the commands for performing related tasks on tabs across the upper portion of the program window.

Ribbon tabs The tabs on the Office Ribbon that display the names of the task-oriented groups of commands.

Rich Text Format (RTF) A universal file format, using the *.rtf* file extension, that can be read by many word processing programs.

Right outer join A join used when you want to display all of the records on the *many* side of a one-to-many relationship, whether or not there are matching records in the table on the *one* side of the relationship. This should not occur if referential integrity has been enforced because all orders should have a related customer.

Right-click The action of clicking the right mouse button one time.

Rotation handle A green circle that displays on the top side of a selected object.

RTF *See* Rich Text Format.

Sans serif A font design with no lines or extensions on the ends of characters.

Scale The range of numbers in the data series that controls the minimum, maximum, and incremental values on the value axis.

Scaling (Excel) The group of commands by which you can reduce the horizontal and vertical size of the printed data by a percentage or by the number of pages that you specify.

Scope The location within which a defined name is recognized without qualification—usually either to a specific worksheet or to the entire workbook.

ScreenTip A small box that that displays useful information when you perform various mouse actions such as pointing to screen elements or dragging.

Scroll bar A vertical or horizontal bar in a window or a pane to assist in bringing an area into view, and which contains a scroll box and scroll arrows.

Scroll box The box in the vertical and horizontal scroll bars that can be dragged to reposition the contents of a window or pane on the screen.

Search box In a folder window, the box in which you can type a word or a phrase to look for an item in the current folder or library.

Select To highlight, by dragging with your mouse, areas of text or data or graphics, so that the selection can be edited, formatted, copied, or moved.

Serif font A font design that includes small line extensions on the ends of the letters to guide the eye in reading from left to right.

Sharpen Increase the clarity of an image.

Shortcut menu A menu that displays commands and options relevant to the selected text or object.

Slide Master Part of a template that stores information about the formatting and text that displays on every slide in a presentation. There are various slide master layouts.

SmartArt graphic A visual representation of your information and ideas.

Soften Decrease the clarity of an image or make it fuzzy.

Sort The action of ordering data, usually in alphabetical or numeric order.

Sort dialog box A dialog box in which you can sort data based on several criteria at once, and which enables a sort by more than one column or row.

Source table The table from which records are being extracted or copied.

Sparklines Tiny charts that fit within a cell and give a visual trend summary alongside your data.

Split The command that enables you to view separate parts of the same worksheet on your screen; splits the window into multiple resizable panes to view distant parts of the worksheet at one time.

Split button A button divided into two parts and in which clicking the main part of the button performs a command and clicking the arrow opens a menu with choices.

Standardization All forms created within the organization will have a uniform appearance; the data will always be organized in the same manner.

Start button The button on the Windows taskbar that displays the Start menu.

Start menu The Windows menu that provides a list of choices and is the main gateway to your computer's programs, folders, and settings.

Static data Data that does not change.

Status bar The area along the lower edge of an Office program window that displays file information on the left and buttons to control how the window looks on the right.

Style set A group of styles that are designed to work together.

Styles window A pane that displays a list of styles and contains tools to manage styles.

Subfolder A folder within a folder.

Subtotal command The command that totals several rows of related data together by automatically inserting subtotals and totals for the selected cells.

Synchronous scrolling The setting that causes two documents to scroll simultaneously.

System tables Tables used to keep track of multiple entries in an attachment field that you cannot view or work with.

Tab delimited text file A file type in which cells are separated by tabs; this type of file can be readily exchanged with various database programs.

Table array A defined range of cells, arranged in a column or a row, used in a VLOOKUP or HLOOKUP function.

Table style A style that applies a consistent look to the borders, shading, and so on of a table.

Tabs On the Office Ribbon, the name of each activity area in the Office Ribbon.

Tags Custom file properties that you create to help find and organize your own files.

Task pane A window within a Microsoft Office application in which you can enter options for completing a command.

Template A predefined file used as a pattern for creating other files.

Text file A file type that separates the cells of each row with tab characters.

Text link A hyperlink applied to a selected word or phrase.

Text pane This always displays to the left of the graphic, is populated with placeholder text, and is used to build a graphic by entering and editing text.

Theme A predesigned set of colors, fonts, lines, and fill effects that look good together and that can be applied to your entire document or to specific items.

Theme template A stored, user-defined set of colors, fonts, and effects that can be shared with other Office programs.

Tick mark labels Identifying information for a tick mark generated from the cells on the worksheet used to create the chart.

Timeline A graphical representation that displays the number of seconds the animation takes to complete.

Title bar The bar at the top edge of the program window that indicates the name of the current file and the program name.

Toggle button A button that can be turned on by clicking it once, and then turned off by clicking it again.

Toolbar In a folder window, a row of buttons with which you can perform common tasks, such as changing the view of your files and folders or burning files to a CD.

Totals query A query that calculates subtotals across groups of records.

Track A song from a CD.

Track Changes A feature that makes a record of the changes made to a document.

Transition sound A prerecorded sound that can be applied and will play as slides change from one to the next.

Transition speed The timing of the transition between all slides or between the previous slide and the current slide.

Transitions Motion effects that occur when a presentation moves from slide to slide in Slide Show view and affect how content is revealed.

Trendline A graphic representation of trends in a data series, such as a line sloping upward to represent increased sales over a period of months.

Trigger A portion of text, a graphic, or a picture that, when clicked, causes the audio or video to play.

Triple-click The action of clicking the left mouse button three times in rapid succession.

Trusted Documents A security feature in Office 2010 that remembers which files you have already enabled; you might encounter this feature if you open a file from an e-mail or download files from the Internet.

Trusted source A person or organization that you know will not send you databases with malicious content.

Two Pages A zoom setting that decreases the magnification to display two pages of a document.

Two-variable data table A data table that changes the values in two cells.

Type argument An optional argument in the PMT function that assumes that the payment will be made at the end of each time period.

Unequal join A join that is used to combine rows from two data sources based on field values that are not equal; can be created only in SQL view.

Unlocked [cells] Cells in a template that may be filled in.

Unmatched records Records in one table that have no matching records in a related table.

Update query An action query that is used to add, change, or delete data in fields of one or more existing records.

URL (Uniform Resource Locator) Defines the address of documents and resources on the Web.

USB flash drive A small data storage device that plugs into a computer USB port.

Validation list (Excel) A list of values that are acceptable for a group of cells; only values on the list are valid and any value *not* on the list is considered invalid.

Validation rule An expression that precisely defines the range of data that will be accepted in a field.

Validation text The error message that displays when an individual enters a value prohibited by the validation rule.

Vertical axis The axis that displays along the left side of a chart; also referred to as the *Y-axis*.

Vertical change bar Displays in the left margin next to each line of text that contains a revision.

Vertical Value axis (y-axis) This displays along the left side of the chart to identify the numerical scale on which the charted data is based.

View Side by Side Displays two open documents, in separate windows, next to each other on the screen.

Views button In a folder window, a toolbar button with which you can choose how to view the contents of the current location.

VLOOKUP An Excel function that looks up values that are displayed vertically in a column.

Walls and floor The areas surrounding a 3-D chart that give dimension and boundaries to the chart.

Web browser Software that interprets HTML files, formats them into Web pages, and then displays them. Also referred to as a *browser*.

Web page A file coded in HTML that can be viewed on the Internet using a Web browser.

Web Page format A file type that saves a Word document as an HTML file, with some elements of the Web page saved in a folder, separate from the Web page itself.

Web site A group of related Web pages published to a specific location on the Internet.

Wildcard A character, such as an asterisk or question mark, used to search for an unknown term.

Window A rectangular area on a computer screen in which programs and content appear, and which can be moved, resized, minimized, or closed.

Windows Explorer The program that displays the files and folders on your computer, and which is at work any time you are viewing the contents of files and folders in a window.

Windows taskbar The area along the lower edge of the Windows desktop that contains the Start button and an area to display buttons for open programs.

With Previous A custom animation that starts the animation effect at the same time as the previous effect in the list.

Word Options A collection of settings that you can change to customize Word.

X-axis *See* Horizontal axis.

XML Paper Specification (XPS) Microsoft's file format that preserves document formatting and enables file sharing. Files can be opened and viewed on any operating system or computer that is equipped with Microsoft Viewer. Files cannot be easily edited.

XPS (XML Paper Specification) A file type, developed by Microsoft, that provides an accurate visual representation of a document across applications and platforms.

Y-axis *See* Vertical axis.

Zero-length string An entry created by typing two quotation marks with no spaces between them ("") to indicate that no value exists for a required text or memo field.

Zoom The action of increasing or decreasing the viewing area on the screen.

Index

Symbols and Numbers

A

D

E

F

G

H

I

M

P

Q

R

S

T

SINGLE PC LICENSE AGREEMENT AND LIMITED WARRANTY

READ THIS LICENSE CAREFULLY BEFORE OPENING THIS PACKAGE. BY OPENING THIS PACKAGE, YOU ARE AGREEING TO THE TERMS AND CONDITIONS OF THIS LICENSE. IF YOU DO NOT AGREE, DO NOT OPEN THE PACKAGE. PROMPTLY RETURN THE UNOPENED PACKAGE AND ALL ACCOMPANYING ITEMS TO THE PLACE YOU OBTAINED THEM. *THESE TERMS APPLY TO ALL LICENSED SOFTWARE ON THE DISK EXCEPT THAT THE TERMS FOR USE OF ANY SHAREWARE OR FREEWARE ON THE DISKETTES ARE AS SET FORTH IN THE ELECTRONIC LICENSE LOCATED ON THE DISK:*

1. GRANT OF LICENSE and OWNERSHIP: The enclosed computer programs ("Software") are licensed, not sold, to you by Prentice-Hall, Inc. ("We" or the "Company") and in consideration of your purchase or adoption of the accompanying Company textbooks and/or other materials, and your agreement to these terms. We reserve any rights not granted to you. You own only the disk(s) but we and/or our licensors own the Software itself. This license allows you to use and display your copy of the Software on a single computer (i.e., with a single CPU) at a single location for academic use only, so long as you comply with the terms of this Agreement. You may make one copy for back up, or transfer your copy to another CPU, provided that the Software is usable on only one computer.

2. RESTRICTIONS: You may not transfer or distribute the Software or documentation to anyone else. Except for backup, you may not copy the documentation or the Software. You may not network the Software or otherwise use it on more than one computer or computer terminal at the same time. You may not reverse engineer, disassemble, decompile, modify, adapt, translate, or create derivative works based on the Software or the Documentation. You may be held legally responsible for any copying or copyright infringement which is caused by your failure to abide by the terms of these restrictions.

3. TERMINATION: This license is effective until terminated. This license will terminate automatically without notice from the Company if you fail to comply with any provisions or limitations of this license. Upon termination, you shall destroy the Documentation and all copies of the Software. All provisions of this Agreement as to limitation and disclaimer of warranties, limitation of liability, remedies or damages, and our ownership rights shall survive termination.

4.DISCLAIMER OF WARRANTY: THE COMPANY AND ITS LICENSORS MAKE NO WARRANTIES ABOUT THE SOFTWARE, WHICH IS PROVIDED "AS-IS." IF THE DISK IS DEFECTIVE IN MATERIALS OR WORKMANSHIP, YOUR ONLY REMEDY IS TO RETURN IT TO THE COMPANY WITHIN 30 DAYS FOR REPLACEMENT UNLESS THE COMPANY DETERMINES IN GOOD FAITH THAT THE DISK HAS BEEN MISUSED OR IMPROPERLY INSTALLED, REPAIRED, ALTERED OR DAMAGED. THE COMPANY DISCLAIMS ALL WARRANTIES, EXPRESS OR IMPLIED, INCLUDING WITHOUT LIMITATION, THE IMPLIED WARRANTIES OF MERCHANTABILITY AND FITNESS FOR A PARTICULAR PURPOSE. THE COMPANY DOES NOT WARRANT, GUARANTEE OR MAKE ANY REPRESENTATION REGARDING THE ACCURACY, RELIABILITY, CURRENTNESS, USE, OR RESULTS OF USE, OF THE SOFTWARE.

5. LIMITATION OF REMEDIES AND DAMAGES: IN NO EVENT, SHALL THE COMPANY OR ITS EMPLOYEES, AGENTS, LICENSORS OR CONTRACTORS BE LIABLE FOR ANY INCIDENTAL, INDIRECT, SPECIAL OR CONSEQUENTIAL DAMAGES ARISING OUT OF OR IN CONNECTION WITH THIS LICENSE OR THE SOFTWARE, INCLUDING, WITHOUT LIMITATION, LOSS OF USE, LOSS OF DATA, LOSS OF INCOME OR PROFIT, OR OTHER LOSSES SUSTAINED AS A RESULT OF INJURY TO ANY PERSON, OR LOSS OF OR DAMAGE TO PROPERTY, OR CLAIMS OF THIRD PARTIES, EVEN IF THE COMPANY OR AN AUTHORIZED REPRESENTATIVE OF THE COMPANY HAS BEEN ADVISED OF THE POSSIBILITY OF SUCH DAMAGES. SOME JURISDICTIONS DO NOT ALLOW THE LIMITATION OF DAMAGES IN CERTAIN CIRCUMSTANCES, SO THE ABOVE LIMITATIONS MAY NOT ALWAYS APPLY.

6. GENERAL: THIS AGREEMENT SHALL BE CONSTRUED IN ACCORDANCE WITH THE LAWS OF THE UNITED STATES OF AMERICA AND THE STATE OF NEW YORK, APPLICABLE TO CONTRACTS MADE IN NEW YORK, AND SHALL BENEFIT THE COMPANY, ITS AFFILIATES AND ASSIGNEES. This Agreement is the complete and exclusive statement of the agreement between you and the Company and supersedes all proposals, prior agreements, oral or written, and any other communications between you and the company or any of its representatives relating to the subject matter. If you are a U.S. Government user, this Software is licensed with "restricted rights" as set forth in subparagraphs (a)-(d) of the Commercial Computer-Restricted Rights clause at FAR 52.227-19 or in subparagraphs (c)(1)(ii) of the Rights in Technical Data and Computer Software clause at DFARS 252.227-7013, and similar clauses, as applicable.

Should you have any questions concerning this agreement or if you wish to contact the Company for any reason, please contact in writing:

Multimedia Production,
Higher Education Division,
Prentice-Hall, Inc.,
1 Lake Street,
Upper Saddle River NJ 07458.